А Б В Г Д Е Ж З И Й К Л М Н О П Р С Т У Ф–Ч Ш–Я

Langenscheidt's Pocket Russian Dictionary

Russian-English
English-Russian

Edited by the

Langenscheidt Editorial Staff

Compiled with contributions by
Irina A. Walshe

Printed in Germany

Preface

This newly-revised Russian/English Pocket Dictionary with its 45,000 references is an ideal tool for all those who work with the Russian and English languages at beginner's or intermediate level. The dictionary offers coverage of everyday language and also details the latest developments in Russian and English. Hundreds of up-to-date Russian and English words have been incorporated into the present edition of this well-known dictionary, making it ideal for everyday use in the modern world – in all walks of life and also at school. The dictionary contains the most important terminology from such specialist areas as trade and commerce, technology, and medicine.

Isolated words are often only clearly understood in context. So a large number of multi-word lexical units, loose combinations such as collocations as well as set phrases such as idiomatic expressions, are given to show the full spectrum of a word's meaning and to illustrate how the two languages (Russian and English) correspond in context.

Translations referring to different word classes of the same headword are indicated by arabic numbers. Synonymous translation variants are seperated by commas, and semantically distinct alternatives by semicolons.

In addition to the main vocabulary, this dictionary contains special quick-reference sections for geographical names and current abbreviations in both Russian and English.

Words need grammar to back them up. *Langenscheidt's Pocket Dictionary Russian* gives detailed information on the conjugation and declension of Russian verbs, nouns and adjectives. Each Russian verb, noun or adjective in the dictionary includes a reference to a corresponding standard verb, noun or adjective in the grammar appendix, which is then fully conjugated or inflected.

English pronunciation in this dictionary follows the principles laid down by Jones / Gimson and is based on the alphabet of the *International Phonetic Association* (IPA).

Russian words can be pronounced properly if the stress is known. Therefore every Russian word has an appropriate stress mark. Shift of stress, as far as it takes place within the inflection, is also indicated. A detailed account of Russian pronunciation with the help of the symbols of the IPA's phonetic transcription can be found on pages 11–17.

It is hoped that this dictionary will be a rich source of information for you as well as an indispensable part of the materials you use to learn Russian or English.

Langenscheidt Publishers

Contents

How to Use the Dictionary

1. **Arrangement.** Strict alphabetical order has been maintained throughout the dictionary.

   A number of prefixed words, especially verbs, are not explicitly listed because of the limited size of the dictionary, and in such cases it may prove useful to drop the prefix and look up the primary form, e. g.:

   поблагодари́ть → благодари́ть

   Compounds not found at their alphabetical place should be reduced to their second component in order to find out their main meaning, e. g.:

   термоя́дерный → я́дерный = nuclear

   The tilde (~) serves as a mark of repetition. The tilde in bold type replaces either the headword or the part of the headword preceding the vertical bar; e. g.:

   изме́н|а ...; **~е́ние** = **измене́ние**

   In the English-Russian part the tilde in multi-word lexical units is used to replace the whole headword, e.g.:

   mobil|e ...; ***~ phone*** = ***mobile phone***

   In the Russian-English part the tilde in idioms is used to relace the part preceding the vertical bar, e. g.:

   коль|циво́й ...; **~цо́** ...; ***обруча́льное ~цо́*** = ***обруча́льное кольцо́***

   The tilde with a circle (ⸯ): when the first letter changes from a capital to a small letter or vice-versa, the usual tilde is replaced by the tilde with a circle.

   In brackets a hyphen (-) has been used instead of the tilde, e. g.:

   брать [беру́, -рёшь; брал, -á ...] = [беру́, берёшь; брал, брала́ ...]

   Of the two main aspects of a Russian verb the imperfective form appears first, in boldface type, followed, in acute-angled brackets < >, by its perfective counterpart.

   An English adjective marked with □ takes the regular adverbial form, i.e. by affixing ...ly to the adjective or by changing ...le into ...ly or ...y into ...ily.

2. **Pronunciation.** As a rule the pronunciation of individual Russian headwords has been given only in cases and places that differ from the standard pronunciation of Russian vowel and consonant letters, e. g.:

   лёгкий (-xk-) - «гк» is pronounced «хк».

3. **Stress.** The accent mark (´) is placed above the stressed vowel of a Russian entry (or any other) word with more than one syllable and printed in full, as well as of run-on words, provided their accentuated vowel is not covered by the tilde or hyphen (= marks of repetition), e. g.:

   дока́з|ывать ..., <~áть> = <доказáть>

   Since ё is always stressed the two dots over it represent implicitly the accent mark.

   Wherever the accent mark precedes the tilde (´~) the second-last syllable of the part for which the tilde stands is stressed, e. g.:

уведом|ля́ть ..., <~ить> = <уве́домить>

An accent mark over the tilde (~́) implies that the last (or sole) syllable of the part replaced by the tilde is to be stressed.

Example:

наход|и́ть ...; **~́ка** = **нахо́дка**
прода|ва́ть ..., <~́ть> = <прода́ть>

In special cases of phonetic transcription, however, the accent mark precedes the stressed syllable, cf. **анте́нна** (-'tɛn-). This usage is in accordance with IPA rules.

Two accents in a word denote two equally possible modes of stressing it, thus:

и́на́че = **ина́че** *or* **и́наче**

Quite a number of predicative (or short) adjectives show a shift, or shifts, of stress as compared with their attributive forms. Such divergences are recorded as follows:

хоро́ший [17; хоро́ш, -а́] = [17; хоро́ш, хороша́, хорошо́ (*pl.* хороши́)]

The same system of stress designation applies, to accent shifts in the preterite forms of a number of verbs, e. g.:

да|ва́ть ..., <~ть> [... дал, -а́, -о; ... (дан, -а́)] = [... дал, дала́, да́ло (*pl.* да́ли); ... (дан, дана́, дано́, даны́)]

Insertion of the "epenthetic" o, e, between the two last stem consonants in masculine short forms has been noted in all adjectives where this applies, e. g.:

лёгкий ... [16; лёгок, легка́; *a.* лёгки] = [16; лёгок, легка́, легко́ (*pl.* легки́ *or* лёгки)]

If the stress in all short forms conforms to that of the attributive adjective the latter is merely provided with the abbreviation *sh.* (for *short form*) which indicates at the same time the possibility of forming such predicative forms, e. g.:

бога́тый [14 *sh.*] = [14; бога́т, бога́та, бога́то, бога́ты]

4. **Inflected forms.** All Russian inflected parts of speech appearing in the dictionary are listed in their appropriate basic forms, i. e. nominative singular (nouns, adjectives, numerals, certain pronouns) or infinitive (verbs). The gender of Russian nouns is indicated by means of one of three abbreviations in italics (*m*, *f*, *n*) after the headword.* Each inflected entry is followed, in square brackets [ ], by a figure which serves as reference to a definite paradigm within the system of conjugation and declension listed at the end of this book. Any variants of these paradigms are stated after the reference figure of each headword in question.

---

* For users of part II: Any Russian noun ending in a consonant *or* -й is of masculine gender;
those ending in -а *or* -я are of feminine gender;
those ending in -о *or* -е are of neuter gender.
In cases where this rule does not apply, as well as in nouns ending in -ь, the gender is indicated.

Example:

ло́жка *f* [5; *g/pl.*: -жек], like **ло́жа** *f* [5], is declined according to paradigm 5, except that in the genitive plural the former example inserts the "epenthetic" е between the two last stem consonants: ло́жек; cf. **ло́дка** *f* [5; *g/pl.*: -док] = [*g/pl.*: ло́док].

кусо́к *m* [1; -ска́] = the "epenthetic" о is omitted in the oblique cases of the singular and in all cases of the plural; cf. **коне́ц** *m* [1; -нца́] = [конца́, концу́, etc.].

As the prefixed forms of a verb follow the same inflection model and (with the exception of perfective aspects having the stressed prefix вы́-) mode of accentuation as the corresponding unprefixed verb, differences in stress, etc. have in cases of such aspect pairs been marked but once, viz. with the imperfective form.

5. **Government.** Case government, except for the accusative, is indicated with the help of Latin and Russian abbreviations. Emphasis has been laid on differences between the two languages, including the use of prepositions. Whenever a special case of government applies only to one of several meanings of a word, this has been duly recorded in connection with the meaning concerned. To ensure a clear differentiation of person and thing in government, the English and Russian notes to that effect show the necessary correspondence in sequence.

6. **Semantic distinction.** If a word has different meanings and, at the same time, different forms of inflection or aspect, this has been indicated by numbers (e. g. бить, коса́, коси́ть); otherwise a semicolon separates different meanings, a comma mere synonyms. Sense indicators in italics serve to specify individual shades of meanings, e. g. **поднима́ть** ... *трево́гу, пла́ту* raise; *ору́жие* take up; *флаг* hoist; *я́корь* weigh; *паруса́* set; *шум* make; **приёмный** ... *часы́* office; *экза́мен* entrance; *оте́ц, сын* foster.

In a number of Russian verbs the perfective aspect indicated (particularly with the prefixes <за-> and <по->) has, strictly speaking, the connotations "to begin to do s. th." (the former) and "to do s. th. for a (little) while" (the latter); but since these forms are very often rendered in English by means of the equivalent verb without any such additions they have occasionally been given as simple aspect counterparts without explicit indication as to their aforesaid connotations.

7. **Orthography.** In both the Russian and English parts newest spelling standards have been applied, and in the latter differences between American and British usage noted wherever possible and feasible.

Words at the end of a line which are always hyphenated are indicated by repetition of the hyphen (at the end of the first line and the beginning of the next line).

In parts of words or additions given in brackets a hyphen is placed within the bracket.

Abbreviations Used in the Dictionary

English Abbreviations

a.	*also* та́кже
abbr.	*abbreviation* сокраще́ние
ac.	*accusative* (*case*) вини́тельный паде́ж
adj.	*adjective* и́мя прилага́тельное
adv.	*adverb* наре́чие
ae.	*aeronautics* авиа́ция
agric.	*agriculture* се́льское хозя́йство
Am.	*Americanism* американи́зм
anat.	*anatomy* анато́мия
arch.	*architecture* архитекту́ра
astr.	*astronomy* астроно́мия
attr.	*attributive usage* атрибути́вное употребле́ние (т.е. в ка́честве определе́ния)
Bibl.	*Biblical* библе́йский
biol.	*biology* биоло́гия
Brt.	*British* (*English*) *usage* брита́нское (англи́йское) словоупотребле́ние
bot.	*botany* бота́ника
b.s.	*bad sense* в дурно́м смы́сле
chem.	*chemistry* хи́мия
cine.	*cinema* кинематогра́фия
cj.	*conjunction* сою́з
coll.	*colloquial usage* разгово́рный язы́к
collect.	*collective* (*noun*) собира́тельное и́мя (существи́тельное)
com.	*commonly* обыкнове́нно
comm.	*commercial term* торго́вля
comp.	*comparative* (*form*) сравни́тельная сте́пень
compds.	*compounds* сло́жные слова́
comput.	*computer* компью́терная те́хника
contp.	*contemptuously* пренебрежи́тельно
cul.	*culinary term* кулина́рия
dat.	*dative* (*case*) да́тельный паде́ж
dim.	*diminutive* уменьши́тельная фо́рма
dipl.	*diplomacy* диплома́тия
e.	*endings stressed* (*throughout*) ударе́ние (сплошь) на оконча́ниях
eccl.	*ecclesiastical term* церко́вное выраже́ние
econ.	*economy* эконо́мика
educ.	*education* шко́ла, шко́льное де́ло, педаго́гика
e.g.	*for example* наприме́р
el.	*electrical engineering* электроте́хника
esp.	*especially* осо́бенно
etc.	*et cetera* (*and so on*) и т. д. (и так да́лее)
euph.	*euphemism* эвфеми́зм
f	*feminine* (*gender*) же́нский род
fig.	*figurative usage* в перено́сном значе́нии
fin.	*financial term* фина́нсы, ба́нковое де́ло
f/pl.	*feminine plural* мно́жественное число́ же́нского ро́да
ft.	*future* (*tense*) бу́дущее вре́мя
gen.	*genitive* (*case*) роди́тельный паде́ж
geogr.	*geography* геогра́фия
geol.	*geology* геоло́гия
ger.	*gerund* геру́ндий (деепри-ча́стие)
g/pl.	*genitive plural* роди́тельный паде́ж мно́жественного числа́
g. pr. (*pt.*)	*present* (*past*) *gerund* дееприча́стие настоя́щего (проше́дшего) вре́мени
gr.	*grammar* грамма́тика
hist.	*history* исто́рия
hort.	*horticulture* садово́дство
hunt.	*hunting* охо́та
impers.	*impersonal* (*form*) безли́чная фо́рма, безли́чно
impf.	*imperfective* (*aspect*) несоверше́нный вид
(*im*)*pf.*	*imperfective and perfective* (*aspect*) несоверше́нный и соверше́нный вид
indecl.	*indeclinable word* несклоня́емое сло́во
inf.	*infinitive* инфинити́в, неопределённая фо́рма глаго́ла

instr. *instrumental* (*case*) твори́тельный падёж
int. *interjection* междоме́тие
interr. *interrogative*(*ly*) вопроси́тельная фо́рма, вопроси́тельно
iro. *ironically* ирони́чески
irr. *irregular* непра́вильная фо́рма
iter. *iterative*, *frequentative* (*aspect*) многокра́тный вид
joc. *jocular* шутли́во
ling. *linguistics* лингви́стика
lit. *literary* кни́жное выраже́ние
m *masculine* (*gender*) мужско́й род
math. *mathematics* матема́тика
med. *medicine* медици́на
mil. *military term* вое́нный те́рмин
min. *mineralogy* минерало́гия
mot. *motoring* автомобили́зм
m/pl. *masculine plural* мно́жественное число́ мужско́го ро́да
mst. *mostly* бо́льшей ча́стью
mus. *musical term* му́зыка
n *neuter* (*gender*) сре́днний род
naut. *nautical term* судохо́дство
no. *number* но́мер
nom. *nominative* (*case*) имени́тельный падёж
n/pl. *neuter plural* мно́жественное число́ сре́днего ро́да
o. a. *one another* друг дру́га, друг дру́гу
obs. *obsolete* устаре́вшее сло́во, выраже́ние
once *semelfactive* (*aspect*) однокра́тный вид
o. s. *oneself* себя́, себе́, -ся
P *popular* просторе́чие
p. *participle* прича́стие
p. *person* лицо́
P. *person* челове́к
paint. *painting* жи́вопись
part. *1. particle* части́ца; *2. particular*(*ly*) осо́бенно
part. g. *partitive genitive* роди́тельный раздели́тельный
pej. *pejorative* пейорашиьно, неодобри́шельно
pers. *person*(*al form*) лицо́, ли́чная фо́рма
pf. *perfective* (*aspect*) соверше́нный вид
pharm. *pharmacy* фармаце́втика
philos. *philosophy* филосо́фия
phot. *photography* фотогра́фия
phys. *physics* фи́зика
pl. *plural* мно́жественное число́
poet. *poetic* поэти́ческое сло́во, выраже́ние
pol. *politics* поли́тика
poss. *possessive* (*form*) притяжа́тельная фо́рма
p. pr. a. (*p.*) *present participle active* (*passive*) действи́тельное (страда́тельное) прича́стие настоя́щего вре́мени
p. pt. a. (*p.*) *past participle active* (*passive*) действи́тельное (страда́тельное) прича́стие проше́дшего вре́мени
pr. *present* (*tense*) настоя́щее вре́мя
pred. *predicative usage* предикати́вное употребле́ние (т. е. в ка́честве имено́й ча́сти сказу́емого)
pref. *prefix* приста́вка
pron. *pronoun* местоиме́ние
prp. *preposition* предло́г
pt. *preterite*, *past* (*tense*) проше́дшее вре́мя
rail. *railway* железнодоро́жное де́ло
refl. *reflexive* (*form*) возвра́тная фо́рма
rhet. *rhetoric* рито́рика
s. b. *somebody* кто-(кого́-, кому́-)нибудь
s. b.'s. *somebody's* че́й-нибудь
sew. *sewing* шве́йное де́ло
sg. *singular* еди́нственное число́
sh. *short* (*predicative*) *form* кра́ткая фо́рма
sl. *slang* жарго́н
st. *stem stressed* (*throughout*) ударе́ние (сплошь) на осно́ве
s. th. *something* что́-либо
su. *substantive*, *noun* и́мя

существи́тельное
tech. *technical* техни́ческий те́рмин
tel. *telephony* телефо́н
th. *thing* вещь, предме́т
thea. *theater* теа́тр
typ. *typography* типогра́фское де́ло
univ. *university* университе́т
usu. *usually* обы́чно
v/aux. *auxiliary verb* вспомога́тельный глаго́л
vb. *verb* глаго́л
v/i. *intransitive verb* неперехо́дный глаго́л
v/refl. *reflexive verb* возвра́тный глаго́л
v/t. *transitive verb* перехо́дный глаго́л
zo. *zoology* зооло́гия

Russian Abbreviations

И именительный паде́ж nominative (case).
Р роди́тельный паде́ж genitive (case).
Д да́тельный паде́ж dative (case).
В вини́тельный паде́ж accusative (case).
Т твори́тельный паде́ж instrumental (case).
П предло́жный паде́ж prepositional *or* locative (case).
и т. д. (и так да́лее) etc. (et cetera).
и т. п. (и тому́ подо́бное) and the like.
лат. лати́нский язы́к Latin.
тж. та́кже also.

Russian Pronunciation

I. Vowels

1. All vowels in stressed position are half-long in Russian.

2. In unstressed position Russian vowels are very short, except in the first pretonic syllable, where this shortness of articulation is less marked. Some vowel letters (notably о, е, я), when read in unstressed position, not only differ in length (quantity), but also change their timbre, i.e. acoustic quality.

Russian letter		Explanation of its pronunciation	Transcription symbol
а	stressed	= **a** in 'f**a**ther', but shorter: ма́ма ['mamə] *mamma*	a
	unstressed	1. = **a** in the above examples, but shorter – in first pretonic syllable: карма́н [kar'man] *pocket*	a
		2. = **a** in '**a**go, **a**bout' – in post-tonic or second, etc. pretonic syllable(s): ата́ка [a'takə] *attack* каранда́ш [kəran'daʃ] *pencil*	ə
		3. = **i** in 's**i**t' – after ч, щ in first pretonic syllable: часы́ [ţʃ̡ɪ'sɨ] *watch* щади́ть [ʃ̡ţʃ̡ɪ'd̡iţ] *spare*	ɪ
е	Preceding consonant (except ж, ш, ц) is soft.		
	stressed	1. = **ye** in '**ye**t' – in initial position, i.e. at the beginning of a word, or after a vowel, ъ, ь (if not ё) before a hard consonant: бытие́ [bɨţi'jɛ] *existence* ел [jɛɫ] *(I) ate* нет [ņɛt] *no*	jɛ/ɛ
		2. = **e** in 's**e**t' – after consonants, soft or hard (ж, ш, ц), before a hard consonant, as well as in final position, i.e. at the end of a word, after consonants: на лице́ [naļi'tsɛ] *on the face* шест [ʃɛst] *pole*	ɛ
		3. = **ya** in **Ya**le; before a soft consonant: ель [jeļ] *fir* петь [p̡eţ] *to sing*	je/e
	unstressed	1. = s**i**t; in initial position and after a vowel preceded by (j) ещё [jɪ'ʃ̡ţʃ̡ɔ] *still* зна́ет ['znajɪt] *(he, she, it) knows* река́ [r̡ɪ'ka] *river*	jɪ/ɪ

Russian letter	Explanation of its pronunciation	Transcription symbol
	2. = **ы** (cf.) after ж, ш, ц: жена́ [ʒɨ'na] *wife* цена́ [tsɨ'na] *price*	ɨ
ё	Preceding consonant (except ж, ш, ц) is soft. only stressed = **yo** in be**yo**nd ёлка ['jɔɫkə] *fir tree* даёт [da'jɔt] (*he, she, it*) *gives* лёд [ļɔt] *ice*	jɔ/ɔ
и	Preceding consonant (except ж, ш, ц) is soft. 1. stressed = like **ee** in s**ee**n, but shorter – in the instr/sg. of он/оно́ and the oblique forms of они́ initial и- may be pronounced (ji-): и́ва ['ivə] *willow* юри́ст [ju'ŗist] *lawyer* их [ix] *or* [jix] *of them* (*g/pl.*)	i/ji
	2. unstressed = like **ee** in s**ee**n, but shorter – in first pretonic syllable: мину́та [m̦i'nutə] *minute*	i
	= **i** in s**i**t – in post-tonic or second, etc. pretonic syllable(s): хо́дит ['xɔd̦it] (*he, she, it*) *goes*	ı
	3. stressed and unstressed = **ы** (cf.) after ж, ш, ц: ши́на ['ʃɨnə] *tire* цили́ндр [tsɨ'ļindr] *cylinder*	ɨ
о	stressed = **o** in **o**bey: том [tɔm] *volume*	ɔ
	unstressed 1. = **o** in **o**bey; in final position of foreign words кака́о [ka'kaɔ] *cocoa*	ɔ
	2. = **a** in f**a**ther, but shorter – in first pretonic syllable: Москва́ [mas'kva] *Moscow*	a
	3. = **a** in **a**go, **a**bout – in post-tonic or second, etc. pretonic syllable(s): со́рок ['sɔrək] *forty* огоро́д [əga'rɔt] *kitchen garden*	ə
у	stressed and unstressed= like **oo** in b**oo**m, but shorter бу́ду ['budu] (*I*) *will be*	u
ы	stressed and unstressed= a retracted variety of **i**, as in h**i**ll; no English equivalent: вы [vɨ] *you*	
э	stressed and unstressed 1. = **e** in s**e**t э́то ['ɛtə] *this* эскóрт [ɛs'kɔrt] *escort*	

Russian letter	Explanation of its pronunciation	Transcription symbol
	2. = resembles the English sound **a** in p**a**le (but without the i-component) – before a soft consonant э́ти ['eţı] *these*	e
ю	Preceding consonant is soft. stressed and unstressed = like **yu** in **yu**le, but shorter рабо́таю [ra'bɔtəju] *(I) work* сюда́ [şu'da] *here*	ju/u
я	Preceding consonant is soft.	ja/a
	stressed 1. = **ya** in **ya**rd, but shorter – in initial position, after a vowel and before a hard consonant: я́ма ['jamə] *pit* моя́ [ma'ja] *my* мя́со ['ṃasə] *meat*	
	2. = **a** in b**a**d – in interpalatal position, i.e. between soft consonants: пять [ṗæţ] *five*	æ
	unstressed 1. = **a** in '**a**go' (preceded by j after vowels) – in final position: со́я [sɔjə] *soya bean* неде́ля [ņı'ḍeļə] *week*	jə/ə
	2. = **i** in 's**i**t', but preceded by (j) – in initial position, i.e. also after a vowel and ъ: язы́к [jı'zɨk] *tongue* та́ять ['tajıţ] *to thaw* мясни́к [ṃış'ņik] *butcher*	jı/ı

II. Semivowel

Russian letter	Explanation of its pronunciation	Transcription symbol
й	1. = **y** in **y**et – in initial position, i.e. also after a vowel, in loan words: йод [jɔt] *iodine* майо́р [ma'jɔr] *major*	j
	2. = in the formation of diphthongs as their second element:	j
ай	= (i) of (ai) in t**i**me: май [maj] *May*	aj
ой	stressed = **oi** in n**oi**se: бой [bɔj] *fight*	ɔj
	unstressed = **i** in t**i**me: война́ [vaj'na] *war*	aj
уй	= **u** in r**u**le + (j): бу́йвол ['bujvəł] *buffalo*	uj
ый	= ы (cf.) + (j): вы́йти ['vɨjţı] *to go out* кра́сный ['krasnɨj] *red*	ɨj

Russian letter		Explanation of its pronunciation	Transcription symbol
ий		= и (cf.) + (j):	ij
	stressed	австри́йка [af'sţrijkə] *Austrian woman*	
	unstressed	си́ний ['şiņıj] *blue*	
ей	stressed	= (j+) **a** in p**a**le:	jej/ej
		ей [jej] *to her*	
		ле́йка ['ļejkə] *watering-can*	
	unstressed	= **ee** in s**ee**n, but shorter + (j):	ıj
		сейча́с [şı(j)'ţʃas] *now*	
юй		= to (cf.) + (j):	juj/uj
		малю́й! [ma'ļuj] *paint!*	
яй	stressed	= (j+) **a** in b**a**d + (j):	jæj/æj
		я́йца ['jæjtsə] *eggs*	
		лентя́й ['ļın'ţæj] *lazy bones*	
	unstressed	**yi** in **Yi**ddish:	jı
		яйцо́ [jı(j)'tsɔ] *egg*	

III. Consonants

1. As most Russian consonants may be palatalized (or 'softened') there is, in addition to the series of normal ('hard') consonants, an almost complete set of 'soft' parallel sounds. According to traditional Russian spelling, in writing or printing this 'softness' is marked by a combination of such palatalized consonants with the vowels е, ё, и, ю, я or, either in final position or before a consonant, the so-called 'soft sign' (ь). In phonetic transcription palatalized consonants are indicated by means of a small hook, or comma, attached to them. As a rule a hard consonant before a soft one remains hard; only з, с may be softened before palatalized з, с, д, т, н.
2. The following consonants are always hard: ж, ш, ц.
3. The following consonants are always soft: ч, щ.
4. The voiced consonants б, в, г, д, ж, з are pronounced voicelessly (i.e. = п, ф, к, т, ш, с) in final position.
5. The voiced consonants б, в, г, ж, з, when followed by (one of) their voiceless counterparts п, ф, к, т, ш, с, are pronounced voicelessly (regressive assimilation) and vice versa: voiceless before voiced is voiced (except that there is no assimilation before в).
6. The articulation of doubled consonants, particularly those following a stressed syllable, is marked by their lengthening.

Russian letter		Explanation of its pronunciation	Transcription symbol
б	hard	= **b** in **b**ad: брат [brat] *brother*	b
	soft	= as in al**b**ion:	ḅ
		бе́лка ['ḅełkə] *squirrel*	

Russian letter			Explanation of its pronunciation	Transcription symbol
в	hard		= **w** in **v**ery: водá [va'da] *water*	v
	soft		= as in **v**iew: вéна ['ᶌɛnə] *vein*	ᶌ
г	hard		= **g** in **g**un: газ [gas] *gas*	g
	soft		= as in ar**g**ue: гимн [ᶃimn] *anthem*	ᶃ
		Note:	= (v) in endings -ого, -его: больнóго [baᶅ'nɔvə] *of the sick* сúнего ['ᶊiᶇɪvə] *of the blue* ничегó [ᶇɪƫᶋɪ'vɔ] *nothing*	v
			= (x) in бог *God* and in the combination -гк-, -гч-: мягкий ['ᶆaxᶄɪj] *soft* мя́гче ['ᶆaxƫᶋɛ] *softer*	x
д	hard		= **d** in **d**oor: дáма ['damə] *lady*	d
	soft		= as in **d**ew: дю́на ['ᶁunə] *dune* In the combination -здн- д is mute: пóздно ['pɔznə] *late*	ᶁ
ж	hard		= **s** in mea**s**ure, but hard: жáжда ['ʒaʒdə] *thirst*	ʒ
		жч	= щ: мужчúна [mu'ᶋƫᶋinə] *man*	ᶋƫᶋ
з	hard		= **z** in **z**oo: закóн [za'kɔn] *law*	z
	soft		= as in pre**s**ume: зелёный [ᶎɪ'ᶅɔnɨj] *green*	ᶎ
		зж	= hard or soft doubled ж: пóзже ['pɔʒʒɛ] *or* ['pɔʓʓɛ] *later*	ʒʒ/ʓʓ
		зч	= щ: извóчик [iz'vɔᶋƫᶋɪk] *coachman*	ᶋƫᶋ
к	hard		= **c** in **c**ome (unaspirated!): как [kak] *how*	k
	soft		= like **k** in **k**ey: кéпка ['ᶄɛpkə] *cap*	ᶄ
л	hard		= **ll** in General American call: лáмпа ['łampə] *lamp*	ł
	soft		= **ll** in mi**ll**ion: лúлия ['ᶅiᶅɪjə] *lily*	ᶅ
м	hard		= **m** in **m**an: мать [maƫ] *mother*	m
	soft		= as in **m**ute: метр [ᶆɛtr] *meter*	ᶆ
н	hard		= **n** in **n**oise: нос [nɔs] *nose*	n
	soft		= **n** in **n**ew: нéбо ['ᶇɛbə] *heaven*	ᶇ
п	hard		= **p** in **p**art (unaspirated!): пáпа ['papə] *daddy*	p
	soft		= as in scor**p**ion: пить [ᶈiƫ] *to drink*	ᶈ
р	hard		= trilled **r**: рот [rɔt] *mouth*	r
	soft		= as in O**ri**ent: ряд [ᶉat] *row*	ᶉ

Russian letter		Explanation of its pronunciation	Transcription symbol
с	hard	= **s** in **s**ad: сорт [sɔrt] *sort*	s
	soft	= as in a**ss**ume: си́ла ['şiłə] *force*	ş
	сч	= щ: сча́стье ['ʃ̡ţʃ̡æşţjɛ] *happiness*	ʃ̡ţʃ̡
т	hard	= **t** in **t**ent (unaspirated!): такт [takt] *measure*	t
	soft	= as in **t**une: тепе́рь [ţı'peŗ] *now*	ţ
		= -стн-, -стл- – in these combinations -т- is mute: изве́стно [iz'v̡ɛsnə] *known* счастли́вый [ʃ̡ţʃ̡ış'ļivɨj] *happy*	
ф	hard	= **f** in **f**ar: фо́рма ['fɔrmə] *form*	f
	soft	= as in **f**ew: фи́рма ['f̡irmə] *firm*	f̡
х	hard	= **ch** as in Scottish lo**ch**: ах! [ax] *ah!*	x
	soft	= like **ch** in German i**ch**, no English equivalent: хи́мик ['x̡im̡ık] *chemist*	x̡
ц	always hard	= **ts** in **ts**ar: царь [tsaŗ] *tsar*	ts
ч	always soft	= **ch** in **ch**eck: час [ţʃ̡as] *hour*	ţʃ̡
ш	always hard	= **sh** in **sh**ip, but hard: шар [ʃar] *ball*	ʃ
щ	always soft	= **sh** + **ch** in **ch**eck, cf. fre**sh ch**eeks, or = doubled (ʃ̡ʃ̡) as in sure: щи [ʃ̡ţʃ̡i] *or* [ʃ̡ʃ̡i] *cabbage soup*	ʃ̡ţʃ̡ *or* ʃ̡ʃ̡

IV. Surds

ъ hard sign = The *jer* or ‘hard sign’ separates a hard (final) consonant of a prefix and the initial vowel, preceded by (j), of the following root, thus marking both the hardness of the preceding consonant and the distinct utterance of (j) before the vowel: предъяви́ть [pŗıdjı'v̡iţ] ‘to show, produce’ съезд [sjɛst] ‘congress’.

ь soft sign = The *jer* or ‘soft sign’ serves to represent the palatal or soft quality of a (preceding) consonant in final position or before another consonant, cf.:

брат [brat] ‘brother’ and брать [braţ] ‘to take’ по́лка ['pɔłkə] ‘shelf’ and по́лька ['pɔļkə] ‘polka, Pole (= Polish woman)’.

Russian letter	Explanation of its pronunciation	Transcription symbol
	It is also used before vowels to indicate the softness of a preceding consonant as well as the pronunciation of (j) with the respective vowel, e. g.: семья́ [şım̡'ja] 'family' – *cf.* се́мя ['şem̡ə] 'seed', and in foreign words, such as батальо́н [bəta'l̡jɔn] 'battalion'.	

English Pronunciation

Vowels

[ɑː] *father* ['fɑːðə]
[æ] *man* [mæn]
[e] *get* [get]
[ə] *about* [ə'baʊt]
[ɜː] *first* [fɜːst]
[ɪ] *stick* [stɪk]
[iː] *need* [niːd]
[ɒ] *hot* [hɒt
[ɔː] *law* [lɔː]
[ʌ] *mother* ['mʌðə]
[ʊ] *book* [bʊk]
[uː] *fruit* [fruːt]

Diphthongs

[aɪ] *time* [taɪm]
[aʊ] *cloud* [klaʊd]
[eɪ] *name* [neɪm]
[eə] *hair* [heə]
[ɪə] *here* [hɪə]
[ɔɪ] *point* [pɔɪnt]
[əʊ] *oath* [əʊθ]
[ʊə] *tour* [tʊə]

Consonants

[b] *bag* [bæg]
[d] *dear* [dɪə]
[f] *fall* [fɔːl]
[g] *give* [gɪv]
[h] *hole* [həʊl]
[j] *yes* [jes]
[k] *come* [kʌm]
[l] *land* [lænd]
[m] *mean* [miːn]
[n] *night* [naɪt]
[p] *pot* [pɒt]
[r] *right* [raɪt]
[s] *sun* [sʌn]
[t] *take* [teɪk]
[v] *vain* [veɪn]
[w] *wait* [weɪt]
[z] *rose* [rəʊz]
[ŋ] *bring* [brɪŋ]
[ʃ] *she* [ʃiː]
[tʃ] *chair* [tʃeə]
[dʒ] *join* [dʒɔɪn]
[ʒ] *leisure* ['leʒə]
[θ] *think* [θɪŋk]
[ð] *the* [ðə]
['] means that the following syllable is stressed: *ability* [ə'bɪlətɪ]

The Russian Alphabet

printed		written		pronounced	transcribed	printed		written		pronounced	transcribed
А	а	А	а	а	a	П	п	П	п	пэ	pɛ
Б	б	Б	б	бэ	bɛ	Р	р	Р	р	эр	ɛr
В	в	В	в	вэ	vɛ	С	с	С	с	эс	ɛs
Г	г	Г	г	гэ	gɛ	Т	т	Т	т	тэ	tɛ
Д	д	Д	д	дэ	dɛ	У	у	У	у	у	u
Е	е	Е	е	е	jɛ	Ф	ф	Ф	ф	эф	ɛf
Ё	ё	Ё	ё	ё	jɔ	Х	х	Х	х	ха	xa
Ж	ж	Ж	ж	жэ	ʒɛ	Ц	ц	Ц	ц	цэ	tsɛ
З	з	З	з	зэ	zɛ	Ч	ч	Ч	ч	че	t̡ʃ̡e
И	и	И	и	и	i	Ш	ш	Ш	ш	ша	ʃa
Й	й	Й	й	и[1])		Щ	щ	Щ	щ	ща	ʃ̡t̡ʃ̡a
К	к	К	к	ка	ka	Ъ	ъ	–	ъ	[2])	
Л	л	Л	л	эль	ɛl̡	Ы	ы	–	ы	ы[3])	ɨ
М	м	М	м	эм	ɛm	Ь	ь	–	ь	[4])	
Н	н	Н	н	эн	ɛn	Э	э	Э	э	э[5])	ɛ
О	о	О	о	о	ɔ	Ю	ю	Ю	ю	ю	iu
						Я	я	Я	я	я	ia

[1]) и кра́ткое short i
[2]) твёрдый знак hard sign
[3]) *or* еры́
[4]) мя́гкий знак soft sign
[5]) э оборо́тное reversed e

Important English Irregular Verbs

alight	alighted, alit	alighted, alit
arise	arose	arisen
awake	awoke	awoken, awaked
be (am, is, are)	was (were)	been
bear	bore	borne
beat	beat	beaten
become	became	become
begin	began	begun
behold	beheld	beheld
bend	bent	bent
beseech	besought, beseeched	besought, beseeched
bet	bet, betted	bet, betted
bid	bade, bid	bidden, bid
bind	bound	bound
bite	bit	bitten
bleed	bled	bled
blow	blew	blown
break	broke	broken
breed	bred	bred
bring	brought	brought
broadcast	broadcast	broadcast
build	built	built
burn	burnt, burned	burnt, burned
burst	burst	burst
bust	bust(ed)	bust(ed)
buy	bought	bought
cast	cast	cast
catch	caught	caught
choose	chose	chosen
cleave (*cut*)	clove, cleft	cloven, cleft
cling	clung	clung
come	came	come
cost	cost	cost
creep	crept	crept
crow	crowed, crew	crowed
cut	cut	cut
deal	dealt	dealt
dig	dug	dug
do	did	done
draw	drew	drawn
dream	dreamt, dreamed	dreamt, dreamed
drink	drank	drunk
drive	drove	driven
dwell	dwelt, dwelled	dwelt, dwelled
eat	ate	eaten
fall	fell	fallen
feed	fed	fed
feel	felt	felt
fight	fought	fought
find	found	found
flee	fled	fled

fling	flung	flung
fly	flew	flown
forbear	forbore	forborne
forbid	forbad(e)	forbidden
forecast	forecast(ed)	forecast(ed)
forget	forgot	forgotten
forgive	forgave	forgiven
forsake	forsook	forsaken
freeze	froze	frozen
get	got	got, *Am.* gotten
give	gave	given
go	went	gone
grind	ground	ground
grow	grew	grown
hang	hung, (*v/t*) hanged	hung, (*v/t*) hanged
have	had	had
hear	heard	heard
heave	heaved, hove	heaved, hove
hew	hewed	hewed, hewn
hide	hid	hidden
hit	hit	hit
hold	held	held
hurt	hurt	hurt
keep	kept	kept
kneel	knelt, kneeled	knelt, kneeled
know	knew	known
lay	laid	laid
lead	led	led
lean	leaned, leant	leaned, leant
leap	leaped, leapt	leaped, leapt
learn	learned, learnt	learned, learnt
leave	left	left
lend	lent	lent
let	let	let
lie	lay	lain
light	lighted, lit	lighted, lit
lose	lost	lost
make	made	made
mean	meant	meant
meet	met	met
mow	mowed	mowed, mown
pay	paid	paid
plead	pleaded, pled	pleaded, pled
prove	proved	proved, proven
put	put	put
quit	quit(ted)	quit(ted)
read [riːd]	read [red]	read [red]
rend	rent	rent
rid	rid	rid
ride	rode	ridden
ring	rang	rung
rise	rose	risen
run	ran	run
saw	sawed	sawn, sawed

say	said	said
see	saw	seen
seek	sought	sought
sell	sold	sold
send	sent	sent
set	set	set
sew	sewed	sewed, sewn
shake	shook	shaken
shear	sheared	sheared, shorn
shed	shed	shed
shine	shone	shone
shit	shit(ted), shat	shit(ted), shat
shoe	shod	shod
shoot	shot	shot
show	showed	shown
shrink	shrank	shrunk
shut	shut	shut
sing	sang	sung
sink	sank	sunk
sit	sat	sat
slay	slew	slain
sleep	slept	slept
slide	slid	slid
sling	slung	slung
slink	slunk	slunk
slit	slit	slit
smell	smelt, smelled	smelt, smelled
smite	smote	smitten
sow	sowed	sown, sowed
speak	spoke	spoken
speed	sped, speeded	sped, speeded
spell	spelt, spelled	spelt, spelled
spend	spent	spent
spill	spilt, spilled	spilt, spilled
spin	spun, span	spun
spit	spat	spat
split	split	split
spoil	spoiled, spoilt	spoiled, spoilt
spread	spread	spread
spring	sprang, sprung	sprung
stand	stood	stood
stave	staved, stove	staved, stove
steal	stole	stolen
stick	stuck	stuck
sting	stung	stung
stink	stunk, stank	stunk
strew	strewed	strewed, strewn
stride	strode	stridden
strike	struck	struck
string	strung	strung
strive	strove	striven
swear	swore	sworn
sweep	swept	swept
swell	swelled	swollen

swim	swam	swum
swing	swung	swung
take	took	taken
teach	taught	taught
tear	tore	torn
tell	told	told
think	thought	thought
thrive	throve	thriven
throw	threw	thrown
thrust	thrust	thrust
tread	trod	trodden
understand	understood	understood
wake	woke, waked	woken, waked
wear	wore	worn
weave	wove	woven
wed	wed(ded)	wed(ded)
weep	wept	wept
wet	wet(ted)	wet(ted)
win	won	won
wind	wound	wound
wring	wrung	wrung
write	wrote	written

Russian-English

A

а 1. *cj.* but; ***а то*** or (else), otherwise; ***а что?*** why (so)?; **2.** *int.* ah!; **3.** *part., coll.* eh?

аб|ажу́р *m* [1] lampshade; **~ба́т** *m* [1] abbot; **~ба́тство** *n* [9] abbey; **~за́ц** *m* [1] paragraph; **~онеме́нт** *m* [1] subscription; **~оне́нт** *m* [1] subscriber; **~о́рт** *m* [1] abortion; **~рико́с** *m* [1] apricot; **~солю́тный** [14; -тен, -тна] absolute; **~стра́ктный** [14; -тен, -тна] abstract; **~су́рд** *m* [1] absurdity; ***довести́ до ~су́рда*** carry to the point of absurdity; **~су́рдный** [14; -ден, -дна] absurd; **~сце́сс** *m* [1] abscess

аван|га́рд *m* [1] avant-garde; **~по́ст** *m* [1] outpost; **~с** *m* [1] advance (of money); **~сом** (payment) in advance; **~тю́ра** *f* [5] adventure, shady enterprise; **~тюри́ст** *m* [1] adventurer; **~тюри́стка** *f* [5; *g/pl.*: -ток] adventuress

авар|и́йный [14] emergency...; **~ия** *f* [7] accident; *mot., ae.* crash; *tech.* breakdown

а́вгуст *m* [1] August

авиа|ба́за *f* [5] air base; **~биле́т** *m* [1] airline ticket; **~констру́ктор** *m* [1] aircraft designer; **~ли́ния** *f* [7] airline; **~но́сец** *m* [1; -сца] aircraft carrier; **~по́чта** *f* [5] air mail; **~тра́сса** *f* [5] air route; **~цио́нный** [14] air-(craft)...; **~ция** *f* [7] aviation, aircraft *pl.*

аво́сь *part. coll.* perhaps, maybe; ***на ~*** on the off chance

австр|али́ец *m* [1; -и́йца], **~али́йка** *f* [5; *g/pl.*: -и́ек], **~али́йский** [16] Australian; **~и́ец** *m* [1; -йца], **~и́йка** *f* [5; *g/pl.*: -и́ек], **~и́йский** [16] Austrian

автобиогр|афи́ческий [16], **~афи́чный** [14; -чен, -чна] autobiographic(al); **~а́фия** *f* [7] autobiography

авто́бус *m* [1] (motor) bus

авто|вокза́л *m* [1] bus *or* coach station; **~го́нки** *f/pl.* [5; *gen.*: -нок] (car) race; **~граф** *m* [1] autograph; **~заво́д** *m* [1] car factory, automobile plant; **~запра́вочный** [14]; ***~запра́вочная ста́нция*** filling station; **~кра́тия** *f* [7] autocracy; **~магистра́ль** *f* [8] highway; **~ма́т** *m* [1] automaton; ***иго́рный*** slot machine; *mil.* submachine gun; *coll.* telephone box *or* booth; **~мати́ческий** [16], **~мати́чный** [14; -чен, -чна] automatic; **~ма́тчик** *m* [1] submachine gunner; **~маши́на** *f* [5] → ***~моби́ль***; **~мобили́ст** *m* [1] motorist; **~моби́ль** *m* [4] (motor)car; ***го́ночный ~моби́ль*** racing car, racer; **~но́мия** *f* [7] autonomy; **~отве́тчик** *m* [1] answering machine; **~портре́т** *m* [1] self-portrait

а́втор *m* [1] author; **~изова́ть** [7] *(im)pf.* authorize; **~ите́т** *m* [1] authority; **~ский** [16] author's; ***~ское пра́во*** copyright; **~ство** *n* [9] authorship

авто|ру́чка *f* [5; *g/pl.*: -чек] fountain pen; **~стоя́нка** *f* [5; *g/pl.*: -нок] parking (space); **~стра́да** *f* [5] high-speed, multilane highway

ага́ (*int.*) aha!; (oh,) I see!

аге́нт *m* [1] agent; **~ство** *n* [9] agency

агити́ровать [7], <с-> *pol.* agitate; agitation, campaign; *coll.* (***убежда́ть***) (try to) persuade

агра́рный [14] agrarian

агрега́т *m* [1] *tech.* unit, assembly

агресс|и́вный [14; -вен, -вна] aggressive; **~ия** *f* [7] aggression

агро|но́м *m* [1] agronomist; **~номи́ческий** [16] agronomic(al); **~но́мия** *f* [7] agronomy

ад *m* [1; в ~у́] hell

ада́птер (-tɛr) *m* [1] *el.* pickup

адвока́т *m* [1] lawyer, attorney (at

law), *Brt.* barrister; solicitor; **~у́ра** *f* [5] the legal profession
адеква́тный [14; -тен, -тна] (*совпада́ющий*) coincident; adequate
адми|нистрати́вный [14] administrative; **~нистра́ция** *f* [7] administration; **~ра́л** *m* [1] admiral
а́дрес *m* [1; *pl.*: -á, *etc. e.*] address (***не по ~у*** Д at the wrong address); **~а́т** *m* [1] addressee; (*грузополуча́тель*) consignee; **~ова́ть** [7] (*im*)*pf.* address, direct
а́дски *coll.* awfully, terribly
а́дский [16] hellish, infernal
адъюта́нт *m* [1] aide-de-camp
адюльте́р *m* [1] adultery
ажиота́ж *m* [1] hullabaloo; **~ный** [14; -жен, -жна]: ***~ный спрос*** unusually high demand (for ***на*** В)
аз *m* [1 *e.*]: **~ы́** *pl.* basics, elements; *coll.* ***с ~о́в*** from scratch
аза́рт *m* [1] passion, heat, enthusiasm; ***войти́ в ~*** get excited; **~ный** [14; -тен, -тна] passionate, enthusiastic; ***~ные и́гры*** games of chance
а́збу|ка *f* [5] alphabet; **~чный** [14] alphabetic(al); ***~чная и́стина*** truism
азербайджа́|нец *m* [1; -нца], **~нка** *f* [5; *g/pl.*: -нок] Azerbaijani(an); **~ский** [16] Azerbaijani(an)
азиа́т *m* [1], **~ка** *f* [5; *g/pl.*: -ток], **~ский** [16] Asian, Asiatic
азо́т *m* [1] nitrogen; **~ный** [14] nitric
а́ист *m* [1] stork
ай *int.* ah!; oh!; *при бо́ли* ouch!
айва́ *f* [5], quince
а́йсберг *m* [1] iceberg
акаде́м|ик *m* [1] academician; **~и́ческий** [16] academic; **~ия** *f* [7] academy; ***Акаде́мия нау́к*** academy of sciences; ***Акаде́мия худо́жеств*** academy of arts
ака́ция *f* [7] acacia
аквала́нг *m* [1] aqualung
акваре́ль *f* [8] water colo(u)r
акклиматизи́ровать(ся) [7] (*im*)*pf.* acclimatize
аккомпан|еме́нт *m* [1] *mus.*, *fig.* accompaniment; **~и́ровать** [7] *mus.* accompany
акко́рд *m* [1] *mus.* chord
аккредит|и́в *m* [1] letter of credit; **~ова́ть** [7] (*im*)*pf.* accredit
аккумул|и́ровать [7] (*im*)*pf.* accumulate; **~я́тор** *m* [1] battery
аккура́тный [14; -тен, -тна] (*исполни́тельный*) accurate; punctual; *рабо́та и т. д.* tidy, neat
аксессуа́ры *m* [1] accessories
акт *m* [1] act(ion); *thea.* act; document; *parl.* bill; **~ёр** *m* [1] actor
акти́в *m* [1] *fin.* asset(s); **~ный** [14; -вен, -вна] active
актри́са *f* [5] actress
актуа́льный [14; -лен, -льна] topical, current
аку́ла *f* [5] shark
аку́сти|ка *f* [5] acoustics; **~ческий** [16] acoustic(al)
акуше́р|ка *f* [5; *g/pl.*: -рок] midwife; **~ство** *n* [9] obstetrics, midwifery
акце́нт *m* [1] accent; (*ударе́ние*) stress
акци|оне́р *m* [1] stockholder, *Brt.* shareholder; **~оне́рный** [14] joint-stock (company); **~они́ровать** [7] turn into a joint-stock company; **´~я¹** *f* [7] share; *pl. a.* stock; **´~я²** *f* [7] action
алба́н|ец *m* [1; -ца], **~ка** *f* [5; *g/pl.*: -ок], **~ский** [16] Albanian
а́лгебра *f* [5] algebra
алеба́стр *m* [1] alabaster
але́ть [8] blush, grow red; *заря́ и т. д.* glow
алиме́нты *m/pl.* [1] alimony
алкого́л|ик *m* [1] alcoholic; **~ь** *m* [4] alcohol
аллегори́ческий [16] allegorical
аллерг|е́н *m* [1] allergen; **~ик** *m* [1] person prone to allergies; **~и́ческий** [16] allergic; **~и́я** *f* [7] allergy
алле́я *f* [6; *g/pl.*: -е́й] avenue, lane
алма́з *m* [1], **~ный** [14] (uncut) diamond
алта́рь *m* [4 *e.*] altar
алфави́т *m* [1] alphabet; **~ный** [14] alphabetical
а́лчн|ость *f* [7] greed(iness); **~ый** [14; -чен, -чна] greedy (for ***к*** Д)
а́лый [14 *sh.*] red
альбо́м *m* [1] album; sketchbook
альмана́х *m* [1] literary miscellany
альпини́|зм *m* [1] mountaineering; **~ст** *m* [1], **~стка** *f* [5; *g/pl.*: -ток] mountaineer
альт *m* [1 *e.*] alto; *инструме́нт* viola

алюми́ний *m* [3] alumin(i)um
амба́р *m* [1] barn; ***для хране́ния зерна́*** granary
амбулато́рный [14]: ~ ***больно́й*** outpatient
америка́н|ец *m* [1; -нца], **~ка** *f* [5; *g/pl.*: -ок], **~ский** [16] American
ами́нь *part.* amen
амнисти́|ровать [7] *(im)pf.*; **~я** *f* [7] amnesty
амортиз|а́тор *m* [1] shock absorber; **~а́ция** *f* [7] amortization, depreciation
амо́рфный [14; -фен, -фна] amorphous
амплиту́да *f* [5] amplitude
амплуа́ *n* [*indecl.*] *thea.* type, role
а́мпула *f* [5] ampoule
ампут|а́ция *f* [7] amputation; **~и́ровать** [7] *(im)pf.* amputate
амфи́бия *f* [7] amphibian
амфитеа́тр *m* [1] amphitheater (-tre); *thea.* circle
ана́ли|з *m* [1] analysis; **~зи́ровать** [7] *(im)pf.*, <про-> analyze, -se
аналог|и́чный [14; -чен, -чна] analogous, similar; **~ия** *f* [7] analogy
анана́с *m* [1] pineapple
ана́рхия *f* [7] anarchy
анато́мия *f* [7] anatomy
анга́р *m* [1] hangar
а́нгел *m* [1] angel
анги́на *f* [5] tonsillitis
англи́|йский [16] English; **~ст** *m* [1] specialist in English studies; **~ча́нин** *m* [1; *pl.*: -ча́не, -ча́н] Englishman; **~ча́нка** *f* [5; *g/pl.*: -нок] Englishwoman
анекдо́т *m* [1] anecdote; **~и́чный** [14; -чен, -чна] anecdotal; (*маловероя́тный*) improbable
ане|ми́я *f* [7] anemia; **~стези́я** (-nɛstɛ-) *f* [7] anaesthesia
ани́с *m* [1] anise
анке́та *f* [5] questionnaire; (*бланк*) form
аннекс|и́ровать [7] *(im)pf.* annex; **~ия** *f* [7] annexation
аннули́ровать [7] *(im)pf.* annul, cancel
анома́лия *f* [7] anomaly
анони́мный [14; -мен, -мна] anonymous
анса́мбль *m* [4] ensemble, *thea.* company
антагони́зм *m* [1] antagonism
антаркти́ческий [16] Antarctic
анте́нна (-'tɛn-) *f* [5] aerial, antenna
антибио́тик *m* [1] antibiotic
антиква́р *m* [1] antiquary; dealer in antique goods; **~иа́т** *m* [1] antiques; **~ный** [14] antiquarian
антило́па *f* [5] antelope
анти|пати́чный [14; -чен, -чна] antipathetic; **~па́тия** *f* [7] antipathy; **~санита́рный** [14] insanitary; **~семити́зм** *m* [1] anti-Semitism; **~се́птика** *f* [5] antisepsis, *collect.* antiseptics
анти́чн|ость *f* [8] antiquity; **~ый** [14] ancient, classical
антоло́гия *f* [7] anthology
антра́кт *m* [1] *thea.* intermission, *Brt.* interval
антропо́л|ог *m* [1] anthropologist; **~о́гия** *f* [7] anthropology
анчо́ус *m* [1] anchovy
аню́тины [14]: ~ ***гла́зки*** *m/pl.* [1; *g/pl.*: -зок] pansy
апат|и́чный [14; -чен, -чна] apathetic; **~ия** *f* [7] apathy
апелл|и́ровать [7] *(im)pf.* appeal (**к** Д to); **~яцио́нный** [14] (*court*) of appeal; ***~яцио́нная жа́лоба*** = **~я́ция** *f* [7] *law* appeal
апельси́н *m* [1] orange
аплоди́|ровать [7], <за-> applaud; **~сме́нты** *m/pl.* [1] applause
апло́мб *m* [1] self-confidence, aplomb
апоге́й *m* [3] *ast.* apogee; *fig.* climax
апо́стол *m* [1] apostle
апофео́з *m* [1] apotheosis
аппара́т *m* [1] apparatus; *phot.* camera; **~у́ра** *f collect.* [5] apparatus, gear, *comput.* hardware
аппе́нд|икс *m* [1] *anat.* appendix; **~ици́т** *m* [1] appendicitis
аппети́т *m* [1] appetite; ***прия́тного ~а!*** bon appétite!; **~ный** [14; -и́тен, -и́тна] appetizing
апре́ль *m* [4] April
апте́ка *f* [5] drugstore, *Brt.* chemist's shop; **~рь** *m* [4] druggist, *Brt.* (pharmaceutical) chemist
апте́чка *f* [5; *g/pl.*: -чек] first-aid kit
ара́|б *m* [1], **~бка** *f* [5; *g/pl.*: -бок]

Arab; **~бский** (**~ви́йский**) [16] Arabian, Arabic, Arab (*League*, *etc.*); **~п** *m* [1] *obs.* Moor, Negro

арби́тр *m* [1] arbiter; umpire, referee; **~а́ж** *m* [1] *law* arbitration, arbitrage

арбу́з *m* [1] watermelon

аргенти́н|ец *m* [1; -нца], **~ка** *f* [5; *g/pl.*: -нок], **~ский** [16] Argentine

аргуме́нт *m* [1] argument; **~а́ция** *f* [7] reasoning, argumentation; **~и́ровать** [7] (*im*)*pf.* argue

аре́на *f* [5] arena

аре́нд|а *f* [5] lease, rent; ***сдава́ть*** (***брать***) ***в ~у*** lease (rent); **~а́тор** *m* [1] lessee, tenant; **~ова́ть** [7] (*im*)*pf.* rent, lease

аре́ст *m* [1] arrest; **~о́ванный** *su.* [14] prisoner; **~о́вывать** [1], <~ова́ть> [7] arrest

аристокра́тия *f* [7] aristocracy

аритми́я *f* [7] *med.* arrhythmia

арифме́т|ика *f* [5] arithmetic; **~и́ческий** [16] arithmetic(al)

а́рия *f* [7] aria

а́рка *f* [5; *g/pl.*: -рок] arc; arch

арка́да *f* [5] arcade

аркти́ческий [16] Arctic

армату́ра *f* [5] fittings, armature

а́рмия *f* [7] army

армян|и́н *m* [1; *pl.*: -мя́не, -мя́н], **~ка** *f* [5; *g/pl.*: -нок], **~ский** [16] Armenian

арома́т *m* [1] aroma, perfume, fragrance; **~и́ческий** [16], **~ный** [14; -тен, -тна] aromatic, fragrant

арсена́л *m* [1] arsenal

арте́ль *f* [8] workmen's *or* peasants' cooperative, association

арте́рия *f* [7] artery

арти́кль *m* [4] *gr.* article

артилле́р|ия *f* [7] artillery; **~и́ст** *m* [1] artilleryman; **~и́йский** [16] artillery...

арти́ст *m* [1] artist(e); actor; **~ка** *f* [5; *g/pl.*: -ток] artist(e); actress

артишо́к *m* [1] artichoke

а́рфа *f* [5] harp

архео́лог *m* [1] archeologist; **~и́ческий** [16] archeologic(al); **~ия** *f* [7] archeology

архи́в *m* [1] archives *pl.*

архиепи́скоп *m* [1] archbishop

архипела́г *m* [1] archipelago

архите́кт|ор *m* [1] architect; **~у́ра** *f* [5] architecture; **~у́рный** [14] architectural

арши́н *m* [1; *g/pl.*: арши́н]: ***ме́рить на свой ~*** measure by one's own yardstick

асбе́ст *m* [1] asbestos

аске́т *m* [1] ascetic; **~и́ческий** [16] ascetic(al)

аспира́нт *m* [1] postgraduate; **~у́ра** *f* [5] postgraduate study

ассамбле́я *f* [6; *g/pl.*: -ле́й]: ***Генера́льная ~ Организа́ции Объединённых На́ций*** United Nations' General Assembly

ассигнова́|ть [7] (*im*)*pf.* assign, allocate, allot; **~ние** *n* [12] assignment, allocation, allotment

ассимил|и́ровать [7] (*im*)*pf.* assimilate, (**-ся** o.s.); **~я́ция** *f* [7] assimilation

ассисте́нт *m* [1], **~ка** *f* [5; *g/pl.*: -ток] assistant; *univ.* junior member of research staff

ассортиме́нт *m* [1] assortment, range

ассоци|а́ция *f* [7] association; **~и́ровать** [7] associate

а́стма *f* [5] asthma

а́стра *f* [5] aster

астроно́м *m* [1] astronomer; **~и́ческий** [16] astronomic(al) (*a. fig.*); **~ия** *f* [7] astronomy

асфа́льт *m* [1] asphalt

ата́к|а *f* [5] attack, charge; **~ова́ть** [7] (*im*)*pf.* attack, charge

атама́н *m* [1] ataman (*Cossack chieftain*)

ателье́ (-tɛ-) *n* [*indecl.*] studio, atelier

атланти́ческий [16] Atlantic...

а́тлас[1] *m* [1] atlas

атла́с[2] *m* [1] satin

атле́т *m* [1] athlete; **~ика** *f* [5] athletics; **~и́ческий** [16] athletic

атмосфе́р|а *f* [5] atmosphere; **~ный** [16] atmospheric

а́том *m* [1] atom; **~ный** [14] atomic

атрибу́т *m* [1] attribute

аттеста́т *m* [1] certificate; ***~ зре́лости*** school-leaving certificate

ауди|е́нция *f* [7] audience; **~то́рия** *f* [7] lecture hall; (***слу́шатели***) audience

аукцио́н *m* [1] auction (**с** P by)
афе́р|а *f* [5] speculation, fraud, shady deal; **~и́ст** *m* [1], **~и́стка** *f* [5; *g/pl.*: -ток] speculator, swindler
афи́ш|а *f* [5] playbill, poster; **~и́ровать** [7] *impf.* parade, advertise, make known
афори́зм *m* [1] aphorism
африка́н|ец *m* [1; -нца], **~ка** *f* [5; *g/pl.*: -нок], **~ский** [16] African
ах *int.* ah!; **~ать** [1], *once* <**~нуть**> [20] groan, sigh; (*удиви́ться*) be amazed
ахине́|я *f* [7] *coll.* nonsense; ***нести́ ~ю*** talk nonsense
ацетиле́н *m* [1] acetylene
аэро́|бус *m* [1] airbus; **~дина́мика** *f* [5] aerodynamics; **~дро́м** *m* [1] airdrome (*Brt.* aero-); **~по́рт** *m* [1] airport; **~сни́мок** *m* [1; -мка] aerial photograph; **~ста́т** *m* [1] balloon; **~съёмка** *f* [5; *g/pl.*: -мок] aerial survey

Б

б → ***бы***
ба́б|а *f* [5] married peasant woman; ***сне́жная ~а*** snowman; **~а-яга́** *f* old witch (*in Russian folk-tales*), hag; **~ий** [18]: ***~ье ле́то*** Indian summer; ***~ьи ска́зки*** *f/pl.* old wives' tales; **~ка** *f* [5; *g/pl.*: -бок] grandmother; **~очка** *f* [5; *g/pl.*: -чек] butterfly; **~ушка** *f* [5; *g/pl.*: -шек] grandmother, granny
бага́ж *m* [1 *e.*] baggage, *Brt.* luggage; ***ручно́й ~*** small baggage; ***сдать в ~*** check one's baggage, *Brt.* register one's luggage; **~ни́к** *m* [1] *mot.* trunk, *Brt.* boot; **~ный** [14]: ***~ный ваго́н*** baggage car, *Brt.* luggage van
багров|е́ть [8], <по-> turn crimson, turn purple; **~ый** [14 *sh.*] purple, crimson
бадминто́н *m* [1] badminton
ба́за *f* [5] base, basis, foundation; *учрежде́ние* depot, center (-tre)
база́р *m* [1] market, bazaar; *coll.* uproar, row; **~ный** [14] market...
бази́ровать [7] *impf.* base (***на*** П on); **~ся** rest *or* base (***на*** П on)
ба́зис *m* [1] basis
байда́рка *f* [5; *g/pl.*: -рок] canoe, kayak
ба́йка *f* [5] flannelette
байт *m* [1] *comput.* byte
бак *m* [1] *naut.* forecastle; container, receptacle; tank, cistern
бакал|е́йный [14]: ***~е́йный магази́н*** grocery, grocer's store (*Brt.* shop); ***~е́йные това́ры*** *m/pl.* = **~е́я** *f* [6] groceries *pl.*
ба́кен *m* [1] beacon
бак|енба́рды *f/pl.* [5], **~и** *m/pl.* [1; *gen.*: бак] side-whiskers
баклажа́н *m* [1] aubergine
баклу́ши: ***бить ~*** *coll.* idle, dawdle, fritter away one's time
бактерио́лог *m* [1] bacteriologist; **~и́ческий** [16] bacteriological; **~ия** *f* [7] bacteriology
бакте́рия *f* [7] bacterium
бал *m* [1; на ~ý; *pl. e.*] ball, dance (***на*** П at)
балага́н *m* [1] booth (*at fairs*); *fig.* farce; noise and bustle
балагу́р *m* [1] *coll.* joker; **~ить** *coll.* [13] jest, crack jokes
балала́йка *f* [5; *g/pl.*: балала́ек] balalaika
баламу́тить [15], <вз-> *coll.* stir up, trouble
бала́нс *m* [1] balance (*a. comm.*); ***торго́вый бала́нс*** balance of trade; **~и́ровать** [7] balance; **~овый** [14] balance...
балахо́н *m* [1] *coll.* loose overall; shapeless garment
балбе́с *m* [1] *coll.* simpleton, booby
балда́ *m/f* [5] sledgehammer; *coll.* blockhead, dolt

бале|ри́на *f* [5] ballerina; **~т** *m* [1] ballet
ба́лка[1] *f* [5; *g/pl.*: -лок] beam, girder
ба́лка[2] *f* [5; *g/pl.*: -лок] gully, ravine
балка́нский [16] Balkan...
балко́н *m* [1] balcony
балл *m* [1] grade, mark (*in school*); point (*sport*)
балла́да *f* [5] ballad
балла́ст *m* [1] ballast
баллисти́ческий [16] ballistic
балло́н *m* [1] balloon (*vessel*); container, cylinder
баллоти́роваться [7] run (**в** B for), be a candidate (**в**, ***на*** B for)
бало́в|анный [14 *sh.*] *coll.* spoiled; **~а́ть** [7] (*a.* **-ся**) be naughty; trifle with; <из-> spoil, coddle; **~ень** *m* [4; -вня] darling, pet; **~ство́** *n* [9] mischievousness; spoiling, pampering
балти́йский [16] Baltic...
бальза́м *m* [1] balsam, balm
балюстра́да *f* [5] balustrade
бамбу́к *m* [1] bamboo
бана́ль|ность *f* [8] banality; commonplace; **~ный** [14; -лен, -льна] banal, trite
бана́н *m* [1] banana
ба́нда *f* [5] band, gang
банда́ж *m* [1 *e.*] bandage; truss
бандеро́ль *f* [8] wrapper for mailing (*newspapers, etc.*); designation for printed matter, book post
банди́т *m* [1] bandit, gangster; **~и́зм** *m* [1] gangsterism
банк *m* [1] bank
ба́нка *f* [5; *g/pl.*: -нок] jar; (***консе́рвная***) **~** can, *Brt.* tin
банке́т *m* [1] banquet
банки́р *m* [1] banker
банкно́т *m* [1] bank note
банкро́т *m* [1] bankrupt; **~иться** [15], <о-> go bankrupt; **~ство** *n* [9] bankruptcy
бант *m* [1] bow
ба́нщик *m* [1] bathhouse attendant
ба́ня *f* [6] (Russian) bath(s)
бапти́ст *m* [1] Baptist
бар *m* [1] (snack) bar; **~мен** *m* [1] barman
бараба́н *m* [1] drum; **~ить** [13], <про-> (beat the) drum; **~ный** [14]: ***~ный бой*** drum beat; ***~ная перепо́нка*** eardrum; **~щик** *m* [1] drummer
бара́к *m* [1] barracks; hut
бара́н *m* [1] ram; P idiot, ass; **~ий** [18] sheep's; mutton; ***согну́ть в ~ий рог*** to make s.b. knuckle under; **~ина** *f* [5] mutton
бара́нка *f* [5; *g/pl.*: -нок] ring-shaped roll; *coll.* steering wheel
барахло́ *n* [9] old clothes; disused goods and chattels, *Brt.* lumber; trash, junk
бара́хтаться [1] *coll.* flounder
барбари́с *m* [1] barberry
бард *m* [1] bard (*poet and singer*)
барда́к *m* [1] *coll.* complete chaos; P brothel
барелье́ф *m* [1] bas-relief
ба́ржа *f* [5] barge
ба́рий *m* [3] barium
ба́рин *m* [1; *pl.*: ба́ре *or* ба́ры, бар] member of landowning gentry in prerevolutionary Russia; *coll.* refers to s.b. affecting an air of superiority
барито́н *m* [1] baritone
барка́с *m* [1] launch, long boat
баро́кко *n* [*indecl.*] baroque
баро́метр *m* [1] barometer
баррика́да *f* [5] barricade
барс *m* [1] snow leopard
ба́р|ский [16] lordly; ***жить на ~скую но́гу*** live in grand style
барсу́к *m* [1 *e.*] badger
ба́рхат *m* [1] velvet; **~ный** [14] velvet(y)
ба́рыня *f* [6] barin's wife; *coll.* refers to s.b. acting in a haughty manner
бары́ш *m* [1 *e.*] profit, gain(s)
ба́рышня *f* [6; *g/pl.*: -шень] *iro. or joc.* young lady, miss
барье́р *m* [1] barrier
бас *m* [1; *pl. e.*] *mus.* bass
баск *m* [1] Basque
баскетбо́л *m* [1] basketball
басно|пи́сец *m* [1; -сца] fabulist; **~сло́вный** [14; -вен, -вна] legendary; *coll.* fabulous, incredible
ба́сня *f* [6; *g/pl.*: -сен] fable
бассе́йн *m* [1]: ***~ реки́*** river basin; ***пла́вательный ~*** swimming pool
ба́ста that will do; no more of this!
бастио́н *m* [1] bastion
бастова́ть [7], <за-> (be *or* go on) strike

батальо́н *m* [1] battalion
батаре́|йка *f* [5; *g/pl*.: -ре́ек] (dry cell) battery; **~я** *f* [6; *g/pl*.: -е́й] *mil., tech.* battery; ***~я парово́го отопле́ния*** (central heating) radiator
бати́ст *m* [1] cambric; **~овый** [14] of cambric
бато́н *m* [1] long loaf of bread
ба́тюшка *m* [5; *g/pl*.: -шек] *coll.* father; (*as mode of address to priest*) father
бахва́л P *m* [1] braggart; **~иться** [13] boast, brag; **~ьство** *n* [9] bragging, vaunting
бахрома́ *f* [5] fringe
бахчево́дство *n* [9] melon growing
бациллоноси́тель *m* [4] bacillus-carrier
ба́шенка *f* [5; *g/pl*.: -нок] turret
башка́ P *f* [5] head, noddle
башкови́тый [14 *sh*.] *coll.* brainy
башма́к *m* [1 *e*.] shoe; ***быть под ~о́м*** be under the thumb of
ба́шня *f* [6; *g/pl*.: -шен] tower; *mil.* turret
баю́кать [1], <у-> lull; rock (to sleep)
бая́н *m* [1] (*kind of*) accordion
бде́ние *n* [12] vigil, watch
бди́тель|ность *f* [8] vigilance; **~ный** [14; -лен, -льна] vigilant, watchful
бег *m* [1; на -у́] run(ning); *pl*. [**бега́** *etc. e*.] race(s); ***~ с барье́рами*** hurdle race; ***~ на коро́ткие диста́нции*** sprint; ***на ~у́*** while running; → ***бего́м***
бе́ганье *n* [12] running (*a. for s.th., on business*)
бе́гать [1], <по-> run (around); *coll.* shun (*a.* p. **от** P); *fig.* run after (*a.* p. **за** T); ***~ вза́пуски*** *coll.* race
бегемо́т *m* [1] hippopotamus
бегле́ц *m* [1 *e*.] runaway
бе́гл|ость *f* [8] *ре́чи* fluency; cursoriness; **~ый** [14] fluent; cursory
бег|ово́й [14] race...; **~о́м** on the double; **~отня́** *coll. f* [6] running about, bustle; **~ство** *n* [9] flight, escape; *пани́ческое* stampede; ***обрати́ть в ~ство*** put to flight
бегу́н *m* [1 *e*.] runner, trotter
беда́ *f* [5; *pl*.: бе́ды] misfortune, disaster, trouble; ***что за ~?*** what does it matter?; ***не беда́*** it doesn't matter; ***~ не велика́*** there's no harm in that; ***в то́м-то и ~*** that's the trouble; the trouble is (that)...; ***на беду́*** *coll.* unluckily; ***про́сто ~!*** it's awful!
бе́д|ненький [16] poor, pitiable; **~не́ть** [8], <о-> grow (become) poor; **~ность** *f* [8] poverty; **~нота́** *f* [5] *collect.* the poor; **~ный** [14; -ден, -дна́, -дно] poor (T in); **~ня́га** *coll. m/f* [5], **~ня́жка** *coll. m/f* [5; *g/pl*.: -жек] poor fellow, wretch; **~ня́к** *m* [1 *e*.] poor man, pauper
бедро́ *n* [9; бёдра, -дер, -драм] thigh; hip; loin
бе́дств|енный [14 *sh*.] disastrous, calamitous; ***~енное положе́ние*** disastrous situation; **~ие** *n* [12] distress, disaster; ***стихи́йное ~ие*** natural disaster; **~овать** [7] suffer want, live in misery
бежа́ть [4; бегу́, бежи́шь, бегу́т; беги́; бегу́щий] <по-> (be) run(ning *etc*.); flee; avoid, shun (*a. p.* **от** P); ***~ сломя́ го́лову*** *coll.* run for one's life
бе́жевый [14] beige
бе́женец *m* [1; -нца], **~ка** *f* [5; *g/pl*.: -нок] refugee
без, **~о** (P) without; in the absence of; less; (*in designations of time*) to: ***~ че́тверти час*** a quarter to one; ***~о всего́*** without anything; ***без вас*** *a.* in your absence
безавари́йный [14; -йен, -йна] *tech.* accident-free
безала́берный *coll.* [14; -рен, -рна] disorderly, slovenly
безалкого́льный [14] nonalcoholic
безапелляцио́нный [14; -о́нен, -о́нна] categorical, peremptory
безбе́дный [14; -ден, -дна] well-off, comfortable
безбиле́тный [14] ticketless; ***~ пассажи́р на корабле́*** stowaway, passenger traveling without a ticket
безбо́жн|ый [14; -жен, -жна] irreligious; *coll.* shameless, scandalous; ***~ые це́ны*** outrageous prices
безболе́зненный [14 *sh*.] painless
безборо́дый [14] beardless
безбоя́зненный [14 *sh*.] fearless

Б

безбра́чие *n* [12] celibacy
безбре́жный [14; -жен, -жна] boundless
безве́рие *n* [12] unbelief
безве́стный [14; -тен, -тна] unknown, obscure
безве́тр|енный [14 *sh.*], **~ие** *n* [12] calm
безви́нный [14; -и́нен, -и́нна] guiltless, innocent
безвку́с|ица *f* [5] tastelessness, bad taste; **~ный** [14; -сен, -сна] tasteless, insipid
безвла́стие *n* [12] anarchy
безво́дный [14; -ден, -дна] arid
безвозвра́тный [14; -тен, -тна] irrevocable, irretrievable
безвозме́здный (-mezn-) [14] gratuitous; without compensation
безволо́сый [14] hairless, bald
безво́льный [14; -лен, -льна] lacking willpower, weak-willed
безвре́дный [14; -ден, -дна] harmless
безвре́менный [14] premature, untimely
безвы́ездный (-jiznyj) [14] uninterrupted, continuous
безвы́ходный [14; -ден, -дна] **1.** permanent; **2.** desperate, hopeless
безголо́вый [14] headless; *fig.* stupid, brainless
безгра́мотн|ость *f* [8] illiteracy, ignorance; **~ый** [14; -тен, -тна] illiterate, ignorant
безграни́чный [14; -чен, -чна] boundless, limitless
безда́рный [14; -рен, -рна] untalented, ungifted; (*of a work of art*) feeble, undistinguished
безде́йств|ие *n* [12] inaction; **~овать** [7] be inactive, idle
безде́л|ица *f* [5], **~ка** *f* [5; *g/pl.*: -лок] trifle, bagatelle; **~у́шка** *f* [5; *g/pl.*: -шек] knickknack
безде́ль|е *n* [12] idleness; **~ник** *m* [1], **~ница** *f* [5] idler; good-for-nothing; **~ничать** [1] idle, lounge
безде́нежье *n* [10] lack of money, impecuniousness
безде́тный [14; -тен, -тна] childless
безде́ятельный [14; -лен, -льна] inactive, sluggish
бе́здна *f* [5] abyss, chasm; *fig. coll.* lots (of)
бездоказа́тельный [14; -лен, -льна] unsubstantiated
бездо́мный [14; -мен, -мна] homeless
бездо́нный [14; -до́нен, -до́нна] bottomless; *fig.* unfathomable
бездоро́жье *n* [12] impassability; absence of roads; prohibitive road conditions
бездохо́дный [14; -ден, -дна] unprofitable
безду́мный [14; -мен, -мна] unthinking, thoughtless
безду́шный [14; -шен, -шна] heartless, soulless
безе́ *n* [*indecl.*] meringue
безжа́лостный (biʒʒ-sn-) [14; -тен, -тна] ruthless, merciless
безжи́зненный (biʒʒ-) [14] lifeless; inanimate; *fig.* dull
беззабо́тный [14; -тен, -тна] carefree, lighthearted; careless
беззаве́тный [14; -тен, -тна] selfless; unreserved
беззако́н|ие *n* [12] lawlessness; unlawful act; **~ность** *f* [8] illegality; **~ный** [14; -о́нен, -о́нна] illegal, unlawful
беззасте́нчивый [14 *sh.*] shameless; impudent; unscrupulous
беззащи́тный [14; -тен, -тна] defenseless; unprotected
беззвёздный (-zn-) [14; -ден, -дна] starless
беззву́чный [14; -чен, -чна] soundless, silent, noiseless
беззло́бный [14; -бен, -бна] good-natured, kind
беззу́бый [14] toothless; *fig.* feeble
безли́кий [16 *sh.*] featureless, faceless
безли́чный [14; -чен, -чна] without personality; impersonal
безлю́дный [14; -ден, -дна] deserted, uninhabited; (*малонаселённый*) sparsely populated
безме́рный [14; -рен, -рна] immeasurable; immense
безмо́зглый [14] *coll.* brainless, stupid
безмо́лв|ие *n* [12] silence; **~ный** [14; -вен, -вна] silent, mute

безмяте́жный [14; -жен, -жна] serene, tranquil, untroubled
безнадёжный [14; -жен, -жна] hopeless
безнадзо́рный [14; -рен, -рна] uncared for; neglected
безнака́занный [14 *sh.*] unpunished
безнали́чный [14] cashless, without cash transfer; **~ *расчёт*** *fin.* clearing
безнра́вственный [14 *sh.*] immoral
безоби́дный [14; -ден, -дна] inoffensive; harmless
безо́блачный [14; -чен, -чна] cloudless; serene
безобра́з|ие *n* [12] ugliness; outrage; disgrace; ***~ие!*** scandalous!, shocking!; **~ничать** [1] behave outrageously; get up to mischief; **~ный** [14; -зен, -зна] ugly; shameful, disgusting
безогово́рочный [14; -чен, -чна] unconditional, unreserved
безопа́с|ность *f* [8] safety; security; ***Сове́т ~ности*** Security Council; **~ный** [14; -сен, -сна] safe, secure (***от*** Р from); ***~ная бри́тва*** safety razor
безору́жный [14; -жен, -жна] unarmed; *fig.* defenseless
безостано́вочный [14; -чен, -чна] unceasing; nonstop...
безотве́тный [14; -тен, -тна] without response; ***любо́вь*** unrequited; (***кро́ткий***) meek
безотве́тственный [14 *sh.*] irresponsible
безотка́зный [14; -зен, -зна] without a hitch; troublefree; *tech.* faultless; reliable
безотлага́тельный [14; -лен, -льна] undelayable, urgent
безотноси́тельно *adv.* irrespective (***к*** Д of)
безотра́дный [14; -ден, -дна] cheerless
безотчётный [14; -тен, -тна] not liable to account; not subject to control; inexplicable; **~ *страх*** unaccountable fear
безоши́бочный [14; -чен, -чна] faultless; correct; unerring
безрабо́т|ица *f* [5] unemployment; **~ный** [14] unemployed
безра́достный [14; -тен, -тна] joyless; dismal
безразде́льный [14; -лен, -льна] undivided; whole-hearted
безразли́ч|ие *n* [12] (***к*** Д) indifference; **~ный** [14; -чен, чна] indifferent; ***э́то мне ~но*** it is all the same to me
безрассу́дный [14; -ден, -дна] reckless, rash
безрезульта́тный [14; -тен, -тна] futile, unsuccessful, ineffectual
безро́потный [14; -тен, -тна] uncomplaining humble, meek, submissive
безрука́вка *f* [5; *g*/*pl.*: -вок] sleeveless jacket *or* blouse
безуда́рный [14; -рен, -рна] unaccented, unstressed
безу́держный [14; -жен, -жна] unrestrained; impetuous
безукори́зненный [14 *sh.*] irreproachable, impeccable
безу́м|ец *m* [1; -мца] *fig.* madman, lunatic; madcap; **~ие** *n* [12] madness, folly; **~ный** [14; -мен, -мна] crazy, insane; nonsensical, absurd; ill-considered, rash
безумо́лчный [14; -чен, -чна] incessant, uninterrupted
безу́мство *n* [9] madness; foolhardiness
безупре́чный [14; -чен, -чна] blameless, irreproachable
безусло́в|но certainly, surely; **~ный** [14; -вен, -вна] absolute, unconditional; (***несомне́нный***) indisputable, undoubted
безуспе́шный [14; -шен, -шна] unsuccessful
безуста́нный [14; -а́нен, -а́нна] tireless; indefatigable
безуте́шный [14; -шен, -шна] inconsolable
безуча́стный [14; -тен, -тна] apathetic, unconcerned
безъя́дерный [14] nuclear-free
безымя́нный [14] nameless, anonymous; **~ *па́лец*** ring finger
безыску́сный [14; -сен, -сна] artless, unaffected, unsophisticated
безысхо́дный [14; -ден, -дна] hopeless, desperate

бейсбо́л *m* [14] baseball
беко́н *m* [1] bacon
белёсый [14] whitish
беле́ть [8], <по-> grow *or* turn white; *impf.* (*a.* **-ся**) appear *or* show white
белиберда́ *f* [14] *coll.* nonsense, rubbish
белизна́ *f* [5] whiteness
бели́ла *n/pl.* [9]: ***свинцо́вые ~*** white lead; ***ци́нковые ~*** zinc white
бели́ть [13; белю́, бели́шь, белённый] **1.** <вы́-> bleach; **2.** <по-> whitewash
бе́лка *f* [5; *g/pl.*: -лок] squirrel
белко́вый [14] albuminous
беллетри́стика *f* [5] fiction
белобры́сый [14] *coll.* flaxen-haired, tow-haired
белова́тый [14 *sh.*] whitish
бело|ви́к *m* [1 *e.*], **~во́й** [14]: ***~во́й экземпля́р*** fair copy; **~гварде́ец** *m* [1; -е́йца] White Guard (*member of troops fighting against the Red Guards and the Red Army in the Civil War 1918–1920*)
бело́к *m* [1; -лка́] albumen, protein; white (*of egg or eye*)
бело|кро́вие *n* [12] leukemia; **~ку́рый** [14 *sh.*] blond, fair; **~ру́с** *m* [1], **~ру́ска** *f* [5; *g/pl.*: -сок], **~ру́сский** [16] Byelorussian; **~сне́жный** [14; -жен, -жна] snow-white
белу́га *f* [5] white sturgeon
бе́л|ый [14; бел, -а́, -о] white; ***~ый свет*** (wide) world; ***~ые стихи́*** *m/pl.* blank verse; ***средь ~а дня*** *coll.* in broad daylight
бель|ги́ец *m* [1; -ги́йца], **~ги́йка** *f* [5; *g/pl.*: -ги́ек], **~ги́йский** [16] Belgian
бельё *n* [12] linen; ***ни́жнее ~*** underwear
бельмо́ *n* [9; *pl.*: бе́льма, бельм] wall-eye; ***она́ у меня́ как ~ на глазу́*** she is a thorn in my side
бельэта́ж *m* [1] *thea.* dress circle; second (*Brt.* first) floor
бемо́ль *m* [4] flat
бенефи́с *m* [1] benefit(-night)
бензи́н *m* [1] gasoline, *Brt.* petrol
бензо|ба́к *m* [1] gasoline *or* petrol tank; **~коло́нка** (*a.* ***запра́вочная ~***) [5; *g/pl.*: -нок] gas *or* petrol pump, *coll.* gas *or* filling station
бенуа́р *m* [1] *thea.* parterre box
бе́рег [1; на -гу́; *pl.*: -га́, *etc. e.*] bank, *морско́й*, shore, coast; (*су́ша*) land; ***вы́йти*** (***вы́ступить***) ***из ~о́в*** overflow the banks; ***приста́ть к ~у*** land; **~ово́й** [14] coast(al), shore...
бережли́вый [14 *sh.*] economical
бе́режный [14; -жен, -жна] cautious, careful
берёза *f* [5] birch tree; rod *or* bundle of twigs for flogging
березня́к *m* [1 *e.*] birch grove
берёзовый [14] birch(en)
бере́мен|ная [14] pregnant; **~ность** *f* [8] pregnancy
бере́т *m* [1] beret
бере́чь [26 г/ж: берегу́, бережёшь] **1.** <по-> guard, watch (over); **2.** <по-, с-> spare, save, take care of; **3.** <с-> [сбережённый] keep; preserve; **-ся** take care (of o.s.); ***береги́сь!*** take care!, look out!
берло́га *f* [5] den, lair
берцо́вый [14]: ***~вая кость*** shinbone
бес *m* [1] demon, evil spirit
бесе́д|а *f* [5] conversation, talk; **~ка** *f* [5; *g/pl.*: -док] arbo(u)r, summerhouse; **~овать** [7] converse
бесёнок *m* [2; -нка; *pl.*: бесеня́та] imp
беси́ть [15], <вз-> [взбешённый] enrage, madden; **-ся** (fly into a) rage; (*резви́ться*) romp
бесконе́ч|ность *f* [8] infinity; ***до ~ности*** endlessly; **~ный** [14; -чен, -чна] *разгово́р и т. д.* endless, infinite; *простра́нство, любо́вь* unlimited, boundless, eternal; ***~но ма́лый*** infinitesimal
бесконтро́льный [14; -лен, -льна] uncontrolled, unchecked
бескоры́ст|ие *n* [12] unselfisheness; **~ный** [14; -тен, -тна] disinterested
бескра́йний [15; -а́ен, -а́йна] boundless
бескро́вный [14; -вен, -вна] anemic, pale, lacking vitality
бескульту́рье *n* [10] lack of culture
беснова́ться [7] be possessed, rage, rave

бесо́вщина *f* [5] devilry

беспа́мятство *n* [9] unconsciousness, frenzy, delirium

беспарти́йный [14] *pol.* independent; non-party (man)

бесперебо́йный [14; -бо́ен, -бо́йна] uninterrupted, regular

беспереса́дочный [14] direct (*train*), through...

бесперспекти́вный [14; -вен, -вна] having no prospects, hopeless

беспе́ч|ность *f* [8] carelessness; **~ный** [14; -чен, -чна] careless

беспла́т|ный [14; -тен, -тна] free (of charge), gratuitous; **~но** gratis

беспло́д|ие *n* [12] barrenness, sterility; **~ный** [14; -ден, -дна] barren, sterile; *fig.* fruitless, vain

бесповоро́тный [14; -тен, -тна] unalterable, irrevocable, final

бесподо́бный [14; -бен, -бна] incomparable, matchless

беспозвоно́чный [14] invertebrate

беспок|о́ить [13], <(п)о-> upset, worry; (*меша́ть*) disturb, bother, trouble; **-ся** worry, be anxious (**о** П about); **~о́йный** [14; -ко́ен, -ко́йна] restless; uneasy; **~о́йство** *n* [9] unrest; trouble; anxiety; ***прости́те за ~о́йство*** sorry to (have) trouble(d) you

бесполе́зный [14; -зен, -зна] useless

беспо́мощный [14; -щен, -щна] helpless

беспоря́до|к *m* [1; -дка] disorder, confusion; *pl.* disturbances, riots; **~чный** [14; -чен, -чна] disorderly, untidy

беспоса́дочный [14]: **~ *перелёт*** nonstop flight

беспо́чвенный [14 *sh.*] groundless, unfounded

беспо́шлинный [14] duty-free

беспоща́дный [14; -ден, -дна] pitiless, ruthless, relentless

беспреде́льный [14; -лен, -льна] boundless, infinite, unlimited

беспредме́тный [14; -тен, -тна] aimless

беспрекосло́вный [14; -вен, -вна] absolute, unquestioning, implicit

беспрепя́тственный [14 *sh.*] unhampered, unhindered, free

беспреры́вный [14; -вен, -вна] uninterrupted, continuous

беспреста́нный [14; -а́нен, -а́нна] incessant, continual

беспри́быльный [14; -лен, -льна] unprofitable

беспризо́рный [14; -рен, -рна] homeless, uncared-for

бесприме́рный [14; -рен, -рна] unprecedented, unparalleled

беспринци́пный [14; -пен, -пна] unprincipled, unscrupulous

беспристра́ст|ие *n* [12] impartiality; **~ный** (-sn-) [14; -тен, -тна] impartial, unprejudiced, unbias(s)ed

беспричи́нный [14; -и́нен, -и́нна] groundless; unfounded

беспрню́тный [14; -тен, -тна] homeless

беспробу́дный [14; -ден, -дна] *сон* deep; *пья́нство* unrestrained

беспросве́тный [14; -тен, -тна] pitch-dark; *fig.* hopeless

беспроце́нтный [14] interest-free; bearing no interest

беспу́тный [14; -тен, -тна] dissolute

бессвя́зный [14; -зен, -зна] incoherent, rambling

бессерде́чный [14; -чен, -чна] heartless, unfeeling, callous

бесси́|лие *n* [12] debility; impotence; **~льный** [14; -лен, -льна] weak, powerless, impotent

бессла́вный [14; -вен, -вна] infamous, ignominious, inglorious

бессле́дный [14; -ден, -дна] without leaving a trace, complete

бесслове́сный [14; -сен, -сна] speechless, dumb; silent

бессме́нный [14; -е́нен, -е́нна] permanent

бессме́рт|ие *n* [12] immortality; **~ный** [14; -тен, -тна] immortal

бессмы́сл|енный [14 *sh.*] senseless; meaningless; **~ица** *f* [5] nonsense

бессо́вестный [14; -тен, -тна] unscrupulous

бессодержа́тельный [14; -лен, -льна] empty, insipid, dull

бессозна́тельный [14; -лен, -льна] unconscious; (*непроизво́льный*) involuntary

бессо́нн|ица *f* [5] insomnia; **~ый** [14] sleepless
бесспо́рный [14; -рен, -рна] indisputable; doubtless, certain
бессро́чный [14; -чен, -чна] without time-limit; indefinite
бесстра́ст|ие *n* [12] dispassionateness, impassiveness; **~ный** [14; -тен, -тна] dispassionate, impassive
бесстра́ш|ие *n* [12] fearlessness; **~ный** [14; -шен, -шна] fearless, intrepid
бессты́д|ный [14; -ден, -дна] shameless, impudent; (*непристо́йный*) indecent; **~ство** *n* [9] impudence, insolence
бессчётный [14] innumerable
беста́ктн|ость *f* [8] tactlessness; tactless action; **~ый** [14; -тен, -тна] tactless
бесталáнный [14; -а́нен, -а́нна] untalented; ill-starred
бе́стия *f* [7] brute, beast; rogue
бестолко́вый [14 *sh.*] muddle-headed, confused; *челове́к* slow-witted
бе́столочь *f* [8] *coll.* nitwit
бестре́петный [14; -тен, -тна] intrepid, undaunted
бестсе́ллер *m* [1] bestseller
бесхара́ктерный [14; -рен, -рна] lacking character, weak-willed
бесхи́тростный [14; -тен, -тна] artless, naive, ingenuous, unsophisticated
бесхо́зный [14] *coll.* ownerless
бесхозя́йствен|ность *f* [8] careless and wasteful management; **~ный** [14] wasteful
бесцве́тный [14; -тен, -тна] colo(u)rless, insipid
бесце́льный [14; -лен, -льна] aimless; *разгово́р* idle
бесце́н|ный [14; -е́нен, -е́нна] invaluable, priceless; **~ок** *m* [1; -нка]: ***за ~ок*** *coll.* for a song or a trifling sum
бесцеремо́нный [14; -о́нен, -о́нна] unceremonious, familiar
бесчелове́чн|ость *f* [8] inhumanity; **~ый** [14; -чен, -чна] inhuman, cruel
бесче́ст|ный [14; -тен, -тна] dishonest; (*непоря́дочный*) dishono(u)rable; **~ье** *n* [10] dishono(u)r, disgrace
бесчи́нство [9] excess, outrage; **~вать** [7] behave outrageously
бесчи́сленный [14 *sh.*] innumerable, countless
бесчу́вств|енный [14 *sh.*] insensible, callous, hard-hearted; **~ие** *n* [12] insensibility (**к** Д); unconsciousness, swoon
бесшаба́шный [14; -шен, -шна] *coll.* reckless, careless; wanton
бесшу́мный [14; -мен, -мна] noiseless, quiet
бето́н *m* [1] concrete; **~и́ровать** [7], <за-> concrete; **~ный** [14] concrete...
бечёвка *f* [5; *g/pl.*: -вок] string
бе́шен|ство *n* [9] **1.** *med.* hydrophobia; **2.** fury, rage; **~ый** [14] **1.** *соба́ка* rabid; **2.** furious, frantic, wild; **3.** *цена́* enormous
библе́йский [16] Biblical; Bible...
библиографи́ческий [16] bibliographic(al)
библиоте́|ка *f* [5] library; **~карь** *m* [4] librarian; **~чный** [14] library...
би́блия *f* [7] Bible
би́вень *m* [4; -вня] tusk
бигуди́ *n/pl.* [*indecl.*] hair curlers
бидо́н *m* [1] can; churn; milkcan
бие́ние *n* [12] beat, throb
бижуте́рия *f* [7] costume jewel(le)ry
би́знес *m* [1] business; **~ме́н** *m* [1] businessman
бизо́н *m* [1] bison
биле́т *m* [1] ticket; card; note, bill; ***обра́тный ~*** round-trip ticket, *Brt.* return-ticket
билья́рд *m* [1] billiards
бино́кль *m* [4] binocular(s), ***театра́льный ~*** opera glasses; ***полево́й ~*** field glasses
бинт *m* [1 *e.*] bandage; **~ова́ть** [7], <за-> bandage, dress
био́граф *m* [1] biographer; **~и́ческий** [16] biographic(al); **~ия** *f* [7] biography
био́лог *m* [1] biologist; **~и́ческий** [16] biological; **~ия** *f* [7] biology
биори́тм *m* [1] biorhythm
биохи́мия *f* [7] biochemistry

би́ржа *f* [5] (stock) exchange; **~ труда́** labor registry office, *Brt.* labour exchange
биржеви́к *m* [1 *e.*] → **бро́кер**
би́рка *f* [5; *g/pl.*: -рок] name-tag, nameplate
бирюза́ *f* [5] turquoise
бис *int.* encore!
би́сер *m* [1] *coll.* (glass) beads *pl.*
бискви́т *m* [1] sponge cake
бит *m* [1] *comput.* bit
би́тва *f* [5] battle
бит|ко́м → **наби́тый**; **~о́к** *m* [1; -тка́] (mince) meat ball
бить [бью, бьёшь; бей!; би́тый] **1.** <по-> beat; **2.** <про-> [проби́л, -би́ла, проби́ло] *часы́* strike; **3.** <раз-> [разобью́, -бьёшь] break, smash; **4.** <у-> shoot; kill; trump (*card*); **5.** *no pf.* spout; **~ в глаза́** strike the eye; **~ трево́гу** *fig.* raise the alarm; **~ отбо́й** *mst. fig.* beat a retreat; **~ ключо́м 1.** bubble; **2.** boil over; **3.** sparkle; **4.** abound in vitality; **про́бил его́ час** his hour has come; **би́тый час** *m* one solid hour; **-ся** fight; *се́рдце* beat; struggle, toil (**над** Т); **-ся голово́й о(б) сте́ну** *fig.* beat one's head against a brick wall; **-ся об закла́д** bet; **она́ бьётся как ры́ба об лёд** she is exerting herself in vain
бифште́кс *m* [1] (beef) steak
бич *m* [1 *e.*] whip; *fig.* scourge
бла́го *n* [9] good; blessing; **всех благ**! *coll.* all the best; **2ве́щение** *n* [12] Annunciation
благови́дный [14; -ден, -дна] *fig.* seemly, *предло́г* specious
благоволи́ть [13] *old use* be favourably disposed (**к** Д); <со-> *iro.* deign
благово́н|ие *n* [12] fragrance; **~ный** [14] fragrant
благогове́йный [14; -ве́ен, -ве́йна] reverent, respectful; **~ве́ние** *n* [12] awe (of), reverence, respect (for) (**пе́ред** Т); **~ве́ть** [8] (**пе́ред** Т) worship, venerate
благодар|и́ть [13], <по-, от-> (В **за** В) thank (*a. p.* for s.th.); **~ность** *f* [8] gratitude; thanks; **не сто́ит ~ности** you are welcome, don't mention it; **~ный** [14; -рен, -рна] grateful, thankful (Д/**за** В to *a. p.* for s.th.); **~я́** (Д) thanks *or* owing to
благода́т|ный [14; -тен, -тна] *кли́мат* salubrious; *край* rich; **~ь** *f* [8] blessing; **кака́я тут ~ь!** it's heavenly here!
благоде́тель *m* [4] benefactor; **~ница** *f* [5] benefactress
благодея́ние *n* [12] good deed
благоду́ш|ие *n* [12] good nature, kindness; **~ный** [14; -шен, -шна] kindhearted, benign
благожела́тель|ность *f* [8] benevolence; **~ный** [14; -лен, -льна] benevolent
благозву́ч|ие *n* [12], **~ность** *f* [8] euphony, sonority; **~ный** [14; -чен, -чна] sonorous, harmonious
благ|о́й [16] good; **~о́е наме́рение** good intentions
благонадёжный [14; -жен, -жна] reliable, trustworthy
благонаме́ренный [14 *sh.*] well-meaning, well-meant
благополу́ч|ие *n* [12] well-being, prosperity, happiness; **~ный** [14; -чен, -чна] happy; safe
благоприя́т|ный [14; -тен, -тна] favo(u)rable, propitious; **~ствовать** [7] (Д) favo(u)r, promote
благоразу́м|ие *n* [12] prudence, discretion; **~ный** [14; -мен, -мна] prudent, judicious
благоро́д|ный [14; -ден, -дна] noble; *иде́и и т. д.* lofty; *мета́лл* precious; **~ство** *n* [9] nobility
благоскло́нный [14; -о́нен, -о́нна] favo(u)rable, well-disposed (to [-ward(s)] a p. **к** Д)
благосло|ве́ние *n* [12] benediction, blessing; **~вля́ть** [28], <~ви́ть> [14 *e.*; -влю́, -ви́шь] bless; **~вля́ть свою́ судьбу́** thank one's lucky stars
благосостоя́ние *n* [12] prosperity
благотвори́тельный [14] charitable, charity...
благотво́рный [14; -рен, -рна] beneficial, wholesome, salutary
благоустро́енный [14 *sh.*] well-equipped, comfortable; with all amenities
благоуха́|ние *n* [12] fragrance, odo(u)r; **~ть** [1] be fragrant, smell sweet

благочести́вый [14 *sh.*] pious

блаже́н|ный [14 *sh.*] blissful; **~ство** *n* [9] bliss; **~ствовать** [7] enjoy felicity

блажь *f* [8] caprice, whim; *дурь* folly

бланк *m* [1] form; ***запо́лнить ~*** fill in a form

блат P *m* [1] profitable connections; ***по ~́у*** on the quiet, illicitly, through good connections; **~но́й** P [14]: ***~но́й язы́к*** thieves' slang, cant

бледне́ть [8], <по-> turn pale

бледнова́тый [14 *sh.*] palish

бле́д|ность *f* [8] pallor; **~ный** [14; -ден, -дна́, -о] pale, *fig.* colo(u)rless, insipid; ***~ный как полотно́*** as white as a sheet

блёк|лый [14] faded, withered; **~нуть** [21], <по-> fade, wither

блеск *m* [1] luster, shine, brilliance; glitter; *fig.* splendo(u)r

блест|е́ть [11; *a.* бле́щешь], *once* <блесну́ть> shine; glitter; flash; ***не всё то зо́лото, что ~и́т*** all that glitters is not gold; **~́ки** (bl̦oski) *f/pl.* [5; *gen.*: -ток] spangle; **~я́щий** [17 *sh.*] shining, bright; *fig.* brilliant

блеф *m* [1] bluff

бле́ять [27], <за-> bleat

ближ|а́йший [17] (→ ***бли́зкий***) the nearest, next; **~́е** nearer; **~́ний** [15] near(by); *su.* fellow creature

близ (Р) near, close; **~́иться** [15; 3rd *p. only*], <при-> approach (a p. **к** Д); **~́кий** [16; -зок, -зка́, -о; *comp.*: бли́же], near, close (**к** Д); **~́кие** *pl.* folk(s), one's family, relatives; **~́ко от** (Р) close to, not far from; **~лежа́щий** [17] nearby, neighbo(u)ring

близне́ц *m* [1 *e.*] twin

близору́кий [16 *sh.*] shortsighted

бли́зость *f* [8] nearness, proximity; *об отноше́ниях* intimacy

блин *m* [1 *e.*] kind of pancake; **~чик** *m* [1] pancake

блиста́тельный [14; -лен, -льна] brilliant, splendid, magnificent

блиста́ть [1] shine

блок *m* [1] **1.** bloc, coalition; **2.** *tech.* pulley; unit

блок|а́да *f* [5] blockade; **~и́ровать** [7] *(im)pf.* block (up)

блокно́т *m* [1] notebook, writing pad

блонди́н *m* [1] blond; **~ка** *f* [5; *g/pl.*: -нок] blonde

блоха́ *f* [5; *nom/pl.*: бло́хи] flea

блуд *m* [1] *coll.* fornication; **~́ный** [14]: ***~́ный сын*** prodigal son

блужда́ть [11], <про-> roam, wander

блу́з|а *f* [5] (working) blouse, smock; **~ка** *f* [5; *g/pl.*: -зок] (ladies') blouse

блю́дечко *n* [9; *g/pl.*: -чек] saucer

блю́до *n* [9] dish; *еда́* course

блю́дце *n* [11; *g/pl.*: -дец] saucer

блюсти́ [25], <со-> observe, preserve, maintain; **~тель** *m* [4]: ***~тель поря́дка*** *iro.* arm of the law

бля́ха *f* [5] name plate; number plate

боб *m* [1 *e.*] bean; haricot; ***оста́ться на ~а́х*** get nothing for one's pains

бобёр [1; -бра] beaver (*fur*)

боби́на *f* [5] bobbin, spool, reel

бобо́в|ый [14]: ***~ые расте́ния*** *n/pl.* legumes

бобр *m* [1 *e.*], **~о́вый** [14] beaver

бо́бслей *m* [3] bobsleigh

бог (bɔx) *m* [1; *vocative*: бо́же *from g/pl. e.*] God; god, idol; ***~ весть, ~ (его́) зна́ет*** *coll.* God knows; ***Бо́же (мой)*** oh God!, good gracious!; ***дай Ձ*** God grant; I (let's) hope (so); ***ра́ди Ձа*** for God's (goodness') sake; ***сла́ва Ձу!*** thank God!; ***сохрани́ (не дай, изба́ви, упаси́) Ձ (бо́же)*** God forbid!

богат|е́ть [8], <раз-> grow (become) rich; **~́ство** *n* [9] wealth; **~́ый** [14 *sh.*; *comp.*: бога́че] rich, wealthy

богаты́рь *m* [4 *e.*] (epic) hero

бога́ч *m* [1 *e.*] rich man

боге́ма *f* [5] (artists leading a) Bohemian life

боги́ня *f* [6] goddess

Богома́терь *f* [8] the Blessed Virgin, Mother of God

Богоро́дица *f* [5] the Blessed Virgin, Our Lady

богосло́в *m* [1] theologian; **~ие** *n* [12] theology, divinity; **~ский** [16] theological

богослуже́ние *n* [12] divine ser-

vice; worship, liturgy
боготвори́ть [13] worship, idolize; deify
бода́ть [1], <за->, *once* <боднýть> [20] (*a.* **~ся**) butt (*a.* o.a.)
бо́др|ость *f* [8] vivacity, sprightliness; **~ствовать** [20] be awake; **~ый** [14; бодр, -á, -o] sprightly, brisk, vigorous
боеви́к *m* [1 *e.*] member of revolutionary fighting group; *coll.* hit; **~ *сезо́на*** hit of the season
боев|о́й [14] battle..., fighting, war-..., military; live (*shell etc.*); pugnacious, militant; ***~ы́е де́йствия*** operations, hostilities; ***~о́й па́рень*** dashing fellow
бое|голо́вка *f* [5; *g/pl.*: -вок] warhead; **~припа́сы** *m/pl.* [1] ammunition; **~спосо́бный** [14; -бен, -бна] battleworthy, effective
бое́ц *m* [1; бойцá] soldier, fighter
Бо́же → ***бог***; **≗ский** [16] fair, just; **≈ственный** [14 *sh.*] divine, **~ство́** *n* [9] deity, divinity
бо́ж|ий [18] God's, divine; ***я́сно как ~ий день*** as clear as day
божи́ться [16 *e.*; -жýсь, -жи́шься], <по-> swear
бо́жья коро́вка *f* [5; *g/pl.*: -вок] ladybird
бой *m* [3; бо́я, в бою́; *pl.*: бои́, боёв, *etc. e.*] battle, combat, fight; ***брать*** (***взять***) ***бо́ем*** *or* **с бо́ю** take by assault (storm); ***рукопа́шный ~*** close fight; ***~ часо́в*** the striking of a clock; **≈кий** [16; бо́ек, бойкá, бо́йко; *comp.*: бо́йч(е)е] brisk, lively; ***ме́сто*** busy; ***речь*** voluble, glib; **≈кость** *f* [8] liveliness
бойкоти́ровать [7] (*im.*)*pf.* boycott
бо́йня *f* [6; *g/pl.*: бо́ен] slaughterhouse; *fig.* massacre, slaughter
бок *m* [1; на бокý; *pl.*: бокá, *etc. e.*] side; ***нá ~***, **≈ом** sideways; ***~ о́ ~*** side by side; ***под бо́ком*** *coll.* close by
бока́л *m* [1] wineglass, goblet
боково́й [14] side, lateral
бокс *m* [1] boxing; **~ёр** *m* [1] boxer; **~и́ровать** [7] box
болва́н *m* [1] dolt, blockhead
болга́р|ин *m* [4; *pl.*: -ры, -р] Bulgarian; **~ка** *f* [5; *g/pl.*: -рок], **~ский** [16] Bulgarian

бо́лее (→ ***бо́льше***) more (than P); ***~ высо́кий*** higher; ***~ или ме́нее*** more or less; ***~ того́*** what is more; ***тем ~, что*** especially as; ***не ~*** at (the) most
боле́зненный [14 *sh.*] sickly, ailing; *fig.* morbid; painful (*a. fig.*)
боле́знь *f* [8] sickness, illness; disease; (*mental*) disorder; sick (*leave...* ***по*** Д)
боле́льщик *m* [1] *sport*: fan
боле́ть [8] **1.** be sick, be down (T with); *за де́ло; о ко́м-то* be anxious (***за*** В, ***о*** П for, about), apprehensive; *sport* support, be a fan (***за*** В of); **2.** [9; 3rd *p. only*] hurt, ache; ***у меня́ боли́т голова́*** (***зуб***, ***го́рло***) I have a headache (a toothache, a sore throat)
болеутоля́ющ|ий [17]: ***~ее сре́дство*** anodyne, analgesic
боло́т|истый [14 *sh.*] boggy, swampy; **~ный** [14] bog..., swamp...; **~о** *n* [9] bog, swamp
болт *m* [1 *e.*] bolt
болта́ть [1] **1.** <вз-> shake up; **2.** (**-ся**) dangle; **3.** *coll.* <по-> [20] chat(ter); **~ся** *coll.* loaf *or* hang about
болтли́вый [14 *sh.*] talkative
болтовня́ *f* [6] *coll.* idle talk, gossip
болту́н *m* [1; -нá] *coll.*, **~ья** *f* [6] babbler, chatterbox
боль *f* [8] pain, ache
больни́|ца *f* [5] hospital; ***вы́писаться из ~цы*** be discharged from hospital; ***лечь в ~цу*** go to hospital; **~чный** [14] hospital...; ***~чный лист*** medical certificate
бо́льн|о painful(ly); P very; ***мне ~о*** it hurts me; ***глаза́м бо́льно*** my eyes smart; **~о́й** [14; бо́лен, больнá] sick, ill, sore; *su.* patient; *fig.* delicate, burning; tender; ***стациона́рный ~о́й*** inpatient
бо́льше bigger, more; ***~ всего́*** most of all; above all; ***~ не*** no more *or* longer; ***как мо́жно ~*** as much (many) as possible; **~ви́зм** *m* [1] Bolshevism; **~ви́к** *m* [1 *e.*] Bolshevik; **~ви́стский** (-visski-) [16] Bolshevist(ic)
бо́льш|ий [17] bigger, greater; ***по ~ей ча́сти*** for the most part; ***са́мое***

~ее at most; **~инство́** *n* [9] majority; most; **~о́й** [16] big, large, great; *coll. взро́слый* grownup; **~у́щий** [17] *coll.* huge

бо́мб|а *f* [5] bomb; **~ардирова́ть** [7] bomb, shell; bombard (*a. fig.*); **~ардиро́вка** *f* [5; *g/pl.*: -вок] bombardment, bombing; **~ардиро́вщик** *m* [1] bomber; **~ёжка** *coll. f* [5; *g/pl.*: -жек] → ***~ардиро́вка***; **~и́ть** [14 *e.*; -блю́, -би́шь (раз-) бомблённый], <раз-> bomb

бомбоубе́жище *n* [11] air-raid *or* bomb-proof shelter

бор *m* [1; в бору́] pine wood *or* forest; ***разгоре́лся сыр ~*** passions flared up

бордо́ *n* [*indecl.*] claret; **~вый** [14] dark purplish red

бордю́р *m* [1] border, trimming

боре́ц *m* [1; -рца́] fighter, wrestler; *fig.* champion, partisan

борза́я *f* [14] *su.* borzoi, greyhound

бормота́ть [3], <про-> mutter

бо́ров *m* [1; *from g/pl. e.*] boar

борода́ *f* [5; *ac/sg.*: бо́роду; *pl.* бо́роды, боро́д, -а́м] beard

борода́вка *f* [5; *g/pl.*: -вок] wart

борода́|тый [14 *sh.*] bearded; **~ч** *m* [1 *e.*] bearded man

борозд|а́ *f* [5; *pl.*: бо́розды, боро́зд, -да́м] furrow; **~и́ть** [15 *e.*; -зжу́, -зди́шь], <вз-> furrow

борон|а́ *f* [5; *ac/sg.*: бо́рону; *pl.*: бо́роны, боро́н, -на́м] harrow; **~и́ть** [13], **~нова́ть** [7], <вз-> harrow

боро́ться [17; боря́сь] fight, struggle (***за*** B for, ***про́тив*** P against) wrestle

борт *m* [1; на ~у́; *nom/pl.*: -та́] *naut.* side; board; ***на ~у́ су́дна*** on board a ship; ***бро́сить за ~*** throw overboard; ***челове́к за ~ом!*** man overboard!

борщ *m* [1 *e.*] borsch(t), red-beet soup

борьба́ *f* [5] *sport* wrestling; *fig.* fight, struggle

босико́м barefoot

босо́й [14; бос, -а́, -о] barefooted; ***на бо́су но́гу*** wearing shoes on bare feet

босоно́гий [16] → ***босо́й***

босоно́жка *f* [5; *g/pl.*: -жек] sandal

бота́ни|к *m* [1] botanist; **~ка** *f* [5] botany; **~ческий** [16] botanic(al)

ботва́ *f* [5] leafy tops of root vegetables, *esp.* beet leaves

боти́нок *m* [1; *g/pl.*: -нок] shoe, *Brt.* (lace) boot

бо́цман *m* [1] boatswain

бо́чк|а *f* [5; *g/pl.*: -чек] cask, barrel; **~овый** [14]: ***~овое пи́во*** draught beer

бочко́м sideway(s), sidewise

бочо́нок *m* [1; -нка] (small) barrel

боязли́вый [14 *sh.*] timid, timorous

боя́зн|ь *f* [8] fear, dread; ***из ~и*** for fear of, lest

боя́р|ин *m* [4; *pl.*: -ре, -р], **~ыня** *f* [6] boyar(d) (*member of old nobility in Russia*)

боя́рышник *m* [1] hawthorn

боя́ться [бою́сь, бои́шься; бо́йся, бо́йтесь!], <по-> be afraid (P of), fear; ***бою́сь сказа́ть*** I don't know exactly, I'm not quite sure

бра *n* [*indecl.*] lampbracket, sconce

бра́во *int.* bravo

бразды́ *f/pl.* [5] *fig.* reins

брази́|лец *m* [1; -льца] Brazilian; **~льский** [16], **~лья́нка** *f* [5; *g/pl.*: -нок] Brazilian

брак[1] *m* [1] marriage; matrimony

брак[2] *m* [1] (*no pl.*) defective articles, rejects, spoilage

бракова́ть [7], <за-> scrap, reject

браконье́р *m* [1] poacher

бракосочета́ние *n* [12] wedding

брани́ть [13], <по-, вы́-> scold, rebuke; **~ся** quarrel; swear

бра́нн|ый [14] abusive; ***~ое сло́во*** swearword

брань *f* [8] abuse, invective

брасле́т *m* [1] bracelet; watchband

брат *m* [1; *pl.*: бра́тья, -тьев, -тьям] brother; (*mode of address*) old boy!; ***на ~а*** a head, each

бра́тец *m* [1; -тца] *iro.* dear brother

бра́тия *f* [7] *coll. joc.* company, fraternity

бра́т|ский [16; *adv.*: (по-)бра́тски] brotherly, fraternal; ***~ская моги́ла*** communal grave; **~ство** *n* [9] brotherhood, fraternity, fellowship

брать [беру́, -рёшь; брал, -а́, -о; ...

бра́нный], <взять> [возьму́, -мёшь; взял, -á, -о; взя́тый (взят, -á, -о)] take; **~ *напрока́т*** hire; **~ *приме́р*** (**с** P) take (*a p.*) as a model; **~ *верх над*** (T) be victorious over, conquer; **~ *обра́тно*** take back; **~ *сло́во*** take (have) the floor; (**с** P) **~ *сло́во*** make (s.o.) promise; **~ *свой слова́ обра́тно*** take back what one has said; **~ *себя́ в ру́ки*** *fig.* collect o.s., pull o.s. together; **~ *на себя́*** assume; **~ *за пра́вило*** make it a rule; ***он взял и уе́хал*** he left unexpectedly; ***возьми́те напра́во!*** turn (to the) right!; → *a.* ***взима́ть***; ***с чего́ ты взял?*** what makes you think that?; **-ся** [бра́лся, -ла́сь, -ло́сь] <взя́ться> [взя́лся, -ла́сь, взяло́сь, взяли́сь] (***за*** В) undertake; (*приступи́ть*) set about; (*хвата́ть*) take hold of, seize; **~ *за́ руки*** join hands; **~ *за кни́гу*** (***рабо́ту***) set about *or* start reading a book (working); ***отку́да э́то берётся?*** where does that come from?; ***отку́да у него́ де́ньги беру́тся?*** wherever does he get his money from?; ***отку́да ни возьми́сь*** all of a sudden

бра́чн|ый [14] matrimonial, conjugal; **~*ое свиде́тельство*** marriage certificate

брев|ёнчатый [14] log...; **~но́** *n* [9; *pl.*: брёвна, -вен, -внам] log; beam

бред *m* [1] delirium; *coll.* nonsense; **~ить** [15], <за-> be delirious; *fig.* rave; be crazy, dream (**о** П about); **~ни** *f/pl.* [6; *gen.*: -ней] nonsense

брéзг|ать [1] (T) be squeamish, fastidious (about); (*гнуша́ться*) disdain; **~ли́вость** *f* [8] squeamishness, disgust; **~ли́вый** [14 *sh.*] squeamish, fastidious (***к*** Д about)

брезе́нт *m* [1] tarpaulin

бре́зжить [16], **~ся** glimmer; (*рассвета́ть*) dawn

бре́мя *n* [3; *no pl.*] load, burden (*a. fig.*)

бренча́ть [4 *e.*; -чу́, -чи́шь] clink, jingle; *на гита́ре* strum

брести́ [25], <по-> drag o.s. along; saunter

брете́лька *f* [5; *g/pl.*: -лек] shoulderstrap

брешь *f* [8] breach; gap

брига́|да *f* [5] brigade (*a. mil.*), team, group of workers; **~ди́р** *m* [1] foreman

бри́джи *pl.* [*gen.*: -жей] breeches

бриллиа́нт *m* [1], **~овый** [14] brilliant, (cut) diamond

брита́н|ец *m* [1; -нца] Briton, Britisher; **~ский** [16] British

бри́тва *f* [5] razor; ***безопа́сная ~*** safety razor

брить [бре́ю, бре́ешь; брей(те)!; бре́я; брил; бри́тый], <вы-, по-> shave; **~ся** *v/i.* get shaved, (have a) shave; **~ё** *n* [10] shaving

бри́финг *m* [1] *pol.* briefing

бров|ь *f* [8; *from g/pl. e.*] eyebrow; ***хму́рить ~и*** frown; ***он и ~ью не повёл*** *coll.* he did not turn a hair; ***попа́сть не в ~ь, а в глаз*** *coll.* hit the nail on the head

брод *m* [1] ford

броди́ть¹ [15], <по-> wander, roam

броди́ть² [15] (*impers.*) ferment

бродя́|га *m* [5] tramp, vagabond; **~чий** [17] vagrant; *соба́ка* stray

броже́ние *n* [12] fermentation; *fig.* agitation, unrest

бро́кер *m* [1] broker

бром *m* [1] bromine

броне|та́нковый [14]: **~*та́нковые ча́сти*** *f/pl.* armo(u)red troops; **~транспортёр** *m* [1] armo(u)red personnel carrier

бро́нз|а *f* [5] bronze; **~овый** [14] bronze...

брони́ровать [7], <за-> reserve, book

бро́нх|и *m/pl.* [1] bronchi *pl.* (*sg.* **~** bronchus); **~и́т** *m* [1] bronchitis

броня́ *f* [6; *g/pl.*: -не́й] armo(u)r

бро́ня *f* [6; *g/pl.*: -ней] reservation

броса́ть [1], <бро́сить> throw, (*a. naut.*) cast, fling (*a.* out) (В *or* Т/***в*** В s.th. at); (*поки́нуть*) leave, abandon, desert; (*прекрати́ть де́лать*) give up, quit, leave off; **~ *взгля́д*** cast a glance; ***бро́сь(те)...!*** *coll.* (oh) stop ...!; **-ся** dash, rush, dart (off **-ся *бежа́ть***); fall up(on) (***на*** В); go to (***в*** В); **~ *в глаза́*** strike the eye

бро́ский [16] bright, loud

бро́совый [14] catchpenny; under (price)

Б

бросо́к *m* [1; -ска́] hurl, throw; (*ры́во́к*) spurt
бро́шка *f* [5; *g/pl.*: -шек] brooch
брошю́ра *f* [5] brochure, pamphlet
брус *m* [1; *pl.*: бру́сья, бру́сьев, бру́сьям] (square) beam; bar; *pl.* ***паралле́льные бру́сья*** parallel bars
брусни́ка *f* [5] cowberry
брусо́к *m* [1; -ска́] **1.** bar, ingot; **2.** (*a.* ***точи́льный ~***) whetstone
бру́тто [*indecl.*] gross (weight)
бры́з|гать [1 *or* 3], *once* <~нуть> [20] splash, spatter, sprinkle; gush; **~ги** *f/pl.* [5] splashes, spray
брык|а́ться [1], *once* <~ну́ться> [20] kick; *fig.* rebel
брюз|га́ *m/f* [5] *coll.* grumbler, grouch; **~гли́вый** [14 sh.] peevish, grouchy; **~жа́ть** [4 *e.*; -жу́, -жи́шь], <за-> grumble, grouch
брю́ква *f* [5] swede
брю́ки *f/pl.* [5] trousers, pants
брюне́т *m* [1] dark-haired man; **~ка** *f* [5; *g/pl.*: -ток] brunette
брюссе́ль|ский [16]: ***~ская капу́ста*** *f* Brussels sprouts
брю́хо P *n* [9] belly, paunch
брюш|и́на *f* [5] peritoneum; **~но́й** [14] abdominal; ***~но́й тиф*** *m* typhoid fever
бря́кать [1], *once* <бря́кнуть> [20] *v/i.* clink, clatter; *v/t. fig. coll.* drop a clanger
бу́бен *m* [1; -бна; *g/pl.*: бу́бен] (*mst. pl.*) tambourine; **~чик** *m* [1] jingle, small bell
бу́блик *m* [1] slightly sweetened ring-shaped bread roll
бу́бны *f/pl.* [5; *g/pl.*: бубён, -бнам] (*cards*) diamonds
буго́р *m* [1; -гра́] hill(ock)
бугри́стый [14] hilly; *доро́га* bumpy
бу́дет (→ ***быть***) (*impers.*): ***~ тебе́ ворча́ть*** stop grumbling
буди́льник *m* [1] alarm clock
буди́ть [15] **1.** <раз-> (a)wake, waken; **2.** <про-> [пробуждённый] *fig.* (a)rouse; ***~ мысль*** set one thinking
бу́дка *f* [5; *g/pl.*: -док] booth, box
бу́дни *m/pl.* [1; *gen.*: -дней] weekdays; *fig.* everyday life; monotony; **~чный** [14] everyday; humdrum
будора́жить [16], <вз-> excite
бу́дто as if, as though (*a.* ***~ бы, ~ б***) that, allegedly
бу́дущ|ее *n* [17] future; ***в ближа́йшем ~ем*** in the near future; **~ий** [17] future (*a. gr.*) ***в ~ем году́*** next year; **~ность** *f* [8] future
бу́ер *m* [1; *pl.*: -ра, *etc. e.*] iceboat, ice yacht
бузина́ *f* [5] elder
буй *m* [3] buoy
бу́йвол *m* [1] buffalo
бу́йный [14; бу́ен, буйна́, -о] violent, vehement; (*необу́зданный*) unbridled; *расти́тельность* luxuriant
бу́йство *n* [9] rage, violence; **~вать** [7] behave violently, rage
бук *m* [1] beech
бу́к|ва *f* [5] letter; ***прописна́я*** (***строчна́я***) ***~ва*** upper-(lower)-case letter (**с** P with); **~ва́льный** [14] literal, verbal; **~ва́рь** *m* [4 *e.*] primer; **~вое́д** *m* [1] pedant
буке́т *m* [1] bouquet (*a. of wine*), bunch of flowers
букини́ст *m* [1] secondhand bookseller; **~и́ческий** [16]: ***~и́ческий магази́н*** secondhand bookshop
бу́ковый [14] beechen, beech...
букси́р *m* [1] tug(boat); ***взять на букси́р*** take in tow; **~ный** [14] tug...; **~ова́ть** [7] tow
була́вка *f* [5; *g/pl.*: -вок] pin; ***англи́йская ~*** safety pin
була́т *m* [1] Damascus steel; *fig.* sword; **~ный** [14] steel...; damask...
бу́лка *f* [5; *g/pl.*: -лок] small loaf; roll; white bread
бу́лоч|ка *f* [5; *g/pl.*: -чек] roll; bun; **~ная** *f* [14] bakery, baker's shop
булы́жник *m* [1] cobblestone
бульва́р *m* [1] boulevard, avenue; **~ный** [14]: ***~ный рома́н*** dime novel, *Brt.* penny dreadful; ***~ная пре́сса*** tabloids; gutter press
бу́лькать [1] gurgle
бульо́н *m* [1] broth; stock
бума́|га *f* [5] paper; document; ***це́нные ~ги*** securities; **~жка** *f* [5; *g/pl.*: -жек] slip of paper; **~жник** *m* [1] wallet; **~жный** [14] paper...
бундеста́г *m* [1] Bundestag

бунт *m* [1] revolt, mutiny, riot; **~а́рь** *m* [4 *e.*] → **~овщи́к**
бунтов|а́ть [7] rebel, revolt; <вз-> instigate; **~ско́й** [14] rebellious, mutinous; **~щи́к** *m* [1 *e.*] mutineer, rebel
бура́в *m* [1 *e.*] gimlet, auger; **~ить** [14], <про-> bore, drill
бура́н *m* [1] snowstorm, blizzard
бурда́ *coll. f* [5] slops
буреве́стник *m* [1] (storm) petrel
буре́ние *n* [12] drilling, boring
буржуаз|и́я *f* [7] bourgeoisie; **~́ный** [14] bourgeois
бури́ть [13], <про-> bore, drill
бу́ркать [1], *once* <-кнуть> mutter
бурли́ть [13] rage; (*кипе́ть*) seethe
бу́рный [14; -рен, -рна] stormy, storm...; *рост* rapid; boisterous, violent (*a. fig.*)
буру́н *m* [1 *e.*] surf, breaker
бурча́|нье *n* [12] grumbling; *в животе́* rumbling; **~ть** [4 *e.*; -чу́, -чи́шь] (*бормота́ть*) mumble; (*ворча́ть*) grumble; rumble
бу́рый [14] brown, tawny; **~ *медве́дь*** brown bear; **~ *у́голь*** brown coal, lignite
бурья́н *m* [1] tall weeds
бу́ря *f* [6] storm (*a. fig.*); **~ *в стака́не воды́*** storm in a teacup
бу́сы *f/pl.* [5] *coll.* (glass)beads
бутафо́рия *f* [7] *thea.* properties *pl.*; *в витри́не* dummies; *fig.* window dressing
бутербро́д (-tɛr-) *m* [1] sandwich
буто́н *m* [1] bud
бу́тсы *f/pl.* [5] football boots
буты́л|ка *f* [5; *g/pl.*: -лок] bottle; **~очка** *f* [5; *g/pl.*: -чек] small bottle; **~ь** *f* [8] large bottle; *оплетённая* carboy
бу́фер *m* [1; *pl.*: -pá, *etc. e.*] buffer
буфе́т *m* [1] sideboard; bar, lunchroom, refreshment room; **~чик** *m* [1] counter assistant; barman; **~чица** *f* [5] counter assistant; barmaid
бух *int.* bounce!, plump!
буха́нка *f* [5; *g/pl.*: -нок] loaf
бу́хать [1], *once* <бу́хнуть> thump, bang
бухга́лтер (bu'ha) *m* [1] bookkeeper; accountant; **~́ия** *f* [7] bookkeeping; **~ский** [16] bookkeeper('s)..., bookkeeping...; **~ский учёт** accounting
бу́хнуть [21] **1.** <раз-> swell; **2.** → ***бу́хать***
бу́хта[1] *f* [5] bay
бу́хта[2] *f* [5] coil (of rope)
бушева́ть [6; бушу́ю, -у́ешь] roar, rage, storm
бушла́т *m* [1] (sailor's) peajacket
буя́нить [13] brawl, kick up a row
бы, *short* **б**, *is used to render subjunctive and conditional patterns*: *a*) *with the preterite, e.g.* ***я сказа́л ~, е́сли ~*** (***я***) ***знал*** I would say it if I knew it; (*similary*: *should*, *could*, *may*, *might*); *b*) *with the infinitive*, *e.g.*: ***всё ~ ему́ знать*** *iro.* he would like to know everything; ***не вам ~ говори́ть!*** you had better be quiet!; c) *to express a wish* ***я ~ съел чего́-нибудь*** I could do with s.th. to eat
быва́лый [14] experienced
быва́|ть [1] **1.** occur, happen; ***как ни в чём не ~ло*** as if nothing had happened; ***она́ ~ло, гуля́ла*** she would (*or* used to) go for a walk; ***бо́ли как не ~ло*** *coll.* the pain had (*or* has) entirely disappeared; **2.** <по-> (**у** P) be (at), visit, stay (with)
бы́вший [17] former, ex-...
бык[1] *m* [1 *e.*] *мо́ста* pier
бык[2] *m* [1 *e.*] bull
были́на *f* [5] Russian epic
были́нка *f* [5; *g/pl.*: -нок] blade of grass
бы́ло (→ ***быть***) (*after verbs*) already; ***я уже́ заплати́л ~ де́ньги*** I had already paid the money, (but)...; almost, nearly, was (were) just going to...; ***я чуть ~ не сказа́л*** I was on the point of saying, I nearly said
был|о́й [14] bygone, former; **~о́е** *n* past; **~ь** *f* [8] true story *or* occurrence
быстро|но́гий [16] swift(-footed); **~та́** *f* [5] quickness, swiftness, rapidity; **~хо́дный** [14; -ден, -дна] fast, high-speed
бы́стрый [14; быстр, -á, -o] quick, fast, swift
быт *m* [1; в быту́] everyday life; ***семе́йный ~*** family life; ***~ дереве́нской жи́зни*** way of life in the country; **~и́е** *n* [12] existence, social

being; ***Книга** 2ия* *Bibl.* Genesis; **~ность** *f* [8] ***в мою ~ность*** in my time; **~овой** [14] everyday, social, popular, genre; ***~овые приборы*** household appliances

быть [3rd *p. sg. pr.*: → ***есть***; 3rd *p. pl.*: суть; *ft.*: буду, -дешь; будь[те]!; будучи; был, -á, -о; нé был, -о, -и] be; (→ ***будет, бывать, было***); **~** (Д) ... will (inevitably) be *or* happen; ***мне было*** (***будет***) ... (***года*** *or* ***лет***) I was (I'll be) ... (years old); ***как же ~?*** what is to be done?; ***так и ~!*** all right!; agreed!; ***будь что будет*** come what may; ***будь по-вашему!*** have it your own way!; ***будьте добры*** (***любезны***), ... be so kind as..., would you please...; ***у меня было много свободного времени*** I had a lot of time

бюджет *m* [1], **~ный** [14] budget

бюллетень *m* [4] bulletin; ballot paper; *coll.* sick-leave certificate

бюро *n* [*indecl.*] office, bureau; ***справочное ~*** inquiry office; information office; ***~ путешествий*** travel agency *or* bureau

бюрократ *m* [1] bureaucrat; **~ический** [16] bureaucratic; ***~ическая волокита*** *f* [5] red tape; **~ия** *f* [7] bureaucracy

бюст *m* [1] bust; **~гальтер** (-'haļ-tɛr) *m* [1] bra(ssière)

бязь *f* [8] calico

В

в, во 1. (В); (*direction*) to, into; for; ***в окно*** out of (in through) the window; (*time*) in; at; on; within; ***в среду*** on Wednesday; ***в два часа*** at two o'clock; (*measure, price, etc.*) at, of; ***в день*** a *or* per day; ***длиной в четыре метра*** four meters long; ***в десять раз больше*** ten times as much; **2.** (П): *положение* in, at, on; *время* in; ***в конце*** (***начале***) ***года*** at the end (beginning) of the year; (*расстояние*) ***в пяти километрах от*** (Р) five kilometers from

ва-банк: (*cards*) ***идти ~*** stake everything

вагон *m* [1] car(riage *Brt.*); **~овожатый** [14] (*Brt.* tram) driver; **~-ресторан** *m* dining car

важн|ичать [1] put on (*or* give *o.s.*) airs; **~ость** *f* [8] importance; conceit; **~ый** [14; важен, -жнá, -о, важны] important, significant; *надменный и т. д.* haughty, pompous; *coll.* ***не ~о*** rather bad; ***это не ~о*** that doesn't matter *or* is of no importance

ваза *f* [5] vase, bowl

вазелин *m* [1] vaseline

вакан|сия *f* [7] vacancy; **~тный** [14; -тен, -тна] vacant

вакуум *m* [1] vacuum

вакцина *f* [5] vaccine

вал *m* [1; на ~у́; *pl. e.*] **1.** *крепостной* rampart; *насыпь* bank; **2.** billow, wave; **3.** *tech.* shaft

валежник *m* [1] brushwood

валенок *m* [1; -нка] felt boot

валерьян|ка *coll.* *f* [5], **~овый** [14]: ***~овые капли*** *f/pl.* tincture of valerian

валет *m* [1] (*cards*) knave, jack

валик *m* [1] **1.** *tech.* roller; **2.** bolster

валить [13; валю, валишь; валенный], <по-, с-> **1.** overturn, tumble (down; *v/i.* **-ся**), *лес* fell; *в кучу* heap (up); dump; **2.** [3rd *p. only*: -ит] *о толпе* flock, throng; ***снег ~ит*** it is snowing heavily

валовой [14] gross, total

валторна *f* [5] French horn

валун *m* [1 *e.*] boulder

вальдшнеп *m* [1] woodcock

вальс *m* [1] waltz; **~ировать** [7], <про-> waltz

валют|а *f* [5] (foreign) currency; ***твёрдая ~а*** hard currency; **~ный**

[14] currency..., exchange...; **~ный курс** *m* rate of exchange

валя́ть [28], <по-> roll, drag; P ***валя́й!*** OK, go ahead!; ***валя́й отсю́да!*** beat it!; ***~ дурака́*** idle; play the fool; **-ся** *о челове́ке* wallow, loll; *о предме́тах* lie about (in disorder)

вандали́зм *m* [1] vandalism

вани́ль *f* [8] vanilla

ва́нн|а *f* [5] tub; bath; ***со́лнечная ~а*** sun bath; ***приня́ть ~у*** take a bath; **~ая** *f* [14] bath(room)

ва́рвар *m* [1] barbarian; **~ский** [16] barbarous; **~ство** *n* [9] barbarity

ва́режка *f* [5; *g/pl.*: -жек] mitten

вар|е́ние *n* [12] → ***ва́рка***; **~е́ник** *m* [1] (*mst. pl.*) boiled pieces of dough with stuffing; **~ёный** [14] cooked, boiled; **~е́нье** *n* [10] jam, confiture

вариа́нт *m* [1] variant, version

вари́ть [13; варю́, ва́ришь; ва́ренный], <с-> cook; boil; brew; *v/i.* **~ся**: ***~ в со́бственном соку́*** stew in one's own juice

ва́рка *f* [5] cooking; boiling

варьете́ *n* (-tɛ) [*indecl.*] variety show

варьи́ровать [7] vary

варя́г *m* [1] *hist.* Varangian; *coll., joc.* alien, stranger

василёк *m* [1; -лька́] cornflower

ва́та *f* [5] absorbent cotton, *Brt.* cotton wool

вата́га *f* [5] gang, band, troop

ватерли́ния (-tɛ-) *f* [7] waterline

ва́тный [14] quilted; wadded

ватру́шка *f* [5; *g/pl.*: -шек] curd tart, cheesecake

ва́фля *f* [6; *g/pl.*: -фель] waffle, wafer

ва́хт|а *f* [5] *naut.* watch; ***стоя́ть на ~е*** keep watch; **~енный** [14] sailor on duty; **~ёр** *m* [1] janitor, *Brt.* porter

ваш *m*, **~а** *f*, **~е** *n*, *pl.* **~и** [25] your; yours; ***по-~ему*** in your opinion; (***пусть бу́дет***) ***по-~ему*** (have it) your own way; (just) as you like; ***как по-~ему?*** what do you think?; → ***наш***

вая́|ние *n* [12] sculpture; **~тель** *m* [4] sculptor; **~ть** [28], <из-> sculpture, cut, model

вбе|га́ть [1], <~жа́ть> [4; -гу́, -жи́шь, -гу́т] run *or* rush into

вби|ва́ть [1], <~ть> [вобью́, вобьёшь; вбе́й(те)!; вбил; вби́тый]; drive (*or* hammer) in; ***~ть себе́ в го́лову*** get into one's head; **~ра́ть** [1], <вобра́ть> [вберу́, -рёшь] absorb, imbibe

вблизи́ nearby; close (to P)

вбок to one side, sideways

вброд: ***переходи́ть ~*** ford, wade

ввал|ивать [1], <~и́ть> [ввалю́, вва́лишь; вва́ленный] throw; heave (in[to]); dump; **-ся** fall or tumble in; burst in(to); ***толпо́й*** flock in

введе́ние *n* [12] introduction

ввезти́ → ***ввози́ть***

ввер|га́ть [1], <~нуть> [21]: ***~а́ть в отча́яние*** drive to despair

вверя́ть [14], <~ить> entrust, commit, give in charge

ввёртывать [1], <ввerте́ть> [11; вверчу́, вве́ртишь] *once* <вверну́ть> [20; ввёрнутый] screw in; *fig.* put in (a word *etc.*)

вверх up(ward[s]); ***~ по ле́стнице*** upstairs; ***~ дном*** (*or* ***нога́ми***) upside down; ***~ торма́шками*** head over heels; ***ру́ки ~!*** hands up!; **~у́** above; overhead

ввести́ → ***вводи́ть***

ввиду́ in view (of P), considering; ***~ того́, что*** as, since, seeing

ввин|чивать [1], <~ти́ть> [15 *e.*; -нчу́, -нти́шь] screw in

ввод *m* [1] *tech.* input

ввод|и́ть [15], <ввести́> introduce; bring *or* usher (in); ***~и́ть в заблужде́ние*** mislead; ***~и́ть в курс де́ла*** acquaint with an affair; ***~и́ть в строй*** (*or* ***де́йствие, эксплуата́цию***) put into operation; **~ный** [14] introductory; ***~ное сло́во*** *or* ***предложе́ние*** *gr.* parenthesis

ввоз *m* [1] import(s); importation; **~и́ть** [15], <ввезти́> [24] import

вво́лю (P) *coll.* plenty of; to one's heart's content

ввя́з|ываться [1], <~а́ться> [3] meddle, interfere (***в*** B with); get involved (in)

вглубь deep into, far into

вгля́д|ываться [1], <~е́ться> [11] (***в*** B) peer (into), look narrowly (at)

вгоня́ть [28], <вогна́ть> [вгоню́, вго́нишь; вогна́л, -а́, -о; во́гнанный (во́гнан, -а́, -о)] drive in (to)
вдава́ться [5], <вда́ться> [вда́мся, вда́шься, *etc.* → ***дать***] jut out into; ***~ в подро́бности*** go (into)
вда́в|ливать [1], <~и́ть> [14] press (in)
вдал|еке́, **~и́** far off, far (**от** Р from); **~ь** into the distance
вдви|га́ть [1], <~нуть> [20] push in
вдво́|е twice (as ..., *comp.*: ***~е бо́льше*** twice as much *or* many); *vb.* + **~е** *a.* double; **~ём** both *or* two (of us, *etc.*, *or* together); **~йне́** twice (as much, *etc.*); doubly
вде|ва́ть [1], <~ть> [вде́ну, вде́нешь; вде́тый] (***в*** В) put into, thread
вде́л|ывать, <~ать> [1] set (in[to])
вдоба́вок in addition (to); into the bargain, to boot
вдов|а́ *f* [5; *pl. st.*] widow; **~е́ц** *m* [1; -вца́] widower
вдо́воль *coll.* in abundance; quite enough; plenty of
вдо́вый [14 *sh.*] widowed
вдого́нку after, in pursuit of
вдоль (Р, ***по*** Д) along; lengthwise; ***~ и попере́к*** in all directions, far and wide
вдох *m* [1] breath, inhalation; ***сде́лайте глубо́кий ~*** take a deep breath
вдохнов|е́ние *n* [12] inspiration; **~е́нный** [14; -ве́нен, -ве́нна] inspired; **~ля́ть** [28], <~и́ть> [14 *e.*; -влю́, -ви́шь] inspire; **-ся** get inspired (Т with *or* by)
вдре́безги to smithereens
вдруг 1. suddenly, all of a sudden; **2.** what if, suppose
вду|ва́ть [1], <~ть> [18] blow into, inflate
вду́м|чивый [14 *sh.*] thoughtful; **~ываться**, <~аться> [1] (***в*** В) ponder (over), reflect ([up]on)
вдыха́ть [1], <вдохну́ть> [20] inhale; *fig.* inspire (with)
вегета|риа́нец *m* [1; -нца] vegetarian; **~ти́вный** [14] vegetative
ве́д|ать [1] **1.** know; **2.** (Т) be in charge of, manage; **~е́ние**[1] *n* [12] running, directing; ***~е́ние книг*** bookkeeping; **~ение**[2] *n* [12]: ***в его́ ~ении*** in his charge, competence; **~омо** known; ***без моего́ ~ома*** without my knowledge; **~омость** *f* [8; *from g/pl. e.*] list, roll, register; *периоди́ческое изда́ние* bulletin; ***инвента́рная ~омость*** inventory; **~омство** *n* [9] department
ведро́ *n* [9; *pl.*: вёдра, -дер, -драм] bucket, pail; ***~ для му́сора*** garbage can, *Brt.* dustbin
веду́щий *m* [17] leading; basic
ведь indeed, sure(ly); why, well; then; you know, you see; ***~ уже́ по́здно*** it is late, isn't it?
ве́дьма *f* [5] witch, hag
ве́ер *m* [1; *pl.*: -ра́ *etc. e.*] fan
ве́жлив|ость *f* [8] politeness; **~ый** [14 *sh.*] polite
везде́ everywhere; **~хо́д** *m* [1] all-terrain vehicle
везе́ние *n* [12] luck; ***како́е ~!*** what luck!
везти́ [24], <по-, с-> *v/t.* drive (be driving, *etc.*), transport; ***са́нки и т. д.*** pull; ***ему́*** (***не***) ***везёт*** *coll.* he is (un)lucky
век *m* [1; на веку́; *pl.*: века́, *etc. e.*] **1.** century; age; **2.** life(time); ***сре́дние ~а́*** *pl.* Middle Ages; ***на моём ~у́*** in my life(time); ***~ с тобо́й мы не вида́лись*** we haven't met for ages
ве́ко *n* [9; *nom/pl.*: -ки] eyelid
веково́й [14] ancient, age-old
ве́ксель *m* [4; *pl.*: -ля́, *etc. e.*] bill of exchange, promissory note
веле́ть [9] (*im*)*pf.*; *pt. pf. only* order, tell (Д/В p. s.th.)
велика́н *m* [1] giant
вели́к|ий [16; вели́к, -а́, -о́] great; (too) large *or* big; *only short form*; ***от ма́ла до ~а*** everybody, young and old; ***Пётр ~ий*** Peter the Great
велико|ду́шие *n* [12] magnanimity; **~ду́шный** [14; -шен, -шна] magnanimous, generous; **~ле́пие** *n* [12] splendo(u)r, magnificence; **~ле́пный** [14; -пен, -пна] magnificent, splendid
велича́вый [14 *sh.*] majestic, stately
вели́ч|ественный [14 *sh.*] majestic, grand, stately; **~ество** *n* [9]

majesty; **~ие** *n* [12] grandeur; greatness; **~ина́** *f* [5; *pl. st.*: -чины] size; magnitude, quantity; *math.* value; *об учёном и т. д.* celebrity; **~ино́й в** *or* (**с** B) ... big *or* high
вело|го́нки *f/pl.* [5; *gen.*: -нок] cycle race; **~дро́м** *m* [1] cycling track
велосипе́д *m* [1] bicycle; ***е́здить на ~е*** cycle; **~и́ст** *m* [1] cyclist; **~ный** [14] (bi)cycle..., cycling...
вельве́т *m* [1], **~овый** [14] velveteen
ве́на *f* [5] *anat.* vein
венг|е́рка *f* [5; *g/pl.*: -рок], **~е́рский** [16]; **~р** *m* [1] Hungarian
венери́ческий [16] venereal
вене́ц *m* [1; -нца] crown; *орео́л* halo; *fig.* consummation
венециа́нский [16] Venetian
ве́нзель *m* [4; *pl.*: -ля́] monogram
ве́ник *m* [1] broom, besom
вено́к *m* [1; -нка́] wreath, garland
вентил|и́ровать [7], <про-> ventilate, air; **~я́тор** *m* [1] ventilator, fan
венча́|льный [14] wedding..., **~ние** *n* [12] wedding (ceremony); **~ть** [1] **1.** <у-> crown; **2.** <об-, по-> marry; **-ся** get married (in church)
ве́ра *f* [5] faith, belief, trust (in **в** B); religion
вера́нда *f* [5] veranda(h)
ве́рба *f* [5] willow
верблю́|д *m* [1] camel; **~жий** [18]: ***~жья шерсть*** *f* camel's hair
ве́рбн|ый [14]: ***2ое воскресе́нье*** *n* Palm Sunday
вербов|а́ть [7], <за-, на-> enlist, recruit; *на рабо́ту* engage, hire; **~ка** *f* [5; -вок] recruiting
верё|вка *f* [5; *g/pl.*: -вок] rope, cord, string; **~вочный** [14] rope...
верени́ца *f* [5] row file, line
ве́реск *m* [1] heather
верещ́ать [16 *e.*; -щу́, -щи́шь] chirp; *coll.* squeal
верзи́ла *coll. m* [5] lanky fellow
ве́рить [13], <по-> believe (in **в** B); believe, trust (acc. Д); ***~ на́ слово*** take on trust; **-ся** (*impers.*): (***мне***) ***не ве́рится*** one (I) can hardly believe it
вермише́ль *f* [8] *coll.* vermicelli
ве́рно *adv.* **1.** & **2.** → ***ве́рный*** **1. 2.**; **3.** probably; **~сть** *f* [8] **1.** faith(fulness), fidelity, loyalty; **2.** correctness, accuracy
верну́ть(ся) [20] *pf.* → ***возвраща́ть(ся)***
ве́рн|ый [14; -рен, -рна́, -о] **1.** *друг* faithful, true, loyal; **2.** (*пра́вильный*) right, correct; (*то́чный*) accurate, exact; **3.** (*надёжный*) safe, sure, reliable; **4.** (*неизбе́жный*) inevitable, certain; ***~е́е*** (***сказа́ть***) or rather
вероисповеда́ние *n* [12] creed; denomination
вероло́м|ный [14; -мен, -мна] perfidious, treacherous; **~ство** *n* [9] perfidy, treachery
веротерпи́мость *f* [8] toleration
вероя́т|ность *f* [8] probability; ***по всей ~ности*** in all probability; **~ный** [14; -тен, -тна] probable, likely
ве́рсия *f* [7] version
верста́к *m* [1 *e.*] workbench
ве́рт|ел *m* [1; *pl.*: -ла́] spit, skewer; **~е́ть** [11; верчу́, ве́ртишь], <по-> turn, twist; **-ся 1.** turn, revolve; **2.** *на сту́ле* fidget; ***-ся на языке́*** be on the tip of one's tongue; ***-ся под нога́ми*** be (or get) in the way; **~ика́льный** [14; -лен, -льна] vertical; **~олёт** *m* [1] helicopter
ве́рующий *m* [17] *su.* believer
верфь *f* [8] shipyard
верх *m* [1; на верху́; *pl. e.*] top, upper part; *fig.* height; ***взять ~*** gain the upper hand, win; **~и́** *pl.* top-ranking officials; **1.** ***в ~а́х*** summit...; **2.** *о зна́ниях* superficial knowledge; **~ний** [15] upper
верхо́в|ный [14] supreme, high; ***~ная власть*** supreme power; ***~ный суд*** supreme court; **~о́й** [14] riding...; rider; horseman; ***~а́я езда́*** *f* riding; **~ье** *n* [10; *g/pl.*: -ьев] upper reaches
верхо́м *adv.* astride, on horseback; ***е́здить ~*** ride, go on horseback
верху́шка *f* [5; *g/pl.*: -шек] top, apex; high-ranking officials
верши́на *f* [5] peak, summit
верши́ть [16 *e.*; -шу́, -ши́шь; -шённый], <за-, с-> **1.** manage, control; **2.** run (T); **3.** accomplish, decide

В

вес *m* [1] weight; **на ~** by weight; **удельный ~** *phys.* specific gravity; **иметь ~** *fig.* carry weight; **на ~ золота** worth its weight in gold; **~ом в** (B) weighting...

вес|ели́ть [13], <раз-> amuse, divert, (**-ся** enjoy o.s.); **~ёлость** *f* [8] gaeity, mirth; **~ёлый** [14; весел, -а́, -о] gay, merry, cheerful; **как ~ело!** it's such fun!; **ему́ ~ело** he is enjoying himself, is of good cheer; **~е́лье** *n* [10] merriment, merry-making, fun; **~ельча́к** *m* [1 *e.*] convivial fellow

весе́нний [15] spring...

ве́с|ить [15] *v/i.* weigh; **~кий** [16; ве́сок, -ска] weighty

весло́ *n* [9; *pl.*: вёсла, -сел] oar

весн|а́ *f* [5; *pl.*: вёсны, вёсен] spring (in [the] T); **~у́шка** *f* [5; *g/pl.*: -шек] freckle

весов|о́й [14] **1.** weight...; balance-...; **2.** sold by weight; **~щи́к** *m* [1 *e.*] weigher

весо́мый [14] *fig.* weighty

ве́сти[1] *f/pl.* [8] news

вести́[2] [25], <по->; **1.** (be) lead(ing *etc.*), conduct, guide; **2.** *разгово́р* carry on; **3.** *дневни́к* keep; **4.** *маши́ну* drive; **~ (своё) нача́ло** originate (**от** P in); **~ себя́** behave (*o.s.*); **и у́хом не ведёт** pays no attention at all; **~сь** be conducted *or* carried on; **так уж у нас повело́сь** that's a custom among us

вестибю́ль *m* [4] entrance hall

ве́ст|ник *m* [1] bulletin; **~очка** *f* [5; *g/pl.*: -чек] *coll.* news; **~ь** *f* [8; *from g/pl. e.*] news, message; **пропа́сть без ~и** be missing

весы́ *m/pl.* [1] scales, balance; ♎ Libra

весь *m*, **вся** *f*, **всё** *n*, *pl.*: **все** [31] **1.** *adj.* all, the whole; full (**в** B at); **2.** *su. n* all over; everything, *pl. e.* everybody; **вот и всё** that's all; **лу́чше всего́** (**всех**) best of all, the best; **пре́жде всего́** first and foremost; **при всём том** for all that; **во всём ми́ре** all over the world; **по всей стране́** throughout the country; **всего́ хоро́шего!** good luck!; **во всю** → **си́ла**; **3. всё** *adv.* always, all the time; only, just; **всё** (**ещё**) **не** not yet; **всё бо́льше** (**и бо́льше**) more and more; **всё же** nevertheless, yet

весьма́ very, extremely, highly; **~ вероя́тно** most probably

ветв|и́стый [14 *sh.*] branchy, spreading; **~ь** *f* [8; *from g/pl. e.*] branch (*a. fig.*), bough

ве́тер *m* [1; -тра] wind; **встре́чный ~** contrary *or* head wind; **попу́тный ~** fair wind; **броса́ть де́ньги** (**слова́**) **на ~** waste money (words); *old use* **держа́ть нос по ве́тру** be a timeserver

ветера́н *m* [1] veteran

ветерина́р *m* [1] veterinary surgeon, *coll.* vet; **~ный** [14] veterinary

ветеро́к *m* [1; -рка́] light wind, breeze, breath

ве́тка *f* [5; *g/pl.*: -ток] branch(let), twig; *rail.* branch line

ве́то *n* [*indecl.*] veto; **наложи́ть ~** veto

ве́тр|еный [14 *sh.*] windy (*a. fig.* = flippant); **~яно́й** [14] wind...; **~яна́я ме́льница** windmill; **~яный** [14]: **~яная о́спа** chicken pox

ве́тх|ий [16; ветх, -а́, -о] *дом* old, dilapidated; *оде́жда* worn out, shabby; decrepit; **~ость** *f* [8] decay, dilapidation; **приходи́ть в ~ость** fall into decay

ветчина́ *f* [5] ham

ветша́ть [1], <об-> decay, become dilapidated

ве́ха *f* [5] landmark, milestone *mst. fig.*

ве́чер *m* [1; *pl.*: -ра́, *etc. e.*] **1.** evening; **2. ~ па́мяти** commemoration meeting; **~ом** in the evening; **сего́дня ~ом** tonight; **вчера́ ~ом** last night; **под ~** toward(s) the evening; **~е́ть** [8; *impers.*] decline (*of the day*); **~и́нка** *f* [5; *g/pl.*: -нок] (evening) party, soirée; **~ко́м** *coll.* = **~ом**; **~ний** [15] evening..., night...; **~я** *f* [6]: **Та́йная ~я** the Last Supper

ве́чн|ость *f* [8] eternity; (**це́лую**) **~ость** *coll.* for ages; **~ый** [14; -чен, -чна] eternal, everlasting; perpetual

ве́ша|лка *f* [5; *g/pl.*: -лок] (coat) hanger; (*петля́*) tab; peg, rack; *coll.*

cloakroom; **~ть** [1] **1.** <повéсить> [15] hang (up); **-ся** hang o.s.; **2.** <взвéсить> [15] weigh
вещáние *n* [12] → ***рáдио~***
вещ|éственный [14] material, substantial; **~ествó** *n* [9] matter, substance; **~úца** *f* [8] knickknack; piece; **~ь** *f* [8; *from g/pl. e.*] thing; object; (*произведéние*) work, piece, play; *pl.* belongings; baggage, *Brt.* luggage
вéя|ние *n* [12] *fig.* trend, tendency, current; ***~ние врéмени*** spirit of the times; **~ть** [27] *v/i.* blow, flutter, <по-> smell, breathe of
вжи|вáться [1], <~ться> [-вýсь, *etc.* → ***жить***] accustom o.s. (***в*** В to)
взад *coll.* back(ward[s]); ***~ и вперёд*** back and forth, to and fro; up and down
взаúмн|ость *f* [8] reciprocity; **~ый** [14; -мен, -мна] mutual, reciprocal
взаимо|вы́годный [14; -ден, -дна] mutually beneficial; **~дéйствие** *n* [12] interaction; *сотрýдничество* cooperation; **~дéйствовать** [7] interact, cooperate; **~отношéние** *n* [12] interrelation; *людéй* relationship, relations *pl.*; **~пóмощь** *f* [8] mutual aid; **~понимáние** *n* [12] mutual understanding
взаймы́: ***брать ~*** borrow (***у***, ***от*** Р from); ***давáть ~*** lend
вза|мéн (Р) instead of, in exchange for; **~пертú** locked up, under lock and key
взбáл|мошный *coll.* [14; -шен, -шна] eccentric, extravagant; **~тывать**, <взболтáть> [1] shake *or* stir up
взбе|гáть [1], <~жáть> [4; взбегý, -жúшь, -гýт] run up
взбивáть [1], <взбить> [взобью́, -бьёшь; взбил, -а; взбúтый] whip, beat up
взбирáться, <взобрáться> [взберýсь, -рёшься; взобрался, -лáсь, -лóсь] climb, clamber up (***на*** В s.th.)
взбúты|й [14]: ***~е слúвки*** whipped cream
взболтáть → ***взбáлтывать***
взбудорáживать [1] → ***будорáжить***
взбунтовáться → ***бунтовáть***
взбух|áть [1], <~нуть> [21] swell
взвáливать [1], <взвалúть> [13; взвалю́, -áлишь; -áленный] load, lift, hoist (onto), *обя́занности и т. д.* charge (***на*** В with)
взвестú → ***взводúть***
взвé|шивать [1], <~сить> [15] weigh; **-ся** weigh o.s
взвивáть [1], <~ть> [взовью́, -вьёшь, *etc.* → ***вить***] whirl up; **-ся** soar up, rise; *fig.* flare up
взвизг|ивать [1], <~нуть> [20] cry out, squeak, scream; *о собáке* yelp
взвин|чивать [1], <~тúть> [15 *e.*; -нчý, -нтúшь; -úнченный] excite; *цéны* raise
взвить → ***взвивáть***
взвод *m* [1] platoon
взводúть [15], <взвестú> [25]: ***~ курóк*** cock (*firearm*)
взволнó|ванный [14 *sh.*] excited; *испы́тывающий беспокóйство* uneasy; **~вáть(ся)** → ***волновáть***
взгля|д *m* [1] look; glance; gaze, stare; *fig.* view, opinion; ***на мой ~д*** in my opinion; ***на пéрвый ~д*** at first sight; ***с пéрвого ~да*** on the face of it; *любóвь* at first sight, at once; **~дывать** [1], *once* <~нýть> [19] (***на*** В) (have a) look, glance (at)
взгромо|ждáть [1], <~здúть> [15 *e.*; -зжý, -здúшь, -мождённый] load, pile up; **-ся** clamber, perch (on ***на*** В)
взгрустнýть [20; -ну, -нёшь] *coll.* feel sad
вздёр|гивать [1], <~нуть> [20] jerk up; ***~нутый нос*** *m* turned-up nose
вздор *m* [1] nonsense; ***нестú ~*** talk nonsense; **~ный** [14; -рен, -рна] foolish, absurd; *coll.* (*сварлúвый*) quarrelsome, cantankerous
вздорожá|ние *n* [12] rise in price(s); **~ть** → ***дорожáть***
вздох *m* [1] sigh; ***испустúть послéдний ~*** breathe one's last; **~нýть** → ***вздыхáть***
вздрáгивать [1], *once* <вздрóгнуть> [20] start, wince; shudder
вздремнýть *coll.* [20] *pf.* have a nap, doze

взду|ва́ть [1], <∼ть> [18] **1.** *це́ны* run up; **2.** *v/i.* **-ся** swell; **3.** *coll.* give a thrashing; **∼́тие** *n* [12] swelling

взду́ма|ть [1] *pf.* conceive the idea, take it into one's head; **-ся**; ***ему́ ∼лось = он ∼л***; ***как ∼ется*** at one's will

взды|ма́ть [1] raise, *клу́бы ды́ма* whirl up; **∼ха́ть** [1], *once* <вздохну́ть> [20] sigh; ***∼ха́ть*** (***по***, **о** П) long (for); *pf. coll.* pause for breath

взи|ма́ть [1] levy, raise (from **с** Р); ***∼ма́ть штраф*** collect; **∼ра́ть** [1] (***на*** В) look (at); ***невзира́я на*** without regard to, notwithstanding

взла́мывать, <взлома́ть> [1] break *or* force open

взлёт *m* [1] upward flight; *ae.* take off; ***∼но-поса́дочная полоса́*** landing strip, runway

взлет|а́ть [1], <∼е́ть> [11] fly up, soar; *ae.* take off

взлом *m* [1] breaking in; **∼а́ть** → ***взла́мывать***; **∼́щик** *m* [1] burglar

взмах *m* [1] *руки́ пловца́* stroke; *косы́* sweep; **∼́ивать** [1], *once* <∼ну́ть> [20] swing, *руко́й* wave, *кры́льями* flap

взмет|а́ть [3], *once* <∼ну́ть> [20] *пыль* whirl *or* throw up

взмо́рье *n* [10] seashore, seaside

взнос *m* [1] payment; fee; *при поку́пке в рассро́чку* installment

взну́зд|ывать [1], <∼а́ть> bridle

взобра́ться → ***взбира́ться***

взойти́ → ***восходи́ть*** & ***всходи́ть***

взор *m* [1] look; gaze; eyes *pl.*

взорва́ть → ***взрыва́ть***

взро́слый [14] grown-up, adult

взрыв *m* [1] explosion; *fig.* outburst; **∼а́тель** *m* [4] (detonating) fuse; **∼а́ть** [1], <взорва́ть> [-ву́, -вёшь; взо́рванный] blow up; *fig.* enrage; **-ся** explode; fly into a rage; **∼но́й** [14], **∼́чатый** [14] explosive (*su.*: ***∼́чатое вещество́***), *coll.* **∼ча́тка**

взрыхля́ть [28] → ***рыхли́ть***

взъе|зжа́ть [1], <∼́хать> [взъе́ду, -дешь; въезжай(те)!] ride *or* drive up; **∼ро́шивать** [1], <∼ро́шить> [16 *st.*] dishevel, tousle; **-ся** become dishevel(l)ed

взыва́ть [1], <воззва́ть> [-зову́, -зовёшь; -зва́л, -а́, -о] appeal (to ***к*** Д); ***∼ о по́мощи*** call for help

взыск|а́ние *n* [12] **1.** penalty, exaction, levy; **2.** (*вы́говор*) reprimand; **∼а́тельный** [14; -лен, -льна] exacting, exigent; **∼́ивать** [1], <∼а́ть> [3] (**с** Р) levy, exact

взя́т|ие *n* [12] seizure, capture; **∼ка** *f* [5; *g/pl.*: -ток] **1.** bribe; ***дать ∼ку*** bribe; **2.** *ка́рты* trick; **∼очник** *m* [1] bribe taker, corrupt official; **∼очничество** *n* [9] bribery; **∼ь** → ***брать***

вибр|а́ция *f* [7] vibration; **∼и́ровать** [7] vibrate

вид *m* [1] **1.** look(s), appearance, air; **2.** sight, view; **3.** kind, sort; species; **4.** *gr.* aspect; ***в ∼́е*** (Р) in the form of, as, by way of; ***в любо́м ∼́е*** in any shape; ***под ∼́ом*** under the guise (of Р); ***при ∼́е*** at the sight of; ***на ∼у́*** (***у*** Р) in sight; visible (to); **с** (*or* ***по***) ***∼́у*** by sight; judging from appearance; ***ни под каки́м ∼́ом*** on no account; ***у него́ хоро́ший ∼*** he looks well; ***де́лать ∼*** pretend; (***не***) ***теря́ть*** *or* ***выпуска́ть из ∼́у*** (not) lose sight of (keep in view); **∼́ы** *pl.* prospects (for ***на*** В)

вида́ть *coll.* [1], <у-, по-> see; ***его́ давно́ не ∼*** I *or* we haven't seen him for a long time; **∼ся** (*iter.*) meet, see (o.a.; *a p.* **с** Т)

ви́дение[1] *n* [12] vision, view; ***моё ∼ пробле́мы*** the way I see it

виде́ние[2] *n* [12] vision, apparition

видео|за́пись *f* [8] video (tape) recording; **∼кассе́та** *f* [5] video cassette; **∼магнитофо́н** *m* [1] video (tape) recorder

ви́деть [11 *st.*], <у-> see; catch sight of; ***∼ во сне*** dream (of В); ***ви́дишь*** (***-ите***) ***ли?*** you see?; **-ся** → ***вида́ться*** (*but a. once*)

ви́дим|о apparently, evidently; ***∼о-не∼о*** *coll.* lots of, immense quantity; **∼ость** *f* [8] **1.** visibility; **2.** *fig.* appearance; ***всё э́то одна́ ∼*** there is nothing behind this; **∼ый** [14 *sh.*] **1.** visible; **2.** [14] apparent

видн|е́ться [8] be visible, be seen; **∼́о** it can be seen; it appears; apparently; (***мне***) ***ничего́ не ∼́о*** I don't *or* can't see anything; **∼́ый 1.** [14; -ден, -дна́, -дно] visible, conspicuous; **2.** [14] distinguished, promi-

nent; *coll. мужчи́на* portly
видоизмен|éние *n* [12] modification, alteration; variety; **~я́ть** [1], <**~и́ть**> [13] alter, change
ви́за *f* [5] visa
визави́ [*indecl.*] **1.** opposite; **2.** person face-to-face with another
византи́йский [16] Byzantine
виз|г *m* [1] scream, shriek; *живóтного* yelp; **~гли́вый** [14 *sh.*] shrill; given to screaming; **~жа́ть** [4 *e.*; -жý, -жи́шь], <за-> shriek; yelp
визи́ровать [7] (*im*)*pf.* visa
визи́т *m* [1] visit, call; ***нанести́ ~*** make an official visit; **~ный** [14]: ***~ная ка́рточка*** *f* calling *or* visiting card
ви́л|ка *f* [5; *g/pl.*: -лок] **1.** fork; **2.** (***штéпсельная***) **~ка** *el.* plug; **~ы** *f/pl.* [5] pitchfork
ви́лла *f* [5] villa
виля́ть [28], <за->, *once* <вильнýть> [20] wag (one's tail *хвостóм*); *о дорóге* twist and turn; *fig.* prevaricate; be evasive
вин|á *f* [5; *pl. st.*] **1.** guilt; fault; blame; **2.** (*причи́на*) reason; ***вменя́ть в ~ý*** impute (to Д); ***сва́ливать ~ý*** lay the blame (on ***на*** В); ***э́то не по моéй ~é*** it's not my fault
винегрéт *m* [1] Russian salad with vinaigrette
вини́т|ельный [14] *gr.* accusative (case); **~ь** [13] blame (***за*** В for), accuse (***в*** П of)
ви́н|ный [14] wine...; **~ó** *n* [9; *pl. st.*] wine
винова́т|ый [14 *sh.*] guilty (of ***в*** П); ***~!*** sorry!, excuse me!; (I beg your) pardon!; ***вы в э́том*** (***не***) ***~ы*** it's (not) your fault; ***я ~ пéред ва́ми*** I must apologize to you, (*a.* ***кругóм ~***) it's all my fault
винóв|ник *m* [1] **1.** culprit; **2.** ***~ник торжества́*** hero; **~ный** [14; -вен, -вна] guilty (of ***в*** П)
виногра́д *m* [1] **1.** vine; **2.** *collect.* grapes *pl.*; **~арство** *n* [9] viticulture; **~ник** *m* [1] vineyard; **~ный** [14] (of) grape(s), grape...
винодéлие *n* [12] winemaking
винт *m* [1 *e.*] screw; **~и́к** *m* [1] small screw; ***у негó ~иков не хвата́ет*** *coll.* he has a screw loose; **~óвка** *f* [5; *g/pl.*: -вок] rifle; **~овóй** [14] screw...; spiral; ***~ова́я лéстница*** spiral (winding) stairs
виньéтка *f* [5; *g/pl.*: -ток] vignette
виолончéль *f* [8] (violon)cello
вира́ж *m* [1 *e.*] bend, curve, turn
виртуóз *m* [1] virtuoso; **~ный** [14; -зен, -зна] masterly
ви́рус *m* [1] virus
ви́селица *f* [5] gallows
висéть [11] hang
ви́ски *n* [*indecl.*] whisk(e)y
вискóза *f* [5] *tech.* viscose; *ткань* rayon
ви́снуть *coll.* [21], <по-> *v/i.* hang
висóк *m* [1; -ска́] *anat.* temple
високóсный [14]: ***~ год*** leap year
вися́чий [17] hanging; suspension-...; ***~ замóк*** padlock
витами́н *m* [1] vitamin; **~ный** [14] vitaminic
вит|а́ть [1]: ***~а́ть в облака́х*** have one's head in the clouds; **~иева́тый** [14] affected, bombastic
витóк *m* [1; -тка] coil, spiral
витра́ж *m* [1] stained-glass window
витри́на *f* [5] shopwindow; showcase
вить [вью, вьёшь; вéй(те)!; вил, -á, -о; ви́тый], <с-> [совью́, совьёшь] wind, twist; ***~ гнездó*** build a nest; **-ся 1.** wind; *о пы́ли* spin, whirl; **2.** *о растéнии* twine, creep; *о волоса́х* curl; **3.** *о пти́це* hover
ви́тязь *m* [4] *hist.* valiant warrior
вихóр *m* [1; -хра́] forelock
вихрь *m* [4] whirlwind
ви́це-... (*in compds.*) vice-...
вишн|ёвый [14] cherry...; **~я** *f* [6; *g/pl.*: -шен] cherry
вка́пывать [1], <вкопа́ть> dig in; *fig.* ***как вкóпанный*** stock-still, rooted to the ground
вка́т|ывать [1], <**~и́ть**> [15] roll in, wheel in
вклад *m* [1] deposit; *капита́ла* investment, *fig.* contribution (***в*** В to); **~ка** *f* [5; *g/pl.*: -док] insert; **~чик** *m* [1] depositor; investor; **~ывать** [1], <вложи́ть> [16] put in, insert, enclose; *дéньги* invest; deposit
вклé|ивать [1], <**~ить**> [13] glue *or* paste in; **~йка** *f* [5; *g/pl.*: -éек] gluing in; sheet, *etc.*, glued in

В

вкли́ни|вать(ся) [1], <~ть(ся)> [13; *a. st.*] drive a wedge into
включ|а́ть [1], <~и́ть> [16 *e.*; -чу́, -чи́шь; -чённый] include; insert; *el.* switch *or* turn on; **-ся** join (**в** В s.th.); **~а́я** including; **~е́ние** *n* [12] inclusion; insertion; *el.* switching on, **~и́тельно** included
вкол|а́чивать [1], <~оти́ть> [15] drive *or* hammer in
вконе́ц *coll.* completely, altogether
вкопа́ть → ***вка́пывать***
вкось askew, aslant, obliquely; ***вкривь и ~*** pell-mell; amiss
вкра́|дчивый [14 *sh.*] insinuating, ingratiating; **~дываться** [1], <~сть(ся)> [25] creep *or* steal in; *fig.* insinuate o.s.
вкра́тце briefly, in a few words
вкруту́ю: ***яйцо́ ~*** hard-boiled egg
вкус *m* [1] taste (*a. fig.*), flavo(u)r; ***прия́тный на ~*** savo(u)ry; ***быть*** (***прийти́сь***) ***по вку́су*** be to one's taste; relish (*or* like) s.th.; ***име́ть ~*** (Р) taste (of); ***о ~ах не спо́рят*** tastes differ; ***э́то де́ло ~а*** it is a matter of taste; **~ный** [14; -сен, -сна́] tasty; (***э́то***) ***~но*** it tastes good *or* nice
вла́га *f* [5] moisture
владе́|лец *m* [1; -льца] owner, proprietor, possessor; **~ние** *n* [12] ownership, possession (of Т); **~ть** [8], <за-, о-> (Т) own, possess; *ситуа́цией* control; *языко́м* have command (Т of); ***~ть собо́й*** control o.s.
влады́ка *m* [5] *eccl.* Reverend
вла́жн|ость *f* [8] humidity; **~ый** [14; -жен, -жна́, -о] humid, damp, moist
вла́мываться [1], <вломи́ться> [14] break in
вла́ст|вовать [7] rule, dominate; **~ели́н** *m* [1] *mst. fig.* lord, master; **~и́тель** *m* [4] sovereign, ruler; **~ный** [14; -тен, -тна] imperious, commanding, masterful; ***в э́том я не ~ен*** I have no power over it; **~ь** *f* [8; *from g/pl. e.*] authority, power; rule, regime; control; *pl.* authorities
влачи́ть [16 *e.*; -чу́, -чи́шь]: ***~ жа́лкое существова́ние*** hardly make both ends meet, drag out a miserable existence
вле́во (to the) left
влез|а́ть [1], <~ть> [24 *st.*] climb *or* get in(to); climb up
влет|а́ть [1], <~е́ть> [11] fly in; *вбежа́ть* rush in
влеч|е́ние *n* [12] inclination, strong attraction; *к кому́-л.* love; **~ь** [26], <по-, у-> drag, pull; *fig.* attract, draw; ***~ь за собо́й*** involve, entail
вли|ва́ть [1], <~ть> [волью́, -льёшь; вле́й(те)!; вли́тый (-та́, -о)] pour in; **-ся** flow *or* fall in; **~па́ть** *coll.* [1], <~пнуть> [20] *fig.* get into trouble; find o.s. in an awkward situation; **~я́ние** *n* [12] influence; **~я́тельный** [14; -лен, -льна] influential; **~я́ть** [28], <по-> (have) influence
влож|е́ние *n* [12] enclosure; *fin.* investment; **~и́ть** → ***вкла́дывать***
вломи́ться → ***вла́мываться***
влюб|лённость *f* [8] (being in) love; **~лённый** enamo(u)red; *su.* lover; **~ля́ться** [28], <~и́ться> [14] fall in love (**в** В with); **~чивый** [14 *sh.*] amorous
вмен|я́емый [14 *sh.*] responsible, accountable; **~я́ть** [28], <~и́ть> [13] consider (**в** В as), impute; ***~я́ть в вину́*** blame; ***~я́ть в обя́занность*** impose as duty
вме́сте together, along with; ***~ с тем*** at the same time
вмести́|мость *f* [8] capacity; **~тельный** [14; -лен, -льна] capacious, spacious; **~ть** → ***вмеща́ть***
вме́сто (Р) instead, in place (of)
вмеш|а́тельство *n* [9] interference, intervention; *хирурги́ческое* operation; **~ивать** [1], <~а́ть> [1] (В/ **в** В) (in; with); *fig.* involve (in); **-ся** interfere, intervene, meddle (**в** В in)
вме|ща́ть [1], <~сти́ть> [15 *e.*; -ещу́, -ести́шь; -ещённый] **1.** (*помести́ть*) put, place; **2.** *зал и т. д.* hold, contain, accommodate; **-ся** find room; hold; go in
вмиг in an instant, in no time
вмя́тина *f* [5] dent
внача́ле at first, at the beginning
вне (Р) out of, outside; beyond; ***быть ~ себя́*** be beside o.s.; ***~ вся́ких сомне́ний*** beyond (any) doubt

внебра́чный [14] extramarital; *ребёнок* illegitimate
внедр|е́ние *n* [12] introduction; **~я́ть** [28], <~и́ть> [13] introduce; **-ся** take root
внеза́пный [14; -пен, -пна] sudden, unexpected
внекла́ссный [14] out-of-class
внеочередно́й [14] out of turn, extra(ordinary)
внес|е́ние *n* [12] entry; **~ти́** → ***вноси́ть***
вне́шн|ий [15] outward, external; *pol.* foreign; **~ость** *f* [8] (*нару́жность*) appearance, exterior
внешта́тный [14] *сотру́дник* not on permanent staff, freelance
вниз down(ward[s]); **~у́ 1.** (P) beneath, below; **2.** down(stairs)
вник|а́ть [1], <~нуть> [19] (***в*** B) get to the bottom (of), fathom
внима́|ние *n* [12] attention; care; ***приня́ть во ~ние*** take into consideration; ***принима́я во ~ние*** taking into account, in view of; ***оста́вить без ~ния*** disregard; **~тельность** *f* [8] attentiveness; **~тельный** [14; -лен, -льна] attentive; **~ть** [1], <внять> [*inf. & pt. only*; внял, -á, -о] (Д) *old use.* hear *or* listen (to)
вничью́: (*sport*) ***сыгра́ть ~*** draw
вновь 1. again; **2.** newly
вноси́ть [15], <внести́> [25; -с-: -су́, -сёшь; внёс, внесла́] carry *or* bring in; *в спи́сок и т. д.* enter, include; *де́ньги* pay (in); contribute; *попра́вки* make (correction); *предложе́ние* submit, put forward
внук *m* [1] grandson; **~и** grandchildren
вну́тренн|ий [15] inner, inside, internal, interior; *мо́ре и т. д.* inland...; (*оте́чественный*) home...; **~ость** *f* [8] interior; (*esp. pl.*) internal organs, entrails
внутр|и́ (P) in(side); within; **~ь** (P) in(to), inward(s), inside
внуч|а́та *m/f pl.* [2] → ***вну́ки***; **~ка** *f* [5; *g/pl.*: -чек] granddaughter
внуш|а́ть [1], <-и́ть> [16 *e.*; -шу́, -ши́шь; -шённый] (Д/В) suggest; *наде́жду, страх* inspire (*a p.* with); *уваже́ние и т. д.* instill; **~е́ние** *n* [12] suggestion; *вы́говор* reprimand; **~и́тельный** [14; -лен, -льна] imposing, impressive; **~и́ть** → **~а́ть**
вня́т|ный [14; -тен, -тна] distinct, intelligible; **~ь** → ***внима́ть***
вобра́ть → ***вбира́ть***
вовл|ека́ть [1], <-е́чь> [26] draw in; (*впу́тывать*) involve
во́время in *or* on time, timely
во́все: **~ не**(**т**) not (at all)
вовсю́ *coll.* with all one's might; ***стара́ться ~*** do one's utmost
во-вторы́х second(ly)
вогна́ть → ***вгоня́ть***
во́гнутый [14] concave
вод|а́ *f* [5; *ac/sg.*: во́ду; *pl.*: во́ды, вод, во́дам] water; ***в му́тной ~е́ ры́бу лови́ть*** fish in troubled waters; ***вы́йти сухи́м из ~ы*** come off cleanly; ***как в ~у опу́щенный*** dejected, downcast; ***толо́чь ~у*** (***в сту́пе***) beat the air
водвор|я́ть [28], <~и́ть> [13] *поря́док* establish
водеви́ль *m* [4] vaudeville, musical comedy
води́тель *m* [4] driver; **~ский** [16]: ***~ские права́*** driving licence
вод|и́ть [15], <по-> **1.** lead, conduct, guide; **2.** *маши́ну* drive; **3.** move (T); **-ся** be (found), live; ***как ~и́тся*** as usual; ***э́то за ним ~и́тся*** *coll.* that's typical of him
во́дка *f* [5; *g/pl.*: -док] vodka
во́дный [14] water...; ***~ спорт*** aquatic sports
водо|воро́т *m* [1] whirpool, eddy; **~ём** *m* [1] reservoir; **~измеще́ние** *n* [12] *naut.* displacement, tonnage
водо|ла́з *m* [1] diver; **Ꙩле́й** *m* [3] Aquarius; **~лече́ние** *n* [12] hydropathy, water cure; **~напо́рный** [14]: ***~напо́рная ба́шня*** *f* water tower; **~непроница́емый** [14 *sh.*] watertight, waterproof; **~па́д** *m* [1] waterfall; **~по́й** *m* [3] watering place; watering (*of animals*); **~прово́д** *m* [1] water supply; *в до́ме* running water; **~прово́дчик** *coll.* *m* [1] plumber; **~разде́л** *m* [1] watershed; **~ро́д** *m* [1] hydrogen; **~ро́дный** [14]: ***~ро́дная бо́мба*** hydrogen bomb; **~росль** *f* [8] alga, seaweed; **~снабже́ние** *n* [12] wa-

В

ter supply; **~сто́к** *m* [1] drain(age), drainpipe; **~сто́чный** [14]: ***~сто́чный жёлоб*** gutter; **~храни́лище** *n* [11] reservoir

водру|жа́ть [1], <~зи́ть> [15 *e.*; -ужу́, -узи́шь; -ужённый] hoist

вод|яни́стый [14 *sh.*] watery; wishy-washy; **~я́нка** *f* [5] dropsy; **~яно́й** [14] water...

воева́ть [6] wage *or* carry on war, be at war

воеди́но together

военача́льник *m* [1] commander

воениз‌|а́ция *f* [7] militarization; **~и́ровать** [7] *(im)pf.* militarize

вое́нно|-возду́шный [14]: ***~-возду́шные си́лы*** *f/pl.* air force(s); **~-морско́й** [14]: ***~-морско́й флот*** navy; **~пле́нный** *m* [14] *su.* prisoner of war; **~слу́жащий** [17] serviceman

вое́нн|ый [14] **1.** military, war...; **2.** military man, soldier; ***~ый врач*** *m* medical officer; ***~ый кора́бль*** *m* man-of-war, warship; ***~ое положе́ние*** martial law (under ***на*** П); ***поступи́ть на ~ую слу́жбу*** enlist, join; ***~ые де́йствия*** *n/pl.* hostilities

вож|а́к *m* [1 *e.*] (gang) leader; **~дь** *m* [4 *e.*] chief(tain); leader; **~жи** *f/pl.* [8; *from g/pl. e.*] reins; ***отпусти́ть ~жи*** *fig.* slacken the reins

воз *m* [1; на -у́; *pl. e.*] cart(load); *coll. fig.* heaps; ***а ~ и ны́не там*** nothing has changed

возбу|ди́мый [14 *sh.*] excitable; **~ди́тель** *m* [4] stimulus, agent; **~жда́ть** [1], <~ди́ть> [15 *e.*; -ужу́, -уди́шь] excite, stir up; *интере́с, подозре́ние* arouse; incite; *наде́жду* raise; *law* ***~ди́ть де́ло про́тив кого́-л.*** bring an action against s.o.; **~жда́ющий** [17] stimulating; **~жде́ние** *n* [12] excitement; **~ждённый** [14] excited

возвести́ → ***возводи́ть***

возв|оди́ть [15], <~ести́> [25] (***в*** *or* ***на*** В) put up, raise, erect; *в сан* elect; *на престо́л* elevate (to)

возвра́|т *m* [1] **1.** → ***~ще́ние***; ***1. & 2.***; **2.** relapse; **~ти́ть(ся)** → **~ща́ть(ся)**; **~тный** [14] back...; *med.* recurring; *gr.* reflexive; **~ща́ть** [1], <~ти́ть> [15 *e.*; -ащу́, -ати́шь; -ащённый] return; give back; *владе́льцу* restore; *долг* reimburse; *здоро́вье* recover; **-ся** return, come back (***из*** *or* **с** Р from); revert (***к*** Д to); **~ще́ние** *n* [12] **1.** return; **2.** *об иму́ществе* restitution

возв|ыша́ть [1], <~ы́сить> [15] raise, elevate; **-ся** rise; tower (over ***над*** Т); **~ыше́ние** *n* [12] rise; elevation; **~ы́шенность** *f* [8] **1.** *fig.* loftiness; **2.** *geogr.* height; **~ы́шенный** [14] high, elevated, lofty

возгл|авля́ть [28], <~а́вить> [14] (be at the) head

во́зглас *m* [1] exclamation, (out)cry

возд|ава́ть [5], <~а́ть> [-да́м, -да́шь, *etc.* → ***дава́ть***] render; (*отплати́ть*) requite; ***~а́ть до́лжное*** give s.b. his due (Д for)

воздвиг|а́ть [1], <~нуть> [21] erect, construct, raise

возде́йств|ие *n* [12] influence, pressure; **~овать** [7] *(im)pf.* (***на*** В) (*ока́зывать влия́ние*) influence; (*де́йствовать, влия́ть*) act upon, affect

возде́л|ывать, <~ать> [1] cultivate, till

воздержа́ние *n* [12] abstinence; abstention

возде́рж|анный [14 *sh.*] abstemious, temperate; **~иваться** [1], <~а́ться> [4] abstain (***от*** Р from); ***при двух ~а́вшихся*** *pol.* with two abstentions

во́здух *m* [1] air; ***на откры́том*** (***све́жем***) ***~е*** in the open air, outdoors; **~оплава́ние** *n* [12] aeronautics

возду́ш|ный [14] air..., aerial; **1.** ***~ная трево́га*** *f* air-raid warning; ***~ное сообще́ние*** aerial communication; ***~ные за́мки*** *m/pl.* castles in the air; **2.** [14; -шен, -шна] airy, light

воззва́|ние *n* [12] appeal; **~ть** → ***взыва́ть***

вози́ть [15] carry, transport; *на маши́не* drive; **-ся** (**с** Т) busy o.s. with, mess (around) with; (*де́лать ме́дленно*) dawdle; *о де́тях* romp, frolic

возл|ага́ть [1], <~ожи́ть> [16] (***на***

В) lay (on); entrust (with); ***~ага́ть наде́жды на*** (В) rest one's hopes upon

во́зле (P) by, near, beside

возложи́ть → ***возлага́ть***

возлю́блен|ный [14] beloved; *m* (*su.*) lover; **~ная** *f* [14] mistress, sweetheart

возме́здие *n* [12] requital

возме|ща́ть [1], <~сти́ть> [15 *e.*: -ещу́, -ести́шь; -ещённый] compensate, make up (for); **~ще́ние** *n* [12] compensation, indemnity; *law* damages

возмо́жн|о it is possible; possibly; ***о́чень ~о*** very likely; **~ость** *f* [8] possibility; ***по*** (***ме́ре***) ***~ости*** as (far as) possible; **~ный** [14; -жен, -жна] possible; ***сде́лать всё ~ое*** do everything possible

возмужа́лый [14] mature, grown up

возму|ти́тельный [14; -лен, -льна] scandalous, shocking; **~ща́ть**, <~ти́ть> [15 *e.*; -щу́, -ути́шь] rouse indignation; **-ся** be shocked *or* indignant (T at); **~ще́ние** *n* [12] indignation; **~щённый** [14] indignant (at)

вознагра|жда́ть [1], <~ди́ть> [15 *e.*; -ажу́, -ади́шь; -аждённый] (*награди́ть*) reward; recompense (for); **~жде́ние** *n* [12] reward, recompense; (*опла́та*) fee

вознаме́ри|ваться [1], <~ться> [13] form the idea of, intend

Вознесе́ние *n* [12] Ascension

возник|а́ть [1], <~нуть> [21] arise, spring up, originate, emerge; ***у меня́ ~ла мысль ...*** a thought occurred to me ...; **~нове́ние** *n* [12] rise, origin, beginning

возня́ *f* [6] **1.** fuss; bustle; romp; ***мыши́ная ~*** petty intrigues; **2.** (*хло́поты*) trouble, bother

возобнов|ле́ние *n* [12] renewal; (*продолже́ние*) resumption; **~ля́ть** [28], <~и́ть> [14 *e.*; -влю́, -ви́шь; -влённый] *знако́мство, уси́лия* renew, resume

возра|жа́ть [1], <~зи́ть> [15 *e.*; -ажу́, -ази́шь] **1.** object (to ***про́тив*** P); **2.** return, retort (***на*** В to); (***я***) ***не ~жа́ю*** I don't mind; **~же́ние** *n* [12] objection; rejoinder

во́зраст *m* [1] age (**в** П at); **~а́ние** *n* [12] growth, increase; **~а́ть** [1], <~и́> [24; -ст-: -расту́; -ро́с, -ла́; -ро́сший] grow, increase, rise

возро|жда́ть [1], <~ди́ть> [15 *e.*; -ожу́, -оди́шь; -ождённый] revive (*v/i.* **-ся**); **~жде́ние** *n* [12] rebirth, revival; ***эпо́ха ~жде́ния*** Renaissance

во́ин *m* [1] warrior, soldier; **~ский** [16] military; ***~ская обя́занность*** service; **~ственный** [14 *sh.*] bellicose

вои́стину in truth

вой *m* [3] howl(ing), wail(ing)

во́йло|к *m* [1]: **~чный** [14] felt

войн|а́ *f* [5; *pl. st.*] war (***на*** П at); warfare; ***идти́ на ~у́*** go to war; ***объяви́ть ~у́*** declare war; ***втора́я мирова́я ~а́*** World War II

войска́ *n* [9; *pl. e.*] army; *pl.* troops, (land, *etc.*) forces

войти́ → ***входи́ть***

вокза́л [1]: ***железнодоро́жный ~*** railroad (*Brt.* railway) station; ***морско́й ~*** port arrival and departure building; ***речно́й ~*** river-boat station

вокру́г (P) (a)round; (***ходи́ть***) ***~ да о́коло*** beat about the bush

вол *m* [1 *e.*] ox

волды́рь *m* [4 *e.*] blister; bump

волейбо́л *m* [1] volleyball

во́лей-нево́лей willy-nilly

во́лжский [16] (of the) Volga

волк *m* [1; *from g/pl. e.*] wolf; ***смотре́ть ~ом*** *coll.* scrowl

волн|а́ *f* [5; *pl. st.*, *from dat. a. e.*] wave; ***дли́нные***, ***сре́дние***, ***коро́ткие ~ы*** long, medium, short waves; **~е́ние** *n* [12] agitation, excitement; *pl.* disturbances, unrest; *на море́* high seas; **~и́стый** [14 *sh.*] *во́лосы* wavy; *ме́стность* undulating; **~ова́ть** [7], <вз-> (**-ся** be[come]) agitate(d), excite(d); (*трево́житься*) worry; **~у́ющий** [17] disturbing; exciting, thrilling

волоки́та *f* [5] *coll.* red tape; a lot of fuss and trouble

волокн|и́стый [14 *sh.*] fibrous; **~о́** *n* [9; *pl.*: -о́кна, -о́кон, *etc. st.*] fiber, *Brt.* fibre

во́лос *m* [1; *g/pl.*: -ло́с; *from dat. e.*] (*a. pl.*) hair; **~а́тый** [14 *sh.*] hairy; **~о́к** *m* [1; -ска́] hairspring; ***быть на ~о́к*** (*or* ***на ~ке́***) ***от сме́рти*** *coll.* be on the verge (within a hair's breadth *or* within an ace) of death; ***висе́ть на ~ке́*** hang by a thread

волосяно́й [14] hair...

волочи́ть [16], <по-> drag, pull, draw; **-ся** drag o.s., crawl along

во́лч|ий [18] wolfish; wolf('s)...; **~и́ца** *f* [5] she-wolf

волчо́к *m* [1; -чка́] top (*toy*)

волчо́нок *m* [2] wolf cub

волше́б|ник *m* [1] magician; **~ни́ца** *f* [5] sorceress; **~ный** [14] magic, fairy...; [-бен, -бна] *fig.* enchanting; **~ство́** *n* [9] magic, wizardry; *fig* enchantment

волы́нк|а *f* [5; *g/pl.*: -нок] bagpipe

во́льн|ость *f* [8] liberty; ***позволя́ть себе́ ~ости*** take liberties; **~ый** [14; -лен, -льна́] free, easy, unrestricted; ***~ая пти́ца*** one's own master

вольт *m* [1] volt

вольфра́м *m* [1] tungsten

во́л|я *f* [6] **1.** will; ***си́ла ~и*** willpower; **2.** liberty, freedom; ***~я ва́ша*** (just) as you like; ***не по свое́й ~е*** against one's will; ***по до́брой ~е*** of one's own free will; ***отпусти́ть на ~ю*** set free; ***дать ~ю*** give free rein

вон 1. there; ***~ там*** over there; **2.** ***~!*** get out!; ***пошёл ~!*** out *or* away (with you)!; ***вы́гнать ~*** turn out; ***~*** (***оно́***) ***что!*** you don't say!; so that's it!

вонза́ть [1], <~и́ть> [15 *e.*; -нжу́, -зи́шь; -зённый] thrust, plunge, stick (into)

вон|ь *f* [8] stench, stink; **~ю́чий** [17 *sh.*] stinking; **~я́ть** [28] stink, reek (of T)

вообра|жа́емый [14 *sh.*] imaginary, fictitious; **~жа́ть** [1], <~зи́ть> [15 *e.*; -ажу́, -ази́шь; -аже́нный] (*a.* ***~жа́ть себе́***) imagine, fancy; ***~жа́ть себя́*** imagine o.s. (T s.b.); ***~жа́ть о себе́*** be conceited; **~же́ние** *n* [12] imagination; fancy

вообще́ in general, on the whole; at all

воодушев|ле́ние *n* [12] enthusiasm; **~ля́ть** [28], <~и́ть> [14 *e.*; -влю́, -ви́шь; -влённый] (**-ся** feel) inspire(d by T)

вооруж|а́ть [1], <~и́ть> [16 *e.*; -жу́, -жи́шь; -жённый] **1.** arm, equip (T with); **2.** stir up (***про́тив*** P against); **~е́ние** *n* [12] armament, equipment

воо́чию with one's own eyes

во-пе́рвых first(ly)

вопи́|ть [14 *e.*; -плю́, -пи́шь], <за-> cry out, bawl; **~ю́щий** [17] crying, flagrant

вопло|ща́ть [1], <~ти́ть> [15 *e.*; -ощу́, -оти́шь, -ощённый] embody, personify; **~щённый** *a.* incarnate; **~ще́ние** *n* [12] embodiment, incarnation

вопль *m* [4] howl, wail

вопреки́ (Д) contrary to; in spite of

вопро́с *m* [1] question; ***под ~ом*** questionable, doubtful; ***~ не в э́том*** that's not the question; ***спо́рный ~*** moot point; ***что за ~!*** of course!; **~и́тельный** [14] interrogative; ***~и́тельный знак*** question mark; ***~и́тельный взгляд*** inquiring look; **~ник** *m* [1] questionnaire

вор *m* [1; *from g/pl. e.*] thief

ворва́ться → ***врыва́ться***

воркова́ть [7], <за-> coo; *fig.* bill and coo

вороб|е́й *m* [3 *e.*; -бья́] sparrow; ***стре́ляный ~е́й*** *coll.* old hand

воров|а́ть [7] steal; **~ка** *f* [5; *g/pl.*: -вок] (female) thief; **~ско́й** [16] thievish; thieves'...; **~ство́** *n* [9] theft; *law* larceny

во́рон *m* [1] raven; **~а** *f* [5] crow; ***бе́лая ~а*** rara avis; ***воро́н счи та́ть*** *coll. old use* stand about gaping

воро́нка *f* [5; *g/pl.*: -нок] **1.** funnel; **2.** *от бо́мбы, снаря́да* crater

вороно́й [14] black; *su. m* black horse

во́рот *m* [1] **1.** collar; **2.** *tech.* windlass; **~а** *n/pl.* [9] gate; **~и́ть** [15]: ***~и́ть нос*** turn up one's nose (at); **~ни́к** *m* [1 *e.*] collar; **~ничо́к** *m* [1; -чка́] (small) collar

во́рох *m* [1; *pl.*: -ха́; *etc. e.*] pile, heap; *coll.* lots, heaps

воро́|чать [1] **1.** move, roll, turn; **2.**

coll. manage, boss (T); **-ся** toss; turn; stir; **~ши́ть** [16 *e.*; -шу́, -ши́шь; -шённый] turn (over)
ворч|а́ние *n* [12] grumbling; *живо́тного* growl; **~а́ть** [4 *e.*; -чу́, -чи́шь], <за-, п(р)о-> grumble; growl; **~ли́вый** [14 *sh.*] grumbling, surly; **~у́н** *m* [1 *e.*], **~у́нья** *f* [6] grumbler
восвоя́си *coll. iro.* home
восемна́дца|тый [14] eighteenth; **~ть** [35] eighteen; → ***пять, пя́тый***
во́семь [35; восьми́, *instr.* восемью́] eight; → ***пять, пя́тый***; **~десят** [35; восьми́десяти] eighty; **~со́т** [36; восьмисо́т] eight hundred; **~ю** eight times
воск *m* [1] wax
воскл|ица́ние *n* [12] exclamation; **~ица́тельный** [14] exclamatory; ***~ица́тельный знак*** exclamation mark; **~ица́ть** [1], <~и́кнуть> [20] exclaim
восково́й [14] wax(en)
воскр|еса́ть [1], <~е́снуть> [21] rise (from ***из*** P); recover; ***Христо́с ~е́с(е)!*** Christ has arisen! (*Easter greeting*); (*reply*:) ***вои́стину ~е́с(е)!*** (He has) truly arisen!; **~есе́ние** *n* [12] resurrection; **~есе́нье** *n* [10] Sunday (on: ***в*** B; *pl.* ***по*** Д); **~еша́ть** [1], <~еси́ть> [15 *e.*; -ешу́, -еси́шь; -ешённый] resurrect, revive
воспал|е́ние *n* [12] inflammation; ***~е́ние лёгких*** (***по́чек***) pneumonia (nephritis); **~ённый** [14 *sh.*] inflamed; **~и́тельный** [14] inflammatory; **~я́ть** [28], <~и́ть> [13] inflame; (*v/i.* **-ся**)
воспе|ва́ть [1], <~ть> [-пою́, -поёшь; -пе́тый] sing of, praise
воспит|а́ние *n* [12] education, upbringing; (good) breeding; **~анник** *m* [1], **~анница** *f* [5] pupil; **~анный** [14 *sh.*] well-bred; ***пло́хо ~анный*** ill-bred; **~а́тель** *m* [4] educator; (private) tutor; **~а́тельный** [14] educational, pedagogic(al); **~ывать** [1], <~а́ть> bring up; educate; *прививать* cultivate, foster
воспламен|я́ть [28], <~и́ть> [13] set on fire (*v/i.* **-ся**) *a fig.*; inflame
восполн|я́ть [28], <~ить> [13] fill in; make up (for)
воспо́льзоваться → ***по́льзоваться***
воспомина́ние *n* [12] remembrance, recollection, reminiscence; *pl. a.* memoirs
воспрепя́тствовать [7] *pf.* hinder, prevent (from Д)
воспре|ща́ть [1], <~ти́ть> [15 *e.*; -ещу́, -ети́шь; -ещённый] prohibit, forbid; ***вход ~щён!*** no entrance!; ***кури́ть ~ща́ется!*** no smoking!
воспри|и́мчивый [14 *sh.*] receptive, impressionable; *к заболева́нию* susceptible (***к*** Д to); **~нима́ть** [1], <~ня́ть> [-приму́, -и́мешь; -и́нял, -а́, -о; -и́нятый] take in, understand; **~я́тие** *n* [12] perception
воспроизв|еде́ние *n* [12] reproduction; **~оди́ть** [15], <~ести́> [25] reproduce
воспря́нуть [20] *pf.* cheer up; ***~ ду́хом*** take heart
воссоедин|е́ние *n* [12] reun(ification)ion; **~я́ть** [28], <~и́ть> [13] reunite
восста|ва́ть [5], <~ть> [-ста́ну, -ста́нешь] rise, revolt
восстан|а́вливать [1], <~ови́ть> [14] **1.** reconstruct, restore; **2.** *про́тив* antagonize; **~ие** *n* [12] insurrection, revolt; **~ови́ть** → ***~а́вливать***; **~овле́ние** *n* [12] reconstruction, restoration
восто́к *m* [1] east; the East, the Orient; ***на ~*** (to[ward] the) east, eastward(s); ***на ~е*** in the east; ***с ~а*** from the east; ***к ~у от*** (P) (to the) east of
восто́р|г *m* [1] delight, rapture; ***я в ~ге*** I am delighted (***от*** P with); ***приводи́ть*** (***приходи́ть***) ***в ~г*** = ***~га́ть(ся)*** [1] *impf.* be delight(ed) (T with); **~женный** [14 *sh.*] enthusiastic, rapturous
восто́чный [14] east(ern, -erly); oriental
востре́бова|ние *n* [12]: ***до ~ния*** to be called for, poste restante; **~ть** [7] *pf.* call for, claim
восхвал|е́ние *n* [12] praise, eulogy; **~я́ть** [28], <~и́ть> [13; -алю́, -а́лишь] praise, extol
восхи|ти́тельный [14; -лен,

-льна] delightful; **~щáть** [1], <~ти́ть> [15 *e.*; -ищу́, -ити́шь; -ищённый] delight, transport; **-ся** (Т) be delighted with; admire; **~щéние** *n* [12] admiration; delight; ***приводи́ть*** (***приходи́ть***) ***в ~щéние*** → **~щáть(ся)**

восхó|д *m* [1] rise; ascent; **~ди́ть** [15], <взойти́> [взойду́, -дёшь; взошёл] rise, ascend; go back to; ***э́тот обы́чай ~дит*** (***к*** Д) this custom goes back (to); **~ждéние** *n* [12] sunrise

восьм|ёрка *f* [5; *g/pl.*: -рок] eight (→ ***двóйка***); **~еро** [37] eight (→ ***двóе***)

восьми|деся́тый [14] eightieth; → ***пя́т***(***идеся́т***)***ый***; **~лéтний** [14] eight-year-old; **~сóтый** [14] eight hundredth

восьмóй [14] eighth; → ***пя́тый***

вот *part.* here (is); there; now; well; that's...; ***~ и всё*** that's all; ***~*** (***онó***) ***как*** *or* ***чтó*** you don't say!, is that so?; ***~ те***(***бé***) ***раз*** *or* ***нá*** well I never!; a pretty business this!; ***~ какóй ...*** such a ...; ***~ человéк!*** what a man!; ***~-~!*** yes, indeed!; ***~-~*** (at) any moment

воткну́ть → ***втыкáть***

вóтум *m* [1]: ***~*** (***не***)***довéрия*** (Д) vote of (no) confidence (in)

воцар|я́ться [28], <~и́ться> [13] (*fig., third person only*) set in; ***~и́лось молчáние*** silence fell

вошь *f* [8; вши; вóшью] louse

вощи́ть [16 *e.*], <на-> wax

вою́ющий [17] belligerent

впа|дáть [1], <~сть> [25; впал, -а] (***в*** В) fall (flow, run) in(to); **~дéние** *n* [12] flowing into; *реки́* mouth, confluence; **~дина** *f* [5] cavity; *глазнáя* socket; *geogr.* hollow; **~лый** [14] hollow, sunken; **~сть** → ***~дáть***

впервы́е for the first time

вперёд forward; ahead (Р of), on(ward); *зарáнее* in advance, beforehand; → *a.* ***взад***

впереди́ in front, ahead (Р of); before

вперемéжку alternately

впечатл|éние *n* [12] impression; **~и́тельный** [14; -лен, -льна] impressionable, sensitive; **~я́ющий** [17 *sh.*] impressive

впи|вáться [1], <~ться> [вопью́сь, -пьёшься; впи́лся, -áсь, -ось] (***в*** В) stick (into); *укуси́ть* sting, bite; ***~ глазáми*** fix one's eyes (on)

впис|ывать [1], <~áть> [3] enter, insert

впи́т|ывать [1], <~áть> soak up *or* in; *fig.* imbibe, absorb

впи́х|ивать *coll.* [1], *once* <~ну́ть> [20] stuff *or* cram in(to) (***в*** В)

вплавь by swimming

впле|тáть [1], <~сти́> [25; -т-: вплету́, -тёшь] interlace, braid

вплот|ну́ю (***к*** Д) close, (right) up to; *fig. coll.* seriously; **~ь** *fig.* (***до*** Р) (right) up to; even (till)

вполгóлоса in a low voice

вполз|áть [1], <~ти́> [24] creep *or* crawl in(to), up

вполнé quite, fully, entirely

впопыхáх → ***второпя́х***

впóру: ***быть ~*** fit

впорхну́ть [20; -ну́, -нёшь] *pf.* flutter *or* flit in(to)

впослéдствии afterward(s), later

впотьмáх in the dark

впрáвду *coll.* really, indeed

впрáве: ***быть ~*** have a right

вправ|ля́ть [28], <~ить> [14] *med.* set; *рубáшку* tuck in; ***~ мозги́*** make s.o. behave more sensibly

впрáво (to the) right

впредь henceforth, in future; ***~ до*** until

впрóголодь half-starving

впрок 1. for future use; **2.** to a p.'s benefit; ***э́то ему́ ~ не пойдёт*** it will not profit him

впросáк: ***попáсть ~*** make a fool of o.s.

впрóчем however, but; or rather

впры́г|ивать [1], *once* <~нуть> [20] jump in(to) *or* on; (***в, на*** В)

впры́с|кивать [1], *once* <~нуть> [20] *mst. tech.* inject

впря|гáть [1], <~чь> [26 г/ж; → ***напря́чь***] harness, put to (***в*** В)

впус|к *m* [1] admission; **~кáть** [1], <~ти́ть> [15] let in, admit

впусту́ю in vain, to no purpose

впу́т|ывать, <~ать> [1] entangle, involve (***в*** В in); **-ся** become entangled

впя́теро five times (→ ***вдво́е***); **~м** five (together)
враг *m* [1 *e.*] enemy
враж|да́ *f* [5] enmity; **~де́бность** *f* [8] animosity; **~де́бный** [14; -бен, -бна] hostile; **~дова́ть** [7] be at odds (**с** T with); **~еский** [16], **~ий** [18] (the) enemy('s)...
вразбро́д *coll.* separately; without coordination
вразре́з: ***идти́ ~*** be contrary (**с** T to)
вразум|и́тельный [14; -лен, -льна] intelligible, clear; **~ля́ть** [1], <~и́ть> [14] make understand, make listen to reason
враньё *n coll.* [12] lies, fibs *pl.*, idle talk
врас|пло́х unawares, by surprise; **~сыпну́ю**: ***бро́ситься ~сыпну́ю*** scatter in all directions
враст|а́ть [1], <~и́> [24 -ст-: -сту́; врос, -ла́] grow in(to)
врата́рь *n* [4 *e.*] goalkeeper
врать *coll.* [вру, врёшь; врал, -á, -о], <со-> lie; (*ошиби́ться*) make a mistake; *о часа́х и т. д.* be inaccurate
врач *m* [1 *e.*] doctor, physician; ***зубно́й ~*** dentist; **~е́бный** [14] medical
вращ|а́ть [1] (В *or* Т) turn, revolve, rotate; (*v/i.* **-ся в** П associate with); **~а́ющийся** revolving; moving; **~е́ние** *n* [12] rotation
вред *m* [1 *e.*] harm, damage; ***во ~*** (Д) to the detriment (of); **~и́тель** *m* [4] *agric.* pest; **~и́ть** [15 *e.*; -ежу́, -еди́шь], <по-> (do) harm, (cause) damage (Д to); **~ный** [14; -ден, -дна́, -о] harmful, injurious (Д *or* ***для*** Р to)
врез|а́ть [1], <~ать> [3] (**в** В) cut in(to); set in; **-ся** run in(to); project into; *в па́мять* impress (on)
вре́менный [14] temporary, transient, provisional
вре́м|я *n* [13] time; *gr.* tense; ***~я го́да*** season; ***во́ ~я*** (Р) during; ***в настоя́щее ~я*** at (the) present (moment); ***в пе́рвое ~я*** at first; ***~я от ~ени, ~ена́ми*** from time to time, (every) now and then, sometimes; ***в ско́ром ~ени*** soon; ***в то*** (***же***) ***~я*** at that (the same) time; ***в то ~я как*** whereas; ***за после́днее ~я*** lately, recently; ***на ~я*** for a (certain) time, temporarily; ***со ~енем, с тече́нием ~ени*** in the course of time, in the long run; ***тем ~енем*** meanwhile; ***ско́лько ~ени?*** what's the time?; ***ско́лько ~ени э́то займёт?*** how long will it take?; ***хорошо́ провести́ ~я*** have a good time; **~яисчисле́ние** *n* [12] chronology; **~я(пре)провожде́ние** *n* [12] pastime
вро́вень level with, abreast (with **с** Т)
вро́де like, such as, kind of
врождённый [14 *sh.*] innate; *med.* congenital
вроз(н)ь separately, apart
врун *coll. m* [1 *e.*], **~ья** *coll. f* [6] liar
вруч|а́ть [1], <~и́ть> [16] hand over; deliver; (*вве́рить*) entrust
вры|ва́ть [1], <~ть> [22; -ро́ю, -ро́ешь] dig in(to); **-ся**, <ворваться> [-вусь, -вёшься; -вался, -лась] rush in(to); enter (by force)
вряд: ***~ ли*** hardly, scarcely
вса́дни|к *m* [1] horseman; **~ца** *f* [5] horsewoman
вса́|живать [1], <~ди́ть> [15] thrust *or* plunge in(to); hit; **~сывать** [1], <всоса́ть> [-су́, -сёшь] suck in *or* up; absorb
всё, все → ***весь***
все|ве́дущий [17] omniscient; **~возмо́жный** [14] of all kinds *or* sorts, various
всегда́ always; **~шний** *coll.* [15] usual, habitual
всего́ (-vɔ) altogether, in all; sum, total; ***~*** (***то́лько, лишь, -на́всего***) only, merely; ***пре́жде ~*** above all
всел|е́нная *f* [14] universe; **~я́ть** [28], <~и́ть> [13] settle, move in(to) (*v/i.* **-ся**); *fig.* inspire
все|ме́рный every (or all) ... possible; **~ме́рно** in every possible way; **~ми́рный** [14] world...; universal; **~могу́щий** [17 *sh.*] → ***~си́льный***; **~наро́дный** [14; -ден, -дна] national, nationwide; *adv.*: **~наро́дно** in public; **~нощная** *f* [14] vespers *pl.*; **~о́бщий** [17] universal, general; **~объе́млющий** [17 *sh.*] compre-

hensive, all-embracing; **~ору́жие** *n* [12]: ***во ~ору́жии*** fully prepared (for), in full possession of all the facts; **~росси́йский** [16] All-Russian

всерьёз *coll.* in earnest, seriously

все|си́льный [14; -лен, -льна] all-powerful; **~сторо́нний** [15] all-round, thorough

всё-таки for all that, still

всеуслы́шанье: ***во ~*** publicly

всеце́ло entirely, wholly

вска́|кивать [1], <вскочи́ть> [16] jump *or* leap (***на*** В up/on); start (**с** Р from); *о пры́щике, ши́шке* come up, swell (up); **~пывать**, <вскопа́ть> [1] dig up

вскара́бк|иваться, <~аться> [1] (***на*** В) scramble, clamber (up, onto)

вска́рмливать [1], <вскорми́ть> [14] raise, rear *or* bring up

вскачь at full gallop

вскип|а́ть [1], <~е́ть> [10 *е.*; -плю́, -пи́шь] boil up; *fig.* fly into a rage

вскло́(ко́)|чивать [1], <~чить> [16] tousle; ***~ченные*** *or* ***~чившиеся во́лосы*** *m/pl.* dishevel(l)ed hair

всколыхну́ть [20] stir up, rouse

вскользь in passing, cursorily

вскопа́ть → ***вска́пывать***

вско́ре soon, before long

вскорми́ть → ***вска́рмливать***

вскочи́ть → ***вска́кивать***

вскри́|кивать [1], <~ча́ть> [4 *е.*; -чу́, -чи́шь], *once* <~кнуть> [20] cry out, exclaim

вскружи́ть [16; -жу́, -у́жи́шь] *pf.*; ~ (Д) ***го́лову*** turn a p.'s head

вскры|ва́ть [1], <~ть> **1.** open; (*обнару́жить*) *fig.* reveal; **2.** *med.* dissect; **-ся 1.** open; be disclosed; **2.** *med.* burst, break; **~тие** *n* [12] *mst. med.* dissection, autopsy

всласть *coll.* to one's heart's content

вслед (***за*** Т, Д) (right) after, behind, following; **~ствие** (Р) in consequence of, owing to; ***~ствие э́того*** consequently

вслепу́ю *coll.* blindly, at random

вслух aloud

вслу́ш|иваться, <~аться> [1] (***в*** В) listen attentively (to)

всма́триваться [1], <всмотре́ться> [9; -отрю́сь, -о́тришься] (***в*** В) peer (at); observe closely, scrutinize

всмя́тку: ***яйцо́ ~*** soft-boiled egg

всо́|вывать [1], <всу́нуть> [20] put, slip (***в*** В into); **~са́ть** → ***вса́сывать***

вспа́|хивать [1], <~ха́ть> [3] plow (*Brt.* plough) *or* turn up; **~шка** *f* [5] tillage

всплес|к *m* [1] splash; **~кивать** [1], <~ну́ть> [20] splash; ***~ну́ть рука́ми*** throw up one's arms

всплы|ва́ть [1], <~ть> [23] rise to the surface, surface; *fig.* come to light, emerge

всполоши́ть [16 *е.*; -шу́, -ши́шь; -шённый] *pf.* alarm; (*v/i.* **-ся**)

вспом|ина́ть [1], <~нить> [13] (В *or* **о** П) remember, recall; (Д + **-ся** = И + *vb.*); **~ога́тельный** [14] auxiliary

вспорхну́ть [20] *pf.* take wing

вспоте́ть [8] (break out in a) sweat

вспры́г|ивать [1], *once* <~нуть> [20] jump *or* spring (up/on ***на*** В)

вспры́с|кивать [1], <~нуть> [20] sprinkle; wet; *coll.* *поку́пку* celebrate

вспу́г|ивать [1], *once* <~ну́ть> [20] frighten away

вспух|а́ть [1], <~нуть> [21] swell

вспыл|и́ть [13] *pf.* get angry, flare up; **~ьчивость** *f* [8] irascibility; **~ьчивый** [14 *sh.*] hot-tempered

вспы́|хивать [1], <~хнуть> [20] **1.** burst into flames; blaze up, flare up; *огонёк* flash; (*покрасне́ть*) blush; **2.** *от гне́ва* burst into a rage; *о войне́* break out; **~шка** *f* [5; *g/pl.*: -шек] flare, flash; outburst; outbreak

вста|ва́ть [5], <~ть> [вста́ну, -нешь] stand up; get up, rise (from **с** Р); arise; **~вка** *f* [5; *g/pl.*: -вок] insertion; insert; **~вля́ть** [28], <~вить> [14] set *or* put in, insert; **~вно́й** [14] inserted; ***~вны́е зу́бы*** *m/pl.* false teeth

встрепену́ться [20] *pf.* start; (*оживи́ться*) become animated

встрёпк|а Р *f* [5] reprimand; ***зада́ть ~у*** (Д) bawl out, scold (a p.)

встре́|тить(ся) → ***~ча́ть(ся)***; **~ча** *f*

[5] meeting, encounter; *приём* reception; ***тёплая ~ча*** warm welcome; **~ча́ть** [1], <~тить> [15 *st.*] **1.** meet (*v/t.*, with В) encounter; *случа́йно* come across; **2.** *прибы́вших* meet, receive, welcome ***~ча́ть Но́вый год*** see the New Year in; celebrate the New Year; *v/i.* **-ся 1.** meet (**с** Т o.a., with); **2.** (*impers.*) occur, happen; there are (were); **~чный** [14] counter...; contrary; head (*wind*); (coming from the) opposite (direction); *маши́на* oncoming; ***пе́рвый ~чный*** the first person one meets; anyone; ***пе́рвый ~чный и попере́чный*** every Tom, Dick and Harry

встря́|ска *f* [5; *g/pl.*: -сок] shock; **~хивать** [1], *once* <~хну́ть> [20] shake (up); *fig.* stir (up); **-ся** *v/i. coll.* cheer up

вступ|а́ть [1], <~и́ть> [14] *стать чле́ном* (**в** В) enter, join; set foot in, step (into); *в до́лжность* assume; ***~и́ть в брак*** marry; ***~и́ть в де́йствие*** come into force; ***~и́ть на трон*** ascend the throne; **-ся** (*за* В) intercede (for), project; take a p.'s side; **~и́тельный** [14] introductory; opening; *экза́мен и т. д.* entrance...; **~ле́ние** *n* [12] *на престо́л* accession; *в кни́ге и т. д.* introduction

всу́|нуть → ***всо́вывать***; **~чивать** *coll.* [1], <~чи́ть> [16] foist (В/Д s.th. on)

всхлип *m* [1], **~ывание** *n* [12] sob(bing); **~ывать** [1], *once* <~нуть> [20 *st.*] sob

всход|и́ть [15], <взойти́> [взойду́, -дёшь; взошёл; *g. pt.*: взойдя́] go *or* climb (**на** В [up] on), ascend, rise; *agric.* come up, sprout; **~ы́** *m/pl.* [1] standing *or* young crops

всхо́жесть *f* [8] germinating capacity

всхрапну́ть [20] *coll. joc. pf.* have a nap

всыпа́ть [1], <~ать> [2 *st.*] pour *or* put (**в** В into); P upbraid; give s.b. a thrashing

всю́ду everywhere, all over

вся́|кий [16] **1.** any; every; anyone; everyone; ***без ~кого сомне́ния*** beyond any doubt; ***во ~ком случа́е*** at any rate; **2.** = **~ческий** [16] all kinds *or* sorts of, sundry; every possible; **~чески** in every way; ***~чески стара́ться*** try one's hardest, try all ways; **~чина** *coll. f* [5]: ***~кая ~чина*** odds and ends

вта́|йне in secret; **~лкивать** [1], <втолкну́ть> [20] push *or* shove in(to); **~птывать** [1], <втопта́ть> [3] trample into; **~скивать** [1], <~щи́ть> [16] pull *or* drag in, into, up

вте|ка́ть [1], <~чь> [26] flow in(to)

вти|ра́ть [1], <втере́ть> [12; вотру́, -рёшь; втёр] rub in; ***~ра́ть очки́*** (Д) throw dust in (p.'s) eyes; **-ся** *coll.* ***в дове́рие*** worm into; **~скивать** [1], <~снуть> [20] squeeze o.s. in(to)

втихомо́лку *coll.* on the sly

втолкну́ть → ***вта́лкивать***

втопта́ть → ***вта́птывать***

втор|га́ться [1], <~гнуться> [21] (**в** В) intrude, invade, penetrate; *в чужи́е дела́* meddle (with); **~же́ние** *n* [12] invasion, incursion; **~ить** [13] *mus.* sing (*or* play) the second part; echo; repeat; **~и́чный** [14] second, repeated; *побо́чный* secondary; **~и́чно** once more, for the second time; **~ник** *m* [1] Tuesday (**в** В, *pl.*: **по** Д on); **~о́й** [14] second; ***из ~ы́х рук*** second-hand; → ***пе́рвый & пя́тый***; **~оку́рсник** *m* [1] sophomore, *Brt.* second-year student

второпя́х hurriedly, in haste

второстепе́нный [14; -е́нен, -е́нна] secondary, minor

в-тре́тьих third(ly)

втри́дорога: *coll.* triple the price; ***плати́ть ~*** pay through the nose

втро́|е three times (as ..., *comp.*: → ***вдво́е***); *vb.* **~е** *a.* treble; **~ём** three (of us *or* together); **~йне́** three times (as much *etc.*), treble

вту́лка *f* [5; *g/pl.*: -лок] *tech.* sleeve

втыка́ть [1], <воткну́ть> [20] put *or* stick in(to)

втя́|гивать [1], <~ну́ть> [19] draw *or* pull in(to), on; *вовле́чь* involve, engage; **-ся** (**в** В) *fig. в рабо́ту* get used (to)

В

вуáль *f* [8] veil

вуз *m* [1] (***вы́сшее учéбное заведéние*** *n*) institution of higher education

вулкáн *m* [1] volcano; **~и́ческий** [16] volcanic

вульгáрный [14; -рен, -рна] vulgar

вундерки́нд *m* [1] child prodigy

вход *m* [1] entrance; entry; ***~а нет*** no entry; ***плáта за ~*** entrance *or* admission fee

входи́ть [15], <войти́> [войду́, -дёшь; вошёл, -шлá; вошéдший *g. pt.*: войдя́] (***в*** В) enter, go, come *or* get in(to); (*помещáться*) go in(to), have room for; hold; be a member of; be included in; ***~ во вкус*** (P) take a fancy to; ***~ в довéрие к*** (Д) gain a p.'s confidence; ***~ в положéние*** (P) appreciate a p.'s position; ***~ в привы́чку*** (*в поговóрку*) become a habit (proverbial); ***~ в*** (***состáв*** P) form part (of), belo (to)

входнóй [14] entrance..., admission...

вхолостýю: ***рабóтать ~*** run idle

вцеп|ля́ться [28], <~и́ться> [14] (***в*** В) grasp, catch hold of

вчерá yesterday; **~шний** [5] yesterday's, of yesterday

вчернé in rough; in draft form

вчéтверо four times (as ..., *comp.*: → ***вдвóе***); **~м** four (of us *etc.*)

вчи́тываться [1] (***в*** В) *impf. only* try to grasp the meaning of

вшéстеро six times (→ ***вдвóе***)

вши|вáть [1], <~ть> [вошью́, -шьёшь; → ***шить***] sew in(to); **~вый** [14] *mst. coll. fig.* lousy

въе|дáться [1], <~сться> [→ ***есть***] eat (in[to]); **~дливый** [14 *sh.*] *coll.* corrosive, acid

въе|зд *m* [1] entrance, entry; **~зднóй** [14]: ***~зднáя ви́за*** entry visa; **~зжáть** [1], <~хать> [въéду, -дешь; въезжáй(те)!] enter, ride *or* drive in(to), up, on (***в, на*** В); move in(to); **~сться** → ***~дáться***

вы [21] you (polite form *a.* 2); ***~ с ним*** you and he; ***у вас*** (***был***) you have (had)

выб|áлтывать *coll.* [1], <~олтать> blab *or* let out; **~егáть** [1], <~ежать> [4; вы́бегу, -ежишь] run out; **~ивáть** [1], <~ить> [вы́бью, -бьешь, *etc.*, → ***бить***] **1.** beat *or* knock out; *стеклó и т. д.* break; smash; (*изгнáть*) drive out, *mil.* dislodge; ***~ить из колéй*** unsettle; **-ся** break out *or* forth; ***~ся из сил*** be(come) exhausted, fatigued; ***~ся из колéй*** go off the beaten track; **~ирáть** [1], <~рать> [вы́беру, -решь; -бранный] choose, pick out; (*избирáть*) elect; take out; *минýтку* find; **-ся** get out; *на концéрт и т. д.* find time to go; **~ить** → ***~ивáть***

вы́боина *f* [5] dent; *на дорóге* pothole; rut

вы́бор *m* [1] choice, option; (*отбóр*) selection; *pl.* election(s); ***на ~*** (*or* ***по ~у***) at a p.'s discretion; random (*test*); ***всеóбщие ~ы*** *pl.* general election; ***дополни́тельные ~ы*** by-election; **~ка** *f* [5; *g/pl.*: -рок] selection; *pl.* excerpts; *statistics* sample; **~ный** [14] electoral; elected

выбр|áсывать [1], <~осить> [15] throw (out *or* away); discard; (*исключи́ть*) exclude, omit; ***~áсывать*** (***зря***) ***дéньги*** waste money; **-ся** throw o.s. out; **~ать** → ***выбирáть***; **~ить** [-ею, -еешь; -итый] *pf.* shave clean; (*v/i.* **-ся**); **~осить** → ***~áсывать***

выб|ывáть [1], <~ыть> [-буду, -будешь] leave; *из игры́* drop out

выв|áливать [1], <~алить> [13] discharge, throw out; **-ся** fall out; **~áривать** [1], <~арить> [13] (*экстраги́ровать*) extract; boil (down); **~éдывать**, <~едать> [1] find out, (try to) elicit; **~езти** → ***~ози́ть***

выв|ёртывать [1], <~ернуть> [20] unscrew; *дéрево* tear out; *рýку и т. д.* dislocate; *наизнáнку* turn (inside out); *v/i.* **-ся**; slip out; extricate o.s.

вы́вес|ить → ***вывéшивать***; **~ка** *f* [5; *g/pl.*: -сок] sign(board); *fig.* screen, pretext; **~ти** → ***выводи́ть***

выв|éтривать [1], <~етрить> [13] (remove by) air(ing); **-ся** *geol.* weather; disappear ***~ся из пáмяти*** be effaced from memory; **~éшивать** [1], <~есить> [15] hang out *or* put out; **~и́нчивать** [1], <~интить> [15] unscrew

вы́вих *m* [1] dislocation; **~нуть** [20] *pf.* dislocate, put out of joint

вы́вод *m* [1] **1.** *во́йск* withdrawal; conclusion; ***сде́лать ~*** draw a conclusion; **~и́ть** [15], <вы́вести> [25] **1.** take, lead *or* move (out, to); **2.** conclude; **3.** *птенцо́в* hatch; *сорт расте́ния* cultivate; **4.** *пятно́* remove, *насеко́мых* extirpate; **5.** *бу́квы* write *or* draw carefully; **6.** *о́браз* depict; **~и́ть** (B) ***из себя́*** make s.b. lose his temper; **-ся**, <-сь> disappear; **~ок** *m* [1; -дка] brood

вы́воз *m* [1] export; *му́сора* removal; **~и́ть** [15], <вы́везти> [24] remove, take *or* bring out; export

выв|ора́чивать *coll.* [1], <~оротить> [15] → ***вывёртывать***

выг|а́дывать, <~адать> [1] gain *or* save (B/***на*** П s.th. from)

вы́гиб *m* [1] bend, curve; **~а́ть** [1], <вы́гнуть> [20] *о ко́шке* arch; curve, bend

вы́гля|деть [11 *st.*] *impf.* look (s.th. T, like ***как***); ***как она́ ~дит?*** what does she look like?; ***он ~дит моло́же свои́х лет*** he doesn't look his age; **~дывать** [1], *once* <~нуть> [20 *st.*] look *or* peep out (of ***в*** B, ***из*** P)

вы́гнать → ***выгоня́ть***

вы́гнуть → ***выгиба́ть***

выгов|а́ривать [1], <´~орить> [13] **1.** pronounce; utter; **2.** *impf. coll.* (Д) tell off; **´~ор** *m* [1] **1.** pronunciation; **2.** reproof, reprimand

вы́год|а *f* [5] (*при́быль*) profit; (*преиму́щество*) advantage; (*по́льза*) benefit; **~ный** [14; -ден, -дна] profitable; advantageous (Д, ***для*** P to)

вы́гон *m* [1] pasture; **~я́ть** [28], <вы́гнать> [вы́гоню, -нишь] turn *or* drive out; *coll. с рабо́ты* fire

выгор|а́живать [1], <´~одить> [15] fence off; P shield, absolve from blame; **~а́ть** [1], <´~еть> [9] **1.** burn down; **2.** (*вы́цвести*) fade; **3.** *coll.* (*получи́ться*) click, come off

выгр|ужа́ть [1], <~узить> [15] unload, discharge; *с су́дна* disembark; (*v/i.* **-ся**); **~узка** [5; *g/pl.*: -зок] unloading; disembarkation

выдава́ть [5], <вы́дать> [-дам, -дашь, *etc.* → ***дать***] **1.** give (out), pay (out); **2.** *про́пуск* issue; **3.** *преда́ть* betray; **4.** *друго́му госуда́рству* extradite; **~** (***себя́***) ***за*** (B) pass (o.s. off) as; **~** (***за́муж***) ***за*** (B) give (a girl) in marriage to; **-ся 1.** (*выступа́ть*) stand out; **2.** *coll. день и т. д.* happen *or* turn out

выд|а́вливать [1], <~авить> [14] press *or* squeeze out (*a. fig.*); ***~авить улы́бку*** force a smile; **~а́лбливать** [1], <~олбить> [14] hollow out, gouge out

вы́да|ть → ***~ва́ть***; **~ча** *f* [5] **1.** (*разда́ча*) distribution; *сда́ча* delivery; *де́нег* payment; **2.** issue; **3.** disclosure; **4.** extradition; ***день ~чи зарпла́ты*** payday; **~ю́щийся** [17; -щегося *etc.*] outstanding, prominent, distinguished

выдви|га́ть [1], <´~нуть> [20] **1.** pull out; **2.** *предложе́ние* put forward, propose; *на до́лжность* promote; *кандида́та* nominate; **-ся 1.** slide in and out; **2.** *esp. mil.* move forward; **3.** *по слу́жбе* advance; **4.** *impf.* → **~жно́й** [14] pull-out..., sliding; (*tech.*) telescopic

выд|еле́ние *n* [12] discharge, secretion; **~елка** *f* [5; *g/pl.*: -лок] *о ка́честве* workmanship; *ко́жи* dressing; **~е́лывать**, <~елать> [1] work, make *ко́жу*; **~еля́ть** [28], <~елить> [13] **1.** mark out, single out; (*отме́тить*) emphasize; **2.** *зе́млю и т. д.* allot; satisfy (*coheirs*); **3.** *med.* secrete; **4.** *chem.* isolate; **-ся** *v/i.* 1, 4; (*отлича́ться*) stand out, rise above; excel; **~ёргивать**, <~ернуть> [20] pull out

выде́рж|ивать [1], <´~ать> [4] stand, bear, endure; *экза́мен* pass; *разме́ры и т. д.* observe; ***´~ать хара́ктер*** be firm; **´~анный** self-possessed; (*после́довательный*) consistent; *о вине́* mature; **´~ка** *f* [5; *g/pl.*: -жек] **1.** self-control; **2.** (*отры́вок*) excerpt, quotation; **3.** *phot.* exposure

выд|ира́ть *coll.* [1], <~рать> [-деру, -ерешь] tear out; *зуб* pull; *pf.* thrash; **~олбить** → ***~а́лбливать***; **~охнуть** → ***~ыха́ть***; **~ра** *f*

В

[5] otter; **~рать** → ***~ира́ть***; **~умка** *f* [5; *g/pl.*: -мок] invention; made-up story, fabrication; **~у́мывать**, <~у-мать> [1] invent, contrive, devise
выд|ыха́ть [1], <~охнуть> [20] breathe out; **-ся** become stale; *fig.* be played out
вы́езд *m* [1] departure; *из го́рода* town/city gate
выезжа́ть [1], <вы́ехать> [вы́еду, -едешь; -езжа́й(те)!] *v/i.* (**из/с** Р) **1.** leave, depart; **2.** *на маши́не, ло́шади* drive *or* ride out, on(to); **3.** *из кварти́ры* leave *or* move (from)
вы́емка *f* [5; *g/pl.*: -мок] excavation; *я́мка* hollow
вы́ехать → ***выезжа́ть***
вы́ж|ать → ***~има́ть***; **~дать** → ***выжида́ть***; **~ива́ние** *n* [12] survival; **~ива́ть** [1], <~ить> [-иву, -ивешь; -итый] survive; go through; stay; *coll. из до́ма и т. д.* oust, drive out; ***~ить из ума́*** be in one's dotage; *fig.* take leave of one's senses; **~ига́ть** [1], <~ечь> [26 г/ж: -жгу, -жжешь, -жгут; -жег, -жженный] burn out; burn down; scorch; **~ида́ть** [1], <~дать> [-жду, -ждешь; -жди(те)!] (Р *or* В) wait for *or* till (after); **~има́ть** [1], <~ать> [-жму, -жмешь; -жатый] squeeze, press *or о белье́* wring out; *sport* lift (weights); **~ить** → ***~ива́ть***
вы́звать → ***вызыва́ть***
выздор|а́вливать [1], <´~оветь> [10] recover; **~а́вливающий** [17] convalescent; **~овле́ние** *n* [12] recovery
вы́з|ов *m* [1] call, summons; (*приглаше́ние*) invitation; *mst. fig.* challenge; **~у́бривать** [1] → ***зубри́ть*** **2**; **~ыва́ть** [1], <~вать> [-ову, -овешь] **1.** call (to; for *thea.*; up *tel.*); *врача́* send for; **2.** summon (**к** Д to, **в суд** before a court) **3.** challenge (to **на** В); **4.** (*приводи́ть*) rouse, cause; *воспомина́ния* evoke; **-ся** undertake *or* offer; **~ыва́ющий** [17] defiant, provoking
выи́гр|ывать, <´~ать> [1] win (from **у** Р); (*извле́чь вы́году*) gain, benefit; **´~ыш** *m* [1] win(ning[s]), gain(s), prize; profit; ***быть в ´~ыше*** have won (profited); **´~ышный** [14] *положе́ние* advantageous, effective
вы́йти → ***выходи́ть***
вык|а́лывать [1], <~олоть> [17] put out; prick out; **~а́пывать**, <~опать> [1] dig out *or* up; **~ара́бкиваться**, <~арабкаться> [1] scramble *or* get out; **~а́рмливать** [1], <~ормить> [14] bring up, rear; **~а́тывать** [1], <~атить> [15] push *or* wheel out; ***~атить глаза́*** Р stare
выки́|дывать [1], *once* <´~нуть> [20] **1.** throw out *or* away; discard; (*опусти́ть*) omit; **2.** *бе́лый флаг* hoist (up); **3.** *coll. фо́кус* play (trick); **´~дыш** *m* [1] miscarriage
вы́кл|адка *f* [5; *g/pl.*: -док] *math.* computation, calculation; *mil.* pack *or* kit; **~а́дывать** [1], <вы́ложить> [16] **1.** *де́ньги* lay out; tell; **2.** (*отде́лать*) face with masonry
выключ|а́тель *m* [4] *el.* switch; **~а́ть** [1], <´~ить> [16] switch *or* turn off; *двига́тель* stop; **~е́ние** *n* [12] switching off, stopping
вык|о́вывать [1], <~овать> [7] forge; *fig.* mo(u)ld; **~ола́чивать** [1], <~олотить> [15] *ковёр* beat *or* knock out; *долги́ и т. д.* exact; **~олоть** → ***~а́лывать***; **~опать** → ***~а́пывать***; **~ормить** → ***~а́рмливать***; **~орчёвывать** [1], <~орчевать> [7] root up *or* out
выкр|а́ивать [1], <~оить> [13] *sew.* cut out; *coll. вре́мя* spare; *де́ньги* find; **~а́шивать** [1], <~асить> [15] paint, dye; **~и́кивать** [1], *once* <~икнуть> [20] cry *or* call (out); **~оить** → ***~а́ивать***; **~ойка** *f* [5; *g/pl.*: -оек] pattern
выкр|ута́сы *coll. m/pl.* [1] *о поведе́нии* vagaries, crotchets; **~у́чивать** [1], <~утить> [15] twist; *бельё* wring (out); *coll.* unscrew; **-ся** *coll. ла́мпочку и т. д.* slip out
вы́куп *m* [1] redemption; *зало́жника и т. д.* ransom; **~а́ть** [1], <~ить> [14] *вещь* redeem; ransom; **~ать** → ***купа́ть***
выку́р|ивать [1], <´~ить> [13] smoke
выл|а́вливать [1], <~овить> [14] fish out, draw out; **~азка** *f* [5; *g/pl.*: -зок] *mil.* sally; **~а́мывать**, <~о-

мать> [1] break open

выл|еза́ть [1], <~езть> [24] climb *or* get out; *о волоса́х* fall out; **~епля́ть** [28], <~епить> [14] model, fashion

вы́лет *m* [1] *ae.* taking off, flight; **~а́ть** [1], <~еть> [11] fly out; *ae.* take off, (**в** В for); rush out *or* up; (*вы́валиться*) fall out; slip (a *p.'s* memory ***~еть из головы́***); ***~еть в трубу́*** go broke

выл|е́чивать [1], <~ечить> [16] cure, heal (*v/i.* **-ся**); **~ива́ть** [1], <~ить> [-лью, -льешь; → ***лить***] pour out; **~итый** [14] the image of, just like (И s.b.)

вы́л|овить → ***~а́вливать***; **~о-жить** → ***выкла́дывать***; **~омать** → ***~а́мывать***; **~упля́ться** [28], <~иться> [14] hatch

вым|а́зывать [1], <~азать> [3] smear; daub (**-ся** o.s.) (Т with); **~а́ливать** [1], <~олить> [13] get *or* obtain by entreaties; ***~а́ливать проще́ние*** beg for forgiveness; **~а́нивать** [1], <~анить> [13] lure (***из*** Р out of); coax *or* cheat (***у*** Р/В a p. out of s.th.); **~а́ривать** [1], <~орить> [13] exterminate; **~а́чивать** [1], <~очить> [16] *дождём* drench; *в жи́дкости* soak; **~а́щивать** [1], <~остить> [15] pave **~е́нивать** [1], <~енять> [28] exchange (for ***на*** В); **~ереть** → ***~ира́ть***; **~ета́ть** [1], <~ести> [25; -т-*st.*: -ету, -етешь] sweep (out); **~еща́ть** [1], <~естить> [15] avenge o.s. (on Д); *зло́бу* vent (***на*** П on p.); **~ира́ть** [1], <~ереть> [12] die out, become extinct

вымога́т|ельство *n* [9] blackmail, extortion; **~ь** [1] extort (В *or* Р/**у** Р s. th. from)

вым|ока́ть [1], <~окнуть> [21] get wet through; ***~окнуть до ни́тки*** get soaked to the skin; **~олвить** [14] *pf.* utter, say; **~олить** → ***~а́ливать***; **~орить** → ***~а́ривать***; **~остить** → ***~а́щивать***; **~очить** → ***~а́чивать***

вы́мпел *m* [1] pennant, pennon

вым|ыва́ть [1], <~ыть> [22] wash (out, up); **~ысел** *m* [1; -сла] invention; fantasy; *ложь* falsehood; **~ыть** → ***~ыва́ть***; **~ышля́ть** [28], <~ыслить> [15] think up, invent; **~ышленный** *a.* fictitious

вы́мя *n* [13] udder

вын|а́шивать [1]: ***~а́шивать план*** nurture a plan; **~ести** → ***~оси́ть***

вын|има́ть [1], <~уть> [20] take *or* draw out, produce

вын|оси́ть [15], <~ести> [24; -с-: -су, -сешь; -с, -сла, -сло] **1.** carry *or* take out (away), remove; **2.** (*терпе́ть*) endure, bear; **3.** *благода́рность* express; pass (*a. law*); ***~оси́ть сор из избы́*** wash one's dirty linen in public; **~о́сливость** *f* [8] endurance; **~о́сливый** [14 *sh.*] sturdy, hardy, tough

вын|ужда́ть [1], <~удить> [15] force, compel; extort (В/**у** *or* **от** Р s.th. from); **~ужденный** [14 *sh.*] forced; of necessity; ***~ужденная поса́дка*** emergency landing

вы́нырнуть [20] *pf.* come to the surface, emerge; *coll.* turn up (unexpectedly)

вы́пад *m* [1] *fencing* lunge; thrust; *fig.* attack

выпа|да́ть [1], <~сть> [25] **1.** fall *or* drop (out); (*вы́скользнуть*) slip out; **2.** fall (Д to, *a.* ***на до́лю*** to *a p.'s* lot); devolve on

вып|а́ливать [1], <~алить> [13] *coll.* blurt out; shoot (***из*** Р with); **~а́лывать** [1], <~олоть> [17] weed (out); **~а́ривать** [1], <~арить> [13] steam; clean, disinfect; (*chem.*) evaporate

вып|ека́ть [1], <~ечь> [26] bake; **~ива́ть** [1], <~ить> [-пью, -пьешь; → ***пить***] drink (up); *coll.* be fond of the bottle; **~ить** (***ли́шнее***) *coll.* have one too many; ***~ить ча́шку ча́ю*** have a cup of tea; **~ивка** *coll. f* [5; *g/pl.*: -вок] booze

вы́п|иска *f* [5; *g/pl.*: -сок] **1.** writing out, copying; **2.** *из те́кста* extract; statement (of account *из счёта*); **3.** order; subscription; **4.** *из больни́цы* discharge; *с ме́ста жи́тельства* notice of departure; **~и́сывать** [1], <~исать> [3] **1.** write out (*or* down); copy; **2.** → ***выводи́ть 6.***; **3.** *журна́л и т. д.* order; subscribe; **4.** discharge; **-ся** sign out; ***-ся из больни́цы*** leave hospital

вы́пла|вка *f* [5] smelting; **⁓кать** [3] *pf.* cry (one's eyes *глаза́*) out; **⁓та** *f* [5] payment; **⁓чивать** [1], <⁓тить> [15] pay (out *or* off)

выпл|ёвывать [1], *once* <⁓юнуть> [20] spit out; **⁓ёскивать** [1], <⁓ескать> [3], *once* <⁓еснуть> [20] dash *or* splash (out); ***⁓еснуть с водо́й ребёнка*** throw the baby out with the bathwater

выпл|ыва́ть [1], <⁓ыть> [23] swim out; surface; emerge, appear

выпол|а́скивать [1], <´⁓оскать> [3] rinse; *го́рло* gargle; **⁓за́ть** [1], <´⁓зти> [24] creep *or* crawl out; **⁓не́ние** *n* [12] fulfil(l)ment, execution, realization; **⁓ня́ть** [1], <´⁓нить> [13] carry out, fulfil(l); execute; **´⁓оть** → ***выпа́лывать***

вы́пр|авка *f* [5; *g/pl.:* -вок]: ***вое́нная ⁓авка*** soldierly bearing; **⁓авля́ть** [28], <⁓авить> [14] set right *or* straighten out; *ру́копись и т. д.* correct; **⁓а́шивать** [1], <⁓осить> [15] try to get *or* obtain, solicit; **⁓ова́живать** *coll.* [1], <⁓оводить> [15] send s.o. packing, turn out; **⁓ы́гивать** [1], <⁓ынуть> [20] jump out; **⁓яга́ть** [1], <⁓ячь> [26 г/ж: -ягу, -яжешь; -яг] unharness; **⁓ямля́ть** [28], <⁓ямить> [14] straighten; **-ся** become straight; *спи́ну* straighten

вы́пукл|ость *f* [8] protuberance; prominence, bulge; **⁓ый** [14] convex; prominent; *fig.* expressive; distinct

вы́пуск *m* [1] output; issue; publication; (*часть рома́на*) instal(l)ment; *о студе́нтах* graduate class; **⁓а́ть** [1], <вы́пустить> [15] let out; *law* release; *това́ры* produce, issue, publish; (*исключи́ть*) omit, leave out; graduate; ***⁓а́ть в прода́жу*** put on sale; **⁓ни́к** *m* [1 *e.*] graduate; **⁓но́й** [14] graduate..., graduation..., final, leaving; *tech.* discharge...; exhaust...

вып|у́тывать, <⁓утать> [1] disentangle *or* extricate (**-ся** o.s.); **⁓у́чивать** [1], <⁓учить> [16] **1.** bulge; **2.** P → ***тара́щить***

вып|ы́тывать, <⁓ытать> [1] find out, (try to) elicit

выпя́|ливать P [1], <⁓лить> [13] → ***тара́щить***; **⁓чивать** *coll.* [1], <´⁓тить> [15] stick *or* thrust out; *fig.* emphasize

выраб|а́тывать, <´⁓отать> [1] manufacture, produce; *план и т. д.* elaborate, work out; develop; **´⁓отка** *f* [15; *g/pl.:* -ток] manufacture, production; output

выр|а́внивать [1], <⁓овнять> [28] **1.** level; smooth out; **2.** align; (*ура́внивать*) equalize; **-ся** straighten; become even

выра|жа́ть [1], <´⁓зить> [15] express, show; ***⁓жа́ть слова́ми*** put into words; **⁓жа́ться** [1], <´⁓зиться> [15] **1.** express o.s.; **2.** manifest itself (**в** П in); **⁓же́ние** *n* [12] expression; **⁓зи́тельный** [14; -лен, -льна] expressive; *coll.* significant

выр|аста́ть [1], <⁓асти> [24 -ст-: -асту; → ***расти́***] **1.** grow (up); increase; (*преврати́ться*) develop into; **2.** (*появи́ться*) emerge, appear; **⁓а́щивать** [1], <⁓астить> [15] *расте́ние* grow; *живо́тных* breed; *ребёнка* bring up; *fig. чемпио́на* train; **⁓вать 1.** → **⁓ыва́ть**; **2.** → ***рвать 3***

вы́рез *m* [1] notch; cut; ***пла́тье с глубо́ким ⁓ом*** low-necked dress; **⁓а́ть** [1], <⁓ать> [15] **1.** cut out, clip; **2.** *из де́рева* carve; (*гравирова́ть*) engrave; **3.** slaughter; **⁓ка** *f* [5; *g/pl.:* -зок] cutting out, clipping; *cul.* tenderloin; **⁓но́й** [14] carved

вы́ро|док *m* [1; -дка] *coll.* monster; **⁓жда́ться** [1], <⁓диться> [15] degenerate; **⁓жде́ние** *n* [12] degeneration

вы́ронить [13] *pf.* drop

вы́росший [17] grown

выр|уба́ть [1], <⁓убить> [14] cut down *or* fell; **⁓уча́ть** [1], <⁓учить> [16] **1.** come to s.o.'s help *or* rescue; **2.** *за това́р* make, net; **⁓учка** *f* [5] rescue; assistance, help; *comm.* proceeds; ***прийти́ на ⁓учку*** come to the aid (Д of)

выр|ыва́ть [1], <⁓вать> [-ву, -вешь] **1.** pull out; tear out; **2.**

snatch (***из*** P, ***у*** P from); *fig.* extort (B/***у*** P s.th. from a p.); **-ся** break away; tear o.s. away (***из*** P from); break loose; escape; **~ывáть**, <~ыть> [22] dig out, up

вы́с|адка *f* [5; *g/pl.*: -док] disembarkation, landing; **~áживать** [1], <~адить> [15] **1.** land, disembark; **2.** help out; make *or* let a p. get off; **3.** *растéния* transplant; **-ся** *v/i.*; *a.* get out, off

выс|áсывать [1], <~осать> [-осу, -осешь] suck out; **~вéрливать** [1], <~верлить> [13] bore, drill; **~вобождáть** [1], <~вободить> [15] free, disentangle

выс|еввáть [1], <~еять> [27] sow; **~екáть** [1], <~ечь> [26] **1.** hew, carve; **2.** → ***сечь***; **~елéние** *n* [12] eviction; **~елять** [28], <~елить> [13] evict; **~еять** → ***~евáть***; **~и́живать** [1], <~идеть> [11] sit out, stay; *яйцó* hatch

выск|áбливать [1], <~облить> [13] scrape clean; *удали́ть* erase; **~áзывать** [1], <~азать> [3] express, tell, state; ***~азать предположéние*** suggest; **-ся** express o.s.; express one's opinion, thoughts, *etc.* (***о*** П about); speak (***за*** B for; ***прóтив*** P against); **~áкивать** [1], <~очить> [16] jump, leap *or* rush out; **~áльзывать, ~ользáть** [1], <~ользнуть> [20] slip out; **~облить** → ***~áбливать***; **~очить** → ***~áкивать***; **~очка** *m/f* [5; *g/pl.*: -чек] upstart; **~ребáть** [1], <~рести> [25 -б-: → ***скрести́***] scrape out (off); (*удали́ть*) scratch out

вы́сл|ать → ***высылáть***; **~éживать** [1], <~едить> [15] track down; **~у́живать** [1], <~ужить> [16] obtain by *or* for service; **-ся** curry favo(u)r (***пéред*** T with s.b.); **~у́шивать**, <~ушать> [1] listen (to), hear (out); *med.* auscultate

высм|éивать [1], <~еять> [27] deride, ridicule

выс|óвывать [1], <~унуть> [20 *st.*] put out; **-ся** lean out

высóкий [16; высóк, -á, -óкó; *comp.*: вы́ше] high; tall (*a.* ***~ рóстом***); *fig.* lofty

высоко|кáчественный [14] (of) high-quality; **~квалифици́рованный** [14] highly skilled; **~мéрие** *n* [12] haughtiness; **~мéрный** [14; -рен, -рна] haughty, arrogant; **~пáрный** [14; -рен, -рна] bombastic, high-flown; **~превосходи́тельство** [9] *hist.* Excellency; **~производи́тельный** [14; -лен, -льна] *рабóта* highly productive; *оборýдование* high-efficiency

вы́сосать → ***высáсывать***

высо|тá *f* [5; *g/pl.*: -óты, *etc. st.*] height; *mus.* pitch; *geogr.* eminence; hill; altitude; *ýровень* level; ***оказáться на ~тé*** be equal to (the occasion); ***высотóй в*** (B) ... or ...; ***в ~тý ...*** high

вы́сох|нуть → ***высыхáть***; **~ший** [17] dried up, withered

выс|очáйший [17] highest; *достижéние* supreme; **~óчество** *n* [9] *hist.* Highness; **~паться** → ***высыпáться***

вы́спренний [15] bombastic

вы́став|ить → ***~лять***; **~ка** *f* [5; *g/pl.*: -вок] exhibition, show; **~лять** [28], <~ить> [14] **1.** (*вы́нуть*) put (take) out; **2.** *карти́ну и т. д.* exhibit, display; represent (***себя*** o.s.); **3.** *оцéнку* give a mark; *mil.* post; *вы́гнать* turn out; ***~лять напокáз*** show, parade; **-ся** exhibit; **~очный** [14] (of the) exhibition, show...

выстр|áивать(ся) [1] → ***стрóить(ся)***; **~ел** *m* [1] shot; (noise) report; ***на*** (***расстоя́ние, -ии***) ***~ел(а)*** within gunshot; **~елить** → ***стреля́ть***

вы́ступ *m* [1] projection; **~áть** [1], <~ить> [14] **1.** step forth, forward; come *or* stand out; *слёзы и т. д.* appear; **2.** *в похóд* set out; **3.** speak (sing, play) in public; ***~áть с рéчью*** (***в прéниях***) address an audience, deliver a speech; take the floor; **~лéние** *n* [12] setting out; *pol.* speech; appearance (in public); *thea.* performance, turn

вы́сунуть(ся) → ***высóвывать(ся)***

высу́ш|ивать [1], <~ить> [16] dry up, *coll.* emaciate

выс|чи́тывать [1], <~читать> calculate, compute; *coll.* deduct

В

вы́сш|ий [17] highest, supreme, higher (*a. educ.*), superior; **~ая** ***ме́ра наказа́ния*** capital punishment

выс|ыла́ть [1], <~́лать> [вы́шлю, -лешь] send, send out, *pol.* exile; *из страны́* deport; **~́ылка** *f* [15] dispatch; exile, expulsion; **~ыпа́ть** [1], <~́ыпать> [2] pour out *or* in, on; *v/i. о лю́дях* spill out; **~ыпа́ться** [1], <вы́спаться> [-сплюсь, -спишься] sleep one's fill, have a good night's rest; **~ыха́ть** [1], <~́охнуть> [21] dry up, wither; **~ь** *f* [8] height, summit

выт|а́лкивать, *coll.* <~́олкать> [1], *once* <~́толкнуть> [20 *st.*] throw out; **~а́пливать** [1], <~́опить> [14] **1.** heat; **2.** *о жи́ре* melt (down); **~а́скивать** [1], <~́ащить> [16] drag off *or* out; *coll. укра́сть* pilfer

выт|ека́ть [1], <~́ечь> [26] flow out; *fig.* follow, result; **~́ереть** → **~ира́ть**; **~́ерпеть** [14] *pf.* endure, bear; ***не ~́ерпел*** couldn't help; **~есня́ть** [28], <~́еснить> [13] force, push out; *оппоне́нта* oust, supplant; **~́ечь** → **~ека́ть**

выт|ира́ть [1], <~́ереть> [12] dry, wipe (**-ся** o.s.); wear out

вы́точенный [14] chiseled; *tech.* turned

вы́тр|ебовать [7] *pf.* ask for, demand, order, summon; *доби́ться тре́бованием* obtain on demand; **~яса́ть** [1], <~́ясти> [24 -с-] shake out

выть [22], <вз-> howl

выт|я́гивать [1], <~́януть> [20 *st.*] draw, pull *or* stretch (out); elicit; *све́дения* endure, bear; **-ся** stretch, extend (o.s.); *вы́расти* grow (up); **~́яжка** *f chem.* extract

выу́|живать [1], <´~дить> [15] catch, dig out (*a. fig.*)

выу́ч|ивать [1], <´~ить> [16] learn, memorize (В + *inf. or* Д); teach (a p. to ... *or* s.th.); **-ся** learn (Д/ **у** Р s.th. from); ***-ся на врача́*** become a doctor

вых|а́живать [1], <~́одить> [15] *больно́го* nurse, restore to health; **~ва́тывать** [1], <~́ватить> [15] snatch away, from, out; pull out, draw

вы́хлоп *m* [1] exhaust; **~но́й** [14] exhaust...

вы́ход *m* [1] **1.** exit; way out (*a. fig.*); *чу́вствам* outlet; **2.** departure; withdrawal, *на пе́нсию* retirement; **3.** *кни́ги* appearance, publication; *thea.* entrance (on stage); **4.** *проду́кции* yield, output; ***~ за́муж*** marriage (of woman); ***~ в отста́вку*** retirement, resignation; **~ец** *m* [1; -дца] immigrant, native of; ***быть ~цем из*** come from

выходи́ть [15], <вы́йти> [вы́йду, -дешь; вы́шел] **1.** go *or* come out; leave; withdraw; retire; **2.** *о кни́ге* appear, be published *or* issued; **3.** *получи́ться* come off; turn out, result; happen, arise, originate; ***вы́шло!*** it's worked!; ***вы́йти в отста́вку*** (***на пе́нсию***) retire, resign; ***~ за преде́лы*** (Р) transgress the bounds of; ***~*** (***за́муж***) ***за*** (В) marry (*v/t.*; *of woman*); ***~ из себя́*** be beside o.s.; ***~ из терпе́ния*** lose one's temper (patience); ***окно́ выхо́дит на у́лицу*** window facing the street; ***~ из стро́я*** fail; be out of action; ***из него́ вы́шел ...*** he has become ...; ***из э́того ничего́ не вы́йдет*** nothing will come of it

вы́ход|ить → ***выха́живать***; **~ка** *f* [5; *g/pl.*: -док] trick, prank; excess; **~но́й** [14] exit...; outlet...; ***~но́й день*** *m* day off; (have a **быть** Т); ***~но́е посо́бие*** gratuity

вы́холенный [14] well-groomed

выцве|та́ть [1], <´~сти> [25 -т-: -ету] fade

выч|ёркивать [1], <~́еркнуть> [20] cross *or* strike out; *из па́мяти* erase, obliterate; **~е́рпывать**, <~́ерпать> [1], *once* <~́ерпнуть> [20 *st.*] bail, scoop (out); **~́есть** → **~ита́ть**; **~́ет** *m* [1] deduction; ***за ~́ом*** (Р) less, minus

вычисл|е́ние *n* [12] calculation; **~я́ть** [1], <´~ить> [13] calculate, compute

вычи|стить → **~ща́ть**; **~та́емое** *n* [14] subtrahend; **~та́ние** *n* [12] subtraction; **~та́ть** [1], <вы́честь> [25 -т-: -чту; -чел, -чла; *g. pt.*: вычтя] deduct; subtract; **~ща́ть** [1], <´~стить> [15] clean, scrub, scour; brush

вы́чурный [14; -рен, -рна] ornate, flowery; fanciful

вы́швырнуть [20 *st.*] *pf.* throw out

вы́ше higher; above; *сил и т. д.* beyond; ***она́ ~ меня́*** she is taller than I (am); ***э́то ~ моего́ понима́ния*** that's beyond my comprehension

вы́ше... above...

выш|иба́ть [1], <˘~ибить> [-бу, -бешь; -б, -бла; -бленный] *coll.* (*вы́бить*) knock out; (*вы́гнать*) kick out; **~ива́ние** *n* [12] embroidery; **~ива́ть** [1], <˘~ить> [-шью, -шьешь] embroider; **˘~ивка** *f* [5; *g/pl.*: -вок] embroidery

вышина́ *f* [5] height; → ***высота́***

вы́шка *f* [5; *g/pl.*: -шек] tower; ***бурова́я ~*** derrick; ***диспе́тчерская ~*** *ae.* control tower

выяв|ля́ть [28], <´~ить> [14] display, make known; uncover, reveal

выясн|е́ние *n* [12] clarification; **~я́ть** [28], <´~ить> [13] clear up, find out, ascertain; **-ся** turn out; come to light

вью́|га *f* [5] snowstorm; **~щиийся** [17] curly; ***~щееся расте́ние*** *n* creeper, climber

вя́жущий [17] astringent

вяз *m* [1] elm

вяза́льн|ый [14] knitting...; ***~ый крючо́к*** crochet hook; ***~ная спи́ца*** knitting needle

вя́зан|ка *f* [5; *g/pl.*: -нок] knitted garment; fag(g)ot; **´~ный** [14] knitted; **~ье** *n* [10] (*a.* **~ие** *n* [12]) knitting; *крючко́м* crochet

вяз|а́ть [3], <с-> **1.** tie, bind (together); **2.** knit; *крючко́м* crochet; **-ся** *impf.* (*соотве́тствовать*) agree, be in keeping; ***разгово́р не ~а́лся*** the conversation flagged; **˘~кий** [16; -зок, -зка́, -о] viscous; *о по́чве* swampy, marshy; **˘~нуть** [21], <за-, у-> get stuck in; sink into

вя́лить [13], <про-> dry; dry-cure, jerk (*meat, fish*)

вя́|лый [14 *sh.*] *цвето́к* withered, faded; *физи́чески* flabby; *fig.* sluggish; dull (*a. comm.*); **~нуть** [20], <за-, у-> wither, fade

Г

габари́т *m* [1] *tech.* clearance-related dimension, size

га́вань *f* [8] harbo(u)r

га́га *f* [5] *zo.* eider

гада́|лка *f* [5; *g/pl.*: -лок] fortune-teller; **~ние** *n* [12] fortune-telling; *дога́дка* guessing, conjecture; **~ть** [1] **1.** <по-> tell fortunes (with cards ***на ка́ртах***); **2.** *impf.* guess, conjecture

га́д|ина *f* [5] *coll.* loathsome person, cur; **~ить** [15] **1.** <на-, за-> soil; (Д) harm; **2.** <из-> P botch; **~кий** [16; -док, -дка́, -о; *comp.*: га́же] nasty, ugly, disgusting, repulsive; **~ли́вый** [14 *sh.*]: ***~ли́вое чу́вство*** feeling of disgust; **~ость** *f* [8] *coll.* filth; low *or* dirty trick; **~ю́ка** *f* [5] *zo.* viper (*a.* P *fig.*), adder

га́ечный ключ *m* [1; *g/pl.*: -е́й] spanner, wrench

газ *m* [1] **1.** gas; ***дать ~*** *mot.* step on the gas; ***на по́лном ~у́*** at full speed (throttle); *pl.* *med.* flatulence; **2.** *ткань* gauze

газе́ль *f* [8] gazelle

газе́т|а *f* [5] newspaper; **~ный** [14] news...; ***~ный кио́ск*** *m* newsstand, *Brt.* news stall; **~чик** *m* [1] *coll.* journalist

газиро́ван|ный [14]: ***~ная вода́*** soda water

га́з|овый [14] **1.** gas...; ***~овая коло́нка*** geyser; water heater; ***~овая плита́*** gas stove; **~овщи́к** *m* [1] *coll.* gasman

газо́н *m* [1] lawn; **~окоси́лка** *f* [5; *g/pl.*: -лок] lawnmower
газо|обра́зный [14; -зен, -зна] gaseous; **~прово́д** *m* [1] gas pipeline
Г
га́йка *f* [5; *g/pl.*: га́ек] *tech.* nut
галантер|е́йный [14]: ***~е́йный магази́н*** notions store, haberdashery; ***~е́йные това́ры*** *m/pl.* = **~е́я** *f* [6] notions *pl.*, haberdashery
галд|ёж *m* [1 *e.*] row, hubbub; **~е́ть** [11], <за-> clamo(u)r, din
гал|ере́я *f* [6] gallery; **~ёрка** *coll. f* [5] *thea.* gallery, "the gods" (*occupants of gallery seats*)
галиматья́ *f* [7] *coll.* balderdash, nonsense; **сплошна́я ~** sheer nonsense
галифе́ *pl.* [*indecl.*] riding breeches *pl.*
га́лка *f* [5; *g/pl.*: -лок] jackdaw
гало́п *m* [1] gallop; ***~ом*** at a gallop; **~и́ровать** [7] gallop
га́лочка *f* [5] tick; ***для ~и*** for purely formal purposes
гало́ши *f/pl.* [5] galoshes, rubbers
га́лстук *m* [1] (neck)tie
галу́н *m* [1 *e.*] galloon, braid
гальван|изи́ровать [7] (*im*)*pf.* galvanize; **~и́ческий** [16] galvanic
га́лька *f* [5; *g/pl.*: -лек] pebble
гам *m* [1] *coll.* din, row, rumpus
гама́к *m* [1 *e.*] hammock
га́мма *f* [5] *mus.* scale; ***кра́сок*** range; ***~-излуче́ние*** gamma rays
гангре́на *f* [5] gangrene
га́нгстер *m* [1] gangster
гандбо́л *m* [1] handball
ганте́ли (-'tɛ-) *f/pl.* [8] (*sport*) dumbbells
гара́ж *m* [1 *e.*] garage
гарант|и́ровать [7] (*im*)*pf.*, **~ия** *f* [7] guarantee
гардеро́б *m* [1] wardrobe, *a. collect.*; **~ная** *f* [14] check-, cloakroom; **~щик** *m* [1], **~щица** *f* [5] cloakroom attendant
гарди́на *f* [5] curtain
гармо́|ника *f* [5] (*kind of*) accordion; ***губна́я ~*** mouth organ, harmonica; **~ни́ровать** [7] harmonize, be in harmony (**с** T with); **~ни́ст** *m* [1] accordionist; harmonist; **~ни́чный** [14; -чен, -чна] harmonious; **~ния** *f* [7] harmony; **~нь** *f* [8], **~шка** *f* [5; *g/pl.*: -шек] → **~ника**
гарни|зо́н *m* [1] garrison; **~р** *m* [1], **~ровать** [7] (*im*)*pf.*, *cul.* garnish; **~ту́р** *m* [1] set; ***ме́бели*** suite
гарпу́н *m* [1 *e.*], **~ить** [13] harpoon
гарь *f* [8] (s.th.) burnt, chared; ***па́хнет ~ю*** there is a smell of smoke
гаси́ть [15], <по-, за-> extinguish, put *or* blow out; ***и́звесть*** slake; ***~ почто́вую ма́рку*** frank a postage stamp
га́снуть [21], <по-, у-> grow feeble, die away; *fig.* fade, wither
гастрол|ёр *m* [1] guest actor *or* artiste; *coll.* casual worker moving from town to town; **~и́ровать** [7] tour; perform on tour; **~и** *f/pl.* [8] tour
гастроно́м *m* [1] *a.* = ***~и́ческий магази́н*** *m* grocery store *or* shop; **~и́ческий** [16] gastronomic(al); **~ия** *f* [7] provisions; delicacies *pl.*
гвалт *coll. m* [1] rumpus, uproar
гвард|е́ец *m* [1; -е́йца] guardsman; **~ия** *f* [7] Guards *pl.*
гво́зд|ик *dim.* → **~ь**; **~и́ка** *f* [5] carnation, pink; (spice) clove; **~ь** *m* [4 *e.*; *pl.*: гво́зди, -де́й] tack, nail; *fig.* ***програ́ммы*** main feature
где where; *coll.* → ***куда́***; ***~-~*** = ***ко́е-где́***; → ***ни***; ***~*** = ***~-либо***, ***~-нибудь***, ***~-то*** anywhere; somewhere; ***~-то здесь*** hereabout(s)
гей! *int.* hi!
гекта́р *m* [1] hectare
ге́лий *m* [3] helium
ген *m* [1] gene
генеало́гия *f* [7] genealogy
генера́|л *m* [1] general; **~лите́т** *m* [1] *collect.* generals; *coll.* top brass; **~льный** [14] general; ***~льная репети́ция*** *f* dress rehearsal; **~тор** *m* [1] generator
гене́ти|ка *f* [5] genetics; **~ческий** [16] genetic, genic
ген|иа́льный [14: -лен, -льна] of genius; ingenious; **~ий** *m* [3] genius
генита́лии *m/pl.* [3] genitals
геноци́д *m* [1] genocide
гео́|граф *m* [1] geographer; **~графи́ческий** [16] geographic(al); **~гра́фия** *f* [7] geography; **~лог** *m*

[1] geologist; **~ло́гия** *f* [7] geology; **~ме́трия** *f* [7] geometry
георги́н(**а** *f* [5]) *m* [1] dahlia
гера́нь *f* [8] geranium
герб *m* [1 *e.*] (coat of) arms; emblem; **~овый** [14] heraldic; stamp(ed)
геркуле́с *m* [1] **1.** man of herculian strength; **2.** rolled oats; porridge
герма́нский [16] German, *ling.* Germanic
гермети́ческий [16] airtight
герои́зм *m* [1] heroism
герои́н *m* [1] heroin
геро|и́ня *f* [6] heroine; **~и́ческий** [16] heroic; **~й** *m* [3] hero; **~йский** [16] heroic
гиаци́нт *m* [1] hyacinth
ги́бель *f* [8] death; ***корабля́ и т. д.*** loss; (***разруше́ние***) ruin, destruction; **~ный** [14; -лен, -льна] disastrous, fatal
ги́бк|ий [16; -бок, -бка́, -о́; *comp.*: ги́бче] supple, pliant, flexible (*a. fig.*); **~ость** *f* [8] flexibility
ги́б|лый [14]: ***~лое де́ло*** hopeless case; ***~лое ме́сто*** godforsaken place; **~нуть** [21], <по-> perish
гига́нт *m* [1] giant; **~ский** [16] gigantic, huge
гигие́н|а *f* [5] hygiene; **~и́ческий** [16], **~и́чный** [14; -чен, -чна] hygienic
гигроскопи́ческий [16; -чен, -чна] hygroscopic
гид *m* [1] guide
гидравли́ческий [16] hydraulic
гидро|пла́н *m* [1] seaplane, hydroplane; **~(электро)-ста́нция** *f* [7] hydroelectric (power) station
гие́на *f* [5] hyena
ги́льза *f* [5] (cartridge) case; (cylinder) sleeve
гимн *m* [1] hymn; ***госуда́рственный*** anthem
гимна|зи́ст *m* [1] pupil; **~зия** *f* [7] high school, *Brt.* grammar school; **~ст** *m* [1] gymnast; **~стёрка** *f* [5; *g/pl.*: -рок] *mil.* blouse, *Brt.* tunic; **~стика** *f* [5] gymnastics; **~сти́ческий** [16] gymnastic; ***~сти́ческий зал*** gymnasium
гипе́рбола[1] *f* [5] *math.* hyperbola
гипе́рбол|а[2] *f* [5] hyperbole; exaggeration; **~и́ческий** [16] hyperbolic, exaggerated
гипертони́я *f* [7] high blood-pressure, hypertension
гипно́|з *m* [1] hypnosis; **~тизи́ровать** [7], <за-> hypnotize
гипо́теза *f* [5] hypothesis
гипс *m* [1] *min.* gypsum; *tech.* plaster of Paris; **~овый** [14] gypseous, plaster...
гирля́нда *f* [5] garland
ги́ря *f* [6] weight
гита́р|а *f* [5] guitar; **~и́ст** *m* [1] guitarist
глава́[1] *f* [5; *pl. st.*] chapter
глав|а́[2] *f* [5; *pl. st.*] head; (***быть, стоя́ть***) ***во ~е́*** (be) at the head; lead (**с** T by); ***поста́вить во ~у́ угла́*** consider to be of the greatest importance; **~а́рь** *m* [4 *e.*] (ring-) leader
главе́нство *n* [9] supremacy; domination; **~вать** [7] command, hold sway (over)
главнокома́ндующий *m* [17] commander in chief; ***Верхо́вный ~*** Commander in Chief; Supreme Commander
гла́вн|ый [14] chief, main, principal, central; head...; ... in chief; ***~ое*** (***де́ло***) the main thing; above all; ***~ым о́бразом*** mainly, chiefly
глаго́л *m* [1] *gr.* verb; **~ьный** [14] verbal
глад|и́льный [14] ironing; ***~и́льная доска́*** ironing board; **~ить** [15] **1.** <вы́-> iron, press; **2.** <по-> stroke, caress; *coll.* ***~ить по голо́вке*** indulge; favo(u)r; ***~ить про́тив ше́рсти*** rub the wrong way; **~кий** [16; -док, -дка́; *comp.*: гла́же] smooth (*a. fig.*); ***во́лосы*** lank; ***ткань*** plain; **~ко** smoothly, successfully; ***всё прошло́ ~ко*** everything went off smoothly; **~ь** *f* [8] smoothness; smooth surface; ***тишь да ~ь*** *coll.* peace and quiet
глаз *m* [1; в ~у́; *pl.*: -а́, глаз, -а́м] eye; look; ***зре́ние*** (eye)sight; *coll.* ***присмо́тр*** heed, care; ***в ~а́*** (Д) to s.b.'s face; ***в мои́х ~а́х*** in my view *or* opinion; ***за ~а́*** in s.b.'s absence, behind one's back; more than enough; ***на ~*** approximately, by eye; ***на ~а́х***

(*poss. or* **у** P) in s.b.'s presence; ***не в бровь, а в ~*** *coll.* hit the mark; ***с ≈у на ~*** privately, tête-à-tête; ***невооружённым ≈ом*** with the naked eye; ***темнó, хоть ~ вы́коли*** *coll.* it is pitch-dark; **~áстый** *coll.* [14 *sh.*] sharp-sighted; **~éть** P [8] stare, gape; **~нóй** [14] eye..., optic; ***~нóй врач*** *m* ophthalmologist; ***~нóе я́блоко*** eyeball; **~óк** *m* [1; -зкá] **1.** [*pl. st.*: -зок] *dim.* → ***глаз***; ***аню́тины ≈ки*** *pl.* pansy; **2.** [*pl. e.*: -зки́, -зкóв] *bot.* bud; *в двери́* peephole

глазомéр *m* [1]: ***хорóший ~*** good eye

глазу́нья *f* [6] fried eggs *pl.*

глазур|овáть [7] (*im*)*pf.* glaze; **≈ь** *f* [8] glaze, icing

глáнда *f* [5] tonsil

глас *m* [1]: ***~ вопию́щего в пусты́не*** voice of one crying in the wilderness

гла|си́ть [15 *e.*; *3. sg. only*] say, read, run; **≈сность** *f* [8] public(ity), openness; **≈сный** [14] open, public; (*a. su.*) vowel

глéтчер *m* [1] glacier

гли́н|а *f* [5] clay; loam; **~истый** [14 *sh.*] clayey; loamy; **~озём** *m* [1] *min.* alumina; **~яный** [14] clay- *or* earthenware-related

глист *m* [1 *e.*], **~á** *f* [5] (intestinal) worm; (***лéнточный***) **~** tapeworm

глицери́н *m* [1] glycerin(e)

глоб|áльный [14; -лен, -льна] global, worldwide; **≈ус** *m* [1] globe

глодáть [3], <об-> gnaw (at, round)

глот|áть [1], <про~и́ть> [15], *once* <≈ну́ть> [20] swallow; *coll. жáдно* devour; **≈ка** *f* [5; *g/pl.*: -ток] throat; ***во всю ≈ку*** → ***гóлос***; **~óк** *m* [1; -ткá] mouthful, gulp (T of)

глóхнуть [21] **1.** <о-> grow deaf; **2.** <за-> *о зву́ке* fade, die away; *о сáде и т. д.* grow desolate, become wild

глуб|инá *f* [5] depth; *векóв* antiquity *fig.* profundity; *лéса* heart of the forest; T/**в** B ...., *or* ... **в** B ... deep; **~и́нка** *f* [5] remote places; **~óкий** [16; -бóк, -бокá, -бóкó; *comp.*: глу́бже] deep; low; remote; *fig.* profound; complete; *стáрость* extreme old age; ***~óкой зимóй*** (***нóчью***) in the dead of winter (late at night)

глубоко|мы́сленный [14 *sh.*] thoughtful, profound; **~мы́слие** *n* [12] thoughtfulness, profundity; **~уважáемый** [14] highly-esteemed; *в письмé* dear

глубь *f* [8] → ***глубинá***

глум|и́ться [14 *e.*; -млю́сь, -ми́шься] sneer, mock, scoff (**над** T at); **~лéние** *n* [12] mockery

глуп|éть [8], <по-> become stupid; **~éц** *m* [1; -пцá] fool, blockhead; **~и́ть** [14 *e.*; -плю́, -пи́шь] fool; **≈ость** *f* [8] stupidity, foolishness; nonsense; **≈ый** [14; глуп, -á, -о] foolish, silly, stupid

глух|áрь *m* [4 *e.*] wood grouse; **~óй** [14; глух, -á, -о; *comp.*: глу́ше] deaf (*a. fig.*; **к** Д to; → ***слепóй***); *звук* dull, muffled; *мéсто* desolate, wild; out-of-the-way; *arch.* solid, blind; ***~óй нóчью*** late at night, in the dead of night; **~онемóй** [14] deaf-mute; **~отá** *f* [5] deafness

глуш|и́тель *m* [4] *tech.* silencer, muffler; **~и́ть** [16 *e.*; -шу́, -ши́шь, -шённый] **1.** <о-> deafen, stun; **2.** <за-> *о зву́ке* muffler; *боль* mitigate; *подави́ть* smother, suppress (*a. bot.*); *tech.* switch off, throttle; ***~и́ть мотóр*** stop the engine; **~ь** *f* [8] out-of-the-way place

глы́ба *f* [5] lump, clod; block

глюкóза *f* [5] glucose

гля|дéть [11; гля́дя], <по->, *once* <≈нуть> [20] look, glance (**на** B at); peep (**из** P out of, from); ***тогó и ~ди́ ...*** it looks as though; ***идти́ кудá глазá ~дя́т*** follow one's nose; ***на ночь ≈дя*** late in the evening

гля́н|ец *m* [1; -нца] luster; polish; **~цев(и́т)ый** [14 (*sh.*)] glossy, lustrous; glazed paper; **~уть** → ***глядéть***

гнать [гоню́, гóнишь; гони́мый; гнал, -á, -о, <по-> **1.** *v/t.* drive; urge on; *из дóма* turn out; **2.** *hunting* pursue, chase; (*a.* **~ся за** T; *fig.* strive for); **3.** *coll. v/i.* speed along

гнев *m* [1] anger; **≈аться** [1], <раз-, про-> be(come) angry (**на** B with);

∼ный [14; -вен, -вна́, -о] angry
гнедо́й [14] sorrel, bay
гнезд|и́ться [15] nest; **∼о́** *n* [9; *pl.*: гнёзда, *etc. st.*] nest, aerie; *el.* socket
гнёт *m* [1] *fig.* oppression, yoke
гни|е́ние *n* [12] decay, rot, putrefaction; **∼ло́й** [14; гнил, -á, -о] rotten, putrid; **∼ль** *f* [8] rottenness; **∼ть** [гнию́, -ёшь; гнил, -á, -о], <с-> rot, decay, putrefy
гно|и́ть, (-ся) [13] let rot, fester; **∼й** *m* [3] pus; **∼йный** [14] purulent
гнуса́вить [14] snuffle; twang
гну́сн|ость *f* [8] vileness; **∼ый** [14; -сен, -сна́, -о] vile, foul
гнуть [20], <со-> bend, curve; bow; *coll. клони́ть* drive (**к** Д at)
гнуша́ться [1], <по-> (Р *or* Т) scorn, despise, disdain
гобеле́н *m* [1] tapestry
гобо́й *m* [3] oboe
го́вор *m* [1] talk; hum; murmur; accent; dialect; **∼и́ть** [13], <по-, сказа́ть> [3] speak *or* talk (**о** П, **про** В about, of; **с** Т to *or* with p.); say, tell; ***∼я́т, ∼и́тся*** they say, it is said; ***∼и́ть по-ру́сски*** speak Russian; ***ина́че ∼я́*** in other words; ***не ∼я́ уже́ о*** (П) let alone; ***по пра́вде*** (***со́вести***) ***∼я́*** tell the truth; ***что вы ∼и́те!*** you don't say!; ***что*** (***как***) ***ни ∼и́*** whatever you (one) may say; ***что и ∼и́ть, и не ∼и́(те)!*** yes, of course!, sure!; **∼ли́вый** [14 *sh.*] talkative
говя́|дина *f* [5], **∼жий** [18] beef
го́голь-мо́голь *m* [4] eggflip
го́гот *m* [1], **∼а́ть** [3], <за-> *гусе́й* cackle; Р roar (with laughter)
год *m* [1; *pl.*: -ды, -да́, *from g/pl. e.* & лет, *etc.* 9 *e.*] year (***в* ∼** a year, per annum); ***в ∼а́х*** elderly, old; ***в ∼ы*** during; ***в те ∼ы*** in those days; ***в э́том*** (***про́шлом***) ***∼у́*** this (last) year; ***из ∼а в ∼*** year in year out; ***∼ от ∼у*** year by year; ***кру́глый ∼*** all (the) year round; (**с**) ***∼а́ми*** for years; as years went on; ***спустя́ ∼*** a year later
годи́т|ься [15 *e.*; гожу́сь, годи́шься], <при-> be of use (***для*** Р, **к** Д, ***на*** В for), do; fit; *pf.* come in handy; ***э́то*** (***никуда́***) ***не ∼ся*** that's no good (for anything), that won't do, it's (very) bad
годи́чный [4] annual
го́дный [14; -ден, -дна́, -о, го́дны́] fit, suitable; *де́йствующий* valid; *поле́зный* useful, good; ***ни на что не ∼*** good-for-nothing
годов|а́лый [14] one-year-old, yearling; **∼о́й** [14] annual, yearly; **∼щи́на** *f* [5] anniversary
гол *m* [1] *sport* goal; ***заби́ть ∼*** score (a goal)
гол|ени́ще *n* [11] bootleg; **∼ень** *f* [8] shin, shank
голла́нд|ец *m* [1; -дца] Dutchman; **∼ка** *f* [5; *g/pl.*: -док] Dutchwoman; **∼ский** [16] Dutch
голов|а́ *f* [5; *ac/sg.*: ∼у; *pl.*: го́ловы, голо́в, -ва́м] head; mind, brain; ***как снег на́ ∼у*** all of a sudden; ***лома́ть ´∼у*** rack one's brains; ***с ∼ы́ до ног*** from head to toe; ***на свою́ ∼у*** *coll.* to one's own detriment; ***пове́сить ´∼у*** become discouraged *or* despondent; ***∼а́ идёт кру́гом*** (***у*** Р s.b.'s) thoughts are in a whirl; **∼ка** *f* [5; *g/pl.*: -вок] small head; *винта́* head; *лу́ка и т. д.* bulb, clove; **∼но́й** [14] head...; ***∼на́я боль*** *f* headache; ***∼но́й плато́к*** head-scarf; ***∼но́й убо́р*** headgear, head-dress
голово|круже́ние *n* [12] giddness; **∼кружи́тельный** [14] dizzy, giddy; **∼ло́мка** [5; *g/pl.*: -мок] puzzle; **∼мо́йка** [5; *g/pl.*: -мо́ек] *coll.* dressing-down; **∼ре́з** *coll.* *m* [1] daredevil; *банди́т* cutthroat, thug; **∼тя́п** *coll.* *m* [1] booby, bungler
го́лод *m* [1] hunger; starvation; famine; **∼а́ть** [1] hunger, starve; go without food, fast; **∼ный** [14; го́лоден, -дна́, -о, го́лодны́] hungry, starving; **∼о́вка** *f* [5; *g/pl.*: -вок] hunger strike
гололе́дица *f* [5] ice-crusted ground
го́лос *m* [1; *pl.*: -са́, *etc. e.*] voice; *на вы́борах* vote; ***пра́во ∼а*** suffrage; ***во весь ∼*** at the top of one's voice; ***в оди́н ∼*** unanimously; ***∼а́ за и про́тив*** the yeas (ayes) & nays; **∼ло́вный** [14; -вен, -вна] unfounded; **∼ова́ние** *n* [12] voting, poll(ing); ***та́йное ∼ова́ние*** secret vote; **∼ова́ть** [7], <про-> vote; *coll.* thumb a lift (by raising one's hand);

~ово́й [14] vocal (cords **свя́зки** *f/pl.*)
голуб|е́ц *m* [1; -бца́] cabbage-roll; **~о́й** [14] (sky) blue; **~ушка** *f* [5; *g/pl.*: -бок(шек)], **~чик** *m* [1] *often iro.* (my) dear; **´~ь** *m* [4] pigeon; **~я́тня** *f* [6; *g/pl.*: -тен] dovecote
го́л|ый [14; гол, -á, -o] naked, nude; bare (*a. fig.*); **~ь** *f* [8]: **~ь на вы́думки хитра́** necessity is the mother of invention
гомеопа́тия *f* [7] homeopathy
го́мон *coll. m* [1] din, hubbub
гондо́ла *f* [5] gondola (*a. ae.*)
гон|е́ние *n* [12] persecution; **~ка** *f* [5; *g/pl.*: -нок] rush; chase; *coll.* haste; *pl.* race(s); *naut.* regatta; **~ка вооруже́ний** arms race
го́нор *m* [1] *coll.* arrogance, airs *pl.*
гонора́р *m* [1] honorarium, fee; **а́вторский** royalties
го́ночный [14] race..., racing
гонча́р *m* [1 *e.*] potter; **~ный** [14] potter's; **~ные изде́лия** *n/pl.* pottery
го́нчая *f* [17] hound
гоня́ть(ся) [1] drive, *etc.*, → **гнать**
гор|а́ *f* [5; *ac/sg.*: го́ру, *pl.*: го́ры, гор, гора́м] mountain; **ку́ча** heap, pile; **ката́ться с ~ы́** toboggan; **в ~у** *or* **на́ ~у** uphill; *fig.* up(ward); **по́д ~у** *or* **с ~ы́** downhill; **под ~о́й** at the foot of a hill (*or* mountain); **не за ~а́ми** not far off, soon; **пир ~о́й** sumptuous feast; **стоя́ть ~о́й** (**за** B) defend s.th. *or* s.b. with might & main; **как у меня́ ~а́ с плеч свали́лась** as if a load had been taken off my mind
гора́здо *used with the comp.* much, far
горб *m* [1 *e.*; на ~у́] hump, hunch; **~а́тый** [14 *sh.*] humpbacked; curved; **нос** aquiline; **~ить** [14], <c-> stoop, bend, curve (*v/i.* **-ся**); **~у́н** *m* [1 *e.*] hunchback; **~у́ша** *f* [5] humpback salmon; **~у́шка** *f* [5; *g/pl.*: -шек] crust (*of a loaf*)
горд|ели́вый [14 *sh.*] haughty, proud; **~е́ц** *m* [1 *e.*] proud man; **~и́ться** [15 *e.*; горжу́сь, горди́шься], <воз-> be(come) proud (T of); **~ость** *f* [8] pride; **~ый** [14; горд, -á, -o] proud (T of)
го́р|е *n* [10] grief, sorrow; misfortune, disaster; **с ~я** out of grief; **ему́ и ~я ма́ло** *coll.* he doesn't care a bit; **с ~ем попола́м** *coll.* hardly, with difficulty; **~ева́ть** [6], <по-> grieve; (**сожале́ть**) regret (**о** П s.th.)
горе́л|ка *f* [5; *g/pl.*: -лок] burner; **~ый** [14] burnt
го́рест|ный [14; -тен, -тна] sorrowful, mournful; **~ь** *f* [8] → **го́ре**
гор|е́ть [9], <c-> burn (*a. fig.*), be alight, be on fire; (**свети́ться**) glow, gleam; **не ~и́т** *coll.* there's no hurry; **де́ло ~и́т** *coll.* the matter is very urgent
го́рец *m* [1; -рца] mountain-dweller; highlander
го́речь *f* [8] bitter taste; *fig.* bitterness; **утра́ты** grief
горизо́нт *m* [1] horizon; skyline; **~а́льный** [14; -лен, -льна] horizontal, level
гори́стый [14 *sh.*] mountainous; hilly
го́рка *f* [5; *g/pl.*: -рок] *dim.* → **гора́** hillock
горла́нить P [13], <за-, про-> bawl
го́рл|о *n* [9] throat; gullet; **сосу́да** neck (*a.* **~ышко** *n* [9; *g/pl.*: -шек]); **дел по ~о** *coll.* up to the eyes in work; **я сыт по ~о** *coll.* I've had my fill (*fig.* I'm fed up with [T]); **во всё ~о** → **го́лос**
горн *m* [1] horn, bugle; **~и́ст** *m* [1] bugler
го́рничная *f* [14] (house)maid
горнопромы́шленный [14] mining
горноста́й *m* [3] ermine
го́рн|ый [14] mountain(ous), hilly; *min.* rock...; mining; **~ое де́ло** *n* mining; **~я́к** *m* [1 *e.*] miner; mining engineer
го́род *m* [1; *pl.*: -да́, *etc. e.*] town; city (large town; *coll.* downtown); **за ~(ом)** go (live) out of town; **~и́ть** P [15], <на-> **вздор** *etc.* talk nonsense; **~о́к** *m* [1; -дка́] small town; **~ско́й** [14] town..., city..., urban, municipal; → **горсове́т**
горожа́н|ин *m* [1; *pl.*: -жа́не, -жа́н] townsman; *pl.* townspeople; **~ка** *f* [5; *g/pl.*: -нок] townswoman

горо́|х *m* [1] *расте́ние* pea; *collect.* peas *pl.*; **~ховый** [14] pea(s)...; ***чу́чело ~ховое** n*, ***шут ~ховый** m coll. fig.* scarecrow; buffoon, merry-andrew; **~шек** *m* [1; -шка] *collect.* green peas *pl.*; **~шин(к)а** *f* [5 (*g/pl.*: -нок)] pea

горсове́т (**городско́й сове́т**) *m* [1] city *or* town council

го́рст|очка *f* [5; *g/pl.*: -чек] very small group of people, *dim. of* **~ь** *f* [8; *from g/pl. e.*] *о ладо́ни* hollow; *земли́ и т. д.* handful (*a. fig.*)

горта́н|ный [14] guttural; **~ь** *f* [8] larynx

горчи́|чник *m* [1] mustard poultice; **~ца** *f* [5] mustard

горшо́к *m* [1; -шка́] pot, jug

го́рьк|ий [16; -рек, -рька́, -о; *comp.*: го́рьче, го́рше] bitter (*a. fig.*); ***~ий пья́ница** coll. m* inveterate drunkard

горю́ч|ее *n* [17] liquid fuel; gasoline, *Brt.* petrol; **~ий** [17 *sh.*] combustible; *old use* bitter (tears)

горя́ч|ий [17; горя́ч, -а́] hot (*a. fig.*); (*вспы́льчивый*) fiery, hot-tempered; *любо́вь, покло́нник* ardent, passionate; *спор* heated; *след* warm; *приём* hearty; *вре́мя* busy; ***~ая то́чка; по ~им следа́м*** hot on the trail; *fig.* without delay; **~и́ть** [16 *e.*; -чу́, -чи́шь], <раз-> excite, irritate; (*a. fig.*); **-ся** get *or* be excited; **~ка** *f* [5] fever (*a. fig.*); ***поро́ть ~ку*** *coll.* act impetuosly; **~ность** *f* [8] zeal, enthusiasm; impulsiveness

гос = **госуда́рственный** state...

госпитал|изи́ровать [7] hospitalize; **~ь** *m* [4] *esp. mil.* hospital

господ|и́н *m* [1; *pl.*: -пода́, -по́д, -да́м] gentleman; Mr.; *pl.* (ladies &) gentlemen; ***уважа́емые ~а́** в письме́* Dear Sirs; **~ство** *n* [9] rule; (*пре-восхо́дство*) supremacy; (*преоблада́ние*) predominance; **~ствовать** [7] rule, reign; (pre)dominate, prevail (***над*** T over); (*возвыша́ться*) command; **℞ь** *m* [Го́спода, -ду; *vocative*: -ди] Lord, God (*a. as int.*, → ***Бог***)

госпожа́ *f* [5] Mrs.; Miss

гостеприи́м|ный [14; -мен, -мна] hospitable; **~ство** *n* [9] hospitality

гост|и́ная *f* [14] drawing room, living room; **~и́нец** *m* [1; -нца] present, gift; **~и́ница** *f* [5] hotel; inn; **~и́ть** [15 *e.*; гощу́, гости́шь] be on a visit, stay with (***у*** P); **~ь** *m* [4; *from g/pl. e.*] guest; visitor (*f* **~ья** [6]); ***идти́*** (***е́хать***) ***в ~и*** go to see (***к*** Д s.b.); ***быть в ~ях*** (***у*** P) → **~и́ть**

госуда́рственн|ый [14] state...; public; *изме́на* high (*treason*); ***~ переворо́т** m* coup d'état; ***~ый строй** m* political system, regime: ***~ая слу́жба*** public *or* civil service

госуда́р|ство *n* [9] state; **~ь** *m* [4] *hist.* sovereign

готова́льня *f* [6; *g/pl.*: -лен] (case of) drawing utensils *pl.*

гото́в|ить [14] **1.**<при-> cook; prepare (**-ся к** Д o.s. *or* get ready for); **2.** <под-> prepare, train; **3.** <за-> store up; lay in (stock); **~ность** *f* [8] readiness; preparedness, willingness; **~ый** [14 *sh.*] ready (**к** Д *or inf.* for), on the point of; finished; willing; *оде́жда* ready-made

гофриро́ванн|ый [14]: ***~ое желе́зо*** corrugated iron

граб *m* [1] hornbeam

граб|ёж *m* [1 *e.*] robbery; **~и́тель** *m* [4] robber; **~и́тельский** [16] *це́ны* exorbitant; **~ить** [14], <о-> rob, plunder

гра́бли *f/pl.* [6; *gen.*: -бель, -блей] rake

грав|ёр *m* [1] engraver; **~ий** *m* [3] gravel; **~ирова́ть** [7], <вы́-> engrave; **~иро́вка** *f* [5; *g/pl.*: -вок] engraving, etching, print, (*a.* **~ю́ра** *f* [5])

град *m* [1] hail (*a. fig.* = shower); ***вопро́сы посы́пались ~ом*** he was showered with questions; ***~ идёт*** it is hailing; **~ом** thick and fast, profusely

гра́дус *m* [1] degree (***в*** B of); ***под ~ом*** P under the weather; **~ник** *m* [1] thermometer

гражд|ани́н *m* [1; *pl.*: гра́ждане, -ан], **~а́нка** *f* [5; *g/pl.*: -нок] citizen (*address mst. without name*); **~а́нский** [16] civil (*a. war*); civic (*a. right*); **~а́нство** *n* [9] citizenship; citizens *pl.*: ***дать*** (***получи́ть***) ***пра́во ~а́нства*** give or (be given) civic rights; (*fig.*) gain general (public) recognition; ***принять ... ~анство*** become a ... citizen

грамм *m* [1] gram(me)

граммáт|ика *f* [5] grammar; **~и́ческий** [16] grammatical

грáмот|а *f* [5] reading & writing; ***вери́тельная ~а*** credentials; ***э́то для меня́ кита́йская ~а*** *coll.* it's Greek to me; **~ность** *f* [8] literacy; **~ный** [14; -тен, -тна] literate; *специали́ст* competent, expert

гранáт *m* [1] pomegranate; *min.* garnet; **~а** *f* [5] shell; *ручна́я* grenade

грандио́зный [14; -зен, -зна] grandiose; mighty, vast

гранёный [14] facet(t)ed; cut

грани́т *m* [1] granite

грани́|ца *f* [5] border, frontier; boundary; *fig.* limit, verge; ***за ~цу*** (***~цей***) go (be) abroad; ***из-за ~цы*** from abroad; ***перейти́ все ~цы*** pass all bounds; **~чить** [16] border *or* verge (**с** T [up]on)

гра́н|ка *f* [5; *g/pl.*: -нок] *typ.* galley (proof); **~ь** *f* [8] → ***грани́ца***; *math.* plane; *драгоце́нного ка́мня* facet; edge; *fig.* verge

граф *m* [1] earl (*Brt.*); count

граф|á *f* [5] column; **~ик** *m* [1] diagram, graph; *временно́й* schedule; **~ика** *f* [5] graphic arts; (*произведе́ния*) drawings

графи́н *m* [1] decanter, carafe

графи́ня *f* [6] countess

графи́|т *m* [1] graphite; **~ть** [14 *e.*; -флю́, -фи́шь; -флённый], <раз-> line *or* rule (paper); **~ческий** [16] graphic(al)

граци|о́зный [14; -зен, -зна] graceful; **~я** *f* [7] grace(fulness)

грач *m* [1 *e.*] *zo.* rook

греб|ёнка *f* [5; *g/pl.*: -нок] comb; ***стри́чь всех под одну́ ~ёнку*** reduce everyone to the same level; **~ень** *m* [4; -бня] comb; *волны́, горы́* crest; **~е́ц** *m* [1; -бца́] oarsman; **~ешо́к** *m* [1; -шка́] → **~ень**; **~ля** *f* [6] rowing; **~но́й** [14] row(ing)...

грёза *f* [5] *rare* (day) dream

гре́зить [15] *impf.* dream (**о** П of)

гре́йдер *m* [1] *tech.* grader; *coll.* earth road

грейпфру́т *m* [1] grapefruit

грек *m* [1] Greek

гре́лка *f* [5; *g/pl.*: -лок] hot-water bottle; ***электри́ческая ~*** heating pad, electric blanket

грем|е́ть [10 *e.*; гремлю́, -ми́шь], <про-, за-> thunder, peal (*a.* *о го́лосе, колокола́х, etc.*); *теле́га, ключи́* rattle, clank, tinkle; *посу́дой* clatter; **~у́чий** [17]: ***~у́чая змея́*** *f* rattlesnake

гре́нки *m/pl.* [1 *e.*] toast (*sg.*: -нок)

грести́ [26 -б-: гребу́; грёб, гребла́], <по-> row; scull; *гра́блями* rake

греть [8; ...гре́тый], <со-, на-, разо-, обо-, подо-> warm (**-ся** o.s.) (up); heat; ***-ся на со́лнце*** sun

грех *m* [1 *e.*] sin; (*недоста́ток*) fault; *coll.* → ***грешно́***; ***с ~о́м попола́м*** just manage; → ***го́ре***; ***есть тако́й ~*** *coll.* well, I own it; ***как на ~*** *coll.* unfortunately

гре́|цкий [16]: ***~цкий оре́х*** *m* walnut; **~ча́нка** *f* [5; *g/pl.*: -нок], **~ческий** [16] Greek

греч|и́ха, ~ка *f* [5] buckwheat; **~невый** [14] buckwheat...

греш|и́ть [16 *e.*; -шу́, -ши́шь], <со-> sin (***про́тив*** P *a.* against); ***~и́ть про́тив и́стины*** distort the truth; **~ник** *m* [1], **~ница** *f* [5] sinner; **~но́** (it's a) shame (on Д); **~ный** [14; -шен, -шна́, -о́] sinful; F *sh.*: sorry

гриб *m* [1 *e.*] mushroom; **~о́к** *m* [1; -бка́] *dim.* → ***гриб***; fungus

гри́ва *f* [5] mane

гри́венник *coll.* *m* [1] ten-kopeck coin

гриль *m* [4] grill

грим *m* [1] *thea.* makeup

грима́с|а *f* [5] grimace; **~ничать** [1] make faces *or* grimaces

гримирова́ть [7], <за-, на-> make up (*v/i.* **-ся**)

грипп *m* [1] influenza

гриф *m* [1]: ***~ секре́тности*** inscription designating the degree of confidentiality

гроб *m* [1; в -у́ *pl.*: -ы́, -а, *etc. e.*] coffin; **~ни́ца** *f* [5] tomb; **~ово́й** [14] coffin...; tomb...; ***~ово́е молча́ние*** deathly silence

гроза́ *f* [5; *pl. st.*] (thunder) storm (*a. fig.*); menace; terror
грозд|ь *m* [4; *pl.*: -ди, -дей, *etc. e.*, -дья, -дьев] *виногра́да* bunch; *я́год, цвето́в* cluster
грози́ть [15 *e.*; грожу́, -зи́шь], <по-> threaten (Д/Т a p. with) (*a.* **-ся**)
гро́з|ный [14; -зен, -зна́, -о] menacing, threatening; *челове́к* formidable; *coll. го́лос* stern, severe; **~ово́й** [14] stormy; ***~ова́я ту́ча*** thundercloud
гром *m* [1; *from g/pl. e.*] thunder (*a. fig.*); ***~ греми́т*** it thunders; ***как ~ среди́ я́сного не́ба*** like a bolt from the blue; ***как ~ом поражённый*** *fig.* thunderstruck
грома́д|а *f* [5] bulk, mass of; **~ный** [14; -ден, -дна] vast, huge; *успе́х и т. д.* tremendous
громи́|ть [14 *e.*; -млю́, -ми́шь; -млённый], <раз-> smash, crush; *врага́* rout, smash
гро́мк|ий [16; -мок, -мка́, -о; *comp.*: гро́мче] loud; noisy; *fig.* famous, great, noted; *слова́* pompous
громо|во́й [14] thunder...; *го́лос* thunderous; **~гла́сный** [14; -сен, -сна] loud; *mst. adv.* publicly, openly; **~зди́ть(ся)** [15 *e.*; -зжу́, -зди́шь] → ***взгроможда́ть(ся)***; **~здкий** [16; -док, -дка] bulky, cumbersome; **~отво́д** *m* [1] lightning rod *or* conductor
громыха́ть *coll.* [1] rumble; *посу́дой* clatter; *о пу́шках* boom
гроссме́йстер *m* [1] *chess* grand master
грот *m* [1] grotto
гроте́ск *m* [1], **~ный** [14] grotesque
гро́х|нуть *coll.* [20] *pf.* crash, bang down (*v/i.* **-ся** fall with a crash); **~от** *m* [1] din; **~ота́ть** [3], <за-> rumble; *пу́шек* roar
грош *m* [1 *e.*]: ***ни ~а́*** not a farthing; ***~ цена́*** *or* ***~а́ ло́маного не сто́ит*** not worth a pin; ***ни в ~ не ста́вить*** not care a straw (В for); **~о́вый** [14] *fig.* (dirt-)cheap
груб|е́ть [8], <за-, о-> coarsen, become rude; **~и́ть** [14 *e.*; -блю́, -би́шь], <на-> be rude (Д to); **~ия́н** *coll. m* [1] rude fellow, boor; **~ость** *f* [8] rudeness; **~ый** [14; груб, -а́, -о] *материа́л* coarse; *игра́, рабо́та* rough; rude; *оши́бка и т. д.* gross
гру́да *f* [5] pile, heap
груд|и́нка *f* [5; *g/pl.*: -нок] brisket; bacon; **~но́й** [14]: ***~на́я кле́тка*** *f* thorax; ***~но́й ребёнок*** infant in arms; **~ь** *f* [8; в, на -ди́; *from g/pl. e.*] breast; chest; ***стоя́ть ~ью*** (***за*** В) champion, defend
груз *m* [1] load (*a. fig.*); *перевози́мый* freight; *naut.* cargo
грузи́н *m* [1; *g/pl.*: грузи́н], **~ка** *f* [5; *g/pl.*: -нок] Georgian; **~ский** [16] Georgian
грузи́ть [15 *e.*; -ужу́, -у́зишь], <на-, за-, по-> load, freight
гру́з|ный [14; -зен, -зна́, -о] massive, heavy; **~ови́к** *m* [1 *e.*] truck, *Brt.* lorry; **~ово́й** [14] freight..., goods...; *naut.* cargo; ***~ово́й автомоби́ль*** *m* → ***~ови́к***; **~оподъёмность** *f* [8] carrying capacity; *naut.* tonnage; **~получа́тель** *m* [4] consignee; **~чик** *m* [1] loader; *naut.* docker, stevedore
грунт *m* [1] soil, earth; ground (*a. paint.*); **~ово́й** [14] *о воде́* subsoil; *доро́га* dirt road
гру́пп|а *f* [5] group; **~ирова́ть(ся)** [7], <с-> (form a) group
груст|и́ть [15 *e.*; -ущу́, -сти́шь], <взгрустну́ть> [20] be sad; long for (***по*** П); **~ный** [14; -тен, -тна́, -о] sad, sorrowful; *coll.* grievous, distressing; ***мне ~о*** I feel sad; **~ь** *f* [8] sadness, grief, melancholy
гру́ша *f* [5] pear (*a.* tree)
гры́жа *f* [5] hernia, rupture
грыз|ня́ *f* [6] squabble, **~ть** [24; *pt. st.*] gnaw (*a. fig.*), nibble; bite; *оре́хи* crack; **-ся** fight, squabble; **~у́н** *m* [1 *e.*] *zo.* rodent
гряд|а́ *f* [5; *nom/pl. st.*] ridge, range; *agric.* bed (*a.* **~ка** *f* [5; *g/pl.*: -док])
гряду́щий [17] future, coming; ***на сон ~*** before going to bed
гряз|ево́й [14] mud...; **~езащи́тный** [14] antisplash; **~елече́бница** *f* [5] therapeutic mud baths; **~и** *f/pl.* [8] (curative) mud; **~ни́ть** [13], <за-> soil (*a. fig.*); **-ся** get dirty; **~нуть** [21], <по-> sink (mud, *etc.*, *fig.*); **~ный** [14; -зен, -зна́, -о,

Г

гря́зны́] dirty (*a. fig.*); muddy; **~ь** *f* [8; в -зи́] dirt, mud; ***в ~и́*** dirty; ***не уда́рить лицо́м в ~*** manage to do s.th. successfully; ***смеша́ть с ~ью*** sling mud (В at)

гря́нуть [19 *st.*] *pf. гром* burst out; *вы́стрел* ring, roar; *война́* break out; *пе́сня* burst, start

Д

губ|а́ *f* [5; *nom/pl. st.*] lip; *зали́в, у́стье* bay; ***у него́ ~а́ не ду́ра*** his taste isn't bad; he knows which side his bread is buttered on

губерн|а́тор *m* [1] governor; **~ия** *f* [7] *hist.* province

губи́т|ельный [14; -лен, -льна] ruinous; pernicious; **~ь** [14], <по-, с-> destroy, ruin; *вре́мя* waste

гу́б|ка *f* [5; *g/pl.*: -бок] **1.** *dim.* → **~а́**; **2.** sponge; **~но́й** [14] labial; ***~на́я пома́да*** *f* lipstick

гуд|е́ть [11], <за-> buzz; *о гудке́* honk, hoot, whistle; *coll. боле́ть* ache; **~о́к** *m* [1; -дка́] honk, hoot, signal; horn; siren; whistle

гул *m* [1] boom, rumble; *голосо́в* hum; **~кий** [16; -лок, -лка́, -о] *гро́мкий* booming, loud; resonant

гуля́|нье *n* [10] walk(ing); *ма́ссовое* open-air merrymaking, fête; **~ть** [28], <по-> [20] go for a walk (*a.* ***идти́ ~ть***), stroll; *fig. о ве́тре и т. д.* sweep; *coll.* carouse, go on a spree

гуля́ш *m* [1; *g/pl.*: -е́й] goulash, stew

гуманита́рны|й [14]: ***~е нау́ки*** the humanities

гума́нн|ость *f* [8] humanity; **~ый** [14; -а́нен, -а́нна] humane

гурма́н *m* [1] gourmet

гур|т *m* [1 *e.*] herd, drove (cattle); **~ьба́** *f* [5] crowd (Т in)

гу́сеница *f* [5] caterpillar

гуси́ный [14] goose (*a.* gooseflesh *ко́жа*)

густ|е́ть [8], <за-> thicken; **~о́й** [14; густ, -а́, -о; *comp.*: гу́ще] thick, dense; deep, rich (*colo(u)r, sound*)

гус|ь *m* [4; *from g/pl. e.*] goose; *fig.* ***хоро́ш ~ь*** *b.s.* fine fellow indeed!; ***как с ~я вода́*** like water off a duck's back, thick-skinned; **~ько́м** in single file

гу́ща *f* [5] grounds *pl.*; *оса́док* sediment; *ле́са* thicket; *fig.* in the center (-tre) of things

Д

да 1. *part.* yes; oh (yes), indeed (*a. interr.*); (oh) but, now, well; *imperative* do(n't)...!; *tags*: aren't, don't, *etc.*; may, let; **2.** *cj.* (*a.* ***~ и***) and; but; ***~ и то́лько*** nothing but; and that's all; ***~ что вы!*** you don't say!

да́бы *old use* (in order) that *or* to

да|ва́ть [5], <~ть> [дам, дашь, даст, дади́м, дади́те, даду́т (...-) дал, -а́, -о; (...)да́нный (дан, -а́)] give; (*позво́лить*) let; (*дарова́ть*) bestow; *кля́тву* take, pledge; make (way); ***~ва́й(те)!*** come on!; *with vb.* (*a.* ***~й(те)***) let us (me); ***ни ~ть ни взять*** exactly alike; ***~ва́ть ход де́лу*** set s.th. going; further s.th.; **-ся** let o.s. (***в*** В *be caught, cheated*); *с трудо́м и т. д.* (turn out to) be (*e.g.* hard for Д); (can) master (И s.th.)

дави́ть [14] **1.** <на-> press; squeeze (<вы́-> out); **2.** <за-, раз-> crush; Р (*сбить маши́ной*) run over, knock down; **3.** <по-> oppress; suppress; **4.** <при-, с-> press (down *or* together), jam, compress; crush, trample; **5.** <у-> strangle; **-ся** choke; (*пове́ситься*) hang o.s.

да́в|ка *f* [5] throng, jam; **~ле́ние** *n* [12] pressure (*a. fig.*)

да́вн|(и́шн)ий [15] old; of long standing; **~о́** long ago; for a long time, long since; **~опроше́дший** [17] remote, long past; **~ость** *f* [8] antiquity; *law* prescription; **срок ∠ости** term of limitation; **∼ы́м-∼о́** very long ago, ages ago

да́же (*a.* **∼ и**) even; **∼ не** not even

да́л|ее → **да́льше**; **и так ∼ее** and so on (*or* forth); **∼ёкий** [16; -лёк, -лека́, -леко́ -лёко; *comp.*: да́льше] far (away), distant (**от** P from); long (way); *fig.* wide (of); strange (to); **он не о́чень ∼ёкий челове́к** he is not very clever; **∼еко́, ∼ёко** far (off, away); a long way (**до** P to); (Д) **∼еко́ до** (P) far from, much inferior to; **∼еко́ не** by no means; **∼еко́ за** (B) long after; **о во́зрасте** well over; **∼еко́ иду́щий** [17] far-reaching; **∼ь** *f* [8; в ∼и́] distance; open space; **∼ьне́йший** [17] further; **в ∼ьне́йшем** in future, henceforth; **∼ьний** [15] distant (*a. kin*); remote; → *a.* **∼ёкий**; **∼ьневосто́чный** [14] Far Eastern

дально|бо́йный [14] *mil.* long range; **∼ви́дность** *f* [8] foresight; **∼ви́дный** [14; -ден, -дна] *fig.* farsighted; **∼зо́ркий** [16; -рок, -рка] far-, long-sighted; **´∼сть** *f* [8] distance; *mil.*, *tech.* (long-)range

да́льше farther; further (more); then, next; (**чита́йте**) **∼!** go on (reading)

да́м|а *f* [5] lady; (dance) partner; *cards* queen; **∼ба** *f* [5] dam, dike; **∼ка** *f* [5; *g/pl.*: -мок] king (*in draughts*); **∼ский** [16] ladies', women's

да́н|ный [14] given, present, in question; **∼ные** *pl.* data, facts; statistics; **обрабо́тка ∼ных** data processing

дань *f* [8] tribute (*a. fig.*); **отдава́ть ∼** appreciate, recognize

дар *m* [1; *pl. e.*] gift (*a. fig.*); **∼и́ть** [13], <по-> give (Д/В a p. s.th.), present (B/T a p. with); **∼моёд** *coll.* *m* [1] sponger; **∼ова́ние** *n* [12] donation, giving; talent; **∼ови́тый** [14 *sh.*] gifted, talented; **∼ово́й** [14] gratis, free

да́ром *adv.* gratis, for nothing; (**напра́сно**) in vain; **пропа́сть ∼** be wasted; **э́то ему́ ∼ не пройдёт** he will smart for this

да́т|а *f* [5] date; **∼ельный** [14] *gr.* dative (*case*); **∼и́ровать** [7] (*im*)*pf.* (**за́дним число́м** ante)date

да́т|ский [16] Danish; **∼ча́нин** *m* [1; *pl.*: -ча́не, -ча́н], **∼ча́нка** *f* [5; *g/pl.*: -нок] Dane

да́тчик *m* [1] *tech.* sensor

да́ть(ся) → **дава́ть(ся)**

да́ч|а *f* [5] dacha, cottage, summer residence, villa; **на ∼е** in a dacha; out of town; in the country; **∼ник** *m* [1] summer resident; **∼ный** [14] suburban; country...; garden (suburb **посёлок**)

два *m*, *n*, **две** *f* [34] two; → **пять**, **пя́тый**; **в ∼ счёта** *coll.* in a jiffy

двадцат|иле́тний [15] twenty-year; twenty-year-old; **∠ый** [14] twentieth; → **пя́т(идеся́т)ый**; **´∼ь** [35; -ти́] twenty; → **пять**

два́жды twice; **∼ два** *math.* two by two; **я́сно как ∼ два** (**четы́ре**) plain as day

двена́дцат|и... (*in compds.*) twelve...; dodec(a)...; duodecimal, duodenary; **∼ый** [14] twelfth; → **пя́тый**; **∼ь** [35] twelve; → **пять**

двер|но́й [14] door...; **∼но́й проём** doorway; **∠ца** *f* [5; *g/pl.*: -рец] (*cupboard*, *etc.*) door; **∼ь** *f* [8; в -ри́; *from g/pl. e.*; *instr. a.* -рьми́] door (*a. pl.* **∠и**)

две́сти [36] two hundred

дви́|гатель *m* [4] engine, motor; **∼гать** [13], <∼нуть> [20] (B/T) move, set in motion; stir; **-ся** move, advance; **отпра́виться** set out; start; **∼же́ние** *n* [12] movement (*a. pol.*); stir; *phys.* motion; traffic; *fig.* emotion; **приводи́ть** (**приходи́ть**) **в ∼же́ние** set going (start [moving]); **∼жимый** [14 *sh.*] prompted, moved; movable; **∼жу́щий** [17]: **∼жущая си́ла** driving force; **∼нуть** → **∼гать**

дво́е [37] two (in a group, together); **нас бы́ло ∼** there were two of us; **∼то́чие** *n* [12] *gr.* colon

двои́т|ься [13], <раз-> divide into two; **у меня́ в глаза́х ∼ся** I see double

дво́й|ка *f* [5; *g/pl.*: дво́ек] two (*a.* boat; team; bus, *etc.*, *no.* 2; cards: *a.* deuce); pair; (mark) = **пло́хо**; **∼ни́к** *m* [1 *e.*] double; **∼но́й** [14] double (*a. fig.*); **~ня** *f* [6; *g/pl.*: дво́ен] twins *pl.*; **~ственный** [14 *sh.*]: ***~ственное отноше́ние*** mixed feelings

двои́чный [14; -чен, -чна] binary

двор *m* [1 *e.*] (court) yard; farm (-stead); *короле́вский* court; ***на ~е́*** outside, outdoors; **~е́ц** *m* [1; -рца́] palace; ***♀ бракосочета́ний*** Wedding Palace; ***♀ культу́ры*** Palace of Culture; **~ни́к** *m* [1] janitor, (yard and) street cleaner; *mot.* windshield (*Brt.* windscreen) wiper; **~ня́га** *coll. f* [5], **~ня́жка** *coll. f* [5; *g/pl.*: -жек] mongrel; **~цо́вый** [14] court..., palace...; ***~цо́вый переворо́т*** palace revolution; **~яни́н** *m* [1; *pl.*: -я́не, -я́н] nobleman; **~я́нка** *f* [5; *g/pl.*: -нок] noblewoman; **~я́нский** [16] of the nobility; of noble birth; **~я́нство** *n* [9] nobility

двою́родн|ый [14]: ***~ый брат*** *m*, ***~ая сестра́*** *f* cousin

двоя́к|ий [16 *sh.*] double, twofold; **~о** in two ways

дву|бо́ртный [14] double-breasted; **~гла́вый** [14] double-headed; **~жи́льный** [14] sturdy, tough; *tech.* twin-core; **~кра́тный** [14] double; done twice; **~ли́чие** *n* [12] duplicity, double-dealing; **~ли́чный** [14; -чен, -чна] two-faced; **~смы́сленный** [14 *sh.*] ambiguous; **~ство́лка** *f* [5; *g/pl.*: -лок] double-barrel(l)ed gun; **~ство́льный** [14]: ***~ство́льное ружьё*** *n* → **~ство́лка**; **~ство́рчатый** [14]: ***~ство́рчатая дверь*** *f* folding doors; **~сторо́нний** [15] bilateral; *движе́ние* two-way; *ткань* reversible

двух|... (→ *a.* **дву...**): **~дне́вный** [14] two days; **~коле́йный** [14] double-track; **~колёсный** [14] two-wheel(ed); **~ле́тний** [15] two-years-old; two-years'; **~ме́стный** [14] two-seat(er); **~ме́сячный** [14] two months' *or* two-months-old; **~мото́рный** [14] twin-engine(d); **~неде́льный** [14] two weeks', *Brt. a.* a fortnight's; **~со́тый** [14] two hundredth; **~эта́жный** [14] two-storied (*Brt.* -reyed)

двуязы́чный [14; -чен, -чна] bilingual

деба́ты *m/pl.* [1] debate

де́бет *m* [1] *comm.* debit; ***занести́ в ~*** = **~ова́ть** [7] (*im*)*pf.* debit (sum against *or* to a p. В/Д)

дебито́р *m* [1] debtor

дебо́ш *m* [1] shindy, riot

де́бр|и *f/pl.* [8] thickets; the wilds; ***запу́таться в ~ях*** get bogged down (P in)

дебю́т *m* [1] debut; *chess* opening

де́ва *f* [5]: ***♀ Мари́я*** the Virgin; ♀ Virgo; (***ста́рая***) **~** (old) maid

девальва́ция *f* [7] devaluation

дева́ть [1], <деть> [де́ну, -нешь] put, leave, mislay; ***куда́ ~*** *a.* what to do with, how to spend; **-ся** go, get; *vb.*+ И = put, leave + *obj.*; be (*pr.*); ***куда́ мне ~ся?*** where shall I go *or* stay?; ***куда́ он де́лся?*** what has become of him?

де́верь *m* [4; *pl.*: -рья́, -ре́й, -рья́м] brother-in-law (*husband's brother*)

деви́з *m* [1] motto

дев|и́ца *f* [5] *iro.* young lady, girl; **~и́чий** [18] maidenly; girlish; **~очка** *f* [5; *g/pl.*: -чек] (little) girl; **~ственный** [14 *sh.*] maiden, virgin...; *лес и т. д.* primeval; **~ушка** *f* [5; *g/pl.*: -шек] young lady, unmarried girl (*a. form of address*); **~чо́нка** *f* [5; *g/pl.*: -нок] girl

девя|но́сто [35] ninety; **~но́стый** [14] ninetieth; → ***пят***(***идеся́т***)***ый***; **~тисо́тый** [14] nine hundredth; **~тка** [5; *g/pl.*: -ток] nine (→ ***дво́йка***); **~на́дцатый** [14] ninetieth; → ***пять***, ***пя́тый***; **~на́дцать** [35] nineteen; → ***пять***; **~тый** [14] ninth; → ***пя́тый***; **´~ть** [35] nine; → ***пять***; **~тьсо́т** [36] nine hundred; **´~тью** nine times

дегенера́т *m* [1] degenerate

деград|а́ция *f* [7] degradation; **~и́ровать** [7] (*im*)*pf.* degrade

де́д|(**ушка** *m* [5; *g/pl.*: -шек]) *m* [1] grandfather; old man; *pl.* **~ы** *a.* forefathers; ***~-моро́з*** *m* Santa Claus, Father Christmas

дееприча́стие *n* [12] *gr.* gerund

дежу́р|ить [13] be on duty; be on watch; **~ный** *m* [14] (*p.*) duty..., on duty; **~ство** *n* [9] duty, (night) watch

дезерти́р *m* [1] deserter; **~овать** [7] (*im*)*pf.* desert; **~ство** *n* [9] desertion
дезинф|е́кция *f* [7] disinfection; **~ици́ровать** [7] (*im*)*pf.* disinfect
дезинформ|а́ция *f* [7] misinformation; **~и́ровать** [7] (*im*)*pf.* misinform
дезодора́нт *m* [1] deodorant; air freshener
дезорганизова́ть [7] (*im*)*pf.* disorganize
де́йств|енный [14 *sh.*] effective; *сре́дство* efficacious; **~ие** *n* [12] action; activity; *mil.*, *tech.*, *math.* operation; *thea.* act; *лека́рства и т. д.* effect; (*влия́ние*) influence, impact; ***ме́сто ~ия*** scene; ***свобо́да ~ий*** free play; **~и́тельно** really, indeed; **~и́тельность** *f* [8] reality, (real) life; **~и́тельный** [14; -лен, -льна] real, actual; *биле́т и т. д.* valid; *mil.*, *gr.* active (*service*; *voice*); **~овать** [7], <по-> act, work (***на*** В on); operate, function; apply; have effect (***на*** В on); get (on one's nerves); **~ующий** [17] active; acting; ***~ующее лицо́*** character, personage
дека́брь *m* [4 *e.*] December
дека́да *f* [5] decade
дека́н *m* [1] *acad.* dean; **~а́т** *m* [1] dean's office
декла|ми́ровать [7], <про-> recite, declaim; **~ма́ция** *f* [7] declaration
декольт|е́ (dɛ-'tɛ) *n* [*indecl.*] décolleté; **~и́рованный** [14 *sh.*] low-cut; *thea.*
декора́|тор *m* [1] (interior) decorator; *thea.* scene-painter; **~ция** *f* [7] decoration; *thea.* scenery
декре́т *m* [1] decree, edict; *coll.* maternity leave
де́ла|нный [14 *sh.*] affected, forced; **~ть** [1], <с-> make, do; *coll.* ***~ть не́чего*** it can't be helped; **-ся** (T) be-come, grow, turn; happen (**с** T with, to), be going on; ***что с ним сде́лалось?*** what has become of him?
делега́|т *m* [1] delegate; **~ция** *f* [7] delegation
дел|ёж *coll. m* [1 *e.*] distribution, sharing; **~е́ние** *n* [12] division (*a. math.*); ***на шкале́*** point, degree (*scale*)
деле́ц *m* [1; -льца́] *mst. pej.* smart operator; *pers.* on the make
деликате́с *m* [1] *cul.* delicatessen
делика́тн|ость *f* [8] tact(fulness), delicacy; **~ый** [14; -тен, -тна] delicate
дели́|мое *n* [14] *math.* dividend; **~тель** *m* [4] *math.* divisor; **~ть** [13; делю́, де́лишь] **1.** <раз-, по-> (***на*** В) divide (in[to]), *a.* by; **2.** <по-> share (*a.* **-ся** [T/**с** T s.th. with s.b.], exchange; confide [s.th. to], tell; *math.* be divisible)
де́л|о *n* [9; *pl. e.*] affair, matter, concern; affair(s), work, business (***по*** Д on); (*де́яние*) deed, act(ion); *law* case, (*a. fig.*) cause; ***говори́ть ~о*** talk sense; ***де́лать ~о*** *fig.* do serious work; ***то и ~о*** continually, time and again; ***в чём ~о?*** what's the matter?; ***в том то и ~о*** that's just the point; ***како́е вам ~о?, э́то не ва́ше ~о*** that's no business of yours; ***ме́жду ~ом*** in between; ***на ~е*** in practice; ***на*** (*or* ***в***) ***са́мом ~е*** in reality, in fact; really, indeed; ***пусти́ть в ~о*** use; ***по ~а́м*** on business; ***как ~а́?*** how are you?; ***~о идёт*** → ***идти́***
делов|и́тый [14 *sh.*], **~о́й** [14] businesslike; efficient; *a.* business...; work(ing)
де́льный [14] businesslike; (*разу́мный*) sensible
де́льта *f* [5] delta
дельфи́н *m* [1] dolphin
демаго́г *m* [1] demagogue; **~ия** *f* [7] demagoguery
демаркацио́нный [14] (*adj. of*) demarcation
демилитаризова́ть [7] (*im*)*pf.* demilitarize
демобилизова́ть [7] (*im*)*pf.* demobilize
демокра́т *m* [1] democrat; **~и́ческий** [16] democratic; **~ия** *f* [7] democracy
демонстр|ати́вный [14; -вен, -вна] demonstrative, done for effect; **~а́ция** *f* [7] demonstration; **~и́ровать** [7] (*im*)*pf.*, *a.* <про-> demonstrate; ***фильм*** show

демонта́ж *m* [1] dismantling
де́мпинг *m* [1] *econ.* dumping
де́нежный [14] money..., monetary, pecuniary; currency...; *coll.* moneyed
день *m* [4; дня] day; ***в ~*** a *or* per day; ***в э́тот ~*** (on) that day; ***~ за днём*** day after day; ***изо дня́ в ~*** day by day; ***~ ото дня́*** with every passing day; ***весь ~*** all day (long); ***на днях*** the other day; in the next few days (*a.* ***со дня на́ ~***); ***три часа́ дня*** 3 p.m., 3 o'clock in the afternoon; → ***днём***; ***~ рожде́ния*** birthday
де́ньги *f/pl.* [*gen.*: де́нег; *from. dat. e.*] money
департа́мент *m* [1] department
депози́т *m* [1] deposit
депута́т *m* [1] deputy, delegate
дёр|гать [1], *once* <~нуть> [20] pull, tug (*a.* ***за*** В at), jerk; ***о те́ле*** twitch; ***отрыва́ть от де́ла*** worry, harrass; ***чёрт меня́ ~нул*** why the devil did I do it
дерев|ене́ть [8], <за-, о-> stiffen; grow numb; **~е́нский** [16] village..., country..., rural, rustic; ***~е́нский жи́тель*** *m* villager; **~ня** *f* [6; *g/pl.*: -ве́нь, *etc. e.*] village; ***не го́род*** country(side); **´~о** *n* [9; *pl.*: -е́вья, -е́вьев] tree; *sg.* wood; ***кра́сное ´~о*** mahogany; ***чёрное ´~о*** ebony; ***резьба́ по ´~у*** wood carving; **~я́нный** [14] wooden (*a. fig.*)
держа́ва *f* [5] *pol.* power
держа́ть [4] hold; keep; support; have (*a. comm.* in stock); ***~ пари́*** bet; ***~ в ку́рсе*** keep posted; ***~ в неве́дении*** keep in the dark; ***~ себя́ (кого́-либо) в рука́х*** (have) control (over) o.s. (*a p.*); ***~ себя́*** conduct o.s., behave = **-ся 1.** ***~ язы́к за зуба́ми*** hold one's tongue; **2.** <у~ся> (***за*** В, Р) hold (on[to]); *fig.* stick (to); keep; (***вы́держивать***) hold out, stand
дерз|а́ть [1], <~ну́ть> [20] dare, venture; **~кий** [16; -зок, -зка́, -о; *comp.* -зче] impudent, insolent; (***сме́лый***) bold, daring, audacious; **~ость** *f* [8] impudence, cheek; daring, audacity
дёрн *m* [1] turf
дёрнуть → ***дёргать***
дес|а́нт *m* [1] landing; troops *pl.* (landed) (***а́вия...*** airborne); **~е́рт** *m* [1] dessert; **~на́** *f* [5; *pl.*: дёсны, -сен, *etc. st.*] *anat.* gum; **~е́ртный** [14] (*adj. of*) dessert; ***вино́*** sweet; **~пот** *m* [1] despot
десяти|дне́вный [14] ten days; **~кра́тный** [14] tenfold; **~ле́тие** *n* [12] decade; ***годовщи́на*** tenth anniversary; **~ле́тний** [15] ten-years; ten-year-old
десят|и́чный [14] decimal; **~ка** *f* [5; *g/pl.*: -ток] ten (→ ***дво́йка***); **~ок** *m* [1; -тка] ten; *pl.* dozens of, many; → ***идти́***; ***не ро́бкого ~ка*** plucky, not a coward; **~ый** [14] tenth (*a., f.*, part; 3, 2-read: ***три це́лых и две ~ых*** = *3. 2*); → ***пят(идеся́т)ый***; ***с пя́того на ~ое*** discursively, in a rambling manner; **´~ь** [35 *e.*] ten; → ***пять & пя́тый***; **~ью** ten times
дета́ль *f* [8] detail; *tech.* part, component; **~но** in detail; **~ный** [14; -лен, -льна] detailed, minute
дет|вора́ *f* [5] *coll.* → **~и**; **~ёныш** *m* [1] young one; cub, *etc.*; **~и** *n/pl.* [-е́й, -ям, -ьми́, -ях] children, kids; ***дво́е (тро́е, че́тверо***, *etc.*) **~е́й** two (three, four) children; *sg.*: ***дитя́*** (*a.* ***ребёнок***); **~ский** [16] child(ren)'s, infant(ile); childlike; childish; ***~ский дом*** children's home; ***~ский сад*** kindergarten; **~ская** *f* nursery; **~ство** *n* [9] childhood
де́ть(ся) → ***дева́ть(ся)***
дефе́кт *m* [1] defect; **~ный** [14] defective, faulty
дефици́т *m* [1] *econ.* deficit; ***това́ров*** shortage; ***това́р*** commodity in short supply; **~ный** [14; -тен, -тна] *econ.* showing a loss; in short supply, scarce
деш|еве́ть [8], <по-> fall in price; become cheaper; **~еви́зна, ~ёвка** *f* [5] cheapness, low price(s); ***купи́ть по ~ёвке*** buy cheap; **~ёвый** [14; дёшев, дешева́, дёшево; *comp.*: деше́вле] cheap (*a. fig.*)
де́ятель *m* [4]: ***госуда́рственный ~*** statesman; ***нау́чный ~*** scientist; ***обще́ственный ~*** public figure; ***полити́ческий ~*** politician; ~-

ность *f* [8] activity, -ties *pl.*; work; **~ный** [14; -лен, -льна] active

джин *m* [1] gin

джи́нсы [1] *pl.* jeans

джу́нгли *f/pl.* [*gen.*: -лей] jungle

диабе́т *m* [1] diabetes; **~ик** *m* [1] diabetic

диа́|гноз *m* [1] diagnosis; **~гона́ль** *f* [8] diagonal; **~ле́кт** *m* [1] dialect; **~ле́ктный** [14] dialect..., dialectal; **~ло́г** *m* [1] dialogue; **~метр** *m* [1] diameter; **~пазо́н** *m* [1] range (*a. fig.*); **~позити́в** *m* [1] *phot.* slide; **~фра́гма** *f* [5] diaphragm; *phot.* aperture

дива́н *m* [1] divan, sofa

диве́рсия *f* [7] *mil.* diversion; sabotage

дивиде́нд *m* [1] dividend

диви́зия *f* [7] *mil.* division

ди́вный [14; -вен, -вна] wonderful; amazing

дие́т|а (-'ɛta) *f* [5] diet; **~и́ческий** [16] dietetic

ди́зель *m* [4] diesel engine; **~ный** [14] diesel...

дизентери́я *f* [7] dysentery

дик|а́рь *m* [4 *e.*] savage (*a. fig.*); *coll.* shy, unsociable person; **~и́й** [16; дик, -á, -о] wild; savage (*a. fig.*); ***поведе́ние и т. д.*** odd, bizarre, absurd; **~ость** *f* [8] wildness; savagery; absurdity

дикт|а́нт *m* [1] → **~о́вка**; **~а́тор** *m* [1] dictator; **~а́торский** [16] dictatorial; **~ату́ра** *f* [5] dictatorship; **~ова́ть** [7], <про-> dictate; **~о́вка** *f* [5; *g/pl.*: -вок] dictation; **~ор** *m* [1] (radio, TV) announcer

ди́кция *f* [7] articulation, enunciation

диле́мм|а *f* [5] dilemma; ***стоя́ть пе́ред диле́ммой*** face a dilemma

дилета́нт *m* [1] dilettante, dabbler; **~ский** [16] dilettantish

динам|и́зм *m* [1] dynamism; **~ика** *f* [5] dynamics; **~и́т** *m* [1] dynamite; **~и́чный** [14; -чен, -чна] dynamic

дина́стия *f* [7] dynasty

дипло́м *m* [1] diploma; *univ.* degree; *coll.* degree work, research

диплома́т *m* [1] **1.** diplomat; **2.** *coll.* (attaché) case; **~и́ческий** [16] diplomatic; **~и́чный** [14; -чен, -чна] *fig.* diplomatic, tactful; **~ия** *f* [7] diplomacy

дире́к|тор *m* [1; *pl.*: -pá, *etc. e.*] manager, director; (*шко́лы*) principal, headmaster; **~ция** *f* [7] management, directorate

дириж|а́бль *m* [4] dirigible, airship; **~ёр** *m* [1] *mus.* conductor; **~и́ровать** [7] (Т) conduct

дисгармо́ния *f* [7] *mus. and fig.* disharmony, discord

диск *m* [1] disk

диск|валифици́ровать [7] (*im*)*pf.* disqualify; **~редити́ровать** [7] (*im*)*pf.* discredit; **~римина́ция** *f* [7] discrimination

диску́ссия *f* [7] discussion

дисп|ансе́р (-'sɛr) *m* [1] health clinic; **~е́тчер** *m* [1] (traffic) controller; *ae.* flight control officer; **~ут** *m* [1] dispute, disputation

дис|серта́ция *f* [7] dissertation, thesis; **~сона́нс** *m* [1] *mus. and fig.* dissonance, discord; **~та́нция** *f* [7] distance; ***сойти́ с ~та́нции*** withdraw; **~тилиро́ванный** [14 *sh.*] distilled; **~ципли́на** *f* [5] discipline

дитя́ *n* [-я́ти; *pl.* → **де́ти**] child

диф|ира́мб *m* [1] dithyramb; (*fig.*) eulogy; ***петь ~ира́мбы*** sing praises (to Д); **~тери́т** *m* [1], **~тери́я** *f* [7] diphtheria

дифференц|иа́л *m* [1], **~иа́льный** [14] *math*, *tech.* differential; **~и́ровать** [7] (*im*)*pf.* differentiate

дич|а́ть [1], <о-> run wild, grow wild; *fig.* become unsociable; **~и́ться** [16 *e.*; -чу́сь, -чи́шься] be shy *or* unsociable; shun (a p. P); **~ь** *f* [8] game, wild fowl; *coll.* (*чушь*) nonsense, bosh

длин|а́ *f* [5] length; ***в ~у́*** (at) full length, lengthwise; ***~о́й в*** (В) ***...*** *or* ***... в ~у́*** long; **~но...** (*in compds.*) long-...; **~ный** [14; -и́нен, -и́нна, -и́нно́] long, too long; *coll.* (*высо́кий*) tall

дли́т|ельный [14; -лен, -льна] long, protracted, lengthy; **~ься** [13], <про-> last

для (Р) for, to; because of; ***~ того́, что́бы*** (in order) to, that... may; ***~ чего́?*** what for; ***я́щик ~ пи́сем*** mail (*Brt.* letter) box

Д

днев|а́ть [6]: ***~а́ть и ночева́ть где́-л.*** spend all one's time somewhere; **~ни́к** *m* [1 *e.*] journal, diary (*vb.*: ***вести́*** keep); **~но́й** [14] day('s), daily; day(light ***свет*** *m*)

днём by day, during the day

дн|о *n* [9; *pl.*: до́нья, -ньев] bottom; ***вверх ~ом*** upside down; ***золото́е ~о*** *fig.* gold mine; ***вы́пить до ~а*** drain to the dregs; ***идти́ ко ~у*** *v/i.* (***пусти́ть на ~о*** *v/t.*) sink

до (Р) *place*: to, as far as, up (*or* down) to; *time*: till, until, to; before; *degree*: to, up to; *age*: under; *quantity*: up to, about; ***~ того́*** so (much); (Д) ***не ~ того́*** not be interested in, have no time, *etc.*, for, to

доба́в|ить → ***~ля́ть***; **~ле́ние** *n* [12] addition; supplement; **~ля́ть** [28], <~ить> [14] add; **~очный** [14] additional, extra; supplementary, accessory

добе|га́ть [1], <~жа́ть> [-егу́, -ежи́шь, -егу́т] run up to, reach (***до*** Р)

доб|ива́ть [1], <~и́ть> [-бью́, -бьёшь, -бе́й(те)!; -би́тый] deal the final blow, kill, finish off; completely smash; **-ся** (Р) (try to) get, obtain *or* reach; (*стреми́ться*) strive for; *пра́вды и т. д.* find out (about); ***он ~и́лся своего́*** he gained his ends; **~ира́ться** [1], <~ра́ться> [-беру́сь, -рёшься] (***до*** Р) get to, reach

до́блест|ный [14; -тен, -тна] valiant, brave; **~ь** *f* [8] valo(u)r

добро́ *n* [9] good deed; *coll.* property; **~м** kindly, amicably; ***~ бы*** it would be a different matter if; ***~ пожа́ловать!*** welcome!; ***жела́ть добра́*** wish *s.o.* well; **~во́лец** *m* [1; -льца] volunteer; **~во́льный** [14; -лен, -льна] voluntary; **~де́тель** *f* [8] virtue; **~ду́шие** *n* [12] good nature; **~ду́шный** [14; -шен, -шна] good-natured; **~жела́тельный** [14; -лен, -льна] benevolent; **~жела́тельство** *n* [9] benevolence; **~ка́чественный** [14 *sh.*] of good quality; *med.* benign; **~серде́чный** [14; -чен, -чна] good-hearted; **~со́вестный** [14; -тен, -тна] conscientious; **~сосе́дский** [16] friendly, neighbo(u)rly

добр|ота́ *f* [5] kindness; **~о́тный** [14; -тен, -тна] of good *or* high quality; **≈ый** [14; добр, -а́, -о, добры́] kind, good; *coll.* solid; ***≈ых два часа́*** two solid hours; ***≈ое у́тро*** (***≈ый день, ве́чер***)***!*** good morning (afternoon, evening); ***в ≈ый час!***, ***всего́ ≈ого!*** good luck!; ***по ≈ой во́ле*** of one's own free will; ***чего́ ≈ого*** after all; ***бу́дь(те) ~(ы́)!*** would you be so kind as to

добы|ва́ть [1], <≈ть> [-бу́ду, -бу́дешь; добы́л, -а́, до́бытый (добы́т, добы́та, добы́то)] get, obtain, procure; extract, mine, quarry; **≈ча** *f* [5] procurement; extraction, mining; (*награ́бленное*) booty, spoils; *живо́тного* prey (*a. fig.*); *hunt.* bag, catch

довезти́ → ***довози́ть***

дове́р|енность *f* [8] (***на*** В) power of attorney; → **~ие**; **~енный** [14] person empowered to act for s.b.; proxy, agent; ***~енное де́ло*** work entrusted; **~ие** *n* [12] confidence, trust (***к*** Д in); **~и́тельный** [14; -лен, -льна] confidential; **~ить** → ***~я́ть***; **~чивый** [14 *sh.*] trusting, trustful; **~ша́ть** [1], <~ши́ть> [16 *e.*; -шу́, -ши́шь] finish, complete; **~ше́ние** *n* [12]: ***в ~ше́ние всего́*** to crown it all, to boot; **~я́ть** [28], <~ить> [13] trust (Д a p.); confide *or* entrust (В/Д s.th. to); entrust (Д/В a p. with); **-ся** (Д) *a.* trust, rely on

дов|ести́ → ***~оди́ть***; **≈од** *m* [1] argument; **~оди́ть** [15], <~ести́> [25] (***до*** Р) see (a p. to); lead (up [to]); *до конца́* bring (to); *до отча́яния и т. д.* drive, make; ***~ до све́дения*** inform, bring to the notice (Р of)

довое́нный [14] prewar

дов|ози́ть [15], <~езти́> [24] (***до*** Р) take *or* bring ([right up] to)

дово́ль|но enough, sufficient; (*до не́которой сте́пени*) rather, pretty, fairly; **~ный** [14; -лен, -льна] content(ed), satisfied (with Т); **~ствие** *n* [12] *mil.* ration, allowance; **~ствоваться** [7] content o.s. (Т with)

догад|а́ться → ***≈ываться***; **≈ка** *f*

[5; *g/pl.*: -док] guess, conjecture **\~ливый** [14 *sh.*] quick-witted; **\~ываться**, <\~а́ться> [1] (**о** П) guess, surmise

до́гма *f* [5], **\~т** *m* [1] dogma

догна́ть → ***догоня́ть***

догов|а́ривать [1], <\~ори́ть> [13] finish saying *or* telling; **-ся** (**о** П) agree (upon), arrange; ***\~а́ривающиеся сто́роны*** *f/pl.* contracting parties; **\~о́р** *m* [1] contract; *pol.* treaty; **\~ори́ть(ся)** → ***\~а́ривать(ся)***; **\~о́рный** [14] contract(ual); *цена́* agreed

дог|оня́ть [28], <\~на́ть> [-гоню́, -го́нишь; → ***гнать***] catch up (with); ***до како́го-л. ме́ста*** drive *or* bring to; *impf. a.* pursue, try to catch up, be (on the point of) overtaking; **\~ора́ть** [1], <\~оре́ть> [9] burn down; *fig.* fade, die out

дод|е́лывать, <\~е́лать> [1] finish, complete; **\~у́мываться**, <\~у́маться> [1] (**до** Р) find, reach; hit upon (*s.th.*, by thinking)

доезжа́|ть [1], <дое́хать> [-е́ду, -е́дешь] (**до** Р) reach; ***не \~я*** short of

дожд|а́ться → ***дожида́ться***; **\~еви́к** *m* [1 *e.*] raincoat; **\~ево́й** [14] rain(y); ***\~ево́й червь*** earthworm; **\~ли́вый** [14 *sh.*] rainy; **\~ь** *m* [4 *e.*] rain (***под*** Т, ***на*** П in); ***\~ь идёт*** it is raining

дож|ива́ть [1], <\~и́ть> [-живу́, -вёшь; до́жи́л, -а́, -о́ (дожи́т, -а́, -о)] *impf.* live out (one's time, years, *etc.*); (**до** Р) *pf.* live (till *or* up to); *до собы́тия* (live to) see; (*докати́ться*) come to; **\~ида́ться** [1], <\~да́ться> [-ду́сь, -дёшься; → ***ждать***] (Р) wait (for, till); *pf. a.* see

до́за *f* [5] dose

дозвони́ться [13] *pf.* ring s.b. (**до** *or* **к**) by means of telephone or doorbell until one gets an answer; get through to s.b. by telephone; gain access to s.b. by doorbell

доигрываться [1; -аюсь, -аешься], <\~а́ться> get o.s. into *or* land o.s. in trouble

доиск|иваться *coll.* [1], <\~а́ться> [3] (Р) (try to) find (out)

дои́ть(ся) [13], <по-> (give) milk

дойти́ → ***доходи́ть***

док *m* [1] *naut.* dock

доказ|а́тельство *n* [9] proof, evidence; **\~ывать** [1], <\~а́ть> [3] prove; argue

док|а́нчивать [1], <\~о́нчить> [16] finish, complete

дока́тываться [1], <\~ти́ться> [15; -ачу́сь, -а́тишься] roll up to; *о звуке* reach; *о челове́ке* come to (Р)

до́кер *m* [1] docker

докла́д *m* [1] report; lecture (**о** П on); paper; address, talk; **\~на́я** [14] (*a.* ***запи́ска*** *f*) memorandum, report; **\~чик** *m* [1] lecturer; speaker; **\~ывать** [1], <доложи́ть> [16] report (В s.th. *or* **о** П on); announce (**о** П a p.)

доко́нчить → ***дока́нчивать***

до́ктор *m* [1; *pl.*: -ра, *etc. e.*] doctor

доктри́на *f* [5] doctrine

докуме́нт *m* [1] document, paper

долби́ть [14 *e.*; -блю́, -би́шь, -блённый] **1.** <вы́-, про-> hollow (out); chisel; *о пти́це* peck (*bird*); **2.** Р <в-> *в го́лову* inculcate, cram

долг *m* [1; *pl. e.*] debt; *sg.* duty; (*после́дний*) (last) respects *pl.*; ***в \~*** → ***взаймы́***; ***в \~у́*** indebted (*a. fig.*, **у** Р, ***пе́ред*** Т to); **\~ий** [16; до́лог, долга́, -о; *comp*: до́льше] long; **\~о** long, (for) a long time *or* while

долго|ве́чный [14; -чен, -чна] perennial, lasting; **\~во́й** [14]: ***\~во́е обяза́тельство*** *n* promissory note; **\~вре́менный** [14 *sh.*] (very) long; **\~вя́зый** [14] *coll.* lanky; **\~жда́нный** [14] long-awaited; **\~ле́тие** *n* [12] longevity; **\~ле́тний** [15] long-standing; of several years; **\~сро́чный** [14] long-term; **\~та́** *f* [5; *pl.*: -го́ты, *etc. st.*] duration; *geogr.* longitude

дол|ета́ть [1], <\~ете́ть> [11] (**до** Р) fly (to, as far as), reach; *a.* = ***доноси́ться***

до́лж|ен *m*, **\~на́** *f*, **\~но́** *n* (→ **\~но**), **\~ны́** *pl.* **1.** must [*pt.*: \~ен был, \~на́ была́, *etc.* had to]; **2.** (Д) owe (a p.)

долж|ни́к *m* [1 *e.*] debtor; **\~но́** one (it) should *or* ought to (be...); proper(ly); **\~но́** = ***\~но́ быть*** probably, apparently; **\~ностно́й** [14] official; **\~ность** *f* [8] post office; **\~ный** [14]

due (*a. su.* **∠ное** *n*), proper; **~ным о́бразом** duly
доли|ва́ть [1], <**∠ть**> [-лью́, -льёшь; → **лить**] fill (up), add
доли́на *f* [5] valley
до́ллар *m* [1] dollar
доложи́ть → **докла́дывать**
доло́й *coll.* off, down; **~ ...** (B)**!** down *or* off with ...!; **с глаз ~ из се́рдца вон** out of sight, out of mind
долото́ *n* [9; *pl. st.*: -ло́та] chisel
до́льше (*comp.* of **до́лгий**) longer
до́ля *f* [6; *from g/pl. e.*] **1.** lot, fate; **2.** part, portion; share; **пра́вды** grain; **льви́ная ~** the lion's share
дом *m* [1; *pl.*: -á, *etc. e.*] house, building; **оча́г** home; (**дома́шние**) household; **вы́йти и́з ~у** leave (one's home), go out; **на́ ~ = ~о́й**; **на ~у́ = ∠а** at home; **как ∠а** at one's ease; (**у** P) **не все ∠а** (be) a bit off (one's head), nutty; **~ о́тдыха** holiday home; **~а́шний** [15] home..., house(hold)..., private; **живо́тное** domestic; *pl. su.* folks; **~а́шняя еда́** home cooking; **∠енный** [14]: **∠енная печь** *f* → **∠на**; **∠ик** *m* [1] *dim.* → **дом**
домини́ровать [7] (pre)dominate
домино́ *n* [*indecl.*] dominoes
домкра́т *m* [1] jack
до́мна *f* [5; *g/pl.*: -мен] blast furnace
домовладе́лец *m* [1; -льца] house owner
домога́ться [1] (P) strive for, solicit
домо́|й home; **~ро́щенный** [14] homespun; crude, primitive; **~се́д** *m* [1] stay-at-home; **~хозя́йка** *f* [5; *g/pl.*: -зя́ек] housewife
домрабо́тница *f* [5] domestic (servant), maid
до́мысел *m* [1; -сла] conjecture
донага́ *adv.*: **разде́ть ~** leave nothing on; *coll. fig.* fleece
доне|се́ние *n* [12] *mst. mil.* dispatch, report; **~сти́(сь)** → **доноси́ть(ся)**
донжуа́н *m* [1] Don Juan, philanderer
до́н|изу to the bottom; **~има́ть** [1], <**~я́ть**> [дойму́, -мёшь; → **заня́ть**] weary, exhaust (T with)
до́нор *m* [1] donor (*mst. of blood*)
доно́с *m* [1] *law* denunciation, information (**на** B against); **~и́ть** [15], <**донести́**> [24; -су́, -сёшь] **1.** carry *or* bring ([up] to); **2.** report (**о** П *s.th.*, about, on); denounce, inform (against **на** B); *a.* **-ся** (**до** P) waft (to); **о зву́ке** reach, (re)sound; **~чик** *m* [1] informer
донско́й [16] (*adj. of river* **Дон**) Don...
доня́ть → **донима́ть**
допи|ва́ть [1], <**∠ть**> [-пью́, -пьёшь; → **пить**] drink up
до́пинг *m* [1] stimulant; *fig.* boost, shot in the arm; *sport* use of illicit substances
допла́|та *f* [5] additional payment, extra (*or* sur)charge; **~чивать** [1], **~ти́ть** [15] pay in addition
допо́длинно for sure
дополн|е́ние *n* [12] addition; supplement; *gr.* object; **~и́тельный** [14] additional; supplementary; extra; *adv. a.* in addition; more; **~я́ть** [28], <**~ить**> [13] add to, complete, embellish; **изда́ние** enlarge
допото́пный [14] *joc.* old-fashioned, antediluvian
допр|а́шивать [1], <**~оси́ть**> [15] *law* interrogate, examine; *impf.* question; **~о́с** *m* [1] *law* interrogation, examination; *coll.* questioning; **~оси́ть** → **~а́шивать**
до́пу|ск *m* [1] access, admittance; *tech.* tolerance; **~ска́ть** [1], <**~сти́ть**> [15] admit (*a.* of), concede; **разреша́ть** allow; (**терпе́ть**) tolerate; (**предполага́ть**) suppose; **оши́бку** make; **~сти́мый** [14 *sh.*] admissible, permissible; **~ще́ние** *n* [12] assumption
допы́т|ываться, <**~а́ться**> [1] *coll.* (try to) find out
дораб|а́тывать, <**~о́тать**> [1] complete, finish off; **-ся** exhaust o.s. with work (**до изнеможе́ния**)
дореволюцио́нный [14] prerevolutionary, before the revolution
доро́г|а *f* [5] road, way (*a. fig.*); (**путеше́ствие**) passage; trip, journey; **желе́зная ~а** railroad, *Brt.* railway; **по ~е** on the way; **туда́ ему́ и ~а** *coll.* it serves him right; → *a.* **путь**
дорого|ви́зна *f* [5] dearness, ex-

pensiveness; **~й** [16; до́рог, -á, -o; *comp.*: доро́же] dear (*a. fig.*), expensive

доро́дный [14; -ден, -дна] portly

дорож|а́ть [1], <вз-, по-> become dearer, rise in price; **~и́ть** [16 *e.*; -жу́, -жи́шь] (Т) esteem (highly), (set a high) value (on)

доро́ж|ка *f* [5; *g/pl.*: -жек] path; *ковро́вая* runner; ***бегова́я ~ка*** race track; **~ный** [14] road..., travel..., traffic

доса́|да *f* [5] vexation; annoyance; ***кака́я ~да!*** how annoying!, what a pity!; **~ди́ть** → ***~жда́ть***; **~дный** [14; -ден, -дна] annoying, vexatious; (*приско́рбный*) deplorable; (***мне***) **~дно** it is annoying (annoys me); **~довать** [7] feel *or* be annoyed *or* vexed (***на*** В at, with); **~жда́ть** [1], <~ди́ть> [15 *e.*; -ажу́, -ади́шь] vex, annoy (Д/Т a p. with)

доск|á *f* [5; *ac/sg*: до́ску; *pl.*: до́ски, до́сок, до́скам] board, plank; (*a.* ***кла́ссная ~á***) blackboard; *мемориа́льная* plate; ***ша́хматная ~á*** chessboard; ***поста́вить на одну́ ~у*** put on the same level

доскона́льный [14; -лен, -льна] thorough

досло́вный [14] literal, verbatim

досм|а́тривать [1], <~отре́ть> [9; -отрю́, -о́тришь] see up to *or* to the end (***до*** Р); *на тамо́жне* examine; **~о́тр** *m* [1] (customs) examination; **~отре́ть** → ***~а́тривать***

доспе́хи *m/pl.* [1] *hist.* armo(u)r

досро́чный [14] ahead of schedule, early

дост|ава́ть [5], <~а́ть> [-ста́ну, -ста́нешь] take (out, *etc.*); get; procure; ([***до***] Р) touch; reach (to); **-ся** (Д) fall to a *p.'s* lot; ***по насле́дству*** inherit; (*быть нака́занным*) catch it; **~а́вить** → ***~авля́ть***; **~а́вка** *f* [5; *g/pl.*: -вок] delivery; conveyance; ***с ~а́вкой*** (***на́ дом***) carriage paid; free to the door; **~авля́ть** [28], <~а́вить> [14] deliver, hand; bring; *fig.* cause, give; **~а́ток** *m* [1; -тка] prosperity; sufficiency; ***жить в ~а́тке*** be comfortably off; **~а́точно** sufficiently; (Р) (be) enough, sufficient; suffice; **~а́точный** [14; -чен, -чна] sufficient

дости|га́ть [1], <~гнуть>, <~чь> [21; -г-: -сти́гну, -гнешь] (Р) reach, arrive at, attain (*a. fig.*); *о це́нах* amount *or* run up (to); **~же́ние** *n* [12] attainment, achievement; **~жи́мый** [14 *sh.*] attainable

достове́рный [14; -рен, -рна] trustworthy, reliable

досто́|инство *n* [9] dignity; (*положи́тельное ка́чество*) merit, virtue; (*це́нность, сто́имость*) worth, value; **~йный** [14; -о́ин, -о́й-на] worthy (*a.* of Р); well-deserved; **~примеча́тельность** *f* [8] (*mst. pl.*) place of interest; ***осмо́тр ~примеча́тельностей*** sight-seeing; **~я́ние** *n* [12] property (*a. fig.*); ***стать ~я́нием обще́ственности*** become public property

до́ступ *m* [1] access; **~ный** [14; -пен, -пна] accessible (*a. fig.*); approachable, affable; (*поня́тный*) comprehensible; *цена́* moderate

досу́г *m* [1] leisure; ***на ~е*** at leisure, during one's spare time

до́с|уха (quite) dry; **~ы́та** to one's fill

дота́ция *f* [7] state subsidy

дотла́: utterly; ***сгоре́ть ~*** burn to the ground

дото́шный [14; -шен, -шна] meticulous

дотр|а́гиваться [1], <~о́нуться> [20] (***до*** Р) touch

до́х|лый [14] *живо́тное* dead; Р *о челове́ке* puny; **~ля́тина** *f* [5] carrion; feeble person; **~нуть¹** [21], <из-, по-> (*of animals*) die; Р (*of human beings*) *coll.* croak, kick the bucket; **~ну́ть²** → ***дыша́ть***

дохо́д *m* [1] income, revenue; (*вы́ручка*) proceeds *pl.*; **~и́ть** [15], <дойти́> [дойду́, -дёшь; → **идти́**] (***до*** Р) go *or* come (to), arrive (at), reach: *hist.* come down to; *о це́нах* rise *or* run up to; **~ный** [14; -ден, -дна] profitable

доце́нт *m* [1] senior lecturer, assistant professor, *Brt.* reader

доче́рн|ий [15] daughter's; ***~яя компа́ния*** affiliate

до́чиста (quite) clean; *coll.* completely

дочи́т|ывать, <~а́ть> finish reading *or* read up to (**до** P)
до́ч|ка *f* [5; *g/pl.*: -чек] *coll.* = **~ь** *f* [до́чери, *etc.* = 8; *pl.*: до́чери, -ре́й, *etc. e.*; *instr.*: -рьми́] daughter
дошко́льн|ик *m* [1] child under school age; **~ый** *m* [1] preschool
дощ|а́тый [14] of boards, plank...; **~е́чка** *f* [5; *g/pl.*: -чек] *dim.* → ***доска́***
доя́рка *f* [5; *g/pl.*: -рок] milkmaid
драгоце́нн|ость *f* [8] jewel, gem (*a. fig.*); precious thing *or* possession; **~ый** [14; -це́нен, -це́нна] precious (*a.* stone), costly, valuable
дразни́ть [13; -ню́, дра́знишь] **1.** <по-> tease, mock; **2.** <раз-> excite, tantalize
дра́ка *f* [5] scuffle, fight
драко́н *m* [1] dragon; **~овский** [16] draconian, extremely severe
дра́ма *f* [5] drama; *fig.* tragedy; **~ти́ческий** [16] dramatic (*a. fig.*); **~ту́рг** *m* [1] playwright, dramatist
драп|ирова́ть [7], <за-> drape; **~овый** [14] (of thick) woolen cloth (***драп***)
дра|ть [деру́, -рёшь; драл, -а́, -о; ...дра́нный], <со-> (→ ***сдира́ть***) pull (off); tweak (*p.'s* ear B/***за*** B); *coll.* → ***выдира́ть*** & ***раздира́ть***; **-ся**, <по-> scuffle, fight, struggle; **~чли́вый** [14 *sh.*] pugnacious
дребе|де́нь *coll. f* [8] trash; **~зг** *coll. m* [1] tinkle, jingle, rattle; **~зжа́ть** [4; -зжи́т], <за-> tinkle, jingle, rattle
древ|еси́на *f* [5] timber; **~е́сный** [14]: ***~е́сный спирт*** methyl alcohol; ***~е́сный у́голь*** charcoal; **~ко** *n* [9; *pl.*: -ки, -ков] flagpole
дре́вн|ий [15; -вен, -вня] ancient (*a. su.*), antique; aged, (very) old; **~ость** *f* [8] antiquity (*a. pl.*= -ties)
дрейф *m* [1] *naut.*, **~ова́ть** [7] drift
дрем|а́ть [2], <за-> doze (off), slumber; **~о́та** *f* [5] drowsiness, sleepiness; **~у́чий** [17] dense (*a. fig.*)
дрессирова́ть [7], <вы́-> train
дроб|и́ть [14 *e.*; -блю́, -би́шь; -блённый], <раз-> break in pieces, crush; (*дели́ть*) divide *or* split up; **~ный** [14; -бен, -бна] *math.* fractional; **~ь** *f* [8] *coll.* (small) shot; *бараба́нная math.* [*from g/pl. e.*] fraction; ***десяти́чная ~ь*** decimal
дров|а́ *n pl.* [9] firewood; **~яни́к** *m* [1], **~яно́й** [14]: ***~ сара́й*** woodshed
дро́|гнуть 1. [21] (*зя́бнуть*) shiver *or* shake (with cold); <про-> be chilled to the bone; **2.** [20 *st.*] *pf. го́лос* quaver; (*заколеба́ться*) waver, falter; flinch; ***не ~гнув*** without flinching; **~жа́ть** [4 *e.*; -жу́, -жи́шь], <за-> tremble, shake, shiver (**от** P with); *о пла́мени и т. д.* flicker, glimmer; dread (s.th. ***пе́ред*** T); be anxious (***за*** B about); tremble (for s.o.); grudge (***над*** T); **~жжи** *f/pl.* [8; *from gen. e.*] yeast; **~жь** *f* [8] trembling, shiver; vibration
дрозд *m* [1 *e.*] thrush; ***чёрный ~*** blackbird
друг *m* [1; *pl.*: друзья́, -зе́й, -зья́м] friend (*a. address*); ***~ ~а*** each (one an)other; ***~ за ~ом*** one after another; ***~ с ~ом*** with each other; **~о́й** [16] (an)other, different; else, next, second; (***н***)***и тот*** (***н***)***и ~о́й*** both (neither); ***на ~о́й день*** the next day
дру́ж|ба *f* [5] friendship; **~елю́бный** [14; -бен, -бна] amicable, friendly; **~еский** [16], **~ественный** [14 *sh.*] friendly; *comput.* user-friendly; **~и́ть** [16; -жу́, -у́жишь] be friends, be on friendly terms (**с** T with); **~и́ще** *m* [11] old chap *or* boy; **~ный** [14; -жен, -жна́, -о; дру́жны] friendly, on friendly terms; (*совме́стный*) joint, concerted; *bot.*, *mil.*, *etc.* vigorous; *adv. a.* together; at once
дря́|блый [14; дрябл, -а́, -о] limp, flabby; **~зги** *coll. f/pl.* [5] squabbles; **~нно́й** P [14] wretched, worthless, trashy; **~нь** *coll. f* [8] rubbish, trash (*a. fig.*); P *вещь* rotten thing; *челове́к* rotter; **~хлый** [14; дряхл, -а́, -о] decrepit; *coll. дом и т. д.* dilapidated
дуб *m* [1; *pl. e.*] oak; **~и́на** *f* [5] club, cudgel; P boor, dolt; **~и́нка** *f* [5; *g/pl.*: -нок] (policeman's) club; **~лёр** *m* [1], **~лика́т** *m* [1] duplicate; reserve; *thea.* understudy; **~ли́ровать** [7] *impf.* duplicate; *thea.* understudy a part; *cine.* dub; **~о́вый** [14] oak(en)

дуг|а́ *f* [5; *pl. st.*] arc (*a. el.*); ***согну́ть в ~у́*** bring under, compel; ***~о́й*** arched

ду́дк|а *f* [5; *g/pl.*: -док] pipe; *coll.* ***~и!*** not on your life!; ***пляса́ть под чью́-л. ~у*** dance to s.b.'s tune

ду́ло *n* [9] muzzle; barrel (gun)

ду́ма *f* [5] **1.** *old use* thought; meditation; **2.** *pol.* duma, parliament; (*in Russia*) duma = council; elective legislative assembly; ***~ть*** [1], <по-> think (**о** П about, of); reflect (***над*** T, **о** П on); (+ *inf.*) intend to, be going to; care (**о** П about); ***как ты ~ешь?*** what do you think?; ***мно́го о себе́ ~ть*** be conceited; ***не до́лго ~я*** without hesitation; **-ся** seem, appear; ***~ется, он прав*** I think he is right; ***мне ~ется, что*** I think that ...

дун|ове́ние *n* [12] waft, breath; ***~уть → дуть***

дупло́ *n* [9; *pl. st.*: ду́пла, -пел, -плам] *де́рева* hollow; *в зу́бе* cavity (*in tooth*)

ду́р|а *f* [5] silly woman; ***~а́к*** *m* [1 *e.*] fool, simpleton; ***~а́к ~ако́м*** arrant fool; ***сваля́ть ~ака́*** do something foolish; ***~а́цкий*** [16] foolish, silly, idiotic; ***~а́чество*** *coll. n* [9] tomfoolery; ***~а́чить*** [16], <о-> fool, hoax; **-ся** play the fool; ***~е́ть*** *coll.* [8], <о-> become stupefied; ***~и́ть*** *coll.* [13]: ***~и́ть го́лову*** confuse, deceive; → ***~а́читься***; be naughty *or* obstinate

дурма́н *m* [1] *fig.* narcotic; ***~ить*** [13], <о-> stupefy

дурн|е́ть [8], <по-> grow plain *or* ugly; ***~о́й*** [14; ду́рен, -рна́, -о] bad; *о вне́шности* plain, ugly; ***мне ~о*** I feel (am) sick *or* unwell; ***~ота́*** *coll. f* [5] giddiness; nausea

дурь *coll. f* [8] folly, caprice

ду́т|ый [14] *fig. авторите́т* inflated; *ци́фры* distorted; ***~ь*** [18], <по->, *once* <ду́нуть> [20] blow; ***ду́ет*** there is a draught (draft); **-ся**, <на-> swell; *coll.* sulk; be angry with (***на*** В)

дух *m* [1] *вре́мени* spirit; *боево́й* courage; (*привиде́ние*) ghost; ***здоро́вый ~ в здоро́вом те́ле*** a sound mind in a sound body; (***не***) ***в ~е*** in a good (bad) temper *or* in high (low) spirits; ***в моём ~е*** to my taste; ***па́дать ~ом*** lose heart; ***прису́тствие ~а*** presence of mind; Р ***~ом*** in a jiffy *or* trice; old use ***во весь ~, что есть ~у*** at full speed; ***~и́*** *m/pl.* [1 *e.*] perfume

духов|е́нство *n* [9] *coll.* clergy; ***~ка*** *f* [5; *g/pl.*: -вок] oven; ***~ный*** [14] spiritual; *состоя́ние* mental; ecclesiastical, clerical, religious; ***~ный мир*** inner world; ***~о́й*** [14] *mus.* wind (*instrument*); ***~о́й орке́стр*** *m* brass band

духота́ *f* [5] sultriness, stuffiness

душ *m* [1] shower; ***приня́ть ~*** take a shower

душ|а́ *f* [5; *ac/sg.*: ду́шу; *pl. st.*] soul; *fig.* heart; *hist.* serf; ***в ~е́*** at heart; ***~а́ в ~у*** at one; in harmony; ***в глубине́ ~и́*** in one's heart of hearts; ***~и́ не ча́ять*** adore; ***~а́ о́бщества*** life and soul of the party; ***не по ~е́*** not to like (the idea of) *or* care; ***от*** (***всей***) ***~и́*** from (with all) one's heart; ***~а́ в пя́тки ушла́*** have one's heart in one's mouth

душ|евнобольно́й [14] mentally ill *or* deranged (person); ***~е́вный*** [14] sincere, heartfelt, cordial; ***~ераздира́ющий*** [17] heart-rending

душ|и́стый [14 *sh.*] fragrant; *горо́шек* sweet (*peas*); ***~и́ть*** [16] **1.** <за-> strangle; smother (*a. fig.*); **2.** <на-> perfume (**-ся** o.s.); ***~ный*** [14; -шен, -шна́, -о] stuffy, sultry

дуэ́|ль *f* [8] *hist.* duel (*a. fig.*); ***~т*** *m* [1] duet

ды́б|ом (*stand*) on end (*of hair*); ***~ы́***: (***встать*** *etc.*) ***на ~ы*** rear (*a.* up); *fig.* resist, revolt (against)

дым *m* [1] smoke; ***~и́ть*** [14 *e.*; -млю́, -ми́шь], <на-> *or* ***~и́ться*** smoke; ***~ка*** *f* [5] haze; ***~ный*** [14] smoky; ***~ово́й*** [14]: ***~ова́я труба́*** chimney; *naut.* funnel; ***~о́к*** *m* [1; -мка́] small puff of smoke

дымохо́д *m* [1] flue

ды́ня *f* [6] (musk) melon

дыр|а́ *f* [5; *pl. st.*], ***~ка*** *f* [5; *g/pl.*: -рок] hole; ***~я́вый*** [14 *sh.*] having a hole, full of holes; *coll.* ***па́мять***

bad; **~ я́вая головá** *coll.* forgetful person

дыхá|ние *n* [12] breath(ing); ***искýсственное ~ние*** artificial respiration; **~тельный** [14] respiratory; ***~тельное гóрло*** windpipe

дышáть [4], <по->, *coll.* (*a.* once) <дохнýть> [20] breathe (T s.th.); *a.* devote *o.s.* to; ***~ свéжим вóздухом*** take the air; ***éле ~*** *or* ***~ на лáдан*** have one foot in the grave; *о вещáх* be completely worn out *or* very old

дья́вол *m* [1] devil; **~ьский** [16] devilish, diabolical

дья́кон *m* [1] deacon

дю́жин|а *f* [5] dozen

дю́|йм *m* [1] inch; **~на** *f* [5] dune

дя́дя *m* [6; *g/pl.*: -дей] uncle (*a. coll. as mode of address by child to any adult male*)

дя́тел *m* [1; -тла] woodpecker

E

Е

Евáнгелие *n* [12] *collect.* the Gospels

еврéй *m* [3] Jew; **~ка** *f* [5; *g/pl.*: -рéек] Jewess; **~ский** [16] Jewish

европ|éец *m* [1; -пéйца], **~éйка** *f* [5; *g/pl.*: -пéек], **~éйский** [16] European; **Ꞩéйский Союз** European Union

éгерь *m* [4; *pl.*: *a.* -ря́, *etc.*] hunter, huntsman; chasseur

егúп|етский [16] Egyptian; **~тя́нин** *m* [1; *pl.*: -я́не, -я́н], **~тя́нка** *f* [5; *g/pl.*: -нок] Egyptian

егó (ji'vɔ) his; its; → ***он***

едá *f* [5] food, meal

едвá (*a.* ***~ ли***) hardly, scarcely; → *a.* ***éле***; no sooner; ***~ не*** almost, nearly; ***~ ли не*** perhaps

един|éние *n* [12] unity, union; **~úца** *f* [5] *math.* one; *часть, величинá* unit; *coll. оцéнка* very bad; *pl.* (a) few; **~úчный** [14; -чен, -чна] single, isolated

еди́но|... (→ *a.* ***однó***): **~бóрство** *n* [9] (single) combat; **~влáстие** *n* [12] autocracy; **~врéменный** [14] once only; *посóбие* extraordinary; **~глáсие** *n* [12] unanimity; **~глáсный** [14; -сен, -сна] unanimous; **~глáсно** unanimously; **~дýшие** *n* [12] unanimity; **~дýшный** [14; -шен, -шна] unanimous; **~ли́чный** [14] individual, personal; **~мы́шленник** *m* [1] like-minded p., associate, confederate; **~обрáзный** [14; -зен, -зна] uniform

еди́нствен|ный [14 *sh.*] only, single, sole; ***~ный в своём рóде*** unique; ***~ое числó*** *gr.* singular

еди́н|ство *n* [9] unity; *взгля́дов и т. д.* unanimity; **~ый** [14 *sh.*] one, single, common; (*тóлько оди́н*) only (one, sole); (*объединённый*) one whole; united; ***все до ~ого*** all to a man

éдкий [16; -док, -дкá, -о] caustic

едóк *m* [1 *e.*] (*coll.* big) eater; ***на кáждого ~á*** per head; ***пять ~óв в семьé*** five mouths to feed

её her; its; → ***онá***

ёж *m* [1 *e.*] hedgehog

ежеви́ка *f* [5] blackberry, -ries *pl.*

еже|гóдный [14] annual; **~днéвный** [14] daily, everyday; **~мéсячный** [14] monthly; **~минýтный** [14] (occurring) every minute; (*непреры́вный*) continual; **~недéльник** *m* [1], **~недéльный** [14] weekly; **~чáсный** [14] hourly

ёжиться [16], <съ-> shiver (from cold, fever); shrink (from fear); *от смущéния* be shy, hem and haw

ежóв|ый [14]: ***держáть в ~ых рукави́цах*** rule with a rod of iron

езд|á *f* [5] ride, drive; **ᷓить** [15], go (T by), ride, drive; (*посещáть регуля́рно*) come, visit; travel

ей: ***~-бóгу*** *int./coll.* really, indeed

éле (*a.* **éле-éле**) hardly, scarcely, barely; ***слегкá*** slightly; ***с трудóм*** with (great) difficulty
елéйный [14] *fig.* unctuous
ёлка *f* [5; *g/pl.*: ёлок] fir; ***рождéственская*** (***новогóдняя***) **~** Christmas (New Year's) tree *or* (children's) party (***на*** В to, for; ***на*** П at)
ел|óвый [14] fir; **~ь** *f* [8] fir; **~ьник** *m* [1] fir-grove; *collect.* firwood
ёмк|ий [16; ёмок, ёмка] capacious; **~ость** *f* [8] capacity; ***~ость запоминáющего устрóйства*** storage capacity; *comput.* memory capacity
енóт *m* [1] raccoon
епúскоп *m* [1] bishop
ералáш *m* [1] *coll.* jumble, muddle
éре|сь *f* [8] heresy; *fig.* nonsense
ёрзать [1] *coll.* fidget
ерóшить [16] → ***взъерóшивать***
ерундá *f* [5] *coll.* nonsense; trifle(s)
ёрш *m* [1 *e.*] **1.** *zo.* ruff; **2.** *coll.* mixture of vodka with beer *or* wine
éсли if; in case; once (*a.* **~ уж**[**é**]); ***а*** *or* ***и*** **~** if ever; whereas; ***~ и*** *or* (***дá***)***же*** even though; ***ах*** *or* ***о***, **~ *б***(***ы***)... oh, could *or* would...; ***~ бы не*** but for; ***~ тóлько*** provided
естéств|енно naturally, of course; **~енный** [14 *sh.*] natural; ***~енные наýки*** natural sciences; **~ó** *n* [9] ***человéка*** nature; essence; **~ознáние** *n old use* [12] natural science
есть¹ [ем, ешь, ест, едúм, едúте, едя́т; éшь(те)!; ел; ...éденный] **1.** <съ-, по-> eat (*pf. a.* up), have; **2.** <разъ-> eat away (*of rust*); *chem.* corrode
есть² → ***быть*** am, is, are; there is (are); ***у меня́ ~ ...*** I have ...; ***так и ~*** I thought as much
ефрéйтор *m* [1] *mil.* private first class, *Brt.* lance-corporal
éха|ть [éду, éдешь; поезжáй!], <по-> (be) go(ing, *etc.*) (by Т), ride, drive (Т *or* ***в***, ***на*** П in, on); (***в***, ***на*** В) leave (for), go (to); (***за*** Т) go for, fetch; ***по~ли!*** → ***идтú***
ехúд|ный [14; -ден, -дна] caustic, spiteful; malicious; **~ство** *n* [9] spite, malice; innuendo
ещё (**не**) (not) yet; (***всё***) **~** still (*a.* with *comp.*); another, more (and more **~ *и* ~**); ***~ раз*** once more; again; ***кто ~?*** who else?; ***о врéмени*** as early (late, *etc.*); ***~ бы!*** (to be) sure! I should think so!, of course!; ***покá ~*** for the time being; ***это ~ ничегó*** it could have been worse; ***он ~ мóлод*** he is still young

Ж

ж → **же**
жáб|а *f* [5] toad; **~ра** *f* [5] gill
жáворонок *m* [1; -нка] lark
жáдн|ичать [1], <по-> be greedy *or* avaricious; **~ость** *f* [8] greed(iness), avarice; **~ый** [14; -ден, -днá, -о] greedy (***на*** В, ***до*** Р, ***к*** Д of), avaricious
жáжда *f* [5] thirst (*a. fig.*, Р *or inf.* for); **~ть** [-ду, -дешь] thirst, crave (Р *or inf.* for)
жакéт *m* [1] (lady's) jacket
жалéть [8], <по-> **1.** pity, feel sorry for; (**о** П) regret; **2.** (Р *or* В) spare; (***скупúться***) grudge
жáлить [13], <у-> sting, bite
жáлк|ий [16; -лок, -лкá, -о; *comp.*: жáльче] pitiable; (***несчáстный***) pathetic, wretched; **~о** → ***жаль***
жáло *n* [9] sting (*a. fig.*)
жáлоб|а *f* [5] complaint; **~ный** [14; -бен, -бна] mournful, plaintive
жáлова|нье *n* [10] *old use* pay, salary; **~ть** [7]: ***не ~ть*** not like; <по-> *mst. iro.* come (to visit, see a p. ***к*** Д); **-ся** (***на*** В) complain (of, about)
жáлост|ливый [14 *sh.*] *coll.* compassionate; **~ный** [14; -тен, -тна]

mournful; (*соболéзнующий*) compassionate; **~ь** *f* [8] pity, compassion

жаль it is a pity (***как ~*** what a pity); (*as adv.*) unfortunately; (Д ~ В): ***мне ~ егó*** I am sorry for *or* I pity him; *a.* regret; grudge

жанр *m* [1] genre; **~овый** [14] genre...; ***~овая живопись*** genre-painting

жар *m* [1; в ~ý] heat; *med.* fever; *fig.* ardo(u)r; **~á** *f* [5] heat, hot weather; **~еный** [14] roast, broiled; fried, grilled; → *a.* **~кóе**; **~ить** [13], <за-, из-> roast; fry; *coll.* *о сóлнце* burn; **~кий** [16; -рок, -ркá, -о; *comp.*: жáрче] hot; *fig.* heated, ardent, vehement, intense; ***мне ~о*** I am hot; **~кóе** *n* [16] roast meat; **~опонижáющий** [17] *med.* febrifugal

жасмúн *m* [1] jasmin(e)

жáт|ва *f* [5] harvest(ing); **~венный** [14] reaping

жать¹ [жну, жнёшь; ...жáтый], <с-> [сожнý], <по-> reap, cut, harvest

жать² [жму, жмёшь; ...жáтый], <с->, <по-> press, squeeze; ***~ рýку*** shake hands (Д with); *об óбуви и т. д.* pinch; **-ся** shrink (**от** Р with); crowd, huddle up, snuggle; (*быть в нерешúтельности*) hesitate, waver

жвáч|ка *f* [5] chewing, rumination; *coll.* chewing gum; **~ный** [14]: ***~ные*** (***живóтные***) *n/pl.* ruminants

жгут *m* [1 *e.*] *med.* tourniquet

жгýчий [17 *sh.*] burning; smarting

ждать [жду, ждёшь; ждал, -á, -о], <подо-> wait (for Р); (*ожидáть*) expect, await; ***врéмя не ждёт*** time presses; ***~ не дождáться*** wait impatiently (Р for)

же 1. *conj.* but, and; whereas, as to; **2.** → ***ведь***; *a. do + vb.*; ***э́то ~*** the (this) very, same *мéсто, врéмя и т. д.*; ***э́тот ~ человéк*** this very man; ***что ~ ты молчáл?*** why on earth didn't you tell me about it?; ***скажú ~ чтó-нибудь!*** for goodness' sake say something!; ***когдá ~ онá уйдёт*** whenever will she leave?

жевá|ть [7 *e.*; жую, жуёшь] chew; **~тельный** [14] *движéние мышцы* masticatory; *резúнка* chewing

жезл *m* [1 *e.*] *мáршальский* staff; rod

желá|ние *n* [12] wish, desire; ***по*** (***соглáсно***) ***~нию*** at, by (as) request(ed); **~нный** [14] desired; wished for; *гость и т. д.* welcome; (*любúмый*) beloved; **~тельный** [14; -лен, -льна] desirable, desired; ***мне ~тельно*** I am anxious to; **~ть** [1], <по-> wish (Д/Р a p. s.th.), desire; ***э́то оставля́ет ~ть лýчшего*** it leaves much to be desired; **~ющие** *pl.* [17] those interested in, those wishing to ...

желé *n* [*indecl.*] jelly (*a. fish, meat*)

железá *f* [5; *pl.*: жéлезы, желёз, железáм] *anat.* gland

желез|нодорóжник *m* [1] railroad (*Brt.* railway-) man; **~нодорóжный** [14] railroad..., *Brt.* railway...; **~ный** [14] iron; ***~ная дорóга*** railway; **~о** *n* [9] iron; ***крóвельное ~о*** sheet iron; ***куй ~о, покá горячó*** strike while the iron is hot; **~обетóн** *m* [1] reinforced concrete

жёлоб *m* [1; *pl.*: -бá, *etc. e.*] gutter; chute

желт|éть [8], <по-> grow *or* turn yellow; *impf.* (*a.* **-ся**) appear yellow; **~изнá** *f* [5] yellow(ness); **~овáтый** [14 *sh.*] yellowish; **~óк** *m* [1; -ткá] yolk; **~ýха** *f med.* [5] jaundice

жёлтый [14; жёлт, -á, -о] yellow

желýдо|к *m* [1; -дка] stomach; **~чный** [14] gastric, stomach

жёлудь *m* [4; from *g/pl. e.*] acorn

жёлч|ный [14] gall...; ***~ный пузы́рь*** gall bladder; [жёлчен, -á, -о] *fig.* irritable; **~ь** *f* [8] bile, gall (*a. fig.*)

жемáн|иться [13] *coll.* mince; be prim; behave affectedly; **~ный** [14; -áнен, -áнна] affected, mincing, prim; **~ство** *n* [9] primness, prudery, affectedness

жéмч|уг *n* [1; *pl.*: -гá, *etc. e.*] *coll.* pearls *pl.*; **~ýжина** *f* [5] pearl; **~ýжный** [14] pearly

жен|á *f* [5; *pl. st.*: жёны] wife; **~áтый** [14 *sh.*] married (*man*; **на** П to a p.); **~úть** [13; женю, жéнишь] (*im*)*pf.* marry (*a man* **на** П to); **-ся** marry (*v/t.* **на** П; *of men*); **~úтьба** *f* [5] marriage (**на** П to); **~úх** *m* [1 *e.*]

fiancé; bridegroom; **~оненавистник** *m* [1] misogynist, woman hater; **~оподобный** [14; -бен, -бна] effeminate; **⁓ский** [16] female, lady's, woman's, women's, girl's; *gr.* feminine; **⁓ственный** [14 *sh.*] feminine, womanly; **⁓щина** *f* [5] woman

жердь *f* [8; *from g/pl. e.*] pole

жереб|ёнок *m* [2] foal, colt; **~éц** *m* [1; -бцá] stallion

жёрнов *m* [1; *pl. e.*: -вá] millstone

жéртв|а *f* [5] victim; sacrifice; (*a.* = ***приносить в ~у***); **~овать** [7], <по-> (T) sacrifice (*v/t.*: o.s. ***собой***); (B) give

жест *m* [1] gesture; **~икулировать** [7] gesticulate

жёсткий [16; -ток, -ткá, -о; *comp.*: -тче] hard; *словá, услóвия* harsh; *мясо* tough; *материáл* stiff, rigid; *критика, мéры* severe

жестóк|ий [16; жестóк, -á, -о] cruel; (*ужáсный*) terrible, dreadful; *морóз* fierce; *действительность* grim; **~осéрдие** *n* [12] hard-heartedness; **~ость** *f* [8] cruelty, brutality

жест|ь *f* [8] tin (plate); **~янóй** [14] tin...

жетóн *m* [1] counter; token

жечь, <с-> [26; г/ж: (со)жгу, -жжёшь, -жгут; (с)жёг, (со)жглá; сожжённый] burn (*a. fig.*); torment

живит|ельный [14; -лен, -льна] life-giving, vivifying; *вóздух* crisp, bracing

живность *f* [8] *coll.* small (domestic) animals, poultry and fowl

жив|óй [14; жив, -á, -о] living; alive (*pred.*); (*дéятельный и т. д.*) lively, vivacious; *ум* quick; (*подвижный*) nimble; *воображéние* lively, vivid; ***в ~ых*** alive; ***как ~óй*** true to life; ***~ и здорóв*** safe and sound; ***ни ~ ни мёртв*** more dead than alive; petrified with fear *or* astonishment; ***задéть за ~óе*** cut to the quick; ***принимáть ~óе учáстие*** take an active part; feel keen sympathy (with); **~описец** *m* [1; -сца] painter; **~описный** [14; -сен, -сна] picturesque; **⁓опись** *f* [8] painting; **⁓ость** *f* [8] liveliness, vivacity; animation

живóт *m* [1 *e.*] abdomen, stomach, belly; **~óрный** [14; -рен, -рна] vivifying; **~новóдство** *n* [9] cattle breeding; **~ное** *n* [14] animal; **~ный** [14] animal; *fig.* bestial, brutal; ***~ный мир*** animal kingdom; ***~ный страх*** blind fear

жив|отрепéщущий [17] actual, topical, of vital importance; *fig.* burning; **~учий** [17 *sh.*] (*вынóсливый*) hardy, tough; *традиция и т. д.* enduring; **~ьём** alive

жидк|ий [16; -док, -дкá, -о; *comp.*: жиже] liquid, fluid; (*водянистый*) watery, weak; *кáша и т. д.* thin; *вóлосы и т. д.* sparse, scanty; **~ость** *f* [8] liquid

жижа *f* [5] *coll.* liquid; (*грязь*) slush; (*бульóн*) broth

жизне|нность *f* [8] viability; vitality; **~нный 1.** [14 *sh.*] (of) life('s), wordly; vivid; **2.** [14] (*жизненно вáжный*) vital; **~рáдостный** [14; -тен, -тна] cheerful, joyful; **~спосóбный** [14; -бен, -бна] viable

жизн|ь *f* [8] life; (***никогдá***) ***в ⁓и не ...*** never (in one's life); ***óбраз ⁓и*** way of life; ***провести в ~ь*** put into practice; ***при ⁓и*** in *a p.'s* lifetime; alive; ***вопрóсы ⁓и и смéрти*** vital question

жил|а *f* [5] *coll.* sinew, tendon; vein (*a. geol.*); **~éт** *m* [1], **~éтка** *f* [5; *g/pl.*: -ток] vest, *Brt.* waistcoat; **~éц** *m* [1; -льцá] lodger, roomer; tenant; **~истый** [14 *sh.*] sinewy, wiry; *мясо* stringy; **~ище** *n* [11] dwelling, lodging(s); **~ищный** [14] housing; **~ка** *f* [5; *g/pl.*: -лок] *dim.* → ***~а***; veinlet; *на листьях, мрáморе* vein (*a. fig.*); **~óй** [14]: ***~óй дом*** dwelling, house; **~плóщадь** *f* [8] living space; **~ьё** *n* [10] habitation; dwelling; lodging(s)

жир *m* [1; в -у; *pl. e.*] fat; grease; ***рыбий ~*** cod-liver oil; **~éть** [8], <о-, раз-> grow fat; **⁓ный** [14; -рен, -рнá, -о] fat; (of) grease, greasy; *землá* rich soil; *typ.* bold(-faced); **~овóй** [14] fat(ty)

жит|éйский [16] wordly, (of) life('s); everyday; **⁓ель** *m* [4], **⁓ельница** *f* [5] inhabitant, resident; **⁓ельство** *n* [9] residence; ***вид на ⁓ельство*** residence per-

mit; **~ие́** *n* [12] life, biography (*mst. of a saint*)
жи́тница *f* [5] *fig.* granary
жить [живу́, -вёшь; жил, -á, -о; нé жил(и)] live (T, **на** B [up]on; T *a.* for); (*прожива́ть*) reside, lodge; ***как живёте?*** how are you (getting on)?; ***жи́л(и)-бы́л(и) ...*** once upon a time there was (were) ...; **~ся:** ***ей хорошо́ живётся*** she is well off; **~ё(-бытьё)** *coll. n* [10] life, living
жмот *m* [1] *coll.* skinflint, miser
жму́рить [13], <за-> screw up, tighten, narrow (one's eyes **-ся**)
жрать P *coarse* [жру, жрёшь, жрал, -á, -о], <со-> devour, gorge, gobble
жре́бий *m* [3] lot (*a. fig.*= destiny); ***броса́ть*** (***тяну́ть***) **~** cast (draw) lots; ***~ бро́шен*** the die is cast
жрец *m* [1 *e.*] (pagan) priest (*a. fig.*)
жужжа́|ние *n* [12], **~ть** [4 *e.*; жужжу́, -и́шь] buzz, hum
жу|к *m* [1 *e.*] beetle; ***ма́йский ~к*** cockchafer; **~ли́к** *coll. m* [1] (*моше́нник*) swindler, cheat, trickster; (*вор*) filcher, pilferer; **~льничать** [1], <с-> cheat, trick
жура́вль *m* [4 *e.*] (*zo., well*) crane
жури́ть *coll.* [13], <по-> scold mildly, reprove
журна́л *m* [1] magazine, periodical, journal; diary; *naut.* log(book); **~и́ст** *m* [1] news(paper)man, journalist; **~и́стика** *f* [5] journalism
журча́|ние *n* [12], **~ть** [-чи́т] purl, murmur
жу́т|кий [14; -ток, -тка́, -о] weird, uncanny, sinister; ***мне ~ко*** I am terrified; *coll.* **~ь** *f* [8] horror; (***меня́***) ***пря́мо ~ь берёт*** I feel terrified
жюри́ *n* [*indecl.*] jury (prizes)

З

за 1. (B): (*direction*) behind; over, across, beyond; out of; (*distance*) at; (*time*) after; over, past; before (*a.* **~ ... до** P); ***ему́ ~ со́рок*** he is over forty; (with) in, for, during; (*object*[*ive*], *favo*[*u*]*r*, *reason*, *value*, *substitute*) for; ***~то, ~ что*** because; ***~ что?*** what for? why?; **2.** (T): (*position*) behind; across, beyond; at, over; after (*time & place*); because of; with; ***~ мной ...*** *a.* I owe ...; ***ко́мната ~ мной*** I'll take (*or* reserve) the room
заба́в|а *f* [5] amusement, entertainment; **~ля́ть** [28], <(по)~ить> [13] amuse (**-ся** o.s., be amused at T); **~ный** [14; -вен, -вна] amusing, funny
забасто́в|ка *f* [5; *g/pl.*: -вок] strike, walkout; ***всео́бщая ~ка*** general strike; **~очный** [14] strike...; **~щик** *m* [1] striker
забве́ние *n* [12] oblivion
забе́|г *m* [1] *sport* heat, race; **~га́ть** [1], <~жа́ть> [4; забегу́, -ежи́шь, -егу́т; -еги́!] run in(to), get; *далеко́* run off; *coll.* drop in (**к** Д on); ***~га́ть вперёд*** anticipate, forestall
забере́менеть [8] *pf.* become pregnant
заб|ива́ть [1], <~и́ть> [-бью, -бьёшь; → **бить**] drive in; *гвоздя́ми* nail up; *гол* score; (*засори́ть*) block (up); *фонта́н* spout forth; *трево́гу* sound; *coll.* *го́лову* stuff; **-ся** *coll.* (*спря́таться*) hide, get; *pf.* begin to beat; get clogged (T with)
заб|ира́ть [1], <~ра́ть>, [-беру́, -рёшь; → **брать**] take (*a., coll.*, away); *в плен* capture (*a. fig.*), seize; arrest; (*отклони́ться*) turn, steer; **-ся** climb *or* creep (in, up); *та́йно* steal in, penetrate; (*спря́таться*) hide; *далеко́* get
заби́|тый [14] browbeaten, cowed, downtrodden; **~ть** → **~ва́ть**; **~я́ка** *m/f* [5] bully, squabbler
заблаго|вре́менно in good time;

in advance; **~вре́менный** [14] done ahead of time; timely; **~рассу́диться** [15; *impers.* Д with] think fit
забл|уди́ться [15] *pf.* lose one's way, go astray; **~у́дший** [17] *fig.* gone astray; **~ужда́ться** [1] be mistaken, err; **~ужде́ние** *n* [12] error, mistake; (*ло́жное мне́ние*) delusion; ***ввести́ в ~ужде́ние*** mislead
забол|ева́ть [1], <**~е́ть**> [8] fall sick *or* ill (of T), be taken ill with; *о бо́ли* begin to ache; *su.*: **~ева́ние** *n* [12] → ***боле́знь***
забо́р *m* [1] fence
забо́т|а *f* [5] care (**о** П about, of), concern, anxiety, worry, trouble; ***без ~ жизнь*** carefree; **~иться** [15], <по-> (**о** П) care (for), take care of, look after; worry, be anxious (about); **~ливый** [14 *sh.*] *хозя́ин* careful, provident; *по отноше́нию к кому́-л.* attentive, thoughtful, solicitous
забр|а́сывать [1] **1.** <**~оса́ть**> (T) (*запо́лнить*) fill up; *вопро́сами и т. д.* shower (T with); *камня́ми* pelt; **2.** <**~о́сить**> [15] throw, fling (*a. fig.*), cast; *де́ло, ребёнка и т. д.* neglect; **~а́ть** → ***забира́ть***; **~еда́ть** [1], <**~ести́**> [25] wander *or* get (in[to], far); **~оса́ть, ~о́сить** → **~а́сывать**; **~о́шенный** [14] neglected; deserted; *ребёнок* unkempt
забры́згать [1] *pf.* splash; *гря́зью* bespatter
заб|ыва́ть [1], <**~ы́ть**> [-бу́ду, -бу́дешь] forget (o.s. **-ся** *перейти́ грани́цу дозво́ленного*; *a.* nap, doze); **~ы́вчивый** [14 *sh.*] forgetful; absent-minded; **~ытьё** *n* [10; в -тьи́] (*беспа́мятство*) unconsciousness, swoon; (*дремо́та*) drowsiness; (*лёгкий сон*) slumber
зава́л *m* [1] obstruction, blockage; **~ивать** [1], <**~и́ть**> [13; -алю́, -а́лишь] fill *or* heap (up); cover; *доро́гу* block, obstruct, close; *рабо́той* overburden (with T); *экза́мен coll.* fail; *де́ло* ruin; **-ся** fall; *стена́* collapse
зава́р|ивать [1], <**~и́ть**> [13; -арю́, -а́ришь] brew, make (tea); pour boiling water (over); *coll. fig.* ***~и́ть ка́шу*** stir up trouble
зав|еде́ние *n* [12] establishment, institution; ***вы́сшее учё́бное ~еде́ние*** higher education(al) institution; **~е́довать** [7] (T) be in charge *or* the head *or* chief of, manage; **~е́домый** [14] undoubted; ***~е́домо зна́я*** being fully aware; ***дава́ть ~е́домо ло́жные показа́ния*** commit perjury; **~е́дующий** *m* [17] (T) chief, head; director; **~езти́** → ***~ози́ть***
зав|ере́ние *n* [12] assurance; **~е́рить** → ***~еря́ть***; **~ерну́ть** → ***~ёртывать***; **~ерте́ть** [11; -ерчу́, -е́ртишь] *pf.* start turning (*v/i.* **-ся**); **~ёртывать** [1], <**~ерну́ть**> [20] wrap up; *за́ угол* turn (*a.* up; *кран и т. д.* off); screw up; (*зайти́*) drop in; **~ерша́ть** [1], <**~ерши́ть**> [16 *e.*; -шу́, -ши́шь, -шённый] finish, complete; **-ся** *успе́хом* crown; **~ерше́ние** *n* [12] conclusion, end; completion; **~еря́ть** [28], <**~е́рить**> [13] assure (В/**в** П *ap.*of); attest, authenticate; *по́дпись* witness a signature
заве́|са *f* [5] *секре́тности fig.* veil; ***дымова́я ~са*** smoke screen; **~сить** → ***~шивать***; **~сти́** → ***заводи́ть***
заве́т *m* [1] *Bibl.* (**Ве́тхий** Old, **Но́вый** New) Testament; **~ный** [14]: ***~ная мечта́*** cherished ambition
заве́|шивать [1], <**~сить**> [15] cover, hang with, curtain
завеща́|ние *n* [12] testament, will; **~ть** [1] *im*(*pf.*) leave, bequeath
завзя́тый [14] *coll. кури́льщик* inveterate; incorrigible
зав|ива́ть [1], <**~и́ть**> [-вью́, -вьёшь; → ***вить***] *во́лосы* wave, curl; wind round; **~и́вка** *f* [5; *g/pl.*: -вок] wave (*in hair*)
зави́д|ный [14; -ден, -дна] enviable; **~овать** [7], <по-> envy (Д/**в** П *a p.* a *th.*), be envious (of)
зави́н|чивать [1], <**~ти́ть**> [15 *e.*; -нчу́, -нти́шь] screw up, down *or* tight
зави́с|еть [11] depend (***от*** P on); **~имость** *f* [8] dependence; ***в ~имости от*** (P) depending on; **~имый** [14 *sh.*] dependent

3

зави́ст|ливый [14 *sh.*] envious; **´~ь** *f* [8] envy (**к** Д of, at)
зави|то́й [14] curly; **~то́к** *m* [1; -тка́] curl, ringlet; **~ть** → **~ва́ть**
завлад|ева́ть [1], <~е́ть> [8] (T) take possesion *or* hold of, seize, capture (*a. fig.*)
завл|ека́тельный [14; -лен, -льна] enticing, tempting; **~ека́ть** [1], **~е́чь** [26] (al)lure, entice, tempt
заво́д[1] *m* [1] works, factory, plant, mill (**на** П/В at/to); ***ко́нский ~*** stud farm
заво́д[2] *m* [1] winding mechanism; **~и́ть** [15], <завести́> [25] **1.** (*приводи́ть*) take, bring, lead; **2.** *де́ло* establish, set up, found; *привы́чку, дру́жбу и т. д.* form, contract; *маши́ну и т. д.* get, procure, acquire; *разгово́р и т. д.* start (*a. мото́р*), begin; *соба́ку и т. д.* keep; **3.** *часы́* wind up; **-ся**, <завести́сь> appear; (*возбуди́ться*) become excited; get, have; **~но́й** [14] *tech.* starting; *игру́шка* mechanical; *че-лове́к* full of beans; **~ский**, **~ско́й** [16] works...; factory...
заво|ева́ние *n* [12] conquest; *fig.* (*mst. pl.*) achievement(s); **~ева́тель** *m* [4] conqueror; **~ёвывать** [1], <~ева́ть> [6] conquer; (*доби́ться*) win, gain
зав|ози́ть [15], <~езти́> [24] take, bring, drive; *coll.* deliver
завол|а́кивать [1], <~о́чь> [26] obscure; *слеза́ми* cloud; get cloudy
завор|а́чивать [1], <~оти́ть> [15] turn (up, down); roll up
завсегда́тай *m* [3] habitué, regular
за́втра tomorrow
за́втрак *m* [1] breakfast (***за*** T at; ***на*** B, ***к*** Д for); **~кать** [1], <по-> (have *or* take) breakfast
за́втрашний [15] tomorrow's; ***~ день*** tomorrow; *fig.* (near) future
за́вуч *m* [1; *g/pl.*: -ей] (= ***заве́дующий уче́бной ча́стью***) director of studies (*at school*)
завыва́ть [1], <завы́ть> [22] howl
зав|яза́ть [3], <~я́знуть> [21] sink in, stick; *coll. fig.* get involved in; ***~яза́ть*** → ***~я́зывать***; ***~я́зка*** *f* [5; *g/pl.*: -зок] string, tie; *нача́ло* beginning, starting point; *рома́на и т. д.* opening; **~я́зывать** [1], <~яза́ть> [3] tie (up), bind, fasten; *fig. разгово́р и т. д.* begin, start; **´~язь** *bot. f* [8] ovary; **~я́нуть** → ***вя́нуть***
заг|ада́ть → ***~а́дывать***; ***~а́дить*** → ***~а́живать***; **~а́дка** *f* [5; *g/pl.*: -док] riddle, enigma; **~а́дочный** [14; -чен, -чна] enigmatic; mysterious; **~а́дывать**, <~ада́ть> [1] *зага́дку* propose; *coll. замы́слить* plan; **~а́живать** [1], <~а́дить> [15] soil, befoul
зага́р *m* [1] sunburn, tan
загво́здка *f* [5; *g/pl.*: -док] hitch; snag
заги́б *m* [1] bend; *страни́цы* dog-ear; **~а́ть** [1], <загну́ть> [20] bend, fold (over), turn up; *pf. coll.* exaggerate
загла́в|ие *n* [12] title; **~ный** [14] title...; ***~ная бу́ква*** capital letter
загла́|живать [1], <~дить> [15] smooth; *утюго́м* press, iron; *fig.* make up (*or* amends) for; expiate
загл|о́хнуть → ***гло́хнуть 2.*** **~о́хший** [17] *сад* overgrown; **~уша́ть** [1], <~уши́ть> [16] → ***глуши́ть 2.***
загля́|дывать [1], <~ну́ть> [19] glance; peep in; *в кни́гу* look (through, up); look in; (*навести́ть*) drop in *or* call (**к** Д on); **~дываться** [1], <~де́ться> [11] (***на*** B) gaze, gape *or* stare (at), feast one's eyes *or* gloat (up[on])
заг|на́ть → ***~оня́ть***; **~ну́ть** → ***~иба́ть***; **~ова́ривать** [1], <~овори́ть> [13] **1.** *v/i.* begin *or* start to talk *or* speak; **2.** *v/t.* tire with one's talk; **3. -ся** *сли́шком увле́чься разгово́ром* be carried away by a conversation; ramble, be confused; **´~овор** *m* [1] conspiracy, plot; **~овори́ть** → ***~ова́ривать***; **~ово́рщик** *m* [1] conspirator, plotter
заголо́вок *m* [1; -вка] heading, headline
заго́н *m* [1] enclosure; ***быть в ~е*** *fig.* be kept down, suffer neglect
загоня́ть [28], <загна́ть> [-гоню́, -го́нишь; → ***гнать***] drive (in, off); (*изму́чить*) exhaust, fatigue
загор|а́живать [1], <~оди́ть> [15, 15 *e.*; -рожу́, -ро́дишь] enclose,

fence in; *доро́гу* block (up); **-ся** *от ве́тра* protect; **~а́ть** [1], <~е́ть> [9] sunbathe; become sunburnt; **-ся** catch fire; begin to burn; *свет* light up; *от гне́ва* blaze up; *щёки* blush; *спор* break out; **~е́лый** [14] sunburnt; **~оди́ть** → **~а́живать**; **~о́дка** *coll. f* [5; *g/pl.*: -док] fence, enclosure; partition; **´~одный** [14] *дом и т. д.* country; out-of-town

загот|а́вливать [1] & **~овля́ть** [28], <~о́вить> [14] prepare; *впрок* store up; lay in; **~о́вка** *f* [5; *g/pl.*: -вок] procurement, storage, laying in

загра|ди́тельный [14] *mil. ого́нь* barrage; **~жда́ть** [1], <~ди́ть> [15 *e.*; -ажу́, -ади́шь; -аждённый] block, obstruct; **~жде́ние** *n* [12] block(ing), obstruction; ***про́волочное* ~жде́ние** barbed-wire entanglement

грани́ц|а — **загрaни́ц|а** *f* [5] *collect.* foreign countries; ***жить* ~ей** live abroad

загрaни́чный [14] foreign, from abroad

загре|ба́ть [1], <~сти́> → ***грести́***

загро́бн|ый [14] beyond the grave; *го́лос* sepulchral; ***~ый мир*** the other world; ***~ая жизнь*** the beyond

загромо|жда́ть [1], <~зди́ть> [15 *e.*; -зжу́, -зди́шь; -мождённый] block (up), (en)cumber, crowd; *fig.* cram, overload

загрубе́лый [14] callous, coarse

загр|ужа́ть [1], <~узи́ть> [15 *e.*; -ужу́, -у́зи́шь] (T) load; *coll. рабо́той* keep busy, assign work to; be occupied with work; **~у́зка** *f* [5] loading; workload; **~ыза́ть** [1], <~ы́зть> [24; *pt. st.*; загры́зенный] bite (*fig.* worry) to death

загрязн|е́ние *n* [12] pollution, contamination; ***~е́ние окружа́ющей среды́*** environmental pollution; **~я́ть** [28], <~и́ть> [13] (**-ся** become) soil(ed); pollute(d), contaminate(d)

ЗАГС, загс *m* [1] (*abbr.* ***отде́л за́писей а́ктов гражда́нского состоя́ния***) registry office

зад *m* [1; на -у́; *pl. e.*] back, rear *or* hind part; buttocks; ***живо́тного*** rump; *pl.* things already known *or* learned; ***~ом наперёд*** back to front

зад|а́бривать [1], <~о́брить> [13] (B) cajole, coax, wheedle

зад|ава́ть [5], <~а́ть> [-да́м, -да́шь, *etc.*, → ***дать***; за́дал, -а́, -о́; за́данный (за́дан, -а́, -о́)] *зада́ние* set, assign; *вопро́с* ask; ***~ава́ть тон*** set the tone; *coll.* ***я тебе́ ~а́м!*** you'll catch it!; **-ся** [*pt.*: -да́лся, -ла́сь] ***це́лью*** (***мы́слью***) take it into one's head to do, set one's mind on doing

зада́в|ливать [1], <~и́ть> [14] crush; P *маши́ной* run over, knock down; (*задуши́ть*) strangle

зада́ние *n* [12] assignment, task; *ва́жное* mission; ***дома́шнее ~*** homework

зада́ток *m* [1; -тка] advance, deposit; *pl.* instincts, inclinations

зада́|ть → ***~ва́ть***; **~ча** *f* [5] problem (*a. math.*); task; (*цель*) object(ive), aim, end; **~чник** *m* [1] book of (mathematical) problems

задв|ига́ть [1], <~и́нуть> [20] push (into, *etc.*); *я́щик* shut; *задви́жку* slide; **~и́жка** *f* [5; *g/pl.*: -жек] bolt; **~ижно́й** [14] sliding (*door*)

зад|ева́ть [1], <~е́ть> [-е́ну, -е́нешь; -е́тый] **1.** be caught (***за*** B on), brush against, touch; *fig.* hurt, wound; *med.* affect; ***~е́ть за живо́е*** cut to the quick; **2.** *coll.* (*подева́ть*) mislay; **~е́лывать**, <~е́лать> [1] block up, close (up); wall up

задёр|гать [1] *pf. coll.* worry, harass; **~гивать** [1], <~нуть> [20] *занаве́ску* draw

задержа́ние *n* [12] arrest

заде́рж|ивать [1], <~а́ть> [4] detain, delay; arrest; *вы́плату и т. д.* withhold, stop; (*заме́длить*) slow down; **-ся** stay; be delayed; linger; stop; be late; **~ка** *f* [5; *g/pl.*: -жек] delay; (*a. tech.*) trouble, setback

задёрнуть → ***задёргивать***

заде́ть → ***задева́ть***

зад|ира́ть [1], <~ра́ть> [-деру́, -рёшь; → ***драть***] lift or pull (up); *impf.* provoke, pick a quarrel (with); ***~(и)ра́ть нос*** be haughty, turn up one's nose

за́дний [15] back, hind; *mot.* reverse (*gear*)

задо́лго (**до** Р) long before

зад|олжа́ть [1] *pf.* (*наде́лать долго́в*) run into debt; (Д) owe; **~о́лженность** *f* [8] debts *pl.*

за́дом backward(s); → **зад**

задо́р *m* [1] fervo(u)r; ***ю́ношеский ~*** youthful enthusiasm; **~ный** [14; -рен, -рна] fervent, ardent

задра́ть → ***задира́ть***

зад|ува́ть [1], <~у́ть> [18] blow out; *ве́тер* begin to blow; *impf.* blow (in)

заду́|мать → ***~мывать***; **~мчи́вый** [14 *sh.*] thoughtful, pensive; **~мывать**, <~мать> [1] conceive; (*реши́ть*) resolve, decide; (*намерева́ться*) plan, intend; **-ся** think (**о** П about, of); reflect, meditate (**над** Т on); ***глубоко́ ~маться*** be lost in thought; *coll.* (*колеба́ться*) hesitate; **~ть** → ***~вать***

задуше́вный [14] sincere, intimate

зад|ыха́ться [1], <~охну́ться> [21] gasp, pant; choke (*a. fig.* **от** Р with)

зае́зд *m* [1] *sport* lap, round

заезжа́ть [1], <зае́хать> [-е́ду, -е́дешь; -езжа́й!] call on (*on the way*), drive, go *or* come (**к** Д to [see, *etc.*] *or* **в** В into); pick up, fetch (**за** Т)

заём *m* [1; за́йма] loan

за|е́хать → ***~езжа́ть***; **~жа́ть** → ***~жима́ть***; **~же́чь** → ***~жига́ть***

заж|ива́ть [1], <~и́ть> [-иву́; -вёшь; за́жил, -а́, -о́] **1.** heal, (*затя́гиваться*) close up; **2.** begin to live

за́живо alive

зажига́|лка *f* [5; *g/pl.*: -лок] (cigarette) lighter; **~ние** *n* [12] ignition; **~тельный** [14] incendiary; *fig.* stirring, rousing; **~ть** [1], <заже́чь> [26 г/ж: -жгу́, -жжёшь; → **жечь**] light, kindle (*a. fig.*); *спи́чку* strike; *свет* turn on; **-ся** light (up); catch fire; become enthusiastic (Т about)

зажи́м *m* [1] clamp; *tech.* terminal; *fig.* suppression; **~а́ть** [1], <зажа́ть> [-жму́, -жмёшь; -жа́тый] press, squeeze; clutch; *fig. кри́тику* suppress; *рот* stop; *нос* hold; *у́ши* close

зажи́|точный [14; -чен, -чна] prosperous; **~точность** *f* [8] prosperity; **~ть** → ***~ва́ть***

зазева́ться [1] stand gaping at

зазем|ле́ние *n* [12], **~ля́ть** [28], <~ли́ть> [13] *el.* ground, *Brt.* earth

зазна|ва́ться [5], <~ться> [1] be(come) conceited; put on airs

зазо́р *m* [1] *tech.* clearance, gap

заз|о́рный [14; -рен, -рна] shameful, scandalous; **~ре́ние** *n* [12]: ***без ~ре́ния*** (***со́вести***) without remorse *or* shame

зазу́бр|ивать [1] → ***зубри́ть***; **~ина** *f* [5] notch

заи́грывать *coll.* [1] (**с** Т) flirt, make advances (to); (*заи́скивать*) ingratiate o.s. (with)

зайк|а *m/f* [5] stutterer; **~а́ние** *n* [12] stuttering, stammering; **~а́ться** [1], *once* <~ну́ться> [20] stutter; stammer; *coll.* (give a) hint (**о** П at), suggest, mention in passing

заи́мствова|ние *n* [12] borrowing; loan word (*a.* ***~нное сло́во***); **~ть** [7] *impf.*, *a.* <по-> borrow, adopt

заиндеве́лый [14] frosty, covered with hoar-frost

заинтересо́в|ывать(ся) [1], <~а́ть(ся)> [7] (be[come]) interest(ed in Т), rouse a p.'s interest (**в** П in); ***я ~ан***(**а**) I am interested (**в** П in)

заи́скивать [1] ingratiate o.s. (**у** Р with)

зайти́ → ***заходи́ть***

закавка́зский [16] Transcaucasian

закады́чный [14] bosom (friend)

зака́з *m* [1] order; ***дать***, ***сде́лать ~*** (***на*** В/Д) place an order (for... with); ***на ~*** to order; *об оде́жде* (made) to measure; **~а́ть** → ***~ывать***; **~но́й** [14]: ***~но́е*** (***письмо́***) registered (letter); **~чик** *m* [1] customer; **~ывать** [1], <~а́ть> [3] order (***себе́*** o.s.)

зака́л|ка *f* [5] tempering; *fig.* hardening; (*выно́сливость*) endurance, hardiness; **~я́ть** [28], <~и́ть> [13] temper; *fig.* harden; **~ённый** *мета́лл* tempered (*metal*); *fig.* hardened

зак|а́лывать [1], <~оло́ть> [17] kill, slaugter; *штыко́м и т. д.* stab;

була́вкой pin (up); ***у меня́ ~оло́ло в боку́*** I have a stitch in one's side; **~а́нчивать** [1], <~о́нчить> [16] finish, conclude; **~а́пывать** [1], <~опа́ть> [1] bury; *я́му* fill up

зака́т *m* [1] sunset; *fig.* decline; **~ывать** [1] **1.** <~а́ть> roll up; **2.** <~и́ть> [15] roll (***в, под*** B into, under, *etc.*); *глаза́* screw up; ***~и́ть истéрику*** go into hysterics; **-ся** roll; *о со́лнце* set (*of sun etc.*); *fig.* end; *смéхом, слеза́ми* burst (out laughing *or* into tears)

зака́шлять [28] *pf.* start coughing; **-ся** have a fit of coughing

заква́ска *f* [5] ferment; leaven; *fig.* breed

заки́|дывать [1] **1.** <~да́ть> [1] *coll. я́му* fill up, cover; *fig. вопро́сами* ply; *камня́ми* pelt; **2.** <~нуть> [20] throw (***в, на, за*** B in[to], on, over, behind, *etc.*); *сеть* throw out; *го́лову* throw back; fling, cast; ***~нуть у́дочку*** *fig.* put out feelers

зак|ипа́ть [1], <~ипе́ть> [10; -пи́т] begin to boil; → ***кипе́ть***; **~иса́ть** [1], <~и́снуть> [21] turn sour

закла́д|ка *f* [5; *g/pl.*: -док] bookmark; **~ывать** [1], <заложи́ть> [16] put (*a.* in, *etc.*), lay (*a.* out [*сад*], the foundation [*фунда́мент*] of, found), place; (*заде́ть*) mislay; (*загромозди́ть*) heap, pile (T with); wall up; *в ломба́рд* pawn; *страни́цу* mark, put in; *impers. нос, у́ши* stuff

закл|ёвывать [1], <~ева́ть> [6 *e.*; -клюю́, -юёшь] *fig. coll.* bait, hector, torment; **~е́ивать** [1], <~е́ить> [13] glue *or* paste up (over); *конве́рт* seal; **~ёпка** *f* [5; *g/pl.*: -пок], **~ёпывать**, <~епа́ть> [1] rivet

заклина́|ние *n* [12] entreaty *mst. pl.*; **~ть** [1] entreat

заключ|а́ть [1], <~и́ть> [16 *e.*; -чу́, -чи́шь; -чённый] enclose, put; *в тюрьму́* confine, imprison; conclude (= finish, with T; = infer, from ***из*** P, ***по*** Д – ***что***; *v/t.*: *догово́р* [= make] *мир и т. д.*); *impf.* (*a.* ***в себе́***) contain; **~а́ться** [1] consist (***в*** П in); (*зака́нчиваться*) end (T with); **~е́ние** *n* [12] confinement, imprisonment (*a. тюре́мное*); (*вы́вод*) conclusion; **~ённый** [14] prisoner; **~и́тельный** [14] final, concluding

закля́тый [14] sworn; ***~ враг*** enemy

закол|а́чивать [1], <~оти́ть> [15] drive in; *гвоздя́ми* nail up; *до́сками* board up; **~до́вывать** [1], <~дова́ть> bewitch, charm; ***~до́ванный круг*** vicious circle; ***~оти́ть*** → ***~а́чивать***; ***~о́ть*** → ***зака́лывать***

зако́лка *f* [5; *g/pl.*: -лок] hairpin

зако́н *m* [1] law; (*пра́вило*) rule; ***нару́шить ~*** break the law; ***по*** (***вопреки́***) **~у** according (contrary) to law; **~ность** *f* [8] legality, lawfulness; **~ный** [14; -о́нен, -о́нна] legal, lawful, legitimate

законо|да́тель *m* [4] legislator; **~да́тельный** [14] legislative; **~да́тельство** *n* [9] legislation; **~ме́рность** *f* [8] regularity; **~ме́рный** [14; -рен, -рна] regular; normal; **~прое́кт** *m* [1] bill, draft

зако́|нчить → ***зака́нчивать***; **~па́ть** → ***зака́пывать***; **~пте́лый** [14] sooty; **~рене́лый** [14] deeprooted, inveterate, ingrained; **~рю́чка** *f* [5; *g/pl.*: -чек] *на письме́* flourish; *fig.* hitch; **~у́лок** *m* [1; -лка] alleyway, (*Brt.*) (narrow) lane; *coll. уголо́к* nook; **~чене́лый** [14] numb with cold

закра́|дываться [1], <~сться> [25; *pt. st.*] creep in *mst. fig.*; **~шивать** [1], <~сить> [15] paint over

закрепля́ть [28], <~и́ть> [14 *e.*; -плю́, -пи́шь; -плённый] secure, fasten, (*a. phot.*) fix; *успе́хи* consolidate; assign (***за*** T to)

закрепо|ща́ть [1], <~сти́ть> [15 *e.*; -ощу́, -ости́шь; -ощённый] enserf

закро́йщи|к *m* [1], **~ца** *f* [5] cutter

закругл|е́ние *n* [12] rounding (off); curve; **~я́ть** [28], <~и́ть> [13] round (off); **-ся** *coll. joc.* round off

закру́|чивать [1], <~ти́ть> [15] turn (round, off, up); twist

закр|ыва́ть [1], <~ы́ть> [22] shut, close; *на замо́к* lock (up); *кры́шкой и т. д.* cover, hide; *кран* turn off; ***~ыва́ть глаза́*** (***на*** B) shut one's eyes (to); **~ы́тие** *n* [12] closing, shutting; ***вре́мя ~ы́тия*** closing time; **~ы́ть** → **~ыва́ть**; **~ы́тый** [14] closed; (*та́йный*) secret; *пла́тье* high-necked; ***в ~ы́том помеще́нии*** indoor(s)

закули́сный [14] occuring behind the scenes; secret

закуп|а́ть [1], <~и́ть> [14] buy (*a.* in), purchase; **~ка** *f* [5; *g/pl.*: -пок] purchase

закупо́р|ивать [1], <~ить> [13] *буты́лку* cork (up); *бо́чку* bung (up); **´~ка** *f* [5; *g/pl.*: -рок] corking; *med.* embolism

заку́почн|ый [14]: ***~ая цена́*** purchase price

заку́пщик *m* [1] purchasing agent, buyer

заку́р|ивать [1], <~и́ть> [13; -урю́, -у́ришь] light a cigarette *etc.*; ***~и́(те)!*** have a cigar(ette)!

заку́с|ка *f* [5; *g/pl.*: -сок] hors d'œuvres; ***на ~ку*** *a.* for the last bit; *coll.* as a special treat; **~очная** *f* [14] snackbar; **~ывать** [1], <~и́ть> [15] bite (*a.* one's lip[s]); take *or* have a snack; eat (s.th. [*with, after a drink*] T); ***~и́ть удила́*** *fig.* get the bit between one's teeth

заку́т|ывать, <~ать> [1] wrap up

зал *m* [1] hall; room; ***спорти́вный ~*** gymnasium

зал|ега́ние *n* [12] *geol.* deposit(ion); **~ега́ть** [1], <~е́чь> [26; -ля́гу, -ля́жешь] *geol.* lie; ***в заса́ду*** hide; (*заболе́ть*) take to one's bed

заледене́лый [14] icy, ice cold; covered with ice

зал|ежа́лый [14] stale, spoiled (by long storage); **~ёживаться** [1], <~ежа́ться> [4 *e.*; -жу́сь, -жи́шься] lie (too) long (*a. goods, & spoil thus*); **~ежь** *f* [8] *geol.* deposit

зал|еза́ть [1], <~е́зть> [24 *st.*] climb up, in(to) *etc.*; hide; (*прони́кнуть*) steal *or* get in(to); ***~е́зть в карма́н*** pick s.o.'s pocket; ***~е́зть в долги́*** run into debt; **~епля́ть** [28], <~епи́ть> [14] stop, close; (*закле́ить*) glue *or* paste up; stick over; **~ета́ть** [1], <~ете́ть> [11] fly in(to), up, far, off, beyond; ***~ете́ть высоко́*** rise in the world

зале́|чивать [1], <~чи́ть> [16] heal; *coll.* doctor to death; **~чь** → **~га́ть**

зали́в *m* [1] gulf, bay; **~ива́ть** [1], <~и́ть> [-лью́, -льёшь; за́ли́л, -а́, -о; за́ли́тый] (T) flood, overflow; pour (all) over, cover; (*влива́ть*) fill; *ого́нь* extinguish; **-ся** break into *or* shed (tears **слеза́ми**), burst out (laughing **сме́хом**); *о пти́це* trill, warble; **~ивно́е** *n* [14] *su.* fish *or* meat in aspic; **~ивно́й** [14]: ***~ивно́й луг*** water-meadow; **~и́ть** → **~ива́ть**

зал|о́г *m* [1] pledge (*a. fig.*); security; *gr.* voice; *fig.* guarantee; ***отда́ть в ~о́г*** pawn; ***под ~о́г*** on the security; **~ожи́ть** → **закла́дывать, ~о́жник** *m* [1], **~о́жница** *f* [5] hostage

залп *m* [1] volley; salvo; ***вы́пить ~ом*** at one draught; *прочита́ть* at one sitting; *произнести́* without pausing for breath

зама́|зка *f* [5] putty; **~зывать** [1], <~зать> [3] (*запа́чкать*) smear, soil; *кра́ской* paint over; *ще́ли* putty; *coll. fig.* veil, hush up; **~лчивать** [1], <замолча́ть> [4 *e.*; -чу́, -чи́шь] conceal, keep secret; **~нивать** [1], <~ни́ть> [13; -маню́, -ма́нишь] lure, decoy, entice; **~нчивый** [14 *sh.*] alluring, tempting; **~хиваться** [1], *once* <~хну́ться> [20] lift one's arm (*etc.* T/***на*** B against), threaten (with); **~шка** *coll. f* [5; *g/pl.*: -шек] *mst. pl.* habit, manner

замедл|е́ние *n* [12] slowing down, delay; **~я́ть** [28], <~ить> [13] slow down, reduce; *ско́рость* decelerate; *разви́тие* retard

заме́|на *f* [5] substitution (T/P of/for), replacement (T by); *law* commutation; substitute; **~ни́мый** [14 *sh.*] replaceable, exchangeable; **~ни́тель** *m* [4] substitute; **~ня́ть** [28], <~ни́ть> [13; -меню́, -ме́нишь; -менённый] replace (T by), substitute (T/B *p., th.* for); *law* commute (for, into)

замере́ть → ***замира́ть***

замерза́|ние *n* [12] freezing; ***то́чка ~ния*** freezing point; ***на то́чке ~ния*** *fig.* at a standstill; **~ть** [1], <замёрзнуть> [21] freeze (up); be fro-

zen (to death, *a. coll.* = feel very cold)
за́мертво (as, if) dead, unconscious
замести́ → ***замета́ть***
замести́|тель *m* [4] deputy; vice...; **~ть** → ***замеща́ть***
заме|та́ть [1], <~сти́> [25; -т-: -мету́] sweep (up); *сне́гом* drift, cover; *доро́гу* block up; *следы́* wipe out
заме́|тить → ***~ча́ть***; **~тка** *f* [5; *g/pl.*: -ток] mark; (*за́пись*) note; *в газе́те* paragraph, short article, item; ***взять на ~тку*** make a note (of); **~тный** [14; -тен, -тна] noticeable, perceptible; marked, appreciable; *успе́х, челове́к* outstanding, remarkable; **~тно** *a.* one (it) can (be) see(n), notice(d); **~ча́ние** *n* [12] remark, observation; *pl.* criticism; *вы́говор* reproof, rebuke; **~ча́тельный** [14; -лен, -льна] remarkable, outstanding; wonderful; noted (T for); **~ча́ть** [1], <~тить> [15] notice, mark; (*сказа́ть*) observe, remark
замеша́тельств|о *n* [9] confusion, embarrassment; ***в ~е*** confused, disconcerted, embarrased; ***привести́ в ~о*** throw into confusion
зам|е́шивать, <~еша́ть> [1] involve, entangle; ***~е́шан(а) в*** (П) *a.* mixed up with; **~е́шкаться** [1] *pf.* linger, tarry; **~еща́ть** [1], <~ести́ть> [15 *e.*; -ещу́, -ести́шь; -ещённый] replace; substitute; act for, deputize; *вака́нсию* fill; **~еще́ние** *n* [12] substitution (*a. math., chem.*); replacement; deputizing; filling
зам|ина́ть *coll.* [1], <~я́ть> [-мну́, -мнёшь; -мя́тый] put a stop to; ***~я́ть разгово́р*** change the subject; **-ся** falter, halt; be(come)confused; **~и́нка** *f* [5; *g/pl.*: -нок] hesitation (*in speech*); hitch; **~ира́ть** [1], <~ере́ть> [12; за́мер, -рла́, -о] be(come) *or* stand stockstill, transfixed (**от** P with); stop; *о зву́ках* fade, die away; ***у меня́ се́рдце ~е́рло*** my heart stood still
за́мкнутый [14 *sh.*] exclusive; *жизнь* unsociable; *челове́к* reserved; → ***замыка́ть***
за́м|ок¹ *m* [1; -мка] castle; ***возду́шные ~ки*** castles in the air
зам|о́к² *m* [1; -мка́] lock; *на ожере́лье* clasp; ***на ~ке́*** *or* ***под ~ко́м*** under lock and key
замо́л|вить [14] *pf.*: ***~вить сло́в(е́чк)о*** *coll.* put in a word (**за** B, **о** П for a *p.*); **~ка́ть** [1], <~кнуть> [21] fall silent, stop (speaking *etc.*), cease, break off; *шаги́ и т. д.* die away *or* off; **~ча́ть** [4 *e.*; -чу́, -чи́шь] *pf.* **1.** *v/i.* → ***~ка́ть***; **2.** *v/t.* → ***зама́лчивать***
замор|а́живать [1], <~о́зить> [15] freeze, ice; **~о́зки** *m/pl.* [1] (light morning *or* night) frost; **~ский** [16] oversea(s)

З

за́муж → ***выдава́ть & выходи́ть***; **~ем** married (**за** T to, *of women*); **~ество** *n* [9] marriage (*of women*); **~ний** [15]: ***~няя (же́нщина)*** married (woman)
замуро́в|ывать [1], <~а́ть> [7] immure; wall up
заму́ч|ивать [1], <~ить> [16] torment the life out of; bore to death; *измота́ть* fatigue, exhaust
за́мш|а *f* [5], **~евый** [14] chamois, suede
замыка́|ние *n* [12]: ***коро́ткое ~ние*** *el.* short circuit; **~ть** [1], <замкну́ть> [20] (en)close; **-ся** isolate o.s. (**в** B *or* T in); ***-ся в себе́*** become unsociable
за́м|ысел *m* [1; -сла] project, plan, design; scheme, idea; **~ы́слить** → ***~ышля́ть***; **~ыслова́тый** [14 *sh.*] intricate, ingenious; fanciful; **~ышля́ть** [28], <~ы́слить> [15] plan, intend; contemplate; *план и т. д.* conceive
замя́ть(ся) → ***замина́ть(ся)***
за́нав|ес *m* [1] curtain (*a. thea.*); **~е́сить** → ***~е́шивать***; **~е́ска** *f* [5; *g/pl.*: -сок] (*window*) curtain; **~е́шивать** [1], <~е́сить> [15] curtain
зан|а́шивать [1], <~оси́ть> [15] wear out; **~ести́** → ***~оси́ть***
занима́|тельный [14; -лен, -льна] interesting, entertaining, amusing; *челове́к* engaging; **~ть** [1], <заня́ть> [займу́, -мёшь; за́нял, -а́, -о; заня́вший; за́нятый (за́нят, -а́, -о)] **1.** borrow (**у** P from); **2.** (T) occupy, (*a. time*) take; *ме́сто, пост* fill, take up; interest, engross, ab-

sorb; *развлека́ть* entertain; **-ся** [заня́лся́, -ла́сь] **1.** occupy *or* busy o.s. (with); (*a.* sport) engage in; *кем-то* attend (to); *учи́ться* learn, study; set about, begin to; **2.** *v/i.* *ого́нь* blaze *or* flare up; *заря́* break, dawn; → *a.* ***заря́***

за́ново anew, afresh

зано́|за *f* [5] splinter; **~зи́ть** [15 *e.*; -ожу́, -ози́шь] *pf.* get a splinter (in)

зано́с *m* [1] drift; **~и́ть** [15] **1.** <занести́> [24; -с-: -су́, -сёшь] bring, carry; *в протоко́л и т. д.* note down, enter, register; (*a. impers.*) (be) cast, get; *доро́ги* drift, cover, block up; *ру́ку* lift, raise; ***куда́ её занесло́?*** where on earth has she got to?; **2.** *pf.*, → ***зана́шивать***; **~чивый** [14 *sh.*] arrogant, haughty

зану́д|а *coll. m/f* [5] bore; **~ливый** [14 *sh.*] boring, tiresome

заня́т|ие *n* [12] occupation, work, business; excercise (T of); *pl.* studies, lessons; **~ный** [14; -тен, -тна] → *coll.* ***занима́тельный***; **~ь(ся)** → ***занима́ть(ся)***; **~о́й** [14] busy; **~ый** [14; за́нят, -а́, -о] occupied, busy, engaged

заодно́ together; at one; (*попу́тно*) at the same time, besides, too

заостр|я́ть [28], <~и́ть> [13] sharpen; *fig.* stress; **-ся** become pointed *or* sharp

зао́чн|ик [1] *univ.* student taking a correspondence course; **~ый** [14] in a *p.'s* absence; ***~ое обуче́ние*** instruction by correspondence; ***~ое реше́ние*** *n law* judg(e)ment by default

за́пад *m* [1] west; ♀ the West; → ***восто́к***; **~а́ть** [1], <запа́сть> [25; -па́л, -а] fall behind; *в па́мять и т. д.* impress (*a.* ***на*** *or* ***в*** B on); **~ный** [14] west(ern, -erly)

западн|я́ *f* [6; *g/pl.*: -не́й] trap; ***попа́сть в ~ю́*** *mst. fig.* fall into a trap

запа́|здывать, <запозда́ть> [1] be late (***на*** B for), be slow (***с*** T with); **~ивать** [1], <~я́ть> [28] solder (up); **~ко́вывать** [1], <~кова́ть> [7] pack (up), wrap up

запа́л *m* [1] *mil.*, *mining* touchhole, fuse; impulse; fit of passion; **~ьчивый** [14 *sh.*] quick-tempered, irascible

запа́с *m* [1] stock (*a. fig.*, *слов и т. д.* = store, supply, (*a. mil.*) reserve); ***у нас два часа́ в ~е*** we have two hours in hand; ***про ~*** in store *or* reserve; **~а́ть** [1], <~ти́> [24 -с-: -су́, -сёшь]; **-ся**, <~ти́сь> provide o.s. (with T); **~ливый** [14 *sh.*] provident; **~но́й**, **~ный** [14] spare (*a. tech.*); reserve... (*a. mil.*); ***~ный вы́ход*** emergency exit; **~ть** → ***запада́ть***

за́п|ах *m* [1] smell, odo(u)r, scent; **~а́хивать** [1] **1.** <~аха́ть> [3] plow (*Brt.* plough) *or* turn up; **2.** <~ахну́ть> [20] wrap (**-ся** o.s.) (***в*** B, T in); *дверь* slam; **~а́ять** → ***~а́ивать***

запе|ва́ла *m/f* [5] leader (of choir); *coll.* initiator, leader; **~ва́ть** [1], <~ть> [-пою́, -поёшь; -пе́тый] start singing; *impf.*: lead a choir; **~ка́нка** *f* [5; *g/pl.*: -нок] baked pudding; **~ка́ть** [1], <~чь> [26] bake; **-ся** *кровь* clot, coagulate; *гу́бы* crack; **~ре́ть** → ***запира́ть***

запеча́т|ать → ***~ывать***; **~лева́ть** [1], <~ле́ть> [8] embody, render; *в па́мяти* imprint, impress (***в*** П on), retain; **~ывать**, <~ать> [1] seal (up)

запе́чь → ***запека́ть***

запи|ва́ть, <~ть> [1 -пью́, -пьёшь; → ***пить***] wash down (T with), drink *or* take (with, after); *pf.* take to drink

зап|ина́ться [1], <~ну́ться> [20] *rare* stumble (***за*** *or* ***о*** B over, against); *о ре́чи* falter, pause, hesitate; **~и́нка** *f* [5]: ***без ~и́нки*** fluently, smoothly

запира́|тельство *n* [9] disavowal, denial; **~ть** [1], <запере́ть> [12; за́пер, -ла́, -о; за́пертый (за́перт, -а́, -о)] lock (up; *a.* ***~ть на ключ***, ***замо́к***); **-ся** lock o.s. in

запис|а́ть → ***~ывать***; **~ка** *f* [5; *g/pl.*: -сок] note, short letter; *докладна́я* memorandum; *pl.* *воспомина́ния* notes, memoirs; *труды́* transactions, proceedings; **~но́й** [14]: ***~на́я кни́жка*** notebook; **~ывать** [1], <~а́ть> [3] write down, note (down); record (*тж. на* *плёнку и т. д.*); *в чле́ны и т. д.* enter, enrol(l), register; **-ся** enrol(l), register, enter one's name; make an appointment (***к врачу́*** with a doctor); **´~ь** *f* [8] entry; enrol(l)ment; registration; record(ing)

запи́ть → ***запива́ть***

запи́х|ивать *coll.* [1], <~а́ть> [1], *once* <~ну́ть> [20] cram, stuff

запла́ка|нный [14 *sh.*] tearful, in tears, tear-stained; **~ть** [3] *pf.* begin to cry

запла́та *f* [5] patch

запле́сневелый [14] mo(u)ldy

запле|та́ть [1], <~сти́> [25 -т-: -плету́, -тёшь] braid, plait; **-ся**: ***но́ги ~та́ются*** be unsteady on one's legs; ***язы́к ~та́ется*** slur, falter

заплы́|в *m* [1] *water sports* round, heat, **~ва́ть¹** [1], <~ть> [23] swim far out

заплы|ва́ть² [23], <~ть> *об отёке* swell, puff up

запну́ться → ***запина́ться***

запове́д|ник *m* [1] reserve, preserve; ***госуда́рственный ~ник*** national park; sanctuary; **~ный** [14] prohibited, reserved; *мечта́ и т. д.* secret, precious; **~ь** ('za-) *f* [8] *Bibl.* commandment

запод|а́зривать [1], <~о́зрить> [13] suspect (***в*** П of)

запозда́|лый [14] (be) late(d), tardy; **~ть** → ***запа́здывать***

запо́|й *m* [3] periodic hard drinking

заполз|а́ть [1], <~ти́> [24] creep into, under

заполн|я́ть [28], <~ить> [13] fill (up); *бланк* fill out (*Brt.* in)

заполя́р|ный [14] polar, transpolar; **~ье** *n* [10; *g/pl.*: -ий] polar regions

запом|ина́ть [1], <~нить> [13] remember, keep in mind; *стихи́ и т. д.* memorize; **~ина́ющий** [17]: ***~ина́ющее устро́йство*** computer memory, storage; **-ся** (Д) remember, stick in one's mind

за́понка *f* [5; *g/pl.*: -нок] cuff link; collar button (*Brt.* stud)

запо́р *m* [1] bar, bolt; lock; *med.* constipation; ***на ~е*** bolted, locked

запороши́ть [16 *e.*; *3rd p. only*] powder *or* cover (with snow T)

запоте́лый *coll.* [14] moist, sweaty; *о стекле́* misted

заправ|и́ла *m* [5] *coll.* boss, leader; **~ля́ть** [28], <~ить> [14] put, tuck (in); *блю́до* (T) dress, season; *горю́чим* tank (up), refuel; **~ка** *f* [5; *g/pl.*: -вок] refuel(l)ing; seasoning, condiment; **~очный** [14]: ***~очная ста́нция*** *f* filling (gas) station; **~ский** [16] true, real

запр|а́шивать [1], <~оси́ть> [15] ask, inquire (**у** Р/**о** П for/about); (*a.* Р) request; *coll. це́ну* charge, ask (**с** Р)

запре́|т *m* [1] → ***~ще́ние***; ***наложи́ть ~т*** place a ban (**на** В on); **~ти́тельный** [14] prohibitive; **~ти́ть** → ***~ща́ть***; **~тный** [14] forbidden; ***~тная зо́на*** *mil.* restricted area; **~ща́ть** [1], <~ти́ть> [15 *e.*; -ещу́, -ети́шь; -ещённый] forbid, prohibit, ban; **~ще́ние** *n* [12] prohibition; *law* injunction

заприхо́довать [7] *pf.* enter, book

запроки́|дывать [1], <~нуть> [20] throw back

запро́с *m* [1] inquiry (**о** П about); *pl. потре́бности* needs, interests; **~и́ть** → ***запра́шивать***; **´~то** without formality

запру́|да *f* [5] dam, weir; **~живать** [1], <~ди́ть> **1.** [15 & 15 *e.*; -ужу́, -у́ди́шь] dam up; **2.** [15 *e.*; -ужу́, -у́ди́шь] *coll.* block up, crowd

запр|яга́ть [1], <~я́чь> [26 г/ж: -ягу́, -я́жешь; → ***напря́чь***] harness; **~я́тывать** [1], <~я́тать> [3] hide, conceal; put (away); **~я́чь** → ***запряга́ть***

запу́г|ивать, <~а́ть> [1] intimidate; **~анный** (in)timid(ated)

за́пус|к *m* [1] start; *раке́ты* launching; **~ка́ть** [1], <~ти́ть> [15] **1.** neglect; **2.** *tech.* start, set going; *змея́* fly; *раке́ту* launch; *coll.* (*a.* T/**в** В) fling, hurl (s.th. at) put, thrust; **~те́лый** [14] desolate; **~ти́ть** → ***~ка́ть***

запу́|тывать, <~тать> [1] (**-ся** become, get) tangle(d, *etc.*); *fig.* confuse, perplex; complicate; *coll.* ***~таться в долга́х*** be deep in debt; **~танный** *тж.* intricate; ***~танный вопро́с*** knotty question; **~щен-**

ный [14] deserted, desolate; neglected, uncared-for, unkempt
запыха́ться *coll.* [1] *pf.* pant, be out of breath
запя́стье *n* [10] wrist; *poet.* bracelet
запята́я *f* [14] comma; *coll.* snag
зараб|а́тывать, <~о́тать> [1] earn; ***~а́тывать на жи́знь*** earn one's living; **-ся** *coll.* overwork; work late *or* long; **´~отный** [14]: ***´~отная пла́та*** wages *pl.*; *слу́жащего* salary; pay; **´~оток** [1; -тка] earnings *pl.*
зара|жа́ть [1], <~зи́ть> [15 *e.*; -ражу́, -рази́шь; -ражённый] infect (*a. fig.*); **-ся** become infected (Т with), catch; **~же́ние** *n* [12] infection; ***~же́ние кро́ви*** blood poisoning
зара́з *coll.* at once; at one sitting
зара́|за *f* [5] infection; contagion; **~зи́тельный** [14; -лен, -льна] *mst. fig.* infectious; **~зи́ть** → ***~жа́ть***; **~зный** [14; -зен, -зна] infectious, contagious
зара́нее beforehand, in advance; ***~ ра́доваться*** (Д) look forward to
зара|ста́ть [1], <~сти́> [24; -сту́, -стёшь; → ***расти́***] be overgrown (with)
за́рево *n* [9] blaze, glow, gleam
заре́з *m* [1] *coll.* disaster; ***до ~у, по ~*** *coll.* (*need s.th.*) very badly
заре|ка́ться [1], <~чься> [26] forswear, promise to give up; **~комендова́ть** [7]: ***~комендова́ть себя́*** (Т) show o.s., prove o.s. (to be)
заржа́вленный [14] rusty
зарисо́вка *f* [5; *g/pl.*: -вок] drawing, sketch
зарни́ца *f* [5] summer (heat) lightning
зар|оди́ть(ся) → ***~ожда́ть(ся)***; **~о́дыш** *m* [1] embryo, f(o)etus, germ (*a. fig.*); ***подави́ть в ~о́дыше*** nip in the bud; **~ожда́ть** [1], <~оди́ть> [15 *e.*; -ожу́, -оди́шь; -ождённый] generate, engender; **-ся** arise; conception
заро́к *m* [1] vow, pledge, promise
зарони́ть [13; -роню́, -ро́нишь] *pf. fig.* rouse; infuse
за́росль *f* [8] underbrush; thicket
зар|пла́та *f* [5] *coll.* → ***~або́тный***
заруб|а́ть [1], <~и́ть> [14] kill; ***~и́(те) на носу́*** (***на лбу́, в па́мяти***)! mark it well!
зарубе́жный [14] foreign
зар|убить → ***~уба́ть***; **~у́бка** *f* [5; *g/pl.*: -бок] incision, notch; **~убцева́ться** [7] *pf.* cicatrize
заруч|а́ться [1], <~и́ться> [16 *e.*; -учу́сь, -учи́шься] (Т) secure; ***~и́ться согла́сием*** obtain consent
зар|ыва́ть [1], <~ы́ть> [22] bury; ***~ы́ть тала́нт в зе́млю*** bury one's talent
зар|я́ *f* [6; *pl.*: зо́ри, зорь, заря́м, зо́рям] (***у́тренняя***) ***~я́*** (*a. fig.*) dawn; ***вече́рняя ~я́*** evening glow; ***на ~е́*** at dawn *or* daybreak (*a.* ***с ~ёй***); *fig.* at the earliest stage *or* beginning; ***от ~и́ до ~и́*** from morning to night, all day (night); ***~я́ занима́ется*** dawn is breaking
заря́|д *m* [1] charge (*mil.*, *el.*); *fig.* *бо́дрости* store; **~ди́ть** → ***~жа́ть***; **~дка** *f* [5] *el.* charge, charging; *sport*: gymnastics *pl.*, exercises; **~жа́ть** [1], <~ди́ть> [15 & 15 *e.*; -яжу́, -я́ди́шь; -я́женный & -яжённый] *mil.*, *phot.* load; *el.* charge; *pl. coll.* set in, go on & on
заса́|да *f* [5] ambush; ***попа́сть в ~ду*** be ambushed; **~живать** [1], <~ди́ть> [15] plant (Т with); *coll.* *в тюрьму́* confine; *за рабо́ту и т. д.* compel (*to do s.th.*); **-ся**, *coll.* <засе́сть> [25; -ся́ду, -дешь; -се́л] sit down; *в заса́де* hide, lie in ambush; (***за*** В) begin to, bury *o.s.* in
заса́л|ивать [1], <засоли́ть> [13; -олю́, -о́ли́шь, -о́ленный] salt; *мя́со* corn
зас|а́ривать [1] & **засоря́ть** [28], <~ори́ть> [13] litter; *трубу́ и т. д.* clog; *сорняка́ми* become weedy; ***~ори́ть глаз***(***а́***) have (get) s.th. in one's eye(s)
зас|а́сывать [1], <~оса́ть> [-су́, -сёшь, -о́санный] suck in; *о боло́те* engulf, swallow up
заса́харенный [14] candied, crystallized
засвет|и́ть(ся) [13; -све́тится] *pf.* light (up); **´~ло** by daylight; before dark
засвиде́тельствовать [7] *pf.* testify; attest, authenticate

засе́|в *m* [1] sowing; **~ва́ть** [1], <~ять> [27] sow
заседа́|ние *n* [12] *law, parl.* session; meeting; (*prp.*: in, at **на** П); **~тель** *m* [4]: ***наро́дный ~тель*** *approx.* juryman; **~ть** [1] **1.** be in session; sit; meet; **2.** <засе́сть> [-ся́ду, -дешь; -се́л] stick
засе|ка́ть [1], <~чь> [26] **1.** [-сёк, -ла́; -сечённый] notch; *вре́мя* mark, note; ***~чь на ме́сте преступле́ния*** catch red-handed
засел|е́ние *n* [12] settlement, colonization; **~я́ть** [28], <~и́ть> [13] people, populate; *дом* occupy, inhabit
засе́|сть → ***заса́живаться*** & ***~да́ть*** **2.**; **~чь** → ***~ка́ть***; **~ять** → ***~ва́ть***
заси́|живать [11], <~де́ть> [11] ***~женный*** [***му́хами***] flyblow(n); **-ся** sit *or* stay (too) long; sit up late
заскору́злый [14] hardened, calloused
засло́н|ка *f* [5; *g/pl.*: -нок] (stove) damper; *tech.* slide valve; **~я́ть** [28], <~и́ть> [13] shield, screen; *свет* shut off; stand in s.o.'s light; *fig.* put into the background
заслу́|га *f* [8] merit, desert; ***он получи́л по ~гам*** (it) serves him right; **~женный** [14] merited, (well-)deserved, just; *челове́к* worthy, hono(u)red (*a. in titles*); **~живать** [1], <~жи́ть> [16] merit, deserve (*impf. a.* P); *coll.* earn
заслу́ш|ивать, <~ать> [1] hear; **-ся** listen (T, P to) with delight
засм|а́триваться [1], <~отре́ться> [9; -отрю́сь, -о́тришься] (***на*** В) feast one's eyes ([up]on), look (at) with delight
засме́|ивать [1; -ею́, -ёшь], <~я́ть> [27 *e.*] ridicule
засну́ть → ***засыпа́ть* 2**
зас|о́в *m* [1] bar, bolt; **~о́вывать** [1], <~у́нуть> [20] put, slip, tuck; (*заде́ть куда́-то*) mislay; **~оли́ть** → ***~а́ливать* 2**
засор|е́ние *n* [12] littering, obstruction, clogging up; **~и́ть**, **~я́ть** → ***заса́ривать***
засоса́ть → ***заса́сывать***
засо́х|ший [17] dry, dried up; *bot.* dead; **~нуть** → ***засыха́ть***
за́спанный *coll.* [14] looking sleepy
заста́|ва *f* [5]: ***пограни́чная ~ва*** frontier post; **~ва́ть** [5], <~ть> [-а́ну, -а́нешь] *до́ма и т. д.* find; *неожи́данно* surprise; ***~ть на ме́сте преступле́ния*** catch red-handed; **~вля́ть** [28], <~вить> [14] **1.** compel, force, make; ***~вить ждать*** keep waiting; ***~вить замолча́ть*** silence; **2.** (T) block (up); fill; **~ре́лый** [14] inveterate; *med.* chronic; **~ть** → ***~ва́ть***
заст|ёгивать [1], <~егну́ть> [20; -ёгнутый] button up (*a.* **-ся** o.s. up); *пря́жкой, крючка́ми* buckle, clasp, hook (up); **~ёжка** *f* [5; *g/pl.*: -жек] fastener; clasp, buckle
застекл|я́ть [28], <~и́ть> [13] glaze, fit with glass
засте́нчивый [14 *sh.*] shy, bashful
засти|га́ть [1], <~гнуть>, <~чь> [21 -г-: -и́гну, -и́гнешь; -и́г, -и́гла; -и́гнутый] surprise, catch; ***~гнуть враспло́х*** take unawares
заст|ила́ть [1], <~ла́ть> [-телю́, -те́лешь; за́стланный] cover; *глаза́, не́бо* cloud
засто́|й *m* [3] stagnation; *econ.* depression; **~йный** [14] stagnant, chronic; **~льный** [14] table...; drinking; **~я́ться** [-ою́сь, -ои́шься] *pf. пе́ред карти́ной и т. д.* stand *or* stay too long; *о воде́ и т. д.* be(come) stagnant *or* stale
застр|а́ивать [1], <~о́ить> [13] build on (up, over); **~ахо́вывать** [1], <~ахова́ть> [7] insure; *fig.* safeguard; **~ева́ть** [1], <~я́ть> [-я́ну, -я́нешь] stick; *coll.* (*задержа́ться*) be delayed; **~е́ливать** [1], <~ели́ть> [13; -елю́, -е́лишь; -е́ленный] shoot, kill; **~е́льщик** *m* [1] skirmisher; *fig.* instigator; initiator; **~о́ить** → ***~а́ивать***; **~о́йка** *f* [5; *g/pl.*: -о́ек] building (on); ***пра́во на ~о́йку*** building permit; **~я́ть** → ***~ева́ть***
за́ступ *m* [1] spade
заступ|а́ться [1], <~и́ться> [14] (***за*** В) take s.b.'s side; protect; intercede for; **~ник** *m* [1], **~ница** *f* [5] defender, protector; **~ничество** *n* [9] intercession

засты|ва́ть [1], <~ть> [-ы́ну, -ы́нешь] cool down; *жир и т. д.* congeal; *на ме́сте* stiffen, stand stockstill; ***кровь ~ыла у него в жи́лах*** his blood ran cold
засу́нуть → ***засо́вывать***
за́суха *f* [5] drought
засу́ч|ивать [1], <~и́ть> [16] turn *or* roll up
засу́ш|ивать [1], <~и́ть> [16] dry (up); **~ливый** [14 *sh.*] dry
засчи́т|ывать, <~а́ть> [1] take into account; include, reckon
зас|ыпа́ть [1] **1.** <~ы́пать> [2] (T) fill up; (*покры́ть*) cover; *fig.* heap, ply, overwhelm; *цвета́ми и т. д.* strew; **2.** <~ну́ть> [20] fall asleep; **~ыха́ть** [1], <~о́хнуть> [21] dry up; wither
зата́|ивать [1], <~и́ть> [13] conceal, hide; *дыха́ние* hold; *оби́ду* bear; **~ённый** *a.* secret
зат|а́пливать [1] **~опля́ть** [28], <~опи́ть> [14] **1.** *печь* light; **2.** flood; *су́дно* sink; **~а́птывать** [1], <~опта́ть> [3] trample, tread (down); **~а́скивать** [1] **1.** <~аска́ть> [1] wear out; **~а́сканный** worn, shabby; *выраже́ние* hackneyed; **2.** <~ащи́ть> [16] drag, pull (off, away); (*заде́ть куда́-л.*) mislay; *в го́сти* take s.o. to one's (*or* somebody's) place
затв|ердева́ть [1], <~ерде́ть> [8] harden
затво́р *m* [1] *винто́вки* lock, bolt; *phot.* shutter; **~я́ть** [28], <~и́ть> [13; -орю́, -ори́шь; -о́ренный] shut, close; **-ся** shut o.s. up
зат|ева́ть *coll.* [1], <~е́ять> [27] start, undertake; ***что он ~е́ял?*** what is he up to?; **~е́йливый** [14 *sh.*] ingenious, intricate; **~ека́ть** [1], <~е́чь> [26] flow (in, *etc.*); (*распу́хнуть*) swell up; *но́ги* be(come) numb, be asleep
зате́м then; *по э́той причи́не* for that reason, that is why; ***~ чтобы*** in order to (*or* that)
затемн|е́ние *n* [12] darkening; *mil.* blackout; *med. в лёгких* dark patch; **~я́ть** [28], <~и́ть> [13] darken, overshadow, (*a. fig.*) obscure
затер|е́ть → ***затира́ть***; **~я́ть** [28] *pf.* lose; **-ся** get *or* be lost; *о ве́щи* disappear; *селе́ние и т. д.* lost *or* inconspicuous in the midst of
затеса́ться [3] (**в** В) worm o.s. into
зате́|чь → ***затека́ть***; **~я** *f* [6] plan, undertaking; escapade; **~ять** → ***~ва́ть***
зат|ира́ть *coll.* [1], <~ере́ть> [12] *mst. fig.* impede, give no chance to get on; **~иха́ть** [1], <~и́хнуть> [21] become silent *or* quiet, stop (speaking, *etc.*); *звук* die away, fade; (*успоко́иться*) calm down, abate; **~и́шье** *n* [10] lull, calm
заткну́ть → ***затыка́ть***
затм|ева́ть [1], <~и́ть> [14 *e.*; *no* 1st *p. sg.*; -ми́шь], **~е́ние** *n* [12] eclipse; ***на него́ нашло́ ~е́ние*** his mind went blank
зато́ but (then, at the same time), but on the other hand
затова́ривание *comm. n* [12] glut
затоп|и́ть, ~ля́ть → ***зата́пливать***; **~та́ть** → ***зата́птывать***
зато́р *m* [1] obstruction; ***~ у́личного движе́ния*** traffic jam
заточ|а́ть [1], <~и́ть> [16 *e.*; -чу́, -чи́шь, -чённый] *old use* confine, imprison; **~е́ние** *n* [12] confinement, imprisonment
затра́|вливать [1], <~ви́ть> [14] hunt *or* chase down; *fig.* persecute; bait; **~гивать** [1], <затро́нуть> [20] touch (*a. fig.*, [up]on); affect; ***затро́нуть чьё-л. самолю́бие*** wound s.o.'s pride
затра́|та *f* [5] expense, outlay; **~чивать** [1], <~тить> [15] spend
затро́нуть → ***затра́гивать***
затрудн|е́ние *n* [12] difficulty, trouble; embarrassment; ***в ~е́нии*** *a.* at a loss; **~и́тельный** [14; -лен, -льна] difficult, hard; embarrassing; ***~и́тельное положе́ние*** predicament; **~я́ть** [28], <~и́ть> [13] embarrass, (cause) trouble; *что́-л.* render (more) difficult; *кого́-л.* inconvenience; *что́-л.* aggravate, complicate; **-ся** *a.* be at a loss (**в** П, Т for)
зату|ма́нивать(ся) [1], <~ма́нить(ся)> [13] fog, dim, cloud; **~ха́ть** [1], <~хнуть> [21] die away,

fade; *ого́нь* go out; **~шёвывать** [1], <~шева́ть> [6] shade; *fig. coll.* veil; gloss over; **~ши́ть** [16] → ***ту-ши́ть***

за́тхлый [14] musty, fusty

зат|ыка́ть [1], <~кну́ть> [20] stop up, plug, (*про́бкой*) cork; ***~кну́ть кого́-л. за по́яс*** *coll.* outdo s.o.; **~ы́лок** *m* [1; -лка] back of the head

заты́чка *f* [5; *g/pl.*: -чек] stopper, plug

затя́|гивать [1], <~ну́ть> [19] tighten, draw tight; (*засоса́ть*) draw in, *etc.*; (*покры́ть*) cover; *ра́ну* close; *вре́мя* protract, delay; ***~гивать пе́сню*** *coll.* strike up a song; **~жка** *f* [5; *g/pl.*: -жек] protraction, delaying; ***сде́лать ~жку*** draw, inhale, take a whiff; **~жно́й** [14] long, lengthy, protracted

зау|ны́вный [14; -вен, -вна] doleful, mournful; **~ря́дный** [14; -ден, -дна] common(place), ordinary, mediocre; **~се́ница** *f* [5] hangnail

зау́треня *f* [6] matins *pl.*

зау́ч|ивать [1], <~и́ть> [16] memorize

захва́т *m* [1] seizure, capture; usurpation; **~ывать** [1], <~и́ть> [15] grasp; take (along with one, *a.* **с собо́й**); (*завладе́ть*) seize, capture; usurp; *fig.* absorb, captivate, thrill; (*засти́гнуть*) catch; *дух* take (away [*breath*], by [*surprise*], *etc.*); **~нический** [16] agressive; **~чик** *m* [1] invader, aggressor; **~ывать** → ***~и́ть***

захвора́ть [1] *pf.* fall sick *or* ill

захл|ёбываться [1], <~ебну́ться> [20] choke, stifle (Т, **от** Р with); *fig.* ***от* *гне́ва*** be beside o.s.; **~ёстывать** [1], <~естну́ть> [20; -хлёснутый] swamp, overwhelm; flow over; **~о́пывать(ся)** [1], <~о́пнуть(ся)> [20] slam, bang

захо́д *m* [1] (**со́лнца** sun)set; *в порт* call; *ae.* approach; **~и́ть** [5], <зайти́> [зайду́, -дёшь; *g. pt.*: зайдя́; → ***идти́***] go *or* come in *or* to (see, *etc.*), call *or* drop in (**к** Д, **в** В on, at); pick up, fetch (***за*** Т); *naut.* call, enter; *куда́-то* get; *за́ у́гол* turn, *ши́рму и т. д.* go behind (***за*** В); *astr.* set; ***речь зашла́ о*** (П) (we, *etc.*) began (came) to (*or* had a) talk (about)

захолу́ст|ный [14] remote, provincial; **~ье** *n* [10] out-of-the-way place

захуда́лый [14] *coll.* shabby, impoverished

зацеп|ля́ть [28], <~и́ть> [14] (*a.* ***за*** В) catch, hook on, grapple; (*соедини́ть*) fasten; **-ся** → ***задева́ть***

зачаро́в|ывать [1], <~а́ть> [7] charm, enchant

зачасти́|ть [15; -щу́, -сти́шь; -и́вший] *pf.* take to doing; begin to visit often (***в го́сти и т. д.***); ***~л дождь*** it began to rain heavily

зачасту́ю *coll.* often, frequently

зача́|тие *n* [12] conception; **~ток** *m* [1; -тка] embryo; rudiment; **~точный** [14] rudimentary; **~ть** [-чну́, -чнёшь; зача́л, -а́, -о; зача́тый (зача́т, -а́, -о)] *pf.* conceive

заче́м why, wherefore, what for; **~-то** for some reason or other

зач|ёркивать [1], <~еркну́ть> [20; -чёркнутый] cross out, strike out; **~ёрпывать** [1], <~ерпну́ть> [20; -чёрпнутый] scoop, draw up; *суп* ladle; **~ерстве́лый** [14] stale; **~е́сть** → ***~и́тывать***; **~ёсывать** [1], <~еса́ть> [3] comb (back); **~ёт** *m* [1] reckoning; *educ.* test; credit; *coll.* ***э́то не в ~ёт*** this does not count

зач|и́нщик *m* [1] instigator; **~исля́ть** [28], <~и́слить> [13] enrol(l), enlist; *в штат* take on the staff; *comm.* enter; **~и́тывать** [1], <~е́сть> [25 -т-: -чту, -чтёшь; → ***проче́сть***] reckon, charge, account; *educ.* credit; **~и́тывать**, <~ита́ть> [1] read (to, aloud); *coll.* *взя́тую кни́гу* not return; **-ся** (*увле́чься*) be(come) absorbed (Т in); go on reading for too long

заш|ива́ть [1], <~и́ть> [-шью, -шьёшь; → ***шить***] sew up; **~нуро́вывать** [1], <~нурова́ть> [7] lace (up); **~то́панный** [14] darned

защёлк|а *f* [5; *g/pl.*: -лок] latch; **~ивать** [1], <~нуть> [20] snap, latch

защем|ля́ть [28], <~и́ть> [14 *e.*;

-емлю́, -еми́шь; -емлённый] pinch, jam; *impers. fig.* ache

защи́|та *f* [5] defense (*Brt.* -nce), protection, cover; *sport, law* the defense (-nce); **~ти́ть** → **~ща́ть**; **~тник** *m* [1] defender; protector; *law* advocate (*a. fig.*), counsel for the defense (-nce); *sport* (full)back; **~тный** [14] protective, safety...; *цвет* khaki...; *шлем* crash; **~ща́ть** [1], <~ти́ть> [15; -ищу́, -ити́шь; -ищённый] (**от** Р) defend (from, against); *от дождя́ и т. д.* protect (from); uphold, back, stand up for; advocate; *диссерта́цию* maintain, support; *impf. law* defend, plead (for)

заяв|и́ть → **~ля́ть**; **~ка** *f* [5; *g/pl.*: -вок] application (for **на** В); claim; request; **~ле́ние** *n* [12] declaration, statement; (*про́сьба*) petition, application (for **о** П); **~ля́ть** [28], <~и́ть> [14] (*a.* **о** П) declare, announce, state; *права́* claim; (*сообщи́ть*) notify, inform

зая́длый *coll.* [14] → **завзя́тый**

за́я|ц *m* [1; за́йца] hare; *coll.* stowaway; *в авто́бусе и т. д.* bilker; **~чий** [18] hare('s)...; **~чья губа́** harelip

зва́|ние *n* [12] *mil.* rank (*тж. академи́ческое*); *чемпио́на и т. д.* title; standing; **~ный** [14] invited; **~ть** [зову́, зовёшь; звал, -а́, -о; (...) зва́нный (зван, -а́, -о)] **1.** <по-> call; invite ([*a.* **~ть в го́сти**] **к** Д, **на** В to); **2.** <на-> (Т) (be) called; **как Вас зову́т?** what is your (first) name?; **меня́ зову́т Петро́м** *or* **Пётр** my name is Peter

звезда́ *f* [5; *pl.* звёзды, *etc. st.*] star (*a. fig.*); **морска́я ~** *zo.* starfish

звёзд|ный [14] star..., stellar; *не́бо* starry; *ночь* starlit; **~очка** *f* [5; *g/pl.*: -чек] starlet; asterisk

звен|е́ть [9], <за-, про-> ring, jingle, clink; **у меня́ ~и́т в уша́х** my ears are ringing

звено́ *n* [9; *pl.*: зве́нья, -ьев] link; *fig.* team, section, *произво́дства* branch

звери́н|ец *m* [1; -нца] menagerie; **~ый** [14] animal; *fig.* savage, brutal; → **зве́рский**

зверово́дство *n* [9] fur-farming

зве́р|ский [16] → **звери́ный**; *fig.* brutal; *coll. mst. adv.* (*о́чень*) awful(ly), dog(-tired); **~ство** [9] brutality; *pl.* atrocities; **~ь** *m* [4; *from g/pl. e.*] (wild) animal, beast; *fig.* brute

звон *m* [1] ring, jingle, peal, chime; **~а́рь** *m* [4 *e.*] bell ringer; rumo(u)rmonger; **~и́ть** [13], <по-> ring (*v/t.* **в** В), chime, peal; (Д) telephone, call up; **вы не туда́ звони́те** you've got the wrong number; **~кий** [16; зво́нок, -нка́, -о; *comp.*: зво́нче] sonorous, clear; resonant; *gr.* voiced; **~о́к** *m* [1; -нка́] bell; (*звук*) ring

звук *m* [1] sound; **пусто́й ~** empty words; **~ово́й** [14] sound...; **~оза́пись** *f* [8] sound recording; **~онепроница́емый** [14] soundproof; **~ооперáтор** *m* [1] *cine.* sound producer

звуч|а́ние *n* [12] sounding; **~а́ть** [4 *e.*; 3rd *p. only*], <про-> (re)sound; *звоно́к* bell, ring; **~ный** [14; -чен, -чна́, -о] sonorous, clear; resonant

звя́к|ать [1], <~нуть> [20] jingle, tinkle

зги: (*only in phr.*) **ни зги не ви́дно** it is pitch-dark

зда́ние *n* [12] building

зде|сь (*of place*) here; (*on mail*) local; **~сь нет ничего́ удиви́тельного** there is nothing surprising in this; **~шний** [15] local; **я не ~шний** I am a stranger here

здоро́в|аться [1], <по-> (**с** Т) greet *or* salute (o.a.); wish good morning, *etc.*; **~аться за́ руку** shake hands; **~о**[1]**!** hi!, hello!; **´~о**[2] awfully; well done; **~ый** [14 *sh.*] *com.* healthy (*a. su.*), sound (*a. fig.*); *пи́ща* wholesome; *кли́мат* salubrious; P strong; in good health; **бу́дь(те) ~(ы)!** good-by(e)!, good luck!; (*ва́ше здоро́вье!*) your health!; **~ье** *n* [10] health; **как ва́ше ~ье?** how are you?; **за ва́ше ~ье!** your health!, here's to you!; **на ~ье!** good luck (health)!; **е́шь(те) на ~ье!** help yourself, please!

здра́в|ница *f* [5] health resort, sanatorium; **~омы́слящий** [17] sane,

sensible; **~оохране́ние** *n* [12] public health service; **~ствовать** [7] be in good health; ***~ствуй(те)!*** hello!, hi!, good morning! (*etc.*); *при знако́мстве* how do you do?; **~ый** [14 *sh.*] → ***здоро́вый***; *fig.* sound, sane, sensible; ***~ый смысл*** common sense; ***в ~ом уме́*** in one's senses; ***~ и невреди́м*** safe and sound
зе́бра *f* [5] zebra
зев *m* [1] *anat.* pharynx; **~а́ка** *m/f* [5] gaper; **~а́ть** [1], *once* <~ну́ть> [20] yawn; ***~а́ть по сторона́м*** stand about gaping; ***не ~а́й!*** look out!; **~о́к** *m* [1; -вка́] yawn; **~о́та** *f* [5] yawning
зелен|е́ть [8], <за-, по-> grow, turn *or* be green; *impf.* (*a.* **-ся**) appear *or* show green; **~ова́тый** [14 *sh.*] greenish
зелён|ый [14; зе́лен, -а́, -о] green (*a. fig.*), verdant; ***~ая у́лица*** *fig.* green light; ***~ юне́ц*** *coll.* greenhorn
зе́л|ень *f* [8] verdure; green; *cul.* potherbs, greens *pl.*; **~ье** *n* [10] *coll.* potion, alcoholic drink
зе́мельный [14] land...; ***~ уча́сток*** plot of land
землевладе́|лец *m* [1; -льца] landowner; **~ние** *n* [12] land ownership
земледе́л|ец *m* [1; -льца] farmer; **~ие** *n* [12] agriculture, farming; **~ьческий** [16] agricultural
земле|ме́р *m* [1] (land)surveyor; **~по́льзование** *n* [12] land tenure; **~трясе́ние** *n* [12] earthquake; **~черпа́лка** *f* [5; *g/pl.*: -лок] dredger, excavator
земли́стый [14 *sh.*] earthy; *цвет лица́* ashy, sallow
земл|я́ *f* [6; *ac/sg.*: зе́млю; *pl.*: зе́мли, земе́ль, зе́млям] earth (as planet **2я́**); land; (*пове́рхность, по́чва*) ground, soil; ***на ~ю*** to the ground; **~я́к** *m* [1 *e.*] (fellow) countryman; **~яни́ка** *f* [5] (wild) strawberry, -ries *pl.*; **~я́нка** *f* [5; *g/pl.*: -нок] *mil.* dugout; **~яно́й** [14] earth(en); ***~яны́е рабо́ты*** excavations
земново́дный [14] amphibious
земно́й [14] (of the) earth, terrestrial; earthly; *fig.* earthy, mundane
зени́т *m* [1] zenith (*a. fig.*); **~ный** [14] *mil.* anti-aircraft...
зени́ц|а *f* [5]: ***бере́чь как ~у о́ка*** cherish
зе́ркал|о *n* [9; *pl. e.*] looking glass, mirror (*a. fig.*); **~ьный** [14] *fig.* (dead-)smooth; ***~ьное стекло́*** plate glass
зерн|и́стый [14 *sh.*] grainy, granular; **~о́** *n* [9; *pl.*: зёрна, зёрен, зёрнам] grain (*a. coll.*), corn (*a. fig.*), seed; ***~о́ и́стины*** grain of truth; ***ко́фе в зёрнах*** coffee beans; **~ово́й** [14] grain...; *su. pl.* cereals
зефи́р *m* [1] sweetmeat (*of egg-white, sugar and gelatin(e)*)
зигза́г *m* [1], **~ообра́зный** [14; -зен, -зна] zigzag
зим|а́ *f* [5; *ac/sg.*: зи́му; *pl. st.*] winter (T in [the]; ***на*** B for the); **~ний** [15] winter..., wintry; **~ова́ть** [7], <за-, пере-> winter, hibernate
зия́ть [28] gape
злак *m* [1] *pl.* gramineous plants; ***хле́бные ~и*** *pl.* cereals
зла́то... *obs. or poet.* gold(en)
злить [13], <обо-, разо-> anger, make angry; (*раздража́ть*) vex, irritate; **~ся** be(come) *or* feel angry (***на*** B with); be in a bad temper
зло *n* [9; *pl. gen.* зол *only*] evil; (***меня́***) ***~ берёт*** it annoys me
зло́б|а *f* [5] malice, spite; rage; ***~а дня*** topic of the day; **~ный** [14; -бен, -бна] spiteful, malicious; **~одне́вный** [14; -вен, -вна] topical, burning; **~ствовать** [7] → ***зли́ться***
злов|е́щий [17 *sh.*] ominous; **~о́ние** *n* [12] stench; **~о́нный** [14; -о́нен, -о́нна] stinking, fetid; **~ре́дный** [14; -ден, -дна] pernicious, noxious
злоде́|й *m* [3] villian; **~ский** [16] *преступле́ние* vile, outrageous; *за́мысел и т. д.* malicious; **~йство** *n* [9], **~я́ние** *n* [12] outrage, villainy, crime
злой [14; зол, зла, зло] wicked, evil; *язы́к, де́йствие* malicious, spiteful; angry (with ***на*** B); *соба́ка* fierce; *нрав* severe; ***~ ге́ний*** evil genius
зло|ка́чественный [14 *sh.*] *med.*

malignant; **~ключéние** *n* [12] misfortune; **~намéренный** [14 *sh.*] malevolent; **~пáмятный** [14; -тен, -тна] rancorous; **~полýчный** [14; -чен, -чна] unfortunate, ill-fated; **~рáдный** [14; -ден, -дна] gloating

злослóви|е *n* [12], **~ть** [14] nalicious gossip, backbiting

злóст|ный [14; -тен, -тна] malicious, spiteful; malevolent; *закоренéлый* inveterate; **~ь** *f* [8] spite, rage

зло|счáстный [14; -тен, -тна] → ***~полýчный***

З

злоумы́шленник *m* [1] plotter; malefactor

злоупотреб|лéние *n* [12], **~ля́ть** [28], <~и́ть> [14 *e.*; -блю́, -би́шь] (T) *влáстью, довéрием* abuse; *спиртны́м* drink too much

зме|и́ный [14] snake('s), serpent('s), serpentine; **~и́ться** [13] meander, wind (o.s.); **~й** *m* [3]: ***воздýшный ~й*** kite; **~я́** *f* [6; *pl. st.*: змéи, змей] snake, serpent (*a. fig.*)

знак *m* [1] sign, mark; *дрýжбы и т. д.* token; symbol; (*предзнаменовáние*) omen; (*значóк*) badge; signal; ***дорóжный ~*** road sign; ***~и*** *pl.* ***препинáния*** punctuation marks; ***в ~*** (P) in token *or* as a sign of

знакóм|ить [14], <по-> introduce (B/**с** T *a p.* to); *a.* <о-> acquaint (**с** T with); **-ся** (**с** T) *p.*: meet, make the acquaintance of, (*a. th.*) become acquainted with; *th.*: familiarize o.s. with, go into; **~ство** *n* [9] acquaintance (-ces *pl.*); **~ый** [14 *sh.*] familiar, acquainted (**с** T with); know; *su.* acquaintance; **~ьтесь, ...,** meet...

знаменáтель *m* [4] denominator; **~ный** [14; -лен, -льна] memorable, remarkable; (*вáжный*) significant, important

знамéн|ие *n* [12]: ***~ие врéмени*** sign of the times; **~и́тость** *f* [8] fame, renown; *p.*: celebrity; **~и́тый** [14 *sh.*] famous, renowned, celebrated (T by, for); **~овáть** [7] *impf.* mark, signify

знáмя *n* [13; *pl.*: -мёна, -мён] banner, flag; *mil.* standard; colo(u)rs

знáни|е *n* [12] (*a. pl.* ~я) knowledge; ***со ~ем дéла*** capable, competently

знáт|ный [14; -тен, -тнá, -o] *род и т. д.* noble; **~óк** *m* [1 *e.*] expert; *ценитель* connoisseur

знать[1] [1] know; ***дать ~*** (Д) let know; ***дать себя́*** (***о себé***) ***~*** make itself felt (send news); ***кто егó знáет*** goodness knows

знать[2] *f* [8] *hist.* nobility, notables *pl.*

знач|éние *n* [12] meaning, sense; *math.* value; significance, importance (*vb.*: ***имéть*** be of); **~и́тельный** [14; -лен, -льна] considerable; large; (*вáжный*) important, significant; **~ить** [16] mean, signify; (*имéть значéние*) matter; **~ит** consequently, so; well (then); **-ся** be mentioned, be registered; *impers.* (it) say(s); **~óк** *m* [1; -чкá] badge; (*помéтка*) sign

знобúт|ь: ***меня́ ~*** I feel shivery

зной *m* [3] heat, sultriness; **~ный** [14; знóен, знóйна] sultry, hot

зоб *m* [1] crop, craw (*of birds*); *med.* goiter (-tre)

зов *m* [1] call

зóдчество *n* [9] architecture

золá *f* [5] ashes *pl.*

золóвка *f* [5; *g/pl.*: -вок] sister-in-law (*husband's sister*)

золотú|стый [14 *sh.*] golden; **~ть** [15 *e.*; -очý, -оти́шь], <по-, вы-> gild

зóлот|о *n* [9] gold; ***на вес ~а*** worth its weight in gold; **~óй** [14] gold(en) (*a. fig.*); ***~óе дно*** gold mine; ***~óй запáс*** *econ.* gold reserves; ***~ы́е рýки*** golden hands; ***~áя серединá*** golden mean

золочёный [14] gilt, gilded

Зóлушка *f* [5; *g/pl.*: -шек] Cinderella

зóн|а *f* [5] zone; **~áльный** [14] zonal, regional

зонд *m* [1] probe, sound; **~и́ровать** [7] sound; ***~и́ровать пóчву*** *fig.* explore the ground

зонт, ~ик *m* [1] umbrella; sunshade; ***складнóй ~ик*** telescopic umbrella

зоó|лог *m* [1] zoologist; **~логи́ческий** [16] zoological; **~лóгия** *f* [7] zoology; **~пáрк** *m* [1] zoo(logical garden)

зо́ркий [16; зо́рок, -рка́, -о; *comp.*: зо́рче] sharp-sighted (*a. fig.*); observant, watchful, vigilant
зрачо́к *m* [1; -чка́] *anat.* pupil
зре́л|ище *n* [11] sight; spectacle; show; **~ость** *f* [8] ripeness; *о челове́ке* maturity; **~ый** [14; зрел, -а́, -о] ripe, mature; ***по ~ому размышле́нию*** on reflection
зре́ни|е *n* [12] (eye)sight; ***по́ле ~я*** field of vision, eyeshot; *fig.* horizon; ***обма́н ~я*** optical illusion; ***то́чка ~я*** point of view; standpoint, angle (*prp.*: **с *то́чки ~я = под угло́м ~я*** from ...)
зреть [8], <со-, вы́-> ripen, mature
зри́тель *m* [4] spectator, onlooker, observer; **~ный** [14] visual, optic; ***~ный зал*** hall, auditorium; ***~ная па́мять*** visual memory
зря *coll.* in vain, to no purpose, (all) for nothing; ***~ ты э́то сде́лал*** you should not have done it
зря́чий [17] sighted (*opp. blind*)
зуб *m* [1; *from g/pl. e.*; зу́бья, зу́бьев] tooth; *tech. a.* cog; ***до ~о́в*** to the teeth; ***не по ~а́м*** too tough (*a. fig.*); ***сквозь ~ы*** through clenched teeth; ***име́ть ~*** (***на*** В) have a grudge against; **~а́стый** [14 *sh.*] *fig.* sharp-tongued; **~е́ц** *m* [1; -бца́] *tech.* → ***зуб***; **~и́ло** *n* [9] chisel; **~но́й** [14] tooth, dental; ***~но́й врач*** *m* dentist; ***~на́я боль*** toothache; ***~на́я щётка*** toothbrush; **~овраче́бный** [14]: ***~овраче́бный кабине́т*** dental surgery
зу́бр *m* [1] European bison; *fig.* diehard; *coll.* pundit
зубр|ёжка *f* [5] cramming; **~и́ть 1.** [13], <за-> notch; ***зазу́бренный*** jagged; **2.** [13; зубрю́, зубри́шь], <вы́-, за-> [зазу́бренный] cram, learn by rote
зу́бчатый [14] *tech.* cog (wheel)..., gear...; jagged
зуд *m* [1], **~е́ть** *coll.* [9] itch; urge; *fig.* complain constantly, talk boringly
зу́ммер *m* [1] buzzer
зы́б|кий [16; зы́бок, -бка́, -о; *comp.*: зы́бче] unsteady, unstable (*a. fig.*) vague; **~ь** *f* [8] ripples *pl.*
зы́чный [14; -чен, -чна; *comp.*: -чнее] loud, shrill
зя́б|нуть [21], <(пр)о-> feel chilly; **~ь** *f* [8] winter tillage *or* cold
зять *m* [4; *pl. e.*: зятья́, -ьёв] son- *or* brother-in-law (*daughter's or sister's husband*)

И

и 1. *cj.* and; and then, and so; but; (even) though, much as; (that's) just (what... is *etc.*), (this) very *or* same; **2.** *part.* oh; too, (n)either; even; ***и ... и ...*** both ... and
и́бо *c.j.* for
и́ва *f* [5; *pl. st.*] willow; ***плаку́чая ~*** weeping willow
и́волга *f* [5] oriole
игл|а́ *f* [5] needle (*a. tech.*); *bot.* thorn, prickle; *zo.* quill, spine, bristle; **~отерапи́я** *f* [7], **~ука́лывание** *n* [12] acupuncture
игнори́ровать [7] (*im*)*pf.* ignore
и́го *n* [9] *fig.* yoke
иго́л|ка *f* [5; *g/pl.*: -лок] → ***игла́***; ***как на ~ках*** on tenterhooks; ***с ~(оч)ки*** brand-new, spick-and-span; **~ьный** [14] needle('s)...; ***~ьное у́шко*** eye of a needle
иго́рный [14] gambling; card...
игра́ *f* [5; *pl. st.*] play; game (***в*** В of); sparkle; ***~ слов*** play on words, pun; ***~ не сто́ит свеч*** it isn't worth while; ***~ воображе́ния*** pure fantasy; **~льный** [14] *ка́рта* playing; **~ть** [1], <по-, сыгра́ть> play (***в*** В, ***на*** П); *в аза́ртные и́гры* gamble; sparkle (wine, *etc.*); *thea. a.* act; ***~ть своей жи́знью*** risk one's life; ***э́то***

не ~ет ро́ли it does not matter
игри́|вый [14 *sh.*] playful; **~стый** [14 *sh.*] sparkling
игро́к *m* [1 *e.*] player; gambler
игру́шка *f* [5; *g/pl.*: -шек] toy; *fig.* plaything
идеа́л *m* [1] ideal; **~изи́ровать** [7] (*im*)*pf.* idealize; **~и́зм** *m* [1] idealism; **~и́ст** *m* [1] idealist; **~исти́ческий** [16] idealistic; **~ьный** [14; -лен, -льна] ideal
идентифика́тор *m* [1] *comput.* name
идео́лог *m* [1] ideologist; **~и́ческий** [16] ideologic(al); **~́ия** *f* [7] ideology
иде́я *f* [6] idea
иди́лл|ия *f* [7] idyl(l); **~и́ческий** [16] idyllic
идио́ма *f* [5] idiom
идио́т *m* [1] idiot; **~и́зм** *m* [1] idiocy; **~ский** [16] idiotic
и́дол *m* [1] idol (*a. fig.*)
идти́ [иду́, идёшь; шёл, шла; ше́дший; идя́, *coll.* и́дучи], <пойти́> [пойду́, -дёшь; пошёл, -шла́] (be) go(ing, *etc.*; *a. fig.*), walk; come; (***за*** Т) follow, *a.* go for, fetch; leave; (*дви́гать[ся]*) move (*a.* chess, Т), flow, drift (***в, на*** В); *шко́лу и т. д.* enter; *а́рмию и т. д.* join, become; (*происходи́ть*) proceed, be in progress, take place; *thea. фильм* be on; *доро́га* lead (*о ка́рте* ***с*** Р); (***на*** В) attack; *о това́ре* sell; (***в, на, под*** В) be used, spent (for); (***к*** Д) suit; (***за*** В) marry; ***~ в счёт*** count; ***~ на вёслах*** row; ***пойти́ в отца́*** take after one's father; ***идёт!*** all right!, done!; ***пошёл*** (***пошли́***)! (let's) go!; ***де́ло*** (***речь***) ***идёт о*** (П) the question *or* matter is (whether), it is a question *or* matter of; ... is at stake; ***ему́ идёт*** *or* ***пошёл шесто́й год*** (***деся́ток***) he is over five (fifty)
иезуи́т *m* [1] Jesuit (*a. fig.*)
иера́рхия *f* [7] hierarchy
иеро́глиф *m* [1] hieroglyph(ic)
иждиве́н|ец *m* [1; -нца] dependent (-dant); **~ие** *n* [12]: ***быть на ~ии*** (Р) be s.o.'s dependent (-dant)
из, ~о (Р) from, out of; of; for, through; with; in; by; ***что ж ~ э́того?*** what does that matter?
изба́ *f* [5; *pl. st.*] (peasant's) house, cottage
избав|и́тель *m* [4] rescuer, deliverer; **~́ить** → **~ля́ть**; **~ле́ние** *n* [12] deliverance, rescue; **~ля́ть** [28], <~́ить> [14] (**от** Р from) (*освободи́ть*) deliver, free; (*спасти́*) save; *от бо́ли* relieve; **-ся** (**от** Р) get rid of
избало́ванный [14 *sh.*] spoilt
избе|га́ть [1], <~жа́ть> [4; -егу́, -ежи́шь, -егу́т], <~́гнуть> [21] (Р) avoid, shun; *сме́рти* escape; (*уклони́ться*) evade; **~жа́ние** *n* [12]: ***во ~жа́ние*** (Р) (in order) to avoid
изб|ива́ть [1], <~и́ть> [изобью́, -бьёшь; → ***бить***] beat unmercifully; **~ие́ние** *n* [12] beating; massacre
избира́тель *m* [4] voter, elector; *pl. a.* electorate; constituency; **~ный** [14] electoral; ballot..., election; ***~ный уча́сток*** polling station; ***~ный о́круг*** constituency
изб|ира́ть [1], <~бра́ть> [-беру́, -рёшь; → ***брать***] choose; elect (В/**в** И *pl. or* /Т); **~́ранный** *a.* select(ed); ***~́ранные сочине́ния*** selected works
изби́|тый [14 *sh.*] *fig.* hackneyed, trite; **~ть** → ***~ва́ть***
избра́|ние *n* [12] election; **~нник** *m* [1] (young) man of her choice; **~ть** → ***избира́ть***
избы́т|ок *m* [1; -тка] surplus; abundance, plenty; ***в ~ке, с ~ком*** in plenty, plentiful(ly); ***в ~ке чу́вств*** *fig.* overcome by emotion; **~очный** [14; -чен, -чна] superfluous, surplus...
и́звер|г *m* [1] monster, cruel person; **~же́ние** *n* [12] eruption
изверну́ться → ***извора́чиваться***
извести́ → ***изводи́ть***
изве́ст|ие *n* [12] news *sg.*; information; *pl. a.* bulletin; ***после́дние ~ия*** *rad.* news(cast), the latest news; **известить** → ***извеща́ть***
извёстк|а *f* [5], **~о́вый** [14] lime
изве́стн|ость *f* [8] reputation, fame; ***по́льзоваться*** (***мирово́й***) ***~остью*** be (world-)renowned *or* famous *or* well-known; ***ста́вить*** (В) ***в ~ость*** bring s.th. to a p.'s notice (**о** П); **~ый** [14; -тен, -тна] known (for

Т; as ***как***, ***за*** В), familiar; well-known, renowned, famous; notorious; (*не́который*) certain; ***наско́лько мне ~о*** as far as I know; (***мне***) ***~о*** it is known (I know); ***ему́ э́то хорошо́ ~о*** he is well aware of this

извест|ня́к *m* [1 *e.*] limestone; **´~ь** *f* [8] lime

изве|ща́ть [1], <~сти́ть> [15 *e.*; -ещу́, -ести́шь; -ещённый] inform (**о** П of); notify; *comm. a.* advise; **~ще́ние** *n* [12] notification, notice; *comm.* advice

изви|ва́ться [1] wind, meander, twist; *о те́ле, змее́ и т. д.* wriggle; **´~лина** *f* [5] bend, curve; turn; *мо́зга* convolution; **´~листый** [14 *sh.*] winding, tortuous

извин|е́ние *n* [12] apology, excuse; **~и́тельный** [14; -лен, -льна] pardonable; [*no sh.*] apologetic; **~я́ть** [28], <~и́ть> [13] excuse, pardon; forgive (Д/В a p. a th.); ***~и́(те)!*** excuse me!, I am sorry!; ***нет, уж ~и́(те)!*** oh no!, on no account!; **-ся** apologize (***пе́ред*** Т, ***за*** В to/for); **~я́юсь!** *coll.* → ***~и́(те)!***

извле|ка́ть [1], <~е́чь> [26] take *or* draw out; extract (*a. math.*); *вы́году* derive; **~че́ние** *n* [12] extract(ion)

извне́ from outside

изводи́ть *coll.* [15], <извести́> [25] (*израсхо́довать*) use up; (*изму́чить*) exhaust, torment

изво́л|ить [13] *iro.* please, deign; **~ь(те)** + *inf.* (would you) please + *vb*

извор|а́чиваться [1], <изверну́ться> [20] *coll.* dodge; (try to) wriggle out; **~о́тливый** [14 *sh.*] resourceful; shrewd

извра|ща́ть [1], <~ти́ть> [15 *e.*; -ащу́, -ати́шь; -ащённый] *фа́кты* misconstrue, distort; *о челове́ке* pervert

изги́б *m* [1] bend, curve, turn; *fig.* shade; **~а́ть** [1], <изогну́ть> [20] bend, curve, crook (*v/i.* **-ся**)

изгла́|живать [1], <~дить> [15] (**-ся** be[come]) efface(d), erase(d); ***~дить из па́мяти*** blot out of one's memory

изгна́|ние *n* [12] *old use, lit.* banishment; exile; **~нник** *m* [1] exile; **~ть** → ***изгоня́ть***

изголо́вье *n* [10] *крова́ти* head

изг|оня́ть [28], <~на́ть> [-гоню́, -го́нишь; -гна́л, -ла́] drive out; oust; expel; exile, banish

и́згородь *f* [8] fence; *зелёная* hedge(row)

изгот|а́вливать [1], **~овля́ть** [28], <~о́вить> [14] make, produce, manufacture; **~овле́ние** *n* [12] manufacture; making; *mil.* preparation

изда|ва́ть [5], <´~ть> [-да́м, -да́шь, *etc.*, → ***дать***; и́зданный (и́здан, -а́, -о)] publish; *прика́з* issue; *за́пах* exhale; *звук* utter, emit; *law* promulgate

и́зда|вна for a long time; from time immemorial; ***~лека́, ~лёка ~ли*** from afar; from a distance

изда́|ние *n* [12] publication; edition; issue; **~тель** *m* [4] publisher; **~тельство** *n* [9] publishing house, publishers *pl.*; **~ть** → ***издава́ть***

издева́т|ельство *n* [9] jeering, scoffing, sneering (***над*** Т at); **~ься** [1] jeer, sneer, mock (***над*** Т at); bully

изде́лие *n* [12] product, article; (needle)work; *pl. a.* goods

издёргать [1] harass, harry; **-ся** overstrain one's nerves; worry one's head off

издерж|а́ться [4] *pf. coll.* spend a lot of (*or* run short of) money; **´~ки** *f/pl.* [5; *gen*: -жек] expenses; *law* costs

издыха́ть [1] → ***до́хнуть***

изж|ива́ть [1], <~и́ть> [-живу́, -вёшь; -жи́тый, *coll.* -то́й (изжи́т, -а́, -о)] (gradually) overcome; ***~и́ть себя́*** be(come) outdated, have had one's day; **~о́га** *f* [5] heartburn

и́з-за (Р) from behind; from; because of; over; for (the sake of); ***~ чего́?*** why?, for what reason?; ***~ э́того*** for that reason

излага́ть [1], <изложи́ть> [16] state, set forth, expound, word

излеч|е́ние *n* [12] cure, (medical) treatment; (*выздоровле́ние*) recovery; **´~ивать** [1], <~и́ть> [16] cure; **~и́мый** [14 *sh.*] curable

изл|ива́ть [1], <**~и́ть**> [изолью́, -льёшь; → **лить**]: **~и́ть ду́шу** unbosom *o.s.*; *гнев* give vent (*to anger*)

изли́ш|ек *m* [1; -шка] surplus, *a.* **~ество** *n* [9] excess; **~не** unnecessarily; **~ний** [15; -шен, -шня, -не] superfluous, excessive; (*нену́жный*) needless

изл|ия́ние *n* [12] outpouring, effusion; **~и́ть** [28] → **~ива́ть**

изловчи́ться *coll.* [16 *e.*; -чу́сь, -чи́шься] *pf.* contrive

излож|е́ние *n* [12] exposition, account; **~и́ть** → **излага́ть**

изло́манный [14] broken; warped; *жизнь, хара́ктер* spoilt, deformed

излуч|а́ть [1] radiate; **~е́ние** *n* [12] radiation

излу́чина *f* [5] *реки́* → **изги́б**

излю́бленный [14] favo(u)rite

изме́н|а *f* [5] treason (Д to); *супру́жеская* unfaithfulness; **~е́ние** *n* [12] change, alteration, modification; **~и́ть** → **~я́ть**; **~ник** *m* [1] traitor; **~чивый** [14 *sh.*] changeable, variable; *о челове́ке, настрое́нии* fickle; **~я́ть** [28], <**~и́ть**> [13; -еню́, -е́нишь] **1.** *v/i.* change (*v/i.* **-ся**) alter; modify; vary; **2.** *v/i.* (Д) betray; be(come) unfaithful (to); *кля́тве и т. д.* break, violate; *па́мять* fail

измер|е́ние *n* [12] measurement; *math.* dimension; **~и́мый** [14 *sh.*] measurable; **~и́тельный** [14]: **~и́тельный прибо́р** measuring instrument, gauge; **~я́ть** [28], <**~ить**> [13 *st.*] measure; *температу́ру* take; *глубину́* fathom (*a. fig.*)

измождённый [14 *sh.*] *вид* emaciated; (*изнурённый*) exhausted

измо́р: **взять кого́-нибудь ~ом** *fig.* worry s.o. into doing s.th

и́зморозь *f* [8] rime, hoar-frost

и́зморось *f* [8] drizzle

изму́чи|вать [1], <**~ть**> [16] (**-ся** be[come]) fatigue(d), exhaust(ed), wear (worn) out

измышле́ние *n* [12] fabrication, invention

изна́нка *f* [5] back, inside; *тка́ни* wrong side; *fig.* seamy side

изнаси́лов|ание *n* [12], **~ать** [7] *pf.* rape, assault, violation

изна́шивать [1], <**износи́ть**> [15] wear out; *v/i.* **-ся**

изне́женный [14] coddled

изнем|ога́ть [1], <**~о́чь**> [26; г/ж: -огу́, -о́жешь, -о́гут] be(come) exhausted *or* enervated; **~ога́ть от уста́лости** feel dead tired; **~оже́ние** *n* [12] exhaustion, weariness

изно́с *m* [1] wear (and tear); **рабо́тать на ~** wear o.s. out with work; **~и́ть** → **изна́шивать**

изно́шенный [14 *sh.*] worn (out); threadbare

изнур|е́ние *n* [12] exhaustion, fatigue; **~и́тельный** [14; -лен, -льна] *труд* hard, exhausting; *боле́знь* wasting; **~я́ть** [28], <**~и́ть**> (**-ся** be[come]) fatigue(d), exhauste(d)

изнутри́ from within; on the inside

изны|ва́ть [1] *impf.* (**от** Р): **~ва́ть от жа́жды** be dying of thirst; **~ва́ть от ску́ки** be bored to death

изоби́л|ие *n* [12] abundance, plenty (Р *a.* **в** П of); **~овать** [7] abound (Т in); **~ьный** [14; -лен, -льна] rich, abundant (Т in)

изоблич|а́ть [1], <**~и́ть**> [16 *e.*; -чу́, -чи́шь; -чённый] unmask; *impf.* reveal, show

изобра|жа́ть [1], <**~зи́ть**> [15 *e.*; -ажу́, -ази́шь; -ажённый] represent, portray, depict; describe; express; **~жа́ть из себя́** (В) make o.s. out to be; **~же́ние** *n* [12] representation; description; *о́браз* image, picture; **~зи́тельный** [14]: **~зи́тельное иску́сство** fine arts

изобре|сти́ → **~та́ть**; **~та́тель** *m* [4] inventor; **~та́тельный** [14; -лен, -льна] inventive, resourceful; **~та́ть** [1], <**~сти́**> [25 -т-: -брету́, -тёшь] invent; **~те́ние** *n* [12] invention

изо́гнут|ый [14 *sh.*] bent, curved; **~ь** → **изгиба́ть**

изо́дранный [14] *coll.* → **изо́рванный**

изол|и́ровать [7] (*im*)*pf.* isolate; *el. a.* insulate; **~я́тор** *m* [1] *el.* insulator; *med.* isolation ward; *в тюрьме́* cell, jail for imprisonment during investigation; **~я́ция** *f* [7] isolation; *el.* insulation

изо́рванный [14] torn, tattered

изощр|ённый [14] refine, subtle; **~я́ться** [28], <~и́ться> [13] exert o.s., excel (**в** П *or* T in); ***~ря́ться в остроу́мии*** sparkle with wit
из-под (P) from under; from; from the vicinity of; ***буты́лка ~ молока́*** milk bottle
изразе́ц *m* [1; -зца́] (Dutch) tile
и́зредка occasionally; *места́ми* here and there
изре́з|ывать [1], <~ать> [3] cut up
изре|ка́ть [1], <~чь> *iro.* pronounce; **~че́ние** *n* [12] aphorism, maxim
изруб|а́ть [1], <~и́ть> [14] chop, mince; cut (up)
изря́дный [14; -ден, -дна] *су́мма* large, fair; *моро́з* rather severe; *подле́ц* real scoundrel
изуве́ч|ивать, [1], <~ить> [16] mutilate
изум|и́тельный [14; -лен, -льна] amazing, wonderful; **~и́ть(ся)** → ***~ля́ть***(***ся***); **~ле́ние** *n* [12] amazement; **~ля́ть** [28], <~и́ть> [14 *e.*; -млю́, -ми́шь, -млённый] (**-ся** Д be) amaze(d), astonish(ed), surprise(d at)
изумру́д *m* [1] emerald
изуч|а́ть [1], <~и́ть> [16] study, learn; (*ознако́миться*) familiarize o.s. with; (*овладе́ть*) master; *тща́тельно* scrutinize; **~е́ние** *n* [12] study
изъе́здить [15] *pf.* travel all over
изъяв|и́тельный [14] *gr.* indicative; **~ля́ть** [28], <~и́ть> [14] express, show; *согла́сие* give
изъя́н *m* [1] defect, flaw
изыма́ть [1], <изъя́ть> [изыму́, изы́мешь] withdraw, confiscate
изыска́ние *n* [12] *mst. mining* prospecting
изы́сканный [14 *sh.*] refined, elegant; *еда́ и т. д.* choice, exquisite
изы́ск|ивать [1], <~а́ть> [3] find
изю́м *m* [1] *coll.* raisins *pl.*; sultanas; **~инка** *f* [5]: **с *~инкой*** piquant
изя́щн|ый [14; -щен, -щна] graceful, elegant
ик|а́ть [1], <~ну́ть> [20] hiccup
ико́н|а *f* [5] icon; **´~опись** *f* [8] icon painting
ико́та *f* [5] hiccup
икра́[1] *f* [5] (hard) roe, spawn, caviar; ***зерни́стая ~*** soft caviar; ***па́юсная ~*** pressed caviar
икра́[2] *f* [5] *mst. pl.* [*st.*] calf (*of leg*)
ил *m* [1] silt
и́ли or; or else; **~ ... ~ ...** either... or
иллю|зия *f* [7] illusion; **~мина́ция** *f* [7] illumination; **~мини́ровать** [7] (*im*)*pf.* illuminate; **~стра́ция** *f* [7] illustration; **~стри́ровать** [7] (*im*)*pf.* illustrate
имби́рь *m* [4 *e.*] ginger
име́ние *n* [12] estate, landed property
имени́|ны *f*/*pl.* [5] name day; name-day party; **~тельный** [14] *gr.* nominative; **~тый** [14 *sh.*] eminent, distinguished
и́менно just, very (*adj.*), exactly, in particular; (*a.* **а ~**, **и ~**) namely, to wit, that is to say; (*a.* **вот ~**) *coll.* indeed
именова́ть [7], <на-> call, name
име́ть [8] have, possess; **~ *де́ло* с** (T) have to do with; **~ *ме́сто*** take place; **~ *в виду́*** have in mind, mean, intend; (*не забыва́ть*) remember, bear in mind; **-ся** *под руко́й* be at, in *or* on hand; (**у** P) have there is, are, *etc.*
имита́ция *f* [7] imitation
иммигра́нт *m* [1] immigrant
иммуните́т *m* [1] immunity
императ|ор *m* [1] emperor; **~ри́ца** *f* [5] empress
импе́р|ия *f* [7] empire; **~ский** [16] imperial
и́мпорт *m* [1], **~и́ровать** [7] (*im*)*pf.* import; **~ный** [14] imported
импоте́нция *f* [7] sexual impotence
импровизи́ровать [7] (*im*)*pf.* <сымпровизи́ровать> improvise
и́мпульс *m* [1] impulse; *el.* pulse; **~и́вный** [14; -вен, -вна] impulsive
иму́щ|ество *n* [9] property; belongings *pl.*; ***недви́жимое ~ество*** real estate; **~ий** [17] well-to-do; ***власть ~ие*** the powers that be
и́мя *n* [13] (*esp.* first, Christian) name (*a. fig. gr.*; parts of speech = *Lat.* nomen); ***и́мени***: ***шко́ла им. Че́хова*** Chekhov school; **во ~** for the sake of; **от *и́мени*** in the name

of (P); ***на ~*** addressed to, for; ***по и́мени*** named; in name (only); (know) by name; ***называ́ть ве́щи свои́ми имена́ми*** call a spade a spade
и́наче differently; otherwise, (or) else; ***так и́ли ~*** one way *or* another, anyhow
инвали́д *m* [1] invalid; ***~ труда́*** (***войны́***) disabled worker (veteran, *Brt.* ex-serviceman)
инвент|ариза́ция *f* [7] stock-taking; **~а́рь** *m* [4 *e.*] *спи́сок* inventory; stock, equipment; implements
инд|е́ец *m* [1; -е́йца] (American) Indian; **~е́йка** *f* [5; *g/pl.*: -е́ек] turkey; **~е́йский** [16] (American) Indian; **~иа́нка** *f* [5; *g/pl.*: -нок] *fem.* of **~е́ец**, **~и́ец**

И

индиви́д *m* [1] individual; **~уа́льность** *f* [8] individuality; **~уа́льный** [14; -лен, -льна] individual
инди́|ец *m* [1; -йца] Indian, **~йский** [16] Indian
инду́с *m* [1], **~ка** *f* [5; *g/pl.*: -сок], **~ский** [16] Hindu
инд|устриа́льный [14] industrial; **~у́стрия** *f* [7] industry
индю́к *m* [1 *e.*] turkey (cock)
и́ней *m* [3] hoar-frost
ине́р|тность *f* [8] inertness, inaction; **~тный** [14; -тен, -тна] inert; **~ция** *f* [7] inertia; *phys.* ***по ~ции*** under one's own momentum; *fig.* mechanically
инжене́р *m* [1] engineer; **~-строи́тель** *m* [1/4] civil engineer
инициа́|лы *m/pl.* [1] initials; **~ти́ва** *f* [5] initiative; **~ти́вный** [14; -вен, -вна] enterprising, full of initiative; **~тор** *m* [1] initiator, organizer
инкруста́ция *f* [7] inlay, incrustation
иногда́ sometimes, now and then
иногоро́дний [15] nonresident, person from another town
ино́|й [14] (an)other, different; (*не́который и т. д.*) some, many a; ***~й раз*** sometimes; ***не кто ~й*** (***не что ~е***), ***как ...*** none other than
иноро́дн|ый [14], heterogeneous; ***~ное те́ло*** *med.* foreign body
иносказа́тельный [14; -лен, -льна] allegorical
иностра́н|ец *m* [1; -нца], **~ка** *f* [5; *g/pl.*: -нок] foreigner; **~ный** [14] foreign; → *a.* ***министе́рство***
инсинуа́ция *f* [7] insinuation
инспе́к|тор *m* [1] inspector; **~ция** *f* [7] inspection
инста́нция *f* [7] *pl.* (official) channels; *pol.* level of authority; *law* instance
инсти́нкт *m* [1] instinct; **~и́вный** [14; -вен, -вна] instinctive
институ́т *m* [1] institute; *бра́ка и т. д.* institution
инстру́кция *f* [7] instruction, direction; ***~ по эксплуата́ции*** manual
инструме́нт *m* [1] *mus. etc.* instrument; *рабо́чий* tool
инсу́льт *m* [1] *med.* stroke
инсцени́р|овать [7] *(im)pf.* adapt for the stage *or* screen; *fig.* feign; **~о́вка** *f* [5; *g/pl.*: -вок] dramatization
интегра́ция *f* [7] integration
интелле́кт *m* [1] intellect; **~уа́льный** [14; -лен, -льна] intellectual
интеллиге́н|т *m* [1] intellectual; **~тность** *f* [8] intelligence and good breeding; **~тный** [14; -тен, -тна] cultured, well-educated; **~ция** *f* [7] intelligentsia, intellectuals *pl.*
интенси́вный (-tɛn-) [14; -вен, -вна] intense, (*a. econ.*) intensive
интерва́л *m* [1] interval; *typ.* space
интервью́ (-tɛr-) *n* [*indecl.*], ***брать, взять ~***, **~и́ровать** (-tɛr-) [7] *(im)pl.* interview
интере́с *m* [1] interest (***к*** Д in; ***име́ть ~ для*** P be of/to; ***в ~ах*** P in the/of); use; **~ный** [14; -сен, -сна] interesting; *о вне́шности* handsome, attractive; ***~но, кто э́то сказа́л?*** I wonder who said this?; **~ова́ть** [7], <за-> (**-ся** be[come]) interest(ed), take an interest (T in)
интерна́т *m* [1]: ***шко́ла-~*** boarding school
интернациона́льный [14; -лен, -льна] international
интерпрета́ция *f* [7] interpretation
интерфе́йс *m* [1] *comput.* interface
интерье́р *m* [1] *art* interior
инти́мн|ость *f* [8] intimacy; **~ый** [14; -мен, -мна] intimate

интона́ция *f* [7] intonation

интри́г|а *f* [5] intrigue; **~а́н** *m* [1] intriguer; **~а́нка** *f* [5; *g/pl.*: -нок] intrigante; **~ова́ть** [7], <за-> intrigue

интуи|ти́вный [14; -вен, -вна] intuitive; **~ция** *f* [7] intuition

интури́ст *m* [1] foreign tourist

инфа́ркт *m* [1] infarction

инфе́кция *f* [7] infection

инфля́ция *f* [7] inflation

информ|а́ция *f* [7] information; **~и́ровать** [7] (*im*)*pf.*, <про-> inform

инциде́нт *m* [1] *mst. mil.*, *pol.* incident

ипподро́м *m* [1] racetrack (course)

и́рис[1] *m* [1] *bot.* iris

ири́с[2] *m* [1], **~ка** *f* [5; *g/pl.*: -сок] toffee

ирла́нд|ец *m* [1; -дца] Irishman; **~ка** *f* [5; *g/pl.*: -док] Irishwoman; **~ский** [16] Irish

ирон|изи́ровать [7] speak ironically (about ***над*** T); **~и́ческий** [16] ironic(al); **~ия** *f* [7] irony

иск *m* [1] *law* suit, action

иска|жа́ть [1], <~зи́ть> [15 *e.*; -ажу́, -ази́шь; -ажённый] distort, twist; misrepresent; **~же́ние** *n* [12] distortion

иска́ть [3], <по-> (B) look for; (*mst.* P) seek

исключ|а́ть [1], <~и́ть> [16 *e.*; -чу́, -чи́шь; -чённый] exclude, leave out; *из шко́лы* expel; **~а́я** (P) except(ing); **~ено́** ruled out; **~е́ние** *n* [12] exclusion; expulsion; exception (***за*** T with the; ***в ви́де*** P as an); **~и́тельный** [14; -лен, -льна] exceptional; ***~и́тельная ме́ра наказа́ния*** capital punishment; *coll.* excellent; *adv. a.* solely, only; **~и́ть** → ***~а́ть***

иско́мый [14] sought-after, looked-for

иско́нный [14] primordial

ископа́ем|ый [14] (*a. fig. su. n*) fossilized; *pl. su.* minerals; ***поле́зные ~ые*** mineral resources

искорен|я́ть [28], <~и́ть> [13] eradicate, extirpate

и́скоса askance; sideways; ***взгляд ~*** sidelong glance

и́скра *f* [5] spark(le); flash; ***~ наде́жды*** glimmer of hope

и́скренн|ий [15; -ренен, -ренна, -е/о, -и/ы] sincere, frank, candid; ***~е Ваш*** yours sincerely; **~ость** *f* [8] sincerity, frankness

и́скр|истый [14 *sh.*] sparking; **~и́ться** [13] sparkle, scintillate

искуп|а́ть [1], <~и́ть> (B) atone for; make up for; **~ле́ние** *n* [12] atonement

искуси́ть → ***искуша́ть***

иску́с|ный [14; -сен, -сна] skil(l)ful; expert; skilled; **~ственный** [14 *sh.*] artificial; *зу́бы и т. д.* false; *же́мчуг и т. д.* imitation; **~ство** *n* [9] fine arts; *мастерство́* skill, trade, craft

иску|ша́ть [1], <~си́ть> [15 *e.*; -ушу́, -уси́шь] tempt; ***~ша́ть судьбу́*** tempt fate; **~ше́ние** *n* [12] temptation; ***подда́ться ~ше́нию*** yield to temptation; **~шённый** [14 *sh.*] experienced

исла́м *m* [1] Islam

испа́н|ец *m* [1; -нца], **~ка** *f* [5; *g/pl.*: -нок] Spaniard; **~ский** [16] Spanish

испар|е́ние *n* [12] evaporation; *pl. a.* vapo(u)r(s); **~я́ть** [28], <~и́ть> [13] evaporate (*v/i.* **-ся**, *a. fig.*)

испе|пеля́ть [28], <~пели́ть> [13] *lit.* burn to ashes; ***~пеля́ющий взгляд*** annihilating look; **~щря́ть** [28], <~щри́ть> [13] mottle, spot (with), cover all over (with)

испи́с|ывать [1], <~а́ть> [3] write on, cover with writing; *тетра́дь* fill (up); **~ан** full of notes, *etc.*

испове́доваться [7] (*im*)*pf.* confess (***пе́ред*** T to a p.; **в** П *s.th.*)

и́споведь *f* [8] confession (*eccl.* [*prp.*: **на** В/П to/at] *a. fig.*)

и́спод|воль *coll.* gradually; **~ло́бья** (*недове́рчиво*) distrustfully; (*нахму́рившись*) frowningly; **~тишка́** *coll.* in an underhand way

испоко́н: ***~ ве́ку*** (***веко́в***) → ***и́здавна***

исполи́н *m* [1] giant; **~ский** [16] gigantic

исполн|е́ние *n* [12] execution; fulfil(l)ment, performance; *обя́занности* discharge; **~и́мый** [14 *sh.*] realizable; practicable; **~и́тель** *m* [4] executor; *thea.*, *mus.* performer; *law* bailiff; **соста́в ~и́телей** *thea.*

cast; **~и́тельный** [14] executive; [-лен, -льна] efficient and reliable; **~я́ть** [28], <**~́ить**> [13] carry out, execute; *долг* fulfil(l), do; *обеща́ние* keep; *thea.*, *mus.* perform; **-ся** come true; *лет* be: ***ей ~́илось пять лет*** she is five; *прошло́* pass (since [***с тех пор***] ***как***)

испо́льзова|ние *n* [12] use, utilization; **~ть** [7] *(im)pf.* use, utilize

испо́р|тить → ***по́ртить***; **~ченный** [14 *sh.*] spoilt; (*тж. ребёнок*) broken; *о челове́ке* depraved

исправ|и́тельно-трудово́й [1]: ***~и́тельно-трудова́я коло́ния*** *approx.* reformatory; **~ле́ние** *n* [12] correction; repair; *челове́ка* reform; **~ля́ть** [28], <**~́ить**> [14] correct; improve; reform; repair; **-ся** reform

испра́вн|ость *f* [8] good (working) order; ***в ~ости*** = **~ый** [14; -вен, -вна] intact, in good working order

испражн|е́ние *n* [12] *med.* defecation; *pl.* f(a)eces; **~я́ться** [28], <**~и́ться**> [13] defecate

испу́г *m* [1] fright; **~а́ть** → ***пуга́ть***

испус|ка́ть [1], <**~ти́ть**> [15] *зву́ки* utter; *за́пах* emit; ***~ти́ть дух*** give up the ghost

испыт|а́ние *n* [12] test, trial; (*a. fig.*) ordeal; examination (***на*** П at); **~́анный** [14] tried; **~а́тельный** [14] test; *срок* probationary; **~у́ющий** [17] *взгляд* searching; **~́ывать**, <**~а́ть**> [1] try (*a. fig.*), test; (*подве́ргнуться*) experience, undergo; *боль и т. д.* feel

иссле́дова|ние *n* [12] investigation, research; *geogr.* exploration; *med.* examination; *chem.* analysis; *нау́чное* treatise, paper, essay (***по*** Д on); **~тель** *m* [4] research worker, researcher; explorer; **~тельский** [16] research... (*a.* ***нау́чно-~тельский***); **~ть** [7] *(im)pf.* investigate; explore; do research into; examine (*a. med.*); *chem.* analyze (*Brt.* -yse)

исступл|е́ние *n* [12] *о слу́шателях и т. д.* ecstasy, frenzy; (*я́рость*) rage; **~ённый** [14] frantic

исс|яка́ть [1], <**~я́кнуть**> [21] *v/i.* dry (*v/i.* up); *fig. a.* exhaust, wear out (*v/i.* o.s. *or* become ...)

ист|ека́ть [1], <**~е́чь**> [26] *вре́мя* elapse; *срок* expire, become due; ***~ека́ть кро́вью*** bleed to death; **~е́кший** [17] past, last

исте́р|ика *f* [5] hysterics *pl.*; **~и́ческий** [16], **~и́чный** [14; -чен, -чна] hysterical; **~и́я** *f* [7] hysteria

исте́ц *m* [1; -тца́] plaintiff; *в бракоразво́дном проце́ссе* petitioner

истече́ни|е *n* [12] *сро́ка* expiration; *вре́мени* lapse; ***по ~и*** (P) at the end of

исте́чь → ***истека́ть***

и́стин|а *f* [5] truth; ***изби́тая ~а*** truism; **~ный** [14; -инен, -инна] true, genuine; *пра́вда* plain

истлева́ть [1], <**~е́ть**> [8] rot, decay; *об у́глях* die away

исто́к *m* [1] source (*a. fig.*)

истолк|ова́ние *n* [12] interpretation; commentary; **~о́вывать** [1], <**~ова́ть**> [7] interpret, expound

исто́м|а *m* [5] languor; **~и́ться** [14 *e.*; -млю́сь, -ми́шься] (be[come]) tire(d), weary (-ied)

истопта́ть [3] *pf.* trample; *о́бувь* wear out

исто́р|ик *m* [1] historian; **~и́ческий** [16] historical; *собы́тие и т. д.* historic; **~ия** *f* [7] history; *расска́з* story; *coll.* event, affair, thing; ***ве́чная ~ия!*** the same old story!; ***~ия боле́зни*** case history

источ|а́ть [1], <**~и́ть**> [16 *e.*; -чу́, -чи́шь] give off, impart; *за́пах* emit; **~́ник** *m* [1] spring; (*a. fig.*) source

истощ|а́ть [1], <**~и́ть**> [16 *e.*; -щу́, -щи́шь; -щённый] (**-ся** be[come]) exhaust(ed); *запа́сы* use(d) up; *ресу́рсы* deplete; **~ённый** [14 *sh.*] *челове́к* emaciated

истра́чивать [1] → ***тра́тить***

истреб|и́тель *m* [4] destroyer; *ae.* fighter plane; **~и́тельный** [14] *война́* destructive; fighter...; **~и́ть** → **~ля́ть**; **~ле́ние** *n* [12] destruction; *тарака́нов и т. д.* extermination; **~ля́ть** [28], <**~и́ть**> [14 *e.*; -блю́, -би́шь; -блённый] destroy, annihilate; exterminate

и́стый [14] true, genuine

истяза́ние *n* [12], **~ть** [1] torture

исхо́д *m* [1] end, outcome, result; *Bibl.* Exodus; ***быть на ~е*** be com-

ing to an end; *о проду́ктах и т. д.* be running short of; **~и́ть** [15] (*из* P) come, emanate (from); (*происходи́ть*) originate; (*осно́вываться*) proceed (from); **~ный** [14] initial; ***~ное положе́ние*** (***~ная то́чка***) point of departure
исхуда́лый [14] emaciated, thin
исцара́пать [1] *pf.* scratch (all over)
исцел|е́ние *n* [12] healing; (*выздоровле́ние*) recovery; **~я́ть** [28], <~и́ть> [13] heal, cure; **-ся** recover
исчез|а́ть [1], <~нуть> [21] disappear, vanish; **~нове́ние** *n* [12] disappearance; **~нуть** → ***~а́ть***
исче́рп|ывать, <~ать> [1] exhaust, use up; *вопро́с и т. д.* settle; **~ывающий** exhaustive
исчисл|е́ние *n* [12] calculation; calculus; **~я́ть** [28], <~ить> [13] calculate
ита́к thus, so; well, then, now
италья́н|ец *m* [1; -нца], **~ка** *f* [5; *g/pl.*: -нок], **~ский** [16] Italian
ито́г *m* [1] sum, total; result; ***в ~е*** in the end; *подвести́* sum up; **~о́** (-'vɔ) altogether; in all; total
их → ***они́***, (*a. possessive adj.*) their(s)
ишь *int. coll.* P (just) look!; listen!
ище́йка *f* [5; *g/pl.*: -еек] bloodhound
ию́|ль *m* [4] July; **~нь** *m* [4] June

Й

йог *m* [1] yogi; **~а** yoga
йод *m* [1] iodine; **~ный** [14]: ***~ный раство́р*** tincture of iodine
йо́|та *f* [5]: ***ни на ~ту*** not a jot

К

к, ко (Д) to, toward(s); *о вре́мени тж.* by; for; ***~ тому́ же*** besides
-ка *coll.* (*after vb.*) just, will you
каба́к *m* [1 *e.*] *hist.* tavern *fig. coll.* hubbub and disorder
кабала́ *f* [5] *hist.* debt-slavery; *fig.* bondage
каба́н *m* [1 *e.*] (*a.* wild) boar
кабачо́к *m* [1; *g/pl.*: -чков] vegetable marrow
ка́бель *m* [4] cable
каби́н|а *f* [5] cabin, booth; *ae.* cockpit; *водителя* cab; **~е́т** *m* [1] study, office; *med.* (consulting) room; *pol.* cabinet
каблу́к *m* [1 *e.*] heel (*of shoe*); ***быть под ~о́м*** *fig.* be under s.o.'s thumb
кабота́ж *m* [1] coastal trade
кавале́р *m* [1] bearer of an order; *old use* boyfriend; *в та́нце* partner
кавале|ри́йский [16] cavalry...; **~ри́ст** *m* cavalryman; **~ия** *f* [7] cavalry
ка́верзный *coll.* [14] tricky
кавка́з|ец *m* [1; -зца] Caucasian; **~ский** [16] Caucasian
кавы́чк|и *f/pl.* [5; *gen.*: -чек] quotation marks; ***в ~ах*** *fig. coll.* so-called
ка́дка *f* [5; *g/pl.*: -док] tub, vat
ка́дмий *m* [3] cadmium
кадр *m* [1] *cine.* frame, still; close-up
ка́др|овый [14] *mil.* regular; *рабо́чий* skilled; **~ы** *pl.* skilled workers; experienced personnel
кады́к *m* [1 *e.*] Adam's apple

каждодне́вный [14] daily
ка́ждый [14] every, each; *su.* everybody, everyone
ка́ж|ется, ~ущийся, → **каза́ться**
каза́к *m* [1 *e.*; *pl. a.* 1] Cossack
каза́рма *f* [5] *mil.* barracks *pl.*
каза́|ться [3], <по-> (Т) seem, appear, look; ***мне ка́жется*** (***~лось***), ***что ...*** it seems (seemed) to me that; ***он, ка́жется, прав*** he seems to be right; *тж.* apparently; ***ка́жущийся*** seeming; ***~лось бы*** one would think; it would seem
каза́х *m* [1], **~ский** [16] Kazak(h)
каза́|цкий [16], **~чий** [18] Cossack('s)...
каза́шка *f* [5; *g/pl.*: -шек] Kazak(h) woman
каз|ённый [14] *подхо́д и т. д.* formal; bureaucratic; *бана́льный* commonplace; ***на ~ённый счёт*** at public expense; **~на́** *f* [5] treasury, exchequer; **~наче́й** *m* [3] treasurer
казн|и́ть [13] (*im*)*pf.* execute, put to death; *impf. fig.* ***~и́ть себя́, -ся*** torment o.s. with remorse; **~ь** *f* [8] execution
кайма́ *f* [5; *g/pl.*: каём] border; hem
как how; as; like; what; since; *coll.* when, if; (+ *su.*, *adv.*) very (much), awfully; (+ *pf.*, *vb.*) suddenly; ***я ви́дела, как он шёл ...*** I saw him going ...; ***~ бу́дто, ~ бы*** as if, as it were; ***~ бы мне*** (+ *inf.*) how am I to ...; ***~ ни*** however; ***~ же!*** sure!; ***~*** (***же***) ***так?*** you don't say !; ***~ ..., так и ...*** both ... and ...; ***~ когда́*** *etc.* that depends; ***~ не*** (+ *inf.*) of course ...; ***~ мо́жно скоре́е*** (***лу́чше***) as soon as (in the best way) possible
кака́о *n* [*indecl.*] cocoa
ка́к-нибудь somehow (or other); anyhow; sometime
како́в [-ва́, -о́] how; what; what sort of; (such) as; ***~!*** just look (at him)!; ***~о́?*** what do you say?; **~о́й** [14] which
како́й [16] what, which; *тж.* how; such as; *coll.* any; that; ***ещё ~!*** and what ... (*su.*)!; ***како́е там!*** not at all!; ***~-либо, ~-нибудь*** any, some; *coll.* no more than, (only) about ***~-то*** some, a
ка́к-то *adv.* somehow; somewhat; *coll.* (*тж.* ***~ раз***) once, one day
каламбу́р *m* [1] pun
каланча́ *f* [5; *g/pl.*: -че́й] watchtower; *fig. coll. о челове́ке* beanpole
кала́ч *m* [1 *e.*] small (*padlock-shaped*) white loaf; ***тёртый ~*** *fig. coll.* cunning, fellow
кале́ка *m/f* [5] cripple
календа́рь *m* [4 *e.*] calendar
калёный [14] red-hot; *оре́хи* roasted
кале́чить [16], <ис-> cripple, maim
кали́бр *m* [1] caliber (-bre); *tech.* gauge
ка́лий *m* [3] potassium
кали́на *f* [5] snowball tree
кали́тка *f* [5; *g/pl.*: -ток] wicket-gate
кали́ть [13] **1.** <на-, рас-> heat *оре́хи*; roast; **2.** <за-> *tech.* temper
кало́рия *f* [7] calorie
ка́лька *f* [5; *g/pl.*: -лек] tracing paper; *fig. ling.* loan translation, calque
калькул|я́тор *m* [1] calculator; **~я́ция** *f* [7] calculation
кальсо́ны *f/pl.* [5] long underpants
ка́льций *m* [3] calcium
ка́мбала *f* [5] flounder
камен|е́ть [8], <о-> turn (in)to stone, petrify; **~и́стый** [14 *sh.*] stony; **~ноу́гольный** [14]: ***~ноу́гольный бассе́йн*** coalfield; **´~ный** [14] stone...; *fig.* stony; ***соль*** rock; ***´~ный у́голь*** coal; **~оло́мня** *f* [6; *g/pl.*: -мен] quarry; **´~щик** *m* [1] bricklayer; **´~ь** *m* [4; -мня; *from g/pl. e.*] stone; rock; *fig.* weight; ка́мнем like a stone; ***´~ь преткнове́ния*** stumbling block
ка́мер|а *f* [5] *тюре́мная*; cell; *tech.* chamber; *phot.* camera; *mot.* inner tube; ***~а хране́ния*** left luggage office; **~ный** [14] *mus.* chamber...
ками́н *m* [1] fireplace
камо́рка *f* [5; *g/pl.*: -pok] closet, small room
кампа́ния *f* [7] *mil.*, *pol.* campaign
камфара́ *f* [5] camphor
камы́ш *m* [1 *e.*], **~о́вый** [14] reed
кана́ва *f* [5] ditch; *сто́чная* gutter
кана́д|ец *m* [1; -ца], **~ка** [5; *g/pl.*: -ок], **~ский** [16] Canadian
кана́л *m* [1] canal; *radio, TV, fig.* channel; **~иза́ция** *f* [7] *городска́я* sewerage

канаре́йка *f* [5; *g/pl*.: -е́ек] canary
кана́т *m* [1], **~ный** [14] rope; cable
канва́ *f* [5] canvas; *fig*. basis; outline
кандида́т *m* [1] candidate; kandidat (*in former USSR, holder of postgraduate higher degree before doctorate*); **~у́ра** *f* [5] candidature
кани́кулы *f/pl*. [5] vacation, *Brt. a*. holidays (***на*** П, ***в*** В during)
канитéль *coll. f* [8] tedious and drawn-out procedure
канона́да *f* [5] cannonade
кано́э *n* [*indecl*.] canoe
кант *m* [1] edging, piping
кану́н *m* [1] eve
ка́нуть [20] *pf*.: ***как в во́ду ~*** disappear without trace; ***~ в ве́чность*** (***в Ле́ту***) sink into oblivion
канцеля́р|ия *f* [7] office; **~ский** [16] office...; ***~ские това́ры*** stationery
ка́нцлер *m* [1] chancellor
ка́п|ать [1 & 2], *once* <~нуть> [20] drip, drop, trickle; *дождь* fall; **~елька** [5; *g/pl*.: -лек] droplet; *sg. coll*. bit, grain
капита́л *m* [1] *fin*. capital; *акционе́рный* stock; *оборо́тный* working capital; **~и́зм** *m* [1] capitalism; **~и́ст** *m* [1] capitalist; **~исти́ческий** [16] capitalist(ic); **~овложе́ние** *n* [12] investment; **~ьный** [14] fundamental, main; ***~ьный ремо́нт*** major repairs
капита́н *m* [1] *naut*., *mil*., *sport* captain; *торго́вого су́дна* skipper
капитул|и́ровать *f* [7] (*im*)*pf*. capitulate; **~я́ция** *f* [7] capitulation
капка́н *m* [1] trap (*a. fig*.)
ка́пл|я *f* [6; *g/pl*.: -пель] drop; *sg. coll*. bit, grain; **~ями** drops by; ***как две ~и воды́*** as like as two peas
капо́т *m* [1] *mot*. hood, *Brt*. bonnet
капри́з *m* [1] whim, caprice; **~ничать** *coll*. [1] be capricious; *о ребёнке* play up; **~ный** [14; -зен, -зна] capricious, whimsical; wil(l)ful
ка́псула *f* [5] capsule
капу́ста *f* [5] cabbage; ***ки́слая ~*** sauerkraut; ***цветна́я ~*** cauliflower
капюшо́н *m* [1] hood
ка́ра *f* [5] punishment
караби́н *m* [1] carbine
кара́бкаться [1], <вс-> climb
карава́й *m* [3] (big) loaf
карава́н *m* [1] caravan; *корабле́й и т. д.* convoy
кара́емый [14 *sh*.] *law*. punishable
кара́куля *f* [6] *f* scribble
кара́кул|ь *m* [4], **~евый** [14] astrakhan
караме́ль *f* [8] caramel(s)
каран|да́ш *m* [1 *e*.] pencil; **~ти́н** *m* [1] quarantine
карапу́з *coll. m* [1] chubby tot
кара́сь *m* [4 *e*.] crucian
карате́ *n* [*indecl*.] karate
кара́|тельный [14] punitive; **~ть** [1], <по-> punish
карау́л *m* [1] sentry, guard; ***стоя́ть на ~е*** be on guard; *int*. **~!** help!; **~ить** [13], <по-> guard, watch (*coll*. ...out, for); **~ьный** [14] sentry... (*a. su*.); ***~ьное помеще́ние*** guardroom
карбу́нкул *m* [1] carbuncle
карбюра́тор *m* [1] carburet(t)or
каре́л *m* [1] Karelian; **~ка** [5; *g/pl*.: -ок] Karelian
каре́та *f* [5] *hist*. carriage, coach
ка́рий [15] (dark) brown
карикату́р|а *f* [5] caricature, cartoon; **~ный** [14] caricature...; [-рен, -рна] comic(al), funny
карка́с *m* [1] frame(work), skeleton
ка́рк|ать [1], *once* <-нуть> [20] croak (*coll., fig*.), caw
ка́рлик *m* [1] dwarf; **~овый** [14] dwarf...; dwarfish
карма́н *m* [1] pocket; ***э́то мне не по ~у*** *coll*. I can't afford that; ***э́то бьёт по ~у*** that costs a pretty penny; ***держи́ ~*** (***ши́ре***) that's a vain hope; ***она́ за сло́вом в ~е ле́зет*** she has a ready tongue; **~ный** [14] pocket...; ***~ный вор*** pickpocket
карнава́л *m* [1] carnival
карни́з *m* [1] cornice; *для што́р* curtain fixture
ка́рт|а *f* [5] map; *naut*. chart; (playing) card; ***ста́вить*** (***всё***) ***на ~у*** stake (have all one's eggs in one basket); **~а́вить** [14] mispronounce *Russ. r or l* (*esp. as uvular* r *or* u, v); **~ёжник** *m* [1] gambler (*at cards*)
карти́н|а *f* [5] picture (***на*** П in);

cine. movie; *art* painting; scene (*a. thea.*); **~ка** [5; *g/pl.*: -нок] (small) picture, illustration; **~ный** [14] picture...
картóн *m* [1] cardboard; **~ка** [5; *g/pl.*: -нок] (cardboard) box
картотéка *f* [5] card index
картóфель *m* [4] *collect.* potatoes *pl.*
кáрточ|ка *f* [5; *g/pl.*: -чек] card; *coll.* photo; season ticket; **~ный** [14] card(s)...; ***~ный дóмик*** house of cards
картóшка *coll. f* [5; *g/pl.*: -шек] potato(es)
карусéль *f* [8] merry-go-round
кáрцер *m* [1] cell, lockup
карьéр *m* [1] full gallop (at T); ***с мéста в ~*** at once; **~а** *f* [5] career; **~úст** *m* [1] careerist
касá|тельная *f* [14] *math.* tangent; **~ться** [1], <коснýться> [20] touch (*a. fig.*); concern; *coll.* be about, deal *or* be concerned with; ***дéло ~ется = дéло идёт о → идтú***; **что ~ется ...** as regards, as to
кáска *f* [5; *g/pl.*: -сок] helmet
каскáд *m* [1] cascade
каспúйский [16] Caspian
кáсса *f* [5] pay desk *or* office; (*a.* ***билéтная ~***) *rail.* ticket window, *Brt.* booking office; *thea.* box office; *дéньги* cash; *в магазúне* cash register; ***сберегáтельная ~*** savings bank
кассац|иóнный [14] → ***апелляциóнный***; **~ия** *law* [7] cassation
кассéт|а *f* [5], **~ный** [14] cassette
кассúр *m* [1], **~ша** *f* [5] cashier
кáста *f* [5] caste (*a. fig.*)
кастóровый [14] castor
кастрúровать [7] (*im*)*pf.* castrate
кастрюля *f* [6] saucepan; pot
катаклúзм *m* [1] cataclysm
катализáтор *m* [1] catalyst
каталóг *m* [1] catalogue
катáние *n* [10] driving, riding, skating, *etc.* (→ ***катáть***[***ся***])
катастрóф|а *f* [5] catastrophe; **~úческий** [16] catastrophic
катáть [1] roll (*a. tech.*); <по-> (take for a) drive, ride, row, *etc.*; **-ся** (go for a) drive, ride (*a. верхóм, etc.*), row (*на лóдке*); skate (*на конькáх*); sled(ge) (*на санях*), *etc.*; roll

катег|орúческий [16], **~орúчный** [14; -чен, -чна] categorical; **~óрия** *f* [7] category
кáтер *m* [1; *pl., etc. e.*] *naut.* cutter; ***моторный ~*** motor-launch
катúть [15], <по-> roll, wheel (*v/i* **-ся**; sweep; *слёзы* flow; *вóлны* roll; → ***катáться***)
катóк *m* [1; -тка] (skating) rink
катóл|ик *m* [1], **~úчка** *f* [5; *g/pl.*: -чек], **~úческий** [16] (Roman) Catholic
кáтор|га *f* [5] penal servitude, hard labo(u)r; *fig.* very hard work, drudgery; **~жный** [14] hard, arduous
катýшка *f* [5; *g/pl.*: -шек] spool; *el.* coil
каучýк *m* [1] caoutchouc, india rubber
кафé *n* [*indecl.*] café
кáфедра *f* [5] *в цéркви* pulpit; department (*of English, etc.*); *univ.* chair
кáфель *m* [4] (Dutch) tile
качá|лка *f* [5; *g/pl.*: -лок] rocking chair; **~ние** *n* [12] rocking; swing(ing); *нéфти, воды* pumping; **~ть** [1] **1.** <по->, *once* <качнýть> [20] rock; swing; shake (*a.* one's head ***головóй***), toss; *naut.* roll, pitch; (**-ся** *v/i.*; stagger, lurch); **2.** <на-> pump
качéли *f/pl.* [8] swing; seesaw
кáчеств|енный [14] qualitative; high-quality; **~о** *n* [9] quality; **в ~е** (P) in one's capacity as, in the capacity of
кáч|ка *f* [5] rolling *naut.* (***бортовáя*** *or* ***боковáя ~ка***); pitching (***килевáя ~ка***); **~нýть(ся)** → ***~áть(ся)***
кáш|а *f* [5] ***грéчневая ~а*** buckwheat gruel; ***мáнная ~а*** semolina; ***овсяная ~а*** porridge; ***рúсовая ~а*** boiled rice; *coll. fig.* mess, jumble; ***заварúть ~у*** stir up trouble
кашалóт *m* [1] sperm whale
кáш|ель *m* [4; -шля], **~лять** [28], *once* <~лянуть> [20] cough
каштáн *m* [1], **~овый** [14] chestnut
каюта *f* [5] *naut.* cabin, stateroom
кáяться [27], <по-> (**в** П) repent
квадрáт *m* [1], **~ный** [14] square
квáк|ать [1], *once* <~нуть> [20] croak

квалифи|ка́ция *f* [7] qualification(s); **~ци́рованный** [14] qualified, competent; *рабо́чий* skilled, trained

кварта́л *m* [1] quarter (= 3 months); block, *coll.* building (*betw. 2 cross streets*); **~ьный** [14] quarter(ly)

кварти́р|а *f* [5] apartment, *Brt.* flat; ***двухко́мнатная ~а*** two-room apt./flat; **~а́нт** *m* [1], **~а́нтка** *f* [5; *g/pl.*: -ток] lodger; **~ный** [14] housing, house-...; ***~ная пла́та*** = **квартпла́та** *f* [5] rent; **~осъёмщик** *m* [1] tenant

квас *m* [1; -а, -у; *pl. e.*] kvass (*Russ. drink*); **~́ить** [15], <за-> sour

ква́шеный [14] sour, fermented

кве́рху up, upward(s)

квит|а́нция *f* [7] receipt; ***бага́жная ~а́нция*** (luggage) ticket; **~́(ы)** *coll.* quits, even, square

кво́рум *m* [1] *parl.* quorum

кво́та *f* [5] quota, share

кедр *m* [1] cedar; ***сиби́рский ~*** Siberian pine; **~о́вый** [14]: ***~о́вый оре́х*** cedar nut

кекс *m* [1] cake

келе́йно privately; in camera

кельт *m* [1] Celt; **~́ский** [16] Celtic

ке́лья *f* [6] *eccl.* cell

кем T → ***кто***

ке́мпинг *m* [1] campsite

кенгуру́ *m* [*indecl.*] kangaroo

ке́пка *f* [5; *g/pl.*: -ок] (peaked) cap

кера́м|ика *f* [5] ceramics; **~и́ческий** [16] ceramic

кероси́н *m* [1], **~овый** [14] kerosene

кета́ *f* [5] Siberian salmon

кефа́ль *f* [8] grey mullet

кефи́р *m* [1] kefir

киберне́тика *f* [5] cybernetics

кив|а́ть [1], *once* <~ну́ть> [20] nod; point (to ***на*** В); **~о́к** [1; -вка́] nod

кида́|ть(ся) [1], *once* <ки́нуть(ся)> [20] → ***броса́ть(ся)***; ***меня́ ~ет в жар и хо́лод*** I'm hot and cold all over

киев|ля́нин *m* [1; *pl.*: -я́не, -я́н], **~ля́нка** *f* [5; *g/pl.*: -но́к] person from Kiev; **~ский** [16] Kiev...

кий *m* [3; кия́; *pl.*: кии́, киёв] cue

кило́ *n* [*indecl.*] → ***~гра́мм***; **~ва́тт (-ча́с)** *m* [1; *g/pl.*] kilowatt(-hour); **~гра́мм** *m* [1] kilogram(me); **~ме́тр** *m* [1] kilometer (*Brt.* -tre)

киль *m* [4] keel; **~ва́тер** (-tɛr) *m* [1] wake

ки́лька *f* [5; *g/pl.*: -лек] sprat

кинемато́гр|аф *m* [1], **~а́фия** *f* [7] cinematography

кинеско́п *m* [1] television tube

кинжа́л *m* [1] dagger

кино́ *n* [*indecl.*] movie, motion picture, *Brt.* the pictures, cinema (**в** В/П to/at); *coll.* screen, film; **~актёр** *m* [1] screen (*or* film) actor; **~актри́са** *f* [5] screen (*or* film) actress; **~журна́л** *m* [1] newsreel; **~звезда́** *coll.* *f* [5; *pl.* -звёзды] filmstar; **~карти́на** *f* [5] film; **~ле́нта** *f* [5] reel, film (copy); **~опера́тор** *m* [1] cameraman; **~плёнка** *f* [5; *g/pl.*: -нок] film (strip); **~режиссёр** *m* [1] film director; **~сеа́нс** *m* [1] show, performance; **~сту́дия** *f* [7] film studio; **~сцена́рий** *m* [3] scenario; **~съёмка** *f* [5 *g/pl.*: -мок] shooting (*of a film*), filming; **~теа́тр** *m* [1] movie theater, cinema; **~хро́ника** *f* [5] newsreel

ки́нуть(ся) → ***кида́ть(ся)***

кио́ск *m* [1] kiosk, stand; ***газе́тый ~*** newsstand

ки́па *f* [5] pile, stack; *това́ров* bale, pack

кипари́с *m* [1] cypress

кипе́|ние *n* [12] boiling; ***то́чка ~ния*** boiling point; **~ть** [10 *e.*; -плю́, -пи́шь], <за-, вс-> boil; *от возмуще́ния* seethe; be in full swing (*о рабо́те и т. д.*)

кипу́ч|ий [17 *sh.*] *жизнь* busy, lively, vigorous, exuberant, vehement, seething; *де́ятельность* tireless

кипят|и́льник *m* [1] boiler; **~и́ть** [15 *e.*; -ячу́, -яти́шь], <вс-> boil (up; *v/i.* **-ся**); *coll.* be(come) excited; **~о́к** *m* [1; -тка́] boiling (hot) water

кирги́з *m* [1], **~ский** [16] Kirghiz

кири́ллица *f* [5] Cyrillic alphabet

кирка́ *f* [5; *g/pl.*; -рок] pick(ax[e])

кирпи́ч *m* [1 *e.*], **~ный** [14] brick

кисе́ль *m* [4 *e.*] (kind of) blancmange

кисл|ова́тый [14 *sh.*] sourish; **~оро́д** *m* [1] oxygen; **~ота́** [5; *pl. st.*: -о́ты] sourness, acidity; **~о́тный**

К

[14] acid; **~́ый** [14; -сел, -сла́, -о] sour, acid...

ки́снуть [21], <с-, про-> turn sour; *coll. fig.* mope

ки́ст|очка *f* [5; *g/pl.*: -чек] brush; *dim. of* **~ь** *f* [8; *from g/pl. e.*] brush; *виногра́да* cluster, bunch; *руки́* hand

кит *m* [1 *e.*] whale

кита́|ец *m* [1; -тайца] Chinese; **~йский** [16] Chinese; **~я́нка** *f* [5; *g/pl.*: -нок] Chinese

ки́тель *m* [4; *pl.* -ля, *etc. e.*] *mil.* jacket

кич|и́ться [16 *e*; -чу́сь, -чи́шься] put on airs; *хва́статься* boast (of T); **~ли́вый** [14 *sh.*] haughty, conceited

кише́ть [киши́т] teem, swarm (with T; *тж.* ***кишмя́ ~***)

киш|е́чник [1] bowels, intestines *pl.*; **~е́чный** [14] intestinal, enteric; **~ка́** *f* [5; *g/pl.*: -о́к] intestine (small ***то́нкая***, large ***то́лстая***), gut; *pl. coll.* bowels; *для воды́* hose

клавиату́ра *f* [5] keyboard (*тж. tech.*)

кла́виш *m* [1], **~а** *f* [5] *mus.*, *tech.* key

клад *m* [1] treasure (*a. fig.*); **~́бище** *n* [11] cemetery; **~́ка** *f* [5] laying, (*brick-*, *stone*)work; **~ова́я** *f* [14] *в доме* pantry, larder; stock- *or* storeroom; **~овщи́к** *m* [1 *e.*] storekeeper

кла́ня|ться [28], <поклони́ться> [13; -оню́сь, -о́нишься] (Д) bow (to); *old use* *приве́тствовать* greet

кла́пан *m* [1] *tech.* valve; *на оде́жде* flap

класс *m* [1] class; *шко́лы* grade, *Brt.* form; classroom; **~́ик** *m* [1] classic; **~ифици́ровать** [7] *(im)pf.* class(ify); **~и́ческий** [16] classic(al); **~́ный** [14] class; *coll.* classy; **~́овый** [14] *pol. soc.* class

класть [кладу́, -дёшь; клал] **1.** <положи́ть> [16] (***в***, ***на***, *etc.*, B) put, lay (down, on, *etc.*); *в банк* deposit; ***в осно́ву*** (***в*** B take as basis); ***положи́ть коне́ц*** put an end (to Д); ***положи́ть под сукно́*** shelve; **2.** <сложи́ть> [16] *ору́жие* lay (down)

клева́ть [6 *e.*; клюю́, клюёшь], *once* <клю́нуть> [20] peck, pick; *о ры́бе* bite; ***~ но́сом*** *coll.* nod

кле́вер *m* [1] clover, trefoil

клевет|а́ *f* [5], **~а́ть** [3; -вещу́, -ве́щешь], <о-> *v/t.*, <на-> (***на*** B) slander; **~ни́к** *m* [1 *e.*] slanderer; **~ни́ческий** 16] slanderous

клеёнка *f* [5] oilcloth

кле́|ить [13], <с-> glue, paste; **-ся** stick; *coll.* work, get on *or* along; **~й** *m* [3; на клею́] glue, paste; **~йкий** [16; кле́ек, кле́йка] sticky, adhesive

клейм|и́ть [14 *e.*; -млю́, -ми́шь], <за-> brand; *fig. a.* stigmatize; **~о́** *n* [9; *pl. st.*] brand; *fig.* stigma, stain; ***фабри́чное ~о́*** trademark

клён *m* [1] maple

клепа́ть [1], <за-> rivet

клёпка *f* [5; *g/pl.*: -пок] riveting

кле́т|ка *f* [5; *g/pl.*: -ток] cage; square, check; *biol.* (*a.* **~очка**) cell; ***в ~(оч)ку*** check(er)ed; *Brt.* chequered; ***грудна́я ~ка*** thorax; **~ча́тка** *f* [5] cellulose; **~чатый** [14] checkered (*Brt.* chequered)

кле|шня́ *f* [6; *g/pl.*: -не́й] claw; **~щ** *m* [1; *g/pl.*: -ще́й] tick; **~́щи́** *f/pl.* [5; *gen.*: -ще́й, *etc. e.*] pincers

клие́нт *m* [1] client; **~у́ра** *f* [5] *collect.* clientele

кли́зма *f* [5] enema

кли́ка *f* [5] clique

кли́макс *m* [1] climacteric, menopause

кли́мат *m* [1] climate; **~и́ческий** [16] climatic

клин *m* [3; *pl.*: кли́нья, -ьев] wedge; gusset; **~́ом** (*борода́ и т. д.*) pointed; ***свет не ~́ом сошёлся*** the world is large; there is always a way out

кли́ника *f* [5] clinic

клино́к *m* [1; -нка] blade

кли́ренс *m* [1] *tech.* clearance

кли́ринг *m* [1] *fin.* clearing

клич *m* [1] call; cry; **~́ка** *f* [5; *g/pl.*: -чек] *живо́тного* name; (*про́звище*) nickname

клише́ *n* [*indecl.*] cliché (*a. fig.*)

клок *m* [1 *e. pl.*: -о́чья, -ьев; клоки́, -ко́в] *воло́с* tuft; shred, rag, tatter

клокота́ть [3] seethe (*тж. fig.*), bubble

клон|и́ть [13; -оню́, -о́нишь], <на-,

с-> bend, bow; *fig.* incline; drive (*or* aim) at (**к** Д); ***меня́ ~ит ко сну*** I am nodding off; (**-ся** *v/i.*; *a.* decline; approach)
клоп *m* [1 *e.*] bedbug
кло́ун *m* [1] clown
клочо́к *m* [1; -чка] *бума́ги* scrap; *земли́* patch
клуб[1] *m* [1; *pl. e.*] *ды́ма* cloud, puff; *a.* **~ок**; **~**[2] *m* [1] club(house); **~ень** *m* [4; -бня] tuber, bulb; **~и́ться** [14 *e.*; *3rd p. only*] *дым* wreathe, puff (up); *пыль* whirl
клубни́ка *f* [5] (*cultivated*) strawberry, -ries *pl.*
клубо́к *m* [1; -бка́] *ше́рсти* ball; *противоре́чий* tangle
клу́мба *f* [5] (flower) bed
клык *m* [1 *e.*] *моржа́* tusk; *челове́ка* canine (tooth); *живо́тного* fang
клюв *m* [1] beak, bill
клю́ква *f* [5] cranberry, -ries *pl.*; ***разве́систая ~*** *mythology* s.th. improbable, nonsensical
клю́нуть → ***клева́ть***
ключ *m* [1 *e.*] key (*a. fig.*, clue); *tech.* [***га́ечный ~***] = wrench, spanner; *mus.* clef; (*родни́к*) spring; **~и́ца** *f* [5] clavicle, collarbone
клю́шка *f* [5; *g/pl.*: -шек] (golf) club; (hockey) stick
кля́нчить *coll.* [16] beg for
кляп *m* [1] gag
кля|сть [-яну́, -нёшь, -ял, -а́, -о] → ***проклина́ть***; **-ся** <покля́сться> swear (***в*** П s.th.; Т by); **~тва** *f* [5] oath; ***дать ~тву***; (*or* ***~твенное обеща́ние***) take an oath, swear
кля́уза *f* [5] intrigue; cavil; slander
кля́ча *f* [5] *pej.* (*horse*) jade
кни́г|а *f* [5] book; **~опеча́тание** *n* [12] (book-)printing, typography; **~охрани́лище** *n* [11] book depository; library
кни́ж|ка *f* [5; *g/pl.*: -жек] book(let); *записна́я* notebook; *че́ковая* check (*Brt.* cheque)book; ***сберега́тельная ~ка*** savings bank book; **~ный** [14] book...; *о сло́ве* bookish; **~о́нка** *f* [5; *g/pl.*: -нок] trashy book
кни́зу down, downward(s)
кно́пк|а *f* [5; *g/pl.*: -пок] thumbtack, *Brt.* drawing pin; *el.* (push) button; (snap), fastener; ***нажа́ть на все ~и*** *fig.* pull all wires
кнут *m* [1 *e.*] whip
кня|ги́ня *f* [6] princess (*prince's consort*); **~жна́** *f* [5; *g/pl.*: -жо́н]) princess (*prince's unmarried daughter*); **~зь** *m* [4; *pl.*: -зья́; -зе́й] prince; ***вели́кий ~зь*** grand duke
коа|лицио́нный [14] coalition...; **~ли́ция** *f* [7] coalition
кобе́ль *m* [4 *e.*] (male) dog
кобура́ *f* [5] holster
кобы́ла *f* [5] mare; *sport* horse
ко́ваный [14] wrought (*iron.*)
кова́р|ный [14; -рен, -рна] crafty, guileful, insidious; **~ство** *n* [9] craftiness, guile, wile
кова́ть [7 *e.*; кую́, куёшь] **1.** <вы́-> forge; **2.** <под-> shoe (*horse*)
ковёр *m* [1; -вра́] carpet, rug
кове́ркать [1], <ис-> distort; *сло-ва́* mispronounce; *жизнь* spoil, ruin
коври́жка *f* [5; *g/pl.*: -жек] gingerbread
ковче́г *m* [1]: ***Но́ев ~*** Noah's Ark
ковш *m* [1 *e.*] scoop; *землечерпа́лки* bucket
ковы́ль *m* [4 *e.*] feather grass
ковыля́ть [28] hobble; *о ребёнке* toddle
ковыря́ть [28], <по-> pick, poke
когда́ when; while, as; *coll.* if; ever; sometimes; → ***ни***; **~ *как*** it depends; **~-либо**; **~-нибудь** (at) some time (or other), one day; *interr.* ever; **~-то** once, one day, sometime
ко́|готь *m* [4; -гтя; *from g/pl. e.*] claw
код *m* [1], **~и́ровать** [7], <за-> code
ко́е-где́ here and there, in some places; **~-ка́к** anyhow, somehow; with (great) difficulty; **~-како́й** [16] some; any; **~-когда́** off and on; **~-кто́** [23] some(body); **~-куда́** here and there, (in)to some place(s), somewhere; **~-что́** [23] something; a little
ко́ж|а *f* [5] skin; *материа́л* leather; ***из ~и*** (***во́н***) ***лезть*** *coll.* do one's utmost; ***~а да ко́сти*** skin and bone; **~аный** [14] leather...; **~и́ца** *f* [5] skin, peel; rind; (*a.* **~ура́** *f* [5]); cuticle

коз|а́ *f* [5; *pl. st.*] (she-)goat; **~ёл** [1; -зла́] (he-)goat; ***~ёл отпуще́ния*** scapegoat; **~ий** [18] goat...; **~лёнок** *m* [2] kid; **~лы** *f/pl.* [5; *gen.*: -зел] *для пи́лки* trestle

ко́зни *f/pl.* [8] intrigues, plots

коз|ырёк *m* [1; -рька́] peak (*of cap*); **~ырь** *m* [4; *from g/pl. e.*] trump; **~ыря́ть** *coll.* [28], *once* <~ырну́ть> [20] (*хва́статься*) boast

ко́йка *f* [5; *g/pl.*: ко́ек] bed, bunk-bed; *naut.* berth

коке́т|ка *f* [5; *g/pl.*: -ток] coquette; **~ливый** [14 *sh.*] coquettish; **~ничать** [1] flirt (with); **~ство** *n* [9] coquetry

коклю́ш *m* [1] whooping cough

ко́кон *m* [1] cocoon

кок|о́с *m* [1] coco; *пло́д* coconut; **~о́совый** [14] coco(nut)...

кокс *m* [1] coke

К

кол 1. [1 *e.*; ко́лья, -ев] stake, picket; **2.** [*pl.* 1 *e.*] ***ни ~а́ ни двора́*** neither house nor home

колбаса́ *f* [5; *pl. st.*: -а́сы] sausage

колго́тки *f* [5; *g/pl.*: -ток] *pl.* panty hose, *Brt.* tights *pl.*

колдо́бина *f* [5] rut, pothole

колд|ова́ть [7] practice (-ise) witchcraft; conjure; **~овство́** *n* [9] magic, sorcery; **~у́н** *m* [1 *e.*] sorcerer, wizard; **~у́нья** *f* [6] sorceress, witch, enchantress

колеб|а́ние *n* [12] oscillation; vibration; *fig.* (*сомне́ние*) hesitation; (*a. comm.*) fluctuation; **~а́ть** [2 *st.*: -е́блю, *etc.*; -е́бли(те); -е́бля], <по->, *once* <~ну́ть> [20] shake (*a. fig.*); **-ся** shake; (*a. comm.*) fluctuate; waver, hesitate; oscillate, vibrate

коле́н|о *n* [*sg.*: 9; *pl.*: 4] knee; ***стать на ~и*** kneel; ***по ~и*** knee-deep; ***ему́ мо́ре по ~о*** he doesn't care a damn; [*pl.*: -нья, -ев; *pl. a.* 9] *tech.* bend, crank; **~чатый** [14] *tech. вал* crank (shaft)

колес|и́ть *coll.* [15 *e.*; -ешу́, -еси́шь] travel about, rove; **~ница** *f* [5] chariot; **~о́** *n* [9; *pl. st.*: -лёса] wheel; ***кружи́ться, как бе́лка в ~е́*** run round in circles; ***вставля́ть кому́-нибудь па́лки в колёса*** put a spoke in a p.'s wheel

коле|я́ *f* [6; *g/pl.*: -ле́й] rut, (*a. rail*) track (*both a. fig.*); ***вы́битый из ~и́*** unsettled

коли́бри *m/f* [*indecl.*] hummingbird

ко́лики *f/pl.*[5] colic

коли́честв|енный [14] quantitative; *gr.* cardinal (*number*); **~о** *n* [9] quantity; number; amount

ко́лка *f* [5] splitting, chopping

ко́лк|ий [16; ко́лок, колка́, ~о] prickly; *fig.* biting; **~ость** *f* [8] sharpness

колле́г|а *m/f* [5] colleague; **~ия** *f* [7] board, collegium; ***~ия адвока́тов*** the Bar

коллекти́в *m* [1] group, body; **~иза́ция** *f* [7] *hist.* collectivization; **~ный** [14] collective, joint

коллек|ционе́р *m* [1] collector; **~ция** [7] collection

коло́д|а *f* [5] block; *карт* pack, deck; **~ец** [1; -дца] well; **~ка** *f* [5; *g/pl.*: -док] last; *tech.* (*brake*) shoe

ко́локол *m* [1; *pl.*: -ла́, *etc. e.*] bell; **~о́льня** *f* [6; *g/pl.*: -лен] bell tower, belfry; **~о́льчик** *m* [1] (little) bell; *bot.* bluebell

коло́ния *f* [7] colony

коло́н|ка *f* [5; *g/pl.*: -нок] *typ.* column; (*apparatus*) water heater, *Brt.* geyser; *a. dim. of* **~на** *f* [5] column (*arch. a.* pillar)

колори́т *m* [1] colo(u)ring; colo(u)r; **~ный** [14; -тен, -тна] colo(u)rful, picturesque

ко́лос *m* [1; *pl.*: -ло́сья, -ьев], (*agric.*) ear, spike; **~и́ться** [15 *e.*; 3rd *p. only*] form ears

колосса́льный [14; -лен, льна] colossal, fantastic

колоти́ть [15] knock (**в** В, ***по*** Д at, on)

коло́ть [17] **1.** <рас-> split, cleave; *оре́хи* crack; **2.** <на-> (Р) chop; **3.** <у->, *once* <кольну́ть> [20] prick; *fig. coll.* taunt; **4.** <за-> stab; *живо́тное* kill, slaughter (*animals*); *impers.* have a stitch in one's side

колпа́к *m* [1 *e.*] cap; shade; bell glass

колхо́з *m* [1] collective farm, kolkhoz; **~ный** [14] kolkhoz...; **~ник** *m* [1], **~ница** *f* [5] collective farmer

колыбе́ль *f* [8] cradle; **~ный** [14]: ***~ная*** (***пе́сня***) *f* lullaby

колых|а́ть [3 *st.*: -ы́шу, *etc.*, *or* 1], <вс->, *once* <~ну́ть> [20] sway, swing; *ли́стья* stir; *пла́мя* flicker; **-ся** *v/i.*

ко́лышек *m* [1; -шка] peg

кольну́ть → ***коло́ть*** *3. & impers.*

коль|цево́й [14] ring...; circular; **~цо́** *n* [9; *pl. st., gen.*: коле́ц] ring; circle; ***обруча́льное ~цо́*** wedding ring; *hist.* **~чу́га** *f* [5] shirt of mail

колю́ч|ий [17 *sh.*] thorny, prickly; *про́волока* barbed; *fig.* → ***ко́лкий***; **~ка** *f* [5; *g/pl.*: -чек] thorn, prickle; barb

коля́ска *f* [5; *g/pl.*: -сок] *мотоци́кла* side-car; *де́тская* baby carriage, *Brt.* pram; *инвали́дная* wheelchair

ком *m* [1; *pl.*: ко́мья, -ьев] lump, clod

кома́нда *f* [5] command, order; *naut.* crew; *sport* team; ***пожа́рная ~*** fire brigade

команди́р *m* [1] commander; **~ова́ть** [7] *(im)pf.*, *a.* <от-> send (on a mission); **~о́вка** *f* [5; *g/pl.*: -вок] business trip; ***она́ в ~о́вке*** she is away on business

кома́нд|ный [14] command(ing); **~ование** *n* [12] command; **~овать** [7] ([***над***] T) command (*a.* [give] order[s], <с->); *coll.* order about **~ующий** [17] (T) commander

кома́р *m* [1 *e.*] mosquito, gnat

комба́йн *m* [1] *agric.* combine

комбин|а́т *m* [1] industrial complex; group of complementary enterprises; ***~ат бытово́го обслу́живания*** multiple (consumer-)services establishment; **~а́ция** *f* [7] combination; *econ.* merger; **~и́ровать** [7], <с-> combine

коме́дия *f* [7] comedy; farce

коменда́|нт *m* [1] *mil.* commandant; superintendent; *общежи́тия* warden; **~нтский** [16]: ***~нтский час*** curfew; **~ту́ра** *f* [5] commandant's office

коме́та *f* [5] comet

ком|и́зм *m* [1] comic side; **~ик** *m* [1] comedian, comic (actor)

комисса́р *m* [1] commissar; commissioner; **~иа́т** *m* [1] commissariat

коми|ссио́нный [14] commission (*a. comm.*; *pl. su.* = sum); **~ссия** *f* [7] commission (*a. comm.*), committee; **~те́т** *m* [1] committee

коми́ч|еский [16], **~ный** [14; -чен, -чна] comic(al), funny

ко́мкать [1], <ис-, с-> crumple

коммент|а́рий *m* [3] comment(ary); **~а́тор** *m* [1] commentator; **~и́ровать** [7] *(im)pf.* comment (on)

коммер|са́нт *m* [1] merchant; businessman; **~ческий** [16] commercial

комму́н|а *f* [5] commune; **~а́льный** [14] communal; municipal; ***~а́льная кварти́ра*** (*coll.* ***~а́лка***) communal flat; **~и́зм** *m* [1] communism; **~ика́ция** *f* [7] communication (*pl. mil.*); **~и́ст** *m* [1], **~и́стка** *f* [5; *g/pl.*: -ток], **~исти́ческий** [14] communist

коммута́тор *m* [1] *el.* switchboard

ко́мнат|а *f* [5] room; **~ный** [14] room...; *bot.* house...

комо́к *m* [1; -мка́] lump, clod

компа́н|ия *f* [7] company (*a. comm*); ***води́ть ~ию с*** (T) associate with; **~ьо́н** *m* [1] *comm.* partner; companion

компа́ртия *f* [7] Communist Party

ко́мпас *m* [1] compass

компенс|а́ция *f* [7] compensation; **~и́ровать** [7] *(im)pf.* compensate

компете́н|тный [14; -тен, -тна] competent; **~ция** [7] competence; scope

ко́мплек|с *m* [1], **~сный** [14] complex; **~т** *m* [1] (complete) set; **~тный** [14], **~това́ть** [7], <у-> complete

комплиме́нт *m* [1] compliment

компози́тор *m* [1] *mus.* composer

компости́ровать [7], <про-> punch

компо́т *m* [1] compote, stewed fruit

компре́сс *m* [1] compress

компром|ети́ровать [7], <с->, **~и́сс** *m* [1] compromise (*v/i. a.* ***идти́ на ~и́сс***)

компью́тер *m* [1] computer

комсомо́л *m* [1] *hist.* Komsomol (Young Communist League); **~ец** *m* [1; -льца], **~ка** *f* [5; *g/pl.*: -лок], **~ьский** [16] Komsomol

комфо́рт *m* [1] comfort, convenience; **~а́бельный** [14; -лен, -льна] comfortable, convenient
конве́йер *m* [1] (belt) conveyor; assembly line
конве́нция *f* [7] convention, agreement
конве́рсия *f* [7] *econ.* conversion
конве́рт *m* [1] envelope
конв|ои́р *m* [1], **~ои́ровать** [7], **~о́й** *m* [3], **~о́йный** [14] convoy, escort
конгре́сс *m* [1] congress
конденс|а́тор (-dɛ-) *m* [1] ***па́ра*** condenser; *el.* capacitor; **~и́ровать** [7] (*im*)*pf.* condense; evaporate (*milk*)
конди́тер|ская *f* [16]: ***~ский мага́зин*** confectioner's shop; ***~ские изде́лия*** *pl.* confectionery
кондиционе́р *m* [1] air conditioner
конево́дство *n* [9] horse-breeding
конёк *m* [1; -нька́] skate; *coll.* hobby
кон|е́ц *m* [1; -нца́] end; close; point; *naut.* rope; ***без ~ца́*** endless(ly); ***в ~е́ц*** (***до ~ца́***) completely; ***в ~це́*** (P) at the end of; ***в ~це́ ~цо́в*** at long last; ***в оди́н ~е́ц*** one way; ***в о́ба ~ца́*** there and back; ***на худо́й ~е́ц*** at (the) worst; ***под ~е́ц*** in the end; ***тре́тий с ~ца́*** last but two
коне́чно (-ʃnə-) of course, certainly
коне́чности *f/pl.* [8] extremities
коне́чн|ый [14; -чен, -чна] *philos.*, *math.* finite; final, terminal; ***цель и т. д.*** ultimate
конкре́тный [14; -тен, -тна] concrete, specific
конкур|е́нт *m* [1] competitor; rival; **~ентноспосо́бный** [14; -бен, -бна] competitive; **~е́нция** *coll.* *f* [7] competition; **~и́ровать** [7] compete; **´~с** *m* [1] competition
ко́нн|ица *f* [5] *hist.* cavalry; **~ый** [14] horse...; (of) cavalry
конопля́ *f* [6] hemp; **~ный** [14] hempen
коносаме́нт *m* [1] bill of lading
консерв|ати́вный [14; -вен, -вна] conservative; **~ато́рия** *f* [7] conservatory, *Brt.* school of music, conservatoire; **~и́ровать** [7] (*im*)*pf.*, *a.* <за-> conserve, preserve; can, *Brt.* tin; **´~ный** [14], **´~ы** *m/pl.* [1] canned (*Brt.* tinned) food
ко́нский [16] horse (*hair*, *etc.*)
консолида́ция *f* [7] consolidation
конспе́кт *m* [1] summary, abstract; synopsis; notes made at a lecture; **~и́ровать** [7] make an abstract (of P); make notes at a lecture
конспир|ати́вный [14; -вен, -вна] secret; **~а́ция** *f* [7], conspiracy
конст|ати́ровать [7] (*im*)*pf.* establish, ascertain; **~иту́ция** *f* [7] constitution
констр|уи́ровать [7] (*im*)*pf.* *a.* <с-> design; **~укти́вный** [14; -вен, -вна] constructive; **~у́ктор** *m* [1] designer; constructor; **~у́кция** *f* [7] design; construction, structure
ко́нсул *m* [1] consul; **~ьский** [16] consular; **~ьство** *n* [9] consulate; **~ьта́ция** *f* [7] consultation; advice; ***юриди́ческая консульта́ция*** legal advice office; **~ьти́ровать** [7], <про-> advise; **~ся** consult (with **с** T)
конта́кт *m* [1] contact; **~ный** [14] *tech.* contact...; [-тен, -тна] *coll.* sociable
континге́нт *m* [1] quota, contingent
контине́нт *m* [1] continent
конто́ра *f* [5] office
контраба́нд|а *f* [5] contraband, smuggling; ***занима́ться ~ой*** smuggle; **~и́ст** *m* [1] smuggler
контр|аге́нт *m* [1] contractor; **~адмира́л** *m* [1] rear admiral
контра́кт *m* [1] contract
контра́льто *n* [9] contralto
контра́ст *m* [1], **~и́ровать** [7] contrast
контрата́ка *f* [5] counterattack
контрибу́ция *f* [7] contribution
контрол|ёр *m* [1] inspector (*rail. a.* ticket collector); **~и́ровать** [7], <про-> control, check; **´~ь** *m* [4] control, checking; **´~ьный** [14] control..., check...; ***´~ьная рабо́та*** test (*in school*, *etc.*)
контр|разве́дка *f* [5] counterespionage, counterintelligence; **~револю́ция** *f* [7] counterrevolution
конту́з|ить [15] *pf.*; **~ия** *f* [7] contusion; shell-shock

ко́нтур *m* [1] contour, outline
конура́ *f* [5] kennel
ко́нус *m* [1] cone; **~ообра́зный** [14; -зен, -зна] conic(al)
конфедера|ти́вный [14] confederative; **~ция** *f* [7] confederation
конфере́нция *f* [7] conference (at ***на*** П)
конфе́та *f* [5] candy, *Brt.* sweet(s)
конфи|денциа́льный [14; -лен, -льна] confidential; **~скова́ть** [7] (*im*)*pf.* confiscate
конфли́кт *m* [1] conflict
конфу́з|ить [15], <с-> (**-ся** be- [come]) embarrass(ed), confuse(d); **~ливый** *coll.* [14 *sh.*] bashful, shy
конц|ентра́т *m* [1] concentrated product; **~ентрацио́нный** [14] *coll.*, → **~ла́герь**; **~ентри́ровать** [7], <с-> concentrate(**-ся** *v/i.*); **~е́рт** *m* [1] concert (**на** П at); *mus.* concerto; **~ла́герь** *m* [4] concentration camp
конч|а́ть [1], <~ить> [16] finish, end, (**-ся** *v/i.*); *univ.*, *etc.* graduate from; **-ся** *срок* terminate, expire; **~ено!** enough!; **~ик** *m* [1] tip; point; **~и́на** *f* [5] decease
коньюнкту́р|а *f* [5] *comm.* state of the market; **~щик** *m* [1] timeserver
конь *m* [4 *e.*; *nom/pl. st.*] horse; *poet.* steed; *chess* knight; **~ки́** *m/pl.* [1] (***ро́ликовые*** roller) skates; **~кобе́жец** *m* [1; -жца] skater; **~кобе́жный** [14] skating
конья́к *m* [1 *e.*; *part.g.*: -у́] cognac
ко́н|юх *m* [1] groom; **~ю́шня** *f* [6; *g/pl.*: -шен] stable
коопер|ати́в *m* [1] cooperative (store, society); **~а́ция** *f* [7] cooperation; ***потреби́тельская ~а́ция*** consumers' society
координа́ты *f/pl.* [5] *math.* coordinates; *coll.* particulars for making contact (*address*, *telephone and fax numbers etc.*)
координи́ровать [7] (*im*)*pf.* coordinate
копа́ть [1], <вы́-> dig (up); **-ся** *impf.* dig, root; *в веща́х* rummage (about); *в саду́ и т. д.* putter about; (*ме́дленно де́лать*) dawdle
копе́йка *f* [5; *g/pl.*: -е́ек] kopeck
копи́лка *f* [5; *g/pl.*: -лок] money box
копир|ова́льный [14]: ***~ова́льная бума́га*** *f* (*coll.* **~ка**) carbon paper; **~ова́ть** [7], <с-> copy; **~о́вщик** *m* [1] copyist
копи́ть [14], <на-> accumulate, save; store up
ко́п|ия *f* [7] copy (*vb.* ***снять ~ию с*** Р); **~на́** *f* [5; *pl.*: ко́пны, -пён, -пна́м] stack; *волос* shock
ко́поть *f* [8] lampblack; soot
копоши́ться [16 *e.*; -шу́сь, -ши́шься], <за-> *coll.* *о лю́дях* putter about, mess around
копти́ть [15 *e.*; -пчу́, -пти́шь, -пчённый], <за-> smoke
копы́то *n* [9] hoof
копьё *n* [10; *pl. st.*] spear; lance
кора́ *f* [5] bark; *земли́ и т. д.* crust
кораб|лекруше́ние *n* [12] shipwreck; **~лестрое́ние** *n* [12] shipbuilding; **~ль** *m* [4 *e.*] ship
кора́лл *m* [1] coral; **~овый** [14] coral..., coralline
Кора́н *m* [1] Koran
коре́|ец *m* [1; -е́йца], **~йский** [16] Korean
корен|а́стый [14 *sh.*] thickset, stocky; **~и́ться** [13] be rooted in; **~но́й** [14] native; (*основно́й*) fundamental; *зуб* molar; **´~ь** *m* [4; -рня; *from g/pl. e.*] root; ***в ко́рне*** radically; ***пусти́ть ко́рни*** take root; ***вы́рвать с ко́рнем*** pull up by the roots; **~ья** *n/pl.* [*gen.*: -ьев] roots
корешо́к *m* [1; -шка́] rootlet; *кни́ги* spine; *квита́нции* stub, counterfoil
корея́нка *f* [5; (*g/pl.*: -нок)] Korean
корзи́н(к)а *f* [5 (*g/pl.*: -нок)] basket
коридо́р *m* [1] corridor, passage
кори́нка *f* [5; *no pl.*] currant(s)
корифе́й *m* [3] *fig.* luminary
кори́ца *f* [5] cinnamon
кори́чневый [14] brown
ко́рка *f* [5; *g/pl.*: -рок] *хле́ба и т. д.* crust; *кожура́* rind, peel
корм *m* [1; *pl.*: -ма́ *etc. e.*] fodder
корма́ *f* [5] *naut.* stern
корм|и́лец *m* [1; льца] breadwinner; **~и́ть** [14], <на-, по-> feed; ***~и́ть гру́дью*** nurse; <про-> *fig.* maintain, support; **-ся** live on (Т); **~ле́ние** *n* [12] feeding; nursing
корнепло́ды *m/pl.* [1] root crops

К

коро́б|ить [14], <по-> warp (*a. fig.*); jar upon, grate upon: **~ка** *f* [5; *g/pl.*: -бок] box, case

коро́в|а *f* [5] cow; ***до́йная ~а*** milch cow; **~ий** [18] cow...; **~ка** *f* [5; *g/pl.*: -вок]: ***бо́жья ~ка*** ladybird; **~ник** *m* [1] cowshed

короле́в|а *f* [5] queen; **~ский** [16] royal, regal; **~ство** *n* [9] kingdom

коро́ль *m* [4 *e.*] king

коромы́сло *n* [9; *g/pl.*: -сел] yoke; (*a. scale*) beam

коро́н|а *f* [5] crown; **~а́ция** coronation; **~ка** *f* [5; *g/pl.*: -нок] (*of tooth*) crown; **~ова́ние** *n* [12] coronation; **~ова́ть** [7] (*im*)*pf.* crown

корот|а́ть *coll.* [1], <с-> while away; **~кий** [16; ко́роток, -тка́, ко́ротко́, ко́ротки́; *comp.*: коро́че] short, brief; ***на ~кой ноге́*** on close terms; ***коро́че*** (***говоря́***) in a word, in short, in brief; ***~ко и я́сно*** (quite) plainly; ***ру́ки ~ки́!*** just try!

ко́рпус *m* [1] body; [*pl.*: -са́, *etc. c.*] frame, case; building; (*a. mil.*, *dipl.*) corps; ***су́дна*** hull

коррект|и́ва *f* [5] correction; **~и́ровать** [7], <про-> correct; *typ.* proofread; **~ный** [14; -тен, -тна] correct, proper; **~ор** *m* [1] proofreader; **~у́ра** *f* [5] proof(reading)

корреспонд|е́нт *m* [1] correspondent; **~е́нция** *f* [7] correspondence

корсе́т *m* [1] corset, *Brt. a.* stays *pl.*

корт *m* [1] (tennis) court

корте́ж *f* [5; *g/pl.*: -жей] cortège; motorcade

ко́ртик *m* [1] dagger

ко́рточк|и *f/pl.* [5; *gen.*: -чек]: ***сесть*** (***сиде́ть***) ***на ~и*** (***~ах***) squat

корчева́|ние *n* [12] rooting out; **~ть** [7], <вы́-, рас-> root out

ко́рчить [16], <с-> *impers.* (**-ся**) writhe (***от бо́ли*** with pain); convulse; (*no pf.*) *coll.* ***ро́жи*** make faces; (*a.* ***~ из себя́***) pose as

ко́ршун *m* [1] kite

корыст|ный [14; -тен, -тна] selfish, self-interested; *a.* = **~олюби́вый** [14 *sh.*] greedy, mercenary; **~олю́бие** *n* [12] self-interest, cupidity; **~ь** *f* [8] gain, profit; cupidity

коры́то *n* [9] trough

корь *f* [8] measles

ко́рюшка *f* [5; *g/pl.*: -шек] smelt

коря́вый [14 *sh.*] knotty, gnarled; rugged, rough; ***по́черк*** crooked; ***речь*** clumsy

коса́ *f* [5; *ac/sg.*: ко́су; *pl. st.*] **1.** plait, braid; **2.** [*ac/sg. a.* косу́] scythe; spit (*of land*)

ко́свенный [14] oblique, indirect (*a. gr.*); *law.* circumstantial

коси́|лка *f* [5; *g/pl.*: -лок] mower machine; **~ть**, <с-> **1.** [15; кошу́, ко́сишь] mow; **2.** [15 *e.*; кошу́, коси́шь] squint; **-ся**, <по-> *v/i.*; *a.* look askance (***на*** В at); **~чка** *f* [5; *g/pl.*: -чек] *dim.* → ***коса́* 1**

косма́тый [14 *sh.*] shaggy

косм|е́тика *f* [5] cosmetics *pl.*; **~ети́ческий** [16] cosmetic; **~и́ческий** [16] cosmic; ***кора́бль*** spaceship, spacecraft; **~она́вт** *m* [1] cosmonaut, astronaut

ко́сн|ость *f* [8] sluggishness, inertness, stagnation; **~у́ться** [14] → ***каса́ться***; **~ый** [14; -сен, -сна] sluggish, inert, stagnant

косо|гла́зый [14 *sh.*] cross- *or* squint-eyed; **~й** [14; кос, -а́, -о] slanting, oblique; sloping; *coll.* ***улы́бка*** wry; **~ла́пый** [14 *sh.*] pigeon-toed; *coll.* неуклю́жий clumsy

костёр *m* [1; -тра́] (camp)fire, bonfire

кост|и́стый [14 *sh.*] bony; **~ля́вый** [14 *sh.*] scrawny, raw-boned; ***ры́ба***; **~очка** *f* [5; *g/pl.*: -чек] bone; *bot.* pit, stone; ***перемыва́ть ~очки*** gossip (Д about)

костыль [4 *e.*] crutch

кост|ь *f* [8; в -ти́; *from g/pl. e.*] bone; ***промо́кнуть до ~е́й*** get soaked to the skin

костю́м *m* [1] suit; dress; costume

костя́|к *m* [1 *e.*] skeleton; *fig.* backbone; **~но́й** [14] bone...

косу́ля *f* [6] roe deer

косы́нка *f* [5; *g/pl.*: -нок] kerchief

кося́к *m* [1 *e.*] (door)post; ***птиц*** flock; ***ры́бы*** school

кот *m* [1 *e.*] tomcat; → *a.* ***ко́тик***; ***купи́ть ~а́ в мешке́*** buy a pig in a poke; ***~ напла́кал*** *coll.* very little

кот|ёл *m* [1; -тла́] boiler, cauldron;

~ело́к *m* [1; -лка́] kettle, pot; *mil.* mess tin; *шля́па* bowler
котёнок *m* [2] kitten
ко́тик *m* [1] *dim.* → **кот**; fur seal; *мех* sealskin; *adj.*: **~овый** [14]
котле́та *f* [5] cutlet; burger; rissole chop
котлови́на *f* [5] *geogr.* hollow, basin
кото́р|ый [14] which; who; that; what; many a; one; ***~ый раз*** how many times; ***~ый час?*** what time is it?; ***в ~ом часу́?*** (at) what time?
котте́дж *n* [1; *g/pl.* -ей] small detached house
ко́фе *m* [*indecl.*] coffee; ***раствори́мый ~*** instant coffee; **~ва́рка** *f* [5; *g/pl.*: -рок] coffeemaker; **~йник** *m* [1] coffeepot; **~мо́лка** *f* [5; *g/pl.*: -лок] coffee mill; **~йный** [14] coffee...
ко́фт|а *f* [5] (woman's) jacket; (***вя́заная ~а***) jersey, cardigan; **~очка** *f* [5; *g/pl.*: -чек] blouse
коча́н *m* [1 *e.*] head (*of cabbage*)
кочев|а́ть [7] be a nomad; wander, roam; move from place to place; **~ник** *m* [1] nomad
кочене́ть [8], <за-, о-> grow numb (**от** P with), stiffen
кочерга́ *f* [5; *g/pl.*: -рёг] poker
ко́чка *f* [5; *g/pl.*: -ек] hummock; tussock
коша́чий [18] cat('s); feline
кошелёк *m* [1; -лька́] purse
ко́шка *f* [5; *g/pl.*: -шек] cat
кошма́р *m* [1] nightmare; **~ный** [14; -рен, -рна] nightmarish; horrible, awful
кощу́нств|енный [14 *sh.*] blasphemous; **~о** *n* [9] blasphemy; **~овать** [7] blaspheme
коэффицие́нт *m* [1] *math.*, *el.* coefficient; factor; ***~ поле́зного де́йствия*** efficiency
краб *m* [1] *zo.* crab
кра́деный [14] stolen (goods *n su.*)
краеуго́льный [14] basic; *fig.* *ка́мень* corner(stone)
кра́жа *f* [5] theft; ***~ со взло́мом*** burglary
край *m* [3; с кра́ю; в ~аю́: *pl.*: -а́я, -аёв, *etc. e.*] edge; (b)rim; brink (*a. fig.* = edge); end; fringe, border, outskirt; region, land, country; **~ний** [15] outermost, (*a. fig.*) utmost, extreme(ly, utterly, most, very, badly **~не**); ***в ~нем слу́чае*** as a last resort; in case of emergency; **~ность** *f* [8] extreme; (*о положе́нии*) extremity; ***до ~ности = ~не***; ***впада́ть в*** (***доходи́ть до***) ***~ности*** go to extremes
крамо́ла *f* [5] *obs.* sedition
кран *m* [1] *tech.* tap; (stop)cock; crane
кра́пать [1 *or* 2 *st.*] drip, trickle
крапи́в|а *f* [5] (stinging) nettle; **~ница** *f* [5] nettle rash
кра́пинка *f* [5; *g/pl.*: -нок] speck, spot
крас|а́ *f* [5] → **~ота́**; **~а́вец** *m* [1; -вца] handsome man; **~а́вица** *f* [5] beautiful woman; **~и́вый** [14 *sh.*] beautiful; handsome; *a.* ***слова́ и т. д.*** *iro.* pretty
крас|и́тель *m* [4] dye(stuff); **~ить** [15], <(п)о-, вы́-, рас-> paint, colo(u)r, dye; *coll.* <на-> paint, make-up; **~ка** *f* [5; *g/pl.*: -сок] colo(u)r, paint, dye
красне́ть [8], <по-> redden, grow *or* turn red; ***от стыда́*** blush; *impf.* be ashamed; (*a.* **-ся**) appear *or* show red
красно|арме́ец *m* [1; -ме́йца] *hist.* Red Army man; **~ба́й** *m* [3] *coll.* phrasemaker; rhetorician; glib talker; **~ва́тый** [14 *sh.*] reddish; **~речи́вый** [14 *sh.*] eloquent; **~ре́чие** *n* [12] eloquence; **~та́** *f* [5] redness; **~щёкий** [16 *sh.*] ruddy
красну́ха *f* [5] German measles
кра́с|ный [14; -сен, -сна́, -о] red (*a. fig.*); ***~ная строка́*** *f typ.* (*first line of*) new paragraph, new line; ***~ная цена́*** *f coll.* outside price; ***~ное словцо́*** *n coll.* witticism; ***проходи́ть ~ной ни́тью*** run through (*of motif, theme, etc.*)
красова́ться [7] stand out *or* impress because of beauty; *coll.* flaunt, show off
красота́ *f* [5; *pl. st.*: -со́ты] beauty
кра́сочный [14; -чен, -чна] colo(u)rful
красть [25 *pt. st.*; кра́денный], <у-> steal (**-ся** *v/i.*, *impf.*; *a.* prowl, slink)

К

кра́тер *m* [1] crater

кра́тк|ий [16; -ток, -тка́, -о; *comp*.: кра́тче] short, brief, concise; ***и́ ~ое*** *the letter* й; → *a.* ***коро́ткий***; **~овре́менный** [14; -енен, -енна] of short duration; (*преходя́щий*) transitory; **~осро́чный** [14; -чен, -чна] short; *ссу́да и т. д.* short-term; **~ость** *f* [8] brevity

кра́тный [14; -тен, -тна] divisible without remainder

крах *m* [1] failure, crash, ruin

крахма́л *m* [1], **~ить** [13], <на-> starch; **~ьный** [14] starch(ed)

кра́шеный [14] painted; dyed

креве́тка *f* [5; *g/pl*.: -ток] *zo.* shrimp

креди́т *m* [1] credit; ***в ~*** on credit; **~ный** [14], **~ова́ть** [7] *(im)pf.* credit; **~о́р** *m* [1] creditor; **~оспосо́бный** [14; -бен, -бна] creditworthy; solvent

кре́йс|ер *m* [1] cruiser; **~и́ровать** [7] cruise; ply

крем *m* [1] cream; ***~ для лица́*** face cream; ***~ для о́буви*** shoe polish

крем|ато́рий *m* [3] crematorium; **~а́ция** *f* [7] cremation; **~и́ровать** [7] cremate

кремл|ёвский [16], **2ь** *m* [4 *e.*] Kremlin

кре́мний [3] *chem.* silicon

крен *m* [1] *naut.* list, heel; *ae.* bank

кре́ндель *m* [4 *from g/pl. e.*] pretzel

крени́ть [13], <на-> list (**-ся** *v/i.*)

креп *m* [1] crepe, crape

креп|и́ть [14 *e.*; -плю́, -пи́шь] fix, secure; *fig.* strengthen; **-ся** hold out, bear up; **~кий** [16; -пок, -пка́, -о; *comp*.: кре́пче] strong; sturdy; *здоро́вье* sound, robust; ***~кий оре́шек*** hard nut to crack; **~ко** *a.* strongly, firmly; **~нуть** [21], <о-> grow strong(er)

крепост|но́й [14] *hist. su.* serf; ***~но́е пра́во*** serfdom; **´~ь** *f* [8; *from g/pl. e.*] fortress; → ***кре́пкий*** strength; firmness, *etc.*

кре́сло *n* [9; *g/pl*.: -сел] armchair

крест *m* [1 *e.*] cross (*a. fig.*); ***~-на~*** crosswise; **~и́ны** *f/pl.* [5] baptism, christening; **~и́ть** [15; -щённый] *(im)pf.*, <о-> baptize, christen; <пере-> cross (**-ся** o.s.); **~ник** *m* [1] godson; **~ница** *f* [5] goddaughter; **~ный** [14] **1.** (of the) cross; **2.** **~ный** (***оте́ц***) godfather; **~ная** (***мать***) godmother

крестья́н|ин *m* [1; *pl.*: -я́не, -я́н] peasant; **~ка** *f* [5; *g/pl.*: -нок] peasant woman; **~ский** [16] farm(er['s]), peasant...; country...; **~ство** *n* [9] *collect.* peasants; peasantry

крети́н *m* [1] cretin; *fig. coll.* idiot

креще́ние *n* [12] baptism, christening; 2 Epiphany

крив|а́я *f* [14] *math.* curve; **~изна́** *f* [5] crookedness, curvature; **~и́ть** [14 *e.*; -влю́, -ви́шь, -влённый], <по-, с-> (**-ся** be[come]) crook(ed), (bent); <с-> (**-ся**) make a wry face; ***~и́ть душо́й*** act against one's conscience *or* convictions; **~ля́нье** *n* [12] affectation; **~ля́ться** [18] (make) grimace(s); mince; **~о́й** [14; крив, -а́, -о] crooked (*a. fig.*), wry; curve(d); P one-eyed; **~оно́гий** [16 *sh.*] bandy-legged, bowlegged; **~ото́лки** *coll. m/pl.* [1] rumo(u)rs, gossip

кри́зис *m* [1] crisis

крик *m* [1] cry, shout; outcry; ***после́дний ~ мо́ды*** the latest word in fashion; **~ли́вый** [14 *sh.*] shrill; clamorous; loud; **~нуть** → ***крича́ть***

кри|мина́льный [14] criminal; **~ста́лл** *m* [1] crystal; **~ста́льный** [14; -лен, -льна] crystalline; *fig.* crystal-clear

крите́рий *m* [3] criterion

кри́ти|к *m* [1] critic; **~ка** *f* [5] criticism; *lit., art* critique, review; **~кова́ть** [7] criticize; **~ческий** [16], **~чный** [14; -чен, -чна] critical

крича́ть [4 *e.*; -чу́, -чи́шь], <за->, *once* <кри́кнуть> [20] cry (out), shout (***на*** B at); scream

кров *m* [1] roof; shelter

крова́|вый [14 *sh.*] bloody; **~ть** *f* [8] bed

кро́вельщик *m* [1] roofer

кровено́сный [14] blood (*vessel*)

кро́вля *f* [6; *g/pl.*: -вель] roof(ing)

кро́вный [14] (*adv.* by) blood; (*жи́зненно ва́жный*) vital

крово|жа́дный [14; -ден, -дна]

bloodthirsty; **~излия́ние** *n* [12] *med.* h(a)emorrhage; **~обраще́ние** *n* [12] circulation of the blood; **~пи́йца** *m/f* [5] bloodsucker; **~подтёк** *m* [1] bruise; **~проли́тие** *n* [12] bloodshed; **~проли́тный** [14; -тен, -тна] → ***крова́вый***; **~смеше́ние** *n* [12] incest; **~тече́ние** *n* [12] bleeding; → ***~излия́ние***; **~точи́ть** [16 *e.*; -чи́т] bleed

кров|ь *f* [8; -ви] blood (*a. fig.*); **~яно́й** [14] blood...

кро|и́ть [13; кро́енный], <вы́-, с-> cut (out); **~́йка** *f* [5] cutting (out)

крокоди́л *m* [1] crocodile

кро́лик *m* [1] rabbit

кро́ме (Р) except, besides (*a.* **~** ***того́***), apart (*or* aside) from; but

кромса́ть [1], <ис-> hack

кро́на *f* [5] crown (*of tree*); (*unit of currency*) crown, krone, krona

кропи́ть [14 *e.*; -плю́, -пи́шь, -плённый], <о-> sprinkle

кропотли́вый [14 *sh.*] laborious, toilsome; painstaking, assiduous

кроссво́рд *m* [1] crossword puzzle

кроссо́вки *f* [5; *g/pl.*: -вок] running shoes; *Brt.* trainers

крот *m* [1 *e.*] *zo.* mole

кро́ткий [16; -ток, -тка́, -о; *comp.*: кро́тче] gentle, meek

кро́|ха *f* [5; *ac/sg.*: кро́ху; *from dat/pl. e.*] crumb; ***о коли́честве*** bit; **~́хотный** *coll.* [14; -тен, -тна], **~́шечный** *coll.* [14] tiny; **~ши́ть** [16], <на-, по-, из-> crumb(le); (***ме́лко руби́ть***) chop; **~́шка** *f* [5; *g/pl.*: -шек] crumb; *coll.* little one; ***ни ~́шки*** not a bit

круг *m* [1; в, на -у́; *pl. e.*] circle (*a. fig.*); ***интере́сов и т. д.*** sphere, range; **~лова́тый** [14 *sh.*] roundish; **~лоли́цый** [14 *sh.*] chubby-faced; **~́лый** [14; кругл, -а́, -о] round; *coll.* ***дура́к*** perfect; ***~́лая су́мма*** round sum; ***~́лые су́тки*** day and night; **~ово́й** [14] circular; ***пору́ка*** mutual; **~оборо́т** *m* [1] circulation; ***собы́тий*** succession; **~озо́р** *m* [1] prospect; range of interests; **~о́м** round; ***вокру́г*** around, (round) about; **~осве́тный** [14] round-the-world

кру́ж|ево *n* [9; *pl. e.*; *g/pl.*: кру́жев] lace; **~и́ть** [16 & 16 *e.*; кружу́, кру́жишь], <за-, вс-> turn (round), whirl; circle; spin; ***плута́ть*** stray about; (**-ся** *v/i.*); ***вскружи́ть го́лову*** (Д) turn s.o.'s head; ***голова́ ~ится*** (**у** Р) feel giddy; **~ка** *f* [5; *g/pl.*: -жек] mug; tankard; ***пи́ва*** glass

кру́жный *coll.* [14] traffic circle, *Brt.* roundabout

кружо́к *m* [1; -жка́] (small) circle; *lit. pol.* study group

круп *m* [1] ***ло́шади*** croup

круп|а́ *f* [5] groats *pl.*; *fig.* ***снег*** sleet; **~и́нка** *f* [5; *g/pl.*: -нок] grain (*a. fig.* = **~и́ца** *f* [5])

кру́пный [14; -пен, -пна́, -о] big, large(-scale), great; (***выдаю́щийся***) outstanding; (***ва́жный***) important, serious; *cine.* close (up); *fig.* **~ *разгово́р*** high words

крутизна́ *f* [5] steep(ness)

крути́ть [15], <за-, с-> twist; twirl; roll (up); turn; whirl; Р *impf.* be insincere *or* evasive; trick; ***любо́вь*** have a love affair (with)

круто́|й [14; крут, -а́, -о; *comp.*: кру́че] steep, (***ре́зкий***) sharp, abrupt; (***неожи́данный***) sudden; ***яйцо́*** hard (*a.* -boiled); ***ме́ра и т. д.*** harsh; **´~сть** *f* [8] harshness

круше́ние *n* [12] wreck; ***наде́жд*** ruin; collapse; *a. rail.* derailment

крыжо́вник *m* [1] gooseberry bush; *collect.* gooseberries

крыл|а́тый [14 *sh.*] winged (*a. fig.*); **~о́** *n* [9; *pl.*: кры́лья; -льев] wing (*a. arch.*, *ae.*, *pol.*); **~ьцо́** *n* [9; *pl.* кры́льца, -ле́ц, -льца́м] steps *pl.*; porch

кры́мский [16] Crimean

кры́са *f* [5] rat

крыть [22], <по-> cover, roof; ***кра́ской*** coat; ***в ка́ртах*** trump; **-ся** *impf.* (**в** П) lie *or* be in; be concealed

крыш|а *f* [5] roof; **~ка** *f* [5; *g/pl.*: -шек] lid, cover; Р (Д p.'s) end

крюк *m* [1 *e.*; *pl. a.*; крю́чья, -ев] hook; *coll.* detour

крюч|кова́тый [14 *sh.*] hooked; **~котво́рство** *n* [9] chicanery; pettifoggery; **~о́к** *m* [1; -чка́] hook; ***для вяза́ния*** crochet hook

кряж *m* [1] mountain range; chain of hills

кря́к|ать [1], *once* <~нуть> [20] quack
кряхте́ть [11] groan, grunt
кста́ти to the point (*or* purpose); opportune(ly), in the nick of time; apropos; besides, too, as well; incidentally, by the way
кто [23] who; **~ ..., ~ ...** some..., others ...; ***~ бы ни*** whoever; ***~ бы то ни́ был*** who(so)ever it may be; ~ *coll.* = **~-либо**, **~-нибудь**, **~-то** [23] anyone; someone
куб *m* [1] *math.* cube
ку́барем *coll.* head over heels
ку́б|ик *m* [1] (small) cube; *игру́шка* brick, block (*toy*); **~и́ческий** [16] cubic
ку́бок *m* [1; -бка] goblet; *приз* cup
кубоме́тр *m* [1] cubic meter (-tre)
кувши́н *m* [1] jug; pitcher
кувши́нка *f* [5; *g/pl.* -нок] water lily
кувырк|а́ться [1], *once* <~ну́ться> [20] somersault, tumble; **~о́м** → ***ку́барем***
куда́ where (... to); what ... for; *coll.* (*a.* ~ **как**[**о́й**], *etc.*) very, awfully, how; at all; by far, much; (*a.* + Д [& *inf.*]) how can ...; ***~ ни*** wherever; (*a.* ***~ тут***, ***там***) (that's) impossible!, certainly not!, what an idea!, (*esp.* ***~ тебе́!***) rats!; **~ ..., ~ ...** to some places ..., to others ...; ***~ вы*** (*i. e.* ***идёте***)?; where are you going?; ***хоть ~*** P fine; couldn't be better; → ***ни ~*** = **~-либо**, **~-нибудь**, **~-то** any-, somewhere
куда́хтать [3] cackle, cluck
куде́сник *m* [1] magician, sorcerer
ку́др|и *f/pl.* [-е́й, *etc. e.*] curls; **~я́вый** [14 *sh.*] curly(-headed); *де́рево* bushy
кузн|е́ц *m* [1 *e.*] (black)smith; **~е́чик** *m* [1] *zo.* grasshopper; **~ица** *f* [5] smithy
ку́зов *m* [1; *pl.*: -ва́, *etc. e.*] body (*of car, etc.*)
кукаре́кать [1] crow
ку́киш P *m* [1] *coll.* (*gesture of derision*) fig, fico
ку́к|ла *f* [5; *g/pl.*: -кол] doll; **~олка** *f* [5; *g/pl.*: -лок] **1.** *dim.* → **~ла**; **2.** *zo.* chrysalis; **~ольный** [14] doll('s); ***~ольный теа́тр*** puppet show
кукуру́з|а *f* [5] corn, *Brt.* maize; **~ный** [14] corn...; ***~ные хло́пья*** cornflakes
куку́шка *f* [5; *g/pl.*: -шек] cuckoo
кула́к *m* [1 *e.*] fist; *hist.* kulak (*prosperous farmer or peasant*)
кулёк *m* [1; -лька́] (paper) bag
кули́к *m* [1 *e.*] curlew; snipe
кулина́р|ия *f* [7] cookery; **~ный** [14] culinary
кули́са *f* [5] *thea.* wing, side; ***за ~ми*** behind the scenes
кули́ч *m* [1 *e.*] Easter cake
куло́н *m* [1] pendant
кулуа́ры *m/pl.* [1] *sg. not used* lobbies
куль *m* [4 *e.*] sack, bag
культ *m* [1] cult; **~иви́ровать** [7] cultivate; **~у́ра** *f* [5] culture; standard (***земледе́лия*** of farming); ***зерновы́е ~у́ры*** cereals; **~у́рный** [14; -рен, -рна] cultural; cultured, well-bred
культя́ *f* [7 *e.*] *med.* stump
кума́ч *m* [1 *e.*] red calico
куми́р *m* [1] idol
кумовство́ *n* [9] *fig.* favo(u)ritism; nepotism
куни́ца *f* [5] marten
купа́|льный [14] bathing; ***~льный костю́м*** bathing suit, *Brt.* bathing costume; **~льщик** *m* [1] bather; **~ть(ся)** [1], <вы́-, ис-> (take a) bath; bathe
купе́ (-'pɛ) *n* [*indecl.*] *rail.* compartment
купе́|ц *m* [1; -пца́] merchant; **~ческий** [16] merchant('s); **~чество** *n* [9] *collect.* merchants
купи́ть → ***покупа́ть***
купле́т *m* [1] couplet, stanza; song
ку́пля *f* [6] purchase
ку́пол *m* [1; *pl.*: -ла] cupola, dome
ку́пчая *f* [14] *hist.* deed of purchase
купю́ра *f* [5] bill, banknote; ***в те́ксте*** cut, excision
курга́н *m* [1] burial mound, barrow
ку́р|ево *coll. n* [9] tobacco, cigarettes; **~е́ние** *n* [12] smoking; **~и́льщик** *m* [1] smoker
кури́ный [14] chicken...; hen's; *coll.* *па́мять* short; *med.* night (*слепота́* blindness)

кури́|тельный [14] smoking; **~ть** [13; курю́, ку́ришь], <по-, вы-> smoke (**-ся** *v/i.*)
ку́рица *f* [5; *pl.*: ку́ры, *etc. st.*] hen; *cul.* chicken
курно́сый [14 *sh.*] snub-nosed
куро́к *m* [1; -рка́] cock (*of weapon*)
куропа́тка *f* [5; *g/pl.*: -ток] partridge
куро́рт *m* [1] health resort
курс *m* [1] course (*naut.*, *ae.*, *med.*, *educ.*; ***держа́ть ~ на*** (B) head for; *a. univ.* year); *fin.* rate of exchange; *fig.* line, policy; ***держа́ть*** (***быть***) ***в ~е*** (P) keep (be) (well) posted on; **~а́нт** *m* [1] *mil.* cadet; **~и́в** *m* [1] *typ.* italics; **~и́ровать** [7] ply; **~о́р** *m* [1] *computer* cursor
ку́ртка *f* [5; *g/pl.*: -ток] jacket
курча́вый [14 *sh.*] curly(-headed)
курь|ёз *m* [1] curious; amusing; **~е́р** *m* [1] messenger; courier
куря́щий *m* [17] smoker
кус|а́ть [1], <укуси́ть> [15] bite (**-ся** *v/i.*, *impf.*), sting; **~о́к** *m* [1; -ска́] piece, bit, morsel; scrap; ***мы́ла*** cake; ***пирога́ и т. д.*** slice; ***на ~ки́*** to pieces; ***зараба́тывать на ~о́к хле́ба*** earn one's bread and butter; **~о́чек** *m* [1; -чка] *dim.* → **~о́к**
куст *m* [1 *e.*] bush, shrub; **~а́рник** *m* [1] *collect.* bush(es), shrub(s)
куста́р|ный [14] handicraft...; hand(made); *fig.* primitive, crude; **~ь** *m* [4 *e.*] craftsman
ку́тать(ся) [1], <за-> muffle *or* wrap o.s. (up, in)
кут|ёж *m* [1 *e.*], **~и́ть** [15] carouse
ку́х|ня *f* [6; *g/pl.*: ку́хонь] kitchen; ***ру́сская и т. д.*** cuisine, cookery; **~онный** [14] kitchen...
ку́цый [14 *sh.*] dock-tailed; short
ку́ч|а *f* [5] heap, pile; a lot of; ***~ами*** in heaps, in crowds; ***вали́ть всё в одну́ ~у*** lump everything together; ***класть в ~у*** pile up; **~ер** *m* [1; *pl.*: -ра, *etc. e.*] coachman; **~ка** *f* [5; *g/pl.*: -чек] *dim.* → **~а**; small group
куша́к *m* [1 *e.*] belt, girdle, sash
ку́ша|нье *n* [10] dish; food; **~ть** [1], <по-> eat (up <с->)
куше́тка *f* [5; *g/pl.*: -ток] couch
кюве́т *m* [1] drainage ditch

Л

лабири́нт *m* [1] labyrinth, maze
лабор|а́нт *m* [1], **~а́нтка** *f* [5; *g/pl.*: -ток] laboratory assistant; **~ато́рия** *f* [7] laboratory
ла́ва *f* [5] lava
лави́на *f* [5] avalanche
лави́ровать [7] *naut.* tack; (*fig.*) maneuver (-noeuvre)
лавр *m* [1] laurel; **~о́вый** [14] (of) laurel(s)
ла́гер|ь 1. [4; *pl.*: -ря́, *etc . e.*] camp (*a.*, *pl.*: -ри, *etc. st.*, *fig.*); ***располага́ться*** (***стоя́ть***) ***~ем*** camp (out), be encamped; **~ный** [14] camp...
лад *m* [1; в ~у́; *pl. e.*]: (***не***) ***в ~у́*** (***~а́х***) → (***не***) ***~ить***; ***идти на ~*** work (well), get on *or* along; **~ан** *m* [1] incense; ***дыша́ть на ~ан*** have one foot in the grave; **~ить** *coll.* [15], <по-, с-> get along *or* on (well), *pf. a.* make it up; (***спра́виться***) manage; ***не ~ить*** *a.* be at odds *or* variance; **-ся** *coll. impf.* → ***идти́ на ~***, ***~ить***; ***~но*** *coll.* all right, O.K.; **~ный** [14; -ден, -дна́, -о] *coll.* fine, excellent
ладо́|нь *f* [8], P *f* [5] palm; ***как на ~ни*** spread before the eyes; ***бить в ~ши*** clap (one's hands)
ладья́ *f* [6] *obs.* boat; *chess*: rook
лаз|е́йка *f* [5; *g/pl.*: -е́ек] loophole; **~ить** [15] climb (*v/t.* ***на*** B); clamber
лазу́р|ный [14; -рен, -рна], **~ь** *f* [8] azure
лай *m* [3] bark(ing), yelp; **~ка** *f* [5;

g/pl.: ла́ек] **1.** Eskimo dog; **2.** *ко́жа* kid; **~ковый** [14] kid...
лак *m* [1] varnish, lacquer; **~овый** [14] varnish(ed), lacquer(ed); *ко́жа* patent leather...
лака́ть [1], <вы́-> lap
лаке́й *m* [3] *fig.* flunk(e)y; **~ский** [16] *fig.* servile
лакирова́ть [7], <от-> lacquer, varnish
ла́ком|иться [14], <по-> (T) enjoy, relish (*a. fig.*), eat with delight; **~ка** *coll. m/f* [5] lover of dainties; ***быть ~кой*** *a.* have a sweet tooth; **~ство** *n* [9] dainty, delicacy; *pl.* sweetmeats; **~ый** [14 *sh.*] dainty; ***~ый кусо́(че)к*** *m* tidbit, *Brt.* titbit
лакони́ч|еский [16], **~ный** [14; -чен, -чна] laconic(al)
ла́мп|а *f* [5] lamp; **~а́да** *f* [5 (*g/pl.*:] lamp (*for icon*); **~овый** [14] lamp...; **~очка** *f* [5; *g/pl.*: -чек] bulb
ландша́фт *m* [1] landscape
ла́ндыш *m* [1] lily of the valley
лань *f* [8] fallow deer; hind, doe
ла́па *f* [5] paw; *fig.* clutch
лапша́ *f* [5] noodles *pl.*; noodle soup
ларёк *m* [1; -рька́] kiosk, stand
ла́ск|а *f* [5] caress; **~а́тельный** [14] endearing, pet; *a.* ***~овый***; **~а́ть** [1], <при-> caress; pet, fondle; **-ся** endear o.s. (***к*** Д to); *о соба́ке* fawn (*of dog*); **~овый** [14 *sh.*] affectionate, tender; caressing; *ве́тер* soft
ла́сточка *f* [5; *g/pl.*: -чек] swallow
лата́ть *coll.* [1], <за-> patch, mend
латви́йский [16] Latvian
лати́нский [16] Latin
лату́нь *f* [8] brass
ла́ты *f/pl.* [5] *hist.* armo(u)r
латы́нь *f* [8] Latin
латы́ш *m* [1 *e.*], **~ка** *f* [5; *g/pl.*: -шек] Lett; **~ский** [16] Lettish
лауреа́т *m* [1] prizewinner
ла́цкан *m* [1] lapel
лачу́га *f* [5] hovel, shack
ла́ять [27], <за-> bark
лгать [лгу, лжёшь, лгут; лгал, -а́, -о], <со-> lie, tell lies
лгун *m* [1 *e.*], **~ья** *f* [6] liar
лебёдка *f* [5; *g/pl.*: -док] winch
лебе|ди́ный [14] swan...; **´~дь** *m* [4; *from g/pl.*: *e.*] (*poet. a. f*) swan; **~зи́ть** *coll.* [15 *e.*; -бежу́, -бези́шь] fawn (***перед*** T upon)
лев *m* [1; льва́] lion; ♌ Leo
лев|ша́ *m/f* [5; *g/pl.*: -ше́й] left-hander; **~ый** [14] left (*a. fig.*), left-hand; *тка́ни* wrong (*side*; on **с** P)
лега́льный [14; -лен, -льна] legal
леге́нд|а *f* [5] legend; **~а́рный** [14; -рен, -рна] legendary
легио́н *m* [1] legion (*mst. fig = a great number of people*)
лёгкий (-xk-) [16; лёгок, легка́; *a.* лёгки; *comp.*: ле́гче] light (*a. fig.*); *нетру́дный* easy; *прикоснове́ние* slight; (Д) ***легко́*** + *inf.* it is very well for ... + *inf.*; ***лёгок на поми́не*** *coll.* talk of the devil!
легкоатле́т *m* [1] track and field athlete
легко|ве́рный (-xk-) [14; -рен, -рна] credulous; **~ве́сный** [14; -сен, -сна] lightweight; *fig.* shallow; **~во́й** [14]: ***легково́й автомоби́ль*** *a.* ***~ва́я*** (***а́вто***)***маши́на*** auto(mobile), car
лёгкое *n* [16] lung
легкомы́сл|енный (-xk-) [14 *sh.*] light-minded, frivolous; thoughtless; **~ие** *n* [12] levity; frivolity; flippancy
лёгкость (-xk-) *f* [8] lightness; easiness; ease
лёд *m* [1; льда́, на льду́] ice
лед|ене́ть [8], <за-, о-> freeze, ice (up, over); grow numb (*with cold*); **~ене́ц** *m* [1; -нца́] (sugar) candy; **~ени́ть** [13], <о(б)-> freeze, ice; *се́рдце* chill; **~ни́к** *m* [1 *e.*] glacier; **~нико́вый** [14] glacial; ice...; **~око́л** *m* [1] icebreaker; **~охо́д** *m* [1] pack ice; **~яно́й** [14] ice...; ice-cold; icy (*a. fig.*)
лежа́|ть [4 *e.*; лёжа] lie; (*быть располо́женным*) be (situated); rest, be incumbent; ***~ть в осно́ве*** (***в*** П form the basis); **~чий** [17] lying; ***~чий больно́й*** (in)patient
ле́звие *n* [12] edge; razor blade
лезть [24 *st.*: ле́зу; лезь!; лез, -ла], <по-> (be) climb(ing, *etc.*; *v/t.*); creep; (*прони́кнуть*) penetrate; *coll.* reach into; (***к*** Д [**с** T]) importune, press; *о волоса́х* fall out; (***на*** B) fit (*v/t*); P *не в своё де́ло* meddle
лейбори́ст *m* [1] *pol.* Labo(u)rite

ле́й|ка *f* [5; *g/pl.*: ле́ек] watering can; **~копла́стырь** *m* [4] adhesive plaster; **~тена́нт** *m* [1] (second) lieutenant; **~тмоти́в** *m* [1] leitmotif
лека́р|ственный [14] medicinal; **~ство** *n* [9] drug, medicine, remedy (***против*** P for)
ле́ксика *f* [5] vocabulary
ле́к|тор *m* [1] lecturer; **~то́рий** *m* [3] lecture hall; **~ция** *f* [7] lecture (at ***на*** П; *vb.*: ***слу́шать*** [***чита́ть***] attend [give, deliver])
леле́ять [27] pamper; *fig.* cherish
лён *m* [1; льна́] flax
лени́в|ец *m* [1; -вца] → ***лентя́й***; **~ица** *f* [5] → ***лентя́йка***; **~ый** [14 *sh.*] lazy, idle; ***вя́лый*** sluggish
лени́ться [13; леню́сь, ле́нишься], be lazy
ле́нта *f* [5] ribbon; band; *tech.* tape
лентя́й *m* [3], **~ка** *f* [5; *g/pl.*: -я́ек] lazybones; sluggard; **~ничать** *coll.* [1] idle
лень *f* [8] laziness, idleness; *coll.* (***мне***) ~ I am too lazy to ...
леопа́рд *m* [1] leopard
лепе|сто́к *m* [1; -тка́] petal; **~т** *m* [1], **~та́ть** [4], <про-> babble, prattle
лепёшка *f* [5; *g/pl.*: -шек] scone
леп|и́ть [14], <вы́-, с-> sculpture, model, mo(u)ld; *coll.* <на-> stick (***на*** В to); **~ка** model(l)ing; **~но́й** [14] mo(u)lded; ***~но́е украше́ние*** stucco mo(u)lding
ле́пт|а *f* [5]: ***внести́ свою́ ~у*** make one's own contribution to s.th
лес *m* [1] [из лесу, из ле́са; в лесу́: *pl.*: леса́, *etc. e.*] wood, forest; ***материа́л*** lumber, *Brt.* timber; *pl.* scaffolding; ***~ом*** through a (the) wood
леса́ *f* [5; *pl.*: лёсы, *etc. st.*] (fishing) line
леси́стый [14 *sh.*] woody, wooded
ле́ска *f* [5; *g/pl.*: -сок] → ***леса́***
лес|ни́к *m* [1 *e.*] ranger, forester; **~ни́чество** *n* [9] forest district; **~ни́чий** *m* [17] forest warden; **~но́й** [14] forest...; wood(y); lumber...; timber...
лесо|во́дство *n* [9] forestry; **~насажде́ние** *n* [12] afforestation; wood; **~пи́льный** [14]: ***~пи́льный заво́д*** = **~пи́льня** *f* [6; *g/pl.*: -лен] sawmill; **~ру́б** *m* [1] lumberman, woodcutter
ле́стница (-sn-) *f* [5] (flight of) stairs *pl.*, staircase; ***приставна́я*** ladder; ***пожа́рная ~*** fire escape
ле́ст|ный [14; -тен, -тна] flattering; **~ь** *f* [8] flattery
лёт *m* [1]: ***хвата́ть на лету́*** grasp quickly, be quick on the uptake
лета́, лет → ***ле́то***; → *a.* ***год***
лета́тельный [14] flying
лета́ть [1] fly
лете́ть [1], <по-> (be) fly(ing)
ле́тний [15] summer...
лётный [14] ***пого́да*** flying; ***~ соста́в*** aircrew
ле́т|о *n* [9; *pl. e.*] summer (T in [the]; ***на*** B for the); *pl.* years, age (***в*** B at); ***ско́лько вам ~?*** how old are you? (→ ***быть***); ***в ~а́х*** elderly, advanced in years; **~опись** *f* [8] chronicle; **~осчисле́ние** *n* [12] chronology; era
лету́чий [17 *sh.*] *chem.* volatile; ***~ая мышь*** *zo.* bat
лётчи|к *m* [1], **~ца** *f* [5] pilot, aviator, flier, air(wo)man; **~к-испыта́тель** test pilot
лече́бн|ица *f* [5] clinic, hospital; **~ый** [14] medic(in)al
леч|е́ние *n* [12] *med.* treatment; **~и́ть** [16] treat; **-ся** undergo treatment, be treated; treat (one's ... **от** P)
лечь → ***ложи́ться***; → *a.* ***лежа́ть***
ле́ший *m* [17] *Russian mythology* wood goblin; P Old Nick
лещ *m* [1 *e.*] *zo.* bream
лж|е... false; pseudo...; **~ец** *m* [1 *e.*] mock...; liar; **~и́вость** *f* [8] mendacity; **~и́вый** [14 *sh.*] false, lying; mendacious
ли, (*short, after vowels, a.*) **ль 1.** (*interr. part.*) ***зна́ет ~ она́ ...?*** (= ***она́ зна́ет ...?***) does she know...?; **2.** (*cj.*) whether, if; ***..., ~, ...~*** whether ..., or...
либера́л *m* [1], **~ьный** [14; -лен, -льна] liberal
ли́бо or; ***~ ..., ~ ...*** either ... or ...
либре́тто *n* [*indecl.*] libretto

Л

ли́вень *m* [4; -вня] downpour, cloudburst
ливре́я *f* [6; *g/pl.*: -ре́й] livery
ли́га *f* [5] league
ли́дер *m* [1] *pol., sport* leader
лиз|а́ть [3], *once* <**~**ну́ть> lick
лик *m* [1] face; countenance; *о́браз* image; *eccl.* assembly; ***причи́слить к ~у святы́х*** canonize
ликвиди́ровать [7] *(im)pf.* liquidate
ликёр *m* [1] liqueur
ликова́ть [7], <воз-> exult
ли́лия *f* [7] lily
лило́вый [14] lilac(-colo[u]red)
лими́т *m* [1] quota, limit; **~и́ровать** [7] *(im)pf.* limit
лимо́н *m* [1] lemon; **~а́д** *m* [1] lemonade; **~ный** [14] lemon; ***~ная кислота́*** citric acid
ли́мфа *f* [5] lymph
лингви́стика *f* [5] → ***языкозна́ние***
лине́й|ка *f* [5; *g/pl.*: -е́ек] line, ruler; **~ный** [14] linear
ли́н|за *f* [5] lens; ***конта́ктные ~зы*** contact lenses; **~ия** *f* [7] line (*a. fig.*; ***по*** Д in); **~ко́р** *m* [1] battleship; **~ова́ть** [7], <на-> rule; **~о́леум** *m* [1] linoleum
линчева́ть [7] *(im)pf.* lynch
линь *m* [4 *e.*] *zo.* tench
ли́н|ька *f* [5] mo(u)lt(ing); **~я́лый** *coll.* [14] *о тка́ни* faded; mo(u)lted; **~я́ть** [28], <вы́-, по-> fade; mo(u)lt
ли́па *f* [5] linden, lime tree
ли́п|кий [16; -пок, -пка́, -о] sticky, adhesive; *пла́стырь* sticking; **~нуть** [21], <при-> stick
ли́р|а *f* [5] lyre; **~ик** *m* [1] lyric poet; **~ика** *f* [5] lyric poetry; **~и́ческий** [16], **~и́чный** [14; -чен, -чна] lyric(al)
лис|(и́ц)а́ *f* [5; *pl. st.*] fox (silver... ***черно-бу́рая***); **~ий** [18] fox...; foxy
лист *m* **1.** [1 *e.*] sheet; (*исполни́тельный*) writ; **2.** [1 *e.*; *pl. st.*: ли́стья, -ев] *bot.* leaf; *coll. a.* → ***~ва́***; **~а́ть** *coll.* [1] leaf *or* thumb through; **~ва́** *f* [5] *collec.* foliage, leaves *pl.*; **~венница** *f* [5] larch; **~венный** [14] deciduous; **~ик** *m* [1] *dim.* → **~**; **~о́вка** *f* [5 *g/pl.*: -вок] leaflet; **~о́к** *m* [1; -тка́] *dim.* → **~**; slip; **~ово́й** [14] sheet...; *желе́зо и т. д.*
лите́йный [14]: ***~ цех*** foundry
литер|а́тор *m* [1] man of letters; writer; **~ату́ра** *f* [5] literature; **~ату́рный** [14; -рен, -рна] literary
лито́в|ец *m* [1; -вца], **~ка** *f* [5; *g/pl.*: -вок], **~ский** [16] Lithuanian
лито́й [14] cast
литр *m* [1] liter (*Brt.* -tre)
лить [лью, льёшь; лил, -а́, -о; лей(те)! ли́тый (лит, -а́, -о)] pour; *слёзы* shed; *tech.* cast; ***дождь льёт как из ведра́*** it's raining cats and dogs; **-ся** flow, pour; *пе́сня* sound; *слёзы и т. д.* stream; **~ё** *n* [10] founding, cast(ing)
лифт *m* [1] elevator, *Brt.* lift; **~ёр** *m* [1] lift operator
ли́фчик *m* [1] bra(ssière)
лих|о́й [14; лих, -а́, -о] *coll.* bold, daring; dashing; **~ора́дка** *f* [5] fever; **~ора́дочный** [14; -чен, -чна] feverish; **~ость** *f* [8] *coll.* swagger; spirit; dash
лицев|а́ть [7], <пере-> face; turn; **~о́й** [14] face...; front...; *сторона́* right; ***~о́й счёт*** personal account
лицеме́р *m* [1] hypocrite; **~ие** *n* [12] hypocrisy; **~ный** [14; -рен, -рна] hypocritical; **~ить** [13] dissemble
лице́нзия *f* [7] license (*Brt.* -ce) (В for ***на***)
лиц|о́ *n* [9; *pl. st.*] face; countenance (*change v/t.* ***в*** П); front; person, individual(ity); ***в ~о́*** by sight; to s.b.'s face; ***от ~а́*** (Р) in the name of; ***~о́м к ~у́*** face to face; ***быть*** (Д) ***к ~у́*** suit *or* become a p.; ***нет ~а́*** be bewildered; ***должностно́е ~о́*** official
личи́нка *f* [5; *g/pl.*: -нок] larva; maggot
ли́чн|ость *f* [8] personality; person, individual; **~ый** [14] personal; private
лиша́й *m* [3 *e.*] *bot.* lichen (*a.* **~ник**); *med.* herpes
лиш|а́ть [1], <**~**и́ть> [16 *e.*; -шу́, -ши́шь, -шённый] deprive; strip (of Р); *насле́дства* disinherit; ***~а́ть себя́ жи́зни*** commit (*suicide*); ***~ённый*** *a.* devoid of, lacking; **-ся** (Р) lose; ***~и́ться чу́вств*** faint; **~е́-**

ние *n* [12] (de)privation; loss; *pl.* privations, hardships; **~е́ние прав** disfranchisement; **~е́ние свобо́ды** imprisonment; **~и́ть(ся)** → **~а́ть(ся)**

ли́шн|ий [15] superfluous, odd, excessive, over...; sur...; *запасно́й* spare; extra; *нену́жный* needless, unnecessary; *su.* outsider; **~ее** undue (*things, etc.*); *вы́пить* (*a.* a glass) too much; **... с ~им** over ...; **~ий раз** once again; **не ~е** + *inf.* (p.) had better

лишь (*a.* + **то́лько**) only; merely, just; as soon as, no sooner ... than, hardly; **~ бы** if only, provided that

лоб *m* [1; лба; во, на лбу́] forehead

лови́ть [14], <пойма́ть> [1] catch; *в западню́* (en)trap; *слу́чай* seize; **~ на сло́ве** take at one's word; *по ра́дио* pick up

ло́вк|ий [16; ло́вок, ловка́, -о; *comp.*: ло́вче] dexterous, adroit, deft; **~ость** *f* [8] adroitness, dexterity

ло́в|ля *f* [6] catching; *ры́бы* fishing; **~у́шка** *f* [5; *g/pl.*: -шек] trap; (*сило́к*) snare

логари́фм *m* [1] *math.* logarithm

ло́г|ика *f* [5] logic; **~и́ческий** [16], **~и́чный** [11; -чен, -чна] logical

ло́гов|ище *n* [11], **~о** *n* [9] lair, den

ло́д|ка *f* [5; *g/pl.*: -док] boat; **подво́дная ~ка** submarine

лоды́жка *f* [5; *g/pl.*: -жек] ankle

ло́дырь *coll. m* [4] idler, loafer

ло́жа *f* [5] *thea.* box

ложби́на *f* [5] narrow, shallow gully; *fig. coll.* cleavage

ло́же *n* [11] channel, bed (*a. of. river*)

ложи́ться [16 *e.*; -жу́сь, -жи́шься], <лечь> [26] [г/ж: ля́гу, лгут; ля́г(те)!; лёг, легла́] lie down; **~ в** (B) go to (*bed, a.* **~** [**спать**]); **~ в больни́цу** go to hospital

ло́жка *f* [5; *g/pl.*: -жек] spoon; **ча́йная ~** teaspon; **столо́вая ~** tablespoon

ло́ж|ный [14; -жен, -жна] false; **~ный шаг** false step; **~ь** *f* [8; лжи; ло́жью] lie, falsehood

лоза́ *f* [5; *pl. st.*] *виногра́дная* vine

ло́зунг *m* [1] slogan

локализова́ть [7] (*im*)*pf.* localize

локо|моти́в *m* [1] locomotive, railway engine; **´~н** *m* [1] curl, lock; **´~ть** *m* [4; -ктя; *from g/pl. e.*] elbow

лом *m* [1; *from g/pl.: e.*] crowbar; *металлоло́м* scrap (metal); **~аный** [14] broken; **~а́ть** [1], <по-, с-> break (*a.* up); *дом* pull down; **~а́ть себе́ го́лову** rack one's brains (**над** T over); **-ся** break; <по-> P clown, jest; put on airs

ломба́рд *m* [1] pawnshop

лом|и́ть [14] *coll.* → **~а́ть**; *impers.* ache, feel a pain in; **-ся** bend, burst; *в дверь и т. д.* force (*v/t.* **в** B), break (into); **~ка** *f* [15] breaking (up); **~кий** [16; ло́мок, ломка́, -о] brittle, fragile; **~о́та** *f* [5] rheumatic pain, ache *pl.*; **~о́ть** *m* [4; -мтя́] slice; **~тик** *m* [1] *dim.* → **~о́ть**

ло́н|о *n* [9] *се́мьи* bosom; **на ~е приро́ды** in the open air

ло́па|сть *f* [8; *from g/pl. e.*] blade; *ae.* vane; **~та** *f* [8] shovel, spade; **~тка** *f* [5; *g/pl.*: -ток] **1.** *dim.* → **~та**; **2.** *anat.* shoulder blade

ло́паться [1], <-нуть> [20] break, burst; split, crack; **чуть не ~ от сме́ха** split one's sides with laughter

лопу́х *m* [1 *e.*] *bot.* burdock; *coll.* fool

лоск *m* [1] luster (-tre), gloss, polish

лоску́т *m* [1 *e.*; pl. *a.*: -ку́тья, -ьев] rag, shred, scrap

лос|ни́ться [13] be glossy, shine; **~оси́на** *f* [5] *cul.* **~о́сь** *m* [1] salmon

лось *m* [4; *from g/pl. e.*] elk

лотере́я *f* [6] lottery

лото́к *m* [1; -тка́] street vendor's tray *or* stall; **продава́ть с лотка́** sell in the street

лохм|а́тый [14 *sh.*] shaggy, dishevel(l)ed; **~о́тья** *n/pl.* [*gen.*: -ьев] rags

ло́цман *m* [1] *naut.* pilot

лошад|и́ный [14] horse...; **~и́ная си́ла** horsepower; **´~ь** *f* [8; *from g/pl. e., instr.*: -дьми́ & -дя́ми] horse

лощи́на *f* [5] hollow, depression

лоя́льн|ость *f* [8] loyalty; **~ый** [14; -лен, -льна] loyal

лу|бо́к *m* [1; -бка́] cheap popular print; **~г** *m* [1; на -у́; *pl.* -а́, *etc. e.*] meadow

лу́ж|а *f* [5] puddle, pool; ***сесть в ~у*** *coll.* get into a mess
лужа́йка *f* [5; *g/pl.*: -а́ек] (small) glade
лук *m* [1] **1.** *collect.* onion(s); **2.** bow (*weapon*)
лука́в|ить [14], <с-> dissemble, be cunning; **~ство** *n* [9] cunning, slyness, ruse; **~ый** [14 *sh.*] crafty, wily; (*игри́вый*) saucy, playful
лу́ковица *f* [5] onion; *bot.* bulb
лун|а́ *f* [5] moon; **~а́тик** *m* [1] sleepwalker, somnambulist; **~ный** [14] moon(lit); *astr.* lunar
лу́па *f* [5] magnifying glass
лупи́ть [14] thrash, flog
лупи́ться [14], <об-> peel, scale (off)
луч *m* [1 *e.*] ray, beam; **~ево́й** [14] radial; radiation (***боле́знь*** sickness); **~еза́рный** [14; -рен, -рна] resplendent; **~и́стый** [14 *sh.*] radiant
лу́чш|е *adv.*, *comp.* → ***хорошо́***; **~ий** [17] better; best (***в ~ем слу́чае*** at ...)
лущи́ть [16 *e.*; -щу́, -щи́шь], <вы́-> shell, husk
лы́ж|а *f* [5] ski; snowshoe (*vb.*: ***ходи́ть***, *etc.*, ***на ~ах***); **~ник** *m* [1], **~ница** *f* [5] skier; **~ный** [14] ski...
лы́с|ый [14 *sh.*] bald; **~ина** *f* [5] bald spot, bald patch
ль → ***ли***
льви́|ный [14] lion's; ***~ный зев*** *bot.* snapdragon; **~ца** *f* [5] lioness
льго́т|а *f* [5] privilege; **~ный** [14; -тен, -тна] privileged; (*сни́женный*) reduced; preferential; favo(u)rable
льди́на *f* [5] ice floe
льну́ть [20], <при-> cling, stick (to); *fig. coll.* have a weakness (for)
льняно́й [14] flax(en); *ткань* linen...
льст|е́ц *m* [1 *e.*] flatterer; **~и́вый** [14 *sh.*] flattering; **~и́ть** [15], <по-> flatter; delude (o.s. **себя́** with T)
любе́зн|ичать *coll.* [1] (**с** T) pay court (**с** T to), flirt, pay compliments (**с** T to); **~ость** *f* [8] courtesy; kindness; (*услу́га*) favo(u)r; *pl.* compliments; **~ый** [14; -зен, -зна] polite, amiable, kind; obliging
люби́м|ец *m* [1; -мца], **~ица** *f* [5] favo(u)rite, pet; **~ый** [14] beloved, darling; favo(u)rite, pet
люби́тель *m* [4], **~ница** *f* [5] lover, fan; amateur; **~ский** [16] amateur
люби́ть [14] love; like, be (<по-> grow) fond of; *pf.* fall in love with
любов|а́ться [7], <по-> (T *or* **на** B) admire, (be) delight(ed) (in); **~ник** *m* [1] lover; **~ница** *f* [5] mistress; **~ный** [14] love...; *отноше́ние* loving, affectionate; ***~ная связь*** love affair; **~ь** *f* [8; -бви́, -бо́вью] love (**к** Д of, for)
любо|зна́тельный [14; -лен, -льна] inquisitive, curious; *ум* inquiring; **~й** [14] either, any(one *su.*); **~пы́тный** [14; -тен, -тна] curious, inquisitive; interesting; ***мне ~пы́тно ...*** I wonder ...; **~пы́тство** *n* [9] curiosity; interest; ***пра́здное ~пы́тство*** idle curiosity
лю́бящий [17] loving, affectionate
люд *m* [1] *collect. coll.*, **~и** [-е́й, -ям, -ьми́, -ях] people; ***вы́йти в ~и*** get on in life; ***на ~ях*** in the presence of others, in company; **~ный** [14; -ден, -дна] crowded; **~oе́д** *m* [1] cannibal; *в ска́зках* ogre
люк *m* [1] hatch(way); manhole
лю́стра *f* [5] chandelier, luster (*Brt.* -tre)
лютера́н|ин *m* [1; *nom./pl.* -ра́не, g. -ра́н], **~ка** *f* [5; *g/pl.*: -нок], **~ский** [16] Lutheran
лю́тик *m* [1] buttercup
лю́тый [14; лют, -а́, -о; *comp.*: -те́е] fierce, cruel
люце́рна *f* [5] alfalfa, lucerne
ляг|а́ть(ся) [1], <~ну́ть> [20] kick
лягуш|а́тник *m* [1] wading pool for children; **~ка** *f* [5; *g/pl.*: -шек] frog
ля́жка *f* [5; *g/pl.*: -жек] *coll.* thigh, haunch
лязг *m* [1], **~ать** [1] clank, clang; *зуба́ми* clack
ля́мк|а *f* [5; *g/pl.*: -мок] strap; ***тяну́ть ~у*** *fig. coll.* drudge, toil

М

мавзоле́й *m* [3] mausoleum
магази́н *m* [1] store, shop
магистра́ль *f* [8] main; *rail.* main line; *во́дная* waterway; thoroughfare; trunk (line)
маги́ческий [16] magic(al)
ма́гний *m* [3] *chem.* magnesium
магни́т *m* [1] magnet; **~офо́н** *m* [1] tape recorder
магомета́н|ин *m* [1; *pl.*: -а́не, -а́н], **~ка** *f* [5; *g/pl.*: -нок] Mohammedan
ма́з|ать [3] **1.** <по-, на-> (*па́чкать*) smear; *esp. eccl.* anoint; *ма́слом и т. д.* spread, butter; **2.** <с-> oil, lubricate; **3.** *coll.* <за-> soil; *impf.* daub; **~ня́** *coll. f* [6] daub(ing); **~о́к** *m* [1; -зка́] dab; stroke; *med.* smear; swab; **~у́т** *m* [1] heavy fuel oil; **~ь** *f* [8] ointment
май *m* [3] May
ма́й|ка *f* [5; *g/pl.*: ма́ек] undershirt, T-shirt; sports shirt; **~оне́з** *m* [1] mayonnaise; **~о́р** *m* [1] major; **~ский** [16] May(-Day)...
мак *m* [1] poppy
макаро́ны *m* [1] macaroni
мак|а́ть [1], *once* <~ну́ть> [20] dip
маке́т *m* [1] model; *mil.* dummy
ма́клер *m* [1] *comm.* broker
макну́ть → ***мака́ть***
максим|а́льный [14; -лен, -льна] maximum; **´~ум** *m* [1] maximum; at most
маку́шка *f* [5; *g/pl.*: -шек] top; *головы́* crown
малева́ть [6], <на-> *coll.* paint, daub
мале́йший [17] least, slightest
ма́ленький [16] little, small; (*ни́зкий*) short; trifling, petty
мали́н|а *f* [5] raspberry, -ries *pl.*; **~овка** *f* [5; *g/pl.*: -вок] robin (redbreast); **~овый** [14] raspberry-...; crimson
ма́ло little (*a.* **~ что**); few (*a.* **~ кто**); a little; not enough; less; ***~ где*** in few places; ***~ когда́*** seldom; *coll.* ***~ ли что*** much, many things, anything; (*a.*) yes, but ...; that doesn't matter, even though; ***~ того́*** besides, and what is more; ***~ того́, что*** not only (that)
мало|ва́жный [14; -жен, -жна] insignificant, trifling; **~ва́то** *coll.* little, not (quite) enough; **~вероя́тный** [14; -тен, -тна] unlikely; **~габари́тный** [14; -тен, -тна] small; **~гра́мотный** [14; -тен, -тна] uneducated, ignorant; *подхо́д и т. д.* crude, faulty; **~доказа́тельный** [14; -лен, -льна] unconvincing; **~ду́шный** [14; -шен, -шна] pusillanimous; **~зна́чащий** [17 *sh.*] → ***~ва́жный***; **~иму́щий** [17 *sh.*] poor; **~кро́вие** *n* [12] an(a)emia; **~ле́тний** [15] minor, underage; little (one); **~литра́жка** *f* [5; *g/pl.*: -жек] *coll.* compact (car); mini car; **~лю́дный** [14; -ден, -дна] poorly populated (*or* attended); **~-ма́льски** *coll.* in the slightest degree; at all; **~общи́тельный** [14; -лен, -льна] unsociable; **~о́пытный** [14; -тен, тна] inexperienced; **~-пома́лу** *coll.* gradually, little by little; **~приго́дный** [14; -ден, -дна] of little use; **~ро́слый** [14 *sh.*] undersized; **~содержа́тельный** [14; -лен, льна] uninteresting, shallow, empty
ма́л|ость *f* [8] *coll.* trifle; a bit; **~оце́нный** [14; -е́нен, -е́нна] of little value, inferior; **~очи́сленный** [14 *sh.*] small (in number), few; **~ый** [14; мал, -а́; *comp.*: ме́ньше] small, little; *ро́стом* short; → ***~енький***; *su.* fellow, guy; ***без ~ого*** almost, all but; ***от ~а до вели́ка*** young and old; ***с ~ых лет*** from childhood; **~ы́ш** *coll. m* [1 *e.*] kid(dy), little boy
ма́льч|ик *m* [1] boy, lad; **~и́шеский** [16] boyish; mischievous; **~и́шка** *coll. m* [5; *g/pl.*: -шек] urchin; greenhorn; **~уга́н** *coll. m* [1] → ***малы́ш***; *a.* → ***~и́шка***
малю́тка *m/f* [5; *g/pl.*: -ток] baby, tot
маля́р *m* [1 *e.*] (house) painter
малярия́ *f* [7] *med.* malaria

М

ма́м|а *f* [5] mam(m)a, mother; **~а́ша** *coll. f* [5], *coll. f* **~очка** *f* [5; *g/pl.*: -чек] mommy, mummy
ма́нго *n* [*indecl.*] mango
мандари́н *m* [1] mandarin(e), tangerine
манда́т *m* [1] mandate
ман|ёвр *m* [1], **~еври́ровать** [7] maneuver, *Brt.* manoeuvre; **~е́ж** *m* [1] riding school; *цирк* arena; **~еке́н** *m* [1] mannequin (*dummy*)
мане́р|а *f* [5] manner; **~ный** [14; -рен, -рна] affected
манже́т(к)а *f* [(5; *g/pl.*: -ток)] cuff
манипули́ровать [7] manipulate
мани́ть [13; маню́, ма́нишь], <по-> (T) beckon; *fig.* entice, tempt
ма́н|ия *f* [7] (***вели́чия*** megalo)mania; **~ки́ровать** [7] (*im*)*pf.* (T) neglect
ма́нная [14]: **~ *крупа́*** semolina
мара́зм *m* [1] *med.* senility; *fig.* nonsense, absurdity
мара́ть *coll.* [1], <за-> soil, stain; <на-> scribble, daub; <вы́-> delete
марганцо́вка *f* [5; -вок] *chem.* potassium manganate
маргари́н *m* [1] margarine
маргари́тка *f* [5; *g/pl.*: -ток] daisy
маринова́ть [7], <за-> pickle
ма́рк|а *f* [5; *g/pl.*: -рок] (postage) stamp; make; grade, brand, trademark; **~е́тинг** *m* [1] marketing; **~си́стский** [16] Marxist
ма́рля *f* [6] gauze
мармела́д *m* [1] fruit jelly (*candied*)
ма́рочный [14] *вино́* vintage
март *m* [1], **~овский** [16] March
марты́шка *f* [5; *g/pl.*: -шек] marmoset
марш *m* [1], **~ирова́ть** [7] march; **~ру́т** *m* [1] route, itinerary; **~ру́тный** [14]: ***~ру́тное такси́*** fixed-route taxi
ма́ск|а *f* [5; *g/pl.*: -сок] mask; **~ара́д** *m* [1] (*a.* ***бал-~ара́д***) masked ball, masquerade; **~ирова́ть** [7], <за->, **~иро́вка** *f* [5; *g/pl.*: -вок] mask; disguise, camouflage
ма́сл|еница *f* [5] Shrovetide; **~ёнка** *f* [5; *g/pl.*: -нок] butter dish; **~еный** [14] → **~яный**; **~ина** *f* [5] olive; **~и́чный** [14] olive...; oil ...; **~о** *n* [9; *pl.*: -сла́, -сел, -сла́м] (*a.* ***сли́вочное ~о***) butter; (*a.* ***расти́тельное ~о***) oil; ***как по ~у*** *fig.* swimmingly; **~озаво́д** creamery; **~яный** [14] oil(y); butter(y); greasy; *fig.* unctuous
ма́сс|а *f* [5] mass; bulk; *людей* multitude; *coll.* a lot; **~а́ж** *m* [1], **~и́ровать** [7] (*pt. a. pf.*) massage; **~и́в** *m* [1] *го́рный* massif; **~и́вный** [14; -вен, -вна] massive; **~овый** [14] mass...; popular...
ма́стер *m* [1; *pl.*: -ра́, *etc. e.*] master; (*бригади́р*) foreman; (*уме́лец*) craftsman; (*знато́к*) expert; ***~ на все ру́ки*** jack-of-all-trades; **~и́ть** *coll.* [13], <с-> work; make; **~ска́я** *f* [16] workshop; *худо́жника и т. д.* atelier, studio; **~ско́й** [16] masterly (*adv.* **~ски́**); **~ство́** *n* [9] trade, craft; skill, craftsmanship
масти́тый [14 *sh.*] venerable; eminent
масть *f* [8; *from g/pl. e.*] colo(u)r (*of animal's coat*); *ка́рты* suit
масшта́б *m* [1] scale (on **в** П); *fig.* scope; caliber (-bre); repute
мат *m* [1] **1.** *sport* mat; **2.** *chess* checkmate; **3.** foul language
матема́ти|к *m* [1] mathematician; **~ка** *f* [5] mathematics; **~ческий** [16] mathematical
материа́л *m* [1] material; **~и́зм** *m* [1] materialism; **~и́ст** *m* [1] materialist; **~исти́ческий** [16] materialistic; **~ьный** [14; -лен, -льна] material; economic; financial
матери́к *m* [1 *e.*] continent
матери́|нский [16] mother('s), motherly, maternal; **~нство** *n* [9] maternity; **´~я** *f* [7] matter; *ткань* fabric, material
ма́тка *f* [5; *g/pl.*: -ток] *anat.* uterus
ма́товый [14] dull, dim, mat
матра́с *m* [1] mattress
ма́трица *f* [5] *typ.* matrix; die, mo(u)ld; *math.* array of elements
матро́с *m* [1] sailor, seaman
матч *m* [1] *sport* match
мать *f* [ма́тери, *etc.* = 8; *pl.*: ма́тери, -ре́й, *etc. e.*] mother
мах *m* [1] stroke, swing; **с** (***одного́***) **~у** at one stroke *or* stretch; at once; ***дать ~у*** miss one's mark, make a

blunder; **~а́ть** [3, *coll.* 1], *once* <~ну́ть> [20] (T) wave; ***хвосто́м*** wag; ***кры́льями*** flap; *pf. coll.* go; ***~ну́ть руко́й на*** (B) give up; **~ови́к** *m* [1 *e.*], **~ово́й** [14]: ***~ово́е колесо́*** flywheel
махо́рка *f* [5] coarse tobacco
махро́вый [14] *bot.* double; Turkish *or* terry-cloth (***полоте́нце*** towel); *fig.* dyed-in-the-wool
ма́чеха *f* [5] stepmother
ма́чта *f* [5] mast
маши́н|а *f* [5] machine; engine; *coll.* car; ***стира́льная ~а*** washing machine; ***шве́йная ~а*** sewing-machine; **~а́льный** [14; -лен, -льна] mechanical, perfunctory; **~и́ст** *m* [1] *rail.* engineer, *Brt.* engine driver; **~и́стка** *f* [5; *g/pl.*: -ток] (girl) typist; **~ка** *f* [5; *g/pl.*: -нок] (***пи́шущая***) typewriter; **~ный** [14] machine..., engine...; **~опись** *f* [8] typewriting; **~острое́ние** *n* [12] mechanical engineering
мая́к *m* [1 *e.*] lighthouse; beacon; leading light
ма́я|тник *m* [1] pendulum; **~ться** P [27] drudge; ***от бо́ли*** suffer; **~чить** *coll.* [16] loom
мгла *f* [5] gloom, darkness; heat mist
мгнове́н|ие *n* [12] moment; instant; ***в ~ие о́ка*** in the twinkling of an eye; **~ный** [14; -е́нен, -е́нна] momentary, instantaneous
ме́б|ель *f* [8] furniture; **~лиро́вка** *f* [5] furnishing(s)
мёд *m* [1; *part.g.*: мёду; в меду́; *pl. e.*] honey
меда́ль *f* [8] medal; **~о́н** *m* [1] locket, medallion
медве́|дица *f* [5] she-bear; *astr.* **Ꙩдица** Bear; **~дь** *m* [4] bear (*coll. a. fig.*); **~жий** [18] bear('s)...; ***услу́га*** bad (*service*); **~жо́нок** *m* [2] bear cub
ме́ди|к *m* [1] physician, doctor; medical student; **~каме́нты** *m/pl.* [1] medication, medical supplies; **~ци́на** *f* [5] medicine; **~ци́нский** [16] medical
ме́дл|енный [14 *sh.*] slow; **~и́тельный** [14; -лен, -льна] sluggish, slow, tardy; **~ить** [14], <про-> delay, linger; be slow, tarry; hesitate
ме́дный [14] copper...
мед|осмо́тр *m* [1] medical examination; **~пу́нкт** *m* [1] first-aid station; **~сестра́** *f* [5; *pl. st.*: -сёстры, -сестёр, -сёстрам] (*medical*) nurse
меду́за *f* [5] jellyfish
медь *f* [8] copper; *coll.* copper (*coin*)
меж → **~ду**; **~а́** *f* [5; *pl.*: ме́жи, меж, межа́м] boundary; **~доме́тие** *n* [12] *gr.* interjection; ***~контипента́льный*** intercontinental
ме́жду (T) between; among(st); ***~ тем*** meanwhile, (in the) meantime; ***~ тем как*** whereas, while; **~горо́дный** [14] *tel.* long-distance..., *Brt.* trunk...; interurban; **~наро́дный** [14] international
межплане́тный [14] interplanetary
мексик|а́нец *m* [1; -нца], **~а́нка** *f* [5; *g/pl.*: -нок], **~а́нский** [16] Mexican
мел *m* [1; в ~у́] chalk; ***для побе́лки*** whitewash
меланхо́л|ик *m* [1] melancholic; **~и́ческий** [16], **~и́чный** [14; -чен, -чна] melancholy, melancholic; **~ия** *f* [7] melancholy
меле́ть [8], <об-> grow shallow
ме́лк|ий [16; -лок, -лка́, -о; *comp.*: ме́льче] small, little; ***интере́сы*** petty; ***песо́к*** fine; ***река́*** shallow; ***таре́лка*** flat; ***~ий дождь*** drizzle; **~ота́** *f* [8] small fry
мелоди́|ческий [16] melodic; melodious; **~чный** [14; -чен, -чна] melodious; **´~я** *f* [7] melody
ме́лоч|ность *f* [8] pettiness, small-mindedness, paltriness; **~ный** [14; -чен, -чна] petty, paltry; **~ь** *f* [8; *from g/pl. e.*] trifle; trinket; *coll.* small fry; ***де́ньги*** (small) change; *pl.* details, particulars
мел|ь *f* [8] shoal, sandbank; ***на ~и́*** aground; *coll.* in a fix
мельк|а́ть [1], <~ну́ть> [20] flash; gleam; flit; fly (past); pass by fleetingly; ***~о́м*** for a brief moment; ***взгляну́ть ~о́м*** cast a cursory glance
ме́льни|к *m* [1] miller; **~ца** *f* [5] mill

М

мельхио́р *m* [1] cupronickel, German silver
мельч|а́ть [1], <из-> become (**~и́ть** [16 *e.*; -чу́, -чи́шь] make) small(er) *or* shallow(er); become petty
мелюзга́ *coll. f* [5] → **ме́лочь** *coll.*
мемориа́л *m* [1], **~ный** [14] memorial; ***~ная доска́*** memorial plaque
мемуа́ры *m/pl.* [1] memoirs
ме́нее less; ***~ всего́*** least of all; ***тем не ~*** nevertheless
ме́ньш|е less; smaller; *a.* ***ме́нее***; **~ий** [17] smaller, lesser; younger; least; **~инство́** *n* [9] minority
меню́ *n* [*indecl.*] menu, bill of fare
меня́ть [28], <по-, об-> exchange, barter (***на*** В for); change (→ ***пере~***); **-ся** *v/i.* (Т/**с** Т s.th. with)
ме́р|а *f* [5] measure; degree, way; ***по ~е*** (Р) *or* ***того́ как*** according to (*a.* ***в ~у*** Р); as far as; while the ..., the ... (+ *comp.*); ***по кра́йней*** (***ме́ньшей***) ***~е*** at least
мере́нга *f* [5] meringue
мере́щиться [16], <по-> (Д) seem (*to hear, etc.*); appear (to), imagine
мерз|а́вец *coll. m* [1; -вца] swine, scoundrel; **~кий** [16; -зок, -зка́, -о] vile, disgusting, loathsome, foul
мёрз|лый [14] frozen; **~нуть** [21], <за-> freeze; feel cold
ме́рзость *f* [8] vileness, loathsomeness
ме́рин *m* [1] gelding; ***врать как си́вый ~*** lie in one's teeth
ме́р|ить [13], <с-> measure; <при-, по-> *coll.* try on; **~ка** *f* [5; *g/pl.*: -рок]: ***снять ~ку*** take s.o.'s measure
ме́ркнуть [21], <по-> fade, darken
мерлу́шка *f* [5; *g/pl.*: -шек] lambskin
ме́р|ный [14; -рен, -рна] measured; rhythmical; **~оприя́тие** *n* [12] measure; action
ме́ртв|енный [14 *sh.*] deathly (pale); **~е́ть** [8], <о-> deaden; *med.* mortify; grow *or* turn numb (pale, desolate); **~е́ц** *m* [1 *e.*] corpse
мёртв|ый [14; мёртв, мертва́, мёртво; *fig.*: мертво́, мертвы́] dead; ***~ая то́чка*** dead point, dead center (-tre) *fig.*; ***на ~ой то́чке*** at a standstill

мерца́|ние *n* [12], **~ть** [1] twinkle
меси́ть [15], <за-, с-> knead
ме́сса *f* [5] *mus.* mass
мести́ [25 -т-; мету́, метёшь; мётший], <под-> sweep, whirl
ме́стн|ость *f* [8] region, district, locality, place; **~ый** [14] local; ***~ый жи́тель*** local inhabitant
ме́ст|о *n* [9; *pl. e.*] place, site; ***сиде́ние*** seat; *coll. old use* job, post; ***в те́ксте*** passage *pl. a.*; → **~ность;** ***о́бщее*** (*or* ***изби́тое***) **~о** platitude, commonplace; (***заде́ть за***) ***больно́е ~о*** tender spot (touch on the raw); (***не***) ***к ~у*** in (out of) place; ***не на ~е*** in the wrong place; ***~а́ми*** in (some) places, here and there; ***спа́льное ~о*** berth; **~ожи́тельство** *n* [9] residence; **~оиме́ние** *n* [12] *gr.* pronoun; **~онахожде́ние, ~оположе́ние** *n* [12] location, position; **~опребыва́ние** *n* [12] whereabouts; residence; **~орожде́ние** *n* [12] deposit; ***нефтяно́е*** field
месть *f* [8] revenge
ме́ся|ц *m* [1] month; moon; ***в ~ц*** a month, per month; ***медо́вый ~ц*** honeymoon; **~чный** [14] month's; monthly
мета́лл *m* [1] metal; **~и́ст** *m* [1] metalworker; **~и́ческий** [16] metal(lic); **~урги́я** *f* [7] metallurgy
метаморфо́за *f* [5] metamorphosis; change in s.o.'s behavio(u)r, outlook, etc.
мета́ть [3] **1.** <на-, с-> baste, tack; **2.** [3], *once* <~ну́ть> [20] throw; ***~а́ть икру́*** spawn; **-ся** toss (*in bed*); rush about
мете́ль [8] snowstorm, blizzard
метеоро́лог *m* [1] meteorologist; **~и́ческий** [16] meteorological; **~ия** *f* [7] meteorology
ме́т|ить [15], <по-> mark; (***в***, ***на*** В) aim, drive at, mean; **~ка** [5; *g/pl.*: -ток] mark(ing); **~кий** [16; -ток, -тка́, -о] well-aimed; ***стрело́к*** good; keen, accurate, steady; pointed; (***выраже́ние***) apt, to the point
мет|ла́ *f* [5; *pl. st.*: мётлы, мётел; мётлам] broom; **~ну́ть** → ***мета́ть***

ме́тод *m* [1] method; **~и́ческий** [16], **~и́чный** [14; -чен, -чна] methodic(al), systematic(al)
метр *m* [1] meter, *Brt.* metre
ме́трика *f* [5] *obs.* birth certificate
метри́ческ|ий [16]: ***~ая систе́ма*** metric system
метро́ *n* [*indecl.*], **~полите́н** *m* [1] subway, *Brt.* tube, underground
мех *m* [1; *pl.*: -xá, *etc.*, *e.*] fur; ***на ~у́*** fur-lined
механ|и́зм *m* [1] mechanism, gear; **~ик** *m* [1] mechanic; *naut.* engineer; **~ика** *f* [5] mechanics; **~и́ческий** [16] mechanical
мехов|о́й [14] fur...; **~щи́к** *m* [1 *e.*] furrier
меч *m* [1 *e.*] sword; ***Дамо́клов ~*** sword of Damocles
мече́ть *f* [8] mosque
мечта́ *f* [5] dream, daydream, reverie; **~тель** *m* [4] (day)dreamer; **~тельный** [14; -лен, -льна] dreamy; **~ть** [1] dream (**о** П of)
меша́|ть [1], <раз-> stir; <с-, пере-> mix; *о чу́вствах* mingle; <по-> disturb; (*препя́тствовать*) hinder, impede, prevent; ***вам не ~ет*** (***~ло бы***) you'd better; **-ся** meddle, interfere (***в*** В with); ***не ~йтесь не в своё де́ло!*** mind your own business!
ме́шк|ать *coll.* [1], <про-> → ***ме́длить***; **~ова́тый** [14 *sh.*] (*clothing*) baggy
мешо́к *m* [1; -шкá] sack, bag
мещан|и́н *m* [1; *pl.*: -áне, -áн], **~ский** [16] *hist.* (petty) bourgeois, Philistine; narrow-minded
мзда *f* [5] *archaic*, *now joc.* recompense, payment; *iro.* bribe
миг *m* [1] moment, instant; **~ом** *coll.* in a trice (*or* flash); **~áть** [1], *once* <~нýть> [20] blink, wink; *звёзды* twinkle; *огоньки́* glimmer
мигре́нь *f* [8] migraine
ми́зерный [14; -рен, -рна] scanty, paltry
мизи́нец [1; -нца] little finger
микро́б *m* [1] microbe
микроско́п *m* [1] microscope
микрофо́н *m* [1] microphone
миксту́ра *f* [5] medicine (*liquid*), mixture
ми́ленький *coll.* [16] lovely; dear; (*as form of address*) darling
милици|оне́р *m* [1] policeman; militiaman; **´~я** *f* [7] police; militia
милли|а́рд *m* [1] billion; **~ме́тр** *m* [1] millimeter (*Brt.* -tre); **~о́н** *m* [1] million
мило|ви́дный [14; -ден, -дна] nice-looking; **~се́рдие** *n* [12] charity, mercy; **~се́рдный** [14; -ден, -дна] charitable, merciful; **´~стыня** *f* [6] alms; **´~сть** *f* [8] mercy; (*одолже́ние*) favo(u)r; ***´~сти про́сим!*** welcome!; *iro.*, *coll.* ***по твое́й*** (***ва́шей***) ***ми́лости*** because of you
ми́лый [14; мил, -á, -o] nice, lovable, sweet; (my) dear, darling
ми́ля *f* [6] mile
ми́мо (Р) past, by; ***бить ~*** miss; **~лётный** [14; -тен, -тна] fleeting, transient; **~хо́дом** in passing; incidentally
ми́на *f* [5] **1.** *mil.* mine; **2.** mien, expression
минда́|лина *f* [5] almond; *anat.* tonsil; **~ль** *m* [4 *e.*] *collect.* almond(s); **~льничать** *coll.* [1] be too soft (towards **с** Т)
миниатю́р|а *f* [5], **~ный** [14; -рен, -рна] miniature...; *fig.* tiny, diminutive
ми́нимум *m* [1] minimum; ***прожи́точный ~*** living wage; *adv.* at the least
минист|е́рство *n* [9] *pol.* ministry; ***~е́рство иностра́нных*** (***вну́тренних***) ***дел*** Ministry of Foreign (Internal) Affairs; **~р** *m* [1] minister, secretary
мин|ова́ть [7] (*im*)*pf.*, <~у́ть> [20] pass (by); *pf.* be over; escape; (Д) **~у́ло** (*о во́зрасте*) → ***испо́лниться***; **~у́вший**, **~у́вшее** *su.* past
мино́рный [14] *mus.* minor; *fig.* gloomy, depressed
ми́нус *m* [1] *math.* minus; *fig.* shortcoming
мину́т|а *f* [5] minute; moment, instant (***в*** В at; ***на*** В for); ***сию́ ~у*** at once, immediately; at this moment; ***с ~ы на ~у*** (at) any moment; → ***пя́тый***, ***пять***; **~ный** [14] minute('s); moment('s), momentary

ми́нуть → ***минова́ть***
мир *m* [1] **1.** peace; **2.** [*pl. e.*] world; *fig.* universe, planet; ***не от ~а сего́*** otherworldly
мир|и́ть [13], <по-, при-> reconcile (to с T); **-ся** make it up, be(come) reconciled; <при-> resign o.s. to; put up with; **~ный** [14; -рен, -рна] peace...; peaceful
мировоззре́ние *n* [12] weltanschauung, world view; ideology
мирово́й [14] world('s); worldwide, universal; *coll.* first-class
миро|люби́вый [14 *sh.*] peaceable; peaceloving; **~тво́рческий** [16] peacemaking
ми́ска *f* [5; *g/pl.*: -сок] dish, tureen; bowl
ми́ссия *f* [7] mission; *dipl.* legation
ми́стика *f* [5] mysticism
мистифика́ция *f* [7] mystification; hoax
ми́тинг *m* [1] *pol.* mass meeting; **~ова́ть** [7] *impf. coll.* hold (*or* take part in) a mass meeting
митрополи́т *m* [1] *eccl.* metropolitan
миф *m* [1] myth; **~и́ческий** [16] mythic(al); **~оло́гия** *f* [7] mythology
ми́чман *m* [1] warrant officer
мише́нь *f* [8] target
ми́шка *coll. m* [5; *g/pl.*: -шек] (*pet name used for*) bear; (***плю́шевый***) teddy bear
мишура́ *f* [5] tinsel
младе́н|ец *m* [1; -нца] infant, baby; **~чество** *n* [9] infancy
мла́дший [17] younger, youngest; junior
млекопита́ющее *n* [17] *zo.* mammal
мле́чный [14] milk..., milky (*a.* ♀, *ast.*); ***~ сок*** latex
мне́ни|е *n* [12] opinion (***по*** Д in); ***обще́ственное ~е*** public opinion; ***по моему́ ~ю*** to my mind
мни́|мый [14 *sh.*, *no m*] imaginary; (*ло́жный*) sham; **~тельный** [14; -лен, -льна] (*подозри́тельный*) hypochondriac(al); suspicious
мно́гие *pl.* [16] many (people, *su.*)
мно́го (P) much, many; a lot (*or* plenty) of; ***ни ~ ни ма́ло*** *coll.* neither more nor less; **~ва́то** *coll.* rather too much (many); **~веково́й** [14] centuries-old; **~гра́нный** [14; -а́нен, -а́нна] many-sided; **~де́тный** [14; -тен, -тна] having many children; **~значи́тельный** [14; -лен, -льна] significant; **~кра́тный** [14; -тен, -тна] repeated; *gr.* frequentative; **~ле́тний** [15] long-standing, of many years; *план и т. д.* long-term...; *bot.* perennial **~лю́дный** [14; -ден, -дна] crowded, populous; *ми́тинг* mass...; **~национа́льный** [14; -лен, -льна] multinational; **~обеща́ющий** [17] (very) promising; **~обра́зный** [14; -зен; -зна] varied, manifold; **~сло́вный** [14; -вен, -вна] wordy; **~сторо́нний** [15; -о́нен, -о́ння] many-sided; **~страда́льный**; [14; -лен, -льна] long-suffering; **~то́чие** *n* [12] ellipsis; **~уважа́емый** [14] dear (*address*); **~цве́тный** [14; -тен, -тна] multicolo(u)red; **~чи́сленный** [14 *sh.*] numerous; **~эта́жный** [14] many-storied (*Brt.* -reyed)
мно́ж|ественный [14 *sh.*] *gr.* plural; **~ество** *n* [9] multitude; a great number; **~имое** *n* [14] *math.* multiplicand; **~итель** *m* [4] multiplier, factor; **~ить**, <по-> → ***умножа́ть***
мобилизова́ть [7] (*im*)*pf.* mobilize
моби́льный [14; -лен, -льна] mobile
моги́л|а *f* [5] grave; **~ьный** [14] tomb...
могу́|чий [17 *sh.*], **~щественный** [14 *sh.*] mighty, powerful; **~щество** *n* [9] might, power
мо́д|а *f* [5] fashion, vogue; **~ели́рование** *n* [12] *tech.* simulation; **~е́ль** (-dɛl) *f* [8] model; **~елье́р** *m* [1] fashion designer; **~е́м** (-dɛ-) *m* [1] *comput.* modem; **~ернизи́ровать** (-dɛr-) [7] (*im*)*pf.* modernize; **~ифици́ровать** [7] (*im*)*pf.* modify; **~ный** [14; -ден, -дна́, -о] fashionable, stylish; *пе́сня* popular
мо́ж|ет быть perhaps, maybe; **~но** (***мне***, *etc.*) one (I, *etc.*) can *or* may; it is possible; → ***как***
можжеве́льник *m* [1] juniper
моза́ика *f* [5] mosaic

мозг *m* [1; -а (-у); в ~у́; *pl. e.*] brain; ***ко́стный*** marrow; ***спинно́й*** cord; ***шевели́ть ~а́ми*** *coll.* use one's brains; ***уте́чка ~о́в*** brain drain; **~ово́й** [14] cerebral

мозо́|листый [14 *sh.*] horny, calloused; **~лить** [13]: ***~лить глаза́*** Д *coll.* be an eyesore to; **~ль** *f* [8] callus; corn

мо|й *m*, **~я́** *f*, **~ё** *n*, **~и́** *pl.* [24] my; mine; *pl. su. coll.* my folks; → ***ваш***

мо́к|нуть [21], <про-> become wet; soak; **~ро́та** *f* [5] *med.* phlegm; **~рый** [14; мокр, -á, -о] wet

мол *m* [1] jetty, pier, mole

молв|а́ *f* [5] rumo(u)r; talk; **~ить** [14] *(im)pf. obs.*, <про-> say, utter

молдава́н|ин *m* [1; *pl.*: -ва́не, -а́н], **~ка** *f* [5; *g/pl.*: -нок] Moldavian

моле́бен *m* [1; -бна] *eccl.* service; public prayer

моле́кул|а *f* [5] molecule; **~я́рный** [14] molecular

моли́т|ва *f* [5] prayer; **~венник** *m* [1] prayer book; **~ь** [13; молю́, мо́лишь] (**о** П) implore, entreat, beseech (for); **~ься**, <по-> pray (Д to; **о** П for); *fig.* idolize (**на** В)

молни|ено́сный [14; -сен, сна] instantaneous; **´~я** *f* [7] lightning; (*застёжка*) zipper, zip fastener

молод|ёжь *f* [8] *collect.* youth, young people *pl.*; **~е́ть** [8], <по-> grow (look) younger; **~е́ц** *coll. m* [1; -дца́] fine fellow, brick; (*оце́нка*) *as int.* well done!; **~и́ть** [15 *e.*; -ложу́, -лоди́шь] make look younger; **~ня́к** *m* [1 *e.*] *о живо́тных* offspring; *о ле́се* undergrowth; **~о-жёны** *m/pl.* [1] newly wedded couple; **~о́й** [14; мо́лод, -á, -о; *comp.*: моло́же] young; *карто́фель, ме́сяц* new: *pl. a.* = **~ожёны**; **´~ость** *f* [8] youth, adolescence; **~цева́тый** [14 *sh.*] smart; *шаг* sprightly

моложа́вый [14 *sh.*] youthful, young-looking

моло́к|и *f/pl.* [5] milt, soft roe; **~о́** *n* [9] milk; ***сгущённое ~о́*** condensed milk; **~осо́с** *coll. m* [1] greenhorn

мо́лот *m* [1] sledgehammer; **~о́к** *m* [1; -тка́] hammer; ***с ~ка́*** by auction; **~ь** [17; мелю́, ме́лешь, меля́], <пере-, с-> grind; *coll.* talk (*вздор* nonsense); **~ьба́** *f* [5] threshing (time)

моло́чн|ик *m* [1] milk jug; **~ый** [14] milk...; dairy...

мо́лча silently, tacitly; in silence; **~ли́вый** [14 *sh.*] taciturn; *согла́сие* tacit; **~ние** *n* [12] silence; **~ть** [4 *e.*; мо́лча] be (*or* keep) silent; (***за***)***молчи́!*** shut up!

моль *f* [8] (clothes) moth

мольба́ *f* [5] entreaty; (*моли́тва*) prayer

моме́нт *m* [1] moment, instant (**в** В at); (*черта́, сторона́*) feature, aspect; **~а́льный** [14] momentary, instantaneous

мона́рхия *f* [7] monarchy

мона|сты́рь *m* [4 *e.*] monastery; *же́нский* convent; **~х** *m* [1] monk; **~хиня** *f* [6] nun (*a.*, F, **~шенка** *f* [5; *g/pl.*: -нок]); **~шеский** [16] monastic; monk's

монго́льский [16] Mongolian

моне́т|а *f* [5] coin; ***той же ~ой*** in a p.'s own coin; ***за чи́стую ~у*** in good faith; ***зво́нкая ~а*** hard cash; **~ный** [14] monetary; ***~ный двор*** mint

монито́р *m* [1] *tech.* monitor

моно|ло́г *m* [1] monologue; **~полизи́ровать** [7] *(im)pf.* monopolize; **~по́лия** *f* [7] monopoly; **~то́нный** [14; -то́нен, -то́нна] monotonous

монт|а́ж *m* [1] assembly, installation, montage; **~ёр** *m* [1] fitter; electrician; **~и́ровать** [7], <с-> *tech.* assemble, mount, fit; *cine.* arrange

монуме́нт *m* [1] monument; **~а́льный** [14; -лен, -льна] monumental (*a. fig.*)

мопе́д *m* [1] moped

мора́ль *f* [8] morals, ethics *pl.*; morality; moral; ***чита́ть ~*** *coll.* lecture, moralize; **~ный** [14; -лен, -льна] moral; ***~ное состоя́ние*** morale

морг *m* [1] morgue

морг|а́ть [1], <~ну́ть> [20] blink (Т); ***и гла́зом не ~ну́в*** *coll.* without batting an eyelid

мо́рда *f* [5] muzzle, snout

мо́ре *n* [10; *pl. e.*] sea; seaside (**на** П at); **~м** by sea; **~пла́вание** *n* [12]

М

navigation; **~пла́ватель** *m* [4] navigator, seafarer
морж *m* [1 *e.*], **~о́вый** [14] walrus; *coll.* out-of-doors winter bather
мори́ть [13], <за-, у-> exterminate; ***~ го́лодом*** starve; exhaust
морко́в|ь *f* [8], *coll.* **~ка** *f* [5; *g/pl.*: -вок] carrot(s)
моро́женое *n* [14] ice cream
моро́з *m* [1] frost; **~и́льник** *m* [1] deepfreeze; **~ить** [15], <за-> freeze; **~ный** [14; -зен, -зна] frosty
мороси́ть [15; -си́т] drizzle
моро́чить *coll.* [16] fool, pull the wool over the eyes of
морс *m* [1]: fruit drink; ***клю́квенный ~*** cranberry juice
морско́й [14] sea..., maritime; naval; nautical; seaside...; ***~ волк*** sea dog, old salt
мо́рфий *m* [3] morphine, morphia
морфоло́гия *f* [7] morphology
морщи́|на *f* [5] wrinkle; **~нистый** [14 *sh.*] wrinkled; **´~ть** [16], <на-, с-> wrinkle, frown (*v/i.* **-ся**); ***ткань*** crease
моря́к *m* [1 *e.*] seaman, sailor
моск|ви́ч *m* [1 *e.*], **~ви́чка** *f* [5; *g/pl.*: -чек] Muscovite; **~о́вский** [16] Moscow...
моски́т *m* [1] mosquito
мост *m* [1 & 1 *e.*; на ~у́; *pl. e.*] bridge; **~и́ть** [15 *e.*; мощу́, мости́шь, мощённый], <вы́-> pave; **~ки́** *m/pl.* [1 *e.*] footbridge; **~ова́я** *f* [14] *old use* carriage way
мот *m* [1] spendthrift, prodigal
мот|а́ть [1], <на-, с-> reel, wind; *coll.* <по->, *once* <~ну́ть> shake, wag; (***трясти́***) jerk; *coll.* <про-> squander; ***~а́й отсю́да!*** scram!; **-ся** *impf.* dangle; P knock about
моти́в[1] *m* [1] *mus.* tune; motif
моти́в[2] *m* [1] motive, reason; **~и́ровать** [7] (*im*)*pf.* give a reason (for), justify
мото́к *m* [1; -тка] skein, hank
мото́р *m* [1] motor, engine
мото|ро́ллер *m* [1] motor scooter; **~цикл** [1], **-е́т** *m* [1] motorcycle; **~циклист** *m* [1] motorcyclist
мотылёк *m* [1; -лька́] moth
мох *m* [1; мха & мо́ха, во (на) мху́: *pl.*: мхи, мхов] moss
мохна́тый [14 *sh.*] shaggy, hairy
моч|а́ *f* [5] urine; **~а́лка** *f* [5; *g/pl.*: -лок] washing-up mop; loofah; bath sponge; **~ево́й** [14]: ***~ево́й пузы́рь*** *anat.* bladder; **~и́ть** [16], <на-, за-> wet, moisten; soak, steep (*v/i.* **-ся**; *a.* urinate); **´~ка** *f* [5; -чек] lobe (*of the ear*)
мочь[1] [26 г/ж: могу́, мо́жешь, мо́гут; мог, -ла́; могу́щий], <с-> can, be able; may; ***я не могу́ не*** + *inf.* I can't help ...ing; ***мо́жет быть*** maybe, perhaps; ***не мо́жет быть!*** that's impossible!
моч|ь[2] P *f* [8]: ***во всю ~ь, изо всей ´~и, что есть ´~и*** with all one's might; ***´~и нет*** it's unbearable
моше́нни|к *m* [1] swindler, cheat; **~чать** [1], <с-> swindle; **~чество** *n* [9] swindling, cheating
мо́шка *f* [5; *g/pl.*: -шек] midge
мо́щи *f/pl.* [*gen.*: -ще́й, *etc. e.*] relics
мо́щ|ность *f* [8] power; *tech.* capacity; ***предприя́тия*** output; **~ный** [14; мо́щен, -щна́, -о] powerful, mighty; **~ь** *f* [8] power, might; strength
мрак *m* [1] dark(ness); gloom
мра́мор *m* [1] marble
мрачн|е́ть [8], <по-> darken; become gloomy; **´~ый** [14; -чен, -чна́, -о] dark; gloomy, somber (*Brt.* -bre)
мсти́|тель *m* [4] avenger; **~тельный** [14; -лен, -льна] revengeful; **~ть** [15], <ото-> revenge o.s., take revenge (Д on); (***за*** В) avenge a p.
мудр|ёный *coll.* [14; -ён, -ена́; -ене́е] difficult, hard, intricate; (***замыслова́тый***) fanciful; ***не ~ено́, что*** (it's) no wonder; **~е́ц** *m* [1 *e.*] sage; **~и́ть** *coll.* [13], <на-> complicate matters unnecessarily; **´~ость** *f* [8] wisdom; ***зуб ´~ости*** wisdom tooth; **´~ствовать** *coll.* [7] → **~и́ть**; **´~ый** [14; мудр, -а́, -о] wise
муж *m* **1.** [1; *pl.*: -жья́, -же́й, -жья́м] husband; **2.** *rare* [1; *pl.*: -жи́, -же́й, -жа́м] man; **~а́ть** [1], <воз-> mature, grow; **-ся** *impf.* take courage; **´~ественный** [14 *sh.*] steadfast; manly; **´~ество** *n* [9] courage, fortitude; **~и́к** *m* [1 *e.*] peasant; P man; **~ско́й** [16] male, masculine (*a. gr.*); (gentle)man('s); **~чи́на** *m* [5] man

музе́й *m* [3] museum
му́зык|а *f* [5] music; **~а́льный** [14; -лен, -льна] musical; **~а́нт** *m* [1] musician
му́ка¹ *f* [5] pain, torment, suffering, torture(s); *coll.* trouble
мука́² *f* [5] flour
мультфи́льм *m* [1] animated cartoon
му́мия *f* [7] mummy
мунди́р *m* [1] full-dress uniform; ***карто́фель в ~е*** *coll.* potatoes cooked in their jackets *or* skin
мундшту́к (-nʃ-) *m* [1 *e.*] cigarette holder; *mus.* mouthpiece
муниципалите́т *m* [1] municipality; town council
мурав|е́й *m* [3; -вья́; *pl.*: -вьи́, -вьёв] ant; **~е́йник** *m* [1] ant hill
мура́шки: **~** (**от** Р) ***бе́гают по спине́*** (**у** Р) F (s.th.) gives (a p.) the creeps
мурлы́кать [3 & 1] purr; *coll.* ***пе́сню*** hum
муска́т *m* [1] nutmeg; ***вино́*** muscat; **~ный** [14]: ***~ный оре́х*** nutmeg
му́скул *m* [1] muscle; **~ату́ра** *f* [5] *collect.* muscles; muscular system; **~и́стый** [14 *sh.*] muscular
му́сор *m* [1] rubbish, refuse; sweepings; **~ить** [13], <за-, на-> *coll.* litter; **~опрово́д** *m* [1] refuse chute
муссо́н *m* [1] monsoon
мусульма́н|ин *m* [1; *pl.*: -а́не, -а́н], **~ка** *f* [5; *g/pl.*: -нок] Muslim
мут|и́ть [15; мучу́, му́ти́шь], <вз-, по-> make muddy; *fig.* trouble; fog; ***меня́ ~и́т*** *coll.* I feel sick; **-ся** = ***~не́ть*** [8], <по-> grow turbid; blur; **~ный** [14; -тен, -тна́, -о] muddy (*a. fig.*); troubled (*waters*); dull; blurred; foggy; **~о́вка** *f* [5; *g/pl.*: -вок] whisk; **~ь** *f* [8] dregs *pl.*; murk
му́фта *f* [5] muff; *tech.* (***~ сцепле́ния***) clutch sleeve, coupling sleeve
му́фтий *m* [3] *eccl.* Mufti
му́х|а *f* [5] fly; **~омо́р** *m* [1] fly agaric (*mushroom*); *coll.* decrepit old person
муч|е́ние *n* [12] → ***му́ка***; **~еник** *m* [1] martyr; **~и́тель** *m* [4] tormentor; **~и́тельный** [14; -лен, -льна] painful, agonizing; **~ить** [16], Р **~ать** [1], <за-, из-> torment, torture; *fig.* vex, worry; **-ся** suffer (*pain*); *fig.* suffer torments; ***над зада́чей и т. д.*** take great pains (over), toil
му́шк|а *f* [5; *g/pl.*: -шек] ***ружья́*** (fore)sight; ***взять на ~у*** take aim (at)
мча́ть(ся) [4], <по-> rush *or* speed (along)
мши́стый [14 *sh.*] mossy
мще́ние *n* [12] vengeance
мы [20] we; ***~ с ним*** he and I
мы́л|ить [13], <на-> soap; ***~ить го́лову*** (Д) *coll.* give s.o. a dressing-down, scold; **~о** *n* [9; *pl. e.*] soap; **~ьница** *f* [5] soap dish; **~ьный** [14] soap(y); ***~ьная пе́на*** lather, suds
мыс *m* [1] *geogr.* cape, promontory
мы́сл|енный [14] mental; **~имый** [14 *sh.*] conceivable; **~и́тель** *m* [4] thinker; **~ить** [13] think (**о** of, about); reason; (***представля́ть***) imagine; **~ь** *f* [8] thought, idea (**о** П of); ***за́дняя ~ь*** ulterior motive
мыта́рство *n* [9] hardship, ordeal
мы́ть(ся) [22], <по-, у-, вы́-> wash (o.s.)
мыча́ть [4 *e.*; -чу́, -чи́шь] moo, low; *coll.* mumble
мышело́вка *f* [5; *g/pl.*: -вок] mouse-trap
мы́шечный [14] muscular
мы́шк|а *f* [5; *g/pl.*: -шек]: ***под ~ой*** under one's arm
мышле́ние *n* [12] thinking, thought
мы́шца *f* [5] muscle
мышь *f* [8; *from g/pl. e.*] mouse
мышья́к *m* [1 *e.*] *chem.* arsenic
мэр *m* [1] mayor
мя́гк|ий (-xk-) [16; -гок, -гка́, -о; *comp.*: мя́гче] soft; ***движе́ние*** smooth; ***мя́со и. т. д.*** tender; *fig.* mild, gentle; lenient; ***~ое кре́сло*** easy chair; ***~ий ваго́н*** *rail.* first-class coach *or* car(riage); **~осерде́чный** [14; -чен, -чна] soft-hearted; **~ость** *f* [8] softness; *fig.* mildness **~оте́лый** [14] *fig.* flabby, spineless
мя́к|иш *m* [1] soft part (*of loaf*); **~нуть** [21], <на-, раз-> become soft; **~оть** *f* [8] flesh; ***плода́*** pulp
мя́мл|ить Р [13] mumble; **~я** *m* & *f* [6] *coll.* mumbler; irresolute person; milksop

M

мяс|истый [14 *sh.*] fleshy; pulpy; **~ни́к** *m* [1 *e.*] butcher; **~но́й** [14] meat...; butcher's; **~́о** *n* [9] meat; flesh **~ору́бка** *f* [5; *g/pl.*: -бок] mincer
мя́та *f* [8] mint
мяте́ж *m* [1 *e.*] rebellion, mutiny; **~ник** *m* [1] rebel, mutineer
мять [мну, мнёшь; мя́тый], <с-, по-, из-> [сомну́; изомну́] (c)rumple, press; knead; *траву́ и т. д.* trample;. **-ся** be easily crumpled; *fig. coll.* waver, vacillate
мяу́к|ать [1], *once* <~нуть> mew
мяч *m* [1 *e.*] ball; **~́ик** [1] *dim.* → ***мяч***

Н

на[1] **1.** (В): (*направле́ние*) on, onto; to, toward(s); into, in; (*дли́тельность, назначе́ние и т. д.*) for; till; *math.* by; **~ *что?*** what for? **2.** (П): (*расположе́ние*) on, upon; in, at; with; for; **~ *ней ...*** she has ... on
на[2] *int. coll.* there, here (you are); *a.* ***вот тебе́ на!*** well, I never!
набав|ля́ть [28], <~́ить> [14] raise, add to, increase
наба́т *m* [1]: ***бить в ~*** *mst. fig.* sound the alarm
набе́|г *m* [1] incursion, raid; **~га́ть** [1], <~жа́ть> [4; -егу́, -ежи́шь, -егу́т; -еги́(те)!] run (into ***на*** В); (*покрыва́ть*) cover; **~гаться** [1] *pf.* be exhausted with running about
набекре́нь *coll.* aslant, cocked
на́бережная *f* [14] embankment, quay
наби|ва́ть [1], <~́ть> [-бью, -бьёшь; → ***бить***] stuff, fill; **~́вка** *f* [5; *g/pl.*: -вок] stuffing, padding
набира́ть [1], <набра́ть> [-беру́, -рёшь; → ***брать***] gather; *на рабо́ту* recruit; *tel.* dial; *typ.* set; take (many, much); *высоту́, ско́рость* gain; **-ся** (*наби́ться*) become crowded; P (*напи́ться*) get soused; ***-ся сме́лости*** pluck up one's courage
наби́|тый [14 *sh.*] (Т) packed; P ***~тый дура́к*** arrant fool; ***битко́м ~тый***; *coll.* crammed full; **~ть** → ***~ва́ть***
наблюд|а́тель *m* [4] observer; **~а́тельный** [14; -лен, -льна] observant, alert; *пост* observation; **~а́ть** [1] (*v/t.* & ***за*** Т) observe; watch; (*a.* ***про-***); see to (it that); **-ся** be observed *or* noted; **~е́ние** *n* [12] observation; supervison
набо́йк|а *f* [5; *g/pl.*: -бо́ек] heel (*of shoe*); ***набива́ть*** <***~би́ть***> **~у** put a heel on, heel
на́бок to *or* on one side, awry
наболе́вший [16] sore, painful (*a. fig.*)
набо́р *m* [1] *на ку́рсы и т. д.* enrol(l)ment; (***компле́кт***) set, kit; typesetting
набр|а́сывать [1] **1.** <~оса́ть> [1] sketch, design, draft; **2.** <~о́сить> [15] throw over *or* on (***на*** В); **-ся** fall (up)on
набра́ть → ***набира́ть***
набрести́ [25] *pf. coll.* come across (***на*** В); happen upon
набро́сок *m* [1; -ска] sketch, draft
набух|а́ть [1], <~́нуть> [21] swell
нава́л|ивать [1], <~и́ть> [13; -алю́, -а́лишь, -а́ленный] heap; *рабо́ту* load (with); **-ся** fall (up)on
нава́лом *adv.* in bulk; *coll.* loads of
наве́д|ываться, <~аться> [1] *coll.* call on (**к** Д)
наве́к, **~и** forever, for good
наве́рн|о(е) probably; for certain, definitely; (*a., coll.* **~яка́**) for sure, without fail
наве́рстывать, <наверста́ть> [1] make up for

наве́рх up(ward[s]); *по ле́стнице* upstairs; **~у́** above; upstairs
наве́с *m* [1] awning; annex (*with sloping roof*); shed, carport
навеселе́ *coll.* tipsy, drunk
навести́ → ***наводи́ть***
навести́ть → ***навеща́ть***
наве́тренный [14] windward
наве́чно forever, for good
наве|ща́ть [1], <~сти́ть> [15 *e.*; -ещу́, -ести́шь; -ещённый] call on
на́взничь backwards, on one's back
навзры́д: ***пла́кать ~*** sob
навига́ция *f* [7] navigation
навис|а́ть [1], <~нуть> [21] hang (over); *опа́сность и т. д.* impend, threaten
навле|ка́ть [1], <~ЧЬ> [26] (***на*** В) bring on, incur
наводи́ть [15], <навести́> [25] (***на*** В) direct (at); point (at), turn (to); lead (to), bring on *or* about, cause, raise (→ ***нагоня́ть***); make; construct; ***~ на мысль*** come up with an idea; ***~ поря́док*** put in order; ***~ ску́ку*** bore; ***~ спра́вки*** inquire (***о*** П after)
наводн|е́ние *n* [12] flood, inundation; **~я́ть** [28], <~и́ть> [13] flood with (*a. fig.*), inundate with
наво́з *m* [1], **~ить** [15], <у-> dung, manure
на́волочка *f* [5; *g/pl.*: -чек] pillowcase
навостри́ть [13] *pf.* *у́ши* prick up
навря́д (**ли**) hardly, scarcely
навсегда́ forever; ***раз и ~*** once and for all
навстре́чу toward(s); ***идти́ ~*** (Д) go to meet; *fig.* meet halfway
навы́ворот Р (*наизна́нку*) inside out; ***де́лать ши́ворот-~*** put the cart before the horse
на́вык *m* [1] experience, skill (***в*** П in)
навя́з|ывать [1], <~а́ть> [3] *мне́ние, во́лю* impose, foist ([up]on; Д *v/i.* **-ся**); **~чивый** [14 *sh.*] obtrusive; ***~чивая иде́я*** idée fixe
наг|иба́ть [1], <~ну́ть> [20] bend, bow, stoop (*v/i.* **-ся**)
нагишо́м *coll.* stark naked
нагл|е́ть [8], <об-> become impudent; **~е́ц** *m* [1 *e.*] impudent fellow; **~ость** *f* [8] impudence, insolence; ***верх ~ости*** the height of impudence; ***~ухо*** tightly; **~ый** [14; нагл, -á, -о] impudent, insolent, *coll.* cheeky
нагляд|е́ться [11]: ***не ~е́ться*** never get tired of looking (at); **~ный** [14; -ден, -дна] clear, graphic; (*очеви́дный*) obvious; *посо́бие* visual; ***~ный уро́к*** object lesson
нагна́ть → ***нагоня́ть***
нагнета́ть [1]: ***~ стра́сти*** stir up passions
нагное́ние *n* [12] suppuration
нагну́ть → ***нагиба́ть***
нагов|а́ривать [1], <~ори́ть> [13] say, tell, talk ([too] much *or* a lot of ...); *coll.* slander (a p. ***на*** В, ***о*** П); (*записа́ть*) record; **~ори́ться** *pf.* talk o.s. out; ***не ~ори́ться*** never get tired of talking
наго́й [14; наг, -á, -о] nude, naked, bare
нагон|я́й *coll. m* [3] scolding, upbraiding; **~я́ть** [28], <нагна́ть> [-гоню́, -го́нишь; → ***гнать***] overtake, catch up (with); (*навёрстывать*) make up (for); ***~я́ть страх, ску́ку***, *etc.* ***на*** (В) frighten, bore, *etc.*
нагота́ *f* [5] nudity; nakedness
нагот|а́вливать [1], <~о́вить> [14] prepare; (*запасти́сь*) lay in; **~о́ве** in readiness, on call
награ́бить [14] *pf.* amass by robbery, plunder (a lot of)
награ́|да *f* [5] reward (***в*** В as a); (*знак отли́чия*) decoration; **~жда́ть** [1], <~ди́ть> [15 *e.*; -ажу́, -ади́шь; -аждённый] (Т) reward; decorate; *fig.* endow with
нагрева́т|ельный [14] heating; **~ь** [1] → ***греть***
нагромо|жда́ть [1], <~зди́ть> [15 *e.*; -зжу́, зди́шь; -ождённый] pile up, heap up
нагру́дник *m* [1] bib, breastplate
нагру|жа́ть [1], <~зи́ть> [15 & 15 *e.*; -ужу́, -у́зи́шь; -у́женный] load (with Т); *coll.* *рабо́той a.* burden, assign; **~зка** *f* [5; *g/pl.*: -зок] load(ing); *coll. a* burden, job, assignment; *преподава́теля* teaching load

нагря́нуть [20] *pf. о гостя́х* appear unexpectedly, descend (on)
над, **~о** (Т) over, above; *смея́ться* at; about; *труди́ться* at, on
нада́в|ливать [1], <~и́ть> [14] (*a.* ***на*** В) press; squeeze; *со́ку* press out
надба́в|ка *f* [5; *g/pl.*: -вок] addition; extra charge; *к зарпла́те* increment, rise; **~ля́ть** [28], <~ить> [14] *coll.* → ***набавля́ть***
надви|га́ть [1], <~нуть> [20] move, push, pull (up to, over); ***~га́ть ша́пку*** pull one's hat over one's eyes; **-ся** approach, draw near; (*закры́ть*) cover
на́двое in two (parts *or* halves); ambiguously; ***ба́бушка ~ сказа́ла*** it remains to be seen
надгро́бие *n* [12] tombstone
наде|ва́ть [1], <~ть> [-е́ну, -е́нешь; -е́тый] put on (*clothes, etc.*)
наде́жд|а *f* [5] hope (***на*** В of); ***подава́ть ~ы*** show promise
надёжный [14; -жен, -жна] reliable, dependable; (*про́чный*) firm; (*безопа́сный*) safe
наде́л|ать [1] *pf.* make (a lot of); (*причиня́ть*) do, cause, inflict; **~я́ть** [28], <~и́ть> [13] *умо́м и т. д.* endow with
наде́ть → ***надева́ть***
наде́яться [27] (***на*** В) hope (for); (*полага́ться*) rely (on)
надзо́р *m* [1] supervision; *мили́ции и т. д.* surveillance
надл|а́мывать, <~омáть> [1] *coll.*, <~оми́ть> [14] crack; *fig.* overtax, break down
надлежа́|ть [4; *impers.* + *dat. and inf.*] it is necessary; **~щий** [17] appropriate, suitable; ***~щим о́бразом*** properly, duly
надлома́ть → ***надла́мывать***
надме́нный [14; -е́нен, -е́нна] haughty
на́до it is necessary (for Д); (Д) (one) must (*go, etc.*); need; want; ***так ему́ и ~*** it serves him right; **~бность** *f* [8] need (***в*** П for), necessity; affair, matter (***по*** Д in); ***по ме́ре ~бности*** when necessary
надо|еда́ть [1], <~е́сть> [-е́м, -е́шь, *etc.*, → ***есть***[1]] (Д, Т) tire; *вопро́сами и т. д.* bother, pester; ***мне ~е́л...*** I'm tired (of) fed up (with); **~е́дливый** [14 *sh.*] tiresome; *челове́к* troublesome, annoying
надо́лго for (a) long (time)
надорва́ть → ***надрыва́ть***
надпи́|сывать [1], <~са́ть> [3] inscribe; *конве́рт и т. д.* superscribe; **´~сь** *f* [8] inscription
надре́з *m* [1] cut, incision; **~а́ть** *and* **~ывать** [1], <~ать> [3] cut, incise
надруга́тельство *n* [9] outrage
надры́в *m* [1] rent, tear; *fig.* strain; **~а́ть** [1], <надорва́ть> [-ву́, -вёшь; надорва́л, -а́, -о; -о́рванный] tear; *здоро́вье* undermine; (over)strain (o.s. себя́, **-ся**; be[come] worn out *or* exhausted; let o.s. go; ***~а́ть живо́т от сме́ха***, ***~а́ться*** (***со́ смеху***) split one's sides (with laughter)
надстр|а́ивать [1], <~о́ить> [13] build on; raise the height of; **~о́йка** [5; *g/pl.*: -ро́ек] superstructure
наду|ва́ть [1], <~ть> [18] inflate; (*обма́нывать*) dupe; ***~ть гу́бы*** pout; **-ся** *v/i. coll.* (*оби́деться*) be sulky (***на*** В with); **~вно́й** [14] inflatable, air...; **~ть** → ***~ва́ть***
надý́м|анный [14] far-fetched, strained; **~ать** *coll.* [1] *pf.* think (of), make up one's mind
надý́тый [1] (*оби́женный*) sulky
наеда́ться [1], <нае́сться> [-е́мся, -е́шься, *etc.*, → ***есть***[1]] eat one's fill
наедине́ alone, in private
нае́зд *m* [1] (***~ом*** on) short *or* flying visit(s); **~ник** *m* [1] rider
нае|зжа́ть [1], <~хать> [нае́ду, -е́дешь] (***на*** В) run into *or* over; *coll.* come (occasionally), call on (***к*** Д)
наём *m* [1; на́йма] *рабо́тника* hire; *кварти́ры* rent; **~ник** *m* [1] *солда́т* mercenary; **~ный** [14] hired
нае́|сться → ***~да́ться***; **~хать** → ***~езжа́ть***
нажа́ть → ***нажима́ть***
нажда́|к *m* [1 *e.*], **~чный** [14] emery
нажи́|ва *f* [5] gain, profit; **~ва́ть** [1], <~ть> [-живу́, -вёшь; на́жил, -а́, -о; нажи́вший; на́житый (на́жит,

-á, -o)] earn, gain; *добро́* amass; *состоя́ние, враго́в* make; *ревмати́зм* get; **~вка** *f* [5; *g/pl.*: -вок] bait

нажи́м *m* [1] pressure (*a. fig.*); **~а́ть** [1], <нажа́ть> [-жму́, -жмёшь; -жа́тый] (*a.* **на** В) press, push (*a. coll. fig.* = urge, impel; influence)

нажи́ть → ***нажива́ть***

наза́д back(ward[s]); **~!** get back!; ***тому́ ~*** ago

назва́|ние *n* [12] name; title; **~ть** → ***называ́ть***

назе́мный [14]: ***~ тра́нспорт*** overland transport

назида́|ние *n* [12] edification (for p.'s **в** В/Д); **~тельный** [14; -лен, -льна] edifying

на́зло́ Д out of spite, to spite (s.b.)

назнач|а́ть [1], <~ить> [16] appoint (p. s.th. В/Т), designate; *вре́мя и т. д.* fix, settle; *лека́рство* prescribe; *день и т. д.* assign; **~е́ние** *n* [12] appointment; assignment; (*цель*) purpose; prescription; (*ме́сто ~е́ния*) destination

назо́йливый [14 *sh.*] importunate

назре|ва́ть [1], <~ть> [8] ripen, mature; *fig.* be imminent *or* impending; ***~ло вре́мя*** the time is ripe

назубо́к *coll.* by heart, thoroughly

называ́|ть [1], <назва́ть> [-зову́, -зовёшь; -зва́л, -á, -o; на́званный (на́зван, -á, -o)] call, name; (*упомяну́ть*) mention; ***~ть себя́*** introduce o.s.; ***~ть ве́щи свои́ми имена́ми*** call a spade a spade; ***так ~емый*** so-called; **-ся** call o.s., be called; ***как ~ется ...?*** what is (*or* do you call) ...?

наи... *in compds.* of all, very; **~бо́лее** most, ...est of all

наи́в|ность *f* [8] naiveté; **~ый** [14; -вен, -вна] naive, ingenuous

наизна́нку inside out

наизу́сть by heart

наиме́нее least ... of all

наименова́ние *n* [12] name; title

наискосо́к obliquely

найти́|е *n* [12]: ***по ~ю*** by intuition

найти́ → ***находи́ть***

наказ|а́ние *n* [12] punishment (**в** В as a); penalty; *coll.* nuisance; **~у́емый** [14 *sh.*] punishable; **~ывать** [1], <~а́ть> [3] punish

нака́л *m* [1] incandescence; **~ивать** [1], <~и́ть> [13] incandesce; ***стра́сти ~и́лись*** passions ran high; **~ённый** incandescent, red-hot; *атмосфе́ра* tense

нак|а́лывать [1], <~оло́ть> [17] *дров* chop

накану́не the day before; **~** (P) on the eve (of)

нака́пливать [1] & **~опля́ть** [28], <~опи́ть> [14] accumulate, amass; *де́ньги* save up

наки́|дка *f* [5; *g/pl.*: -док] cape, cloak; **~дывать** [1] **1.** <~да́ть> [1] throw about; **2.** <~нуть> [20] throw on; *coll.* (*наба́вить*) add; raise; **-ся** (**на** В) *coll.* fall (up)on

на́кипь *f* [8] *пе́на* scum (*a. fig.*); *оса́док* scale

наклад|на́я *f* [14] invoice, waybill; **~но́й** [14]: ***~ные расхо́ды*** overhead, expenses, overheads; **~ывать** *and* **налага́ть** [1], <наложи́ть> [16] (**на** В) lay (on), apply (to); put (on), set (to); *взыска́ние, штраф* impose; *отпеча́ток* leave; (*напо́лнить*) fill, pack, load

накле́|ивать [1], <~ить> [13; -éю] glue *or* paste on; *ма́рку* stick on; **~йка** *f* [5; *g/pl.*: -éек] label

накло́н *m* [1] incline; slope; **~е́ние** *n* [12] *gr.* inclination; mood; **~и́ть** → **~я́ть**; **~ный** [14] inclined, slanting; **~я́ть** [28], <~и́ть> [13; -оню́, -о́нишь; -онённый] bend, tilt; bow, stoop; incline; **-ся** *v/i.*

накова́льня *f* [6; *g/pl.*: -лен] anvil

наколо́ть → ***нака́лывать***

наконе́|ц (***~ц-то*** oh) at last, finally; at length; **~чник** *m* [1] tip, point

накоп|ле́ние *n* [12] accumulation; **~ля́ть, ~и́ть** → ***нака́пливать***

накрахма́ленный [14] starched

на́крепко fast, tight

накры|ва́ть [1], <~ть> [22] cover; *стол* (*a.* В) lay (*the table*); Р *престу́пника* catch, trap

накуп|а́ть [1], <~и́ть> [14] (P) buy up (a lot)

наку́р|ивать [1], <~и́ть> [13; -урю́, -у́ришь; -у́ренный] fill with smoke *or* fumes

налага́ть → ***накла́дывать***

нала́|живать [1], <~дить> [15] put

Н

right *or* in order, get straight, fix; *дела́* get things going; *отноше́ния* establish

нале́во to *or* on the left of; → ***напра́во***

нале|га́ть [1], <~чь>; [26; г/ж: -ля́гу, -ля́жешь, -ля́гут; -лёг, -гла́; -ля́г(те)!] (***на*** В) lean (on); press (against, down); *fig. на рабо́ту и т. д.* apply o.s. (to)

налегке́ *coll.* with no baggage (*Brt.* luggage)

налёт *m* [1] *mil., ae.* raid, attack; *med.* fur; (*a. fig.*) touch; **~а́ть** [1], <~е́ть> [11] (***на*** В) fly (at, [*a.* knock, strike] against); swoop down; raid, attack; (*набро́ситься*) fall ([up]on); *о ве́тре, бу́ре* spring up; **~чик** *m* [1] bandit

нале́чь → ***налега́ть***

нали|ва́ть [1], <~ть> [-лью́, -льёшь; -ле́й(те)!; на́ли́л, -а́, -о; -ли́вший; на́ли́тый (на́ли́т, -а́, -о)] pour (out); fill; *p. pt. p.* (*a.* **~то́й**) ripe, jucy; *о те́ле* firm; (**-ся** *v/i.*; *a.* ripen); **~вка** *f* [5; *g/pl.*: -вок] (fruit) liqueur; **~м** *m* [1] burbot

налито́й, **нали́ть** → ***налива́ть***

налицо́ present, on hand

нали́ч|ие *n* [12] presence; **~ность** *f* [8] cash-in-hand; *a* → **~ие**; ***в ~ности*** → ***налицо́***; **~ный** [14] (*a. pl., su.*); *де́ньги* ready cash (*a.* down Т); (*име́ющийся*) present, on hand; ***за ~ные*** for cash

налог *m* [1] tax; *на това́ры* duty; **~оплате́льщик** *m* [1] taxpayer

нало́ж|енный [14]: ***~енным платежо́м*** cash (*or* collect) on delivery; **~и́ть** → ***накла́дывать***

налюбова́ться [7] *pf.* (Т) gaze to one's heart's content; ***не ~*** never get tired of admiring (o.s. ***собо́й***)

нама́|зывать [1] → ***ма́зать***; **~тывать** [1] → ***мота́ть***

нам|ёк *m* [1] (***на*** В) allusion (to), hint (at); **~ека́ть** [1], <~екну́ть> [20] (***на*** В) allude (to), hint (at)

намер|ева́ться [1] intend → (***я*** I, *etc.*) **~ен(а)**; **~ение** *n* [12] intention, design; purpose (**с** Т on); **~енный** [14] intentional, deliberate

намета́ть → ***намётывать***

наме́тить → ***намеча́ть***

нам|ётка *f* [5; *g/pl.*: -ток], **~ётывать** [1], <~ета́ть> [3] *sew.* baste, tack

наме|ча́ть [1], <~тить> [15] (*плани́ровать*) plan, have in view; (*отбира́ть*) nominate, select

намно́го much, (by) far

намок|а́ть [1], <~нуть> [21] get wet

намо́рдник *m* [1] muzzle

нанести́ → ***наноси́ть***

нани́з|ывать [1], <~а́ть> [3] string, thread

нан|има́ть [1], <~я́ть> [найму́, -мёшь; на́нял, -а́, -о; -я́вший; на́нятый (на́нят, -а́, -о)] rent, hire; *рабо́чего* take on, engage; **-ся** *coll.* take a job

на́ново anew, (over) again

наноси́ть [15], <нанести́> [24 -с-: несу́, -сёшь; -нёс, -несла́] bring (much, many); *водо́й* carry, waft, deposit, wash ashore; *кра́ску и т. д.* lay on, apply; *на ка́рту и т. д.* plot, draw; (*причиня́ть*) inflict (on Д), cause; *визи́т* pay; *уда́р* deal

наня́ть(ся) → ***нанима́ть(ся)***

наоборо́т the other way round, vice versa, conversely; on the contrary

наобу́м *coll.* at random, haphazardly; without thinking

наотре́з bluntly, categorically

напа|да́ть [1], <~сть> [25; *pt. st.*: -па́л, -а; -па́вший] (***на*** В) attack, fall (up)on; (*случа́йно обнару́жить*) come across *or* upon; hit on; *страх* come over, seize, grip; **~да́ющий** *m* [17] assailant; *sport* forward; **~де́ние** *n* [12] attack; assault; **~дки** *f/pl.* [5; *gen.*: -док] accusations; (*приди́рки*) carping, faultfinding *sg.*

нап|а́ивать [1], <~ои́ть> [13] *водо́й и т. д.* give to drink; *спиртны́м* make drunk

напа́|сть **1.** *coll.* *f* [8] misfortune, bad luck; **2.** → ***~да́ть***

напе́|в *m* [1] melody, tune; **~ва́ть** [1] hum, croon

напере|бо́й *coll.* vying with one another; **~го́нки́** *coll.*: ***бежа́ть ~го́нки́*** racing one another; **~ко́р** (Д) in spite *or* defiance (of), counter (to); **~ре́з** cutting (across s.b.'s way Д, Р);

~чёт each and every; *as pred.* not many, very few
напёрсток *m* [1; -тка] thimble
напи|ва́ться [1], <~~ться> [-пью́сь, -пьёшься; -пи́лся, -пила́сь; пе́йся, -пе́йтесь!] drink, quench one's thirst; (*опьяне́ть*) get drunk
напи́льник *m* [1] (*tool*) file
напи́|ток *m* [1; -тка] drink, beverage; ***прохлади́тельные*** (***спиртны́е***) **~тки** soft (alcoholic) drinks; **~ться** → ***~ва́ться***
напи́х|ивать, <~~а́ть> [1] cram into, stuff into
наплы́в *m* [1] *покупа́телей и т. д.* influx
нанова́л outright, on the spot
наподо́бие (Р) like, resembling
напои́ть → ***напа́ивать***
напока́з for show; → ***выставля́ть***
наполн|я́ть [28], <~~ить> [13] (Т) fill; crowd; *p. pt. p. a.* full
наполови́ну half; (*do*) by halves
напом|ина́ние *n* [12] reminding, reminder; **~ина́ть** [1], <~~нить> [13] remind (a. p. of Д/**о** П)
напо́р *m* [1] pressure (*a. fig.*); **~истость** [8] push, vigo(u)r
напосле́док *coll.* in the end, finally
напра́в|ить(ся) → **~ля́ть(ся)**; **~ле́ние** *n* [12] direction (**в** П, ***по*** Д in); *fig.* trend, tendency; **~ля́ть** [28], <~ить> [14] direct, aim; send, refer to; assign, detach; **-ся** head for; (*coll.*) get going, get under way; turn (***на*** В to)
напра́во (**от** Р) to the right, on the right
напра́сн|ый [14; -сен, -сна] vain; (*необосно́ванный*) groundless, idle; **~о** in vain; (*незаслу́женно*) wrongly
напр|а́шиваться [1], <~~оси́ться> [15] (***на*** В) (pr)offer (o.s. for), solicit; *на оскорбле́ния* provoke; *на комплиме́нты* fish (for); *impf. вы́воды и т. д.* suggest itself
наприме́р for example, for instance
напро|ка́т for hire; ***взять***(***дать***) **~ка́т** hire (out); **~лёт** *coll.* (all)... through(out); without a break; **~ло́м** *coll.*: ***идти́ ~ло́м*** force one's way; (*act*) regardless of obstacles
напроси́ться → ***напра́шиваться***
напро́тив (Р) opposite; on the contrary; → *a.* ***наперекóр*** *and* ***наоборо́т***
напря|га́ть [1], <~~чь> [26; г/ж: -ягу́, -яжёшь; -пря́г] strain (*a. fig.*); exert; *му́скулы* tense; **~же́ние** *n* [12] tension (*a. el.* voltage), strain, exertion, effort; close attention; **~жённый** [14 *sh.*] *отноше́ния* strained; *труд и т. д.* (in)tense; *внима́ние* keen, close
напрями́к *coll.* straight out; outright
напря́чь → ***напряга́ть***
напу́ганный [14] scared, frightened
напус|ка́ть [1], <~ти́ть> [15] let in, fill; set on (***на*** В); *coll.* (***~ка́ть на себя́***) put on (*airs*); Р *стра́ху* cause; **-ся** *coll.* fly at, go for (***на*** В); **~кно́й** [14] affected, assumed, put-on
напу́тств|енный [14] farewell..., parting; **~ие** *n* [12] parting words
напы́щенный [14 *sh.*] pompous; *стиль* high-flown
наравне́ (**с** Т) on a level with; equally; together (*or* along) with
нараспа́шку *coll.* unbuttoned; (***душа́***) **~** frank, candid
нараспе́в with a singsong voice
нараст|а́ть [1], <~~и́> [24; -стёт; → ***расти́***] grow; *о проце́нтах* accrue; increase; *о зву́ке* swell
нарасхва́т *coll.* like hot cakes
нарез|а́ть [1], <~~ать> [3] cut; *мя́со* carve; *ло́мтиками* slice; **~ывать** → **~а́ть**
нарека́ние *n* [12] reprimand, censure
наре́чие[1] *n* [12] dialect
наре́чие[2] *gr.* adverb
нарица́тельный [14] *econ.* nominal; *gr.* common
нарко́|з *m* [1] narcosis, an(a)esthesia; **~ма́н** *m* [1] drug addict; **~тик** *m* [1] narcotic
наро́д *m* [1] people, nation; **~ность** *f* [8] nationality; **~ный** [14] people's, popular, folk...; national; ***~ное хозя́йство*** national economy
наро́ст *m* [1] (out)growth
нароч|и́тый [14 *sh.*] deliberate, intentional; *adv.* = **~но** *a.* on purpose; *coll.* in fun; *coll. a.* → ***на́зло́***; **´~ный** [14] courier

нáрты *f/pl.* [5] sledge (*drawn by dogs or reindeer*)

нарýж|ность *f* [8] exterior; outward appearance; **~ный** [14], external; *спокóйствие и т. д.* outward(s); **~у** outside, outward(s); ***вы́йти ~у*** *fig.* come to light

наруш|áть [1], <~ить> [16] disturb; *прáвило и т. д.* infringe, violate; *тишинý и т. д.* break; **~éние** *n* [12] violation, transgression, breach; disturbance; **~и́тель** *m* [4] *грани́цы* trespasser; *спокóйствия* disturber; *закóна* infringer; **~ить** → **~áть**

нарци́сс *m* [1] daffodil

нáры *f/pl.*[5] plank bed

навры́в *m* [1] abcess; → ***гнои́ть***; **~áть** [1], <нарвáть> *med.* come to a head

нарá|д *m* [1] *одéжда* attire, dress; **~ди́ть** → **~жáть**; **~дный** [14; -ден, -дна] well-dressed; elegant; smart

нарядý (**с** T) together (*or* along) with, side by side; at the same time; *a.* → ***наравнé***

наря|жáть [1], <~ди́ть> [15 & 15 *e.*; -яжý, -я́ди́шь; -я́женный & -яжённый] dress up (as) (*v/i.* **-ся**)

наса|ждáть [1], <~ди́ть> [15] (im)plant (*a. fig.*); → *a.* **~живать**; **~ждéние** *n* [12] *mst. pl.* specially planted trees, bushes; **~живать** [1], <~жáть>, <~ди́ть> [15] plant (many); *на рýчку* haft

насви́стывать [1] whistle

наседáть [1] *impf.* press (*of crowds, etc.*)

насекóмое *n* [14] insect

насел|éние *n* [12] population; *гóрода* inhabitants; **~ённый** [14; -лён, -ленá, -ленó] populated; ***~ённый пункт*** (*official designation*) locality, built-up area; **~я́ть** [28], <~и́ть> [13] people, settle; *impf.* inhabit, live in

наси́женный [14] snug; familiar, comfortable

наси́|лие *n* [12] violence, force; (*принуждéние*) coercion; **~ловать** [7] violate, force; rape; (*a.* **из-**); **~лу** *coll.* → ***éле***; **~льно** by force; forcibly; **~льственный** [14] forcible; *смерть* violent

наск|áкивать [1], <~очи́ть> [16] (**на** B) *fig. coll.* fly at, fall (up)on; *кáмень и т. д.* run *or* strike against; (*столкнýться*) collide (with)

насквóзь throughout; *coll.* through and through

наскóлько as (far as); how (much); to what extent

нáскоро *coll.* hastily, in a hurry

наскочи́ть → ***наскáкивать***

наскýчить *coll.* [16] *pf.*, → ***надоедáть***

насла|ждáться [1], <~ди́ться> [15 *e.*; -ажýсь, -ади́шься] (T) enjoy (o.s.), (be) delight(ed); **~ждéние** *n* [12] enjoyment; delight; pleasure

наслéд|ие *n* [12] heritage, legacy; → *a.* **~ство**; **~ник** *m* [1] heir; **~ница** *f* [5] heiress; **~ный** [14] *принц* crown...; **~овать** [7] *(im)pf.*, <у-> inherit; (Д) succeed to; **~ственность** *f* [8] heredity; **~ственный** [14] hereditary; *имýщество* inherited; **~ство** *n* [9] inheritance; → *a.* **~ие**; *vb.* + **в ~ство** (*or* **по ~ству**) inherit

наслоéние *n* [12] stratification

насл|ýшаться [1] *pf.* (P) listen to one's heart's content; ***не мочь ~ýшаться*** never get tired of listening to; *a.* = **~ы́шаться** [4] (P) hear a lot (of) *or* much; → ***понаслы́шке***

насмáрку: ***пойти́ ~*** come to nothing

нáсмерть to death (*a. fig.*), mortally; ***стоя́ть ~*** fight to the last ditch

насме|хáться [1] mock, jeer; sneer (at ***над*** T); **~шка** *f* [5; *g/pl.*: -шек] mockery, ridicule; **~шливый** [14 *sh.*] derisive, mocking; **~шник** *m* [1], **~шница** *f* [5] scoffer, mocker

нáсморк *m* [1] cold (*in the head*); ***подхвати́ть ~*** catch a cold

насмотрéться [9; -отрю́сь, -óтришься] *pf.* → ***наглядéться***

насóс *m* [1] pump

нáспех hastily, carelessly

наста|вáть [5], <~ть> [-стáнет] come; **~вить** → **~вля́ть**; **~влéние** *n* [12] (*поучéние*) admonition, guidance; **~вля́ть** [28], <~вить> [14] **1.** put, place, set (many P); **2.** (*поучáть*) instruct; teach (Д, **в** П s.th.) **~ивать** [1], <настоя́ть> [-стою́, -стои́шь] insist (***на*** П on);

чай и т. д. draw, extract; ***настоя́ть на своём*** insist on having it one's own way; **~ть → *~ва́ть***
на́стежь wide open
насти|га́ть [1], <~гнуть> & <~чь> [21; -г-: -и́гну] overtake; catch (up with)
наст|ила́ть [1], <~ла́ть> [-телю́, -те́лешь; на́стланный] lay, spread; *до́сками* plank; *пол* lay
насто́й *m* [3] infusion, extract; **~ка** *f* [5; *g/pl.*: -óек] liqueur; *a.* → ~
насто́йчивый [14 *sh.*] persevering; *тре́бование* urgent, insistent, persistent; (*упо́рный*) obstinate
насто́ль|ко so (*or* as [much]); **~ный** [14] table...
насторо|а́живаться [1], <~ожи́ться> [16 *e.*; -жу́сь, -жи́шься] prick up one's ears; become suspicious; **~оже́** on the alert, on one's guard
настоя́|ние *n* [12] insistence, urgent request (***по*** Д at); **~тельный** [14; -лен, -льна] urgent, pressing, insistent; **~ть → *наста́ивать***
настоя́щ|ий [17] present (*time*) (***в*** В at); *a. gr.* ***~ее вре́мя*** present tense; true, real, genuine; ***по-~ему*** properly
настр|а́ивать [1], <~о́ить> [13] build (many P); *инструме́нт, орке́стр, ра́дио* tune (up, in); *про́тив* set against; *a.* ***нала́живать*** adjust; ***~ого*** strictly; **~ое́ние** *n* [12] mood, spirits *pl.*, frame (of mind); **~о́ить** → ***~а́ивать***; **~о́йка** *f* [5; *g/pl.*: -óек] tuning
наступ|а́тельный [14] offensive; **~а́ть** [1], <~и́ть> [14] tread *or* step (***на*** В on); (*нача́ться*) come, set in; *impf. mil.* attack, advance; (*приближа́ться*) approach; **~ле́ние** *n* [12] offensive, attack, advance; coming, approach: *дня* daybreak; *су́мерек* nightfall (**с** Т at)
насту́рция [7] nasturtium
насу́пить(ся) [14] *pf.* frown
на́сухо dry
насу́щный [14; -щен, -щна] vital; ***~ хлеб*** daily bread
насчёт (Р) *coll.* concerning, about
насчи́т|ывать, <~а́ть> [1] number (= *to have or contain*); **-ся** *impf.* there is (are)
насып|а́ть [1], <~ать> [2] pour; fill; **~ь** *f* [8] embankment
насы|ща́ть [1], <~тить> [15] satisfy; *вла́гой* saturate; **~ще́ние** *n* [12] satiation; saturation
нат|а́лкивать [1], <~олкну́ть> [20] (***на*** В) push (against, on); *coll.* prompt, suggest; **-ся** strike against; (*случа́йно встре́тить*) run across
натвори́ть *coll.* [13] *pf.* do, get up to
нат|ира́ть [1], <~ере́ть> [12] (Т) rub; *мозо́ль* get; *пол* wax, polish
на́тиск *m* [1] pressure; *mil.* onslaught, charge
наткну́ться → ***натыка́ться***
натолкну́ть(ся) → ***ната́лкивать-ся***
натоща́к on an empty stomach
натра́в|ливать [1], <~и́ть> [14] set (***на*** В on), incite
на́трий *m* [3] *chem.* sodium
нату́|га *coll.* *f* [5] strain, effort; **~го** *coll.* tight(ly)
нату́р|а *f* [5] (*хара́ктер*) nature; (artist's) model (= **~щик** *m* [1], **~щица** [5]): **с *~ы*** from nature *or* life; **~а́льный** [14; -лен, -льна] natural
нат|ыка́ться [1], <~кну́ться> [20] (***на*** В) run *or* come across
натя́|гивать [1], <~ну́ть> [19] stretch, draw tight; pull (***на*** В on); draw in (*reins*); **~жка** *f* [5; *g/pl.*: -жек] forced *or* strained interpretation; ***допусти́ть ~жку*** stretch a point; **с *~жкой*** *a.* at a stretch; **~нутый** [14] tight; *отноше́ния* strained; *улы́бка* forced; **~ну́ть** → ***~гивать***
наугáд at random, by guessing
нау́ка *f* [5] science; *coll.* lesson
наутёк: *coll.* ***пусти́ться ~*** take to one's heels
нау́тро the next morning
научи́ть [16] teach (В/Д a p. s.th.); **-ся** learn (Д s.th.)
нау́чный [14; -чен, -чна] scientific
нау́шники *m/pl.* [1] ear- *or* headphones; earmuffs
наха́|л *m* [1] impudent fellow; **~льный** [14; -лен, -льна] impudent, insolent; **~льство** *n* [12] impudence, insolence
нахва́т|ывать, <~а́ть> *coll.* [1] (Р)

Н

pick up, come by, get hold of; hoard; *a.* **-ся**
нахлы́нуть [20] *pf.* flow; gush (over, into); *чу́вства* sweep over
нахму́ривать [1] → ***хму́рить***
наход|и́ть [15], <найти́> [найду́, дёшь; нашёл, -шла́; -ше́дший; на́йденный; *g. pt.*: найдя́] **1.** find (*a. fig.* = think, consider).; *impf. удово́льствие* take; **2.** come (over ***на*** B); (*закры́ть*) cover; *тоска́ и т. д.*; be seized with; (**-ся**, <найти́сь>) be (found, there, [*impf.*] situated, located); (*име́ться*) happen to have; (*не растеря́ться*) not be at a loss; **~ка** *f* [5; *g/pl.*: -док] find; *coll.* discovery; *coll. fig.* godsend; ***стол ~ок*** lost-property office; **~чивый** [14 *sh.*] resourceful; quick-witted, smart
наце́нка *f* [5; *g/pl.*: -нок] markup
национал|из(и́р)ова́ть [7] (*im*)*pf.* nationalize; **~и́зм** *m* [1] nationalism; **~ьность** *f* [8] nationality; **~ьный** [14; -лен, -льна] national
на́ция *f* [7] nation
нача́|ло *n* [9] beginning (at a П); (*исто́чник*) source, origin; (*осно́ва*) basis; principle; **~льник** *m* [1] head, chief, superior; **~льный** [14] initial, first; *стро́ки* opening; **~льство** *n* [9] (the) authorities; command(er[s], chief[s], superior[s]); (*администра́ция*) administration, management; **~тки** *m/pl.* [1] elements; **~ть(ся)** → ***начина́ть(ся)***
начеку́ on the alert, on the qui vive
на́черно roughly, in draft form
начина́|ние *n* [12] undertaking; **~ть** [1], <нача́ть> [-чну́, -чнёшь; на́чал, -а́, -о; нача́вший; на́чатый (на́чат, -а́, -о)] begin, start (**с** P *or* T with); **-ся** *v/i.*; **~ющий** [17] beginner
начиная *as prep.* (**с** P) as (from), beginning (with)
начи́н|ка [5; *g/pl.*: -нок] *mst. cul.* filling, stuffing; **~я́ть** [28] <~и́ть> [13] fill, stuff (with T)
начисле́ние *n* [12] additional sum, extra charge
на́чисто clean; → ***на́бело***; (*по́лностью*) fully
начи́т|анный [14 *sh.*] well-read; **~а́ться** [1] (P) read (a lot of); *доста́точно* read enough (of); ***не мочь ~а́ться*** never get tired of reading
наш *m*, **~а** *f*, **~е** *n*, **~и** *pl.* [25] our; ours; ***по ~ему*** to our way of thinking; ***~а взяла́!*** we've won!
нашаты́р|ный [14]: ***~ный спирт*** *m* liquid ammonia; *coll. a.* **~ь** *m* [4 *e.*] *chem.* ammonium chloride
наше́ствие *n* [12] invasion, inroad
наши|ва́ть [1], <~ть> [-шью́, -шьёшь; → ***шить***] sew on (***на*** B *or* П) *or* many...; **~вка** *f* [5; *g/pl.*: -вок] *mil.* stripe, chevron
нащу́п|ывать, <~ать> [1] find by feeling *or* groping; *fig.* discover; detect
наяву́ while awake, in reality
не not; no; ***~ то*** *coll.* or else, otherwise
неаккура́тный [14; -тен, -тна] (*небре́жный*) careless; (*неря́шливый*) untidy; *в рабо́те* inaccurate; unpunctual
небе́сный [14] celestial, heavenly; *цвет* sky-blue; (*боже́ственный*) divine; → ***небосво́д***
неблаго|ви́дный [14; -ден, -дна] unseemly; **~да́рность** *f* [8] ingratitude; **~да́рный** [14; -рен, -рна] ungrateful; **~полу́чный** [14; -чен, чна] unfavorable, adverse, bad; *adv.* not successfully, not favo(u)rably; **~прия́тный** [14; -тен, -тна] unfavo(u)rable, inauspicious; **~разу́мный** [14; -мен, -мна] imprudent; unreasonable; **~ро́дный** [14; -ден, -дна] ignoble; **~скло́нный** [14; -о́нен, -о́нна] unkindly; ill-disposed; ***судьба́ ко мне ~скло́нна*** fate has not treated me too kindly
не́бо¹ *n* [9; *pl.*: небеса́, -е́с] sky (in ***на*** П); heaven(s); ***под откры́тым ~м*** in the open air
нёбо² *n* [9] *anat.* palate
небога́тый [14 *sh.*] of modest means; poor
небольш|о́й [17] small; short; ***... с ~и́м*** ... odd
небо|сво́д *m* [1] firmament; *a.* **~скло́н** *m* [1] horizon; **~скрёб** *m* [1] skyscraper
небре́жный [14; -жен, -жна] careless, negligent; slipshod

небы|ва́лый [14] unheard-of, unprecedented; **~ли́ца** *f* [5] fable, invention

нева́жн|ый [14; -жен, -жна, -о] unimportant, trifling; *coll.* poor, bad; ***э́то ~о*** it does not matter

невдалеке́ not far off *or* from (**от** P)

невдомёк: ***мне бы́ло ~*** it never occurred to me

неве́|дение *n* [12] ignorance; **~домый** [14 *sh.*] unknown; **~жа** *m/f* [5] boor; **~жда** *m/f* [5] ignoramus; **~жество** *n* [9] ignorance; **~жливость** *f* [8] incivility; **~жливый** [14 *sh.*] impolite, rude

неве́р|ие *n* [12] *в свои́ си́лы* lack of self-confidence; **~ный** [14; -рен, -рна, -о] incorrect; *fig.* false; *друг* unfaithful; *похо́дка и т. д.* unsteady; *su.* infidel; **~оя́тный** [14; -тен, -тна] improbable; incredible

невесо́мый [14 *sh.*] imponderable; weightless (*a. fig.*)

неве́ст|а *f* [5] fiancée, bride; *coll.* marriageable girl; **~ка** *f* [5; *g/pl.*: -ток] daughter-in-law; sister-in-law (*brother's wife*)

невз|го́да *f* [5] adversity, misfortune; **~ира́я** (***на*** B) in spite of, despite; without respect (of p.'s); **~нача́й** *coll.* unexpectedly, by chance; **~ра́чный** [14; -чен, -чна] plain, unattractive; **~ыска́тельный** [14] unpretentious, undemanding

неви́д|анный [14] singular, unprecedented; **~имый** [14 *sh.*] invisible

неви́нный [14; -и́нен, -и́нна] innocent, virginal

невку́сный [14; -сен, -сна] unpalatable

невме|ня́емый [14 *sh.*] *law* irresponsible; *coll.* beside o.s. **~ша́тельство** *n* [9] nonintervention

невнима́тельный [14; -лен, -льна] inattentive

невня́тный [14; -тен, -тна] indistinct, inarticulate

не́вод *m* [1] seine, sweep-net

невоз|врати́мый [14 *sh.*], **~вра́тный** [14; -тен, -тна] irretrievable, irreparable, irrevocable; **~мо́жный** [14; -жен, -жна] impossible; **~мути́мый** [14 *sh.*] imperturbable

нево́л|ить [13] force, compel; **~ьный** [14; -лен, -льна] involuntary; (*вы́нужденный*) forced; **~я** *f* [6] captivity; *coll. необходи́мость* need, necessity; ***охо́та пу́ще ~и*** where there's a will, there's a way

невоо|брази́мый [14 *sh.*] unimaginable; **~ружённый** [14] unarmed; ***~ружённым гла́зом*** with the naked eye

невоспи́танный [14 *sh.*] ill-bred

невосполни́мый [14 *sh.*] irreplaceable

невпопа́д *coll.* → ***некста́ти***

невреди́мый [14 *sh.*] unharmed, sound

невы́|годный [14; -ден, -дна] unprofitable; *положе́ние* disadvantageous; **~держанный** [14 *sh.*] inconsistent, uneven; *сыр и т. д.* unripe; **~носи́мый** [14 *sh.*] unbearable, intolerable; **~полне́ние** *n* [12] nonfulfil(l)ment; **~полни́мый** → ***неисполни́мый***; **~рази́мый** [14 *sh.*] inexpressible, ineffable; **~рази́тельный** [14; -лен, -льна] inexpressive; **~со́кий** [16; -со́к, -а́, -со́ко́] low, small; *челове́к* short; *ка́чество* inferior

не́где there is nowhere (+ *inf.*); **~ сесть** there is nowhere to sit

негла́сный [14; -сен, -сна] secret; *рассле́дование* private

него́д|ный [14; -ден, -дна, -о] unsuitable; unfit; *coll.* worthless; **~ова́ние** *n* [12] indignation; **~ова́ть** [7] be indignant (***на*** B with); **~я́й** *m* [3] scoundrel, rascal

негр *m* [1] Negro

негра́мотн|ость → ***безгра́мотность***; **~ый** → ***безгра́мотный***

негритя́н|ка *f* [5; *g/pl.*: -нок] Negress; **~ский** [16] Negro...

неда́|вний [15] recent; ***с ~вних*** (***~вней***) ***пор***(***ы́***) of late; **~вно** recently; **~лёкий** [16; -ёк, -ека́, -еко́ *and* -ёко] near(by), close; short; not far (off); (*неда́вний*) recent; (*глупова́тый*) dull, stupid; **~льнови́дный** [14] lacking foresight, shortsighted; **~ром** not in vain, not without reason; justly

недви́жимость *f* [8] *law* real estate

неде|йстви́тельный [14; -лен, -льна] invalid, void; **~ли́мый** [14] indivisible
неде́л|ьный [14] a week's, weekly; **~я** *f* [6] week; ***в ~ю*** a *or* per week; ***на э́той*** (***про́шлой***, ***бу́дущей***) ***~е*** this (last, next) week; ***че́рез ~ю*** in a week's time
недобро|жела́тельный [14; -лен, -льна] malevolent, ill-disposed; **~ка́чественный** [14 *sh.*] inferior, low-grade; **~со́вестный** [14; -тен, -тна] *конкуре́нция* unscrupulous, unfair; *рабо́та* careless
недо́брый [14; -до́бр, -á, -о] unkind(ly), hostile; *предзнаменова́ние* evil, bad
недове́р|ие *n* [12] distrust; **~чи́вый** [14 *sh.*] distrustful (***к*** Д of)
недово́ль|ный [14; -лен, -льна] (Т) dissatisfied, discontented; **~ство** *n* [9] discontent, dissatisfaction
недога́дливый [14 *sh.*] slow-witted
недоеда́|ние *n* [12] malnutrition; **~ть** [1] be underfed *or* undernourished
недо́лго not long, short; ***~ и*** (+ *inf.*) one can easily; ***~ ду́мая*** without hesitation
недомога́ть [1] be unwell *or* sick
недомо́лвка *f* [5; *g/pl.*: -вок] reservation, innuendo
недооце́н|ивать [1], <~и́ть> [13] underestimate, undervalue
недо|пусти́мый [14 *sh.*] inadmissible, intolerable; **~ра́звитый** [14 *sh.*] underdeveloped; **~разуме́ние** *n* [12] misunderstanding (***по*** Д through); **~рого́й** [16; -до́рог, -á, -о] inexpensive
недослы́шать [1] *pf.* fail to hear all of
недосмо́тр *m* [1] oversight, inadvertence (***по*** Д through); **~е́ть** [9; -отрю́, -о́тришь; -о́тренный] *pf.* overlook (*s.th.*)
недост|ава́ть [5], <~а́ть> [-ста́нет] *impers.*: (Д) (be) lack(ing), want(ing), be short *or* in need of (Р) *кого́-л.*; miss; ***э́того ещё ~ава́ло!***; and that too!; **~а́ток** *m* [1; -тка] lack, shortage (Р, ***в*** П of); deficiency; defect, shortcoming; ***физи́ческий ~а́ток*** deformity; **~а́точный** [14; -чен, -чна] insufficient, deficient, inadequate; *gr.* defective; **~а́ть** → **~ава́ть**
недо|стижи́мый [14 *sh.*] unattainable; **~сто́йный** [14; -о́ин, -о́йна] unworthy; **~сту́пный** [14; -пен, -пна] inaccessible
недосу́г *coll. m* [1] lack of time (***за*** Т, ***по*** Д for); ***мне ~*** I have no time
недосяга́емый [14 *sh.*] unattainable
недоум|ева́ть [1] be puzzled, be perplexed; **~е́ние** *n* [12] bewilderment; ***в ~е́нии*** in a quandary
недочёт *m* [1] deficit; *изъя́н* defect
не́дра *n/pl.* [9] *земли́* bowels, depths (*a. fig.*)
не́друг *m* [1] enemy, foe
недружелю́бный [14; -бен, -бна] unfriendly
неду́г *m* [1] ailment
недурно́й [14; -ду́рен & -рён, -рна́, -о] not bad; *собо́й* not bad-looking
недю́жинный [14] out of the ordinary, uncommon
нестé́ственный [14 *sh.*] unnatural; *смех* affected; *улы́бка* forced
нежела́|ние *n* [12] unwillingness; **~тельный** [14; -лен, -льна] undesirable
не́жели *lit.* → **чем** than
нежена́тый [14] single, unmarried
нежило́й [14] not fit for habitation
не́ж|ить [16] luxuriate; **~ничать** *coll.* [1] caress, spoon; **~ность** *f* [8] tenderness; *pl.* display of affection **~ный** [14; -жен, -жна́, -о] tender, affectionate; *о ко́же, вку́се* delicate
незаб|ве́нный [14 *sh.*], **~ыва́емый** [14 *sh.*] unforgettable; **~у́дка** *f* [5; *g/pl.*: -док] *bot.* forget-me-not
незави́сим|ость *f* [8] independence; **~ый** [14 *sh.*] independent
незада́чливый *coll.* [14 *sh.*] unlucky
незадо́лго shortly (***до*** Р before)
незако́нный [14; -о́нен, -о́нна] illegal, unlawful, illicit; *ребёнок и т. д.* illegitimate
незаме|ни́мый [14 *sh.*] irreplaceable; **~тный** [14; -тен, -тна] imperceptible, inconspicuous; *челове́к*

plain, ordinary; **~ченный** [14] unnoticed

неза|мыслова́тый *coll.* [14 *sh.*] simple, uncomplicated; **~па́мятный** [14]: **с *~па́мятных времён*** from time immemorial; **~те́йливый** [14 *sh.*] plain, simple; **~уря́дный** [14; -ден, -дна] outstanding, exceptional

не́зачем there is no need *or* point

незва́ный [14] uninvited

нездоро́в|иться [14]: ***мне ~ится*** I feel (am) unwell; **~ый** [14 *sh.*] sick; morbid (*a. fig.*); ***кли́мат и т. д.*** unhealthy

незло́бивый [14 *sh.*] forgiving

незнако́м|ец *m* [1; -мца], **~ка** *f* [5; *g/pl.*: -мок] stranger; **~ый** [14] unknown, unfamiliar

незна́|ние *n* [12] ignorance; **~чи́тельный** [14; -лен, -льна] insignificant

незр|е́лый [14 *sh.*] unripe; *fig.* immature; **~и́мый** [14 *sh.*] invisible

незы́блемый [14 *sh.*] firm, stable, unshak(e)able

неиз|бе́жный [14; -жен, -жна] inevitable; **~ве́стный** [14; -тен, -тна] unknown; *su. a.* stranger; **~глади́мый** [14 *sh.*] indelible; **~лечи́мый** [14 *sh.*] incurable; **~ме́нный** [14; -е́нен, -е́нна] invariable; immutable; **~мери́мый** [14 *sh.*] immeasurable, immense; **~ъясни́мый** [14 *sh.*] inexplicable

неим|е́ние *n* [12]: ***за ~е́нием*** (P) for want of; **~ове́рный** [14; -рен, -рна] incredible; **~у́щий** [17] poor

неис|кренний [15; -енен, -енна] insincere; **~кушённый** [14; -шён, -шена́] inexperienced, innocent; **~полне́ние** *n* [12] ***зако́на*** failure to observe (*the law*); **~полни́мый** [14 *sh.*] impracticable

неиспр|ави́мый [14 *sh.*] incorrigible; **~а́вность** *f* [8] disrepair; carelessness; **~а́вный** [14; -вен, -вна] out of order, broken, defective; ***плате́льщик*** unpunctual

неиссяка́емый [14 *sh.*] inexhaustible

неистов|ство *n* [9] rage, frenzy; **~ствовать** [7] rage; **~ый** [14 *sh.*] frantic, furious

неис|тощи́мый [14 *sh.*] inexhaustible; **~треби́мый** [14 *sh.*] ineradicable; **~цели́мый** [14 *sh.*] incurable; **~черпа́емый** [14 *sh.*] → ***~тощи́мый***; **~числи́мый** [14 *sh.*] innumerable

нейло́н *m* [1], **~овый** [14] nylon (...)

нейтрал|ите́т *m* [1] neutrality; **~ьный** [14; -лен, -льна] neutral

неказ́истый *coll.* [14 *sh.*] → ***невзра́чный***

не́|кий [24 *st.*] a certain, some; **~когда** there is (***мне ~когда*** I have) no time; once; **~кого** [23] there is (***мне ~кого*** I have) nobody *or* no one (to *inf.*); **~компете́нтный** [14; -тен, -тна] incompetent; **~корре́ктный** [-тен, -тна] impolite, discourteous; **~который** [14] some (*pl.* ***из*** P of); **~краси́вый** [14 *sh.*] plain, unattrative; ***поведе́ние*** unseemly, indecorous

некроло́г *m* [1] obituary

некста́ти inopportunely; (***неуме́стно***) inappropriately

не́кто somebody, someone; a certain

не́куда there is nowhere (+ *inf.*); ***мне ~ пойти́*** I have nowhere to go; *coll.* ***ху́же и т. д. ~*** could not be worse, *etc.*

некуря́щий [17] nonsmoker, nonsmoking

нел|а́дный *coll.* [14; -ден, -дна] wrong, bad; ***будь он ~а́ден!*** blast him!; **~ега́льный** [14; -лен, -льна] illegal; **~е́пый** [14 *sh.*] absurd

нело́вкий [16; -вок, -вка́, -о] awkward, clumsy; ***ситуа́ция*** embarrassing

нело́вко *adv.* → ***нело́вкий***; ***чу́вствовать себя́ ~*** feel ill at ease

нелоги́чный [14; -чен, -чна] illogical

нельзя́ (it is) impossible, one (***мне*** I) cannot *or* must not; ***~!*** no!; ***как ~ лу́чше*** in the best way possible, excellently; ***~ не*** → ***не***(***мочь***)

нелюди́мый [14 *sh.*] unsociable

нема́ло (P) a lot, a great deal (of)

неме́дленный [14] immediate

неме́ть [8], <о-> grow dumb, numb

не́м|ец *m* [1; -мца], **~е́цкий** [16], **~ка** *f* [5; *g/pl.*: -мок] German

неми́лость *f* [8] disgrace, disfavour
немину́емый [14 *sh.*] inevitable
немно́|гие *pl.* [16] (a) few, some; **~го** a little; *слегка́* slightly, somewhat; **~гое** *n* [16] few things, little; **~гим** a little; **~ж(еч)ко** *coll.* a (little) bit, a trifle
немо́й [14; нем, -á, -o] dumb, mute
немо|лодо́й [14; -мо́лод, -á, -o] elderly; **~та́** *f* [5] dumbness, muteness
не́мощный [14; -щен, -щна] infirm
немы́слимый [14 *sh.*] inconceivable, unthinkable
ненави́|деть [11], <воз-> hate; **~стный** [14; -тен, -тна] hateful, odious; **~сть** ('n̦e-) *f* [8] hatred (**к** Д of)
нена|гля́дный [14] *coll.* beloved; **~дёжный** [14; -жен, -жна] unreliable; (*непро́чный*) unsafe, insecure; **~до́лго** for a short while; **~ме́ренный** [14] unintentional; **~паде́ние** *n* [12] nonaggression; **~́стный** [14; -тен, -тна] rainy, foul; **~́стье** *n* [10] foul weather; **~сы́тный** [14; -тен, -тна] insatiable
нен|орма́льный [14; -лен, -льна] abnormal; *coll.* crazy; **~у́жный** [14; -жен, -жна́, -o] unnecessary
необ|ду́манный [14 *sh.*] rash, hasty; **~ита́емый** [14 *sh.*] uninhabited; *о́стров* desert; **~озри́мый** [14 *sh.*] immense, boundless; **~осно́ванный** [14 *sh.*] unfounded; **~рабо́танный** [14] *земля́* uncultivated; **~у́зданный** [14 *sh.*] unbridled, ungovernable
необходи́м|ость *f* [8] necessity (**по** П of), need (Р, **в** П for); **~ый** [14 *sh.*] necessary (П; **для** Р for), essential; → **ну́жный**
необ|щи́тельный [14; -лен, -льна] unsociable, reserved; **~ъясни́мый** [14 *sh.*] inexplicable; **~ъя́тный** [14; -тен, -тна] immense, unbounded; **~ыкнове́нный** [14; -е́нен, -е́нна] unusual, uncommon; **~ы́ч(а́й)ный** [14; -ч(а)ен, -ч(а́й)на] extraordinary, exceptional; **~яза́тельный** [14; -лен, -льна] optional; *челове́к* unreliable
неограни́ченный [14 *sh.*] unrestricted
неод|нокра́тный [14] repeated; **~обре́ние** *n* [12] disapproval; **~обри́тельный** [14; -лен, -льна] disapproving; **~оли́мый** → **непреодоли́мый**; **~ушевлённый** [14] inanimate
неожи́данн|ость *f* [8] unexpectedness, surprise; **~ый** [14 *sh.*] unexpected, sudden
нео́н *m* [1] *chem.* neon; **~овый** [14] neon...
неоп|ису́емый [14 *sh.*] indescribable; **~ла́ченный** [14 *sh.*] unpaid, unsettled; **~ра́вданный** [14] unjustified; **~ределённый** [14; -ёнен, -ённа] indefinite (*a. gr.*), uncertain, vague; **~ровержи́мый** [14 *sh.*] irrefutable; **~́ытный** [14; -тен, -тна] inexperienced
неос|ведомлённый [14; -лён, -лена́, -лены́] ill-informed; **~ла́бный** [14; -бен, -бна] unremitting, unabated; **~мотри́тельный** [14; -лен, -льна] imprudent; **~пори́мый** [14 *sh.*] undisputable; **~торо́жный** [14; -жен, -жна] careless, incautious; imprudent; **~уществи́мый** [14 *sh.*] impracticable; **~яза́емый** [14 *sh.*] intangible
неот|врати́мый [14 *sh.*] inevitable; **~ёсанный** [14 *sh.*] unpolished; *coll. челове́к* uncouth; **´~куда** → **не́где**; **~ло́жный** [14; -жен, -жна] pressing, urgent; **~лу́чный** ever-present → **постоя́нный**; **~рази́мый** [14 *sh.*] irresistible; *до́вод* irrefutable; **~сту́пный** [14; -пен, -пна] persistent; importunate; **~чётливый** [14 *sh.*] indistinct, vague; **~ъе́млемый** [14 *sh.*] *часть* integral; *пра́во* inalienable
неохо́т|а *f* [5] reluctance; (**мне**) **~а** *coll.* I (*etc.*) am not in the mood; **~но** unwillingly
не|оцени́мый [14 *sh.*] inestimable; invaluable; **~перехо́дный** [14] *gr.* intransitive
неплатёжеспосо́бный [14; -бен, -бна] insolvent
непо|беди́мый [14 *sh.*] invincible; **~воро́тливый** [14 *sh.*] clumsy, slow; **~го́да** *f* [5] foul weather; **~греши́мый** [14 *sh.*] infallible; **~далёку** not far (away *or* off);

~да́тливый [14 *sh.*] unyielding, intractable
непод|ви́жный [14; -жен, -жна] motionless, fixed, stationary; **~де́льный** [14; -лен, -льна] genuine, unfeigned; *и́скренний* sincere; **~ку́пный** [14; -пен, -пна] incorruptible; **~оба́ющий** [17] improper, unbecoming; **~ража́емый** [14 *sh.*] inimitable; **~ходя́щий** [17] unsuitable; **~чине́ние** *n* [12] insubordination
непо|зволи́тельный [14; -лен, -льна] not permissible; **~колеби́мый** [14 *sh.*] (*надёжный*) firm, steadfast; (*сто́йкий*) unflinching; **~ко́рный** [14; -рен, -рна] refractory; **~ла́дка** *coll. f* [5; *g/pl.*: -док] *tech.* defect, fault; **~лный** [14; -лон, -лна́, -о] incomplete; *рабо́чий день* short; **~ме́рный** [14; -рен, -рна] excessive, inordinate
непоня́т|ливый [14 *sh.*] slow-witted; **~ный** [14; -тен, -тна] unintelligible, incomprehensible; *явле́ние* strange, odd
непо|прави́мый [14 *sh.*] irreparable, irremediable; **~ря́дочный** [14; -чен, -чна] dishono(u)rable; disreputable; **~се́дливый** [14 *sh.*] fidgety; **~си́льный** [14; -лен, -льна] beyond one's strength; **~сле́довательный** [14; -лен, -льна] inconsistent; **~слу́шный** [14; -шен, -шна] disobedient
непо|сре́дственный [14 *sh.*] immediate, direct; (*есте́ственный*) spontaneous; **~стижи́мый** [14 *sh.*] inconceivable; **~стоя́нный** [14; -я́нен, -я́нна] inconstant, changeable, fickle; **~хо́жий** [17 *sh.*] unlike, different (***на*** В from)
непра́в|да *f* [5] untruth, lie; (it is) not true; ***все́ми пра́вдами и ~дами*** by hook or by crook; **~доподо́бный** [14; -бен, -бна] improbable; implausible; **~ильный** [14; -лен, -льна] incorrect, wrong; irregular (*a. gr.*); improper (*a. math.*); **~ый** [14; непра́в, -а́, -о] mistaken; (*несправедли́вый*) unjust
непре|взойдённый [14 *sh.*] unsurpassed; **~дви́денный** [14] unforeseen; **~дубеждённый** [14] unbiased; **~кло́нный** [14; -о́нен, -о́нна] inflexible; obdurate, inexorable; **~ло́жный** [14; -жен, жна] *и́стина* indisputable; **~ме́нный** [14; -е́нен, -е́нна] indispensable, necessary; **~ме́нно** → ***обяза́тельно***; **~одоли́мый** [14 *sh.*] insuperable; *стремле́ние* irresistible; **~река́емый** [14 *sh.*] indisputable; **~ры́вный** [14; -вен, -вна] uninterrupted, continuous; **~ста́нный** [14; -а́нен, -а́нна] incessant
непри|вы́чный [14; -чен, -чна] unaccustomed; (*необы́чный*) unusual; **~гля́дный** [14; -ден, -дна] *вне́шность* homely; unattractive; ungainly; **~го́дный** [14; -ден, -дна] unfit; useless; **~е́млемый** [14 *sh.*] unacceptable; **~коснове́нный** [14; -е́нен, -е́нна] inviolable; *mil. запа́с* emergency; **~кра́шенный** [14] unvarnished; **~ли́чный** [14; -чен, -чна] indecent, unseemly; **~ме́тный** [14; -тен, -тна] imperceptible; *челове́к* unremarkable; **~мири́мый** [14 *sh.*] irreconcilable; **~нуждённый** [14 *sh.*] unconstrained; relaxed, laid-back; **~сто́йный** [14; -о́ен, -о́йна] obscene, indecent; **~сту́пный** [14; -пен, -пна] inaccessible; *кре́пость* impregnable; *челове́к* unapproachable, haughty; **~тво́рный** [14; -рен, -рна] genuine, unfeigned; **~тяза́тельный** [14; -лен, -льна] modest, unassuming
неприя́|зненный [14 sh.] inimical, unfriendly; **~знь** *f* [8] hostility
неприя́|тель *m* [4] enemy; **~тельский** [16] hostile, enemy('s); **~тность** *f* [8] unpleasantness; trouble; **~тный** [14; -тен, -тна] disagreeable, unpleasant
непро|гля́дный [14; -ден, -дна] *тьма* pitch-dark; **~должи́тельный** [14; -лен, -льна] short, brief; **~е́зжий** [17] impassable; **~зра́чный** [14; -чен, -чна] opaque; **~изводи́тельный** [14; -лен, -льна] unproductive; **~изво́льный** [14; -лен, -льна] involuntary; **~мока́емый** [14 *sh.*] waterproof; **~ница́емый** [14 *sh.*] impenetrable, imper-

meable; *улы́бка и т. д.* inscrutable; **~сти́тельный** [14; -лен, -льна] unpardonable; **~ходи́мый** [14 *sh.*] impassable; *coll.* complete; **~́чный** [14; -чен, -чна, -о] flimsy; *мир* unstable

нерабо́чий [17] nonworking, free, off (*day*)

нера́в|енство *n* [9] inequality; **~номе́рный** [14; -рен, -рна] uneven; **~ный** [14; -вен, -вна́, -о] unequal

нера́ди́вый [14 *sh.*] careless, negligent

нераз|бери́ха *coll. f* [5] muddle, confusion; **~бо́рчивый** [14 *sh.*] illegible; *fig.* undiscriminating; *в сре́дствах* unscrupulous; **~вито́й** [14; -ра́звит, -а́, -о] undeveloped; *ребёнок* backward; **~личи́мый** [14 *sh.*] indistinguishable; **~лу́чный** [14; -чен, -чна] inseparable; **~реши́мый** [14 *sh.*] insoluble; **~ры́вный** [14; -вен, -вна] indissoluble; **~у́мный** [14; -мен, -мна] injudicious

нерасположе́ние *n* [12] *к челове́ку* dislike; disinclination (to, for)

нерациона́льный [14; -лен, -льна] unpractical

нерв *m* [1] nerve; **~и́ровать** [7], **~́ничать** [1] to get on one's nerves; become fidgety *or* irritated; **~(о́з)ный** [14; -вен, -вна́, -о (-зен, -зна)] nervous; high-strung

нереа́льный [14; -лен, -льна] unreal; (*невыполни́мый*) impracticable

нереши́тельн|ость *f* [8] indecision; ***в ~ости*** undecided; **~ый** [14; -лен, -льна] indecisive, irresolute

нержаве́ющ|ий [15] rust-free; ***~ая сталь*** stainless steel

неро́|бкий [16; -бок, -бка́, -о] not timid; brave; **~вный** [14; -вен, -вна́, -о] uneven, rough; *пульс* irregular

неря́|ха *m/f* [5] sloven; **~шливый** [14 *sh.*] slovenly; *в рабо́те* careless, slipshod

несамостоя́тельный [14; -лен, -льна] not independent

несбы́точный [14; -чен, -чна] unrealizable

не|своевре́менный [14; -енен, -енна] inopportune, untimely; tardy; **~свя́зный** [14; зен, зна] incoherent; **~сгора́емый** [14] fireproof; **~сде́ржанный** [14 *sh.*] unrestrained; **~серьёзный** [14; -зен, -зна] not serious, frivolous; **~сказа́нный** *lit.* [14 *sh.*, *no m*] indescribable; **~скла́дный** [14; -ден, -дна] *челове́к* ungainly; *речь* incoherent; **~склоня́емый** [14 *sh.*] *gr.* indeclinable

не́сколько [32] a few; some, several; *adv.* somewhat

не|скро́мный [14; -мен, -мна́, -о] immodest; **~слы́ханный** [14 *sh.*] unheard-of; (*беспримéрный*) unprecedented; **~сме́тный** [14; -тен, -тна] innumerable, incalculable

несмотря́ (***на*** В) in spite of, despite, notwithstanding; (al)though.

несно́сный [14; -сен, -сна] intolerable

несо|блюде́ние *n* [12] nonobservance; **~вершеннолéтие** *n* [12] minority; **~верше́нный** [14; -éнен, -éнна] *gr.* imperfective; **~верше́нство** *n* [9] imperfection; **~вмести́мый** [14 *sh.*] incompatible; **~гла́сие** *n* [12] disagreement; **~измери́мый** [14 *sh.*] incommensurable; **~круши́мый** [14 *sh.*] indestructible; **~мне́нный** [14; -éнен, -éнна] undoubted; ***~мне́нно*** *a.* undoubtedly, without doubt; **~отве́тствие** *n* [12] discrepancy; **~разме́рный** [14; -éрен, -éрна] disproportionate; **~стоя́тельный** [14; -лен, -льна] *должни́к* insolvent; (*необосно́ванный*) groundless, unsupported

несп|око́йный [14; -óен, -óйна] restless, uneasy; **~осо́бный** [14; -бен, -бна] incapable (***к*** Д, ***на*** В of); **~раведли́вость** *f* [8] injustice, unfairness; **~раведли́вый** [14 *sh.*] unjust, unfair; **~роста́** *coll.* → ***нeда́ром***

несрав|не́нный [14; -éнен, -éнна] *and* **~и́мый** [14 *sh.*] incomparable, matchless

нестерпи́мый [14 *sh.*] intolerable

нести́ [24; -с-: -су́], <по-> (be) carry(ing, *etc.*); bear; bring; *убы́тки и т.*

д. suffer; *о зáпахе и т. д.* smell (of T); drift, waft; (**-ся** *v/i.*; *a.* be heard; spread); <c-> lay (eggs **-сь**); talk *чушь*; несёт (*сквозúт*) there's a draft (*Brt.* draught)

не|стрóйный [14; -óен, -óйна, -о] *звýки* discordant; *ряды́* disorderly; **~сурáзный** *coll.* [14; -зен, -зна] senseless, absurd; **~сусвéтный** [14] unimaginable; *чушь* sheer

несчáст|ный [14; -тен, -тна] unhappy, unfortunate; ***~ный слýчай*** accident; **~ье** *n* [12] misfortune; disaster; accident; ***к ~ью*** unfortunately

несчётный [14; -тен, -тна] innumerable

нет 1. *part.*: no; ***~ ещё*** not yet; **2.** *impers. vb.* [*pt.* нé было, *ft.* не бýдет] (P) there is (are) no; ***у меня́*** (*etc.*) **~** I (*etc.*) have no(ne); ***егó*** (***её***) **~** (s)he is not (t)here *or* in; ***на ~ и судá нет*** well, it can't be helped

нетактúчный [14; -чен, -чна] tactless

нетвёрдый [14; -вёрд, -вердá] unsteady; shaky (*a. fig.*)

нетерп|елúвый [14 *sh.*] impatient; **~éние** *n* [12] impatience; **~úмый** [14 *sh.*] intolerant; (*невыносúмый*) intolerable

не|тлéнный [14; -éнен, -éнна] imperishable; **~трéзвый** [14; трезв, -á, -о] drunk (*a.* ***в ~трéзвом вúде***); **~трóнутый** [14 *sh.*] untouched; *fig.* chaste, virgin; **~трудоспосóбный** [14; -бен, -бна] disabled

нéт|то [*indecl.*] *comm.* net; **~у** *coll.* → ***нет*** *2*

неу|важéние *n* [12] disrespect (**к** Д for); **~вéренный** [14 *sh.*] uncertain; **~вядáемый** [14 *sh.*] *rhet.* unfading; everlasting; **~вя́зка** [5; *g/pl.*: -зок] *coll.* misunderstanding; (*несогласóванность*) discrepancy, lack of coordination; **~гасúмый** [14 *sh.*] inextinguishable; **~гомóнный** [14; -óнен, -óнна] restless, untiring

неудáч|а *f* [5] misfortune; failure; ***потерпéть ~у*** fail; **~ливый** [14 *sh.*] unlucky; **~ник** *m* [1] unlucky person, failure; **~ный** [14; -чен, -чна] unsuccessful, unfortunate

неуд|ержúмый [14 *sh.*] irrepressible; **~ивúтельно** (it is) no wonder

неудóб|ный [14; -бен, -бна] uncomfortable; *врéмя* inconvenient; *положéние* awkward, embarrassing; **~ство** *n* [9] inconvenience

неудов|летворúтельный [14; -лен, -льна] unsatisfactory; **~летворённость** *f* [8] dissatisfaction, discontent; **~óльствие** *n* [12] displeasure

неужéли *interr. part.* really?, is it possible?

неу|жúвчивый [14 *sh.*] unsociable, unaccommodating; **~клóнный** [14; -óнен, -óнна] steady; **~клю́жий** [17 *sh.*] clumsy, awkward; **~кротúмый** [14 sh.] indomitable; **~ловúмый** [14 sh.] elusive; (*éле замéтный*) imperceptible; **~мéлый** [14 *sh.*] unskil(l)ful, awkward; **~мéние** *n* [12] inability; **~мéренный** [14 *sh.*] intemperate, immoderate; **~мéстный** [14; -тен, -тна] inappropriate; **~молúмый** [14 *sh.*] inexorable; **~мы́шленный** [14 *sh.*] unintentional; **~потребúтельный** [14; -лен, -льна] not in use, not current; **~рожáй** *m* [3] bad harvest; **~стáнный** [14; -áнен, -áнна] tireless, unwearying; *a.* → ***~томúмый***; **~стóйка** [5; *g/pl.*: -оек] forfeit; **~стóйчивый** [14 *sh.*] unstable; unsteady; *погóда* changeable; **~страшúмый** [14 *sh.*] intrepid, dauntless; **~стýпчивый** [14 *sh.*] unyielding, tenacious; **~толúмый** [14 *sh.*] unquenchable; **~томúмый** [14 *sh.*] tireless, indefatigable

нéуч *coll. m* [1] ignoramus

неу|чтúвый [14 *sh.*] uncivil; **~ю́тный**; [14; -тен, -тна] comfortless; **~язвúмый** [14 *sh.*] invulnerable

нефт|епровóд *m* [1] pipeline; **~ь** *f* [8] (mineral) oil, petroleum; **~янóй** [14] oil...

не|хвáтка *f* [5; *g/pl.*: -ток] shortage; **~хорóший** [17; -рóш, -á] bad; **~хотя** unwillingly; **~цензýрный** [14; -рен, -рна] unprintable; ***~цензýрное слóво*** swearword; **~чáянный** [14] *встрéча* unexpected; (*случáйный*) accidental; (*неумы́шленный*) unintentional

не́чего [23]: (***мне***, *etc.*) + *inf.* (there is *or* one can), (I have) nothing to...; (one) need not, (there is) no need; (it is) no use; stop ...ing

не|челове́ческий [16] inhuman; *уси́лия* superhuman; **~че́стный** [14; -тен, -тна́, -o] dishonest; **~чёт-ный** [14] odd (*number*)

нечист|опло́тный [14; -тен, -тна] dirty; *fig.* unscrupulous; **~ота́** *f* [5; *pl. st.*: -о́ты] dirtiness; *pl.* sewage; **~ый** [14; -чи́ст, -á, -o] unclean, dirty; impure; *по́мыслы и т. д.* evil, vile, bad, foul

не́что something

не|чувстви́тельный [14; -лен, -льна] insensitive, insensible (**к** Д to); **~ща́дный** [14; -ден, -дна] merciless; **~я́вка** *f* [5] nonappearance; **~я́ркий** [16; -я́рок, -ярка́, -o] dull, dim; *fig.* mediocre; **~я́сный** [14; -сен, -сна́, -o] not clear; *fig.* vague

ни not a (single ***оди́н***); **~ ..., ~** neither ... nor; ... ever (*e.g.* ***кто*** [***бы***] **~** who-ever); ***кто*** (***что***, ***когда́***, ***где***, ***куда́***) ***бы то ~ был***(***о***) whosoever (what-, when-, wheresoever); ***как ~*** + *vb. a.* in spite of *or* for all + *su.*; ***как бы*** (***то***) **~** ***было*** anyway, whatever happens; ***~ за что ~ про что***, for no apparent reason

нигде́ nowhere

ни́ж|е below, beneath; *ро́стом* shorter; **~еподписа́вшийся** *m* [17] (the) undersigned; **~ний** [15] lower; under...; *эта́ж* first, *Brt.* ground

низ *m* [1; *pl. e.*] bottom, lower part; **~а́ть** [3], <на-> string, thread

низи́на *f* [5] hollow, lowland

ни́зк|ий [16; -зок, -зка́, -o; *comp.*: ни́же] low; *fig.* mean, base; *ро́ст* short; **~оро́слый** [14 *sh.*] undersized, stunted; *куста́рник* low; **~осо́ртный** [14; -тен, -тна] low-grade; *това́р* of inferior quality

ни́зменн|ость *f* [8] *geogr.* lowland, plain; **~ый** [14 *sh.*] low-lying

низо́|вье *n* [10; *g/pl.*: -вьев] lower reaches (*of a river*); **´~сть** *f* [8] meanness

ника́к by no means, not at all; **~о́й** [16] no ... (at all *coll.*)

ни́кел|ь *m* [4] nickel; **~иро́ван-ный** [14 *sh.*] nickel-plated

никогда́ never

ни|ко́й: *now only in* ***~ко́им о́бразом*** by no means *and* ***ни в ко́ем слу́чае*** on no account; **~кто́** [23] nobody, no one, none; **~куда́** nowhere; → *a.* ***годи́ться***, ***го́дный***; **~кчёмный** *coll.* [14] good-for-nothing; **~ма́ло** → ***ско́лько***; **~от-ку́да** from nowhere; **~почём** *coll.* very cheap, easy, *etc.*; **~ско́лько** not in the least, not at all

нисходя́щий [17] descending

ни́т|ка *f* [5; *g/pl.*: -ток], **~ь** [8] thread; *же́мчуга* string; *хлопчато-бума́жная* cotton; **~ь** *a.* filament; ***до ~ки*** *coll.* to the skin; ***ши́то бе́-лыми ~ками*** be transparent; ***на живу́ю ~ку*** carelessly, superficially

ничего́ nothing; not bad; so-so; no(t) matter; ***~!*** never mind!, that's all right!; ***~ себе́!*** well (I never)!

нич|е́й *m*, **~ья́** *f*, **~ьё** *n*, **~ьи́** *pl.* [26] nobody's; *su. f* ***в игре́*** draw

ничко́м prone

ничто́ [23] nothing → ***ничего́***; **~жество** *n* [9] nonentity; **~жный** [14; -жен, -жна] insignificant, tiny; *причи́на* paltry

нич|у́ть *coll.* → ***нисколько***; **~ья́** → **~е́й**

ни́ша *f* [5] niche

ни́щ|ая *f* [17], **~енка** *coll.* [5; *g/pl.*: -нок] beggar woman; **~енский** [16] beggarly; **~ета́** *f* [5] poverty, destitution; **~ий 1.** [17; нищ, -á, -e] beggarly; **2.** *m* [17] beggar

но but, yet, still, nevertheless

нова́тор *m* [1] innovator

нове́лла *f* [5] short story

но́в|енький [16; -нек] (brand-) new; **~изна́** *f* [5], **~и́нка** [5; *g/pl.*: -нок] novelty; **~ичо́к** *m* [1; -чка́] novice, tyro

ново|бра́чный [14] newly married; **~введе́ние** *n* [12] innovation; **~го́дний** [15] New Year's (Eve ***~го́дний ве́чер***); **~лу́ние** *n* [12] new moon; **~рождённый** [14] newborn (child); **~се́лье** *n* [10] house-warming; ***справля́ть*** <**~вить**> ***~се́лье*** give a house-warming party

но́в|ость *f* [8] (piece of) news; novelty; **~шество** *n* [9] innovation, novelty; **~ый** [14; нов, -á, -о] new; novel; (*после́дний*) fresh; **2ый год** *m* New Year's Day; **с 2ым го́дом!** Happy New Year!; **что ~ого?** what's (the) new(s)?

ног|á *f* [5; *ac/sg*.: но́гу; *pl*.: но́ги, ног, нога́м, *etc. e*.] foot, leg; ***идти́ в ~у со вре́менем*** keep abreast of the times; ***со всех ~*** as fast as one's legs will carry one; ***стать на́ ~и*** *вы́здороветь* recover; become independent; ***положи́ть ~у на́ ~у*** cross one's legs; ***ни ~о́й*** (**к** Д) never set foot (*in s.o.'s house*); ***~и унести́*** (have a narrow) escape; ***под ~а́ми*** underfoot

но́готь *m* [4; -гтя; *from g/pl*.: *e*.] (finger-, toe-) nail

нож *m* [1 *e*.] knife; ***на ~а́х*** at daggers drawn; **~ик** *m* [1] *coll*. → **нож**; **~ка** *f* [5; *g/pl*.: -жек] *dim*. → **нога́**; *сту́ла и т. д.* leg; **~ницы** *f/pl*. [5] (pair of) scissors; *econ*. discrepancy; **~но́й** [14] foot...; **~ны** *f/pl*. [5; *gen*.: -жен] sheath

ноздря́ [6; *pl*.: но́здри, ноздре́й, *etc. e*.] nostril

ноль *m*. = **нуль** *m* [4] naught; zero

но́мер *m* [1; *pl*.: -рá, *etc. e*.] number ([with] **за** Т); (*разме́р*) size; *в оте́ле* room; *програ́ммы* item, turn; trick; ***вы́кинуть ~*** do an odd *or* unexpected thing; (*a., dim*., **~о́к** *m* [1; -рка́]) cloakroom ticket

номина́льный [14; -лен, -льна] nominal

норá *f* [5; *ac/sg*.: -рý; *pl. st*.] hole, burrow, lair

норве́|жец *m* [1; -жца], **~жка** *f* [5; *g/pl*.: -жек], **~жский** [16] Norwegian

но́рка *f* [5; *g/pl*.: -рок] *zo*. mink

но́рм|а *f* [5] norm, standard; *вы́работки и т. д.* rate; **~ализова́ть** [7] (*im*)*pf*. standardize; **~а́льный** [14; -лен, -льна] normal

нос *m* [1; в, на носý; *pl. e*.] nose; *пти́цы* beak; *ло́дки*, bow, prow; ***води́ть за ~*** lead by the nose; (*вско́ре*) ***на ~ý*** at hand; ***у меня́ идёт кровь ~ом*** my nose is bleeding; **~ик** *m* [1] *dim*. → **нос**; spout

носи́|лки *f/pl*. [5; -лок] stretcher; **~льщик** *m* [1] porter; **~тель** *m med*. [4] carrier; **~ть** [15] carry, bear, *etc*.; → **нести́**; wear (*v/i*. **-ся**); *coll*. **-ся** run about; (**с** Т) *a*. have one's mind occupied with

носово́й [14] *звук* nasal; *naut*. bow; ***~ плато́к*** handkerchief

носо́к *m* [1; -ска́] sock; *боти́нка* toe

носоро́г *m* [1] rhinoceros

но́т|а *f* [5] note; *pl. a*. music; ***как по ~ам*** without a hitch

нота́риус *m* [1] notary (public)

нота́ция *f* [7] reprimand, lecture

ноч|ева́ть [7], <пере-> pass (*or* spend) the night; **~ёвка** *f* [5; *g/pl*.: -вок] overnight stop (*or* stay *or* rest); *a*. → **~ле́г**; **~ле́г** *m* [1] night's lodging, night quarters; *a*. → **~ёвка**; **~но́й** [14] night(ly), (*a. bot., zo*.) nocturnal; **~ь** *f* [8; в ночи́; *from g/pl. e*.] night; **~ью** at (*or* by) night (= *a*. ***в ~ь, по ~а́м***); ***~ь под ...*** (В) ... night

но́ша *f* [5] load, burden

ноя́брь *m* [4 *e*.] November

нрав *m* [1] disposition, temper; *pl*. ways, customs; (***не***) ***по ~у*** (Д) (not) to one's liking; **~иться** [14], <по-> please (a p. Д); ***она́ мне ~ится*** I like her; **~оуче́ние** *n* [12] moral admonition; **~ственность** *f* [8] morals *pl*., morality; **~ственный** [14 *sh*.] moral

ну (*a*. **~-ка**) well *or* now (then **же**)! come (on)!, why!, what!; the deuce (take him *or* it ***~ его́***)!; (*a*. ***да ~?***) indeed?, really?, you don't say!; ha?; ***~ да*** of course, sure; ***~ так что́ же?*** what about it?

ну́дный [14; ну́ден, -á, -о] tedious, boring

нужд|á *f* [5; *pl. st*.] need, want (**в** П of); ***в слу́чае ~ы́*** if necessary; ***в э́том нет ~ы́*** there is no need for this; **~а́ться** [1] (**в** П) (be in) need (of); *в деньга́х* be hard up, needy

ну́жн|ый [14; ну́жен, -жна́, -о, ну́жны] necessary (Д for); (Д) **~о** + *inf*. must (→ ***на́до***)

нуль → ***ноль***

нумер|а́ция *f* [7] numeration; numbering; **~ова́ть** [7], <за-, про-> number

ну́трия *f* [7] *zo*. coypu; *мех* nutria

Н

ны́н|е *obs.* now(adays), today; **~ешний** *coll.* [15] present *coll.* today's; **~че** *coll.* → **~е**
ныр|я́ть [28], *once* <~ну́ть> [20] dive
ныть [22] ache; *coll.* whine, make a fuss
нюх [1], **~ать** [1], <по-> *о живо́тном* smell, scent
ня́н|чить [16] nurse, tend; **-ся** *coll.* fuss over, busy o.s. (**с** T with); **~я** *f* [6] (**~ька** [5; -нек]) nurse, *Brt. a.* nanny

О

о, **об**, **обо 1.** (П) about, of; on; **2.** (B) against, (up)on; ***бок о́ бок*** side by side; ***рука́ о́б руку*** hand in hand
о! *int.* oh!, o!
о́б|а *m* & *n*, **~е** *f* [37] both
обагр|я́ть [28], <~и́ть> [13]: ***~и́ть ру́ки в крови́*** steep one's hands in blood
обанкро́титься → ***банкро́титься***
обая́|ние *n* [12] spell, charm; **~тельный** [14; -лен, -льна] charming
обва́л *m* [1] collapse; landslide; *сне́жный* avalanche; **~иваться** [1], <~и́ться> [13; обва́лится] fall in *or* off; **~я́ть** [1] *pf.* roll
обвари́ть [13; -арю́, -а́ришь] scald; pour boiling water over
обве́|сить [15] *coll.* → ***~шивать***
обвести́ → ***обводи́ть***
обве́тренный [14 *sh.*] weather-beaten; *гу́бы* chapped
обветша́лый [14] decayed
обве́ш|ивать, <~ать> [1] **1.** hang, cover (T with); **2.** *pf.* <обве́сить> [1] give short weight to; cheat
обви|ва́ть [1], <~ть> [обовью́, -вьёшь; → ***вить***] wind round; ***~ть ше́ю рука́ми*** throw one's arms round s.o.'s neck
обвин|е́ние *n* [12] accusation, charge; *law* indictment; the prosecution; **~и́тель** *m* [4] accuser; *law* prosecutor; **~и́тельный** [14] accusatory; *заключе́ние* of 'guilty'; **~я́ть** [28] <~и́ть> [13] (***в*** П) accuse (of), charge (with); **~я́емый** accused; (*отве́тчик*) defendant
обви́слый *coll.* [14] flabby
обви́|ть → ***~ва́ть***
обводи́ть [13], <обвести́> [25] lead, see *or* look (round, about); enclose, encircle *or* border (T with); ***~ вокру́г па́льца*** twist round one's little finger
обвор|а́живать [1], <~ожи́ть> [16 *e.*; -жу́, -жи́шь, -жённый] charm, fascinate; **~ожи́тельный** [14; -лен, -льна] charming, fascinating; ***~ожи́ть*** → ***~а́живать***
обвя́з|ывать [1], <~а́ть> [3] *верёвкой* tie up *or* round
обгоня́ть [28], <обогна́ть> [обгоню́, -о́нишь; обо́гнанный] (out) distance, outstrip (*a. fig.*); pass, leave behind
обгрыз|а́ть [1], <~ть> [24; *pt. st.*] gnaw (at, round, away)
обд|ава́ть [5], <~а́ть> [-а́м, -а́шь; → ***дать***; о́бдал, -а́, -о; о́бданный (о́бдан, -а́, -о)] pour over; ***~ать кипятко́м*** scald; ***~ать гря́зью*** bespatter with mud
обдел|я́ть [28], <~и́ть> [13; -елю́, -е́лишь] deprive of one's due share (of T)
обдира́ть [1], <ободра́ть> [обдеру́, -рёшь; ободра́л, -а́, -о; обо́дранный] *кору́* bark, *обо́и и т. д.* tear (off); *ту́шу* skin; *коле́но* scrape; *fig. coll.* fleece
обду́м|ать → ***~ывать***; **~анный** [14 *sh.*] well considered; **~ывать**, <~ать> [1] consider, think over
обед *m* [1] dinner (***за*** T at, ***на*** B, ***к***

Д for), lunch; ***до*** (***по́сле***) ***~а*** in the morning (afternoon); **~ать** [1], <по-> have dinner (lunch), dine; **~енный** [14] dinner..., lunch...
обедне́вший [17] impoverished
обез|бо́ливание *n* [12] an(a)esthetization; **~вре́живать** [1], <~вре́дить> [15] render harmless; neutralize; **~до́ленный** [14] unfortunate, hapless; **~зара́живание** *n* [12] disinfection; **~лю́деть** [8] *pf.* become depopulated, deserted; **~обра́живать** [1], <~обра́зить> [15] disfigure; **~опа́сить** [15] *pf.* secure (**от** P against); **~ору́живать** [1], <~ору́жить> [16] disarm (*a. fig.*); **~у́меть** [8] *pf.* lose one's mind, go mad
обезья́н|а *f* [5] monkey; ape; **~ий** [18] monkey('s); apish, apelike; **~ичать** *coll.* [1] ape
обели́ск *m* [1] obelisk
обер|ега́ть [1], <~е́чь> [26; г/ж: -гу, -жёшь] guard, *v/i.* **-ся**, protect o.s.; (against, from **от** P)
оберну́ть(ся) → ***обёртывать(ся)***
обёрт|ка *f* [5; *g/pl.*: -ток] *книги* cover; **~очный** [14] wrapping (*or* brown) paper; **~ывать** [1], <оберну́ть> [20] wrap (up); wind; ***~ывать лицо́*** turn one's face toward(s); **-ся** turn (round, *coll.* back)
обескура́ж|ивать [1], <~ить> [16] discourage, dishearten
обеспе́ч|ение *n* [12] securing; *о за́йме* (**под** B on) security, guarantee; *поря́дка* maintenance; *социа́льное* security; **~енность** *f* [8] (adequate) provision; *зажи́точность* prosperity; **~енный** [14] well-to-do; well provided for; **~ивать** [1], <~ить> [16] (*снабжа́ть*) provide (for; with T); *мир и т. д.* secure, guarantee; ensure
обесси́л|еть [8] *pf.* become enervated, exhausted; **~ивать** [1], <~ить> [13] enervate, weaken
обесцве́|чивать [1], <~тить> [15] discolo(u)r, make colo(u)rless
обесце́н|ивать [1], <~ить> [13] depreciate
обесче́стить [15] *pf.* dishono(u)r; *себя́* disgrace o.s
обе́т *m* [1] vow, promise; **~ова́нный** [14]: ***~ова́нная земля*** the Promised Land
обеща́|ние *n* [12], **~ть** [1] (*im*)*pf.*, *coll. a.* <по-> promise
обжа́лование *n* [12] *law* appeal
обж|ига́ть [1], <~е́чь> [26; г/ж: обожгу́, -жжёшь, обжёг, обожгла́; обожжённый] burn; scorch; *гли́ну* bake; **-ся** burn o.s. (*coll.* one's fingers)
обжо́р|а *coll. m/f* [5] glutton; **~ливый** *coll.* [14 *sh.*] gluttonous; **~ство** *coll. n* [9] gluttony
обзав|оди́ться [15], <~ести́сь> [25] provide o.s. (T with), acquire, set up
обзо́р *m* [1] survey; review
обзыва́ть [1], <обозва́ть> [обзову́, -ёшь; обозва́л, -а́, -о; обо́званный] call (*names* T)
оби|ва́ть [1], <~ть> [обобью́, обобьёшь; → ***бить***] upholster; **~вка** *f* [5] upholstery
оби́|да *f* [5] insult; ***не в ~ду будь ска́зано*** no offense (-nce) meant; ***не дать в ~ду*** let not be offended; **~деть(ся)** → ***~жа́ть(ся)***; **~дный** [14; -ден, -дна] offensive, insulting; ***мне ~дно*** it is a shame *or* vexing; it offends *or* vexes me; I am sorry (for **за** B); **~дчивый** [14 *sh.*] touchy; **~дчик** *coll. m* [1] offender; **~жа́ть** [1], <~деть> [11] (**-ся** be), offend(ed), (*a.* be angry with *or* at **на** B); wrong; overreach (→ *a.* ***обделя́ть***); **~женный** [14 *sh.*] offended (*a.* → ***~жа́ть(ся)***)
оби́лие *n* [12] abundance, plenty
оби́льный [14; -лен, -льна] abundant (T in), plentiful, rich (in)
обиня́к *m* [1 *e.*] *only in phrr.* ***говори́ть ~а́ми*** beat about the bush; ***говори́ть без ~о́в*** speak plainly
обира́ть *coll.* [1], <обобра́ть> [оберу́, -ёшь; обобра́л, -а́, -о; обо́бранный] rob
обита́|емый [14 *sh.*] inhabited; **~тель** *m* [4] inhabitant; **~ть** [1] live, dwell, reside
оби́ть → ***обива́ть***
обихо́д *m* [1] use, custom, practice; ***предме́ты дома́шнего ~а*** household articles; **~ный** [14; -ден, -дна] everyday; *язы́к* colloquial

О

обкла́дывать [1], <обложи́ть> [16] *поду́шками* lay round; *ту́чами* cover; *med.* fur; → ***облага́ть***

обкра́дывать [1], <обокра́сть> [25; обкраду́, -дёшь; *pt. st.*: обкра́денный] rob

обла́ва *f* [5] *на охо́те* battue; *поли́ции* raid; roundup

облага́|емый [14 *sh.*] taxable; **~ть** [1], <обложи́ть> [16] *нало́гом* impose (*tax* T)

облагор|а́живать [1], <~о́дить> [15] ennoble, refine

облада́|ние *n* [12] possession (of T); **~тель** *m* [4] possessor; **~ть** [1] (T) possess, have; be in (***хоро́шим здоро́вьем***) good health

о́блак|о *n* [9; *pl.*: -ка́, -ко́в] cloud; ***вита́ть в ~а́х*** be up in the clouds

обл|а́мывать [1], <~ома́ть> [1] & <~оми́ть> [14] break off

обласка́ть [1] *pf.* treat kindly

област|но́й [14] regional; **´~ь** *f* [8; *from g/pl. e.*] region; *fig.* province, sphere, field

облач|а́ться [1], <~чи́ться> [16] *eccl.* put on one's robes; *coll. joc.* array oneself

облачи́ться → ***облача́ться***

о́блачный [14; -чен, -чна] cloudy

обле|га́ть [1], <~́чь> [26; г/ж: → ***лечь***] fit closely

облегч|а́ть [1], <~и́ть> [16 *e.*; -чу́, -чи́шь, -чённый] lighten; (*упрости́ть*) facilitate; *боль* ease, relieve

обледене́лый [14] ice-covered

облéзлый *coll.* [14] mangy, shabby

обле|ка́ть [1], <~́чь> [26] *полномо́чиями* invest (T with); (*вы́разить*) put, express

облеп|ля́ть [28], <~и́ть> [14] stick all over (*or* round); (*окружи́ть*) surround; *о му́хах и т. д.* cover

облет|а́ть [1], <~е́ть> [11] fly round (*or* all over, past, in); *ли́стья* fall; *о слу́хах и т. д.* spread

обле́чь [1] → ***облега́ть & облека́ть***

обли|ва́ть [1], <~́ть> [оболью́, -льёшь; обле́й!; о́блил, -а́, -о; о́бли́тый (о́бли́т, -а́, -о)] pour (s.th. T) over; ***~́ть гря́зью*** *coll.* fling mud (at); **-ся** [*pf.*: -и́лся, -ила́сь, -и́лось] (T) pour over o.s.; *слеза́ми* shed; *по́том* be dripping; *or кро́вью* covered; *се́рдце* bleed

облига́ция *f* [7] *fin.* bond, debenture

обли́з|ывать [1], <~а́ть> [3] lick (off); **-ся** lick one's lips (*or* o.s.)

о́блик *m* [1] aspect, look; appearance

обли́|ть(ся) → ***~ва́ть(ся)***; **~цо́вывать** [1], <~цева́ть> [7] face (with), revet

облич|а́ть [1], <~и́ть> [16 *e.*; -чу́, -чи́шь, -чённый] unmask; (*раскрыва́ть*) reveal; (*обвини́ть*) accuse (***в*** П of); **~и́тельный** [14; -лен, -льна] accusatory, incriminating; **~и́ть** → ***~а́ть***

облож|е́ние *n* [12] taxation; **~и́ть** → ***обкла́дывать*** *and* ***облага́ть***; **~́ка** [5; *g/pl.*: -жек] cover; (*су́пер* ~) dustcover, folder

облок|а́чиваться [1], <~оти́ться> [15 & 15 *e.*; -кочу́сь, -ко́тишься] lean one's elbow (***на*** B on)

облом|а́ть, **~и́ть** → ***обла́мывать***; **~́ок** *m* [1; -мка] fragment; *pl.* debris, wreckage

облуч|а́ть [1], <~и́ть> [16 *e.*; -чу́, -чи́шь, -чённый] irradiate

облюбова́ть [7] *pf.* take a fancy to, choose

обма́з|ывать [1], <~ать> [3] besmear; plaster, putty, coat, cement

обма́к|ивать [1], <~ну́ть> [20] dip

обма́н *m* [1] deception; deceit, *mst. law* fraud; ***~ зре́ния*** optical illusion; **~ный** [14] deceitful, fraudulent; **~у́ть(ся)** → ***~ывать(ся)***; **~чивый** [14 *sh.*] deceptive; **~щик** *m* [1], **~щица** *f* [5] cheat, deceiver; **~ывать** [1], <~у́ть> [20] (**-ся** be) deceive(d), cheat; be mistaken (in ***в*** П)

обм|а́тывать, <~ота́ть> [1] wind (round); **~а́хивать** [1], <~ахну́ть> [20] *пыль* wipe, dust; *ве́ером* fan

обме́н *m* [1] exchange (in/for ***в/на*** B); interchange (T, P of); **~ивать** [1], <~я́ть> [28] exchange (***на*** B for; **-ся** T s.th.)

обм|е́ривать → ***ме́рить***; **~ета́ть** [1], <~ести́> [25 -т-: обмету́] sweep (off), dust; **~озго́вывать** [1], <~ва́ть> [7] *coll.* think over

обмóлв|иться [14] *pf.* make a slip of the tongue; (*упомянýть*) mention, say; **~ка** *f* [5; *g/pl.*: -вок] slip of the tongue

обморóзить [15] *pf.* frostbite

óбморок *m* [1] fainting spell, swoon

обмот|áть → *обмáтывать*; **~ка** *f* [5; *g/pl.*: -ток] *el.* winding

обмундировá|ние *n* [12], **~ть** [7] *pf.* fit out with uniform

обмы|вáть [1], <**~ть**> [22] bathe, wash (off); *coll. покýпку и т. д.* celebrate

обнадёж|ивать [1], <**~ить**> [16] (re)assure, encourage, give hope to

обнаж|áть [1], <**~и́ть**> [16 *e.*; -жý, -жи́шь; -жённый] *гóлову* bare, uncover; *fig.* lay bare; *шпáгу* draw, unsheathe; **~ённый** [14; -жён, -жена́] naked, bare; nude (*a. su*)

обнарóдовать [7] *pf.* promulgate

обнарýж|ивать [1], <**~ить**> [16] (*вы́явить*) disclose, show, reveal; (*найти́*) discover, detect; **-ся** appear, show; come to light; be found, discovered

обнести́ → *обноси́ть*

обн|имáть [1], <**~я́ть**> [обнимý, обни́мешь; óбнял, -á, -о; óбнятый (óбнят, -á, -о)] embrace, hug, clasp in one's arms

обнóв|(к)а *f* [5; (*g/pl.*: -вок)] *coll.* new; article of clothing; **~и́ть** → **~ля́ть**; **~лéние** *n* [12] *репертуáра и т. д.* renewal; (*ремóнт и т. д.*) renovation; **~ля́ть** [28], <**~и́ть**> [14 *e.*; -влю́, -ви́шь; -влённый] renew; renovate; update; repair

обн|оси́ть [15], <**~ести́**> [24; -с-: -сý] pass (round); *coll.* serve; (T) fence in, enclose; **-ся** *coll. impf.* wear out one's clothes

обню́х|ивать, <**~ать**> [1] sniff around

обня́ть → *обнимáть*

обобрáть → *обирáть*

обобщ|áть [1], <**~и́ть**> [16 *e.*; -щý, -щи́шь; -щённый] generalize; **~и́ть** → **~áть**

обога|щáть [1], <**~ти́ть**> [15 *e.*; -ащý, -ти́шь; -ащённый] enrich; *рудý* concentrate

обогнáть → *обгоня́ть*

обогнýть → *огибáть*

обоготворя́ть [28] → *боготвори́ть*

обогревáть [1] → *греть*

óбод *m* [1; *pl.*: обóдья, -дьев] rim, felloe; **~óк** *m* [1; -дкá] rim

обóдр|анный [14 *sh.*] *coll.* ragged, shabby; **~áть** → *обдирáть*; **~éние** *n* [12] encouragement; **~я́ть** [28], <**~и́ть**> [13] cheer up, reassure; **-ся** take heart, cheer up

обожáть [1] adore, worship

обожеств|ля́ть [28], <**~и́ть**> [14 *e.*; -влю́, -ви́шь; -влённый] deify

обожжённый [14; -ён, -енá] burnt

обозвáть → *обзывáть*

обознач|áть [1], <**~ить**> [16] denote, designate, mark; **-ся** appear; **~éние** *n* [12] designation; *знак* sign, symbol

обозр|евáть [1], <**~éть**> [9], **~éние** *n* [12] survey; *mst. lit.* review

обó|и *m/pl.* [3] wallpaper; **~йти́(сь)** → *обходи́ть(ся)*; **~крáсть** → *обкрáдывать*

оболóчка *f* [5; *g/pl.*: -чек] cover(ing), envelope; *anat. сли́зистая и т. д.* membrane; *рáдужная* (*роговáя*) ~ iris (cornea)

оболь|сти́тель *m* [4] seducer; **~сти́тельный** [14; -лен, -льна] seductive; **~щáть** [1], <**~сти́ть**> [15 *e.*; -льщý, льсти́шь; -льщённый] seduce; (**-ся** be) delude(d; flatter o.s.)

обомлéть [8] *pf. coll.* be stupefied

обоня́ние *n* [12] (sense of) smell

оборáчивать(ся) → *обёртывать(ся)*

оборв|áнец *coll. m* [1; -нца] ragamuffin; **~анный** [14 *sh.*] ragged; **~áть** → *обрывáть*

обóрка *f* [5; *g/pl.*: -рок] frill, ruffle

оборóн|а *f* [5] defense (*Brt.* defence); **~и́тельный** [14] defensive; **~ный** [14] defense..., armament...; **~ная промы́шленность** defense industry; **~оспосóбность** *f* [8] defensive capability; **~я́ть** [28] defend

оборóт *m* [1] turn; *tech.* revolution, rotation; *fin.* circulation; *comm.* turnover; *сторонá* back, reverse; (**см.**) **на ~е** please turn over (PTO); **ввести́ в ~** put into circulation; **взять когó-нибудь в ~** *fig. coll.*

get at s.o.; take s.o. to task; **~и́ть(ся)** P [15] *pf.* → ***оберну́ть(ся)***; **~ливый** [14 *sh.*] *coll.* resourceful; **~ный** [14] *сторона́* back, reverse; *fig.* seamy (*side*); ***~ный капита́л*** working capital

обору́дова|ние *n* [12] equipment; ***вспомога́тельное ~ние*** *comput.* peripherals, add-ons; **~ть** [7] (*im*)*pf.* equip, fit out

обосн|ова́ние *n* [12] substantiation; ground(s); **~о́вывать** [1], <~ова́ть> [7] prove, substantiate; **-ся** settle down

обос|обля́ть [28], <~о́бить> [14] isolate; **-ся** keep aloof, stand apart

обостр|я́ть [28], <~и́ть> [13] (**-ся** become); (*уху́дшить*) aggravate(d), strain(ed); *о чу́вствах* become keener; *med.* become acute

обою́дный [14; -ден, -дна] mutual, reciprocal

обраб|а́тывать, <~о́тать> [1] work, process; *agr.* till; *текст и т. д.* elaborate, finish, polish; *chem. etc.* treat; (*адапти́ровать*) adapt; *coll.* work upon, win round ***кого́-л.***; *p. pr. a.* *промы́шленность* manufacturing; **~о́тка** *f* [5; *g/pl.*: -ток] processing; *agric.* cultivation; elaboration; adaptation

о́браз *m* [1] manner, way (T in), mode; shape, form; *lit.* figure, character; image; [*pl.*: -á, *etc. e.*] icon; ***каки́м*** (***таки́м***) ***~ом*** how (thus); ***нико́им ~ом*** by no means; ***~ жи́зни*** way of life; **~е́ц** *m* [1; -зца́] specimen, sample; (*приме́р*) model, example; *материа́ла* pattern; **~ный** [14; -зен, -зна] graphic, picturesque, vivid; **~ова́ние** *n* [12] *сло́ва и т. д.* formation; education **~о́ванный** [14 *sh.*] educated; **~ова́тельный** [14; -лен, -льна] educational (*qualification*); **~о́вывать** [1], <~ова́ть> [7] form; **-ся** (*v/i.*) arise; constitute; **~у́мить(ся)** [14] *pf. coll.* bring (come) to one's senses; **~цо́вый** [14] exemplary, model...; **~чик** *m* [1] → **~е́ц**

обрам|ля́ть [28], <~ить> [14 *st.*], *fig.* <~и́ть> [14 *e.*; -млю́, -ми́шь; -млённый] frame

обраст|а́ть [1], <~и́> [24; -ст-: -сту́; обро́с, -ла́] *мхом и т. д.* become overgrown with, covered with

обра|ти́ть → **~ща́ть**; **~тный** [14] back, return...; reverse, (*a. math.* inverse; *law* retroactive; ***~тная связь*** *tech.* feedback (*a. fig.*); **~тно** back; **~ща́ть** [1], <~ти́ть> [15 *e.*; -ащу́, -ати́шь; -ащённый] turn; *взор* direct; *eccl.* convert; draw *or* pay *or* (***на себя́***) attract (*attention*; to ***на*** B); ***не ~ща́ть внима́ния*** (***на*** B) disregard; **-ся** turn (***в*** B to); address o.s. (***к*** Д to); apply (to; for ***за*** T); appeal; ***-ся в бе́гство*** take to flight; *impf.* (**с** T) treat, handle; *дви́гаться* circulate; **~ще́ние** *n* [12] address, appeal; *оборо́т* circulation; (**с** T) treatment (of), management; manners

обре́з *m* [1] edge; ***де́нег в ~*** just enough money; **~а́ть** [1], <~ать> [3] cut (off); cut short; *но́гти и т. д.* pare; *ве́тки* prune; *coll.* (*прерва́ть*) snub, cut short; **~ок** *m* [1; -зка] scrap; *pl.* clippings **~ывать** [1] → ***~а́ть***

обре|ка́ть [1], <~чь> [26] condemn, doom (to ***на*** B, Д)

обремен|и́тельный [14; -лен, -льна] burdensome; **~я́ть** [28], <~и́ть> [13] burden

обре|чённый [14] doomed (to ***на*** B); **~чь** → ***~ка́ть***

обрисо́в|ывать [1], <~а́ть> [7] outline, sketch; **-ся** loom, appear

обро́сший [17] covered with

обруб|а́ть [1], <~и́ть> [14] chop (off), lop; **~ок** *m* [1; -бка] stump, block

о́бруч *m* [1; *from g/pl.*: *e.*] hoop; **~а́льный** [14] wedding...; **~а́ться** [1], <~и́ться> [16 *e.*; -чу́сь, -чи́шься] be(come) engaged (to **с** T); **~е́ние** *n* [12] betrothal

обру́ш|ивать [1], <~ить> [16] bring down; **-ся** fall in, collapse; fall (up)on (***на*** B)

обры́в *m* [1] precipice; *tech.* break; **~а́ть** [1], <оборва́ть> [-ву́, -вёшь; -ва́л, -вала́, -о; обо́рванный] tear *or* pluck (off); break off, cut short; **-ся** *a.* fall (from **с** P); **~истый** [14 *sh.*] steep; abrupt; **~ок** *m* [1; -вка] scrap, shred; **~очный** [14; -чен,

-чна] scrappy
обры́зг|ивать, <~ать> [1] sprinkle
обрю́зглый [14] flabby, bloated
обря́д *m* [1] ceremony, rite
обса́живать [1], <обсади́ть> [15] plant round (T with)
обсервато́рия *f* [7] observatory
обсле́дова|ние *n* [12] (P) inspection (of), inquiry (into), investigation (of); medical examination; **~ть** [7] *(im)pf.* inspect, examine, investigate
обслу́ж|ивание *n* [12] service; *tech.* servicing, maintenance; operation; **~ивать** [1], <~и́ть> [16] serve, attend; *tech.* service
обсо́хнуть → ***обсыха́ть***
обста|вля́ть [28], <~вить> [14] surround (with); furnish (T with); *coll.* outwit, deceive **~но́вка** *f* [5; *g/pl.*: -вок] furniture; (*обстоя́тельства*) situation, conditions *pl.*
обстоя́тель|ный [14; -лен, -льна] detailed, circumstantial; *coll. челове́к и т. д.* thorough; **~ство** *n* [9] circumstance (***при*** П, ***в*** П under, in); ***по ~ствам*** depending on circumstances
обстоя́ть [-ои́т] be, get on; stand; ***как обстои́т де́ло с*** (T)? how are things going?
обстре́л *m* [1] bombardment, firing; **~ивать** [1], <~я́ть> [28] fire at, on; shell
обстру́кция *f* [7] *pol.* obstruction, filibustering
обступ|а́ть [1], <~и́ть> [14] surround
об|сужда́ть [1], <~суди́ть> [15; -ждённый] discuss; **~сужде́ние** *n* [12] discussion; **~суши́ться** [16] *pf.* dry o.s.; **~счита́ть** [1] *pf.* cheat; **-ся** miscalculate
обсып|а́ть [1], <~ать> [2] strew, sprinkle
обс|ыха́ть [1], <~о́хнуть> [21] dry
обт|а́чивать [1], <~очи́ть> [16] turn; **~ека́емый** [14] streamlined; *отве́т* vague; **~ере́ть** → **~ира́ть**; **~ёсывать** [1], <~еса́ть> [3] hew; **~ира́ть** [1], <~ере́ть> [12; оботру́; обтёр; *g. pt. a.*: -тёрши & -терёв] rub off *or* down, wipe (off), dry; *coll.* wear thin
обточи́ть → ***обта́чивать***
обтрёпанный [14] shabby, *обшлага́* frayed
обтя́|гивать [1], <~ну́ть> [19] *ме́бель* cover (T with); *impf.* be close-fitting; **~жка** *f* [5]: ***в ~жку*** close-fitting dress
обу|ва́ть [1], <~ть> [18] put (**-ся** one's) shoes on; **´~вь** *f* [8] footwear, shoes *pl.*
обу́гл|иваться [1], <~иться> [13] char; carbonize
обу́за *f* [5] *fig.* burden
обу́зд|ывать [1], <~а́ть> [1] bridle, curb
обусло́в|ливать [1], <~ить> [14] make conditional (T on); cause
обу́ть(ся) → ***обува́ть(ся)***
о́бух *m* [1] *топора́* head; ***его́ как ~ом по голове́*** he was thunderstruck
обуч|а́ть [1], <~и́ть> [16] teach (Д s.th.), train; **-ся** (Д) learn, be taught; **~е́ние** *n* [12] instruction, training; education
обхва́т *m* [1] arm's span; circumference; **~ывать** [1], <~и́ть> [15] clasp (T in), embrace, enfold
обхо́д *m* [1] round; *полице́йского* beat; ***де́лать ~*** make one's round(s); ***пойти́ в ~*** make a detour; **~и́тельный** [14; -лен, -льна] affable, amiable; **~и́ть** [15], <обойти́> [обойду́, -дёшь; → ***идти́***] go round; visit (all [one's]); (*вопро́с*) avoid, evade; *зако́н* circumvent; pass over (T in); (**-ся**, <-сь>) cost (***мне*** me); (*спра́виться*) manage, make, do with(out) (***без*** P); there is (*no ... without*); treat (**с** T s.b.); **~ный** [14] roundabout
обш|а́ривать [1], <~а́рить> [13] rummage (around); **~ива́ть** [1], <~и́ть> [обошью́, -шьёшь; → ***шить***] sew round, border (T with); *до́сками и т. д.* plank, face, *coll.* clothe; **~и́вка** *f* [5] trimming, *etc.* (*vb.*)
обши́|рный [14; -рен, -рна] vast, extensive; (*многочи́сленный*) numerous; **~ть** → **~ва́ть**
обща́ться [1] associate (**с** T with)
обще|досту́пный [14; -пен, -пна]

О

popular; *a.* → ***досту́пный***; **~жи́тие** *n* [12] hostel; society, community; communal life; **~изве́стный** [14; -тен, -тна] well-known

обще́ние *n* [12] intercourse; relations

общепри́нятый [14 *sh.*] generally accepted, common

обще́ств|енность *f* [8] community, public; **~енный** [14] social, public; ***~енное мне́ние*** public opinion; **´~о** *n* [9] society; company (*a. econ*); association; community; ***акционе́рное ´~о*** joint-stock company; **~ове́дение** *n* [12] social science

общеупотреби́тельный [14; -лен, -льна] current, in general use

о́бщ|ий [17; о́бщ, -á, -е] general; common (in ***~его***); public; total, (***в ~ем*** on the) whole; **~ина** *f* [5] *eccl. pol., etc.* group, community; **~и́тельный** [14; -лен, -льна] sociable, affable; **~ность** *f* [8] community

объе|да́ть [1], <**~́сть**> [-éм, -éшь, *etc.* → **есть**] eat *or* gnaw round, away; **-ся** overeat

объедин|е́ние *n* [12] association, union; *де́йствие* unification; **~я́ть** [28], <**~и́ть**> [13] unite, join ; **-ся** (*v/i.*) join, unite (with)

объе́дки *coll. m/pl.* [1] leftovers

объе́|зд *m* [1] detour, by-pass; *vb.* + ***в ~зд*** = **~зжа́ть** [1] **1.** <**~хать**> [-éду, -éдешь] go, drive round; travel through *or* over; visit (all [one's]); **2.** <**~здить**> [15] break in (*horses*); **~кт** *m* [1] object; **~кти́вный** [14; -вен, -вна] objective

объём *m* [1] volume; (*величина́*) size; *зна́ний и т. д.* extent, range; **~истый** [14 *sh.*] *coll.* voluminous, bulky

объе́сть(ся) → ***объеда́ть(ся)***

объе́хать → ***объезжа́ть*** *1*

объяв|и́ть → ***~ля́ть***; **~ле́ние** *n* [12] announcement, notice; *рекла́ма* advertisement; *войны́* declaration; **~ля́ть** [28], <**~и́ть**> [14] declare (s.th. *a.* **о** П; s.b. [to be] s.th. В/Т), tell, anounce, proclaim; *благода́рность* express

объясн|е́ние *n* [12] explanation; declaration (of love ***в любви́***); **~и́мый** [14 *sh.*] explicable, accountable; **~и́тельный** [14] explanatory; **~я́ть** [28], <**~и́ть**> [13] explain, illustrate; account for; **-ся** explain o.s.; be accounted for; have it out (**с** T with); *impf.* make o.s. understood (T by)

объя́тия *n/pl.* [12] embrace (*vb.*: ***заключи́ть в ~***); ***с распростёртыми ~ми*** with open arms

обыва́тель *m* [4] philistine; **~ский** [16] narrow-minded; philistine...

обы́гр|ывать, <**~а́ть**> [1] beat (*at a game*); win

обы́денный [14] everyday, ordinary

обыкнове́н|ие *n* [12] habit; ***по ~ию*** as usual; **~ный** [14; -éнен, -éнна] ordinary; *де́йствия* usual, habitual

о́быск *m* [1], **~́ивать** [1], <**~а́ть**> [3] search

обы́ч|ай *m* [3] custom; *coll.* habit; **~ный** [14; -чен, -чна] customary, usual, habitual

обя́занн|ость *f* [8] duty; ***во́инская ~ость*** military service; ***исполня́ющий ~ости*** (P) acting; **~ый** [14 *sh.*] obliged; indebted; ***он вам обя́зан жи́знью*** he owes you his life

обяза́тель|ный [14; -лен, -льна] obligatory, compulsory; **~но** without fail, certainly; **~ство** *n* [9] obligation; *law* liability; engagement; ***вы́полнить свои́ ~ства*** meet one's obligations

обя́з|ывать [1], <**~а́ть**> [3] oblige; bind, commit; **-ся** engage, undertake, pledge o. s

овдове́вший [17] widowed

овёс *m* [1; овсá] oats *pl*

ове́чий [18] sheep('s)

овлад|ева́ть [1], <**~е́ть**> [8] (T) seize, take possession of; get control over; *зна́ниями* master; ***~е́ть собо́й*** regain one's self-control

о́вощ|и *m/pl.* [1; *gen.*: -щéй, *etc. e.*] vegetables; **~но́й** [14]: ***~но́й магази́н*** place selling fresh fruits and vegetables; (*chiefly Brt.*) greengrocer's

овра́г *m* [1] ravine
овся́нка *f* [5; *g/pl.*: -нок] oatmeal
овц|а́ *f* [5; *pl. st.*; *g/pl.*: ове́ц] sheep; **~ево́дство** *n* [9] sheepbreeding
овча́рка *f* [5; *g/pl.*: -рок] sheepdog; ***неме́цкая ~*** Alsatian (dog)
овчи́на *f* [5] sheepskin
огиба́ть [1], <обогну́ть> [20] turn *or* bend (round)
оглавле́ние *n* [12] table of contents
огла́|ска *f* [5] publicity; **~ша́ть** [1], <~си́ть> [15 *e.*; -ашу́, -аси́шь, -ашённый] announce, make public; **-ся** *кри́ками и т. д.* fill; resound; ring; **~ше́ние** *n* [12] proclamation; publication
оглуш|а́ть [1], <~и́ть> [16 *e.*; -шу́, -ши́шь, -шённый] deafen; stun; **~и́тельный** [14; -лен, -льна] deafening; stunning
огля́|дка *coll. f* [5] looking back; ***без ~дки*** without turning one's head; ***с ~дкой*** carefully; **~дывать** [1], <~де́ть> [11] examine, look around; **-ся 1.** look round; *fig.* to adapt o.s.; **2.** *pf.*: <~ну́ться> [20] look back (***на*** B at)
о́гне|нный [14] fiery; **~опа́сный** [14; -сен, -сна] inflammable; **~сто́йкий** [16; -о́ек, -о́йка] → ***~упо́рный***; **~стре́льный** [14] fire (*arm*); **~туши́тель** *m* [4] fire extinguisher; **~упо́рный** [14; -рен, -рна] fireproof
огов|а́ривать [1], <~ори́ть> [13] (*оклевета́ть*) slander; *усло́вия* stipulate; **-ся** make a slip of the tongue; → ***обмо́лвиться***; **~о́рка** *f* [5; *g/pl.*: -рок] slip of the tongue; reservation, proviso
огол|я́ть [28], <~и́ть> [13] bare
огонёк *m* [1; -нька́] (small) light; *fig.* zest, spirit
ого́нь *m* [4; огня́] fire (*a. fig.*); light; ***из огня́ да в по́лымя*** out of the frying pan into the fire; ***пойти́ в ~ и во́ду*** through thick and thin; ***тако́го днём с огнём не найдёшь*** impossible to find another like it
огор|а́живать [1], <~оди́ть> [15 & 15 *e.*; -ожу́, -о́ди́шь; -о́женный] enclose, fence (in); **~о́д** *m* [1] kitchen garden; **~о́дник** *m* [1] market *or* kitchen gardener; **~о́дничество** *n* [9] market gardening
огорч|а́ть [1], <~и́ть> [16 *e.*; -чу́, -чи́шь; -чённый] grieve (**-ся** *v/i.*), (be) vex(ed), distress(ed T); **~е́ние** *n* [9] grief, affliction; **~и́тельный** [14; -лен, -льна] grievous; distressing
огра|бле́ние *n* [12] burglary, robbery; **~да** *f* [5] fence; *ка́менная* wall; **~жда́ть** [1], <~ди́ть> [15 *e.*; -ажу́, -ади́шь; -аждённый] *обре́чь* guard, protect; **~жде́ние** *n* [12] barrier; railing
огранич|е́ние *n* [12] limitation; restriction; **~енный** [14 *sh.*] confined; *сре́дства* limited; *челове́к* narrow(-minded); **~ивать** [1], <~ить> [16] confine, limit, restrict (o.s. **-ся**; to T); content o.s. with; not go beyond; **~и́тельный** [14; -лен, -льна] restrictive, limiting
огро́мный [14; -мен, -мна] huge, vast; *интере́с и т. д.* enormous, tremendous
огрубе́лый [14] coarse, hardened
огрыз|а́ться *coll.* [1], *once* <~ну́ться> [20] snap (at); **~ок** *m* [1; -зка] bit, end; *карандаша́* stump, stub
огу́льный *coll.* [14; -лен, -льна] wholesale, indiscriminate; (*необосно́ванный*) unfounded
огуре́ц *m* [1; -рца́] cucumber
ода́лживать [1], <одолжи́ть> [16 *e.*; -жу́, -жи́шь] lend (Д/В a. p. s.th.); *coll. взять* borrow
одар|ённый [14 *sh.*] gifted; talented; **~ивать** [1], <~и́ть> [13] give (presents) to (T); *fig.* (*impf.* **~я́ть** [28]) endow (T with)
оде|ва́ть [1], <~ть> [-е́ну, -е́нешь; -е́тый] dress in; clothe in (**-ся** *v/i.* dress o.s., clothe o.s.); **~жда** *f* [5] clothes *pl.*, clothing
одеколо́н *m* [1] eau de cologne
одеревене́лый [14] numb
оде́рж|ивать [1], <~а́ть> [4] gain, win; ***~а́ть верх над*** (T) gain the upper hand (over); **~и́мый** [14 *sh.*] (T) obsessed (by); *стра́хом* ridden (by)
оде́ть(ся) → ***одева́ть(ся)***
одея́ло *n* [9] blanket, cover(let); *стёганое* quilt
оди́н *m*, **одна́** *f*, **одно́** *n*, **одни́** *pl.*

О

[33] one; alone; only; a, a certain; some; *~ мой друг* a friend of mine; *одно́ su.* one thing, thought, *etc.*; *~ на ~* tête-à-tête; *все до одного́* (*or* *все как ~*) all to a (*or* the last) man
один|а́ковый [14 *sh.*] identical (with), the same (as); **~надцатый** [14] eleventh; → *пятый*; **~надцать** [35] eleven; → *пять*; **~о́кий** [16 *sh.*] lonely, lonesome; (*незаму́жняя и т. д.*) single; **~о́чество** *n* [9] solitude, loneliness; **~о́чка** *m/f* [5; *g/pl.*: -чек] lone person; one-man boat (*or coll.* cell); **~о́чкой, в ~о́чку** alone; **~о́чный** [14] single; *заключе́ние* solitary; individual; one-man...
одио́зный [14; -зен, -зна] odious, offensive
одича́лый [14] (having gone) wild
одна́жды once, one day
одна́ко, (*a.* **~ж[е]**) however; yet, still; but, though
одно|...: ~бо́кий [16 *sh.*] *mst. fig.* one-sided; **~бо́ртный** [14] single-breasted; **~вре́ме́нный** [14] simultaneous; **~зву́чный** [14; -чен, -чна] monotonous; **~зна́чный** [14; -чен, -чна] synonymous; *math.* simple; **~имённый** [14; -ёнен, -ённа] of the same name; **~кла́ссник** *m* [1] classmate; **~коле́йный** [14] single-track; **~кра́тный** [14; -тен, -тна] occurring once, single; **~ле́тний** [15] one-year(-old); *bot.* annual; **~ле́ток** *m* [1; -тка] of the same age (as); **~ме́стный** [14] single-seater; **~обра́зный** [14; -зен, -зна] monotonous; **~ро́дный** [14; -ден, -дна] homogeneous; **~сло́жный** [14; -жен, -жна] monosyllabic; *fig.* terse, abrupt; **~сторо́нний** [15; -о́нен, -о́нняя] one-sided (*a. fig.*); unilateral; *движе́ние* one-way; **~фами́лец** *m* [1; -льца́] namesake; **~цве́тный** [14; -тен, -тна] monochromatic; **~эта́жный** [14] one-storied (*Brt.* -reyed)
одобр|е́ние *n* [12] approval; **~и́тельный** [14; -лен, -льна] approving; **~я́ть** [28], <~ить> [13] approve (of)
одол|ева́ть [1], <~е́ть> [8] overcome, defeat; *fig.* master; cope with; *страх и т. д.* (be) overcome (by)
одолж|е́ние *n* [12] favo(u)r, service; **~и́ть** → *ода́лживать*
одува́нчик *m* [1] dandelion
оду́м|ываться, <~аться> [1] change one's mind
одура́чивать → *дура́чить*
одур|ма́нивать [1], <~ма́нить> [13] stupefy
одутлова́тый [14 *sh.*] puffy
одухотворённый [14 *sh.*] inspired
одушев|лённый [14] *gr.* animate; **~ля́ть** [28], <~и́ть> [14 *e.*; -влю́, -ви́шь; -влённый] animate; (*воодушеви́ть*) inspire
оды́шка *f* [5] short breath
ожере́лье *n* [10] necklace
ожесточ|а́ть [1], <~и́ть> [16 *e.*; -чу́, -чи́шь; -чённый] harden; embitter **~е́ние** [12] bitterness; **~ённый** [14 *sh.*] *a.* hardened, fierce, bitter
ожи|ва́ть [1], <~ть> [-иву́, -ивёшь; о́жил, -а́, -о] revive; **~ви́ть(ся)** → **~*вля́ть(ся)***; **~вле́ние** *n* [12] animation; **~влённый** [14 *sh.*] animated, lively; **~вля́ть** [28], <~ви́ть> [14 *e.*; -влю́, -ви́шь, -влённый] revive; enliven, animate; **-ся** quicken, revive; brighten
ожида́|ние *n* [12] expectation; ***зал ~ния*** waiting room; ***обману́ть ~ния*** disappoint; **~ть** [1] wait (for P); expect; ***как мы и ~ли*** just as we expected
ожи́ть → *ожива́ть*
ожо́г *m* [1] burn; *кипятко́м* scald
озабо́|чивать [1], <~тить> [15] disquiet, alarm; **~ченный** [14 *sh.*] anxious, worried (T about); (*поглощённый*) preoccupied
озагла́в|ливать [1], <~ить> [14] give a title to; head (*a chapter*)
озада́ч|ивать [1], <~ить> [16] puzzle, perplex
озар|я́ть [28], <~и́ть> [13] (**-ся** be[come]) illuminate(d), light (lit) up; brighten, lighten
озвере́ть [8] *pf.* become furious
оздоров|ля́ть [1], <~и́ть> [14] *обстано́вку и т. д.* improve
о́зеро *n* [9; *pl.*: озёра, -ёр] lake
ози́мый [14] winter (*crops*)
озира́ться [1] look round
озлоб|ля́ть [28], <~ить> [14] (**-ся**

О

become) embitter(ed); **~ле́ние** *n* [12] bitterness, animosity
ознак|омля́ть [28], <~о́мить> [14] familiarize (**-ся** o.s., **с** T with)
ознамен|ова́ние *n* [12] marking, commemoration (**в** B in); **~о́вывать** [1], <~ова́ть> [7] mark, commemorate, celebrate
означа́ть [1] signify, mean
озно́б *m* [1] chill; shivering; ***чу́вствовать ~*** feel shivery
озор|ни́к *m* [1 *e.*], **~ни́ца** *f* [5] *coll.* → ***шалу́н(ья)***; *coll.* **~нича́ть** [1] → ***шали́ть***; **~но́й** *coll.* [14] mischievous, naughty; **~ство́** *coll. n* [9] mischief, naughtiness
ой *int.* oh! o dear!
ока́з|ывать [1], <~а́ть> [3] show; render, do; *влия́ние* exert; *предпочте́ние* give; **-ся** (T) turn out (to be), be found; find o.s
окайм|ля́ть [28], <~и́ть> [14 *e.*; -млю́, -ми́шь, -млённый] border
окамене́лый [14] petrified
ока́нчивать [1], <око́нчить> [16] finish, end (**-ся** *v/i.*)
ока́пывать [1], <окопа́ть> [1] dig round; entrench (**-ся** o.s.)
океа́н *m* [1], **~ский** [16] ocean
оки́|дывать [1], <~нуть> [20] (***взгля́дом***) take in at a glance
окис|ля́ть [28], <~ли́ть> [13] oxidize; **´~ь** *f* [8] *chem.* oxide
оккуп|ацио́нный [14] occupation-...; **~и́ровать** [7] *(im)pf.* occupy
окла́д *m* [1] salary; salary scale
окла́дистый [14 *sh.*] (*of a beard*) full
окле́и|вать [1], <~ть> [13] paste over (with); *обо́ями* paper
о́клик *m* [1], **~ать** [1], <~нуть> [20] call, hail
окно́ *n* [9; *pl. st*: о́кна, о́кон, о́кнам] window (*look* through **в** B); *school sl.* free period
о́ко *n* [9; *pl.*: о́чи, оче́й, *etc. e.*] *mst. poet.* eye
око́вы *f/pl.*: [5] fetters (*mst. fig.*)
околдова́ть [7] *pf.* bewitch
окол|ева́ть [1], <~е́ть> [8] die (*of animals*)
о́кол|о (P) (*приблизи́тельно*) about, around, nearly; (*ря́дом*) by, at, near; nearby
око́нный [14] window...
оконч|а́ние *n* [12] end(ing *gr.*) close, termination; *рабо́ты* completion ([up]on **по** П); *univ.* graduation; **~а́тельный** [14; -лен, -льна] final, definitive; **~ить** → ***ока́нчивать***
око́п *m* [1] *mil.* trench; **~а́ть(ся)** → ***ока́пывать(ся)***
о́корок *m* [1; *pl.*: -ка, *etc. e.*] ham
око|стене́лый [14] ossified (*a. fig.*); **~чене́лый** [14] numb (with cold)
око́ш|ечко *n* [9; *g/pl.*: -чек], **~ко** [9; *g/pl.*: -шек] *dim.* → ***окно́***
окра́ина *f* [5] outskirts *pl.*
окра́|ска *f* [5] painting; dyeing; colo(u)ring; *fig.* tinge; **~шивать** [1], <~сить> [15] paint; dye; stain; tint
окре́стн|ость (*often pl.*) *f* [8] environs *pl.*, neighbo(u)rhood; **~ый** [14] surrounding; in the vicinity
окрова́вленный [14] bloodstained, bloody
о́круг *m* [1; *pl.*: -га́, *etc. e.*] region, district; circuit
округл|я́ть [28], <~и́ть> [13] round (off); **~ый** [14 *sh.*] rounded
окруж|а́ть [1], <~и́ть> [16 *e.*; -жу́, -жи́шь; -жённый] surround; **~а́ющий** [17] surrounding; **~е́ние** *n* [12] *среда́* environment; *mil.* encirclement; *лю́ди* milieu, circle, company; **~и́ть** → **~а́ть**; **~но́й** [14] district...; circular; **~ность** *f* [8] circumference
окрыл|я́ть [28], <~и́ть> [13] *fig.* encourage, lend wings, inspire
октя́брь *m* [4 *e.*], **~ский** [16] October; *fig.* Russian revolution of October 1917
окун|а́ть [1], <~у́ть> [20] dip, plunge (*v/i.* **-ся**; dive, *a. fig.*)
о́кунь *m* [4; *from g/pl. e.*] perch (*fish*)
окуп|а́ть [1], <~и́ть> [14], (**-ся** be) offset, recompense(d), compensate(d)
оку́рок *m* [1; -рка] cigarette end, stub, butt
оку́т|ывать, <~ать> [1] wrap (up); *fig.* shroud, cloak
ола́дья *f* [6; *g/pl.*: -дий] *cul.* fritter
оледене́лый [14] frozen, iced

оле́нь *m* [4] deer; **се́верный ~** reindeer
оли́в|а *f* [5], **~ка** *f* [5; *g/pl.*: -вок], olive (tree); **~ковый** [14] olive...
олимп|иа́да *f* [5] Olympiad, Olympics; **~и́йский** [16] Olympic; ***~и́йские и́гры*** Olympic Games
олицетвор|е́ние *n* [12] personification, embodiment; **~я́ть** [28], <**~и́ть**> [13] personify, embody
о́лов|о *n* [9], tin; **~я́нный** [14] tin, tin-bearing, stannic
о́лух *m* [1] *coll.* blockhead, dolt
ольх|а́ *f* [5], **~о́вый** [14] alder (tree)
ома́р *m* [1] lobster
оме́ла *f* [5] mistletoe
омерз|е́ние *n* [12] loathing; **~и́тельный** [14; -лен, -льна] sickening, loathsome
омертве́лый [14] stiff, numb; *med.* necrotic
омле́т *m* [1] omelet(te)
омоложе́ние *n* [12] rejuvenation
омо́ним *m* [1] *ling.* homonym
омрач|а́ть [1], <**~и́ть**> [16 *e.*; -чу́, -чи́шь; -чённый] darken, sadden (*v/i.* **-ся**)
о́мут *m* [1] whirlpool; deep place (*in river or lake*); ***в ти́хом ~е че́рти во́дятся*** still waters run deep
омы|ва́ть [1], <**~ть**> [22] wash (*of seas*)
он *m*, **~а́** *f*, **~о́** *n*, **~и́** *pl.* [22] he, she, it, they
онда́тра [5] muskrat; *мех* musquash
онеме́лый [14] dump; numb
опа|да́ть [1], <**~сть**> [25; *pt. st.*] fall (off); (*уменьша́ться*) diminish, subside
опа́здывать, <опозда́ть> [1] be late (***на*** В, ***к*** Д for); ***на пять мину́т*** arrive 5 min. late; *на по́езд* miss; *impf. only* be slow (*of timepieces*)
опал|я́ть [28], <**~и́ть**> [13] singe
опас|а́ться [1] (P) fear, apprehend; beware (of); **~е́ние** *n* [12] fear, apprehension, anxiety; **~ка** *f* [5; *g/pl.*: -сок]: ***с ~кой*** cautiously, warily; **~ливый** [14 *sh.*] wary; anxious; **~ность** [8] danger, peril; risk (**с** T/ ***для*** P at/of); ***с ~ностью для себя́*** at a risk to himself; **~ный** [14; -сен, -сна] dangerous (***для*** P to); **~ть** → ***опада́ть***
опе́к|а *f* [5] guardianship, (*a. fig.*) tutelage; *над иму́ществом* trusteeship; **~а́ть** [1] be guardian (trustee) of; patronize; **~а́емый** [14] ward; **~у́н** *m* [1 *e.*], **~у́нша** *f* [5] guardian; trustee
о́пера *f* [5] opera
опер|ати́вный [14] *руково́дство* efficient; *med.* surgical; **~а́тор** *m* [1] operator; **~ацио́нный** [14] operating; ***~ацио́нная*** *su.* operating room; **~а́ция** *f* [7] operation; ***перенести́ ~а́цию*** be operated on
опер|ежа́ть [1], <**~ди́ть**> [15] outstrip (*a. fig.* = outdo, surpass); **~ние** *n* [12] plumage; **~ться** → ***опира́ться***
опери́ровать [7] (*im*)*pf.* operate
о́перный [14] opera(tic); ***~ теа́тр*** opera house
опер|я́ться [28], <**~и́ться**> [13] fledge
опеча́т|ка *f* [5; *g/pl.*: -ток] misprint, erratum; **~ывать**, <**~ать**> [1] seal (up)
опе́шить *coll.* [16] *pf.* be taken aback
опи́лки *f/pl.* [5; *gen.*: -лок] sawdust
опира́ться [1], <опере́ться> [12; обопру́сь, -рёшься, опёрся, оперла́сь] lean (***на*** В against, on), *a. fig.* = rest, rely ([up]on)
опис|а́ние *n* [12] description; **~а́тельный** [14] descriptive; **~а́ть** → ***~ывать***; **~ка** *f* [5; *g/pl.*: -сок] slip of the pen; **~ывать** [1], <**~а́ть**> [3] describe (*a. math.*); list, make an inventory (of); *иму́щество* distrain; **-ся** make a slip of the pen; **´~ь** *f* [8] list, inventory; distraint
опла́к|ивать [1], <**~ать**> [3] bewail, mourn (over)
опла́|та *f* [5] pay(ment); (*вознагражде́ние*) remuneration, settlement; **~чивать** [1], <**~ти́ть**> [15] pay (for); *счёт* settle; ***~ти́ть убы́тки*** pay damages
оплеу́ха *coll. f* [5] slap in the face
оплодотвор|е́ние *n* [12] impregnation; fertilization; **~я́ть** [28], <**~и́ть**> [13] impregnate; fertilize, fecundate

опло́т *m* [1] bulwark, stronghold
опло́шность *f* [8] blunder
опове|ща́ть [1], <~сти́ть> [15 *e.*; -ещу́, -ести́шь; -ещённый] notify; inform
опозда́|ние *n* [12] lateness; delay; *vb.* + **с ~нием = ~ть** → ***опа́здывать***
опозн|ава́тельный [14] distinguishing; **~ава́ть** [5], <~а́ть> [1] identify
о́ползень *m* [4; -зня] landslide
ополч|а́ться [1], <~и́ться> [16 *e.*; -чу́сь, -чи́шься] take up arms (against); *fig.* turn (against)
опо́мниться [13] *pf.* come to *or* recover one's senses
опо́р *m* [1]: ***во весь ~*** at full speed, at a gallop
опо́р|а *f* [5] support, prop, rest; **~ный** [14] *tech.* bearing, supporting
опоро́|жнить [13] *pf.* empty; **~чивать** [1], <~чить> [16] defile
опошл|я́ть [28], <~ить> [13] vulgarize
опоя́с|ывать [1], <~ать> [3] gird
оппозици|о́нный [14], **´~я** *f* [7] opposition...
оппон|е́нт *m* [1] opponent; **~и́ровать** [7] (Д) oppose; *univ.* act as opponent at defense of dissertation, *etc.*
опра́ва *f* [5] ***ка́мня*** setting; ***очко́в и т. д.*** rim, frame
оправд|а́ние *n* [12] justification, excuse; *law* acquittal; **~а́тельный** [14] justificatory; ***пригово́р*** 'not guilty'; **~ывать** [1], <~а́ть> [1] justify, excuse; *law* acquit; ***~а́ть дове́рие*** come up to expectations; **-ся** *a.* prove (*or* come) true
оправ|ля́ть [28], <~ить> [14] ***ка́мень*** set; **-ся** recover (*a.* o.s.)
опра́шивать [1], <опроси́ть> [15] interrogate, cross-examine
определ|е́ние *n* [12] determination; *ling., etc.* definition; decision; *gr.* attribute; **~ённый** [14; -ёнен, -ённа] definite; certain; ***в ~ённых слу́чаях*** in certain cases; **~я́ть** [28], <~и́ть> [13] determine; define; **-ся** take shape; (***проясни́ться***) become clearer
опров|ерга́ть [1], <~е́ргнуть> [21] refute; disprove; **~ерже́ние** *n* [12] refutation; denial
опроки́|дывать [1], <~нуть> [20] overturn, upset, ***о ло́дке*** capsize (**-ся** *v/i.*); ***пла́ны*** upset
опро|ме́тчивый [14 *sh.*] rash, precipitate; **~метью**: ***вы́бежать ~метью*** rush out headlong
опро́с *m* [1]: interrogation; cross-examination; referendum; ***~ обще́ственного мне́ния*** opinion poll; **~и́ть** → ***опра́шивать***; **~ный** [14] *adj. of* ~; ***~ный лист*** questionnaire
опры́с|кивать, <~ать> [1] sprinkle, spray
опря́тный [14; -тен, -тна] tidy
о́птика *f* [5] optics
опто́|вый [14], **´~м** *adv.* wholesale
опубликов|а́ние *n* [12] publication; **~ывать** [1] → ***публикова́ть***
опус|ка́ть [1], <~ти́ть> [15] lower; let down; ***го́лову*** hang; ***глаза́*** look down; (***исключи́ть***) omit; ***~ти́ть ру́ки*** lose heart; **-ся** sink; ***о температу́ре*** fall; ***о со́лнце, температу́ре*** go down; *fig.* come down (in the world); *p. pt. a.* down and out
опуст|е́лый [14] deserted; **~и́ться** → ***опуска́ть(ся)***; **~оша́ть** [1], <~оши́ть> [16 *e.*; -шу́, -ши́шь; -шённый] devastate; **~оше́ние** *n* [12] devastation; **~оши́тельный** [14; -лен, -льна] devastating
опу́т|ывать, <~ать> [1] entangle (*a. fig.*); ensnare
опух|а́ть [1], <~нуть> [21] swell; **´~оль** *f* [8] swelling; tumo(u)r
опу́шка *f* [5; *g/pl.*: -шек] edge (*of a forest*)
опыл|я́ть [28], <~и́ть> [13] pollinate
о́пыт *m* [1] ***жи́зненный и т. д.*** experience; experiment; **~ный** [14] [-тен, -тна] experienced; experiment(al); empirical
опьяне́ние *n* [12] intoxication
опя́ть again; *a. coll.*, ***~-таки*** (and) what is more; but again; however
ора́ва *coll. f* [5] gang, horde, mob
ора́кул *m* [1] oracle
ора́нже|вый [14] orange...; **~ре́я** *f* [6] greenhouse
ора́ть *coll.* [ору́, орёшь] yell, bawl

орби́т|а *f* [5] orbit; ***вы́вести на ~у*** put into orbit
о́рган[1] *m* [1] *biol., pol.* organ
орга́н[2] *m* [1] *mus.* organ
организ|а́тор *m* [1] organizer; **~м** *m* [1] organism; **~ова́ть** [7] (*im*)*pf.* (*impf. a.* **~о́вывать** [1]) arrange, organize (*v/i.* **-ся**)
органи́ч|еский [16] organic; **~ный** [14; -чен, -чна]: ***~ное це́лое*** integral whole
о́ргия *f* [7] orgy
орда́ *f* [5; *pl. st.*] horde
о́рден *m* [1; *pl.*: -на́, *etc. e.*] order, decoration
о́рдер *m* [1; *pl.*: -ра́, *etc. e.*] *law* warrant, writ
орёл *m* [1; орла́] eagle; ***~ или ре́шка?*** heads or tails?
орео́л *m* [1] halo, aureole
оре́х *m* [1] nut; ***гре́цкий ~*** walnut; ***лесно́й ~*** hazelnut; ***муска́тный ~*** nutmeg; **~овый** [14] nut...; (*wood*) walnut
оригина́льный [14; -лен, -льна] original
ориенти́р|оваться [7] (*im*)*pf.* orient o.s. (***на*** В by), take one's bearings; **~о́вка** *f* [5; *g/pl.*: -вок] orientation, bearings *pl.*; **~о́вочный** [14; -чен, -чна] approximate
орке́стр *m* [1] orchestra; band
орли́ный [14] aquiline
орна́мент *m* [1] ornament, ornamental design
оро|ша́ть [1], <~си́ть> [15; -ошу́, -оси́шь; -ошённый] irrigate; **~ше́ние** *n* [12] irrigation
ору́д|ие *n* [12] tool (*a. fig.*); instrument, implement; *mil.* gun; **~ийный** [14] gun...; **~овать** *coll.* [7] (Т) handle, operate
оруж|е́йный [14] arms...; **~ие** *n* [12] weapon(s), arm(s); ***холо́дное*** (*cold*) steel
орфогра́ф|ия *f* [7] spelling; **~и́ческий** [16] orthographic(al)
орхиде́я *f* [6] *bot.* orchid
оса́ *f* [5; *pl. st.*] wasp
оса́|да *f* [5] siege; **~ди́ть** → ***~жда́ть*** *and* ***~живать***; **~док** *m* [1; -дка] precipitation, sediment; *fig.* aftertaste; **~жда́ть** [1], <~ди́ть> [15 & 15 *e.*; -ажу́, -а́ди́шь; -аждённый] besiege; ***~жда́ть вопро́сами*** ply with questions; **~живать** [1], <~ди́ть> [15] check, snub
оса́н|истый [14 *sh.*] dignified, stately; **~ка** *f* [5] carriage, bearing
осв|а́ивать [1], <~о́ить> [13] (*овладева́ть*) assimilate, master; *но́вые зе́мли и т. д.* open up; **-ся** accustom o.s. (**в** П to); familiarize o.s. (**с** Т with)
осведом|ля́ть [28], <~ить> [14] inform (**о** П of); **-ся** inquire (**о** П after, for; about); **~лённый** [14] informed; versed (in)
освеж|а́ть [1], <~и́ть> [16 *e.*; -жу́, -жи́шь; -жённый] refresh; freshen *or* touch up; *fig.* brush up; **~а́ющий** [17 *sh.*] refreshing
осве|ща́ть [1], <~ти́ть> [15 *e.*; -ещу́, -ети́шь; -ещённый] light (up), illuminate; *fig.* elucidate, cast light on; cover, report on (*in the press*)
освиде́тельствова|ние *n* [12] examination; **~ть** [7] *pf.* examine
осви́ст|ывать [1], <~а́ть> [3] hiss (off)
освобо|ди́тель *m* [4] liberator; **~ди́тельный** [14] emancipatory, liberation; **~жда́ть** [1], <~ди́ть> [15 *e.*; -ожу́, -оди́шь; -ождённый] (set) free, release; liberate, *рабо́в и т. д.* emancipate; *от упла́ты* exempt; *ме́сто* clear; ***~ди́ть от до́лжности*** relieve of one's post; **~жде́ние** *n* [12] liberation; release, emancipation; exemption
осво|е́ние *n* [12] assimilation; mastering; *земе́ль* opening up; **~ить(ся)** → ***осва́ивать(ся)***
освя|ща́ть [1], <~ти́ть> [15 *e.*; -ящу́, -яти́шь; -ящённый] *eccl.* consecrate
осе|да́ть [1], <~сть> [25; ося́дет; осе́л; → **сесть**] subside, settle; **~длый** [14] settled
осёл *m* [1; осла́] donkey, ass (*a. fig.*)
осени́ть → ***осеня́ть***
осе́н|ний [15] autumnal, fall...; **´~ь** *f* [8] fall, autumn (in [the] Т)
осен|я́ть [28], <~и́ть> [13] overshadow; ***~и́ть кресто́м*** make the sign of the cross; ***меня́ ~и́ла***

мысль it dawned on me, it occurred to me

осéсть → ***оседáть***

осётр *m* [1 *e.*] sturgeon

осетрúна *f* [5] *cul.* sturgeon

осéчка *f* [5; *g/pl.*: -чек] misfire

осúли|вать [1], <~ть> [13] → ***одолевáть***

осúн|а *f* [5] asp; **~овый** [14] asp

осúпнуть [21] *pf.* grow hoarse

осиротéлый [14] orphan(ed); *fig.* deserted

оскáли|вать [1], <~ть> [13]: ***~ть зýбы*** bare one's teeth

оскандáли|ваться [1], <-иться> [13] *coll.* disgrace o.s.; make a mess of s. th.

осквер|нять [28], <~úть> [13] profane, desecrate, defile

оскóлок *m* [1; -лка] splinter, fragment

оскорб|úтельный [14; -лен, -льна] offensive, insulting; **~лéние** *n* [12] insult, offence; **~лять** [28], <~úть> [14 *e.*; -блю, -бúшь; -блённый] (**-ся** feel) offend(ed), insult(ed)

оскуд|евáть [1], <~éть> [8] grow scarce

ослаб|евáть [1], <~éть> [8] grow weak *or* feeble; *натяжéние* slacken; *вéтер и т. д.* abate; **~úть** → **~лять**; **~лéние** *n* [12] weakening; slackening; relaxation; **~лять** [28], <~úть> [14] weaken, slacken; *внимáние и т. д.* relax, loosen

ослеп|úтельный [14; -лен, -льна] dazzling; **~лять** [28], <~úть> [14 *e.*; -плю, -пúшь; -плённый] blind; dazzle; **~нуть** [21] *pf.* go blind

осложн|éние *n* [12 complication; **~ять** [28], <~úть> [13] (**-ся** be[come]) complicate(d)

ослýш|иваться, <~аться> [1] disobey

ослы́шаться [4] *pf.* mishear

осм|áтривать [1], <~отрéть> [9; -отрю, -óтришь; -óтреный] view, look around; examine, inspect; see; **-ся** look round; *fig.* take one's bearings; see how the land lies

осмé|ивать [1], <~ять> [27 *e.*; -ею, -еёшь; -еянный] mock, ridicule, deride

осмéли|ваться [1], <~ться> [13] dare, take the liberty (of), venture

осмея|ние *n* [12] ridicule, derision; **~ть** → ***осмéивать***

осмóтр *m* [1] examination, inspection; *достопримечáтельностей* sight-seeing; **~éть(ся)** → ***осмáтривать(ся)***; **~úтельность** *f* [8] circumspection; **~úтельный** [14; -лен, -льна] circumspect

осмы́сл|енный [14 *sh.*] sensible; intelligent; **~ивать** [1] *and* **~ять** [28], <~ить> [13] comprehend, grasp, make sense of

оснá|стка *f* [5] *naut.* rigging (out, up); **~щáть** [1], <~стúть> [15 *e.*; -ащý, -астúшь; -ащённый] rig; equip; **~щéние** *n* [12] rigging, fitting out; equipment

оснóв|а *f* [5] basis, foundation, fundamentals; *gr.* stem; **~áние** *n* [12] foundation, basis; *math.*, *chem.* base; (*причúна*) ground(s), reason; argument; **~áтель** *m* [4] founder; **~áтельный** [14; -лен, -льна] well-founded, sound, solid; (*тщáтельный*) thorough; **~áть** → **~ывать**; **~нóй** [14] fundamental, basic, principal, primary; ***в ~нóм*** on the whole; **~оположник** *m* [1] founder; **~ывать**, <~áть> [7] found; establish; **-ся** be based, rest (on)

осóба *f* [5] person; personage; ***вáжная ~*** bigwig

осóбенн|ость *f* [8] peculiarity; feature; **~ый** [14] (e)special, particular, peculiar

особня́к *m* [1 *e.*] private residence, detached house

особнякóм by o.s., separate(ly); ***держáться ~*** keep aloof

осóб|ый [14] → ***~енный***

осозн|авáть [5], <~áть> [1] realize

осóка *f* [5] *bot.* sedge

óсп|а *f* [5] smallpox; ***ветрянáя ~а*** chickenpox

осп|áривать [1], <~óрить> [13] contest, dispute; *звáние чемпиóна и т. д.* contend (for)

оставáться [5], <остáться> [-áнусь, -áнешься] (T) remain, stay; be left; keep, stick (to); be(come); have to; go, get off; (***за*** T) get, win; *прáво и т. д.* reserve; ***долг*** owe; ~

без (P) lose, have no (left); **~ с** ***но́сом*** *coll.* get nothing

остав|ля́ть [28], <**~**ить> [14] leave; abandon; (*отказа́ться*) give up; drop, stop; *в поко́е* leave (*alone*); keep; ***~ля́ть за собо́й*** reserve

остально́|й [14] remaining; *pl. a.* the others; *n & pl. a. su.* the rest (**в ~м** in other respects; as for the rest)

остан|а́вливать [1], <**~**ови́ть> [14] stop, bring to a stop; *взгляд* rest, fix; **-ся** stop; *в оте́ле и т. д.* put up (**в** П at); *в ре́чи* dwell (**на** П on); **~ки** *m/pl.* [1] remains; **~ови́ть**(**ся**) → ***~а́вливать***(***ся***); **~о́вка** *f* [5; *g/pl.*: -вок] stop(page); *авто́бусная* bus stop; ***~о́вка за ...*** (T) (*only*) ... is holding up

оста́|ток *m* [1; -тка] remainder (*a. math*), rest; *тка́ни* remnant; *pl.* remains; **~ться** → ***~ва́ться***

остекл|я́ть [28], <**~**и́ть> [13] glaze

остервене́лый [14] frenzied

остер|ега́ться [1], <**~**е́чься> [26 г/ж: -егу́сь, -ежёшься, -егу́тся] (P) beware of, be careful of

о́стов *m* [1] frame, framework; *anat.* skeleton

остолбене́лый *coll.* [14] dumbfounded

осторо́жн|ость *f* [8] care; caution; ***обраща́ться с ~остью!*** handle with care!; **~ый** [14; -жен, -жна] cautious, careful; (*благоразу́мный*) prudent; ***~о!*** look out!

остри|га́ть [1], <**~**чь> [26; г/ж: -игу́, -ижёшь, -игу́т] cut; *ове́ц* shear; *но́гти* pare; **~ё**; *n* [12; *g/pl.*: -иёв] point; spike; **~ть** [13], <за-> sharpen; <с-> joke; be witty; **~чь** → ***~га́ть***

о́стров *m* [1; *pl.*: -ва́, *etc. e.*] island; isle; **~итя́нин** *m* [1; -я́не, -я́н] islander; **~о́к** *m* [1; -вка́] islet

остро|гла́зый *coll.* [14 *sh.*] sharp-sighted; **~коне́чный** [14; -чен, -чна] pointed; **~та́**[1] *f* [5; *pl. st*; -о́ты] sharpness, keenness, acuteness; **~та**[2] *f* [5] witticism; joke; **~у́мие** *n* [12] wit; **~у́мный** [14; -мен, -мна] witty; *реше́ние* ingenious

о́стр|ый [14; остр, (*coll. a.* остёр), -á, -o] sharp, pointed; *интере́с* keen; *у́гол и т. д.* acute; critical; **~я́к** *m* [1 *e.*] wit(ty fellow)

оступ|а́ться [1], <**~**и́ться> [14] stumble

остыва́ть [1] → ***сты́нуть***

осу|жда́ть [1], <**~**ди́ть> [15; -уждённый] censure, condemn; *law* convict; **~жде́ние** *n* [12] condemnation; *law* conviction

осу́нуться [20] *pf.* grow thin

осуш|а́ть [1], <**~**и́ть> [16] drain; dry (up); (*опорожни́ть*) empty

осуществ|и́мый [14 *sh.*] feasible; practicable; **~ля́ть** [28], <**~**и́ть> [14 *e.*; -влю́, -ви́шь; -влённый] bring about, realize; **-ся** be realized, fulfilled, implemented; *мечта́* come true; **~ле́ние** *n* [12] realization

осчастли́вить [14] *pf.* make happy

осып|а́ть [1], <**~**ать> [2] strew (with); shower (on); *звёздами* stud (with); *fig.* heap (on); **-ся** crumble; fall

ось *f* [8; *from g/pl. e.*] axis; axle

осяза́|емый [14 *sh.*] tangible; **~ние** *n* [12] sense of touch; **~тельный** [14] tactile; [-лен, -льна] palpable; **~ть** [1] touch, feel

от, ото (P) from; of; off; against; for, with; in; *и́мени* on behalf of

ота́пливать [1], <отопи́ть> [14] heat

отбав|ля́ть [28], <**~**ить> [14]: *coll.* ***хоть ~ля́й*** more than enough, in plenty

отбе|га́ть [1], <**~**жа́ть> [4; -бегу́, -бежи́шь, -бегу́т] run off

отби|ва́ть [1], <**~**ть> [отобью́, -бьёшь; → ***бить***] beat, strike (*or* kick) off; *mil.* repel; *coll. де́вушку* take away (**у** P from;) *край* break away; *охо́ту* discourage s.o. from sth.; **-ся** ward off (**от** P); *от гру́ппы* get lost; drop behind; break off; *coll.*; (*изба́виться*) get rid of

отбивна́я *f* [14]: *cul.* **~** ***котле́та*** *su.* chop

отбира́ть [1], <отобра́ть> [отберу́, -рёшь; отобра́л, -á, -o; ото́бранный] (*забра́ть*) take (away); seize; (*вы́брать*) select, pick out; *биле́ты* collect

отби́ть(**ся**) → ***отбива́ть***(***ся***)

о́тблеск *m* [1] reflection, gleam

О

отбо́й *m* [3]: ***нет отбо́ю от*** (P) have very many

отбо́р *m* [1] selection, choice; **~ный** [14] select, choice; **~очный** [14]: ***~очное соревнова́ние*** *sport* knock-out competition

отбр|а́сывать [1], <**~о́сить**> [15] throw off *or* away; *mil.* throw back; *иде́ю* reject; *тень* cast; **~о́сы** *m/pl.* [1] refuse, waste

отбы|ва́ть [1], <**~ть**> [-бу́ду, -бу́дешь; о́тбыл, -а́, -о] **1.** *v/i.* leave, depart (***в*** В for); **2.** *v/t. срок и т. д.* serve, do (time); **~тие** *n* [12] departure

отва́|га *f* [5] bravery, courage; **~живаться** [1], <**~житься**> [16] have the courage to, venture to, dare to; **~жный** [14; -жен, -жна] valiant, brave

отва́л: ***до ~а*** *coll.* one's fill; **~иваться** [1], <**~и́ться**> [13; -али́тся] fall off; slip

отварно́й [14] *cul.* boiled

отвезти́ → ***отвози́ть***

отверг|а́ть [1], <**~нуть**> [21] reject, turn down; repudiate, spurn

отвердева́ть [1] → ***тверде́ть***

отверну́ть(ся) → ***отвёртывать*** *and* ***отвора́чивать(ся)***

отвёрт|ка [5; *g/pl.*: -ток] screwdriver; **~ывать** [1], <отверну́ть> [20; отвёрнутый], <отверте́ть> *coll.* [11] unscrew

отве́с|ный [14; -сен, -сна] precipitous, steep, sheer; **~ти́** → ***отводи́ть***

отве́т *m* [1] answer, reply (***в ~ на*** В in reply to); ***быть в ~е*** be answerable (***за*** for)

ответвл|е́ние *n* [12] branch, offshoot; **~я́ться** [28] branch off

отве́|тить → **~ча́ть**; **~тственность** *f* [8] responsibility; **~тственный** [14 *sh.*] responsible (to ***пе́ред*** Т); **~тчик** *m* [1] defendant; **~ча́ть** [1], <**~тить**> [15] (***на*** В) answer, reply (to); (***за*** В) answer, account (for); (*соотве́тствовать*) (Д) answer, suit, meet

отви́н|чивать [1], <**~ти́ть**> [15 *e.*; -нчу́, -нти́шь; -и́нченный] unscrew

отвис|а́ть [1], <**~нуть**> [21] hang down, flop, sag; **~лый** [14] loose, flopping, sagging

отвле|ка́ть [1], <**~чь**> [26] divert, distract; **~чённый** [14 *sh.*] abstract

отвод|и́ть [15], <отвести́> [25] lead, take; *глаза́* avert; *уда́р* parry; *кандидату́ру* reject; *зе́млю* allot; ***~и́ть ду́шу*** *coll.* unburden one's heart

отво|ёвывать [1], <**~ева́ть**> [6] (re)conquer, win back; **~зи́ть** [15], <отвезти́> [24] take, drive away

отвора́чивать [1], <отверну́ть> [20] turn off; **-ся** turn away

отвори́ть(ся) → ***отворя́ть(ся)***

отворо́т *m* [1] lapel

отвор|я́ть [28], <**~и́ть**> [13; -орю́, -о́ришь; -о́ренный] open (*v/i.* **-ся**)

отвра|ти́тельный [14; -лен, -льна] disgusting, abominable; **~ща́ть** [1], <**~ти́ть**> [15 *e.*; -ащу́, -ати́шь; -ащённый] avert; **~ще́ние** *n* [12] aversion, disgust (***к*** Д for, at)

отвык|а́ть [1], <**~нуть**> [21] (***от*** P) get out of the habit of, grow out of, give up

отвя́з|ывать [1], <**~а́ть**> [3] (**-ся** [be]come) untie(d), undo(ne); *coll.* (*отде́лываться*) get rid of (***от*** P); ***отвяжи́сь!*** leave me alone!

отга́д|ывать [1], <**~а́ть**> guess; **~ка** *f* [5; *g/pl.*: -док] solution (to a riddle)

отгиба́ть [1], <отогну́ть> [20] unbend; turn up (*or* back)

отгов|а́ривать [1], <**~ори́ть**> [13] dissuade (***от*** P from); **~о́рка** *f* [5; *g/pl.*: -рок] excuse, pretext

отголо́сок *m* [1; -ска] → ***о́тзвук***

отгоня́ть [28], <отогна́ть> [отгоню́, -о́нишь; ото́гнанный; → ***гнать***] drive (*or* frighten) away; *fig. мысль* banish, suppress

отгор|а́живать [1], <**~оди́ть**> [15 & 15 *e.*; -ожу́, -о́ди́шь; -о́женный] fence in; *в до́ме* partition off

отгру|жа́ть [1], <**~зи́ть**> [15 & 15; *e.*; -ужу́, -у́зи́шь; -у́женный & -ужённый] ship, dispatch

отгрыз|а́ть [1], <**~ть**> [24; *pt. st.*] bite off, gnaw off

отда|ва́ть [5], <**~ть**> [-да́м, -да́шь, *etc.*, → ***дать***; о́тдал, -а́, -о] give back, return; give (away); *в шко́лу* send (***в*** В to); *долг* pay; ***~ва́ть честь*** (Д) *mil.* salute; *coll.* sell;

О

~ва́ть до́лжное give s.o. his due; ***~ва́ть прика́з*** give an order; *impf.* smell or taste (Т of); **-ся** devote o.s. to; *чу́вство* surrender, give o.s. to; *о зву́ке* resound

отда́в|ливать [1], <~и́ть> [14] crush; (*наступи́ть*) tread on

отдал|е́ние *n* [12]: ***в ~е́нии*** in the distance; **~ённый** [14 *sh.*] remote; **~я́ть** [28], <~и́ть> [13] move away; *встре́чу* put off, postpone; *fig.* alienate; **-ся** move away (**от** Р from); *fig.* become estranged; digress

отда́|ть(ся) → ***отдава́ть***(***ся***); **~ча** *f* [5] return; *mil.* recoil; *tech.* output, efficiency

отде́л *m* [1] department; *в газе́те* section; **~ *ка́дров*** personnel department; **~ать(ся)** → ***~ывать***(***ся***); **~е́ние** *n* [12] separation; department, division; branch (office); *mil.* squad; *в столе́ и т. д.* compartment; *в больни́це* ward; *конце́рта* part; *coll.* (police) station; ***~е́ние свя́зи*** post office; **~и́мый** [14 *sh.*] separable; **~и́ть(ся)** → ***~я́ть***(***ся***); **~ка** *f* [5; *g/pl.*: -лок] finishing; *оде́жды* trimming; **~ывать**, <~ать> [1] finish, put the final touches to; decorate; **-ся** get rid of (**от** Р); get off, escape (Т with); **~ьность** *f* [8]: ***в ~ьности*** individually; **~ьный** [14] separate; individual; **~я́ть** [28], <~и́ть> [13; -елю́, -е́лишь] separate (*v/i.* **-ся от** Р from; come off)

отдёр|гивать [1], <~нуть> [20] draw back; pull aside

отдира́ть [1], <отодра́ть> [отдеру́, -рёшь; отодра́л, -а́, -о; ото́дранный] tear *or* rip (off); *pf. coll.* thrash

отдохну́ть → ***отдыха́ть***

отду́шина *f* [5] (air) vent (*a. fig.*)

о́тдых *m* [1] rest, relaxation; holiday; **~а́ть** [1], <отдохну́ть> [20] rest, relax

отдыша́ться [4] *pf.* get one's breath back

отёк *m* [1] swelling, edema

оте|ка́ть [1], <~чь> [26] swell

оте́ль *m* [4] hotel

оте́ц *m* [1; отца́] father

оте́че|ский [16] fatherly; paternal; **~ственный** [14] native, home...; *война́* patriotic; **~ство** *n* [9] motherland, fatherland, one's (native) country

оте́чь → ***отека́ть***

отжи|ва́ть [1], <~ть> [-живу́; -вёшь; о́тжил, -а́, -о; о́тжи́тый (о́тжи́т, -а́, -о)] (have) live(d, had) (one's time *or* day); *о тради́ции и т. д.* become obsolete, outmoded; die out

о́тзвук *m* [1] echo, repercussion; *чу́вство* response

о́тзыв *m* [1] opinion, judg(e)ment (**по** Д on *or* about), reference; comment, review; *диплома́та* recall; **~а́ть** [1], <отозва́ть> [отзову́, -вёшь; ото́званный] take aside; recall; **-ся** respond, answer; speak (**о** П of *or* to); (re)sound; (*вы́звать*) call forth (Т s.th.); (*влия́ть*) affect (**на** В s.th.); **~чивый** [14 *sh.*] responsive

отка́з *m* [1] refusal, denial, rejection (**в** П, Р of); renunciation (**от** Р of); *tech.* failure; ***без ~а*** smoothly; ***по́лный до ~а*** cram-full; ***получи́ть ~*** be refused; **~ывать** [1], <~а́ть> [3] refuse, deny (a p. s.th. Д/**в** П); *tech.* fail; **-ся** (**от** Р) refuse, decline, reject; renounce, give up; (***я***) ***не откажу́сь*** *coll.* I wouldn't mind

отка́|лывать [1], <отколо́ть> [17] break *or* chop off; *була́вку* unpin, unfasten; **-ся** break off; come undone; *fig.* break away; **~пывать**, <откопа́ть> [1] dig up, unearth; **~рмливать** [1], <откорми́ть> [14] fatten up; **~тывать** [1], <~ти́ть> [15] roll, haul (away) (**-ся** *v/i.*); **~чивать**, <~ча́ть> [1] pump out; resuscitate; **~шливаться** [1], <~шляться> [28] clear one's throat

отки|дно́й [14] *сиде́ние* tip-up; **~дывать** [1], <~нуть> [20] throw away; turn back, fold back; **-ся** lean back recline

откла́дывать [1], <отложи́ть> [16] lay aside; *де́ньги* save; (*отсро́чить*) put off, defer, postpone

откле́|ивать [1], <~ить> [13] unstick; **-ся** come unstuck

о́тклик *m* [1] response; comment;

→ *a.* ***óтзвук***; **~áться** [1], <~нуться> [20] (***на*** B) respond (to), answer; comment (on)

отклон|éние *n* [12] deviation; *от тéмы* digression; *предложéния* rejection; **~я́ть** [28], <~и́ть> [13; -оню́, -óнишь] decline, reject; **-ся** deviate; digress

отключáть [4], <~чи́ть> [16] *el.* cut off, disconnect; *p. p .p.* dead

отк|олóть → ***~áлывать***; **~опáть** → ***~áпывать***; **~орми́ть** → ***~áрмливать***

откóс *m* [1] slope, slant, escarp

откровéн|ие *n* [12] revelation; **~ный** [14; -éнен, -éнна] frank, candid, blunt, outspoken

откры|вáть [1], <~ть> [22] open; *кран* turn on; *нóвую планéту* discover; *тáйну* disclose, reveal; *пáмятник* unveil; *учреждéние* inaugurate; **-ся** open; *комý-л.* unbosom o.s.; **~тие** *n* [12] opening; discovery; revelation; inauguration; unveiling; **~тка** *f* [5; *g/pl.*: -ток] (*с ви́дом* picture) post card; **~тый** [14] open; *слýшания и т. д.* public; **~ть(ся)** → ***~вáться***

откýда where from?; whence; ***~ вы?*** where do you come from? ***~ вы знáете?*** how do you know ...?; **~-нибудь, ~-то** (from) somewhere or other

откуп|áться [1], <~и́ться> [14] pay off

откупóри|вать [1], <~ть> [13] uncork; open

откýс|ывать [1], <~и́ть> [15] bite off

отлагáтельств|о *n* [9]: ***дéло не тéрпит ~а*** the matter is urgent

отлагáться [1], <отложи́ться> [16] *geol.* be deposited

отлáмывать, <отломáть> [1], <отломи́ть> [14] break off (*v/i.* **-ся**)

отл|ёт *m* [1] *птиц* flying away; **~етáть** [1], <~етéть> [11] fly away *or* off; *coll.* come off

отли́в[1] *m* [1] ebb (tide)

отли́в[2] *m* [1] play of colo(u)rs, shimmer

отли|вáть[1] [1], <~ть> [отолью́, -льёшь; óтли́л, -á, -о; → ***лить***] pour off, in, out (some... P); *tech.* found, cast

отливáть[2] *impf.* (T) shimmer, play

отлич|áть [1], <~и́ть> [16 *e.*; -чý, -чи́шь; -чённый] distinguish (***от*** P from); **-ся** *a. impf.* differ; be noted (T for); **~ие** *n* [12] distinction, difference; ***в ~ие от*** (P) as against; ***знáки ~ия*** decorations; **~и́тельный** [14] distinctive; **~ник** *m* [1], **~ница** *f* [5] excellent pupil, *etc.*; **~ный** [14; -чен, -чна] excellent, perfect; *от чегó-л.* different; *adv. a.* very good (*as su. a mark* → ***пятёрка***)

отлóгий [16 *sh.*] sloping

отлож|éние *n* [12] deposit; **~и́ть(ся)** → ***отклáдывать*** & ***отлагáться***; **~нóй** [14] *воротни́к* turndown

отлом|áть, <~и́ть> → ***отлáмывать***

отлуч|áться [1], <~и́ться> [16 *e.*; -чýсь, -чи́шься] (***из*** P) leave, absent o.s. (from); **~ка** *f* [5] absence

отмáлчиваться [1] keep silent

отмá|тывать [1], <отмотáть> [1] wind *or* reel off, unwind; **~хиваться** [1], <~хнýться> [20] disregard, brush aside

óтмель *f* [8] shoal, sandbank

отмéн|а *f* [5] *закóна* abolition; *спектáкля* cancellation; *прикáза* countermand; **~ный** [14; -éнен, -éнна] → ***отли́чный***; **~я́ть** [28], <~и́ть> [14; -еню́, -éнишь] abolish; cancel; countermand

отмер|éть → ***отмирáть***; **~зáть** [1], <отмёрзнуть> [21] be frostbitten

отмéр|ивать [1] & **~я́ть** [28], <~ить> [13] measure (off)

отмéстк|а *coll. f* [5]: ***в ~у*** in revenge

отмé|тка *f* [5; *g/pl.*: -ток] mark, *шкóльная тж.* grade; **~чáть** [1], <~тить> [15] mark, note

отмирáть [1], <отмерéть> [12; отомрёт; óтмер, -рлá, -о; отмéрший] *об обы́чае* die away *or* out

отмор|áживать [1], <~óзить> [15] frostbite

отмотáть → ***отмáтывать***

отмы|вáть [1], <~ть> [22] clean; wash (off); **~кáть** [1], <отомкнýть> [20] unlock, open; **~чка** *f* [5; *g/pl.*: -чек] master key; picklock

О

отнéкиваться *coll.* [1] deny, disavow
отнести́(сь) → ***относи́ть(ся)***
отнима́ть [1], <отня́ть> [-ниму́, -ни́мешь; о́тнял, -á, -о; о́тнятый (о́тнят, -á, -о)] take away (***у*** P from); ***врéмя*** take; amputate; ***~ от груди́*** wean; **-ся** *coll.* be paralyzed
относи́тельн|ый [14; -лен, -льна] relative; **~о** (P) concerning, about
отно|си́ть [15], <отнести́> [24; -с-, -есу́; -ёс, -еслá] take (Д, ***в*** В, ***к*** Д to); ***вéтром и т. д.*** carry (off, away); ***на мéсто*** put; *fig.* refer to; ascribe; **-ся**, <отнести́сь> (***к*** Д) treat, be; *impf.* concern; refer; belong; date from; be relevant; ***э́то к дéлу не ~си́тся*** that's irrelevant; **~шéние** *n* [12] attitude (toward[s] ***к*** Д); treatment; relation; *math.* ratio; respect (***в*** П, ***по*** Д in, with); ***по ~шéнию*** (***к*** Д) as regards, to(ward[s]); ***имéть ~шéние*** (***к*** Д) concern, bear a relation to
отны́не *old use* henceforth
отню́дь: ***~ не*** by no means
отня́ть(ся) → ***отнима́ть(ся)***
отобра|жа́ть [1], <~зи́ть> [15 *e.*; -ажу́, -ази́шь; -ажённый] represent; reflect
ото|бра́ть → ***отбира́ть***; **~всю́ду** from everywhere; **~гна́ть** → ***отгоня́ть***; **~гну́ть** → ***отгиба́ть***; **~грева́ть** [1], <~грéть> [8; -грéтый] warm (up); **~двига́ть** [1], <~дви́нуть> [20 *st.*] move aside, away (*v/i.* **-ся**)
отодра́ть → ***отдира́ть***
отож(д)еств|ля́ть [28], <~и́ть> [14; -влю́, -ви́шь; -влённый] identify
ото|зва́ть(ся) → ***отзыва́ть(ся)***; **~йти́** → ***отходи́ть***; **~мкну́ть** → ***отмыка́ть***; **~мсти́ть** → ***мстить***
отоп|и́ть [28] → ***ота́пливать***; **~лéние** *n* [12] heating
оторва́ть(ся) → ***отрыва́ть(ся)***
оторопéть [8] *pf. coll.* be struck dumb
отосла́ть → ***отсыла́ть***
отпа|да́ть [1], <~́сть> [25; *pt. st.*] (***от*** P) fall off *or* away; *fig.* (***минова́ть***) pass
отпе|ва́ние *n* [12] funeral service; **~́тый** [14] *coll.* inveterate, out-and-out; **~рéть(ся)** → ***отпира́ть(ся)***
отпеча́т|ок *m* [1; -тка] (im)print; impress; *a. fig.* ***~ок па́льца*** fingerprint; **~ывать**, <~ать> [1] print; type; **-ся** imprint, impress
отпи|ва́ть [1], <~́ть> [отопью́, -пьёшь; о́тпил, -á, -о; -пéй(те)!] drink (some... P); **~́ливать** [1], <~ли́ть> [13] saw off
отпира́ть [1], <отперéть> [12; отопру́, -прёшь; о́тпер, -рлá, -о; отперший; о́тпертый (-ерт, -á, -о)] unlock, unbar, open; **-ся**[1] open
отпира́ться[2] deny; disown
отпи́ть → ***отпива́ть***
отпи́х|ивать *coll.* [1], *once* <~ну́ть> [20] push off; shove aside
отпла́|та *f* [5] repayment, requital; **~чивать** [1], <~ти́ть> [15] (re)pay, requite
отплы|ва́ть [1], <~́ть> [23] sail, leave; swim (off); **~́тие** *n* [12] sailing off, departure
о́тповедь *f* [8] rebuff, rebuke
отпо́р *m* [1] repulse, rebuff
отпоро́ть [17] *pf.* rip (off)
отправ|и́тель *m* [4] sender; **~́ить(ся)** → ***~ля́ть(ся)***; **~́ка** *coll. f* [5] sending off, dispatch; **~лéние** *n* [12] dispatch; departure; **~ля́ть** [28], <~́ить> [14] send, dispatch, forward; mail; *impf. only* exercise, perform (*duties*, *functions*, *etc.*); **-ся** set out; go; leave, depart (***в***, ***на*** В for); **~но́й** [14] starting...
отпра́шиваться [1], <отпроси́ться> [15] ask for leave; *pf.* ask for and obtain leave
отпры́г|ивать [1], *once* <~нуть> [20] jump, spring back (*or* aside)
о́тпрыск *m* [1] *bot. and fig.* offshoot, scion
отпря́нуть [20 *st.*] *pf.* recoil
отпу́г|ивать [1], <~ну́ть> [20] scare away
о́тпуск *m* [1; *pl.* -ка́, *etc. e.*] holiday(s), leave (*a. mil.*), vacation (on: *go* ***в*** В; *be* ***в*** П); ***~ по болéзни*** sick leave; **~а́ть** [1], <отпусти́ть> [15] **1.** let go; release, set free; dismiss; slacken; ***бо́роду*** grow; *coll.* ***шу́тку*** crack; **2.** ***това́р*** serve; **~ни́к** *m* [1 *e.*] vacationer, holiday maker; **~но́й**

[14] **1.** vacation..., holiday...; **2.** *econ. цена́* selling

отпуще́н|ие *n* [12] ***козёл ~ия*** scapegoat

отраб|а́тывать, <~о́тать> [1] *долг и т. д.* work off; finish work; *p. pt. p. a. tech.* waste, exhaust

отра́в|а *f* [5] poison; *fig.* bane; **~ле́ние** *n* [12] poisoning; **~ля́ть** [28], <~и́ть> [14] poison; *fig.* spoil

отра́д|а *f* [5] comfort, joy, pleasure; **~ный** [14; -ден, -дна] pleasant, gratifying, comforting

отра|жа́ть [1], <~зи́ть> [15 *e.*; -ажу́, -ази́шь; -ажённый] repel, ward off; *в зе́ркале, о́бразе* reflect, mirror; **-ся** (*v/i.*) (***на*** П) affect; show

о́трасль *f* [8] branch

отра|ста́ть [1], <~сти́> [24; -ст-: -сту́; → ***расти́***] grow; **~́щивать** [1], <~сти́ть> [15 *e.*; -ащу́, -асти́шь; -ащённый] (let) grow

отре́бье *n* [10] *obs.* waste; *fig.* rabble

отре́з *m* [1] length (*of cloth*); **~а́ть**, **~ывать** [1], <~ать> [3] cut off; *coll.* give a curt answer

отрезв|ля́ть [28], <~и́ть> [14 *e.*; -влю́, -ви́шь; -влённый] sober

отре́з|ок *m* [1; -зка] piece; *доро́ги* stretch; *вре́мени* space; *math.* segment; **~ывать** → ***~а́ть***

отре|ка́ться [1], <~́чься> [26] (***от*** P) disown, disavow; *от убежде́ний и т. д.* renounce; ***~́чься от престо́ла*** abdicate

отре|че́ние *n* [12] renunciation; abdication; **~́чься** → ***~ка́ться***; **~шённый** [14] estranged, aloof

отрица́|ние *n* [12] negation, denial; **~тельный** [14; -лен, -льна] negative; **~ть** [1] deny; (*law*) ***~ть вино́вность*** plead not guilty

отро́|г *m* [1] *geogr.* spur; **´~ду** *coll.* in age; from birth; in one's life; **~дье** *n* [10] *coll. pej.* spawn; **~сток** *m* [1; -тка] *bot.* shoot; *anat.* appendix; **~́чество** *n* [9] boyhood; adolescence

отруб|а́ть [1], <~и́ть> [14] chop off

о́труби *f/pl.* [8; *from g/pl. e.*] bran

отры́в *m* [1]: ***в ~е*** (***от*** P) out of touch (with); **~а́ть** [1] **1.** <оторва́ть> [-рву́, -вёшь; -ва́л, -а́, -о; ото́рванный] tear off; *от рабо́ты* tear away; separate; **-ся** (***от*** P) come off; tear o.s. away; *от друзе́й* lose contact (with); ***не ~а́ясь*** without rest; **2.** <отры́ть> [22] dig up, out; **~истый** [14 *sh.*] abrupt; **~но́й** [14] perforated; tear-off (*sheet, block, calendar etc.*); **~ок** *m* [1; -вка] fragment; extract, passage; **~очный** [14; -чен, -чна] fragmentary, scrappy

отры́жка *f* [5; *g/pl.*: -жек] belch(ing), eructation

отры́ть → ***отрыва́ть***

отря́|д *m* [1] detachment; *biol.* class; **~хивать** [1], *once* <~хну́ть> [20] shake off

отсве́чивать [1] be reflected; shine (with T)

отсе́|ивать [1], <~ять> [27] sift, screen; *fig.* eliminate; **~ка́ть** [1], <~чь> [26; *pt.*: -се́к, -секла́; -сечённый] sever; cut off; **~че́ние** *n* [12]: ***дава́ть го́лову на ~че́ние*** *coll.* stake one's life

отси́|живать [1], <~де́ть> [11; -жу́, -ди́шь] sit out; *в тюрьме́* serve; *но́гу* have pins and needles (in one's leg)

отск|а́кивать [1], <~очи́ть> [16] jump aside, away; *мяч* rebound; *coll.* break off, come off

отслу́ж|ивать [1], <~и́ть> [16] *в а́рмии* serve (one's time); *оде́жда и т. д.* be worn out

отсове́товать [7] *pf.* dissuade (from)

отсо́хнуть → ***отсыха́ть***

отсро́ч|ивать [1], <~ить> [16] postpone; **~ка** *f* [5; *g/pl.*: -чек] postponement, delay; *law* adjournment

отста|ва́ть [5], <~́ть> [-а́ну, -а́нешь] (***от*** P) lag *or* fall behind; be slow (***на пять мину́т*** 5 min.); *обо́и и т. д.* come off; *coll. pf.* leave alone

отста́в|ка *f* [5] resignation; retirement; (*увольне́ние*) dismissal; ***в ~ке*** = ***~но́й***; **~ля́ть** [28], <~ить> [14] remove, set aside; **~но́й** [14] *mil.* retired

отст|а́ивать[1] [1], <~оя́ть> [-ою́, -ои́шь] defend; *права́ и т. д.* uphold, maintain; stand up for

О

отст|áивать[2] [1], <~оя́ть> stand (through), remain standing
отстá|лость *f* [8] backwardness; **~лый** [14] backward; **~ть** → ***~вáть***
отстёгивать [1], <отстегнýть> [20; -ёгнутый] unbutton, unfasten
отстоя́ть [1] *pf.* be at a distance (of Р)
отстоя́ть(ся) → ***отстáивать(ся)***
отстр|áивать [1], <~óить> [13] finish building; build (up); **~аня́ть** [28], <~ани́ть> [13] push aside, remove; *от дóлжности* dismiss; **-ся** (**от** Р) dodge; shirk; keep aloof; **~óить** → ***~áивать***
отступ|áть [1], <~и́ть> [14] step back; *mil.* retreat, fall back; *в ýжасе* recoil; *fig.* back down; go back on; *от прáвила* deviate; **~лéние** *n* [12] retreat; deviation; *в изложéнии* digression
отсýтств|ие *n* [12] absence; ***в её ~ие*** in her absence; ***за ~ием*** for lack of; ***находи́ться в ~ии*** be absent; **~овать** [7] be absent; be lacking
отсчи́т|ывать, <~áть> [1] count (out); count (off)
отсыл|áть [1], <отослáть> [-ошлю́, -шлёшь; отóсланный] send (off, back); refer (**к** Д to); **~ка** *f* [5; *g/pl.*: -лок] → ***ссы́лка***
отсып|áть [1], <~ать> [2] pour (out); measure (out)
отсы|рéлый [14] damp; **~хáть** [1], <отсóхнуть> [21] dry up; wither
отсю́да from here; (*слéдовательно*) hence; (*fig.*) from this
оттá|ивать [1], <~ять> [27] thaw out; **~лкивать** [1], <оттолкнýть> [20] push away, aside; *fig.* antagonize; *друзéй* alienate; **~лкивающий** [17] repulsive, repellent; **~скивать** [1], <~щи́ть> [16] drag away, aside; **~чивать** [1], <оттачи́ть> [16] whet, sharpen; *стиль и т. д.* perfect; **~ять** → ***~ивать***
оттéн|ок *m* [1; -нка] shade, nuance (*a. fig.*); tinge; **~я́ть** [28], <~и́ть> [13] shade; (*подчеркнýть*) set off, emphasize
óттепель *f* [8] thaw
оттесня́ть [28], <~и́ть> [13] push back, aside; *mil.* drive back
óттиск *m* [1] impression, offprint
отто|гó therefore, (*a.* ***~гó и***) that's why; ***~гó что*** because; **~лкнýть** → ***оттáлкивать***; **~пы́рить** *coll.* [13] *pf.* bulge, protrude, stick out (*v/i.* **-ся**); **~чи́ть** → ***оттáчивать***
оттýда from there
оття́|гивать [1], <~нýть> [20; -я́нутый] draw out, pull away (*mil.*) draw off (back); *coll. решéние* delay; ***он хóчет ~нýть врéмя*** he wants to gain time
отуч|áть [1], <~и́ть> [16] break (**от** Р of), cure (of); wean; **-ся** break o.s. (of)
отхлы́нуть [20] *pf.* flood back, rush back
отхóд *m* [1] departure; withdrawal; *fig.* deviation; **~и́ть** [15], <отойти́> [-ойдý, -дёшь; отошёл, -шлá; отойдя́] move (away, off); leave, depart; deviate; *mil.* withdraw; (*успокóиться*) recover; **~ы** *m/pl.* [1] waste
отцве|тáть [1], <~сти́> [25; -т-: -етý] finish blooming, fade (*a. fig.*)
отцеп|ля́ть [28], <~и́ть> [14] unhook; uncouple; *coll.* ***~и́сь!*** leave me alone!
отцóв|ский [16] paternal; fatherly; **~ство** *n* [9] paternity
отчá|иваться [1], <~яться> [27] despair (of **в** П); be despondent
отчáли|вать [1], <~ть> [13] cast off, push off; *coll.* ***~вай!*** beat it!; scram!
отчáсти partly, in part
отчáя|ние *n* [12] despair; **~нный** [14 *sh.*] desperate; **~ться** → ***отчáиваться***
óтче: ♀ ***наш*** Our Father; Lord's Prayer
отчегó why; ***~-то*** that's why
отчекáн|ивать [1], <~ить> [13] mint, coin; say distinctly
óтчество *n* [9] patronymic
отчёт *m* [1] account (**о**, **в** П of), report (on); (**от**)***давáть себé ~ в*** (П) realize *v/t.*; **~ливый** [14 *sh.*] distinct, clear; **~ность** *f* [8] accounting
отчи́|зна *f* [5] fatherland; **´~й** [17]: ***´~й дом*** family home; **´~м** *m* [1] stepfather
отчисл|éние *n* [12] (*вы́чет дéнег*)

deduction; *студе́нта* expulsion; **~я́ть** [28], <~ить> [13] deduct; dismiss
отчи́т|ывать *coll.*, <~а́ть> [1] *coll.* read a lecture to; tell off; **-ся** give *or* render an account (to ***пе́ред*** T)
от|чужда́ть [1] *law.* alienate; estrange; **~шатну́ться** [20] *pf.* start *or* shrink back; recoil; **~швырну́ть** *coll.* [20] *pf.* fling (away); throw off; **~ше́льник** *m* [1] hermit; *fig.* recluse
отъе́|зд *m* [1] departure; **~зжа́ть** [1], <~хать> [-е́ду, -е́дешь] drive (off), depart
отъя́вленный [14] inveterate, thorough, out-and-out
оты́гр|ывать, <~а́ть> [1] win back, regain; **-ся** regain one's lost money
оты́ск|ивать [1], <~а́ть> [3] find; track down; **-ся** turn up; appear
отяго|ща́ть [1], <~ти́ть> [15 *e.*; -щу́, -оти́шь; -ощённый] burden
отягч|а́ть [4], <~и́ть> [16] make worse, aggravate
офиц|е́р *m* [1] officer; **~е́рский** [16] office(r's, -s'); **~иа́льный** [14; -лен, -льна] official; **~иа́нт** *m* [1] waiter; **~иа́нтка** *f* [5] waitress
оформ|ля́ть [28], <~ить> [14] *кни́гу* design; *докуме́нты* draw up; *витри́ну* dress; *брак* register; ***~ить на рабо́ту*** take on the staff
офо́рт *m* [1] etching
ох *int.* oh!, ah!; **~анье** *n* [10] *col.* moaning, groaning
оха́пка *f* [5; *g/pl.*: -пок] armful
о́х|ать [1], *once* <~нуть> [20] groan
охва́т|ывать [1], <~и́ть> [15] enclose; *о чу́встве* seize, grip; *вопро́сы* embrace; *пла́менем* envelop; *fig.* comprehend
охла|дева́ть, <~де́ть> [8] grow cold (toward); *a. fig.* lose interest in; **~жда́ть** [1], <~ди́ть> [15 *e.*; -ажу́, -ади́шь; -аждённый] cool; **~жде́ние** *n* [12] cooling
охмеле́ть [8] *coll.* get tipsy
о́хнуть → ***о́хать***
охо́та[1] *f* [5] *coll.* desire (for), mind (to)
охо́т|а[2] *f* [5] (***на*** B, ***за*** T) hunt(ing) (of, for); chase (after); **~иться** [15] (***на*** B, ***за*** T) hunt; chase (after); **~ник**[1] *m* [1] hunter
охо́тник[2] *m* [1] volunteer; lover (of ***до*** P)
охо́тничий [18] hunting, shooting; hunter's
охо́тн|о willingly, gladly, with pleasure; ***~нее*** rather; ***~нее всего́*** best of all
охра́н|а *f* [5] guard(s); *прав* protection; ***ли́чная ~а*** bodyguard; **~я́ть** [28], <~и́ть> [13] guard, protect (**от** P from, against)
охри́п|лый *coll.* [14], **~ший** [17] hoarse
оце́н|ивать [1], <~и́ть> [13; -еню́, -е́нишь] value (***в*** B at); estimate; *ситуа́цию* appraise; (*по досто́инству*) appreciate; **~ка** *f* [5; *g/pl.*: -нок] evaluation, estimation; appraisal; appreciation; *шко́льная* mark
оцепене́|лый [14] torpid, benumbed; *fig.* petrified, stupefied; **~ние** *n* [12]: ***в ~нии*** petrified
оцеп|ля́ть [28], <~и́ть> [14] encircle, cordon off
оча́г *m* [1 *e.*] hearth (*a. fig.*); *fig.* center (-tre), seat
очаров|а́ние *n* [12] charm, fascination; **~а́тельный** [14; -лен, -льна] charming; **~ывать** [1], <~а́ть> [7] charm, fascinate, enchant
очеви́д|ец *m* [1; -дца] eyewitness; **~ный** [14; -ден, -дна] evident, obvious
о́чень very; (very) much
очередно́й [14] next (in turn); yet another; latest
о́черед|ь *f* [8; *from g/pl. e.*] turn (***по ~и*** in turns); order, succession; line (*Brt.* queue); *mil.* volley; ***ва́ша ~ь*** *or* ***~ь за ва́ми*** it is your turn; ***на ~и*** next; ***в свою́ ~ь*** in (for) my, *etc.*, turn (part)
о́черк *m* [1] sketch; essay
очерня́ть [28] → ***черни́ть***
очерстве́лый [14] hardened, callous
очер|та́ние *n* [12] outline, contour; **~чивать** [1], <~ти́ть> [15] outline, sketch; ***~тя́ го́лову*** *coll.* headlong
очи́|стка *f* [5; *g/pl.*: -ток] clean(s)-ing; *tech.* refinement; *pl.* peelings; ***для ~стки со́вести*** clear one's conscience; **~ща́ть** [1], <~стить>

[15] clean(se); clear; peel; purify; *tech.* refine

очк|ú *n/pl.* [1] spectacles, eyeglasses; ***защúтные ~и*** protective goggles; **~ó** *n* [9; *pl.*: -кú, -кóв] *sport*: point; *cards*: spot, *Brt.* pip; **~овтирáтельство** *coll. n* [9] eyewash, deception

очнýться [20] *pf.* → ***опóмниться***

очутúться [15; *1 st. p. sg. not used*] find o.s.; come to be

ошалéлый *coll.* [14] crazy, mad

ошéйник *m* [1] collar (*on a dog only*)

ошелом|лять [28], <~úть> [14 *e.*; -млю́, -мúшь; -млённый] stun, stupefy

ошиб|áться [1], <~úться> [-бýсь, -бёшься; -úбся, -úблась] be mistaken, make a mistake, err; be wrong *or* at fault; **´~ка** *f* [5; *g/pl.*: -бок] mistake (**по** Д by), error, fault; **´~очный** [14; -чен, -чна] erroneous, mistaken

ошпáр|ивать [1], <~ить> [13] scald

ощýп|ывать, <~ать> [1] feel, grope about; touch; **´~ь** *f* [8]: ***на ´~ь*** to the touch; ***двúгаться на ´~ь*** grope one's way; **´~ью** *adv.* gropingly; *fig.* blindly

ощу|тúмый [14 *sh.*], **~тúтельный** [14; -лен, -льна] palpable, tangible; felt; (*замéтный*) appreciable; **~щáть** [1], <~тúть> [15 *e.*; -ущý, -утúшь; -ущённый] feel, sense; experience; **-ся** be felt; **~щéние** *n* [12] sensation; feeling

П

павиáн *m* [1] baboon

павильóн *m* [1] pavilion; exhibition hall

павлúн *m* [1], **~ий** [18] peacock

пáводок *m* [1; -дка] flood, freshet

пá|губный [14;-бен, -бна] ruinous, pernicious; **~даль** *f* [8] carrion

пáда|ть [1] **1.** <упáсть> [25; *pt. st.*] fall; *ценá* drop; **2.** <пасть> [15] *fig.* fall; ***~ть дýхом*** lose heart

пад|éж[1] *m* [1 *e.*] *gr.* case; **~ёж**[2] *m* [1 *e.*] *скотá* murrain; epizootic; **~éние** *n* [12] fall; *fig.* downfall; **´~кий** [16; -док, -дка] (**на** В) greedy (for), having a weakness (for)

пáдчерица *f* [5] stepdaughter

паёк *m* [1; пайкá] ration

пáзух|а *f* [5] bosom (***за*** В, ***за*** Т in); *anat.* sinus; ***держáть кáмень за ~ой*** harbo(u)r a grudge (against)

пай *m* [3; *pl. e.*: пай, паёв] share; **´~щик** *m* [1] shareholder

пакéт *m* [1] parcel, package, packet; paper bag

пáкля *f* [6] (*material*) tow, oakum

паковáть [7], <у-, за-> pack

пáк|ость *f* [8] filth, smut; dirty trick; **~т** *m* [1] pact, treaty

палáт|а *f* [5] chamber (*often used in names of state institutions*); *parl.* house; *больнúчная* ward; ***оружéйная ~а*** armo(u)ry; **~ка** *f* [5; *g/pl.*: -ток] tent; ***в ~ках*** under canvas

палáч *m* [1 *e.*] hangman, executioner; *fig.* butcher

пáл|ец *m* [1; -льца] finger; *ногú* toe; ***смотрéть сквозь пáльцы*** connive (**на** В at); ***знать как свой пять ~ьцев*** have at one's fingertips; **~исáдник** *m* [1] (small) front garden

палúтра *f* [5] palette

палúть [13] **1.** <с-> burn, scorch; **2.** <о-> singe; **3.** <вы́-> fire, shoot

пáл|ка *f* [5; *g/pl.*: -лок] stick; *трость* cane; ***из-под ~ки*** *coll.* under constraint; ***это ~ка о двух концáх*** it cuts both ways; **~очка** *f* [5; *g/pl.*: -чек] (small) stick; *mus.* baton; *волшéбная* wand; *med.* bacillus

палóмни|к *m* [1] pilgrim; **~чество** *n* [9] pilgrimage

пáлтус *m* [1] halibut

П

пáлуба *f* [5] deck
пальбá *f* [5] firing; fire
пáльма *f* [5] palm (tree)
пальтó *n* [*indecl.*] (over)coat
пáмят|ник *m* [1] monument, memorial; **~ный** [14; -тен,-тна] memorable, unforgettable; **~ть** *f* [8] memory (***на*, о** П in/of); remembrance; recollection (**о** П of); ***на ~ь*** *a.* by heart; ***без ~и*** *coll.* mad (**от** Р about s.o.)
панéль *f* [8] panel; panel(l)ing
пáника *f* [5] panic
панихúда *f* [5] funeral service; ***граждáнская ~*** civil funeral
пансионáт *m* [1] boardinghouse
пантéра *f* [5] panther
пáнты *f/pl.* [5] antlers of young Siberian stag
пáнцирь *m* [4] coat of mail
пáпа[1] *coll. m* [5] papa, dad(dy)
пáпа[2] *m* [5] pope
пáперть *f* [8] porch (*of a church*)
папирóса *f* [5] *Russian cigarette*
пáпка *f* [5; *g/pl.*: -пок] folder; file
пáпоротник *m* [1] fern
пар [1; в -у; *pl. e.*] **1.** steam; **2.** fallow
пáра *f* [5] pair, couple
парáграф *m* [1] *тéкста* section; *договóра и т. д.* article
парáд *m* [1] parade; **~ный** [14] *фóрма* full; *дверь* front
парадóкс *m* [1] paradox; **~áльный** [14; -лен, -льна] paradoxical
парали|зовáть [7] (*im*)*pf.* paralyze (*a. fig.*); **~ч** *m* [1] paralysis
паралéль *f* [8] parallel; ***провестú ~*** draw a parallel; (*мéжду*) between
парашют (-'ʃut) *m* [1] parachute; **~úст** [1] parachutist
парéние *n* [12] soar(ing), hover(ing)
пáрень *m* [4; -рня; *from g/pl. e.*] lad, boy; *coll.* chap
парú *n* [*indecl.*] bet, wager (*vb.*: ***держáть ~***)
париж|áнин *m* [1; *pl.*: -áне, -áн], **~áнка** *f* [5; *g/pl.*: -нок] Parisian
парúк *m* [1 *e.*] wig; **~мáхер** *m* [1] haidresser, barber; **~мáхерская** *f* [16] hairdressing salon, barber's (shop)
парú|ровать [7] (*im*)*pf.*, *a.* <от-> parry; **~ть**[1] [13] soar, hover
пáрить[2] [13] steam (*in a bath*: **-ся**)
паркéт *m* [1], **~ный** [14] parquet
парлáмент *m* [1] parliament; **~áрий** *m* [3] parliamentarian; **~ский** [16] parliamentary
парнúк *m* [1 *e.*], **~óвый** [14] hotbed; ***~óвый эффéкт*** greenhouse effect
парнúшка *m* [5; *g/pl.*: -шек] *coll.* boy, lad, youngster
пáрный [14] paired; twin...
паро|вóз *m* [1] steam locomotive; **~вóй** [14] steam...; **~дúровать** [7] (*im*)*pf.*, **~дия** *f* [7] parody
парóль *m* [4] password, parole
парóм *m* [1] ferry(boat); ***переправлять на ~е*** ferry; **~щик** *m* [1] ferryman
парохóд *m* [1] steamer; **~ный** [14] steamship...; **~ство** *n* [9] steamship line
пáрт|а *f* [5] school desk; **~éр** (-'tɛr) *m* [1] *thea.* stalls; **~изáн** *m* [1] guerilla, partisan; **~итýра** *f* [5] *mus.* score; **~ия** *f* [7] party; *comm.* lot, consignment, batch; *sport* game; set; match; *mus.* part; **~нёр** *m* [1], **~нёрша** *f* [5] partner
пáрус *m* [1; *pl.*: -сá, *etc. e.*] sail; ***на всех ~áх*** under full sail; **~úна** *f* [5] sailcloth, canvas, duck; **~úновый** [14] canvas...; **~ник** *m* [1] = ***~ное сýдно*** *n* [14/9] sailing ship
парфюмéрия *f* [7] perfumery
парч|á *f* [5], **~óвый** brocade
паршúвый [14 *sh.*] mangy; *coll.* *настроéние* bad
пас *m* [1] pass (*sport*, *cards*); ***я ~*** count me out
пáсека *f* [5] apiary
пáсквиль *m* [4] lampoon
пáсмурный [14; -рен, -рна] dull, cloudy; *вид* gloomy
пасовáть [7] pass (*sport*; *cards*, <с->); *coll.* give in, yield (***пéред*** Т to)
пáспорт *m* [1; *pl.*: -тá, *etc. e.*], **~ный** [14] passport
пассажúр *m* [1], **~ка** *f* [5; *g/pl.*: -рок], **~ский** [16] passenger
пассúв *m* [1] *comm.* liabilities *pl.*; **~ный** [14; -вен, -вна] passive
пáста *f* [5] paste; ***зубнáя ~*** toothpaste

П

пáст|бище *n* [11] pasture; **~ва** *f* [5] *eccl.* flock; **~и́** [24 -с-] graze (*v/i.* **-сь**), pasture; **~у́х** *m* [1 *e.*] herdsman, shepherd; **~ь 1.** → ***пáдать***; **2.** *f* [8] jaws *pl.*, mouth

Пáсха *f* [5] Easter (***на*** B for); Easter pudding (*sweet dish of cottage cheese*); **~льный** [14] Easter...

пáсынок *m* [1; -нка] stepson

патéнт *m* [1], **~овáть** [7] (*im*)*pf.*, *a.* <за-> patent

пáтока *f* [5] molasses, *Brt. a.* treacle

патр|ио́т *m* [1] patriot; **~иоти́ческий** [16] patriotic; **~о́н** *m* [1] cartridge, shell; (lamp) socket; **~онтáш** *m* [1] cartridge belt, pouch; **~ули́ровать** [7], **~у́ль** *m* [4 *e.*] *mil.* patrol

пáуза *f* [5] pause

пау́к *m* [1 *e.*] spider

паути́на *f* [5] cobweb

пáфос *m* [1] pathos; enthusiasm, zeal (for)

пах *m* [1; в -у́] *anat.* groin

пахáть [3], <вс-> plow (*Brt.* plough), till

пáхн|уть¹ [20] smell (T of); **~у́ть²** [20] *pf. coll.* puff, blow

пáхот|а *f* [5] tillage; **~ный** [14] arable

паху́чий [17 *sh.*] odorous, strong-smelling

пациéнт *m* [1], **~ка** *f* [5; *g*/*pl.*: -ток] patient

пáчка *f* [5; *g*/*pl.*: -чек] pack(et), package; ***пи́сем*** batch

пáчкать [1], <за-, ис-, вы-> soil

пáшня *f* [6; *g*/*pl.*: -шен] tillage, field

паштéт *m* [1] pâté

пая́льник *m* [1] soldering iron

пая́ть [28], <за-> solder

пев|éц *m* [1; -вца], **~и́ца** *f* [5] singer; **~у́чий** [17 *sh.*] melodious; **~чий** [17] singing; ***~чая пти́ца*** songbird; *su. eccl.* choirboy

педагóг *m* [1] pedagogue, teacher; **~ика** *f* [5] pedagogics; **~и́ческий** [16]: ***~и́ческий институ́т*** teachers' training college; **~и́чный** [14; -чен, -чна] sensible

педáль *f* [8] treadle, pedal

педáнт *m* [1] pedant; **~и́чный** [14; -чен, -чна] pedantic

педиáтр *m* [1] p(a)ediatrician

пейзáж *m* [1] landscape

пекáр|ня *f* [6; *g*/*pl.*: -рен] bakery; **~ь** *m* [4; *a.* -ря́, *etc. e.*] baker

пелен|á *f* [5] shroud; **~áть** [1], <за-, с-> swaddle

пелён|ка *f* [5; *g*/*pl.*: -нок] diaper, *Brt. a.* nappy; **с ~ок** *fig.* from the cradle

пельмéни *m*/*pl.* [-ней] *cul.* kind of ravioli

пéна *f* [5] foam, froth; ***мы́льная*** lather, soapsuds

пéние *n* [12] singing; ***петухá*** crow

пéн|истый [14 *sh.*] foamy, frothy; **~иться** [13], <вс-> foam, froth; **~ка** *f* [5; *g*/*pl.*: -нок] ***на молокé и т. д.*** skin; ***снять ~ки*** skim (**с** P); *fig.* take the pickings (of)

пенси|онéр *m* [1] pensioner; **~о́нный** [14], **´~я** *f* [7] pension

пень *m* [4; пня] stump

пеньк|á *f* [5] hemp; **~о́вый** [14] hemp(en)

пéня *f* [6; *g*/*pl.*: -ней] fine (*penalty*)

пеня́|ть *coll.* [28]: blame; ***~й на себя́!*** it's your own fault!

пéпел [1; -пла] ashes *pl.*; **~и́ще** *n* [11] site of a fire; **~ьница** *f* [5] ashtray; **~ьный** [14] ashy; ***цвет*** ashgrey

пéрвен|ец *m* [1; -нца] first-born; **~ство** *n* [9] first place; *sport* championship

перви́чный [14; -чен, -чна] primary

перво|бы́тный [14; -тен, -тна] primitive, primeval; **~исто́чник** *m* [1] primary source; origin; **~клáссный** [14] first-rate *or* -class; **~ку́рсник** *m* [1] freshman; **-нá-перво** P *coll.* first of all; **~начáльный** [14; -лен, -льна] original; primary; **~очереднóй** [14] first and foremost; immediate; **~сóртный** → ***~клáссный***; **~степéнный** [14; -éнен, -éнна] paramount, of the first order

пéрв|ый [14] first; former; earliest; ***~ый этáж*** first (*Brt.* ground) floor; ***~ое врéмя*** at first; ***~ая пóмощь*** first aid; ***~ый рейс*** maiden voyage; ***из ~ых рук*** firsthand; ***на ~ый взгляд*** at first sight; **~ое** *n* first course (*meal*; ***на*** B for); ***~ым дé-***

лом (**до́лгом**) *or* **в ~ую о́чередь** first of all, first thing; *coll.* **~е́йший** the very first; → **пя́тый**

перга́мент *m* [1] parchment

переб|ега́ть [1],<~ежа́ть> [4; -егу́, -ежи́шь, -егу́т] run over (*or* across); **~е́жчик** *m* [1] traitor, turncoat; **~ива́ть** [1], <~и́ть> [-бью́, -бьёшь, → **би́ть**] interrupt

переб|ива́ться, <~и́ться> *coll.* make ends meet

переб|ира́ть [1],<~ра́ть> [-беру́, -рёшь; -бра́л, -а́, -о; -е́бранный] look through; sort out (*a. fig.*); turn over, think over; *impf. mus.* finger; **-ся** move (**на, в** B into); cross (*v/t.* **че́рез** B)

переб|и́ть 1. → **~ива́ть**; **2.** *pf.* kill, slay; *посу́ду* break; **~о́й** *m* [3] interruption, intermission; **~оро́ть** [17] *pf.* overcome, master

пребр|а́нка F *f* [5; *g/pl.*: -нок] wrangle; **~а́сывать** [1],<~о́сить> [15] throw over; *mil.*, *comm.* transfer, shift; **-ся**; *слова́ми* exchange (*v/t.* T); **~а́ть(ся)** → **перебира́ть(ся)**; **~о́ска** *f* [5; *g/pl.*: -сок] transfer

перева́л *m* [1] pass; **~ивать** [1], <~и́ть> [13; -алю́, -а́лишь; -а́ленный] transfer, shift (*v/i.* **-ся**; *impf.* waddle); *coll.* cross, pass; *impers.* **ему́ ~и́ло за 40** he is past 40

перева́р|ивать [1], <~и́ть> [13; -арю́, -а́ришь; -а́ренный] digest; *coll. fig.* **она́ его́ не ~ивает** she can't stand him

пере|везти́ → **~вози́ть**; **~вёртывать** [1], <~верну́ть> [20; -вёрнутый] turn over (*v/i.* **-ся**); **~ве́с** *m* [1] preponderance; **~вести́(сь)** → **переводи́ть(ся)**; **~ве́шивать** [1], <~ве́сить> [15] hang (elsewhere); reweigh; *fig.* outweigh; **-ся** lean over; **~вира́ть** [1], <~вра́ть> [-вру́, -врёшь; -е́вранный] *coll.* garble; misquote; misinterpret

перево́д *m* [1] transfer; translation (**с** P/**на** B from/into); *де́нег* remittance; *почто́вый* (money *or* postal) order; **~и́ть** [15], <перевести́> [25] lead; transfer; translate (**с**/**на** B from/into) interpret; remit; set (*watch*, *clock*; *usu.* **стре́лку**); **~и́ть дух** take a breath; **-ся**, <-сь> be transferred, move; **~ный** [14] translated; (*a. comm.*) transfer...; **~чик** *m* [1], **~чица** *f* [5] translator; interpreter

перевоз|и́ть [15], <перевезти́> [24] transport, convey; *ме́бель* remove; *че́рез ре́ку и т. д.* ferry (over); **~ка** *f* [5; *g/pl.*: -зок] transportation, conveyance, ferrying, *etc.*

пере|вооруже́ние *n* [12] rearmament; **~вора́чивать** [1] → **~вёртывать**; **~воро́т** *m* [1] revolution; *госуда́рственный* coup d'état; **~воспита́ние** *n* [12] reeducation; **~вра́ть** → **~вира́ть**; **~вы́боры** *m/pl.* [1] reelection

перевя́з|ка *f* [5; *g/pl.*: -зок] dressing, bandage; **~очный** [14] dressing...; **~ывать** [1], <~а́ть> [3] tie up; *ра́ну и т. д.* dress, bandage

переги́б *m* [1] bend, fold; *fig.* exaggeration; **~а́ть** [1], <перегну́ть> [20] bend; **~а́ть па́лку** go too far; **-ся** lean over

перегля́|дываться [1], *once* <~ну́ться> [19] exchange glances

пере|гна́ть → **~гоня́ть**; **~гно́й** *m* [3] humus; **~гну́ть(ся)** → **~гиба́ть(ся)**

перегов|а́ривать [1], <~ори́ть> [13] talk (s. th) over (**о** T), discuss; **~о́ры** *m/pl.* [1] negotiations; **вести́ ~о́ры** (**с** T) negotiate (with)

перег|о́нка *f* [5] distillation; **~оня́ть** [28], <~на́ть> [-гоню́, -го́нишь; -гна́л, -а́, -ой; -е́гнанный] **1.** outdistance, leave behind; *fig.* overtake, outstrip, surpass, outdo; **2.** *chem.* distil

перегор|а́живать [1], <~оди́ть> [15 & 15 *e.*; -рожу́, -роди́шь] partition (off); **~а́ть** [1], <~е́ть> [9] *ла́мпочка*, *про́бка* burn out; **~о́дка** *f* [5; *g/pl.*: -док] partition

перегр|ева́ть [1], <~е́ть> [8; -е́тый] overheat; **~ужа́ть** [1], <~узи́ть> [15 & 15 *e.*; -ужу́, -у́зишь], overload; **~у́зка** *f* [5; *g/pl.*: -зок] *двигателя* overload; *о рабо́те* overwork; **~уппирова́ть** [7] *pf.* regroup; **~уппиро́вка** *f* [5; -вок] regrouping; **~ыза́ть** [1], <~ы́зть> [24; *pt. st.*: -ы́зенный] gnaw through

П

пéред[1], **~о** (T) before; in front of; ***извини́ться ~ кем-л.*** apologize to s.o.

перёд[2] *m* [1; пéреда; *pl*.: -дá, *etc. e*.] front

перед|авáть [5], <~áть> [-дáм, -дáшь, *etc*. → ***дáть***; *pt*. пéредал, -á, -о] pass, hand (over), deliver; give (*a*. ***привéт***); *radio*, *TV* broadcast, transmit; ***содержáние*** render; tell; ***по телефóну*** take a message (for Д, *on the phone*); **-ся** *med*. be transmitted, communicated; **~áтчик** *m* [1] transmitter; **~áть(ся)** → ***~авáть(ся)***; **~áча** *f* [5] delivery, handing over; transfer; broadcast, (*a. tech*.) transmisssion; *mot*. gear

передв|игáть [1], <~и́нуть> [20] move, shift; **~ижéние** *n* [12] movement; ***грýзов*** transportation; **~ижнóй** [14] travel(l)ing, mobile

передéл|ка [5; *g/pl*.: -лок] alteration; *coll*. ***попáсть в ~ку*** get into a pretty mess; **~ывать**, <~ать> [1] do again; alter; ***~ать мнóго дел*** do a lot

перéдн|ий [15] front..., fore...; **~ик** *m* [1] apron; **~яя** *f* [15] (entrance) hall, lobby

передов|и́ца *f* [5] leading article, editorial; **~óй** [14] foremost; *mil*. frontline; ***~áя статья́*** → ***передови́ца***

пере|дохнýть [20] *pf*. pause for breath *or* a rest; **~дрáзнивать** [1], <дразни́ть> [13; -азню́, -áзнишь] mimic; **~дря́га** *coll*. *f* [5] fix, scrape; **~дýмывать**, <~дýмать> [1] change one's mind; *coll*. → ***обдýмать***; **~дышка** *f* [5; *g/pl*.: -шек] breathing space, respite

пере|éзд *m* [1] *rail*., *etc*. crossing; ***в другóе мéсто*** move (**в**, **на** В [in]to); **~езжáть** [1], <~éхать> [-éду, -éдешь; -éзжай!] **1.** *v/i*. cross (*v/t*. ***чéрез*** В); move (В, **на** В [in]to); **2.** *v/t*. ***маши́ной*** run over

переж|дáть → ***~идáть***; **~ёвывать** [1], <~евáть> [7 *e*.; -жую́, -жуёшь] masticate, chew; *fig*. repeat over and over again; **~ивáние** *n* [12] emotional experience; worry *etc*.; **~ивáть**, <~и́ть> [-живý, -вёшь; пéрежил, -á, -о; пéрежи́тый (пéрежи́т, -á, -о)] experience; live through, endure; ***жить дóльше*** survive, outlive; **~идáть** [1], <~дáть> [-ждý, -ждёшь; -ждáл, -á, -о] wait (till s.th. is over); **~и́ток** *m* [1; -тка] survival

перезаклю|чáть [1], <~и́ть> [16 *e*.; -чý, -чи́шь; -чённый]: ***~и́ть дóговóр*** (***контрáкт***) renew a contract

перезрéлый [14] overripe; *fig*. past one's prime

переиз|бирáть [1], <~брáть> [-берý, -рёшь; -брáл, -á, -о; -избранный] reelect; **~брáние** *n* [12] reelection; **~давáть** [5], <~дáть> [-дáм,-дáшь, *etc*. → ***дать***; -дáл, -á, -о] reprint, republish; **~дáние** *n* [12] republication; new edition, reprint; ***~дáть*** → ***~давáть***

переименовáть [7] *pf*. rename

переинáчи|вать *coll*. [1], <~ть> [16] alter, modify; (***искази́ть***) distort

перейти́ → ***переходи́ть***

переки́|дывать [1], <~нуть> [20] throw over (чéрез В); **-ся** exchange (*v/t*. Т); ***огóнь*** spread

переки|пáть [1], <~пéть> [10 *e*.; 3rd *p. only*] boil over

пéрекись *f* [8] *chem*. peroxide; ***~ водорóда*** hydrogen peroxide

перекладі|ина *f* [5] crossbar, crossbeam; **~ывать** [1], <переложи́ть> [16] put, lay (elsewhere); move, shift; interlay (Т with); → ***перелагáть***

перекл|икáться [1], <~и́кнуться> [20] call to o.a.; have s.th. in common (**с** Т with); reecho (*v/t*. **с** Т)

переключ|áтель *m* [4] switch; **~áть** [1], <~и́ть> [16; -чý, -чи́шь; -чённый] switch over (*v/i*. **-ся**); ***внимáние*** switch; **~éние** *n* [12] switching over; ***~и́ть*** → ***~áть***

перекóшенный [14] twisted, distorted; ***дверь и т. д.*** warped; wry

перекрёст|ный [14] cross...; ***~ный огóнь*** cross-fire; ***~ный допрóс*** cross-examination; **~ок** *m* [1; -тка] crossroads, crossing

перекр|ывáть [1], <~ы́ть> [22]

cover again; *рекóрд и т. д.* exceed, surpass; *закры́ть* close; *рéку* dam; **~ы́тие** *n* [12] *arch.* ceiling; floor

перекýс|ывать [1], <~и́ть> [15] bite through; *coll.* have a bite *or* snack

перел|агáть [1], <~ожи́ть> [16]: ***~ожи́ть на мýзыку*** set to music

перел|áмывать [1] **1.** <~оми́ть> [14] break in two; *fig.* overcome; change; **2.** <~омáть> [1] break

перел|езáть [1], <~éзть> [24 *st.*; -лéз] climb over, get over (***чéрез*** В)

перел|ёт *m* [1] *птиц* passage; *ae.* flight; **~етáть** [1], <~етéть> [11] fly over (across); migrate; overshoot; **~ётный** [14]: ***~ётная пти́ца*** bird of passage *a. fig.*, migratory bird

перели́|в *m* [1] *гóлоса* modulation; *цвéта* play; **~вáние** *n* [12] *med.* transfusion; **~вáть** [1], <~ть> [-лью́, -льёшь, *etc.*, → **лить**] decant, pour from one vessel into another; *med.* transfuse; ***~вáть из пустóго в порóжнее*** mill the wind; **-ся** overflow; *impf. о цвéте* play, shimmer

перели́ст|ывать, <~áть> [1] *страни́цы* turn over; *кни́гу* look *or* leaf through

перели́ть → ***переливáть***

перелицевáть [7] *pf.* turn, make over

перелож|éние *n* [12] transposition; arrangement; *на мýзыку* setting to music; **~и́ть** → ***переклáдывать***, ***перелагáть***

перелóм *m* [1] break, fracture; *fig.* crisis, turning point; **~áть**, **~и́ть** → ***перелáмывать***

перем|áлывать [1], <~олóть> [17; -мелю́, -мéлешь; -меля́] grind, mill; **~ежáть(ся)** [1] alternate

перемéн|а *f* [5] change; *в шкóле* break; **~и́ть(ся)** → ***~я́ть(ся)***; **~ный** [14] variable; *el.* alternating; **~чивый** *coll.* [14] changeable; **~я́ть** [28], <~и́ть> [13; -еню́, -éнишь] change (*v/i.* **-ся**)

переме|сти́ть(ся) → ***~щáть(ся)***; **~шивать**,<~шáть> [1] intermingle, intermix; *coll.* mix (up); **-ся**: ***у меня́ в головé всё ~шáлось*** I feel confused; **~щáть** [1], <~сти́ть> [15 *e.*; -ещу́, -ести́шь; -ещённый] move, shift (*v/i.* **-ся**)

переми́рие *n* [12] armistice, truce

перемолóть → ***перемáлывать***

перенаселéние *n* [12] overpopulation

перенести́ → ***переноси́ть***

перен|имáть [1], <~я́ть> [-ейму́, -мёшь; переня́л, -á, -о; пéренятый (пéренят, -á, -о)] adopt; *манéру и т. д.* imitate

перенóс *m* [1] *typ.* word division; ***знак ~а*** hyphen; **~и́ть**, <перенести́> [24 -с-] transfer, carry over; (*испытáть*) bear, endure, stand; (*отложи́ть*) postpone, put off (till ***на*** В); **~ица** *f* [5] bridge (*of nose*)

перенóс|ка *f* [5; *g/pl.*: -сок] carrying over; **~ный** [14] portable; figurative

переня́ть → ***перенимáть***

переоборýдова|ть [7] (*im*)*pf*; refit, reequip; **~ние** *n* [12] reequipment

переод|евáться [1], <~éться> [-éнусь, -нешься] change (one's clothes); **~éтый** [14 *sh.*] *a.* disguised

переоцéн|ивать [1], <~и́ть> [13; -еню́, -éнишь] overestimate, overrate; (*оцени́ть зáново*) revalue; **~ка** *f* [5; *g/pl.*: -нок] overestimation; revaluation

пéрепел *m* [1; *pl.*: -лá, *etc. e.*] *zo.* quail

перепечáт|ка *f* [5; *g/pl.*: -ток] reprint; **~ывать**, <~ать> [1] reprint; *на маши́нке* type

перепи́с|ка *f* [5; *g/pl.*: -сок] correspondence; **~ывать** [1], <~áть> [3] rewrite, copy; ***~áть нáбело*** make a fair copy; **-ся** *impf.* correspond (**с** Т with); **~ь** ('pe-) *f* [8] census

переплáчивать [1], <~ти́ть> [15] overpay

перепл|етáть [1], <~ести́> [25 -т-] *кни́гу* bind; interlace, intertwine (*v/i.* **-ся** <-сь>); **~ёт** *m* [1] binding, book cover; **~ётчик** *m* [1] bookbinder; **~ывáть** [1], <~ы́ть> [23] swim *or* sail (***чéрез*** В across)

П

переполз|áть [1], <~тú> [24] creep, crawl

перепóлн|енный [14 *sh.*] overcrowded; *жúдкостью* overflowing; overfull; **~ять** [28], <~ить> [13] overfill; **-ся** (*v/i.*) be overcrowded

переполó|х *m* [1] commotion, alarm, flurry; **~шúть** *coll.* [16 *e.*; -шý, -шúшь; -шённый] *pf.* (**-ся** get) alarm(ed)

перепóнка [5; *g/pl.* -нок] membrane; *птúцы* web; ***барабáнная ~*** eardrum

перепрáв|а *f* [5] crossing, passage; *брод* ford; temporary bridge; **~лять** [28], <~ить> [14] carry (over), convey, take across; transport (to); *mail* forward; **-ся** cross, get across

перепрод|авáть [5], <~áть> [-дáм, -дáшь, *etc.* → ***дать***; *pt.*: -óдáл, -лá, -о] resell; **~áжа** *f* [5] resale

перепрыг|ивать [1], <~нуть> [20] jump (over)

перепýг *coll.* *m* [1] fright (of **с ~у**); **~áть** [1] *pf.* (**-ся** get) frighten(ed)

перепýтывать [1] → ***пýтать***

перепýтье *n* [10] *fig.* crossroad(s)

перераб|áтывать, <~óтать> [1] work into; remake; *кнúгу* revise; **~óтка** *f* [5; *g/pl.*: -ток] processing; remaking; revision; ***~óтка вторúчного сырья́*** recycling

перерас|тáть [1], <~тú> [24; -ст-; -рóс, -слá] (*видоизменúться*) grow, develop; *о рóсте* outstrip; **~хóд** *m* [1] excess expenditure

перерез|áть *and* **~ывать** [1], <~áть> [3] cut (through); cut off, intercept; kill (all *or* many of)

переро|ждáться [1], <~дúться> [15 *e.*; -ожýсь, -одúшься; -ождённый] *coll.* be reborn; *fig.* regenerate; *biol.* degenerate

переруб|áть [1], <~úть> [14] hew *or* cut through

переры́в *m* [1] interruption; break, interval; ***~ на обéд*** lunch time

пересá|дка *f* [5; *g/pl.*: -док] *bot.*, *med.* transplanting; *med.* grafting; *rail.* change; **~живáть** [1], <~дúть> [15] transplant; graft; make change seats; **-ся**, <пересéсть> [25; -сяду, -сядешь, -сéл] take another seat, change seats; *rail.* change (*trains*)

пересд|авáть [5], <~áть> [-дáм, -дáшь, *etc.*, → ***дать***] repeat (*exam.*)

пересе|кáть [1], <~чь> [26; *pt.* -сéк, -секлá] traverse; intersect, cross (*v/i.* **-ся**)

пересел|éнец *m* [1; -нца] migrant; (re)settler; **~éние** *n* [12] (e)migration; **~я́ть** [28], <~úть> [13] (re)move (*v/i.* **-ся**; [e]migrate)

пересéсть → ***пересáживаться***

пересе|чéние *n* [12] crossing; intersection; **~чь** → ***~кáть***

пересúли|вать [1], <~ть> [13] overpower; *fig.* master, subdue

перескáз *m* [1] retelling; **~ывать** [1], <~áть> [3] retell

перескак|áкивать [1], <~очúть> [16] jump (over **чéрез** В); *при чтéнии* skip over

переслáть → ***пересылáть***

пересм|áтривать [1], <~отрéть> [9; -отрю́, -óтришь; -óтренный] reconsider, *плáны* revise; *law* review; **~óтр** *m* [1] reconsideration, revision; *law* review

пересо|лúть [13; -солю́, -óлúшь] *pf.* put too much salt (**в** В in); *coll.* *fig.* go too far; **~хнуть** → ***пересыхáть***

переспáть → ***спать***; oversleep; *coll.* spend the night; sleep with s.o.

переспр|áшивать [1], <~осúть> [15] repeat one's question

перессóриться [13] *pf.* quarrel (*mst. with everybody*)

перест|авáть [5], <~áть> [-áну, -áнешь] stop, cease, quit; **~авля́ть** [28], <~áвить> [14] put (elsewhere), (*тж. часы́*) set, move; *мéбель* rearrange; **~анóвка** *f* [5; *g/pl.*: -вок] transposition; rearrangement; *math.* permutation; **~áть** → ***~авáть***

перестр|áивать [1], <~óить> [13] rebuild, reconstruct; *рабóту* reorganize; *сúлы* regroup; **-ся** (*v/i.*) adapt, change one's views; **~éливаться** [1], **~éлка** *f* [5; *g/pl.*: -лок] firing; skirmish; **~óить** → ***~áивать***; **~óйка** *f* [5; *g/pl.*: -óек] rebuilding, reconstruction; reorganization; perestroika

преступ|а́ть [1], <~и́ть> [14] step over, cross; *fig*. transgress
пересчи́т|ывать, <~а́ть> [1] (re)count; count up
перес|ыла́ть [1], <~ла́ть> [-ешлю́, -шлёшь; -е́сланный] send (over), *де́ньги* remit; *письмо́* forward; **~ы́лка** *f* [5; *g/pl*.: -лок] remittance; ***сто́имость ~ы́лки*** postage; carriage; **~ыха́ть** [1], <~о́хнуть> [21] dry up; *го́рло* be parched
перета́|скивать [1], <~щи́ть> [16] drag *or* carry (***че́рез*** В over, across)
перет|я́гивать [1], <~януть> [19] draw (*fig. на свою́ сто́рону* win) over; *верёвкой* cord
переубе|жда́ть [1], <~ди́ть> [15 *e*.; *no 1st. p. sg*.; -ди́шь, -еждённый] make s.o. change his mind
переу́лок *m* [1; -лка] lane, alleyway; side street
переутомл|е́ние *n* [12] overstrain; overwork; **~ённый** [14 *sh*.] overtired
переучёт *m* [1] stock-taking
перехва́т|ывать [1], <~и́ть> [15] intercept, catch; *coll. де́нег* borrow; *перекуси́ть* have a quick snack
перехитри́ть [13] *pf*. outwit
перехо́д *m* [1] passage; crossing; *fig*. transition; **~и́ть** [15], <перейти́> [-йду́, -дёшь; -шёл, -шла́; → ***идти́***] cross, go over; pass (on), proceed; (***к*** Д to); turn (***в*** В [in]to); *грани́цы* exceed, transgress; **~ный** [14] transitional; *gr*. transitive; intermittent; **~я́щий** [17] *sport* challenge (*cup*, *etc*.)
пе́рец *m* [1; -рца] pepper; ***стручко́вый ~*** paprika
пе́речень *m* [4; -чня] list; enumeration
пере|чёркивать [1], <~черкну́ть> [20] cross out; **~че́сть** → ***~счи́тывать & ~чи́тывать***; **~числя́ть** [28], <~чи́слить> [13] enumerate; *де́ньги* transfer; **~чи́тывать**, <~чита́ть> [1] & <~че́сть> [-чту́, -чтёшь, -чёл, -чла́] reread; read (many, all ...); **~чить** *coll*. [16] contradict; oppose; **´~чница** *f* [5] pepper-pot; **~шагну́ть** [20] *pf*. step over; cross; **~ше́ек** *m* [1; -ше́йка] isthmus; **~шёптываться** [1] whisper (to one another); **~шива́ть** [1], <~ши́ть> [-шью́, -шьёшь, *etc*., → ***шить***] *sew* alter; **~щеголя́ть** *coll*. [28] *pf*. outdo
пери́ла *n/pl*. [9] railing; banisters
пери́на *f* [5] feather bed
пери́од *m* [1] period; *geol*. age; **~ика** *f* [5] *collect*. periodicals; **~и́ческий** [16] periodic(al); *math*. recurring
перифери́я *f* [7] periphery; outskirts *pl*. (***на*** П in); the provinces
перламу́тр *m* [1] mother-of-pearl
перло́вый [14] pearl (*крупа́* barley)
перна́тые *pl*. [14] *su*. feathered, feathery (*birds*)
перо́ *n* [9; *pl*.: пе́рья, -ьев] feather, plume; pen; ***ни пу́ха ни пера́!*** goodluck!; **~чи́нный** [14]: ***~чи́нный но́ж(ик)*** penknife
перро́н *m* [1] *rail*. platform
перс|и́дский [16] Persian; **~ик** *m* [1] peach; **~о́на** *f* [5] person; **~она́л** *m* [1] personnel; staff; **~пекти́ва** *f* [5] perspective; *fig*. prospect, outlook; **~пекти́вный** [14; -вен, -вна] with prospects; forward-looking, promising
пе́рстень *m* [4; -тня] ring (*with a precious stone, etc*.)
пе́рхоть *f* [8] dandruff
перча́тка *f* [5; *g/pl*.: -ток] glove
пёс *m* [1; пса] dog
пе́сенка *f* [5; *g/pl*.: -нок] song
песе́ц *m* [1; песца́] Arctic fox; ***бе́лый*** (***голубо́й***) **~** white (blue) fox (fur)
пе́сн|ь *f* [8] (*poet*., *eccl*.), **~я** *f* [6; *g/pl*.: -сен] song; *coll*. ***до́лгая ~*** long story; ***ста́рая ~*** it's the same old story
песо́|к *m* [1; -ска́] sand; *са́харный* granulated sugar; **~чный** [14] sand(y); ***~чное пече́нье*** shortbread
пессимисти́ч|еский [16], **~ный** [14; -чен, -чна] pessimistic
пестр|е́ть [8] *оши́бками* be full (of); **~и́ть** [13], **~ый** ('pɔ-) [14; пёстр, пестра́, пёстро & пестро́] variegated, parti-colo(u)red, motley (*a. fig*.); gay
песч|а́ный [14] sand(y); **~и́нка** *f* [5; *g/pl*.: -нок] grain (of sand)

петли́ца *f* [5] buttonhole; tab
пе́тля *f* [6; *g/pl*.: -тель] loop (*a., ae.*, ***мёртвая ~***); *для крючка́* eye; stitch; *дверна́я* hinge; ***спусти́ть пе́тлю*** drop a stitch
петру́шка *f* [5] parsley
пету́|х *m* [1 *e.*] rooster, cock; **~ши́ный** [14] cock(s)...
петь [пою́, поёшь; пе́тый] **1.** <с-, про-> sing; **2.** <про-> *пету́х* crow
пехо́т|а *f* [5], **~ный** [14] infantry; **~и́нец** *m* [1; -нца] infantryman
печа́л|ить [13], <о-> grieve (*v/i.* **-ся**); **~ь** *f* [8] grief, sorrow; **~ьный** [14; -лен, -льна] sad, mournful, sorrowful
печа́т|ать [1], <на-> print; *на маши́нке* type; **-ся** *impf.* be in the press; appear in (***в*** П); **~ник** *m* [1] printer; **~ный** [14] printed; printing; **~ь** *f* [8] seal, stamp (*a. fig.*); *пре́сса* press; *ме́лкая, чёткая* print, type; ***вы́йти из ~и*** be published
печён|ка *f* [5; *g/pl*.: -нок] *cul.* liver; **~ый** [14] baked
пе́чень *f* [8] *anat.* liver
пече́нье *n* [10] cookie, biscuit
пе́чка *f* [5; *g/pl*.: -чек] → ***печь***[1]
печь[1] *f* [8; в -чи́; *from g/pl. e.*] stove; oven; *tech.* furnace; kiln
печь[2] [26], <ис-> bake; *со́лнце* scorch
пеш|ехо́д *m* [1], **~ехо́дный** [14] pedestrian; **~ка** *f* [5; *g/pl*.: -шек] *in chess* pawn (*a. fig.*); **~ко́м** on foot
пеще́ра *f* [5] cave
пиан|и́но *n* [*indecl.*] upright (piano); **~и́ст** *m* [1] pianist
пивна́я *f* [14] pub, saloon
пи́во *n* [9] beer; ***све́тлое ~*** pale ale; **~ва́р** *m* [1] brewer; **~ва́ренный** [14]: ***~ва́ренный заво́д*** brewery
пигме́нт *m* [1] pigment
пиджа́к *m* [1 *e.*] coat, jacket
пижа́ма *f* [5] pajamas (*Brt.* py-) *pl.*
пик *m* [1] peak; ***часы́ ~*** rush hour
пика́нтный [14; -тен, -тна] piquant, spicy (*a. fig.*)
пика́п *m* [1] pickup (van)
пике́т *m* [1], **~и́ровать** [7] (*im*)*pf.* picket
пи́ки *f/pl.* [5] spades (*cards*)
пики́ровать *ae.* [7] (*im*)*pf.* dive
пи́кнуть [20] *pf.* peep; ***он и ~ не успе́л*** before he could say knife; ***то́лько пи́кни!*** (*threat implied*) just one peep out of you!
пил|а́ *f* [5; *pl. st.*], **~и́ть** [13; пилю́, пи́лишь] saw; **~о́т** *m* [1] pilot
пилю́ля *f* [6] pill
пингви́н *m* [1] penguin
пино́к *m* [1; -нка́] *coll.* kick
пинце́т *m* [1] pincers, tweezers *pl.*
пио́н *m* [1] peony
пионе́р *m* [1] pioneer
пипе́тка [5; *g/pl*.; -ток] *med.* dropper
пир [1; в ~у́; *pl. e.*] feast
пирами́да *f* [5] pyramid
пира́т *m* [1] pirate
пиро́|г *m* [1 *e.*] pie; **~жное** *n* [14] pastry; (fancy) cake; **~жо́к** *m* [1; -жка́] pastry; patty
пир|у́шка *f* [5; *g/pl*.: -шек] carousal, binge, revelry; **~шество** *n* [9] feast, banquet
писа́|ние *n* [12] writing; (*свяще́нное*) Holy Scripture; **~тель** *m* [4] writer, author; **~тельница** *f* [5] authoress; **~ть** [3], <на-> write; *карти́ну* paint
писк *m* [1] chirp, squeak; **~ли́вый** [14 *sh.*] squeaky; **~нуть** → ***пища́ть***
пистоле́т *m* [1] pistol
пи́сч|ий [17]: ***~ая бума́га*** writing paper, note paper
письмен|ность *f* [8] *collect.* literary texts; written language; **~ный** [14] written; in writing; *стол и т. д.* writing
письмо́ *n* [9; *pl. st., gen.*: пи́сем] letter; writing (***на*** П in); ***делово́е ~*** business letter; ***заказно́е ~*** registered letter
пита́|ние *n* [12] nutrition; nourishment; feeding; **~тельный** [14; -лен, -льна] nutritious, nourishing; **~ть** [1] nourish (*a. fig.*), feed (*a. tech.*); *наде́жду и т. д.* cherish; *не́нависть* bear against (***к*** Д); **-ся** feed *or* live (Т on)
пито́м|ец *m* [1; -мца], **~ица** *f* [5] foster child; charge; pupil; alumnus; **~ник** *m* [1] nursery
пить [пью, пьёшь; пил, -а́, -о; пе́й(те)!; пи́тый; пит, пита́, пи́то], <вы-> drink (*pf. a.* up; ***за*** В to); have, take; ***мне хо́чется ~*** I feel

П

thirsty; **~ё** *n* [10] drink(ing); **~ево́й** *вода́* [14] drinking
пи́хта *f* [5] fir tree
пи́цц|а *f* [5] pizza; **~ери́я** *f* [7] pizzeria
пи́чкать *coll.* [1], <на-> *coll.* stuff, cram (with T)
пи́шущ|ий [17]: ***~ая маши́нка*** typewriter
пи́ща *f* [5] food (*a. fig.*)
пища́ть [4 *e.*; -щу́, -щи́шь], <за->, *once* <пи́скнуть> [20] peep, squeak, cheep
пище|варе́ние *n* [12] digestion; **~во́д** *m* [1] *anat.* (o)esophagus, gullet; **~во́й** [14]: ***~вы́е проду́кты*** foodstuffs
пия́вка *f* [5; *g/pl.*: -вок] leech
пла́ва|ние *n* [12] swimming; *naut.* navigation; (*путеше́ствие*) voyage, trip; **~ть** [1] swim; float; sail, navigate
пла́в|ить [14], <рас-> smelt; **~ки** *pl.* [5; *g/pl.*: -вок] swimming trunks; **~кий** [16]: ***~кий предохрани́тель*** fuse; **~ни́к** *m* [1 *e.*] fin, flipper
пла́вный [14; -вен, -вна] *речь и т. д.* fluent; *движе́ние и т. д.* smooth
плаву́ч|есть *f* [8] buoyancy; **~ий** [17] *док* floating
плагиа́т *m* [1] plagiarism
плака́т *m* [1] poster
пла́к|ать [3] weep, cry (***от*** P for; ***о*** П); **-ся** *coll.* complain (***на*** B of); **~са** *coll. m/f* [5] crybaby; **~си́вый** *coll.* [14 *sh.*] *го́лос* whining
плам|ене́ть [8] blaze, flame; **~енный** [14] flaming, fiery; *fig. a.* ardent; **~я** *n* [13] flame; blaze
план [1] plan; scheme; plane; ***уче́бный ~*** curriculum; ***пере́дний ~*** foreground; ***за́дний ~*** background
планёр, **пла́нер** *ae. m* [1] *ae.* glider
плане́та *f* [5] planet
плани́ров|ать [7] **1.** <за-> plan; **2.** <с-> *ae.* glide; **~ка** *f* [5; *g/pl.*: -вок] planning; *па́рка и т. д.* lay(ing)-out
пла́нка *f* [5; *g/pl.*: -нок] plank; *sport* (cross)bar
пла́но|вый [14] planned; plan(ning); **~ме́рный** [14; -рен, -рна] systematic, planned
планта́ция *f* [7] plantation
пласт *m* [1 *e.*] layer, stratum
пла́ст|ика *f* [5] plastic arts *pl.*; eurhythmics; **~и́нка** *f* [5; *g/pl.*: -нок] plate; record, disc; **~и́ческий** [16]: ***~и́ческая хирурги́я*** plastic surgery; **~ма́сса** *f* [5] plastic; **~ырь** *m* [4] plaster
пла́т|а *f* [5] pay(ment); fee; wages *pl.*; *за прое́зд* fare; *за кварти́ру* rent; **~ёж** *m* [1 *e.*] payment; **~ёжеспосо́бный** [14; -бен, -бна] solvent; **~ёжный** [14] of payment; **~ина** *f* [5] platinum; **~и́ть** [15], <за-, у-> pay (T in; ***за*** B for); settle (*account* ***по*** Д); **-ся**, <по-> *fig.* pay (T with, ***за*** B for); **~ный** [14] paid; be paid for
плато́к *m* [1; -тка́] handkerchief
платфо́рма *f* [5] platform (*a. fig.*)
пла́т|ье *n* [10; *g/pl.*: -ьев] dress, gown; **~яно́й** [14] clothes...; ***~яно́й шкаф*** wardrobe
пла́ха *f* [5] (*hist.* executioner's) block
плац|да́рм *m* [1] base; *mil.* bridgehead; **~ка́рта** *f* [5] ticket for a reserved seat *or* berth
пла|ч *m* [1] weeping; **~че́вный** [14; -вен, -вна] deplorable, pitiable, lamentable; **~шмя́** flat, prone
плащ *m* [1 *e.*] raincoat; cloak
плебисци́т *m* [1] plebiscite
плева́ть [6 *e.*; плюю́, плюёшь], *once* <плю́нуть> [20] spit (out); not care (***на*** B for)
плево́к [1; -вка] spit(tle)
плеври́т *m* [1] pleurisy
плед *m* [1] plaid, blanket
плем|енно́й [14] tribal; *скот* brood..., *ло́шадь* stud...; **~я** *n* [13] tribe; breed; *coll.* brood; ***на ~я*** for breeding
племя́нни|к *m* [1] nephew; **~ца** *f* [5] niece
плен *m* [1; в ~у́] captivity; ***взять*** (***попа́сть***) ***в ~*** (be) take(n) prisoner
плен|а́рный [14] plenary; **~и́тельный** [14; -лен, -льна] captivating, fascinating; **~и́ть(ся)** → **~я́ть(ся)**
плёнка *f* [5; *g/pl.*: -нок] film; *для за́писи* tape
пле́н|ник *m* [1], **~ный** *m* [14] captive, prisoner; **~я́ть** [28], <~и́ть> [13] (**-ся** be) captivate(d)

П

плéнум *m* [1] plenary session
плéсень *f* [8] mo(u)ld
плеск *m* [1], **~áть** [3], *once* <плеснýть> [20], **-ся** *impf.* splash
плéсневеть [8], <за-> grow mo(u)ldy, musty
пле|сти́ [25 -т-: плетý], <с-, за-> braid, plait; weave; *coll.* ***~сти́ небыли́цы*** spin yarns; ***~сти́ интри́ги*** intrigue (against); *coll.* ***что ты ~тёшь?*** what on earth are you talking about?; **-сь** drag, lag; **~тёный** [14] wattled; wicker...; **~тéнь** *m* [4; -тня́] wattle fence
плётка *f* [5; *g/pl.*: -ток], **плеть** *f* [8; *from g/pl. e.*] lash
плеч|ó *n* [9; *pl.*: плéчи, плеч, -чáм] shoulder; *tech.* arm; **с(*о всегó*) *~á*** with all one's might; (И) ***не по ~ý*** (Д) not be equal to a th.; → *a.* ***горá*** *coll.*
плешь *f* [8] bald patch
плит|á *f* [5; *pl. st.*] slab, (flag-, grave)stone; *металли́ческая* plate; (*kitchen*) range; (*gas*) cooker, stove; **~ка** *f* [5; *g/pl.*: -ток] tile; *шоколáда* bar; cooker, stove; electric hotplate
плов|éц *m* [1; -вцá] swimmer
плод *m* [1 *e.*] fruit; **~и́ть** [15 *e.*; пложý, -ди́шь], <рас-> propagate, multiply (*v/i.* **-ся**); **~ови́тый** [14 *sh.*] fruitful, prolific (*a. fig.*); **~овóдство** *n* [9] fruit growing; **~óвый** [14] fruit...; ***~óвый сад*** orchard; **~оносный** [14; -сен, -сна] fruit-bearing; **~орóдие** *n* [12] fertility; **~орóдный** [14; -ден, -дна] fertile; **~отвóрный** [14; -рен, -рна] fruitful, productive; *влия́ние* good, positive
плóмб|а *f* [5] (lead) seal; *зубнáя* filling; **~и́ровать** [7], <о-> seal; <за-> fill, stop
плóск|ий [16; -сок, -скá, -о; *comp.*: плóще] flat (*a. fig.* = stale, trite), level; **~огóрье** *n* [10] plateau, tableland; **~огýбцы** *pl.* [1; *g/pl.*: -цев] pliers; **~ость** *f* [8; *from g/pl. e.*] flatness; plane (*a. math.*); platitude
плот *m* [1 *e.*] raft; **~и́на** *f* [5] dam, dike; **~ник** *m* [1] carpenter
плóтн|ость *f* [8] density (*a. fig.*); solidity; **~ый** [14; -тен, -тнá, -о] compact, solid; *ткань* dense, close, thick; *о сложéнии* thickset
плот|оя́дный [14; -ден, -дна] carnivorous; *взгляд* lascivious; **~ский** [16] carnal; **~ь** *f* [8] flesh
плох|óй [16; плох, -á, -о; *comp.*: хýже] bad; **~о** bad(ly); *coll.* bad mark; → ***двóйка & едини́ца***
площáд|ка *f* [5; *g/pl.*: -док] ground, area; *дéтская* playground; *sport* court; platform; *лéстничная* landing; ***пусковáя ~ка*** launching pad; ***строи́тельная ~ка*** building site; **´~ь** *f* [8; *from g/pl. e.*] square; area (*a. math.*); space; ***жилáя ´~ь*** → ***жилплóщадь***
плуг *m* [1; *pl. e.*] plow, *Brt.* plough
плут *m* [1 *e.*] rogue; trickster, cheat; **~áть** [1] *coll.* stray; **~овáть** [7], <с-> trick, cheat; **~овствó** *n* [9] trickery, cheating
плыть [23] (be) swim(ming); float(ing); *на кораблé* sail(ing); ***~ по течéнию*** *fig.* swim with the tide; → ***плáвать***
плю́нуть → ***плевáть***
плюс (*su. m* [1]) plus; *coll.* advantage
плюш *m* [1] plush
плющ *m* [1 *e.*] ivy
пляж *m* [1] beach
пляс|áть [3], <с-> dance; **~ка** *f* [5; *g/pl.*: -сок] (folk) dance; dancing
пневмати́ческий [16] pneumatic
пневмони́я *f* [7] pneumonia
по 1. (Д); on, along; through; all over; in; by; according to, after; through; owing to; for; over; across; upon; each, at a time (*2, 3, 4, with* В; ***по два***) **2.** (В) to, up to; till, through; for; **3.** (П) (up)on; ***~ мне*** for all I care; ***~ чáсу в день*** an hour a day
по- (in *compds.*): → ***рýсский, ваш***
побáиваться [1] be a little afraid of (Р)
побéг *m* [1] escape, flight; *bot.* shoot, sprout
побег|ýшки: ***быть на ~ýшках*** *coll.* run errands (**у** Р for)
побé|да *f* [5] victory; **~ди́тель** *m* [4] victor; winner; **~ди́ть** → ***~ждáть***; **~дный** [14], **~донóсный** [14; -сен,-сна] victorious; **~ждáть** [1], <~ди́ть> [15 *e.*; *1st p.*

П

sg. not used; -ди́шь, -еждённый] be victorious (B over), win (*a.* victory), conquer, defeat; beat; *страх, сомне́ния* overcome
побере́жье *n* [10] coast, seaboard, littoral
побла́жка *coll. f* [5; *g/pl.*: -жек] indulgence
побли́зости close by; (**от** P) near
побо́и *m/pl.* [3] beating; **~ще** *n* [11] bloody battle
побо́р|ник *m* [1] advocate; **~о́ть** [17] *pf.* conquer; overcome; beat
побо́чный [14] *эффе́кт* side; *проду́кт* by-(*product*); *old use* *сын, дочь* illegitimate
побу|ди́тельный [14]: ***~ди́тельная причи́на*** motive; **~жда́ть** [1], <**~ди́ть**> [15 *e.*; -ужу́, -уди́шь; -уждённый] induce, prompt, impel; **~жде́ние** *n* [12] motive, impulse, incentive
пова́д|иться *coll.* [15] *pf.* fall into the habit (of [visiting] *inf.*); **~ка** [5; *g/pl.*: -док] *coll.* habit
пова́льный [14] indiscriminate; *увлече́ние* general
по́вар *m* [1; *pl.*: -pá, *etc. e.*] culinary; cook; **~енный** [14] *кни́га* cook (*book*, *Brt.* cookery book); *соль* (*salt*) table
пове|де́ние *n* [12] behavio(u)r, conduct; **~ли́тельный** [14; -лен, -льна] *тон* peremptory; *gr.* imperative
поверг|а́ть [1], <**~нуть**> [21] *в отча́яние* plunge into (**в** B)
пове́р|енный [14]: ***~енный в дела́х*** chargé d'affaires; **~ить** → ***ве́рить***; **~ну́ть(ся)** → ***повора́чивать(ся)***
пове́рх (P) over, above; **~ностный** [14; -тен, -тна] *fig.* superficial; surface...; **~ность** *f* [8] superficiality
пове́рье *n* [10] popular belief, superstition
пове́сить(ся) → ***ве́шать(ся)***
повествова́|ние *n* [12] narration, narrative; **~тельный** [14] *стиль* narrative; ***~тельное предложе́ние*** *gr.* sentence; **~ть** [7] narrate (*v/t.* **о** П)
пове́ст|ка *f* [5; *g/pl.*: -ток] *law* summons; (*уведомле́ние*) notice; ***~ка дня*** agenda; **´~ь** *f* [8; *from g/pl. e.*] story, tale
по-ви́димому apparently
пови́дло *n* [9] jam
пови́н|ность *f* [8] duty; **~ный** [14; -и́нен, -и́нна] guilty; **~ова́ться** [7] (*pt. a. pf.*) (Д) obey; comply with; **~ове́ние** *n* [12] obedience
по́вод *m* **1.** [1] ground, cause; occasion (on ***по*** Д); ***по ~у*** (P) as regards, concerning; **2.** [1; в -ду́: *pl.*: -о́дья, -о́дьев] rein; ***на ~у́*** (**у** P) be under s.b.'s thumb; **~о́к** *m* [1; -дка́ и т. д.; *pl.* -дки́ и т. д.] (dog's) lead
пово́зка *f* [5; *g/pl.*: -зок] vehicle, conveyance; (*not equipped with springs*) carriage; cart
повор|а́чивать [1], <поверну́ть> [20] turn (*v/i.* **-ся**; ***~а́чивайся!*** come on!); **~о́т** *m* [1] turn; **~о́тливый** [14 *sh.*] nimble, agile; **~о́тный** [14] turning (*a. fig.*)
повре|жда́ть [1], <**~ди́ть**> [15 *e.*; -ежу́, -еди́шь; -еждённый] damage; *но́гу и т. д.* injure, hurt; **~жде́ние** *n* [12] damage; injury
поврем|ени́ть [13] *pf.* wait a little; **~е́нный** [14] *опла́та* payment on time basis (*by the hour*, *etc.*)
повсе|дне́вный [14; -вен, -вна] everyday, daily; **~ме́стный** [14; -тен, -тна] general, universal; **~ме́стно** everywhere
повста́н|ец *m* [1; -нца] rebel, insurgent; **~ческий** [16] rebel(lious)
повсю́ду everywhere
повтор|е́ние *n* [12] repetition; *материа́ла* review; *собы́тий* recurrence; **~ный** [14] repeated, recurring; **~я́ть** [28], <**~и́ть**> [13] repeat (**-ся** o.s.); review
повы|ша́ть [1], <**~сить**> [15] raise, increase; *по слу́жбе* promote; **-ся** rise; *в зва́нии* advance; **~ше́ние** *n* [12] rise; promotion; **~шенный** [14] increased, higher; *температу́ра* high
повя́з|ка *f* [5; *g/pl.*: -зок] *med.* bandage; band, armlet
пога|ша́ть [1], <**~си́ть**> [15] put out, extinguish; *долг* pay; *ма́рку* cancel
погиб|а́ть [1], <**~нуть**> [21] perish; be killed, fall; **~ший** [17] lost, killed

погло|ща́ть [1], <~ти́ть> [15; -ощу́; -ощённый] swallow up, devour; (*впи́тывать*) absorb (*a. fig.*)

погля́дывать [1] cast looks (***на*** В at)

погов|а́ривать [1]: ***~а́ривают*** there is talk (**о** П of); ***~о́рка*** [5; *g/pl.*: -рок] saying, proverb

пого́|да *f* [5] weather (***в*** В, ***при*** П in); ***э́то ~ды не де́лает*** this does not change anything; ***~ди́ть*** *coll.* [15 *e.*; -гожу́, -годи́шь] *pf.* wait a little; ***~дя́*** later; ***~ло́вный*** [14] general, universal; ***~ло́вно*** without exception; ***~ло́вье*** *n* [10] livestock

пого́н *m* [1] *mil.* shoulder strap

пого́н|я *f* [6] pursuit (***за*** Т of); pursuers *pl.*; ***~я́ть*** [28] drive *or* urge (on); drive (*for a certain time*)

пограни́чн|ый [14] border...; ***~ик*** *m* [1] border guard

по́гре|б [1; *pl.*: -ба́, *etc. e.*] cellar; ***~ба́льный*** [14] funeral; ***~бе́ние*** *n* [12] burial; funeral; ***~му́шка*** *f* [5; *g/pl.*: -шек] rattle; ***~шность*** *f* [8] error, mistake

погру|жа́ть [1], <~зи́ть> [15 & 15 *e.*; -ужу́, -у́зишь; -у́женный & -ужённый] immerse; sink, plunge, submerge (*v/i.* **-ся**); ***~жённый*** *a.* absorbed, lost (***в*** В in); load, ship; ***~же́ние*** *n* [12] *подло́дки* diving; *аппара́та* submersion; ***~зка*** [5; *g/pl.*: -зок] loading, shipment

погряз|а́ть [1], <~нуть> [21] get stuck (***в*** Т in)

под, **~о 1.** (В) (*направле́ние*) under; toward(s), to; (*во́зраст, вре́мя*) about; on the eve of; à la, in imitation of; for, suitable as; **2.** (Т) (*расположе́ние*) under, below, beneath; near, by; *сраже́ние* of; *для* (used) for; ***по́ле ~ ро́жью*** rye field

пода|ва́ть [5], <~ть> [-да́м, -да́шь, *etc.*, → ***дать***] give; serve (*a. sport*); *заявле́ние* hand (*or* send) in; *жа́лобу* lodge; *приме́р* set; *ру́ку по́мощи* render; ***~ть в суд*** (***на*** В) bring an action against; ***не ~ва́ть ви́ду*** give no sign; **-ся** move; yield

подав|и́ть → ***~ля́ть***; ***~и́ться*** *pf.* [14] choke; ***~ле́ние*** *n* [12] suppression; ***~ля́ть*** [28], <~и́ть> [14] suppress; repress; depress; crush; ***~ля́ющий*** *a.* overwhelming

пода́вно *coll.* so much *or* all the more

пода́гра *f* [5] gout; podagra

пода́льше *coll.* a little farther

пода́|рок *m* [1; -рка] present, gift; ***~тливый*** [14 *sh.*] (com)pliant; ***~ть(ся)*** → ***~ва́ть(ся)***; ***~ча*** *f* [5] serve; *sport* service; *материа́ла* presentation; *воды́, га́за* supply; *tech.* feed(ing); ***~чка*** *f* [5; *g/pl.*: -чек] sop; *fig.* tip

подбе|га́ть [1], <~жа́ть> [4; -бегу́, -бежи́шь, -бегу́т] run up (***к*** Д to)

подби|ва́ть [1], <~ть> [подобью́, -бьёшь, *etc.*, → ***бить***] line (Т with); *подмётку* (re)sole; hit, injure; *coll.* instigate, incite; ***~тый*** *coll. глаз* black

под|бира́ть [1], <~обра́ть> [подберу́, -рёшь; подобра́л, -а́, -о; подо́бранный] pick up; *ю́бку* tuck up; *живо́т* draw in; (*отбира́ть*) pick out, select; **-ся** sneak up (***к*** Д to); ***~би́ть*** → ***~бива́ть***; ***~бо́р*** *m* [1] selection; assortment; ***на ~бо́р*** choice, well-matched, select

подборо́док *m* [1; -дка] chin

подбр|а́сывать [1], <~о́сить> [15] throw *or* toss (up); jolt; *в ого́нь* add; (*подвезти́*) give a lift

подва́л *m* [1] basement; cellar

подвезти́ → ***подвози́ть***

подвер|га́ть [1], <~гнуть> [21] subject, expose; ***~гнуть испыта́нию*** put to the test; ***~гнуть сомне́нию*** call into question; **-ся** undergo; ***~женный*** [14 *sh.*] subject to

подве́с|ить → ***подве́шивать***; ***~но́й*** [14] hanging, pendant; *мост* suspension; *мото́р* outboard

подвести́ → ***подводи́ть***

подве́тренный [14] *naut.* leeward; sheltered side

подве́|шивать [1], <~сить> [15] hang (under; on); suspend (from)

по́двиг *m* [1] feat, exploit, deed

подви|га́ть [1], <~нуть> [20] move little (*v/i.* **-ся**); ***~жно́й*** [14] *mil.* mobile; *rail.* rolling; ***~жность*** *f* [8] mobility; *челове́ка* agility; ***~нуть(ся)*** → ***~га́ть(ся)***

подвла́стный [14; -тен, -тна] subject to, dependent on

подводи́ть [15], <подвести́> [25] lead ([up] to); *фундáмент* lay; build; *coll.* let a p. down (*обманýть и т. д.*); **~ итóги** sum up

подвóдн|ый [14] underwater; submarine; **~ая лóдка** submarine; **~ый кáмень** reef; *fig.* unexpected obstacle

подвóз *m* [1] supply; **~и́ть** [15], <подвезти́> [24] bring, transport; *когó-л.* give a p. a lift

подвы́пивший *coll.* [17] tipsy, slightly drunk

подвя́з|ывать [1], <~áть> [3] tie (up)

под|гибáть [1], <~огнýть> [20] tuck (under); bend (*a.* **-ся**); ***нóги ~гибáются от устáлости*** I am barely able to stand (*with tiredness*)

подгля́д|ывать [1], <~éть> [11] peep at, spy on

подгов|áривать [1], <~ори́ть> [13] instigate, put a p. up to

под|гоня́ть [28], <~огнáть> [подгоню́, -гóнишь, → ***гнать***] drive to *or* urge on, hurry; *к фигýре и т. д.* fit, adapt (to)

подгор|áть [1], <~éть> [9] burn slightly

подготов|и́тельный [14] preparatory; *рабóта* spadework; **~ка** *f* [5; *g/pl.*: -вок] preparation, training (***к*** Д for); **~ля́ть** [28], <~ить> [14] prepare; ***~ить пóчву*** *fig.* pave the way

подда|вáться [5], <~ться> [-дáмся, -дáшься, *etc.*, → ***дать***] yield; ***не ~вáться описáнию*** defy *or* beggar description

поддáк|ивать [1], <~нуть> [20] say yes (to everything), consent

пóдда|нный *m* [14] subject; **~нство** *n* [9] nationality, citizenship; **~ться** → ***~вáться***

поддéл|ка [5; *g/pl.*: -лок] *бумáг, пóдписи, дéнег и т. д.* forgery, counterfeit; **~ывать**, <~ать> [1] forge; **~ьный** [14] counterfeit...; sham...

поддéрж|ивать [1], <~áть> [4] support; back (up); *поря́док* maintain; *разговóр и т. д.* keep up; **~ка** *f* [5; *g/pl.*: -жек] support; backing

подéл|ать *coll.* [1] *pf.* do; ***ничегó не ~аешь*** there's nothing to be done; → *a.* ***дéлать***; *coll.* **~óм**: ***~óм емý*** it serves him right

подéржанный [14] secondhand; worn, used

поджáр|ивать [1], <~ить> [13] fry, roast, grill slightly; brown; *хлеб* toast

поджáрый [14 *sh.*] lean

поджáть → ***поджимáть***

под|жéчь → ***~жигáть***; **~жигáть** [1], <~жéчь> [26; подожгý; -ожжёшь; поджёг, подожглá; подожжённый] set on fire (*or* fire to)

под|жидáть [1], <~ождáть> [-дý, -дёшь; -áл, -á, -о] wait (for Р, В)

под|жимáть [1], <~жáть> [подожмý, -мёшь; поджáтый] draw in; *нóги* cross (one's legs); *гýбы* purse (one's lips); ***~жáть хвост*** have one's tail between one's legs; ***врéмя ~жимáет*** time is pressing

поджóг *m* [1] arson

подзаголóвок *m* [1; -вка] subtitle

подзадóр|ивать *coll.* [1], <~ить> [13] egg on, incite (***на*** В, ***к*** Д to)

подза|ты́льник *m* [1] cuff on the back of the head; **~щи́тный** *m* [14] *law* client

подзéмный [14] underground, subterranean; ***~ толчóк*** tremor

под|зывáть [1], <~озвáть> [подзовý, -ёшь; подозвáл, -á, -о; подóзванный] call, beckon

под|карáуливать *coll.* [1], <~карáулить> [13] → ***подстерегáть***; **~кáрмливать** [1], <~корми́ть> [14] *скот* feed up, fatten; *растéния* give extra fertilizer; **~кáтывать** [1], <~кати́ть> [15] roll *or* drive up; **~кáшиваться** [1], <~коси́ться> [15] give way

подки́|дывать [1], <~нуть> [20] → ***подбрáсывать***; **~дыш** *m* [1] foundling

подклáд|ка [5; *g/pl.*: -док] lining; **~ывать** [1], <подложи́ть> [16] lay (under); (*добáвить*) add; ***подложи́ть свинью́*** *approx.* play a dirty trick on s.o

подклé|ивать [1], <~ить> [13] glue, paste

подключ|áть [4], <~и́ть> [16] *tech.* connect, link up; *fig.* include, attach

подко́в|а *f* [5] horseshoe; **~ывать** [1], <**~а́ть**> [7 *e.*; -кую, -куёшь] shoe; give a grounding in; **~анный** [14] *a.* versed in
подко́жный [14] hypodermic
подкоси́ть|ся → ***подка́шивать-ся***
подкра́|дываться [1], <**~сться**> [25] steal *or* sneak up (***к*** Д to); **~шивать** [1], <**~сить**> [15] touch up one's make-up (*a.* **-ся**)
подкреп|ля́ть [28], <**~и́ть**> [14 *e.*; -плю́, -пи́шь, -плённый] reinforce, support; *fig.* corroborate; **-ся** fortify o.s.; **~ле́ние** *n* [12] *mil.* reinforcement
по́дкуп *m* [1], **~а́ть** [1], <**~и́ть**> [14] suborn; bribe; *улы́бкой и т. д.* win over, charm
подла́|живаться [1], <**~диться**> [15] adapt o.s. to, fit in with; humo(u)r, make up to
по́дле (Р) beside, by (the side of); nearby
подлеж|а́ть [4 *e.*; -жу́, -жи́шь] be subject to; be liable to; (И) ***не ~и́т сомне́нию*** there can be no doubt (about); **~а́щий** [17] subject (Д to); liable to; **~а́щее** *n gr.* subject
подле|за́ть [1], <**~зть**> [24 *st.*] creep (under; up); **~сок** *m* [1; -ска и т. д.] undergrowth; **~та́ть** [1], <**~те́ть**> [11] fly up (to)
подле́ц *m* [1 *e.*] scoundrel, rascal
подли|ва́ть [1], <**~ть**> [подолью́, -льёшь; подле́й! подли́л, -а, -о; подли́тый (-ли́т, -а́, -о)] add to, pour on; **~вка** *f* [5; *g/pl.*: -вок] gravy; sauce
подли́з|а *coll. m/f* [5] toady; **~ываться** *coll.* [1], <**~а́ться**> [3] flatter, insinuate o.s. (***к*** Д with), toady (to)
по́длинн|ик *m* [1] original; **~ый** [14; -инен, -инна] original; authentic, genuine; true, real
подли́ть → ***подлива́ть***
подло́|г *m* [1] forgery; **~жи́ть** → ***подкла́дывать***; **~жный** [14; -жен, -жна] spurious, false
по́дл|ость *f* [8] meanness; baseness; low-down trick; **~ый** [14; подл, -а́, -о] mean, base, contemptible
подма́з|ывать [1], <**~ать**> [3] grease (*a.*, *coll. fig.*); **-ся** *coll.* insinuate o.s., curry favo(u)r (***к*** Д with)
подма́н|ивать [1], <**~и́ть**> [13; -аню́, -а́нишь] beckon, call to
подме́н|а *f* [5] substitution (*of s.th. false for s.th. real*), exchange; **~ивать** [1], <**~и́ть**> [13; -еню́, -е́нишь] substitute (Т/В s.th./for), (ex)change
подме|та́ть [1], <**~сти́**> [25; -т-: -мету́] sweep; **~тить** → ***подмеча́ть***
подмётка *f* [5; *g/pl.*: -ток] sole
подме|ча́ть [1], <**~тить**> [15] notice, observe, perceive
подме́ш|ивать, <**~а́ть**> [1] mix *or* stir (into), add
подми́г|ивать [1], <**~ну́ть**> [20] wink (Д at)
подмо́га *coll. f* [5] help, assistance
подмок|а́ть [1], <**~нуть**> get slightly wet
подмо́стки *m/pl.* [1] *thea.* stage
подмо́ченный [14] slightly wet; *coll. fig.* tarnished
подмы|ва́ть [1], <**~ть**> [22] wash (*a.* out, away); undermine; *impf. coll.* (*impers.*) ***меня́ так и ~ва́ет ...*** I can hardly keep myself from ...
поднести́ → ***подноси́ть***
поднима́ть [1], <подня́ть> [-ниму́, -ни́мешь; по́днятый (-нят, -а́, -о)] lift; pick up (**с** Р from); hoist; *трево́гу, пла́ту* raise; *ору́жие* take up; *флаг* hoist; *я́корь* weigh; *паруса́* set; *шум* make; ***~ нос*** put on airs; ***~ на́ ноги*** rouse; ***~ на́ смех*** ridicule; **-ся** [*pt.*: -ня́лся́, -ла́сь] (**с** Р from) rise; go up (stairs ***по ле́стнице***); *coll.* climb (hill ***на холм***); *спор и т. д.* arise; develop
подного́тная *coll. f* [14] all there is to know; the ins and outs *pl.*
подно́ж|ие *n* [12] foot, bottom (*of a hill, etc.*) (at **у** Р); pedestal; **~ка** *f* [5; *g/pl.*: -жек] footboard; *mot.* running board; (*wrestling*) tripping up one's opponent
подно́|с *m* [1] tray; **~си́ть** [15], <поднести́> [24 -с-] bring, carry, take; present (Д); **~ше́ние** *n* [12] gift, present
подня́т|ие *n* [12] lifting; raising, hoisting, *etc.*, →; ***поднима́ть***(**ся**);

~ь(ся) → ***поднима́ть(ся)***

подоб|а́ть: *impf.* (*impers.*) **~а́ет** it becomes; befits; **ˊ~ие** *n* 12] resemblance; image (*a. eccl.*); *math.* similarity; **ˊ~ный** [14; -бен, -бна] similar (Д to); such; ***и тому́ ˊ~ное*** and the like; ***ничего́ ˊ~ного*** nothing of the kind; ***ˊ~но тому́ как*** just as; **~остра́стный** [14; -тен, -тна] servile

подо|бра́ть(ся) → ***подбира́ть(ся)***; **~гна́ть** → ***подгоня́ть***; **~гну́ть(ся)** → ***подгиба́ть(ся)***; **~грева́ть** [1], <-греть> [8; -етый] warm up, heat up; rouse; **~двига́ть** [1], <-дви́нуть> [20] move (***к*** Д [up] to) (*v/i.* **-ся**); **~жда́ть** → ***поджида́ть & ждать***; **~зва́ть** → ***подзыва́ть***

подозр|ева́ть [1], <заподо́зрить> [13] suspect (***в*** П of); **~е́ние** *n* [12] suspicion; **~и́тельный** [14; -лен, -льна] suspicious

подойти́ → ***подходи́ть***

подоко́нник *m* [1] window sill

подо́л *m* [1] hem (*of skirt*)

подо́лгу (for a) long (time)

подо́нки *pl.* [*sg.* 1; -нка] dregs; *fig.* scum, riffraff

подо́пытный [14; -тен, -тна] experimental; ***~ кро́лик*** *fig.* guinea-pig

подорва́ть → ***подрыва́ть***

подоро́жник *m* [1] *bot.* plantain

подо|сла́ть → ***подсыла́ть***; **~спе́ть** [8] *pf.* come (in time); **~стла́ть** → ***подстила́ть***

подотчётный [14; -тен, -тна] accountable to

подохо́дный [14]: ***~ нало́г*** income tax

подо́шва *f* [5] sole (*of foot or boot*); *холма́ и т. д.* foot, bottom

подпа|да́ть [1], <ˊ~сть> [25; *pt. st.*] fall (under); **~ли́ть** [13] *pf. coll.* → ***подже́чь***; singe; *coll.* **ˊ~сть** → ***~да́ть***

подпира́ть [1], <подпере́ть> [12; подопру́, -прёшь] support, prop up

подпис|а́ть(ся) → ***ˊ~ывать(ся)***; **ˊ~ка** *f* [5; *g/pl.*: -сок] subscription (***на*** В to; for); signed statement; **~но́й** [14] subscription...; **ˊ~чик** *m* [1] subscriber; **ˊ~ывать(ся)** [1], <~а́ть(ся)> [3] sign; subscribe (***на*** В to; for); **ˊ~ь** *f* [8] signature (for ***на*** В); ***за ˊ~ью*** (Р) signed by

подплы|ва́ть [1], <ˊ~ть> [23] swim up to; sail up to [***к*** Д]

подпо|лза́ть [1], <~лзти́> [24] creep *or* crawl (***под*** В under; ***к*** Д up to); **~лко́вник** *m* [1] lieutenant colonel; **ˊ~лье** [10; *g/pl.*: -ьев] cellar; (*fig.*) underground work *or* organization; **ˊ~льный** [14] underground...; **ˊ~р(к)а** *f* [5 (*g/pl.*: -рок)] prop; **ˊ~чва** *f* [5] subsoil; **~я́сывать** [1], <~я́сать> [3] belt; gird

подпр|ы́гивать [1], *once* <~ы́гнуть> [20] jump up

подпус|ка́ть [1], <~ти́ть> [15] allow to approach

подра|ба́тывать [1], <~бо́тать> [1] earn additionally; put the finishing touches to

подр|а́внивать [1], <~овня́ть> [28] straighten; level; *и́згородь* clip; *во́лосы* trim

подража́|ние *n* [12] imitation (in/of ***в*** В/Д); **~тель** *m* [4] imitator (of Д); **~ть** [1] imitate, copy (*v/t.* Д)

подраздел|е́ние *n* [12] subdivision; subunit; **~я́ть** [28], <~и́ть> [13] (**-ся** be) subdivide(d) (into ***на*** В)

подра|зумева́ть [1] mean (***под*** Т by), imply; **-ся** be implied; be meant, be understood; **~ста́ть** [1], <~сти́> [24 -ст-; -ро́с, -ла́] grow (up); grow a little older; ***~ста́ющее поколе́ние*** the rising generation

подрез|а́ть & ˊ~ывать [1], <ˊ~ать> [3] cut; clip, trim

подро́бн|ость *f* [8] detail; ***вдава́ться в ~ости*** go into details; **~ый** [14; -бен, -бна] detailed, minute; **~о** in detail, in full

подровня́ть → ***подра́внивать***

подро́сток *m* [1; -стка] juvenile, teenager; youth; young girl

подруб|а́ть [1], <~и́ть> [14] **1.** cut; **2.** *sew.* hem

подру́га [5] (girl) friend

по-дру́жески (in a) friendly (way)

подружи́ться [16 *e.*; -жу́сь, -жи́шься] *pf.* make friends (**с** Т with)

П

подрумя́ниться [13] *pf.* rouge; *cul.* brown

подру́чный [14] improvised; *su.* assistant; mate

подры́|в *m* [1] undermining; blowing up; **~ва́ть** [1] **1.** <~ть> [22] *здоро́вье и т. д.* sap, undermine; **2.** <подорва́ть> [-рву́, -рвёшь; -рва́л, -а́, -о; подо́рванный] blow up, blast, *fig.* undermine; **~вно́й** [14] *де́ятельность* subversive; ***~вно́й заря́д*** charge

подря́д 1. *adv.* successive(ly), running; one after another; **2.** *m* [1] contract; **~чик** *m* [1] contractor

подс|а́живать [1], <~адить> [15] help sit down; *расте́ния* plant additionally; **-ся**, <~е́сть> [25; -ся́ду, -ся́дешь; -сел] sit down (***к*** Д near, next to)

подсве́чник *m* [1] candlestick

подсе́сть → ***подса́живаться***

подска́з|ывать [1], <~а́ть> [3] prompt; **~ка** *coll. f* [5] prompting

подскак|а́ть [3] *pf.* gallop (***к*** Д up to); **~ивать** [1], <подскочи́ть> [16] run (***к*** Д [up] to); jump up

под|сла́щивать [1], <~сласти́ть> [15 *e.*; -ащу́, -асти́шь; -ащённый] sweeten; **~сле́дственный** *m* [14] *law* under investigation; **~слепова́тый** [14 *sh.*] weak-sighted; **~слу́шивать**, <~слу́шать> [1] eavesdrop, overhear; **~сма́тривать** [1], <~смотре́ть> [9; -отрю́, -о́тришь] spy, peep; **~сме́иваться** [1] laugh (***над*** Т at); **~смотре́ть** → ***сма́тривать***

подсне́жник *m* [1] *bot.* snowdrop

подсо́|бный [14] subsidiary, by-..., side...; *рабо́чий* auxiliary; **~вывать** [1], <подсу́нуть> [20] shove under; *coll.* palm (Д [off] on); **~зна́тельный** [14; -лен, -льна] subconscious; **~лнечник** *m* [1] sunflower; **~хнуть** → ***подсыха́ть***

подспо́рье *coll. n* [10] help, support; ***быть хоро́шим ~м*** be a great help

подста́в|ить → **~ля́ть**; **~ка** *f* [5; *g/pl.*: -вок] support, prop, stand; **~ля́ть** [28], <~ить> [14] put, place, set (***под*** В under); *math.* substitute; (*подвести́*) *coll.* let down; ***~ля́ть но́гу*** or (***но́жку***) (Д) trip (a p.) up; **~но́й** [14] false; substitute; ***~но́е лицо́*** figurehead

подстан|о́вка *f* [5; *g/pl.*: -вок] *math.* substitution; **~ция** *f* [7] *el.* substation

подстер|ега́ть [1], <~е́чь> [26 г/ж: -регу́, -режёшь; -рёг, -регла́] lie in wait for, be on the watch for; ***его́ ~ега́ла опа́сность*** he was in danger

подстил|а́ть [1], <подостла́ть> [подстелю́, -е́лешь; подо́стланный & подстеленный] spread (***под*** В under)

подстр|а́ивать [1], <~о́ить> [13] build on to; *coll. fig.* bring about by secret plotting; connive against

подстрек|а́тель *m* [4] instigator; **~а́тельство** *n* [9] instigation; **~а́ть** [1], <~ну́ть> [20] incite (***на*** В to); stir up, provoke

подстр|е́ливать [1], <~ели́ть> [13; -елю́, -е́лишь] hit, wound; **~ига́ть** [1], <~и́чь> [26 г/ж: -игу́, -ижёшь; -и́г, -и́гла; -и́женный] cut, crop, clip; trim, lop; **~о́ить** → ***подстра́ивать***; **~о́чный** [14] interlinear; foot(*note*)

по́дступ *m* [1] approach (*a. mil.*); **~а́ть** [1], <~и́ть> [14] approach (*v/t.* ***к*** Д); rise; press

подсуд|и́мый *m* [14] defendant; **~ность** *f* [8] jurisdiction

подсу́нуть → ***подсо́вывать***

подсч|ёт *m* [1] calculation, computation, cast; **~и́тывать**, <~ита́ть> [1] count (up), compute

подсы|ла́ть [1], <подосла́ть> [-шлю́, -шлёшь; -о́сланный] send (secretly); **~па́ть** [1], <~пать> [2] add, pour; **~ха́ть** [1], <подсо́хнуть> [21] dry (up)

подта́|лкивать [1], <подтолкну́ть> [20] push; nudge; **~со́вывать** [1], <~сова́ть> [7] shuffle garble; **~чивать** [1], <подточи́ть> [16] eat (away); wash (out); sharpen; *fig.* undermine

подтвер|жда́ть [1], <~ди́ть> [15 *e.*; -ржу́, -рди́шь; -рждённый] confirm, corroborate; acknowledge; **-ся** prove (to be) true; **~жде́ние** [12] confirmation; acknowledg(e)ment

под|тере́ть → ***~тира́ть***; **~тёк** *m* [1] bloodshot spot; **~тира́ть** [1], <~тере́ть> [12; подотру́; подтёр] wipe (up); **~толкну́ть** → ***~та́лкивать***; **~точи́ть** → ***~та́чивать***

подтру́н|ивать [1], <~и́ть> [13] tease, banter, chaff (*v/t.* ***над*** T)

подтя́|гивать [1], <~ну́ть> [19] pull (up); draw (in *reins*); tighten; raise (*wages*); wind *or* key up; egg on; join in (*song*); **-ся** chin; brace up; improve, pick up; **~жки** *f/pl.* [5; *gen.*: -жек] suspenders, *Brt.* braces

поду́мывать [1] think (**о** П about)

подуч|а́ть [1], <~и́ть> [16] → ***учи́ть***

поду́шка *f* [5; *g/pl.*: -шек] pillow; cushion, pad

подхали́м *m* [1] toady, lickspittle

подхва́т|ывать [1], <~и́ть> [15] catch; pick up; take up; join in

подхо́д *m* [1] approach (*a. fig.*); **~и́ть** [15], <подойти́> [-ойду́, -дёшь; -ошёл; -шла́; *g. pt.* -ойдя́] (**к** Д) approach, go (up to); arrive, come; (Д) suit, fit; **~я́щий** [17] suitable, fit(ting), appropriate; convenient

подцеп|ля́ть [28], <~и́ть> [14] hook on; couple; *fig.* pick up; *на́сморк* catch (a cold)

подча́с at times, sometimes

подч|ёркивать [1], <~еркну́ть> [20; -ёркнутый] underline; stress

подчин|е́ние *n* [12] subordination (*a. gr.*); submission; subjection; **~ённый** [14] subordinate; **~я́ть** [28], <~и́ть> [13] subject, subordinate; put under (Д s.b.'s) command; **-ся** (Д) submit (to); *прика́зу* obey

под|шива́ть [1], <~ши́ть> [подошью́, -шьёшь; → ***шить***] sew on (**к** Д to); hem; file (*papers*); **~ши́пник** *m* [1] *tech.* bearing; **~ши́ть** → ***~шива́ть***; **~шу́чивать** [1], <~шути́ть> [15] play a trick (***над*** T on); chaff, mock (***над*** T at)

подъе́|зд *m* [1] entrance, porch; *доро́га* drive; approach; **~зжа́ть** [1], <~хать> [-е́ду, -е́дешь] (**к** Д) drive or ride up (to); approach; *coll.* drop in (on); *fig.* get round s.o., make up to s.o.

подъём *m* [1] lift(ing); ascent, rise (*a. fig.*); enthusiasm; *но́ги* instep; ***лёгок*** (***тяжёл***) ***на ~*** nimble (slow); **~ник** *m* [1] elevator, lift, hoist; **~ный** [14]: ***~ный мост*** drawbridge

подъе́|хать → ***~зжа́ть***

под|ыма́ть(ся) → ***~нима́ть(ся)***

поды́ск|ивать [1], <~а́ть> [3] *impf.* seek, look for; *pf.* seek out, find; (*вы́брать*) choose

подыто́ж|ывать [1], <~ить> [16] sum up

поеда́ть [1], <пое́сть> → ***есть***[1]

поеди́нок *m* [1; -нка] duel (with weapons ***на*** П) (*mst. fig.*)

по́езд *m* [1; *pl.*: -да́, *etc. e.*] train; **~ка** *f* [5; *g/pl.*: -док] trip, journey; tour

пожа́луй maybe, perhaps; I suppose; **~ста** please; certainly, by all means; *в отве́т на благода́рность* don't mention it; → *a.* (***не́ за***) ***что***

пожа́р *m* [1] fire (***на*** В/П to/at); conflagration; **~ище** *n* [11] scene of a fire; *coll.* big fire; **~ник** *m* [1] fireman; **~ный** [14] fire...; *su.* → ***~ник***; → ***кома́нда***

пожа́ть → ***пожима́ть*** & ***пожина́ть***

пожела́ни|е *n* [12] wish, desire; ***наилу́чшие ~я*** best wishes

пожелте́лый [14] yellowed

поже́ртвование *n* [12] donation

пожи|ва́ть [1]: ***как*** (***вы***) ***~ва́ете?*** how are you (getting on)? **~ви́ться** [14 *e.*; -влю́сь, -ви́шься] *pf. coll.* get s.th. at another's expense; live off; **~зненный** [14] life...; **~ло́й** [14] elderly

пожи|ма́ть [1], <пожа́ть> [-жму́, -жмёшь; -жа́тый] → ***жать***[1]; press, squeeze; ***~ма́ть ру́ку*** shake hands; ***~ма́ть плеча́ми*** shrug one's shoulders; **~на́ть** [1], <пожа́ть> [-жну́, -жнёшь; -жа́тый] → ***жать***[2]; **~ра́ть** P [1], <пожра́ть> [-жру́, -рёшь; -а́л, -а́, -о] eat up, devour; **~тки** *coll. m/pl.* [1] belongings, (one's) things

по́за *f* [5] pose, posture, attitude

поза|вчера́ the day before yesterday; **~ди́** (Р) behind; past; **~про́шлый** [14] the ... before last

позвол|е́ние *n* [12] permission (**с** Р with), leave (by); **~и́тельный** [14; -лен, -льна] permissible; **~я́ть** [28], <~ить> [13] allow (*a.* of), per-

П

mit (Д); ***~ять себé*** allow o.s.; venture; *расхóды* afford; **´~ь(те)** may I? let me

позвонó|к *m* [1; -нкá] *anat.* vertebra; **~чник** *m* [1] spinal (*or* vertebral) column, spine, backbone; **~чный** [14] vertebral; vertebrate

пóздн|ий [15] (-zn-) (**~о** *a.* it is) late

поздорóвит|ься *coll. pf.*: ***емý не ~ся*** it won't do him much good

поздрав|ѝтель *m* [4] congratulator; **~ѝтельный** [14] congratulatory; **´~ить** → ***~лять***; **~лéние** *n* [12] congratulation; *pl.* compliments of ... (**с** Т); **~лять** [28], <**´~ить**> [14] (**с** Т) congratulate (on), wish many happy returns of ... (*the day, occasion, event, etc.*); send (*or* give) one's compliments (of the season)

пóзже later; ***не ~*** (Р) ... at the latest

позитѝвный [14; -вен, -вна] positive

позѝци|я *f* [7] *fig.* stand, position, attitude (***по*** Д on); ***занять твёрдую ~ю*** take a firm stand

позна|вáть [5], <**´~ть**> [1] perceive; (come to) know; **´~ние** *n* [12] perception; *pl.* knowledge; *philos.* cognition

позолóта *f* [5] gilding

позóр *m* [1] shame, disgrace, infamy; **~ить** [13], <о-> dishono(u)r, disgrace; **~ный** [14; -рен, -рна] shameful, disgraceful, infamous, ignominious

поимённый [14] of names; nominal; by (roll) call

пóис|ки *m/pl.* [1] search (***в*** П in), quest; **´~тине** truly, really

по|ѝть [13], <на-> *скот* water; give to drink (s.th. Т)

пой|мáть → ***ловѝть***; **~тѝ** → ***идтѝ***

покá for the time being (*a.* **~ что**); meanwhile; *cj.* while; **~ (не)** until; **~!** *coll.* so long!, (I'll) see you later!

покáз *m* [1] demonstration; showing; **~áние** (*usu. pl.*) *n* [12] evidence; *law* deposition; *techn.* reading (*on a meter, etc.*); **~áтель** *m* [4] *math.* exponent; index; *выпуска продýкции и т. д.* figure; **~áтельный** [14; -лен, -льна] significant; revealing; **~áть(ся)** → ***~ывать(ся)***; **~нóй** [14] ostentatious; for show; **~ывать** [1], <**~áть**> [3] *фильм и т. д.* show; demonstrate; point; (**на** В at); *tech.* indicate, read; ***~áть себя*** (Т) prove o.s. *or* one's worth; ***и вѝду не ~ывать*** seem to know nothing; look unconcerned; **-ся** appear, seem (Т); come in sight; ***-ся врачý*** see a doctor

покáт|ость *f* [8] declivity; slope, incline; **~ый** [14 *sh.*] slanting, sloping; *лоб* retreating

покаяние *n* [12] confession; repentance

поки|дáть [1], <**´~нуть**> [20] leave, quit; (*брóсить*) abandon, desert

покла|дáя: ***не ~дáя рук*** indefatigably; **´~дистый** [14 *sh.*] complaisant; accommodating; **´~жа** *f* [5] load; luggage

поклóн *m* [1] bow (*in greeting*); *fig.* ***послáть ~ы*** send regards *pl.*; **~éние** *n* [12] (Д) worship; **~ѝться** → ***клáняться***; **~ник** *m* [1] admirer; **~яться** [28] (Д) worship

покóиться [13] rest, lie on; (*оснóвываться*) be based on

покó|й *m* [3] rest, peace; calm; ***остáвить в ~е*** leave alone; ***приёмный ~й***; casualty ward; **~йник** *m* [1], **~йница** *f* [5] the deceased; **~йный** [14; -óен, -óйна] the late; *su.* → ***~йник, ~йница***

поколéние [12] generation

покóнчить [16] *pf.* ([**с**] Т) finish; (**с** Т) do away with; *дурнóй привы́чкой* give up; **~ с собóй** commit suicide

покор|éние *n* [12] *прирóды* subjugation; **~ѝтель** *m* [4] subjugator; **~ѝть(ся)** → ***~ять(ся)***; **´~ность** *f* [8] submissiveness, obedience; **´~ный** [14; -рен, -рна] obedient, submissive; **~ять** [28], <**~ѝть**> [13] subjugate; subdue; *сéрдце* win; **-ся** submit; *необходѝмости и т. д.* resign o.s.

покóс *m* [1] (hay)mowing; meadow (-land)

покрѝкивать *coll.* [1] shout (***на*** В at)

покрóв *m* [1] cover

покровѝтель *m* [4] patron, protector; **~ница** *f* [5] patroness, protectress; **~ственный** [14] protective;

patronizing; *тон* condescending; **~ство** *n* [9] protection (of Д); patronage; **~ствовать** [7] (Д) protect; patronize
покро́й *m* [3] *оде́жды* cut
покры|ва́ло *n* [9] coverlet; **~ва́ть** [1], <~ть> [22] (T) cover (*a.* = defray); *кра́ской* coat; *cards* beat, trump; **-ся** cover o.s.; *сы́пью* be(come) covered; **~тие** *n* [12] cover(ing); coat(ing); defrayal; **~шка** *f* [5; -шек] *mot.* tire (*Brt.* tyre)
покуп|а́тель *m* [4], **~а́тельница** *f* [5] buyer; customer; **~а́тельный** [14] purchasing; **~а́ть** [1], <купи́ть> [14] buy, purchase (from **у** P); **~ка** *f* [5; *g/pl.*: -пок] purchase; ***идти́ за ~ками*** go shopping; **~но́й** [14] bought, purchased
поку|ша́ться [1], <~си́ться> [15 *e.*; -ушу́сь, -уси́шься] attempt (*v/t.* ***на*** B); *на чьи́-л. права́* encroach ([up]on); **~ше́ние** *n* [12] attempt (***на*** B [up]on)
пол[1] *m* [1; на́ ~; на ~ý; *pl. e.*] floor
пол[2] *m* [1; *from g/pl. e.*] sex
пол[3]**(...)** [*g/sg., etc.*: ~(у)...] half (...)
полага́|ть [1], <положи́ть> [16] think, suppose, guess; ***на́до ~ть*** probably; ***поло́жим, что ...*** suppose, let's assume that; **-ся** rely (on ***на*** B); (Д) ***~ется*** must; be due *or* proper; ***как ~ется*** properly
по́л|день *m* [*gen.*: -(у́)дня: *g/pl.*: -дён] noon (**в** B at); → ***обе́д***; ***по́сле ~у́дня*** in the afternoon; **~доро́ги** → ***~пути́***; **~дю́жины** [*gen.*: -удю́жины] half (a) dozen
по́ле *n* [10; *pl. e.*] field (*a. fig.*; ***на***, ***в*** П in, ***по*** Д, T across); ground; (*край листа́*) *mst. pl.* margin; **~во́й** [14] field...; *цветы́* wild
поле́зный [14; -зен, -зна] useful, of use; *сове́т и т. д.* helpful; *для здоро́вья* wholesome, healthy
полем|изи́ровать [7] engage in polemics; **~ика** *f* [5], **~и́ческий** [16] polemic
поле́но *n* [9; *pl.*: -нья, -ньев] log
полёт *m* [1] flight; ***бре́ющий ~*** low-level flight
по́лз|ать [1], **~ти́** [24] creep, crawl; **~ко́м** on all fours; **~у́чий** [17]: ***~у́чее расте́ние*** creeper, climber
поли|ва́ть [1], <~ть> [-лью́, -льёшь, → ***лить***] water; *pf.* start raining (*or* pouring); **~вка** *f* [5] watering
полиго́н *m* [1] *mil.* firing range
поликли́ника *f* [5] polyclinic; *больни́чная* outpatient's department
полиня́лый [14] faded
поли|рова́ть [7], <от-> polish; **~ро́вка** *f* [5; *g/pl.*: -вок] polish(ing)
по́лис *m* [1]: ***страхово́й ~*** insurance policy
политехни́ческий [16]: ***~ институ́т*** polytechnic
политзаключённый *m* [14] political prisoner
поли́т|ик *m* [1] politician; **~ика** *f* [5] policy; politics *pl.*; **~и́ческий** [16] political
поли́ть → ***полива́ть***
полиц|е́йский [16] police(man *su.*); **~ия** *f* [7] police
поли́чн|ое *n* [14]: ***пойма́ть с ~ым*** catch red-handed
полиэтиле́н *m* [1], **~овый** [14] polyethylene (*Brt.* polythene)
полк *m* [1 *e.*; в ~ý] regiment
по́лка *f* [5; *g/pl.*: -лок] shelf
полко́в|ник *m* [1] colonel; **~о́дец** *m* [1; -дца] (*not a designation of military rank*) commander, military leader, warlord; one who leads and supervises; **~о́й** [14] regimental
полне́йший [17] utter, sheer
полне́ть [8], <по-> grow stout
полно|ве́сный [14; -сен, -сна] of full weight; weighty; **~вла́стный** [14; -тен, -тна] sovereign; **~во́дный** [14; -ден, -дна] deep; **~кро́вный** [14; -вен, -вна] full-blooded; **~лу́ние** *n* [12] full moon; **~мо́чие** *n* [12] authority, (full) power; **~мо́чный** [14; -чен, -чна] plenipotentiary; → ***полпре́д***; **~пра́вный** [14; -вен, -вна]: ***~пра́вный член*** full member; **´~стью** completely, entirely; **~та́** *f* [5] fullness; *информа́ции* completeness; (*ту́чность*) corpulence; ***для ~ты́ карти́ны*** to complete the picture; **~це́нный** [14; -е́нен, -е́нна] full (value)...; *fig. специали́ст* full-fledged

П

по́лночь *f* [8; -(у́)ночи] midnight
по́лн|ый [14; по́лон, полна́, по́лно́; полне́е] full (of P *or* T); (***наби́тый***) packed; complete, absolute; perfect (*a. right*); (***ту́чный***) stout; **~ое собра́ние сочине́ний** complete works; **~ы́м-~о́** *coll.* chock-full, packed (with P); lots of
полови́к *m* [1 *e.*] mat
полови́н|а *f* [5] half (***на*** B by); **~а (в ~е) пя́того** (at) half past four; **два с ~ой** two and a half; **~ка** *f* [5; *g/pl.*: -нок] half; **~чатый** [14] *fig.* determinate
полови́ца *f* [5] floor; board
полово́дье *n* [10] high tide (*in spring*)
полов|о́й[1] [14] floor...; **~а́я тря́пка** floor cloth; **~о́й**[2] [14] sexual; **~а́я зре́лость** puberty; **~ы́е о́рганы** *m/pl.* genitals
поло́гий [16; *comp.*: поло́же] gently sloping
полож|е́ние *n* [12] position, location; situation; (***состоя́ние***) state, condition; ***социа́льное*** standing; (***пра́вила***) regulations *pl.*; thesis; **семе́йное ~е́ние** marital status; **~и́тельный** [14; -лен, -льна] positive; ***отве́т*** affirmative; **~и́ть(ся)** → **класть 1. & полага́ть(ся)**
поло́мка *f* [5; *g/pl.*: -мок] breakage; breakdown
полоса́ [5; *ac/sg.*: по́лосу́; *pl.*: по́лосы, поло́с, -са́м] stripe, streak; strip; belt, zone; field; period; **~ неуда́ч** a run of bad luck; **~тый** [14 *sh.*] striped
полоска́ть [3], <про-> rinse; gargle; **-ся** paddle; ***о фла́ге*** flap
по́лость *f* [8; *from g/pl. e.*] *anat.* cavity; **брюшна́я ~** abdominal cavity
полоте́нце *n* [11; *g/pl.*: -нец] towel (T on); **ку́хонное ~** dish towel; **махро́вое ~** Turkish towel
поло́тн|ище *n* [11] width; **~о́** *n* [9; *pl.*: -о́тна, -о́тен, -о́тнам], **~я́ный** [14] linen(...)
поло́ть [17], <вы-, про-> weed
пол|пре́д *m* [1] plenipotentiary; **~пути́** halfway (*a.* **на ~пути́**); **~сло́ва** [9; *gen.*: -(у)сло́ва] **ни ~** not a word; (a few) word(s); **останови́ться на ~(у)сло́ве** stop short; **~со́тни** [6; *g/sg.*: -(у)со́тни; *g/pl.*: -лусотен] fifty
полтор|а́ *m* & *n*, **~ы́** *f* [*gen.*: -у́тора, -ры (*f*)] one and a half; **~а́ста** [*obl. cases*; -у́тораста] a hundred and fifty
полу|боти́нки *old use m/pl.* [1; *g/pl.*: -нок] (low) shoes; **~го́дие** *n* [12] half year, six months; **~годи́чный**, **~годово́й** [14] half-yearly; **~гра́мотный** [14; -тен, -тна] semiliterate; **~де́нный** [14] midday...; **~живо́й** [14; -жи́в, -а́, -о] half dead; **~защи́тник** *m* [1] *sport* halfback; **~кру́г** *m* [1] semicircle; **~ме́сяц** *m* [1] half moon, crescent; **~мра́к** *m* [1] twilight, semidarkness; **~но́чный** [14] midnight...; **~оборо́т** *m* [1] half-turn; **~о́стров** *m* [1; *pl.*: -ва́, *etc. e.*] peninsula; **~проводни́к** *m* [1] semiconductor, transistor; **~стано́к** *m* [1; -нка] *rail.* stop; **~тьма́** *f* [5] → **~мра́к**; **~фабрика́т** *m* [1] semifinished product *or* foodstuff
получ|а́тель *m* [4] addressee, recipient; **~а́ть** [1], <~и́ть> [16] receive, get; ***разреше́ние и т. д.*** obtain; ***удово́льствие*** derive; **-ся**; (***оказа́ться***) result; prove, turn out; **~е́ние** *n* [12] receipt; **~чка** *coll. f* [5; *g/pl.*: -чек] pay(day)
полу|ша́рие *n* [12] hemisphere; **~шу́бок** *m* [1; -бка] knee-length sheepskin coat
пол|цены́: **за ~цены́** at half price; **~часа́** *m* [1; *g/sg.*: -уча́са] half (an) hour
по́лчище *n* [11] horde; *fig.* mass
по́лый [14] hollow
полы́нь *f* [8] wormwood
полынья́ *f* [6] polnya, patch of open water in sea ice
по́ль|за *f* [5] use; benefit (**на**, **в** B, **для** P for), profit, advantage; **в ~у** (P) in favo(u)r of; **~ова́тель** *m* [4] user; **~ова́ться** [7], <вос~ова́ться> (T) use, make use of; avail o.s. of; ***репута́цией и т. д.*** enjoy, have; ***слу́чаем*** take
по́ль|ка *f* [5; *g/pl.*: -лек] **1.** Pole, Polish woman; **2.** polka; **~ский** [16] Polish
полюбо́вный [14] amicable
по́люс *m* [1] pole (*a. el*)

поля́|к *m* [1] Pole; **~на** *f* [5] *леснáя* glade; clearing; **~рный** [14] polar
помáда *f* [5] pomade; ***губнáя ~*** lipstick
помалéньку *coll.* so-so; in a small way; (*постепéнно*) little by little
помáлкивать *coll.* [1] keep silent *or* mum
помá|рка [5; *g/pl.*: -рок] blot; correction
поместú ть(ся) → ***помещáть(ся)***
помéстье *n* [10] *hist.* estate
пóмесь *f* [8] crossbreed, mongrel
помёт *m* [1] dung; (*приплóд*) litter, brood
помé|тить → ***~чáть***; **~тка** *f* [5; *g/pl.*: -ток] mark, note; **~ха** *f* [5] hindrance; obstacle; *pl. only radio* interference; **~чáть** [1], <**~тить**> [15] mark, note
помéш|анный *coll.* [14 *sh.*] crazy; mad (about ***на*** П); **~áтельство** *n* [9] insanity; **~áть** → ***мешáть***; **-ся** *pf.* go mad; be mad (***на*** П about)
поме|щáть [1], <**~стúть**> [15 *e.*; -ещý, -естúшь; -ещённый] place; (*поселúть*) lodge, accommodate; *капитáл* invest; insert, publish; **-ся** locate; lodge; find room; (*вмещáть*) hold; be placed *or* invested; *impf.* be (located); **~щéние** *n* [12] premise(s), room; investment; **~щик** *m* [1] *hist.* landowner, landlord
помидóр *m* [1] tomato
помúл|ование *n* [12], **~овать** [7] *pf. law* pardon; forgiveness; ***~уй бог!*** God forbid!
помúмо (Р) besides, apart from
помúн *m* [1]: ***лёгок на ~е*** talk of the devil; **~áть** [1], <**помянýть**> [19] speak about, mention; commemorate; ***не ~áть лúхом*** bear no ill will (toward[s] a p. В); **~ки** *f/pl.* [5; *gen.*: -нок] commemoration (for the dead); **~ýтно** every minute; constantly
пóмнит|ь [13], <**вс-**> remember (***о*** П); ***мне ~ся*** (as far as) I remember; ***не ~ь себя́ от рáдости*** be beside o.s. with joy
помо|гáть [1], <**~чь**> [26; г/ж: -огý, -óжешь, -óгут; -óг, -оглá] (Д) help; aid, assist; *о лекáрстве* relieve, bring relief
помó|и *m/pl.* [3] slops; *coll.* **~йка** *f* [5; *g/pl.*: -óек] rubbish heap
помóл *m* [1] grind(ing)
помóлвка *f* [5; *g/pl.*: -вок] betrothal, engagement
помóст *m* [1] dais; rostrum; scaffold
помóчь → ***помогáть***
помóщ|ник *m* [1], **~ница** *f* [5] assistant; helper, aide; **´~ь** *f* [8] help, aid, assistance (***с*** Т, ***при*** П with, ***на*** В/Д to one's); relief; ***машúна скóрой ´~и*** ambulance; ***пéрвая ´~ь*** first aid
пóмпа *f* [5] pomp
помутнéние *n* [12] dimness; turbidity
пóмы|сел *m* [1; -сла] thought; (*намéрение*) design; **~шля́ть** [28], <**~слить**> [13], think (***о*** П of), contemplate
помянýть → ***поминáть***
помя́тый [14] (c)rumpled; *травá* trodden
понá|добиться [14] *pf.* (Д) be, become necessary; **~слы́шке** *coll.* by hearsay
поне|вóле *coll.* willy-nilly; against one's will; **~дéльник** *m* [1] Monday (***в*** В, *pl.* ***по*** Д on)
понемнó|гу, *coll.* **~жку** (a) little; little by little, gradually; *coll. a.* (*так-себé*) so-so
пони|жáть [1], <**~зить**> [15] lower; (*ослáбить, умéньшить*) reduce (*v/i.* **-ся**; fall, sink); **~жéние** *n* [12] fall; reduction; drop
поник|áть [1], <**~нуть**> [21] droop, hang (one's head головóй); *цветы́* wilt
понимá|ние *n* [12] comprehension, understanding; conception; ***в моём ~нии*** as I see it; **~ть** [1], <**поня́ть**> [поймý, ~мёшь; пóнял, -á, -о; пóнятый (пóнят, -á, -о)] understand, comprehend; realize; (*ценúть*) appreciate; ***~ю*** (***~ешь***, ***~ете*** [***ли***]) I (you) see
понóс *m* [1] diarrh(o)ea
поносúть [15] revile, abuse
понóшенный [14 *sh.*] worn, shabby
понтóн [1], **~ный** [14] pontoon
пону|ждáть [1], <**~дúть**> [15; -у-, -ждённый] force, compel

понука́ть [1] *coll.* urge on, spur
пону́р|ить [13] hang; **~ый** [14 *sh.*] downcast
по́нчик *m* [1] doughnut
поны́не *obs.* until now
поня́т|ие *n* [12] idea, notion; concept(ion); (***я***) ***не име́ю ни мале́йшего ~ия*** I haven't the faintest idea; **~ливый** [14 *sh.*] quick-witted; **~ный** [14; -тен, -тна] understandable; intelligible; clear, plain; **~ь** → ***понима́ть***
поо́|даль at some distance; **~ди́ночке** one by one; **~черёдный** [14] taken in turns
поощр|е́ние *n* [12] encouragement; ***материа́льное ~е́ние*** bonus; **~я́ть** [28], <~и́ть> [13] encourage
попа|да́ние *n* [12] hit; **~да́ть** [1], <~́сть> [25; *pt. st.*] (***в***, ***на*** В) (*оказа́ться*) get; fall; find o.s.; *в цель* hit; *на по́езд* catch; *coll.* (Д *impers.*) catch it; ***не ~́сть*** miss; ***как ~́ло*** anyhow, at random, haphazard; ***кому́ ~́ло*** to the first comer (= ***пе́рвому ~́вшемуся***); **-ся** (***в*** В) be caught; fall (into a trap ***на у́дочку***); *coll.* (Д + *vb.* + И) *статья́ и т. д.* come across, chance (up)on, meet; (*быва́ть*) occur, there is (are); strike (Д ***на глаза́*** a p.'s eye); ***вам не ~да́лась моя́ кни́га***? did you happen to see my book?
попа́рно in pairs, two by two
попа́сть → ***попада́ть***(***ся***)
попер|ёк (Р) across, crosswise; *доро́ги* in (*a p.'s way*); **~еме́нно** in turns; **~е́чный** [14] transverse; diametrical
попеч|е́ние *n* [12] care, charge (in ***на*** П); **~и́тель** *m* [4] guardian, trustee
попира́ть [1] trample (on); (*fig.*) flout
поплаво́к *m* [1; -вка́] float (*a. tech*)
попо́йка *coll. f* [5; *g/pl.*: -о́ек] booze
попол|а́м in half; half-and-half; fifty-fifty; **~знове́ние** *n* [12]: ***у меня́ бы́ло ~знове́ние*** I had half a mind to ...; **~ня́ть** [28], <~́нить> [13] replenish, supplement; *зна́ния* enrich
пополу́дни in the afternoon, p. m.
попра́в|ить(***ся***) → **~ля́ть**(***ся***); **~ка** *f* [5; *g/pl.*: -вок] correction; *parl.* amendment; (*улучше́ние*) improvement; recovery; **~ля́ть** [28], <~ить> [14] adjust; correct, (a)mend; improve; *здоро́вье* recover (*v/i.* **-ся**); put on weight
по-пре́жнему as before
попрек|а́ть [1], <~ну́ть> [20] reproach (with T)
по́прище *n* [11] field (***на*** П in); walk of life, profession
по́про|сту plainly, unceremoniously; ***~сту говоря́*** to put it plainly; **~ша́йка** *coll. m/f* [5; *g/pl.*: -а́ек] beggar; cadger
попуга́й *m* [3] parrot
популя́рн|ость *f* [8] popularity; **~ый** [14; -рен, -рна] popular
попус|ти́тельство *n* [9] tolerance; connivance; **´~ту** *coll.* in vain, to no avail
попу́т|ный [14] accompanying; *ве́тер* fair, favo(u)rable; (***~но*** in) passing, incidental(ly); **~чик** *m* [1] travel(l)ing companion; *fig. pol.* fellow-travel(l)er
попыт|а́ть *coll.* [1] *pf.* try (one's luck ***сча́стья***); **~́ка** [5; *g/pl.*: -ток] attempt
пор|а́[1] *f* [5; *ac/sg.*: по́ру; *pl. st.*] time; season; ***в зи́мнюю ~́у*** in winter (time); (***давно́***) ***~а́*** it's (high) time (for Д); ***до ~ы́, до вре́мени*** for the time being; not forever; ***до*** (***с***) ***каки́х ~?*** how long (since when)?; ***до сих ~*** so far, up to now (here); ***до тех ~***(, ***пока́***) so (*or* as) long (as); ***с тех ~*** (***как***) since then (since); ***на пе́рвых ~ах*** at first, in the beginning; ***~о́й*** at times; ***вече́рней ~ой*** → ***ве́чером***
по́ра[2] *f* [5] pore
пора|боща́ть [1], <~ти́ть> [15 *e.*; -ощу́, -оти́шь; -ощённый] enslave, enthrall
поравня́ться [28] *pf.* draw level (***с*** T with), come up (to), come alongside (of)
пора|жа́ть [1], <~зи́ть> [15 *e.*; -ажу́, -ази́шь; -ажённый] strike (*a. fig.* = amaze; *med.* affect); defeat; **~же́ние** *n* [12] defeat; *law* disenfranchisement; **~зи́тельный** [14; -лен, -льна] striking; **~зи́ть** →

П

~жа́ть; **~ни́ть** [13] *pf.* wound, injure
порва́ть(**ся**) → ***порыва́ть***(***ся***)
поре́з [1], **~ать** [3] *pf.* cut
поре́й *m* [3] leek
по́ристый [14 *sh.*] porous
порица́|ние [12], **~ть** [1] blame, censure
по́ровну in equal parts, equally
поро́г *m* [1] threshold; *pl.* rapids
поро́|да *f* [5] breed, species, race; *о челове́ке* stock; *geol.* rock; **~ди́стый** [14 *sh.*] thoroughbred; **~жда́ть** [1], <**~ди́ть**> [15 *e.*; -ожу́, -оди́шь; -ождённый] engender, give rise to, entail
поро́жний *coll.* [15] empty; idling
по́рознь *coll.* separately; one by one
поро́к *m* [1] vice; *ре́чи* defect; *се́рдца* disease
поролóн *m* [1] foam rubber
поросёнок *m* [2] piglet
поро́|ть [17] **1.** <pac-> undo, unpick; *impf. coll.* talk (***вздор*** nonsense); **2.** *coll.* <вы-> whip, flog; **´~х** *m* [1] gunpowder; **~хово́й** [14] gunpowder...
поро́ч|ить [16], <о-> discredit; *репута́цию* blacken, defame; **~ный** [14; -чен, -чна] *круг* vicious; *иде́я и т. д.* faulty; *челове́к* depraved
порошо́к *m* [1; -шка́] powder
порт *m* [1; в ~у́; *from g/pl. e.*] port; harbo(u)r
порт|ати́вный [14; -вен, -вна] portable; **~ить** [15], <ис-> spoil; **-ся** (*v/i.*) break down
порт|ни́ха *f* [5] dressmaker; **~но́й** *m* [14] tailor
порто́в|ый [14] port..., dock...; ***~ый го́род*** seaport
портре́т *m* [1] portrait; (*похо́жесть*) likeness
портсига́р *m* [1] cigar(ette) case
португа́л|ец *m* [1; -льца] Portuguese; **~ка** *f* [5; *g/pl.*: -лок], **~ьский** [16] Portuguese
порт|упе́я *f* [6] *mil.* sword belt; shoulder belt; **~фе́ль** *m* [4] brief case; *мини́стра* (*functions and office*) portfolio
пору́|ка *f* [5] bail (***на*** В *pl.* on), security; guarantee; ***кругова́я ~ка*** collective guarantee; **~ча́ть** [1], <**~чи́ть**> [16] charge (Д/В a p. with); commission, bid, instruct (+ *inf.*); entrust; **~че́ние** *n* [12] commission; instruction; *dipl.* mission; (*a. comm.*) order (***по*** Д by, on behalf of); **~чик** *m* [1] *obs.* (first) lieutenant; **~чи́тель** *m* [4] guarantor; **~чи́тельство** *n* [9] (*зало́г*) bail, surety, guarantee; **~чи́ть** → ***~ча́ть***
порх|а́ть [1], *once* <**~ну́ть**> [20] flit
по́рция *f* [7] (*of food*) portion, helping
по́р|ча *f* [5] spoiling; damage; **~шень** *m* [4; -шня] (*tech.*) piston
поры́в *m* [1] gust, squall; *гне́ва и т. д.* fit, outburst; *благоро́дный* impulse; **~а́ть** [1], <порва́ть> [-ву́, -вёшь; -а́л, -а́, -о; по́рванный] tear; break off (**с** Т with); **-ся** *v/i.*; *impf.* strive; *a.* → ***рва́ть***(***ся***); **~истый** [14 *sh.*] gusty; *fig.* impetuous, fitful
поря́дко|вый [14] *gr.* ordinal; **~м** *coll.* rather
поря́д|ок *m* [1; -дка] order; (*после́довательность*) sequence; *pl.* conditions; ***~ок дня*** agenda; ***в ~ке исключе́ния*** by way of an exception; ***это в ~ке веще́й*** it's quite natural; ***по ~ку*** one after another; **~очный** [14; -чен, -чна] *челове́к* decent; fair(ly large *or* great)
посад|и́ть → ***сажа́ть*** & ***сади́ть***; **~ка** *f* [5; *g/pl.*: -док] planting; *naut.* embarkation, (*a. rail.*) boarding; *ae.* landing; ***вы́нужденная ~ка*** forced landing; **~очный** [14] landing...
по-сво́ему in one's own way
посвя|ща́ть [1], <**~ти́ть**> [15 *e.*; -ящу́, -яти́шь; -ящённый] devote ([o.s.] to [***себя́***] Д); *кому́-л.* dedicate; *в та́йну* let, initiate (***в*** В into); **~ще́ние** *n* [12] initiation; dedication
посе́в *m* [1] sowing; crop; **~но́й** [14] sowing; ***~на́я пло́щадь*** area under crops
поседе́вший [14] (turned) gray, *Brt.* grey
поселе́нец [1; -нца] settler
посёл|ок *m* [1; -лка] urban settlement; **~я́ть** [28], <**~и́ть**> [13] settle; **-ся** (*v/i.*) put up (***в*** П at)

посереди́не in the middle *or* midst of

посе|ти́тель [4], **~ти́тельница** *f* [5] visitor, caller; **~ти́ть** → **~ща́ть**; **~ща́емость** *f* [8] attendance; **~ща́ть** [1], <~ти́ть> [15 *e.*; -ещу́, -ети́шь; -ещённый] visit, call on; *impf. заня́тия и т. д.* attend; **~ще́ние** *n* [12] visit (P to), call

поси́льный [14; -лен, -льна] one's strength *or* possibilities; feasible

поскользну́ться [20] *pf.* slip

поско́льку so far as, as far as

посла́|ние *n* [12] message; *lit.* epistle; **♀ния** *Bibl.* the Epistles; **~нник** *m* [1] *dipl.* envoy; **~ть** → **посыла́ть**

по́сле 1. (P) after (*a.* **~ того́ как** + *vb.*); **~ чего́** whereupon; **2.** *adv.* after(ward[s]), later (on); **~вое́нный** [14] postwar

после́дний [15] last; *изве́стия, мо́да* latest; (*оконча́тельный*) last, final; *из двух* latter; worst

после́д|ователь *m* [4] follower; **~овательный** [14; -лен, -льна] consistent; successive; **~ствие** *n* [12] consequence; **~ующий** [17] subsequent, succeeding, following

после|за́втра the day after tomorrow; **~сло́вие** *n* [12] epilogue

посло́вица *f* [5] proverb

послуш|а́ние *n* [12] obedience; **~ник** *m* [1] novice; **~ный** [14; -шен, -шна] obedient

посм|а́тривать [1] look (at) from time to time; **~е́иваться** [1] chuckle; laugh (**над** T at); **~е́ртный** [14] posthumous; **~е́шище** *n* [11] laughingstock, butt; **~ея́ние** *n* [12] ridicule

посо́б|ие *n* [12] relief, benefit; textbook, manual; ***нагля́дные ~ия*** visual aids; ***~ие по безрабо́тице*** unemployment benefit

посо́л *m* [1; -сла́] ambassador; **~ьство** *n* [9] embassy

поспа́ть [-сплю́, -спи́шь; -спа́л, -а́, -о] *pf.* (have a) nap

поспе|ва́ть [1], <~ть> [8] (*созрева́ть*) ripen; (*of food being cooked or prepared*) be done; *coll.* → **успева́ть**

поспе́шн|ость *f* [8] haste; **~ый** [14; -шен, -шна] hasty, hurried; (*необду́манный*) rash

посред|и́(не) (P) amid(st), in the middle (of); **~ник** *m* [1] mediator, intermediary, *comm.* middleman; **~ничество** *n* [9] mediation; **~ственность** *f* [8] mediocrity; **~ственный** [14 *sh.*] middling; mediocre; **~ственно** *a.* fair, so-so, satisfactory, C (mark; → **тро́йка**); **~ством** (P) by means of

пост[1] *m* [1 *e.*] post; ***~ управле́ния*** *tech.* control station

пост[2] *m* [1 *e.*] fasting; *eccl.* ***Вели́кий ~*** Lent

поста́в|ить → **~ля́ть & ста́вить**; **~ка** *f* [5; *g/pl.*: -вок] delivery (on *при*); supply; **~ля́ть** [28], <~ить> [14] deliver (*v/t.*; Д p.); supply, furnish; **~щи́к** *m* [1 *e.*] supplier

постан|ови́ть → **~овля́ть**; **~о́вка** *f* [5; *g/pl.*: -вок] *thea.* staging, production; *де́ла* organization; ***~о́вка вопро́са*** the way a question is put; **~овле́ние** *n* [12] resolution, decision; *parl., etc.* decree; **~овля́ть** [28], <~ови́ть> [14] decide; decree; **~о́вщик** *m* [1] stage manager; director (of film); producer (of play)

посте|ли́ть → **стлать**; **~ль** *f* [8] bed; **~пе́нный** [14; -е́нен, -е́нна] gradual

пости|га́ть [1], <~гнуть> & <~чь> [21] comprehend, grasp; *несча́стье* befall; **~жи́мый** [14 *sh.*] understandable; conceivable

пост|ила́ть [1] → **стлать**; **~и́ться** [15 *e.*; пощу́сь, пости́шься] fast; **~и́чь** → **~ига́ть**; **~ный** [14; -тен, -тна́, -о] *coll. мя́со* lean; *fig.* sour; (*ха́нжеский*) sanctimonious

посто́льку: ***~ поско́льку*** to that extent, insofar as

посторо́нни|й [15] strange(r *su.*), outside(r), foreign (*тж. предме́т*); unauthorized; ***~м вход воспрещён*** unauthorized persons not admitted

постоя́н|ный [14; -я́нен, -я́нна] constant, permanent; (*непреры́вный*) continual, continuous; *рабо́та* steady; *el.* direct; **~ство** *n* [9] constancy

пострада́вший [17] victim; *при ава́рии* injured
постре́л *coll. m* [1] little imp, rascal
постри|га́ть [1], <~чь> [26 г/ж: -игу́, -ижёшь, -игу́т] (**-ся** have one's hair) cut; become a monk *or* nun
постро́йка *f* [5; *g/pl.*: -о́ек] construction; *зда́ние* building; building site
поступ|а́тельный [14] forward, progressive; **~а́ть** [1], <~и́ть> [14] act; (**с** T) treat, deal (with), handle; (**в**, ***на*** B) enter, join; *univ.* matriculate; *заявле́ние* come in, be received (***на*** B for); ***~и́ть в прода́жу*** be on sale; **-ся** (T) waive; **~ле́ние** *n* [12] entry; matriculation; receipt; ***~ле́ние дохо́дов*** revenue return; **~ок** *m* [1; -пка] act; (*поведе́ние*) behavio(u)r, conduct; **´~ь** [8] gait, step
посты́|дный [14; -ден, -дна] shameful; **~лый** [14 *sh.*] *coll.* hateful; repellent
посу́да *f* [5] crockery; plates and dishes; ***фая́нсовая*** (***фарфо́ровая***) **~** earthenware (china)
посчастли́ви|ться [14; *impers.*] *pf.*: ***ей ~лось*** she succeeded (in *inf.*) *or* was lucky enough (to)
посыл|а́ть [1], <посла́ть> [пошлю́, -шлёшь; по́сланный] send (for ***за*** T); dispatch; **~ка¹** *f* [5; *g/pl.*: -лок] package, parcel
посы́лка² *f* [5; *g/pl.*: -лок] *philos.* premise
посып|а́ть [1], <~ать> [2] (be-) strew (T over; with); sprinkle (with); **~аться** *pf.* begin to fall; *fig.* rain; *coll. о вопро́сах* shower (*with*)
посяг|а́тельство *n* [9] encroachment; infringement; **~а́ть** [1], <~ну́ть> [20] encroach, infringe (***на*** B on); attempt
пот *m* [1] sweat; ***весь в ~у́*** sweating all over
пота|йно́й [14] secret; **~ка́ть** *coll.* [1] indulge; **~со́вка** *coll. f* [5; *g/pl.*: -вок] scuffle
по-тво́ему in your opinion; as you wish; ***пусть бу́дет ~*** have it your own way
потво́рство *n* [9] indulgence, connivance; **~вать** [7] indulge, connive (Д at)
потёмки *f/pl.* [5; *gen.*: -мок] darkness
потенциа́л *m* [1] potential
потерпе́вший [17] victim
потёртый [14 *sh.*] shabby, threadbare, worn
поте́ря *f* [6] loss; *вре́мени, де́нег* waste
потесни́ть → ***тесни́ть***; **-ся** squeeze up (*to make room for others*)
поте́ть [8], <вс-> sweat, *coll.* toil; *стекло́* <за-> mist over
поте́|ха *f* [5] fun, *coll.* lark; **~шный** [14; -шен, -шна] funny, amusing
поти|ра́ть *coll.* [1] rub; **~хо́ньку** *coll.* slowly; silently; secretly, on the sly
по́тный [14; -тен, -тна; -о] sweaty
пото́к *m* [1] stream; torrent; flow
пото|ло́к *m* [1; -лка́] ceiling; ***взять что́-л. с ~лка́*** spin s.th. out of thin air
пото́м afterward(s); then; **~ок** *m* [1; -мка] descendant, offspring; **~ственный** [14] hereditary; **~ство** *n* [9] posterity, descendants *pl.*
потому́ that is why; ***~ что*** because
пото́п *m* [1] flood, deluge
потреб|и́тель *m* [4] consumer; **~и́ть** → ***~ля́ть***; **~ле́ние** *n* [12] consumption; use; **~ля́ть** [28], <~и́ть> [14 *e.*; -блю́, -би́шь; -блённый] consume; use; **~ность** *f* [8] need, want (***в*** П of), requirement
потрёпанный *coll.* [14] shabby, tattered, worn
потро|ха́ *m/pl.* [1 *e.*] pluck; giblets; **~ши́ть** [16 *e.*; -шу́, -ши́шь; -шённый], <вы-> draw, disembowel
потряс|а́ть [1], <~ти́> [24; -с-] shake (*a. fig.*); **~а́ющий** [17] tremendous; **~е́ние** *n* [12] shock; **~ти́** → ***~а́ть***
поту́|ги *f/pl.* [5] *fig.* (vain) attempt; **~пля́ть** [28], <~пи́ть> [14] *взгляд* cast down; *го́лову* hang; **~ха́ть** [1] → ***ту́хнуть***
потягивать(**ся**) → ***тяну́ть***(***ся***)
поуч|а́ть [1] *coll.* preach at, lecture; **~и́тельный** [14; -лен, -льна] instructive

П

похáбный P [14; -бен, -бна] *coll.* obscene, smutty

похвал|á *f* [5] praise; commendation; **~ьный** [14; -лен, -льна] commendable, praiseworthy

похи|щáть [1], <~тить> [15; -ищу; -йщенный] purloin; *человéка* kidnap; **~щéние** *n* [12] theft; kidnap(p)ing, abduction

похлёбка *f* [5; *g/pl.*: -бок] soup

похмéлье *n* [10] hangover

похóд *m* [1] march; *mil. fig.*, campaign; *турúстский* hike; ***крестóвый ~*** crusade

походúть [15] (***на*** B) be like, resemble

похóд|ка *f* [5] gait; **~ный** [14] *пéсня* marching

похождéние *n* [12] adventure

похóж|ий [17 *sh.*] (***на*** B) like, resembling; similar (to); ***быть ~им*** look like; ***ни на что не ~е*** *coll.* like nothing else; unheard of

по-хозя́йски thriftily; wisely

похо|рóнный [14] funeral...; *марш* dead; ***~рóнное бюрó*** undertaker's office; **´~роны** *f/pl.* [5; -óн, -онáм] funeral, burial (***на*** П at); **~тлúвый** [14 *sh.*] lustful, lewd; **´~ть** *f* [8] lust

поцелу́й *m* [3] kiss (***в*** B on)

пóчва *f* [5] soil, (*a. fig.*) ground

почём *coll.* how much (is/are)...; (*only used with parts of verb* знать) ***~ я знáю, что ...*** how should I know that

почему́ why; ***~-то*** for some reason

пóчерк *m* [1] handwriting

почéрпнуть [20; -éрпнутый] get, obtain

пóчесть *f* [8] hono(u)r

почёт *m* [1] hono(u)r, esteem; **~ный** [14; -тен, -тна] honorary; hono(u)rable; (*карáул* guard) of hono(u)r

почúн *m* [1] initiative; ***по сóбственному ~у*** on his own initiative

почúн|ка *f* [5; *g/pl.*: -нок] repair; ***отдавáть в ~ку*** have s.th. repaired; **~я́ть** [28] → ***чинúть*** *1a*

поч|итáть[1] [1], <~тúть> [-чту́, -тúшь; -чтённый] esteem, respect, hono(u)r; ***~тúть пáмять вставáнием*** stand in s.o.'s memory; **~итáть**[2] [1] *pf.* read (a while)

пóчка *f* [5; *g/pl.*: -чек] **1.** *bot.* bud; **2.** *anat.* kidney

пóчт|а *f* [5] mail, *Brt.* post (***по*** Д by); **~альóн** *m* [1] mailman, *Brt.* postman; **~áмт** *m* [1] main post office (***на*** П at)

почтéн|ие *n* [12] respect (***к*** Д for), esteem; **~ный** [14; -éнен, -éнна] respectable; *вóзраст* venerable

почтú almost, nearly, all but; **~тельность** *f* [8] respect; **~тельный** [14; -лен, -льна] respectful; *coll.* *о расстоя́нии и т. д.* considerable; **~ть** → ***почитáть***

почтóв|ый [14] post(al), mail...; post-office; ***~ый я́щик*** mail (*Brt.* letter) box; ***~ый úндекс*** zip (*Brt.* post) code; ***~ое отделéние*** post office

пóшл|ина *f* [5] customs, duty; **~ость** [8] vulgarity; **~ый** [14; пошл, -á, -о] vulgar

поштýчный [14] by the piece

пощáда *f* [5] mercy

поэ́|зия *f* [7] poetry; **~т** *m* [1] poet; **~тúческий** [16] poetic(al)

поэ́тому therefore; and so

появ|úться → ***~ля́ться***; **~лéние** *n* [12] appearance; **~ля́ться** [28], <~úться> [14] appear; emerge

пóяс *m* [1; *pl.*: -cá, *etc. e.*] belt; zone

поясн|éние *n* [12] explanation; **~úтельный** [14] explanatory; **~úть** → ***~я́ть***; **~úца** *f* [5] small of the back; **~óй** [14] waist...; zonal; *портрéт* half-length; **~я́ть** [28], <~úть> [13] explain

прабáбушка *f* [5; *g/pl.*: -шек] great-grandmother

прáвд|а *f* [5] truth; (***э́то***) **~а** it is true; ***вáша ~а*** you are right; ***не ~а ли?*** isn't it, (s)he?, aren't you, they?, do(es)n't ... (*etc.*)?; **~úвый** [14 *sh.*] true, truthful; **~оподóбный** [14; -бен, -бна] (*вероя́тный*) likely, probable; (*похóжий на прáвду*) probable, likely

прáведн|ик *m* [1] righteous person; **~ый** [14; -ден, -дна] just, righteous, upright

прáвил|о *n* [9] rule; principle; *pl.* regulations; ***как ~о*** as a rule; ***~а ýличного движéния*** traffic regulations; **~ьный** [14; -лен, -льна] correct, right; *черты лица и т. д.* regular

правитель *m* [4] ruler; **~ственный** [14] governmental; **~ство** *n* [9] government

прáв|ить [14] (T) govern, rule; *mot.* drive; *гранки* (proof) read; **~ка** *f* [5] proofreading; **~ление** *n* [12] governing; board of directors; managing *or* governing body

прáвнук *m* [1] great-grandson

прáво[1] *n* [9; *pl. e.*] right (**на** В to; **по** Д of, by); law; ***водительские права*** driving license (*Brt.* licence); **~**[2] *adv. coll.* indeed, really; **~вóй** [14] legal; **~мóчный** [14; -чен, -чна] competent; authorized; (*оправданный*) justifiable; **~нарушитель** *m* [1] offender; **~писáние** *n* [12] orthography, spelling; **~слáвие** *n* [12] Orthodoxy; **~слáвный** [14] Orthodox; **~сýдие** *n* [12] administration of the law; **~тá** *f* [5] rightness

прáвый [14; *fig.* прав, -á, -о] right, correct (*a. fig.*; *a. side*, on *a.* **с** Р), right-hand

прáвящий [17] ruling

прáдед *m* [1] great-grandfather

прáздн|ик *m* [1] (public) holiday; (religious) feast; festival; **с ~иком!** compliments *pl.* (of the season)!; **~ичный** [14] festive, holiday...; **~ование** *n* [12] celebration; **~овать** [7], <от-> celebrate; **~ость** *f* [8] idleness; **~ый** [14; -ден, -дна] idle, inactive

прáкти|к *m* [1] practical worker *or* person; **~ка** *f* [5] practice (**на** П in); ***войти в ~ку*** become customary; **~ковáть** [7] practice (-ise); **-ся** (*v/i.*); be in use *or* used; **~ческий** [16], **~чный** [14; чен, -чна] practical

прáпорщик *m* [1] (*in tsarist army*) ensign; (*in Russian army*) warrant officer

прах *m* [1; *no pl.*] *obs. rhet.* dust; ashes *pl.* (*fig.*); ***всё пошлó ~ом*** our efforts were in vain

прáчечная *f* [14] laundry

пребывá|ние *n* [12], **~ть** [1] stay

превзойти → ***превосходить***

превоз|могáть [1], <~мóчь> [26; г/ж: -огý, -óжешь, -óгут; -óг, -глá] overcome, surmount; **~носить** [15], <~нести> [24 -с-] extol, exalt

превосх|одительство *n* [9] *hist.* Excellency; **~одить** [15], <превзойти> [-йдý, -йдёшь, *etc.*, → ***идти***; -йдённый] excel (in), surpass (in); **~óдный** [14; -ден, -дна] superb, outstanding; *кáчество* superior; superlative *a. gr.*; **~óдство** *n* [9] superiority

превра|тить(ся) → **~щáть(ся)**; **~тность** *f* [8] vicissitude; *судьбы* reverses; **~тный** [14; -тен, -тна] *невéрный* wrong, mis-...; **~щáть** [1], <~тить> [15 *e.*; -ащý, -атишь; -ащённый] change, convert, turn, transform (**в** В into) (*v/i.* **-ся**); **~щéние** *n* [12] change; transformation

превы|шáть [1], <~сить> [15] exceed; **~шéние** *n* [12] excess, exceeding

прегрá|да *f* [5] barrier; obstacle; **~ждáть** [1], <~дить> [15 *e.*; -ажý, -адишь; -аждённый] bar, block, obstruct

пред → ***пéред***

преда|вáть [5], <~ть> [-дáм, -дáшь, *etc.*, → ***дáть***; прéдал, -á, -о; -дáй(те)!; прéданный (-ан, -á, -о)] betray; ***~ть глáсности*** make public; ***~ть забвéнию*** consign to oblivion; ***~ть судý*** bring to trial; **-ся** (Д) indulge (in); devote o.s., give o.s. up (to); *отчáянию* give way to (*despair*); **~ние** *n* [12] legend; tradition; **´~нный** [14 *sh.*] devoted, faithful, true; → ***искренний***; **~тель** *m* [4] traitor; **~тельский** [16] treacherous; **~тельство** *n* [9] *pol.* betrayal, perfidy, treachery; **~ть(ся)** → ***~вáть(ся)***

предвар|ительно as a preliminary, before(hand); **~ительный** [14] preliminary; **~ять** [28], <~ить> [13] (В) forestall; anticipate; *выступлéние и т. д.* preface

предвé|стие → ***предзнаменовáние***; **~стник** *m* [1] precursor, herald; **~щáть** [1] portend, presage

предвзятый [14 *sh.*] preconceived

предвидеть [11] foresee

предвку|шáть [1], <~сить> [15] look forward (to); **~шéние** *n* [12] (pleasurable) anticipation

предводитель *m* [4] leader; *hist.*

П

marshal of the nobility; ringleader, **~ство** *n* [9] leadership
предвосх|ища́ть [1], <**~и́тить**> [15; -ищу́] anticipate, forestall
предвы́борный [14] (pre)election...
преде́л *m* [1] limit, bound(ary) (***в*** П within); ***страны́*** border; *pl.* precincts; ***положи́ть ~*** put an end (to); **~ьный** [14] maximum..., utmost, extreme
предзнаменова́|ние *n* [12] omen, augury, portent; **~ть** [7] *pf.* portend, augur, bode
предисло́вие *n* [12] preface
предл|ага́ть [1], <**~ожи́ть**> [16] offer (a p. s.th. Д/В); ***идéю и т. д.*** propose, suggest; (***веле́ть***) order
предло́|г *m* [1] pretext (on, under ***под*** Т), pretense (under); *gr.* preposition; **~же́ние** *n* [12] offer; proposal, proposition, suggestion; *parl.* motion; *comm.* supply; *gr.* sentence, clause; ***~жи́ть → предла́гать***; **~жный** [14] *gr.* prepositional (*case*)
предме́стье *n* [10] suburb
предме́т *m* [1] object; subject (matter); *comm.* article; ***на ~*** (Р) with the object of; **~ный** [14]: ***~ный указа́тель*** index
предназн|ача́ть [1], <**~а́чить**> [16] (**-ся** be) intend(ed) for, destine(d) for
преднаме́ренный [14 *sh.*] premeditated, deliberate
пре́док *m* [1; -дка] ancestor
предопредел|е́ние *n* [12] predestination; **~я́ть** [28], <**~и́ть**> [13] predetermine
предост|авля́ть [28], <**~а́вить**> [14] (Д) let (a p.) leave (to); give; ***креди́т, пра́во*** grant; ***в распоряже́ние*** place (at a p.'s disposal)
предостер|ега́ть [1], <**~е́чь**> [26; г/ж] warn (**от** Р of, against); **~еже́ние** *n* [12] warning, caution
предосторо́жност|ь *f* [8] precaution(ary measure ***ме́ра ~и***)
предосуди́тельный [14; -лен, -льна] reprehensible, blameworthy
предотвра|ща́ть [1], <**~ти́ть**> [15 *e.*; -ащу́; -ати́шь; -ащённый] avert, prevent; **~ще́ние** *n* [12] prevention
предохран|е́ние *n* [12] protection (**от** Р from, against); **~и́тельный** [14] precautionary; *med.* preventive; *tech.* safety...; **~я́ть** [28], <**~и́ть**> [13] guard, preserve (**от** Р from, against)
предпис|а́ние *n* [12] order, injunction; instructions, directions; **~ывать** [1], <**~а́ть**> [3] order, prescribe
предпол|ага́ть [1], <**~ожи́ть**> [16] suppose, assume; *impf.* (***намерева́ться***) intend, plan; (***быть усло́вием***) presuppose; **~ожи́тельный** [14; -лен,-льна] conjectural; hypothetical; ***да́та*** estimated; **~ожи́ть** → ***~ага́ть***
предпо|сла́ть → ***~сыла́ть***; **~сле́дний** [15] penultimate, last but one; **~сыла́ть** [1], <**~сла́ть**> [-шлю́, -шлёшь; → **слать**] preface (with); **~сы́лка** *f* [5; *g/pl.*: -лок] (pre)condition, prerequiste
предпоч|ита́ть [1], <**~е́сть**> [25; -т-: -чту́, -чтёшь; -чёл, -чла́; -чтённый] prefer; *pt.* + ***бы*** would rather; **~те́ние** *n* [12] preference; predilection; ***отда́ть ~те́ние*** (Д) show a preference for; give preference to; **~ти́тельный** [14; -лен, -льна] preferable
предпри|и́мчивость *f* [8] enterprise; **~и́мчивый** [14 *sh.*] enterprising; **~нима́тель** *m* [4] entrepreneur; employer; **~нима́ть** [1], <**~ня́ть**> [-иму́, -и́мешь; -и́нял, -а́, -о; -и́нятый (-и́нят, -а́, -о)] undertake; **~я́тие** *n* [12] undertaking, enterprise; ***заво́д и т. д.*** plant, works, factory (***на*** П at); ***риско́ванное ~я́тие*** risky undertaking
предраспол|ага́ть [1], <**~ожи́ть**> [16] predispose; **~оже́ние** *n* [12] predisposition (to)
предрассу́док *m* [1; -дка] prejudice
предрешённый [14; -шён, -шена́] predetermined, already decided
председа́тель *m* [4] chairman; president; **~ство** *n* [9] chairmanship; presidency; **~ствовать** [7] preside (***на*** П over), be in the chair
предсказ|а́ние *n* [12] prediction; ***пого́ды*** forecast; (***прорица́ние***) prophecy; **~ывать** [1], <**~а́ть**> [3] foretell, predict; forecast; prophesy

предсмéртный [14] occurring before death

представи́тель *m* [4] representative; → *a.* ***полпрéд***; **~ный** [14; -лен, -льна] representative; *о внéшности* stately, imposing; **~ство** *n* [9] representation; → *a.* ***полпрéдство***

представ|ить(ся) → **~ля́ть(ся)**; **~лéние** *n* [12] *книги и т. д.* presentation; *thea.* performance; *при знакóмстве* introduction; idea, notion; **~ля́ть** [28], <~ить> [14] present; **-ся** present o.s., occur, offer; (*предъявля́ть*) produce; introduce (o.s.); (*a.* **собóй**) represent, be; act (*a.* = feign **-ся** [Т]); (*esp.* **~ля́ть себé**) imagine; (*к звáнию*) propose (**к** Д for); *refl. a.* appear; seem

предст|авáть [5], <~áть> [-áну, -áнешь] appear (before); **~оя́ть**, [-óит] be in store (Д for), lie ahead; (will) have to; **~оя́щий** [17] (forth)coming

преду|беждéние *n* [12] prejudice, bias; **~гáдывать**, <~гадáть> [1] guess; foresee; **~мы́шленный** [14] → ***преднамéренный***

предупре|ди́тельный [14; -лен, -льна] preventive; *человéк* obliging; **~ждáть** [1], <~ди́ть> [15 *e.*; -ежу́, -еди́шь; -еждённый] forestall; anticipate (*p.*); (*предотвращáть*) prevent (*th.*); *об опáсности и т. д.* warn (**о** П of); *об ухóде* give notice (of); **~ждéние** *n* [12] warning; notice; notification; prevention

предусм|áтривать [1], <~отрéть> [9; -отрю́, -óтришь] foresee; (*обеспéчивать*) provide (for), stipulate; **~отри́тельный** [14; -лен, -льна] prudent, far-sighted

предчу́вств|ие *n* [12] presentiment; foreboding; **~овать** [7] have a presentiment (of)

предшéств|енник *m* [1] predecessor; **~овать** [7] (Д) precede

предъяв|и́тель *m* [4] bearer; **~ля́ть** [28], <~и́ть> [14] present, produce, show; *law* **~ля́ть иск** bring a suit *or* an action (**прóтив** Д against); **~лять прáво на** (В) raise a claim to

пре|дыду́щий [17] preceding, previous; **~éмник** *m* [1] successor

прéж|де formerly; (at) first; (P) before (*a.* **~де чем**); **~деврéменный** [14; -енен, -енна] premature, early; **~ний** [15] former, previous

презид|éнт *m* [1] president; **´~иум** *m* [1] presidium

през|ирáть [1] despise; <~рéть> [9] scorn, disdain; **~рéние** *n* [12] contempt (**к** Д for); **~рéть** → **~ирáть**; **~ри́тельный** [14; -лен, -льна] contemptuous, scornful, disdainful

преиму́ществ|енно chiefly, principally, mainly; **~о** *n* [9] advantage; preference; privilege; ***по ~у*** → ***~енно***

прейскурáнт *m* [1] price list

преклон|éние *n* [12] admiration (***пéред*** Т of); **~и́ться** → **~я́ться**; **´~ный** [14] old; advanced; **~я́ться** [28], <~и́ться> [13] revere, worship

прекослóвить [14] contradict

прекрáсный [14; -сен, -сна] beautiful; fine, splendid, excellent; ***~ пол*** the fair sex; *adv. a.* perfectly well

прекра|щáть [1], <~ти́ть> [15 *e.*; -ащу́, -ати́шь; -ащённый] stop, cease, end (*v/i.* **-ся**); (*прерывáть*) break off; **~щéние** *n* [12] cessation, discontinuance

прелéст|ный [14; -тен, -тна] lovely, charming, delightful; **´~ь** *f* [8] charm; *coll.* → **~ный**

прелом|лéние *n* [12] *phys.* refraction; *fig.* interpretation; **~ля́ть** [28], <~и́ть> [14; -млённый] (**-ся** be) refract(ed)

прéлый [14 *sh.*] rotten; musty

прель|щáть [1], <~сти́ть> [15 *e.*; -льщу́, -льсти́шь; -льщённый] (**-ся** be) charm(ed), tempt(ed), attract(ed)

прелю́дия *f* [7] prelude

преми́нуть [19] *pf.* fail (*used only with* **не** + *inf.*:) not fail to

прéмия *f* [7] prize; bonus; *страховáя* premium

премьéр *m* [1] premier, (*usu.* **~-мини́стр**) prime minister; **~а** *f* [5] *thea.* première, first night

пренебр|егáть [1], <~éчь> [26 г/ж]; **~ежéние** *n* [12] (Т) (*невнимáние*) neglect, disregard; (*презрéние*) disdain, scorn, slight; **~ежи́-**

П

тельный [14; -лен, -льна] slighting; scornful, disdainful; **~е́чь** → **~ега́ть**

пре́ния *n/pl.* [12] debate, discussion

преоблада́|ние *n* [12] predominance; **~ть** [1] prevail; *чи́сленно* predominate

преобра|жа́ть [1], <~зи́ть> [15 *e.*; -ажу́, -ази́шь, -ажённый] change, (*vi.* **-ся**); **~же́ние** *n* [12] transformation; **2же́ние** *eccl.* Transfiguration; **~зи́ть(ся)** → **~жа́ть(ся)**; **~зова́ние** *n* [12] transformation; reorganization; reform; **~зо́вывать** [1], <~зова́ть> [7] reform, reorganize; transform

преодолева́ть [1], <~е́ть> [8] overcome, surmount

препара́т *m* [1] *chem., pharm.* preparation

препира́тельство *n* [9] altercation, wrangling

преподава́|ние *n* [12] teaching, instruction; **~тель** *m* [4], **~тельница** *f* [5] teacher; lecturer; instructor; **~ть** [5] teach

преподн|оси́ть [15], <~ести́> [24 -с-] present with, make a present of; ***~ести́ сюрпри́з*** give s.o. a surprise

препрово|жда́ть [1], <~ди́ть> [15 *e.*; -ожу́, -оди́шь; -ождённый] *доку́менты* forward, send, dispatch

препя́тств|ие *n* [12] obstacle, hindrance; ***ска́чки с ~иями*** steeplechase; ***бег с ~иями*** hurdles (race); **~овать** [7], <вос-> hinder, prevent (Д/в П a p. from)

прер|ва́ть(ся) → ***~ыва́ть(ся)***; **~ека́ние** *n* [12] squabble, argument; **~ыва́ть** [1], <~ва́ть> [-ву́, -вёшь; -а́л, -а́, -о; пре́рваный (-ан, -а́, -о)] interrupt; break (off), *v/i.* **-ся**; **~ы́вистый** [14 *sh.*] broken, faltering

пересе|ка́ть [1], <~чь> [26] cut short; *попы́тки* suppress; ***~чь в ко́рне*** nip in the bud; **-ся** break; stop

пресле́дов|ание *n* [12] pursuit; (*притесне́ние*) persecution; *law* prosecution; **~ать** [7] pursue; persecute; *law* prosecute

пресловутый [14] notorious

пресмыка́|ться [1] creep, crawl; *fig.* grovel, cringe (***пе́ред*** Т to); **~ющиеся** *n/pl.* [17] reptiles

пре́сный [14; -сен, -сна́, -о] *вода́* fresh, *fig.* insipid, stale

пресс *m* [1] the press; **~а** *f* [5] the press; **~-конфере́нция** *f* [7] press conference

престаре́лый [14] aged, advanced in years

престо́л *m* [1] throne; *eccl.* altar

преступ|а́ть [1], <~и́ть> [14] break, infringe; **~ле́ние** *n* [12] crime; ***на ме́сте ~ле́ния*** red-handed; **~ник** *m* [1] criminal, offender; **~ность** *f* [8] criminality; crime

пресы|ща́ться [1], <~титься> [15], **~ще́ние** *n* [12] satiety

претвор|я́ть [28], <~и́ть> [13]: ***~я́ть в жизнь*** put into practice, realize

претен|де́нт *m* [1] claimant (to); candidate (for); *на престо́л* pretender; **~дова́ть** [7] (***на*** В) (lay) claim (to); **~зия** *f* [7] claim, pretension (***на*** В, ***к*** Д to); ***быть в ~зии*** (***на*** В [***за*** В]) have a grudge against s.o.

претерп|ева́ть [1], <~е́ть> [10] suffer, endure; (*подве́ргнуться*) undergo

преувел|иче́ние *n* [12] exaggeration; **~и́чивать** [1], <~и́чить> [16] exaggerate

преусп|ева́ть [1], <~е́ть> [8] succeed; (*процвета́ть*) thrive, prosper

при (П) by, at, near; (*би́тва*) of; under, in the time of; in a p.'s possession: by, with, on; about (one **~ *себе́***), with; in (*пого́де и т. д.*); for (all that ***~ всём том***); when, on (-ing); ***~ э́том*** at that; ***быть ни ~ чём*** *coll.* have nothing to do with (it ***тут***), not be a p.'s fault

приба́в|ить(ся) → ***~ля́ть(ся)***; **~ка** [5; *g/pl.*: -вок], **~ле́ние** *n* [12] augmentation, supplement; *семе́йства* addition; **~ля́ть** [28], <~ить> [14] (В *or* Р) add; augment; put on (*weight* **в** П); ***~ля́ть ша́гу*** quicken one's steps; **-ся** increase; be added; (a)rise; grow longer; **~очный** [14] additional; *сто́имость* surplus...

прибалти́йский [16] Baltic

прибе|га́ть [1] **1.** <~жа́ть> [4; -егу́, -ежи́шь, -егу́т] come running; **2.**

<~гнуть> [20] resort, have recourse (**к** Д to); **~регáть** [1], <~рéчь> [26 г/ж] save up, reserve

приби|вáть [1], <~ть> [-бью́, -бьёшь, *etc.*, → **бить**] nail; *пыль и т. д.* lay, flatten; *к бéрегу* throw *or* wash ashore (*mst. impers.*); **~рáть** [1], <прибрáть> [-берý, -рёшь; -брáл -á, -о; прúбранный] tidy *or* clean (up); ***прибрáть к рукáм*** lay one's hands on s.th.; take s.o. in hand; **~ть** → ***~вáть***

прибли|жáть [1], <~зить> [15] approach, draw near (**к** Д; *v/i.* **-ся**); *событие* hasten; *о величúнах* approximate; **~жéние** *n* [12] approach(ing); approximation; **~зúтельный** [14; -лен, -льна] approximate; **~зить(ся)** → ***~жáть*** (***-ся***)

прибóй *m* [3] surf

прибóр *m* [1] apparatus; instrument

прибрáть → ***прибирáть***

прибрéжный [14] coastal, littoral

прибы|вáть [1], <~ть> [-бýду, -дешь; прúбыл, -á, -о] arrive (**в** В in, at); *о водé* rise; **´~ль** *f* [8] profit, gains *pl.*; **´~льный** [14; -лен, -льна] profitable; **~тие** *n* [12] arrival (**в** В in, at; **по** П upon); **~ть** → ***~вáть***

привáл *m* [1] halt, rest

привезтú → ***привозúть***

приверéдливый [14 *sh.*] fastidious; squeamish

привéржен|ец *m* [1; -нца] adherent; **~ность** *f* [8] devotion; **~ный** [14 *sh.*] devoted

привестú → ***приводúть***

привéт *m* [1] greeting(s); regards, compliments *pl.*; *coll.* hello!, hi!; **~ливый** [14 *sh.*] affable; **~ственный** [14] salutatory, welcoming; **~ствие** *n* [12] greeting, welcome; **~ствовать** [7; *pt. a. pf.*] greet, salute; (*одобрять*) welcome

приви|вáть [1], <~ть> [-вью́, -вьёшь, *etc.*, → **вить**] inoculate, vaccinate; *bot.* graft; *привы́чки и т. д. fig.* cultivate, inculcate; **-ся** take; **~вка** *f* [5; *g/pl.*: -вок] inoculation, vaccination; grafting; **~дéние** *n* [12] ghost; **~легирóванный** [14] privileged; *áкции* preferred; **~лéгия** *f* [7] privilege; **~нчивать** [1], <~нтúть> [15 *e.*; -нчý, -нтúшь] screw on; **~ть(ся)** → ***~вáть***(***ся***)

прúвкус *m* [1] aftertaste; smack (of) (*a. fig.*)

привле|кáтельный [14; -лен, -льна] attractive; **~кáть** [1],<~чь> [26] draw, attract; *к рабóте* recruit (**к** Д in); call (*к отвéтственности* to account); bring (*к судý* to trial)

прúвод *m* [1] *tech.* drive, driving gear; **~úть** [15], <привестú> [25] bring; lead; result (**к** Д in); (*цитúровать*) adduce, cite; *math.* reduce; *в порядок* put, set; *в отчáяние* drive; **~нóй** [14] driving (*ремéнь и т. д. belt, etc.*)

привоз|úть [15], <привезтú> [24] bring (*other than on foot*); import; **~нóй** [14] imported

привóлье *n* [10] open space, vast expanse; freedom

привы|кáть [1], <~кнуть> [21] get *or* be(come) accustomed *or* used (**к** Д to); **~чка** *f* [5; *g/pl.*: -чек] habit; custom; **~чный** [14; -чен, -чна] habitual, usual

привя́з|анность *f* [8] attachment (to); **~áть(ся)** → ***~ывать***(***ся***); **~чивый** [14 *sh.*] *coll.* affectionate; (*надоéдливый*) obtrusive; **~ывать** [1], <~áть> [3] (**к** Д) tie, attach (to); **-ся** become attached; *coll.* pester; **´~ь** [8] leash, tether

пригла|сúтельный [14] invitation...; **~шáть** [1], <~сúть> [15 *e.*; -ашý, -асúшь; -ашённый] invite (to *mst* **на** В), ask; *врачá* call; **~шéние** *n* [12] invitation

пригнáть → ***пригонять***

пригов|áривать [1], <~орúть> [13] sentence; condemn; *impf. coll.* keep saying; **~óр** *m* [1] sentence; verdict (*a. fig.*); **~орúть** → ***~áривать***

пригóдный [14; -ден, -дна] → ***гóдный***

пригоня́ть [28], <пригнáть> [-гоню́, -гóнишь; -гнáл, -á, -о; прúгнанный] fit, adjust

пригор|áть [1], <~éть> [9] be burnt; **´~од** *m* [1] suburb; **´~одный** [14] suburban; *пóезд и т. д.* local; **´~шня** *f* [6; *g/pl.*: -ней & -шен] hand(ful)

пригот|а́вливать(ся) [1] → **~овля́ть(ся)**; **~о́вить(ся)** → **~овля́ть(ся)**; **~овле́ние** *n* [12] preparation (**к** Д for); **~овля́ть** [28], <**~о́вить**> [14] prepare; **-ся** (*v/i.*) prepare o.s. (**к** Д for)

прида|ва́ть [5], <**~́ть**> [-да́м, -да́шь, *etc.*, → **дать**; при́дал, -а́, -о; при́данный (-ан, -а́, -о)] add; give; *значе́ние* attach; **~́ное** *n* [14] dowry; **~́точный** [14] supplementary; *gr.* subordinate (*clause*); **~́ть** → **~ва́ть**; **~́ча** *f* [5]: **в ~́чу** in addition

придви|га́ть [1], <**~́нуть**> [20] move up (*v/i.* **-ся**; draw near)

придво́рный [14] court (*of a sovereign or similar dignitary*); courtier (*su. m*)

приде́л|ывать, <**~ать**> [1] fasten, fix (**к** Д to)

приде́рж|ивать [1], <**~а́ть**> [4] hold (back); **-ся** *impf.* (Р) hold, adhere (to)

придир|а́ться [1], <придра́ться> [-деру́сь, -рёшься; -дра́лся, -ла́сь, -а́лось] (**к** Д) find fault (with), carp *or* cavil (at); **~ка** *f* [5; *g/pl.*: -рок] faultfinding, carping; **~́чивый** [14 *sh.*] captious, faultfinding

придира́ться → **придра́ться**

приду́м|ывать, <**~ать**> [1] think up, devise, invent

прие́з|д *m* [1] arrival (**в** В in); **по ~е** on arrival (in, at); **~жа́ть** [1], <прие́хать> [-е́ду, -е́дешь] arrive (*other than on foot* **в** В in, at); **~жий** [17] newly arrived; guest...

приём *m* [1] reception; *в университе́т и т. д.* admission; *лека́рства* taking; (*спо́соб де́йствия*) way, mode; device, trick; method; **в оди́н ~** at one go; **~́лемый** [14 *sh.*] acceptable; *допусти́мый* admissible; **~ная** *f* [14] *su.* reception room; waiting room; **~ник** *m* [1] *tech.* receiver; *для дете́й* reception center, *Brt.* -tre; → **радиоприёмник**; **~ный** *часы́* office; *экза́мен* entrance; *оте́ц, сын* foster

при|е́хать → **~езжа́ть**; **~жа́ть(ся)** → **~жима́ть(ся)**; **~жига́ть** [1], <**~же́чь**> [26 г/ж: -жгу́, -жжёшь, → **жечь**] cauterize; **~жима́ть** [1], <**~жа́ть**> [-жму́, -жмёшь; -а́тый] press, clasp (**к** Д to, on); **-ся** press o.s. (to, against); nestle, cuddle up (to); **~жи́мистый** [14 *sh.*] tightfisted, stingy; **~з** *m* [1] prize

призва́|ние *n* [12] vocation, calling; **~ть** → **призыва́ть**

приземл|я́ться [28], <**~и́ться**> [13] *ae.* land; **~е́ние** *n* [12] landing, touchdown

призёр *m* [1] prizewinner

при́зма *f* [5] prism

призна|ва́ть [5], <**~́ть**> [1] (Т; *a.* **за** В) recognize, acknowledge (as); (*сознава́ть*) see, admit, own; (*счита́ть*) find, consider; **-ся** confess (**в** П s.th.), admit; **~́ться** *or* **~ю́сь** tell the truth, frankly speaking; **´~к** *m* [1] sign; indication; **~́ние** *n* [12] acknowledg(e)ment, recognition; **~́ние в преступле́нии** confession; declaration (**в любви́** of love); **~́тельность** *f* [8] gratitude; **~́тельный** [14; -лен, -льна] grateful, thankful (for **за** В); **~́ть(ся)** → **~ва́ть(ся)**

при́зра|к *m* [1] phantom, specter (*Brt.* -tre); **~чный** [14; -чен, -чна] spectral, ghostly; *наде́жда* illusory

призы́в *m* [1] appeal, call (**на** В for); *mil.* draft, conscription; **~а́ть** [1], <призва́ть> [-зову́, -вёшь; -зва́л, -а́, -о; при́званный] call, move dawn appeal (**на** В for); *mil.* draft, call up (**на** В for); **~ни́к** *m* [1 *e.*] draftee, conscript; **~но́й** [14]: **~но́й во́зраст** call-up age

при́иск *m* [1] mine (*for precious metals*); **золото́й ~** gold field

прийти́(сь) → **приходи́ть(ся)**

прика́з *m* [1] order, command; **~а́ть** → **~ывать**; **~ывать** [1], <**~а́ть**> [3] order, command; give orders

при|ка́лывать [1], <коло́ть> [17] pin, fasten; **~каса́ться** [1], <косну́ться> [20] (**к** Д) touch (lightly); **~ки́дывать**, <**~ки́нуть**> [20] weigh; estimate (approximately); **~ки́нуть в уме́** *fig.* ponder, weigh up; **-ся** pretend *or* feign to be, act (the Т)

прикла́д *m* [1] *винто́вки* butt

приклад|но́й [14] applied; **~́ывать** [1], <приложи́ть> [16] (**к** Д) apply (to), put (on); *к письму и т. д.* enclose (with); *печа́ть* affix a seal

прикле́и|вать [1], <~ть> [13] paste

приключ|а́ться *coll.* [1], <~и́ться> [16 *e.*; 3rd *p. only*] happen, occur; **~е́ние** *n* [12] (**~е́нческий** [16] of) adventure(...)

прико́|вывать [1], <~ва́ть> [7 *e.*; -кую́, -куёшь] chain; *внима́ние и т. д.* arrest; **~ла́чивать** [1], <~лоти́ть> [15] nail (on, to ***к***), fasten with nails; **~ло́ть** → ***прика́лывать***; **~мандирова́ть** [7] *pf.* attach; **~снове́ние** *n* [12] touch, contact; **~сну́ться** → ***прикаса́ться***

прикра́с|а *f* [5] *coll.* embellishment; ***без ~*** unvarnished

прикреп|и́ть(ся) → **~ля́ть(ся)**; **~ля́ть** [28], <~и́ть> [14 *e.*; -плю́, -пи́шь; -плённый] fasten; attach; **-ся** register (at, with ***к*** Д)

прикри́к|ивать [1], <~нуть> [20] shout (at ***на*** В)

прикры|ва́ть [1], <~ть> [22] cover; (*защища́ть*) protect; **~тие** *n* [12] cover, escort (*a. mil*); *fig.* cloak

прила́вок *m* [1; -вка] (*shop*) counter

прилага́|тельное *n* [14] *gr.* adjective (*a.* ***и́мя ~тельное***); **~ть** [1], <приложи́ть> [16] (***к*** Д) enclose; apply (to); *уси́лия* take, make (*efforts*); **~емый** enclosed

прила́|живать [1], <~дить> [15] fit to, adjust to

приле|га́ть [1] **1.** (***к*** Д) (ad)join, border; **2.** <~чь> [26 г/ж: -ля́гу, -ля́жешь, -ля́гут; -лёг, легла́, -ля́г(те)!] lie down (for a while); **3.** *об оде́жде* fit (closely); **~жа́ние** *n* [12] diligence; **~жный** [14; -жен, -жна] industrious; **~пля́ть** [28], <~пи́ть> [14] stick to; **~та́ть** [1], <~те́ть> [11] arrive by air, fly in; **~чь** → ***~га́ть 2***

прили́|в *m* [1] flood, flow; *fig. кро́ви* rush; ***~в эне́ргии*** surge of energy; **~ва́ть** [1], <~ть> [-лью́, -льёшь; → ***лить***] flow to; rush to; **~па́ть** [1], <~пнуть> [21] stick; **~ть** → ***~ва́ть***

прили́ч|ие *n* [12] decency, decorum; **~ный** [14; -чен, -чна] decent, proper; *coll. су́мма и т. д.* decent, fair

прилож|е́ние *n* [12] enclosure (*document with a letter etc.*); *журна́льное* supplement; *сил и т. д.* application (putting to use); *в кни́ге* appendix, addendum; *gr.* apposition; **~и́ть** → ***прикла́дывать*** & ***прилага́ть***

прима́нка *f* [5; *g/pl.*: -нок] bait, lure; (*fig.*) enticement

примен|е́ние *n* [12] application; use; **~и́мый** [14 *sh.*] applicable; **~и́тельно** in conformity with; **~я́ть** [28], <~и́ть> [13; -еню́, -е́нишь; -енённый] apply (***к*** Д to); use, employ

приме́р *m* [1] example; ***привести́ в ~*** cite as an example; ***не в ~*** *coll.* unlike; ***к ~у*** *coll.* → ***наприме́р***; **~ивать** [1], <~ить> [13] try on; fit; **~ка** *f* [5; *g/pl.*: -рок] trying on; fitting; **~ный** [14; -рен, -рна] exemplary; (*приблизи́тельный*) approximate; **~я́ть** [28] → **~ивать**

при́месь *f* [8] admixture; *fig.* touch

приме́|та *f* [5] mark, sign; *дурна́я* omen; ***на ~те*** in view; **~тный** → ***заме́тный***; **~ча́ние** *n* [12] (foot)note; **~ча́тельный** [14; -лен, -льна] notable, remarkable

примир|е́ние *n* [12] reconciliation; **~и́тельный** [14; -лен, -льна] conciliatory; **~я́ть(ся)** [28] → ***мири́ть(ся)***

примити́вный [14; -вен, -вна] primitive, crude

прим|кну́ть → **~ыка́ть**; **~о́рский** [16] coastal, seaside...; **~о́чка** *f* [5; *g/pl.*: -чек] lotion; **~у́ла** *f* [5] primrose; **~ус** *m* [1] *trademark* Primus (stove); **~ча́ться** [4 *e.*; -мчу́сь, -чи́шься] *pf.* come in a great hurry; **~ыка́ть** [1], <~кну́ть> [20] join (*v/t.* ***к*** Д); *о зда́нии и т. д. impf.* adjoin

принадл|ежа́ть [4 *e.*; -жу́, -жи́шь] belong ([***к***] Д to); **~е́жность** *f* [8] belonging (***к*** Р to); *pl.* accessories

принести́ → ***приноси́ть***

принима́ть [1], <приня́ть> [приму́, -и́мешь; при́нял, -а́, -о; при́нятый (-ят, а́, -о)] take (*a.* over; ***за*** В for; *measures*); *предложе́ние* accept; *госте́й* receive; *в шко́лу и т. д.* admit (***в, на*** В [in] to); *зако́н и т. д.* pass, adopt; *обя́занности* assume;

~ на себя́ take (up)on o.s., undertake; *~ на свой счёт* take as referring to o.s.; **-ся** [-ня́лся́, -ла́сь] (**за** В) start, begin; set to, get down to; *coll.* take in hand; *bot.*, *med.* take effect (injections)
приноровиться [14 *e.*; -влю́сь, -ви́шься] *pf. coll.* adapt o.s. to
прин|оси́ть [15], <~ести́> [24 -с-: -есу́; -ёс, -есла́] bring (*a.* forth, in), *плоды́* yield; make (sacrifice **в** В); *~оси́ть по́льзу* be of use *or* of benefit
прину|ди́тельный [14; -лен, -льна] forced, compulsory, coercive; **~жда́ть** [1], <~ди́ть> [15] force, compel, constrain; **~жде́ние** *n* [12] compulsion, coercion, constraint (**по** Д under)
при́нцип *m* [1] principle; *в ~е* in principle; *из ~а* on principle; **~иа́льный** [14; -лен, -льна] of principle; guided by principle
приня́|тие *n* [12] taking, taking up; acceptance; admission (**в, на** В to); *зако́на и т. д.* passing, adoption; **´~тый** [14] customary; **~ть(ся)** → *принима́ть(ся)*
приобре|та́ть [1], <~сти́> [25 -т-] acquire, obtain, get; buy; **~те́ние** *n* [12] acquisition
приоб|ща́ть [1], <~и́ть> [16 *e.*; -щу́, -щи́шь; -щённый] (**к** Д) *докуме́нт* file; introduce (to); **-ся** join (in); consort with
приостан|а́вливать [1], <~ови́ть> [14] call a halt to (*v/i.* **-ся**); *law* suspend
припа́док *m* [1; -дка] fit, attack
припа́сы *m/pl.* [1] supplies, stores; *съестны́е ~* provisions
припая́ть [28] *pf.* solder (**к** Д to)
припе́|в *m* [1] refrain; **~ка́ть** [1], <~чь> [26] *coll.* (*of the sun*) burn, be hot
припи́с|ка *f* [5; *g/pl.*: -сок] postscript; addition; **~ывать** [1], <~а́ть> [3] ascribe, attribute (**к** Д to)
припла́та *f* [5] extra payment
припло́д *m* [1] increase (*in number of animals*)
приплы|ва́ть [1], <~ть> [23] swim; sail (**к** Д up to)
приплю́снутый [14] flat (*nose*)
приподн|има́ть [1], <~я́ть> [-ниму́, -ни́мешь; -по́днял, -а́, -о; -по́днятый (-ят, -а́, -о)] lift *or* raise (**-ся** rise) (a little); **~я́тый** [14] *настрое́ние* elated; animated
приполз|а́ть [1], <~ти́> [24] creep up, in
припом|ина́ть [1], <~нить> [13] remember, recollect; *он тебе́ э́то ~нит* he'll get even with you for this
припра́в|а *f* [5] seasoning; dressing; **~ля́ть** [28], <~ить> [14] season; dress
припух|а́ть [1], <~нуть> [21] swell (a little)
прира|ба́тывать [1], <~бо́тать> [1] earn in addition
припра́вн|ивать [1], <~я́ть> [28] equate (with); place on the same footing (as)
прира|ста́ть [1], <~сти́> [24 -ст-: -стёт; -ро́с, -сла́] take; grow (**к** Д to); increase (**на** В by); **~ще́ние** *n* [12] increment
приро́|да *f* [5] nature; **от ~ды** by nature, congenitally; **по ~де** by nature, naturally; **~дный** [14] natural; *a.* = **~ждённый** [14] (in)born, innate; **~ст** *m* [1] increase, growth
прируч|а́ть [1], <~и́ть> [16 *e.*; -чу́, -чи́шь; -чённый] tame
при|са́живаться [1], <~се́сть> [25; -ся́ду; -се́л] sit down (for a while), take a seat
присв|а́ивать [1], <~о́ить> [13] appropriate; *сте́пень и т. д.* confer ([up] on Д); *~о́ить зва́ние* promote to the rank (of); *~о́ить и́мя* name; **~о́ение** *n* [12] appropriation
присе|да́ть [1], <~сть> [25; -ся́ду, -се́л] sit down; squat; **~ст** *m* [1]: *в оди́н ~ст* at one sitting; **~сть** → *~да́ть* & *приса́живаться*
приско́рб|ие *n* [12] sorrow; regret; **~ный** [14; -бен, -бна] regrettable, deplorable
присла́ть → *присыла́ть*
прислон|я́ть [28], <~и́ть> [13] lean (*v/i.* **-ся**; **к** Д against)
прислу́|га [5] maid; servant; **~жива́ть** [1] wait (up)on (Д), serve;

~шиваться, <~шаться> [1] listen, pay attention (**к** Д to)

присм|а́тривать [1], <~отре́ть> [9; -отрю́, -о́тришь; -о́тренный] look after (**за** Т); *coll. но́вый дом и т. д.* find; **-ся** (**к** Д) peer, look narrowly (at); examine (closely); *к кому́-л.* size s.o. up; *к рабо́те и т. д.* familiarize o.s., get acquainted (with); **~о́тр** *m* [1] care, supervision; surveillance; **~отре́ть(ся)** → ***~а́тривать(ся)***

присоедин|е́ние *n* [12] addition; *pol.* annexation; **~я́ть** [28], <~и́ть> [13] (**к** Д) join (*a.* **-ся**); connect, attach (to); annex, incorporate

приспосо́б|ить(ся) → ***~ля́ть(ся)***; **~ле́ние** *n* [12] adaptation; (*устро́йство*) device; **~ля́ть** [28], <~ить> [14] fit, adapt (**-ся** o.s.; **к** Д, **под** В to, for)

приста|ва́ть [5], <~ть> [-а́ну, -а́нешь] (**к** Д) stick (to); *к кому́-л.* bother, pester; *о ло́дке* put in; *о су́дне* tie up; **~вить** → ***~вля́ть***; **~вка** *f* [5; *g/pl.*: -вок] *gr.* prefix; **~вля́ть** [28], <~вить> [14] (**к** Д) set, put (to), lean (against); (*приде́лать*) add on; **~льный** [14; -лен, -льна] steadfast, intent; **~нь** *f* [8; *from g/pl. e.*] landing stage; quay, wharf, pier; **~ть** → ***~ва́ть***

пристёгивать [1], <пристегну́ть> [20] button (up), fasten

пристр|а́ивать [1], <~о́ить> [13] (**к** Д) add *or* attach (to); settle; place; provide; **-ся** *coll.* → ***устра́иваться***; join

пристра́ст|ие *n* [12] predilection, weakness (**к** Д for); bias; **~ный** [14; -тен, -тна] bias(s)ed, partial (**к** Д to)

пристре́ли|вать [1], <~ть> [13; -стрелю́, -е́лишь] shoot (down)

пристр|о́ить(ся) → ***~а́ивать(ся)***; **~о́йка** *f* [5; *g/pl.*: -о́ек] annex(e); out-house

при́ступ *m* [1] *mil.* assault, onslaught, storm (by Т); *med. fig.* fit, attack; *бо́ли* pang; *боле́зни* bout; **~а́ть** [1], <~и́ть> [14] set about, start, begin

прису|жда́ть [1], <~ди́ть> [15; -уждённый] (**к** Д) *law* sentence to; condemn to; *приз и т. д.* award; **~жде́ние** *n* [12] awarding; adjudication

прису́тств|ие *n* [12] presence (in **в** П; of mind **ду́ха**); **~овать** [7] be present (**на**, **в**, **при** П at); **~ующий** [17] present

прису́щий [17 *sh.*] inherent (in Д)

прис|ыла́ть [1], <~ла́ть> [-шлю́, -шлёшь; при́сланный] send (**за** Т for)

прися́|га *f* [5] oath (**под** Т on); **~га́ть** [1], <~гну́ть> [20] swear (to); **~жный** [14] juror; **суд *~жных*** jury; *coll.* born, inveterate

прита|и́ться [13] *pf.* hide; keep quiet; **~скивать** [1], <~щи́ть> [16] drag, haul (**-ся** *coll.* o.s.; **к** Д [up] to); *coll.* bring (come)

притвор|и́ть(ся) → ***~я́ть(ся)***; **~ный** [14; -рен, -рна] feigned, pretended, sham; **~ство** *n* [9] pretense, -nce; **~я́ть** [28], <~и́ть> [13; -орю́, -о́ришь; -о́ренный] leave ajar; **-ся** [13] feign, pretend (to be Т); be ajar

притесн|е́ние *n* [12] oppression; **~и́тель** *m* [4] oppressor; **~я́ть** [28], <~и́ть> [13] oppress

притих|а́ть [1], <~нуть> [21] become silent, grow quiet; *ве́тер* abate

прито́к *m* [1] tributary; influx (*a. fig.*)

прито́м (and) besides

прито́н *m* [1] den

при́торный [14; -рен, -рна] too sweet, cloying (*a. fig.*)

притр|а́гиваться [1], <~о́нуться> [20] touch (*v/t.* **к** Д)

притуп|ля́ть [28], <~и́ть> [14] (**-ся** become) blunt; *fig.* dull

при́тча *f* [5] parable

притя́|гивать [1], <~ну́ть> [19] drag, pull; *о магни́те* attract; *coll.* → ***привлека́ть***; **~жа́тельный** [14] *gr.* possessive; **~же́ние** *n* [12] (*phys.*) attraction; **~за́ние** *n* [12] claim, pretension (**на** В to); **~ну́ть** → ***~гивать***

приу|ро́чить [16] *pf.* time, date (for *or* to coincide with **к** Д); **~са́дебный** [14]: ***~са́дебный уча́сток*** plot adjoining the (farm)house;

П

~ча́ть [1], <~чи́ть> [16] accustom; train

при|хва́рывать *coll.* [1], <~хвор-ну́ть> [20] be(come *pf.*) unwell

прихо́д *m* [1] **1.** arrival, coming; **2.** *comm.* receipt(s); **3.** *eccl.* parish; **~и́ть** [15], <прийти́> [приду́, -дёшь; пришёл, -шла́, -ше́дший; *g. pt.*: придя́] come (to), arrive (***в***, ***на*** В in, at, ***за*** Т for); ***~и́ть в упа́док*** fall into decay; ***~и́ть в я́рость*** fly into a rage; ***~и́ть в го́лову, на ум***, *etc.* think of, cross one's mind, take into one's head; ***~и́ть в себя́*** (*or* ***чу́вство***) come to (o.s.); **-ся** *ро́дственником* be; *пра́здник* fall (***в*** В on, ***на*** В to); ***мне ~и́тся*** I have to, must; **~ский** [16] parish...

прихож|а́нин *m* [1; *pl.* -а́не, -а́н] parishioner; **~ая** *f* [17] → ***пере́дняя***

прихот|ли́вый [14 *sh.*] *узо́р* fanciful; **´~ь** *f* [8] whim

прихра́мывать [1] limp slightly

прице́л *m* [1] sight; **~иваться** [1], <~иться> [13] (take) aim (at ***в*** В)

прице́п *m* [1] trailer; **~ля́ть** [28], <~и́ть> [14] hook on (***к*** Д to); couple; **-ся** stick, cling; → *a.* ***прис-та́(ва́)ть***

прича́л *m* [1] mooring; **~ивать** [1], <~ить> [13] moor

прича́|стие *n* [12] *gr.* participle; *eccl.* Communion; the Eucharist; **~стный** [14; -тен, -тна] participating *or* involved (***к*** Д in); **~ща́ть** [1], <~сти́ть> [15 *e.*; -ащу́, -асти́шь; -ащённый] administer (**-ся** receive) Communion; **~ще́ние** *n* [12] receiving Communion

причём moreover; in spite of the fact that; while

причёс|ка *f* [5; *g/pl.*: -сок] haircut; hairdo, coiffure; **~ывать** [1], <при-чеса́ть> [3] do, brush, comb (**-ся** one's hair)

причи́н|а *f* [5] cause; reason (***по*** Д for); ***по ~е*** because of; ***по той и́ли ино́й ~е*** for some reason or other; **~я́ть** [28], <~и́ть> [13] cause, do

причи|сля́ть [28], <~сли́ть> [13] rank, number (***к*** Д among); **~та́ние** *n* [12] (ritual) lamentation; **~та́ть** [1] lament; **~та́ться** [1] be due, (p.: **с** Р) have to pay

причу́д|а *f* [5] whim, caprice; *ха-ра́ктера* oddity; **~ливый** [14 *sh.*] odd; quaint; *coll.* whimsical, fanciful

при|ше́лец *m* [1; -льца] newcomer, stranger; a being from space; **~ши́б-ленный** *coll.* [14] dejected; **~ши-ва́ть** [1], <~ши́ть> [-шью́, -шьёшь, *etc.* → ***шить***] (***к*** Д) sew ([on] to); **~щемля́ть** [28], <~щеми́ть> [14 *e.*; -млю́, ми́шь; -млённый] pinch, squeeze; **~ще́пка** *f* [5; *g/pl.*: -пок] clothes-peg; **~щу́ривать** [1], <~щу́рить> [13] → ***жму́рить***

прию́т *m* [1] refuge, shelter; **~и́ть** [15 *e.*; -ючу́, -юти́шь] *pf.* give shelter (*v/i.* **-ся**)

прия́|тель *m* [4], **~тельница** *f* [5] friend; **~тельский** [16] friendly; **~тный** [14; -тен, -тна] pleasant, pleasing, agreeable

про *coll.* (В) about, for, of; **~ себя́** to o.s., (*read*) silently

про́ба *f* [5] *для ана́лиза* sample; *о зо́лоте* standard; *на изде́лии* hallmark

пробе́|г *m* [1] *sport* run, race; **~га́ть** [1], <~жа́ть> [4 *e.*; -егу́, -ежи́шь, -гу́т] run (through, over), pass (by); *расстоя́ние* cover; *глаза́ми* skim

пробе́л *m* [1] blank, gap (*a. fig.*)

проби|ва́ть [1], <~ть> [-бью́, -бьёшь; -бе́й(те)!; проби́л, -а, -о] break through; pierce, punch; **-ся** fight (*or* make) one's way (***сквозь*** В through); *bot.* come up; *со́лнце* shine through; **~ра́ть** [1], <про-бра́ть> [-беру́, -рёшь, → ***брать***] *coll.* scold; *до косте́й* chill (*to the bone*); **-ся** [-бра́лся, -ла́сь, -ло́сь] force one's way (***сквозь*** В through); steal, slip; **~рка** *f* [5; *g/pl.*: -рок] test tube; **~ть(ся)** → **~ва́ть(ся)**

про́бк|а *f* [5; *g/pl.*: -бок] cork (*material of bottle*); stopper, plug; *el.* fuse; *fig.* traffic jam; **~овый** [14] cork...

пробле́ма [5] problem; **~ти́чный** [14; -чен, -чна] problematic(al)

про́блеск *m* [1] gleam; flash; **~ *наде́жды*** ray of hope

про́б|ный [14] trial..., test...; ***эк-земпля́р*** specimen..., sample...; ***~ный ка́мень*** touchstone (a. *fig.*);

~овать [7], <по-> try; *на вкус* taste

пробо́ина *f* [5] hole; *naut.* leak

пробо́р *m* [1] parting (*of the hair*)

пробра́ться → ***пробира́ть*(ся)**

пробу|жда́ть [1], <~ди́ть> [15; -уждённый] waken, rouse; **-ся** awake, wake up; **~жде́ние** *n* [12] awakening

пробы́ть [-бу́ду, -бу́дешь; про́был, -а́, -о] *pf.* stay

прова́л *m* [1] collapse; *fig.* failure; **~ивать** [1], <~и́ть> [13; -алю́, -а́лишь; -а́ленный] *на экза́мене* fail; **~ива́й(те)!** *coll.* beat it!; **-ся**; collapse, fall in; fail, flunk; (*исче́знуть*) *coll.* disappear, vanish

прове́|дать *coll.* [1] *pf.* visit; (*узна́ть*) find out; **~де́ние** *n* [12] carrying out, implementation; **~зти́** → ***провози́ть***; **~рить** → ***~ря́ть***; **~рка** [5; *g/pl.*: -рок] inspection, check(up), examination, control; **~ря́ть** [28], <~рить> [13] inspect, examine, check (up on), control; **~сти́** → ***проводи́ть***; **~тривать** [1], <~трить> [13] air, ventilate

прови|ни́ться [13] *pf.* commit an offense (-nce), be guilty (***в*** П of), offend (***пе́ред*** Т р.; ***в*** П with); **~нциа́льный** [14; -лен, -льна] *mst. fig.* provincial; **~нция** *f* [7] province(s)

про́во|д *m* [1; *pl.*: -да́, *etc. e.*] wire, line; *el.* lead; **~ди́мость** *f* [8] conductivity; **~ди́ть** [15] **1.** <провести́> [25] lead, *a. el. impf.* conduct, guide; (*осуществля́ть*) carry out (*or* through), realize, put (*into practice*); put *or* get through; pass; spend (*вре́мя*; ***за*** Т at); *ли́нию и т. д.* draw; *водопрово́д и т. д.* lay; *поли́тику* pursue; *собра́ние* hold; *coll.* trick, cheat; **2.** → ***~жа́ть***; **~дка** *f* [5; *g/pl.*: -док] installation; *el.* wiring; *tel.* line, wire(s); **~дни́к** *m* [1 *e.*] guide; *rail.*, *el.* conductor (*Brt. rail.* guard); **~жа́ть** [1], <~ди́ть> [15] see (off), accompany; *глаза́ми* follow with one's eyes; **~з** *m* [1] conveyance; transport(ation)

провозгла|ша́ть [1], <~си́ть> [15 *e.*; -ашу́, -аси́шь; -ашённый] proclaim; *тост* propose

провози́ть [15], <провезти́> [24] convey, transport, bring (with one)

провока́|тор *m* [1] agent provocateur; instigator; **~ция** *f* [7] provocation

про́вол|ока *f* [5] wire; **~о́чка** *coll. f* [5; *g/pl.*: -чек] delay (**с** Т in), protraction

прово́р|ный [14; -рен, -рна] quick, nimble, deft; **~ство** *n* [9] quickness, nimbleness, deftness

провоци́ровать [7] (*im*)*pf.*, *a.* <с-> provoke (***на*** В to)

прогада́ть [1] *pf. coll.* miscalculate (***на*** П by)

прога́лина *f* [5] glade

прогл|а́тывать [1], <~оти́ть> [15] swallow, gulp; *coll.* ***~а́тывать язы́к*** lose one's tongue; **~я́дывать** [1] **1.** <~яде́ть> [11] overlook; (*просма́тривать*) look over (*or* through); **2.** <~яну́ть> [19] peep out, appear

прогн|а́ть → ***прогоня́ть***; **~о́з** *m* [1] (***пого́ды***) (weather) forecast; *med.* prognosis

прого|ва́ривать [1], <~вори́ть> [13] say; talk; **-ся** blab (out) (*v/t.* **о** П); **~лода́ться** [1] *pf.* get *or* feel hungry; **~ня́ть** [28], <прогна́ть> [-гоню́, -го́нишь; -гна́л, -а́, -о; про́гнанный] drive (away); *coll. рабо́ты* fire; **~ра́ть** [1], <~ре́ть> [9] burn through; *coll.* (*обанкро́титься*) go bust

прого́рклый [14] rancid

програ́мм|а *f* [5] program(me *Brt.*); **~и́ровать** [1] program(me); **~и́ст** *m* [1] (computer) program(m)er

прогре́сс *m* [1] progress; **~и́вный** [14; -вен, -вна] progressive; **~и́ровать** [7] (make) progress; *о боле́зни* get progressively worse

прогрыз|а́ть [1], <~ть> [24; *pt. st.*] gnaw *or* bite through

прогу́л *m* [1] truancy; absence from work; **~ивать** [1], <~я́ть> [28] shirk (work); play truant; **-ся** take (*or* go for a) walk; **~ка** *f* [5; *g/pl.*: -лок] walk (***на*** В for), stroll, *верхо́м* ride; **~ьщик** *m* [1] shirker; truant; **~я́ть(ся)** → ***~ивать*(ся)**

прода|ва́ть [5], <~ть> [-да́м, -да́шь, *etc.*, → ***дать***; про́дал, -а́, -о; про́данный (про́дан, -а́, -о)] sell;

-ся (*v/i.*); *a.* be for *or* on sale; **~ве́ц** *m* [1; -вца́], **~вщи́ца** *f* [5] seller, sales(wo)man, (store) clerk, *Brt.* shop assistant; **˜жа** *f* [5] sale (**в** П on; **в** В for); **˜жный** [14] for sale; *цена́* sale; [-жен, -жна] venal, corrupt; **˜ть**(**ся**) → **~ва́ть**(**ся**)

продви|га́ть [1], <**˜нуть**> [20] move, push (ahead); **-ся** advance; **~же́ние** *n* [12] advance(ment)

проде́л|ать → **~ывать**; **~ка** *f* [5; *g/pl.*: -лок] trick, prank; **~ывать**, <**~ать**> [1] *отве́рстие* break through, make; *рабо́ту и т. д.* carry through *or* out, do

проде́ть [-де́ну, -де́нешь; -де́нь(-те)!; -де́тый] *pf.* pass, run through; *ни́тку* thread

продл|ева́ть [1], <**~и́ть**> [13] extend, prolong; **~е́ние** *n* [12] extension, prolongation

продово́льств|енный [14] food...; grocery...; **~ие** *n* [12] food(stuffs), provisions *pl.*

продол|гова́тый [14 *sh.*] oblong; **~жа́тель** *m* [4] continuer; **~жа́ть** [1], <**˜жить**> [16] continue, go on; lengthen; prolong; **-ся** last; **~же́ние** *n* [12] continuation; *рома́на* sequel; **~же́ние сле́дует** to be continued; **~жи́тельность** *f* [8] duration; **~жи́тельный** [14; -лен, -льна] long; protracted; **˜жить**(**ся**) → **~жа́ть**(**ся**); **˜ьный** [14] longitudinal

продро́гнуть [21] *pf.* be chilled to the marrow

П

проду́к|т *m* [1] product; *pl. a.* foodstuffs; **~ти́вный** [14; -вен, -вна] productive; fruitful; **~то́вый** [14] grocery (*store*); **~ция** *f* [7] production, output

проду́м|ывать, <**~ать**> [1] think over, think out

про|еда́ть [1], <**~е́сть**> [-е́м, -е́шь, *etc.*, → **есть**[1]] eat through, corrode; *coll.* spend on food

прое́з|д *m* [1] passage, thoroughfare; **~да нет!** "no thoroughfare!"; **~до́м** on the way, en route; **пла́та за ~д** fare; **~ди́ть** → **~жа́ть**; **~дно́й** [14]: **~дно́й биле́т** season ticket; **~жа́ть** [1], <**прое́хать**> [-е́ду, -е́дешь; -езжа́й(те)!] pass, drive *or* ride through (*or* past, by); travel; **-ся** *coll.* take a drive *or* ride; **~жий** [17] (through) travel(l)er; passerby transient; **~жая доро́га** thoroughfare

прое́к|т *m* [1] project, plan, scheme; *докуме́нта* draft; **~ти́ровать** [7], <с-> project, plan; design; **~ция** *f* [7] *math.* projection; view

прое́|сть → **~да́ть**; **~хать** → **~зжа́ть**

проже́ктор *m* [1] searchlight

прожи|ва́ть [1], <**˜ть**> [-иву́, -ивёшь; про́жил, -а́, -о; про́житый (про́жит, -а́, -о)] live; *pf.* spend; **~га́ть** [1], <проже́чь> [26 г/ж: -жгу́, -жжёшь] burn (through); **~га́ть жизнь** *coll.* live fast; **˜точный** [14]: **˜точный ми́нимум** *m* living *or* subsistence wage; **˜ть** → **~ва́ть**

прожо́рлив|ость *f* [8] gluttony, voracity; **~ый** [14 *sh.*] gluttonous

про́за *f* [5] prose; **˜ик** *m* [1] prose writer; **~и́ческий** [16] prosaic; prose...

про́|звище *n* [11] nickname; **по ~звищу** nicknamed; **~зва́ть** → **~зыва́ть**; **~зева́ть** *coll.* [1] *pf.* miss; let slip; **~зорли́вый** [14 *sh.*] perspicacious; **~зра́чный** [14; -чен, -чна] transparent; *a. fig.* limpid; **~зре́ть** [9] *pf.* recover one's sight; begin to see clearly; perceive; **~зыва́ть** [1], <**~зва́ть**> [-зову́, -вёшь; -зва́л, -а́, -о; про́званный] (Т) nickname; **~зяба́ть** [1] vegetate; **~зя́бнуть** [21] *coll.* → **продро́гнуть**

проигр|ывать [1], <**~а́ть**> [1] lose (at play); *coll.* play; **-ся** lose all one's money; **˝ыш** *m* [1] loss (**в** П)

произв|еде́ние *n* [12] work, product(ion); **~вести́** → **~оди́ть**; **~оди́тель** *m* [4] producer; (*animal*) male parent, sire; **~оди́тельность** *f* [8] productivity; *заво́да* output; **~оди́тельный** [14; -лен, -льна] productive; **~оди́ть** [15], <**~ести́**> [25] (**-ся** *impf.* be) make (made), carry (-ried) out, execute(d), effect(ed); (*tech. usu. impf.*) produce(d); *на свет* bring forth; *impf.*

derive(d; **от** P from); **~о́дный** [14] *сло́во* derivative (*a. su. f math.*); **~о́дственный** [14] production...; manufacturing; works...; **~о́дство** *n* [9] production, manufacture; *coll.* plant, works, factory (**на** П at)

произ|во́л *m* [1] arbitrariness; *судьбы́* mercy; tyranny; **~во́льный** [14; -лен, -льна] arbitrary; **~носи́ть** [15], <**~нести́**> [24 -с-] pronounce; *речь* deliver, make; utter; **~ноше́ние** *n* [12] pronunciation; **~ойти́** → ***происходи́ть***

про́ис|ки *m/pl.* [1] intrigues; **~ходи́ть** [15], <произойти́> [-зойдёт; -зошёл, -шла; *g. pt.*: произойдя́] take place, happen; (*возника́ть*) arise, result (**от** P from); *о челове́ке* descend (**от**, **из** P from); **~хожде́ние** *n* [12] origin (by [= birth] **по** Д), descent; **~ше́ствие** *n* [12] incident, occurrence, event

про|йти́(сь) → ***~ходи́ть*** & ***~ха́живаться***

прок *coll. m* [1] → ***по́льза***

прока́з|а *f* [5] **1.** prank, mischief; **2.** *med.* leprosy; **~ник** *m* [1], **~ница** *f* [5] → *coll.* ***шалу́н(ья)***; **~ничать** [1] *coll.* → ***шали́ть***

прока́|лывать [1], <проколо́ть> [17] pierce; perforate; *ши́ну* puncture; **~пывать** [1], <прокопа́ть> [1] dig (through); **~рмливать** [1], <прокорми́ть> [14] support, nourish; feed

прока́т *m* [1] hire (**на** B for); *фи́льма* distribution; **~и́ть(ся)** [15] *pf.* give (take) a drive *or* ride; **~ывать** <**~ать**> [1] mangle; ride; **-ся** → *coll.* ***~и́ться***

прокла́д|ка *f* [5; *g/pl.*: -док] *трубопрово́да* laying; *доро́ги* construction; *tech.* gasket, packing; **~ывать** [1], <проложи́ть> [16] lay (*a.* = build); *fig.* pave; force (one's *way* себе́); *ме́жду* interlay

прокл|ина́ть [1], <**~я́сть**> [-яну́, -янёшь; про́клял, -á, -о; про́клятый (про́клят, -á, -о)] curse, damn; **~я́тие** *n* [12] damnation; **~я́тый** [14] cursed, damned

проко́|л *m* [1] perforation; *mot.* puncture; **~ло́ть** → ***прока́лывать***; **~па́ть** → ***прока́пывать***; **~рми́ть** → ***прока́рмливать***

прокра́|дываться [1], <**~сться**> [25; *pt. st.*] steal, go stealthily

прокуро́р *m* [1] public prosecutor; *на суде́* counsel for the prosecution

про|лага́ть → ***~кла́дывать***; **~ла́мывать**, <**~лома́ть**> [1] & <**~ломи́ть**> [14] break (through; *v/i.* **-ся**); fracture; **~лега́ть** [1] lie; run; **~леза́ть** [1], <**~ле́зть**> [24 *st.*] climb *or* get (in[to], through); **~лёт** *m* [1] flight; *моста́* span; *ле́стницы* well; **~летариа́т** *m* [1] proletariat; **~лета́рий** *m* [3], **~лета́рский** [16] proletarian; **~лета́ть** [1], <**~лете́ть**> [11] fly (covering a certain distance); fly (past, by, over); *fig.* flash, flit

проли́|в *m* [1] strait (*e.g.* ***~в Па-де-Кале́*** Strait of Dover [the Pas de Calais]); **~ва́ть** [1], <**~ть**> [-лью́, -льёшь; ле́й(те)!; про́ли́ло; про́ли́тый (про́ли́т, -á, -о)] spill; (*v/i.* **-ся**); *слёзы, свет* shed; **~вно́й** [14]: ***~вно́й дождь*** pouring rain, pelting rain; **~ть** → ***~ва́ть***

проло́|г *m* [1] prologue; **~жи́ть** → ***прокла́дывать***; **~м** *m* [1] breach; **~ма́ть**, **~ми́ть** → ***прола́мывать***

про́мах *m* [1] miss; blunder (make ***дать*** *or* ***сде́лать*** *a.* slip, fail); *coll.* ***он па́рень не ~*** he is no fool; **~иваться** [1], <**~ну́ться**> [20] miss

промедле́ние *n* [12] delay; procrastination

промежу́то|к *m* [1; -тка] interval (**в** П at; **в** B of); period; **~чный** [14] intermediate

проме|лькну́ть → ***мелькну́ть***; **~нивать** [1], <**~ня́ть**> [28] exchange (**на** B for); **~рза́ть** [1], <промёрзнуть> [21] freeze (through); *coll.* → ***продро́гнуть***

промо|ка́ть [1], <**~кнуть**> [21] get soaked *or* drenched; *impf. only* let water through; not be water proof; **~лча́ть** [4 *e.*; -чу́, -чи́шь] *pf.* keep silent; **~чи́ть** [16] *pf.* get soaked *or* drenched

промтова́ры *m/pl.* [1] manufactured goods (*other than food stuffs*)

промча́ться [4] *pf.* dart, tear *or* fly (past, by)

промы|вáть [1], <´~ть> [22] wash (out, away); *med.* bathe, irrigate

прóмы|сел *m* [1; -сла]: ***нарóдные ~слы*** folk crafts; **´~слóвый** [14]: ***~слóвый сезóн*** fishing (hunting, *etc.*) season; **´~ть** → ***~вáть***

промы́шлен|ник *m* [1] manufacturer, industrialist; **~ность** *f* [8] industry; **~ный** [14] industrial

пронести́(сь) → ***проноси́ть(ся)***

прон|зáть [1], <~зи́ть> [15 *e.*; -нжу́, -нзи́шь; -нзённый] pierce, stab; **~зи́тельный** [14; -лен, -льна] shrill, piercing; *взгляд* penetrating; **~и́зывать** [1], <~изáть> [3] penetrate, pierce

прони|кáть [1], <´~кнуть> [21] penetrate; permeate (***чéрез*** through); get (in); **-ся** be imbued (T with); **~кновéние** *n* [12] penetration; *fig.* fervo(u)r; **~кновéнный** [14; -éнен, -éнна] heartfelt; **~цáемый** [14 *sh.*] permeable; **~цáтельный** [14; -лен, -льна] penetrating, searching; *человéк* acute, shrewd

про|носи́ть [15] **1.** <~нести́> [24 -с-: -есу́; -ёс, -еслá] carry (through, by, away); **-ся**, <-сь> *о пу́ле, кáмне* fly (past, by); pass *or* ***слу́хи*** spread (swiftly); **2.** *pf. coll.* wear out; **~ны́рливый** [14 *sh.*] crafty; pushy; **~ню́хать** [1] *coll.* get wind of

проóбраз *m* [1] prototype

пропагáнда *f* [5] propaganda

пропа|дáть [1], <´~сть> [25; *pt. st.*] get *or* be lost; *дáром* go to waste; be (missing; *a.* ***~сть бéз вести***); *интерéс* lose, vanish; **´~жа** *f* [5] loss; **´~сть¹** → ***~дáть***; **´~сть²** *f* [8] precipice, abyss; ***на краю́ ´~сти*** on the verge of disaster; *coll. мнóго* lots *or* a lot (of)

пропи|вáть [1], <´~ть> [-пью́, -пьёшь; -пéй(те)!; прóпил, -á, -о; прóпи́тый (прóпи́т, -á, -о)] spend on drink

пропис|áть(ся) → ***´~ывать(ся)***; **´~ска** *f* [5; *g/pl.*: -сок] registration; **~нóй** [14] capital, → ***бу́ква***; ***~нáя и́стина*** truism; **´~ывать** [1], <~áть> [3] *med.* prescribe (Д for); register (*v/i.* **-ся**); **´~ью** (*write*) in full

пропи́|тывать, <~тáть> [1] (**-ся** be[come]) steeped in, saturate(d; T with); **~ть** → ***~вáть***

проплы|вáть [1], <´~ть> [23] swim *or* sail (by); float, drift (by, past); *fig. joc.* sail (by, past)

проповéд|ник *m* [1] preacher; **~овать** [1] preach; *fig.* advocate; **´~ь** ('pro-) *f* [8] *eccl.* sermon

пропол|зáть [1], <~зти́> [24] creep, crawl (by, through, under); **´~ка** *f* [5] weeding

пропорционáльный [14; -лен, -льна] proportional, proportionate

прóпус|к *m* [1] **1.** [*pl.*: -ки] omission, blank; (*отсу́тствие*) absence; **2.** [*pl.*: -кá, *etc. e.*] pass, permit; admission; **~кáть** [1], <~ти́ть> [15] let pass (or through), admit; (*опусти́ть*) omit; *заня́тие и т. д.* miss; let slip; *impf.* (*течь*) leak

прора|бáтывать, <~бóтать> *coll.* [1] study; **~стáть** [1], <~сти́> [24 -ст-: -стёт; -рóс, -рослá] germinate; sprout, shoot (*of plant*)

прорвáть(ся) → ***прорывáть(ся)***

прорéз|ать [1], <~áть> [3] cut through; **-ся** *о зубáх* cut (*teeth*)

прорéха *f* [5] slit, tear

прорó|к *m* [1] prophet; **~ни́ть** [13; -оню́, -óнишь; -óненный] *pf.* utter; **~ческий** [16] prophetic; **~чество** *n* [9] prophecy; **~чить** [16] prophesy

проруб|ать [1], <~и́ть> [14] cut (through); **´~ь** *f* [8] hole cut in ice

прор|ы́в *m* [1] break; breach; **~ывáть** [1] **1.** <~вáть> [-ву́, -вёшь; -вáл, -á, -о; прóрванный (-ан, -á, -о)] break through; **-ся** (*v/i.*) break through; burst open; force one's way; **2.** <~ы́ть> [22] dig (through)

про|сáчиваться [1], <~сочи́ться> [16 *e.*; *3rd p. only*] ooze (out), percolate; **~сверли́ть** [13] *pf.* drill, bore (through)

просвé|т *m* [1] *в облакáх* gap; (*щель*) chink; *fig.* ray of hope; **~ти́ть** → ***~щáть*** & ***~чивать*** **2.**; **~тлéть** [8] *pf.* clear up, brighten up; **~чивать** [1] **1.** shine through, be seen; **2.** <~ти́ть> [15] *med.* X-ray; **~щáть** [1], <~ти́ть> [15 *e.*; -ещу́, -ети́шь; -ещённый] enlighten, edu-

cate, instruct; **~ще́ние** *n* [12] education; **Ѻще́ние** Enlightenment
про́|седь *f* [8] streaks of gray (*Brt.* grey), grizzly hair; **~се́ивать** [1], <~се́ять> [27] sift; **~сека** *f* [5] cutting, opening (*in a forest*); **~сёлочный** [14]: ***~сёлочная доро́га*** country road, cart track, unmetalled road; **~се́ять** → ***~се́ивать***
проси́|живать [1], <~де́ть> [11] sit (up); stay, remain (*for a certain time*); *над че́м-л.* spend; **~ть** [15], <по-> ask (В/**о** П; **у** Р/Р p. for), beg, request; (*пригласи́ть*) invite; intercede (***за*** В for); ***прошу́, про́сят*** *a.* please; ***прошу́***! please come in!; **-ся** (***в, на*** В) ask (for; leave [to enter, go]); **~я́ть** [28] *pf.* begin to shine; light up with
проск|ользну́ть [20] *pf.* slip, creep (**в** В in); **~очи́ть** [16] *pf.* rush by, tear by; slip through; fall between *or* through
просл|авля́ть [28], <~а́вить> [14] glorify, make (**-ся** become) famous; **~еди́ть** [15 *e.*; -ежу́, -еди́шь; -ежённый] *pf.* track down; trace; **~ези́ться** [15 *e.*; -ежу́сь, -ези́шься] *pf.* shed (a few) tears
просло́йка *f* [5; *g/pl.*: -оек] layer
про|слу́шать [1] *pf.* hear; (through); *med.* auscultate; *coll.* miss, not catch (*what is said e.g.*); **~сма́тривать** [1], <~смотре́ть> [9; -отрю́, -о́тришь; -о́тренный] survey; view; look through *or* over; (*не заме́тить*) overlook; **~смо́тр** *m* [1] *докуме́нтов* examination, survey; review (*о фи́льме тж.* preview); **~сну́ться** → ***~сыпа́ться***; **~со** *n* [9] millet; **~со́вывать** [1], <~су́нуть> [20] pass or push (through); **~со́хнуть** → ***~сыха́ть***; **~сочи́ться** → ***~са́чиваться***; **~спа́ть** → ***~сыпа́ть***
проспе́кт[1] *m* [1] avenue
проспе́кт[2] *m* [1] prospectus
просро́ч|ивать [1], <~ить> [16] let lapse *or* expire; exceed the time limit; **~ка** *f* [5; *g/pl.*: -чек] expiration; (*превыше́ние сро́ка*) exceeding
прост|а́ивать [1], <~оя́ть> [-ою́, -ои́шь] stand stay (*for a certain time*); *tech.* stand idle; **~а́к** *m* [1 *e.*] simpleton
прост|ира́ть [1], <~ере́ть> [12] stretch (*v/i.* **-ся**), extend
прости́тельный [14; -лен, -льна] pardonable, excusable
проститу́тка *f* [5; *g/pl.*: -ток] prostitute
прости́ть(ся) → ***проща́ть(ся)***
простоду́ш|ие *n* [12] naiveté; **~ный** [14; -шен, -шна] ingenuous, artless; simple-minded
просто́|й[1] [14; прост, -а́, -о; *comp.*: про́ще] simple, plain; easy; *мане́ры и т. д.* unaffected, unpretentious; *о лю́дях* ordinary, common; *math.* prime
просто́й[2] *m* [3] stoppage, standstill
простоква́ша *f* [5] sour milk, yog(h)urt
просто́|р *m* [1] open (space); freedom (***на*** П in); *fig.* scope; **~ре́чие** *n* [12] popular speech; common parlance; **~рный** [14; -рен, -рна] spacious, roomy; **~та́** *f* [5] simplicity; naiveté; **~я́ть** → ***проста́ивать***
простра́н|ный [14; -а́нен, -а́нна] vast; *о ре́чи, письме́* long-winded, verbose; **~ство** *n* [9] space; expanse
простра́ция *f* [7] prostration, complete physical *or* mental exhaustion
простре́л *m* [1] *coll.* lumbago; **~ивать** [1], <~и́ть> [13; -елю́, -е́лишь; -елённый] shoot (through)
просту́|да *f* [5] common cold; **~жа́ть** [1], <~ди́ть> [15] chill; **-ся** catch a cold
просту́пок *m* [1; -пка] misdeed; offense (-ce); *law* misdemeano(u)r
простыня́ *f* [6; *pl.*: про́стыни, -ы́нь, *etc. e.*] (bed) sheet
просу́|нуть → ***просо́вывать***; **~шивать** [1], <~ши́ть> [16] dry thoroughly
просчита́ться [1] *pf.* miscalculate
просыпа́ть [1], <проспа́ть> [-плю́, -пи́шь; -спа́л, -а́, -о] oversleep; sleep; *coll.* miss (by sleeping); **~ся**, <просну́ться> [20] awake, wake up
прос|ыха́ть [1], <~о́хнуть> [21] get dry, dry out
про́сьба *f* [5] request (***по*** П at; **о** П for); please (don't ***не*** + *inf.*) ***у меня́ к вам ~*** I have a favo(u)r to ask you
про|та́лкивать [1], *once* <~тол-

П

кну́ть> [20], *coll.* <~толка́ть> [1] push (through); **-ся** force one's way (through); **~та́птывать** [1], <~топта́ть> [3] *доро́жку* tread; **~та́скивать** [1], <~тащи́ть> [16] carry *or* drag (past, by); *coll.* smuggle in

проте́з ('tes) *m* [1] prosthetic appliance; artificial limb; ***зубно́й ~*** false teeth, dentures

проте|ка́ть [1], <~чь> [26] *impf. only* (*of a river or stream*) flow, run (by); *ло́дка* leak; *pf.* *вре́мя* pass, elapse; take its course; **~кция** *f* [7] patronage; **~ре́ть** → ***протира́ть***; **~ст** *m* [1], **~стова́ть** [7], *v/t.* (*im*)*pf.* & <о-> protest; **~чь** → ***~ка́ть***

про́тив (Р) against; opposite; ***быть*** *or* ***име́ть ~*** (have) object(ion; to), mind; **~иться** [14], <вос-> (Д) oppose, object; **~ник** *m* [1] opponent, adversary; enemy; **~ный**[1] [14; -вен, -вна] repugnant, disgusting, offensive, nasty; **~ный**[2] opposite, contrary; opposing, opposed; ***мне ~но*** *a.* I hate; ***в ~ном слу́чае*** otherwise

противо|ве́с *m* [1] counterbalance; **~возду́шный** [14] antiaircraft...; ***~возду́шная оборо́на*** air defense (-ce); **~де́йствие** *n* [12] counteraction; (*сопротивле́ние*) resistance; **~де́йствовать** [7] counteract; resist; **~есте́ственный** [14 *sh.*] unnatural; **~зако́нный** [14; -о́нен, -о́нна] unlawful, illegal; **~зача́точный** [14] contraceptive; **~показа́ние** *n* [12] *med.* contra-indication; **~поло́жность** *f* [8] contrast, opposition (***в*** В in); antithesis; **~поло́жный** [14; -жен, -жна] opposite; contrary, opposed; **~поставля́ть** [28], <-поста́вить> [14] oppose; **~поставле́ние** *n* [12] opposition; **~раке́тный** [14] antimissile; **~речи́вый** [14 *sh.*] contradictory; **~ре́чие** *n* [12] contradiction; **~ре́чить** [16] (Д) contradict; **~стоя́ть** [-ою́, -ои́шь] (Д) withstand; stand against; **~я́дие** *n* [12] antidote

про|тира́ть [1], <~тере́ть> [12] wear (through); *стекло́* wipe; **~ткну́ть** → ***~тыка́ть***; **~токо́л** *m* [1] (**~токоли́ровать** [7] [*im*]*pf.*, *a.*, <за-> take down the) minutes *pl.*, record; *su. a.* protocol; **~толка́ть**, **~толкну́ть** → ***~та́лкивать***; **~топта́ть** → ***~та́птывать***; **~торённый** [14] *доро́га* beaten well-trodden; **~точи́п** *m* [1] prototype; **~то́чный** [14] flowing, running; **~трезвля́ться** [28], <~трезви́ться> [14 *e.*; -влю́сь, -ви́шься; -влённый] sober up; **~тыка́ть** [1], *once* <~ткну́ть> [20] pierce, skewer; transfix

протя́|гивать [1], <~ну́ть> [19] stretch (out), extend, hold out; (*переда́ть*) pass; **~же́ние** *n* [12] extent, stretch (***на*** П over, along); (*of time*) space (***на*** П for, during); **~жный** [14; -жен, -жна] *звук* drawn-out; **~ну́ть** → ***~гивать***

проучи́ть *coll.* [16] *pf.* teach a lesson

професс|иона́льный [14] professional; trade... (*e.g.* trade union → ***профсою́з***); **~ия** *f* [7] profession, trade (***по*** Д by); **~ор** *m* [1; *pl.*: -pá, *etc. e.*] professor; **~у́ра** *f* [5] professorship; *collect.* the professors

про́филь *m* [4] **1.** profile; **2. *~ учи́лища*** type of school or college

профо́рма *coll. f* [5] form, formality

профсою́з *m* [1], **~ный** [14] trade union

про|ха́живаться [1], <~йти́сь> [-йду́сь, -йдёшься; -шёлся, -шла́сь] (go for a) walk, stroll; *coll.* have a go at s.o. (***на че́й-либо счёт***); **~хво́ст** *coll. m* [1] scoundrel

прохла́д|а *f* [5] coolness; **~и́тельный** [14; -лен, -льна]: ***~и́тельные напи́тки*** soft drinks; **~ный** [14; -ден, -дна] cool (*a. fig.*), fresh

прохо́|д *m* [1] passage, pass; *anat.* duct (***за́дний ~д*** anus); **~ди́мец** *m* [1; -мца] rogue, scoundrel; **~ди́мость** *f* [8] *доро́ги* passability; *anat.* permeability; **~ди́ть** [15], <пройти́> [пройду́, -дёшь; прошёл; ше́дший; про́йденный; *g. pt.*: пройдя́] pass, go (by, through, over, along); take a ... course, be; **~дно́й** [14] *двор* (with a) through passage; **~жде́ние** *n* [12] passage, passing; **~жий** *m* [17] passerby

П

процветать [1] prosper, thrive
проце|ду́ра *f* [5] procedure; **~жи-вать** [1], <~ди́ть> [15] filter, strain; **~нт** *m* [1] percent(age) (**на** В by); (*usu. pl.*) interest; **ста́вка ~нта** rate of interest; **~сс** *m* [1] process; *law* trial (**на** П at); **~ссия** [7] procession
проче́сть → **прочи́тывать**
про́ч|ий [17] other; *n* & *pl. a. su.* the rest; **и ~ее** and so on *or* forth, *etc.*; **ме́жду ~им** by the way, incidentally; **поми́мо всего́ ~его** in addition
прочи́|стить → **~ща́ть**; **~тывать**, <~та́ть> [1] & <проче́сть> [25 -т-: -чту́, -тёшь; -чёл, -чла́; *g. pt.*: -чтя́, -чтённый] read (through); **~ть** [16] intend (for), have s.o. in mind (**в** В as); **успе́х** destine (for); **~ща́ть** [1], <~стить> [15] clean
про́чн|ость *f* [8] durability, firmness; **~ый** [14; -чен, -чна; -о] firm, solid, strong; **мир** lasting; **зна́ния** sound
прочте́ние *n* [12] reading; perusal; *fig.* interpretation
прочь away → **доло́й**; **я не ~** + *inf. coll.* I wouldn't mind ...ing
прош|е́дший [17] past, last (*a. su. n* **~е́дшее** the past); *gr.* past (tense); **~е́ствие** *n* [12] → **истече́ние**; **~лого́дний** [15] last year's; **~лый** [14] past (*a. su. n* **~лое**), bygone; **~мыгну́ть** *coll.* [20] *pf.* slip, whisk (by, past)
прощ|а́й(те)! farewell!, goodby(e)!, adieu!; **~а́льный** [14] farewell...; **слова́** parting; **~а́ние** *n* [12] parting (**при** П, **на** В when, at), leave-taking, farewell; **~а́ть** [1], <прости́ть> [15 *e.*; -ощу́, -ости́шь; -ощённый] forgive (р. Д), excuse, pardon; **-ся** (**с** Т) take leave (of), say goodby (to); **~е́ние** *n* [12] forgiveness, pardon
прояв|и́тель *m* [4] *phot.* developer; **~и́ть(ся)** → **~ля́ть(ся)**; **~ле́ние** *n* [12] manifestation, display, demonstration; *phot.* development; **~ля́ть** [28], <~и́ть> [14] show, display, manifest; *phot.* develop
проясн|я́ться [28], <~и́ться> [13] (*of weather*) clear up (*a. fig.*); brighten
пруд *m* [1 *e.*; в ~у́] pond
пружи́на *f* [5] spring; **скры́тая ~** motive
прут *m* [1; *a. e.*; *pl.*: -ья, -ьев] twig; **желе́зный** rod
пры́|гать [1], *once* <~гнуть> [20] jump, spring, leap; **~гу́н** *m* [1 *e.*] (*sport*) jumper; **~жо́к** *m* [1; -жка́] jump, leap, bound; **в во́ду** dive; **~ткий** [16; -ток, -тка, -о] nimble, quick; **~ть** *coll.* *f* [8] agility; speed (**во всю** at full); **~щ** *m* [1 *e.*], **~щик** *m* [1] pimple
пряди́льный [14] spinning
пря|дь *f* [8] lock, tress, strand; **~жа** *f* [5] yarn; **~жка** *f* [5; *g/pl.*: -жек] buckle
прям|изна́ *f* [5] straightness; **~о́й** [14; прям, -а́, -о] straight (*a.* = bee) line (**~а́я** *su. f*); direct (*a. gr.*); *rail* through...; **у́гол** right; *fig.* straight (-forward), downright, outspoken, frank; **~а́я кишка́** rectum; **~оли-не́йный** [14; -е́ен, -е́йна] rectilinear; *fig.*; → **~о́й** *fig.*; **~ота́** *f* [5] straightforwardness, frankness; **~о-уго́льник** *m* [1] rectangle; **~о-уго́льный** [14] rectangular
пря́н|ик *m* [1] **имби́рный** gingerbread; **медо́вый ~ик** honeycake; **~ость** *f* [8] spice; **~ый** [14 *sh.*] spicy, *fig.* piquant
прясть [25; -ял, -а́, -о], <с-> spin
пря́т|ать [3], <с-> hide (*v/i.* **-ся**), conceal; **~ки** *f/pl.* [5; *gen.*: -ток] hide-and-seek
псал|о́м *m* [1; -лма́] psalm; **~ты́рь** *f* [8] Psalter
псевдони́м *m* [1] pseudonym
псих|иа́тр *m* [1] psychiatrist; **~ика** *f* [5] state of mind; psyche; mentality; **~и́ческий** [16] mental, psychic(al); **~и́ческое заболева́ние** mental illness; **~о́лог** *m* [1] psychologist; **~оло́гия** *f* [7] psychology
птене́ц [1; -нца́] nestling, fledgling
пти́|ца *f* [5] bird; **дома́шняя ~ца** *collect.* poultry; **~цево́дство** *n* [9] poultry farming; **~чий** [18] bird('s); poultry...; **вид с ~чьего полёта** bird's-eye view; **~чка** *f* [5; *g/pl.*: -чек] (**га́лочка**) tick
пу́бли|ка *f* [5] audience; public; **~ка́ция** *f* [7] publication; **~кова́ть**

П

[7], <о-> publish; **~цист** *m* [1] publicist; **~чный** [14] public; ***~чный дом*** brothel

пу́г|ало *n* [9] scarecrow; **~а́ть** [1], <ис-, на->, *once* <~ну́ть> [20] (**-ся** be) frighten(ed; of P), scare(d); **~ли́вый** [14 *sh.*] timid, fearful

пу́говица *f* [5] button

пу́дель *m* [4; *pl. a. etc. e.*] poodle

пу́др|а *f* [5] powder; ***са́харная ~а*** powdered (*Brt.* caster) sugar; **~еница** *f* [5] powder compact; **~ить** [13], <на-> powder

пуз|а́тый P [14 *sh.*] paunchy; **~о** P *n* [9] paunch, potbelly

пузыр|ёк *m* [1; -рька́] vial; *a. dim.* → **~ь** *m* [4 *e.*] bubble; *anat.* bladder; *coll.* ***на ко́же*** blister

пулемёт *m* [1] machine gun

пуль|веризáтор *m* [1] spray(er); **~с** *m* [1] pulse; *coll.* ***щу́пать ~с*** feel the pulse; **~си́ровать** [7] puls(at)e; **~т** *m* [1] conductor's stand; *tech.* control panel *or* desk

пу́ля *f* [6] bullet

пункт *m* [1] point, station; place, spot; ***докуме́нта*** item, clause, article; ***по ~ам*** point by point; **~и́р** *m* [1] dotted line; **~уа́льность** *f* [8] punctuality; accuracy; **~уа́льный** [14; -лен, -льна] punctual; accurate; **~уа́ция** *f* [7] punctuation

пунцо́вый [14] crimson

пунш *m* [1] punch (*drink*)

пуп|о́к *m* [1; -пка́], *coll.* **~** *m* [1 *e.*] navel

П

пурга́ *f* [5] blizzard, snowstorm

пу́рпур *m* [1], **~ный**, **~овый** [14] purple

пуск *m* [1] (*a.* **~ *в ход***) start(ing), setting in operation; **~а́й** → *coll.* ***пусть***; **~а́ть** [1], <пусти́ть> [15] let (go; in[to]), set going, in motion *or* operation [*a.* ***~а́ть в ход***]; start; (*бро́сить*) throw; ***ко́рни*** take root; *fig.* begin; ***в прода́жу*** offer (*for sale*); ***~а́ть под отко́с*** derail; **-ся** (+ *inf.*) *в путь* start (...ing; *v/ct.* ***в*** В), set out (***в*** В on); begin, undertake; enter upon

пуст|е́ть [8], <о-, за-> become empty *or* deserted; **~и́ть** → ***пуска́ть***

пуст|о́й [14; пуст, -ó, -о] empty; ***наде́жда, разгово́р*** vain, idle (talk **~о́е**; *n su.* → *a.* **~я́к**); ***ме́сто*** vacant; ***взгляд*** blank; *geol.* ***поро́да*** barren rock; (*по́лый*) hollow; **~ота́** *f* [5; *pl. st.*: -óты] emptiness; void; *phys.* vacuum

пусты́|нный [14; -ынен, -ынна] uninhabited, deserted; **~ня** *f* [6] desert, wilderness; **~рь** *m* [4 *e.*] waste land; **~шка** *f* [5; *g/pl.*: -шек] *coll.* baby's dummy; *fig.* hollow man

пусть let (him, *etc.* + *vb.*; **~ [он]** + *vb.* 3rd *p.*); even (if)

пустя́|к *coll. m* [1 *e.*] trifle; *pl.* (it's) nothing; ***па́ра ~ко́в*** child's play; **~ко́вый**, **~чный** *coll.* [14] trifling, trivial

пу́та|ница *f* [5] confusion, muddle, mess; **~ть** [1], <за-, с-, пере-> (**-ся** get) confuse(d), muddle(d), mix(ed) up, entangled, ***-ся под нога́ми*** get in the way

путёвка *f* [5; *g/pl.*: -вок] pass, authorization (*for a place on a tour, in a holiday home, etc.*)

путе|води́тель *m* [4] guide(book) (***по*** Д to); **~во́дный** [14] ***звезда́*** lodestar; **~во́й** [14] travel(l)ing; ***~вы́е заме́тки*** travel notes

путеше́ств|енник *m* [1] travel(l)er; **~ие** *n* [12] journey, trip; voyage, ***мо́рем*** cruise; **~овать** [7] travel (***по*** Д through)

пу́т|ник *m* [1] travel(l)er, wayfarer; **~ный** *coll.* [14] → ***де́льный***

путч *m* [1] *pol.* coup, putsch

пут|ь *m* [8 *e.*; *instr/sg.*: -тём] way (*a. fig.*: [in] *that* way **~ём**, *a.* by means of P); road, path; *rail* track, line; (*спо́соб*) means; (*пое́здка*) trip, journey (***в*** В *or* П on); route; ***в*** *or* ***по ~и́*** on the way; in passing; ***нам по ~и́*** I (we) am (are) going the same way (***с*** Т as); ***быть на ло́жном ~и́*** be on the wrong track

пух *m* [1; в -ху́] down, fluff; ***в ~ (и прах)*** (*defeat*) utterly, totally; **~леньки́й** *coll.* [16], **~лый** [14; пухл, -á, -о] chubby, plump; **~нуть** [21], <рас-> swell; **~о́вый** [14] downy

пучи́на *f* [5] gulf, abyss (*a. fig.*)

пучо́к *m* [1; -чка] bunch; *coll.* bun (hairdo)

пу́ш|ечный [14] gun..., cannon...;

~́инка *f* [5; *g/pl.*: -нок] down, fluff; **~́истый** [14 *sh.*] downy, fluffy; **~ка** *f* [5; *g/pl.*: -шек] gun, cannon; **~ни́на** *f* [5] *collect.* furs, pelts *pl.*; **~нóй** [14] fur...; **~óк** *coll. m* [1; -шкá] fluff

пчел|á *f* [5; *pl. st.*: пчёлы] bee; **~овóд** *m* [1] beekeeper; **~овóдство** *n* [9] beekeeping

пшен|и́ца *f* [5] wheat; **~и́чный** [14] wheaten; **~́ный** ('pʃo-) [14] millet...; **~ó** *n* [9] millet

пыл *m* [1] *fig.* ardo(u)r, zeal; ***в ~ý сражéния*** in the heat of the battle; **~áть** [1], <за-> blaze, flame, *o лицé* glow, burn; rage; (T) *гнéвом*; **~есóс** *m* [1] vacuum cleaner; **~и́нка** *f* [5; *g/pl.*: -нок] mote, speck of dust; **~и́ть** [13], <за-> get dusty; **-ся** be(come) dusty; **~́кий** [16; -лок, -лкá, -o] ardent, passionate

пыль *f* [8; в ~ли́] dust; **~́ный** [14; -лен, -льнá, -o] dusty (*a.* = ***в -ли́***); **~цá** *f* [5] pollen

пыт|áть [1] torture; **~áться** [1], <по-> try, attempt; **~́ка** *f* [5; *g/pl.*: -ток] torture; **~ли́вый** [14 *sh.*] inquisitive, searching

пыхтéть [11] puff, pant; *coll.* ***~ над чéм-либо*** sweat over something

пы́шн|ость *f* [8] splendo(u)r, pomp; **~ый** [14; -шен, -шнá, -o] magnificent, splendid, sumptuous; *вóлосы, расти́тельность* luxuriant, rich

пьедестáл *m* [1] pedestal

пьéса *f* [5] *thea.* play; *mus.* piece

пьян|éть [8], <о-> get drunk (*a. fig.*; from, on **от** P); **~́ица** *m/f* [5] drunkard; **~́ство** *n* [9] drunkenness; **~́ствовать** [7] drink heavily; *coll.* booze; **~́ый** [14; пьян, -á, -o] drunk(en), *a. fig.* (**от** P with)

пюрé (-'re) *n* [*indecl.*] purée; ***картóфельное ~*** mashed potatoes *pl.*

пятá *f* [5; *nom/pl. st.*] heel; ***ходи́ть за кéм-л. по ~м*** follow on s.o.'s heels

пят|áк *coll. m* [1 *e.*], **~ачóк** *coll. m* [1; -чкá] five-kopeck (*Brt.* -copeck) coin; **~ёрка** *f* [5; *g/pl.*: -рок] five (→ ***двóйка***); *coll.* → ***отли́чно***; five-ruble (*Brt.* -rouble) note; **~́еро** [37] five (→ ***двóе***)

пяти|деся́тый [14] fiftieth; ***~деся́тые гóды*** *pl.* the fifties; → ***пя́тый***; **~лéтний** [15] five-year (old), of five; **~сóтый** [14] five hundredth

пя́титься [15],<по-> (move) back

пя́тк|а *f* [5; *g/pl.*: -ток] heel (take to one's heels ***показáть ~и***)

пятнáдцат|ый [14] fifteenth; → ***пя́тый***; **~ь** [35] fifteen; → ***пять***

пятни́стый [14 *sh.*] spotted, dappled

пя́тн|ица *f* [5] Friday (on: ***в*** B; *pl.*: ***по*** Д); **~ó** *n* [9; *pl. st.*; *g/pl.*: -тен] spot, stain (*a. fig.*), blot(ch) (*pl.* ***в*** B with); ***роди́мое ~ó*** birthmark

пя́т|ый [14] fifth; (*page, chapter, etc.*) five; ***~ая*** *f su. math.* a fifth (*part*); ***~ое*** *n su.* the fifth (*date*; on P: ***~ого***; → ***числó***); ***~ь мину́т ~ого*** five (minutes) past four; **~ь** [35] five; ***без ~и́ (мину́т) час (два***, *etc.*, [часá], five (minutes) to one (two, *etc.* [o'clock]); ***~ь***, *etc.* (***часóв***) five, etc. (o'clock); **~ьдеся́т** [35] fifty; **~ьсóт** [36] five hundred; **~ью́** five times

Р

раб *m* [1 *e.*], **~á** *f* [5] slave

рабóт|а *f* [5] work (***за*** T; ***на*** П at); job; labo(u)r, toil; *кáчество* workmanship; **~ать** [1] work (***над*** T on; ***на*** B for; T as); labo(u)r, toil; *tech.* run, operate; *магази́н и т. д.* be open; **~ник** *m* [1], **~ница** *f* [5] worker, working (wo)man; day labo(u)rer, (farm)hand; official, functionary; employee; *наýчный*

Р

scientist; **~ода́тель** *m* [4] employer, *coll.* boss; **~оспосо́бный** [14; -бен, -бна] able-bodied; hard-working; **~я́щий** [17*sh.*] industrious

рабо́ч|ий *m* [17] (*esp. industrial*) worker; *adj.*: working, work (*a. day*); workers', labo(u)r...; ***~ая си́ла*** manpower; work force; labo(u)r

ра́б|ский [16] slave...; slavish, servile; **~ство** *n* [9] slavery, servitude; **~ы́ня** *f* [6] → **~á**

ра́в|енство *n* [9] equality; **~ни́на** *f* [5] *geog.* plain; **~но́** alike; as well as; ***всё ~но́*** it's all the same, it doesn't matter; anyway, in any case; ***не всё ли ~но́?*** what's the difference?

равно|ве́сие *n* [12] balance (*a. fig.*), equilibrium; **~ду́шие** *n* [12] indifference (**к** Д to); **~ду́шный** [14; -шен, -шна] indifferent (**к** Д to); **~ме́рный** [14; -рен, -рна] uniform, even; **~пра́вие** *n* [12] equality (of rights); **~пра́вный** [14; -вен, -вна] (enjoying) equal (rights); **~си́льный** [14; -лен, -льна] of equal strength; tantamount to; equivalent; **~це́нный** [14; -е́нен, -е́нна] equal (in value)

ра́вн|ый [14; ра́вен, -вна́] equal (*a. su.*); ***~ым о́бразом*** → **~о́**; ***ему́ нет ~ого*** he is unrivalled; **~я́ть** [28], <с-> equalize; *coll.* compare with, treat as equal to; (*v/i.* **-ся**; *a.* be [equal to Д])

рад [14; ра́да] (be) glad (Д at, of; *a.* to see *p.*), pleased, delighted; ***не ~*** (be) sorry; regret

рада́р *m* [1] radar

ра́ди (Р) for the sake of; for (...'s) sake; for

радиа́тор *m* [1] radiator

радика́л [1], **~ьный** [14; -лен, -льна] radical

ра́дио *n* [*indecl.*] radio (***по*** Д on); **~акти́вность** *f* [8] radioactivity; **~акти́вный** [14; -вен, -вна] radioactive; ***~акти́вное загрязне́ние*** (***оса́дки***) radioactive contamination (fallout); **~веща́ние** *n* [12] broadcasting (system); **~люби́тель** *m* [4] radio amateur; **~переда́ча** *f* [5] (radio) broadcast, transmission; **~приёмник** *m* [1] radio set; receiver; **~слу́шатель** *m* [4] listener; **~ста́нция** *f* [7] radio station; **~телефо́н** *m* [1] radiotelephone

ради́ст *m* [1] radio operator

ра́диус *m* [1] radius

ра́до|вать [7], <об-, по-> (В) gladden, please; **-ся** (Д) rejoice (at), be glad *or* pleased (of, at); **~стный** [14; -тен, -тна] joyful, glad; merry; **~сть** *f* [8] joy, gladness; pleasure

ра́ду|га *f* [5] rainbow; **~жный** [14] iridescent, rainbow...; *fig.* rosy; ***~жная оболо́чка*** *anat.* iris

раду́ш|ие *n* [12] cordiality; kindness; (*гостеприи́мство*) hospitality; **~ный** [14; -шен, -шна] kindly, hearty; hospitable

раз *m* [1; *pl. e., gen.* раз] time ([**в**] В this, *etc.*); one; ***оди́н ~*** once; ***два ~а*** twice; ***ни ~у*** not once, never; ***не ~*** repeatedly; ***как ~*** just (in time *coll.* ***в са́мый*** → *a.* ***впо́ру***), the very; ***вот тебе́ ~*** → ***на²***

разба|вля́ть [28], <~вить> [14] dilute; **~лтывать** *coll.*, <разболта́ть> [1] blab out, give away

разбе́|г *m* [1] running start, run (with, at **с** Р); **~га́ться** [1], <~жа́ться> [4; -егу́сь, -ежи́шься, -егу́тся] take a run; ***в ра́зные сто́роны*** scatter; ***у меня́ глаза́ ~жа́лись*** I was dazzled

разби|ва́ть [1], <~ть> [разобью́, -бьёшь; разбе́й(те)!; -и́тый] break (to pieces), crash, crush; defeat (*a. mil.*); (*раздели́ть*) divide up (into **на** В); *парк* lay out; *пала́тку* pitch; *коле́но и т. д.* hurt badly; *дово́ды и т. д.* smash; **-ся** break; get broken; *на гру́ппы* break up, divide; hurt o.s. badly; **~ра́тельство** *n* [9] examination, investigation; **~ра́ть** [1], <разобра́ть> [разберу́, -рёшь; разобра́л, -á, -о; -о́бранный] take to pieces, dismantle; *дом* pull down; *де́ло* investigate, inquire into; (*различа́ть*) make out, decipher, understand; *ве́щи* sort out; (*раскупа́ть*) buy up; **-ся** (**в** П) grasp, understand; **~тый** [14 *sh.*] broken; *coll.* (*уста́лый*) jaded; **~ть(ся)** → **~ва́ть(ся)**

разбо́й *m* [3] robbery; **~ник** *m* [1] robber; *joc.* (little) rogue; scamp

Р

разболта́ть → ***разба́лтывать***

разбо́р *m* [1] analysis; *произведе́ния* review, critique; *де́ла* investigation, inquiry (into); ***без ~а, ~у*** *coll.* indiscriminately; **~ка** *f* [5] taking to pieces, dismantling; (*сортиро́вка*) sorting (out); **~ный** [14] collapsible; **~чивость** *f* [8] *по́черка* legibility; *о челове́ке* scrupulousness; **~чивый** [14 *sh.*] scrupulous, fastidious; legible

разбр|а́сывать, <~оса́ть> [1] scatter, throw about, strew; **~еда́ться** [1], <~ести́сь> [25] disperse; **~о́д** [1] disorder; **~о́санный** [14] sparse; scattered; **~оса́ть** → ***~а́сывать***

разбух|а́ть [1], <~нуть> [21] swell

разва́л *m* [1] collapse, breakdown; disintegration; **~ивать** [1], <≈и́ть> [13; -алю́, -а́лишь] pull (*or* break) down; disorganize; **-ся** fall to pieces, collapse; *coll. в кре́сле* collapse, sprawl; **~ины** *f pl.* [5] ruins (*coll. a. sg. = p.*)

ра́зве really; perhaps; only; except that

развева́ться [1] fly, flutter, flap

разве́д|ать → ***~ывать***; **~е́ние** *n* [12] breeding; *расте́ний* cultivation; **~ённый** [14] divorced; divorcé(e) *su.*; **~ка** *f* [5; *g/pl.*: -док] *mil.* reconnaissance; intelligence service; *geol.* prospecting; **~чик** *m* [1] scout; intelligence officer; reconnaissance aircraft; **~ывательный** [14] reconnaissance...; **~ывать**, <~ать> [1] reconnoiter (*Brt.* -tre); *geol.* prospect; *coll.* find out

разве|зти́ → ***развози́ть***; **~нча́ть** [1] *pf. fig.* debunk

развёр|нутый [14] (*широкомасшта́бный*) large-scale; detailed; **~тывать** [1], <разверну́ть> [20] unfold, unroll, unwrap; *mil.* deploy; *fig.* develop; (**-ся** *v/i.*; *a.* turn)

разве|сно́й [14] sold by weight; **≈сить** → ***≈шивать***; **~сти́(сь)** → ***разводи́ть(ся)***; **~твле́ние** *n* [12] ramification, branching; **~твля́ться** [28], <~тви́ться> [14 *e.*; 3rd *p. only*] ramify, branch; **≈шивать** [1], <≈сить> [15] weigh (out); *бельё* hang (out); **≈ять** [27] *pf.* disperse; *сомне́ния* dispel

разви|ва́ть [1], <≈ть> [разовью́, -вьёшь; разве́й(те)!; разви́л, -а́, -о; -ви́тый (ра́зви́т, -а́, -о)] develop (*v/i.* **-ся**); evolve; **≈нчивать** [1], <~нти́ть> [15 *e.*; -нчу́, -нти́шь; -и́нченный] unscrew; **≈тие** *n* [12] development, evolution; **~то́й** [14; ра́звит, -а́, -о] developed; *ребёнок* advanced, well-developed; **≈ть(ся)** → ***~ва́ть(ся)***

развле|ка́ть [1],<≈чь> [26] entertain, amuse (**-ся** o.s.); (*развле́чь отвлека́я*) divert; **~че́ние** *n* [12] entertainment, amusement; diversion

разво́д *m* [1] divorce; ***быть в ~е*** be divorced; **~и́ть** [15], <развести́> [25] take (along), bring; divorce (**с** T from); (*раствори́ть*) dilute; *живо́тных* rear, breed; *agric.* plant, cultivate; *ого́нь* light, make; *мост* raise; **-ся**, <-сь> get *or* be divorced (**с** T from); *coll.* multiply, grow *or* increase in number

раз|вози́ть [15], <~везти́> [24] *това́ры* deliver; *госте́й* drive; **~вора́чивать** *coll.* → ***~вёртывать***

развра́|т *m* [1] debauchery; depravity; **~ти́ть(ся)** → ***~ща́ть(ся)***; **~тник** *m* [1] profligate; debauchee, rake; **~тный** [14; -тен, -тна] depraved, corrupt; **~ща́ть** [1], <~ти́ть> [15 *e.*; -ащу́, -ати́шь; -ащённый] (**-ся** become) deprave(d), debauch(ed), corrupt; **~щённость** *f* [8] depravity

развяз|а́ть → ***≈ывать***; **≈ка** *f* [5; *g/pl.*: -зок] *lit.* denouement; outcome; upshot; ***де́ло идёт к ≈ке*** things are coming to a head; **≈ный** [14; -зен, -зна] forward, (overly) familiar; **≈ывать** [1], <~а́ть> [3] untie, undo; *fig. войну́* unleash; *coll. язы́к* loosen; **-ся** come untied; *coll.* (*освободи́ться*) be through (**с** T with)

разгад|а́ть → ***≈ывать***; **≈ка** [5; *g/pl.*: -док] solution; **≈ывать**, <~а́ть> [1] guess; *зага́дку* solve

разга́р *m* [1] (**в** П *or* В) ***в ~е спо́ра*** in the heat of; ***в ~е ле́та*** at the height of; ***в по́лном ~е*** in full swing

раз|гиба́ть [1], <~огну́ть> [20] unbend, straighten (**-ся** o.s.)

разгла́|живать [1], <~дить> [15] smooth out; *швы и т. д.* iron, press; **~ша́ть** [1], <~си́ть> [15 *e.*; -ашу́, -аси́шь; -ашённый] divulge, give away, let out

разгляд|е́ть [11] *pf.* make out; discern; **~ывать** [1] examine, scrutinize

разгне́ванный [14] angry

разгов|а́ривать [1] talk (**с** Т to, with; **о** П about, of), converse, speak; **~о́р** *m* [1] talk, conversation; → ***речь***; ***перемени́ть те́му ~о́ра*** change the subject; **~о́рный** [14] colloquial; **~о́рчивый** [14 *sh.*] talkative, loquacious

разго́н *m* [1] dispersal; *a.* → ***разбе́г***; **~я́ть** [28], <разогна́ть> [разгоню́, -о́нишь; разгна́л, -а́, -о; разо́гнанный] drive away, disperse; *тоску́ и т. д.* dispel; *coll.* drive at high speed; **-ся** gather speed; gather momentum

разгор|а́ться [1], <~е́ться> [9] flare up; *щёки* flush

разгра|бля́ть [28], <~бить> [14], **~бле́ние** *n* [12] plunder, pillage, loot; **~ниче́ние** *n* [12] delimitation, differentiation; **~ни́чивать** [1], <~ни́чить> [16] demarcate, delimit; *обя́занности* divide

разгро́м *m* [1] *mil., etc.* crushing defeat, rout; *coll.* (*по́лный беспоря́док*) havoc, devastation, chaos

разгру|жа́ть [1], <~зи́ть> [15 & 15 *e.*; -ужу́, -у́зи́шь; -у́женный & -ужённый] (**-ся** be) unload(ed); **~зка** *f* [5; *g/pl.*: -зок] unloading

разгу́л *m* [1] (*кутёж*) revelry, carousal; *шовини́зма* outburst of; **~ивать** F [1] stroll, saunter; **-ся**, <~я́ться> [28] *о пого́де* clear up; **~ьный** *coll.* [14; -лен, -льна]: ***~ьный о́браз жи́зни*** life of dissipation

разда|ва́ть [5], <~ть> [-да́м, -да́шь, *etc.* → ***дать***; ро́здал, раздала́, ро́здало; ро́зданный, (-ан, раздана́, ро́здано)] distribute; dispense; give (*cards*: deal) out; **-ся** (re)sound, ring out, be heard; **~вли-ва́ть** [1] → ***дави́ть 2.***; **~ть(ся)** → ***~ва́ть(ся)***; **~ча** *f* [5] distribution

раздва́иваться → ***двои́ться***

раздви|га́ть [1], <~нуть> [20] part, move apart; *занаве́ски* draw back; **~жно́й** [14] *стол* expanding; *дверь* sliding

раздвое́ние *n* [12] division into two, bifurcation; ***~ ли́чности*** *med.* split personality

раздева́|лка *coll.* *f* [5; *g/pl.*: -лок] checkroom, cloakroom; **~ть** [1], <разде́ть> [-де́ну, -де́нешь; -де́тый] undress (*v/i.* **-ся**) strip (of)

разде́л *m* [1] division; *кни́ги* section; **~аться** *coll.* [1] *pf.* get rid *or* be quit (**с** Т о); **~е́ние** *n* [12] division (***на*** В into); **~и́тельный** [14] dividing; *gr.* disjunctive; **~и́ть(ся)** → ***~я́ть(ся)*** & ***дели́ть(ся)***; **~ьный** [14] separate; (*отчётливый*) distinct; **~я́ть** [28], <~и́ть> [13; -елю́, -е́лишь; -елённый] divide (***на*** В into; *a.* [-ed] by); separate; *го́ре и т. д.* share; **-ся** (be) divide(d)

разде́ть(ся) → ***раздева́ть(ся)***

раз|дира́ть *coll.* [1], <~одра́ть> [раздеру́, -рёшь; разодрал, -а́, -о; -о́дранный] *impf.* rend; *pf. coll.* tear up; **~добы́ть** *coll.* [-бу́ду, -бу́дешь] *pf.* get, procure, come by

раздо́лье *n* [10] → ***приво́лье***

раздо́р *m* [1] discord, contention; ***я́блоко ~а*** bone of contention

раздоса́дованный *coll.* [14] angry

раздраж|а́ть [1], <~и́ть> [16 *e.*; -жу́, -жи́шь; -жённый] irritate, provoke; vex, annoy; **-ся** become irritated; **~е́ние** *n* [12] irritation; **~и́тельный** [14; -лен, -льна] irritable, short-tempered; **~и́ть(ся)** → ***~а́ть(ся)***

раздробл|е́ние *n* [12] breaking, smashing to pieces; **~я́ть** [28] → ***дроби́ть***

разду|ва́ть [1], <~ть> [18] fan; blow, blow about; (*распу́хнуть*) swell; (*преувели́чивать*) inflate; exaggerate; **-ся** swell

разду́м|ывать, <~ать> [1] (*переду́мать*) change one's mind; *impf.* deliberate, consider; ***не ~ывая*** without a moment's thought; **~ье** *n* [10] thought(s), meditation; (*сомне́ние*) doubt(s)

разду́ть(ся) → ***раздува́ть(ся)***

раз|ева́ть *coll.* [1], <~и́нуть> [20] open wide; ***~ева́ть рот*** gape; **~жа́лобить** [14] *pf.* move to pity; **~жа́ть** → ***~жима́ть***; **~жёвывать** [1], <~жева́ть> [7 *e.*; -жую́, -жуёшь] chew; **~жига́ть** [1],<~же́чь> [г/ж: -зожгу́, -жжёшь; -жгут; разжёг, -зожгла́; разожжённый] kindle (*a. fig.*); *стра́сти* rouse; *вражду́* stir up; **~жима́ть** [1], <~жа́ть> [разожму́, -мёшь; разжа́тый] unclasp, undo; **~и́нуть** → ***~ева́ть***; **~и́ня** *coll. m/f* [6] scatterbrain; **~и́тельный** [14; -лен, -льна] striking; **~и́ть** [13] reek (T of)

раз|лага́ть [1], <~ложи́ть> [16] break down, decompose; (*v/i.* **-ся**); (become) demoralize(d), corrupt(ed); go to pieces; **~ла́д** *m* [1] discord; **~ла́живаться** [1], <~ла́диться> [1] get out of order; *coll.* go wrong; **~ла́мывать** [1], <~лома́ть> [1], <~ломи́ть> [14] break (in pieces); **~лета́ться** [1], <~лете́ться> [11] fly (away, asunder); *coll.* shatter (to pieces); *наде́жды* come to naught; *о новостя́х и т. д.* spread quickly

разли́|в *m* [1] flood; **~ва́ть** [1], <~ть> [разолью́, -льёшь; → ***лить***; -ле́й(те); -и́л, -а́, -о; -и́тый (-и́т, -а́, -о)] spill; pour out; bottle; *суп и т. д.* ladle; **-ся** (*v/i.*) flood, overflow

различ|а́ть [1],<~и́ть> [16 *e.*; -чу́, -чи́шь; -чённый] (*отлича́ть*) distinguish; (*разгляде́ть*) discern; **-ся** *impf.* differ (T, ***по*** Д in); **~ие** *n* [12] distinction, difference; **~и́тельный** [14] distinctive; **~и́ть** → ***~а́ть***; **~ный** [14; -чен, -чна] different, various, diverse

разлож|е́ние *n* [12] decomposition, decay; *fig.* corruption; **~и́ть(ся)** → ***разлага́ть*** (**-ся**) & ***раскла́дывать***

разлом|а́ть, **~и́ть** → ***разла́мывать***

разлу́|ка *f* [5] separation (**с** T from), parting; **~ча́ть** [1], <~чи́ть> [16 *e.*; -чу́, -чи́шь; -чённый] separate (*v/i.* **-ся**; **с** T from), part

разма́|зывать [1], <~зать> [3] smear, spread; **~тывать** [1], <размота́ть> unwind, uncoil; **~х** *m* [1] swing; span (*ae.* & *fig.*); sweep; *ма́ятника* amplitude; *fig.* scope; **~хивать** [1], *once* <~хну́ть> [20] (T) swing, sway; *са́блей и т. д.* brandish; gesticulate; **-ся** lift (one's hand T); *fig.* do things in a big way; **~шистый** *coll.* [14 *sh.*] *шаг*, *жест* wide; *по́черк* bold

разме|жева́ть [7] *pf.* delimit, demarcate; **~льча́ть** [1], <~льчи́ть> [16 *e.*; -чу́, -чи́шь; -чённый] pulverize

разме́н [1], **~ивать** [1], <~я́ть> [28] (ex)change (***на*** B for); **~ный** [14]: ***~ная моне́та*** small change

разме́р *m* [1] size, dimension(s); rate (***в*** П at), amount; scale; extent; ***в широ́ких ~ах*** on a large scale; ***доска́ ~ом 0.2 х 2 ме́тра*** board measuring 0.2 x 2 meters, *Brt.* -tres; **~енный** [14 *sh.*] measured; **~я́ть** [28], <~ить> [13] measure (off)

разме|сти́ть → ***~ща́ть***; **~ча́ть** [1], <~тить> [15] mark (out); **~шивать** [1], <~ша́ть> [1] stir (up); **~ща́ть** [1], <~сти́ть> [15 *e.*; -ещу́, -ести́шь; -ещённый] place; lodge, accommodate (***в*** П, ***по*** Д in, at, with); (*распредели́ть*) distribute; stow; **~ще́ние** *n* [12] distribution; accommodation; arrangement, order; *гру́за* stowage; *mil.* stationing, quartering; *fin.* placing, investment

рaзми|на́ть [1], <размя́ть> [разомну́, -нёшь; размя́тый] knead; *coll.* *но́ги* stretch (*one's legs*); **~ну́ться** *coll. pf.* [20] *о пи́сьмах* cross; miss o.a.

размнож|а́ть [1], <~ить> [16] multiply; duplicate; (*v/i.* **-ся**); reproduce; breed; **~е́ние** *n* [12] multiplication; mimeographing; *biol.* propagation, reproduction; **~ить(ся)** → ***~а́ть(ся)***

размо|зжи́ть [16 *e.*; -жу́, -жи́шь; -жённый] *pf.* smash; **~ка́ть** [1], <~кнуть> [21] get soaked; **~лвка** *f* [5; *g/pl.*: -вок] tiff, quarrel; **~ло́ть** [17; -мелю́, -ме́лешь] grind; **~та́ть** → ***разма́тывать***; **~чи́ть** [16] *pf.* soak; steep

размы|ва́ть [1], <~ть> [22] *geol.* wash away; erode; **~ка́ть** [1], <разомкну́ть> [20] open (*mil.* order, ranks); disconnect, break (*el.* circuit); **~́ть** → ***~ва́ть***

размышл|е́ние *n* [12] reflection (**о** П on), thought; ***по зре́лому ~е́нию*** on second thoughts; **~я́ть** [28] reflect, meditate (**о** П on)

размягч|а́ть [1], <~и́ть> [16 *e.*; -чу́, -чи́шь; -чённый] soften; *fig.* mollify

раз|мя́ть → ***~мина́ть***; **~на́шивать**, <~носи́ть> [15] *ту́фли* wear in; **~нести́** → ***~носи́ть 1.***; **~нима́ть** [1], <~ня́ть> [-ниму́, -ни́мешь; -ня́л & ро́знял, -а́, -о; -ня́тый (-ня́т, -а́, -о)] *деру́щихся* separate, part

ра́зница *f* [5; *sg. only*; -цей] difference

разнобо́й *m* [3] disagreement; *в де́йствиях* lack of coordination

разно|ви́дность *f* [8] variety; **~гла́сие** *n* [12] discord, disagreement; difference; (*расхожде́ние*) discrepancy; **~кали́берный** *coll.* [14], **~ма́стный** [14; -тен, -тна] → ***~шёрстный***; **~обра́зие** *n* [12] variety, diversity, multiplicity; **~обра́зный** [14; -зен, -зна] varied, various; **~реч...** → ***противореч...***; **~ро́дный** [14; -ден, -дна] heterogeneous

разно́с *m* [1] *по́чты* delivery; *coll.* ***устро́ить ~*** give s.o. a dressing-down; **~и́ть** [15] **1.** <разнести́> [25 -с-] deliver (**по** Д to, at), carry; *слу́хи и т. д.* spread; (*разби́ть*) smash, destroy; *ве́тром* scatter; *coll.* (*распу́хнуть*) swell; **2.** → ***разна́шивать***

разно|сторо́нний [15; -о́нен, -о́нна] many-sided; *fig.* versatile; *math.* scalene; **~́сть** *f* [8] difference; **~́счик** *m* [1] peddler (*Brt.* pedlar); *газе́т* delivery boy; ***~счик телегра́мм*** one delivering telegrams; **~цве́тный** [14; -тен, -тна] of different colo(u)rs; multicolo(u)red; **~шёрстный** [14; -тен, -тна] *coll.* *пу́блика* motley, mixed

разну́зданный [14 *sh.*] unbridled

ра́зн|ый [14] various, different, diverse; **~я́ть** → ***~има́ть***

разо|блача́ть [1], <~блачи́ть> [16 *e.*; -чу́, -чи́шь; -чённый] *eccl.* disrobe, divest; *fig.* expose, unmask; **~блаче́ние** *n* [12] exposure, unmasking; **~бра́ть(ся)** → ***разбира́ть(ся)***; **~гна́ть(ся)** → ***разгоня́ть(ся)***; **~гну́ть(ся)** → ***разгиба́ть(ся)***; **~грева́ть** [1], <~гре́ть> [8; -е́тый] warm (up); **~де́тый** *coll.* [14 *sh.*] dressed up; **~дра́ть** → ***раздира́ть***; **~йти́сь** → ***расходи́ться***; **~мкну́ть** → ***размыка́ть***; **~рва́ть(ся)** → ***разрыва́ть(ся)***

разор|е́ние *n* [12] *fig.* ruin; *в результа́те войны́* devastation; **~и́тельный** [14; -лен, -льна] ruinous; **~и́ть(ся)** → ***~я́ть(ся)***; **~ужа́ть** [1], <~ужи́ть> [16 *e.*; -жу́, -жи́шь; -жённый] disarm (*v/i.* **-ся**); **~уже́ние** *n* [12] disarmament; **~я́ть** [28], <~и́ть> [13] ruin; devastate; (**-ся** be ruined, bankrupt)

разосла́ть → ***рассыла́ть***

разостла́ть → ***расстила́ть***

разочар|ова́ние *n* [12] disappointment; **~о́вывать** [1], <~ова́ть> [7] (**-ся** be) disappoint(ed) (**в** П in)

разра|ба́тывать, <~бо́тать> [1] *agric.* cultivate; work out, develop, elaborate; *mining* exploit; **~бо́тка** *f* [5; *g/pl.*: -ток] *agric.* cultivation; working (out), elaboration; exploitation; **~жа́ться** [1], <~зи́ться> [15 *e.*; -ажу́сь, -ази́шься] *о што́рме, войне́* break out; *сме́хом* burst out laughing; **~ста́ться** [1], <~сти́сь> [24; 3rd *p. only*: -тётся; -ро́сся, -сла́сь] grow (*a. fig.*); *расте́ния* spread

разрежённый [14] *phys.* rarefied; rare

разре́з *m* [1] cut; (*сече́ние*) section; slit; *глаз* shape of the eyes; **~́ать** [1], <~ать> [3] cut (up), slit; **~ыва́ть** [1] → ***~́ать***

разреш|а́ть [1], <~и́ть> [16 *e.*; -шу́, -ши́шь; -шённый] permit, allow; *пробле́му* (re)solve; (*ула́живать*) settle; **-ся** be (re)solved; **~е́ние** *n* [12] permission (**с** Р with); permit; authorization (**на** В for); *пробле́мы* (re)solution; *конфли́ктов и т. д.* settlement; **~и́ть(ся)** → ***~а́ть(ся)***

раз|рисова́ть [7] *pf.* cover with drawings; ornament; **~ро́зненный** [14] broken up (as, e.g., a set); left over *or* apart (from, e.g., a set); odd; **~руба́ть** [1], <~руби́ть> [14] chop; ***~руби́ть го́рдиев у́зел*** cut the Gordian knot

разру́|ха *f* [5] ruin; ***экономи́ческая ~ха*** dislocation; **~ша́ть** [1], <~шить> [16] destroy, demolish; *здоро́вье* ruin; (*расстро́ить*) frustrate; **-ся** fall to ruin; **~ше́ние** *n* [12] destruction, devastation; **~шить(ся)** → ***~ша́ть(ся)***

разры́|в *m* [1] breach, break, rupture; (*взрыв*) explosion; (*промежу́ток*) gap; **~ва́ть** [1] **1.** <разорва́ть> [-ву́, -вёшь; -ва́л, -а́, -о; -о́рванный] tear (to *pieces* ***на*** В); break (off); (**-ся** *v/i., a.* explode); **2.** <~ть> [22] dig up; **~да́ться** [1] *pf.* break into sobs; **~ть** → ***~ва́ть* 2.**; **~хля́ть** [28] → ***рыхли́ть***

разря́|д *m* [1] **1.** category, class; *sport* rating; **2.** *el.* discharge; **~ди́ть** → ***~жа́ть***; **~дка** *f* [5; *g/pl.*: -док] **1.** *typ.* letterspacing; **2.** discharging; unloading; *pol.* détente; **~жа́ть** [1], <~ди́ть> [15 *e.* & 15; -яжу́, -яди́шь; -яжённый & -я́женный] discharge; *typ.* space out; ***~ди́ть атмосфе́ру*** relieve tension

разу|бежда́ть [1], <~беди́ть> [15 *e.*; -ежу́, -еди́шь; -еждённый] (***в*** П) dissuade (from); **-ся** change one's mind about; **~ва́ться** [1], <~ться> [18] take off one's shoes; **~веря́ться** [28], <~ве́риться> [13] (***в*** П) lose faith (in); **~знава́ть** *coll.* [5], <~зна́ть> [1] find out (**о** П, В about); *impf.* make inquiries about; **~кра́шивать** [1], <~кра́сить> decorate; embellish; **~крупня́ть** [28], <~крупни́ть> [14] break up into smaller units

ра́зум *m* [1] reason; intellect; **~е́ть** [8] understand; know; mean, imply (***под*** Т by); **~е́ться** [8]: ***само́ собо́й ~е́ется*** it goes without saying; ***разуме́ется*** of course; **~ный** [14; -мен, -мна] rational; reasonable, sensible; wise

разу́|ться → ***~ва́ться***; **~чивать** [1], <~чи́ть> [16] learn, study, *стихи́ и т. д.* learn; **-ся** forget

разъе|да́ть [1] → ***есть*[1] 2.**; **~диня́ть** [28], <~дини́ть> [13] separate; *el.* disconnect; **~зжа́ть** [1] drive, ride, go about; be on a journey *or* trip; **-ся**, <~ха́ться> [-е́дусь, -е́дешься; -езжа́йтесь!] leave (***по*** Д for); *о супру́гах* separate; *о маши́нах* pass o.a. (**с** Т)

разъярённый [14] enraged, furious

разъясн|е́ние *n* [12] explanation; clarification; **~я́ть** [28], <~и́ть> [13] explain, elucidate

разы́|грывать, <~гра́ть> [1] play; *в лотере́е* raffle; (*подшути́ть*) play a trick (on); **-ся** *о бу́ре* break out; *о страстя́х* run high; happen; **~скивать** [1], <~ска́ть> [3] seek, search (for; *pf.* out = find)

рай *m* [3; в раю́] paradise

рай|о́н *m* [1] district; region, area; **~о́нный** [14] district...; regional; **~сове́т** *m* [1] (***райо́нный сове́т***) district soviet (*or* council)

рак *m* [1] crayfish; *med.* cancer; *astron.* Cancer; ***кра́сный как ~*** red as a lobster

раке́т|а *f* [5] rocket; missile; **~ка** *f* [5; *g/pl.*: -ток] *sport* racket; **~ный** [14] rocket-powered; missile...; **~чик** *m* [1] missile specialist

ра́ковина *f* [5] shell; *на ку́хне* sink; ***ушна́я ~*** helix

ра́м|(к)а *f* [5; (*g/pl.*: -мок)] frame (-work, *a. fig.* = limits; ***в*** П within); **~па** *f* [5] footlights

ра́н|а *f* [5] wound; **~г** *m* [1] rank; **~е́ние** *n* [12] wound(ing); **~еный** [14] wounded (*a. su.*); **~ец** *m* [1; -нца] *шко́льный* schoolbag, satchel; **~ить** [13] (*im*)*pf.* wound, injure (***в*** В in)

ра́н|ний [15] early (*adv.* ***~о***); ***~о или по́здно*** sooner *or* later; **~ова́то** *coll.* rather early; **~ьше** earlier; formerly; (*сперва́*) first; (Р) before; ***как мо́жно ~ьше*** as soon as possible

рап|и́ра *f* [5] foil; **~о́рт** [1], **~ортова́ть** [7] (*im*)*pf.* report; **~со́дия** *f* [7] *mus.* rhapsody

ра́са *f* [5] race

раска́|иваться [1], <~яться> [27] repent (*v/t.*; ***в*** П of); **~лённый** [14], **~ли́ть(ся)** → ***~ля́ть(ся)***; **~лывать** [1], <расколо́ть> [17] split,

P

cleave; crack; (*v/i.* **-ся**); **~лять** [28], <~лить> [13] make (**-ся** become) red-hot, white-hot; **~пывать** [1], <раскопáть> [1] dig out *or* up; **~т** *m* [1] roll, peal; **~тистый** [14 *sh.*] rolling; **~тывать**, <~тáть> [1] (un)roll; *v/i.* **-ся**; **~чивать**, <~чáть> [1] swing; shake; **-ся** *coll.* bestir o.s.; **~яние** *n* [12] repentance (**в** П of); **~яться** → ***~иваться***

раскидистый [14 *sh.*] spreading

раски|дывать [1], <~нуть> [20] spread (out); stretch (out); *шатёр* pitch, set up

раскла|днóй [14] folding, collapsible; **~дýшка** *coll. f* [5; *g/pl.*: -шек] folding *or* folding bed; **~дывать** [1], <разложи́ть> [16] lay *or* spread out, distribute; *костёр* make, light; (*распредели́ть*) apportion

раскó|л *m* [1] *hist.* schism, dissent; *pol.* division, split; **~лóть(ся)** → ***раскáлывать(ся)***; **~пáть** → ***раскáпывать***; **~пка** *f* [5; *g/pl.*: -пок] excavation

раскр|áшивать [1] → ***крáсить***; **~епощáть** [1], <~епости́ть> [15 *e.*; -ощý, -ости́шь; -ощённый] emancipate, liberate; **~епощéние** *n* [12] emancipation, liberation; **~итиковáть** [7] *pf.* severely criticize; **~ичáться** [4 *e.*; -чýсь, -чи́шься] *pf.* shout, bellow (***на*** В at); **~ывáть** [1], <~ы́ть> [22] open wide (*v/i.* **-ся**); uncover, disclose, reveal; ***~ы́ть свóй кáрты*** show one's cards *or* one's hand

раску|пáть [1], <~пи́ть> [14] buy up; **~пóривать** [1], <~пóрить> [13] uncork; open; **~сывать** [1], <~си́ть> [15] bite through; *pf. only* get to the heart of; *coll. когó-л.* see through; *чтó-л.* understand; **~тывать**, <~тать> [1] unwrap

рáсовый [14] racial

распáд *m* [1] disintegration; *радиоакти́вный* decay

распа|дáться [1], <~сться> [25; -пáлся, -лась; -пáвшийся] fall to pieces; disintegrate; break up (***на*** В into); collapse; *chem.* decompose; **~кóвывать** [1], <~ковáть> [7] unpack; **~рывать** [1] → ***порóть***; **~сться** → ***~дáться***; **~хивать** [1] **1.** <~хáть> [3] plow (*Brt.* plough) up; **2.** <~хнýть> [20] throw *or* fling open (*v/i.* **-ся**); **~шóнка** *f* [5; *g/pl.*: -нок] baby's undershirt (*Brt.* vest)

распе|вáть [1] sing for a time; **~кáть** *coll.* [1], <~чь> [26] scold; **~чáтка** *f* [5; *g/pl.*: -ток] *tech.* hard copy; *comput.* printout; **~чáтывать**, <~чáтать> [1] **1.** unseal; open; **2.** print out

распи́|ливать [1], <~ли́ть> [13; -илю́, -и́лишь; -и́ленный] saw up; **~нáть** [1], <распя́ть> [-пнý, -пнёшь; -пя́тый] crucify

распис|áние *n* [12] timetable (*rail.*) ***~áние поездóв***; ***~áние урóков*** schedule (***по*** Д of, for); **~áть(ся)** → **~ывать(ся)**; **~ка** *f* [5; *g/pl.*: -сок] receipt (***под*** В against); **~ывать** [1], <~áть> [3] write, enter; *art* paint; ornament; **-ся** sign (one's name); (acknowledge) receipt (**в** П); *coll.* register one's marriage

распл|авля́ть [28] → ***плáвить***; **~áкаться** [3] *pf.* burst into tears; **~áта** *f* [5] payment; (*возмéздие*) reckoning; **~áчиваться** [1], <~ати́ться> [15] (**с** Т) pay off, settle accounts (with); pay (***за*** В for); **~ескáть** [3] *pf.* spill

распле|тáть [1], <~сти́> [25 -т-] (**-ся**, <-сь> come) unbraid(ed); untwist(ed), undo(ne)

расплы|вáться [1], <~ться> [23] spread; *черни́ла и т. д.* run; *на водé* swim about; *очертáния* blur; ***~ться в улы́бке*** break into a smile; **~вчатый** [14 *sh.*] blurred, vague

расплю́щить [16] *pf.* flatten out, hammer out

распозн|авáть [5], <~áть> [1] recognize, identify; *болéзнь* diagnose

распол|агáть [1], <~ожи́ть> [16] arrange; *войск* dispose; *impf.* (Т) dispose (of), have (at one's disposal); **-ся** settle; encamp; *pf.* be situated; **~агáющий** [17] prepossessing; **~зáться** [1], <~зти́сь> [24] creep *or* crawl away; *слýхи* spread; **~ожéние** *n* [12] arrangement; (dis)position (***к*** Д toward[s]); location, situation; (*влечéние, дóброе*

Р

отноше́ние) inclination, propensity; **~оже́ние ду́ха** mood; **~о́женный** [14 *sh.*] *a.* situated; (well-)disposed (**к** Д toward[s]); inclined; **~ожи́ть(ся)** → **~ага́ть(ся)**

распор|яди́тельность *f* [8] good management; **~яди́тельный** [14; -лен, -льна] capable; efficient; **~яди́ться** → **~яжа́ться**; **~я́док** [1; -дка] order; *в больни́це и т. д.* regulations *pl.*; **~яжа́ться** [1], <~яди́ться> [15 *e.*; -яжу́сь, -яди́шься] order; (T) dispose (of); see to, take care of; *impf.* (*управля́ть*) be the boss; manage; **~яже́ние** *n* [12] order(s), instruction(s); disposal (**в** В; **в** П at); ***име́ть в своём ~яже́нии*** have at one's disposal

распра́в|а *f* [5] violence; reprisal; *крова́вая* massacre; **~ля́ть** [28], <~ить> [14] straighten; smooth; *кры́лья* spread; *но́ги* stretch; **-ся** (**с** Т) deal with; make short work of

распредел|е́ние *n* [12] distribution; **~и́тельный** [14] distributing; *el. щит* switch...; **~я́ть** [28], <~и́ть> [13] distribute; *зада́ния и т. д.* allot; (*напра́вить*) assign (**по** Д to)

распрод|ава́ть [5], <~а́ть> [-да́м, -да́шь; *etc.*, → **дать**; -про́дал, -а́, -о; -про́данный] sell out (*or* off); **~а́жа** *f* [5] (clearance) sale

распрост|ира́ть [1], <~ере́ть> [12] stretch out; *влия́ние* extend (*v/i.* **-ся**); **~ёртый** *a.* open (arms *объя́тия pl.*); outstretched; prostrate, prone; **~и́ться** [15 *e.*; -ощу́сь, -ости́шься] (**с** Т) bid farewell (to); (*отказа́ться*) give up, abandon

распростран|е́ние *n* [12] *слу́хов и т. д.* spread(ing); *зна́ний* dissemination, propagation; ***получи́ть широ́кое ~е́ние*** become popular; be widely practiced; **~ённый** [14] widespread; **~я́ть** [28], <~и́ть> [13] spread, diffuse (*v/i.* **-ся**); propagate, disseminate; extend; *за́пах* give off; **-ся** *coll.* enlarge upon

распро|ща́ться [1] *coll.* → **~сти́ться**

ра́спря *f* [6; *g/pl.*: -рей] strife, conflict; **~га́ть** [1], <~чь> [26 г/ж: -ягу́, -яжёшь] unharness

распу|ска́ть [1], <~сти́ть> [15] dismiss, disband; *parl.* dissolve; *на кани́кулы* dismiss for; *зна́мя* unfurl; *вяза́ние* undo; *во́лосы* loosen; *слу́хи* spread; *ма́сло* melt; *fig.* spoil; **-ся** *цвето́к* open; (*раствори́ться*) dissolve; *coll.* become intractable; let o.s. go; **~тать** → **~тывать**; **~тица** *f* [5] season of bad roads; **~тывать**, <~тать> [1] untangle; **~тье** *n* [10] crossroad(s); **~ха́ть** [1], <~хнуть> [21] swell; **~хший** [17] swollen; **~щенный** [14 *sh.*] spoiled, undisciplined; dissolute

распыл|и́тель *m* [4] spray(er), atomizer; **~я́ть** [28], <~и́ть> [13] spray, atomize; *fig.* dissipate

распя́|тие *n* [12] crucifixion; crucifix; **~ть** → ***распина́ть***

расса́|да *f* [5] seedlings; **~ди́ть** → **~живать**; **~дник** *m* [1] seedbed; *a. fig.* hotbed; **~живать** [1], <~ди́ть> [15] transplant; *люде́й* seat; **-ся**, <рассе́сться> [расся́дусь, -дешься; -се́лся, -се́лась] sit down, take one's seat; *fig.* sprawl

рассве́|т *m* [1] dawn (**на** П at), daybreak; **~та́ть** [1], <~сти́> [25 -т-: -светёт; -свело́] dawn

рассе|дла́ть [1] *pf.* unsaddle; **~ивать** [1], <~ять> [27] sow; *толпу́* scatter, *ту́чи* disperse (*v/i.* **-ся**); *сомне́ния* dispel; **~ка́ть** [1], <~чь> [26] cut through, cleave; (*of a cane, etc.*) swish; **~ля́ть** [28], <~ли́ть> [13] settle in a new location (*v/i.* **-ся**); **~сться** → ***расса́живаться***; **~янность** *f* [8] absentmindedness; **~янный** [14 *sh.*] absentminded; scattered; *phys.* diffused; **~ять(ся)** → ***~ивать(ся)***

расска́з *m* [1] account, narrative; tale, story; **~а́ть** → ***~ывать***; **~чик** *m* [1] narrator; storyteller; **~ывать** [1], <~а́ть> [3] tell; recount, narrate

расслаб|ля́ть [28], <~ить> [14] weaken, enervate (*v/i.* **~еть** [8] *pf.*)

рассл|е́дование *n* [12] investigation, inquiry; **~е́довать** [7] (*im*)*pf.* investigate, inquire into; **~ое́ние** *n* [12] stratification; **~ы́шать** [16] *pf.* catch (*what a p. is saying*); ***не ~ы́шать*** not (quite) catch

Р

рассм|а́тривать [1], <~отре́ть> [-отрю́, -о́тришь; -о́тренный] examine, view; consider; (*различи́ть*) discern, distinguish; **~ея́ться** [27 *e.*; -ею́сь; -еёшься] *pf.* burst out laughing; **~отре́ние** *n* [12] examination (***при*** П at); consideration; **~отре́ть** → ***~а́тривать***

рассо́л *m* [1] brine

расспр|а́шивать [1], <~оси́ть> [15] inquire, ask; **~о́сы** *pl.* [1] inquiries

рассро́чка *f* [5] (payment by) instal(l)ments (**в** В *sg.* by)

расста|ва́ние → ***проща́ние***; **~ва́ться** [5], <~ться> [-а́нусь, -а́нешься] part (**с** Т with); leave; *с мечто́й и т. д.* give up; **~вля́ть** [28], <~вить> [14] place; arrange; set up; (*раздвига́ть*) move apart; **~но́вка** *f* [5; *g/pl.*: -вок] arrangement; punctuation; *персона́л* placing; ***~но́вка полити́ческих сил*** political scene; **~ться** → ***~ва́ться***

расст|ёгивать [1], <~егну́ть> [20] unbutton; unfasten (*v/i.* **-ся**); **~ила́ть** [1], <разостла́ть> [расстелю́, -е́лешь; разо́стланный] spread out; lay (*v/i.* **-ся**); **~оя́ние** *n* [12] distance (at a ***на*** П); ***держа́ться на ~оя́нии*** keep aloof

расстр|а́ивать [1], <~о́ить> [13] upset; disorganize; disturb, spoil; shatter; *пла́ны* frustrate; *mus.* put out of tune; **-ся** be(come) upset, ill-humo(u)red, *etc.*

расстре́л *m* [1] execution by shooting; **~ивать** [1], <~я́ть> [28] shoot

расстро́|ить(ся) → ***расстра́ивать(ся)***; **~йство** *n* [9] disorder, confusion; derangement; frustration; *желу́дка* stomach disorder; *coll.* diarrh(o)ea

расступ|а́ться [1], <~и́ться> [14] make way; *о толпе́* part

рассу|ди́тельность *f* [8] judiciousness; **~ди́тельный** [14; -лен, -льна] judicious, reasonable; **~ди́ть** [15] *pf.* judge; arbitrate; think, consider; decide; **~док** *m* [1; -дка] reason; common sense; **~дочный** [14; -чен, -чна] rational; **~жда́ть** [1] argue, reason; discourse (on); argue (about); discuss; **~жде́ние** *n* [12] reasoning, argument, debate, discussion

рассчи́т|ывать, <~а́ть> [1] calculate, estimate; *с рабо́ты* dismiss, sack; *impf.* count *or* reckon (***на*** В on); (*ожида́ть*) expect; (*намерева́ться*) intend; **-ся** settle accounts, *fig.* get even (**с** Т with); (*расплати́ться*) pay off

рассыл|а́ть [1], <разосла́ть> [-ошлю́, -ошлёшь; -о́сланный] send out (*or* round); **~ка** *f* [5] distribution; dispatch

рассып|а́ть [1], <~ать> [2] scatter, spill; *v/i.* **-ся** crumble, fall to pieces; break up; ***~а́ться в комплиме́нтах*** shower compliments (on Д)

раста́|лкивать, <растолка́ть> [1] push asunder, apart; (*буди́ть*) shake; **~пливать** [1], <растопи́ть> [14] light, kindle; *жир* melt; (*v/i.* **-ся**); **~птывать** [1], <растопта́ть> [3] trample, stamp (on); crush; **~скивать** [1], <~щи́ть> [16], *coll.* <~ска́ть> [1] (*раскра́сть*) pilfer; *на ча́сти* take away, remove little by little; *деру́щихся* separate

раство́р *m* [1] *chem.* solution; *цеме́нта* mortar; **~и́мый** [14 *sh.*] soluble; **~я́ть** [28], <~и́ть> **1.** [13] dissolve; **2.** [13; -орю́, -о́ришь; -о́ренный] open

расте́|ние *n* [12] plant; **~ре́ть** → ***растира́ть***; **~рза́ть** [1] *pf.* tear to pieces; **~рянный** [14 *sh.*] confused, perplexed, bewildered; **~ря́ть** [28] *pf.* lose (little by little); (**-ся** get lost; lose one's head; be[come] perplexed *or* puzzled)

расти́ [24 -ст-: -сту́, -стёшь; рос, -сла́; ро́сший] <вы́-> grow; grow up; (*увели́чиваться*) increase

раст|ира́ть [1], <~ере́ть> [12; разотру́, -трёшь] grind, pulverize; rub in; rub, massage

расти́тельн|ость *f* [8] vegetation; verdure; *на лице́* hair; **~ый** [14] vegetable; ***вести́ ~ый о́браз жи́зни*** vegetate

расти́ть [15 *e.*; ращу́, расти́шь] rear; grow, cultivate

расто|лка́ть → ***раста́лкивать***; **~лкова́ть** [7] *pf.* expound, explain; **~пи́ть** → ***раста́пливать***; **~пта́ть** → ***раста́птывать***; **~пы́рить** [13] *pf.* spread wide; **~ргáть** [1], <~ргнуть> [21] *договóр* cancel, annul; *брак* dissolve; **~ржéние** *n* [12] cancellation; annulment; dissolution; **~рóпный** [14; -пен, -пна] *coll.* smart, deft, quick; **~чáть** [1], <~чи́ть> [16 *e.*; -чý, -чи́шь; -чённый] squander, waste, dissipate; *похвалы́* lavish (Д on); **~чи́тель** *m* [4], squanderer, spendthrift; **~чи́тельный** [14; -лен, -лен] wasteful, extravagant

растра|влять [28], <~ви́ть> [14] irritate; *дýшу* aggravate; ***~ви́ть рáну*** *fig.* rub salt in the wound; **~́та** *f* [5] squandering; embezzlement; **~́тчик** *m* [1] embezzler; **~́чивать** [1], <~́тить> [15] spend, waste; embezzle

растр|епáть [2] *pf.* (**-ся** be[come]) tousle(d, **~ёпанный** [14]), dishevel([l]ed); ***в ~ёпанных чýвствах*** confused, mixed up

растрогáть [1] *pf.* move, touch

растя́|гивать [1], <~нýть> [19] stretch (*v/i.* **-ся**; *coll.* fall flat); *med.* sprain, strain; *словá* drawl; *во врéмени* drag out, prolong; **~жéние** *n* [12] stretching; strain(ing); **~жи́мый** [14 *sh.*] extensible, elastic; *fig.* vague; **~нутый** [14] long-winded, prolix; **~нýться** → ***~гиваться***

рас|формировáть [8] *pf.* disband; **~хáживать** [1] walk about, pace up and down; **~хвáливать** [1], <~хвали́ть> [13; -алю́, -áлишь; -áленный] shower praise on; **~хвáтывать**, *coll.* <~хватáть> [1] snatch away; (*раскупи́ть*) buy up (quickly)

расхи|щáть [1], <~́тить> [15] plunder; misappropriate; **~щéние** *n* [12] theft; misappropriation

расхó|д *m* [1] expenditure (**на** В for), expense(s); *тóплива и т. д.* consumption; **~ди́ться** [15], <разойти́сь> [-ойдýсь, -ойдёшься; -ошéдшийся; *g. pt.*: -ойдя́сь] go away; disperse; break up; *во мнéниях* differ (**с** Т from); *т. ж. о ли́ниях* diverge; (*расстáться*) part, separate; pass (*without meeting*); (*letters*) cross; *товáр* be sold out, sell; *дéньги* be spent, (**у** Р) run out of; **~довать** [7], <из-> spend, expend; *pf. a.* use up; **~ждéние** *n* [12] divergence, difference (**в** П of)

расцарáп|ывать, <~ать> [1] scratch (all over)

расцвé|т *m* [1] bloom, blossoming; *fig.* flowering; heyday, prime; *искýсства и т. д.* flourishing; ***в ~те лет*** in his prime; **~тáть** [1], <~сти́> [25; -т] blo(ss)om; flourish, thrive; **~тка** *f* [5; *g/pl.*: -ток] colo(u)ring, colo(u)rs

расцé|нивать [1], <~ни́ть> [13; -еню́, -éнишь; -енённый] estimate, value, rate; (*считáть*) consider, think; **~нка** *f* [5; *g/pl.*: -нок] valuation; *ценá* price; *об оплáте* rate; **~пля́ть** [28], <~пи́ть> [14] uncouple, unhook; disengage

рас|чесáть → ***~чёсывать***; **~чёска** *f* [5; *g/pl.*: -сок] comb; **~чéсть** → ***рассчитáть***; **~чёсывать** [1], <~чесáть> [3] comb (one's hair **-ся** *coll.*)

расчёт *m* [1] calculation; estimate; settlement (of accounts); payment; (*увольнéние*) dismissal, sack; account, consideration; ***приним́ать в ~*** take into account; ***из ~а*** on the basis (of); ***в ~е*** quits with; ***безнали́чный ~*** payment by written order; by check (*Brt.* cheque); ***~ нали́чными*** cash payment; **~ливый** [14 *sh.*] provident, thrifty; circumspect

рас|чищáть [1], <~чи́стить> [15] clear; **~членя́ть** [28], <~члени́ть> [13] dismember; divide; **~шáтывать**, <~шатáть> [1] loosen (*v/i.* **-ся** become lose); *о нéрвах, здорóвье* (be[come]) impair(ed); shatter(ed); **~шевели́ть** *coll.* [13] *pf.* stir (up)

расши|бáть → ***ушибáть***; **~вáть** [1], <~́ть> [разошью́, -шьёшь; → ***шить***] embroider; **~рéние** *n* [12] widening, enlargement; expansion; **~ря́ть** [28], <~́рить> [13] widen, enlarge; extend, expand; *med.* dilate; ***~́рить кругозóр*** broaden one's mind; **~́ть** → ***~вáть***; **~фрóвывать** [1], <~фровáть> [7] decipher, decode

рас|шнурóвывать [7] *pf.* unlace; **~щéлина** *f* [5] crevice, cleft, crack;

Р

~щепле́ние *n* [12] splitting; *phys.* fission; **~щепля́ть** [28], <~щепи́ть> [14 *e.*; -плю́, -пи́шь; -плённый] split
ратифи|ка́ция *f* [7] ratification; **~ци́ровать** [7] *(im)pf.* ratify
ра́товать [7] *за что́-л.* fight for, stand up for; *про́тив* inveigh against, declaim against
рахи́т *m* [1] rickets
рацион|ализи́ровать [7] *(im)pf.* rationalize, improve; **~а́льный** [14; -лен, -льна] rational (*a. math.*, *no sh.*); efficient
рвану́ть [20] *pf.* jerk; tug (**за** В at); **-ся** dart
рвать [рву, рвёшь; рвал, -á, -о] **1.** <разо-, изо-> [-о́рванный] tear (**на**, **в** В to *pieces*), *v/i.* **-ся**; **2.** <со-> pluck; **3.** <вы́-> pull out; *impers.* (В) vomit, spew; **4.** <пре-> break off; **5.** <взо-> blow up; **~ и мета́ть** *coll.* be in a rage; **-ся** break; (*стреми́ться*) be spoiling for
рве́ние *n* [12] zeal; eagerness
рво́т|а *f* [5] vomit(ing); **~ный** [14] emetic (*a. n, su.*)
реа|билити́ровать [7] *(im)pf.* rehabilitate; **~ги́ровать** [7] (**на** В) react (to); respond (to); **~кти́вный** [14] *chem.* reactive; *tech. ae.* jet-propelled; **~кто́р** *m* [1] *tech.* reactor, pile; **~кционе́р** *m* [1], **~кцио́нный** [14] reactionary; **~кция** *f* [7] reaction
реал|и́зм *m* [1] realism; **~изова́ть** [7] realize; *comm. a.* sell; **~исти́ческий** [16] realistic; **~ьность** *f* [8] reality; **~ьный** [14; -лен, -льна] real; (*осуществи́мый*) realizable
ребёнок *m* [2; *pl. a.* де́ти] child, *coll.* kid; baby; **грудно́й ~** suckling
ребро́ *n* [9; *pl.*: рёбра, рёбер, рёбрам] rib; edge (on **~м**); **поста́вить вопро́с ~м** *fig.* put a question point-blank
ребя́|та *pl. of* **ребёнок**; *coll.* children; (*of adults*) boys and lads; **~ческий** [16], **~чий** *coll.* [18] childish; **~чество** *n* [9] *coll.* childishness; **~читься** *coll.* [16] behave childishly
рёв *m* [1] roar; bellow; howl
рев|а́нш *m* [1] revenge; *sport* return match; **~е́нь** *m* [4 *e.*] rhubarb; **~е́ть** [-ву́, -вёшь] roar; bellow; howl; *coll.* cry
реви́з|ия *f* [7] inspection; *fin.* audit; *нали́чия това́ров и т. д.* revision; **~о́р** *m* [1] inspector; auditor
ревмати́|зм *m* [1] rheumatism; **~ческий** [16] rheumatic
ревн|и́вый [14 *sh.*] jealous; **~ова́ть** [7], <при-> be jealous (**к** Д [В] of [p.'s]); **~ость** *f* [8] jealousy; **~остный** [14; -тен, -тна] zealous, fervent
револ|ьве́р *m* [1] revolver; **~юционе́р** *m* [1], **~юцио́нный** [14] revolutionary; **~ю́ция** *f* [7] revolution
реги́стр *m* [1], **~и́ровать** [7], *pf. and impf.*, *pf. also* <за-> register, record; (*v/i.* **-ся**); register (o.s.); register one's marriage
рег|ла́мент *m* [1] order, regulation *pl.*; **~ре́сс** *m* [1] regression
регул|и́ровать [7], <у-> regulate; adjust; (*esp. pf.*) settle; **~иро́вщик** *m* [1] traffic controller; **~я́рный** [14; -рен, -рна] regular; **~я́тор** *m* [1] regulator
редак|ти́ровать [7], <от-> edit; **~тор** *m* [1] editor; **~ция** *f* [7] editorial staff; editorial office; wording; **под ~цией** edited by
ред|е́ть [8], <по-> thin, thin out; **~и́ска** *f* [5; *g/pl.*: -сок] (*red*) radish
ре́дк|ий [16; -док, -дка́, -о; *comp.*: ре́же] uncommon; *во́лосы* thin, sparse; *кни́га и т. д.* rare; *adv. a.* seldom; **~ость** *f* [8] rarity, curiosity; uncommon (thing); **на ~ость** *coll.* exceptionally
ре́дька *f* [5; *g/pl.*: -дек] radish
режи́м *m* [1] regime(n); routine; (*усло́вия рабо́ты*) conditions
режисс|ёр *m* [1] *cine.* director; *thea.* producer
ре́зать [3] **1.** <раз-> cut (up, open); slice; *мя́со* carve; **2.** <за-> slaughter, kill; **3.** <вы́-> carve, cut (**по** В, **на** П in *wood*); **4.** <с-> *coll.* *на экза́мене* fail; **5.** **-ся** *coll.* cut (one's teeth)
резв|и́ться [14 *e.*; -влю́сь, -ви́шься] frolic, frisk, gambol; **~ый** [14; -резв, -á, -о] frisky, sportive, frolic-

some; quick; *ребёнок* lively
резе́рв *m* [1] *mil., etc.* reserve(s); **~и́ст** *m* [1] reservist; **~ный** [14] reserve
резе́ц *m* [1; -зца́] *зуб* incisor; *tech.* cutter; cutting tool
рези́н|а *f* [5] rubber; **~овый** [14] rubber...; **~ка** *f* [5; *g/pl.*: -нок] eraser; rubber band, (*piece of*) elastic
ре́з|кий [16; -зок, -зка́, -о; *comp.*: ре́зче] sharp, keen; *ве́тер* biting, piercing; *боль* acute; *звук* harsh; shrill; *свет* glaring; *мане́ра* rough, abrupt; **~кость** *f* [8] sharpness, *etc.*, → **~кий**; harsh word; **~но́й** [14] carved; **~ня́** *f* [6] slaughter; **~олю́ция** *f* [7] resolution; instruction; **~о́н** *m* [1] reason; **~она́нс** *m* [1] resonance; (*о́тклик*) response; **~о́нный** *coll.* [14; -о́нен, -о́нна] reasonable; **~ульта́т** *m* [1] result (as a **в** П); **~ьба́** *f* [5] carving, fretwork
резю́м|е *n* [*indecl.*] summary; **~и́ровать** [7] (*im*)*pf.* summarize
рейд[1] *m* [1] *naut.* road(stead)
рейд[2] *m* [1] *mil.* raid
рейс *m* [1] trip; voyage; flight
река́ *f* [5; *ac/sg a. st.*; *pl. st.*; *from dat/pl. a. e.*] river
ре́квием *m* [1] requiem
рекла́м|а *f* [5] advertising; advertisement; publicity; **~и́ровать** [7] (*im*)*pf.* advertise; publicize; boost; **~ный** [14] publicity
реко|мenда́тельный [14] of recommendation; **~менда́ция** *f* [7] (*сове́т*) advice, recommendation; (*докуме́нт*) reference; **~мендова́ть** [7] (*im*)*pf.*, *a.*, <по-> recommend, advise; **~нструи́ровать** [7] (*im*)*pf.* reconstruct; **~рд** *m* [1] record; *установи́ть* **~рд** set a record; **~рдный** [14] record...; record-breaking; **~рдсме́н** *m* [1], **~рдсме́нка** *f* [5; *g/pl.*: -нок] record-holder
ре́ктор *m* [1] president, (*Brt.* vice-) chancellor of a university
рели|гио́зный [14; -зен, -зна] religious; **~гия** *f* [7] religion; **~квия** [7] relic
рельс [1], **~овый** [14] rail; track
реме́нь *m* [4; -мня́] strap, belt
реме́сл|енник *m* [1] craftsman, artisan; *fig.* bungler; **~енный** [14] trade...; handicraft...; **~о́** *n* [9; -мёсла, -мёсел, -мёслам] trade; (handi)craft; occupation
ремо́нт *m* [1] repair(s); maintenance; *капита́льный* overhaul; **~и́ровать** [7] (*im*)*pf.*, **~ный** [14] repair...
рента́бельный [14; -лен, -льна] profitable, cost effective
рентге́новск|ий [16]: **~ий сни́мок** X-ray photograph
реорганизова́ть [7] (*im*)*pf.* reorganize
ре́п|а *f* [5] turnip; ***про́ще па́реной ~ы*** (as) easy as ABC
репа|ра́ция *f* [7] reparation; **~трии́ровать** [7] (*im*)*pf.* repatriate
репе́йник *m* [1] burdock
репертуа́р *m* [1] repertoire, repertory
репети́|ровать [7], <про-> rehearse; **~тор** *m* [1] coach (*teacher*); **~ция** *f* [7] rehearsal
ре́плика *f* [5] rejoinder, retort; *thea.* cue
репорта́ж *m* [1] report(ing)
репортёр *m* [1] reporter
репресс|и́рованный *m* [14] *su.* one subjected to repression; **~ия** *f* [7] *mst. pl.* repressions *pl.*
ресни́ца *f* [5] eyelash
респу́блик|а *f* [5] republic; **~а́нец** *m* [1; -нца], **~а́нский** [16] republican
рессо́ра *f* [5] *tech.* spring
рестора́н *m* [1] restaurant (**в** П at)
ресу́рсы *m/pl.* [5] resources
рефера́т *m* [1] synopsis; essay
рефере́ндум *m* [1] referendum
рефо́рм|а *f* [5], **~и́ровать** [7] (*im*)*pf.* reform; **~а́тор** *m* [1] reformer
рефрижера́тор *m* [1] *tech.* refrigerator; *rail.* refrigerator car, *Brt.* van
реценз|е́нт *m* [1] reviewer; **~и́ровать** [7], <про->, **~ия** *f* [7] review
реце́пт *m* [1] *cul.* recipe; *med.* prescription
рециди́в *m* [1] *med.* relapse; recurrence; *law* repeat offence
ре́ч|ка *f* [5; *g/pl.*: -чек] (small) river; **~но́й** [14] river...
реч|ь *f* [8; *from g/pl. e.*] speech;

Р

(*выступле́ние*) address, speech; ***об э́том не мо́жет быть и ~и*** that is out of the question; → ***идти́***

реш|а́ть [1], <~и́ть> [16 *e.*; -шу́, -ши́шь; -шённый] *пробле́му* solve; (*приня́ть реше́ние*) decide, resolve (*a.* **-ся** [***на*** B on, to], make up one's mind); (*осме́литься*) dare, risk; ***не ~а́ться*** hesitate; **~а́ющий** [17] decisive; **~е́ние** *n* [12] decision; (re)solution; **~ётка** *f* [5; -ток] grating; lattice; trellis; fender; **~ето́** *n* [9; *pl. st.*: -шёта] sieve; **~и́мость** *f* [8] resoluteness; determination; **~и́тельный** [14; -лен, -льна] *челове́к* resolute, firm; decisive; definite; **~и́ть(ся)** → ***~а́ть(ся)***

ржа|ве́ть [8], <за->, **~вчина** *f* [5] rust; **~вый** [14] rusty; **~но́й** [14] rye...; **~ть** [ржёт], <за-> neigh

ри́м|ский [14] Roman; ***~ская ци́фра*** Roman numeral

ри́нуться [20] *pf.* dash; rush; dart

рис *m* [1] rice

риск *m* [1] risk; ***на свой*** (***страх и***) **~** at one's own risk; **с *~ом*** at the risk (***для*** P of); **~о́ванный** [14 *sh.*] risky; **~ова́ть** [7], <~ну́ть> [20] (*usu.* T) risk, venture

рисова́|ние *n* [12] drawing; **~ть** [7], <на-> draw; *fig.* depict, paint; **-ся** act, pose

ри́совый [14] rice...

рису́нок *m* [1; -нка] drawing; design; picture, illustration; figure

ритм *m* [1] rhythm; **~и́чный** [14; -чен, -чна] rhythmical

ритуа́л *m* [1], **~ьный** [14; -лен, -льна] ritual

риф *m* [1] reef

ри́фма *f* [5] rhyme

роб|е́ть [8], <о-> be timid, quail; ***не ~е́й!*** don't be afraid!; **~кий** [16; -бок, -бка́, -o; *comp.*: ро́бче] shy, timid; **~ость** *f* [8] shyness, timidity

ро́бот *m* [1] robot

ров *m* [1; рва; во рву] ditch

рове́сник *m* [1] of the same age

ро́вн|ый [14; -вен, -вна́, -o] even, level, flat; straight; equal; *хара́ктер* equable; **~о** precisely, exactly; *о вре́мени тж.* sharp; *coll.* absolutely; **~я** *f* [5] equal, match

рог *m* [1; *pl. e.*: -га́] horn; antler; **~ *изоби́лия*** horn of plenty; **~а́тый** [14 *sh.*] horned; ***кру́пный ~а́тый скот*** cattle; **~ови́ца** *f* [5] cornea; **~ово́й** [14] horn...

род *m* [1; в, на -у́; *pl. e.*] *biol.* genus; *челове́ческий* human race; (*поколе́ние*) generation; family; (*сорт*) kind; *gr.* gender; (*происхожде́ние*) birth (T by); ***в своём ~е*** in one's own way; ***~ом из***, **с** P come *or* be from; ***о́т ~у*** (Д) *be* ... old; **с ~у** in one's life

роди́|льный [14] maternity (hospital ***дом*** *m*); **~мый** [14] → ***´~нка***; **´~на** *f* [5] native land, home(land) (***на*** П in); **´~нка** *f* [5; *g/pl.*: -нок] birthmark; mole; **~тели** *m/pl.* [4] parents; **~тельный** [14] *gr.* genitive; **~тельский** [16] parental, parent's

роди́ть [15 *e.*; рожу́, роди́шь; -ил, -а (*pf.*: -а́), -o; рождённый] (*im*)*pf.* (*impf. a.* ***рожда́ть***, *coll.* ***рожа́ть*** [1]) bear, give birth to; *fig.* give rise to; **-ся** [*pf.* -и́лся] be born; come into being

родн|и́к *m* [1 *e.*] (*source of water*) spring; **~о́й** [14] own (*by blood relationship*); *го́род и т. д.* native; (my) dear; *pl.* = **~я́** *f* [6] relative(s), relation(s)

родо|нача́льник *m* [1] ancestor, (*a. fig.*) father; **~сло́вный** [14] genealogical; ***~сло́вная*** *f* family tree

ро́дствен|ник *m* [1], **~ница** *f* [5] relative, relation; **~ный** [14 *sh.*] related, kindred; *языки́* cognate; of blood

родств|о́ *n* [9] relationship; ***в ~е́*** related (**с** T to)

ро́ды *pl.* [1] (child)birth

ро́жа *f* [5] **1.** *med.* erysipelas; **2.** P mug

рожд|а́емость *f* [8] birthrate; **~а́ть(ся)** → ***роди́ть(ся)***; **~е́ние** *n* [12] birth (***от*** P by); ***день ~е́ния*** birthday (***в*** B on); **~е́ственский** [16] Christmas...; **~ество́** *n* [9] (*a.* ***~ество́*** [***христо́во***]) Christmas (***на*** B at); ***поздра́вить с ~ество́м христо́вым*** wish a Merry Christmas; ***до*** (***по́сле***) ***Р.хр.*** B.C. (A.D.)

рож|о́к *m* [1; -жка́] feeding bottle; *для о́буви* shoehorn; **~ь** *f* [8; ржи;

instr./sg.: ро́жью] rye
ро́за *f* [5] rose
розе́тка *f* [5; *g/pl.*: -ток] **1.** jam-dish; **2.** *el.* socket, wall plug
ро́зн|ица *f* [5]: ***в ~ицу*** retail; **~ичный** [14] retail...
ро́зовый [14 *sh.*] pink, rosy
ро́зыгрыш *m* [1] (*жеребьёвка*) draw; drawing in a lottery; (*шу́тка*) (practical) joke; ***~ ку́бка*** play-off
ро́зыск *m* [1] search; *law* inquiry; ***уголо́вный ~*** criminal investigation department
ро|и́ться [13] swarm (*of bees*); crowd (*of thoughts*); **~й** [3; в рою́; *pl. e.*: рой, роёв] swarm
рок *m* [1] **1.** fate; **2.** *mus.* rock; **~ер** *m* [1] rocker; **~ово́й** [14] fatal; **~от** *m* [1], **~ота́ть** [3] roar, rumble
роль *f* [8; *from g/pl. e.*] *thea.* part, role; ***э́то не игра́ет ро́ли*** it is of no importance
ром *m* [1] rum
рома́н *m* [1] novel; *coll.* (love) affair; **~и́ст** *m* [1] novelist; **~с** *m* [1] *mus.* romance; **~ти́зм** *m* [1] romanticism; **~тика** *f* [5] romance; **~ти́ческий** [16], **~ти́чный** [14; -чен, -чна] romantic
ром|а́шка *f* [5; *g/pl.*: -шек] *bot.* camomile; **~б** *m* [1] *math.* rhombus
роня́ть [28], <урони́ть> [13; -оню́, -о́нишь; -о́ненный] drop; *ли́стья* shed; *fig.* disparage, discredit
ро́п|от *m* [1], **~та́ть** [3; -пщу́, ро́пщешь] murmur, grumble, complain (about ***на*** B)
роса́ *f* [5; *pl. st.*] dew
роско́ш|ный [14; -шен, -шна] luxurious; sumptuous, luxuriant; **´~ь** *f* [8] luxury; luxuriance
ро́слый [14] big, tall
ро́спись *f* [8] *art* fresco, mural
ро́спуск *m* [1] *parl.* dissolution; *на кани́кулы* breaking up
рост *m* [1] growth; *цен и т. д.* increase, rise; *челове́ка* stature, height; ***высо́кого ~а*** tall
рос|то́к *m* [1; -тка́] sprout, shoot; **~черк** *m* [1] flourish; ***одни́м ~черком пера́*** with a stroke of the pen
рот *m* [1; рта, во рту́] mouth
ро́та *f* [5] *mil.* company
ро́ща *f* [5] grove
роя́ль *m* [4] (grand) piano
ртуть *f* [8] mercury, quicksilver
руба́|нок *m* [1; -нка] plane; **~шка** *f* [5; *g/pl.*: -шек] shirt; ***ни́жняя ~шка*** undershirt (*Brt.* vest); ***ночна́я ~шка*** nightshirt; *же́нская* nightgown
рубе́ж *m* [1 *e.*] boundary; border(line), frontier; ***за ~о́м*** abroad
рубero'ид *m* [1] ruberoid
рубе́ц *m* [1; -бца́] *шов* hem; *на те́ле* scar
руби́н *m* [1] ruby
руби́ть [14] **1.** <на-> chop, cut, hew, hack; **2.** <с-> fell
ру́бка[1] *f* [5] *ле́са* felling
ру́бка[2] *f* [5] *naut.* wheelhouse
ру́бленый [14] minced, chopped
рубль *m* [4 *e.*] ruble (*Brt.* rouble)
ру́брика *f* [5] heading
ру́га|нь *f* [8] abuse; **~тельный** [14] abusive; **~тельство** *n* [9] swearword, oath; **~ть** [1], <вы́-> abuse, swear at; attack verbally; **-ся** swear, curse; abuse o.a.
руд|а́ *f* [5; *pl. st.*] ore; **~ни́к** *m* [1 *e.*] mine, pit; **~око́п** *m* [1] miner
руж|е́йный [14] gun...; **~ьё** *n* [10; *pl. st.*; *g/pl.*: -жей] (hand)gun, rifle
руи́на *f* [5] ruin (*mst. pl.*)
рук|а́ *f* [5; *ac/sg.*: ру́ку; *pl.*: ру́ки, рук, -ка́м] hand; arm; ***~а́ о́б ~у*** hand in hand (arm in arm); ***по́д ~у*** arm in arm; with s.o. on one's arm; ***из ~ вон*** (***пло́хо***) *coll.* wretchedly; ***быть на́ ~у*** (Д) suit (well); ***махну́ть ~о́й*** give up as a bad job; ***на́ ~у нечи́ст*** light-fingered; ***от ~и́*** handwritten; ***пожа́ть ~у*** shake hands (Д with); ***по ~а́м!*** it's a bargain!; ***под ~о́й*** at hand, within reach; ***~о́й пода́ть*** it's no distance (a stone's throw); (***у*** Р) ***~и ко́ротки*** Р not in one's power; ***из пе́рвых ~*** at first hand; ***приложи́ть ~у*** take part in s.th. bad
рука́в *m* [1 *e.*; *pl.*: -ва́, -во́в] sleeve; *реки́* branch; *tech.* hose; **~и́ца** *f* [5] mitten; gauntlet
руковод|и́тель *m* [4] leader; head, manager; ***нау́чный ~и́тель*** supervisor (of studies); **~и́ть** [15] (Т) lead; direct, manage; **~ство** *n* [9] leadership; guidance; *mst. tech.* in-

struction(s); handbook, guide, manual; **~ствовать(ся)** [7] manual; follow; be guided (by T); **~я́щий** [17] leading

руко|де́лие *n* [12] needlework; **~мо́йник** *m* [1] washstand; **~па́шный** [14] hand-to-hand; **´~пись** *f* [8] manuscript; **~плеска́ние** *n* [12] (*mst. pl.*) applause; **~пожа́тие** *n* [12] handshake; **~я́тка** *f* [5; *g/pl.*: -ток] handle, grip; hilt

рул|ево́й [14] steering; *su. naut.* helmsman; **~о́н** *m* [1] roll; **~ь** *m* [4 *e.*] ***су́дна*** rudder, helm; *mot.* steering wheel; ***велосипе́да*** handlebars

румы́н *m* [1], **~ка** *f* [5; *g/pl.*: -нок], **~ский** [16] Romanian

румя́н|ец *m* [1; -нца] ruddiness; blush; **~ить** [13] **1.** <за-> redden; **2.** <на-> rouge; **~ый** [14 *sh.*] ruddy, rosy; ***я́блоко*** red

ру́пор *m* [1] megaphone; *fig.* mouthpiece

руса́лка *f* [5; *g/pl.*: -лок] mermaid

ру́сло *n* [9] (river)bed, (*a. fig.*) channel

ру́сский [16] Russian (*a. su.*); *adv.* ***по-ру́сски*** (in) Russian

ру́сый [14 *sh.*] light brown

рути́н|а *f* [5], **~ный** [14] routine

ру́хлядь *coll. f* [8] lumber, junk

ру́хнуть [20] *pf.* crash down; *fig.* fail

руча́ться [1], <поручи́ться> [16] (***за*** B) warrant, guarantee, vouch for

руче́й *m* [3; -чья́] brook, stream

ру́чка *f* [5; -чек] *dim.* → **рука́**; ***две́ри*** handle, knob; ***кре́сла*** arm; ***ша́риковая ~*** ballpoint pen

ручно́й [14] hand...; ***труд*** manual; ***~ рабо́ты*** handmade; small; ***живо́тное*** tame

ру́шить [16] (*im*)*pf.* pull down; **-ся** collapse

ры́б|а *f* [5] fish; **~а́к** *m* [1 *e.*] fisherman; **~ий** [18] fish...; ***жир*** cod-liver oil; **~ный** [14] fish(y); ***~ная ло́вля*** fishing

рыболо́в *m* [1] fisherman; angler; **~ный** [14] fishing; fish...; ***~ные принадле́жности*** fishing tackle; **~ство** *n* [9] fishery

рыво́к *m* [1; -вка́] jerk; *sport* spurt, dash

рыг|а́ть [1], <~ну́ть> [20] belch

рыда́|ние *n* [12] sob(bing); **~ть** [1] sob

ры́жий [17; рыж, -á, -о] red (haired), ginger

ры́ло *n* [9] snout; P mug

ры́но|к *m* [1; -нка] market (***на*** П in); **~чный** [14] market...

рыс|а́к *m* [1 *e.*] trotter; **~ка́ть** [3] rove, run about; **~ь** *f* [8] **1.** trot (at T); **2.** *zo.* lynx

ры́твина *f* [5] rut, groove; hole

рыть [22], <вы́-> dig; burrow; **~ся** rummage

рыхл|и́ть [13], <вз-, раз-> loosen (*soil*); **~ый** [14; рыхл, -á, -о] friable, loose; ***те́ло*** flabby; podgy

ры́цар|ский [16] knightly, chivalrous; knight's; **~ь** *m* [4] knight

рыча́г *m* [1 *e.*] lever

рыча́ть [4; -чу́, -чи́шь] growl, snarl

рья́ный [14 *sh.*] zealous

рюкза́к *m* [1] rucksack, knapsack

рю́мка *f* [5; *g/pl.*: -мок] (wine)glass

ряби́на *f* [5] mountain ash

ряби́ть [14; -и́т] ***во́ду*** ripple; *impers.* flicker (***в глаза́х у*** P before one's eyes)

ря́б|чик *m* [1] *zo.* hazelhen; **~ь** *f* ripples *pl.*; ***в глаза́х*** dazzle

ря́вк|ать *coll.* [1], *once* <~нуть> [20] bellow, roar (***на*** B at)

ряд *m* [1; в -ý; *pl. e.*; *after* 2, 3, 4, ряда́] row; line; series; ***в ~е слу́чаев*** in a number of cases; *pl.* ranks; *thea.* tier; ***~а́ми*** in rows; ***из ~а вон выходя́щий*** remarkable, extraordinary; **~ово́й** [14] ordinary; *su. mil.* private; **~ом** side by side; (**с** T) beside, next to; next door; close by; ***сплошь и ~ом*** more often than not

ря́са *f* [5] cassock

С

с, со 1. (P) from; since; with; for; **2.** (B) about; **3.** (T) with; of; to; ***мы ~ ва́ми*** you and I; ***ско́лько ~ меня́?*** how much do I owe you?

са́бля *f* [6; *g/pl.*: -бель] saber (*Brt.* -bre)

сабот|а́ж *m* [1], **~и́ровать** [7] (*im*)*pf.* sabotage

сад *m* [1; в ~у́; *pl. e.*] garden; ***фрукто́вый ~*** orchard

сади́ть [15], <по-> → ***сажа́ть***; **~ся**, <сесть> [25; ся́ду, -дешь; сел, -а; се́вший] (***на***, ***в*** B) sit down; *в маши́ну и т. д.* get in(to) *or* on, board *a. rail.*; *naut.* embark; *на ло́шадь* mount; *о пти́це* alight; *ae.* land; *со́лнце* set, sink; *ткань* shrink; set (***за*** B to *work*); run (aground ***на мель***)

садо́в|ник *m* [1] gardener; **~о́дство** *n* [9] gardening, horticulture

са́ж|а *f* [5] soot; ***в ~е*** sooty

сажа́ть [1] (*iter. of* ***сади́ть***) seat; *в тюрьму́* put into; *расте́ния* plant

са́женец *m* [1; -нца и т. д.] seedling; sapling

са́йра *f* [5] saury

сала́т *m* [1] salad; *bot.* lettuce

са́ло *n* [9] fat, lard

сало́н *m* [1] lounge; showroom; saloon; *ae.* passenger cabin; ***космети́ческий ~*** beauty salon

салфе́тка *f* [5; *g/pl.*: -ток] (table) napkin

са́льдо *n* [*indecl.*] *comm.* balance

са́льный [14; -лен, -льна] greasy; *анекдо́т* bawdy

салю́т *m* [1], **~ова́ть** [7] (*im*)*pf.* salute

сам *m*, **~а́** *f*, **~о́** *n*, **~и** *pl.* [30] -self: ***я ~(а́)*** I ... myself; ***мы ~и*** we ... ourselves; ***~о́ собо́й разуме́ется*** it goes without saying; **~е́ц** *m* [1; -мца́] *zo.* male; **~ка** *f* [5; *g/pl.*: -мок] *zo.* female

само|бы́тный [14; -тен, -тна] original; **~ва́р** *m* [1] samovar; **~во́льный** [14; -лен, -льна] unauthorrized; **~го́н** *m* [1] home-brew, moonshine; **~де́льный** [14] homemade

самодержа́вие *n* [12] autocracy

само|де́ятельность *f* [8] independent action *or* activity; *худо́жественная* amateur performances (*theatricals*, *musicals*, *etc.*); **~дово́льный** [14; -лен, -льна] self-satisfied, self-complacent; **~защи́та** *f* [5] self-defense (-nce); **~кри́тика** *f* [5] self-criticism

самолёт *m* [1] airplane (*Brt.* aeroplane), aircraft; ***пассажи́рский ~*** airliner

само|люби́вый [14 *sh.*] proud, touchy; **~лю́бие** *n* [12] pride, self-esteem; **~мне́ние** *n* [12] conceit; **~наде́янный** [14 *sh.*] self-confident, presumptuous; **~облада́ние** *n* [12] self-control; **~обма́н** *m* [1] self-deception; **~оборо́на** *f* [5] self-defense (-nce); **~обслу́живание** *n* [12] self-service; **~определе́ние** *n* [12] self-determination; **~отве́рженный** [14 *sh.*] selfless; **~отво́д** *m* [1] *кандидату́ры* withdrawal; **~поже́ртвование** *n* [12] self-sacrifice; **~сва́л** *m* [1] dump truck; **~сохране́ние** *n* [12] self-preservation

самостоя́тельн|ость *f* [8] independence; **~ый** [14; -лен, -льна] independent

само|су́д *m* [1] lynch *or* mob law; **~уби́йство** *n* [9], **~уби́йца** *m/f* [5] suicide; **~уве́ренный** [14 *sh.*] self-confident; **~управле́ние** *n* [12] self-government; **~у́чка** *m/f* [5; *g/pl.*: -чек] self-taught pers.; **~хо́дный** [14] self-propelled; **~цве́ты** *m/pl.* [1] semiprecious stones; **~це́ль** *f* [8] end in itself; **~чу́вствие** *n* [12] (state of) health

са́м|ый [14] the most, ...est; the very; the (self)same; just, right; early or late; ***~ое большо́е (ма́лое)*** *coll.* at (the) most (least)

сан *m* [1] dignity, office

санато́рий *m* [3] sanatorium

санда́лии *f/pl.* [7] sandals

С

са́ни *f/pl.* [8; *from gen. e.*] sled(ge), sleigh
санита́р *m* [1], **~ка** *f* [5; *g/pl.*: -рок] hospital attendant, orderly; **~ный** [14] sanitary
сан|кциони́ровать [7] *(im)pf.* sanction; **~те́хник** *m* [1] plumber
сантиме́тр *m* [1] centimeter (*Brt.* -tre)
сану́зел *m* [1] lavatory
сапёр *m* [1] engineer
сапо́г *m* [1 *e.*; *g/pl.*: сапо́г] boot
сапо́жник *m* [1] shoemaker
сапфи́р *m* [1] sapphire
сара́й *m* [3] shed
саранча́ *f* [5; *g/pl.*: -че́й] locust
сарафа́н *m* [1] sarafan (*Russian peasant women's dress*)
сард|е́лька *f* [5; *g/pl.*: -лек] (*sausage*) saveloy, polony.; **~и́на** *f* [5] sardine
сарка́зм *m* [1] sarcasm
сатана́ *m* [5] Satan
сати́н *m* [1] sateen, glazed cotton
сати́р|а *f* [5] satire; **~ик** *m* [1] satirist; **~и́ческий** [16] satirical
са́хар *m* [1; *part.g.*: -у] sugar; **~истый** [14 *sh.*] sugary; **~ница** *f* [5] sugar bowl; **~ный** [14] sugar...; ***~ная боле́знь*** diabetes
сачо́к *m* [1; -чка́] butterfly net
сбав|ля́ть [28], <**~ить**> [14] reduce
сбе|га́ть[1] [1], <**~жа́ть**> [4; -егу́, -ежи́шь, -егу́т] run down (from); *pf.* run away, escape, flee; **-ся** come running; **~гать**[2] [1] *pf.* run for, run to fetch (***за*** T)
сбере|га́тельный [14] savings (bank)...; **~га́ть** [1], <**~чь**> [26 г/ж: -регу́, -режёшь, -регу́т] save; preserve; **~же́ние** *n* [12] economy; savings *pl.*
сберка́сса *f* [5] savings bank
сби|ва́ть [1], <**~ть**> [собью́, -бьёшь; сбей!; сби́тый] knock down (*or* off, *a.* **с *ног***); *ae.* shoot down; *сли́вки* whip; *я́йца* beat up; *ма́сло* churn; (*сколоти́ть*) knock together; lead (astray **с *пути́***; **-ся** lose one's way); ***~ть с то́лку*** confuse; *refl. a.* run o.s. off (one's legs **с *ноги́***); flock, huddle (together ***в ку́чу***); **~вчивый** [14 *sh.*] confused; inconsistent; **~ть(ся)** → ***~ва́ть(ся)***
сбли|жа́ть [1], <**~зить**> [15] bring *or* draw together; **-ся** become friends (**с** T with) *or* lovers; **~же́ние** *n* [12] (*a. pol.*) rapprochement; approach(es)
сбо́ку from one side; on one side; (*ря́дом*) next to
сбор *m* [1] collection; gathering; ***~ урожа́я*** harvest; ***~ нало́гов*** tax collection; ***порто́вый ~*** harbo(u)r dues; ***тамо́женный ~*** customs duty; *pl.* preparations; ***в ~е*** assembled; **~ище** *n* [11] mob, crowd; **~ка** *f* [5; *g/pl.*: -рок] *sew.* gather; *tech.* assembly, assembling; **~ник** *m* [1] collection; **~ный** [14] *sport* combined team; **~очный** [14] assembly
сбр|а́сывать [1], <**~о́сить**> [15] throw down; drop; *оде́жду и т. д.* shed; **~од** *m* [1] rabble, riff-raff; **~о́сить** → ***~а́сывать***; **~у́я** *f* [6] harness
сбы|ва́ть [1], <**~ть**> [сбу́ду, -дешь; сбыл, -а́, -о] sell, market; get rid of (*a.* **с *рук***); **-ся** come true; **~т** *m* [1] sale; **~ть(ся)** → ***~ва́ть(ся)***
сва́д|ебный [14], **~ьба** *f* [5; *g/pl.*: -деб] wedding
сва́л|ивать [1], <**~и́ть**> [13; -алю́, -а́лишь] bring down; *де́рево* fell; *в ку́чу* dump; heap up; *вину́* shift (***на*** B to); **-ся** fall down; **~ка** *f* [5; *g/pl.*: -лок] dump; (*дра́ка*) brawl
сва́р|ивать [1], <**~и́ть**> [13; сварю́, сва́ришь, сва́ренный] weld; **~ка** *f* [5], **~очный** [14] welding
сварли́вый [14 *sh.*] quarrelsome
сва́я *f* [6; *g/pl.*: свай] pile
све́д|ение *n* [12] information; ***приня́ть к ~ению*** note; **~ущий** [17 *sh.*] well-informed, knowledgable
свеж|есть *f* [8] freshness; coolness; **~е́ть** [8], <по-> freshen, become cooler; *pf. a.* look healthy; **~ий** [15; свеж, -а́, -о́, свежи́] fresh; cool; *но́вости* latest; *хлеб* new
свезти́ → ***свози́ть***
свёкла *f* [5; *g/pl.*: -кол] red beet
свёк|ор *m* [1; -кра] father-in-law (*husband's father*); **~ро́вь** *f* [8] mother-in-law (*husband's mother*)
свер|га́ть [1], <**~гнуть**> [21] overthrow; dethrone (**с *престо́ла***);

С

~же́ние *n* [12] overthrow; **~ить** → **~я́ть**

сверк|а́ть [1], *once* <~ну́ть> [20] sparkle, glitter; *мо́лнии* flash

сверл|е́ние *n* [12], **~и́льный** [14] drilling; **~и́ть** [13], <про->, **~о́** *n* [9; *pl. st.*: свёрла] drill

свер|ну́ть(ся) → **свёртывать(ся)** & **свора́чивать**; **~стник** → **рове́сник**

свёрт|ок *m* [1; -тка] roll; parcel; bundle; **~ывать** [1], <сверну́ть> [20] roll (up); *за у́гол* turn; (*сократи́ть*) curtail; *строи́тельство* stop; twist; **-ся** coil up; *молоко́* curdle; *кровь* coagulate

сверх (P) above, beyond; over; besides; **~ вся́ких ожида́ний** beyond (all) expectations; **~ того́** moreover; **~звуково́й** [14] supersonic; **~при́быль** *f* [8] excess profit; **~у** from above; **~уро́чный** [14] overtime; **~ъесте́ственный** [14 *sh.*] supernatural

сверчо́к *m* [1; -чка́] *zo.* cricket

свер|я́ть [28], <~ить> [13] compare, collate

све́сить → **све́шивать**

свести́(сь) → **своди́ть(ся)**

свет *m* [1] light; world (**на** П in); **вы́пустить в ~** publish; **чуть ~** at dawn; **~а́ть** [1] dawn; **~и́ло** *n* [9] *poet.* the sun; luminary (*a. fig.*); **~и́ть(ся)** [15] shine

светл|е́ть [8], <по-> brighten; grow light(er); **~о...** light...; **~ый** [14; -тел, -тла́, -о] light, bright; lucid; **~ая голова́** good head; **~я́к** *m* [1 *e.*; -чка́] glowworm

свето|во́й [14] light...; **~фо́р** *m* [1] traffic light

све́тский [16] worldly

светя́щийся [17] luminous

свеча́ *f* [5; *pl.*: све́чи, -е́й, -а́м] candle; *el.* spark(ing) plug; candlepower

све́|шивать [1], <~сить> [15] let down; dangle; **-ся** hang over; *pf.* lean over

сви|ва́ть [1], <~ть> [совью́, -вьёшь; → **вить**] wind, twist; *гнездо́* build

свида́ни|е *n* [12] appointment, meeting, date; **до ~я** good-by(e)

свиде́тель *m* [4], **~ница** *f* [5] witness; **~ство** *n* [9] evidence; testimony; certificate; **~ство о рожде́нии** birth certificate; **~ствовать** [7], <за-> testify; attest *тж. по́дпись*; *impf.* (**о** П) show

свине́ц *m* [1; -нца́] *metal* lead

свин|и́на *f* [5] pork; **~ка** *f* [5; *g/pl.*: -нок] *med.* mumps; **морска́я ~ка** guinea pig; **~о́й** [14] pig..., pork...; **~ство** *n* [9] dirty *or* rotten act

сви́н|чивать [1], <~ти́ть> [15 *e.*; -нчу́, -нти́шь; сви́нченный] screw together, fasten with screws; unscrew

свинь|я́ *f* [6; *pl. st.*, *gen.*: -не́й; *a.* -нья́м] pig, sow; *fig.* swine; **подложи́ть ~ю́ кому́-л.** play a mean trick (on)

свире́п|ствовать [7] rage; **~ый** [14 *sh.*] fierce, ferocious

свиса́ть [1] hang down, droop

свист *m* [1] whistle; hiss; **~а́ть** [13] & **~е́ть** [11], *once* <~нуть> [20] whistle; *pf.* P (*стяну́ть*) pilfer; **~о́к** *m* [1; -тка́] whistle

свистопля́ска *f* [5; *g/pl.*: -сок] turmoil and confusion

сви́т|а *f* [5] retinue, suite; **~ер** (-tɛr) *m* [1] sweater; **~ок** *m* [1; -тка] scroll; **~ь** → **свива́ть**

свихну́ть *coll.* [20] *pf.* sprain; **-ся** go mad

свищ *m* [1 *e.*] *med.* fistula

свобо́д|а *f* [5] freedom, liberty; **вы́пустить на ~у** set free; **~ный** [14; -ден, -дна] free (**от** P from, of); *ме́сто и т. д.* vacant; *вре́мя и т. д.* spare; *до́ступ* easy; *оде́жда* loose; *владе́ние* fluent; exempt (**от** P from); **~омы́слящий** [17] free-thinking; *su.* freethinker, liberal

свод *m* [1] *arch.* arch, vault

своди́ть [15], <свести́> [25] lead; take down (from, off); bring (together); reduce (**к** Д to); *счёты* square; *но́гу* cramp; drive (mad **с ума́**); **~ на нет** bring to nought; **-ся**, <-сь> (**к** Д) come *or* amount (to), result (in)

сво́д|ка *f* [5; *g/pl.*: -док] report, communiqué; **~ный** [14] *табли́ца* summary; *брат* step...; **~чатый** [14] vaulted

свое|во́льный [14; -лен, -льна]

self-willed, wil(l)ful; **~вре́менный** [14; -менен, -менна] timely; **~нра́вный** [14; -вен, -вна] capricious; **~обра́зный** [14; -зен, -зна] original; peculiar, distinctive

свози́ть [15], <свезти́> [24] take, convey

сво|й *m*, **~я́** *f*, **~ё** *n*, **~и́** *pl*. [24] my, his, her, its, our, your, their (*refl.*); one's own; peculiar; ***в ~ё вре́мя*** at one time; in due course; *su. pl.* one's people, folks, relations; ***не ~й*** frantic (*voice* in T); **≈йственный** [14 *sh.*] peculiar (Д to); (Д p.'s) usual; **≈йство** *n* [9] property, quality, characteristic

сво́|лочь *f* [8] scum, swine; **~ра** *f* [5] pack; **~ра́чивать** [1], <сверну́ть> [20] turn (**с** P off); roll (up); **~я́ченица** *f* [5] sister-in-law (*wife's sister*)

свы|ка́ться [1], <≈кнуться> [21] get used (**с** T to); **~сока́** haughtily; **≈ше** from above; (P) over, more than

свяЗ|а́ть(ся) → ***≈ывать(ся)***; **~и́ст** *m* [1] signalman; **≈ка** *f* [5; *g/pl.*: -зок] bunch; *anat.* ligament; *anat.* (*vocal*) cord; *gr.* copula; **≈ный** [14; -зен, -зна] coherent; **≈ывать** [1], <~а́ть> [3] tie (together), bind; connect, join; unite; associate; *teleph.* put through, connect; **-ся** get in touch (with), contact; get involved with (**с** T); **~ь** *f* [8; в -зи́] tie, bond; connection; relation; contact; *полова́я* liaison; communication (radio, telephone, post, *etc.*)

свят|и́ть [15 *e.*; -ячу́, -яти́шь], <о-> consecrate, hallow; **≈ки** *f/pl.* [5; *gen.*: -ток] Christmas (***на*** П at); **~о́й** [14; свят, -а́, -о] holy; sacred (*a. fig.*); *su.* saint; **≈ость** *f* [8] holiness, sanctity; **~ота́тство** *n* [9] sacrilege; **~ы́ня** *f* [6] *eccl.* sacred place; (*fig.*) sacred object

свяще́нн|ик *m* [1] priest; **~ый** [14 *sh.*] holy; sacred

сгиб *m* [1], **~а́ть** [1], <согну́ть> [20] bend, fold; *v/i.* **-ся**

сгла́|живать [1], <~дить> [15] smooth out; **-ся** become smooth

сгнива́ть → ***гнить***

сго́вор *m* [1] *usu. pej* agreement; collusion; **~и́ться** [13] *pf.* agree; come to terms; **≈чивый** [14 *sh.*] compliant, amenable

сго|ня́ть [28], <согна́ть> [сгоню́, сго́нишь; со́гнанный] drive (off); **~ра́ние** *n* [12] combustion; **~ра́ть** [1], <~ре́ть> [9] burn down; ***~ра́ть от стыда́*** burn with shame; **~рячá** in a fit of temper

сгр|еба́ть [1], <~ести́> [24 -б-: сгребу́; сгрёб, сгребла́] rake up; shovel off, from; **~ужа́ть** [1], <~узи́ть> [15 & 15 *e.*; -ужу́, -у́зи́шь; -у́женный & -ужённый] unload

сгу|сти́ть → ***~ща́ть***; **≈сток** *m* [1; -тка] clot; **~ща́ть** [1], <~сти́ть> [15 *e.*; -ущу́, -усти́шь; -ущённый] thicken; condense; ***~ща́ть кра́ски*** lay it on thick, exaggerate; **~щёнка** *f* [5; *g/pl.*: -нок] condensed milk

сда|ва́ть [5], <~ть> [сдам, сдашь *etc.* → ***дать***] deliver, hand in (*or* over); *бага́ж* check, register; *дом и т. д.* rent, let (out); *ка́рты* deal; *экза́мен* pass; *mil.* surrender; **-ся** surrender; ***~ётся...*** for rent (*Brt.* to let); **≈вливать** [1], <~ви́ть> [14] squeeze; **~ть(ся)** → ***~ва́ть(ся)***; **≈ча** *f* [5] *mil.* surrender; (*переда́ча*) handing over; *де́ньги* change

сдвиг *m* [1] shift; *geol.* fault; *fig.* change (for the better), improvement; **~а́ть** [1], <сдви́нуть> [20] move, shift (*v/i.* **-ся**); *бро́ви* knit; push together

сде́л|ка *f* [5; *g/pl.*: -лок] bargain, transaction, deal; **~ьный** [14] piecework

сде́рж|анный [14 *sh.*] reserved, (self-)restrained; **~ивать** [1], <~а́ть> [4] check, restrain; *гнев и т. д.* suppress; *сло́во и т. д.* keep; **-ся** control o.s.

сдира́ть [1], <содра́ть> [сдеру́, -рёшь; содра́л,-а́, -о; со́дранный] tear off (*or* down), strip; *шку́ру* flay (*a. fig.*)

сдо́бн|ый [14] *cul.* rich, short; ***~ая бу́л(оч)ка*** bun

сдружи́ться → ***подружи́ться***

сду|ва́ть [1], <~ть> [16], *once* <≈нуть> [20] blow off (*or* away); **≈ру** *coll.* foolishly

сеа́нс *m* [1] sitting; *cine.* show

С

себесто́имость *f* [8] cost; cost price

себ|я́ [21] myself, yourself, himself, herself, itself, ourselves, yourselves, themselves (*refl.*); oneself; ***к ~е́*** home; into one's room; ***мне не по ~е́*** I don't feel quite myself, I don't feel too well; ***та́к ~е́*** so-so

сев *m* [1] sowing

се́вер *m* [1] north; → ***восто́к***; **~ный** [14] north(ern); northerly; arctic; **~о-восто́к** *m* [1] northeast; **~о-восто́чный** [14] northeast...; **~о-за́пад** *m* [1] northwest; **~о-за́падный** [14] northwest...; **~я́нин** *m* [1; *pl.* -я́не, -я́н ***и т. д.***] northerner

севрю́га *f* [5] stellate sturgeon

сего́дня (şɪv'ɔ-) today; ***~ у́тром*** this morning; **~шний** [15] today's

сед|е́ть [8], <по-> turn gray (*Brt.* grey); **~ина́** *f* [5] gray hair

седл|а́ть [1], **~о** *n* [9; *pl. st.*: сёдла, сёдел, сёдлам] saddle

седо|воло́сый [14 *sh.*], **~́й** [14; сед, -á, -о] gray-haired (*Brt.* grey)

седо́к *m* [1 *e.*] horseman, rider; fare (*passenger*)

седьмо́й [14] seventh; → ***пя́тый***

сезо́н *m* [1] season; **~ный** [14] seasonal

сей *m*, **сия́** *f*, **сие́** *n*, **сии́** *pl. obs.* [29] this; ***по ~ день*** till now; ***на ~ раз*** this time; ***сию́ мину́ту*** at once; right now; ***сего́ го́да*** (***ме́сяца***) of this year (month)

сейф *m* [1] safe

сейча́с now, at present; (*о́чень ско́ро*) presently, (*a.* ***~ же***) immediately, at once; (*то́лько что*) just (now)

сека́тор *m* [1] secateurs, pruning shears

секре́т *m* [1] secret (***по*** Д, ***под*** Т in); **~ариа́т** *m* [1] secretariat; **~а́рь** *m* [4 *e.*] secretary; **~ничать** *coll.* [1] be secretive; **~ный** [14; -тен, -тна] secret; confidential

сек|суа́льный [14; -лен, -льна] sexual; **~́та** *f* [5] sect; **~́тор** *m* [1] sector

секу́нд|а *f* [5] (*of time*) second; **~ный** [14] second...; ***~ная стре́лка*** (*of timepiece*) second hand; **~оме́р** *m* [1] stopwatch

селёдка *f* [5; *g/pl.*: -док] herring

селез|ёнка *f* [5; *g/pl.*: -нок] *anat.* spleen; **´~ень** *m* [4; -зня] drake

селе́кция *f* [7] *agric.* selection, breeding

сели́ть(ся) [13] → ***поселя́ть(ся)***

сел|о́ *n* [9; *pl. st.*: сёла] village (***в*** *or* ***на*** П in); ***ни к ~у́ ни к го́роду*** *coll.* for no reason at all; neither here nor there

сельд|ере́й *m* [3] celery; **~́ь** *f* [8; *from g/pl. e.*] herring

се́ль|ский [16] rural, country..., village...; ***~ское хозя́йство*** agriculture; **~скохозя́йственный** [14] agricultural; **~сове́т** *m* [1] village soviet

сёмга *f* [5] salmon

семе́й|ный [14] family...; having a family; **~ство** *n* [9] family

семена́ → ***се́мя***

семен|и́ть *coll.* [13] (*when walking*) mince; **~но́й** [14] seed...; *biol.* seminal

семёрка [5; *g/pl.*: -рок] seven; → ***дво́йка***

се́меро [37] seven; → ***дво́е***

семе́стр *m* [1] term, semester

се́мечко *n* [9; *pl.*: -чки, -чек, -чкам] *dim. of* **се́мя**; (*pl.*) sunflower seeds

семи|деся́тый [14] seventieth; → ***пя(тидеся́)тый***; **~ле́тний** [15] seventy-year-old; of seventy

семина́р *m* [1] seminar; **~ия** *f* [7] seminary; ***духо́вная ~ия*** theological college

семисо́тый [14] seven hundredth

семна́дцат|ый [14] seventeenth; → ***пя́тый***; **~́ь** [35] seventeen; → ***пять***

семь [35] seven; → ***пять*** & ***пя́тый***; **~́десят** [35] seventy; **~со́т** [36] seven hundred; **~́ю** seven times

семья́ [6; *pl.*: се́мьи, семе́й, се́мьям] family; **~ни́н** *m* [1] family man

се́мя *n* [13; *pl.*: -мена́, -мя́н, -мена́м] seed (*a. fig.*); *biol.* semen

сена́т *m* [1] senate; **~ор** *m* [1] senator

се́ни *f/pl.* [8; *from gen. e.*] entryway (*in a Russian village house*)

се́но *n* [9] hay; **~ва́л** *m* [1] hayloft; **~ко́с** *m* [1] haymaking; → ***коси́лка***

сен|сацио́нный [14; -о́нен, -о́нна] sensational; **~тимента́льный** [14; -лен, -льна] sentimental

сентя́брь *m* [4 *e.*] September

сень *f* [8; в -ни́] *obs. or poet.* canopy, shade; *fig.* protection

сепарат|и́ст *m* [1] separatist; **~ный** [14] separate

се́п|сис *m* [1] *med.* sepsis

се́ра *f* [5] sulfur; *coll.* earwax

серб *m* [1], **~(ия́н)ка** *f* [5; *g/pl.*: -б(ия́н)ок] Serb(ian); **~ский** [16] Serbian

серви́|з *m* [1] service, set; **~рова́ть** [7] *(im)pf.* serve

се́рвис *m* [1] (*consumer*) service

серде́чный [14; -чен, -чна] of the heart; *приём* hearty, cordial; *челове́к* warmhearted; *благода́рность* heartfelt; **~ при́ступ** heart attack

серди́|тый [14 *sh.*] angry, mad (**на** В with, at); **~ть** [15], <рас-> annoy, vex, anger; **-ся** be(come) angry, cross (**на** В with)

се́рдц|е *n* [11; *pl. e.*: -дца́, -де́ц, -дца́м] heart; **в ~а́х** in a fit of temper; **принима́ть бли́зко к ~у** take to heart; **от всего́ ~а** wholeheartedly; **по́ ~у** (Д) to one's liking; **положа́ ру́ку на́ ~е** *coll.* (quite) frankly; **~еби́ение** *n* [12] palpitation; **~еви́на** *f* [5] core, pith, heart

серебр|и́стый [14 *sh.*] silvery; **~и́ть** [13], <по-, вы́-> silver; **-ся** become silvery; **~о́** *n* [9] silver; **~я́ный** [14] silver(y)

середи́на *f* [5] middle; midst; mean

серёжка *f* [5; *g/pl.*: -жек] earring; *bot.* catkin

серéть [8], <по-> turn (*impf.* show) gray (*Brt.* grey)

сержа́нт *m* [1] sergeant

сери́|йный [14] serial; **´~я** *f* [7] series

се́рна *f* [5] *zo.* chamois

се́р|ный [14] sulfuric; sulfur...; **~ова́тый** [14 *sh.*] grayish, *Brt.* greyish

серп *m* [1 *e.*] sickle; *луны́* crescent

серпанти́н *m* [1] paper streamer; road with sharp, U-shaped curves

сертифика́т *m* [1] *ка́чества и т. д.* certificate

се́рфинг *m* [1] surfing

се́рый [14; сер, -á, -о] gray, *Brt.* grey; dull, dim

се́рьги *f/pl.* [5; серёг, серьга́м; *sg. e.*] earrings

серьёзн|ый [14; -зен, -зна] serious, grave; earnest; **~о** *a.* indeed, really

се́ссия *f* [7] session (**на** П in)

сестра *f* [5; *pl.*: сёстры, сестёр, сёстрам] sister; (first) cousin; nurse

сесть → ***сади́ться***

се́т|ка *f* [5; *g/pl.*: -ток] net; *тари́фов и т. д.*; **~овать** [1] complain (**на** В about); **~ча́тка** *f* [5; *g/pl.*: -ток] *anat.* retina; **~ь** *f* [8; в се́ти́; *from g/pl. e.*] net; (*систе́ма*) network

сече́ние *n* [12] section; cutting; ***ке́сарево ~*** cesarean birth

сечь¹ [26; *pt. e.*; сек, секла́] cut (up); **-ся** split; **~²** [26; *pt. st.*; сек, се́кла], <вы́-> whip

се́ялка *f* [5; *g/pl.*: -лок] drill

се́ять [27], <по-> sow (*a. fig.*)

сжа́литься [13] *pf.* (**над** Т) have *or* take pity (on)

сжа́т|ие *n* [12] pressure; compression; **~ый** [14] (*во́здух и т. д.*) compressed; *fig.* compact, concise, terse; **~ь(ся)** → ***сжима́ть(ся)*** & ***жать¹***, ***жать²***

сжига́ть [1], <сжечь> → ***жечь***

сжима́ть [1], <сжать> [сожму́, -мёшь; сжа́тый] (com)press, squeeze; (*кулаки́*) clench; **-ся** contract; shrink; become clenched

сза́ди (from) behind (*as prp.*: Р)

сзыва́ть → ***созыва́ть***

сиби́р|ский [16], **~я́к** *m* [1 *e.*], **~я́чка** *f* [5; *g/pl.*: -чек] Siberian

сига́р(е́т)а *f* [5] cigar(ette)

сигна́л [1], **~изи́ровать** [7] *(im)pf.*, **~ьный** [14] signal, alarm

сиде́лка *f* [5; *g/pl.*: -лок] nurse

сиде́|нье *n* [10] seat; **~ть** [11; си́дя] sit (**за** Т at, over); *до́ма* be, stay; *об оде́жде* fit (**на** П a p.); *на ко́рточках* squat; **-ся**: ***ему́ не сиди́тся на ме́сте*** he can't sit still

сидр *m* [1] cider

сидя́чий [17] *о́браз жи́зни* sedentary; sitting

си́зый [14; сиз, -á, -о] blue-gray, *Brt.* -grey; dove-colo(u)red

си́л|а *f* [5] strength; force (*тж. привы́чки*); power, might; vigo(u)r; intensity; energy; *зву́ка* volume; ***свои́ми ~ами*** unaided, by o.s.; ***в ~у*** (P) by virtue of; ***не в ~ах*** unable; ***не по ~ам, свы́ше чьи́х-л. сил*** beyond one's power; ***изо всех ~*** *coll.* with all one's might; **~а́ч** *m* [1 *e.*] strong man; **~иться** [13] try, endeavo(u)r; **~ово́й** [14] power...

силуэ́т *m* [1] silhouette

си́льн|ый [14; си́лен & силён, -льна́, -о, си́льны́] strong; powerful, mighty; intense; *дождь* heavy; *на́сморк* bad; **~о** *a.* very much; strongly; badly

си́мвол *m* [1] symbol; **~и́ческий** [16], **~и́чный** [14; -чен, -чна] symbolic

симметри́|чный [14; -чен, -чна] symmetrical; **~я** *f* [7] symmetry

симпат|изи́ровать [7] sympathize (with Д); **~и́чный** [14; -чен, -чна] nice, attractive; ***он мне ~и́чен*** I like him; **~ия** *f* [7] liking (***к*** Д for)

симпто́м *m* [1] symptom

симул|и́ровать [7] (*im*)*pf.* feign, sham; simulate; **~я́нт** *m* [1], **~я́нтка** *m* [5; *g/pl.*: -ток] simulator; malingerer

симфони́|ческий [16] symphonic, symphony...; **´~я** *f* [7] symphony

син|ева́ *f* [5] blue; **~ева́тый** [14 *sh.*] bluish; **~е́ть** [8], <по-> turn (*impf.* show) blue; **~ий** [15; синь, синя́, си́не] blue; **~и́ть** [13], <под-> blue; apply blueing to; **~и́ца** *f* [5] titmouse

син|о́д *m* [1] *eccl.* synod; **~о́ним** *m* [1] synonym; **~таксис** *m* [1] syntax; **~тез** *m* [1] synthesis; **~те́тика** *f* [5] synthetic material; **~тети́ческий** [16] synthetic; **~хронизи́ровать** [7] (*im*)*pf.* synchronize; **~хро́нный** [14] synchronous; ***~хро́нный перево́д*** interpretation

синь *f* [8] blue colo(u)r; **~ка** *f* [5; *g/pl.*: -нек] blue; blueing; blueprint

синя́к *m* [1 *e.*] bruise

си́плый [14; сипл, -а́, -о] hoarse

сире́на *f* [5] siren

сире́н|евый [14], **~ь** *f* [8] lilac (colo[u]r)

сиро́п *m* [1] syrup

сирота́ *m/f* [5; *pl. st.*: сиро́ты] orphan

систе́ма *f* [5] system; ***~ управле́ния*** control system; **~ти́ческий** [16], **~ти́чный** [14; -чен, -чна] systematic

си́тец *m* [1; -тца] chintz, cotton

си́то *n* [9] sieve

ситуа́ция *f* [7] situation

сия́|ние *n* [12] radiance; (*нимб*) halo; ***се́верное ~ние*** northern lights; **~ть** [28] shine; *от ра́дости* beam; *от сча́стья* radiate

сказ|а́ние *n* [12] legend; story; tale; **~а́ть** → ***говори́ть***; **~ка** *f* [5; *g/pl.*: -зок] fairy tale; *coll.* tall tale, fib; **~очный** [14; -чен, -чна] fabulous; fantastic; fairy (tale)...

сказу́емое *n* [14] *gr.* predicate

скак|а́ть [3] skip, hop, jump; gallop; race; **~ово́й** [14] race...; racing

скал|а́ [5; *pl. st.*] rock face, crag; cliff; reef; **~и́стый** [14 *sh.*] rocky, craggy; **~ить** [13], <о-> show, bare; *coll.* ***~ить зу́бы*** *impf.* grin; jeer; **~ка** *f* [5; *g/pl.*: -лок] rolling pin; **~ывать** [1], <сколо́ть> [17] pin together; (*от-ка́лывать*) break (off)

скам|е́ечка *f* [5; -чек] footstool; *a. dim. of* **~е́йка** *f* [5; *g/pl.*: -е́ек], **~ья́** *f* [6; *nom/pl. a. st.*] bench; ***~ья́ подсуди́мых*** *law* dock

сканда́л *m* [1] scandal; disgrace; *coll.* shame; **~ить** [13], <на-> row, brawl; **~ьный** [14; -лен, -льна] scandalous

скандина́вский [16] Scandinavian

ска́пливать(ся) [1] → ***скопля́ть(ся)***

скар|б *coll.* [1] belongings; goods and chattels; **~лати́на** *f* [5] scarlet fever

скат *m* [1] slope, pitch

скат|а́ть → ***ска́тывать 2***; **~ерть** *f* [8; *from g/pl. e.*] tablecloth; ***~ертью доро́га*** good riddance!

ска́т|ывать [1] **1.** <~ить> [15] roll (*or* slide) down (*v/i.* **-ся**); **2.** <~а́ть> [1] roll (up)

ска́ч|ка *f* [5; *g/pl.*: -чек] galloping; *pl.* horse race(s); **~о́к** → ***прыжо́к***

ска́шивать [1], <скоси́ть> [15] mow

сква́жина *f* [5] slit, hole; ***замо́чная ~*** keyhole; ***нефтяна́я ~*** oil well

сквер *m* [1] public garden; **~носло́-**

вить [14] use foul language; **~ный** [14; -рен, -рна́, -о] *ка́чество* bad, poor; *челове́к, посту́пок* nasty, foul

сквоз|и́ть [15 *e.*; -и́т] *о све́те* shine through; **~и́т** there is a draft, *Brt.* draught; **~но́й** [14] through...; **~ня́к** *m* [1 *e.*] draft, *Brt.* draught; **~ь** (B) *prp.* through

скворе́|ц *m* [1; -рца́] starling; **~чница** *f* (-ʃn-) [5] nesting box

скеле́т *m* [1] skeleton

скепти́ческий [16] skeptical (*Brt.* sceptical)

ски́|дка *f* [5; *g/pl.*: -док] discount, rebate; **де́лать ~дку** make allowances (**на** for); **~дывать** [1], <~нуть> [20] throw off *or* down; *оде́жду* take *or* throw off; *coll. це́ну* knock off (from); **~петр** *m* [1] scepter, *Brt.* -tre; **~пида́р** *m* [1] turpentine; **~рда́** *f* [5] stack, rick

скис|а́ть [1], <~нуть> [21] turn sour

скита́ться [1] wander, rove

склад *m* [1] **1.** warehouse, storehouse (**на** П in); *mil.* depot; **2.** (*нрав*) disposition, turn of mind; **~ка** *f* [5; *g/pl.*: -док] pleat, fold; *на брю́ках и т. д.* crease; *на лбу* wrinkle; **~но́й** [14] fold(ing), collapsible; camp...; **~ный** [14; -ден, -дна] *речь* coherent, smooth; P well-made (*or* -built); **~чина** *f* [5]: **в ~чину** by clubbing together; **~ывать** [1], <сложи́ть> [16] lay *or* put (together); pile up; pack (up); fold; *чи́сла* add up; *пе́сню* compose; *ору́жие, жизнь* lay down; *сложа́ ру́ки* idle; **-ся** (be) form(ed), develop; *coll.* club together

скле́и|вать [1], <~ть> [13; -е́ю] stick together, glue together (*v/i.* **-ся**)

склеп *m* [1] crypt, vault

скло́ка *f* [5] squabble

склон *m* [1] slope; **~е́ние** *n* [12] *gr.* declension; *astr.* declination; **~и́ть(ся)** → **~я́ть(ся)**; **~ность** *f* [8] inclination (*fig.*; **к** Д to, for), disposition; **~ный** [14; -о́нен, -онна́, -о] inclined (**к** Д to), disposed; **~я́ть** [28] **1.** <~и́ть> [13; -оню́, -о́нишь, -онённый] bend, incline (*a. fig.*; *v/i.* **-ся**; *о со́лнце* sink); (*убеди́ть*) persuade; **2.** <просклоня́ть> *gr.* (**-ся** be) decline(d)

ско́б|а *f* [5; *pl.*: ско́бы, скоб, скоба́м] cramp (iron), clamp; **~ка** *f* [5; *g/pl.*: -бок] cramp; *gr.*, *typ.* bracket, parenthesis; **~ли́ть** [13; -облю́, -обли́шь, -обленный] scrape; plane

скова́ть → **ско́вывать**

сковорода́ *f* [5; *pl.*: ско́вороды, -ро́д, -да́м] frying pan

ско́в|ывать [1], <~а́ть> [7 *e.*; -скую́, скуёшь] forge (together); weld; *fig.* fetter; bind; arrest

сколо́ть → **ска́лывать**

скольз|и́ть [15 *e.*; -льжу́, -льзи́шь], *once* <~нуть> [20] slide, glide, slip; **~кий** [16; -зок, -зка́, -о] slippery

ско́лько [32] how (*or* as) much, many; *coll.* **~ лет, ~ зим** → **ве́чность** *coll.*

сконча́ться [1] *pf.* die, expire

скоп|ля́ть [28], <~и́ть> [14] accumulate, gather (*v/i.* **-ся**), amass; save; **~ле́ние** *n* [12] accumulation; *люде́й* gathering, crowd

скорб|е́ть [10 *e.*; -блю́, -би́шь] grieve (**о** П over); **~ный** [14; -бен, -бна] mournful, sorrowful; **~ь** *f* [8] grief, sorrow

скорлупа́ *f* [5; *pl. st.* -лу́пы] shell

скорня́к *m* [1 *e.*] furrier

скоро|гово́рка *f* [5; *g/pl.*: -рок] tongue twister; *речь* patter; **~пали́тельный** [14 *sh.*] hasty, rash; **~пости́жный** [14; -жен, -жна] sudden; **~спе́лый** [14 *sh.*] early; *fig.* hasty; **~стно́й** [14] (high-) speed...; **´~сть** *f* [8; *from g/pl. e.*] speed; *све́та и т. д.* velocity; *mot.* gear; **со ´~стью** at the rate of; **груз ма́лой ´~стью** slow freight

ско́р|ый [14; скор, -а́, -о] quick, fast, rapid, swift; *по́мощь* first (*aid*); *бу́дущем* near; **~о** *a.* soon; **~е́е всего́** *coll.* most probably; **на ~ую ру́ку** *coll.* in haste, anyhow

скоси́ть → **ска́шивать**

скот *m* [1 *e.*] cattle, livestock; **~и́на** *f* [5] *coll.* cattle; P beast, brute; **~ный** [14]: **~ный двор** cattle yard; **~обо́йня** *f* [6; *g/pl.*: -о́ен] slaughterhouse; **~ово́дство** *n* [9] cattle breeding; **~ский** [16] brutish, bestial

С

скра́|шивать [1], <**~сить**> [15] *fig.* relieve, lighten, smooth over
скребо́к *m* [1; -бка́] scraper
скре́жет [1], **~а́ть** [3] (Т) gnash
скреп|и́ть → **~ля́ть**; **~ка** *f* [5; *g/pl.*: -пок] (paper) clip; **~ле́ние** *n* [12] fastening; **~ля́ть** [28], <**~и́ть**> [14 *e.*; -плю́, -пи́шь; -плённый] fasten together; clamp; make fast; *по́дписью* countersign; **~я́ се́рдце** reluctantly
скрести́ [24 -б-: скребу́; скрёб] scrape; scratch
скре́щива|ть [1], <скрести́ть> [15 *e.*; -ещу́, -ести́шь; -ещённый] cross; clash (*v/i.* **-ся**); **~ение** *n* [12] crossing; intersection
скрип *m* [1] creak, squeak; *сне́га* crunch; **~а́ч** *m* [1 *e.*] violinist; **~е́ть** [10 *e.*; -плю́, -пи́шь], <про->, *once* <**~нуть**> [20] creak, squeak; crunch; *зуба́ми* grit, gnash; **~ка** *f* [5; *g/pl.*: -пок] violin
скро́мн|ость *f* [8] modesty; **~ый** [14; -мен, -мна́, -о] modest; *обе́д* frugal
скру́|чивать [1], <**~ти́ть**> [15] twist; roll; bind
скры|ва́ть [1], <**~ть**> [22] hide, conceal (**от** Р from); **-ся** disappear; (*пря́таться*) hide; **~тность** *f* [8] reserve; **~тный** [14; -тен, -тна] reserved, reticent; **~тый** [14] concealed; latent (*a. phys.*); secret; *смысл* hidden; **~ть(ся)** → **~ва́ть(ся)**
скря́га *m/f* [5] miser, skinflint
ску́дный [14; -ден, -дна] scanty, poor
ску́ка *f* [5] boredom, ennui
скула́ *f* [5; *pl. st.*] cheekbone; **~стый** [14 *sh.*] with high *or* prominent cheek-bones
скули́ть [13] whimper
ску́льпт|ор *m* [1] sculptor; **~у́ра** *f* [5] sculpture
ску́мбрия *f* [7] mackerel
скуп|а́ть [1], <**~и́ть**> [14] buy up, corner
скуп|и́ться [14], <по-> be stingy (*or* sparing), stint (**на** В in, of); **~о́й** [14; скуп, -а́, -о] stingy; sparing (**на** В in); inadequate; taciturn (*на слова́*); *su.* miser; **~ость** *f* [8] stinginess, miserliness
скуч|а́ть [1] be bored (**о** П, **по** Д) long (for), miss; **~ный** (-ʃn-) [14; -чен, -чна́, -о] boring, tedious, dull; (Д) **~но** feel bored
слаб|е́ть [8], <о-> weaken; *о ве́тре и т. д.* slacken; **~и́тельный** [14] laxative (*n a. su.*); **~ово́льный** [14; -лен, -льна] weak-willed; **~ость** *f* [8] weakness, *a. fig.* = foible (**к** Д for); infirmity; **~оу́мный** [14; -мен, -мна] feeble-minded; **~охара́ктерный** [14; -рен, -рна] characterless; of weak character; **~ый** [14; слаб, -а́, -о] weak (*a. el.*); feeble; *звук, схо́дство* faint; *здоро́вье* delicate; *хара́ктер* flabby; *зре́ние* poor
сла́в|а *f* [5] glory; fame, renown; reputation, repute; **~а бо́гу!** thank goodness!; **на ~у** *coll.* first-rate, wonderful, right-on; **~ить** [14], <про-> glorify; praise, extol; **-ся** be famous (Т for); **~ный** [14; -вен, -вна, -о] famous, glorious; *coll.* nice; splendid
славян|и́н *m* [1; *pl.*: -я́не, -я́н], **~ка** *f* [5; *g/pl.*: -нок] Slav; **~ский** [16] Slavic, Slavonic
слага́ть [1], <сложи́ть> [16] *пе́сню* compose; *ору́жие* lay down; *полномо́чия* resign (from); *обя́занности* relieve o.s. (of); → **скла́дывать(ся)**
сла́д|кий [16; -док, -дка́, -о; *comp.*: сла́ще] sweet; sugary; **~ое** *su.* dessert (**на** В for); **~остный** [14; -тен, -тна] sweet, delightful; **~остра́стие** *n* [12] voluptuousness; **~остра́стный** [14] voluptuous; **~ость** *f* [8] sweetness, delight; → **сла́сти**
сла́женный [14 *sh.*] harmonious; *де́йствия* coordinated
слайд *m* [1] slide, transparency
сла́нец *m* [1; -нца] shale, slate
сла́сти *f/pl.* [8; *from gen. e.*] candy *sg.*, *Brt. a.* sweets
слать [шлю, шлёшь], <по-> send
слаща́вый [14 *sh.*] sugary, sickly sweet
сле́ва on, to (*or* from) the left
слегка́ slightly; somewhat; *прикосну́ться* lightly, gently
след *m* [1; *g/sg. e.* & -ду; на -ду́; *pl.*

e.] trace (*a. fig.*); track; footprint; (*за́пах*) scent; **~ом** (right) behind; **его́ и ~ просты́л** *coll.* he vanished into thin air; **~и́ть** [15 *e.*; -ежу́, -еди́шь] (**за** T) watch, follow; (*присма́тривать*) look after; *та́йно* shadow; *за собы́тиями* keep up (**за** T with)

сле́доват|ель *m* [4] investigator; **~ельно** consequently, therefore; so; **~ь** [7] (**за** T; Д) follow; result (**из** P from); be bound for; (Д) *impers.* should, ought to; **как сле́дует** properly, as it should be; **кому́** *or* **куда́ сле́дует** to the proper person *or* quarter

сле́дствие *n* [12] **1.** consequence; **2.** investigation

сле́дующий [17] following, next

сле́жка *f* [5; *g/pl.*: -жек] shadowing

слез|а́ *f* [5; *pl.*: слёзы, слёз, слеза́м] tear; **~а́ть** [1], <~ть> [24 *st.*] come or get down (from); *с ло́шади* dismount; *coll. о ко́же, кра́ске* come off; **~и́ться** [15; -и́тся] water; **~ли́вый** [14 *sh.*] given to crying; tearful, lachrymose; **~оточи́вый** [14] *глаза́* running; *газ* tear; **~ть** → **~а́ть**

слеп|е́нь *m* [4; -пня́] gadfly; **~е́ц** *m* [1; -пца́] blind man; *fig.* one who fails to notice the obvious; **~и́ть 1.** [14 *e.*; -плю́, -пи́шь], <о-> [ослеплённый] blind; *я́рким све́том* dazzle; **2.** [14] *pf.*; *impf.*: **~ля́ть** [28] stick together (*v/i.* **-ся**) → *a.* **лепи́ть**; **~нуть** [21], <о-> go (*or* become) blind; **~о́й** [14; слеп, -á, -о] blind (*a. fig.*); *текст* indistinct; *su.* blind man; **~ок** *m* [1; -пка] mo(u)ld, cast; **~ота́** *f* [5] blindness

сле́сар|ь *m* [4; *pl.*: -ря́, *etc. e.*, & -ри] metalworker; fitter; locksmith

слет|а́ть [1], <~е́ть> [11] fly down, (from); *coll.* fall (down, off); **-ся** fly together

слечь *coll.* [26 г/ж: сля́гу, сля́жешь; сля́г(те)!] *pf.* fall ill; take to one's bed

сли́ва *f* [5] plum

сли́|вать [1], <~ть> [солью́, -льёшь; → **лить**] pour (off, out, together); *о фи́рмах и т. д.* merge, amalgamate (*v/i.* **-ся**)

сли́в|ки *f/pl.* [5; *gen.*: -вок] cream (*a. fig.* = elite); **~очный** [14] creamy; **~очное ма́сло** butter; **~очное моро́женое** ice cream

сли́з|истый [14 *sh.*] mucous; slimy; **~истая оболо́чка** mucous membrane; **~ь** *f* [8] slime; mucus, phlegm

слипа́ться [1] stick together; *о глаза́х* close

сли́т|ный [14] joined; united; **~ное написа́ние слов** omission of hyphen from words; **~но** *a.* together; **~ок** *m* [1; -тка] ingot; **~ь(ся)** → **слива́ться**

слич|а́ть [1], <~и́ть> [16 *e.*; -чу́, -чи́шь; -чённый] compare, collate

сли́шком too; too much; **э́то (уж) ~** *coll.* that beats everything

слия́ние *n* [12] *рек* confluence; *фирм* amalgamation, merger

слова́к *m* [1] Slovak

слова́р|ный [14]: **~ный соста́в** stock of words; **~ь** *m* [4 *e.*] dictionary; vocabulary, glossary; lexicon

слов|а́цкий [16], **~а́чка** *f* [5; *g/pl.*: -чек] Slovak; **~е́нец** *m* [1; -нца], **~е́нка** *f* [5; *g/pl.*: -нок], **~е́нский** [16] Slovene

слове́сн|ость *f* [8] literature; *obs.* philology; **~ый** [14] verbal, oral

сло́вно as if; like; *coll.* as it were

сло́в|о *n* [9; *pl. e.*] word; **~ом** in a word; **~о за ~о** word for word; speech; **к ~у сказа́ть** by the way; **по слова́м** according to; **проси́ть (предоста́вить** Д) **~** ask (give p.) permission to speak; **~оизмене́ние** *n* [12] inflection (*Brt.* -xion); **~оохо́тливый** [14 *sh.*] talkative

слог *m* [1; *from g/pl. e.*] syllable; style

слоёный [14] *те́сто* puff pastry

слож|е́ние *n* [12] *math.* addition; *челове́ка* constitution, build; *полномо́чий* laying down; **~и́ть(ся)** → **скла́дывать(ся)**, **слага́ть(ся)** & **класть 2.**; **~ность** *f* [8] complexity; **в о́бщей ~ности** all in all; **~ный** [14; -жен, -жна́, -о] complicated, complex, intricate; *сло́во* compound

сло|и́стый [14 *sh.*] stratiform; flaky; **~й** *m* [3; *pl. e.*: слои́, слоёв] layer, stratum (in T *pl.*); *кра́ски* coat(ing)

слом *m* [1] demolition, pulling down; **~и́ть** [14] *pf.* break, smash; *fig.* overcome; ***~я́ го́лову*** *coll.* headlong, at breakneck speed
слон *m* [1 *e.*] elephant; bishop (*chess*); **~о́вый** [14]: ***~о́вая кость*** ivory
слоня́ться *coll.* [28] loiter about
слу|га́ *m* [5; *pl. st.*] servant; **~жа́щий** [17] employee; **~жба** *f* [5] service; work; employment; **~жéбный** [14] office...; official; **~жéние** *n* [12] service; **~жи́ть** [16], <по-> serve (a p./th. Д); be in use
слух *m* [1] hearing; ear (***на*** В by; ***по*** Д); rumo(u)r, hearsay; **~ово́й** [14] of hearing; acoustic; ear...
слу́ча|й *m* [3] case; occurrence, event; occasion (***по*** Д on; ***при*** П), opportunity, chance; (*a.* ***несча́стный ~й***) accident; ***во вся́ком ~е*** in any case; ***в проти́вном ~е*** otherwise; ***на вся́кий ~й*** to be on the safe side; ***по ~ю*** on the occasion (of Р); **~йность** *f* [8] chance; **~йный** [14; -áен, -áйна] accidental, fortuitous; casual, chance (**~йно** by chance); **~ться** [1], <случи́ться> [16 *e.*; 3rd *p. or impers.*] happen (**с** Т to); come about; take place; ***что бы не случи́лось*** come what may
слу́ша|тель *m* [4] listener, hearer; student; *pl. collect.* audience; **~ть** [1], <по-> listen (В to); ***лéкции*** attend; **~ю!** (*on telephone*) hello!; **-ся** obey (Р p.); ***совéта*** take
слыть [23], <про-> (Т) have a reputation for
слы́|шать [4], <у-> hear (of, about **о** П); **~шаться** [4] be heard; **~шимость** *f* [8] audibility; **~шно** one can hear; ***мне ~шно*** I can hear; ***что ~шно?*** what's new?; **~шный** [14; -шен, -шна, -о] audible
слюда́ *f* [5] mica
слюн|á *f* [5], **~и** *coll. pl.* [8; *from gen. e.*] saliva, spittle; **~ки** *coll. f/pl.*: (**у** Р) ***от э́того ~ки теку́т*** makes one's mouth water
сля́коть *f* [8] slush
сма́з|ать → **~ывать**; **~ка** *f* [5; *g/pl.*: -зок] greasing, oiling, lubrication; lubricant; **~очный** [14] lubricating; **~ывать** [1], <~ать> [3] grease, oil, lubricate; *coll.* ***очертáния*** slur; blur
сма́|нивать [1], <~ни́ть> [13; сманю́, -áнишь; -áненный & -анённый] lure, entice; **~тывать**, <смотáть> [1] wind, reel; **~хивать** [1], <~хну́ть> [20] brush off (*or* aside); *impf. coll.* (***походи́ть***) have a likeness (***на*** В to); **~чивать** [1], <смочи́ть> [16] moisten
смéжный [14; -жен, -жнá] adjacent
смéл|ость *f* [8] boldness; courage; **~ый** [14; смел, -á, -о] courageous; bold; **~о** *a. coll.* easily; ***могу́ ~о сказáть*** I can safely say
смéн|а *f* [5] shift (**в** В in); change; changing; replacement; successors *pl.*; ***прийти́ на ~у*** → **~и́ться**; **~я́ть** [28], <~и́ть> [13; -еню́, -éнишь; -енённый] (**-ся** be) supersede(d; o.a.), relieve(d), replace(d by Т), substitut(ed; for); give way to
смерк|áться [1], <~нуться> [20] grow dusky *or* dark
смерт|éльный [14; -лен, -льна] mortal; ***исхо́д*** fatal; ***яд*** deadly; **~ность** *f* [8] mortality, death rate; **~ный** [14; -тен, -тна] mortal (*a. su.*); ***грех*** deadly; *law* death...; ***казнь*** capital; **~ь** *f* [8; *from g/pl. e.*] death; *coll.* ***надоéсть до́ ~и*** bore to death; ***при́ ~и*** at death's door
смерч *m* [1] waterspout; tornado
смести́ → ***сметáть***; **~ть** → ***смещáть***
сме|сь *f* [8] mixture; blend, compound; **~та** *f* [5] *fin.* estimate
сметáна *f* [5] sour cream
сме|тáть [1], <~сти́> [25 -т-] sweep off *or* away; sweep into; ***~ с лицá земли́*** wipe off the face of the earth
смéтливый [14 *sh.*] sharp, quick on the uptake
сметь [8], <по-> dare, venture
смех *m* [1] laughter; ***со́ ~у*** with laughter; ***~а рáди*** for a joke, for fun, in jest; ***подня́ть нá ~*** ridicule; → ***шу́тка***
смéш|анный [14] mixed; **~áть(ся)** → ***~ивать(ся)***; **~ивать**, <~áть> [1] mix with, blend with (*v/i.* **-ся**; get *or* be[come]) confuse(d); ***с толпо́й*** mingle with

смеш|и́ть [16 *e.*; -шу́, -ши́шь], <рас-> [-шённый] make laugh; **~но́й** [14; -шо́н, -шна́] laughable, ludicrous; ridiculous; funny; ***мне не ~но́*** I don't see anything funny in it

сме|ща́ть [1], <~сти́ть> [15 *e.*; -ещу́, -ести́шь; -ещённый] displace, shift, remove; **~ще́ние** *n* [12] displacement, removal

смея́ться [27 *e.*; -ею́сь, -еёшься], <за-> laugh (*impf.* ***над*** T at); mock (at); deride; *coll.* *шути́ть* joke

смир|е́ние *n* [12], **~е́нность** *f* [8] humility; meekness; **~и́ть(ся)** → ***~я́ть(ся)***; **~ный** [14; -рен (*coll.* -рён), -рна́, -о] meek, gentle; (*поко́рный*) submissive; **~я́ть** [28], <~и́ть> [13] subdue; restrain, check; **-ся** resign o.s. (**с** T to)

смо́кинг *m* [1] tuxedo, dinner jacket

смол|а́ *f* [5; *pl. st.*] resin; pitch; tar; **~и́стый** [14 *sh.*] resinous; **~и́ть** [13], <вы́-, за-> pitch, tar; **~ка́ть** [1], <~кнуть> [21] grow silent; *звук* cease; **~оду** *coll.* from *or* in one's youth; **~яно́й** [14] pitch..., tar...

сморка́ться [1], <вы́-> blow one's nose

сморо́дина *f* [5] currant(s *pl.*)

смота́ть → ***сма́тывать***

смотр|е́ть [9; -отрю́, -о́тришь; -о́тренный], <по-> look (***на*** B at), gaze; view, see, watch; *больно́го и т. д.* examine, inspect; ***~я́*** depending (***по*** Д on), according (to); ***~е́ть в о́ба*** keep one's eyes open, be on guard; ***~и́ не опозда́й!*** mind you are not late!; **~и́тель** *m* [4] supervisor; *музе́я* custodian, keeper

смочи́ть → ***сма́чивать***

смрад *m* [1] stench; **~ный** [14; -ден, -дна] stinking

сму́глый [14; смугл, -а́, -о] swarthy

смут|и́ть(ся) → ***смуща́ть(ся)***; **~ный** [14; -тен, -тна] vague, dim; *на душе́* restless, uneasy

смущ|а́ть [1], <смути́ть> [15 *e.*; -ущу́, -ути́шь; -ущённый] (**-ся** be[come]) embarrass(ed), confuse(d), perplex(ed); **~е́ние** *n* [12] embarrassment, confusion; **~ённый** [14] embarrassed, confused

смы|ва́ть [1], <~ть> [22] wash off (*or* away); **~ка́ть** [1], <сомкну́ть> [20] close (*v/i.* **-ся**); **~сл** *m* [1] sense, meaning; ***в э́том ~сле*** in this respect; *coll.* ***како́й ~сл?*** what's the point?; **~слить** *coll.* [13] understand; **~ть** → ***~ва́ть***; **~чко́вый** [14] *mus.* stringed; **~чо́к** *m* [1; -чка́] *mus.* bow; **~шлёный** *coll.* [14 *sh.*] clever, bright

смягч|а́ть (-xtʃ-) [1], <~и́ть> [16 *e.*; -чу́, -чи́шь; -чённый] soften (*v/i.* **-ся**); *наказа́ние, боль* mitigate, alleviate; **-ся** *a.* relent; **~а́ющий** *law* extenuating; **~е́ние** *n* [12] mitigation; **~и́ть(ся)** → ***~а́ть(ся)***

смяте́ние *n* [12] confusion

снаб|жа́ть [1], <~ди́ть> [15 *e.*; -бжу́, -бди́шь; -бжённый] supply, furnish, provide (with P); **~же́ние** *n* [12] supply, provision

сна́йпер *m* [1] sharpshooter, sniper

снару́жи on the outside; from (the) outside

снаря́|д projectile, missile, shell; *гимнасти́ческий* apparatus; **~жа́ть** [1], <~ди́ть> [15 *e.*; -яжу́, -яди́шь; -яжённый] equip, fit out (T with); **~же́ние** *n* [12] equipment; outfit; *mil.* munitions *pl.*

снасть *f* [8; *from g/pl. e.*] tackle; *usu. pl.* rigging

снача́ла at first; first; (*сно́ва*) all over again

снег *m* [1; в -у́; *pl. e.*: -а́] snow; ***~ идёт*** it is snowing; **~и́рь** *m* [4 *e.*] bullfinch; **~опа́д** *m* [1] snowfall

снеж|и́нка *f* [5; *g/pl.*: -нок] snowflake; **~ный** [14; -жен, -жна] snow(y); **~о́к** *m* [1; -жка́] *dim.* → ***снег***; light snow; snowball

сни|жа́ть [1], <~зить> [15] lower; (*уме́ньшить*) reduce, decrease; (**-ся** *v/i.*; *a.* fall) (*себесто́имости*) cut production costs; **~же́ние** *n* [12] lowering; reduction, decrease; fall; **~зойти́** → ***~сходи́ть***; **~зу** from below

сним|а́ть [1], <снять> [сниму́, сни́мешь; снял, -а́, -о; сня́тый (снят, -а́, -о)] take (off *or* down); remove, discard; *с рабо́ты* sack, dismiss; *кандидату́ру* withdraw; *фильм* shoot; *ко́мнату* rent; (take a) photograph (of); *урожа́й* reap, gather; *оса́ду* raise; *ко́пию* make; ***~а́ть***

сли́вки skim; **-ся** weigh (***с я́коря*** anchor); have a picture of o.s. taken; *с учёта* be struck off; **~ок** *m* [1; -мка] photograph, photo, print (***на*** П in)

сниска́ть [3] get, win

снисхо|ди́тельный [14; -лен, -льна] condescending; indulgent; **~ди́ть** [15], <снизойти́> [-ойду́, -ойдёшь; → ***идти́***] condescend; **~жде́ние** *n* [12] indulgence, leniency; condescension

сни́ться [13], <при-> *impers.* (Д) dream (of И)

сно́ва (over) again, anew

сно|ва́ть [7 *e.*] scurry about, dash about; **~виде́ние** *n* [12] dream

сноп *m* [1 *e.*] sheaf

сноро́вка *f* [5] knack, skill

снос|и́ть [15], <снести́> [24 -с-: снесу́, снёс] carry (down, away *or* off); take; *зда́ние* pull down, demolish; (*терпе́ть*) endure, bear, tolerate; → *a.* ***нести́***; **~ка** *f* [5; *g/pl.*: -сок] footnote; **~ный** [14; -сен, -сна] tolerable

снотво́рное *n* [14] *su.* soporific

сноха́ *f* [5; *pl. st.*] daughter-in-law

снят|о́й [14]: ***~о́е молоко́*** skimmed milk; **~ь(ся)** → ***снима́ть*(ся)**

соба́|ка *f* [5] dog; hound; **~чий** [18] dog('s), canine

собесе́дник *m* [1] interlocutor

собира́т|ель *m* [4] collector; **~ельный** [14] *gr.* collective; **~ь** [1], <собра́ть> [-беру́, -рёшь; -а́л, -а́, -о; со́бранный (-ан, -а́, -о)] gather, collect; *tech.* assemble; prepare; **-ся** gather, assemble; prepare for, make o.s. (*or* be) ready to start (*or* set out *or* go; ***в путь*** on a journey); (*намерева́ться*) be going to, intend to; collect (***с мы́слями*** one's thoughts); (*с си́лами*) brace up

собла́зн *m* [1] temptation; **~и́тель** *m* [4] tempter; seducer; **~и́тельный** [14; -лен, -льна] tempting, seductive; **~я́ть** [28], <~и́ть> [13] (**-ся** be) tempt(ed); allured, enticed

соблю|да́ть [1], <~сти́> [25] observe, obey, adhere (to); *поря́док* maintain; **~де́ние** *n* [12] observance; maintenance; **~сти́** → ***~да́ть***

соболе́знова|ние *n* [12] sympathy, condolences; **~ть** [7] sympathize (Д with)

со́бо|ль *m* [4; *pl. a.* -ля́, *etc. e.*] sable; **~р** *m* [1] cathedral

собра́|ние *n* [12] meeting (***на*** В at, in), assembly; collection; **~ть(ся)** → ***собира́ть*(ся)**

со́бственн|ик *m* [1] owner, proprietor; **~ость** *f* [8] property; possession, ownership; **~ый** [14] own; *и́мя* proper; personal

собы́тие *n* [12] event, occurrence

сова́ *f* [5; *pl. st.*] owl

сова́ть [7 *e.*; сую́, суёшь], <су́нуть> [20] shove, thrust; *coll.* slip; butt in, poke one's nose into

соверш|а́ть [1], <~и́ть> [16 *e.*; -шу́, -ши́шь; -шённый] accomplish; *преступле́ние и т. д.* commit; *пое́здку и т. д.* make; *сде́лку* strike; **-ся** happen, take place; **~енноле́тие** *n* [12] majority, full age; **~еннолетний** [15] (***стать*** Т come) of age; **~е́нный** [14; -е́нен, -е́нна] perfect(ive *gr.*); *coll.* absolute, complete; *adv. a.* quite; **~е́нство** *n* [9] perfection; ***в ~е́нстве*** *a.* perfectly; **~е́нствовать** [7], <у-> perfect (**-ся** o.s.), improve, develop; **~и́ть** (**-ся**) → ***соверша́ть*(ся)**

со́вест|ливый [14 *sh.*] conscientious; **~но** (р. Д) ashamed; **~ь** *f* [8] conscience; ***по ~и*** honestly, to be honest

сове́т *m* [1] advice; *law* opinion; board; soviet; ***~ Безопа́сности*** Security Council; **~ник** *m* [1] adviser; (*as title of office or post*) councillor; **~овать** [7], <по-> advise (Д р.); **-ся** ask advice, consult (**о** П on); **~ский** [16] soviet (of local bodies); **~чик** *m* [1] adviser

совеща́|ние *n* [12] conference (at ***на*** П), meeting (*a.* in); (*обсужде́ние*) deliberation; **~тельный** [14] deliberative, consultative; **~ться** [1] confer, consult, deliberate

совме|сти́мый [14 *sh.*] compatible; **~сти́ть** → ***~ща́ть***; **~стный** [14] joint, combined; **~стно** common; **~ща́ть** [1], <~сти́ть> [15 *e.*; -ещу́, -ести́шь; -ещённый] combine; *tech.* match

совóк *m* [1; -вкá] shovel; scoop; *для мýсора* dustpan
совокýпн|ость *f* [8] total(ity), aggregate, whole; **~ый** [14] joint
совпа|дáть [1], <**~сть**> [25; *pt. st.*] coincide with; agree with; **~дéние** *n* [12] coincidence, *etc.* → *vb.*
совремéнн|ик *m* [1] contemporary; **~ый** [14; -éнен, -éнна] contemporaneous; of the time (of); present-day; up-to-date; → *a.* **~ик** contemporary
совсéм quite, entirely; at all; ***я егó ~ не знáю*** I don't know him at all
совхóз *m* [1] (***совéтское хозя́йство***) state farm; → ***колхóз***
соглá|сие *n* [12] consent (***на*** В to; **с** Р with); agreement (***по*** Д by); harmony, concord; **~сúться** → ***~шáться***; **~сно** (Д) according to, in accordance with; **~сный** [14; -сен, -сна] agreeable; harmonious; ***я ~сен*** (*f* ***~сна***) I agree (**с** Т with; ***на*** В to); (*a. su.*) consonant; **~совáние** *n* [12] coordination; *gr.* agreement; **~совáть** → ***~сóвывать***; **~совáться** [7] (*im*)*pf.* (**с** Т) conform (to); agree (with); **~сóвывать** [1],<~совáть> [7] coordinate; come to an agreement (**с** Т with); (*a. gr.*) make agree; **~шáться** [1], <~сúться> [15 *e.*; -ашýсь, -асúшься] agree (**с** Т with; ***на*** В to), consent (to); *coll.* (*признавáть*) admit; **~шéние** *n* [12] agreement, understanding; covenant
согнáть → ***сгоня́ть***
согнýть(ся) → ***сгибáть(ся)***
согре|вáть [1], <**~ть**> [28] warm, heat
содéйств|ие *n* [12] assistance, help; **~овать** [7] (*im*)*pf.*, *a.* <по-> (Д) assist, help; *успéху, соглáсию* contribute (to), further, promote
содерж|áние *n* [12] content(s); *семьú и т. д.* maintenance, support, upkeep; **~áтельный** [14; -лен, -льна] pithy, having substance and point; **~áть** [4] contain, hold; maintain, support; keep; **-ся** be contained, *etc.*; **~úмое** [14] contents *pl.*
содрáть → ***сдирáть***
содрог|áние *n* [12], **~áться** [1], *once* <~нýться> [20] shudder
содрýжеств|о *n* [9] community; concord; ***Бритáнское ~о нáций*** the British Commonwealth; ***в тéсном ~е*** in close cooperation (**с** Т with)
соедин|éние *n* [12] joining; conjunction, (at *a.* ***на*** П), connection; combination; *chem.* compound; *tech.* joint; **~úтельный** [14] connective; *a. gr.* copulative; **~я́ть** [28], <~úть> [13] unite, join; connect, link (*by telephone, etc.*); (*v/i.* **-ся**); → ***США***
сожал|éние *n* [12] regret (**о** П for); ***к ~éнию*** unfortunately, to (p.'s) regret; **~éть** [8] (**о** П) regret
сожжéние *n* [12] burning; cremation
сожúтельство *n* [9] cohabitation
созв|áть → ***созывáть***; **~éздие** *n* [12] constellation; **~онúться** *coll.* [13] *pf.* (**с** Т) speak on the phone; arrange s.th. on the phone; phone; **~ýчный** [14; -чен, -чна] in keeping with, consonant with
созда|вáть [5], <**~ть**> [-дáм, -дáшь *etc.*, → ***дать***; сóздал, -á, -о; сóзданный (-ан, -á, -о)] create; produce; found; establish; **-ся** arise, form; ***у меня́ ~лóсь впечатлéние*** I have gained the impression that ...; **~ние** *n* [12] creation; (*существó*) creature; **~тель** *m* [4] creator; founder; **~ть(ся)** → ***~вáть(ся)***
созерцáт|ельный [14; -лен, -льна] contemplative; **~ь** [1] contemplate
созидáтельный [14; -лен, -льна] creative
созна|вáть [5], <**~ть**> [1] realize, be conscious of, see; **-ся** (***в*** П) confess; **~ние** *n* [12] consciousness; ***без ~ния*** unconscious; **~тельный** [14; -лен, -льна] conscious; *отношéние и т. д.* conscientious; **~ть (-ся)** → ***~вáть(ся)***
созы́в *m* [1] convocation; **~áть** [1], <созвáть> [созовý, -вёшь; -звáл, -á, -о; сóзванный] *гостéй* invite; *собрáние* call, convene; *parl.* convoke
соизмерúмый [14 *sh.*] commensurable
сойтú(сь) → ***сходúть(ся)***

С

сок *m* [1; в -ý] juice; *берёзовый и т. д.* sap; **~овыжима́лка** *f* [5; -лок] juice extractor

со́кол *m* [1] falcon

сокра|ща́ть [1], <~ти́ть> [15 *e.*; -ащý, -ати́шь; -ащённый] shorten; abbreviate; abridge; *расхо́ды* reduce, curtail; *p. pt. p. a.* short, brief; **-ся** grow shorter; decrease; *о мы́шцах и т. д.* contract; **~ще́ние** *n* [12] shortening, abbreviation, reduction, curtailment; *те́кста* abridgement; contraction

сокров|е́нный [14 *sh.*] innermost; secret; concealed; **~ище** *n* [11] treasure; **~ищница** *f* [5] treasury

сокруш|а́ть [1], <~и́ть> [16 *e.*; -шý, -ши́шь; -шённый] shatter, smash; **~и́ть врага́** rout the enemy; **-ся** *impf.* grieve, be distressed; **~и́тельный** [14; -лен, -льна] shattering; **~и́ть** → **~а́ть**

солда́т *m* [1; *g/pl.*: солда́т] soldier; **~ский** [16] soldier's

сол|е́ние *n* [12] salting; **~ёный** [14; со́лон, -á, -о] salt(y); corned; pickled; *fig.* spicy; (*short forms only*) hot

солида́рн|ость *f* [8] solidarity; **~ый** [14; -рен, -рна] in sympathy with, at one with; *law* jointly liable

соли́дн|ость *f* [8] solidity; **~ый** [14; -ден, -дна] solid, strong, sound; *фи́рма* reputable, respectable; *coll.* sizable

соли́ст *m* [1], **~ка** *f* [5; *g/pl.*: -ток] soloist

соли́ть [13; солю́, со́ли́шь; со́ленный] **1.** <по-> salt; **2.** <за-> corn; pickle; <на-> *coll.* spite; cause annoyance; do s.o. a bad turn

со́лн|ечный [14; -чен, -чна] sun(ny); solar; **~це** ('son-) *n* [11] sun (**на** П *lie* in); **~цепёк** *m* [1]: **на ~цепёке** in the blazing sun

солове́й *m* [3; -вья́] nightingale

со́лод *m* [1], **~овый** [14] malt

соло́м|а *f* [5] straw; thatch; **~енный** [14] straw...; thatched; grass (*widow*); **~инка** *f* [5; *g/pl.*: -нок] straw; ***хвата́ться за ~инку*** clutch at straws

соло́нка *f* [5; *g/pl.*: -нок] saltcellar

сол|ь *f* [8; *from g/pl. e.*] salt (*a. fig.*); *coll.* **вот в чём вся ~ь** that's the whole point; **~яно́й** [14] salt...; saline

сом *m* [1 *e.*] catfish

сомкну́ть(ся) → ***смыка́ть(ся)***

сомн|ева́ться [1], <усомни́ться> [13] (**в** П) doubt; **~е́ние** *n* [12] doubt (**в** П about); question (**под** Т in); **~и́тельный** [14; -лен, -льна] doubtful; questionable, dubious

сон *m* [1; сна] sleep; dream (in **в** П); **~ли́вый** [14 *sh.*] sleepy; **~ный** [14] sleeping (*a. med.*); sleepy, drowsy; **~я** *coll. m/f* [6; *g/pl.*: -ней] sleepyhead

сообра|жа́ть [1], <~зи́ть> [15 *e.*; -ажý, -ази́шь; -ажённый] consider, weigh, think (over); (*поня́ть*) grasp, understand; **~же́ние** *n* [12] consideration; (*причи́на*) reason; **~зи́тельный** [14; -лен, -льна] sharp, quick-witted; **~зи́ть** → **~жа́ть**; **~зный** [14; -зен, -зна] conformable (**с** Т to); *adv. a.* in conformity (with); **~зова́ть** [7] (*im*)*pf.* (make) conform, adapt (to) (**с** Т); **-ся** conform, adapt (**с** Т to)

сообща́ together, jointly

сообщ|а́ть [1], <~и́ть> [16 *e.*; -щý, -щи́шь; -щённый] communicate (*v/i.* **-ся** *impf.*), report; inform (Д/**о** П p. of); impart; **~е́ние** *n* [12] communication, report; statement; announcement; information; **~ество** *n* [9] association, fellowship; community; **~и́ть** → **~а́ть**; **~ник** *m* [1], **~ница** *f* [5] accomplice

соору|жа́ть [1], <~ди́ть> [15 *e.*; -ужý, -уди́шь; -ужённый] build, construct, erect, raise; **~же́ние** *n* [12] construction, building, structure

соотве́тств|енный [14 *sh.*] corresponding; *adv. a.* according(ly) (Д to), in accordance (with); **~ие** *n* [12] conformity, accordance; **~овать** [7] (Д) correspond, conform (to), agree; **~ующий** [17] corresponding, appropriate; suitable

соотéчественни|к *m* [1], **~ца** *f* [5] compatriot, fellow country (wo)man

соотноше́ние *n* [12] correlation

сопе́рни|к *m* [1] rival; **~чать** [1] compete, vie (with); rival; be a

С

match (for **с** Т); **~чество** *n* [9] rivalry

соп|еть [10 *e.*; соплю, сопишь] breathe heavily through the nose; wheeze; **~ка** *f* [5; *g/pl.*: -пок] hill; volcano; **~ли** P *pl.* [6; *gen.*: -лей, *etc. e.*] snot

сопостав|ление *n* [12] comparison; confrontation; **~лять** [28], <~вить> [14] compare

сопри|касаться [1], <~коснуться> [20] (**с** Т) (*примыкать*) adjoin; (*касаться*) touch; *с людьми* deal with; **~косновение** *n* [12] contact

сопрово|дительный [14] covering (*letter*); **~ждать** [1] **1.** accompany; escort; **2.** <~дить> [15 *e.*; -ожу, -одишь; -ождённый] *примечанием и т. д.* provide (T with); **-ся** *impf.* be accompanied (T by); entail; **~ждение** *n* [12] accompaniment; ***в ~ждении*** (P) accompanied (by)

сопротивл|ение *n* [12] resistance; opposition; **~яться** [28] (Д) resist; oppose

сопряжённый [14; -жён, -жена] connected with; entailing

сопутствовать [14] (Д) accompany

сор *m* [1] dust; litter

соразмерно in proportion (Д to)

сорв|анец *coll. m* [1; -нца] madcap; (*of a child*) a terror; **~ать(ся)** → ***срывать(ся)***; **~иголова** *coll. m/f* [5; *ac/sg.*: сорвиголову; *pl.* → ***голова***] daredevil

соревнова|ние *n* [12] competition; contest; ***отборочные ~ния*** heats, qualifying rounds; **~ться** [7] (**с** Т) compete (with)

сор|ить [13], <на-> litter; *fig. деньгами* squander; **~ный** [14]: ***~ная трава*** = **~няк** *m* [1 *e.*] weed

сорок [35] forty; **~а** *f* [5] magpie

сороко|вой [14] fortieth; → ***пят(идесят)ый***; **~ножка** *f* [5; *g/pl.*: -жек] centipede

сорочка *f* [5; -чек] shirt; undershirt; chemise

сорт *m* [1; *pl.*: -та, *etc. e.*] sort, brand; variety, quality; **~ировать** [7], <рас-> sort out; *по размеру* grade; **~ировка** *f* [5] sorting

сосать [-су, -сёшь; сосанный] suck

сосед *m* [*sg.*: 1; *pl.*: 4], **~ка** *f* [5; *g/pl.*: -док] neighbo(u)r; **~ний** [15] neighbo(u)ring, adjoining; **~ский** [16] neighbo(u)r's; **~ство** *n* [9] neighbo(u)rhood

сосиска *f* [5; *g/pl.*: -сок] sausage; frankfurter

соска *f* [5; *g/pl.*: -сок] (*baby's*) dummy, pacifier

соск|акивать [1], <~очить> [16] jump *or* spring (off, down); come off; **~альзывать** [1], <~ользнуть> [20] slide (down, off); slip (off); **~учиться** [16] *pf.* become bored; miss (***по*** Д); → ***скучать***

сосл|агательный [14] *gr.* subjunctive; **~ать(ся)** → ***ссылаться***; **~уживец** *m* [1; -вца] colleague

сосна *f* [5; *pl. st.*: сосны, сосен, соснам] pine tree

сосок *m* [1; -ска] nipple, teat

сосредоточ|ение *n* [12] concentration; **~ивать** [1], <~ить> [16] concentrate (*v/i.* **-ся**); *p. pt. p. a.* intent

состав *m* [1] composition (*a. chem.*); structure; *студентов и т. д.* body; *thea.* cast; *rail.* train; ***подвижной ~*** rolling stock; ***в ~е*** (P) *a.* consisting of; **~итель** *m* [4] compiler; author; **~ить** → **~лять**; **~ление** *n* [12] *словаря и т. д.* compilation; *документа и т. д.* drawing up; **~лять** [28], <~ить> [14] compose, make (up); put together; *план и т. д.* draw up, work out; compile; (*образовывать*) form, constitute; (*равняться*) amount (*or* come) to; **~ной** [14]: composite; ***~ная часть*** constituent part; component

состоя|ние *n* [12] state, condition; position; (*богатство*) fortune; ***быть в ~нии ...*** *a.* be able to ...; ***я не в ~нии*** I am not in a position ...; **~тельный** [14; -лен, -льна] well-to-do, well-off; (*обоснованный*) sound, well-founded; **~ть** [-ою, -оишь] consist (***из*** P of; ***в*** П in); *членом и т. д.* be (*a.* T); **-ся** *pf.* take place

сострадание *n* [12] compassion, sympathy

состяза|ние *n* [12] contest, compe-

tition; match; **~ться** [1] compete, vie, contend (with)
сосу́д *m* [1] vessel
сосу́лька *f* [5; *g/pl.*: -лек] icicle
сосуществова́|ние *n* [12] coexistence; **~ть** [7] coexist
сотворе́ние *n* [12] creation
со́тня *f* [6; *g/pl.*: -тен] a hundred
сотру́дни|к *m* [1] employee; *pl.* staff; *газе́ты* contributor; colleague; **~чать** [1] collaborate with; contribute to; **~чество** *n* [9] collaboration, cooperation
сотрясе́ние *n* [12] shaking; *мо́зга* concussion
со́ты *m/pl.* [1] honeycomb(s); **~й** [14] hundredth; → ***пя́тый***; ***две це́лых и два́дцать пять ~х*** 2.25
со́ус *m* [1] sauce; gravy
соуча́ст|ие *n* [12] complicity; **~ник** *m* [1] accomplice
со́хнуть [21] **1.** <вы́-> dry; **2.** <за-> *coll.* wither; **3.** *coll. impf.* pine away
сохран|е́ние *n* [12] preservation; conservation; **~и́ть(ся)** → **~я́ть(ся)**; **~ность** *f* [8] safety; undamaged state; ***в ~ности*** *a.* safe; **~я́ть** [28], <~и́ть> [13] keep; preserve; retain; maintain; reserve (for o.s. ***за собо́й***); ***Бо́же сохрани́!*** God forbid!; **-ся** be preserved; ***в па́мяти и т. д.*** remain
социа́л|-демокра́т *m* [1] social democrat; **~-демократи́ческий** [16] social democrat(ic); **~и́зм** *m* [1] socialism; **~и́ст** *m* [1] socialist; **~исти́ческий** [16] socialist(ic); **~ьный** [14] social
соцстра́х *m* [1] social insurance
соче́льник *m* [1] Christmas Eve
сочета́|ние *n* [12] combination; **~ть** [1] combine (*v/i.* **-ся**)
сочин|е́ние *n* [12] composition; writing, work; *нау́чное* thesis; *gr.* coordination; **~я́ть** [28], <~и́ть> [13] compose (*a lit. or mus. work*); write; (*вы́думать*) invent, make up
соч|и́ться [16 *e.*; 3rd *p. only*] exude; ooze (out); *о кро́ви* bleed; **~ный** [14; -чен, -чна] juicy; *fig.* succulent; rich
сочу́вств|енный [14 *sh.*] sympathetic, sympathizing; **~ие** *n* [12] sympathy (**к** Д with, for); **~овать** [7] (Д) sympathize with, feel for; **~ующий** [17] sympathizer
сою́з *m* [1] union; alliance; confederation; league; *gr.* conjunction; **~ник** *m* [1] ally; **~ный** [14] allied
со́я *f* [6] soya bean
спа|д *m* [1] *econ.* recession, slump; **~да́ть** [1], <~сть> [25; *pt. st.*] fall; **~ивать 1.** <~я́ть> [28] solder; **2.** *coll.* <спои́ть> [13] accustom to drinking; **~йка** *f* [5] *fig.* union
спа́льн|ый [14] sleeping; bed...; ***~ое ме́сто*** bunk, berth; **~я** *f* [6; *g/pl.*: -лен] bedroom
спа́ржа *f* [5] asparagus
спас|а́тель *m* [4] one of a rescue team; (*at seaside*) lifeguard; **~а́тельный** [14] rescue...; life-saving; **~а́ть** [1], <~ти́> [24 -с-] save, rescue; ***~ти́ положе́ние*** save the situation; **-ся**, <-сь> save o.s.; *a.* escape (*v/i.* **от** Р); **~е́ние** *n* [12] rescue; escape; salvation
спаси́бо (***вам***) thank you (very much ***большо́е ~***), thanks (***за*** В, ***на*** П for)
спаси́тель *m* [4], ♀ the Savio(u)r; rescuer; **~ный** [14] saving
спас|ти́ → ***~а́ть***; **~ть** → ***спада́ть***
спать [сплю, спишь; спал, -а́, -о] sleep; be asleep; (*a.* ***идти́***, ***ложи́ться ~***) go to bed; *coll.* ***мне не спи́тся*** I can't (get to) sleep
спая́ть → ***спа́ивать 1***
спека́ться [1] *coll.* → ***запека́ться***
спекта́кль *m* [4] *thea.* performance; show
спекул|и́ровать [7] speculate (Т in); **~я́нт** *m* [1] speculator, profiteer; **~я́ция** *f* [7] speculation (in); profiteering; *philos.* speculation
спе́лый [14; спел, -а́, -о] ripe
сперва́ *coll.* (at) first
спе́реди in front (of); at the front, from the front (*as prp.*: Р)
спёртый *coll.* [14 *sh.*] stuffy, close
спеть [8], <по-> ripen; → *a.* ***петь***
спех *coll.* *m* [1]: ***не к ~у*** there is no hurry
специ|ализи́роваться [7] (*im*)*pf.* specialize (***в*** П, ***по*** Д in); **~али́ст** *m* [1] specialist, expert (***по*** Д in); **~а́льность** *f* [8] speciality, special

С

interest, profession (**по** Д by); **~а́льный** [14; -лен, -льна] special; **~фи́ческий** [16] specific

спе́ция *f* [7] *mst. pl.* spice

спецоде́жда *f* [5] working clothes; overalls *pl.*

спеш|и́ть [16 *e.*; -шу́, -ши́шь] hurry (up), hasten; of *clock* be fast (***на пять мину́т*** 5 min.); **~ка** *coll. f* [5] haste, hurry; **~ный** [14; -шен, -шна] urgent, pressing; ***в ~ном поря́дке*** quickly

спин|а́ *f* [5; *ac. sg.*: спи́ну; *pl. st.*] back; **~ка** *f* [5; *g/pl.*: -нок] *of piece of clothing or furniture* back; **~но́й** [14] spinal (***мозг*** cord); vertebral (***хребе́т*** column), back (*bone*)

спи́ннинг *m* [1] (*method of fishing*) spinning

спира́ль *f* [8], **~ный** [14] spiral

спирт *m* [1; *a.* в -у́; *pl. e.*] alcohol, spirit(s *pl.*); **~но́й** [14] alcoholic; *напи́ток тж.* strong

спис|а́ть → ***~ывать***; **~ок** *m* [1; -ска] list, register; **~ывать** [1], <~а́ть> [3] copy; *долг и т. д.* write (off); plagiarize, crib; *naut.* transfer, post (out of)

спи́х|ивать [1], *once* <~ну́ть> *coll.* [20] push (down, aside)

спи́ца *f* [5] spoke; knitting needle

спи́чка *f* [5; *g/pl.*: -чек] match

сплав *m* [1] **1.** alloy; **2.** *ле́са* float(ing); **~ля́ть** [28], <~ить> [14] **1.** alloy; **2.** float

спла́чивать [1], <сплоти́ть> [15 *e.*; -очу́, -оти́шь; -очённый] rally (*v/i.* **-ся**)

сплет|а́ть [1], <сплести́> [25 -т-] plait, braid; (inter)lace; **~е́ние** *n* [12] interlacing; ***со́лнечное ~е́ние*** solar plexus; **~ник** *m* [1], **~ница** *f* [5] scandalmonger; **~ничать** [1], <на-> gossip; **~ня** *f* [6; *g/pl.*: -тен] gossip

спло|ти́ть(ся) → ***спла́чивать(ся)***; **~хова́ть** *coll.* [7] *pf.* blunder; **~че́ние** *n* [12] rallying; **~шно́й** [14] *ма́сса и т. д.* solid, compact; (*непреры́вный*) continuous; *coll.* sheer, utter; **~шь** throughout, entirely, all over; ***~шь и ря́дом*** quite often

сплю́щить [16] *pf.* flatten, laminate

споить → ***спа́ивать 2***

споко́й|ный [14; -о́ен, -о́йна] calm, quiet, tranquil; (*сде́ржанный*) composed; **~но** *coll.* → **сме́ло** *coll.*; ***~ной но́чи***! good night!; ***бу́дьте ~ны!*** don't worry!; **~ствие** *n* [12] calm(ness), tranquillity; composure; *в о́бществе и т. д.* peace, order

сполз|а́ть [1], <~ти́> [24] climb down (from); *fig. coll.* slip (into)

сполна́... wholly, in full

сполосну́ть [20] *pf.* rinse (out)

спо́нсор *m* [1] sponsor

спор *m* [1] dispute, controversy, argument; ***~у нет*** undoubtedly; **~ить** [13], <по-> dispute, argue, debate; *coll. держа́ть пари́* bet (on); **~иться** *coll.* [13] *рабо́та* go well; **~ный** [14; -рен, -рна] disputable, questionable

спорт *m* [1] sport; ***лы́жный ~*** skiing; **~и́вный** [14] sporting, athletic; sport(s)...; ***~и́вный зал*** gymnasium; **~сме́н** *m* [1] sportsman; **~сме́нка** *f* [5; *g/pl.*: -нок] sportswoman

спо́соб *m* [1] method, means; way, mode (Т in); *употребле́ния* directions *pl.* (for *use* Р); **~ность** *f* [8] (cap)ability (**к** Д for), talent; *к языка́м и т. д.* faculty, capacity; power; ***покупа́тельная ~ность*** purchasing power; **~ный** [14; -бен, -бна] (**к** Д) able, talented, clever (at); capable (of; *a.* **на** В); **~ствовать** [7], <по-> (Д) promote, further, contribute to

спот|ыка́ться [1], <~кну́ться> [20] stumble (**о** В against, over)

спохва́т|ываться [1], <~и́ться> [15] suddenly remember

спра́ва to the right (of)

справедли́в|ость *f* [8] justice, fairness; **~ый** [14 *sh.*] just, fair; (*пра́вильный*) true, right

спра́в|ить(ся) → ***~ля́ть(ся)***; **~ка** *f* [5; *g/pl.*: -вок] inquiry (make ***наводи́ть***); information; certificate; **-ся** inquiry (**о** П about); consult (*v/t.* **в** П); (**с** Т) manage, cope with; **~очник** *m* [1] reference book; *телефо́нный* directory; *путеводи́тель* guide; **~очный** [14] (of) *бюро́* inquiries...; *кни́га* reference...

спра́шива|ть [1], <спроси́ть> [15] ask (p. *a.* **у** P; for s.th. *a.* P), inquire; (**с** P) make answer for, call to account; **~ется** one may ask

спрос *m* [1] *econ.* demand (**на** B for); ***без ~а*** *or* ***~у*** *coll.* without permission; **~ *и предложе́ние*** supply and demand

спросо́нок *coll.* half asleep

спроста́: *coll.* **не ~** it's not by chance

спры́|гивать [1], *once* <~гнуть> [20] jump down (from); **~скивать** [1], <~снуть> [20] sprinkle

спря|га́ть [1], <про-> *gr.* (**-ся** *impf.* be) conjugate(d); **~же́ние** *n* [12] *gr.* conjugation

спу́г|ивать [1], <~ну́ть> [20; -ну́, -нёшь] frighten off

спус|к *m* [1] lowering; descent; *склон* slope; *корабля́* launch(ing); *воды́* drain(ing); ***не дава́ть ~ку*** (Д) *coll.* give no quarter; **~ка́ть** [1], <~ти́ть> [15] lower, let down; launch; drain; *соба́ку* unchain, set free; *куро́к* pull; *о ши́не* go down; **-ся** go (*or* come) down (*stairs по ле́стнице*), descend; **~тя́** (B) later, after

спу́тни|к *m* [1], **~ца** *f* [5] travelling companion; *жи́зни* companion; **~к** *astr.* satellite; *иску́сственный тж.* sputnik

спя́чка *f* [5] hibernation

сравн|е́ние *n* [12] comparison (**по** Д/**с** T in/with); *lit.* simile; **~ивать** [1] **1.** <~и́ть> [13] compare (**с** T; *v/i.* **-ся** to, with); **2.** <~я́ть> [28] level, equalize; **~и́тельный** [14] comparative; **~и́ть(ся)** → ***~ивать*(ся)**; **~я́ть** → ***~ивать* 2**

сра|жа́ть [1], <~зи́ть> [15 *e.*; -ажу́, -ази́шь; -ажённый] smite; overwhelm; **-ся** fight, battle; *coll.* contend, play; **~же́ние** *n* [12] battle; **~зи́ть(ся)** → ***~жа́ть*(ся)**

сра́зу at once, straight away

срам *m* [1] shame, disgrace; **~и́ть** [14 *e.*; -млю́, -ми́шь], <о-> [осрамлённый] disgrace, shame, compromise; **-ся** bring shame upon o.s

сраст|а́ться [1], <~и́сь> [24 -ст-; сро́сся, срosла́сь] *med.* grow together, knit

сред|а́ *f* **1.** [5; *ac/sg.*: сре́ду; *nom/pl. st.*] Wednesday (on: **в** B, *pl.*: **по** Д); **2.** [5; *ac/sg.*: -ду́; *pl.st.*] environment, surroundings *pl.*, milieu; *phys.* medium; midst; ***в на́шей ~е́*** in our midst; **~и́** (P) among, in the middle (of), amid(st); **~изе́мный** [14], **~иземномо́рский** [16] Mediterranean; **~невеко́вый** [14] medieval; **~ний** [15] middle; medium...; central; (*посре́дственный*) middling; average... (**в** П on); *math.* mean; *gr.* neuter; *шко́ла* secondary

средото́чие *n* [12] focus, center (*Brt.* -tre)

сре́дство *n* [9] means ([**не**] **по** Д *pl.* within [beyond] one's); (*лека́рство*) remedy; *pl. a.* facilities

сре́з|ать & **~ывать** [1], <~ать> [3] cut off; *coll. на экза́мене* fail (*v/i.* **-ся**)

сровня́ть → ***сра́внивать* 2**

сро|к *m* [1] term (T/**на** B for/of), date, deadline; time (**в** B; **к** Д in, on), period; ***продли́ть ~к ви́зы*** extend a visa; **~чный** [14; -чен, -чна́, -о] urgent, pressing; at a fixed date

сруб|а́ть [1], <~и́ть> [14] cut down, fell; *дом* build of logs

сры|в *m* [1] frustration; derangement; *перегово́ров* breakdown; **~ва́ть** [1], <сорва́ть> [-ву, -вёшь; сорва́л, -а́, -о; со́рванный] tear off; *цветы́ и т. д.* pluck, pick; *пла́ны и т. д.* disrupt, frustrate; *злость* vent; **-ся** (**с** P) come off; break away (*or* loose); fall down; *coll. с ме́ста* dart off; *о пла́нах* fail, miscarry

сса́ди|на *f* [5] scratch, abrasion; **~ть** [15] *pf.* graze

сса́живать [1], <ссади́ть> [15; -жу́, -дишь] help down; help alight; make get off (*public transport*)

ссо́р|а *f* [5] quarrel; **~иться** [13], <по-> quarrel, falling-out

ссу́д|а *f* [5] loan; **~и́ть** [15] *pf.* lend, loan

ссыл|а́ть [1], <сосла́ть> [сошлю́, -лёшь; со́сланный] exile, deport, banish; **-ся** (**на** B) refer to, cite; **~ка** *f* [5; *g/pl.*: -лок] **1.** exile; **2.** reference (**на** B to)

ссыпа́|ть [1], <~ть> [2] pour

стабил|из(и́р)овать [7] (*im*)*pf.*

stabilize; **~ьный** [14; -лен, -льна] stable, firm
ста́вень *m* [4; -вня] shutter (*for window*)
ста́в|ить [14], <по-> put, place, set, stand; *часы́ и т. д.* set; *па́мятник и т. д.* put (*or* set) up; *на ло́шадь* stake, (**на** В) back; *thea.* stage; *усло́вия* make; *в изве́стность* inform, bring to the notice of; **~ить в тупи́к** nonplus; **~ка** *f* [5; *g/pl.*: -вок] (*учётная и т. д.*) rate; (*зарпла́та*) wage, salary; **сде́лать ~ку** gamble (on **на** В); **~ленник** *m* [1] protegé; **~ня** *f* [6; *g/pl.*: -вен] → **~ень**
стадио́н *m* [1] stadium (**на** П in)
ста́дия *f* [7] stage
ста́до *n* [9; *pl. e.*] herd, flock
стаж *m* [1] length of service
стажёр *m* [1] probationer; student in special course not leading to degree
стака́н *m* [1] glass
ста́лкивать [1], <столкну́ть> [20] push (off, away); **-ся** (**с** Т) come into collision with; *a. fig.* conflict with; *с ке́м-л.* come across; run into
сталь *f* [8] steel; **нержаве́ющая ~** stainless steel; **~но́й** [14] steel...
стаме́ска *f* [5; *g/pl.*: -сок] chisel
станда́рт *m* [1] standard; **~ный** [14; -тен, -тна] standard...
стани́ца *f* [5] Cossack village
станови́ться [14], <стать> [ста́ну, -нешь] *impf.* (Т) become, grow, get; stand; stop; **~ в о́чередь** get in line, *Brt.* queue up; *pf.* begin to; start; *лу́чше* feel; **во что бы то ни ста́ло** at all costs, at any cost
стано́к *m* [1; -нка] machine; *тока́рный* lathe; *печа́тный* press; **тка́цкий ~** loom
ста́нция *f* [7] station (**на** П at); *tel.* exchange
ста́птывать [1], <стопта́ть> [3] trample; (*сноси́ть*) wear out
стара́|ние *n* [12] pains *pl.*, care; endeavo(u)r; **~тельный** [14; -лен, -льна] assiduous, diligent; painstaking; **~ться** [1], <по-> endeavo(u)r, try (hard)
стар|е́ть [21] **1.** <по-> grow old, age; **2.** <у-> grow obsolete; **~и́к** *m* [1 *e.*] old man; **~ина́** *f* [5] olden times, days of yore (**в** В in); *coll.* old man *or* chap; **~и́нный** [14] ancient, antique; old; *обы́чай* time-hono(u)red; **~ить** [13], <со-> make (**-ся** grow) old
старо|мо́дный [14; -ден, -дна] old-fashioned, out-of-date; **~ста** *m* *кла́сса* prefect, monitor; **~сть** *f* [8] old age (in one's **на** П **лет**)
стартова́ть [7] (*im*)*pf. sport* start; *ae.* take off
стар|у́ха *f* [5] old woman; **~ческий** [16] old man's; senile; **~ший** [17] elder, older, senior; eldest, oldest; *по до́лжности* senior, superior; head, chief; *лейтена́нт* first; **~шина́** *m* [5] *mil.* first sergeant (*naut.* mate); **~шинство́** *n* [9] seniority
ста́р|ый [14; стар, -á, -о; *comp.*: ста́рше *or* -ре́е] old; *времена́* olden; **~ьё** *n* [10] *coll.* old clothes *pl.*; junk, *Brt.* lumber
ста́|скивать [1], <~щи́ть> [16] drag off, pull off; drag down; take, bring; *coll.* filch
стати́ст *m* [1], **~ка** *f* [5; *g/pl.*: -ток] *thea.* supernumerary; *film* extra; **~ика** *f* [5] statistics; **~и́ческий** [16] statistical
ста́т|ный [14; -тен, -тна, -о] well-built; **~уя** *f* [6; *g/pl.*: -уй] statue; **~ь**[1] *f* [8]: **с како́й ~и?** *coll.* why (should I, *etc.*)?
стать[2] → **станови́ться**; **~ся** *coll.* (*impers.*) happen (to **с** Т); **мо́жет ~ся** it may be, perhaps
статья́ *f* [6; *g/pl.*: -те́й] article; *догово́ра и т. д.* clause, item, entry; *coll.* matter (another *осо́бая*)
стациона́р *m* [1] permanent establishment; **лече́бный ~** hospital; **~ный** [14] permanent, fixed; **~ный больно́й** in-patient
ста́чка *f* [5; *g/pl.*: -чек] strike
стащи́ть → **ста́скивать**
ста́я *f* [6; *g/pl.*: стай] flight, flock; *волко́в* pack
ста́ять [27] *pf.* thaw, melt
ствол *m* [1 *e.*] trunk; *ружья́* barrel
сте́бель *m* [4; -бля; *from g/pl. e.*] stalk, stem
стёганый [14] quilted
сте|ка́ть [1], <~чь> [26] flow

С

(down); **-ся** flow together; (*собира́ться*) gather, throng

стек|ло́ [9; *pl.*: стёкла, стёкол, стёклам] glass; *око́нное* pane; ***пере́днее ~ло́*** windshield (*Brt.* windscreen); **~ля́нный** [14] glass...; glassy; **~о́льщик** *m* [1] glazier

стел|и́ть(ся) *coll.* → ***стла́ть*(ся)**; **~ла́ж** *m* [1 *e.*] shelf; **~ька** *f* [5; *g/pl.*: -лек] inner sole

стен|а́ *f* [5; *as/sg.*: сте́ну; *pl.*: сте́ны, стен, стена́м] wall; **~газе́та** *f* [5] (***стенна́я газе́та***) wall newspaper; **~д** *m* [1] stand; **~ка** *f* [5; *g/pl.*: -нок] wall; ***как об ~ку горо́хом*** like talking to a brick wall; **~но́й** [14] wall...

стеногра́|мма *f* [5] shorthand (verbatim) report *or* notes *pl.*; **~фи́стка** *f* [5; *g/pl.*: -ток] stenographer; **~фия** *f* [7] shorthand

сте́пень *f* [8; *from g/pl. e.*] degree (to **до** P), extent; *math.* power

степ|но́й [14] steppe...; **~ь** *f* [8; в -пи́; *from g/pl. e.*] steppe

сте́рва P *f* [5] (*as term of abuse*) bitch

сте́рео- *combining form* stereo-; **~ти́п** *m* [1], **~ти́пный** [14; -пен, -пна] stereotype

стере́ть → ***стира́ть***

стере́чь [26 г/ж: -егу́, -ежёшь; -ёг, -егла́] guard, watch (over)

сте́ржень *m* [4; -жня] *tech.* rod, pivot

стерил|изова́ть [7] (*im*)*pf.* sterilize; **~ьный** [14; -лен, -льна] sterile, free of germs

стерпе́ть [10] *pf.* endure, bear

стесн|е́ние *n* [12] constraint; **~и́тельный** [14; -лен, -льна] shy; **~я́ть** [28], <**~и́ть**> [13] constrain, restrain; (*смуща́ть*) embarrass; (*меша́ть*) hamper; **~я́ться**, <по-> feel (*or* be) shy, self-conscious *or* embarrassed; (P) be ashamed of; (*колеба́ться*) hesitate

стеч|е́ние *n* [12] confluence; *обстоя́тельств* coincidence; *наро́да* concourse; **~ь(ся)** → ***стека́ть*(ся)**

стиль *m* [4] style; ***но́вый ~*** New Style (*according to the Gregorian calendar*); ***ста́рый ~*** Old Style (*according to the Julian calendar*)

сти́мул *m* [1] stimulus, incentive

стипе́ндия *f* [7] scholarship, grant

стир|а́льный [14] washing; **~а́ть** [1] **1.** <стере́ть> [12; сотру́, -трёшь; стёр(ла); стёрши & стере́в] wipe *or* rub off; erase, efface, blot out; *но́гу* rub sore; **2.** <вы-> wash, launder; **~ка** *f* [5] wash(ing), laundering; ***отда́ть в ~ку*** send to the wash

сти́с|кивать [1], <**~нуть**> [20] squeeze, clench; *в объя́тиях* hug

стих (*a.* -и́ *pl.*) *m* [1 *e.*] verse; *pl. a.* poem(s); **~а́ть** [1], <**~нуть**> [21] *ве́тер и т. д.* abate; subside; (*успоко́иться*) calm down, become quiet; **~и́йный** [14; -и́ен, -и́йна] elemental; *fig.* spontaneous; *бе́дствие* natural; **~и́я** *f* [7] element(s); **~нуть** → ***~а́ть***

стихотворе́ние *n* [12] poem

стлать & *coll.* **стели́ть** [стелю́, сте́лешь], <по-> [по́стланный] spread, lay; *посте́ль* make; **-ся** *impf.* (be) spread; drift; *bot.* creep

сто [35] hundred

стог *m* [1; в сто́ге & в стогу́; *pl.*: -а́, *etc. e.*] *agric.* stack, rick

сто́и|мость *f* [8] cost; value, worth (... T/**в** B); **~ть** [13] cost; be worth; (*заслу́живать*) deserve; ***не ~т*** *coll.* → ***не́ за что***

стой! stop!, halt!

сто́й|ка *f* [5; *g/pl.*: сто́ек] stand; *tech.* support; *в ба́нке* counter; *в рестора́не* bar; **~кий** [16; сто́ек, стойка́, -о; *comp.*: сто́йче] firm, stable, steady; (*in compounds*) ...proof; **~кость** *f* [8] firmness; steadfastness

сток *m* [1] flowing (off); drainage, drain

стол *m* [1 *e.*] table (***за*** T at); (*пита́ние*) board, fare; diet; ***~ нахо́док*** lost property office

столб *m* [1 *e.*] post, pole; *ды́ма* pillar; **~е́ц** *m* [1; -бца́], **~ик** *m* [1] column (*in newspaper, etc.*); **~ня́к** *m* [1 *e.*] *med.* tetanus

столе́тие *n* [12] century; (*годовщи́на*) centenary

сто́лик *m* [1] *dim.* → **стол**; small table

столи́|ца *f* [5] capital; **~чный** [14] capital...; metropolitan

столкн|ове́ние *n* [12] collision; *fig. mil.* clash; **~у́ть(ся)** → ***ста́лкивать(ся)***

столо́в|ая *f* [14] dining room; café, restaurant; *на предприя́тии* canteen; **~ый** [14]: ***~ая ло́жка*** table spoon; ***~ый серви́з*** dinner service

столп *m* [1 *e.*] *arch.* pillar, column

столь so; **~ко** [32] so much, so many; ***~ко же*** as much *or* many

столя́р *m* [1 *e.*] joiner, cabinetmaker; **~ный** [14] joiner's

стон *m* [1], **~а́ть** [-ну́, сто́нешь; стона́я], <про-> groan, moan

стоп! stop!; ***~ сигна́л*** *mot.* stoplight; **~а́ 1.** [5 *e.*] foot; ***идти́ по чьи́м-л. стопа́м*** follow in s.o.'s footsteps; **~ка** *f* [5; *g/pl.*: -пок] pile, heap; **~о́рить** [13], <за-> stop; bring to a standstill; **~та́ть** → ***ста́птывать***

сто́рож *m* [1; *pl.*: -á; *etc. e.*] guard, watchman; **~ево́й** [14] watch...; on duty; *naut.* escort...; patrol...; **~и́ть** [16 *e.*; -жу́, -жи́шь] guard, watch (over)

сторон|а́ *f* [5; *ac/sg.*: сто́рону; *pl.*: сто́роны, сторо́н, -на́м] side (on *a.* **по** Д; **с** Р); (*направле́ние*) direction; part (**с** Р on); (*ме́стность*) place, region, country; *в суде́ и т. д.* party; distance (**в** П at; **с** Р from); ***в ~у*** aside, apart (*a.* joking ***шу́тки***); ***в ~е́ от*** at some distance (from); ***с одно́й ~ы́*** on the one hand; ***... с ва́шей ~ы́*** *a.* ... of you; ***со свое́й ~ы́*** on my part; **~и́ться** [13; -оню́сь, -о́нишься], <по-> make way, step aside; (*избега́ть*) (Р) avoid, shun; **~ник** *m* [1] adherent, follower, supporter

сто́чный [14] waste...; *во́ды* sewage

стоя́нка *f* [5; *g/pl.*: -нок] stop (**на** П at); ***автомоби́льная ~*** parking place *or* lot; *naut.* anchorage; ***~ такси́*** taxi stand (*Brt.* rank)

стоя́|ть [стою́, стои́шь; сто́я] stand; be; stop; stand up (**за** В for), defend, insist (**на** П on); ***сто́йте!*** stop!; *coll.* wait!; **~чий** [17] *положе́ние* upright; *вода́* stagnant; *воротни́к* stand-up

сто́ящий [17] worthwhile; *челове́к* worthy, deserving

страда́|лец *m* [1; -льца] sufferer; *iro.* martyr; **~ние** *n* [12] suffering; **~тельный** [14] *gr.* passive; **~ть** [1], <по-> suffer (**от** Р, Т from); ***он ~ет забы́вчивостью*** he has a poor memory

стра́жа *f* [5] guard, watch; ***~ поря́дка*** *mst. pl.* the militia

стран|а́ *f* [5; *pl. st.*] country; **~и́ца** *f* [5] page (→ ***пя́тый***); **~ность** *f* [8] strangeness, oddity; **~ный** [14; -а́нен, -а́нна, -о] strange, odd; **~ствовать** [7] wander, travel

страст|но́й [14] *неде́ля* Holy; *пя́тница* Good; **~ный** (-sn-) [14; -тен, -тна́, -о] passionate, fervent; ***он ~ный люби́тель джа́за*** he's mad about jazz; **~ь** *f* [8; *from g/pl. e.*] passion (**к** Д for)

стратег|и́ческий [16] strategic; **~ия** *f* [7] strategy

стра́ус *m* [1] ostrich

страх *m* [1] fear (**от**, **со** Р for); risk, terror (**на** В at); **~ова́ние** *n* [12] insurance (*fire...* **от** Р); **~ова́ть** [7], <за-> insure (**от** Р against); *fig.* safeguard o.s. (against); **~о́вка** *f* [5; *g/pl.*: -вок] insurance (rate); **~ово́й** [14] insurance...

страш|и́ть [16 *e.*; -шу́, -ши́шь], <у-> [-шённый] (**-ся** be) frighten(ed; at Р; fear, dread, be afraid of); **~ный** [14; -шен, -шна́, -о] terrible, frightful, dreadful; *coll.* awful; **Ѕный суд** the Day of Judg(e)ment; ***мне ~но*** I'm afraid, I fear

стрекоза́ *f* [5; *pl. st.*: -о́зы, -о́з, -о́зам] dragonfly

стрел|а́ *f* [5; *pl. st.*] arrow; *a. fig.* shaft, dart; **~ка** *f* [5; *g/pl.*: -лок] (*of a clock or watch*) hand; *ко́мпаса и т. д.* needle; *на рису́нке* arrow; **~ко́вый** [14] shooting...; (of) rifles *pl.*; **~о́к** *m* [1; -лка́] marksman, shot; **~ьба́** *f* [5; *pl. st.*] shooting, fire; **~я́ть** [28], <вы́стрелить> [13] shoot, fire (**в** В, **по** Д at; *gun* **из** Р)

стрем|гла́в headlong; **~и́тельный** [14; -лен, -льна] impetuous, headlong, swift; **~и́ться** [14 *e.*; -млю́сь, -ми́шься] (**к** Д) aspire (to), strive (for); **~ле́ние** *n* [12] aspiration (to), striving (for), urge, desire (to)

стремя́нка *f* [5; *g/pl.*: -нок] stepladder

стресс *m* [1] *psych.* stress

стриж *m* [1 *e.*] sand martin

стри́|жка *f* [5] haircut(ting); *ове́ц* shearing; *ногте́й* clipping; **~чь** [26; -игу́, -ижёшь; *pl.st.*], <по-, о-(об-)> cut; shear; clip, (*подровня́ть*) level, trim; **-ся** have one's hair cut

строга́ть [1], <вы́-> plane

стро́г|ий [16; строг, -á, -о; *comp.*: стро́же] severe; strict; *стиль и т. д.* austere; *взгляд* stern; ***~о говоря́*** strictly speaking; **~ость** *f* [8] severity; austerity; strictness

строе|во́й [14] building...; ***~во́й лес*** timber; **~ние** *n* [12] construction, building; structure

строи́тель *m* [4] builder, constructor; **~ный** [14] building...; ***~ная площа́дка*** building *or* construction site; **~ство** *n* [9] construction

стро́ить [13], <по-> build (up), construct; *пла́ны и т. д.* make, scheme; play *fig.* (***из*** P); **-ся** <вы́-, по-> be built; build (*a house*, *etc.*); *в о́чередь* form

строй *m* **1.** [3; в строю́; *pl. e.*: строи́, строёв] order, array; line; **2.** [3] system, order, regime; ***ввести́ в ~*** put into operation; **~ка** *f* [5; *g/pl.*: -óек] construction; building site; **~ность** *f* [8] proportion; *mus.* harmony; *о сложе́нии* slenderness; **~ный** [14; -óен, -ойна́, -о] slender, slim; well-shaped; *mus.*, *etc.* harmonious, well-balanced

строка́ [5; *ac/sg.*: стро́ку́; *pl.* стро́ки, строк, стро́кам] line; ***кра́сная ~*** *typ.* indent

стропи́ло *n* [9] rafter, beam

стропти́вый [14 *sh.*] obstinate, refractory

строфа́ *f* [5; *nom/pl. st.*] stanza

строч|и́ть [16 & 16 *e.*; -очу́, -о́чи́шь; -о́ченный & -очёный] stitch, sew; *coll.* (*писа́ть*) scribble, dash off; **~ка** *f* [5; *g/pl.*: -чек] line; *sew.* stitch

стру́|жка *f* [5; *g/pl.*: -жек] shavings *pl.*; **~и́ться** [13] stream, flow; **~йка** *f* [5; *g/pl.*: -у́ек] *dim.* → ***~я́***

структу́ра *f* [5] structure

струн|а́ *f* [5; *pl. st.*] *mus.*, **~ный** [14] string

стрюч|ко́вый → ***бобо́вый***; **~о́к** *m* [1; -чка́] pod

струя́ *f* [6; *pl. st.*: -у́и] stream (T in); jet; *во́здуха* current; ***бить струёй*** spurt

стря́|пать *coll.* [1], <со-> cook; concoct; **~хивать** [1], <~хну́ть> [20] shake off

студе́н|т *m* [1], **~тка** *f* [5; *g/pl.*: -ток] student, undergraduate; **~ческий** [16] students'...

сту́день *m* [4; -дня] aspic

сту́дия *f* [7] studio, atelier

сту́жа *f* [7] hard frost

стук *m* [1] *в дверь* knock; rattle, clatter, noise; **~нуть** → ***стуча́ть***

стул *m* [1; *pl.*: сту́лья, -льев] chair; seat; *med.* stool

ступ|а́ть [1], <~и́ть> [14] step, tread, go; **~е́нь** *f* **1.** [8; *pl.*: ступе́ни, ступе́ней] step (*of stairs*); rung (*of ladder*); **2.** [8; *pl.*: ступе́ни, -не́й, *etc. e.*] stage, grade; *раке́ты* rocket stage; **~е́нька** *f* [5; *g/pl.*: -нек] = 2.; ***~и́ть*** → ***~а́ть***; **~ка** *f* [5; *g/pl.*: -пок] (small) mortar; **~ня́** *f* [6; *g/pl.*: -не́й] foot, sole (*of foot*)

сту|ча́ть [4 *e.*; -чу́, -чи́шь], <по->, *once* <~кнуть> [20] knock (*door* ***в*** B at; *a.* **-ся**); rap, tap; *о се́рдце и т. д.* throb; (*зуба́ми*) chatter; clatter, rattle; ***~ча́т*** there's a knock at the door; **~кнуть** → ***испо́лниться***

стыд *m* [1 *e.*] shame; **~и́ть** [15 *e.*; -ыжу́, -ыди́шь], <при-> [пристыжённый] shame, make ashamed; **-ся**, <по-> be ashamed (P of); **~ли́вый** [14 *sh.*] shy, bashful; ***~но!*** (for) shame!; ***мне ~но*** I am ashamed (***за*** B of p.)

стык *m* [1] joint, juncture (***на*** П at); **~о́вка** *f* [5; *g/pl.*: -вок] docking (*of space vehicles*), rendezvous

сты́(ну)ть [21], <о-> (become) cool

сты́чка *f* [5; *g/pl.*: -чек] skirmish; scuffle

стюарде́сса *f* [5] stewardess, air hostess

стя́|гивать [1], <~ну́ть> [19] tighten; pull together; *mil.* gather, assemble; pull off; *coll.* pilfer

суб|бо́та *f* [5] Saturday (on: ***в*** В *pl.*; ***по*** Д); **~си́дия** *f* [7] subsidy
субтропи́ческий [16] subtropical
субъе́кт *m* [1] subject; *coll.* fellow; **~и́вный** [14; -вен, -вна] subjective
сувени́р *m* [1] souvenir
суверен|ите́т *m* [1] sovereignty; **~́ный** [14; -е́нен, -е́нна] sovereign
суг|ро́б *m* [1] snowdrift; **~у́бо** *adv.* especially; ***э́то ~у́бо ча́стный вопро́с*** this is a purely private matter
суд *m* [1 *e.*] (*сужде́ние*) judg(e)ment; court (of law); trial (***отда́ть под ~*** put on trial; ***преда́ть ~у́*** bring to trial, prosecute; (*правосу́дие*) justice
суда́к *m* [1 *e.*] pike perch
суда́р|ыня *f* [6] *obs.* (*mode of address*) madam; **´~ь** *m* [4] *obs.* (*mode of address*) sir
суд|е́бный [14] judicial, legal; forensic; law...; (of the) court; **~и́ть** [15; суждённый] **1.** <по-> judge (***по*** Д by); *fig.* form an opinion (***о*** П of); **2.** (*im*)*pf.* try, judge; **~́я по** (Д) judging by
су́д|но *n* [9; *pl.*: суда́, -о́в] *naut.* ship, vessel; ***~но на возду́шной поду́шке*** hovercraft; ***~но на возду́шных кры́льях*** hydrofoil
судопроизво́дство *n* [9] legal proceedings
су́доро|га *f* [5] cramp, convulsion, spasm; **~жный** [14; -жен, -жна] convulsive, spasmodic
судо|строе́ние *n* [12] shipbuilding; **~строи́тельный** [14] shipbuilding...; ship(yard); **~хо́дный** [14; -ден, -дна] navigable; **~хо́дство** *n* [9] navigation
судьб|а́ *f* [5; *pl.*: су́дьбы, су́деб, су́дьбам] destiny, fate; ***благодари́ть ~у́*** thank one's lucky stars
судья́ *m* [6; *pl.*: су́дьи, судей, су́дьям] judge; *sport* referee, umpire
суеве́р|ие *n* [12] superstition; **~ный** [14; -рен, -рна] superstitious
сует|а́ *f* [5], **~и́ться** [15 *e.*; суечу́сь, суети́шься] bustle, fuss; **~ли́вый** [14 *sh.*] bustling, fussy
суж|де́ние *n* [12] opinion, judg(e)ment; **~е́ние** *n* [12] narrowing; **~́ивать** [1], <су́зить> [15] narrow (*v/i.*: **-ся**; taper); *пла́тье* take in
сук *n* [1 *e.*; на ~у́; *pl.*: су́чья, -ьев & -и́, -о́в] bough; *в древеси́не* knot
су́к|а *f* [5] bitch (*also as term of abuse*); **~ин** [19]: ***~ин сын*** son of a bitch
сукно́ *n* [9; *pl. st.*: су́кна, су́кон, су́кнам] broadcloth; heavy, coarse cloth; ***положи́ть под ~*** *fig.* shelve
сули́ть [13], <по-> promise
султа́н *m* [1] sultan
сумасбро́д|ный [14; -ден, -дна] wild, extravagant; **~ство** *n* [9] madcap *or* extravagant behavio(u)r
сумасше́|дший [17] mad, insane; *su.* madman; **~дший дом** *fig.* madhouse; **~ствие** *n* [12] madness, lunacy
сумато́ха *f* [5] turmoil, confusion, hurly-burly
сум|бу́р *m* [1] → ***пу́таница***; **~́ерки** *f/pl.* [5; *gen.*: -рек] dusk, twilight; **~́ка** *f* [5; *g/pl.*: -мок] (hand)bag; *biol.* pouch; **~́ма** *f* [5] sum (***на*** В/***в*** В for/of), amount; **~ма́рный** [14; -рен, -рна] total; **~ми́ровать** [7] (*im*)*pf.* sum up
су́мочка *f* [5; *g/pl.*: -чек] handbag
су́мра|к *m* [1] twilight, dusk; gloom; **~чный** [14; -чен, -чна] gloomy
сунду́к *m* [1 *e.*] trunk, chest
су́нуть(ся) → ***сова́ть(ся)***
суп *m* [1; *pl. e.*], **~ово́й** [14] soup(...)
суперобло́жка *f* [5; *g/pl.*: -жек] dust jacket
супру́|г *m* [1] husband; **~га** *f* [5] wife; **~жеский** [16] matrimonial, conjugal; *жизнь* married; **~жество** *n* [9] matrimony, wedlock
сургу́ч *m* [1 *e.*] sealing wax
суро́в|ость *f* [8] severity; **~ый** [14 *sh.*] harsh, rough; *кли́мат и т. д.* severe; stern; *дисципли́на* rigorous
суррога́т *m* [1] substitute
суста́в *m* [1] *anat.* joint
су́тки *f/pl.* [5; *gen.*: -ток] twenty-four-hour period; ***кру́глые ~*** round the clock
су́точный [14] day's, daily; twenty-four-hour, round-the-clock; *pl. su.* daily allowance
суту́лый [14 *sh.*] round-shouldered

сут|ь *f* [8] essence, crux, heart; ***по ~и де́ла*** as a matter of fact
суфле́ *n* [*indecl.*] soufflé
сух|а́рь *m* [4 *e.*] *сдо́бный* rusk, zwieback; dried piece of bread; **~ожи́лие** *n* [12] sinew; **~о́й** [14; сух, -á, -о; *comp.*: су́ше] dry; *кли́мат* arid; *де́рево* dead; *fig.* cool, cold; *докла́д* boring, dull; ***~о́е молоко́*** dried milk; **~опу́тный** [14] land...; **~ость** *f* [8] dryness, *etc.* → **~о́й**; **~оща́вый** [14 *sh.*] lean; skinny; **~офру́кты** *pl.* [1] dried fruit
сучо́к *m* [1; -чка́] *dim.* → **сук**
су́ш|а *f* [5] (dry) land; **~ёный** [14] dried; **~и́лка** *m* [5; *g/pl.*: -лок] *coll.* dish drainer; **~и́ть** [16], <вы́-> dry; **~ка** *f* [5; *g/pl.*: -шек] drying; dry, ring-shaped cracker
суще́ств|енный [14 *sh.*] essential, substantial; **~и́тельное** [14] noun, substantive (*a.* **и́мя ~и́тельное**); **~о́** *n* [9] creature, being; *суть* essence; ***по ~у́*** at bottom; to the point; **~ова́ние** *n* [12] existence, being; ***сре́дства к ~ова́нию*** livelihood; **~ова́ть** [7] exist, be; live, subsist
су́щ|ий [17] *coll.* *пра́вда* plain; *вздор* absolute, sheer, downright; **~ность** *f* [8] essence, substance; ***в ~ности*** in fact; really and truly
сфе́ра *f* [5] sphere; field, realm
схват|и́ть(ся) → **~ывать(ся)**; **~ка** *f* [5; *g/pl.*: -ток] skirmish, fight, combat; scuffle; *a. pl.* contractions, labo(u)r, birth pangs; **~ывать** [1], <~и́ть> [15] seize (***за*** В by), grasp (*a. fig.*), grab; snatch; (*пойма́ть*) catch (*a cold, etc.*); **-ся** seize; *coll.* grapple (with)
схе́ма *f* [5] diagram, chart (in ***на*** П), plan, outline; **~ти́ческий** [16] schematic; *fig.* sketchy
сход|и́ть [15], <сойти́> [сойду́, -дёшь; сошёл, -шла́, *g. pt.*: сойдя́] go (*or* come) down, descend (from **с** Р); *о ко́же и т. д.* come off; *о сне́ге* melt; *coll.* pass (***за*** В for); Р do; pass off; ***ей всё ~ит с рук*** she can get away with anything; **~и́ть** *pf.* go (& get *or* fetch ***за*** Т); → **ум**; **-ся**, <-сь> meet; gather; become friends; agree (***в*** П upon); (*совпа́сть*) coincide; *coll.* click; **~ни** *f/pl.* [6; *gen.*: -ней] gangplank, gangway; **~ный** [14; -ден, -дна, -о] similar (**с** Т to), like; *coll.* *цена́* reasonable; **~ство** *n* [9] similarity (**с** Т to), likeness
сцеди́ть [15] *pf.* pour off; draw off
сце́н|а *f* [5] stage; scene (*a. fig.*); **~а́рий** *m* [3] scenario, script; **~и́ческий** [16] stage..., scenic
сцеп|и́ть(ся) → **~ля́ть(ся)**; **~ка** [5; *g/pl.*: -пок] coupling; **~ле́ние** *n* [12] *phys.* adhesion; cohesion; *tech.* clutch, coupling; **~ля́ть** [28], <~и́ть> [14] link; couple (*v/i.* **-ся**: *coll.* quarrel, grapple)
счаст|ли́вец *m* [1; -вца] lucky man; **~ли́вый** [14; сча́стли́в, -а, -о] happy; fortunate; lucky; ***~ли́вого пути́!*** bon voyage!; ***~ли́во*** *coll.* good luck!: ***~ли́во отде́латься*** have a narrow escape; **~ье** *n* [10] happiness; luck; good fortune; ***к ~ью*** fortunately
сче́сть(ся) → **счита́ть(ся)**
счёт *m* [1; на ~е & счету́; *pl.*: счета́, *etc. e.*] count, calculation; *в ба́нке* account (***в*** В; ***на*** В on); *счёт к опла́те* bill; *sport* score; ***в два ~а*** in a jiffy, in a trice; ***в коне́чном ~е*** ultimately; ***за ~*** (Р) at the expense (of); ***на э́тот ~*** on this score, in this respect; ***ска́зано на мой ~*** aimed at me; ***быть на хоро́шем ~у́*** (***у*** Р) be in good repute
счёт|чик *m* [1] meter; counter; **~ы** *pl.* [1] abacus *sg.*; ***свести́ ~ы*** square accounts, settle a score (with)
счита́|ть [1], <со-> & <счесть> [25; сочту́, -тёшь; счёл, сочла́; сочтённый; *g. pt.*: сочтя́] count; (*pf.* счесть) (Т, ***за*** В) consider, regard (*a.* as), hold, think; ***~я*** *a.* including; **´~нные** *pl.* very few; **-ся** (Т) be considered (*or* reputed) to be; (**с** Т) consider, respect
сши|ва́ть [1], <~ть> [сошью́, -шьёшь; сше́й(те)!; сши́тый] sew (together)
съед|а́ть [1], <съесть> → ***есть 1***; **~о́бный** [14; -бен, -бна] edible
съез|д *m* [1] congress (***на*** П at); **~дить** [15] *pf.* go; (***за*** Т) fetch; (***к*** Д) visit; **~жа́ть** [1], <съе́хать> [съе́ду, -дешь] go *or* drive (*or* slide) down; **-ся** meet; gather

съёмка *m* [5; *g/pl.*: -мок] survey; *фильма* shooting
съёмный [14] detachable
съестно́й [14] food...
съе́хать(ся) → **съезжа́ть(ся)**
сы́|воротка *f* [5; *g/pl.*: -ток] whey; *med.* serum; **~гра́ть** → **игра́ть**
сы́знова *coll.* anew, (once) again
сын *m* [1; *pl.*: сыновья́, -ве́й, -вья́м; *fig. pl.* сыны́] son; *fig. a.* child; **~о́вний** [15] filial; **~о́к** *coll. m* [1; -нка́] (*as mode of address*) sonny
сы́п|ать [2], <по-> strew, scatter; pour; **-ся** pour; *уда́ры, град* hail; *дождь, град* pelt; **~но́й** [14]: **~но́й тиф** typhus; spotted fever; **~у́чий** [17 *sh.*] *те́ло* dry; **~ь** *f* [8] rash
сыр *m* [1; *pl. e.*] cheese; **ката́ться как ~ в ма́сле** live off the fat of the land; **~е́ть** [8], <от-> become damp; **~е́ц** *m* [1; -рца́]: **шёлк-~е́ц** raw silk; **~ник** *m* [1] curd fritter; **~ный** [14] cheese...; **~ова́тый** [14 *sh.*] dampish; rare, undercooked; **~о́й** [14; сыр, -á, -о] damp; moist; (*не варёный*) raw; *нефть* crude; *хлеб* sodden; **~ость** *f* [8] dampness; humidity; **~ьё** *n* [10] *collect.* raw material
сыт|ный [14; сы́тен, -тна́, -о] substantial, copious; **~ый** [14; сыт, -á, -о] satisfied, full
сыч *m* [1 *e.*] little owl
сы́щик *m* [1] detective
сюда́ here; hither
сюже́т *m* [1] subject; plot
сюи́та *f* [5] *mus.* suite
сюрпри́з *m* [1] surprise

Т

та → **тот**
таба́|к *m* [1 *e.*; *part.g.*: -у́] tobacco; **~чный** [14] tobacco...
та́бе|ль *m* [1] table; time-keeping *or* attendance record (*in a factory, school, etc.*); **~ле́тка** *f* [5; *g/pl.*: -ток] pill, tablet; **~ли́ца** *f* [5] table; **~ли́ца умноже́ния** multiplication table; **электро́нная ~ли́ца** *comput.* spreadsheet; **~ло́** *n* [*indecl.*] indicator *or* score board; **~о́р** *m* [1 *e.*] camp; Gypsy encampment
табу́н *m* [1 *e.*] herd, drove
табуре́тка *f* [5; *g/pl.*: -ток] stool
таджи́к *m* [1], **~ский** [16] Tajik
таз *m* [1; в -у́; *pl. e.*] basin; *anat.* pelvis
таи́нств|енный [14 *sh.*] mysterious; secret(ive); **´~о** *n* [9] sacrament
таи́ть [13] hide, conceal; **-ся** be in hiding; *fig.* lurk
тайга́ *f* [5] *geog.* taiga
тай|ко́м secretly; behind (one's) back (**от** P); **~м** *m* [1] *sport* half, period; **~мер** *m* [1] timer; **~на** *f* [5] secret; mystery; **~ни́к** *m* [1 *e.*] hiding (place); **~ный** [14] secret; stealthy
так so, thus; like that; (**~ же** just) as; so much; just so; then; well; yes; one way...; → *a.* **пра́вда**; *coll.* properly; **не ~** wrong(ly); **~ и** (*both*...) and; **~ как** as, since; **и ~** even so; without that; **~же** also, too; **~же не** neither, nor; **а ~же** as well as; **~и** *coll.* all the same; indeed; **~ называ́емый** so-called; alleged; **~ово́й** [14; -ко́в, -кова́] such; (a)like; same; **был(á) ~о́в(á)** disappeared, vanished; **~о́й** [16] such; so; **~о́е** *su.* such things; **~о́й же** the same; as...; **~о́й-то** such-and-such; so-and-so; **что (э́то) ~о́е?** *coll.* what's that?; what did you say?, what's on?; **кто вы ~о́й (~а́я)? = кто вы?**
та́кса[1] *f* [5] statutory price; tariff
та́кса[2] *f* [5] dachshund
такси́ *n* [*indecl.*] taxi(cab); **~ст** *m* [1] taxi driver
такт *m* [1] *mus.* time, measure, bar; *fig.* tact; **~ика** *f* [5] tactics *pl.* & *sg.*; **~и́ческий** [16] tactical; **~и́чность** *f* [8] tactfulness; **~и́чный** [14; -чен, -чна] tactful

тала́нт *m* [1] talent, gift (**к** Д for); man of talent; gifted person; **~ливый** [14 *sh.*] talented, gifted
та́лия *f* [7] waist
тало́н *m* [1] coupon
та́лый [14] thawed; melted
там there; when; **~ же** in the same place; ibid; **~ ви́дно бу́дет** we shall see; **~ и сям** here, there, and everywhere; **как бы ~ ни́ было** at any rate
та́мбур *m* [1] *rail.* vestibule
тамо́ж|енный [14] customs...; **~ня** [6; *g/pl.*: -жен] customs house
та́мошний [15] *coll.* of that place
та́н|ец *m* [1; -нца] dance (*go* dancing **на** В; *pl.*); **~к** *m* [1] tank; **~кер** *m* [1] tanker; **~ковый** [14] tank...
танц|ева́льный [14] dancing...; **~ева́ть** [7], <с-> dance; **~о́вщик** *m* [1], **~о́вщица** *f* [5] (ballet) dancer; **~о́р** *m* [1] dancer
та́почка *f* [5; *g/pl.*: -чек] *coll.* slipper; *sport* sneaker, *Brt.* trainer
та́ра *f* [5] packing, packaging
тарака́н *m* [1] cockroach
тарахте́ть *coll.* [11] rumble, rattle
тара́щить [16], <вы́->: **~ глаза́** goggle (at **на** В; with *suprise* **от** Р)
таре́лка *f* [5; *g/pl.*: -лок] plate; *глубо́кая* soup plate; **лета́ющая ~** flying saucer; **чу́вствовать себя́ не в свое́й ~е** feel out of place; feel ill at ease
тари́ф *m* [1] tariff; **~ный** [14] tariff...; standard (*wages*)
таска́ть [1] carry; drag, pull; *coll.* steal; Р wear; **-ся** wander, gad about
тасова́ть [7], <с-> shuffle (cards)
тата́р|ин *m* [1; *pl.*: -ры, -р, -рам], **~ка** *f* [5; *g/pl.*: -рок], **~ский** [16] Ta(r)tar
тахта́ *f* [5] ottoman
та́чка *f* [5] wheelbarrow
тащи́ть [16] **1.** <по-> drag, pull, carry; <при-> bring; **2.** *coll.* <с-> steal, pilfer; **-ся** *coll.* trudge, drag o.s. along
та́ять [27], <рас-> thaw, melt; *fig.* fade, wane, languish (**от** Р with)
тварь *f* [8] creature; *collect.* creatures; (*a. pej.* miscreant)
тверде́ть [8], <за-> harden
твёрд|ость *f* [8] firmness, hardness; **~ый** [14; твёрд, тверда,-о] hard; solid; firm; (*a. fig.*) stable, steadfast; *зна́ния* sound, good; *це́ны* fixed, *coll.* sure; **~о** *a.* well, for sure; **~о обеща́ть** make a firm promise
тво|й *m*, **~я́** *f*, **~ё** *n*, **~и́** *pl.* [24] your; yours; *pl. su. coll.* your folks; → **ваш**
твор|е́ние *n* [12] creation; work; (*существо́*) creature; being; **~е́ц** *m* [1; -рца́] creator, author; **~и́тельный** [14] *gr.* instrumental (case); **~и́ть** [13], <со-> create, do; **-ся** *coll.* be (going) on; **~о́г** *m* [1 *e.*] curd(s); **~о́жник** curd pancake
тво́рче|ский [16] creative; **~ство** *n* [9] creation; creative work(s)
теа́тр *m* [1] theater (*Brt.* -tre; **в** П at); the stage; **~а́льный** [14; -лен, -льна] theatrical; theater..., drama...
тёзка *f* [5; *g/pl.*: -зок] namesake
текст *m* [1] text; words, libretto
тексти́ль *m* [4] *collect.* textiles *pl.*; **~ный** [14] textile; *комбина́т* weaving
теку́|щий [17] current; *ме́сяц* the present; *ремо́нт* routine; **~щие собы́тия** current affairs
телеви́|дение *n* [12] television, TV; **по ~дению** on TV; **~зио́нный** [14] TV; **~зор** *m* [1] TV set
теле́га *f* [5] cart
телегра́мма *f* [5] telegram
телегра́ф *m* [1] telegraph (office); **~и́ровать** [7] (*im*)*pf.* (Д) telegraph, wire, cable; **~ный** [14] telegraph(ic); telegram...; by wire
теле́жка *f* [5; *g/pl.*: -жек] handcart
те́лекс *m* [1] telex
телёнок *m* [2] calf
телепереда́ча *f* [5] telecast
телеско́п *m* [1] telescope
теле́сный [14] *наказа́ние* corporal; *поврежде́ния* physical; flesh-colo(u)red
телефо́н *m* [1] telephone (**по** Д by); **звони́ть по ~у** call, phone, ring up; **~-автома́т** *m* [1] telephone booth, *Brt.* telephone box; **~и́ст** *m* [1], **~и́стка** *f* [5; *g/pl.*: -ток] telephone operator; **~ный** [14] tele(phone)...
Теле́ц *m* [1] *astr.* Taurus
те́ло *n* [9; *pl. e.*] body; **инoро́дное ~** foreign body; **всем ~м** all over; **~сложе́ние** *n* [12] build; **~охра-**

Т

нитель *m* [4] bodyguard
теля́|тина *f* [5], **~чий** [18] veal
тем → ***тот***
тém(áтик)а *f* [5] subject, topic, theme(s)
тембр ('tɛ-) *m* [1] timbre
темн|éть [8] **1.** <по-> darken; **2.** <с-> grow *or* get dark; **3.** (*a.* **-ся**) appear dark; loom
тёмно... (*in compds.*) dark...
темнотá *f* [5] darkness; dark
тёмный [14; тёмен, темнá] dark; *fig.* obscure; gloomy; (*подозри́тельный*) shady, dubious; (*си́лы*) evil; (*невéжественный*) ignorant
темп ('tɛ-) *m* [1] tempo; rate, pace, speed
темперáмент *m* [1] temperament; spirit; **~ный** [14; -тен, -тна] energetic; vigorous; spirited
температу́ра *f* [5] temperature
тéмя *n* [13] crown, top of the head
тенденци|óзный (tɛndɛ-) [-зен, -зна] biased; **~я** (tɛn'dɛ-) *f* [7] tendency
тéндер *fin.* ('tɛndɛr) *m* [1] *naut. rail.* tender
тени́стый [14 *sh.*] shady
тéннис *m* [1] tennis; ***настóльный ~*** table tennis; **~и́ст** *m* [1] tennis player
тéнор *m* [1; *pl.*: -рá, *etc. e.*] *mus.* tenor
тень *f* [8; в тени́; *pl.*: тéни, тенéй; *etc. e.*] shade; shadow; ***ни тéни сомнéния*** not a shadow of doubt
теор|éтик *m* [1] theorist; **~ети́ческий** [16] theoretical; **~ия** *f* [7] theory
тепéр|ешний [1] *coll.* present; **~ь** now, nowadays, today
тепл|éть [8; 3rd *p. only*], <по-> grow warm; **~и́ться** [13] *mst. fig.* gleam, flicker, glimmer; **~и́ца** *f* [5], **~и́чный** [14] greenhouse, hothouse; **~ó 1.** *n* [9] warmth; *phys.* heat; warm weather; **2.** *adv.* → ***тёплый***; **~овóз** *m* [1] diesel locomotive; **~овóй** [14] (of) heat, thermal; **~отá** *f* [5] warmth; *phys.* heat; **~охóд** *m* [1] motor ship
тёплый [14; тёпел, теплá, -ó & тёпло] warm (*a. fig.*); (***мне***) ***теплó*** it is (I am) warm
терапи́я *f* [7] therapy
тере|би́ть [14 *e.*; -блю́, -би́шь] pull (at); pick (at); tousle; *coll.* (*надоедáть*) pester; **~ть** [12] rub; *на тёрке* grate
терзá|ние *n* [12] *lit.* torment, agony; **~ть** [1] **1.** <ис-> torment, torture; **2.** <рас-> tear to pieces
тёрка *f* [5; *g/pl.*: -рок] grater
тéрмин *m* [1] term
термó|метр *m* [1] thermometer; **´~с** ('tɛ-) *m* [1] vacuum flask; **~я́дерный** [14] thermonuclear
тёрн *m* [1] *bot.* blackthorn, sloe
терни́стый [14 *sh.*] thorny
терп|ели́вый [14 *sh.*] patient; **~éние** *n* [12] patience; **~éть** [10], <по-> suffer, endure; (*мири́ться*) tolerate, bear, stand; ***врéмя не ~ит*** there is no time to be lost; (Д) ***не*** **-ся** *impf.* be impatient *or* eager; **~и́мость** *f* [8] tolerance (**к** Д toward[s]); **~и́мый** [14 *sh.*] tolerant; *услóвия и т. д.* tolerable, bearable
тéрпкий [16; -пок, -пкá, -о; *comp.*: тéрпче] tart, astringent
террáса *f* [5] terrace
террит|ориáльный [14] territorial; **~óрия** *f* [7] territory
террóр *m* [1] terror; **~изи́ровать** & **~изовáть** [7] *im(pf.)* terrorize
тёртый [14] ground, grated
теря́ть [28], <по-> lose; *врéмя* waste; *листву́* shed; *надéжду* give up; ***не ~ из ви́ду*** keep in sight; *fig.* bear in mind; **-ся** get lost; disappear, vanish; (*смущáться*) become flustered, be at a loss
тесáть [3], <об-> hew, cut
тесн|и́ть [13], <с-> press, crowd; **-ся** crowd, throng; jostle; **~отá** *f* [5] crowded state; narrowness; crush; **~ый** [14; тéсен, теснá, -о] crowded; cramped; narrow; *fig.* tight; close; *отношéния* intimate; ***мир тéсен*** it's a small world
тéст|о *n* [9] dough, pastry; **~ь** *m* [4] father-in-law (*wife's father*)
тесьмá *f* [5; *g/pl.*: -сём] tape; ribbon
тéтерев *m* [1; *pl.*: -á, *etc. e.*] *zo.* black grouse, blackcock
тетивá *f* [5] bowstring
тётка *f* [5; *g/pl.*: -ток] aunt; (*as term of address to any older woman*) ma'am, lady

тетрáд|ь *f* [8], **~ка** *f* [5; *g/pl.*: -док] exercise book, notebook, copybook
тётя *coll. f* [6; *g/pl.*: -тей] aunt
тéхн|ик *m* [1] technician; **~ика** *f* [5] engineering; *исполнéния и т. д.* technique; equipment; **~икум** *m* [1] technical college; **~ѝческий** [16] technical; engineering...; ***~ѝческое обслýживание*** maintenance; ***~ѝческие услóвия*** specifications; **~ологѝческий** [16] technological; **~олóгия** *f* [7] technology
теч|éние *n* [12] current; stream (***вверх*** [***вниз***] ***по*** Д up[down]); course (**в** В in; **с** Т/Р in/of *time*); *fig.* trend; tendency; **~ь** [26] **1.** flow, run; stream; *врéмя* pass; (*протекáть*) leak; **2.** *f* [8] leak (spring ***дать***)
тёща *f* [5] mother-in-law (*wife's mother*)
тибéтец *m* [1; -тца] Tibetan
тигр *m* [1] tiger; **~ѝца** *f* [5] tigress
тѝка|нье [10], **~ть** [1] *of clock* tick
тѝна *f* [5] slime, mud, ooze
тип *m* [1] type; *coll.* character; **~ѝчный** [14; -чен, -чна] typical; **~ográфия** *f* [7] printing office
тир *m* [1] shooting gallery
тирáда *f* [5] tirade
тирáж *m* [1 *e.*] circulation; edition; *лотерéи* drawing; ***~óм в 2000*** edition of 2,000 copies
тирáн *m* [1] tyrant; **~ить** [13] tyrannize; **~ѝя** *f* [7], **~ство** *n* [9] tyranny
тирé *n* [*indecl.*] dash
тѝс|кать [1], <~нуть> [20] squeeze, press; **~кѝ** *m/pl.* [1 *e.*] vise, *Brt.* vice; grip; ***в ~кáх*** in the grip of (Р); **~нёный** [14] printed
титр *m* [1] *cine.* caption, subtitle, credit
тѝтул *m* [1] title; **~ьный лист** [14] title page
тиф *m* [1] typhus
тѝ|хий [16; тих, -á, -о; *comp.*: тѝше] quiet, still; calm; soft, gentle; *ход* slow; **~ше!** be quiet!, silence!; **~шинá** *f* [5] silence, stillness, calm; **~шь** [8; в тишѝ] quiet, silence
ткa|нь *f* [8] fabric, cloth; *anat.* tissue; **~ть** [тку, ткёшь; ткал, ткáлá, -о], <со-> [сóтканный] weave; **~цкий** [16] weaver's; weaving; **~ч** *m* [1 *e.*], **~чѝха** *f* [5] weaver
ткнýть(ся) → ***тыкать(ся)***
тлé|ние *n* [12] decay, putrefaction; *углéй* smo(u)ldering; **~ть** [8], <ис-> smo(u)lder; decay, rot, putrefy; *о надéжде* glimmer
то 1. [28] that; ***~ же*** the same; ***к ~мý*** (***же***) in addition (to that), moreover; add to this; ***ни ~ ни сё*** *coll.* neither fish nor flesh; ***ни с ~гó ни с сегó*** *coll.* all of a sudden, without any visible reason; ***до ~гó*** so; ***онá до ~гó разозлѝлась*** she was so angry; ***до ~гó врéмени*** before (that); **2.** (*cj.*) then; ***~ ... ~*** now ... now; ***не ~ ... не ~ ...*** *or* ***~ ли ... ~ ли ...*** either ... or ..., half ... half ...; ***не ~, чтóбы*** not that; ***а не ~*** (or) else; **3.** ***~-~*** just, exactly; ***в тóм-~ и дéло*** that's just it
товáр *m* [1] commodity, article; *pl.* goods, wares; ***~ы ширóкого потреблéния*** consumer goods
товáрищ *m* [1] comrade, friend; mate, companion (***по*** Д in *arms*); colleague; ***~ по шкóле*** schoolmate; ***~ по университéту*** fellow student; **~еский** [16] friendly; **~ество** *n* [9] comradeship, fellowship; *comm.* association, company
товáр|ный [14] goods...; ***~ный склад*** warehouse; *rail.* freight...; **~обмéн** *m* [1] barter; **~оборóт** *m* [1] commodity circulation
тогдá then, at that time; ***~ как*** whereas, while; **~шний** [15] of that (*or* the) time, then
тó есть that is (to say), i.e
тождéств|енный [14 *sh.*] identical; **´~о** *n* [9] identity
тóже also, too, as well; → ***тáкже***
ток *m* [1] current
токáр|ный [14] turner's; *станóк* turning; **´~ь** *m* [4] turner, lathe operator
токсѝчный [14; -чен, -чна] toxic
толк *m* [1; бéз ~у] sense; use; understanding; ***знать ~*** (**в** П) know what one is talking about; ***бéз ~у*** senselessly; ***сбить с ~у*** muddle; **~áть** [1], *once* <~нýть> [20] push, shove, jog; *fig.* induce, prompt; *coll.* urge on, spur; **-ся** push (o.a.); **~овáть** [7] **1.** <ис-> interpret, expound, explain; comment; **2.** <по-> talk (**с** Т to);

~óвый [14] explanatory; [*sh.*] smart, sensible; **~ом** plainly; ***я ~ом не знáю ...*** I don't really know ...; **~отня́** *coll. f* [6] crush, crowding

толо|кнó *n* [9] oat meal; **~чь** [26; -лкý, -лчёшь, -лкýт; -лóк, -лклá; -лчённый], <рас-, ис-> pound, crush

толп|á *f* [5; *pl. st.*], **~и́ться** [14 *e.*; *no 1st. & 2*[nd] *p. sg.*], <с-> crowd, throng

толст|éть [8], <по-, рас-> grow fat; grow stout; **~окóжий** [17 *sh.*] thick-skinned; **~ый** [14; толст, -á, -о; *comp.*: тóлще] thick; heavy; (*тýчный*) stout; fat; **~я́к** *coll. m* [1 *e.*] fat man

толч|ёный [14] pounded; **~ея́** *coll. f* [6] crush, crowd; **~óк** *m* [1; -чкá] push; shove; jolt; ***при землетрясéнии*** shock, tremor; *fig.* impulse, spur

толщин|á *f* [5] fatness; corpulence; thickness; ***~óй в*** (В), ***... в ~ý*** ...thick

толь *m* [4] roofing felt

тóлько only, but; ***как ~*** as soon as; ***лишь*** (*or* ***едвá***) ***~*** no sooner ... than; ***~ бы*** if only; ***~ что*** just now; ***~-~*** *coll.* barely

том *m* [1; *pl.*: -á; *etc. e.*] volume

томáт *m* [1], **~ный** [14] tomato; ***~ный сок*** tomato juice

том|и́тельный [14; -лен, -льна] wearisome; trying; *ожидáние* tedious; *жарá* oppressive; **~ность** *f* [8] languor; **~ный** [14; -мен, -мнá, -о] languid, languorous

тон *m* [1; *pl.*: -á; *etc. e.*] *mus. and fig.* tone

тóнк|ий [16; -нок, -нкá, -о; *comp.*: тóньше] thin; *тáлия и т. д.* slim, slender; *шёлк и т. д.* fine; *вопрóс и т. д.* delicate, subtle; *слух* keen; *гóлос* high; *поли́тик* clever, cunning; **~ость** *f* [8] thinness, *etc.* → **~ий**; delicacy, subtlety; *pl.* details (go into ***вдавáться в*** В; *coll.* split hairs)

тóнна *f* [5] ton; **~ж** *m* [1] (*metric*) ton

тоннéль (-'nε-) *m* [4] tunnel

тóнус *m* [1] *med.* tone

тонýть [19] *v/i.* **1.** <по-, за-> sink; **2.** <у-> drown

тóп|ать [1], *once* <~нуть> [20] stamp; **~и́ть** [14] *v/t.* **1.** <за-, по-> sink; *водóй* flood; **2.** <за-, ис-, на-> stoke (*a stove, etc.*); heat up; **3.** <рас-> melt; **4.** <у-> drown; **~кий** [16; -пок, -пкá, -о] boggy, marshy; **~лёный** [14] melted; *молокó* baked; **~ливо** *n* [9] fuel; ***жи́дкое ~ливо*** fuel oil; **~нуть** → **~ать**

топогрá|фия *f* [7] topography

тóполь *m* [4; *pl.*: -ля́; *etc. e.*] poplar

топóр *m* [1 *e.*] ax(e); **~ный** [14; -рен, -рна] clumsy; coarse, uncouth

тóпот *m* [1] stamp(ing), tramp(ing)

топтáть [3], <по-, за-> trample, tread; <вы́-> trample down; <с-> wear out; **-ся** tramp(le); *coll.* hang about; mark time (*на мéсте*)

топь *f* [8] marsh, bog, swamp

торг *m* [1; на -ý; *pl.*: -и́; *etc. e.*] trading; bargaining, haggling; *pl.* auction (**с** Р by; ***на*** П at); **~áш** *m* [1 *e.*] *pej.* (petty) tradesman; mercenary-minded person; **~овáть** [8] trade, deal (in Т); sell; **-ся**, <с-> (strike a) bargain (**о** П for); **~óвец** *m* [1; -вца] dealer, trader, merchant; **~óвка** *f* [5; *g/pl.*: -вок] market woman; **~óвля** *f* [6] trade, commerce; *наркóтиками* traffic; **~óвый** [14] trade..., trading, commercial, of commerce; *naut.* merchant...; **~пpéд** *m* [1] trade representative; **~прéдство** *n* [9] trade delegation

торжéств|енность *f* [8] solemnity; **~енный** [14 *sh.*] solemn; festive; **~о** *n* [9] triumph; (*прáзднество*) festivity, celebration; **~овáть** [7], <вос-> triumph (***над*** Т over); *impf.* celebrate

тóрмо|з *m* **1.** [1; *pl.*: -á, *etc. e.*] brake; **2.** [1] *fig.* drag; **~зи́ть** [15 *e.*; -ожý, -ози́шь; -ожённый], <за-> (put the) brake(s on); *fig.* hamper; *psych.* inhibit; **~ши́ть** *coll.* [16; -шý, -ши́шь] → ***тереби́ть***

тороп|и́ть [14], <по-> hasten, hurry up (*v/i.* **-ся**; *a.* be in hurry); **~ли́вый** [14 *sh.*] hasty, hurried

торпéд|а *f* [5], **~и́ровать** [7] (*im*)*pf.* torpedo (*a. fig.*); **~ный** [14] torpedo..

торт *m* [1] cake

торф *m* [1] peat; **~янóй** [14] peat...

торчáть [4 *e.*; -чý, -чи́шь] stick up, stick out; *coll.* hang about

торшéр *m* [1] standard lamp

Т

тоск|а́ *f* [5] melancholy; (*томле́ние*) yearning; (*ску́ка*) boredom, ennui; ***~а́ по ро́дине*** homesickness; **~ли́вый** [14] melancholy; *пого́да* dull, dreary; **~ова́ть** [7] grieve, feel sad (*or* lonely); feel bored; yearn *or* long (for ***по*** П *or* Д); be homesick (*по ро́дине*)

тост *m* [1] toast; ***предложи́ть ~*** propose a toast (***за*** В to)

тот *m*, **та** *f*, **то** *n*, **те** *pl.* [28] that, *pl.* those; the one; the other; ***не ~*** wrong; (***н***)***и тот*** (***н***)***и друго́й*** both (neither); ***тот же*** (***са́мый***) the same; ***тем бо́лее*** the more so; ***тем лу́чше*** so much the better; ***тем са́мым*** thereby; → *a.* ***то***

тоталитар|и́зм *m* [1] totalitarianism; **~ный** [14] totalitarian

то́тчас (**же**) immediately, at once

точёный [14] sharpened; *черты́ лица́* chisel(l)ed; *фигу́ра* shapely

точи́|льный [14]: ***~льный брусо́к*** whetstone; **~ть 1.** <на-> whet, grind; sharpen; **2.** <вы́-> turn; **3.** <ис-> eat (*or* gnaw) away

то́чк|а *f* [5; *g/pl.*: -чек] point; dot; *gr.* period, full stop; ***вы́сшая ~а*** zenith, climax (***на*** П at); ***~а с запято́й*** *gr.* semicolon; ***~а зре́ния*** point of view; ***попа́сть в са́мую ~у*** hit the nail on the head; ***дойти́ до ~и*** *coll.* come to the end of one's tether

то́чн|о *adv.* → **~ый**; *a.* → **сло́вно**; indeed; **~ость** *f* [8] accuracy, exactness, precision; ***в ~ости*** → **~о**; **~ый** [14; -чен, -чна́, -о] exact, precise, accurate; punctual; *прибо́р* (of) precision

точь: ***~ в ~*** *coll.* exactly

тошн|и́ть [13]: ***меня́ ~и́т*** I feel sick; I loathe; **~ота́** *f* [5] nausea

то́щий [17; тощ, -á, -о] lean, lank, gaunt; *coll.* empty; *расти́тельность* scanty, poor

трава́ *f* [5; *pl. st.*] grass; *med. pl.* herbs; *со́рная* weed

трав|и́ть [14 *sh.*] **1.** <за-> *fig.* persecute; **2.** <вы́-> exterminate; **~ля** *f* [6; *g/pl.*: -лей] persecution

травян|и́стый [14 *sh.*], **~о́й** [14] grass(y)

траг|е́дия *f* [7] tragedy; **~ик** *m* [1] tragic actor, tragedian; **~и́ческий** [16], **~и́чный** [14; -чен, -чна] tragic

традици|о́нный [14; -о́нен, -о́нна] traditional; **´~я** *f* [7] tradition, custom

тракт *m* [1]: high road, highway; *anat.* ***желу́дочно-кише́чный ~*** alimentary canal; **~ова́ть** [7] treat; discuss; interpret; **~о́вка** [5; *g/pl.*: -вок] treatment; interpretation; **~ори́ст** *m* [1] tractor driver; **~орный** [14] tractor...

тра́льщик *m* [1] trawler; *mil.* mine sweeper

трамбова́ть [7], <у-> ram

трамва́й *m* [3] streetcar, *Brt.* tram(car) (Т, ***на*** П by)

трампли́н *m* [1] *sport* springboard (*a. fig.*); ***лы́жный ~*** ski-jump

транзи́стор *m* [1] *el.* (*component*) transistor

транзи́т *m* [1], **~ный** [14] transit

транс|криби́ровать [7] (*im*)*pf.* transcribe; **~ли́ровать** [7] (*im*)*pf.* broadcast, transmit (*by radio*); relay; **~ля́ция** *f* [7] transmission; **~пара́нт** *m* [1] transparency; banner

тра́нспорт *m* [1] transport; transport(ation; *a.* system [of]); **~и́ровать** [7] (*im*)*pf.* transport, convey; **~ный** [14] (of) transport(ation)...

трансформа́тор *m* [1] *el.* transformer

транше́я *f* [6; *g/pl.*: -е́й] trench

трап *m* [1] *naut.* ladder; *ae.* gangway

тра́сса *f* [5] route, line

тра́т|а *f* [5] expenditure; waste; ***пуста́я ~а вре́мени*** a waste of time; **~ить** [15], <ис-, по-> spend, expend; use up; waste

тра́ур *m* [1] mourning; **~ный** [14 mourning...; *марш и т. д.* funeral...

трафаре́т *m* [1] stencil; stereotype; cliché (*a. fig.*)

трах *int.* bang!

тре́бова|ние *n* [12] demand (***по*** Д on); request, requirement; (*прете́нзия*) claim; *судьи́* order; **~тельный** [14; -лен, -льна] exacting; (*разбо́рчивый*) particular; **~ть** [7], <по-> (Р) demand; require; claim; summon, call for; **-ся** be required (*or* wanted); be necessary

тревó|га *f* [5] alarm, anxiety; *mil. etc.* warning, alert; **~жить** [16] **1.** <вс-, рас-> alarm, disquiet; **2.** <по-> disturb, trouble; **-ся** be anxious; worry; **~жный** [14; -жен, -жна] worried, anxious, uneasy; *извéстия и т. д.* alarm(ing), disturbing

трéзв|ость *f* [8] sobriety; **~ый** [14; трезв, -á, -о] sober (*a. fig.*)

трéнер *m* [1] trainer, coach

трéние *n* [12] friction (*a. fig.*)

тренир|овáть [12], <на-> train, coach; *v/i.* **-ся**; **~óвка** *f* [7] training, coaching

трепáть [2], <по-> *вéтром* tousle; dishevel; blow about; **~ *комý-л. нéрвы*** get on s.o.'s nerves

трéпет *m* [1] trembling, quivering; **~áть** [3], <за-> tremble (**от** P with); quiver, shiver; *о плáмени* flicker; *от ýжаса* palpitate; **~ный** [14; -тен, -тна] quivering; flickering

треск *m* [1] crack, crackle

трескá *f* [5] cod

трéск|аться [1], <по-, трéснуть> [20] crack, split; *о кóже и т. д.* chap; **~отня́** *f* [6] *о рéчи* chatter, prattle; **~ýчий** [17 *sh.*] *морóз* hard, ringing; *fig.* bombastic

трéснуть → ***трéскаться*** & ***трещáть***

трест *m* [1] *econ.* trust

трéт|ий [18] third; **~и́ровать** [7] slight; **~ь** *f* [8; *from g/pl. e.*] (one) third

треугóльн|ик *m* [1] triangle; **~ый** [14] triangular

трéфы *f/pl.* [5] clubs (*cards*)

трёх|годи́чный [14] three-year; **~днéвный** [14] three-day; **~колёсный** [14] three-wheeled; **~лéтний** [15] three-year; three-year-old; **~сóтый** [14] three hundredth; **~цвéтный** [14] tricolo(u)r; **~этáжный** [14] three-storied (*Brt.* -reyed)

трещ|áть [4 *e.*; -щý, -щи́шь] **1.** <за-> crack; crackle; *о мéбели* creak; *coll.* prattle; ***головá ~и́т*** have a splitting headache; **2.** <трéснуть> [20] burst; **~и́на** *f* [5] split (*a. fig.*), crack, cleft, crevice, fissure; *на кóже* chap

три [34] three; → ***пять***

трибýн|а *f* [5] platform; rostrum; tribune; (*at sports stadium*) stand; **~áл** *m* [1] tribunal

тривиáльный [14; -лен, -льна] trivial; trite

тригономéтрия *f* [7] trigonometry

тридцá|тый [14] thirtieth; → ***пятидеся́тый***; **´~ть** [35 *e.*] thirty

три́жды three times

трикотáж *m* [1] knitted fabric; *collect.* knitwear

трилóгия *f* [7] trilogy

тринáдца|тый [14] thirteenth; → ***пя́тый***; **~ть** [35] thirteen; → ***пять***

три́ста [36] three hundred

триýмф *m* [1] triumph; **~áльный** [14] *áрка* triumphal; triumphant

трóга|тельный [14; -лен, -льна] touching, moving; **~ть** [1], *once* <трóнуть> [20] touch (*a. fig.* = affect, move); *coll.* pester; ***не тронь её!*** leave her alone!; **-ся** start; set out (***в путь*** on a journey)

трóе [37] three (→ ***двóе***); **~крáтный** [14; -тен, -тна] thrice-repeated

Трóица *f* [5] Trinity; Whitsun(day); ♀ *coll.* trio

трóй|ка *f* [5; *g/pl.*: трóек] three (→ ***двóйка***); troika (*team of three horses abreast* [+ *vehicle*]); *coll.* (*of school mark* =) ***посрéдственно***; **~нóй** [14] threefold, triple, treble; **~ня** *f* [6; *g/pl.*: трóен] triplets *pl.*

троллéйбус *m* [1] trolley bus

трон *m* [1] throne; **~ный** [14] *речь* King's, Queen's

трóнуть(ся) → ***трóгать(ся)***

троп|á *f* [5; *pl.*: трóпы, троп, -пáм] path, track; **~и́нка** [5; *g/pl.*: -нок] (small) path

тропи́ческий [16] tropical

трос *m* [1] *naut.* line; cable, hawser

трост|ни́к *m* [1 *e.*] reed; *сáхарный* cane; **~никóвый** [14] reed...; cane...; **~ь** *f* [8; *from g/pl. e.*] cane, walking stick

тротуáр *m* [1] sidewalk, *Brt.* pavement

трофéй *m* [3] trophy (*a. fig.*); *pl.* spoils of war; booty; **~ный** [14] *mil.* captured

тро|ю́родный [14] second (cousin **брат** *m*, **сестра́** *f*); **~я́кий** [16 *sh.*] threefold, triple

труб|а́ *f* [5; *pl. st.*] pipe; *печна́я* chimney; *naut.* funnel; *mus.* trumpet; ***вы́лететь в ~у́*** go bust; **~а́ч** *m* [1 *e.*] trumpeter; **~и́ть** [14; -блю́, -би́шь], <про-> blow (the **в** В); **~ка** [5; *g/pl.*: -бок] tube; *для куре́ния* pipe; *teleph.* receiver; **~опрово́д** *m* [1] pipeline; **~очный** [14] *таба́к* pipe

труд *m* [1 *e.*] labo(u)r, work; pains *pl.*, trouble; difficulty (**с** Т with; *a.* hard[ly]); scholarly work; *pl.* (*in published records of scholarly meetings, etc.*) transactions; *coll.* (*услу́га*) service; ***взять на себя́ ~*** take the trouble (to); **~и́ться** [15], <по-> work; toil; **~ность** *f* [8] difficulty; **~ный** [14; -ден, -дна́, -о] difficult, hard; *coll.* heavy; ***де́ло оказа́лось ~ным*** it was heavy going; **~ово́й** [14] labo(u)r...; *день* working; *дохо́д* earned; *стаж* service...; **~олюби́вый** [14 *sh.*] industrious; **~оспосо́бный** [14; -бен, -бна] able-bodied, capable of working; **~я́щийся** [17] working; *su. mst. pl.* working people

тру́женик *m* [1] toiler, worker

труп *m* [1] corpse, dead body

тру́ппа *f* [5] company, troupe

трус *m* [1] coward

тру́сики *no sg.* [1] shorts, swimming trunks, undershorts

тру́с|ить [15], be a coward; <с-> be afraid (of P); **~и́ха** *coll./f* [5] *f* → ***трус***; **~ли́вый** [14 *sh.*] cowardly; **~ость** *f* [8] cowardice

трусы́ *no sg.* = ***тру́сики***

трущо́ба *f* [5] thicket; *fig.* out-of-the-way place; slum

трюк *m* [1] feat, stunt; *fig.* gimmick; *pej.* trick

трюм *m* [1] *naut.* hold

трюмо́ *n* [*indecl.*] pier glass

тря́п|ка *f* [5; *g/pl.*: -пок] rag; *для пы́ли* duster; *pl. coll.* finery; *о челове́ке* milksop; **~ьё** *n* [10] rag(s)

тря́с|ка *f* [5] jolting; **~ти́** [24; -с-], *once* <тряхну́ть> [20] shake (a *p.'s* Д *hand, head, etc.*Т; *a. fig.*); (*impers.*) jolt; **~ти́сь** shake; shiver (with **от** Р)

тряхну́ть → ***трясти́***

тсс! *int.* hush!; ssh!

туале́т *m* [1] toilet, lavatory; dress, dressing

туберкулёз *m* [1] tuberculosis; **~ный** [14] *больно́й* tubercular

туго́|й [14; туг, -а́, -о *comp.*: ту́же] tight, taut; *замо́к* stiff; (*ту́го наби́тый*) crammed; hard (*a.* of hearing *на́ ухо*); *adv. a. открыва́ться* hard; with difficulty; ***у него́ ~ с деньга́ми*** he is short of money

туда́ there, thither; that way

туз *m* [1 *e.*] *cards* ace

тузе́м|ец *m* [1; -мца] native; **~ный** [14] native

ту́ловище *n* [11] trunk, torso

тулу́п *m* [1] sheepskin coat

тума́н *m* [1] fog, mist; *ды́мка* haze (*a. fig.*); **~ный** [14; -а́нен, -а́нна] foggy, misty; *fig.* hazy, vague

ту́мбочка *f* [5; *g/pl.*: -чек] bedside table

ту́ндра *f* [5] *geog.* tundra

туне́ц *m* [1; -нца́ и т. д.] tuna *or* tunny fish

тунне́ль → ***тонне́ль***

туп|е́ть [8], <(п)о-> *fig.* grow blunt; **~и́к** *m* [1 *e.*] blind alley, cul-de-sac; *fig.* deadlock, impasse; ***ста́вить в ~и́к*** reach a deadlock; ***стать в ~и́к*** be at a loss, be nonplussed; **~о́й** [14; туп, -а́, -о] blunt; *math.* obtuse; *fig.* dull, stupid; **~ость** *f* [8] bluntness; dullness; **~оу́мный** [14; -мен, -мна] dull, obtuse

тур *m* [1] *перегово́ров* round; tour; turn (*at a dance*); *zo.* aurochs

турба́за *f* [5] hostel

турби́на *f* [5] turbine

туре́цкий [16] Turkish

тури́|зм *m* [1] tourism; **~ст** *m* [1] tourist

туркме́н *m* [1] Turkmen; **~ский** [16] Turkmen

турне́ (-'nɛ) *n* [*indecl.*] tour (*esp. of performers or sports competitors*)

турни́к *m* [1 *e.*] *sport* horizontal bar

турнике́т [1] turnstile; *med.* tourniquet

турни́р *m* [1] tournament (***на*** П in)

ту́р|ок *m* [1; -рка; *g/pl.*: ту́рок], **~ча́нка** [5; *g/pl.*: -нок] Turk

ту́ск|лый [14; тускл, -á, -о] *свет* dim; dull; **~не́ть** [8], <по-> & **~нуть** [20] grow dim *or* dull; lose luster (-tre); pale (***пе́ред*** T before)

тут here; there; then; ***~!*** present!, here!; ***~ же*** there and then, on the spot; ***~ как ~*** *coll.* there he is; there they are; that's that

ту́тов|ый [14]: ***~ое де́рево*** mulberry tree

ту́фля *f* [6; *g/pl.*: -фель] shoe; *дома́шняя* slipper

ту́х|лый [14; тухл, -á, -о] *яйцо́* bad, rotten; **~нуть** [21] **1.** <по-> *о све́те* go out; *о костре́* go *or* die out; **2.** <про-> go bad

ту́ч|а *f* [5] cloud; rain *or* storm cloud *наро́да* crowd; *мух* swarm; *dim.* **~ка** *f* [5; *g/pl.*: -чек], **~ный** [14; -чен, -чнá, -о] corpulent, stout

туш *m* [1] *mus.* flourish

ту́ша *f* [5] carcass

туш|ёнка *f* [5] *coll.* corned beef *or* pork; **~ёный** [14] stewed; **~и́ть** [16], <по-> **1.** switch off, put out, extinguish; *сканда́л* quell; **2.** *impf.* stew

тушь *f* [8] Indian ink; mascara

тща́тельн|ость *f* [8] thoroughness; care(fulness); **~ый** [14; -лен, -льна] painstaking; careful

тще|ду́шный [14; -шен, -шна] sickly; **~сла́вие** *n* [12] vanity; **~сла́вный** [14; -вен, -вна] vain (-glorious); **~́тный** [14; -тен, -тна] vain, futile; ***~́тно*** in vain

ты [21] you; *obs.* thou; ***быть на ~*** (**с** T) be on familiar terms with s.o.

ты́кать [3], <ткнуть> [20] poke, jab, thrust; (*v/i.* **-ся**) knock (***в*** B against, into)

ты́ква *f* [5] pumpkin

тыл *m* [1; в -ý; *pl. e.*] rear, back

ты́сяч|а *f* [5] thousand; **~еле́тие** *n* [12] millenium; **~ный** [14] thousandth; of thousand(s)

тьма *f* [5] dark(ness); *coll.* a host of, a multitude of

тьфу! *coll.* fie!, for shame!

тю́бик *m* [1] tube (*of toothpaste, etc.*)

тюк *m* [1 *e.*] bale, pack

тюле́нь *m* [4] *zo.* seal

тюль *m* [4] tulle

тюльпа́н *m* [1] tulip

тюр|е́мный [14] prison...; **~е́мный контролёр** jailer, *Brt.* gaoler, warder; **~ьма́** *f* [5; *pl.*: тю́рьмы, -рем, -рьмам] prison, jail, *Brt.* gaol

тюфя́к *m* [1 *e.*] mattress (*filled with straw, etc.*)

тя́вкать *coll.* [1] yap, yelp

тя́г|а *f* [5] *в печи́* draft, *Brt.* draught; *си́ла* traction; *fig.* bent (***к*** Д for); craving (for); **~а́ться** *coll.* [1] (**с** T) be a match (for), vie (with); **~о́стный** [14; -тен, -тна] (*обремени́тельный*) burdensome; (*неприя́тный*) painful; **~ость** *f* [8] burden (*be...* to ***в*** В/Д); **~оте́ние** *n* [12] *земно́е* gravitation; *a.* → ***~а*** *fig.*; **~оте́ть** [8] gravitate (toward[s] ***к*** Д); weigh (upon ***над*** T); **~оти́ть** [15 *e.*; -ощу́, -оти́шь] weigh upon, be a burden to; **-ся** feel a burden (T of); **~у́чий** [17 *sh.*] *жи́дкость* viscous; *речь* drawling

тяж|елове́с *m* [1] *sport* heavyweight; **~елове́сный** [14; -сен, -сна] heavy, ponderous; **~ёлый** [14; -жел, -желá] heavy, difficult, hard; *стиль* laborious; *ране́ние и т. д.* serious; *уда́р, положе́ние* severe, grave; *обстоя́тельства и т. д.* grievous, sad, oppressive, painful; *во́здух* close; (Д) ***~ело́*** feel miserable; **~́есть** *f* [8] heaviness; weight; load; burden; gravity; seriousness; **~́кий** [16; тя́жек, тяжкá, -о] heavy (*fig.*), *etc.*, → ***~ёлый***

тян|у́ть [19] pull, draw; *naut.* tow; *ме́длить* protract; *слова́* drawl (out); (*влечь*) attract; long; have a mind to; would like; *о за́пахе* waft; ***~́ет*** there is a draft (*Brt.* draught) (T of); *coll.* *красть* steal; take (**с** P from); **-ся** stretch (*a.* = extend); last; drag; draw on; reach out (***к*** Д for)

У

у (P) at, by, near; with; (at) ...'s; at ...'s place; ***у меня*** (***был, -á ...***) I have (had); my; *взять, узнáть и т. д.* from, of; *бéрега и т. д.* off; in; ***у себя́*** in (at) one's home *or* room *or* office

убав|ля́ть [28], <~ить> [14] reduce, diminish, decrease; ***~ить в вéсе*** lose weight; *v/i.* **-ся**

убе|гáть [1], <~жáть> [4; -егу́, -жи́шь, -гу́т] run away; *тайко́м* escape

убе|ди́тельный [14; -лен, -льна] convincing; *про́сьба* urgent; **~ждáть** [1], <~ди́ть> [15 *e.*; *no 1st p. sg.*; -еди́шь, -еждённый] convince (**в** П of); (*уговори́ть*) persuade (*impf. a.* try to...); **~ждéние** *n* [12] persuasion; conviction, belief

убеж|áть → ***убегáть***; **~ище** *n* [11] shelter, refuge; *полити́ческое* asylum

убер|егáть [1], <~éчь> [26 г/ж] keep safe, safeguard

уби|вáть [1], <~ть> [убью́, -ьёшь; уби́тый] kill, murder; assassinate; *fig.* drive to despair; ***~вáть врéмя*** kill *or* waste time

уби́й|ственный [14 *sh.*] killing; *взгляд* murderous; **~ство** *n* [9] murder; *полити́ческое* assassination; ***покушéние на ~ство*** murderous assault; **~ца** *m/f* [5] murderer; assassin

убирá|ть [1], <убрáть> [уберу́, -рёшь; убрáл, -á, -о; у́бранный] take (*or* put, clear) away (in); gather, harvest; tidy up; (*украшáть*) decorate, adorn, trim; **-ся** *coll.* clear off; ***~йся*** (***вон***)***!*** get out of here!, beat it!

убить → ***убивáть***

убо́|гий [16 *sh.*] (*бéдный*) needy, poor; *жили́ще* miserable; **~жество** *n* [9] poverty; mediocrity

убо́й *m* [3] slaughter (*of livestock*) (for **на** В)

убо́р *m* [1]: ***головно́й ~*** headgear; **~истый** [14 *sh.*] close; **~ка** *f* [5; *g/pl.*: -рок] harvest, gathering; *ко́мнаты и т. д.* tidying up; **~ная** *f* [14] lavatory, toilet; *thea.* dressing room; **~очный** [14] harvest(ing); **~щица** *f* [5] cleaner (*in offices, etc.*); charwoman

убрá|нство *n* [9] furniture, appointments; interior decor; **~ть**(**ся**) → ***убирáть***(***ся***)

убы|вáть [1], <~ть> [убу́ду, -убу́дешь; у́был, -á, -о] *о водé* subside, fall; (*уменьшáться*) decrease; **´~ль** *f* [8] diminution, fall; **~ток** *m* [1; -тка] loss, damage; **~точный** [14; -чен, -чна] unprofitable; **~ть** → **~вáть**

уваж|áемый [14] respected; dear (*as salutation in letter*); **~áть** [1], **~éние** *n* [12] respect, esteem (*su.* **к** Д for); **~и́тельный** [14; -лен, -льна] *причи́на* valid; *отношéние* respectful

уведом|ля́ть [28], <´~ить> [14] inform, notify, advise (**о** П of); **~лéние** *n* [12] notification, information

увезти́ → ***увози́ть***

увекове́чи|вать [1], <~ть> [16] immortalize, perpetuate

увелич|éние *n* [12] increase; *phot.* enlargement; **~ивать** [1], <~ить> [16] increase; enlarge; extend; *v/i.* **-ся**; **~и́тельный** [14] magnifying

увенчáться [1] *pf.* (T) be crowned

увер|éние *n* [12] assurance (of **в** П); **~енность** *f* [8] assurance; certainty; confidence (**в** П in); **~енный** [14 *sh.*] confident, sure, certain (**в** П of); ***бу́дьте ~ены*** you may be sure, you may depend on it; **~ить** → **~я́ть**

увёрт|ка *coll. f* [5; *g/pl.*: -ток] subterfuge, dodge, evasion; **~ливый** [14 *sh.*] evasive, shifty

увертю́ра *f* [5] overture

увер|я́ть [28], <~ить> [13] assure (**в** П of); *убеди́ть*(*ся*) make believe (sure **-ся**), persuade

уве́систый [14 *sh.*] rather heavy; *coll.* weighty

увести́ → ***уводи́ть***

уве́ч|ить [16], <из-> maim, mutilate; **~ный** [14] maimed, mutilated, crippled; **~ье** *n* [10] mutilation

увещ(ев)á|ние *n* [12] admonition; **~ть** [1] admonish

увúл|ивать [1], <~ьнýть> [20] shirk

увлажн|ять [28], <~úть> [13] wet, dampen, moisten

увле|кáтельный [14; -лен, -льна] fascinating, absorbing; **~кáть** [1], <~чь> [26] carry (away; *a. fig.* = transport, captivate); **-ся** (Т) be carried away (by), be(come) enthusiastic (about); (*погрузúться*) become) absorbed (in); (*влюбúться*) fall (*or* be) in love (with); **~чéние** *n* [12] enthusiasm, passion (for Т)

уво|дúть [15], <увестú> [25] take, lead (away, off); *coll.* (*укрáсть*) steal; **~зúть** [15], <увезтú> [24] take, carry, drive (away, off); abduct, kidnap

увóл|ить → **~ьнять**; **~ьнéние** *n* [12] dismissal (**с** Р from); **~ьнять** [28], <~ить> [13] dismiss (**с** Р from)

увы́! *int.* alas!

увя|дáние *n* [12] withering; *о человéке* signs of aging; **~дáть** [21], <~нуть> [20] wither, fade; **~дший** [17] withered

увяз|áть [1] **1.** <~нуть> [21] get stuck (in); *fig.* get bogged down (in); **2.** → **~ывать(ся)**; **~ка** *f* [5] coordination; **~ывать** [1], <~áть> [3] tie up; (*согласóвывать*) coordinate (*v/i.* **-ся**)

угáд|ывать [1], <~áть> [1] guess

угáр *m* [1] charcoal fumes; *fig.* ecstasy, intoxication

угас|áть [1], <~нуть> [21] *об огнé* die down; *о звýке* die (*or* fade) away; *надéжда* die; *сúлы* fail; *о человéке* fade away

угле|кúслый [14] *chem.* carbonate (of); (**~кúслый газ** carbon dioxide); **~рóд** *m* [1] carbon

угловóй [14] *дом* corner...; angle...; angular

углуб|úть(ся) → **~лять(ся)**; **~лéние** *n* [12] deepening; (*впáдина*) hollow, cavity, hole; *знáний* extension; **~лённый** [14 *sh.*] profound; *a. p. pt. p. of* **~úть(ся)**; **~лять** [28], <~úть> [14 *e.*; -блю́, -бúшь; -блённый] deepen (*v/i.* **-ся**); make (become) more profound, extend; **-ся** *a.* go deep (**в** В into), be(come) absorbed (in)

угнáть → **угонять**

угнет|áтель *m* [4] oppressor; **~áть** [1] oppress; (*мýчить*) depress; **~éние** *n* [12] oppression; (*a.* **~ённость** *f* [8]) depression; **~ённый** [14; -тён, -тенá] oppressed; depressed

угов|áривать [1], <~орúть> [13] (В) (*impf.* try to) persuade; **-ся** arrange, agree; **~óр** *m* [1] agreement; *pl.* persuasion; **~орúть(ся)** → **~áривать(ся)**

угóд|а *f* [5]: **в ~у** (Д) for the benefit of, to please; **~úть** → **угождáть**; **~ливый** [14 *sh.*] fawning, ingratiating, toadyish; **~ник** *m* [1]: **святóй ~ник** saint; **~но** please; **как** (**что**) **вам ~но** just as (whatever) you like; (**что**) **вам ~но?** what can I do for you?; **скóлько** (**душé**) **~но** → **вдóволь & вдáсть**

уго|ждáть [1], <~дúть> [15 *e.*; -ожý, -одúшь] (Д, **на** В) please; *pf. coll.* *в яму* fall (into); *в бедý* get; *в глаз и т. д.* hit

ýгол *m* [1; углá; в, на углý] corner (**на** П at); *math.* angle

уголóвный [14] criminal; **~ кóдекс** criminal law

уголóк *m* [1; -лкá] nook, corner

ýголь *m* [4; ýгля] coal; **как на ~ях** *coll.* on tenterhooks; **~ный** [14] coal...; carbonic

угомонúть(ся) [13] *pf. coll.* calm (down)

угонять [28], <угнáть> [угоню́, угóнишь; угнáл] drive (away, off); *машúну* steal; *самолёт* hijack; **-ся** *coll.* catch up (**за** Т with)

угор|áть [1], <~éть> [9] be poisoned by carbon monoxide fumes

ýгорь[1] *m* [4 *e.*; угря] eel

ýгорь[2] *m* [4 *e.*; угря] *med.* blackhead

уго|щáть [1], <~стúть> [15 *e.*; -ощý, -остúшь; -ощённый] treat (Т), entertain; **~щéние** *n* [12] entertaining; treating (to); refreshments; food, drinks *pl.*

угро|жáть [1] threaten (p. with Д/

Т); **~за** *f* [5] threat, menace
угрызе́ни|е *n* [12]: **~я** *pl.* ***со́вести*** pangs of conscience; remorse
угрю́мый [14 *sh.*] morose, gloomy
уда́в *m* [1] boa, boa constrictor
уда|ва́ться [5], <**~ться**> [уда́стся, -аду́тся; уда́лся, -ала́сь] succeed; ***мне ~ётся*** (***~ло́сь***) (+ *inf.*) I succeed(ed) (in ...ing)
удал|е́ние *n* [12] removal; *зу́ба* extraction; sending away (*sport* off); ***на ~е́нии*** at a distance; **~и́ть(ся)** → **~я́ть(ся)**; **~о́й**, **~ый** [14; уда́л, -á, -о] bold, daring; **~ь** *f* [8], *coll.* **~ьство́** *n* [9] boldness, daring; **~я́ть** [28], <**~и́ть**> [13] remove; *зуб* extract; **-ся** retire, withdraw; move away
уда́р *m* [1] blow (*a. fig.*); (*a. med.*) stroke; *el.* shock (*a. fig.*); (*столкнове́ние*) impact; *ножо́м* slash; *гро́ма* clap; *coll.* form; ***он в ~е*** he's in good form; **~е́ние** *n* [12] stress, accent; **~иться** → ***~я́ться***; **~ный** [14]: ***~ные инструме́нты*** percussion instruments; **~я́ть** [28], <**~ить**> [13] strike (***по*** Д on), hit; knock; beat; sound (*трево́гу*); punch (*кулако́м*); butt (*голово́й*); kick (*ного́й*); *моро́зы* set in; **-ся** strike *or* knock (Т/**о** В with/against); hit (***в*** В); ***-ся в кра́йности*** go to extremes
уда́ться → ***удава́ться***
уда́ч|а *f* [5] success, (good) luck; **~ник** *coll. m* [1] lucky person; **~ный** [14; -чен, -чна] successful; good
удв|а́ивать [1], <**~о́ить**> [13] double (*v/i.* **-ся**)
уде́л *m* [1] lot, destiny; **~и́ть** → ***~я́ть***; **~ьный** [14] *phys.* specific; **~я́ть** [28], <**~и́ть**> [13] devote, spare; allot
уде́рж|ивать [1], <**~а́ть**> [4] withhold, restrain; *в па́мяти* keep, retain; *де́ньги* deduct; **-ся** hold (***за*** В on; to; *a.* out); refrain (from **от** Р)
удешев|ля́ть [28], <**~и́ть**> [14 *e.*; -влю́, -ви́шь, -влённый] become cheaper
удив|и́тельный [14; -лен, -льна] astonishing, surprising; (*необы́чный*) amazing, strange; (***не***) ***~и́тельно*** it is a (no) wonder; **~и́ть(ся)** → ***~ля́ть(ся)***; **~ле́ние** *n* [12] astonishment, surprise; **~ля́ть** [28], <**~и́ть**> [14 *e.*; -влю́, -ви́шь, -влённый] (**-ся** be) astonish(ed at Д), surprise(d, wonder)
удила́ *n/pl.* [9; -и́л, -ила́м]: ***закуси́ть ~*** get (*or* take) the bit between one's teeth
удира́ть *coll.* [1], <удра́ть> [удеру́, -рёшь; удра́л, -á, -о] make off; run away
уди́ть [15] angle (for *v/t.*), fish
удлин|е́ние *n* [12] lengthening; **~я́ть** [28], <**~и́ть**> [13] lengthen, prolong
удо́б|ный [14; -бен, -бна] (*подходя́щий*) convenient; *ме́бель и т. д.* comfortable; ***воспо́льзоваться ~ным слу́чаем*** take an opportunity; **~о...** easily...; **~ре́ние** *n* [12] fertilizer; fertilization; **~ря́ть** [28], <**~рить**> [13] fertilize, manure; **~ство** *n* [9] convenience; comfort
удовлетвор|е́ние *n* [12] satisfaction; **~и́тельный** [14; -лен, -льна] satisfactory; *adv. a.* "fair" (*as school mark*); **~я́ть** [28], <**~и́ть**> [13] satisfy; *про́сьбу* grant; (Д) meet; **-ся** content o.s. (Т with)
удо|во́льствие *n* [12] pleasure; **~рожа́ть** [1], <**~рожи́ть**> [16] raise the price of
удост|а́ивать [1], <**~о́ить**> [13] (**-ся** be) award(ed); deign (*взгля́да, -ом* В to look at p.); **~овере́ние** *n* [12] certificate, certification; ***~овере́ние ли́чности*** identity; **~оверя́ть** [28], <**~ове́рить**> [13] certify, attest; *ли́чность* prove; *по́дпись* witness; convince (***в*** П of; **-ся** o.s.; *a.* make sure); **~о́ить(ся)** → ***~а́ивать(ся)***
удосу́житься *coll.* [16] find time
у́дочк|а *f* [5; *g/pl.*: -чек] fishing rod; ***заки́нуть ~у*** *fig.* cast a line, put a line out; ***попа́сться на ~у*** swallow the bait
удра́ть → ***удира́ть***
удружи́ть [16 *e.*; -жу́, -жи́шь] *coll.* do a service *or* good turn; *iro.* unwittingly do a disservice
удруч|а́ть [1], <**~и́ть**> [16 *e.*; -чу́, -чи́шь; -чённый] deject, depress
удуш|е́ние *n* [12] suffocation; **~ли-**

вый [14 *sh.*] stifling, suffocating; **~ье** *n* [10] asthma; asphyxia
уедин|ение *n* [12] solitude; **~ённый** [14 *sh.*] secluded, lonely, solitary; **~яться** [28], <~ить(ся)> [13] withdraw, go off (by o.s.); seclude o.s.
уезд *m* [1] *hist.*, **~ный** [14] district
уезжать [1], <уехать> [уеду, -едешь] (**в** В) leave (for), go (away; to)
уж 1. *m* [1 *e.*] grass snake; **2.** → **уже**; indeed, well; *do*, *be* (+ *vb.*)
ужас *m* [1] horror; terror, fright; *coll.* → **~ный**, **~но**; **~ать** [1], <~нуть> [20] horrify; **-ся** be horrified *or* terrified (Р, Д at); **~ающий** [17] horrifying; **~ный** [14; -сен, -сна] terrible, horrible, dreadful; awful
уже already; by this time; by now; **~ не** not... any more; (**вот**) **~** for; **~ пора** it's time (to + *inf.*)
ужение *n* [12] angling, fishing
ужи|ваться [1], <~ться> [14; -ивусь, -вёшься; -ился, -илась] get accustomed (**в** П to); get along (**с** Т with); **~вчивый** [14 *sh.*] easy to get on with
ужин *m* [1] supper (**за** Т at; **на** В, **к** Д for); **~ать** [1], <по-> have supper
ужиться → **уживаться**
узакон|ивать [1], <~ить> [13] legalize
узбек *m* [1], **~ский** [16] Uzbek
узд|а *f* [5; *pl. st.*], **~ечка** *f* [5; *g/pl.*: -чек] bridle
узел *m* [1; узла] knot; *rail.* junction; *tech.* assembly; **вещей** bundle; **~ок** *m* [1; -лка] knot; small bundle
узк|ий [16; узок, узка, -о; *comp.*: уже] narrow (*a. fig.*); (**тесный**) tight; **~ое место** bottleneck; weak point; **~околейный** [14] narrow-gauge
узлов|атый [14 *sh.*] knotty; **~ой** [14] (**основной**) central, chief
узна|вать [5], <~ть> [1] recognize (by **по** Д); learn (**от** Р from: p.; **из** Р th.), find out, (get to) know
узник *m* [1] prisoner
узор *m* [1] pattern, design; **с ~ами** = **~чатый** [14 *sh.*] figured; decorated with a pattern
узость *f* [8] narrow(-minded)ness

узы *f/pl.* [5] bonds, ties
уйма *coll. f* [5] lots of, heaps of
уйти → **уходить**
указ *m* [1] decree, edict; **~ание** *n* [12] instruction (**по** Д by), direction; indication (Р, **на** В of); **~атель** *m* [4] **в книге** index; indicator (*a. mot.*); **~ательный** [14] indicating; (**палец**) index finger; *gr.* demonstrative; **~ать** → **~ывать**; **~ка** *f* [5] pointer; *coll.* orders *pl.*, bidding (*of s.o. else*) (**по** Д by); **~ывать** [1], <~ать> [3] point out; point (**на** В to); **путь и т. д.** show; indicate
укач|ивать, <~ать> [1] rock to sleep, lull; *impers.* make (sea)sick
уклад *m* [1] structure; mode, way (**жизни**); **~ка** *f* [5] packing; **рельсов и т. д.** laying; **волос** set(ting); **~ывать** [1], <уложить> [16] put (to bed); lay; stack, pack (up *coll.* **-ся**); place; cover; **-ся** *a.* go into; fit; *coll.* manage; **~ываться в голове** sink in
уклон *m* [1] slope, incline; slant (*a. fig.* = bias, bent, tendency); *pol.* deviation; **~ение** *n* [12] evasion; **~ить(ся)** → **~ять(ся)**; **~чивый** [14 *sh.*] evasive; **~яться** [28], <~иться> [13; -онюсь, -онишься] **от темы и т. д.** digress, deviate; evade (*v/t.* **от** Р)
уключина *f* [5] oarlock (*Brt.* row-)
укол *m* [1] prick; jab; *med.* injection
укомплектов|ывать [1], <~ать> [7] complete, bring up to (full) strength; supply (fully; with Т)
укор *m* [1] reproach
укор|ачивать [1], <~отить> [15 *e.*; -очу, -отишь; -оченный] shorten; **~еняться** [28], <~ениться> [13] take root; **~изна** *f* [5] → **~**; **~изненный** [14] reproachful; **~ить** → **~ять**; **~отить** → **~ачивать**; **~ять** [28], <~ить> [13] reproach (with), blame (for) (**в** П, **за** В)
украдкой furtively
украин|ец *m* [1; -нца], **~ка** *f* [5; *g/pl.*: -нок], **~ский** [16] Ukranian
укра|шать [1], <~сить> [15] adorn; (**-ся** be) decorat(ed); trim; embellish; **~шение** *n* [12] adornment; decoration; ornament; embellishment

укреп|и́ть(ся) → ***~ля́ть(ся)***; **~ле́ние** *n* [12] strengthening; (*положе́ния*) reinforcing; *mil.* fortification; **~ля́ть** [28], <~и́ть> [14 *e.*; -плю́, -пи́шь; -плённый] strengthen; make fast; consolidate; *mil.* fortify; **-ся** strengthen, become stronger

укро́|мный [14; -мен, -мна] secluded; **~п** *m* [1] dill fennel

укро|ти́тель *m* [4], **~ти́тельница** *f* [5] (animal) tamer; **~ща́ть** [1], <~ти́ть> [15 *e.*; -ощу́, -оти́шь; -ощённый] tame; (*уме́рить*) subdue, restrain; **~ще́ние** *n* [12] taming

укрупн|я́ть [28], <~и́ть> [13] enlarge, extend; amalgamate

укры|ва́ть [1], <~́ть> [22] cover; give shelter; (*пря́тать*) conceal, harbo(u)r; **-ся** cover o.s.; hide; take shelter *or* cover; **~́тие** *n* [12] cover, shelter

у́ксус *m* [1] vinegar

уку́с *m* [1] bite; **~и́ть** → ***куса́ть***

уку́т|ывать, <~ать> [1] wrap up (in)

ула́|вливать [1], <уловить> [14] catch; perceive, detect; *coll.* seize (*an opportunity*, *etc.*); (*поня́ть*) grasp; **~живать** [1], <~дить> [15] settle, arrange, resolve

у́лей *m* [3; у́лья] beehive

улет|а́ть [1], <~е́ть> [11] fly (away)

улету́чи|ваться [1], <~ться> [16] evaporate, volatilize; *coll.* disappear, vanish

уле́чься [26 г/ж: ула́гусь, уля́жешься, уля́гутся; улётся *pf.*] lie down, go (to bed); *о пыли и т. д.* settle; (*ути́хнуть*) calm down, abate

ули́ка *f* [5] evidence

ули́тка *f* [5; *g/pl.*: -ток] snail

у́лиц|а *f* [5] street (in, on **на** П); ***на ~е*** *a.* outside, outdoors

улич|а́ть [1], <~и́ть> [16 *e.*; -чу́, -чи́шь, -чённый] (**в** П) catch out in lying; establish the guilt (of); ***~и́ть во лжи*** give s.o. the lie

у́личн|ый [14] street...; ***~ое движе́ние*** road traffic

уло́в *m* [1] catch; **~и́мый** [14 *sh.*] perceptible; **~и́ть** → ***ула́вливать***; **~ка** *f* [5; *g/pl.*: -вок] trick, ruse

уложи́ть(ся) → ***укла́дывать(ся)***

улуч|а́ть *coll.* [1], <~и́ть> [16 *e.*; -чу́, -чи́шь; -чённый] find, seize, catch

улучш|а́ть [1], <~ить> [16] improve; *v/i.* **-ся**; **~е́ние** *n* [12] improvement; **~́ить(ся)** → ***~а́ть(ся)***

улыб|а́ться [1], <~ну́ться> [20], **~́ка** *f* [5; *g/pl.*: -бок] smile (at Д)

ультимат|и́вный [14; -вен, -вна] categorical, express; **~́ум** *m* [1] ultimatum

ультра|звуково́й [14] ultrasonic; **~коро́ткий** [16] ultra-short (frequency)

ум *m* [1 *e.*] intellect; mind; sense(s); ***без ~а́*** mad (about **от** Р); ***за́дним ~о́м кре́пок*** wise after the event; ***быть на ~е́*** (**у** Р) be on one's mind; ***э́то не его́ ~а́ де́ло*** it's not his business; ***сойти́ с ~а́*** go mad; ***сходи́ть с ~а́*** *coll. a.* be mad (about **по** П); *coll.* ***~ за ра́зум захо́дит*** I'm at my wits end

умал|е́ние *n* [12] belittling; **~и́ть** → ***~я́ть***; **~́чивать** [1], <умолча́ть> [4 *e.*; -чу́, -чи́шь] (**о** П) pass over in silence; **~я́ть** [28], <~и́ть> [13] belittle, derogate, disparage

уме́|лый [14] able, capable, skilled; **~ние** *n* [12] skill, ability, know-how

уменьш|а́ть [1], <~́ить> [16 & 16 *e.*; -е́ньшу́, -е́ньши́шь; -е́ньшенный & -шённый] reduce, diminish, decrease (*v/i.* **-ся**); ***~́ить расхо́ды*** cut down expenditures; **~е́ние** *n* [12] decrease, reduction; **~и́тельный** [14] diminishing; *gr.* diminutive; **~́ить(ся)** → ***~а́ть(ся)***

уме́ренн|ость *f* [8] moderation; **~ый** [14 *sh.*] moderate, (*a. geogr.* [*no sh.*]) temperate

умер|е́ть → ***умира́ть***; **~́ить** → ***~я́ть***; **~тви́ть** → ***~щвля́ть***; **~ший** [17] dead; **~щвлять** [28], <~твить> [14; -рщвлю, -ртвишь; -рщвлённый] kill; **~я́ть** [28], <~́ить> [13] become moderate

уме|сти́ть(ся) → ***~ща́ть(ся)***; **~́стный** (-'mesn) [14; -тен, -тна] appropriate; **~́ть** [8], <с-> be able to; know how to; **~ща́ть** [1], <~сти́ть> [15 *e.*; -ещу́, -ести́шь; -ещённый] fit, get (into **в** В); **-ся** find room

умил|е́ние *n* [12] emotion, tender-

У

ness; **~ённый** [14] touched, moved; **~я́ть** [28], <~и́ть> [13] (**-ся** be) move(d), touch(ed)

умира́ть [1], <умере́ть> [12; *pt.*: у́мер, умерла́, -о; уме́рший] die (of, from **от**); **~ от ску́ки** be bored to death

умиротворённый [14; -ена, -ён] tranquil; contented

умн|е́ть [8], <по-> grow wiser; **~ик** *coll. m* [1], **~ица** *m/f* [5] clever person; **~ичать** *coll.* [1] → **мудри́ть**

умнож|а́ть [1], <~ить> [16] multiply (by **на** В); (*увели́чивать*) increase; *v/i.* **-ся**; **~е́ние** *n* [12] multiplication

у́м|ный [14; умён, умна́, у́мно́] clever, smart, wise, intelligent; **~озаключе́ние** *n* [12] conclusion; **~озри́тельный** [14; -лен, -льна] speculative

умол|и́ть → **~я́ть**; **´~к**: **без ´~ку** incessantly; **~ка́ть** [1], <~кнуть> [21] *шум* stop; lapse into silence, become silent; **~ча́ть** → **ума́лчивать**; **~я́ть** [28], <~и́ть> [13; -олю́, -о́лишь] implore (*v/t.*), beseech, entreat (for **о** П)

умопомрачи́тельный [14; -лен, -льна] *coll.* fantastic

умо́р|а *coll. f* [5], **~и́тельный** *coll.* [14; -лен, -льна] side-splitting, hilarious; **~и́ть** *coll.* [13] *pf.* kill; exhaust, fatigue (*a.* with laughing **со́ смеху**)

у́мственный [14] intellectual, mental; *рабо́та* brainwork

умудр|я́ть [28], <~и́ть> [13] teach; make wiser; **-ся** *coll.* contrive, manage

умыва́|льник *m* [1] washbowl, *Brt.* wash-basin; **~ние** *n* [12] washing; wash; **~ть** [1], <умы́ть> [22] (**-ся**) wash (*a.* o.s.)

у́мы|сел *m* [1; -сла] design, intent(ion); **с ~слом** (**без ~ла**) (un-) intentionally; **~ть(ся)** → **~ва́ть** (**-ся**); **~шленный** [14] deliberate; intentional

унести́(сь) → **уноси́ть(ся)**

универ|ма́г *m* [1] (**~са́льный магази́н**) department store; **~са́льный** [14; -лен, -льна] universal; **~са́м** *m* [1] supermarket; **~сите́т** *m* [1] university (at, in **в** П)

уни|жа́ть [1], <~зить> [15] humiliate; **~же́ние** *n* [12] humiliation; **~жённый** [14 *sh.*] humble; **~зи́тельный** [14; -лен, -льна] humiliating; **~зить** → **~жа́ть**

унима́ть [1], <уня́ть> [уйму́, уймёшь; уня́л, -а́, -о; -я́тый (-я́т, -а́, -о)] appease, soothe; *боль* still; **-ся** calm *or* quiet down; *ве́тер и т. д.* subside

уничт|ожа́ть [1], <~о́жить> [16] annihilate, destroy; **~оже́ние** *n* [12] annihilation; **~о́жить** → **~ожа́ть**

уноси́ть [15], <унести́> [24 -с-] carry, take (away, off); **-ся** <сь-> speed away

уны|ва́ть [1] be depressed, be dejected; **~лый** [14 *sh.*] depressed; dejected; **~ние** *n* [12] despondency; depression; dejection

уня́ть(ся) → **унима́ть(ся)**

упа́до|к *m* [1; -дка] decay, decline; **~к ду́ха** depression; **~к сил** breakdown

упаков|а́ть → **~ывать**; **~ка** *f* [5; *g/pl.*: -вок] packing; wrapping; **~щик** *m* [1] packer; **~ывать** [1], <~а́ть> [7] pack (up), wrap up

упа́сть → **па́дать**

упира́ть [1], <упере́ть> [12] rest, prop (against **в** В); **-ся** lean, prop (s.th. Т; against **в** В); *в сте́нку и т. д.* knock *or* run against; (*наста́ивать*) insist on; be obstinate

упи́танный [14 *sh.*] well-fed, fattened

упла́|та *f* [5] payment (in **в** В); **~чивать** [1], <~ти́ть> [15] pay; *по счёту* pay, settle

уплотн|е́ние *n* [12] compression; packing; **~я́ть** [28], <~и́ть> [13] condense, make compact; fill up (with work); *tech.* seal

уплы|ва́ть [1], <~ть> [23] swim or sail (away, off); pass (away), vanish

упова́ть [1] (**на** В) trust (in), hope (for)

упод|обля́ть [28], <~о́бить> [14] liken, become like (*v/i.* **-ся**)

упо|е́ние *n* [12] rapture, ecstasy; **~ённый** [14; -ён, -ена] enraptured; **~и́тельный** [14; -лен,

-льна] rapturous, intoxicating

уползти́ [24] *pf.* creep away

уполномо́ч|енный [14 *sh.*] authorized; **~ивать** [1], <**~ить**> [16] authorize, empower (to **на** В)

упомина́|ние *n* [12] mention (of **о** П); **~ть** [1], <**упомяну́ть**> [19] mention (*v/t.* В, **о** П)

упо́р *m* [1] rest; support, prop; stop; ***де́лать ~*** lay stress *or* emphasis (on ***на*** В); ***в ~*** point-blank, straightforward; ***смотре́ть в ~ на кого́-л.*** look full in the face of s.o.; **~ный** [14; -рен, -рна] persistent, persevering; (*упря́мый*) stubborn, obstinate; **~ство** *n* [9] persistence, perseverance; obstinacy; **~ствовать** [7] be stubborn; persevere, persist (in **в** П)

употреб|и́тельный [14; -лен, -льна] common, customary; *сло́во* in current use; ***~и́ть*** → ***~ля́ть***; **~ле́ние** *n* [12] use; usage; **~ля́ть** [28], <**~и́ть**> [14 *e.*; -блю́, -би́шь; -блённый] (*impf.* **-ся** be) use(d), employ(ed); ***~и́ть все сре́дства*** make every effort; ***~и́ть во зло*** abuse

упра́в|иться → ***~ля́ться***; **~ле́ние** *n* [12] administration (of Р; Т), management; *tech.* control; *gr.* government; *маши́ной* driving; ***орке́стр под ~ле́нием*** orchestra conducted by (Р); **~ля́ть** (Т) manage, operate; rule; govern (*a. gr.*); drive; *naut.* steer; *tech.* control; *mus.* conduct; **-ся**, <**~иться**> *coll.* [14] (**с** Т) manage; finish; **~ля́ющий** [17] manager

упражн|е́ние *n* [12] exercise; practice; **~я́ть** [28] exercise (*v/i.*, *v/refl.* **-ся** ***в*** П: practice (-ise) s.th.)

упраздн|е́ние *n* [12] abolition; liquidation; **~я́ть** [28], <**~и́ть**> [13] abolish; liquidate

упра́шивать [1], <**упроси́ть**> [15] (*impf.*) beg, entreat; (*pf.*) prevail upon

упрёк *m* [1] reproach

упрек|а́ть [1], <**~ну́ть**> [20] reproach (with **в** П)

упро|си́ть → ***упра́шивать***; **~сти́ть** → ***~ща́ть***; **~че́ние** *n* [12] consolidation; **~чивать** [1], <**~чить**> [16] consolidate (*v/i.* **-ся**), stabilize; **~ща́ть** [1], <**~сти́ть**> [15 *e.*; -ощу́, -ости́шь; -ощённый] simplify; **~ще́ние** *n* [12] simplification

упру́г|ий [16 *sh.*] elastic, resilient; **~ость** *f* [8] elasticity

упря́м|иться [14] be obstinate; persist in; **~ство** *n* [9] obstinacy, stubbornness; **~ый** [14 *sh.*] obstinate, stubborn

упря́т|ывать [1], <**~ать**> [3] hide

упу|ска́ть [1], <**~сти́ть**> [15] let go; let slip; let fall; *возмо́жность* miss; **~ще́ние** *n* [12] neglect, ommission

ура́! *int.* hurrah!

уравн|е́ние *n* [12] equalization; *math.* equation; **~ивать** [1] **1.** <**уровня́ть**> [28] level; **2.** <**~я́ть**> [28] level, equalize *fig.*; **~и́ловка** *f* [5; *g/pl.*: -вок] *pej.* egalitarianism (*esp.* with respect to economic rights and wage level[l]ing); **~ове́шивать** [1], <**~ове́сить**> [15] balance; *p. pt. p. a.* well-balanced, composed, calm; ***~я́ть*** → ***~ивать 2***

урага́н *m* [1] hurricane

ура́льский [16] Ural(s)

ура́н *m* [1], **~овый** [14] uranium

урегули́рование *n* [12] settlement; regulation; *vb.* → ***регули́ровать***

урез|а́ть & **~ывать** *coll.* [1], <**~ать**> [3] cut down, curtail; axe; **~о́нить** *coll.* [13] *pf.* bring to reason

у́рна *f* [5] ballot box; refuse bin

у́ров|ень *m* [4; -вня] level (at, on **на** П; **в** В); standard; *tech.* gauge; (*показа́тель*) rate; ***жи́зненный ~ень*** standard of living; **~ня́ть** → ***ура́внивать1***

уро́д *m* [1] monster; *coll.* ugly creature; **~ливый** [14 *sh.*] deformed; ugly; abnormal; **~овать** [7], <**из-**> deform, disfigure; (*кале́чить*) mutilate; maim; **~ство** *n* [9] deformity; ugliness; *fig.* abnormality

урож|а́й *m* [3] harvest, (abundant) crop; **~а́йность** *f* [8] yield (heavy *высо́кая*), productivity; **~а́йный** [14] productive; *год* good year for crops; **~е́нец** *m* [1; -нца], **~е́нка** *f* [5; *g/pl.*: -нок] native (of)

уро́|к *m* [1] lesson; **~н** *m* [1] (*уще́рб*) loss(es); *репута́ции* injury; **~ни́ть** → ***роня́ть***

урча́ть [4 *e.*; -чу́, -чи́шь] *в желу́дке* rumble; *пёс* growl
уры́вками *coll.* by fits and starts; in snatches; at odd moments
ус *m* [1; *pl. e.*] (*mst. pl.*) m(o)ustache
уса|ди́ть → **≈живать**; **≈дьба** *f* [5; *g/pl.*: -деб] farmstead, farm center (-tre); *hist.* country estate, country seat; **≈живать** [1], <**~ди́ть**> [15] seat; set; *дере́вьями и т. д.* plant (with T); **-ся**, <**усе́сться**> [25; уся́дусь, -дешься; уся́дься!; усе́лся, -лась] sit down, take a seat; settle down (to **за** B)
уса́тый [14] with a m(o)ustache; (*of animals*) with whiskers
усв|а́ивать [1], <**~о́ить**> [13] *привы́чку* adopt; *зна́ния* acquire, assimilate; *язы́к и т. д.* master, learn; **~oе́ние** *n* [12] adoption; acquirement, assimilation; mastering, learning
усе́|ивать [1], <**~ять**> [27] sow, cover, litter, strew (with); *звёздами* stud
усе́рд|ие *n* [12] zeal; (*прилежа́ние*) diligence, assiduity; **~ный** [14; -ден, -дна] zealous; diligent, assiduous
усе́сться → **уса́живаться**
усе́ять → **усе́ивать**
усид|е́ть [11] *pf.* remain sitting; keep one's place; sit still; *coll.* (*вы́держать*) hold out, keep a job; **≈чивый** [14 *sh.*] assiduous, persevering
усил|е́ние *n* [12] strengthening, *звука* intensification; *el.* amplification; **≈енный** [14] intensified; *пита́ние* high-caloric; **≈ивать** [1], <**≈ить**> [13] strengthen, reinforce; intensify; *звук* amplify; *боль и т. д.* aggravate; **-ся** increase; **≈ие** *n* [12] effort, exertion; ***приложи́ть все ≈ия*** make every effort; **~и́тель** *m* [4] *el.* amplifier; *tech.* booster; **≈ить(ся)** → **≈ивать(ся)**
ускольз|а́ть [1], <**~ну́ть**> [20] slip (off, away), escape (from **от** P)
ускор|е́ние *n* [12] acceleration; **~я́ть** [28], <**≈ить**> [13] quicken; speed up, accelerate; *v/i.* **-ся**
усла́|вливаться [1], <**усло́виться**> [14] arrange; settle, agree (upon **о** П); **~ть** → **усыла́ть**
усло́в|ие *n* [12] condition (on **с** T, **при** П; under **на** П), term; stipulation; proviso; *pl.* circumstances; **~иться** → **усла́вливаться**; **~ленный** [14 *sh.*] agreed, fixed; **~ность** *f* [8] conditionality; convention; **~ный** [14; -вен, -вна] *рефле́кс* conditional; (*относи́тельный*) relative; ***~ный пригово́р*** suspended, sentence; ***~ный знак*** conventional sign
усложн|я́ть [28], <**~и́ть**> [13] (**-ся** become) complicate(d)
услу́|га *f* [5] service (at **к** Д *pl.*), favo(u)r; **~живать** [1], <**~жить**> [16] do (p. Д) a service or favo(u)r; → *iro.* **удружи́ть**; **~жливый** [14 *sh.*] obliging
усм|а́тривать [1], <**~отре́ть**> [9; -отрю́, -о́тришь; -о́тренный] see (in **в** П); **~еха́ться** [1], <**~ехну́ться**> [20], **~е́шка** *f* [5; *g/pl.*: -шек] smile, grin; **~ире́ние** *n* [12] suppression; **~иря́ть** [28], <**~ири́ть**> [13] pacify; *си́лой* suppress; **~отре́ние** *n* [12] discretion (at **по** Д; to **на** B), judg(e)ment; **~отре́ть** → **~а́тривать**
усну́ть [20] *pf.* go to sleep, fall asleep
усоверше́нствован|ие *n* [12] improvement, refinement; **~ный** [14] improved, perfected
усомни́ться → **сомнева́ться**
усо́пший [17] *lit.* deceased
успе|ва́емость *f* [8] progress (*in studies*); **~ва́ть** [1], <**≈ть**> [8] have (*or* find) time, manage, succeed; arrive, be in time (for **к** Д, **на** B); catch (*train* ***на по́езд***); *impf.* get on, make progress, learn; **не ≈л(а)** (+ *inf.*), **как** no sooner + *pt.* than; **≈ется** *pf. impers.* there is no hurry; **≈х** *m* [1] success; *pl. a.* progress; ***с тем же ≈хом*** with the same result; **≈шный** [14; -шен, -шна] successful; ***≈шно*** *a.* with success
успок|а́ивать [1], <**~о́ить**> [13] calm, soothe; reassure; **-ся** calm down; *ве́тер, боль* subside; become quiet; content o.s. (with **на** П); **~oе́ние** *n* [12] peace; calm; **~ои́тельный** [14; -лен, -льна]

soothing, reassuring; **~óить(ся)** → ***~áивать*(ся)**

уст|á *n/pl.* [9] *obs. or poet* . mouth, lips *pl.*; ***узнáть из пéрвых ~*** learn at first hand; ***у всех на ~áх*** everybody is talking about it

устáв *m* [1] statute(s); regulations *pl.*; ~ *ООН и т. д.* charter

уста|вáть [5], <~ть> [-áну, -áнешь] get tired; **~влять** [28], <~вить> [14] place; cover (with T), fill; *взгляд* direct, fix (*eyes* on **на** B); **-ся** stare (at **на** *or* **в** B); **~лость** *f* [8] weariness, fatigue; **~лый** [14] tired, weary; **~нáвливать** [1], <~новить> [14] set *or* put up; *tech.* mount; arrange; fix; *порядок* establish; (*узнáть*) find out, ascertain; adjust (to **на** B); **-ся** be established; form; *погóда* set in; **~нóвка** *f* [5; *g/pl.*: -вок] *tech.* mounting, installation; *силовáя* plant; *fig.* orientation (toward[s] **на** B); **~новлéние** *n* [12] establishment; **~рéлый** [14] obsolete, out-of-date; **~ть** → ***~вáть***

устилáть [1], <устлáть> [-телю, -тéлешь; ýстланный] cover, pave (with T)

ýстный [14] oral, verbal

устó|и *m/pl.* [3] foundation; **~йчивость** *f* [8] stability; **~йчивый** [14 *sh.*] stable; **~ять** [-ою, -оишь] keep one's balance; stand one's ground; resist (*v/t.* ***прóтив*** P; ***пéред*** T)

устр|áивать [1], <~óить> [13] arrange, organize; (*создавáть*) set up, establish; *сцéну* make; provide (*job* **на** B; *place* in **в** B); *coll. impers.* (*подходить*) suit; **-ся** be settled; settle; get a job (*a.* ***на рабóту***); **~анéние** *n* [12] removal; elimination; **~анять** [28], <~анить> [13] remove; eliminate, clear; **~ашáть** [1] **(-ся)** → ***страшиться***; **~емлять** [28], <~емить> [14 *e.*; -млю, -мишь; -млённый] (**на** B) direct (to, at), fix (on); **-ся** rush; be directed; **~ица** *f* [5] oyster; **~óить(ся)** → ***~áивать*(ся)**; **~óйство** *n* [9] arrangement; organization; *общéственное* structure, system; device; mechanism

устýп *m* [1] *скалы* ledge; projection; terrace; **~áть** [1], <~ить> [14] cede, let (p. Д) have; *в спóре* yield; (*быть хýже*) be inferior to (Д); (*продáть*) sell; ***~áть дорóгу*** (Д) let pass, give way; ***~áть мéсто*** give up one's place; **~ка** *f* [5; *g/pl.*: -пок] concession; cession; **~чивый** [14 *sh.*] compliant, pliant

устыдить [15 *e.*; -ыжý, -ыдишь; -ыжённый] (**-ся** be) ashame(d; of P)

ýстье *n* [10; *g/pl.*: -ьев] (*of a river*) mouth, estuary (at **в** П)

усугуб|лять [28], <~ить> [14 & 14 *e.*; -гýблю, -гýбишь; -гýбленный & -гублённый] increase, intensify; aggravate

усы́ → **ус**; **~лáть** [1], <услáть> [ушлю, ушлёшь; ýсланный] send (away); **~новлять** [28], <~новить> [14 *e.*; -влю, -вишь; -влённый] adopt; **~пать** [1], <~пáть> [2] (be)strew (with P); **~плять** [28], <~пить> [14 *e.*; -плю, -пишь; -плённый] put to sleep (*by means of narcotics, etc.*) lull to sleep; *живóтное* put to sleep; *fig.* lull, weaken, neutralize

утá|ивать [1], <~ить> [13] conceal, keep to o.s.; appropriate; **~йка** *coll.*: ***без ~йки*** frankly; **~птывать** [1], <утоптáть> [3] tread *or* trample (down); **~скивать** [1], <~щить> [16] carry, drag *or* take (off, away); *coll.* walk off with, pilfer

ýтварь *f* [8] *collect.* equipment; utensils *pl.*; ***церкóвная ~*** church plate

утвер|дительный [14; -лен, -льна] affirmative; **~дительно** in the affirmative; **~ждáть** [1], <~дить> [15 *e.*; -ржý, -рдишь; -рждённый] confirm; (*укреплять*) consolidate (*v/i.* **-ся**); *impf.* affirm, assert, maintain; **~ждéние** *n* [12] confirmation; affirmation, assertion; consolidation

уте|кáть [1], <~чь> [26] flow (away); leak; (*of gas, etc.*) escape; *coll.* run away; **~рéть** → ***утирáть***; **~рпéть** [10] *pf.* restrain o.s.; ***не ~рпéл, чтóбы не*** (+ *inf. pf.*) could not help ...ing

утёс *m* [1] cliff, crag

утé|чка *f* [5] leakage (*a. fig.*); *гáза*

escape; ***~чка мозго́в*** brain drain; **~чь** → ***~ка́ть***; **~ша́ть** [1], <~шить> [16] console, comfort; **-ся** *a.* take comfort in (T); **~ше́ние** *n* [12] comfort, consolation; **~ши́тельный** [14; -лен, -льна] comforting, consoling

ути́|ль *m* [4] *collect.* salvage, waste, scrap; **~ра́ть** [1], <утере́ть> [12] wipe; **~ха́ть** [1], <~хнуть> [21] subside, abate; *зву́ки* cease; (*успоко́иться*) calm down

у́тка *f* [5; *g/pl.*: у́ток] duck; *газе́тная* canard; false *or esp.* fabricated report

уткну́ть(ся) *coll.* [20] *pf.* *лицо́м* bury, hide; *в кни́гу* be(come) engrossed; (*наткну́ться*) run up against

утол|и́ть → ***~я́ть***; **~ща́ть** [1], <~сти́ть> [15 *e.*; -лщу́, -лсти́шь; -лщённый] become thicker; **~ще́ние** *n* [12] thickening; **~я́ть** [28], <~и́ть> [13] *жа́жду* slake, quench; *го́лод* appease; *жела́ние* satisfy

утом|и́тельный [14; -лен, -льна] wearisome, tiring; tedious, tiresome; **~и́ть(ся)** → **~ля́ть(ся)**; **~ле́ние** *n* [12] fatigue, exhaustion; **~лённый** [14; -лён, -ена́] tired, weary; **~ля́ть** [28], <~и́ть> [14 *e.*; -млю́, -ми́шь; -млённый] tire, weary (*v/i.* **-ся**; *a.* get tired)

утонч|а́ть [1], <~и́ть> [16 *e.*; -чу́, -чи́шь; -чённый] make thinner; *p. pt. p.* thin; *fig.* refine; make refined (*v/i.* **-ся**)

утоп|а́ть [1] **1.** <утону́ть> → ***тону́ть* 2.**; **2.** drown; **~ленник** *m* [1] drowned man; **~ленница** *f* [5] drowned woman; **~та́ть** → ***ута́птывать***

уточн|е́ние *n* [12] expressing *or* defining more precisely; amplification; elaboration; **~я́ть** [28], <~и́ть> [13] amplify; elaborate

утра́|ивать [1], <утро́ить> [13] treble; *v/i.* **-ся**; **~мбова́ть** [7] *pf.* ram, tamp; **~та** *f* [5] loss; **~чивать** [1], <~тить> [15] lose

у́тренний [15] morning

утри́ровать [7] exaggerate

у́тр|о *n* [9; с, до -а́; к -у́] morning (in the **~ом**; ***по ~а́м***); ***...~а́*** *a...* A.M. → ***день***; **~о́ба** *f* [5] womb; **~о́ить(ся)** → ***~а́ивать(ся)***; **~ужда́ть** [1], <~уди́ть> [15 *e.*; -ужу́, -уди́шь; -уждённый] trouble, bother

утряса́ть [3; -сти́, -су́, -сёшь], <~сти́> [25] *fig.* settle

утю́|г *m* [1] (flat)iron; **~жить** [16], <вы-, от-> iron

уха́ *f* [5] fish soup; **~б** *m* [1] pothole; **~бистый** [14 *sh.*] bumpy

уха́живать [1] (***за*** T) nurse, look after; *за же́нщиной* court, woo

ухва́т|ывать [1], <~и́ть> [15] (***за*** B) seize, grasp; **-ся** snatch; cling to; *fig.* seize, jump at

ухи|тря́ться [28], <~три́ться> [13] contrive, manage; **~щре́ние** *n* [12] contrivance; **~щря́ться** [28] contrive

ухмыл|я́ться *coll.* [28], <~ьну́ться> [20] grin, smirk

у́хо *n* [9; *pl.*: у́ши, уше́й, *etc. e.*] ear (in ***на*** B); ***влюби́ться по́ уши*** be head over heels in love; ***пропуска́ть ми́мо уше́й*** turn a deaf ear (to B); ***держа́ть ~ востро́*** → ***насто́роже***

ухо́д *m* [1] going away, leaving, departure; (***за*** T) care, tending, nursing; **~и́ть** [15], <уйти́> [уйду́, уйдёшь; ушёл, ушла́; уше́дший; *g. pl.*: уйдя́] leave (*v/t.* ***из***, ***от*** P) go away; (*минова́ть*) pass; *от наказа́ния* escape; *от отве́та* evade, *в отста́вку* resign; *на пе́нсию* retire; *coll.* be worn out, spent (for ***на*** B); ***уйти́ в себя́*** shrink into o.s.

ухудш|а́ть [1], <~ить> [16] deteriorate (*v.i.* **-ся**); **~е́ние** *n* [12] deterioration; worsening

уцеле́ть [8] *pf.* come through alive; survive; escape

уцепи́ться [14] *coll.* → ***ухвати́ться***

уча́ст|вовать [7] participate, take part (in ***в*** П); **~вующий** [17] → ***~ник***; **~ие** *n* [12] (***в*** П) participation (in); (*сочу́вствие*) interest (in), sympathy (with); **~и́ть(ся)** → ***учаща́ть(ся)***; **~ливый** [14 *sh.*] sympathizing, sympathetic; **~ник** *m* [1], **~ница** *f* [5] participant, participator; competitor (*sports*); *член* member; **~ок** *m* [1; -тка] *земли́* plot; (*часть*) part, section; ***избира́тельный ~ок*** electoral district; polling station; **´~ь** [8] fate, lot

уча|ща́ть [1], <**~сти́ть**> [15 *e.*; -ащу́, -асти́шь; -ащённый] make (**-ся** become) more frequent

уч|а́щийся *m* [17] schoolchild, pupil, student; **~ёба** *f* [5] studies *pl.*, study; (*подгото́вка*) training; **~е́бник** *m* [1] textbook; **~е́бный** [14] school...; educational; (*посо́бие*) text (*book*), exercise..; ***~е́бный план*** curriculum

уче́н|ие *n* [12] learning; instruction apprenticeship; *mil.* training, practice; teaching, doctrine; **~и́к** *m* [1 *e.*] *and* **~и́ца** *f* [5] pupil; student; *сле́саря и т. д.* apprentice; (*после́довать*) disciple; **~и́ческий** [16] crude, immature

учён|ость *f* [8] learning; erudition; **~ый** [14 *sh.*] learned; ***~ая сте́пень*** (university) degree; *su.* scholar, scientist

уч|е́сть → ***учи́тывать***; **~ёт** *m* [1] calculation; registration; *това́ров* stock-taking; **с *~ётом*** taking into consideration

учи́лище *n* [11] school, college (at **в** П)

учиня́ть [28] → ***чини́ть 2***

учи́тель *m* [4; *pl.*: -ля, *etc. e.*; *fig. st.*], **~ница** *f* [5] teacher, instructor; **~ский** [16] (of) teachers('); **~ская** *as. su.* teachers' common room

учи́тывать [1], <уче́сть> [25; учту́, -тёшь; учёл, учла́; *g. pt.*: учтя́; учтённый] take into account, consider; register; *ве́ксель* discount

учи́ть [16] **1.** <на-, об-, вы́-> teach (p. s.th. В/Д), instruct; train; (*a.* **-ся** Д); **2.** <вы́-> learn, study

учреди́тель *m* [4] founder; **~ный** [14] constituent

учре|жда́ть [1], <**~ди́ть**> [15 *e.*; -ежу́, -еди́шь; -еждённый] found, establish, set up; **~жде́ние** *n* [12] founding, setting up, establishment; (*заведе́ние*) institution

учти́вый [14 *sh.*] polite, courteous

уша́нка *f* [5; *g/pl.*: -нок] cap with earflaps

уши́б *m* [1] bruise; injury; **~а́ть** [1], <**~и́ть**> [-бу́, -бёшь; -и́б(ла); уши́бленный] hurt, bruise (o.s. **-ся**)

ушко́ *n* [9; *pl.*: -ки́, -ко́в] *tech.* eye, lug; (*of a needle*) eye

ушно́й [14] ear...; aural

уще́лье *n* [10] gorge, ravine

ущем|ля́ть [28], <**~и́ть**> [14 *e.*; -млю́, -ми́шь; -млённый] *права́* infringe

уще́рб *m* [1] damage; loss; **в ~** to the detriment

ущипну́ть → ***щипа́ть***

ую́т *m* [1] coziness (*Brt.* cosiness); **~ный** [14; -тен, -тна] snug, cozy (*Brt.* cosy), comfortable

уязв|и́мый [14 *sh.*] vulnerable; **~ля́ть** [28], <**~и́ть**> [14 *e.*; -влю́, -ви́шь; -влённый] *fig.* hurt

уясн|я́ть [28], <**~и́ть**> [13] *себе́* understand

Ф

фа́бри|ка *f* [5] factory (in ***на*** П); mill; **~кова́ть** [7], *pf.* <с-> *fig. coll.* fabricate

фа́була *f* [5] plot, story

фа́за *f* [5] phase

фаза́н *m* [1] pheasant

файл *m* [1] *comput.* file

фа́кел *m* [1] torch

факс *m* [1] fax

факт *m* [1] fact; ***~ тот, что*** the fact is that; **~и́ческий** [16] (f)actual, real; *adv. a.* in fact; **~у́ра** *f* [5] *lit.* style, texture

факульте́т *m* [1] faculty (in ***на*** П); department

фаль|сифици́ровать [7] (*im*)*pf.*

falsify; forge; **~ши́вить** [14], <с-> sing out of tune, play falsely; *coll.* act incincerely, be false; **~ши́вка** *f* [5; *g/pl.*: -вок] forged document; false information; **~ши́вый** [14 *sh.*] false, forged, counterfeit; ***моне́та*** base; **~шь** *f* [8] falseness; ***лицеме́рие*** hypocrisy, insincerity
фами́л|ия *f* [7] surname; ***как ва́ша ~ия?*** what is your name?; **~ья́рный** [14; -рен, -рна] familiar
фанати́|зм *m* [1] fanaticism; **~чный** [14; -чен, -чна] fanatical
фане́ра *f* [5] plywood; veneer
фанта|зёр *m* [1] dreamer, visionary; **~зи́ровать** [7] *impf. only* indulge in fancies, dream; <с-> invent; **~зия** *f* [7] imagination; fancy; (*вы́думка*) invention, fib; *mus.* fantasia; *coll.* (*при́хоть*) whim; **~стика** *f* [5] *lit.* fantasy, fiction; ***нау́чная ~стика*** science fiction; *collect.* the fantastic, the unbelievable; **~сти́ческий** [16], **~сти́чный** [14; -чен, -чна] fantastic
фа́р|а *f* [5] headlight; **~ва́тер** *m* [1] *naut.* fairway; **~маце́вт** *m* [1] pharmacist; **~тук** *m* [1] apron; **~фо́р** [1], **~фо́ровый** [14] china, porcelain; **~ш** *m* [1] stuffing; minced meat; **~широва́ть** [7] *cul.* stuff
фаса́д *m* [1] façade, front
фасов|а́ть [7] *impf.*; **~ка** *f* [5; *g/pl.*: -вок] prepackage
фасо́|ль *f* [8] string (*Brt.* runner) bean(s); **~н** *m* [1] cut, style
фата́льный [14; -лен, -льна] fatal
фаши́|зм *m* [1] fascism; **~ст** *m* [1] fascist; **~стский** [16] fascist...
фая́нс *m* [1], **~овый** [14] faience
февра́ль *m* [4 *e.*] February
федера́|льный [14] federal; **~ти́вный** [14] federative, federal; **~ция** *f* [7] federation
фейерве́рк *m* [1] firework(s)
фельд|ма́ршал *m* [1] *hist.* field marshal; **~шер** *m* [1] doctor's assistant, medical attendant
фельето́н *m* [1] satirical article
фен *m* [1] hairdryer
фено́мен *m* [1] phenomenon
феода́льный [14] feudal
ферзь *m* [4 *e.*] queen (*chess*)
фе́рм|а *f* [5] farm; **~ер** *m* [1] farmer
фестива́ль *m* [4] festival
фетр *m* [1] felt; **~овый** [14] felt...
фехтова́|льщик *m* [1] fencer; **~ние** *n* [12] fencing; **~ть** [7] fence
фиа́лка *f* [5; *g/pl.*: -лок] violet
фи́г|а *f* [5], **~овый** [14] fig
фигу́р|а *f* [5] figure; chess piece (*excluding pawns*); **~а́льный** [14; -лен, -льна] figurative; **~и́ровать** [7] figure, appear; **~ный** [14] figured; ***~ное ката́ние*** figure skating
фи́зи|к *m* [1] physicist; **~ка** *f* [5] physics; **~оло́гия** *f* [7] physiology; **~оно́мия** [7] physiognomy; **~ческий** [14] physical; ***труд*** manual
физкульту́р|а *f* [5] physical training; gymnastics; **~ник** *m* [1] sportsman, **~ница** *f* [5] sportswoman
фик|си́ровать [7], <за-> record in writing; fix; **~ти́вный** [14; -вен, -вна] fictitious; **~ция** *f* [7] fiction; invention, untruth
фила|нтро́п *m* [1] philantropist; **~рмони́ческий** [16] philharmonic; **~рмо́ния** *f* [7] philharmonic society, the philharmonic
филе́ *n* [*indecl.*] tenderloin, fil(l)et
филиа́л *m* [1] branch (*of an institution*)
фи́лин *m* [1] eagle owl
фило́л|ог *m* [1] philologist; **~оги́ческий** [16] philological; **~о́гия** *f* [7] philology
фило́с|оф *m* [1] philosopher; **~о́фия** *f* [7] philosophy; **~о́фский** [16] philosophical; **~о́фствовать** [7] philosophize
фильм *m* [1] film (*vb.* ***снима́ть ~***); ***документа́льный ~*** documentary (film); ***мультипликацио́нный ~*** cartoon; ***худо́жественный ~*** feature film
фильтр *m* [1], **~ова́ть** [7] filter
фина́л *m* [1] final; *mus.* finale
финанс|и́ровать [7] (*im*)*pf.* finance; **~овый** [14] financial; **~ы** *m/pl.* [1] finance(s)
фи́ник *m* [1] date (*fruit*)
фини́фть *f* [8] *art* enamel
фи́ниш *m* [1] *sport* finish; **~ный** [14]: ***~ная пряма́я*** last lap
финн *m* [1], **~ка** *f* [5; *g/pl.*: -ок], **~ский** [16] Finnish
фиоле́товый [14] violet

фи́рма *f* [5] firm
фиска́льный [14] fiscal
фити́ль *m* [4 *e.*] wick; (*igniting device*) fuse; (*detonating device*) *usu.* fuze
флаг *m* [1] flag, colo(u)rs *pl.*
фланг *m* [1], **~овый** [14] *mil.* flank
флане́л|евый [14], **~ь** *f* [8] flannel
флегмати́чный [14; -чен, -чна] phlegmatic
фле́йта *f* [5] flute
фли́|гель *arch. m* [4; *pl.*: -ля, *etc. e.*] wing; outbuilding; **~рт** *m* [1] flirtation; **~ртова́ть** [7] flirt
флома́стер *m* [1] felt-tip pen
флот *m* [1] fleet; ***вое́нно-морско́й ~*** navy; ***вое́нно-возду́шный ~*** (air) force; **~ский** [16] naval
флю|гер *m* [1] weather vane; weathercock; **~с** *m* [1] gumboil
фля́|га *f* [5], **~жка** *f* [5; *g/pl.*: -жек] flask; *mil.* canteen
фойе́ *n* [*indecl.*] lobby, foyer
фо́кус *m* [1] (juggler's *or* conjurer's) trick, sleight of hand; *coll.* caprice; whim; **~ник** *m* [1] juggler, conjurer; **~ничать** *coll.* [1] play tricks; *о ребёнке* play up; behave capriciously
фольга́ *f* [5] foil
фолькло́р *m* [1], **~ный** [14] folklore
фон *m* [1] background (against **на** П)
фона́р|ик *m* [1] flashlight, *Brt.* torch; **~ь** *m* [4 *e.*] lantern; (street) lamp; *coll.* black eye
фонд *m* [1] fund; *pl.* reserves, stock(s); **~овый** [14] stock...
фоне́т|ика *f* [5] phonetics; **~и́ческий** [16] phonetic(al)
фонта́н *m* [1] fountain
форе́ль *f* [8] trout
фо́рм|а *f* [5] form, shape; *tech.* mo(u)ld; cast; *mil.* uniform; dress (*sports*); **~а́льность** *f* [8] formality; **~а́льный** [14; -лен, -льна] formal; **~а́т** *m* [1] size, format (*a. tech.*); **~енный** [14] uniform; *coll.* proper; regular; ***~енная оде́жда*** uniform; **~ирова́ть** [7], <c-> (**-ся** be) form(ed); **~ули́ровать** [7] (*im*)*pf.* & <c-> formulate; **~улиро́вка** [5; *g/pl.*: -вок] formulation
форпо́ст *m* [1] *mil.* advanced post; outpost (*a. fig.*)
форси́ровать [7] (*im*)*pf.* force
фо́|рточка *f* [5; *g/pl.*: -чек] window leaf; **~рум** *m* [1] forum; **~сфор** *m* [1] phosphorus
фото|аппара́т *m* [1] camera; **~граф** *m* [1] photographer; **~графи́ровать** [7], <c-> photograph; **~графи́ческий** [16] photographic; → ***~аппара́т***; **~гра́фия** *f* [7] photograph; photography; photographer's studio
фрагмента́рный [14; -рен, -рна] fragmentary
фра́за *f* [5] phrase
фрак *m* [1] tailcoat, full-dress coat
фра́кция *f* [7] *pol.* faction; (*chem.*) fraction
франт *m* [1] dandy, fop
франц|у́женка *f* [5; *g/pl.*: -нок] Frenchwoman; **~у́з** *m* [1] Frenchman; **~у́зский** [16] French
фрахт *m* [1], **~ова́ть** [7] freight
фре́ска *f* [5] fresco
фронт *m* [1] *mil.* front; **~ово́й** [14] front...; front-line
фрукт *m* [1] (*mst. pl.*) fruit; **~о́вый** [14] fruit...; ***~о́вый сад*** orchad
фу! *int.* (*expressing revulsion*) ugh!; (*expressing surprise*) oh!; ooh!
фунда́мент *m* [1] foundation; *осно́ва* basis; **~а́льный** [14; -лен, -льна] fundamental
функциони́ровать [7] function
фунт *m* [1] pound
фур|а́ж *m* [1 *e.*] fodder; **~а́жка** *f* [5; *g/pl.*: -жек] *mil.* service cap; **~го́н** *m* [1] van; **~о́р** *m* [1] furor(e); **~у́нкул** *m* [1] furuncle, boil
футбо́л *m* [1] football, soccer (*Brt. a.* association football); **~и́ст** *m* [1] soccer player; **~ьный** [14] soccer..., football...
футля́р *m* [1] case, container
фы́рк|ать [1], <~нуть> [20] snort; *coll.* grouse

Х

ха́ки [*indecl.*] khaki
хала́т *m* [1] dressing gown, bathrobe; *врача́* smock; **~ный** *coll.* [14; -тен, -тна] careless, negligent
халту́ра *coll. f* [5] potboiler; hackwork; extra work (*usu.* inferior) chiefly for profit
хам *m* [1] cad, boor, lout
хандр|а́ *f* [5] depression, blues *pl.*; **~и́ть** [13] be depressed *or* in the dumps
ханж|а́ *coll. m/f* [5; *g/pl.*: -же́й] hypocrite; **~́ество́** *n* [9] hypocrisy
хао́|с *m* [1] chaos; **~ти́ческий** [16], **~ти́чный** [14; -чен, -чна] chaotic
хара́ктер *m* [1] character, nature; *челове́ка* temper, disposition; **~изова́ть** [7] (*im*)*pf.* & <о-> characterize; (*опи́сывать*) describe; **~и́стика** *f* [5] character(istic); characterization; (*докуме́нт*) reference; **~́ный** [14; -рен, -рна] characteristic (**для** P of)
ха́риус *m* [1] *zo.* grayling
ха́ря *coll. f* [6] mug (= *face*)
ха́та *f* [5] peasant house
хвал|а́ *f* [5] praise; **~е́бный** [14; -бен, -бна] laudatory; **~ёный** [14] *iro.* much-vaunted; **~и́ть** [13; хвалю́, хва́лишь] praise; **-ся** boast (T of)
хва́ст|аться & *coll.* **~ать** [1], <по-> boast, brag (T of); **~ли́вый** [14 *sh.*] boastful; **~овство́** *n* [9] boasting; **~у́н** *m* [1 *e.*] *coll.* boaster, braggart
хват|а́ть [1] **1.** <(с)хвати́ть> [15] (**за** B) snatch (at); grasp, seize (by); *a., coll.*, (**-ся за** B; lay hold of); **2.** <~и́ть> (*impers.*) (P) suffice, be sufficient; (p. Д, **у** P) have enough; last (*v/t.* **на** B); (**э́того мне**) **~́ит** (that's) enough (for me)
хво́йный [14] coniferous
хвора́ть *coll.* [1] be sick *or* ill
хво́рост *m* [1] brushwood
хвост *m* [1 *e.*] tail; *coll.* (*о́чередь*) line, *Brt.* queue; **в ~е́** get behind, lag behind; **поджа́ть ~** *coll.* become more cautious
хво́я *f* [6] (pine) needle(s *or* branches *pl.*)
хе́рес *m* [1] sherry
хи́жина *f* [5] hut, cabin
хи́лый [14; хил, -а́, -о] weak, sickly, puny
хи́ми|к *m* [1] chemist; **~́ческий** [16] chemical; **~я** *f* [7] chemistry
химчи́стка *f* [5; *g/pl.*: -ток] dry cleaning; dry cleaner's
хини́н *m* [1] quinine
хире́ть [8] weaken, grow sickly; *расте́ние* wither; *fig.* decay
хиру́рг *m* [1] surgeon; **~и́ческий** [16] surgical; **~и́я** *f* [7] surgery
хитр|е́ц *m* [1 *e.*] cunning person; **~и́ть** [13], <с-> use guile; → **мудри́ть**; **~́ость** *f* [8] craft(iness), cunning; (*приём*) artifice, ruse, trick; stratagem; **~́ый** [14; -тёр, -тра́, хи́тро] cunning, crafty, sly, wily; *coll.* artful; (*изобрета́тельный*) ingenious
хихи́кать [1] giggle, titter
хище́ние *n* [12] theft; embezzlement
хи́щн|ик *m* [1] beast (*or* bird) of prey; **~́ический** [14] predatory; *fig.* injurious (*to nature*); **~ый** [16; -щен, -щна] rapacious, predatory; of prey
хладнокро́в|ие *n* [12] composure; **~ный** [14; -вен, -вна] cool(headed), calm
хлам *m* [1] trash, rubbish
хлеб *m* [1] **1.** bread; **2.** [1; *pl.*: -ба́, *etc. e.*] grain, *Brt.* corn; (*пропита́ние*) livelihood; *pl.* cereals; **~́ный** [14] grain..., corn..., cereal...; bread...; **~опека́рня** *f* [6; *g/pl.*: -рен] bakery; **~осо́льный** [14; -лен, -льна] hospitable
хлев *m* [1; в -е & -у́; *pl.*: -а́, *etc. e.*] cattle shed; *fig.* pigsty
хлест|а́ть [3] *once*, <~ну́ть> [20] lash, whip, beat; *о воде́* gush, spurt; *о дожде́* pour
хлоп! *int.* bang! crack!, plop!; → *a.* **~́ать** [1], <по->, *once* <~́нуть> [20] *по спине́* slap; *в ладо́ши* clap; *две́рью и т. д.* bang, slam (*v/t.* T)

хло́пок *m* [1; -пка] cotton
хлопо́к *m* [1; -ка́ *и т. д.*] clap; bang
хлопот|а́ть [3], <по-> (**о** П) busy *or* exert o.s. (**о** П, **за** В on behalf of); *impf. по хозя́йству* toil, bustle (about); **~ли́вый** [14 *sh.*] *о челове́ке* busy, fussy; **~ный** [14] troublesome; exacting; **´~ы** *f/pl.* [5; *g/pl.*: -по́т] trouble(s), efforts (on behalf of, for); cares
хлопчатобума́жный [14] cotton...
хло́пья *n/pl.* [10; *gen.*: -ьев] flakes; *кукуру́зные ~* corn flakes
хлор *m* [1] chlorine; **~истый** [14] chlorine...; chloride...
хлы́нуть [20] *pf.* gush (forth); rush; *дождь* (begin to) pour in torrents
хлыст *m* [1 *e.*] whip; switch
хлю́пать *coll.* [1] squelch
хмель¹ *m* [4] hop(s)
хмель² *m* [4] intoxication
хму́р|ить [13], <на-> frown, knit one's brows; **-ся** frown, scowl; *пого́да* be(come) overcast; **~ый** [14; хмур, -а́, -о] gloomy, sullen; *день* cloudy
хны́кать *coll.* [3] whimper, snivel; *fig.* whine
хо́бби *n* [*indecl.*] hobby
хо́бот *m* [1] *zo.* trunk
ход *m* [1; в (на) -у́ & -е; *pl.*: хо́ды́] motion; (*ско́рость*) speed (**на** П at), pace; *исто́рии и т. д.* course; *подзе́мный* passage; *по́ршня* stroke; *чёрный* entrance; lead (*cards*); move (*chess, etc.*); **на ~у́** in transit; *a.* while walking, *etc.*; ***пусти́ть в ~*** start; motion; *ору́жие* use; ***знать все ~ы́ и вы́ходы*** know all the ins and outs; ***по́лным ~ом*** in full swing; ***~ мы́слей*** train of thought
хода́тай|ство *n* [9] intercession; petition; **~ствовать** [7], <по-> intercede (**у** Р, **за** В with/for); petition (**о** П for)
ход|и́ть [15] go (**в, на** В to); walk; *под па́русом* sail; *по́езд и т. д.* run, ply; *в ша́шках и т. д.* move; visit, attend (*v/t.* **в, на** В; *p.* **к** Д); *о слу́хах* circulate; (*носи́ть*) (**в** П) wear; **~кий** [16; хо́док, -дка́, -о; *comp.*: ходче] *coll.* fast; *това́р* marketable, saleable; in great demand; **~у́льный** [14; -лен, -льна] stilted; **~ьба́** *f* [5] walking; walk; **~я́чий** [17] popular; current; *coll. больно́й* ambulant
хожде́ние *n* [12] going, walking; (*распростране́ние*) circulation
хозя́|ин *m* [1; *pl.*: хозя́ева, хозя́ев] owner; boss, master; *домовладе́лец* landlord; *принима́ющий госте́й* host; **~ева** → **~ин & ~йка**; **~йка** *f* [5; *g/pl.*: -я́ек] mistress; landlady; hostess; housewife; **~йничать** [1] keep house; manage (at will); make o.s. at home; **~йственный** [14 *sh.*] economic(al), thrifty; ***~йственные това́ры*** household goods; **~йство** *n* [9] economy; household; farm
хокке́й *m* [3] hockey; ***~ с ша́йбой*** ice hockey
холе́ра *f* [5] cholera
хо́лить [13] tend, care for
холл *m* [1] vestibule, foyer
хол|м *m* [1 *e.*] hill; **~ми́стый** [14 *sh.*] hilly
хо́лод *m* [1] cold (**на** П in); chill (*a. fig.*); *pl.* [-а́, *etc. e.*] cold (weather) (**в** В in); **~е́ть** [8], <по-> grow cold, chill; **~и́льник** *m* [1] refrigerator; **~ность** *f* [8] coldness; **~ный** [14; хо́лоден, -дна́, -о] cold (*a. fig.*); *geogr.* & *fig.* frigid; (**мне**) **~но** it is (I am) cold
холост|о́й [14; хо́лост] single, unmarried; bachelor('s); *патро́н* blank; *tech. ход* idle; **~я́к** *m* [1 *e.*] bachelor
холст *m* [1 *e.*] canvas
хомя́к *m* [1 *e.*] hamster
хор *m* [1] choir; **~ом** all together
хорва́т *m* [1], **~ка** *f* [5; *g/pl.*: -ток] Croat; **~ский** [16] Croatian
хорёк *m* [1; -рька́] polecat, ferret
хореогра́фия *f* [7] choreography
хорово́д *m* [1] round dance
хорони́ть [13; -оню́, -о́нишь], <по-> bury
хоро́ш|енький [16] pretty; **~е́нько** *coll.* properly, throughly; **~е́ть** [8], <по-> grow prettier; **~ий** [17; хоро́ш, -а́; *comp.*: лу́чше] good; fine, nice; (*a.* **собо́й**) pretty, good-looking, handsome; **~о́** well; *отме́тка* good, B (→ **четвёрка**); all

right!, OK!, good!; **~о́, что вы** it's a good thing you...; **~о́ вам** (+ *inf.*) it is all very well for you to...
хоте́|ть [хочу́, хо́чешь, хо́чет, хоти́м, хоти́те, хотя́т], <за-> (P) want, desire; ***я ~л(а) бы*** I would (*Brt.* should) like; ***я хочу́, что́бы вы*** + *pt.* I want you to...; ***хо́чешь не хо́чешь*** willy-nilly; **-ся** (*impers.*): ***мне хо́чется*** I'd like; *a.* → **~ть**
хоть (*a.* **~ бы**) at least; even; even (if *or* though); if only; **~ ... ~** whether ... whether, (either) or; *coll.* ***~ бы и так*** even if it be so; ***~ убе́й*** for the life of me; *a.* **хотя́**
хотя́ although, though (*a.* **~ и**); **~ бы** even though; if; → *a.* **хоть**
хо́хот *m* [1] guffaw; loud laugh; **~а́ть** [3], <за-> roar (with laughter)
храбр|е́ц *m* [1 *e.*] brave person; **~ость** *f* [8] valo(u)r, bravery; **~ый** [14; храбр, -а, -о] brave, valiant
храм *m* [1] *eccl.* temple, church
хран|е́ние *n* [12] keeping; *това́ров* storage; ***ка́мера ~е́ния*** *rail., ae., etc.*; cloakroom, *Brt.* left-luggage office; *автомати́ческая* left-luggage locker; **~и́лище** *n* [11] storehouse; depository; **~и́тель** *m* [4] keeper, custodian; *музе́я* curator; **~и́ть** [13], <со-> keep; maintain; store *tech. a. of computer*; *па́мяти* preserve; (*соблюда́ть*) observe
храп *m* [1], **~е́ть** [10 *e.*; -плю́, -пи́шь] snore; snorting
хребе́т *m* [1; -бта́] *anat.* spine; spinal column; (mountain) range
хрен *m* [1] horseradish
хрип *m* [1], **~е́ние** *n* [12] wheeze; wheezing; **~е́ть** [10; -плю́, -пи́шь] wheeze; be hoarse; *coll.* speak hoarsely; **~лый** [14; хрипл, -а́, -о] hoarse, husky; **~нуть** [21], <о-> become hoarse; **~ота́** [5] hoarseness; husky voice
христ|иани́н *m* [1; *pl.*: -а́не, -а́н], **~иа́нка** *f* [5; *g/pl.*: -нок], **~иа́нский** [16] Christian; **~иа́нство** *n* [9] Christianity; **Хо́с** *m* [Христа́] Christ
хром *m* [1] chromium; chrome
хром|а́ть [1] limp; be lame; **~о́й** [14; хром, -а́, -о] lame
хро́н|ика *f* [5] chronicle; current events; newsreel; **~и́ческий** [16] chronic(al); **~ологи́ческий** [16] chronological; **~оло́гия** *f* [7] chronology
хру́|пкий [16; -пок, -пка́, -о; *comp.*: хру́пче] brittle, fragile, frail, infirm; **~ста́ль** *m* [4 *e.*] crystal; **~сте́ть** [11] crunch; **~щ** *m* [1 *e.*] cockchafer
худо́ж|ественный [14 *sh.*] artistic; art(s)...; of art; belles(*-lettres*); applied (*arts*); **~ество** *n* [9] (applied) art; **~ник** *m* [1] artist; painter
худ|о́й [14; худ, -а́, -о; *comp.*: худе́е] thin, lean, scrawny; [*comp.*: ху́же] bad, evil; **~ший** [16] worse, worst; → ***лу́чший***
ху́же worse; → ***лу́чше & тот***
хулига́н *m* [1] rowdy, hooligan

Ц

ца́п|ать *coll.* [1], *once* <~нуть> [20] snatch, grab; scratch
ца́пля *f* [6; *g/pl.*: -пель] heron
цара́п|ать [1], <(п)о->, *once* <~нуть> [20], **~ина** *f* [5] scratch
цар|е́вич *m* [1] czarevitch; prince; **~е́вна** *f* [5; *g/pl.*: -вен] princess; **~и́ть** [13] *fig.* reign; **~и́ца** *f* [5] czarina, (Russian) empress; *fig.* queen; **~ский** [16] of the czar(s), czarist; royal; **~ство** *n* [9] realm; kingdom (*a. fig.*); rule; *a.* → **~ствование** *n* [12] reign (**в** В in); **~ствовать** [7] reign, rule; **~ь** *m* [4 *e.*] czar, (Russian) emperor; *fig.* king; ***без ~я́ в голове́*** stupid
цвести́ [25 -т-] bloom, blossom
цвет *m* [1] **1.** [*pl.*: -а́, *etc. e.*] colo(u)r; *fig.* cream, pick; *лица́* complexion; ***защи́тного ~а*** khaki; **2.** [*only pl.*: -ы́, *etc. e.*] flowers; **3.** [*no pl.*: **в -у́** in bloom] blossom, bloom; **~е́ние** *n*

[12] flowering; **~истый** [14 *sh.*] multicolo(u)red, florid; **~ни́к** [1 *e.*] flower bed, garden; **~но́й** [14] colo(u)red; colo(u)r; ***мета́ллы*** nonferrous; ***~на́я капу́ста*** cauliflower; **~о́к** *m* [1; -тка́; *pl. usu.* = 2] flower; **~о́чный** [14] flower...; ***~о́чный магази́н*** florist's; **~у́щий** [17 *sh.*] flowering; *fig.* flourishing; ***во́зраст*** prime (of life)

целе́|бный [14; -бен, -бна] curative, medicinal; **~во́й** [14] special, having a special purpose; **~сообра́зный** [14; -зен, -зна] expedient; **~устремлённый** [14 *sh.*] purposeful

цели|ко́м entirely, wholly; **~на́** *f* [5] virgin lands; virgin soil; **~и́тельный** [14; -лен, -льна] salutary, curative; **~ть(ся)** [13], <при-> aim (***в*** B at)

целлюло́за *f* [5] cellulose

целова́ть(ся) [7], <по-> kiss

це́л|ое [14] whole (***в*** П on the); **~омý дренный** [14 *sh.*] chaste; **~омýдрие** *n* [12] chastity; **~остность** *f* [8] integrity; **~ость** *f* [8]: safety; ***в ~ости*** intact; **~ый** [14; цел, -á, -о] whole, entire, intact; ***~ый и невреди́мый*** safe and sound; ***~ое число́*** whole number, integer; → ***деся́тый*** & ***со́тый***

цель *f* [8] aim, end, goal, object; (***мише́нь***) target; purpose (**с** T, ***в*** П *pl.* for); ***име́ть ~ю*** aim at; **~ность** *f* [8] integrity; **~ный** [14; це́лен, -льна́, -о] of one piece; entire, whole; ***челове́к*** self-contained; ***молоко́*** [*no sh.*] unskimmed

цеме́нт *m* [1] cement; **~и́ровать** [7] *tech.* cement, case-harden

цен|á *f* [5; *ac/sg.*: це́ну; *pl. st.*] price (P of; ***по*** Д/***в*** B at/of), cost; value (Д of *or* one's); ***знать себе́ ~у*** know one's worth; ***~ы́ нет*** (Д) be invaluable; ***любо́й ~о́й*** at any price; **~зу́ра** *f* [5] censorship

цен|и́тель *m* [4] judge, connoisseur; **~и́ть** [13; ценю́, це́нишь], <о-> estimate; value, appreciate; **~ность** *f* [8] value; *pl.* valuables; **~ный** [14; -е́нен, -е́нна] valuable; *fig.* precious, important; ***~ные бума́ги*** *pl.* securities

це́нтнер *m* [1] centner

центр *m* [1] center, *Brt.* centre; **~ализова́ть** [7] (*im*)*pf.* centralize; **~а́льный** [14] central; ***~а́льная газе́та*** national newspaper; **~обе́жный** [14] centrifugal

цеп|ене́ть [8], <о-> become rigid, freeze; be rooted to the spot; *fig.* be transfixed; **~кий** [16; -пок, -пка́, -о] tenacious (*a. fig.*); **~ля́ться** [28] cling (to ***за*** B); **~но́й** [14] chain(ed); **~о́чка** *f* [5; *g/pl.*: -чек] chain; **~ь** *f* [8; в, на -и́; *from g/pl. e.*] chain (*a. fig.*); *mil.* line; *el.* circuit

церемо́н|иться [13], <по-> stand on ceremony; **~ия** *f* [7] ceremony; **~ный** [14] ceremonious

церко́в|ный [14] church...; ecclesiastical; **´~ь** *f* [8; -кви; *instr./sg.*: -ковью; *pl.*: -кви, -ве́й, -ва́м] church (*building and organization*)

цех *m* [1] shop (*section of factory*)

цивилиз|а́ция *f* [7] civilization; **~о́ванный** [14] civilized

цикл *m* [1] cycle; ***ле́кций*** course; **~о́н** *m* [1] cyclone

цико́рий *m* [3] chicory

цили́ндр *m* [1] cylinder; **~и́ческий** [16] cylindrical

цинга́ *f* [5] *med.* scurvy

цини́|зм *m* [1] cynicism; **´~к** *m* [1] cynic; **~чный** [14; -чен, -чна] cynical

цинк *m* [1] zinc; **~овый** [14] zinc...

цино́вка *f* [5; *g/pl.*: -вок] mat

цирк *m* [1], **~ово́й** [14] circus

циркул|и́ровать [7] circulate; **´~ь** *m* [4] (a pair of) compasses *pl.*; **~я́р** *m* [1] (official) instruction

цисте́рна *f* [5] cistern, tank

цитаде́ль (-'dɛ-) *f* [8] citadel; *fig.* bulwark; stronghold

цита́та *f* [5] quotation

цити́ровать [7], <про-> quote

ци́трусовые [14] citrus (trees)

циф|ербла́т *m* [1] dial; ***часо́в*** face; **~ра** *f* [5] figure; number

цо́коль *m* [4] *arch.* socle; *el.* screw base (*of light bulb*)

цыга́н *m* [1; *nom./pl.*: -е & -ы; *gen.*: цыга́н], **~ка** *f* [5; *g/pl.*: -нок], **~ский** [16] Gypsy, *Brt.* Gipsy

цыплёнок *m* [2] chicken

цы́почк|и: ***на ~ах*** (***~и***) on tiptoe

Ц

Ч

чад *m* [1; в -ý] fume(s); *fig.* daze; intoxication; **~и́ть** [15 *e.*; чажý, чади́шь], <на-> smoke

ча́до *n* [9] *obs. or joc.* child

чаевы́е *pl.* [14] tip, gratuity

чай *m* [3; *part.g.*: -ю; в -е & -ю́; *pl. e.*: чаи́, чаёв] tea; ***дать на ~*** tip

ча́йка [5; *g/pl.*: ча́ек] (sea) gull

ча́йн|ик *m* [1] *для зава́рки* teapot; teakettle; **~ый** [14] *ло́жка и т. д.* tea

чалма́ *f* [5] turban

чан *m* [1; *pl. e.*] tub, vat

ча́р|ка *f* [5; *g/pl.*: -рок] *old use* cup, goblet; **~ова́ть** [20] charm; **~оде́й** *m* [3] magician, wizard (*a. fig.*)

час *m* [1; в -е & -ý; *after* 2, 3, 4: -á; *pl. e.*] hour (for *pl.* ***~а́ми***); (one) o'clock (at ***в*** B); time, moment (at ***в*** B); an hour's...; ***второ́й ~*** (it is) past one; ***в пя́том ~ý*** between four and five; (→ ***пять*** & ***пя́тый***); ***кото́рый ~?*** what's the time?; ***с ~у на ~*** soon; ***~ от ~у не ле́гче*** things are getting worse and worse; **~о́вня** *f* [6; *g/pl.*: -вен] chapel; **~ово́й** [14] hour's; watch..., clock...; *su.* sentry, guard; ***~ово́й по́яс*** time zone; ***~ово́й ма́стер*** = **~овщи́к** *m* [1 *e.*] watchmaker

част|и́ца *f* [5] particle; **~и́чный** [14; -чен, -чна] partial; **~ник** *coll.* private trader; owner of a small business; **~ное** *n* [14] *math.* quotient; **~ность** *f* [8] detail; **~ный** [14] private; particular, individual; ***~ная со́бственность*** private property; **~ота́** *f* [5; *pl. st.*: -о́ты] frequency; **~у́шка** *f* [5; *g/pl.*: -шек] humorous or topical two- or four-lined verse; **~ый** [14; част, -á, -о; *comp.*: ча́ще] frequent (*adv. a.* often); *густо́й* thick, dense; *стежки́ и т. д.* close; *пульс и т. д.* quick, rapid; **~ь** *f* [8; *from g/pl. e.*] part (in T; *pl. a.* ***по*** Д); (*до́ля*) share; piece; section; *mil.* unit; ***бо́льшей ~ью***, ***по бо́льшей ~и*** for the most part, mostly; ***разобра́ть на ~и*** take to pieces

час|ы́ *no sg.* [1] *ручны́е* watch; clock; ***по мои́м ~а́м*** by my watch

ча́х|лый [14 *sh.*] sickly; *расти́тельность* stunted; **~нуть** [21], <за-> wither away; *о челове́ке* become weak, waste away

ча́ш|а *f* [5] cup, bowl; *eccl.* chalice; **~ечка** *f* [5] *dim.* → **ча́шка**: ***коле́нная ~ечка*** kneecap; **~ка** *f* [5; *g/pl.*: -шек] cup; *весо́в* pan

ча́ща *f* [5] thicket

ча́ще more (***~ всего́*** most) often

ча́яние *n* [12] expectation, aspiration

чей *m*, **чья** *f*, **чьё** *n*, **чьи** *pl.* [26] whose; ***~ э́то дом?*** whose house is this?

чек *m* [1] check, *Brt.* cheque; *для опла́ты* chit, bill; *опла́ченный* receipt; **~а́нить** [13], <вы́-> mint, coin; *узо́р* chase; **~а́нка** *f* [5; *g/pl.*: -нок] minting, coinage; chasing; **~и́ст** *m* [1] (state) security officer; *hist.* member of the cheka; **~овый** [14] check...

челно́|к *m* [1 *e.*], **~чный** [14] shuttle

чело́ *n* [9; *pl. st.*] *obs.* brow

челове́|к *m* [1; *pl.*: лю́ди; 5, 6, *etc.* -е́к] man, human being; person, individual; ***ру́сский ~к*** Russian; **~колю́бие** *n* [12] philanthropy; **~ческий** [16] human(e); **~чество** *n* [9] mankind, humanity; **~чный** [14; -чен, -чна] humane

че́люсть *f* [8] jaw; (full) denture

чем than; rather than, instead of; ***~ ..., тем ...*** the more ... the more ...; ***~ скоре́е, тем лу́чше*** the sooner, the better; **~ода́н** *m* [1] suitcase

чемпио́н *m* [1] champion; **~а́т** *m* [1] championship

чепуха́ *f* [5] *coll.* nonsense; (*ме́лочь*) trifle

че́пчик *m* [1] baby's bonnet

че́рв|и *f/pl.* [4; *from gen. e.*] & **~ы** *f/pl.* [5] hearts (*cards*)

черви́вый [14 *sh.*] worm-eaten

черво́нец *m* [1; -нца] *hist.* (*gold coin*) chervonets; (*ten-r(o)uble bank note in circulation 1922–47*)

черв|ь [4 *e.*; *nom/pl. st.*: че́рви, черве́й], **~я́к** *m* [1 *e.*] worm
черда́к *m* [1 *e.*] garret, attic, loft
черёд *coll. m* [1 *e.*] (*о́чередь*) turn; (*поря́док*) course
чередова́|ние *n* [12] alternation; **~ть(ся)** [7] alternate (with)
че́рез (В) through; *у́лицу* across, over; *вре́мя* in, after; *е́хать* via; **~** *день a.* every other day
черёмуха *f* [5] bird cherry
че́реп *m* [1; *pl.*: -á, *etc. e.*] skull
черепа́|ха *f* [5] tortoise; *морска́я* turtle; **~ховый** [14] tortoise(shell)...; **~ший** [18] tortoise's, snail's
череп|и́ца *f* [5] tile (*of roof*); **~и́чный** [14] tiled; **~о́к** [1; -пка́] fragment, piece
чере|счу́р too, too much; **~́шня** *f* [6; *g/pl.*: -шен] (sweet) cherry, cherry tree
черкну́ть *coll.* [20] *pf.*: scribble; dash off; **~** ***па́ру*** (*or* ***не́сколько***) ***слов*** drop a line
черн|е́ть [8], <по-> blacken, grow black; *impf.* show up black; **~и́ка** *f* [5] bilberry, -ries *pl.*; **~и́ла** *n/pl.* [9] ink; **~и́ть** [13], <о-> *fig.* blacken, denigrate, slander
черно|ви́к *m* [1 *e.*] rough copy; draft; **~во́й** [14] draft...; rough; **~воло́сый** [14 *sh.*] black-haired; **~гла́зый** [14 *sh.*] black-eyed; **~зём** *m* [1] chernozem, black earth; **~ко́жий** [17 *sh.*] black; *as su.* [-его́] *m* black (man), negro; **~мо́рский** [16] Black Sea...; **~сли́в** *m* [1] prune(s); **~та́** *f* [5] blackness
чёрн|ый [14; чёрен, черна́] black (*a. fig.*); *хлеб* brown; *мета́лл* ferrous; *рабо́та* rough; *ход* back; ***на ~ый день*** for a rainy day; ***~ым по бе́лому*** in black and white
чернь *f* [8] *art* niello
че́рп|ать [1], <~ну́ть> [20] scoop, ladle; *зна́ния, си́лы* derive, draw (from ***из*** Р, ***в*** П)
черстве́ть [8], <за-, по-> grow stale; *fig.* harden
чёрствый [14; чёрств, -á, -о] stale, hard; *fig.* callous
чёрт *m* [1; *pl.* 4: че́рти, -те́й, *etc. e.*] devil; *coll.* **~** ***побери́*** the devil take it; ***на кой ~*** *coll.* what the deuce; ***ни черта́*** *coll.* nothing at all; ***~а с два!*** like hell!
черт|а́ *f* [5] line; trait, feature (*a.* ***~ы́ лица́***); ***в ~е́ го́рода*** within the city boundary
чертёж *m* [1 *e.*] drawing, draft (*Brt.* draught), design; **~ник** *m* [1] draftsman, *Brt.* draughtsman; **~ный** [14] *доска́ и т. д.* drawing (*board, etc.*)
черт|и́ть [15], <на-> draw, design; **~о́вский** [16] *coll.* devilish
чёрточка *f* [5; *g/pl.*: -чек] hyphen
черче́ние *n* [12] drawing
чеса́ть [3] **1.** <по-> scratch; **2.** <при-> *coll.* comb; **-ся** itch
чесно́к *m* [1 *e.*] garlic
чесо́тка *f* [5] scab, rash, mange
че́ст|вование *n* [12] celebration; **~вовать** [7] celebrate, hono(u)r; **~ность** *f* [8] honesty; **~ный** [14; че́стен, -тна́, -о] honest, upright; (*справедли́вый*) fair; **~олюби́вый** [14 *sh.*] ambitious; **~олю́бие** *n* [12] ambition; **~ь** *f* [8] hono(u)r (in ***в*** В); credit; ***э́то де́лает вам ~ь*** it does you credit; *coll.* ***~ь ~ью*** properly, well
чета́ *f* [5] couple, pair; match; ***она́ ему́ не ~*** she is no match for him
четве́р|г *m* [1 *e.*] Thursday (on ***в*** В, *pl.*: ***по*** Д); **~е́ньки** *coll. f/pl.* [5] all fours (on ***на*** В, П); **~ка** *f* [5; *g/pl.*: -рок] four (→ ***тро́йка***); *coll.* (*mark*) → ***хорошо́***; **~́о** [37] four (→ ***дво́е***); **~тый** (-'vɔr-) [14] fourth → ***пя́тый***; **~́ть** *f* [8; *from g/pl. e.*] (one) fourth; *шко́льная* (school-)term; quarter (to ***без*** Р; past one ***второ́го***)
чёткий [16; чёток, четка́, -о] precise; clear; *по́черк* legible; (*то́чный*) exact, accurate
чётный [14] even (*of numbers*)
четы́ре [34] four; → ***пять***; **~жды** four times; **~ста** [36] four hundred
четырёх|ле́тний [15] of four years; four-year; **~ме́стный** [14] four-seater; **~со́тый** [14] four hundredth; **~уго́льник** *m* [1] quadrangle; **~уго́льный** [14] quadrangular
четы́рнадца|тый [14] fourteenth; → ***пя́тый***; **~ть** [35] fourteen; → ***пять***
чех *m* [1] Czech

чехарда́ *f* [5] leapfrog; ***министе́рская ~*** frequent changes in personnel (*esp. in government appointments*)

чехо́л *m* [1; -хла́] case, cover

чечеви́ца *f* [5] lentil(s)

че́ш|ка *f* [5; *g/pl.*: -шек] Czech (woman); **~ский** [16] Czech

чешуя́ *f* [6] *zo.* scales *pl.*

чи́бис *m* [1] *zo.* lapwing

чиж *m* [1 *e.*], *coll.* **~и́к** *m* [1] *zo.* siskin

чин *m* [1; *pl. e.*] *mil.* rank

чин|и́ть [13; чиню́, чи́нишь] a) <по-> mend, repair; b) <о-> *каранда́ш* sharpen, point; ***~и́ть препя́тствие*** (Д) obstruct, impede; **~ный** [14; чи́нен, чинна́, чи́нно] proper; sedate; **~о́вник** *m* [1] official, functionary

чири́к|ать [1], <~нуть> [20] chirp

чи́рк|ать [1], <~нуть> [20] strike

чи́сл|енность *f* [8] number; **~енный** [14] numerical; **~и́тель** *m* [4] *math.* numerator; **~и́тельное** *n* [14] *gr.* numeral (*a.* ***и́мя ~и́тельное***); **~иться** [13] be *or* be reckoned (**в** П *or* **по** Д/Р); **~о́** *n* [9; *pl. st.*: чи́сла, чи́сел, чи́слам] number; date, day; ***како́е сего́дня ~о́?*** what is the date today? (→ ***пя́тый***); **в ~е́** (Р) among, **в том ~е́** including

чи́ст|ить [15] **1.** <по-, вы́-> clean(se); brush; *о́бувь* polish; **2.** <о-> peel; **~ка** [5; *g/pl.*: -ток] clean(s)ing; *pol.* purge; **~окро́вный** [14; -вен, -вна] thoroughbred; **~оплóтный** [14; -тен, -тна] cleanly; *fig.* clean, decent; **~осерде́чный** [14; -чен, -чна] openhearted, frank, sincere; **~ота́** *f* [5] clean(li-)ness; purity; **~ый** [14; чист, -а́, -о; *comp.*: чи́ще] clean; *зо́лото и т. д.* pure; *спирт* neat; *не́бо* clear; *вес* net; *лист* blank; *рабо́та* fine, faultless; *пра́вда* plain; *случа́йность* mere

чита́|льный [14]: ***~льный зал*** reading room; **~тель** *m* [4] reader; **~ть** [1], <про-> & *coll.* <проче́сть> [25; -чту́, -чтёшь; чёл, -чла́; -чтённый] read, recite; give (*lecture* on **о** П), deliver; ***~ть мора́ль*** lecture

чи́тка *f* [5; *g/pl.*: -ток] reading (*usu. by a group*)

чих|а́ть [1], *once* <~нуть> [20] sneeze

член *m* [1] member; (*коне́чность*) limb; part; **~oраздéльный** [14; -лен, -льна] articulate; **~ский** [16] member(ship)...; **~ство** *n* [9] membership

чмо́к|ать *coll.* [1], *once* <~нуть> [20] smack; (*поцелова́ть*) give s.o. a smacking kiss

чо́к|аться [1], *once* <~нуться> [20] clink (glasses Т) (with **с** Т)

чо́|порный [14; -рен, -рна] prim, stiff; **~рт** → ***чёрт***

чрев|а́тый [14 *sh.*] fraught (with Т); **~о** [9] womb

чрез → ***че́рез***

чрез|выча́йный [14; -а́ен, -а́йна] extraordinary; extreme; special; ***~выча́йное положе́ние*** state of emergency; **~ме́рный** [14; -рен, -рна] excessive

чте́|ние *n* [12] reading; *худо́жественное* recital; **~ц** *m* [1 *e.*] reader

чтить → ***почита́ть***[1]

что [23] **1.** *pron.* what (*a.* **~ *за***); that, which; how; (*a.* **а ~?**) why (so?); (*a.* **а ~**) what about; what's the matter; *coll.* **а ~?** well?; **вот ~** the following; listen; that's it; **~ *до меня́*** as for me; **~ *вы*** (***ты***)! you don't say!, what next!; ***не́ за ~*** (you are) welcome, *Brt.* don't mention it; ***ни за ~*** not for the world; ***ну и ~?*** what of that; (***уж***) ***на ~*** *coll.* however; **с чего́ бы э́то?** *coll.* why? why ...?; **~ *и говори́ть*** *coll.* sure; → **ни**; *coll.* → **~нибудь**, **~-то**; **2.** *cj.* that; like, as if; **~** (***ни***) **...**, **то ...** every ... (a) ...

что́б(ы) (in order) that *or* to (*a.* ***с тем, ~***); **~ *не*** lest, for fear that; ***вме́сто того́ ~*** + *inf.* instead of ...ing; ***скажи́ ему́, ~ он*** + *pt.* tell him to *inf.*

что́|-либо, **~-нибудь**, **~-то** [23] something; anything; ***~-то*** *a. coll.* somewhat; somehow, for some reason or other

чу́вств|енный [14 *sh.*] sensuous; (*плóтский*) sensual; **~и́тельность** *f* [8] sensibility; **~и́тельный** [14; -лен, -льна] sensitive; sentimental; sensible (*a.* = considerable, great, strong); **~о** *n* [9] sense; feeling; sensation; *coll.* love; **óрганы ~** organs of sense; **~овать** [7], <по-> feel (*a.* **себя́** [T s.th.]); **-ся** be felt

чугу́н *m* [1 *e.*] cast iron; **~ный** [14] cast-iron...

чуд|а́к *m* [1 *e.*] crank, eccentric; **~а́чество** *n* [9] eccentricity; **~е́сный** [14; -сен, -сна] wonderful, marvel(l)ous; *спасе́ние* miraculous; **~и́ть** [15 *e.*] *coll.* → **дури́ть**; **~иться** [15] *coll.* → **мере́щиться**; **~ный** [14; -ден, -дна] wonderful, marvel(l)ous; **~о** *n* [9; *pl.*: чудеса́, -е́с, -еса́м] miracle, marvel; wonder; *a.* → **~но**; **~о́вище** *n* [11] monster; **~о́вищный** [14; -щен, -щна] monstrous; *поте́ри и т. д.* enormous

чуж|би́на *f* [5] foreign country (in **на** П; *a.* abroad); **~да́ться** [1] (Р) shun, avoid; **~дый** [14; чужд, -а́, -о] foreign; alien; free (from Р); **~о́й** [14] someone else's, others'; alien; strange, foreign; *su. a.* stranger, outsider

чул|а́н *m* [1] storeroom, larder; **~о́к** *m* [1; -лка́; *g/pl.*: -ло́к] stocking

чума́ *f* [5] plague

чурба́н *m* [1] block; *fig.* blockhead

чу́тк|ий [16; -ток, -тка́, -о; *comp.*: чу́тче] sensitive (to **на** В), keen; *сон* light; *слух* quick (of hearing); *челове́к* sympathetic; **~ость** *f* [8] keenness; delicacy (of feeling)

чу́точку *coll.* a wee bit

чуть hardly, scarcely; a little; **~ не** nearly, almost; **~ ли не** *coll.* almost, all but; **~ что** *coll.* on the slightest pretext; **чуть-чуть** → **чуть**

чутьё *n* [10] instinct (for **на** В); flair

чу́чело *n* [9] stuffed animal; **~ горо́ховое** scarecrow; *coll.* dolt

чушь *coll. f* [8] bosh, twaddle

чу́ять [27], <по-> scent, *fig.* feel

Ш

шаба́шник *m* [1] *coll. pej.* moonlighter

шабло́н *m* [1] stencil, pattern, cliché; **~ный** [14] trite, hackneyed

шаг *m* [1; *after* 2, 3, 4: -а́; в -у́; *pl. e.*] step (by step **~ за** Т) (*a. fig.*); *большо́й* stride; *звук* footsteps; *tech.* pitch; **приба́вить ~у** quicken one's pace; **ни ~у** (**да́льше**) not a step futher; **на ка́ждом ~у́** everywhere, at every turn, continually; **~а́ть** [1], *once* <~ну́ть> [20] step, stride; walk; pace; (*че́рез*) cross; *pf.* take a step; **далеко́ ~ну́ть** *fig.* make great progress; **~а́ть взад и вперёд** pace back and forth

ша́йба *f* [5] *tech.* washer; *sport* puck

ша́йка *f* [5; *g/pl.*: ша́ек] gang

шака́л *m* [1] jackal

шала́ш *m* [1] hut

шал|и́ть [13] be naughty, frolic, romp; fool (about), play (pranks); **~и́шь!** *coll.* (*rebuke*) don't try that on me!; none of your tricks!; **~ovли́вый** [14 *sh.*] mischievous, playful; **~опа́й** *coll. m* [3] loafer; **~ость** *f* [8] prank; **~у́н** *m* [1 *e.*] naughty boy; **~у́нья** *f* [6; *g/pl.*: -ний] naughty girl

шалфе́й *m* [3] *bot.* sage

шаль *f* [8] shawl

шальн|о́й [14] mad, crazy; *пу́ля* stray...; **~ы́е де́ньги** easy money

ша́мкать [1] mumble

шампа́нское *n* [16] champagne

шампиньо́н *m* [1] field mushroom

шампу́нь *m* [4] shampoo

шанс *m* [1] chance, prospect (of **на** В)

шанта́ж *m* [1], **~и́ровать** [7] blackmail

ша́пка *f* [5; *g/pl.*: -пок] cap; *typ.* banner headlines

шар *m* [1; *after* 2, 3, 4: -а́; *pl. e.*] sphere; ball; **возду́шный ~** balloon; **земно́й ~** globe

шара́х|аться *coll.* [1], <∼нуться> [20] dash, jump (aside), recoil; *о ло́шади* shy

шарж *m* [1] cartoon, caricature; ***дру́жеский*** **∼** harmless, well-meant caricature

ша́рик *m* [1] *dim.* → ***шар***; **∼овый** [14] → ***ру́чка***; **∼оподши́пник** *m* [1] ball bearing

ша́рить [13], <по-> *в чём-л.* rummage; grope about, feel

ша́р|кать [1], *once* <∼кнуть> [20] shuffle

шарни́р *m* [1] *tech.* hinge, joint

шаро|ва́ры *f/pl.* [5] baggy trousers; **∼ви́дный** [14; -ден, -дна] **∼обра́зный** [14; -зен, -зна] spherical, globe-shaped

шарф *m* [1] scarf, neckerchief

шасси́ *n* [*indecl.*] chassis; *ae.* undercarriage

шат|а́ть [1], *once* <(по)шатну́ть> [20] shake; rock; **-ся** *о зу́бе и т. д.* be loose; *о челове́ке* stagger, reel, totter; *coll.* *без де́ла* lounge *or* loaf, gad about

шатёр *m* [1; -тра́] tent, marquee

ша́т|кий [16; -ток, -тка] shaky, unsteady (*a. fig.*); *ме́бель* rickety; *fig. friend, etc.* unreliable; fickle; **∼ну́ть (-ся)** → **∼а́ть(ся)**

шах *m* [1] shah; check (*chess*)

шахмат|и́ст *m* [1] chess player; **∼ный** [14] chess...; **´∼ы** *f/pl.* [5] chess; ***игра́ть в ´∼ы*** play chess; chessmen

ша́хт|а *f* [5] mine, pit; *tech.* shaft; **∼ёр** *m* [1] miner; **∼ёрский** [16] miner's

ша́шка[1] *f* [5; *g/pl.*: -шек] saber, *Brt.* sabre

ша́шка[2] *f* [5; *g/pl.*: -шек] checker, draughtsman; *pl.* checkers, *Brt.* draughts

шашлы́к *m* [1] shashlik, kebab

швартова́ться [7], <при-> *naut.* moor, make fast

швед *m* [1], **∼ка** *f* [5; *g/pl.*: -док] Swede; **∼ский** [16] Swedish

шве́йн|ый [14] sewing; ***∼ая маши́на*** sewing machine

швейца́р *m* [1] doorman, doorkeeper, porter

швейца́р|ец *m* [1; -рца], **∼ка** *f* [5; *g/pl.*: -рок] Swiss; **♀ия** [7] Switzerland; **∼ский** [16] Swiss

швыр|я́ть [28], *once* <∼ну́ть> [20] hurl, fling (*a.* Т)

шеве|ли́ть [13; -елю́, -е́ли́шь], <по->, *once* <(по)∼льну́ть> [20] stir, move (*v/i.* **-ся**); ***∼ли́ть мозга́ми*** *coll.* use one's wits

шевелю́ра *f* [5] (head of) hair

шеде́вр (-'dɛvr) *m* [1] masterpiece, chef d'œuvre

ше́йка *f* [5; *g/pl.*: ше́ек] neck

ше́лест *m* [1], **∼е́ть** [11] rustle

шёлк *m* [1; *g/sg. a.* -у; в шелку́; *pl.*: шелка́, *etc. e.*] silk

шелкови́|стый [14 *sh.*] silky; **∼ца** *f* [5] mulberry (tree)

шёлковый [14] silk(en); ***как*** **∼** meek as a lamb

шел|охну́ться [20] *pf.* stir; **∼уха́** *f* [5], **∼уши́ть** [16 *e.*; -шу́, -ши́шь] peel, husk; **-ся** *о ко́же* peel

шельмова́ть [7], <о-> *hist.* punish publicly; *coll.* defame, charge falsely

шепеля́в|ить [14] lisp; **∼ый** [14 *sh.*] lisping

шёпот *m* [1] whisper (in a Т)

шеп|та́ть [3], <про->, *once* <∼ну́ть> [20] whisper (*v/i. a.* **-ся**)

шере́нга *f* [5] file, rank

шерохова́тый [14 *sh.*] rough, *fig.* uneven, rugged

шерст|ь *f* [8; *from g/pl. e.*] wool; *живо́тного* coat; *овцы́* fleece; **∼яно́й** [14] wool([l]en)

шерша́вый [14 *sh.*] rough

шест *m* [1 *e.*] pole

ше́ств|ие *n* [12] procession; **∼овать** [7] stride, walk (*as in a procession*)

шест|ёрка *f* [5; *g/pl.*: -рок] six (→ ***тро́йка***); six-oar boat; **∼ерня́** *f* [6; *g/pl.*: -рён] *tech.* pinion; cogwheel; **∼еро** [37] six (→ ***дво́е***); **∼идеся́тый** [14] sixtieth; → ***пя́т(идеся́т)ый***; **∼име́сячный** [14] of six months; six-month; **∼исо́тый** [14] six hundredth; **∼иуго́льник** *m* [1] hexagon; **∼на́дцатый** [14] sixteenth; → ***пя́тый***; **∼на́дцать** [35] sixteen; → ***пять***; **∼о́й** [14] sixth; → ***пя́тый***; **∼ь** [35 *e.*] six; → ***пять***; **∼ьдеся́т** [35] sixty; **∼ьсо́т** [36] six hundred; **∼ью** six times

шеф *m* [1] chief, head; *coll.* boss

ше́я *f* [6; *g/pl.*: -шей] neck

ши́ворот: ***взять за ~*** seize by the collar

шик|а́рный [14; -рен, -рна] chic, smart; **~а́ть** *coll.* [1], *once* <~ну́ть> [20] shush, hush, urge to be quiet

ши́ло *n* [1; *pl.*: -лья, -льев] awl

ши́на *f* [5] tire, *Brt.* tyre; *med.* splint

шине́ль *f* [8] greatcoat

шинкова́ть [7] chop, shred

шип *m* [1 *e.*] thorn; *на о́буви* spike

шипе́|ние *n* [12] hiss(ing); **~ть** [10], <про-> hiss; *о ко́шке* spit; *на сковороде́* sizzle

шипо́вник *m* [1] *bot.* dogrose

шип|у́чий [17 *sh.*] sparkling, fizzy; **~у́чка** *f* [5; *g/pl.*: -чек] *coll.* fizzy drink; **~я́щий** [17] sibilant

шири|на́ *f* [5] width, breadth; ***~но́й в*** (В) *or* **... в ~ну́** ... wide; **´~ть** [13] (**-ся**) widen, expand

шири́нка *f* [5; *g/pl.*: -нок] fly (of trousers)

ши́рма *f* [5] (*mst. pl.*) screen

широ́к|ий [16; широ́к, -ока́, -о́ко́; *comp.*: ши́ре] broad; wide; vast; great; mass...; *наступле́ние и т. д.* large-scale; ***на ~ую но́гу*** in grand style; **~омасшта́бный** [14; -бен, -бна] large-scale; **~опле́чий** [17 *sh.*] broad-shouldered

шир|ота́ *f* [5; *pl. st.*: -о́ты] breadth; *geogr.* latitude; **~потре́б** *coll. m* [1] consumer goods; **~ь** *f* [8] expanse width; extent

шить [шью, шьёшь; ше́й(те)!; ши́тый], <с-> [сошью, -ьёшь, сши́тый] sew (*pf. a.* together); (*вы́шить*) embroider; себе́ have made; **~ё** *n* [10] sewing; needlework; embroidery

ши́фер *m* [1] (roofing) slate

шифр *m* [1] cipher, code; *библиоте́чный* pressmark (*chiefly Brt.*); **~ова́ть** [7], <за-> encipher, encode

шиш *coll. m* [1 *e.*]: ***ни ~а́*** damn all

ши́шка *f* [5; *g/pl.*: -шек] *на голове́* bump, lump; *bot.* cone; *coll.* bigwig

шка|ла́ *f* [5; *pl. st.*] scale; **~ту́лка** *f* [5; *g/pl.*: -лок] casket; **~ф** *m* [1; в -у́; *pl. e.*] cupboard; *платяно́й* wardrobe; ***книжный ~ф*** bookcase

шквал *m* [1] squall, gust

шкив *m* [1] *tech.* pulley

шко́л|а *f* [5] school (*go* to **в** В; *be* at, in **в** П); ***вы́сшая ~а*** higher education establishment(s); ***~а-интерна́т*** boarding school; **~ьник** *m* [1] schoolboy; **~ьница** *f* [5] schoolgirl; **~ьный** [14] school...

шку́р|а *f* [5] skin (*a.* **~ка** *f* [5; *g/pl.*: -рок]), hide

шлагба́ум *m* [1] barrier (*at road or rail crossing*)

шлак *m* [1] slag

шланг *m* [1] hose

шлем *m* [1] helmet

шлёпать [1], *once* <~нуть> [20] slap, spank (*v/i. coll.* **-ся** fall with a plop); plump down

шлифова́ть [7], <от-> grind; (*полирова́ть*) polish

шлю|з *m* [1] sluice, lock; **~пка** *f* [5; *g/pl.*: -пок] launch, boat; *спаса́тельная* lifeboat

шля́п|а *f* [5] hat; **~ка** *f* [5; *g/pl.*: -пок] *dim.* → **~а** hat; *гвоздя́* head

шля́ться *coll.* [1] → ***шата́ться***

шмель *m* [4 *e.*] bumblebee

шмы́гать *coll.* [1], *once* <~ну́ть> [20] whisk, scurry, dart; *но́сом* sniff

шни́цель *m* [4] cutlet, schnitzel

шнур *m* [1 *e.*] cord; **~ова́ть** [7], <за-> lace up; **~о́к** *m* [1; -рка́] shoestring, (shoe) lace

шныря́ть *coll.* [28] dart about

шов *m* [1; шва] seam; *tech.* joint; *в вы́шивке* stitch (*a. med.*)

шок *m* [1], **~и́ровать** [7] shock

шокола́д *m* [1] chocolate

шо́рох *m* [1] rustle

шо́рты *no sg.* [1] shorts

шоссе́ *n* [*indecl.*] highway

шотла́нд|ец *m* [1; -дца] Scotsman, *pl.* the Scots; **~ка** *f* [5; *g/pl.*: -док] Scotswoman; **~ский** [16] Scottish

шофёр *m* [1] driver, chauffeur

шпа́га *f* [5] *sport* épée; sword

шпага́т *m* [1] cord, string; *gymnastics* split(s)

шпа́л|а *rail. f* [5] cross tie, *Brt.* sleeper; **~е́ра** *f* [5] *для виногра́да и т. д.* trellis

шпарга́лка *coll. f* [5; *g/pl.*: -лок] pony, *Brt.* crib (*in school*)

шпигова́ть [7], <на-> lard

шпик *m* [1] lard; fatback; *coll.* secret agent

шпиль *m* [4] spire, steeple
шпи́|лька *f* [5; *g/pl.*: -лек] hairpin; hat pin; tack; *fig.* taunt, caustic remark, (*v/b.*: ***подпусти́ть*** B); **~на́т** *m* [1] spinach
шпио́н *m* [1], **~ка** *f* [5; *g/pl.*: -нок] spy; **~а́ж** *m* [1] espionage; **~ить** [13] spy
шприц *m* [1] syringe
шпро́ты *m* [1] sprats
шпу́лька *f* [5; *g/pl.*: -лек] spool, bobbin
шрам *m* [1] scar
шрифт *m* [1] type, typeface; script
штаб *m* [1] *mil.* staff; headquarters
шта́бель *m* [4; *pl.*: -ля́, *etc. e.*] pile
штамп *m* [1], **~ова́ть** [7], <от-> stamp, impress
шта́нга *f* [5] *sport*: weight; (*пере-кла́дина*) crossbar
штаны́ *coll. m/pl.* [1 *e.*] trousers
штат[1] *m* [1] state (*administrative unit*)
штат[2] *m* [1] staff; **~ный** [14] (on the) staff; **~ский** [16] civilian; *оде́жда* plain
штемпел|ева́ть ('ʃtɛ-) [6], **´~ь** *m* [4; *pl.*: -ля́, *etc. e.*] stamp; postmark
ште́псель ('ʃtɛ-) *m* [4; *pl.*: -ля́, *etc. e.*] plug; **~ный** [14]: ***~ная розе́тка*** socket
штиль *m* [4] *naut.* calm
штифт *m* [1 *e.*] *tech.* joining pin, dowel
што́п|ать [1], <за-> darn, mend; **~ка** *f* [5] darning, mending
што́пор *m* [1] corkscrew; *ae.* spin
што́ра *f* [5] blind; curtain
шторм *m* [1] *naut.* gale; storm
штраф *m* [1] fine; ***наложи́ть ~*** impose a fine; **~но́й** [14] *sport* penalty...; **~ова́ть** [7], <о-> fine
штрейкбре́хер *m* [1] strikebreaker
штрих *m* [1 *e.*] stroke (*in drawing*), hachure; *fig.* trait; ***доба́вить не́сколько ~ов*** add a few touches; **~ова́ть** [7], <за-> shade, hatch
штуди́ровать [7], <про-> study
шту́ка *f* [5] item; piece; *coll.* thing; (*вы́ходка*) trick
штукату́р|ить [13], <о->, **~ка** *f* [5] plaster
штурва́л *m* [1] *naut.* steering wheel
штурм *m* [1] storm, onslaught
шту́рм|ан *m* [1] navigator; **~ова́ть** [7] storm, assail; **~ови́к** *m* [1 *e.*] combat aircraft
шту́чный [14] (by the) piece (*not by weight*)
штык *m* [1 *e.*] bayonet
шу́ба *f* [5] fur (coat)
шум *m* [1] noise; din; *воды́* rush; *ли́стьев* rustle; *маши́ны, в уша́х* buzz; *coll.* hubbub, row, ado; ***~ и гам*** hullabaloo; ***наде́лать ~у*** cause a sensation; **~е́ть** [10 *e.*; шумлю́, шуми́шь] make a noise; rustle; rush; roar; buzz; **~и́ха** *coll. f* [5] sensation, clamo(u)r; **~ный** [14; -мен, -мна́, -о] noisy, loud; sensational; **~о́вка** *f* [5; *g/pl.*: -вок] skimmer; **~о́к** [1; -мка́]: ***под ~о́к*** *coll.* on the sly
шу́р|ин *m* [1] brother-in-law (*wife's brother*); **~ша́ть** [4 *e.*; -шу́, -ши́шь], <за-> rustle
шу́стрый *coll.* [14; -тёр, -тра́, -о] nimble
шут *m* [1 *e.*] fool, jester; *горо́ховый* clown, buffoon; *coll.* ***~ его́ зна́ет*** deuce knews; **~и́ть** [15], <по-> joke, jest; make fun (of ***над*** T); **~ка** *f* [5; *g/pl.*: -ток] joke, jest (in ***в*** B); fun (for ***ра́ди*** P); *coll.* trifle (it's no ***~ка ли***); ***кро́ме ~ок*** joking apart; are you in earnest?; ***не на ~ку*** serious(ly); (Д) ***не до ~ок*** be in no laughing mood; **~ли́вый** *coll.* [14 *sh.*] jocose, playful; **~ни́к** *m* [1 *e.*] joker, wag; **~очный** [14] joking, sportive, comic; *де́ло* laughing; **~я́** jokingly (***не*** in earnest)
шушу́кать(ся) *coll.* [1] whisper
шху́на *f* [5] schooner
ш-ш shush!

Щ

щаве́ль *m* [4 *e.*] *bot.* sorrel

щади́ть [15 *e.*; щажу́, щади́шь], <по-> [-щажённый] spare; have mercy (on)

щё́бень *m* [4; -бня] broken stone or cinders; road metal

щебета́ть [3] chirp, twitter

щего́л *m* [1; -гла́] goldfinch

щегол|ева́тый [14 *sh.*] foppish, dandified; **́~ь** *m* [4] dandy, fop; **~я́ть** [28] overdress; give exaggerated attention to fashion; *coll.* flaunt, parade, show off

ще́др|ость *f* [8] generosity; **~ый** [14; щедр, -á, -о] liberal, generous

щека́ [5; *ac/sg.*: щёку; *pl.*: щёки, щёк, щека́м, *etc. e.*] cheek

щеко́лда *f* [5] latch

щекот|а́ть [3], <по->, **~́ка** *f* [5] tickle; **~ли́вый** [14 *sh.*] ticklish, delicate

щёлк|ать [1], *once* <~нуть> [20] **1.** *языко́м и т. д. v/i.* click (T), *па́льцами* snap; *кнуто́м* crack; *зуба́ми* chatter; *пти́ца* warble, sing; **2.** *v/t.* flick, fillip (on ***по́ лбу***); *оре́хи* crack

щёло|чь *f* [8; *from g/pl. e.*] alkali; **~чно́й** [14] alkaline

щелчо́к *m* [1; -чка́] flick, fillip; crack

щель *f* [8; *from g/pl. e.*] chink, crack, crevice; slit

щеми́ть [14 *e.*; *3rd p. only*, *a. impers.*] *о се́рдце* ache

щено́к *m* [1; -нка́; *pl.*: -нки́ & (2) -ня́та] puppy; *ди́кого живо́тного* whelp

щеп|ети́льный [14; -лен, -льна] scrupulous, punctilious; fussy, finicky; **~́ка** *f* [5; *g/pl.*: -пок] chip; ***худо́й как ~́ка*** thin as a rake

щепо́тка *f* [5; *g/pl.*: -ток] pinch (*of salt, ect.*)

щети́н|а *f* [5] bristle(s); *coll.* stubble; **~иться** [13], <о-> bristle

щётка *f* [5; *g/pl.*: -ток] brush

щи *f/pl.* [5; *gen.*: -щей] shchi (cabbage soup)

щи́колотка *f* [5; *g/pl.*: -ток] ankle

щип|а́ть [2], *once* <(у)~ну́ть> [20], pinch, tweak (*v/t.* ***за*** В), (*тж. от моро́за*) nip, bite; <об-> pluck; *траву́* browse; **~цы́** *m/pl.* [1 *e.*] tongs, pliers, pincers, nippers; *med.* forceps; (nut)crackers; **~́чики** *m/pl.* [1] tweezers

щит *m* [1 *e.*] shield; ***распредели́тельный ~*** switchboard

щитови́дный [14] *железа́* thyroid

щу́ка *f* [5] *zo.* pike (fish)

щу́п|альце *n* [11; *g/pl.*: -лец] feeler, tentacle; **~ать** [1], <по-> feel; probe; touch; <про-> *fig.* sound; **~лый** *coll.* [14; щупл, -á, -о] puny, frail

щу́рить [13] screw up (one's eyes **-ся**)

Э

эваку|а́ция *f* [7] evacuation; **~и́ровать** [7] (*im*)*pf.* evacuate

эволюцио́нный [14] evolutionary

эги́д|а *f* [5]: ***под ~ой*** under the aegis (of P)

эгои́|зм [1] ego(t)ism, selfishness; **~ст** *m* [1], **~стка** *f* [5; *g/pl.*: -ток] egoist; **~сти́ческий** [16], **~сти́чный** [14; -чен, -чна] selfish

эй! *int.* hi!, hey!

эквивале́нт [1], **~ный** [14; -тен, -тна] equivalent

экза́м|ен *m* [1] examination (in ***по*** Д); **~ена́тор** *m* [1] examiner; **~е-**

нова́ть [7], <про-> examine; **-ся** be examined (by **у** P), have one's examination (with); *p. pr. p.* examine
экземпля́р *m* [1] copy; (*образе́ц*) specimen
экзоти́ческий [16] exotic
экип|а́ж *m* [1] *naut., ae.* crew; **~ирова́ть** [7] *(im)pf.* fit out, equip; **~иро́вка** *f* [5; *g/pl.*: -вок] equipping; equipment
эколо́ги|я *f* [7] ecology; **~ческий** [16] ecologic(al)
эконо́м|ика *f* [5] economy; *нау́ка* economics; **~ить** [14], <с-> save; economize; **~и́ческий** [16] economic; **~ия** *f* [7] economy; saving (of P, **в** П); **~ный** [14; -мен, -мна] economical, thrifty
экра́н *m* [1] *cine.* screen; *fig.* film industry; shield, shade
экскава́тор *m* [1] excavator
экскурс|а́нт *m* [1] tourist, excursionist; **~ия** *f* [7] excursion, outing, trip; **~ово́д** *m* [1] guide
экспеди́|тор *m* [1] forwarding agent; **~ция** *f* [7] dispatch, forwarding; expedition
экспер|имента́льный [14] experimental; **~т** *m* [1] expert (in **по** Д); **~ти́за** *f* [5] examination; (expert) opinion
эксплуа|та́тор *m* [1] exploiter; **~та́ция** *f* [7] exploitation; *tech.* operation; ***сдать в ~та́цию*** comission, put into operation; **~ти́ровать** [7] exploit; *tech.* operate, run
экспон|а́т *m* [1] exhibit; **~и́ровать** [7] *(im)pf.* exhibit; *phot.* expose
э́кспорт *m* [1], **~и́ровать** [7] *(im)pf.* export; **~ный** [14] export...
экс|про́мт *m* [1] impromptu, improvisation; ***~про́мтом*** *a.* extempore; **~та́з** *m* [1] ecstasy; **~тра́кт** *m* [1] extract; **~тренный** [14 *sh.*] *вы́пуск* special; urgent; ***в ~тренных слу́чаях*** in case of emergency; **~центри́чный** [14; -чен, -чна] eccentric
эласти́чн|ость *f* [8] elasticity; **~ый** [14; -чен, -чна] elastic
элега́нтн|ость *f* [8] elegance; **~ый** [14; -тен, -тна] elegant, stylish
эле́ктр|ик *m* [1] electrician; **~и́ческий** [16] electric(al); **~и́чество** *n* [9] electricity; **~и́чка** *f* [5; *g/pl.*: -чек] *coll.* suburban electric train; **~ово́з** *m* [1] electric locomotive; **~омонтёр** → **~ик**; **~о́н** *m* [1] electron; **~о́ника** *f* [5] electronics; **~опрово́дка** *f* [5; *g/pl.*: -док] electric wiring; **~оста́нция** *f* [7] electric power station; **~оте́хник** *m* [1] → ***эле́ктрик***; **~оте́хника** *f* [5] electrical engineering
элеме́нт *m* [1] element; *comput.* pixel; *el.* cell, battery; *coll.* type, character; **~а́рный** [14; -рен, -рна] elementary
эма́л|евый [14], **~ирова́ть** [7], **~ь** *f* [8] enamel
эмба́рго *n* [*indecl.*] embargo; ***наложи́ть ~*** place an embargo (on **на** B)
эмбле́ма *f* [5] emblem; *mil.* insignia
эмигр|а́нт *m* [1], **~а́нтка** *f* [5; *g/pl.*: -ток], **~а́нтский** [16] emigrant; émigré; **~и́ровать** [7] *(im)pf.* emigrate
эми́ссия *f* [7] *де́нег* emission
эмоциона́льный [14; -лен, -льна] emotional
энерге́тика *f* [5] power engineering
энерг|и́чный [14; -чен, -чна] energetic; forceful, drastic; **~ия** *f* [7] energy; *fig. a.* vigo(u)r; **~оёмкий** [16; -мок, -мка] power-consuming
энтузиа́зм *m* [1] enthusiasm
энциклопе́д|ия *f* [7] (*a.* **~и́ческий слова́рь** *m*) encyclop(a)edia
эпи|гра́мма *f* [5] epigram; **~деми́ческий** [16], **~де́мия** *f* [7] epidemic; **~зо́д** *m* [1] episode; **~ле́псия** *f* [7] epilepsy; **~ло́г** *m* [1] epilogue; **~тет** *m* [1] epithet; **~це́нтр** *m* [1] epicenter, *Brt.* -tre
э́по|с *m* [1] epic (literature), epos; **~ха** *f* [5] epoch, era, period (in **в** B)
эроти́ческий [16] erotic
эруди́ция *f* [5] erudition
эска́др|а *f* [5] *naut.* squadron; **~и́лья** *f* [6; *g/pl.*: -лий] *ae.* squadron
эс|кала́тор *m* [1] escalator; **~ки́з** *m* [1] sketch; **~кимо́с** *m* [1] Eskimo, Inuit; **~корти́ровать** [7] escort; **~ми́нец** *m* [1; -нца] *naut.* destroyer; **~се́нция** *f* [7] essence; **~тафе́та** *f* [5] relay race; **~тети́ческий** [16] aesthetic

эсто́н|ец *m* [1; -нца], **~ка** *f* [5; *g/pl.*: -нок], **~ский** [16] Estonian
эстра́да *f* [5] stage, platform; → ***варьете́***
эта́ж *m* [1 *e.*] floor, stor(e)y; ***дом в три ~а́*** three-storied (*Brt.* -reyed) house
э́так(ий) *coll.* → ***так(о́й)***
эта́п *m* [1] stage, phase; *sport* lap
э́тика *f* [5] ethics (*a. pl.*)
этике́тка *f* [5; *g/pl.*: -ток] label
этимоло́гия *f* [7] etymology
этногра́фия *f* [7] ethnography
э́т|от *m*, **~а** *f*, **~о** *n*, **~и** *pl.* [27] this, *pl.* these; *su.* this one; the latter; that; it; there
этю́д *m* [1] *mus.* étude, exercise; *art lit.* study, sketch; *chess* problem
эф|е́с *m* [1] (*sword*) hilt; **~и́р** *m* [1] ether; *fig.* air; ***переда́ть в ~и́р*** broadcast; **~и́рный** [14; -рен, -рна] ethereal
эффект|и́вность *f* [8] effectiveness, efficacy; **~и́вный** [14; -вен, -вна] efficacious; **~ный** [14; -тен, -тна] effective, striking
эх! *int.* eh!; oh!; ah!
эшело́н *m* [1] echelon; train

Ю

юбил|е́й *m* [3] jubilee, anniversary; **~е́йный** [14] jubilee...; **~я́р** *m* [1] pers. (*or* institution) whose anniversary is being marked
ю́бка *f* [5; *g/pl.*: ю́бок] culotte, split skirt
ювели́р *m* [1] jewel(l)er; **~ный** [14]) jewel(l)er's
юг *m* [1] south; ***е́хать на ~*** travel south; → ***восто́к***; **~о-восто́к** *m* [1] southeast; **~о-восто́чный** [14] southeast...; **~о-за́пад** *m* [1] southwest; **~о-за́падный** [14] southwest
ю́жный [14] south(ern); southerly
ю́зом *adv.* skidding
ю́мор *m* [1] humo(u)r; **~исти́ческий** [16] humorous; comic
ю́нга *m* [5] sea cadet
ю́ность *f* [8] youth (*age*)
ю́нош|а *m* [5; *g/pl.*: -шей] youth (*person*); **~ество** *n* [9] youth
ю́ный [14; юн, -á, -о] young, youthful
юри|ди́ческий [16] juridical, legal; of the law; ***~ди́ческая консульта́ция*** legal advice office; **~ско́нсульт** *m* [1] legal adviser
юри́ст *m* [1] lawyer; legal expert
ю́рк|ий [16; ю́рок, юрка́, -о] nimble, quick; **~нуть** [20] *pf.* scamper, dart (away)
ю́рта *f* [5] yurt, nomad's tent
юсти́ция *f* [7] justice
юти́ться [15 *e.*; ючу́сь, юти́шься] huddle together; take shelter

Я

я [20] I; ***э́то я*** it's me
я́бед|а *coll. f* [5] tell-tale; **~ничать** [1] tell tales; inform on
я́бло|ко *m* [9; *pl.*: -ки, -к] apple; ***глазно́е*** eyeball; **~ня** *f* [6] apple tree
яв|и́ть(ся) → **~ля́ть(ся)**; **~ка** *f* [5] appearance; attendance; rendez-

vous; *мéсто* place of (secret) meeting; **~лéние** *n* [12] phenomenon; occurrence, event; *thea.* scene; **~лять** [28], <**~ить**> [14] present; display, show; **-ся** appear, turn up; come; (T) be; **~ный** [14; явен, явна] obvious, evident; *вздор* sheer; **~ствовать** [7] follow (*logically*); be clear
ягнёнок *m* [2] lamb
ягод|а *f* [5], **~ный** [14] berry
ягодица *f* [5] buttock
яд *m* [1] poison; *fig. a.* venom
ядерный [14] nuclear
ядовитый [14 *sh.*] poisonous; *fig.* venomous
ядр|ёный *coll.* [14 *sh.*] *здорóвый* strong, stalwart, *морóз* severe; **~ó** *n* [9; *pl. st.*; *g/pl.*: ядер] kernel; *phys.*, nucleus; *fig.* core, pith
язв|а *f* [5] ulcer, sore; *fig.* plague; **~ительный** [14; -лен, -льна] sarcastic, caustic
язык *m* [1 *e.*] tongue; language (in **на** П); speech; ***на рýсском ~é*** (*speak, write, etc.*) in Russian; ***держáть ~ за зубáми*** hold one's tongue; **~овóй** [14] language...; linguistic; **~ознáние** *n* [12] linguistics
языч|еский [16] pagan; **~ество** *n* [9] paganism; **~ник** *m* [1] pagan
язычóк *m* [1; -чкá] *anat.* uvula
яичн|ица *f* [5] (*a.* **~ица-глазýнья**) fried eggs *pl.*; **~ый** [14] egg...
яйцó *n* [9; *pl.*: яйца, яиц, яйцам] egg; ***~ вкрутýю*** (***всмятку***) hard-boiled (soft-boiled) egg
якобы allegedly; as it were
якор|ь *m* [4; *pl.*: -ря́, *etc. e.*] anchor (at ***на*** П); ***стоять на ~е*** ride at anchor
ям|а *f* [5] hole, pit; **~(оч)ка** [5; *g/pl.*: ямо(че)к] dimple
ямщик *m* [1 *e.*] *hist.* coachman
январь *m* [4 *e.*] January
янтáрь *m* [4 *e.*] amber
япóн|ец *m* [1; -нца], **~ка** *f* [5; *g/pl.*: -нок], **~ский** [16] Japanese
яркий [16; ярок, яркá, -о; *comp.*: ярче] *свет* bright; *цвет* vivid, rich; *плáмя* blazing; *fig.* striking, outstanding
яр|лык *m* [1 *e.*] label; **~марка** *f* [5; *g/pl.*: -рок] fair (at ***на*** П)
яровóй [14] *agric.* spring; *as su.* **~óе** spring crop
ярост|ный [14; -тен, -тна] furious, fierce; **~ь** *f* [8] fury, rage
ярус *m* [1] *thea.* circle; *geol.* layer
ярый [14 *sh.*] ardent; vehement
ясень *m* [4] ash tree
ясли *m/pl.* [4; *gen.*: яслей] day nursery, *Brt.* crèche
ясн|овидец *m* [1; -дца] clairvoyant; **~ость** *f* [8] clarity; **~ый** [14; ясен, яснá, -о] clear; bright; *погóда* fine; (*отчётливый*) distinct; (*очевидный*) evident; *ответ* plain
ястреб *m* [1; *pl.*: -бá & -бы] hawk
яхта *f* [5] yacht
ячé|йка *f* [5; *g/pl.*: -éек] *biol. pol.* cell; ***~йка пáмяти*** *computer* storage cell; **~я́** *f* [6; *g/pl.*: ячей] mesh
ячмéнь *m* [4 *e.*] barley; *med.* sty
ящерица *f* [5] lizard
ящик *m* [1] box, case, chest; *выдвигáющийся* drawer; ***почтóвый ~*** mailbox (*Brt.* letter-box); ***откладывать в дóлгий ~*** shelve, put off
ящур *m* [1] foot-and-mouth disease

Я

English-Russian

A

a [eɪ, ə] *неопределённый артикль; как правило, не переводится*; **~ table** стол; **ten r(o)ubles a dozen** десять рублей дюжина

A [eɪ] *su.*: **from ~ to Z** от "А" до "Я"

aback [ə'bæk] *adv.*: **taken ~** поражён, озадачен

abandon [ə'bændən] **1.** (*give up*) отказываться [-заться] от (Р); (*desert*) оставлять [-авить], покидать [-инуть]; **~ o.s.** преда(ва)ться (**to** Д); **2.** непринуждённость *f*; **~ed** покинутый

abase [ə'beɪs] унижать [унизить]; **~ment** [~mənt] унижение

abash [ə'bæʃ] смущать [смутить]

abate [əb'eɪt] *v/t.* уменьшать [-еньшить]; *of wind, etc. v/i.* утихать [утихнуть]

abb|ess ['æbɪs] настоятельница монастыря; **~ey** ['æbɪ] монастырь *m*; **~ot** ['æbət] аббат, настоятель *m*

abbreviat|e [ə'briːvɪeɪt] сокращать [-ратить]; **~ion** [əbriːvɪ'eɪʃn] сокращение

ABC [eiːbiː'siː] азбука, алфавит; (**as**) **easy as ~** легче лёгкого

abdicat|e ['æbdɪkeɪt] отрекаться от престола; *of rights, office* отказываться [-заться] от (Р); **~ion** [æbdɪ'keɪʃn] отречение от престола

abdomen ['æbdəmən] брюшная полость *f*, *coll.* живот

aberration [æbə'reɪʃn] *judg(e)ment or conduct* заблуждение; *mental* помрачение ума; *deviation* отклонение от нормы; *astr.* аберрация

abeyance [ə'beɪəns] состояние неизвестности; **in ~** *law* временно отменённый

abhor [əb'hɔː] ненавидеть; (*feel disgust*) питать отвращение (к Д); **~rence** [əb'hɔrəns] отвращение; **~rent** [~ənt] □ отвратительный

abide [ə'baɪd] [*irr.*]: **~ by** придерживаться (Р); *v/t.* **not ~** не терпеть

ability [ə'bɪlətɪ] способность *f*

abject ['æbdʒekt] □ жалкий; **~ poverty** крайняя нищета

ablaze [ə'bleɪz]: **be ~** пылать; **~ with anger** *of eyes, cheeks* пылать гневом; **~ with light** ярко освещён(ный)

able ['eɪbl] □ способный; **be ~** мочь, быть в состоянии; **~-bodied** [~bɔdɪd] здоровый; годный

abnormal [æb'nɔːməl] ненормальный; аномальный; *med.* **~ psychology** психопатология

aboard [ə'bɔːd] *naut.* на судне, на борту; **go ~** садиться на судно (в самолёт; в автобус, на поезд)

abolish [ə'bɒlɪʃ] отменять [-нить]; *of custom, etc.* упразднять [-нить]

A-bomb ['eɪbɒm] атомная бомба

abomina|ble [ə'bɒmɪnəbl] □ отвратительный; **~ snowman** снежный человек; **~tion** [əbɒmɪ'neɪʃn] отвращение; *coll.* какой-то *or* просто ужас

aboriginal [æbə'rɪdʒənl] = **aborigine** [-'rɪdʒɪnɪ] *as su.* коренной житель, туземец *m*, ка *f*, абориген; *as adj.* коренной, туземный

abortion [ə'bɔːʃn] аборт

abound [ə'baʊnd] быть в изобилии; изобиловать (**in** Т)

about [ə'baʊt] **1.** *prp.* вокруг (Р); около (Р); о (П), об (П), обо (П) насчёт (Р); у (Р); про (В); **2.** *adv.* вокруг, везде; приблизительно; **be ~ to** собираться

above [ə'bʌv] **1.** *prp.* над (Т); выше (Р); свыше (Р); **~ all** прежде всего; **2.** *adv.* наверху, наверх; выше; **3.** *adj.* вышесказанный; **~-board** [~'bɔːd] *adv. & adj.* честный, открытый; **~-mentioned** [~'menʃənd] вышеупомянутый

abrasion [ə'breɪʒn] *of skin* ссадина

abreast [ə'brest] в ряд; **keep ~ of**

fig. быть в ку́рсе; ***keep ~ of the times*** идти́ в но́гу со вре́менем
abridg|e [əˈbrɪdʒ] сокраща́ть [-рати́ть]; **~(e)ment** [~mənt] сокраще́ние
abroad [əˈbrɔːd] за грани́цей, за грани́цу; ***there is a rumo(u)r ~*** хо́дит слух
abrogate [əˈbrəgeɪt] *v/t.* отменя́ть [-ни́ть]; аннули́ровать *(im)pf.*
abrupt [əˈbrʌpt] (*steep*) круто́й; (*sudden*) внеза́пный; (*blunt*) ре́зкий
abscess [ˈæbsɪs] нары́в, абсце́сс
abscond [əbˈskɒnd] *v/i.* скры(ва́)ться, укры́(ва́)ться
absence [ˈæbsəns] отсу́тствие; ***~ of mind*** рассе́янность *f*
absent 1. [ˈæbsənt] □ отсу́тствующий (*a. fig.*); **2.** [æbˈsent] ***~ o.s.*** отлуча́ться [-чи́ться]; **~minded** рассе́янный
absolute [ˈæbsəluːt] □ абсолю́тный; *coll.* по́лный, соверше́нный
absorb [æbˈsɔːb] впи́тывать [впита́ть], поглоща́ть [-лоти́ть] (*a. fig.*); *of gas, etc.* абсорби́ровать *(im)pf.*; **~ing** [~ɪŋ] *fig.* увлека́тельный
abstain [əbˈsteɪn] возде́рживаться [-жа́ться] (***from*** от Р)
abstention [æbˈstenʃən] воздержа́ние
abstinence [ˈæbstɪnəns] уме́ренность *f*; *from drink* тре́звость *f*
abstract 1. [ˈæbstrækt] отвлечённый, абстра́ктный (*a. gr.*); **2.** резюме́, кра́ткий обзо́р; ***in the ~*** теорети́чески; **3.** [æbˈstrækt] (*take out*) извлека́ть [-ле́чь]; (*purloin*) похища́ть [-хи́тить]; резюми́ровать *(im)pf.*; **~ed** [~ɪd] *of person* погружённый в свои́ мы́сли; **~ion** [~kʃn] абстра́кция
abstruse [æbˈstruːs] □ *fig.* непоня́тный, тёмный, мудрёный
abundan|ce [əˈbʌndəns] изоби́лие; **~t** [~dənt] □ оби́льный, бога́тый
abus|e [əˈbjuːs] **1.** (*misuse*) злоупотребле́ние; (*insult*) оскорбле́ние; (*curse*) брань *f*; **2.** [əˈbjuːz] злоупотребля́ть [-би́ть] (T); [вы́-] руга́ть; **~ive** [əˈbjuːsɪv] □ оскорби́тельный
abyss [əˈbɪs] бе́здна
acacia [əˈkeɪʃə] ака́ция
academic|(al □) [ækəˈdemɪk(əl)] академи́ческий; **~ian** [əkædəˈmɪʃn] акаде́мик
accede [ækˈsiːd]: ***~ to*** (*assent*) соглаша́ться [-аси́ться] (с T); *of office* вступа́ть [-пи́ть] в (B)
accelerat|e [əkˈseləreɪt] ускоря́ть [-о́рить]; **~or** [əkˈseləreɪtə] *mot.* педа́ль га́за
accent [ˈæksənt] (*stress*) ударе́ние; (*mode of utterance*) произноше́ние, акце́нт; **~uate** [ækˈsentjʊeɪt] де́лать или ста́вить ударе́ние на (П); *fig.* подчёркивать [-черкну́ть]
accept [əkˈsept] принима́ть [-ня́ть]; соглаша́ться [-гласи́ться] с (T); **~able** [əkˈseptəbl] □ прие́млемый; *of a gift* прия́тный; **~ance** [əkˈseptəns] приня́тие; (*approval*) одобре́ние; *comm.* акце́пт
access [ˈækses] до́ступ; (*way*) прохо́д, прое́зд; ***easy of ~*** досту́пный; ***access code*** *comput.* код до́ступа; **~ory** [ækˈsesərɪ] соуча́стник (-ица); **~ible** [ækˈsesəbl] □ досту́пный, достижи́мый; **~ion** [ækˈseʃn]: ***~ to the throne*** вступле́ние на престо́л
accessory [ækˈsesərɪ] □ **1.** дополни́тельный, второстепе́нный; **2.** *pl.* принадле́жности *f/pl.*; *gloves, etc.* аксессуа́ры
accident [ˈæksɪdənt] (*chance*) случа́йность *f*; (*mishap*) несча́стный слу́чай; *mot., tech.* ава́рия; *rail.* круше́ние; **~al** [æksɪˈdentl] случа́йный
acclaim [əˈkleɪm] **1.** аплоди́ровать; приве́тствовать **2.** приве́тствие; ова́ция
acclimatize [əˈklaɪmətaɪz] акклиматизи́ровать(ся) *(im)pf.*
accommodat|e [əˈkɒmədeɪt] (*adapt*) приспособля́ть [-посо́бить]; предоста́вить жильё (Д); (*hold*) вмеща́ть [вмести́ть]; *comm.* вы́да(ва́)ть ссу́ду; **~ion** [əkɒməˈdeɪʃn] жильё, помеще́ние
accompan|iment [əˈkʌmpənɪmənt] сопровожде́ние; аккомпанеме́нт; **~y** [~pənɪ] *v/t.* (*escort*) сопровожда́ть [-води́ть]; *mus.* аккомпани́ровать (Д)

accomplice [ə'kʌmplɪs] соуча́стник (-ица) (*in crime*)
accomplish [ə'kʌmplɪʃ] (*fulfill*) выполня́ть [вы́полнить]; (*achieve*) достига́ть [-и́гнуть] (Р); (*complete*) заверша́ть [-и́ть]; **~ment** [~mənt] выполне́ние; достиже́ние
accord [ə'kɔːd] **1.** (*agreement*) согла́сие; соглаше́ние; ***of one's own ~*** по со́бственному жела́нию; ***with one ~*** единоду́шно; **2.** *v/i.* согласо́вываться [-сова́ться] (с Т), гармони́ровать (с Т); *v/t.* предоставля́ть [-ста́вить]; **~ance** [-əns] согла́сие; ***in ~ with*** в соотве́тствии с (Т); **~ing** [~ɪŋ]: ***~ to*** согла́сно (Д); **~ingly** [~ɪŋlɪ] *adv.* соотве́тственно; таки́м о́бразом
accost [ə'kɒst] загова́ривать [-вори́ть] с (Т)
account [ə'kaʊnt] **1.** *comm.* счёт; (*report*) отчёт; (*description*) сообще́ние, описа́ние; ***by all ~s*** су́дя по всему́; ***on no ~*** ни в ко́ем слу́чае; ***on ~ of*** из-за (Р); ***take into ~, take ~ of*** принима́ть во внима́ние; ***turn to (good) ~*** испо́льзовать (*im*)*pf.* (с вы́годой); ***call to ~*** призыва́ть к отве́ту; ***~ number*** но́мер счёта; **2.** *v/i.* ***~ for*** отвеча́ть [-е́тить] за (В); (*explain*) объясня́ть [-ни́ть]; *v/t.* (*consider*) счита́ть [счесть] (В/Т); **~able** [ə'kauntəbl] □ (*responsible*) отве́тственный (***to*** пе́ред Т, ***for*** за В); **~ant** [-ənt] квалифици́рованный бухга́лтер
accredit [ə'kredɪt] *of ambassador, etc.* аккредитова́ть (*im*)*pf.*; (*attribute*) припи́сывать [-са́ть]; *credit* выдава́ть [-дать] креди́т
accrue [ə'kruː]: ***~d interest*** наро́сшие проце́нты
accumulat|e [ə'kjuːmjʊleɪt] нака́пливать(ся) [-копи́ть(ся)]; скопля́ть(ся) [-пи́ть(ся)]; **~ion** [əkjuːmjuː'leɪʃn] накопле́ние; скопле́ние
accura|cy ['ækjʊrəsɪ] то́чность *f*; *in shooting* ме́ткость *f*; **~te** [~rɪt] то́чный; *of aim or shot* ме́ткий
accurs|ed [ə'kɜːsɪd], **~t** [-st] прокля́тый
accus|ation [ækjuː'zeɪʃn] обвине́ние; **~e** [ə'kjuːz] *v/t.* обвиня́ть [-ни́ть]; **~er** [~ə] обвини́тель *m*, -ни́ца *f*
accustom [ə'kʌstəm] приуча́ть [-чи́ть] (***to*** к Д); ***get ~ed*** привыка́ть [-вы́кнуть] (***to*** к Д); **~ed** [~d] привы́чный; (*inured*) приу́ченный; (*usual*) обы́чный
ace [eɪs] туз; *fig.* первокла́ссный лётчик, ас; ***be within an ~ of*** быть на волосо́к от (Р)
acerbity [ə'sɜːbətɪ] те́рпкость *f*
acet|ic [ə'siːtɪk] у́ксусный
ache [eik] **1.** боль *f*; **2.** *v/i.* боле́ть
achieve [ə'tʃiːv] достига́ть [-и́гнуть] (Р); **~ment** [~mənt] достиже́ние
acid ['æsid] **1.** кислота́; **2.** ки́слый; *fig.* е́дкий; ***~ rain*** кисло́тный дождь
acknowledg|e [ək'nɒlɪdʒ] *v/t.* подтвержда́ть [-ерди́ть]; *confess* призна́(ва́)ть; **~(e)ment** [~mənt] призна́ние; подтвержде́ние
acorn ['eɪkɔːn] *bot.* жёлудь *m*
acoustics [ə'kaustɪks] аку́стика
acquaint [ə'kweɪnt] *v/t.* [по]знако́мить; ***~ o.s. with*** ознако́миться с (Т); ***be ~ed with*** быть знако́мым с (Т); **~ance** [~əns] знако́мство; *pers.* знако́мый; ***make s.o.'s ~*** познако́миться с ке́м-л.
acquiesce [ækwɪ'es] мо́лча или неохо́тно соглаша́ться (***in*** на В)
acquire [ə' kwaɪə] *v/t.* приобрета́ть [-ести́]
acquisition [ækwɪ'zɪʃn] приобрете́ние
acquit [ə'kwɪt] *law v/t.* опра́вдывать [-да́ть]; ***~ o.s. well*** хорошо́ прояви́ть себя́; **~tal** [~l] оправда́ние
acrid ['ækrɪd] острый, едкий (*a. fig.*)
across [ə'krɒs] **1.** *adv.* попере́к; на ту сто́рону; ***two miles ~*** ширино́й в две ми́ли; **2.** *prp.* че́рез (В)
act [ækt] **1.** *v/i.* де́йствовать; поступа́ть [-пи́ть]; *v/t. thea.* игра́ть [сыгра́ть]; **2.** посту́пок; постановле́ние, закон; *thea.* де́йствие, акт; **~ing** [~ɪŋ] **1.** исполня́ющий обя́занности; **2.** *thea.* игра́
action ['ækʃn] (*conduct*) посту́пок; (*acting*) де́йствие; (*activity*) де́ятельность *f*; *mil.* бой; *law* иск; ***take ~*** принима́ть ме́ры
activ|e ['æktɪv] □ акти́вный; энер-

ги́чный; де́ятельный; **~ity** [æk'tɪvətɪ] де́ятельность *f*, рабо́та; акти́вность *f*; эне́ргия
act|or ['æktə] актёр; **~ress** [-trɪs] актри́са
actual ['æktʃʊəl] □ действи́тельный; факти́ческий; **~ly** факти́чески, на са́мом де́ле
acute [ə'kju:t] □ си́льный, о́стрый; (*penetrating*) проница́тельный
adamant ['ædəmənt] *fig.* непрекло́нный
adapt [ə'dæpt] приспособля́ть [-посо́бить] (***to, for*** к Д); *text* адапти́ровать; **~ *o.s*** адапти́роваться; **~ation** [ædæp'teɪʃn] приспособле́ние; *of text* обрабо́тка; *of organism* адапта́ция
add [æd] *v/t.* прибавля́ть [-а́вить]; *math.* скла́дывать [сложи́ть]; *v/i.* увели́чи(ва)ть (***to*** В)
addict ['ædɪkt]: ***drug* ~** наркома́н; **~ed** [ə'dɪktɪd] скло́нный (***to*** к Д)
addition [ə'dɪʃn] *math.* сложе́ние; прибавле́ние; ***in* ~** кро́ме того́, к тому́ же; ***in* ~ *to*** вдоба́вок к (Д); **~al** [~əl] доба́вочный, дополни́тельный
address [ə'dres] *v/t.* **1.** *a letter* адресова́ть (*im*)*pf.*; (*speak to*) обраща́ться [обрати́ться] к (Д); **2.** а́дрес; обраще́ние; речь *f*; **~ee** [ædre'si:] адреса́т
adept ['ædept] иску́сный; уме́лый
adequa|cy ['ædɪkwəsɪ] соотве́тствие; доста́точность *f*, адеква́тность; **~te** [~kwɪt] (*sufficient*) доста́точный; (*suitable*) соотве́тствующий, адеква́тный
adhere [əd'hɪə] прилипа́ть [-ли́пнуть] (***to*** к Д); *fig.* приде́рживаться (***to*** Р); **~nce** [~rəns] приве́рженность *f*; **~nt** [~rənt] приве́рженец (-нка)
adhesive [əd'hi:sɪv] □ ли́пкий, кле́йкий; **~ *plaster*** лейкопла́стырь *m*; **~ *tape*** ли́пкая ле́нта
adjacent [ə'dʒeɪsənt] □ сме́жный (***to*** с Т), сосе́дний
adjoin [ə'dʒɔɪn] примыка́ть [-мкну́ть] к (Д); прилега́ть *pf.* к (Д)
adjourn [ə'dʒɜ:n] *v/t.* (*suspend proceedings*) закрыва́ть [-ы́ть]; (*carry over*) переноси́ть [-нести́]; (*postpone*) отсро́чи(ва)ть; *parl.* де́лать переры́в; **~ment** [~mənt] отсро́чка; переры́в
administ|er [əd'mɪnɪstə] руководи́ть, управля́ть (Т); **~ *justice*** отправля́ть правосу́дие; **~ration** [ədmɪnɪ'streɪʃn] администра́ция; **~rative** [əd'mɪnɪstrətɪv] администрати́вный; исполни́тельный; **~rator** [əd'mɪnɪstreɪtə] администра́тор
admir|able ['ædmərəbl] превосхо́дный; замеча́тельный; **~ation** [ædmɪ:reɪʃən] восхище́ние; **~e** [əd'maɪə] восхища́ться [-йться] (Т); [по]любова́ться (Т *or* на В)
admiss|ible [əd'mɪsəbl] □ допусти́мый, прие́млемый; **~ion** [əd'mɪʃən] (*access*) вход; (*confession*) призна́ние; **~ *fee*** пла́та за вход
admit [əd'mɪt] *v/t.* (*let in*) впуска́ть [-сти́ть]; (*allow*) допуска́ть [-сти́ть]; (*confess*) призна́(ва́)ть(ся); **~tance** [~əns] до́ступ, вход
admixture [əd'mɪkstʃə] при́месь *f*
admon|ish [əd'mɒnɪʃ] (*exhort*) увещ(ев)а́ть *impf.*; (*warn*) предостерега́ть [-ре́чь] (***of*** от Р); **~ition** [ædmə'nɪʃn] увеща́ние; предостереже́ние
ado [ə'du:] суета́; хло́поты *f/pl.*; ***without much* ~** без вся́ких цере-мо́ний
adolescen|ce [ædə'lesəns] отро́чество; **~t** [~snt] **1.** подростко́вый; **2.** *person* подро́сток
adopt [ə'dɒpt] *v/t.* усыновля́ть [-ви́ть]; *girl* удочеря́ть [-ри́ть]; *resolution, etc.* принима́ть [-ня́ть]; **~ion** [ə'dɒpʃn] усыновле́ние; удочере́ние; приня́тие
ador|able [ə'dɔ:rəbl] обожа́емый, преле́стный; **~ation** [ædə'reɪʃn] обожа́ние; **~e** [ə'dɔ:] *v/t.* обожа́ть
adorn [ə'dɔ:n] украша́ть [укра́сить]; **~ment** [~mənt] украше́ние
adroit [ə'drɔɪt] □ ло́вкий, иску́сный
adult ['ædʌlt] взро́слый, совершенноле́тний
adulter|ate [ə'dʌltəreɪt] (*debase*) [ис]по́ртить; (*dilute*) разбавля́ть [-а́вить]; фальсифици́ровать (*im*)*pf.*; **~y** [~rɪ] наруше́ние супру́жеской ве́рности, адюльте́р

advance [əd'vɑːns] **1.** *v/i. mil.* наступáть; (*move forward*) продвигáться [продви́нуться]; (*a. fig.*) дéлать успéхи; *v/t.* продвигáть [-и́нуть]; *idea, etc.* выдвигáть [вы́двинуть]; плати́ть авáнсом; **2.** *mil.* наступлéние; *in studies* успéх; прогрéсс; *of salary* авáнс; **~d** [əd'vɑːnst] передовóй; *in years* престарéлый, пожилóй; **~ment** [īmənt] успéх; продвижéние

advantage [əd'vɑːntɪdʒ] преимýщество; (*benefit*) вы́года; ***take ~ of*** [вос]пóльзоваться (Т); **~ous** [ædvən'teɪdʒəs, ædvæn~] вы́годный, полéзный, благоприя́тный

adventur|e [əd'ventʃə] приключéние; **~er** [-rə] искáтель приключéний; авантюри́ст; **~ous** [~rəs] предприи́мчивый; авантю́рный

advers|ary ['ædvəsərɪ] (*antagonist*) проти́вник (-ица); (*opponent*) сопéрник (-ица); **~e** ['ædvɜːs] неблагоприя́тный; **~ity** [əd'vɜːsɪti] несчáстье, бедá

advertis|e ['ædvətaɪz] реклами́ровать (*im*)*pf*.; *in newspaper* помещáть [-ести́ть] объявлéние; **~ement** [əd'vɜːtɪsmənt] объявлéние; реклáма; **~ing** ['ædvətaɪzɪŋ] реклáмный

advice [əd'vaɪs] совéт

advis|able [əd'vaɪzəbl] □ желáтельный, целесообрáзный; **~e** [əd'vaɪz] *v/t.* [по]совéтовать (Д), [по-] рекомендовáть; (*inform*) сообщáть [-щи́ть]; **~er** [~ə] *official* совéтник, *professional* консультáнт

advocate 1. ['ædvəkət] сторóнник (-ица); *law* адвокáт, защи́тник; **2.** [~keɪt] поддéрживать, *speak in favo(u)r of* выступáть [вы́ступить] (за В)

aerial ['eərɪəl] антéнна; ***outdoor ~*** нарýжная антéнна

aero... [eərə] áэро...; **~bics** [~bɪks] аэрóбика; **~drome** ['eərədrəʊm] аэродрóм; **~naut** [~nɔːt] аэронáвт; **~nautics** [~nɔːtɪks] аэронáвтика; **~plane** [~pleɪn] самолёт; **~sol** [~sɔl] аэрозóль *m*; **~stat** [~stæt] аэростáт

aesthetic [iːs'θetɪk] эстети́ческий; **~s** [~s] эстéтика

afar [ə'fɑː] *adv.*: вдалекé; ***from ~*** издалекá

affable ['æfəbl] привéтливый

affair [ə'feə] *business* дéло; *love* любóвная связь *f*, ромáн

affect [ə'fekt] *v/t.* [по]влия́ть на (В); задé(вá)ть; *med.* поражáть [-рази́ть]; (*pretend*) притворя́ться [-ри́ться]; **~ation** [æfek'teɪʃən] жемáнство; **~ed** [ə'fektɪd] □ притвóрный; манéрный; **~ion** [ə'fekʃn] привя́занность *f*, любóвь *f*; **~ionate** [ə'fekʃnət] □ нéжный, лáсковый, любя́щий

affiliate [ə'fɪlɪeɪt] **1.** *v/t. join, attach* присоединя́ть [-ни́ть] (как филиáл); **2.** дочéрняя компáния; компáния-филиáл

affinity [ə'fɪnətɪ] *closeness* бли́зость *f*, *relationship* родствó; *attraction* влечéние

affirm [ə'fɜːm] утверждáть [-рди́ть]; **~ation** [æfə'meɪʃn] утверждéние; **~ative** [ə'fɜːmətɪv] □ утверди́тельный

affix [ə'fɪks] прикрепля́ть [-пи́ть] (***to*** к Д)

afflict [ə'flɪkt]: ***be ~ed*** страдáть (***with*** Т, от Р); постигáть [-и́чь *or* -и́гнуть]; **~ion** [ə'flɪkʃn] гóре; недýг

affluen|ce ['æfluəns] изоби́лие, богáтство; **~t** [~ənt] □ оби́льный, богáтый

afford [ə'fɔːd] позволя́ть [-вóлить] себé; ***I can ~ it*** я могý себé э́то позвóлить; *yield, give* (пре-)доставля́ть [-áвить]

affront [ə'frʌnt] **1.** оскорбля́ть [-би́ть]; **2.** оскорблéние

afield [ə'fiːld] *adv.* вдалекé; ***far ~*** далекó

afloat [ə'fləʊt] на водé, на плавý (*a. fig.*)

afraid [ə'freɪd] испýганный; ***be ~ of*** боя́ться (Р)

afresh [ə'freʃ] *adv.* снóва, сы́знова

African ['æfrɪkən] **1.** африкáнец (-нка); **2.** африкáнский

after ['ɑːftə] **1.** *adv.* потóм, пóсле, затéм; позади́; ***shortly ~*** вскóре; **2.** *prp.* за (Т), позади́ (Р); чéрез (В); пóсле (Р); ***time ~ time*** скóлько раз; ***~ all*** в концé концóв; всё же; **3.** *cj.*

с тех пор, как; после того, как; **4.** *adj.* последующий; **~math** ['ɑːftəmæθ] отава; *fig.* последствия *n/pl.*; **~noon** [~'nuːn] время после полудня; **~-taste** (остающийся) привкус; **~-thought** мысль, пришедшая поздно; **~wards** [~wədz] *adv.* впоследствии, потом

again [ə'gen] *adv.* снова, опять; ***~ and ~, time and ~*** неоднократно; снова и снова; ***as much ~*** ещё столько же

against [ə'genst] *prp.* против (Р); о, об (В); на (В); ***as ~*** по сравнению с (Т); ***~ the wall*** у стены, к стене

age [eɪdʒ] **1.** век, возраст; года *m/pl.*; век, эпоха; ***of ~*** совершеннолетний; ***under ~*** несовершеннолетний; **2.** *v/t.* [со]старить; *v/i.* [по]старить; **~d** ['eɪdʒɪd] престарелый

agency ['eɪdʒənsɪ] агентство

agenda [ə'dʒendə] повестка дня

agent ['eɪdʒənt] агент; доверенное лицо; *chem.* средство

aggravate ['ægrəveɪt] (*make worse*) усугублять [-бить]; ухудшать [ухудшить]; (*irritate*) раздражать [-жить]

aggregate ['ægrɪgət] совокупность, общее число; ***in the ~*** в целом

aggress|ion [ə'greʃn] агрессия; **~or** [ə'gresə] агрессор

aghast [ə'gɑːst] ошеломлённый, поражённый ужасом

agil|e ['ædʒaɪl] □ проворный, подвижный, живой; ***~ mind*** живой ум; **~ity** [ə'dʒɪlɪtɪ] проворство; живость *f*

agitat|e ['ædʒɪteɪt] *v/t.* [вз]волновать, возбуждать [-удить]; *v/i.* агитировать (***for*** за В); **~ion** [ædʒɪ'teɪʃn] волнение; агитация

agnail ['ægneɪl] заусеница

ago [ə'gəu]: ***a year ~*** год тому назад; ***long ~*** давно; ***not long ~*** недавно

agonizing ['ægənaɪzɪŋ] мучительный

agony ['ægənɪ] агония; мучение

agree [ə'griː] *v/i.* (*consent, accept*) соглашаться [-ласиться] (***to*** с Т, на В); ***~ [up]on*** (*settle, arrange*) уславливаться [условиться] о (П); (*reach a common decision*) договариваться [-вориться]; **~able** [~əbl] (*pleasing*) приятный; (*consenting*) согласный (***to*** с Т, на В); **~ment** [~mənt] согласие; (*contract, etc.*) соглашение, договор

agricultur|al [ægrɪ'kʌltʃərəl] сельскохозяйственный; **~e** ['ægrɪkʌltʃə] сельское хозяйство; земледелие; **~ist** [ægrɪ'kʌltʃərɪst] агроном

ahead [ə'hed] вперёд, впереди; ***straight ~*** прямо, вперёд

aid [eɪd] **1.** помощь *f*; помощник (-ица); *pl.* (*financial, etc.*) пособия; **2.** помогать [помочь] (Д)

AIDS [eɪdz] *med.* СПИД (синдром приобретённого имунодефицита); **~-infected** инфицированный СПИДом

ail|ing ['eɪlɪŋ] больной, нездоровый; **~ment** ['eɪlmənt] недомогание, болезнь *f*

aim [eɪm] **1.** *v/i* прицели(ва)ться (***at*** в В); *fig.* ***~ at*** иметь в виду; *v/t.* направлять [-равить] (***at*** на В); **2.** цель *f*, намерение; **~less** [eɪmlɪs] □ бесцельный

air¹ [eə] **1.** воздух; ***by ~*** самолётом; авиапочтой; ***go on the ~*** *of person* выступать [выступить] по радио; ***in the ~*** (*uncertain*) висеть в воздухе; *of rumour, etc.* носиться в воздухе; ***clear the ~*** разряжать [-ядить] атмосферу; **2.** (*ventilate*) проветри(ва)ть(ся) (*a. fig.*)

air² [~] вид; ***give o.s. ~s*** важничать

air³ [~] *mus.* мелодия; песня

air|bag подушка безопасности; **~-base** авиабаза; **~conditioned** с кондиционированным воздухом; **~craft** самолёт; **~field** аэродром; **~force** военно-воздушные силы; **~hostess** стюардесса; **~lift** воздушная перевозка; **~line** авиалиния; **~liner** (авиа)лайнер; **~mail** авиапочта; **~man** лётчик, авиатор; **~plane** *Am.* самолёт; **~port** аэропорт; **~-raid** воздушный налёт; **~shelter** бомбоубежище; **~strip** взлётно-посадочная полоса; **~tight** герметический

airy ['eəri] □ полный воздуха; *of plans, etc.* беспечный, легкомысленный

aisle [ɑɪl] *thea.* прохо́д (ме́жду ряда́ми)
ajar [ə'dʒɑː] приоткры́тый
akin [ə'kɪn] ро́дственный, сро́дный (***to*** Д)
alacrity [ə'lækrɪtɪ] гото́вность *f*; рве́ние
alarm [ə'lɑːm] **1.** трево́га; (*fear*) страх; *tech.* трево́жно-предупреди́тельная сигнализа́ция; **2.** [вс]трево́жить, [вз]волнова́ть; **~ clock** буди́льник; **~ing** [~ɪŋ] *adj.*: **~ *news*** трево́жные изве́стия *n/pl.*
album ['ælbəm] альбо́м
alcohol ['ælkəhɒl] алкого́ль *m*; спирт; **~ic** [ælkə'hɒlɪk] **1.** алкого́льный; **2.** алкого́лик; **~ism** ['ælkəhɒlɪzəm] алкоголи́зм
alcove ['ælkəʊv] алько́в, ни́ша
alder ['ɔːldə] ольха́
ale [eɪl] пи́во, эль *m*
alert [ə'lɜːt] **1.** □ (*lively*) живо́й, прово́рный; (*watchful*) бди́тельный; насторо́женный; **2.** сигна́л трево́ги; ***on the ~*** настороже́
algorithm ['ælgərɪðəm] алгори́тм
alien ['eɪlɪən] **1.** иностра́нный; чу́ждый; **2.** иностра́нец *m*, -ка *f*; **~ate** [~eɪt] *law* отчужда́ть; (*estrange*) отдаля́ть [-ли́ть]; (*turn away*) отта́лкивать [-толкну́ть]
alight[1] [ə'laɪt] сходи́ть [сойти́] (с Р)
alight[2] [~] *pred. adj.* (*on fire*) зажжённый; в огне́; (*lit up*) освещённый
align [ə'laɪn] выра́внивать(ся) [вы́ровнять(ся)]; **~ment** [~mənt] выра́внивание; (*arrangement*) расстано́вка
alike [ə'laɪk] **1.** *pred. adj.* (*similar*) подо́бный, похо́жий; (*as one*) одина́ковый; **2.** *adv.* то́чно так же; подо́бно
alimentary [ælɪ'mentərɪ]: **~ *canal*** пищевари́тельный тракт
alimony ['ælɪmənɪ] алиме́нты *m/pl.*
alive [ə'laɪv] (*living*) живо́й; (*alert, keen*) чу́ткий (***to*** к Д); (*infested*) киша́щий (***with*** Т); ***be ~ to*** я́сно понима́ть
all [ɔːl] **1.** *adj.* весь *m*, вся *f*, всё *n*, все *pl*; вся́кий; всевозмо́жный; ***for ~ that*** несмотря́ на то; **2.** всё, все; ***at ~*** вообще́; ***not at ~*** во́все не; ***not at ~!*** не́ за что!; ***for ~ (that) I care*** мне безразли́чно; ***for ~ I know*** наско́лько я зна́ю; **3.** *adv.* вполне́, всеце́ло, соверше́нно; ***~ at once*** сра́зу; ***~ the better*** тем лу́чше; ***~ but*** почти́; ***~ right*** хорошо́, ла́дно
allay [ə'leɪ] успока́ивать [-ко́ить]
allegation [ælɪ'geɪʃn] голосло́вное утвержде́ние
allege [ə'ledʒ] утвержда́ть (без основа́ния)
allegiance [ə'liːdʒəns] ве́рность *f*, пре́данность *f*
allerg|ic [ə'lɜːdʒɪk] аллерги́ческий; **~y** ['ælədʒɪ] аллерги́я
alleviate [ə'liːvɪeɪt] облегча́ть [-чи́ть]
alley ['ælɪ] переу́лок; ***blind ~*** тупи́к
alliance [ə'laɪəns] сою́з
allocat|e ['æləkeɪt] *money* ассигнова́ть; *land, money* выделя́ть [вы́делить] (*distribute*); распределя́ть [-ли́ть]; **~ion** [ælə'keɪʃn] распределе́ние
allot [ə'lɒt] *v/t.* распределя́ть [-ли́ть]; разда́(ва́)ть; **~ment** [~mənt] распределе́ние; до́ля, часть *f*; *Brt.* (*plot of land*) земе́льный уча́сток
allow [ə'laʊ] позволя́ть [-о́лить]; допуска́ть [-сти́ть]; *Am.* утвержда́ть; **~able** [~əbl] □ позволи́тельный; **~ance** [~əns] посо́бие, пе́нсия; *fin.* ски́дка; ***make ~ for*** принима́ть во внима́ние
alloy ['ælɔɪ] сплав
all-purpose многоцелево́й, универса́льный
all-round всесторо́нний
allude [ə'luːd] ссыла́ться [сосла́ться] (***to*** на В); (*hint at*) намека́ть [-кну́ть] (***to*** на В)
allure [ə'ljʊə] (*charm*) привлека́ть [-ле́чь]; (*lure*) завлека́ть [-ле́чь]; **~ing** привлека́тельный, зама́нчивый
allusion [ə'luːʒn] намёк, ссы́лка
ally [ə'laɪ] **1.** соединя́ть [-ни́ть] (***to, with*** с Т); **2.** сою́зник
almighty [ɔːl'maɪtɪ] всемогу́щий
almond [ɑːmənd] минда́ль *m*
almost ['ɔːlməʊst] почти́, едва́ не
alone [ə'ləʊn] оди́н *m*, одна́ *f*, одно́ *n*, одни́ *pl.*; одино́кий (-кая); ***let*** (*или* ***leave***) **~** оста́вить *pf.* в поко́е;

let ~ ... не говоря́ уже́ о ... (П)
along [ə'lɒŋ] **1.** *adv.* вперёд; ***all ~*** всё вре́мя; ***~ with*** вме́сте с (Т); *coll.* ***get ~ with you!*** убира́йтесь; **2.** *prp.* вдоль (Р), по (Д); **~side** [~saɪd] бок о́ бок, ря́дом
aloof [ə'lu:f]: ***stand ~*** держа́ться в стороне́ *or* особняко́м
aloud [ə'laʊd] гро́мко, вслух
alpha|bet ['ælfəbet] алфави́т; **~betic** [ˌ~'etɪk] а́збучный, алфави́тный; **~numeric** *comput.* алфави́тно- *or* бу́квенно-цифрово́й
already [ɔ:l'redɪ] уже́
also ['ɔ:lsəʊ] та́кже, то́же
altar ['ɔ:ltə] алта́рь *m*
alter ['ɔ:ltə] *v/t. & v/i.* меня́т(ся) (*impf.*); изменя́ть(ся) [-ни́ть(ся)]; **~ation** [ɔ:ltə'reɪʃn] измене́ние, переде́лка (***to*** Р)
alternat|e **1.** ['ɔ:ltəneɪt] чередова́ть(ся); **2.** [ɔ:l'tɜ:nɪt] □ переме́нный; ***alternating current*** переме́нный ток; **~ion** [ɔ:ltə'neɪʃn] чередова́ние; **~ive** [ɔ:l'tɜ:nətɪv] **1.** альтернати́вный; переме́нно де́йствующий; **2.** альтернати́ва; вы́бор
although [ɔ:l'ðəʊ] хотя́
altitude ['æltɪtju:d] высота́
altogether [ɔ:ltə'geðə] (*entirely*) вполне́, соверше́нно; (*in general*; *as a whole*) в це́лом, в о́бщем
alumin(i)um [ælju'mɪnɪəm, *Am:* ə'lu:mɪnəm] алюми́ний
always ['ɔ:lweɪz] всегда́
Alzheimer's disease ['æltshɑɪməz] боле́знь Альцге́ймера
am [æm· *в предложе́нии*: əm] [*irr.*] *1st pers. sg. pr. om* **be**
A.M. (*abbr. of* ***ante meridiem***) утра́, у́тром
amalgamate [ə'mælgəmeɪt] *v/t.* объединя́ть [-ни́ть]; *v/i.* объединя́ться [-ни́ться] (***with*** с Т)
amass [ə'mæs] соб(и)ра́ть; (*accumulate*) накопля́ть [-пи́ть]
amateur ['æmətə] люби́тель *m*, -ница *f*; дилета́нт *m*, -ка *f*, *attr.* люби́тельский
amaz|e [ə'meɪz] изумля́ть [-ми́ть], поража́ть [порази́ть]; **~ement** [~mənt] изумле́ние; **~ing** [ə'meɪzɪŋ] удиви́тельный, порази́тельный
ambassador [æm'bæsədə] посо́л
amber ['æmbə] янта́рь *m*
ambigu|ity [æmbɪ'gju:ətɪ] двусмы́сленность *f*; **~ous** [æm'bɪgjʊəs] □ двусмы́сленный
ambitio|n [æm'bɪʃn] честолю́бие; (*aim*) мечта́, стремле́ние; **~us** [~ʃəs] честолюби́вый
amble ['æmbl] идти́ лёгкой похо́дкой, прогу́ливаться
ambulance ['æmbjʊləns] маши́на ско́рой по́мощи
ambush ['æmbʊʃ] заса́да
amenable [ə'mi:nəbl] (*tractable*) □ пода́тливый; (*obedient*) послу́шный; (*complaisant*) сгово́рчивый
amend [ə'mend] исправля́ть(ся) [-а́вить(ся)]; вноси́ть [внести́] попра́вки в (В); **~ment** [~mənt] исправле́ние; попра́вка; **~s** [ə'mendz]: ***make ~ for*** компенси́ровать (В)
amenity [ə'mi:nətɪ] *mst. pl.* удо́бства; *in town* места́ о́тдыха и развлече́ний; *of family life* пре́лести
American [ə'merɪkən] **1.** америка́нец *m*, -нка *f*; **2.** америка́нский
amiable ['eɪmjəbl] □ доброду́шный; (*sweet*) ми́лый
amicable ['æmɪkəbl] □ дружелю́бный, дру́жественный
amid(st) [ə'mɪd(st)] среди́ (Р), посреди́ (Р), ме́жду (Т)
amiss [ə'mɪs] *adv.* непра́вильно; ***take ~*** обижа́ться [оби́деться]
amity ['æmɪtɪ] дру́жба
ammonia [ə'məʊnɪə] аммиа́к; ***liquid ~*** нашаты́рный спирт
ammunition [æmjʊ'nɪʃn] боеприпа́сы *m/pl.*
amnesty ['æmnəstɪ] **1.** амни́стия; **2.** амнисти́ровать (*im*)*pf.*
among(st) [ə'mʌŋ(st)] среди́ (Р), ме́жду (Т *sometimes* Р)
amoral [eɪ'morəl] □ амора́льный
amorous ['æmərəs] □ (*in love*) влюблённый (***of*** в В); (*inclined to love*) влю́бчивый
amount [ə'maʊnt] **1.** ***~ to*** равня́ться (Д); *fig.* быть равноси́льным; ***it ~s to this*** де́ло сво́дится к сле́дующему; **2.** су́мма, коли́чество
ample ['æmpl] (*sufficient*) доста́точный, (*abundant*) оби́льный; (*spacious*) просто́рный

ampli|fier ['æmplıfaıə] *el.* усили́тель *m*; **~fy** [~faı] уси́ли(ва)ть; (*expand*) расширя́ть [-и́рить]; **~tude** [~tju:d] широта́, разма́х; амплиту́да
ampoule ['æmpu:l] а́мпула
amputate ['æmpjʊteıt] ампути́ровать (*im*)*pf.*
amuse [ə'mju:z] забавля́ть, позаба́вить *pf.*, развлека́ть [-е́чь]; **~ment** [~mənt] развлече́ние, заба́ва; **~ park** площа́дка с аттракцио́нами
an [æn, ən] *неопределённый арти́кль*
an(a)emi|a [ə'ni:mıə] анеми́я; **~c** [~mık] анеми́чный
an(a)esthetic [ænıs'θetık] обезбо́ливающее сре́дство; ***general ~*** о́бщий нарко́з; ***local ~*** ме́стный нарко́з
analog|ous [ə'næləgəs] □ аналоги́чный, схо́дный; **~y** [ə'nælədʒı] анало́гия, схо́дство
analysis [ə'næləsıs] ана́лиз
analyze, *Brit.* **-yse** ['ænəlaız] анализи́ровать (*im*)*pf.*, *pf. a.* [про-]
anarchy ['ænəkı] ана́рхия
anatomy [ə'nætəmı] (*science*) анато́мия; (*dissection*) анатоми́рование; (*analysis*) разбо́р; (*human body*) те́ло
ancest|or ['ænsıstə] пре́док; **~ral** [æn'sestrəl] родово́й; **~ry** ['ænsestrı] (*lineage*) происхожде́ние; (*ancestors*) пре́дки *m/pl.*
anchor ['æŋkə] **1.** я́корь *m*; ***at ~*** на я́коре; **2. *come to ~*** станови́ться [стать] на я́корь
anchovy ['æntʃəvı] анчо́ус
ancient [eınʃənt] дре́вний; анти́чный
and [ənd, ən, ænd] и; а
anew [ə'nju:] (*again*) сно́ва; (*in a different way*) по-но́вому, за́ново
angel ['əındʒəl] а́нгел; **~ic(al** □) [æn'dʒelık(l)] а́нгельский
anger ['æŋgə] **1.** гнев; **2.** [рас]серди́ть
angle[1] ['æŋgl] у́гол; (*viewpoint*) то́чка зре́ния
angle[2] [~] уди́ть ры́бу; *fig.* напра́шиваться (***for*** на В); **~r** [~ə] рыболо́в
Anglican ['æŋglıkən] **1.** член англика́нской це́ркви; **2.** англика́нский
angry ['æŋgrı] серди́тый (***with*** на В)
anguish ['æŋgwıʃ] страда́ние, му́ка
angular ['æŋgjʊlə] *mst. fig.* углова́тый; (*awkward*) нело́вкий
animal ['ænıml] **1.** живо́тное; ***pack ~*** вью́чное живо́тное; **2.** живо́тный; ***~ kingdom*** живо́тное ца́рство
animat|e ['ænımeıt] оживля́ть [-ви́ть]; **~ion** [ænı'meıʃn] жи́вость *f*; оживле́ние
animosity [ænı'mɒsətı] вражде́бность *f*
ankle ['æŋkl] лоды́жка
annals ['ænlz] *pl.* ле́топись *f*
annex [ə'neks] аннекси́ровать (*im*)*pf.*; присоединя́ть [-ни́ть]; **~ation** [ænek'seıʃn] анне́ксия
annex(e) ['ænəks] (*to a building*) пристро́йка; крыло́; (*to document, etc.*) приложе́ние
annihilate [ə'naıəleıt] уничтожа́ть [-о́жить], истребля́ть [-би́ть]
anniversary [ænı'vɜ:sərı] годовщи́на
annotat|e ['ænəteıt] анноти́ровать (*im*)*pf.*; снабжа́ть примеча́ниями; **~ion** [ænə'teıʃn] аннота́ция; примеча́ние
announce [ə'naʊns] объявля́ть [-ви́ть]; заявля́ть [-ви́ть]; **~ment** [~mənt] объявле́ние, заявле́ние; *on the radio, etc.* сообще́ние; **~r** [~ə] *radio* ди́ктор
annoy [ə'nɔı] надоеда́ть [-е́сть] (Д); досажда́ть [досади́ть] (Д); раздража́ть; **~ance** [~əns] доса́да; раздраже́ние; неприя́тность *f*
annual ['ænjʊəl] **1.** *publication* □ ежего́дный; годово́й; **2.** *plant* ежего́дник; однолетнее расте́ние
annul [ə'nʌl] аннули́ровать (*im*)*pf.*; отменя́ть [-ни́ть]; *contract* расторга́ть [-о́ргнуть]; **~ment** [~mənt] отме́на, аннули́рование
anodyne ['ænədaın] болеутоля́ющее сре́дство; успока́ивающее сре́дство
anomalous [ə'nɒmələs] □ *adj.* анома́льный
anonymous [ə'nɒnıməs] □ анони́мный
another [ə'nʌðə] друго́й, ещё; ***one***

after ~ оди́н за други́м; ***quite ~ thing*** совсе́м друго́е де́ло
answer ['ɑːnsə] **1.** *v/t.* отвеча́ть [-е́тить] (Д); (*fulfil*) удовлетворя́ть [-ри́ть]; ***~ back*** дерзи́ть; ***~ the bell*** *or* ***door*** открыва́ть дверь на звоно́к; ***~ the telephone*** взять *or* снять тру́бку; *v/i.* отвеча́ть [-е́тить] (**to a p.** Д, **to a question** на вопро́с); ***~ for*** отвеча́ть [-е́тить] за (В); **2.** отве́т (**to** на В); реше́ние *a. math.*; **~able** ['ɑːnsərəbl] □ отве́тственный; **~ing machine** автоотве́тчик
ant [ænt] мураве́й
antagonism [æn'tægənɪzəm] антагони́зм, вражда́
antagonize [æn'tægənaɪz] настра́ивать [-ро́ить] (***against*** про́тив Р)
antenatal [æntɪ'neɪtl]: ***~ clinic*** *approx.* же́нская консульта́ция
antenna [æn'tenə] *Am.* → ***aerial***
anterior [æn'tɪərɪə] *of time* предше́ствующий (**to** Д); *of place* пере́дний
anthem ['ænθəm] хора́л, гимн; ***national ~*** госуда́рственный гимн
anti... [æntɪ…] противо..., анти...
antiaircraft [æntɪ'ɛəkrɑːft] противовозду́шный; ***~ defence*** противовозду́шная оборо́на (ПВО)
antibiotic [~baɪ'ɒtɪk] антибио́тик
anticipat|e [æn'tɪsɪpeɪt] (*foresee*) предви́деть, предчу́вствовать; (*expect*) ожида́ть; предвкуша́ть [-уси́ть]; (*forestall*) предупрежда́ть [-преди́ть]; **~ion** [æntɪsɪ'peɪʃn] ожида́ние; предчу́вствие; ***in ~*** в ожида́нии, в предви́дении
antics ['æntɪks] ша́лости *f/pl.*, прока́зы *f/pl.*, проде́лки *f/pl.*
antidote ['æntɪdəʊt] противоя́дие
antipathy [æn'tɪpəθɪ] антипа́тия
antiqua|ry ['æntɪkwərɪ] антиква́р; **~ted** [~kweɪtɪd] устаре́лый; (*old-fashioned*) старомо́дный
antiqu|e [æn'tiːk] **1.** анти́чный; стари́нный; **2.** ***the ~*** (*art*) анти́чное иску́сство; **~ity** [æn'tɪkwətɪ] дре́вность *f*; старина́; анти́чность *f*
antiseptic [æntɪ'septɪk] антисепти́ческое сре́дство
antlers ['æntləz] *pl.* оле́ньи рога́ *m/pl.*
anvil ['ænvɪl] накова́льня
anxiety [æŋ'zaɪətɪ] (*worry*) беспоко́йство, (*alarm*) трево́га; (*keen desire*) стра́стное жела́ние; (*apprehension*) опасе́ние
anxious ['æŋkʃəs] озабо́ченный; беспоко́ящийся (***about***, ***for*** о П); *of news*, *warning signals*, *etc.* трево́жный
any ['enɪ] **1.** *pron.& adj.* како́й-нибудь; вся́кий, любо́й; ***at ~ rate*** во вся́ком слу́чае; ***not ~*** никако́й; **2.** *adv.* ско́лько-нибудь, нисколько; **~body**, **~one** кто́-нибудь; вся́кий; **~how** ка́к-нибудь; так и́ли ина́че, всё же; **~thing** что́-нибудь; ***~thing but*** то́лько не...; **~ where** где́-нибудь, куда́-нибудь
apart [ə'pɑːt] отде́льно; по́рознь; ***~ from*** кро́ме (Р); **~ment** [~mənt] → ***flat*** *Brt.*; *mst. pl.* апартаме́нты *m/pl.*; *Am.* кварти́ра; ***~ house*** многокварти́рный дом
ape [eɪp] **1.** обезья́на; **2.** подража́ть (Д), [с]обезья́нничать
aperient [ə'pɪərɪənt] слаби́тельное
aperitif [ə'perɪtɪf] аперити́в
aperture ['æpətʃə] отве́рстие; *phot.* диафра́гма
apex ['eɪpeks] верши́на
apiece [ə'piːs] за шту́ку; за ка́ждого, с челове́ка
apolog|etic [əpɒlə'dʒetɪk] (***~ally***): ***be ~*** извиня́ться [-ни́ться] (***about***, ***for*** за В); ***~ air*** винова́тый вид; **~ize** [ə'pɒlədʒaɪz] извиня́ться [-ни́ться] (***for*** за В; ***to*** пе́ред Т); **~y** [~dʒɪ] извине́ние
apoplectic [æpə'plektɪk]: ***~ stroke*** уда́р, инсу́льт
apostle [ə'pɒsl] апо́стол
apostrophe [ə'pɒstrəfɪ] *gr.* апостро́ф
appall *or Brt.* **appal** [ə'pɔːl] ужаса́ть [-сну́ть]
apparatus [æpə'reɪtəs] прибо́р; аппарату́ра, аппара́т; *sport* снаря́ды *m/pl.*
appar|ent [ə'pærənt] (*obvious*) очеви́дный; (*visible*, *evident*) ви́димый; ***for no ~ reason*** без ви́димой причи́ны; **~ently** по-ви́димому; **~ition** [æpə'rɪʃən] при́зрак
appeal [ə'piːl] **1.** апелли́ровать

(*im*)*pf.*; обраща́ться [обрати́ться] (**to** к Д); (*attract*) привлека́ть [-е́чь] (**to** В); *law* обжа́ловать; **2.** воззва́ние, призы́в; привлека́тельность *f*; обжа́лование; **~ing** [~ɪŋ] (*moving*) тро́гательный; (*attractive*) привлека́тельный

appear [ə'pɪə] появля́ться [-ви́ться]; (*seem*) пока́зываться [-за́ться]; *on stage etc.* выступа́ть [вы́ступить]; ***it ~s to me*** мне ка́жется; **~ance** [ə'pɪərəns] появле́ние; вне́шний вид; *person's* вне́шность *f*; **~s** *pl.* прили́чия *n/pl.*; ***keep up ~s*** соблюда́ть прили́чия

appease [ə'pi:z] умиротворя́ть [-ри́ть]; успока́ивать [-ко́ить]

append [ə'pend] прилага́ть [-ложи́ть] (к Д); **~icitis** [əpendɪ'saɪtɪs] аппендици́т; **~ix** [ə'pendɪks] *of a book, etc.* приложе́ние; *anat.* аппе́ндикс

appetite ['æpɪtaɪt] аппети́т (**for** на В); *fig.* влече́ние, скло́нность *f* (**for** к Д)

appetizing ['æpɪtaɪzɪŋ] аппети́тный

applaud [ə'plɔ:d] *v/t.* аплоди́ровать (Д); (*approve*) одобря́ть [одо́брить]

applause [ə'plɔ:z] аплодисме́нты *m/pl*; *fig.* (*approval*) одобре́ние

apple [æpl] я́блоко; ***~ of discord*** я́блоко раздо́ра; **~tree** я́блоня

appliance [ə'plaɪəns] устро́йство, приспособле́ние, прибо́р

applica|ble ['æplɪkəbl] примени́мый, (*appropriate*) подходя́щий (**to** к Д); ***delete where ~*** зачеркни́те, где необходи́мо; **~nt** [~kənt] кандида́т (**for** на В); ***not ~*** не отно́сится (**to** к Д); **~tion** [æplɪ'keɪʃn] примене́ние; заявле́ние; про́сьба (**for** о П); ***send in an ~*** пода́ть заявле́ние, зая́вку

apply [ə'plaɪ] *v/t.* (*bring into action*) прилага́ть [-ложи́ть] (**to** к Д); (*lay or spread on*) прикла́дывать [приложи́ть]; (*use*) применя́ть [-ни́ть] (**to** к Д); ***~ o.s. to*** занима́ться [заня́ться] (Т); *v/i.* (*approach, request*) обраща́ться [обрати́ться] (**for** за Т; **to** к Д); (*concern, relate to*) относи́ться

appoint [ə'pɔɪnt] назнача́ть [-на́чить]; **~ment** [~mənt] назначе́ние; (*meeting*) встре́ча; (*agreement*) договорённость *f*; ***by ~*** по предвари́тельной договорённос ти, по за́писи

apportion [ə'pɔ:ʃn] разделя́ть [-ли́ть]

apprais|al [ə'preɪzl] оце́нка; **~e** [ə'preɪz] оце́нивать [-ни́ть], расце́нивать [-ни́ть]

apprecia|ble [ə'pri:ʃəbl] □ заме́тный, ощути́мый; **~te** [~ieɪt] *v/t.* оце́нивать [-ни́ть]; [о]цени́ть; (*understand*) понима́ть [-ня́ть]; *v/i.* повыша́ться [-вы́ситься] в цене́; **~tion** [əpri:ʃɪ'eɪʃn] (*gratitude*) призна́тельность *f*; оце́нка, понима́ние

apprehen|d [æprɪ'hend] (*foresee*) предчу́вствовать; (*fear*) опаса́ться; (*seize, arrest*) заде́рживать [-жа́ть], аресто́вывать [-ова́ть]; **~sion** [~'henʃn] опасе́ние, предчу́вствие; аре́ст; **~sive** [~'hensɪv] □ озабо́ченный, по́лный трево́ги

apprentice [ə'prentɪs] учени́к; **~ship** [~ʃɪp] уче́ние, учени́чество

approach [ə'prəʊtʃ] **1.** приближа́ться [-бли́зиться] к (Д); (*speak to*) обраща́ться [обрати́ться] к (Д); **2.** приближе́ние; по́дступ; *fig.* подхо́д; **~ing** [~ɪŋ] приближа́ющийся; ***~ traffic*** встре́чное движе́ние

approbation [æprə'beɪʃn] одобре́ние; са́нкция, согла́сие

appropriate **1.** [ə'prəʊprɪeɪt] (*take possession of*) присва́ивать [-сво́ить]; **2.** [~ət] (*suitable*) подходя́щий, соотве́тствующий

approv|al [ə'pru:vl] одобре́ние; утвержде́ние; **~e** [ə'pru:v] одобря́ть [одо́брить]; утвержда́ть [-ди́ть]; санкциони́ровать (*im*)*pf.*

approximate **1.** [ə'prɒksɪmeɪt] приближа́ть(ся) [-бли́зить(ся)] к (Д); **2.** [~mət] приблизи́тельный

apricot ['eɪprɪkɒt] абрико́с

April ['eɪprəl] апре́ль *m*

apron ['eɪprən] пере́дник, фа́ртук

apt [æpt] □ (*suitable*) подходя́щий, (*pertinent*) уме́стный; (*gifted*) спосо́бный; ***~ to*** скло́нный к (Д); **~itude** ['æptɪtju:d], **~ness** [~nɪs]

спосо́бность *f*; скло́нность *f* (***for***, ***to*** к Д); уме́стность *f*
aqualung ['ækwəlʌŋ] аквала́нг
aquarium [ə'kweərɪəm] аква́риум
Aquarius [ə'kweərɪəs] Водоле́й
aquatic [ə'kwætɪk] **1.** водяно́й, во́дный; **2.** **~s** *pl.* во́дный спорт
aqueduct ['ækwɪdʌkt] акведу́к
Arab ['ærəb] ара́б *m*, -ка *f*; **~ic** ['ærəbɪk] **1.** ара́бский язы́к; **2.** ара́бский
arable ['ærəbl] па́хотный
arbit|er ['ɑːbɪtə] (*judge*) арби́тр; (*third party*) трете́йский судья́; **~rariness** ['ɑːbɪtrərɪnɪs] произво́л; **~rary** [ĩtrərɪ] произво́льный; **~rate** ['ɑːbɪtreɪt] выступа́ть в ка́честве арби́тра; **~ration** [ɑːbɪ'treɪʃn] арбитра́ж; **~rator** ['ɑːbɪtreɪtə] трете́йский судья́, арби́тр
arbo(u)r ['ɑːbə] бесе́дка
arc [ɑːk] дуга́; **~ade** [ɑː'keɪd] (*covered passageway*) арка́да; *with shops* пасса́ж
arch¹ [ɑːtʃ] **1.** а́рка; свод; дуга́; **2.** придава́ть фо́рму а́рки; выгиба́ться
arch² [~] **1.** хи́трый, лука́вый; **2.** *pref.* архи...; гла́вный
archaic [ɑː'keɪɪk] (***~ally***) устаре́лый, устаре́вший; дре́вний
archbishop [ɑːtʃ'bɪʃəp] архиепи́скоп
archery ['ɑːtʃərɪ] стрельба́ из лу́ка
architect ['ɑːkɪtekt] архите́ктор; **~ural** [ɑːkɪ'tektʃərəl] архитекту́рный; **~ure** ['ɑːkɪtektʃə] архитекту́ра
archway ['ɑːtʃweɪ] сводча́тый прохо́д
arctic ['ɑːktɪk] аркти́ческий; ***the Arctic*** А́рктика
ardent ['ɑːdənt] □ *mst. fig.* горя́чий, пы́лкий; я́рый
ardo(u)r ['ɑːdə] рве́ние, пыл
arduous ['ɑːdjʊəs] □ тру́дный
are [ɑː; *в предложе́нии*: ə] → ***be***
area ['eərɪə] (*measurement*) пло́щадь *f*; ***~ of a triangle*** пло́щадь треуго́льника; (*region*) райо́н, край, зо́на; (*sphere*) о́бласть
Argentine ['ɑːdʒəntaɪn] **1.** аргенти́нский; **2.** аргенти́нец *m*, -нка *f*
argue ['ɑːgjuː] *v/t.* обсужда́ть [-уди́ть]; доказывать [-за́ть]; ***~ a p. into*** убежда́ть [убеди́ть] в (П); *v/i.* [по]спо́рить (с Т); ***~ against*** приводи́ть до́воды про́тив (Р)
argument ['ɑːgjʊmənt] до́вод, аргуме́нт; (*discussion, debate*) спор; **~ation** [ɑːgjʊmen'teɪʃn] аргумента́ция
arid ['ærɪd] сухо́й (*a. fig.*); засу́шливый
Aries ['eəriːz] Овен
arise [ə'raɪz] (*get up, stand up*) встава́ть [встать]; (*fig., come into being*) возника́ть [-ни́кнуть] (***from*** из Р); явля́ться [яви́ться] результа́том (***from*** из Р); **~n** [ə'rɪzn] *p. pt. от* ***arise***
aristocra|cy [ærɪ'stɒkrəsɪ] аристокра́тия; **~t** ['ærɪstəkræt] аристокра́т; **~tic** [ærɪstə'krætɪk] аристократи́ческий
arithmetic [ə'rɪθmətɪk] арифме́тика
ark [ɑːk]: ***Noah's ~*** Но́ев ковче́г
arm¹ [ɑːm] рука́; (*sleeve*) рука́в
arm² [~] вооружа́ть(ся) [-жи́ть(ся)]; ***~ed forces*** вооружённые си́лы
armament ['ɑːməmənt] вооруже́ние
armchair кре́сло
armful ['ɑːmfʊl] оха́пка
armistice ['ɑːmɪstɪs] переми́рие
armo(u)r ['ɑːmə] *hist.* доспе́хи *m/pl.*; броня́; **~y** [~rɪ] арсена́л; оруже́йная пала́та
armpit ['ɑːmpɪt] подмы́шка
arms [ɑːmz] ору́жие
army ['ɑːmɪ] а́рмия; *fig.* мно́жество
arose [ə'rəʊz] *pt. от* ***arise***
around [ə'raʊnd] **1.** *adv.* всю́ду, круго́м; **2.** *prp.* вокру́г (Р)
arouse [ə'raʊz] [раз]буди́ть (*a. fig.*); *fig.* возбужда́ть [-уди́ть]; *interest, envy etc.* вызыва́ть [вы́звать]
arrange [ə'reɪndʒ] приводи́ть в поря́док; *a party etc.* устра́ивать [-ро́ить]; (*agree in advance*) усла́вливаться [усло́виться]; *mus.* аранжи́ровать (*im*)*pf.*; **~ment** [~mənt] устро́йство; расположе́ние; соглаше́ние, мероприя́тие; *mus.* аранжиро́вка
array [ə'reɪ] *fig. assemblage* мно́жество, *display* колле́кция; це́лый ряд

arrear(s) [ə'rɪə] *mst. pl.* отстава́ние; задо́лженность *f*
arrest [ə'rest] **1.** аре́ст, задержа́ние; **2.** аресто́вывать [-ова́ть], заде́рживать [-жа́ть]
arriv|al [ə'raɪvl] прибы́тие, прие́зд; **~s** *pl.* прибы́вшие *pl.*; **~e** [ə'raɪv] прибы́(ва́)ть; приезжа́ть [-е́хать] (**at** в, на В)
arroga|nce ['ærəgəns] надме́нность *f*, высокоме́рие; **~nt** [~nt] надме́нный, высокоме́рный
arrow ['ærəʊ] стрела́; *as symbol on road sign, etc.* стре́лка
arsenal ['ɑːsənl] арсена́л
arsenic ['ɑːsnɪk] мышья́к
arson ['ɑːsn] *law* поджо́г
art [ɑːt] иску́сство; **fine ~s** изя́щные *or* изобрази́тельные иску́сства
arter|ial [ɑ'tɪərɪəl]: **~ road** магистра́ль *f*; **~y** ['ɑːtərɪ] *anat.* арте́рия
artful ['ɑːtfəl] ло́вкий; хи́трый
article ['ɑːtɪkl] (*object*) предме́т, вещь *f*; (*piece of writing*) статья́; (*clause*) пункт, пара́граф; арти́кль *m*
articulat|e [ɑː'tɪkjʊleɪt] **1.** отчётливо, я́сно произноси́ть; **2.** [~lət] отчётливый; членоразде́льный; **~ion** [ɑːtɪkjʊ'leɪʃn] артикуля́ция
artificial [ɑːtɪ'fɪʃl] иску́сственный
artillery [ɑː'tɪlərɪ] артилле́рия; **~man** [~mən] артиллери́ст
artisan [ɑːtɪ'zæn] реме́сленник
artist ['ɑːtɪst] худо́жник (-ица); (*actor*) актёр, актри́са; **~e** [ɑː'tiːst] арти́ст(ка); **~ic(al** □) [ɑː'tɪstɪk(l)] артисти́ческий, худо́жественный
artless ['ɑːtlɪs] есте́ственный; (*ingenuous*) простоду́шный; (*unskilled*) неиску́сный
as [əz, æz] *cj. a. adv.* когда́; в то вре́мя как; та́к как; хотя́; **~ far ~ I know** наско́лько мне изве́стно; **~ it were** так сказа́ть; ка́к бы; **~ well** та́кже; в тако́й же ме́ре; **such ~** тако́й как; как наприме́р; **~ well ~** и ... и ...; *prp.* **~ for**, **~ to** что каса́ется (Р); **~ from** с (Р)
ascend [ə'send] поднима́ться [-ня́ться]; восходи́ть [взойти́]
ascension [ə'senʃn]: ♀ (**Day**) Вознесе́ние
ascent [ə'sent] восхожде́ние; (*upward slope*) подъём
ascertain [æsə'teɪn] удостоверя́ться [-ве́риться] в (П); устана́вливать [-нови́ть]
ascribe [ə'skraɪb] припи́сывать [-са́ть] (Д/В)
aseptic [eɪ'septɪk] *med.* асепти́ческий, стери́льный
ash[1] [æʃ] *bot.* я́сень *m*; **mountain ~** ряби́на
ash[2] [~] *mst. pl.* **~es** ['æʃɪz] зола́, пе́пел
ashamed [ə'ʃeɪmd] пристыжённый; **I'm ~ of you** мне сты́дно за тебя́; **feel ~ of o.s.** стыди́ться
ash can *Am.* ведро́ для му́сора
ashen ['æʃən] пе́пельного цве́та; (*pale*) бле́дный
ashore [ə'ʃɔː] на бе́рег, на берегу́
ashtray пе́пельница
ashy ['æʃɪ] *of or relating to ashes* пе́пельный
Asian ['eɪʃn] **1.** азиа́тский; **2.** азиа́т *m*, -ка *f*
aside [ə'saɪd] в сто́рону, в стороне́
ask [ɑːsk] *v/t.* (*request*) [по]проси́ть (**a th. of**, **from a p.** что́-нибудь у кого́-нибудь); **~ that** проси́ть, что́бы ...; (*inquire*) спра́шивать [спроси́ть]; **~ (a p.) a question** задава́ть вопро́с (Д); *v/i.* **~ for** [по]проси́ть (В *or* Р *or* о П)
askance [ə'skæns]: **look ~** ко́со посмотре́ть (**at** на В)
askew [ə'skjuː] кри́во
asleep [ə'sliːp] спя́щий; **be ~** спать
asparagus [ə'spærəgəs] спа́ржа
aspect ['æspekt] вид (*a. gr.*); аспе́кт, сторона́
aspen ['æspən] оси́на
asperity [æ'sperətɪ] (*sharpness*) ре́зкость *f*; **with ~** ре́зко; (*severity*) суро́вость *f*
asphalt ['æsfælt] **1.** асфа́льт; **2.** покрыва́ть асфа́льтом
aspir|ation [æspə'reɪʃn] стремле́ние; **~e** [ə'spaɪə] стреми́ться (**to**, **after**, **at** к Д)
aspirin ['æsprɪn] аспири́н
ass [æs] осёл (*a. fig.*); **make an ~ of o.s.** поста́вить себя́ в глу́пое положе́ние; *coll.* сваля́ть дурака́
assail [ə'seɪl] (*attack*) напада́ть [-па́сть] на (В); *fig.* энерги́чно

бра́ться за; *with questions* засыпа́ть [засы́пать] вопро́сами; **~ant** [~ənt] напада́ющий

assassin [əˈsæsɪn] уби́йца *m/f*; **~ate** [~ɪneɪt] уби́(ва́)ть; **~ation** [əsæsɪˈneɪʃn] уби́йство

assault [əˈsɔːlt] **1.** нападе́ние; *mil.* ата́ка, штурм; **2.** напада́ть [напа́сть], набра́сываться [-ро́ситься] на (В)

assembl|e [əˈsembl] (*gather*) собира́ть(ся) [-бра́ть(ся)]; *tech.* [с]монти́ровать, собира́ть [-бра́ть]; **~y** [~i] собра́ние; ассамбле́я; *tech.* сбо́рка

assent [əˈsent] **1.** согла́сие; **2.** соглаша́ться [-ласи́ться] (***to*** на В; с Т)

assert [əˈsɜːt] утвержда́ть [-рди́ть]; **~ion** [əˈsɜːʃn] утвержде́ние

assess [əˈses] оце́нивать [-ни́ть] (*a. fig.*); *taxes etc.* определя́ть [-ли́ть], устана́вливать [-нови́ть]; **~ment** [~mənt] *for taxation* обложе́ние; *valuation* оце́нка

asset [ˈæset] це́нное ка́чество; *fin.* статья́ дохо́да; **~s** *pl. fin.* акти́в(ы); ***~s and liabilities*** акти́в и пасси́в

assiduous [əˈsɪdjʊəs] приле́жный

assign [əˈsaɪn] (*appoint*) назнача́ть [-на́чить]; (*allot*) ассигно́вывать, ассигнова́ть (*im*)*pf.*; (*charge*) поруча́ть [-чи́ть]; *room, etc.* отводи́ть [-вести́]; **~ment** [~mənt] назначе́ние; зада́ние, поруче́ние

assimilat|e [əˈsɪmɪleɪt] ассимили́ровать(ся) (*im*)*pf.*; (*absorb*) усва́ивать [-во́ить]; **~ion** [əsɪmɪˈleɪʃn] ассимиля́ция; усвое́ние

assist [əˈsɪst] помога́ть [-мо́чь] (Д), [по]соде́йствовать (*im*)*pf.* (Д); **~ance** [~əns] по́мощь *f*; **~ant** [~ənt] ассисте́нт(ка); помо́щник (-ица); **~ *professor*** *univ. Am.* ассисте́нт; ***shop* ~** *Brt.* продаве́ц

associa|te [əˈsəʊʃɪeɪt] **1.** обща́ться (***with*** с Т); (*connect*) ассоции́ровать(ся) (*im*)*pf.*; **2.** [~ʃɪət] колле́га *m*; соуча́стник; *comm.* компаньо́н; **~tion** [əsəʊsɪˈeɪʃn] ассоциа́ция; объедине́ние, о́бщество

assort|ed [əˈsɔːtɪd] разнообра́зный; **~ *chocolates*** шокола́д ассорти́ *indecl.*; **~ment** [~mənt] ассортиме́нт

assum|e [əˈsjuːm] (*suppose*) предполага́ть [-ложи́ть]; (*take up*) вступа́ть [-пи́ть]; **~ption** [əˈsʌmpʃn] предположе́ние; *eccl.* ♀ Успе́ние

assur|ance [əˈʃʊərəns] (*promise*) увере́ние; (*confidence*) уве́ренность *f*; (*insurance*) страхо́вка; **~e** [əˈʃʊə] уверя́ть [уве́рить]; **~edly** [~rɪdlɪ] *adv.* коне́чно, несомне́нно

aster [ˈæstə] *bot.* а́стра

astir [əsˈtɜː] в движе́нии; на нога́х

astonish [əˈstɒnɪʃ] удивля́ть [-ви́ть], изумля́ть [-ми́ть]; ***be ~ed*** удивля́ться [-ви́ться] (***at*** Д); **~ing** [~ɪʃɪŋ] удиви́тельный, порази́тельный; **~ment** [~mənt] удивле́ние, изумле́ние

astound [əˈstaʊnd] поража́ть [порази́ть]

astrakhan [æstrəˈkæn] (*lambskin*) кара́куль *m*

astray [əˈstreɪ]: ***go ~*** заблуди́ться, сби́ться с пути́ (*a. fig.*); ***lead s.o. ~*** сбить с пути́ (и́стинного)

astride [əˈstraɪd] верхо́м (***of*** на П)

astringent [əˈstrɪndʒənt] *med.* вя́жущее сре́дство

astro|logy [əˈstrɒlədʒɪ] астроло́гия; **~nomer** [əˈstrɒnəmə] астроно́м; **~nomy** [əˈstrɒnəmɪ] астроно́мия

astute [əˈstjuːt] □ (*cunning*) хи́трый; (*shrewd*) проница́тельный; **~ness** [~nɪs] хи́трость *f*; проница́тельность *f*

asylum [əˈsaɪləm] (*place of refuge*) убе́жище; (*shelter*) прию́т; (*mental institution*) сумасше́дший дом

at [æt, ət] *prp.* в (П, В); у (Р); при (П); на (П, В); о́коло (Р); за (Т); ***~ school*** в шко́ле; ***~ the age of*** в во́зрасте (Р); ***~ first*** снача́ла; ***~ first sight*** с пе́рвого взгля́да; на пе́рвый взгляд; ***~ last*** наконе́ц

ate [et, eit] *pt. om* **eat**

atheism [ˈeɪθɪɪzəm] атеи́зм

athlet|e [ˈæθliːt] спортсме́н, атле́т; **~ic(al** □) [æθˈletɪk(əl)] атлети́ческий; **~ics** [æθˈletɪks] *pl.* (лёгкая) атле́тика

atmospher|e [ˈætməsfɪə] атмосфе́ра (*a. fig.*); **~ic(al** □) [ætməsˈferɪk(əl)] атмосфе́рный

atom [ˈætəm] а́том; ***not an ~ of***

truth нет и до́ли и́стины; **~ic** [ə'tɒmɪk] а́томный; ***~ pile*** а́томный реа́ктор; ***~ power plant*** а́томная электроста́нция; ***~ waste*** отхо́ды а́томной промы́шленности
atone [ə'təʊn]: ***~ for*** загла́живать [-ла́дить], искупа́ть [-пи́ть]
atroci|ous [ə'trəʊʃəs] □ зве́рский, *coll.* ужа́сный; **~ty** [ə'trɒsətɪ] зве́рство
attach [ə'tætʃ] *v/t. com.* прикрепля́ть [-пи́ть]; *document* прилага́ть [-ложи́ть]; *importance, etc.* прида(ва)́ть; *law* налага́ть аре́ст на (В); ***~ o.s. to*** привя́зываться [-за́ться] к (Д); **~ment** [~mənt] (*affection*) привя́занность *f*, (*devotion*) пре́данность *f*
attack [ə'tæk] **1.** *mil.* ата́ка; нападе́ние (*a. mil.*); *in press, etc.* ре́зкая кри́тика; *med.* при́ступ; **2.** *v/t.* атакова́ть (*im*)*pf.*; напада́ть [напа́сть] на (В), набра́сываться [-ро́ситься] на (В); подверга́ть [-ве́ргнуть] ре́зкой кри́тике
attain [ə'teɪn] *v/t.* достига́ть [-и́гнуть] (Р), доби́(ва́)ться; (Р); **~ment** [~mənt] достиже́ние
attempt [ə'tempt] **1.** попы́тка; *on s.o.'s life* покуше́ние; **2.** [по]пыта́ться, [по]про́бовать
attend [ə'tend] (*wait, serve*) обслу́живать [-жи́ть]; (*go to*) посеща́ть [-ети́ть]; *med.* уха́живать за (Т); *be present* прису́тствовать (***at*** на П); (*accompany*) сопровожда́ть *mst. impf.*; (*give care*) быть внима́тельным; **~ance** [ə'tendəns] прису́тствие (***at*** на П); наплы́в пу́блики; посеща́емость *f*; *med.* ухо́д (за Т); **~ant** [~ənt] **1.**: ***~ nurse*** дежу́рная медсестра́; **2.** *in elevator* (*Brt. lift*) лифтёр
attent|ion [ə'tenʃn] внима́ние; **~ive** [~tɪv] внима́тельный
attest [ə'test] (*certify*) удостоверя́ть [-ве́рить]; (*bear witness to*) [за]свиде́тельствовать
attic ['ætɪk] черда́к; манса́рда
attire [ə'taɪə] наря́д
attitude ['ætɪtju:d] отноше́ние, пози́ция; (*pose*) по́за
attorney [ə'tɜ:nɪ] уполномо́ченный, дове́ренный; *at law* пове́ренный в суде́, адвока́т; ***power of ~*** дове́ренность *f*; ***attorney general*** *Am.* мини́стр юсти́ции
attract [ə'trækt] *v/t.* привлека́ть [-вле́чь] (*a. fig.*); *magnet* притя́гивать [-яну́ть]; *fig.* прельща́ть [-льсти́ть]; **~ion** [ə'trækʃn] притяже́ние; *fig.* привлека́тельность *f*; ***the town has many ~s*** в го́роде мно́го достопримеча́тельностей; **~ive** [~tɪv] привлека́тельный, зама́нчивый; **~iveness** [~tɪvnɪs] привлека́тельность *f*
attribute **1.** [ə'trɪbju:t] припи́сывать [-са́ть] (Д/В); (*explain*) объясня́ть [-ни́ть]; **2.** ['ætrɪbju:t] сво́йство, при́знак; *gr.* определе́ние
aubergine ['əʊbəʒi:n] баклажа́н
auction ['ɔ:kʃn] **1.** аукцио́н, торги́ *m/pl.*; ***sell by ~, put up for ~*** продава́ть с аукцио́на; **2.** продава́ть с аукцио́на (*mst.* ***~ off***); **~eer** [ɔ:kʃə'niə] аукциони́ст
audaci|ous [ɔ:'deɪʃəs] (*daring*) отва́жный, де́рзкий; (*impudent*) на́глый; **~ty** [ɔ:'dæsətɪ] отва́га; де́рзость *f*; на́глость *f*
audible ['ɔ:dəbl] вня́тный, слы́шный
audience ['ɔ:dɪəns] слу́шатели *m/pl.*, зри́тели *m/pl.*, пу́блика; (*interview*) аудие́нция (***of, with*** у Р)
audiovisual [ɔ:dɪəʊ'vɪʃʊəl] аудиовизуа́льный
audit ['ɔ:dɪt] **1.** прове́рка фина́нсовой отчётности, ауди́т; **2.** проверя́ть [-е́рить] отчётность *f*; **~or** ['ɔ:dɪtə] бухга́лтер-ревизо́р, контролёр
auditorium [ɔ:dɪ'tɔ:rɪəm] аудито́рия; зри́тельный зал
augment [ɔ:g'ment] увели́чи(ва)ть
August ['ɔ:gəst] а́вгуст
aunt [ɑ:nt] тётя, тётка
auspices ['ɔ:spɪsɪz] *pl.*: ***under the ~*** под эги́дой
auster|e [ɒ'stɪə] □ стро́гий, суро́вый; **~ity** [ɒ'sterətɪ] стро́гость *f*, суро́вость *f*
Australian [ɒ'streɪlɪən] **1.** австрали́ец *m*, -и́йка *f*; **2.** австрали́йский
Austrian ['ɒstrɪən] **1.** австри́ец *m*, -и́йка *f*; **2.** австри́йский

authentic [ɔːˈθentɪk] (**~*ally***) по́длинный, достове́рный
author [ˈɔːθə] а́втор; **~itative** [ɔːˈθɒrɪtətɪv] □ авторите́тный; **~ity** [ɔːˈθɒrɪtɪ] авторите́т; (*right*) полномо́чие; власть *f* (***over*** над Т); ***on the ~ of*** на основа́нии (Р); по утвержде́нию (Р); **~ize** [ˈɔːθəraiz] уполномо́чи(ва)ть; (*sanction*) санкциони́ровать (*im*)*pf.*; **~ship** [~ʃɪp] а́вторство
autobiography [ɔːtəbaɪˈɒgrəfɪ] автобиогра́фия
autogenic [ɔːtəˈdʒenɪk]: ***~ training*** аутоге́нная трениро́вка
autograph [ˈɔːtəgrɑːf] автóграф
automatic [ɔːtəˈmætɪk] (**~*ally***) автомати́ческий; *fig.* машина́льный; ***~ machine*** автома́т
automobile [ˈɔːtəməbiːl] автомаши́на, автомоби́ль *m.*; *attr.* автомоби́льный
autonomy [ɔːˈtɒnəmɪ] автоно́мия
autumn [ˈɔːtəm] о́сень *f*; **~al** [ɔːˈtʌmnəl] осе́нний
auxiliary [ɔːgˈzɪlɪərɪ] вспомога́тельный; (*additional*) дополни́тельный
avail [əˈveɪl] **1.** помога́ть [помо́чь] (Д); ***~ o.s. of*** [вос]по́льзоваться (Т); **2.** по́льза, вы́года; ***of no ~*** бесполе́зный; ***to no ~*** напра́сно; **~able** [əˈveɪləbl] (*accessible*) досту́пный; (*on hand*) име́ющийся (в нали́чии)
avalanche [ˈævəlɑːnʃ] лави́на
avaric|e [ˈævərɪs] ску́пость *f*; (*greed*) жа́дность *f*; **~ious** [ævəˈrɪʃəs] скупо́й; жа́дный
aveng|e [əˈvendʒ] [ото]мсти́ть (Д за В); **~er** [~ə] мсти́тель *m*, -ница *f*
avenue [ˈævənjuː] алле́я; *Am.* широ́кая у́лица, проспе́кт; *fig.* (*approach, way*) путь *m*
aver [əˈvɜː] утвержда́ть [-ди́ть]
average [ˈævərɪdʒ] **1.**: ***on an*** (***the***) ***~*** в сре́днем; **2.** сре́дний; **3.** (в сре́днем) составля́ть [-а́вить]
avers|e [əˈvɜːs] □ нерасполо́женный (***to, from*** к Д); ***I'm not ~ to*** я не прочь, я люблю́; **~ion** [əˈvɜːʃn] отвраще́ние, антипа́тия
avert [əˈvɜːt] отвраща́ть [-рати́ть]; *eyes* отводи́ть [-вести́] (*a. fig.*); *head* отвора́чивать [-верну́ть]
aviation [eɪvɪˈeɪʃn] авиа́ция
avocado [ævəˈkɑːdəʊ], **~ pear** авока́до *indecl.*
avoid [əˈvɔɪd] избега́ть [-ежа́ть]
await [əˈweɪt] ожида́ть (Р)
awake [əˈweɪk] **1.** бо́дрствующий; ***be ~ to*** я́сно понима́ть; **2.** [*irr.*]. *v/t.* (*mst.* **~n** [əˈweɪkən]) [раз]буди́ть; *interest, etc.* пробужда́ть [-уди́ть] (к Д); *v/i.* просыпа́ться [просну́ться]; ***~ to a th.*** осозн(ав)а́ть (В)
award [əˈwɔːd] **1.** награ́да; *univ.* стипе́ндия; **2.** присужда́ть [-уди́ть]
aware [əˈweə]: ***be ~ of*** знать (В *or* о П), сознава́ть (В); ***become ~ of*** почу́вствовать
away [əˈweɪ] прочь; далеко́
awe [ɔː] благогове́ние, тре́пет (***of*** перед Т)
awful [ɔːfʊl] □ стра́шный, ужа́сный (*a. coll.*)
awhile [əˈwaɪl] на не́которое вре́мя; ***wait ~*** подожди́ немно́го
awkward [ˈɔːkwəd] (*clumsy*) неуклю́жий, нело́вкий (*a. fig.*); (*inconvenient, uncomfortable*) неудо́бный
awl [ɔːl] ши́ло
awning [ˈɔːnɪŋ] наве́с, те́нт
awoke [əˈwəʊk] *pt.* и *pt. p. от* ***awake***
awry [əˈraɪ] ко́со, на́бок; ***everything went ~*** всё пошло́ скве́рно
ax(e) [æks] топо́р, колу́н
axis [ˈæksɪs], *pl.* **axes** [~siːz] ось *f*
axle [ˈæksl] *tech.* ось *f*
ay(e) [aɪ] *affirmative vote* го́лос "за"
azure [ˈæʒə] **1.** лазу́рь *f*; **2.** лазу́рный

B

babble ['bæbl] **1.** ле́пет; болтовня́; **2.** [по]болта́тъ; [за]лепета́ть
baboon [bə'bu:n] *zo.* бабуи́н
baby ['beɪbɪ] **1.** младе́нец, ребёнок, дитя́ *n*; **2.** небольшо́й; ма́лый; ~ ***carriage*** де́тская коля́ска; ~ ***grand*** кабине́тный роя́ль; **~hood** ['beɪbɪhud] младе́нчество
bachelor ['bætʃələ] холостя́к; *univ.* бакала́вр
back [bæk] **1.** спина́; *of chair, dress, etc.* спи́нка; *of cloth* изна́нка; *sport* **full~** защи́тник; *of head* заты́лок; *of coin, etc.* обра́тная сторона́; **2.** *adj.* за́дний; обра́тный; отдалённый; **3.** *adv.* наза́д, обра́тно; тому́ наза́д; **4.** *v/t.* подде́рживать [-жа́ть]; подкрепля́ть [-пи́ть]; *fin.* субсиди́ровать, финанси́роватъ; гаранти́ровать; *v/i.* отступа́ть [-пи́ть]; [по]пя́титься; **~bone** позвоно́чник, спинно́й хребе́т; *fig.* опо́ра; **~er** ['bækə] *fin.* субсиди́рующий; гара́нт; **~ground** за́дний план, фон; **~ing** подде́ржка; **~side** (*coll. buttocks*) зад; за́дница; **~stairs** та́йный, закули́сный; **~stroke** пла́вание на спине́; **~ talk** *Am.* де́рзкий отве́т; **~up 1.** подде́ржка, *comput.* резе́рвная ко́пия; **2.** создава́ть [созда́ть] резе́рвную ко́пию; **~ward** ['bækwəd] **1.** *adj.* обра́тный; отста́лый; **2.** *adv.* (*a.* **~ward[s]** [-z]) наза́д; за́дом; наоборо́т; обра́тно
bacon ['beɪkən] беко́н
bacteri|ologist [bæktɪərɪ'ɒlədʒɪst] бактерио́лог; **~um** [bæk'tɪərɪəm], *pl.* **~a** [~rɪə] бакте́рия
bad [bæd] □ плохо́й, дурно́й, скве́рный; (*harmful*) вре́дный; ~ ***cold*** си́льный на́сморк; ~ ***mistake*** серьёзная (гру́бая оши́бка); ***he is ~ly off*** он в невы́годном положе́нии; ***~ly wounded*** тяжелора́неный; *coll.* ***want ~ly*** о́чень хоте́ть
bade [beɪd, bæd] *pt. om* ***bid***
badge [bædʒ] значо́к
badger ['bædʒə] **1.** *zo.* барсу́к; **2.** изводи́ть [извести́]
baffle ['bæfl] (*confuse*) сбива́ть с то́лку
bag [bæg] **1.** *large* мешо́к; су́мка, *small, hand~* су́мочка; **2.** класть [положи́ть] в мешо́к
baggage ['bægɪdʒ] бага́ж; ~ ***check*** *Am.* бага́жная квита́нция
bagpipe ['bægpaɪp] волы́нка
bail [beɪl] **1.** зало́г; (*guarantee*) поручи́тельство; **2.** поруча́ться [-чи́ться]
bait [beɪt] **1.** нажи́вка, прима́нка (*a. fig.*); *fig.* искуше́ние; **2.** прима́нивать [-ни́ть]; *fig.* пресле́довать, изводи́ть [-вести́]
bake [beɪk] [ис]пе́чь(ся); **~er** ['beɪkə] пе́карь *m*; **~er's** (**shop**) бу́лочная; **~ery** [~rɪ] пека́рня; **~ing soda** со́да (питьева́я)
balance ['bæləns] **1.** (*scales*) весы́ *m/pl.*; (*equilibrium*) равнове́сие; *fin.* бала́нс; са́льдо *n indecl.*; *coll.* (*remainder*) оста́ток; ~ ***of power*** полити́ческое равнове́сие; ~ ***of trade*** торго́вый бала́нс; **2.** [с]баланси́ровать (*B*); сохраня́ть равнове́сие; *fin.* подводи́ть бала́нс; *mentally* взве́шивать [-е́сить]; быть в равнове́сии
balcony ['bælkənɪ] балко́н
bald [bɔ:ld] лы́сый, плеши́вый; *fig.* (*unadorned*) неприкра́шенный; **~ly**: ***to put it ~ly*** говоря́ пря́мо
bale [beɪl] ки́па, тюк
balk [bɔ:k] *v/t.* (*hinder*) [вос]препя́тствовать (Д), [по]меша́ть (Д)
ball¹ [bɔ:l] мяч; шар; *of wool* клубо́к; ***keep the ~ rolling*** *of a conversation* подде́рживать разгово́р
ball² [~] бал, танцева́льный ве́чер
ballad ['bæləd] балла́да
ballast ['bæləst] балла́ст
ballbearing(**s** *pl.*) шарикоподши́пник
ballet ['bæleɪ] бале́т
balloon [bə'lu:n] возду́шный шар, аэроста́т
ballot ['bælət] **1.** голосова́ние; **2.** [про]голосова́ть; ~ **box** избира́тельная у́рна; ~ **paper** избира́-

тельный бюллетéнь *m*
ballpoint → ***pen***
ballroom танцевáльный зал
ballyhoo [bælɪˈhuː] шуми́ха
balm [bɑːm] бальзáм; *fig.* утешéние
balmy [ˈbɑːmɪ] □ ароматный; успокои́тельный; *air* благоухáнный
baloney [bəˈləʊnɪ] *Am. sl.* вздор
balsam [ˈbɔːlsəm] бальзáм; *bot.* бальзами́н
balustrade [bæləˈstreɪd] балюстрáда
bamboo [bæmˈbuː] бамбýк
bamboozle *coll.* [bæmˈbuːzl] надý(вá)ть, обмáнывать [-нýть]
ban [bæn] **1.** запрéт; ***be under a ~*** быть под запрéтом; ***raise the ~*** снять запрéт; **2.** налагáть запрéт на (В)
banana [bəˈnɑːnə] банáн
band [bænd] **1.** лéнта; *of robbers, etc.* шáйка, бáнда; грýппа, отря́д; *mus.* оркéстр; **2.**: ***~ together*** объединя́ться [-ни́ться] (***against*** прóтив Р)
bandage [ˈbændɪdʒ] **1.** бинт, повя́зка; **2.** [за]бинтовáть, перевя́зывать [-зáть]
bandit [ˈbændɪt] банди́т
bandmaster [ˈbændmɑːstə] капельмéйстер
bandy [ˈbændɪ] обмéниваться [-ня́ться] (*словáми, мячóм и т.п.*) *coll.* перебрáниваться
bane [beɪn] *fig.* поги́бель, бедá; проклятие
bang [bæŋ] **1.** удáр, стук; **2.** (*hit*) ударя́ть(ся) [удáрить(ся)]; стучáть; *once* [стýкнуть(ся)]; *door* хлóпать, *once* [-пнуть]
banish [ˈbænɪʃ] *from country* высылáть [вы́слать]; *from one's mind* гнать
banisters [ˈbænɪstəz] *pl.* пери́ла *n/pl.*
bank¹ [bæŋk] бéрег
bank² [~] **1.** банк; ***~ of issue*** эмиссиóнный банк; **2.** *fin.* класть (дéньги) в банк; *v/i.* ***~ on*** полагáться [-ложи́ться] на (В); ***~ account*** счёт в бáнке; **~er** [ˈbæŋkə] банки́р; **~ing** [ˈbæŋ-kɪŋ] бáнковое дéло; ***~ rate*** учётная стáвка; **~rupt** [ˈbæŋkrʌpt] **1.** банкрóт; **2.** обанкрóтившийся; неплатёжеспосóбный; **3.** дéлать банкрóтом; **~ruptcy** [ˈbæŋkrʌptsɪ] банкрóтство
banner [ˈbænə] знáмя *n, poet.* стяг, флаг
banquet [ˈbæŋkwɪt] пир; *formal* банкéт
banter [ˈbæntə] подшýчивать [-ути́ть], поддрáзнивать [-ни́ть]
baptism [ˈbæptɪzəm] крещéние
Baptist [ˈbæptɪst] бапти́ст
baptize [bæpˈtaɪz] [о]крести́ть
bar [bɑː] **1.** брусóк, *of chocolate* пли́тка; *across door* засóв; (*bank*) óтмель *f*; *in pub* бар; *mus.* такт; *fig.* прегрáда, препя́тствие; *law* адвокатýра; **2.** запирáть на засóв; (*obstruct*) преграждáть [-ради́ть]; (*exclude*) исключáть [-чи́ть]
barbed [bɑːbd]: ***~ wire*** колючая прóволока
barbar|ian [bɑːˈbeərɪən] **1.** вáрвар; **2.** вáрварский; **~ous** [ˈbɑːbərəs] □ ди́кий; (*cruel*) жестóкий
barbecue [ˈbɑːbɪkjuː] гриль для жáрки мя́са на откры́том вóздухе
barber [ˈbɑːbə] (мужскóй) парикмáхер; **~shop** парикмáхерская
bare [beə] **1.** гóлый, обнажённый; (*empty*) пустóй; ***the ~ thought*** дáже мысль (о П); **2.** обнажáть [-жи́ть], откры́(вá)ть; **~faced** [ˈbeəfeɪst] бессты́дный; **~foot** босикóм; **~-footed** босóй; **~headed** с непокры́той головóй; **~ly** [ˈbeəlɪ] едвá, éле-éле
bargain [ˈbɑːgɪn] **1.** сдéлка; (*sth. bought*) вы́годная покýпка; ***into the ~*** в придáчу; **2.** [по]торговáться (о П, с Т)
barge [bɑːdʒ] **1.** бáржа; **2.**: (***~ into***) *coll.* натáлкиваться [-толкнýться]; влезáть [влезть]; ***~ in*** ввáливаться [-и́ться]
bark¹ [bɑːk] **1.** корá; **2.** *strip* сдирáть корý с (Р)
bark² [~] **1.** *of dog* лай; **2.** [за]лáять
barley [ˈbɑːlɪ] ячмéнь *m*
bar|maid [ˈbɑːmeɪd] официáнтка в бáре; **~man** [~mən] бáрмен
barn [bɑːn] амбáр, сарáй
baron [ˈbærən] барóн; **~ess** [~ɪs] баронéсса

baroque [bə'rɒk, bə'rəʊk] **1.** баро́чный; **2.** баро́кко *n indecl.*
barrack(**s** *pl.*) ['bærək(s)] бара́к; каза́рма
barrel ['bærəl] (*cask*) бо́чка, (*keg*) бочо́нок; *of gun* ствол
barren ['bærən] □ неплодоро́дный, беспло́дный
barricade [bærɪ'keɪd] **1.** баррика́да; **2.** [за]баррикади́ровать
barrier ['bærɪə] барье́р; *rail.* шлагба́ум; *fig.* препя́тствие, поме́ха
barring ['bɑːrɪŋ] *prp.* кро́ме; за исключе́нием
barrister ['bærɪstə] адвока́т
barrow ['bærəʊ] та́чка; ручна́я теле́жка
barter ['bɑːtə] **1.** ба́ртер, обме́н; ба́ртерная сде́лка; **2.** [по]меня́ть, обме́нивать [-ня́ть] (***for*** на В)
base¹ [beɪs] □ по́длый, ни́зкий
base² [~] **1.** осно́ва, ба́зис, фунда́мент; **2.** осно́вывать [-ова́ть] (В на П), бази́ровать
base|ball ['beɪsbɔːl] бейсбо́л; **~less** [~lɪs] необосно́ванный; **~ment** [~mənt] подва́л, подва́льный эта́ж
bashful ['bæʃfəl] □ засте́нчивый, ро́бкий
basic ['beɪsɪk] основно́й; ***~ally*** в основно́м
basin [beɪsn] таз, ми́ска; (*sink*) ра́ковина; *geogr.* бассе́йн
bas|is ['beɪsɪs], *pl.* **~es** [~iːz] основа́ние, осно́ва
bask [bɑːsk]: ***~ in the sun*** гре́ться на со́лнце
basket ['bɑːskɪt] корзи́на; **~ball** баскетбо́л
bass [beɪs] *mus.* **1.** бас; **2.** басо́вый
bassoon [bə'suːn] фаго́т
bastard ['bæstəd] внебра́чный ребёнок
baste [beɪst] *sew.* смётывать [смета́ть]
bat¹ [bæt] *zo.* летучая мышь
bat² [~] **1.** *at games* бита́ (в крике́те); **2.** бить, ударя́ть в мяч
bat³ [~]: ***without ~ting an eyelid*** и гла́зом не моргну́в
batch [bætʃ] па́ртия; *of letters, etc.* па́чка
bath [bɑːθ] **1.** ва́нна; **2.** [вы́-, по]мы́ть, [вы́]купа́ть
bathe [beɪð] [вы́]купа́ться
bathing ['beɪðɪŋ] купа́ние
bath|robe ['bɑːθrəʊb] (купа́льный) хала́т; **~room** ва́нная (ко́мната); **~ towel** купа́льное полоте́нце
batiste [bæ'tiːst] бати́ст
baton ['bætən] *mus.* дирижёрская па́лочка
battalion [bə'tæljən] батальо́н
batter ['bætə] **1.** взби́тое те́сто; **2.** си́льно бить, [по]колоти́ть, изби́ть *pf.*; ***~ down*** взла́мывать [взлома́ть]; **~y** [~rɪ] батаре́я; *mot.* аккумуля́тор; *for clock, etc.* батаре́йка
battle ['bætl] **1.** би́тва, сраже́ние (***of*** под Т); **2.** сража́ться [срази́ться]; боро́ться
battle|field поле сраже́ния; **~ship** лине́йный кора́бль, линко́р
bawdy ['bɔːdɪ] непристо́йный
bawl [bɔːl] крича́ть [кри́кнуть], [за]ора́ть; ***~ out*** выкри́кивать [вы́крикнуть]
bay¹ [beɪ] зали́в, бу́хта
bay² [~] лавро́вое де́рево
bay³ [~] **1.** (*bark*) лай; **2.** [за]ла́ять; ***bring to ~*** *fig.* припере́ть *pf.* к стене́; ***keep at ~*** не подпуска́ть [-сти́ть]
bayonet ['beɪənɪt] *mil.* штык
bay window [beɪ'wɪndəʊ] *arch.* э́ркер
bazaar [bə'zɑː] база́р
be [biː, bɪ] [*irr.*]: **a**) быть, быва́ть; (*be situated*) находи́ться; *of position* лежа́ть, стоя́ть; ***there is, are*** есть; ***~ about to*** соб(и)ра́ться (+ *inf.*); ***~ away*** отсу́тствовать; ***~ at s.th.*** де́лать, быть за́нятым (Т); ***~ off*** уходи́ть [уйти́], отправля́ться [-а́виться]; ***~ on*** идти́ *of a film, etc.*; ***~ going on*** происходи́ть; ***how are you?*** как вы поживаете?, как вы себя́ чу́вствуете? **b**) *v/aux.* (*для образова́ния дли́тельной формы*) ***~ reading*** чита́ть; **c**) *v/aux.* (*для образова́ния пасси́ва*): ***~ read*** чита́ться, быть чи́танным (чита́емым)
beach [biːtʃ] **1.** пляж, взмо́рье; **2.** (*pull ashore*) вы́тащить *pf.* на бе́рег
beacon ['biːkən] сигна́льный ого́нь; мая́к; ба́кен
bead [biːd] бу́сина, би́серина; *of sweat* ка́пля

beads [bi:dz] *pl.* бу́сы *f/pl.*
beak [bi:k] клюв
beam [bi:m] **1.** ба́лка, брус; (*ray*) луч; **2.** сия́ть; излуча́ть [-чи́ть]
bean [bi:n] боб; ***full of ~s*** экспанси́вный, живо́й; ***spill the ~s*** проболта́ться *pf.*
bear[1] [beə] медве́дь *m* (-ве́дица *f*)
bear[2] [~] [*irr.*] *v/t.* носи́ть, нести́; (*endure*) [вы́]терпе́ть, выде́рживать [вы́держать]; (*give birth*) рожда́ть [роди́ть]; ~ ***down*** преодоле́(ва́)ть; ~ ***out*** подтвержда́ть [-рди́ть]; ~ ***o.s.*** держа́ться, вести́ себя́; ~ ***up*** подде́рживать [-жа́ть]; ~ (***up***)***on*** каса́ться [косну́ться] (Р); име́ть отноше́ние (к Д); ***bring to ~*** употребля́ть [-би́ть]
beard [bɪəd] борода́; **~ed** [~ɪd] борода́тый
bearer ['beərə] челове́к, несу́щий груз; *in expedition, etc.* носи́льщик; *of letter* предъяви́тель(ница *f*) *m*
bearing ['beərɪŋ] (*way of behaving*) мане́ра держа́ть себя́; (*relation*) отноше́ние; ***beyond*** (***all***) ~ невыноси́мо; ***find one's ~s*** [с]ориенти́роваться (*a. fig.*); ***lose one's ~s*** заблуди́ться, *fig.* растеря́ться
beast [bi:st] зверь *m*; скоти́на; **~ly** [~lɪ] *coll.* ужа́сный
beat [bi:t] **1.** [*irr.*] *v/t.* [по]би́ть; (*one blow*) ударя́ть [уда́рить]; ~ ***a retreat*** отступа́ть [-пи́ть]; ~ ***up*** изби́(ва́)ть; *eggs, etc.* взби(ва́)ть; ~ ***about the bush*** ходи́ть вокру́г да о́коло; *v/i. drums* бить; *heart* би́ться; *on door* колоти́ть; **2.** уда́р; бой; бие́ние; ритм; **~en** ['bi:tn] **1.** *p. pt.* от ***beat***; **2.** би́тый, побеждённый; *track* проторённый
beautician [bju:'tɪʃn] космето́лог
beautiful ['bju:tɪfl] □ краси́вый, прекра́сный, *day, etc.* чу́дный
beautify ['bju:tɪfaɪ] украша́ть [укра́сить]
beauty ['bju:tɪ] красота́, краса́вица; ~ ***parlo***(***u***)***r***, *Brt.* ~ ***salon*** космети́ческий кабине́т
beaver ['bi:və] бобр
became [bɪ'keɪm] *pt. от* ***become***
because [bɪ'kɒz] потому́ что, так как; ~ ***of*** из-за (Р)
beckon ['bekən] [по]мани́ть
becom|e [bɪ'kʌm] [*irr.* (***come***)] *v/i.* [с]де́латься; станови́ться [стать]; *of clothes v/t.* быть к лицу́, идти́ (Д); подоба́ть (Д); **~ing** [~ɪŋ] □ подоба́ющий; *of dress, etc.* (иду́щий) к лицу́
bed [bed] **1.** посте́ль *f*; кровать *f*; *agric.* гря́дка, клу́мба; *of river* ру́сло; **2.** (*plant*) выса́живать [вы́садить]
bedclothes *pl.* посте́льное бельё
bedding ['bedɪŋ] посте́льные принадле́жности *f/pl.*
bed|ridden ['bedrɪdn] прико́ванный к посте́ли; **~room** спа́льня; **~spread** покрыва́ло; **~time** вре́мя ложи́ться спать
bee [bi:] пчела́; ***have a ~ in one's bonnet*** *coll.* быть поме́шанным на чём-л.
beech [bi:tʃ] бук, бу́ковое де́рево
beef [bi:f] говя́дина; **~steak** бифште́кс; ~ **tea** кре́пкий бульо́н; **~y** [bi:fɪ] му́скулистый
bee|hive у́лей; **~keeping** пчелово́дство; **~line**: ***make a ~*** пойти́ напрями́к, стрело́й помча́ться
been [bi:n, bɪn] *pt. p. от* ***be***
beer [bɪə] пи́во; ***small ~*** сла́бое пи́во, *fig.* ме́лкая со́шка
beet [bi:t] свёкла (*chiefly Brt.*: *beetroot*)
beetle [bi:tl] жук
before [bɪ'fɔ:] **1.** *adv.* впереди́, вперёд; ра́ньше; ~ ***long*** вско́ре; ***long ~*** задо́лго; **2.** *cj.* пре́жде чем; пока не; перед тем как; скоре́е чем; **3.** *prp.* пе́ред (Т); впереди́ (Р); до (Р); **~hand** зара́нее, заблаговре́менно
befriend [bɪ'frend] относи́ться подру́жески к (Д)
beg [beg] *v.t.* [по]проси́ть (Р); умоля́ть [-ли́ть] (***for*** о П); выпра́шивать [вы́просить] (*of* у Р); *v/i.* ни́щенствовать
began [bɪ'gæn] *pt. от* ***begin***
beggar ['begə] **1.** ни́щий, ни́щенка; ***lucky ~*** счастли́вчик; ***poor ~*** бедняга; **2.** разоря́ть [-ри́ть], доводи́ть [-вести́] до нищеты́; ***it ~s all description*** не поддаётся описа́нию
begin [bɪ'gɪn] [*irr.*] нач(ин)а́ть (***with*** с Р); ***to ~ with*** во-пе́рвых; снача́ла, для нача́ла; **~ner** [~ə] начина́ю-

щий, новичо́к; **~ning** [~ıŋ] нача́ло; ***in*** *or* ***at the ~*** внача́ле
begrudge [bı'grʌdʒ] (*envy*) [по]зави́довать (Д в П); жале́ть, скупи́ться
begun [bı'gʌn] *p. pt. om* ***begin***
behalf [bı'hɑ:f]: ***on*** *or* ***in ~ of*** для (Р), ра́ди (Р); от и́мени (Р)
behav|e [bı'heıv] вести́ себя́; держа́ться; поступа́ть [-пи́ть]; **~iour** [~jə] поведе́ние
behind [bı'haınd] **1.** *adv.* позади́, сза́ди; ***look ~*** огляну́ться *pf.*; ***be ~ s.o.*** отстава́ть [-ста́ть] от кого́-л. (***in*** в П); **2.** *prp.* за (Т); позади́ (Р), сза́ди (Р); по́сле (Р)
beige [beıʒ] бе́жевый
being ['bi:ıŋ] бытие́, существова́ние; (*creature*) живо́е существо́; ***for the time ~*** в настоя́щее вре́мя; на не́которое вре́мя, пока́
belated [bı'leıtıd] запозда́лый
belch [beltʃ] **1.** отры́жка; **2.** рыга́ть [рыгну́ть]
belfry ['belfrı] колоко́льня
Belgian ['beldʒən] **1.** бельги́ец *m*, -и́йка *f*; **2.** бельги́йский
belief [bı'li:f] ве́ра (***in*** в В); убежде́ние; ***beyond ~*** (про́сто) невероя́тно; ***to the best of my ~*** по моему́ убежде́нию; наско́лько мне изве́стно
believe [bı'li:v] [по]ве́рить (***in*** в В); **~r** [~ə] ве́рующий
belittle [bı'lıtl] *fig.* умаля́ть [-ли́ть]; принижа́ть [-ни́зить]
bell [bel] ко́локол; звоно́к
belles-lettres [bel'letrə] *pl.* худо́жественная литерату́ра, беллетри́стика
bellicose ['belıkəʊs] □ вои́нственный, агресси́вный
belligerent [bı'lıdʒərənt] **1.** вою́ющая сторона́; **2.** вою́ющий
bellow ['beləʊ] **1.** *of animal* мыча́ние; *of wind, storm* рёв; **2.** реве́ть; ора́ть
belly ['belı] **1.** живо́т, *coll.* брю́хо; **2.** наду́(ва́)ть(ся); **~ful** [~fʊl]: ***have had a ~ful*** *coll., fig.* быть сы́тым по го́рло (***of*** Т)
belong [bı'lɒŋ] принадлежа́ть (Д); относи́ться (к Д); **~ings** [~ıŋz] *pl.* ве́щи *f/pl.*, пожи́тки
beloved [bı'lʌvıd, *pred.* bı'lʌvd] возлю́бленный, люби́мый
below [bı'ləʊ] **1.** *adv.* внизу́; ни́же; **2.** *prp.* ни́же (Р); под (В, Т)
belt [belt] **1.** по́яс, *of leather* реме́нь; зо́на; *tech.* приводно́й реме́нь; *mil.* портупе́я; ***safety ~*** *mot.* реме́нь безопа́сности; *ae.* привязно́й реме́нь; **2.** подпоя́с(ыв)ать; (*thrash*) поро́ть ремнём
bemoan [bı'məʊn] опла́к(ив)ать
bench [bentʃ] скамья́; (*work ~*) верста́к
bend [bend] **1.** сгиб, изги́б; *of road* поворо́т, изги́б; *of river* излу́чина; **2.** [*irr.*] *v/t.* [по-, со]гну́ть; *head, etc.* наклоня́ть [-ни́ть]; *v/i.* наклоня́ться [-ни́ться]; сгиба́ться [согну́ться]
beneath [bı'ni:θ] → ***below***
benediction [benı'dıkʃn] благослове́ние
benefactor ['benıfæktə] благоде́тель; (*donor*) благотвори́тель
beneficial [benı'fıʃl] □ благотво́рный, поле́зный
benefit ['benıfıt] **1.** вы́года, по́льза; (*allowance*) посо́бие; *thea.* бенефи́с; **2.** приноси́ть по́льзу; извлека́ть по́льзу
benevolen|ce [bı'nevələns] благожела́тельность *f*; **~t** [~ənt] □ благожела́тельный
benign [bı'naın] □ добросерде́чный; *climate* благотво́рный; *med.* доброка́чественный
bent [bent] **1.** *pt. и p. pt. om* ***bend***; ***~ on*** поме́шанный на (П); **2.** скло́нность *f*, спосо́бность *f*; ***follow one's ~*** сле́довать свои́м накло́нностям
bequeath [bı'kwi:ð] завеща́ть (*im*)*pf.*
bequest [bı'kwest] насле́дство
bereave [bı'ri:v] [*irr.*] лиша́ть [-ши́ть] (Р); отнима́ть [-ня́ть]
beret ['bereı] бере́т
berry ['beri] я́года
berth [bɜ:θ] *naut.* я́корная стоя́нка; (*cabin*) каю́та; (*sleeping place*) ко́йка; *rail.* спа́льное ме́сто, по́лка; *fig.* (вы́годная) до́лжность
beseech [bı'si:tʃ] [*irr.*] умоля́ть [-ли́ть], упра́шивать [упроси́ть] (+ *inf.*)

beset [bɪ'set] [*irr.* (***set***)] окружáть [-жи́ть]; *with questions, etc.* осаждáть [осади́ть]; ***I was ~ by doubts*** меня́ одолевáли сомнéния
beside [bɪ'saɪd] *prp.* ря́дом с (Т), óколо (Р), близ (Р); ми́мо ***~ o.s.*** вне себя́ (***with*** от Р); ***~ the point*** не по существу́; не относится к делу; **~s** [~z] **1.** *adv.* крóме тогó, сверх тогó; **2.** *prp.* крóме (Р)
besiege [bɪ'siːdʒ] осаждáть [осади́ть]
besought [bɪ'sɔːt] *pt. om* **beseech**
bespatter [bɪ'spætə] забры́зг(ив)ать
best [best] **1.** *adj.* лу́чший; ***~ man*** *at a wedding* шáфер; ***the ~ part*** бóльшая часть; **2.** *adv.* лу́чше всегó, всех; **3.** сáмое лу́чшее; ***to the ~ of ...*** наскóлько ...; ***make the ~ of*** испóльзовать наилу́чшим óбразом; ***at ~*** в лу́чшем слу́чае; ***all the ~!*** всегó сáмого лу́чшего!
bestial ['bestɪəl, 'bestʃəl] □ (*behaviour*) скóтский; *cruelty, etc.* звéрский
bestow [bɪ'stəʊ] одáривать [-ри́ть]; награждáть [-ради́ть] (В/Т); *title* присвáивать [-вóить]
bet [bet] **1.** пари́ *n indecl.*; **2.** [*irr.*] держáть пари́; би́ться об заклáд; ***~ on horses*** игрáть на скáчках
betray [bɪ'treɪ] предá(вá)ть; (*show*) вы́да(вá)ть; **~al** [~əl] предáтельство; **~er** [~ə] предáтель *m*, -ница *f*
betrothal [bɪ'trəʊðl] помóлвка
better ['betə] **1.** *adj.* лу́чший; ***he is ~*** ему́ лу́чше; **2.**: ***change for the ~*** перемéна к лу́чшему; ***get the ~ of*** взять верх над (Т); [пре]одолéть; **3.** *adv.* лу́чше; бóльше; ***so much the ~*** тем лу́чше; ***you had ~ go*** вам бы лу́чше уйти́; ***think ~ of it*** передýмать *pf.*; **4.** *v/t.* улучшáть [улу́чшить]
between [bɪ'twiːn] **1.** *adv.* мéжду; **2.** *prp.* мéжду (Т); ***~ you and me*** мéжду нáми (говоря́)
beverage ['bevərɪdʒ] напи́ток
beware [bɪ'weə] берéчься, остерегáться (Р) *impf.*; ***~ of the dog!*** осторóжно, злáя собáка!
bewilder [bɪ'wɪldə] смущáть [смути́ть]; стáвить в тупи́к; (*confuse*) сбивáть с тóлку; **~ment** [~mənt] смущéние, замешáтельство; путáница
bewitch [bɪ'wɪtʃ] околдóвывать [-довáть], очарóвывать [-ровáть]
beyond [bɪ'jɒnd] **1.** *adv.* вдали́, на расстоя́нии; ***this is ~ me*** э́то вы́ше моегó понимáния; **2.** *prp.* за (В, Т); вне (Р); сверх (Р); по ту стóрону (Р)
bias ['baɪəs] **1.** (*prejudice*) предубеждéние (прóтив Р); (*tendency of mind*) склóнность *f*; **2.** склоня́ть [-ни́ть]; ***~ed opinion*** предвзя́тое мнéние
bib [bɪb] дéтский нагру́дник
Bible [baɪbl] Би́блия
biblical ['bɪblɪkəl] □ библéйский
bicarbonate [baɪ'kɑːbənət]: ***~ of soda*** питьевáя сóда
bicker ['bɪkə] пререкáться (с Т)
bicycle ['baɪsɪkl] **1.** велосипéд; **2.** éздить на велосипéде
bid [bɪd] **1.** [*irr.*] *price* предлагáть [-ложи́ть]; **2.** предложéние, (*at sale*) зая́вка; ***final ~*** окончáтельная ценá; **~den** [bɪdn] *p. pt. om* **bid**
biennial [baɪ'enɪəl] двухлéтний
bifocal [baɪ'fəʊkl] бифокáльный
big [big] большóй, кру́пный; (*tall*) высóкий; *of clothes* вели́к; *coll. fig.* вáжный; *coll. fig.* ***~ shot*** ши́шка; ***talk ~*** [по]хвастáться
bigamy ['bigəmɪ] двоебрáчие
bigot ['bɪgət] слепóй привéрженец, фанáтик
bigwig ['bɪgwɪg] *coll.* ши́шка
bike [baɪk] *coll.* велосипéд
bilateral [baɪ'lætərəl] двусторóнний
bilberry ['bɪlbəri] черни́ка
bile [baɪl] жёлчь *f*; *fig.* жёлчность *f*
bilious ['bɪlɪəs]: ***~ attack*** при́ступ тошноты́; рвóта
bill[1] [bɪl] *of a bird* клюв
bill[2] [~] законопроéкт, билль *m*; счёт; (*poster*) афи́ша; *fin.* вéксель *m*; ***~ of credit*** аккредити́в; ***~ of fare*** меню́; ***that will fill the ~*** э́то подойдёт; ***foot the ~*** оплати́ть счёт *pf.*
billiards ['bɪljədz] *pl.* бильярд
billion ['bɪljən] биллиóн; *Am.* миллиáрд
billow ['bɪləʊ] **1.** вал, большáя волнá; **2.** *of sea* вздымáться; *sails* надувáть [-ду́ть]

bin [bɪn]: ***rubbish* ~** му́сорное ведро́
bind [baɪnd] *v/t.* [с]вяза́ть; свя́зывать [-за́ть]; (*oblige*) обя́зывать [-за́ть]; *book* переплета́ть [-плести́]; **~er** ['baɪndə] переплётчик; **~ing** [~ɪŋ] (*book cover*) переплёт
binoculars [bɪ'nɒkjʊləz] бино́кль *m*
biography [baɪ'ɒgrəfɪ] биогра́фия
biology [baɪ'ɒlədʒɪ] биоло́гия
biosphere ['bɑɪəsfɪə] биосфе́ра
birch [bɜːtʃ] (**~ *tree***) берёза
bird [bɜːd] птица; ***early* ~** ра́няя пта́шка (*о челове́ке*); **~'s-eye** ['bɜːdzaɪ]: **~ *view*** вид с пти́чьего полёта
Biro ['baɪərəʊ] *Brt. trademark* ша́риковая ру́чка
birth [bɜːθ] рожде́ние; (*origin*) происхожде́ние; ***give* ~** рожда́ть [роди́ть]; **~day** день рожде́ния; **~-place** ме́сто рожде́ния; **~rate** рожда́емость *f*
biscuit ['bɪskɪt] пече́нье
bishop ['bɪʃəp] *eccl.* епи́скоп; *chess* слон; **~ric** [~rɪk] епа́рхия
bison ['baɪsn] *zo.* бизо́н, зубр
bit[1] [bɪt] кусо́чек, части́ца; немно́го
bit[2] [~] *comput.* бит, двои́чная ци́фра
bit[3] [~] *pt. от* **~e**
bitch [bɪtʃ] су́ка
bit|e [baɪt] **1.** уку́с; *of fish* клёв; кусо́к; ***have a* ~** перекуси́ть *pf.*; **2.** [*irr.*] куса́ть [укуси́ть]; клева́ть [клю́нуть]; *of pepper, etc.* жечь; *of frost* щипа́ть; **~ing** *wind* прони́зывающий; *remark, etc.* язви́тельный
bitten ['bɪtn] *p. pt. от* ***bite***
bitter ['bɪtə] □ го́рький, ре́зкий; *fig.* го́рький, мучи́тельный; *struggle, person* ожесточённый
blab [blæb] *coll.* разба́лтывать [-болта́ть]
black [blæk] **1.** чёрный; тёмный, мра́чный; **~ *eye*** синя́к под гла́зом; ***in* ~ *and white*** чёрным по бе́лому; ***give s.o. a* ~ *look*** мра́чно посмотре́ть на (В); **2.** *fig.* очерни́ть; **~ *out*** потеря́ть созна́ние; **3.** чёрный цвет; (*Negro*) чернoко́жий; **~berry** ежеви́ка; **~bird** чёрный дрозд; **~board** кла́ссная доска́; **~en** ['blækn] *v/t.* [за]черни́ть; *fig.* [о]черни́ть; *v/i.* [по]черне́ть; **~-guard** ['blægɑːd] негодя́й, подле́ц; **~head** *med.* угри́ *m/pl.*; **~-letter day** несча́стливый день; **~mail 1.** вымога́тельство, шанта́ж; **2.** вымога́ть (*pf.*) де́ньги у (Р); **~out** затемне́ние; *med.* поте́ря созна́ния; **~smith** кузне́ц
bladder ['blædə] *anat.* пузы́рь *m*
blade [bleɪd] ло́пасть *f*; *of knife* ле́звие; **~ *of grass*** трави́нка
blame [bleɪm] **1.** вина́; **2.** вини́ть, обвиня́ть [-ни́ть]; ***he has only himself to* ~** он сам во всем винова́т; **~less** ['bleɪmləs] безупре́чный
blanch [blɑːntʃ] (*grow pale*) побледне́ть *pf.*; *cul.* бланши́ровать
blank [blæŋk] **1.** □ (*empty*) пусто́й; (*expressionless*) невырази́тельный; *of form, etc.* незапо́лненный; **~ *cartridge*** холосто́й патро́н; **2.** (*empty space*) пробе́л; ***my mind was a* ~** у меня́ в голове́ не́ было ни одно́й мы́сли
blanket [blæŋkɪt] шерстяно́е одея́ло; *fig.* покро́в
blare [bleə] *radio* труби́ть, реве́ть
blasphemy ['blæsfəmɪ] богоху́льство
blast [blɑːst] **1.** си́льный поры́в ве́тра; *of explosion* взрыв; ***at full* ~** на по́лную мо́щность; **2.** взрыва́ть [взорва́ть]; *mus.* труби́ть; **~ed** [~ɪd] *coll.* прокля́тый; **~ furnace** до́менная печь *f*
blatant ['bleɪtənt] на́глый, вопию́щий
blaze [bleɪz] **1.** пла́мя *n*; *of flame, passion* вспы́шка; **2.** *v/i.* горе́ть; пыла́ть (*a. fig.*); сверка́ть [-кну́ть]; **~r** ['bleɪzə] спорти́вная ку́ртка
bleach [bliːtʃ] бели́ть
bleak [bliːk] уны́лый, безра́достный; *prospects etc.* мра́чный
blear|y ['blɪərɪ] затума́ненный, нея́сный; **~-eyed** ['blɪərɪaɪd] с му́тными глаза́ми
bleat [bliːt] **1.** бле́яние; **2.** [за]бле́ять
bled [bled] *pt. и pt. p. от* ***bleed***
bleed [bliːd] [*irr.*] *v/i.* кровото́чить; истека́ть [-те́чь] кро́вью; **~ing** ['bliːdɪŋ] кровотече́ние
blemish ['blemɪʃ] недоста́ток; пятно́ (*a. fig.*)

blend [blend] **1.** сме́шивать(ся) [-ша́ть(ся)]; (*harmonize*) сочета́ть(ся) (*im*)*pf.*; **2.** смесь *f*
bless [bles] благословля́ть [-ви́ть]; одаря́ть [-ри́ть]; **~ed** ['blesɪd] *adj.* счастли́вый, блаже́нный; **~ing** ['blesɪŋ] *eccl.* благослове́ние; бла́го, сча́стье
blew [blu:] *pt. от* **blow**
blight [blaɪt] **1.** *disease* головня́; ржа́вчина; мучни́стая роса́ *и т.д.*; то, что разруша́ет (*пла́ны*), отравля́ет (*жизнь и т.д.*); **2.** *hopes, etc.* разби́(ва́)ть
blind [blaɪnd] **1.** □ слепо́й (*fig.* **~ to** к Д); *handwriting* нечёткий, нея́сный; **~ alley** тупи́к; **turn a ~ eye** закрыва́ть [закры́ть] глаза́ (**to** на В); **~ly** *fig.* науга́д, наобу́м; **2.** што́ра; жалюзи́ *n indecl.*; **3.** ослепля́ть [-пи́ть]; **~fold** ['blaɪndfəʊld] завя́зывать глаза́ (Д); **~ness** слепота́
blink [blɪŋk] **1.** (*of eye*) морга́ние, *of light* мерца́ние; **2.** *v/i.* морга́ть [-гну́ть]; мига́ть [мигну́ть]
bliss [blɪs] блаже́нство
blister ['blɪstə] **1.** волды́рь *m*; **2.** покрыва́ться волдыря́ми
blizzard ['blɪzəd] бура́н, си́льная мете́ль *f*
bloat [bləʊt] распуха́ть [-пу́хнуть]; разду́(ва́)ться
block [blɒk] **1.** *of wood* коло́да, чурба́н; *of stone, etc.* глы́ба; *between streets* кварта́л; **~ of apartments** (*Brt.* **flats**) многоэта́жный дом; **2.** (*obstruct*) прегражда́ть [-ади́ть]; **~ in** набра́сывать вчерне́; (*mst.* **~ up**) блоки́ровать (*im*)*pf*; *of pipe* засоря́ться [-ри́ться]
blockade [blɒ'keɪd] **1.** блока́да; **2.** блоки́ровать (*im*)*pf.*
blockhead ['blɒkhed] болва́н
blond(e) [blɒnd] блонди́н *m*, -ка *f*; белоку́рый
blood [blʌd] кровь *f*; **in cold ~** хладнокро́вно; **~shed** кровопроли́тие; **~thirsty** кровожа́дный; **~ vessel** кровено́сный сосу́д; **~y** ['blʌdɪ] окрова́вленный, крова́вый
bloom [blu:m] **1.** цвето́к, цвете́ние; *fig.* расцве́т; **in ~** в цвету́; **2.** цвести́, быть в цвету́
blossom ['blɒsəm] **1.** цвето́к (фрукто́вого де́рева); **2.** цвести́, расцвета́ть [-ести́]
blot [blɒt, blɑ:t] **1.** пятно́ (*a. fig.*); **2.** *fig.* запятна́ть *pf.*
blotch [blɒtʃ] кля́кса, пятно́
blouse [blaʊz] блу́за, блу́зка
blow[1] [bləʊ] уда́р (*a. fig.*)
blow[2] [~] [*irr.*] **1.** [по]ду́ть; **~ up** взрыва́ть(ся) [взорва́ть(ся)]; **~ one's nose** [вы́]сморка́ться; **2.** дунове́ние; **~n** [~n] *pt. p. от* **blow**
blue [blu:] **1.** голубо́й; лазу́рный; (*dark* ~) си́ний; *coll.* (*be sad, depressed*) уны́лый, пода́вленный; **2.** голубо́й цвет; си́ний цвет; **3.** окра́шивать в си́ний, голубо́й цвет; *of washing* [под]сини́ть; **~bell** колоко́льчик
blues [blu:z] *pl.* меланхо́лия, хандра́
bluff[1] [blʌf] (*abrupt*) ре́зкий; (*rough*) грубова́тый; *of headlands, etc.* обры́вистый
bluff[2] [~] **1.** обма́н, блеф; **2.** *v/t.* обма́нывать[-ну́ть]; *v/i.* блефова́ть
blunder ['blʌndə] **1.** гру́бая оши́бка; **2.** де́лать гру́бую оши́бку
blunt [blʌnt] **1.** □ тупо́й; *remark, etc.* ре́зкий; **2.** [за]тупи́ть; *fig.* притупля́ть [-пи́ть]
blur [blɜ:] **1.** (*indistinct outline*) нея́сное очерта́ние; пятно́; **2.** *v/t.* сде́лать нея́сным *pf.*; сма́зывать [-зать]; *tears, etc.* затума́нить *pf.*
blush [blʌʃ] **1.** кра́ска от смуще́ния *или* стыда́; **2.** [по]красне́ть
boar [bɔ:] бо́ров, *hunt.* каба́н
board [bɔ:d] **1.** доска́; (*food*) стол; *of ship* борт; *thea.* сце́на, подмо́стки *m/pl.*; *council* правле́ние; **~ of directors** правле́ние директоро́в; **2.** *v/t.* наст(и)ла́ть; *v/i.* столова́ться; *train, plane, etc.* сади́ться [сесть] на, в (В); **~er** ['bɔ:dər] жиле́ц, оплачива́ющий ко́мнату и пита́ние; **~ing house** пансио́н; **~ing school** шко́ла-интерна́т
boast [bəʊst] **1.** хвастовство́; **2.** горди́ться (Т); (*of, about*) [по]хва́статься (Т); **~ful** ['bəʊstfəl] хвастли́вый
boat [bəʊt] *small* ло́дка, *vessel* су́дно; **~ing** ['bəʊtɪŋ] ката́ние на ло́дке

подпры́гивать [-гнуть]
bobbin ['bɒbɪn] кату́шка; шпу́лька
bode [bəʊd]: (*portend*) **~ *well*** быть хоро́шим знако́м
bodice ['bɒdɪs] лиф
bodily ['bɒdɪlɪ] теле́сный, физи́ческий
body ['bɒdɪ, 'bɑːdɪ] те́ло; (*corpse*) труп; *mot.* ку́зов; **~ building** бо́дибилдинг, культури́зм
bog [bɒg] **1.** боло́то, тряси́на; **2. *get ~ged down*** увяза́ть [увя́знуть]
boggle ['bɒgl] отша́тываться [-ну́ться] отпря́нуть (*out of surprise, fear, or doubt*); ***the mind ~s*** уму́ непостижи́мо
bogus ['bəʊgəs] подде́льный
boil[1] [bɔɪl] *med.* фуру́нкул
boil[2] [~] **1.** кипе́ние; **2.** [с]вари́ть(ся); [вс]кипяти́ть(ся); кипе́ть; **~er** ['bɔɪlə] *tech.* котёл
boisterous ['bɔɪstərəs] □ бу́рный, шу́мный; *child* ре́звый
bold [bəʊld] □ (*daring*) сме́лый; *b.s.* на́глый; *typ.* жи́рный; **~ness** ['bəʊldnɪs] сме́лость *f*; на́глость *f*
bolster ['bəʊlstə] **1.** ва́лик; опо́ра; **2.** (*prop*) подде́рживать [-жа́ть]; подпира́ть [-пере́ть]
bolt [bəʊlt] **1.** болт; *on door* засо́в, задви́жка; (*thunder~*) уда́р гро́ма; ***a ~ from the blue*** гром среди́ я́сного не́ба; **2.** *v/t.* запира́ть на засо́в; *v/i.* нести́сь стрело́й; (*run away*) убега́ть [убежа́ть]
bomb [bɒm] **1.** бо́мба; **2.** бомби́ть
bombard [bɒm'bɑːd]: ***~ with questions*** бомбардирова́ть, забра́сывать [-роса́ть] вопро́сами
bombastic [bɒm'bæstɪk] напы́щенный
bond [bɒnd] *pl. fig.*: **~s** у́зы *f/pl.*; *fin.* облига́ции *f/pl.*
bone [bəʊn] **1.** кость *f*; ***~ of contention*** я́блоко раздо́ра; ***make no ~s about*** *coll.* не [по]стесня́ться; не церемо́ниться с (Т); **2.** вынима́ть, выреза́ть ко́сти
bonfire ['bɒnfaɪə] костёр
bonnet ['bɒnɪt] *baby's* че́пчик; *mot.* капо́т
bonus ['bəʊnəs] *fin.* пре́мия, вознагражде́ние
bony ['bəʊnɪ] костля́вый
book [bʊk] **1.** кни́га; **2.** (*tickets*) зака́зывать, заброни́ровать (*a. room in a hotel*); **~case** кни́жный шкаф; **~ing clerk** ['bʊkiŋklɑːk] *rail.* касси́р; **~ing office** биле́тная ка́сса; **~keeping** бухгалте́рия; **~let** брошю́ра, букле́т; **~seller** продаве́ц книг; ***second-hand ~*** букини́ст
boom[1] [buːm] **1.** *econ.* бум; **2.** *of business* процвета́ть *impf.*
boom[2] [~] **1.** *of gun, thunder, etc.* гул; ро́кот; **2.** бу́хать, рокота́ть
boon [buːn] бла́го
boor [bʊə] гру́бый, невоспи́танный челове́к; **~ish** ['bʊərɪʃ] гру́бый, невоспи́танный
boost [buːst] *trade* стимули́ровать (разви́тие); *tech.* уси́ливать [-лить]; ***it ~ed his morale*** э́то его́ подбодри́ло; (*advertise*) реклами́ровать
boot[1] [buːt]: ***to ~*** в прида́чу, вдоба́вок *adv.*
boot[2] [~] сапо́г, боти́нок; *mot.* бага́жник; **~lace** ['~leɪs] шнуро́к для боти́нок
booth [buːð] кио́ск; ***telephone ~*** телефо́нная бу́дка; ***polling ~*** каби́на для голосова́ния
booty ['buːtɪ] добы́ча
border ['bɔːdə] **1.** грани́ца; (*edge*) край; *on tablecloth, etc.* кайма́; **2.** грани́чить (***upon*** с Т)
bore[1] [bɔː] **1.** расто́ченное отве́рстие; *of gun* кали́бр; *fig.* зану́да **2.** [про]сверли́ть; *fig.* надоеда́ть [-е́сть] (Д); наводи́ть ску́ку на (В)
bore[2] [~] *pt. от* ***bear***[2]
boredom ['bɔːdəm] ску́ка
born [bɔːn] рождённый; *fig.* прирождённый; **~e** [~] *pt. p. от* ***bear***[2]
borough ['bʌrə] (*town*) го́род; (*section of a town*) райо́н
borrow ['bɒrəʊ] *money* брать [взять] взаймы́; занима́ть [-ня́ть] (***from*** у Р); *book* взять почита́ть
Bosnian ['bɒznɪən] **1.** босни́ец *m*, -и́йка *f*; **2.** босни́йский
bosom ['bʊzəm] грудь *f*; *fig.* ло́но; ***~ friend*** закады́чный друг
boss [bɒs] *coll.* **1.** шеф, босс, нача́льник; **2.** кома́ндовать (Т); **~y** ['bɒsɪ] лю́бящий кома́ндовать

botany ['bɒtənɪ] бота́ника
botch [bɒtʃ] по́ртить; сде́лать *pf.* пло́хо и́ли ко́е-как
both [bəʊθ] о́ба, о́бе; и тот и друго́й; *~ ... and ...* как ... так и ...; и ... и ...
bother ['bɒðə] *coll.* **1.** беспоко́йство; *oh ~!* кака́я доса́да!; **2.** вози́ться; надоеда́ть [-е́сть] (Д); [по]беспоко́ить
bottle ['bɒtl] **1.** буты́лка; *for scent* флако́н; ***baby's ~*** рожо́к; ***hot-water ~*** гре́лка; **2.** разлива́ть по буты́лкам; **~ opener** ключ, открыва́лка
bottom ['bɒtəm] **1.** дно; *of boat* дни́ще; ни́жняя часть *f*; *of hill* подно́жье; *coll.* зад; *fig.* осно́ва, суть *f*; ***at the ~*** внизу́; ***be at the ~ of sth.*** быть причи́ной и́ли зачи́нщиком (Р); ***get to the ~ of sth.*** добра́ться до су́ти (Р); **2.** са́мый ни́жний
bough [baʊ] сук; ве́тка, ветвь *f*
bought [bɔːt] *pt.* и *pt. p. от* ***buy***
boulder ['bəʊldə] валу́н
bounce [baʊns] **1.** прыжо́к, скачо́к; ***full of ~*** по́лный эне́ргии; **2.** подпры́гивать [-гнуть]; *of ball* отска́кивать [отскочи́ть]
bound¹ [baʊnd] **1.** грани́ца; преде́л (*a. fig.*); ограниче́ние; **2.** (*limit*) ограни́чивать; (*be the boundary of*) грани́чить (с Т)
bound² [~]: ***be ~*** направля́ться (***for*** в В)
bound³ [~] **1.** прыжо́к, скачо́к; **2.** пры́гать [-гнуть], [по]скака́ть; (*run*) бежа́ть скачка́ми
bound⁴ [~] **1.** *pt. и pt. p. от* ***bind***; **2.** свя́занный; (*obliged*) обя́занный; *of book* переплетённый
boundary ['baʊndərɪ] грани́ца; *between fields* межа́; *fig.* преде́л
boundless ['baʊndlɪs] безграни́чный
bouquet [bʊ'keɪ] буке́т (*a. of wine*)
bout [baʊt] *of illness* при́ступ; *in sports* встре́ча
bow¹ [baʊ] **1.** покло́н; **2.** *v/i.* [со]гну́ться; кла́няться [поклони́ться]; (*submit*) подчиня́ться [-ни́ться] (Д); *v/t.* [со]гну́ть
bow² [bəʊ] лук; (*curve*) дуга́; (*knot*) бант; *mus.* смычо́к
bow³ [baʊ] *naut.* нос
bowels ['baʊəlz] *pl.* кишки́ *f/pl.*; *of the earth* не́дра *n/pl.*
bowl¹ [bəʊl] ми́ска; ва́за
bowl² [~] **1.** шар; *pl.* игра́ в шары́; **2.** *v/t.* [по]кати́ть; *v/i.* игра́ть в шары́; ***be ~ed over*** быть покорённым *или* ошеломлённым (***by*** Т)
box¹ [bɒks] **1.** коро́бка; я́щик; *thea.* ло́жа; **2.** укла́дывать в я́щик
box² [~] *sport* **1.** бокси́ровать; **2.** ***~ on the ear*** пощёчина; **~er** ['~ə] *sportsman, dog* боксёр; **~ing** ['~ɪŋ] *sport* бокс
box office театра́льная ка́сса
boy [bɔɪ] ма́льчик; ю́ноша; **~friend** ['~frend] друг (*де́вушки*); **~hood** ['~hʊd] о́трочество; **~ish** ['bɔɪɪʃ] □ мальчи́шеский
brace [breɪs] **1.** *tech.* коловоро́т, скоба́; ***~ and bit*** дрель; **2.** (*support*) подпира́ть [-пере́ть]; ***~ up*** подбодря́ть [-бодри́ть]; ***~ o.s.*** собра́ться с ду́хом
bracelet ['breɪslɪt] брасле́т
braces [breɪsɪz] *pl. suspenders* подтя́жки *f/pl.*
bracket ['brækɪt] **1.** *tech.* кронште́йн; (*income ~*) катего́рия, гру́ппа; *typ.* ско́бка; **2.** заключа́ть [-чи́ть] в ско́бки; *fig.* ста́вить на одну́ до́ску с (Т)
brag [bræg] [по]хва́статься
braggart ['brægət] хвасту́н
braid [breɪd] **1.** *of hair* коса́; (*band*) тесьма́; *on uniform* галу́н; **2.** заплета́ть [-ести́]; обшива́ть тесьмо́й
brain [breɪn] мозг; (*fig. mst.* **~s**) рассу́док, ум; у́мственные спосо́бности *f/pl.* ***rack one's ~s*** лома́ть себе́ го́лову (над Т); ***use your ~s!*** шевели́ мозга́ми!; **~wave** блестя́щая иде́я; **~y** ['~ɪ] *coll.* башкови́тый
brake [breɪk] **1.** *mot.* то́рмоз; **2.** [за]тормози́ть
branch [brɑːntʃ] **1.** ветвь *f*, ве́тка (*a. rail*), сук (*pl.*: су́чья); *of science* о́трасль; *of bank, etc.* отделе́ние, филиа́л; **2.** разветвля́ть(ся) [-етви́ть(ся)]; расширя́ться [-ши́рить-ся]
brand [brænd] **1.** клеймо́; сорт; торго́вая ма́рка; **2.** *fig.* (*stigmatize*) [за]клейми́ть, [о]позо́рить

brandish ['brændɪʃ] разма́хивать [-хну́ть] (Т)
brand-new [brænd'nju:] *coll.* совершённо но́вый, с иго́лочки
brandy ['brændɪ] конья́к
brass [brɑ:s] лату́нь; *coll.* (*impudence*) на́глость *f*, наха́льство; **~ band** духово́й орке́стр
brassière ['bræsɪə] ли́фчик, бюстга́льтер
brave [breɪv] **1.** хра́брый, сме́лый; **2.** хра́бро встреча́ть; **~ry** ['breɪvərɪ] хра́брость *f*, сме́лость *f*
brawl [brɔ:l] **1.** шу́мная ссо́ра, потасо́вка; **2.** [по]сканда́лить, [по-]дра́ться
brawny ['brɔ:nɪ] си́льный; му́скулистый
brazen ['breɪzn] ме́дный, бронзо́вый; бессты́дный, на́глый (*a.* **~-faced**)
Brazilian [brə'zɪlɪən] **1.** брази́льский; **2.** брази́лец *m*, бразилья́нка *f*
breach [bri:tʃ] **1.** проло́м; *fig.* (*breaking*) разры́в; *of rule*, *etc.* наруше́ние; (*gap*) брешь *f*; **2.** пробива́ть брешь в (П)
bread [bred] хлеб
breadth [bredθ] ширина́; *fig.* широта́ (кругозо́ра); широ́кий разма́х
break [breɪk] **1.** (*interval*) переры́в; па́уза; (*crack*) тре́щина; разры́в; *coll.* шанс; ***a bad ~*** неуда́ча; **2.** [*irr.*] *v/t.* [с]лома́ть; разби́(ва́)ть; разруша́ть [-ру́шить]; (*interrupt*) прер(ы)ва́ть; (*a lock*, *etc.*) взла́мывать [взлома́ть]; ***~ up*** разла́мывать [-лома́ть]; разби́(ва́)ть; *v/i.* пор(ы)ва́ть (с Т); [по]лома́ться, разби́(ва́)ться; ***~ away*** отделя́ться [-ли́ться] (от Р); ***~ down*** *tech.* потерпе́ть *pf.* ава́рию, вы́йти *pf.* из стро́я; ***~ out*** вспы́хивать [-хнуть]; **~able** ['breɪkəbl] ло́мкий, хру́пкий; **~age** ['breɪkɪdʒ] поло́мка; **~down** *of talks*, *etc.* прекраще́ние; *tech.* поло́мка; ***nervous ~*** не́рвное расстро́йство
breakfast ['brekfəst] **1.** за́втрак; **2.** [по]за́втракать
breakup распа́д, разва́л
breast [brest] грудь *f*; ***make a clean ~ of sth.*** чистосерде́чно сознава́ться в чём-л.; **~stroke** *sport* брасс
breath [breθ] дыха́ние; вздох; ***take a ~*** перевести́ *pf.* дух; ***with bated ~*** затаи́в дыха́ние; **~e** [bri:ð] *v/i.* дыша́ть [дохну́ть]; **~er** [bri:ðə] *pause* переды́шка; **~less** ['breθlɪs] запыха́вшийся; *of a day* безве́тренный
bred [bred] *pt. u pt. p. om* ***breed***
breeches ['brɪtʃɪz] *pl.* бри́джи *pl.*
breed [bri:d] **1.** поро́да; **2.** [*irr.*] *v/t.* выводи́ть [вы́вести]; разводи́ть *v/i.* [-вести́], размножа́ться [-о́житься]; [рас]плоди́ться; **~er** ['bri:də] *of animal* производи́тель *m*; скотово́д; **~ing** [~dɪŋ] разведе́ние (живо́тных); *of person* воспита́ние; ***good ~*** воспи́танность *f*
breez|e [bri:z] лёгкий ветеро́к, бриз; **~y** ['bri:zɪ] ве́тренный; *person* живо́й, весёлый
brevity ['brevətɪ] кра́ткость *f*
brew [bru:] *v/t. beer* [с]вари́ть; *tea* зава́ривать [-ри́ть]; *fig.* затева́ть [зате́ять]; **~ery** ['bru:ərɪ] пивова́ренный заво́д
brib|e [braɪb] **1.** взя́тка; по́дкуп; **2.** подкупа́ть [-пи́ть]; дава́ть взятку (Д); **~ery** ['braɪbərɪ] взя́точничество
brick [brɪk] кирпи́ч; *fig.* молодчи́на; сла́вный па́рень *m*; ***drop a ~*** сморо́зить *pf.* глу́пость; (*say*) ля́пнуть *pf.*; **~layer** ка́менщик
bridal ['braɪdl] □ сва́дебный
bride [braɪd] неве́ста; *just married* новобра́чная; **~groom** жени́х; *just married* новобра́чный; **~smaid** подру́жка неве́сты
bridge [brɪdʒ] **1.** мост; ***~ of the nose*** перено́сица; **2.** соединя́ть мо́стом; стро́ить мост че́рез (В); (*overcome*) *fig.* преодоле́(ва́)ть
bridle ['braɪdl] **1.** узда́; **2.** *v/t.* взну́здывать [-да́ть]
brief [bri:f] **1.** коро́ткий, кра́ткий, сжа́тый; **2.** [про]инструкти́ровать; **~case** портфе́ль *m*
brigade [brɪ'geɪd] *mil.* брига́да
bright [braɪt] □ я́ркий; све́тлый, я́сный; (*intelligent*) смышлёный; **~en** ['braɪtn] *v/t.* оживля́ть [-ви́ть]; *v/i. weather* проясня́ться [-ни́ться]; *person*: оживля́ться [-ви́ться]; **~ness** ['~nɪs] я́ркость *f*; блеск
brillian|ce, **~cy** ['brɪljəns, ~sɪ] я́р-

кость *f*; блеск; (*splendo[u]r*) великоле́пие; (*intelligence*) блестя́щий ум; **~t** [~jənt] **1.** □ блестя́щий (*a. fig.*); сверка́ющий; **2.** бриллиа́нт

brim [brɪm] **1.** край; *of hat* поля́ *n/pl.* **2.** наполня́ть(ся) до краёв; **~ *over*** *fig.* перелива́ться [-ли́ться] че́рез край

brine [braɪn] *cul.* рассо́л

bring [brɪŋ] [*irr.*] приноси́ть [-нести́]; доставля́ть [-а́вить]; *in car, etc.* привози́ть [-везти́]; (*lead*) приводи́ть [-вести́]; **~ *about*** осуществля́ть [-ви́ть]; **~ *down*** *prices* снижа́ть [сни́зить]; **~ *down the house*** вы́звать *pf.* бу́рю аплодисме́нтов; **~ *home to*** довести́ что́-нибудь до чьего́-нибудь созна́ния; **~ *round*** приводи́ть [-вести́] в созна́ние; **~ *up*** воспи́тывать [-та́ть]

brink [brɪŋk] (*edge*) край (*a. fig.*); (круто́й) бе́рег; ***on the ~ of war*** на гра́ни войны́

brisk [brɪsk] ско́рый, оживлённый

bristl|e ['brɪsl] **1.** щети́на; **2.** [о]щети́ниться; **~ *with anger*** [рас]серди́ться; **~ *with*** изоби́ловать (T); **~y** [~ɪ] щети́нистый, колю́чий

British ['brɪtɪʃ] брита́нский; ***the ~*** брита́нцы *m/pl.*

brittle ['brɪtl] хру́пкий, ло́мкий

broach [brəʊtʃ] *question* поднима́ть [-ня́ть]; (*begin*) нач(ин)а́ть

broad [brɔːd] □ широ́кий, обши́рный; *of humour* грубова́тый; ***in ~ daylight*** средь бе́ла дня; **~cast** [*irr.* (***cast***)] **1.** *rumour, etc.* распространя́ть [-ни́ть]; передава́ть по ра́дио, трансли́ровать; **2.** радиопереда́ча, трансля́ция; радиовеща́ние

brocade [brə'keɪd] парча́

broil [brɔɪl] жа́рить(ся) на огне́; *coll.* жа́риться на со́лнце

broke [brəʊk] *pt. от* ***break***; ***be ~*** быть без гроша́; ***go ~*** обанкро́титься *pf.*

broken ['brəʊkən] **1.** *pt. p. от* ***break***; **2.** разби́тый, раско́лотый; **~ *health*** надло́мленное здоро́вье

broker ['brəʊkə] бро́кер, ма́клер

bronchitis [brɒŋ'kaɪtɪs] бронхи́т

bronze [brɒnz] **1.** бро́нза; **2.** бро́нзовый; **3.** загора́ть [-ре́ть]

brooch [brəʊtʃ] брошь, бро́шка

brood [bruːd] **1.** вы́водок; *fig.* ора́ва; **2.** *fig.* гру́стно размышля́ть

brook [brʊk] руче́й

broom [bruːm] метла́, ве́ник

broth [brɒθ] бульо́н

brothel ['brɒθl] публи́чный дом

brother ['brʌðə] брат; собра́т; **~hood** [~hʊd] бра́тство; **~-in-law** [~rɪnlɔː] (*wife's brother*) шу́рин; (*sister's husband*) зять *m*; (*husband's brother*) де́верь *m*; **~ly** [~lɪ] бра́тский

brought [brɔːt] *pt. и pt. p. от* **bring**

brow [braʊ] лоб; (*eye~*) бровь *f*; *of hill* верши́на; **~beat** ['braʊbiːt] [*irr.* (***beat***)] запу́гивать [-га́ть]

brown [braʊn] **1.** кори́чневый цвет; **2.** кори́чневый; сму́глый; загоре́лый; **3.** загора́ть [-ре́ть]

browse [braʊz] пасти́сь; *fig.* чита́ть беспоря́дочно, просма́тривать

bruise [bruːz] **1.** синя́к, кровоподтёк; **2.** ушиба́ть [-би́ть]; поста́вить *pf.* (себе́) синяки́

brunt [brʌnt]: ***bear the ~ of sth.*** *fig.* выноси́ть всю тя́жесть чего́-л.

brush [brʌʃ] **1.** *for sweeping, brushing, etc.* щётка; *for painting* кисть *f*; **2.** *v/t.* чи́стить щёткой; причёсывать щёткой; **~ *aside*** отма́хиваться [-хну́ться] (от P); **~ *up*** приводи́ть в поря́док; *fig.* освежа́ть в па́мяти; *v/i.* **~ *by*** прошмы́гивать [-гну́ть]; **~ *against s.o.*** слегка́ заде́ть кого́-либо; **~wood** ['brʌʃwʊd] хво́рост, валёжник

brusque [brʊsk] □ гру́бый; (*abrupt*) ре́зкий

brussels sprouts [brʌsəls'spraʊts] брюссе́льская капу́ста

brut|al ['bruːtl] □ гру́бый; (*cruel*) жесто́кий; **~ality** [bruː'tælətɪ] гру́бость *f*, жесто́кость *f*; **~e** [bruːt] **1.** жесто́кий; ***by ~ force*** гру́бой си́лой; **2.** *animal* живо́тное; *pers.* скоти́на

bubble ['bʌbl] **1.** пузы́рь *m*, *dim.* пузырёк; **2.** пузы́риться; (*boil*) кипе́ть; *of spring* бить ключо́м (*a. fig.*)

buck [bʌk] **1.** *zo.* саме́ц (*оле́ня, за́йца и др.*); **2.** станови́ться на дыбы́; **~ *up*** *coll.* встряхну́ться *pf.*; оживля́ться [-ви́ться]

bucket ['bʌkɪt] ведро́; *of dredging machine* ковш
buckle ['bʌkl] **1.** пря́жка; **2.** *v/t.* застёгивать [-тегну́ть]; *v/i. of metal, etc.* [по]коро́биться; **~ down to** принима́ться за де́ло
buckwheat ['bʌkwi:t] гречи́ха; *cul.* гре́чневая крупа́
bud [bʌd] **1.** по́чка, буто́н; *fig.* заро́дыш; ***nip in the ~*** подави́ть *pf.* в заро́дыше; **2.** *v/i. bot.* дава́ть по́чки; *fig.* разви́(ва́)ться
budge ['bʌdʒ] *mst. v/i.* сдвига́ться [-и́нуться]; шевели́ть(ся) [-льну́ть(ся)]; *fig.* уступа́ть [-пи́ть]
budget ['bʌdʒɪt] **1.** бюдже́т; фина́нсовая сме́та; **2.**: **~ *for*** ассигнова́ть определённую су́мму на что́-то; предусма́тривать [-смотре́ть]
buff [bʌf] тёмно-жёлтый
buffalo ['bʌfələʊ] *zo.* бу́йвол
buffer ['bʌfə] *rail.* бу́фер
buffet[1] ['bʌfɪt] ударя́ть [-а́рить]; **~ *about*** броса́ть из стороны́ в сто́рону
buffet[2] **1.** [~] буфе́т; **2.** ['bʊfeɪ] буфе́тная сто́йка; **~ *supper*** у́жин "а-ля-фурше́т"
buffoon [bə'fu:n] шут
bug [bʌg] клоп; *Am.* насеко́мое; *hidden microphone* подслу́шивающее устро́йство
build [bɪld] **1.** [*irr.*] [по]стро́ить; сооружа́ть [-руди́ть]; *nest* [с]вить; **~ *on*** полага́ться [положи́ться], возлага́ть наде́жды на (В); **2.** (тело)сложе́ние; **~er** ['bɪldə] строи́тель *m*; **~ing** ['~ɪŋ] зда́ние; строи́тельство
built [bɪlt] *pt. и pt. p. от* ***build***
bulb [bʌlb] *bot.* лу́ковица; *el.* ла́мпочка
bulge [bʌldʒ] **1.** вы́пуклость *f*; **2.** выпя́чиваться [вы́пятиться], выдава́ться [вы́даться]
bulk [bʌlk] объём; основна́я часть *f*; ***in ~*** нава́лом; **~y** ['bʌlkɪ] громоздки́й; *person* ту́чный
bull [bʊl] бык; ***take the ~ by the horns*** взять *pf.* быка́ за рога́; ***~ in a china shop*** слон в посу́дной ла́вке
bulldog ['bʊldɒg] бульдо́г
bulldozer ['bʊldəʊʒə] бульдо́зер
bullet ['bʊlɪt] пу́ля
bulletin ['bʊlətɪn] бюллете́нь *m*
bull's-eye ['bʊlzaɪ] я́блочко мише́ни; ***hit the ~*** попа́сть *pf.* в цель (*a. fig.*)
bully ['bʊlɪ] **1.** задира *m*; **2.** задира́ть, запу́гивать [-га́ть]
bum [bʌm] *coll.* за́д(ница); *Am. sl.* ло́дырь *m*; бродя́га *m*
bumblebee ['bʌmblbi:] шмель *m*
bump [bʌmp] **1.** глухо́й уда́р; (*swelling*) ши́шка; **2.** ударя́ть(ся) [уда́рить(ся)]; **~ *into*** ната́лкиваться [-толкну́ться] (*a. fig.*); *of cars, etc.* ста́лкиваться [столкну́ться]; **~ *against*** сту́каться [-кнуться]
bumper ['bʌmpə] *mot.* бу́фер
bumpy ['bʌmpɪ] уха́бистый, неро́вный
bun [bʌn] бу́лочка
bunch [bʌntʃ] *of grapes* гроздь, кисть; *of keys* свя́зка; *of flowers* буке́т; *of people* гру́ппа
bundle ['bʌndl] **1.** у́зел; **2.** *v/t.* (*put together*) собира́ть вме́сте, свя́зывать в у́зел (*a.* **~ *up***)
bungalow ['bʌŋgələʊ] одноэта́жный котте́дж
bungle ['bʌŋgl] неуме́ло, небре́жно рабо́тать; [на] по́ртить; *coll.* завали́ть
bunk[1] [bʌŋk] вздор
bunk[2] [~] ко́йка (*a. naut.*); *rail.* спа́льное ме́сто, по́лка
buoy [bɔɪ] *naut.* ба́кен, буй; **~ant** ['bɔɪənt] □ плаву́чий; (*cheerful*) жизнера́достный; бо́дрый
burden ['bɜ:dn] **1.** но́ша; *fig.* бре́мя *n*, груз; **2.** нагружа́ть [-рузи́ть]; обременя́ть [-ни́ть]; **~some** [~səm] обремени́тельный
bureau ['bjʊərəʊ] конто́ра; бюро́ *n indecl.*; ***information ~*** спра́вочное бюро́; **~cracy** [bjʊə'rɒkrəsɪ] бюрокра́тия
burglar ['bɜ:glər] взло́мщик; **~y** [~rɪ] кра́жа со взло́мом
burial ['berɪəl] по́хороны *f/pl.*; **~ *service*** заупоко́йная слу́жба
burly ['bɜ:lɪ] здорове́нный, дю́жий
burn [bɜ:n] **1.** ожо́г; **2.** [*irr.*] *v/i.* горе́ть; *of food* подгора́ть [-ре́ть]; *sting* жечь; *v/t.* [с]жечь; сжига́ть [сжечь]; **~er** ['bɜ:nə] горе́лка

burnt [bɜ:nt] *pt. и pt. p. от* **burn**
burrow ['bʌrəʊ] **1.** нора́; **2.** [вы́]рыть но́ру
burst [bɜ:st] **1.** (*explosion*) взрыв *a. fig.*; *of anger, etc.* вспы́шка; **2.** [*irr.*] *v/i.* взрыва́ться [взорва́ться]; *dam* прор(ы)ва́ться; *pipe, etc.* ло́паться [ло́пнуть]; **~ *into the room*** врыва́ться [ворва́ться] в ко́мнату; **~ *into tears*** разрыда́ться; *v/t.* взрыва́ть [взорва́ть]
bury ['berɪ] [по]хорони́ть; *a bone, etc. in earth* зары́(ва́)ть
bus [bʌs] авто́бус
bush [bʊʃ] куст, куста́рник; ***beat about*** *or* ***around the* ~** ходи́ть вокру́г да о́коло
business ['bɪznɪs] де́ло; би́знес; торго́вое предприя́тие; ***have no* ~ *to*** *inf.* не име́ть пра́ва (+ *inf.*); **~-like** [~laɪk] делово́й; практи́чный; **~man** бизнесме́н, предпринима́тель; **~ trip** делова́я пое́здка
bus|station автовокза́л; **~stop** авто́бусная остано́вка
bust [bʌst] бюст; же́нская грудь *f*
bustle ['bʌsl] **1.** сумато́ха; суета́; **2.** *v/i.* [по]торопи́ться, [за]суети́ться; *v/t.* [по]торопи́ть
busy ['bɪzɪ] **1.** □ занято́й (***at*** Т); за́нятый (*a. tel.*); **2.** (*mst.* **~ *o.s.***) занима́ться [заня́ться] (***with*** Т)
but [bʌt, bət] **1.** *cj.* но, а; одна́ко; тем не ме́нее; е́сли бы не; **2.** *prp.* кро́ме (Р), за исключе́нием (Р); ***the last* ~ *one*** предпоследний; **~ *for*** без (Р); **3.** *adv.* то́лько, лишь; **~ *now*** то́лько что; ***all* ~** едва́ не ...; ***nothing* ~** ничего́ кро́ме, то́лько; ***I cannot help* ~** *inf.* не могу́ не (+ *inf.*)
butcher ['bʊtʃə] **1.** мясни́к; *fig.* уби́йца *m*; **2.** *cattle* забива́ть; *people* уби́(ва́)ть; **~y** [~rɪ] бо́йня, резня́
butler ['bʌtlə] дворе́цкий
butt [bʌt] **1.** (*blow*) уда́р; *of rifle* прикла́д; (*of cigarette*) оку́рок; *fig. of person* мише́нь для насме́шек; **2.** ударя́ть голово́й; (*run into*) натыка́ться [наткну́ться]; **~ *in*** перебива́ть [-би́ть]
butter ['bʌtə] **1.** (сли́вочное) ма́сло; **2.** нама́зывать ма́слом; **~cup** *bot.* лю́тик; **~fly** ба́бочка
buttocks ['bʌtəks] *pl.* я́годицы *f/pl.*
button ['bʌtn] **1.** пу́говица; *of bell, etc.* (*knob*) кно́пка; **2.** застёгивать [-тегну́ть]; **~hole** петля́
buxom ['bʌksəm] пы́шная, полногру́дая
buy [baɪ] [*irr.*] *v/t.* покупа́ть [купи́ть] (***from*** у Р); **~er** ['baɪə] покупа́тель *m*, -ница *f*
buzz [bʌz] **1.** жужжа́ние; *of crowd* гул; **2.** *v/i.* [за]жужжа́ть
by [baɪ] **1.** *prp.* у (Р), при (П), о́коло (Р); к (Д); вдоль (Р); **~ *the dozen*** дю́жинами; **~ *o.s.*** оди́н *m*, одна́ *f*; **~ *land*** назе́мным тра́нспортом; **~ *rail*** по желе́зной доро́ге; ***day* ~ *day*** день за днём; **2.** *adv.* бли́зко, ря́дом; ми́мо; **~ *and* ~** вско́ре; **~ *the way*** ме́жду про́чим; **~ *and large*** в це́лом; **~-election** ['baɪɪlekʃn] дополни́тельные вы́боры *m/pl.*; **~gone** про́шлый; **~pass** объезд, объездна́я доро́га; **~-product** побо́чный проду́кт; **~stander** ['~stændə] очеви́дец (-дица); **~street** у́лочка
byte [baɪt] *comput.* байт
by|way глуха́я доро́га; **~word** при́тча во язы́цех

C

cab [kæb] такси́ *n indecl.*; *mot., rail.* каби́на
cabbage ['kæbɪdʒ] капу́ста
cabin ['kæbɪn] (*hut*) хи́жина; *ae.* каби́на; *naut.* каю́та
cabinet ['kæbɪnɪt] *pol.* кабине́т; *of*

TV, radio, etc. ко́рпус
cable ['keɪbl] **1.** ка́бель *m*; (*rope*) кана́т; телегра́мма; **~ *television*** ка́бельное телеви́дение; **2.** *tel.* телеграфи́ровать (*im*)*pf.*
cackle ['kækl] **1.** куда́хтанье; гогота́нье; **2.** [за]куда́хтать; *of geese and man* [за]гогота́ть
cad [kæd] негодя́й
cadaverous [kə'dævərəs] исхуда́вший как скеле́т
caddish ['kædɪʃ] по́длый
cadet [kə'det] каде́т, курса́нт
cadge [kædʒ] *v/t.* кля́нчить; *v/i.* попроша́йничать; **~r** ['kædʒə] попроша́йка
café ['kæfeɪ] кафе́ *n indecl.*
cafeteria [kæfɪ'tɪərɪə] кафете́рий; *at factory, univ.* столо́вая
cage [keɪdʒ] *for animals* кле́тка; (*of elevator*) каби́на ли́фта
cajole [kə'dʒəʊl] угова́ривать [-вори́ть]; *coll.* обха́живать; доби́ться *pf.* чего-л. ле́стью и́ли обма́ном
cake [keɪk] кекс, торт; *fancy* пиро́жное; *of soap* кусо́к
calamity [kə'læmətɪ] бе́дствие
calcium ['kælsɪəm] ка́льций
calculat|e ['kælkjʊleɪt] *v/t.* вычисля́ть [вы́числить]; *cost, etc.* подсчи́тывать [-ита́ть]; *v/i.* рассчи́тывать (***on*** на В); **~ion** [kælkjʊ'leɪʃn] вычисле́ние; расчёт; **~or** ['kælkjʊleɪtə] калькуля́тор
calendar ['kælɪndə] календа́рь
calf[1] [kɑːf], *pl.* **calves** [kɑːvz] телёнок (*pl.*: теля́та); (*a.* **~skin**) теля́чья ко́жа, опо́ек
calf[2] [~], *pl.* **calves** *of the leg(s)* [~] икра́
caliber *or* **calibre** ['kælɪbə] кали́бр (*a. fig.*)
calico ['kælɪkəʊ] си́тец
call [kɔːl] **1.** крик, зов, о́клик; *tel.* звоно́к; (*summon*) вы́зов; (*appeal*) призы́в; визи́т, посеще́ние; ***on ~ of nurse, doctor*** дежу́рство на дому́; **2.** *v/t.* [по]зва́ть; оклика́ть [-и́кнуть]; (*summon*) соз(ы)ва́ть; вызыва́ть [вы́звать]; [раз]буди́ть; призыва́ть; **~ *off*** отменя́ть [-ни́ть] (Р); **~ *up*** призыва́ть на вое́нную слу́жбу; **~ *s.o.'s attention to*** привле́чь *pf.* чьё-л. внима́ние (к Д); *v/i.* крича́ть [кри́кнуть]; *tel.* [по]звони́ть; (*visit*) заходи́ть [зайти́] (***at*** в В; ***on a p.*** к Д); **~ *for*** [по]тре́бовать; **~ *for a p.*** заходи́ть [зайти́] за (Т); **~ *in*** *coll.* забега́ть [-ежа́ть] (к Д); **~ *on*** навеща́ть [-ести́ть] (В); приз(ы)ва́ть (***to do*** *etc.* сде́лать *и т.д.*); **~box** ['kɔːlbɒks] *Am.* телефо́н-автома́т, телефо́нная бу́дка; **~er** ['kɔːlə] го́сть(я *f*) *m*
calling ['kɔːlɪŋ] (*vocation*) призва́ние; профе́ссия
call|ous ['kæləs] □ огрубе́лый; мозо́листый; *fig.* бессерде́чный; **~us** ['kæləs] мозо́ль
calm [kɑːm] **1.** □ споко́йный; безве́тренный; **2.** тишина́; *of sea* штиль *m.*; споко́йствие; **3. ~ *down*** успока́ивать(ся) [-ко́ить(ся)]; *of wind, etc.* стиха́ть [-и́хнуть]
calorie ['kælərɪ] *phys.* кало́рия
calve [kɑːv] [о]тели́ться; **~s** *pl. от* ***calf***
cambric ['keɪmbrɪk] бати́ст
came [keɪm] *pt. от* ***come***
camera ['kæmərə] фотоаппара́т; *cine.* киноаппара́т; ***in ~*** при закры́тых дверя́х
camomile ['kæməmaɪl] рома́шка
camouflage ['kæməflɑːʒ] **1.** камуфля́ж, маскиро́вка (*a. mil.*); **2.** [за]маскирова́ть(ся)
camp [kæmp] **1.** ла́герь *m*; **~ *bed*** похо́дная крова́ть; **2.** стать ла́герем; **~ *out*** расположи́ться *pf.* и́ли ночева́ть на откры́том во́здухе
campaign [kæm'peɪn] **1.** *pol., etc.* кампа́ния; **2.** проводи́ть кампа́нию; агити́ровать (***for*** за В, ***against*** про́тив Р)
camphor ['kæmfə] камфара́
camping ['kæmpɪŋ] ке́мпинг (= *a.* **~ *site***)
campus ['kæmpəs] *Am. university grounds and buildings* университе́тский городо́к
can[1] [kæn] *v/aux.* [с]мочь, быть в состоя́нии; [с]уме́ть
can[2] [~] **1.** *for milk* бидо́н; (*tin*) ба́нка; *for petrol* кани́стра; **2.** консерви́ровать (*im*)*pf.*, *pf. a.* [за-]; **~ *opener*** консе́рвный нож
canal [kə'næl] кана́л
canary [kə'neərɪ] канаре́йка

cancel ['kænsl] (*call off*) отменя́ть [-ни́ть]; (*cross out*) вычёркивать [вы́черкнуть]; *agreement, etc.* аннули́ровать (*im*)*pf.*; *stamp* погаша́ть [погаси́ть]; *math.* (*a.* **~ out**) сокраща́ть [-рати́ть]
cancer ['kænsə] *astr.* созве́здие Ра́ка; *med.* рак; **~ous** [~rəs] ра́ковый
candid ['kændɪd] □ и́скренний, прямо́й; **~ camera** скры́тая ка́мера
candidate ['kændɪdət] кандида́т (**for** на В)
candied ['kændɪd] заса́харенный
candle ['kændl] свеча́; **the game is (not) worth the ~** игра́ (не) сто́ит свеч; **~stick** [~stɪk] подсве́чник
cando(u)r ['kændə] открове́нность *f*; и́скренность *f*
candy ['kændɪ] ледене́ц; *Am.* конфе́ты *f/pl.*, сла́сти *f/pl.*
cane [keɪn] *bot.* тростни́к; *for walking* трость *f*
canned [kænd] консерви́рованный
cannon ['kænən] пу́шка; ору́дие
cannot ['kænɒt] не в состоя́нии, → **can**[1]
canoe [kə'nuː] кано́э
canon ['kænən] *eccl.* кано́н; пра́вило
cant [kænt] пусты́е слова́; ханжество́
can't [kɑːnt] = **cannot**
canteen [kæn'tiːn] *eating place* буфе́т; столо́вая
canvas ['kænvəs] *cloth* холст; *for embroidery* канва́; *fig.* карти́на; паруси́на
canvass [~] *v/t.*: **~ opinions** иссле́довать обще́ственное мне́ние; собира́ть голоса́ перед вы́борами
caoutchouc ['kaʊtʃʊk] каучу́к
cap [kæp] **1.** *with peak* ке́пка, *mil.* фура́жка; *without peak* ша́пка; *tech.* колпачо́к; *of mushroom* шля́пка; **~ in hand** в ро́ли проси́теля; **2.** накрыва́ть [-ры́ть] кры́шкой; *coll.* перещеголя́ть *pf.*; **to ~ it all** в доверше́ние всего́
capab|ility [keɪpə'bɪlətɪ] спосо́бность *f*; **~le** ['keɪpəbl] □ спосо́бный (**of** на В); (*gifted*) одарённый
capaci|ous [kə'peɪʃəs] □ вмести́тельный; **~ty** [kə'pæsətɪ] объём, вмести́мость *f*; (*ability*) спосо́бность *f*; *tech.* производи́тельность *f*; *of engine* мо́щность *f*; *el.* ёмкость *f*; **in the ~ of** в ка́честве (Р)
cape[1] [keɪp] плащ
cape[2] [~] *geogr.* мыс
caper ['keɪpə] прыжо́к, ша́лость; **cut ~s** выде́лывать антраша́; дура́читься
capital ['kæpɪtl] **1.** □ (*crime*) кара́емый сме́ртью; (*sentence, punishment*) сме́ртный; **2.** столи́ца; (*wealth*) капита́л; (*a.* **~ letter**) загла́вная бу́ква; **~ism** ['kæpɪtəlɪzəm] капитали́зм; **~ize** ['kæpɪtəlaɪz]: **~ on** обраща́ть в свою́ по́льзу
capitulate [kə'pɪtʃʊleɪt] капитули́ровать, сд(ав)а́ться (**to** Д) (*a. fig.*)
capric|e [kə'priːs] капри́з, прихо́ть; **~ious** [kə'prɪʃəs] □ капри́зный
capsize [kæp'saɪz] *v/i. naut.* опроки́дываться [-ки́нуться]; *v/t.* опроки́дывать [-ки́нуть]
capsule ['kæpsjuːl] *med.* ка́псула
captain ['kæptɪn] *mil., naut., sport* капита́н
caption ['kæpʃn] *title, words accompanying picture* по́дпись к карти́нке; заголо́вок; *cine.* ти́тры *m/pl.*
captiv|ate ['kæptɪveɪt] пленя́ть [-ни́ть], очаро́вывать [-ова́ть]; **~e** ['kæptɪv] пле́нный; *fig.* пле́нник; **~ity** [kæp'tɪvətɪ] плен; нево́ля
capture ['kæptʃə] **1.** пойма́ть; захва́тывать [-ти́ть]; брать в плен; **2.** по́имка; захва́т
car [kɑː] *rail vehicle* ваго́н; *motor vehicle* автомоби́ль, маши́на; **by ~** маши́ной
caramel ['kærəmel] караме́ль *f*
caravan ['kærəvæn] карава́н; дом-автоприце́п
caraway ['kærəweɪ] тмин
carbohydrate [ˌkɑːbəʊ'haɪdreɪt] углево́д
carbon ['kɑːbən] углеро́д; **~ paper** копи́рка
carburet(t)or [kɑːbjʊ'retə] *mot.* карбюра́тор
carcase ['kɑːkəs] ту́ша
card [kɑːd] ка́рта, ка́рточка; **~board** ['kɑːdbɔːd] карто́н
cardigan ['kɑːdɪgən] кардига́н
cardinal ['kɑːdənəl] **1.** □ (*chief*) гла́вный, основно́й; (*most impor-*

tant) кардина́льный; **~ number** коли́чественное числи́тельное; **2.** *eccl.* кардина́л
card|index ['kɑːdɪndeks] картоте́ка; **~ phone** ка́рточный телефо́н
care [keə] **1.** забо́та; (*charge*) попече́ние; (*attention*) внима́ние; (*tending*) присмо́тр (за Т); (*nursing*) ухо́д (за Т); **~ of** (*abbr.* **c/o**) по а́дресу (Р); **take ~ of** [с]бере́чь (В); присмотре́ть за (Т); **handle with ~!** осторо́жно!; **2.** име́ть жела́ние, [за]хоте́ть (**to**: + *inf.*); **~ for**: **a)** [по]забо́титься о (П); **b)** люби́ть (В); *coll.* **I don't ~!** мне всё равно!; **well ~d for** ухо́женный
career [kə'rɪə] **1.** *fig.* карье́ра; **2.** нести́сь, мча́ться
carefree ['keəfriː] беззабо́тный
careful ['keəfl] □ (*cautious*) осторо́жный; (*done with care*) аккура́тный, тща́тельный; внима́тельный (к Д); **be ~ (of, about, with)** забо́титься (о П); стара́ться (+ *inf.*); **~ness** [~nɪs] осторо́жность *f*; тща́тельность *f*
careless ['keəlɪs] □ *work, etc.* небре́жный; *driving, etc.* неосторо́жный; **~ness** [~nɪs] небре́жность *f*
caress [kə'res] **1.** ла́ска; **2.** ласка́ть
caretaker ['keəteɪkə] сто́рож
carfare ['kɑːfeə] *Am.* пла́та за прое́зд
cargo ['kɑːgəʊ] *naut., ae.* груз
caricature ['kærɪkətʃʊə] **1.** карикату́ра; **2.** изобража́ть в карикату́рном ви́де
car jack ['kɑːdʒæk] *lifting device* домкра́т
carnal ['kɑːnl] □ *sensual* чу́вственный, пло́тский; *sexual* полово́й
carnation [kɑː'neɪʃn] гвозди́ка
carnival ['kɑːnɪvl] карнава́л
carol ['kærəl] рожде́ственский гимн
carp[1] [kaːp] *zo.* карп
carp[2] [~] придира́ться
carpent|er ['kɑːpəntə] пло́тник; **~ry** [~trɪ] пло́тничество
carpet ['kɑːpɪt] **1.** ковёр; **2.** устила́ть ковро́м
carriage ['kærɪdʒ] *rail.* ваго́н; перево́зка, транспортиро́вка; *of body* оса́нка; **~ free, ~ paid** опла́ченная доста́вка
carrier ['kærɪə] (*porter*) носи́льщик; *med.* носи́тель инфе́кции; **~s** тра́нспортное аге́нтство; **~ bag** су́мка
carrot ['kærət] морко́вка; *collect.* морко́вь *f*
carry ['kærɪ] **1.** *v/t.* носи́ть, [по]нести́; *in train, etc.* вози́ть, [по]везти́; **~ o.s.** держа́ться, вести́ себя́; *of law, etc.* **be carried** быть при́нятым; **~ s.th. too far** заходи́ть сли́шком далеко́; **~ on** продолжа́ть [-до́лжить]; **~ out** *или* **through** доводи́ть до конца́; выполня́ть [вы́полнить]; *v/i.* *of sound* доноси́ться [донести́сь]
cart [kɑːt] теле́га, пово́зка
cartilage ['kɑːtɪlɪdʒ] хрящ
carton ['kɑːtn] *container* карто́нка; *for milk, etc.* паке́т
cartoon [kɑː'tuːn] карикату́ра, шарж; *animated* мультфи́льм, *coll.* му́льтик
cartridge ['kɑːtrɪdʒ] патро́н
carve [kɑːv] *on wood* ре́зать; *meat* нареза́ть [наре́зать]
carving ['kɑːvɪŋ] *object* резьба́
case[1] [keɪs] я́щик; *for spectacles, etc.* футля́р; (*suit~*) чемода́н; (*attaché ~*) (портфе́ль-)диплома́т
case[2] [~] слу́чай; (*state of affairs*) положе́ние; (*circumstances*) обстоя́тельство; *law* суде́бное де́ло; **in any ~** в любо́м слу́чае; **in ~ of need** в слу́чае необходи́мости; **in no ~** ни в ко́ем слу́чае
cash [kæʃ] **1.** де́ньги, нали́чные де́ньги *f/pl.*; **on a ~ basis** за нали́чный расчёт; **~ on delivery** нало́женным платежо́м; **2.** получа́ть де́ньги по (Д); **~ in on** воспо́льзоваться; **~ier** [kæ'ʃɪə] касси́р(ша)
cask [kɑːsk] бо́чка, бочо́нок
casket ['kɑːskɪt] шкату́лка; *Am. a. = coffin* гроб
casserole ['kæsərəʊl] гли́няная кастрю́ля; запека́нка
cassette [kə'set] кассе́та
cassock ['kæsək] ря́са, сута́на
cast [kɑːst] **1.** (*act of throwing*) бросо́к, мета́ние; *thea.* (*actors*) соста́в исполни́телей; **2.** [*irr.*] *v/t.* броса́ть [бро́сить] (*a. fig.*); *shadow* отбра́сывать; *tech.* *metals* отли́(ва́)ть;

C

thea. roles распределя́ть [-ли́ть]; ~ ***light on*** пролива́ть [-ли́ть] свет на (В); ~ ***lots*** броса́ть жре́бий; ***be ~ down*** быть в уны́нии; *v/i.* ~ ***about for*** разы́скивать
caste [kɑːst] ка́ста
castigate ['kæstɪgeɪt] нака́зывать [-за́ть]; *fig.* жесто́ко критикова́ть
cast iron чугу́н; *attr.* чугу́нный
castle ['kɑːsl] за́мок; *chess* ладья́
castor ['kɑːstə]: ~ ***oil*** касто́ровое ма́сло
castrate [kæ'streɪt] кастри́ровать *(im)pf.*
casual ['kæʒjʊl] □ *(chance)* случа́йный; *(careless)* небре́жный; **~ty** [~tɪ] несча́стный слу́чай; *person* пострада́вший, же́ртва; *pl. mil.* поте́ри
cat [kæt] ко́шка; *(male)* кот
catalog(ue) ['kætəlɒg] **1.** катало́г; **2.** составля́ть [-вить] катало́г, вноси́ть в катало́г
cataract ['kætərækt] *(waterfall)* водопа́д; *med.* катара́кта
catarrh [kə'tɑː] ката́р
catastrophe [kə'tæstrəfɪ] катастро́фа; *natural* стихи́йное бе́дствие
catch [kætʃ] **1.** *of fish* уло́в; *(trick)* подво́х; *on door* задви́жка; **2.** [*irr.*] *v/t.* лови́ть [пойма́ть]; *(take hold of)* схва́тывать [схвати́ть]; *disease* заража́ться [зарази́ться] (Т); *train, etc.* поспе́(ва́)ть к (Д); ~ ***cold*** просту́живаться [-уди́ться]; ~ ***s.o.'s eye*** пойма́ть взгляд (Р); ~ ***up*** догоня́ть [догна́ть]; **3.** *v/i.* зацепля́ться [-пи́ться]; *coll.* ~ ***on*** станови́ться мо́дным; ~ ***up with*** догоня́ть [догна́ть] (В); **~ing** ['kætʃɪŋ] *fig.* зарази́тельный; *med.* зара́зный; **~word** *(popular phrase)* мо́дное слове́чко
categor|ical [kætɪ'gɒrɪkl] □ категори́ческий; **~y** ['kætɪgərɪ] катего́рия, разря́д
cater ['keɪtə]: ~ ***for*** обслу́живать (В)
caterpillar *zo.* ['kætəpɪlə] гу́сеница
catgut ['kætgʌt] струна́; *med.* ке́тгут
cathedral [kə'θiːdrəl] собо́р
Catholic ['kæθəlɪk] **1.** като́лик; **2.** католи́ческий
catkin ['kætkɪn] *bot.* серёжка
cattle ['kætl] кру́пный рога́тый скот; **~-breeding** скотово́дство
caught [kɔːt] *pt.* и *pt. p. от* ***catch***
cauliflower ['kɒlɪflaʊə] цветна́я капу́ста
cause ['kɔːz] **1.** причи́на, основа́ние; *(motive)* по́вод; **2.** причиня́ть [-ни́ть]; *(make happen)* вызыва́ть [вы́звать]; **~less** ['kɔːzlɪs] □ беспричи́нный, необосно́ванный
caution ['kɔːʃn] **1.** *(prudence)* осторо́жность *f*; *(warning)* предостереже́ние; **2.** предостерега́ть [-ре́чь] (***against*** от Р)
cautious ['kɔːʃəs] □ осторо́жный, осмотри́тельный; **~ness** [~nɪs] осторо́жность *f*, осмотри́тельность *f*
cavalry ['kævlrɪ] кавале́рия
cave [keɪv] **1.** пеще́ра; **2.** ~ ***in***: *v/i.* оседа́ть [осе́сть]; *fig., coll.* сда́ться *pf.*
caviar(e) ['kævɪɑː] икра́
cavil ['kævəl] **1.** приди́рка; **2.** прид(и)ра́ться (***at, about*** к Д, за В)
cavity ['kævɪtɪ] впа́дина; по́лость *f*; *in tooth, tree* дупло́
cease [siːs] *v/i.* перест(ав)а́ть; *v/t.* прекраща́ть [-крати́ть]; остана́вливать [-нови́ть]; **~-fire** прекраще́ние огня́; переми́рие; **~less** ['siːsləs] □ непреры́вный, непреста́нный
cedar ['siːdə] кедр
cede [siːd] уступа́ть [-пи́ть] (В)
ceiling ['siːlɪŋ] потоло́к; *attr.* максима́льный; ***price*** ~ преде́льная цена́
celebrat|e ['selɪbreɪt] [от]пра́зднова́ть; **~ed** [~ɪd] знамени́тый; **~ion** [selɪ'breɪʃn] торжества́ *n/pl.*; пра́зднование
celebrity [sɪ'lebrɪtɪ] *pers. and state of being* знамени́тость *f*
celery ['selərɪ] сельдере́й
celestial [sɪ'lestɪəl] □ небе́сный
cell [sel] *pol.* яче́йка; *in prison* ка́мера; *eccl.* ке́лья; *biol.* кле́тка; *el.* элеме́нт
cellar ['selə] подва́л; ***wine*** ~ ви́нный по́греб
cello ['tʃeləʊ] виолонче́ль
Cellophane® ['seləfeɪn] целлофа́н
cement [sɪ'ment] **1.** цеме́нт; **2.** це-

ментировать (*im*)*pf.*; *fig.* ~ ***relations*** укреплять [-пить] связи
cemetery ['semɪtrɪ] кладбище
censor ['sensə] **1.** цензор; **2.** подвергать цензуре; **~ship** ['sensəʃɪp] цензура
censure ['senʃə] **1.** осуждение, порицание; **2.** осуждать [осудить], порицать
census ['sensəs] перепись *f*
cent [sent] *Am. coin* цент
centenary [sen'tiːnərɪ] столетняя годовщина, столетие
center (*Brt.* **-tre**) ['sentə] **1.** центр; (*focus*) средоточие; ***in the*** ~ в середине; **2.** [с]концентрировать(ся); сосредоточи(ва)ть(ся)
centi|grade ['sentɪgreɪd]: ***... degrees*** ~ ... градусов по Цельсию; **~meter** (*Brt. -tre*) [~miːtə] сантиметр; **~-pede** [~piːd] *zo.* сороконожка
central ['sentrəl] □ центральный; главный; ~ ***office*** управление; **~ize** [~laɪz] централизовать (*im*)*pf.*
centre → ***center***
century ['sentʃərɪ] столетие, век
ceramics [sɪ'ræmɪks] керамика
cereal ['sɪərɪəl] хлебный злак
cerebral ['serɪbrəl] мозговой, церебральный
ceremon|ial [serɪ'məʊnɪəl] □ торжественный; **~ious** [~nɪəs] церемонный; **~y** ['serɪmənɪ] церемония
certain ['sɜːtn] □ (*definite*) определённый; (*confident*) уверенный; (*undoubted*) несомненный; некий; некоторый; ***a ~ Mr. Jones*** некий г-н Джоунз; ***to a ~ extent*** до некоторой степени; **~ty** [~tɪ] уверенность *f*; определённость *f*
certi|ficate **1.** [sə'tɪfɪkət] свидетельство; справка; ***birth*** ~ свидетельство о рождении; **2.** [~keɪt] выдать удостоверение (Д); **~fy** ['sɜːtɪfaɪ] удостоверять [-ерить]; **~tude** [~tjuːd] уверенность *f*
cessation [se'seɪʃn] прекращение
CFC ***chlorofluorocarbon*** фреон
chafe [tʃeɪf] *v/t. make sore* натирать [натереть]; *v/i.* раздражаться [-житься]
chaff [tʃɑːf] подшучивать [-шутить] над (Т), подтрунивать [-нить]
chagrin ['ʃægrɪn] **1.** досада, огорчение; **2.** досаждать [досадить] (Д); огорчать [-чить]
chain [tʃeɪn] **1.** цепь *f* (*a. fig.*); *dim.* цепочка; **~s** *pl. fig.* оковы *f/pl.*; узы *f/pl.*; ~ ***reaction*** цепная реакция; **2.** *dog* держать на цепи
chair [tʃeə] стул; ***be in the ~*** председательствовать; **~man** ['tʃeəmən] председатель *m*; **~woman** [~wʊmən] (женщина-)председатель, председательница
chalk [tʃɔːk] **1.** мел; **2.** писать, рисовать мелом; ~ ***up*** (*register*) отмечать [етить]
challenge ['tʃælɪndʒ] **1.** вызов; **2.** вызывать [вызвать]; *s.o.'s right, etc.* оспаривать [оспорить]
chamber ['tʃeɪmbə] (*room*) комната; (*official body*) ~ ***of commerce*** торговая палата; **~maid** горничная; ~ **music** камерная музыка
chamois ['ʃæmwaː] замша
champagne [ʃæm'peɪn] шампанское
champion ['tʃæmpɪən] **1.** чемпион *m*, -ка *f*; защитник *m*, -ница *f*; **2.** защищать [-итить]; бороться за (В); **~ship** первенство, чемпионат
chance [tʃɑːns] **1.** случайность *f*; риск; (*opportunity*) удобный случай; шанс (***of*** на В); ***by*** ~ случайно; ***take a*** ~ рисковать [-кнуть]; **2.** случайный; **3.** *v/i.* случаться [-читься]
chancellor ['tʃɑːnsələ] канцлер
chancy ['tʃɑːnsɪ] *coll.* рискованный
chandelier [ʃændə'lɪə] люстра
change [tʃeɪndʒ] **1.** перемена, изменение; *of linen* смена; ***small*** ~ *money* сдача; ***for a*** ~ для разнообразия; **2.** *v/t.* [по]менять; изменять [-нить]; *money* разменивать [-нять]; *v/i.* [по]меняться; изменяться [-ниться]; *into different clothes* переоде(ва)ться; обмениваться [-нять]; *rail.* пересаживаться [-сесть]; **~able** ['tʃeɪndʒəbl] □ непостоянный, изменчивый
channel ['tʃænl] *river* русло; (*naut. fairway*) фарватер; *geogr.* пролив; *fig.* (*source*) источник; ***through official ~s*** по официальным каналам
chaos ['keɪɒs] хаос, беспорядок

C

chap¹ [tʃæp] **1.** (*split, crack of skin*) трéщина; **2.** [по]трéскаться
chap² [~] *coll.* пáрень *m*
chapel ['tʃæpl] часóвня
chapter ['tʃæptə] главá
char [tʃɑː] (*burn*) обýгли(ва)ть(ся)
character ['kærəktə] харáктер; (*individual*) ли́чность *f*; *thea.* дéйствующее лицó; *lit.* герóй, персонáж; (*letter*) бýква; **~istic** [kærəktə'rɪstɪk] **1.** (**~ally**) характéрный; типи́чный (**of** для Р); **2.** характéрная чертá; свóйство; **~ize** ['kærəktəraɪz] характеризовáть (*im*)*pf.*
charcoal ['tʃɑːkəʊl] древéсный ýголь *m*
charge [tʃɑːdʒ] **1.** плáта; *el.* заря́д; (*order*) поручéние; *law* обвинéние; *mil.* атáка; *fig.* попечéние, забóта; **~s** *pl. comm.* расхóды *m/pl.*; издéржки *f/pl.*; **be in ~ of** руководи́ть (Т); быть отвéтственным (за В); **2.** *v/t. battery* заряжáть [-яди́ть]; поручáть [-чи́ть] (Д); обвиня́ть [-ни́ть] (**with** в П); *price* проси́ть (**for** за В); (*rush*) бросáться ['-ситься]
charisma [kə'rɪzmə] ли́чное обая́ние
charitable ['tʃærətəbl] □ благотвори́тельный; (*kind*) милосéрдный
charity ['tʃærətɪ] милосéрдие; благотвори́тельность *f*
charm [tʃɑːm] **1.** (*trinket*) амулéт; *fig.* чáры *f/pl.*; обая́ние, очаровáние; **2.** заколдóвывать [-довáть]; *fig.* очарóвывать [-овáть]; **~ing** ['tʃɑːmɪŋ] □ очаровáтельный, обая́тельный
chart [tʃɑːt] *naut.* морскáя кáрта; диагрáмма; *pl.* спи́сок шля́геров, бестсéллеров
charter ['tʃɑːtə] **1.** *hist.* хáртия; **~ of the UN** Устáв ООН; **2.** *naut.* [за]фрахтовáть (*сýдно*)
charwoman ['tʃɑːwʊmən] убóрщица, приходя́щая домрабóтница
chase [tʃeɪs] **1.** погóня *f*; *hunt.* охóта; **2.** охóтиться за (Т); преслéдовать; **~ away** прогоня́ть [-гнáть]
chasm [kæzəm] бéздна, прóпасть *f*
chaste [tʃeɪst] □ целомýдренный
chastity ['tʃæstətɪ] целомýдрие; дéвственность *f*
chat [tʃæt] **1.** бесéда; **2.** [по]болтáть, [по]бесéдовать
chattels ['tʃætlz] *pl.* (*mst.* **goods and ~**) имýщество, вéщи *f/pl.*
chatter ['tʃætə] **1.** болтовня́ *f*; щебетáние; **2.** [по]болтáть; **~box, ~er** [~rə] болтýн *m*, -нья *f*
chatty ['tʃætɪ] разговóрчивый
chauffeur ['ʃəʊfə] води́тель *m*; шофёр
cheap [tʃiːp] □ дешёвый; *fig.* плохóй; **~en** ['tʃiːpən] [по]дешевéть; *fig.* унижáть [уни́зить]
cheat [tʃiːt] **1.** *pers.* обмáнщик, плут; (*fraud*) обмáн; **2.** обмáнывать [-нýть]
check [tʃek] **1.** *chess* шах; (*restraint*) препя́тствие; остановка; (*verification, examination*) контрóль *m* (**on** над Т), провéрка (**on** Р); *luggage/baggage ticket* багáжная квитáнция; *bank draft* (*Brt.* **cheque**), *receipt or bill in restaurant, etc.* чек; **2.** проверя́ть [-вéрить]; [про]контроли́ровать; приостанáвливать [-нови́ть]; препя́тствовать; **~ book** чéковая кни́жка; **~er** ['tʃekə] контролёр; **~ers** ['tʃekəz] *pl. Am.* шáшки *f/pl.*; **~mate 1.** шах и мат; **2.** дéлать мат; **~-up** провéрка; *med.* осмóтр
cheek [tʃiːk] щекá (*pl.*: щёки); *coll.* нáглость *f*, дéрзость *f*
cheer [tʃɪə] **1.** весéлье; одобри́тельные вóзгласы *m/pl.*; **2.** *v/t.* подбáдривать [-бодри́ть]; привéтствовать вóзгласами; *v/i.* **~ up** приободри́ться; **~ful** ['tʃɪəfl] □ бóдрый, весёлый; **~less** [~ləs] □ уны́лый, мрáчный; **~y** [~rɪ] □ живóй, весёлый, рáдостный
cheese [tʃiːz] сыр
chemical ['kemɪkl] **1.** □ хими́ческий; **2. ~s** [~s] *pl.* хими́ческие препарáты *m/pl.*, химикáлии *f/pl.*
chemist ['kemɪst] *scientist* хи́мик; *pharmacist* аптéкарь *m*; **~ry** ['kemɪstrɪ] хи́мия; **~'s** *Brt.* аптéка
cherish ['tʃerɪʃ] *hope* лелéять; *in memory* храни́ть; (*love*) нéжно люби́ть
cherry ['tʃerɪ] ви́шня
chess [tʃes] шáхматы *f/pl.*; **~board** шáхматная доскá; **~man** шáхматная фигýра

C

chest [tʃest] ящик, сундýк; *anat.* грудная клéтка; **~ of drawers** комóд; **get s.th. off one's ~** облегчи́ть дýшу
chestnut ['tʃesnʌt] **1.** каштáн; **2.** каштáновый
chew [tʃuː] жевáть; **~ over** (*think about*) размышля́ть; **~ing gum** ['tʃuːɪŋgʌm] жевáтельная рези́нка, *coll.* жвáчка
chic [ʃiːk] элегáнтный
chick [tʃɪk] цыплёнок; **~en** ['tʃɪkɪn] кýрица; *cul.* куря́тина; **~enpox** ветряна́я óспа
chief [tʃiːf] **1.** □ глáвный; **2.** главá, руководи́тель, начáльник, *coll.* шеф; **~ly** глáвным óбразом
child [tʃaɪld] ребёнок, дитя́ *n* (*pl.*: дéти); **~ prodigy** ['prɒdɪdʒɪ] вундерки́нд; **~birth** рóды *m/pl.*; **~hood** ['~hʊd] дéтство; **from ~** с дéтства; **~ish** ['tʃaɪldɪʃ] □ ребя́ческий; **~like** [~laɪk] как ребёнок; **~ren** ['tʃɪldrən] *pl. от* **child**
chill [tʃɪl] **1.** хóлод; *fig.* хóлодность *f*; *med.* простýда; **2.** холóдный; *fig.* расхолáживающий; **3.** *v/t.* охлаждáть [-ладúть]; [о]студи́ть; *v/i.* охлаждáться [-лади́ться]; **~y** ['tʃɪlɪ] холóдный, прохлáдный (*both a. fig.*)
chime [tʃaɪm] **1.** звон колоколóв; бой часóв; **2.** [за]звони́ть; *of clock* проби́ть *pf.*; **~ in** вмéшиваться [-шáться]; *fig.* **~ (in) with** гармонизи́ровать; соотвéтствовать
chimney ['tʃɪmnɪ] дымовáя трубá
chin [tʃɪn] подборóдок
china ['tʃaɪnə] фарфóр
Chinese [tʃaɪ'niːz] **1.** китáец *m*, -áянка *f*; **2.** китáйский
chink [tʃɪŋk] *crevice* щель *f*, трéщина
chip [tʃɪp] **1.** *of wood* щéпка; *of glass* оскóлок; *on plate, etc.* щерби́нка; **~s** *Brt.* картóфель-чи́псы; **2.** *v/t.* отби́ть *pf.* край; *v/i.* отлáмываться [отломáться]
chirp [tʃɜːp] **1.** чири́канье; щебетáние; **2.** чири́кать [-кнуть]; [за-] щебетáть
chisel ['tʃɪzl] **1.** долотó, стамéска; *sculptor's* резéц; **2.** рабóтать долотóм, резцóм; **~led features** тóчёные черты́ лицá
chitchat ['tʃɪt tʃæt] болтовня́
chivalrous ['ʃɪvəlrəs] □ *mst. fig.* ры́царский
chlor|inate ['klɔːrɪneɪt] хлори́ровать; **~oform** ['klɒrəfɔːm] хлорофóрм
chocolate ['tʃɒklɪt] шоколáд; *pl.* шоколáдные конфéты *f/pl.*
choice [tʃɔɪs] **1.** вы́бор; альтернати́ва; **2.** □ отбóрный
choir ['kwaɪə] хор
choke [tʃəʊk] *v/t.* [за]души́ть; (*mst.* **~ down**) глотáть с трудóм; *laughter* дави́ться (**with** от Р); *v/i.* (*suffocate*) задыхáться [-дохнýться]; [по]дави́ться (**on** Т)
choose [tʃuːz] [*irr.*] выбирáть [вы́брать]; (*decide*) предпочитáть [-чéсть]; **~ to** *inf.* хотéть (+ *inf.*)
chop [tʃɒp] **1.** отбивнáя (котлéта); **2.** *v/t. wood, etc.* [на]руби́ть; *parsley, etc.* [на]кроши́ть; **~ down** срубáть [-би́ть]; **~ and change** бесконéчно менять свои взгля́ды, плáны *и т.д.*; **~per** ['tʃɒpə] *tool* топóр; *sl. helicopter* вертолёт; **~py** ['tʃɒpɪ] *sea* неспокóйный
choral ['kɔːrəl] □ хоровóй; **~(e)** [kɒ'rɑːl] хорáл
chord [kɔːd] струнá; *mus.* аккóрд
chore [tʃɔː] нýдная рабóта; повседнéвные делá
chorus ['kɔːrəs] хор; мýзыка для хóра; *of song* припéв, рефрéн; **in ~** хóром
chose [tʃəʊz] *pt. от* **choose**; **~n** [~n] **1.** *pt. p. от* **choose**; **2.** и́збранный
Christ [kraɪst] Христóс
christen ['krɪsn] [о]крести́ть; **~ing** [~ɪŋ] крести́ны *f/pl.*; крещéние
Christian ['krɪstʃən] **1.** христиáнский; **~ name** и́мя (*в отли́чие от фами́лии*); **2.** христиáнин *m*, -áнка *f*; **~ity** [krɪstɪ'ænətɪ] христиáнство
Christmas ['krɪsməs] Рождествó
chromium ['krəʊmɪəm] хром; **~-plated** хроми́рованный
chronic ['krɒnɪk] (**~ally**) хрони́ческий (*a. med.*); **~le** [~l] хрóника, лéтопись *f*
chronolog|ical [ˌkrɒnə'lɒdʒɪkl] □ хронологи́ческий; **~y** [krə'nɒlədʒɪ]

C

хроноло́гия
chubby ['tʃʌbɪ] *coll.* по́лный; *child* пу́хленький
chuck [tʃʌk] броса́ть [бро́сить]; *coll.* швыря́ть [-рну́ть]; **~ *out*** выбра́сывать [вы́бросить]; *from work* вышвы́ривать [вы́швырнуть]
chuckle ['tʃʌkl] посме́иваться
chum [tʃʌm] *coll.* **1.** прия́тель; **2.** быть в дру́жбе
chump [tʃʌmp] коло́да, чурба́н; *sl.* (*fool*) болва́н
chunk [tʃʌnk] *coll. of bread* ло́моть *m*; *of meat, etc.* то́лстый кусо́к
church [tʃɜːtʃ] це́рковь *f*; **~ *service*** богослуже́ние; **~yard** пого́ст, кла́дбище
churlish ['tʃɜːlɪʃ] □ (*ill-bred*) гру́бый; (*bad-tempered*) раздражи́тельный
churn [tʃɜːn]: маслобо́йка; бидо́н
chute [ʃuːt] *slide, slope* спуск; (*rubbish* ~) мусоропрово́д; *for children* го́рка
cider ['saɪdə] сидр
cigar [sɪ'gɑː] сига́ра
cigarette [sɪgə'ret] сигаре́та; (*of Russian type*) папиро́са; **~ holder** мундшту́к
cinch [sɪntʃ] *coll.* не́что надёжное, ве́рное
cinder ['sɪndə]: **~s** *pl.* у́гли; **~ track** *sport* га́ревая доро́жка
cinema ['sɪnɪmə] кинематогра́фия, кино́ *n indecl.*
cinnamon ['sɪnəmən] кори́ца
cipher ['saɪfə] **1.** шифр; (*zero*) нуль *m or* ноль *m*; **2.** зашифро́вывать [-ова́ть]
circle ['sɜːkl] **1.** круг (*a. fig.*); (*ring*) кольцо́; *thea.* я́рус; ***business* ~s** делов́ые круги́; **2.** враща́ться вокру́г (Р); соверша́ть круги́, кружи́ть(ся)
circuit ['sɜːkɪt] (*route*) маршру́т; объе́зд; *el.* цепь *f*, схе́ма
circular ['sɜːkjʊlə] **1.** □ кру́глый; *road* кругово́й; **~ *letter*** циркуля́рное письмо́; **2.** циркуля́р; (*advertisement*) проспе́кт
circulat|e ['sɜːkjʊleɪt] *v/i. rumo(u)r* распространя́ться [-ни́ться]; циркули́ровать (*a. fig.*); **~ing** [~ɪŋ]: **~ library** библиоте́ка с вы́дачей книг на́ дом; **~ion** [sɜːkjʊ'leɪʃn] кровообраще́ние; циркуля́ция; *of newspapers etc.* тира́ж; *fig.* распростране́ние
circum... ['sɜːkəm] *pref.* (*в сло́жных слова́х*) вокру́г, круго́м
circum|ference [sə'kʌmfərəns] окру́жность *f*; перифери́я; **~spect** ['sɜːkəmspekt] □ осмотри́тельный, осторо́жный; **~stance** ['sɜːkəmstəns] обстоя́тельство; **~stantial** [sɜːkəm'stænʃl] □ обстоя́тельный, подро́бный; **~vent** [~'vent] (*law, etc.*) обходи́ть [обойти́]
circus ['sɜːkəs] цирк; *attr.* циркво́й
cistern ['sɪstən] бак; *in toilet* бачо́к
cit|ation [saɪ'teɪʃn] цита́та, ссы́лка, цити́рование; **~e** [saɪt] ссыла́ться [сосла́ться] на (В)
citizen ['sɪtɪzn] граждани́н *m*, -да́нка *f*; **~ship** [~ʃɪp] гражда́нство
citrus ['sɪtrəs]: **~ fruit** ци́трусовые
city ['sɪtɪ] го́род; *attr.* городско́й; ***the* ♀** Си́ти (*делово́й центр в Ло́ндоне*)
civic ['sɪvɪk] гражда́нский; *of town* городско́й
civil ['sɪvl] □ *of a community* гражда́нский (*a. law*); шта́тский; (*polite*) ве́жливый; **~ *servant*** госуда́рственный слу́жащий, *contp.* чино́вник; **~ *service*** госуда́рственная слу́жба; **~ian** [sɪ'vɪljən] шта́тский; **~ity** [sɪ'vɪlətɪ] ве́жливость *f*; **~ization** [sɪvəlaɪ'zeɪʃn] цивилиза́ция
clad [klæd] *pt. u pt. p. от* ***clothe***
claim [kleɪm] **1.** претендова́ть, (*demand*) на (В); [по]тре́бовать; (*assert*) утвержда́ть [-рди́ть]; предъявля́ть права́ на (В); **2.** тре́бование; прете́нзия; *law* иск; **~ *for damages*** иск за причинённый уще́рб; **~ *to be*** выдава́ть себя́ за (В); **~ant** ['kleɪmənt] претенде́нт; *law* исте́ц
clairvoyant [kleə'vɔɪənt] ясновидец
clamber ['klæmbə] [вс]кара́бкаться
clammy ['klæmɪ] □ (*sticky*) ли́пкий; *hands* холо́дный и вла́жный; *weather* сыро́й и холо́дный
clamo(u)r ['klæmə] **1.** шум, кри́ки *m/pl.*; шу́мные проте́сты *m/pl.*; **2.** шу́мно тре́бовать (Р)

clamp [klæmp] **1.** *tech.* скоба́; зажи́м; **2.** скрепля́ть [-пи́ть]; заж(им)а́ть
clandestine [klæn'destɪn] □ та́йный
clang [klæŋ] **1.** лязг; *of bell* звон; **2.** ля́згать [-гнуть]
clank [klæŋk] **1.** звон, лязг, бря́цание; **2.** бря́цать, [за]греме́ть
clap [klæp] **1.** хлопо́к; хло́панье; *of thunder* уда́р; **2.** хло́пать, аплоди́ровать; **~trap** пуста́я болтовня́; (*nonsense*) чепуха́
clarify ['klærɪfaɪ] *v/t. liquid, etc.* очища́ть [очи́стить]; (*make transparent*) де́лать прозра́чным; *fig.* выясня́ть [вы́яснить]; *v/i.* де́латься прозра́чным, я́сным
clarity ['klærətɪ] я́сность *f*
clash [klæʃ] **1.** столкнове́ние; (*contradiction*) противоре́чие; конфли́кт; **2.** ста́лкиваться [столкну́ться]; *of opinions, etc.* расходи́ться [разойти́сь]
clasp [klɑːsp] **1.** пря́жка, застёжка; *fig.* (*embrace*) объя́тия *n/pl.*; **2.** *v/t.* (*fasten*) застёгивать [застегну́ть]; (*hold tightly*) сж(им)а́ть; *fig.* заключа́ть в объя́тия; *hand* пож(им)а́ть
class [klɑːs] **1.** *school* класс; *social* обще́ственный класс; (***evening***) **~es** (вече́рние) ку́рсы; **2.** классифици́ровать *(im)pf.*
classic ['klæsɪk] **1.** кла́ссик; **2.** **~(al** □) [~(əl)] класси́ческий
classi|fication [klæsɪfɪ'keɪʃn] классифика́ция; **~fy** ['klæsɪfaɪ] классифици́ровать *(im)pf.*
clatter ['klætə] **1.** *of dishes* звон; *of metal* гро́хот (маши́н); (*talk*) болтовня́; *of hoofs, etc.* то́пот; **2.** [за]греме́ть; [за]то́пать; *fig.* [по-] болта́ть
clause [klɔːz] *of agreement, etc.* пункт, статья́; *gr.* ***principal/subordinate*** **~** гла́вное/прида́точное предложе́ние
claw [klɔː] **1.** *of animal* ко́готь *m*; *of crustacean* клешня́; **2.** разрыва́ть, терза́ть когтя́ми
clay [kleɪ] гли́на
clean [kliːn] **1.** *adj.* □ чи́стый; (*tidy*) опря́тный; **2.** *adv.* на́чисто; соверше́нно, по́лностью; **3.** [по]чи́стить; **~ *up*** уб(и)ра́ть; приводи́ть в поря́док; **~er** ['kliːnə] убо́рщик *m*, -ица *f*; **~er's** химчи́стка; **~ing** ['kliːnɪŋ] чи́стка; *of room* убо́рка; **~liness** ['klenlɪnɪs] чистопло́тность *f*; **~ly** **1.** *adv.* ['kliːnlɪ] чи́сто; **2.** *adj.* ['klenlɪ] чистопло́тный; **~se** [klenz] очища́ть [очи́стить]
clear [klɪər] **1.** □ све́тлый, я́сный (*a. fig.*); (*transparent*) прозра́чный; *fig.* свобо́дный (***from***, ***of*** от P); *profit, etc.* чи́стый; (*distinct*) отчётливый; (*plain*) я́сный, поня́тный; **2.** *v/t.* убира́ть [-бра́ть]; очища́ть [очи́стить] (***from***, ***of*** от P); расчища́ть [-и́стить]; (*free from blame*) опра́вдывать [-да́ть]; **~ *the air*** разряди́ть атмосфе́ру; *v/i.* (*a.* **~ up**) *of mist* рассе́иваться [-е́яться]; *of sky* проясня́ться [-ни́ться]; **~ance** ['klɪərəns] *comm.* разреше́ние (на прово́з, на вы́воз, *naut.* на вы́ход); **~ing** ['klɪərɪŋ] *tech.* зазор; *mot.* кли́ренс; *in forest* про́сека, поля́на; *fin.* кли́ринг; **~ly** я́сно; (*obviously*) очеви́дно
cleave [kliːv] [*irr.*] *split* раска́лывать(ся) [-коло́ть(ся)]; рассека́ть [-е́чь]; *adhere* прилипа́ть [-ли́пнуть]
clef [klef] *mus.* ключ
cleft [kleft] рассе́лина
clemen|cy ['klemənsɪ] милосе́рдие; снисхожде́ние; **~t** ['klemənt] милосе́рдный; *weather* мя́гкий
clench [klentʃ] заж(им)а́ть; *fists* сж(им)а́ть; *teeth* сти́скивать [сти́снуть]; → ***clinch***
clergy ['klɜːdʒɪ] духове́нство; **~man** [~mən] свяще́нник
clerical ['klerɪkl] □ *eccl.* духо́вный; *of clerks* канцеля́рский
clerk [klɑːk] клерк, конто́рский слу́жащий; *Am.* ***sales*** **~** продаве́ц
clever ['klevə] □ у́мный; (*skilled*) уме́лый; *mst. b.s.* ло́вкий
click [klɪk] **1.** щёлканье; **2.** *lock* щёлкать [-кнуть]; *tongue* прищёлкивать [-кнуть]; *fig.* идти́ гла́дко; **~ *on*** *comput.* щёлкнуть мы́шью
client ['klaɪənt] клие́нт; покупа́тель *m*; **~èle** [kliːən'tel] клиенту́ра
cliff [klɪf] утёс, скала́

C

climate ['klaımıt] кли́мат
climax ['klaımæks] **1.** кульмина́ция; **2.** достига́ть [-и́гнуть] кульмина́ции
climb [klaım] [*irr.*] влез(а́)ть на (В); *mountain* поднима́ться [-ня́ться] (на В); **~er** ['klaımə] альпини́ст; *fig.* карьери́ст; *bot.* выо́щееся расте́ние
clinch [klıntʃ] *fig.* оконча́тельно договори́ться *pf.*, реши́ть *pf.*; ***that ~ed the matter*** э́тим вопро́с был оконча́тельно решён
cling [klıŋ] [*irr.*] (**to**) [при]льну́ть к (Д); **~ *together*** держа́ться вме́сте
clinic ['klınık] кли́ника; поликли́ника; **~al** [~ıkəl] клини́ческий
clink [klıŋk] **1.** звон; **2.** [за]звене́ть; **~ *glasses*** чо́каться [-кнуться]
clip¹ [klıp] **1.** *newspaper* вы́резка; *TV* клип; **2.** выреза́ть [вы́резать]; (*cut*) [о-, под]стри́чь
clip² [~] **1.** скре́пка; **2.**: **~ *together*** скрепля́ть [-пи́ть]
clipp|er ['klıpə]: (*a pair of*) (*nail-*) **~ers** *pl.* маникю́рные но́жницы *f/pl.*; *hort.* сека́тор; **~ings** [~ıŋz] *pl.* газе́тные вы́резки *f/pl.*; обре́зки *m/pl.*
cloak [kləʊk] **1.** плащ; *of darkness* покро́в; *fig.* (*pretext*) предло́г; **2.** покры́(ва́)ть; *fig.* прикры́(ва́)ть; **~room** гардеро́б, *coll.* раздева́лка; *euph.*, *mst. Brt.* туале́т; **~room attendant** гардеро́бщик *m*, -щица *f*
clock [klɒk] часы́ *m/pl.* (*стенные и т.д.*); **~wise** по часово́й стре́лке
clod [klɒd] ком; (*fool*) ду́рень *m*, о́лух
clog [klɒg] засоря́ть(ся) [-ри́ть(ся)], забива́ться [-би́ться]
cloister ['klɔıstə] монасты́рь *m*; *arch.* кры́тая арка́да
close 1. [kləʊs] □ (*restricted*) закры́тый; (*near*) бли́зкий; (*tight*) те́сный; *air* ду́шный, спёртый; (*stingy*) скупо́й; *study*, *etc.* внима́тельный, тща́тельный; **~ *by*** *adv.* ря́дом, поблизости; **~ *to*** о́коло (Р); **2.** [kləʊz] коне́ц; (*conclusion*) заверше́ние; ***come to a ~*** зако́нчиться, заверши́ться; **3.** [kləʊz] *v/t.* закры́(ва́)ть; зака́нчивать [-ко́нчить]; конча́ть [ко́нчить]; заключа́ть [-чи́ть] (речь); *v/i.* закры́(ва́)ться; конча́ться [ко́нчиться]; **~ *in*** приближа́ться [-ли́зиться]; наступа́ть [-пи́ть]; **~ness** ['kləʊsnıs] бли́зость *f*; ску́пость *f*
closet ['klɒzıt] *Am.* чула́н; стенно́й шкаф
close-up: ***take a ~*** снима́ть [снять] кру́пным пла́ном
closure ['kləʊʒə] закры́тие
clot [klɒt] **1.** *of blood* сгу́сток; комо́к; **2.** *mst. of blood* свёртываться [сверну́ться]
cloth [klɒθ], *pl.* **~s** [klɒθs] ткань *f*, материа́л; ***length of ~*** отре́з
clothe [kləʊð] [*a. irr.*] оде́(ва́)ть; *fig.* облека́ть [обле́чь]
clothes [kləʊðz] *pl.* оде́жда; ***change one's ~*** переоде́ться; **~line** верёвка для су́шки белья́; **~peg** прище́пка
clothing ['kləʊðıŋ] оде́жда; ***ready-made ~*** гото́вая оде́жда
cloud [klaʊd] **1.** о́блако, ту́ча; ***have one's head in the ~s*** вита́ть в облака́х; **2.** покрыва́ть(ся) ту́чами, облака́ми; *fig.* омрача́ть(ся) [-чи́ть(ся)]; **~burst** ли́вень *m*; **~less** ['klaʊdləs] □ безо́блачный; **~y** [~ı] □ о́блачный; *liquid* му́тный; *ideas* тума́нный
clove¹ [kləʊv] гвозди́ка (пря́ность)
clove² [~] *pt. от* ***cleave***
clover ['kləʊvə] кле́вер; ***in ~*** жить припева́ючи
clown [klaʊn] кло́ун
club [klʌb] **1.** *society* клуб; (*heavy stick*) дуби́на; *Am.* дуби́нка (полице́йского); **~s** *pl. at cards* тре́фы *f/pl.*; **2.** *v/t.* [по]би́ть; *v/i.* собира́ться вме́сте; **~ *together*** сложи́ться [скла́дываться]; (*share expense*) устра́ивать скла́дчину
clue [kluː] ключ к разга́дке; ***I haven't a ~*** поня́тия не име́ю
clump [klʌmp] **1.** *of bushes* куста́рник; *of trees* ку́па, гру́ппа; **2.** *tread heavily* тяжело́ ступа́ть
clumsy ['klʌmzı] □ неуклю́жий; нело́вкий (*a. fig.*); (*tactless*) беста́ктный
clung [klʌŋ] *pt. и pt. p. от* ***cling***
cluster ['klʌstə] **1.** кисть *f*; гроздь *f*; **2.** расти́ гро́здьями; **~ *round*** окружа́ть [-жи́ть]
clutch [klʌtʃ] **1.** *of car* сцепле́ние;

fall into s.o.'s ~es попа́сть *pf.* в чьи́-л. ла́пы; **2.** (*seize*) схва́тывать [-ти́ть]; ухвати́ться *pf.* (***at*** за В)
clutter ['klʌtə] **1.** беспоря́док; **2.** завали́ть, загромозди́ть
coach [kəʊtʃ] **1.** *Brt.* междугоро́дный авто́бус; (*trainer*) тре́нер; (*tutor*) репети́тор; *rail.* пассажи́рский ваго́н; **2.** [на]тренирова́ть; ната́скивать к экза́мену
coagulate [kəʊ'ægjʊleɪt] свёртываться, коагули́роваться
coal [kəʊl] (ка́менный) у́голь *m*
coalition [kəʊə'lɪʃn] коали́ция
coal|mine, ~ pit у́гольная ша́хта
coarse [kɔːs] □ *material* гру́бый; *sugar, etc.* кру́пный; *fig.* неотёсанный; *joke* непристо́йный
coast [kəʊst] морско́й бе́рег, побере́жье; **~al: ~ *waters*** прибре́жные во́ды; **~er** ['kəʊstə] *naut.* су́дно кабота́жного пла́вания
coat [kəʊt] **1.** (*man's jacket*) пиджа́к; (*over* ~) пальто́ *n indecl.*; (*fur*) мех, шерсть *f*; (*layer of paint, etc.*) слой; **~ *of arms*** герб; **2.** (*cover*) покры́(ва́)ть; **~ hanger** ве́шалка; **~ing** ['kəʊtɪŋ] слой
coax [kəʊks] угова́ривать [уговори́ть]
cob [kɒb] *of maize* поча́ток
cobbler ['kɒblə] сапо́жник
cobblestone ['kɒblstəʊn] булы́жник; *attr.* булы́жный
cobweb ['kɒbweb] паути́на
cock [kɒk] **1.** (*rooster*) пету́х; (*tap*) кран; *in gun* куро́к; **2.** *ears* насторáживать [-рожи́ть]
cockatoo [kɒkə'tuː] какаду́ *m indecl.*
cockchafer ['kɒktʃeɪfər] ма́йский жук
cock-eyed ['kɒkaɪd] *sl.* косогла́зый; косо́й; *Am.* пья́ный
cockpit ['kɒkpɪt] *ae.* каби́на
cockroach ['kɒkrəʊtʃ] *zo.* тарака́н
cock|sure [kɒk'ʃʊə] *coll.* самоуве́ренный; **~tail** ['~teɪl] кокте́йль *m*; **~y** ['kɒkɪ] □ *coll.* наха́льный, де́рзкий
cocoa ['kəʊkəʊ] *powder or drink* кака́о *n indecl.*
coconut ['kəʊkənʌt] коко́с, коко́совый оре́х
cocoon [kə'kuːn] ко́кон
cod [kɒd] треска́
coddle ['kɒdl] [из]ба́ловать, [из]не́жить
code [kəʊd] **1.** *of conduct, laws* ко́декс; *of symbols, ciphers* код; **2.** коди́ровать (*im*)*pf.*
cod-liver: ~ *oil* ры́бий жир
coerc|e [kəʊ'ɜːs] принужда́ть [-ну́дить]; **~ion** [~ʃn] принужде́ние
coexist [kəʊɪg'zɪst] сосуществова́ть (с Т)
coffee ['kɒfɪ] ко́фе *m indecl.*; ***instant ~*** раствори́мый ко́фе; **~ *grinder*** кофемо́лка; **~ *set*** кофе́йный серви́з; **~pot** кофе́йник
coffin ['kɒfɪn] гроб
cog [kɒg] зубе́ц
cogent ['kəʊdʒənt] □ (*convincing*) убеди́тельный
cognac ['kɒnjæk] конья́к
cohabit [kəʊ'hæbɪt] сожи́тельствовать, жить вме́сте
coheren|ce [kəʊ'hɪərəns] связь *f*; свя́зность *f*; согласо́ванность *f*; **~t** [~rənt] □ *story, etc.* свя́зный; поня́тный; согласо́ванный
cohesion [kəʊ'hiːʒn] сцепле́ние; сплочённость *f*
coiffure [kwɑː'fjʊə] причёска
coil [kɔɪl] **1.** кольцо́; *el.* кату́шка; **2.** (*a.* **~ *up***) свёртываться кольцо́м (спира́лью)
coin [kɔɪn] **1.** моне́та; ***pay s.o. back in his own ~*** отплати́ть *pf.* кому́-л. той же моне́той; **2.** (*mint*) чека́нить; **~age** ['kɔɪnɪdʒ] чека́нка
coincide [kəʊɪn'saɪd] совпада́ть [-па́сть]; **~nce** [kəʊ'ɪnsɪdəns] совпаде́ние; *fig.* случа́йное стече́ние обстоя́тельств; ***by sheer ~*** по чи́стой случа́йности
coke[1] [kəʊk] кокс
coke[2] [~] *coll.* ко́ка-ко́ла
colander ['kʌləndə] дуршла́г
cold [kəʊld] **1.** □ холо́дный; *fig.* неприве́тливый; **2.** хо́лод; просту́да; ***catch*** (***a***) **~** простуди́ться; **~ness** ['kəʊldnɪs] *of temperature* хо́лод; *of character, etc.* хо́лодность *f*
colic ['kɒlɪk] *med.* ко́лики *f/pl.*
collaborat|e [kə'læbəreɪt] сотру́дничать; **~ion** [kəlæbə'reɪʃn] сот-

C

ру́дничество; ***in ~ with*** в сотру́дничестве (с Т)

collapse [kəˈlæps] **1.** (*caving in*) обва́л; разруше́ние; *of plans, etc.* круше́ние; *med.* по́лный упа́док сил, колла́пс; **2.** *of a structure* обру́ши(ва)ться, ру́хнуть; *of person* упа́сть без созна́ния

collar [ˈkɒlər] **1.** воротни́к; *dog's* оше́йник; **2.** схвати́ть *pf.* за ши́ворот; *sl. a criminal* схвати́ть *pf.*; **~-bone** *anat.* ключи́ца

collateral [kəˈlætərəl] побо́чный; *evidence* ко́свенный

colleague [ˈkɒliːg] колле́га *f/m*, сослужи́вец *m*, -вица *f*

collect [kəˈlekt] *v/t.* (*get together*) соб(ир)а́ть; *stamps etc.* коллекциони́ровать; (*call for*) заходи́ть [зайти́] за (Т); *o.s.* (*control o.s.*) овладева́ть собо́й; *v/i.* (*gather*) соб(и)ра́ться (*a. fig.*); ***~ on delivery*** *Am.* нало́женным платежо́м; **~ed** [kəˈlektɪd] □ *fig.* споко́йный; ***~ works*** собра́ние сочине́ний; **~ion** [kəˈlekʃn] колле́кция, собра́ние; **~ive** [~tɪv] □ коллекти́вный; совоку́пный; **~or** [~tə] коллекционе́р; *of tickets, etc.* контролёр

college [ˈkɒlɪdʒ] колле́дж; институ́т, университе́т

collide [kəˈlaɪd] ста́лкиваться [столкну́ться]

collie [ˈkɒlɪ] ко́лли *m/f indecl.*

collier [ˈkɒlɪər] углeко́п, шахтёр; **~y** [ˈkɒljərɪ] каменноуго́льня ша́хта

collision [ˈkəlɪʒn] столкнове́ние

colloquial [kəˈləʊkwɪəl] □ разгово́рный

colon [ˈkəʊlən] *typ.* двоето́чие

colonel [ˈkɜːnl] полко́вник

colonial [kəˈləʊnɪəl] колониа́льный

colony [ˈkɒlənɪ] коло́ния

colo(u)r [ˈkʌlə] **1.** цвет; (*paint*) кра́ска; *on face* румя́нец; *fig.* колори́т; **~s** *pl.* госуда́рственный флаг; ***be off ~*** нева́жно себя́ чу́вствовать; **2.** *v/t.* [по]кра́сить; окра́шивать [окра́сить]; *fig.* приукра́шивать [-кра́сить]; *v/i.* [по]красне́ть; **~-blind**: ***be ~*** быть дальто́ником; **~ed** [~d] окра́шенный; цветно́й; **~ful** [~fʊl] я́ркий; **~ing** [~rɪŋ] окра́ска, раскра́ска; *fig.* приукра́шивание; **~less** [~ləs] □ бесцве́тный (*a. fig.*)

colt [kəʊlt] жеребёнок (*pl.*: жеребя́та); *fig.* птене́ц

column [ˈkɒləm] *arch.*, *mil.* коло́нна; *of smoke, etc.* столб; *of figures* столбе́ц

comb [kəʊm] **1.** гре́бень *m*, гребёнка; **2.** *v/t.* расчёсывать [-чеса́ть], причёсывать [-чеса́ть]

combat [ˈkɒmbæt] **1.** бой, сраже́ние; **2.** сража́ться [срази́ться]; боро́ться (*a. fig.*); **~ant** [ˈkɒmbətənt] бое́ц

combin|ation [kɒmbɪˈneɪʃn] сочета́ние; **~e** [kəmˈbaɪn] объединя́ть(ся) [объедини́ть(ся)]; сочета́ть(ся) (*im*)*pf.*; ***~ business with pleasure*** сочета́ть прия́тное с поле́зным

combusti|ble [kəmˈbʌstəbl] горю́чий, воспламеня́емый; **~on** [-tʃən] горе́ние, сгора́ние; ***internal ~ engine*** дви́гатель вну́треннего сгора́ния

come [kʌm] [*irr.*] приходи́ть [прийти́]; *by car, etc.* приезжа́ть [прие́хать]; ***to ~*** бу́дущий; ***~ about*** случа́ться [-чи́ться], происходи́ть [произойти́]; ***~ across*** встреча́ться [-ре́титься] с (Т), ната́лкиваться [наткну́ться] на (В); ***~ back*** возвраща́ться [-ти́ться]; ***~ by*** дост(ав)а́ть (случа́йно); ***~ from*** быть ро́дом из (Р); ***~ off***; (*be successful*) уда́сться *pf.*; *of skin, etc.* сходи́ть [сойти́]; ***~ round*** приходи́ть в себя́; *coll.* заходи́ть [зайти́] к (Д); *fig.* идти на усту́пки; ***~ to*** доходи́ть [дойти́] до (Р); (*equal*) равня́ться (Д), сто́ить (В *or* Р); ***~ up to*** соотве́тствовать (Д); ***~ to know s.o.*** (***sth.***) познако́миться *pf.* (с Т) (узнава́ть [-на́ть] В); ***~ what may*** что бы ни случи́лось

comedian [kəˈmiːdɪən] ко́мик

comedy [ˈkɒmədɪ] коме́дия

comeliness [ˈkʌmlɪnɪs] милови́дность *f*

comfort [ˈkʌmfət] **1.** комфо́рт, удо́бство; *fig.* (*consolation*) утеше́ние; (*support*) подде́ржка; **2.** утеша́ть [уте́шить]; успока́ивать

C

[-ко́ить]; **~able** [~əbl] удо́бный, комфорта́бельный; *income, life* вполне́ прили́чный; **~less** [~lıs] □ неую́тный

comic ['kɒmık] **1.** коми́ческий, смешно́й; юмористи́ческий; **2.** ко́мик; ***the ~s*** ко́миксы

coming ['kʌmıŋ] **1.** прие́зд, прибы́тие; **2.** бу́дущий; наступа́ющий

comma ['kɒmə] запята́я

command [kə'mɑ:nd] **1.** кома́нда, прика́з; (*authority*) кома́ндование; ***have at one's ~*** име́ть в своём распоряже́нии; **2.** прика́зывать [-за́ть] (Д); владе́ть (Т); *mil.* кома́ндовать; **~er** [kə'mɑ:ndə] *mil.* команди́р; *navy* капита́н; **Ձer-in-chief** [~rın'tʃi:f] главнокома́ндующий; **~ment** [~mənt] *eccl.* за́поведь *f*

commemora|te [kə'meməreıt] *anniversary* ознаменова́ть; *event* отмеча́ть [отме́тить]; **~tion** [kəmemə'reıʃn] ознаменова́ние

commence [kə'mens] нач(ин)а́ть (-ся); **~ment** [~mənt] нача́ло, торже́ственное вруче́ние дипло́мов

commend [kə'mend] отмеча́ть [-е́тить], [по]хвали́ть (***for*** за В); рекомендова́ть (*im*)*pf.*

comment ['kɒment] **1.** (*remark*) замеча́ние; *on text, etc.* коммента́рий; ***no ~!*** коммента́рии изли́шни!; **2.** (***on***) комменти́ровать (*im*)*pf.*; отзыва́ться [отозва́ться]; [с]де́лать замеча́ние; **~ary** ['kɒməntrı] коммента́рий; **~ator** ['kɒmənteıtə] коммента́тор

commerc|e ['kɒmɜ:s] торго́вля, комме́рция; **~ial** [kə'mɜ:ʃl] □ торго́вый, комме́рческий; *su. radio, TV* рекла́ма

commiseration [kəmızə'reıʃn] сочу́вствие, соболе́знование

commission [kə'mıʃn] **1.** (*body of persons*) коми́ссия; (*authority*) полномо́чие; (*errand*) поруче́ние; (*order*) зака́з; *comm.* комиссио́нные **2.** зака́зывать [-за́ть]; поруча́ть [-чи́ть]; **~er** [~ʃənə] уполномо́ченный; член коми́ссии

commit [kə'mıt] (*entrust*) поруча́ть [-чи́ть]; вверя́ть [вве́рить]; *for trial, etc.* преда́(ва́)ть; *crime* соверша́ть [-ши́ть]; **~** (***o.s.***) обя́зывать(ся) [-за́ть(ся)]; **~** (***to prison***) заключа́ть [-чи́ть] (в тюрму́); **~ment** [~mənt] (*promise*) обяза́тельство; **~tee** [~ı] коми́ссия; комите́т; ***be on a ~*** быть чле́ном коми́ссии

commodity [kə'mɒdətı] това́р, предме́т потребле́ния

common ['kɒmən] □ о́бщий; (*ordinary*) просто́й, обыкнове́нный; (*mediocre*) зауря́дный; (*widespread*) распространённый; ***it is ~ knowledge that ...*** общеизве́стно, что ...; ***out of the ~*** незауря́дный; ***~ sense*** здра́вый смысл; ***we have nothing in ~*** у нас нет ничего́ о́бщего; **~place 1.** бана́льность *f*; **2.** бана́льный, *coll.* изби́тый; **~s** [~z] *pl.* простонаро́дье; (*mst.* ***House of***) Ձ Пала́та о́бщи́н; **~wealth** [~welθ] госуда́рство, содру́жество; ***the British Ձ of Nations*** Брита́нское Содру́жество На́ций

commotion [kə'məʊʃn] волне́ние, смяте́ние, возня́

communal ['kɒmjʊnl] (*pertaining to community*) обще́ственный, коммуна́льный; ***~ apartment*** *or* ***flat*** коммуна́льная кварти́ра

communicat|e [kə'mju:nıkeıt] *v.t.* сообща́ть [-щи́ть]; перед(ав)а́ть; *v/i.* сообща́ться; **~ion** [kəmju:nı'keıʃn] сообще́ние; коммуника́ция; связь *f*; ***~s satellite*** спу́тник свя́зи; **~ive** [kə'mju:nıkətıv] □ общи́тельный, разгово́рчивый

communion [kə'mju:njən] обще́ние; *sacrament* прича́стие

communiqué [kə'mju:nıkeı] коммюнике́ *n indecl.*

communis|m ['kɒmjʊnızəm] коммуни́зм; **~t 1.** коммуни́ст *m*, -ка *f*; **2.** коммунисти́ческий

community [kə'mju:nətı] о́бщество; ***local ~*** ме́стные жи́тели

commute [kə'mju:t] *law* смягчи́ть наказа́ние; *travel back and forth regularly* е́здить на рабо́ту (*напр. из при́города в го́род*)

compact [kəm'pækt] *adj.* компа́ктный; (*closely packed*) пло́тный; *style* сжа́тый; *v/t.* сж(им)а́ть; уплотня́ть [-ни́ть]; ***~ disc*** компа́кт-диск

companion [kəm'pænjən] това́-

рищ, подру́га; (*travel[l]ing ~*) спу́тник; **~ship** [~ʃɪp] компа́ния; дру́жеские отноше́ния *n/pl.*
company ['kʌmpənɪ] о́бщество; *comm.* компа́ния; акционе́рное о́бщество, фи́рма; (*guests*) го́сти *pl.*; *thea.* тру́ппа; ***have ~*** принима́ть госте́й
compar|able ['kɒmpərəbl] □ сравни́мый; **~ative** [kəm'pærətɪv] □ сравни́тельный; **~e** [kəm'peər] **1.** ***beyond ~*** вне вся́кого сравне́ния; **2.** *v/t.* сра́внивать [-ни́ть], слича́ть [-чи́ть], (***to*** с Т); *v/i.* сра́вниваться [-ни́ться]; ***~ favo(u)rably with*** вы́годно отлича́ться от Р; **~ison** [kəm'pærɪsn] сравне́ние; ***by ~*** по сравне́нию (с Т)
compartment [kəm'pɑːtmənt] отделе́ние; *rail.* купе́ *n indecl.*
compass ['kʌmpəs] ко́мпас; (*extent*) преде́л; (***a pair of***) **~es** *pl.* ци́ркуль *m*
compassion [kəm'pæʃn] сострада́ние, жа́лость *f*; **~ate** [~ʃənət] □ сострада́телный, сочу́вствующий
compatible [kəm'pætəbl] □ совмести́мый (*a. comput.*)
compatriot [kəm'pætrɪət] соотéчественник *m*, -ница *f*
compel [kəm'pel] заставля́ть [-а́вить]; принужда́ть [-нуди́ть]
compensat|e ['kɒmpənseɪt] *v/t.* компенси́ровать; *losses* возмеща́ть [-ести́ть]; **~ion** [kɒmpən'seɪʃn] возмеще́ние, компенса́ция
compete [kəm'piːt] соревнова́ться, состяза́ться; конкури́ровать (***with*** с Т, ***for*** за В)
competen|ce, ~cy ['kɒmpɪtəns, ~ɪ] спосо́бность *f*; компете́нтность *f*; **~t** [~tənt] □ компете́нтный
competit|ion [kɒmpə'tɪʃn] состяза́ние, соревнова́ние; *comm.* конкуре́нция; *of pianists, etc.* ко́нкурс; **~ive** [kəm'petətɪv] конкурентоспосо́бный; **~or** [kəm'petɪtə] конкуре́нт *m*, -ка *f*; (*rival*) сопе́рник *m*, -ица *f*; уча́стник ко́нкурса
compile [kəm'paɪl] составля́ть [-а́вить]
complacen|ce, ~cy [kəm'pleɪsəns, ~ɪ] самодово́льство
complain [kəm'pleɪn] [по]жа́ловаться (***of*** на В); *law* обжа́ловать *pf.*; **~t** [~t] жа́лоба; *med.* боле́знь *f*; *comm.* реклама́ция
complement ['kɒmplɪmənt] **1.** дополне́ние; компле́кт; **2.** дополня́ть [допо́лнить]; [у]комплектова́ть
complet|e [kəm'pliːt] **1.** □ (*whole*) по́лный; (*finished*) зако́нченный; *coll. fool* кру́глый; ***~ stranger*** соверше́нно незнако́мый челове́к; **2.** зака́нчивать [зако́нчить]; **~ion** [~'pliʃn] оконча́ние
complex ['kɒmpleks] **1.** □ (*intricate*) сло́жный; (*composed of parts*) ко́мплексный, составно́й; *fig.* сло́жный, запу́танный; **2.** ко́мплекс; **~ion** [kəm'plekʃn] цвет лица́; **~ity** [~sɪtɪ] сло́жность *f*
compliance [kəm'plaɪəns] усту́пчивость *f*; согла́сие; ***in ~ with*** в соотве́тствии с (Т)
complicat|e ['kɒmplɪkeɪt] усложня́ть(ся) [-ни́ть(ся)]; **~ion** [~'keɪʃn] сло́жность *f*, тру́дность *f*; *pl.* осложне́ния *n/pl.*, *a. med.*
compliment **1.** ['kɒmplɪmənt] комплиме́нт; (*greeting*) приве́т; **2.** [~ment] *v/t.* говори́ть комплиме́нты (Д); поздравля́ть [-а́вить] (***on*** с Т)
comply [kəm'plaɪ] уступа́ть [-и́ть], соглаша́ться [-ласи́ться] (***with*** с Т); (*yield*) подчиня́ться [-ни́ться] (***with*** Д)
component [kəm'pəunənt] **1.** компоне́нт; составна́я часть *f*; **2.** составно́й
compos|e [kəm'pəuz] (*put together*) составля́ть [-а́вить]; (*create*) сочиня́ть [-ни́ть]; *compose o.s.* успока́иваться [-ко́иться]; **~ed** [~d] □ споко́йный, сде́ржанный; **~er** [~ə] компози́тор; **~ition** [kɒmpə'zɪʃn] *art* компози́ция; (*structure*) соста́в; *lit.*, *mus.* сочине́ние; **~ure** [kəm'pəuʒə] самооблада́ние, споко́йствие
compound **1.** ['kɒmpaund] *chem.* соста́в, соедине́ние; *gr.* сло́жное сло́во; **2.** сло́жный; ***~ interest*** сло́жные проце́нты *m/pl.*
comprehend [kɒmprɪ'hend] постига́ть [пости́гнуть], понима́ть [-ня́ть]; (*include*) охва́тывать [охвати́ть]

comprehen|sible [kɒmprɪ'hensəbl] поня́тный, постижи́мый; **~sion** [~ʃn] понима́ние; поня́тливость *f*; **~sive** [~sɪv] □ (*inclusive*) (все)объ-е́млющий; исче́рпывающий; *study* всесторо́нний

compress [kəm'pres] сж(има́)ть; ***~ed air*** сжа́тый во́здух

comprise [kəm'praɪz] состоя́ть; заключа́ть в себе́

compromise ['kɒmprəmaɪz] **1.** компроми́сс; **2.** *v/t.* [c]компромети́ровать; *v/i.* пойти́ *pf.* на компроми́сс

compuls|ion [kəm'pʌlʃn] принужде́ние; **~ory** [~'pʌlsərɪ] *education, etc.* обяза́тельный; принуди́тельный

comput|e [kəm'pju:t] вычисля́ть [вы́числить]; **~er** [~ə] компью́тер

comrade ['kɒmreɪd] това́рищ

con [kɒn] = ***contra*** про́тив: ***the pros and ~s*** (голоса́) за и про́тив

conceal [kən'si:l] скры́(ва́)ть;ута́ивать [-и́ть], ума́лчивать [умолча́ть]

concede [kən'si:d] уступа́ть [-пи́ть]; (*allow*) допуска́ть [-сти́ть]

conceit [kən'si:t] самонаде́янность, самомне́ние; **~ed** [~ɪd] самонаде́янный

conceiv|able [kən'si:vəbl] мы́слимый; постижи́мый; ***it's hardly ~*** вряд ли; **~e** [kən'si:v] *v/i.* представля́ть себе́; *v/t.* заду́м(ыв)ать

concentrate ['kɒnsəntreɪt] сосредото́чи(ва)ть(ся)

conception [kən'sepʃn] конце́пция; за́мысел; *biol.* зача́тие

concern [kən'sɜ:n] **1.** де́ло; (*anxiety*) беспоко́йство; интере́с; *comm.* предприя́тие; ***what ~ is it of yours?*** како́е вам до э́того де́ло? **2.** каса́ться [косну́ться] (P); име́ть отноше́ние к (Д); ***~ o.s. about, with*** [за]интересова́ться, занима́ться [заня́ться] (T); **~ed** [~d] □ заинтересо́ванный; име́ющий отноше́ние; озабо́ченный; **~ing** [~ɪŋ] *prp.* относи́тельно (P)

concert ['kɒnsət] конце́рт; ***act in ~*** де́йствовать согласо́ванно

concerto [kən'tʃeətəʊ] конце́рт

concession [kən'seʃn] усту́пка; *econ.* конце́ссия; *in price* ски́дка

conciliat|e [kən'sɪlɪeɪt] примиря́ть [-ри́ть]; **~or** [~ə] посре́дник

concise [kən'saɪs] □ сжа́тый, кра́ткий; **~ness** [~nɪs] сжа́тость *f*, кра́ткость *f*

conclude [kən'klu:d] *agreement, etc.* заключа́ть [-чи́ть]; (*finish*) зака́нчивать [зако́нчить]; ***to be ~d*** оконча́ние сле́дует

conclusi|on [kən'klu:ʒn] оконча́ние; (*inference*) заключе́ние; вы́вод; ***draw a ~*** сде́лать *pf.* вы́вод; **~ve** [~sɪv] □ (*final*) заключи́тельный; (*convincing*) убеди́тельный

concoct [kən'kɒkt] [со]стря́пать (*a. fig.*); *fig.* приду́м(ыв)ать

concord ['kɒŋkɔ:d] (*agreement*) согла́сие

concrete ['kɒŋkri:t] **1.** конкре́тный; **2.** бето́н; **3.** [за]бетони́ровать

concur [kən'kɜ:] (*agree*) соглаша́ться [-ласи́ться]; (*coincide*) совпада́ть [-па́сть]

concussion [kən'kʌʃn]: сотрясе́ние мо́зга

condemn [kən'dem] осужда́ть [осуди́ть]; (*blame*) порица́ть; пригова́ривать [-вори́ть] (к Д); [за]бракова́ть; **~ation** [kɒndəm'neɪʃn] осужде́ние

condens|ation [kɒnden'seɪʃn] конденса́ция, сгуще́ние; **~e** [kən'dens] сгуща́ть(ся); *fig.* сокраща́ть [-рати́ть]

condescen|d [kɒndɪ'send] снисходи́ть [снизойти́]; **~sion** [~'senʃn] снисхожде́ние; снисходи́тельность *f*

condiment ['kɒndɪmənt] припра́ва

condition [kən'dɪʃn] **1.** усло́вие; (*state*) состоя́ние; **~s** *pl.* (*circumstances*) обстоя́тельства *n/pl.*; усло́вия *n/pl.*; ***on ~ that*** при усло́вии, что; **2.** ста́вить усло́вия; обусло́вливать [-о́вить]; **~al** [~əl] □ усло́вный

condol|e [kən'dəʊl] соболе́зновать (***with*** Д); **~ence** [~əns] соболе́знование

condom ['kɒndəm] презервати́в, кондо́м

condone [kən'dəʊn] проща́ть; (*overlook*) смотре́ть сквозь па́льцы

C

conduct 1. ['kɒndʌkt] поведе́ние; **2.** [kən'dʌkt] вести́ себя́; *affairs* руководи́ть; *mus.* дирижи́ровать; **~or** [kən'dʌktə] *mus.* дирижёр; *el.* проводни́к
cone [kəʊn] ко́нус; *bot.* ши́шка
confectionery [kən'fekʃənərı] конди́терские изде́лия *n/pl.*
confedera|te 1. [kən'fedərət] федерати́вный; **2.** [~] член конфедера́ции; сою́зник; (*accomplice*) соуча́стник, сообщник; **3.** [~reıt] объединя́ться в сою́з; **~tion** [kənfedə'reıʃn] конфедера́ция
confer [kənfɜː] *v/t.* (*award*) присужда́ть [-уди́ть]; *v/i.* (*consult*) совеща́ться; **~ence** ['kɒnfərəns] конфере́нция; совеща́ние
confess [kən'fes] призн(ав)а́ться, созн(ав)а́ться в (П); **~ion** [~'feʃn] призна́ние; *to a priest* и́споведь *f*; *creed*, *denomination* вероисповéдание
confide [kən'faıd] доверя́ть (**in** Д); (*entrust*) вверя́ть [вве́рить]; (*trust*) полага́ться [положи́ться] (**in** на В); **~nce** ['kɒnfıdəns] дове́рие; (*firm belief*) уве́ренность *f*; **~nt** ['kɒnfıdənt] □ уве́ренный; **~ntial** [kɒnfı'denʃəl] конфиденциа́льный; секре́тный
configure [kən'fıgə] *comput.* конфигури́ровать
confine [kən'faın] ограни́чи(ва)ть; *to prison* заключа́ть [-чи́ть]; **be ~d** *of pregnant woman* рожа́ть [роди́ть]; **~ment** [~mənt] ограниче́ние; зак-лючéние; ро́ды *m/pl.*
confirm [kən'fɜːm] подтвержда́ть [-рди́ть]; **~ed bachelor** убеждённый холостя́к; **~ation** [kɒnfə'meıʃn] подтвержде́ние
confiscat|e ['kɒnfıskeıt] конфискова́ть (*im*)*pf.*; **~ion** [ˌkɒnfı'skeıʃn] конфиска́ция
conflagration [kɒnflə'greıʃn] бушу́ющий пожа́р
conflict 1. ['kɒnflıkt] конфли́кт, столкнове́ние; **2.** [kən'flıkt] быть в конфли́кте; *v/i.* противоре́чить
confluence ['kɒnflʊəns] *of rivers* слия́ние
conform [kən'fɔːm] согласо́вывать [-сова́ть] (**to** с Т); (*obey*) подчиня́ться [-ни́ться] (**to** Д); *to standards etc.* удовлетворя́ть [-ри́ть], соотве́тствовать; **~ity** [~ıtı] соотве́тствие; подчине́ние; **in ~ with** в соотве́тствии с (Т)
confound [kən'faʊnd] (*amaze*) поража́ть [порази́ть]; (*stump*) [по]ста́вить в тупи́к; (*confuse*) [с]пу́тать; **~ it!** чёрт побери́!
confront [kən'frʌnt] стоя́ть лицо́м к лицу́ с (Т)
confus|e [kən'fjuːz] [с]пу́тать; (*embarrass*) смуща́ть [-ути́ть]; **~ion** [kən'fjuːʒən] смуще́ние; (*disorder*) беспоря́док; **throw into ~** привести́ в замеша́тельство
congeal [kən'dʒiːl] засты́(ва́)ть
congenial [kən'dʒiːnıəl] □ бли́зкий по ду́ху, прия́тный; *climate* благоприя́тный
congenital [kən'dʒenıtl] врождённый
congestion [kən'dʒestʃən] *traffic* перегру́женность *f*; перенаселённость *f*
conglomeration [kənglɒmə'reıʃn] скопле́ние, конгломера́т
congratulat|e [kən'grætʃʊleıt] поздравля́ть [-а́вить] (**on** с Т); **~ion** [kəngrætʃʊ'leıʃn] поздравле́ние
congregat|e ['kɒŋgrıgeıt] соб(и-)ра́ть(ся); **~ion** [kɒŋgrı'geıʃn] *in Bitte church* собра́ние прихожа́н
congress ['kɒŋgres] конгре́сс; съезд; **~man** *Am.* конгрессме́н
congruous ['kɒŋgrʊəs] □ (*fitting*) соотве́тствующий; гармони́рующий (**to** с Т)
conifer ['kɒnıfə] де́рево хво́йной поро́ды
conjecture [kən'dʒektʃə] **1.** дога́дка, предположе́ние; **2.** предполага́ть [-ложи́ть]
conjugal ['kɒndʒʊgl] супру́жеский
conjunction [kən'dʒʌŋkʃn] соедине́ние; *gr.* сою́з; связь *f*; **in ~ with** совме́стно (с Т)
conjunctivitis [kəndʒʌŋktı'vaıtıs] конъюнктиви́т
conjur|e ['kʌndʒə] **~ up** *fig.* вызыва́ть в воображе́нии; *v/i.* пока́зывать фо́кусы; **~er, ~or** [~rə] фо́кусник
connect [kə'nekt] соединя́ть(ся)

[-ни́ть(ся)]; (*link*) свя́зывать(ся) [-за́ть(ся)]; *tel.* соединя́ть [-ни́ть]; **~ed** [~ɪd] □ свя́занный; ***be ~ with*** име́ть свя́зи (с Т); **~ion** [kə'nekʃn] связь *f*; соедине́ние; ***~s*** свя́зи; (*family*) ро́дственники

connive [kə'naɪv]: ***~ at*** потво́рствовать (Д), попусти́тельствовать

connoisseur [kɒnə'sɜː] знато́к

conquer ['kɒŋkə] *country* завоёвывать [-ева́ть]; (*defeat*) побежда́ть [победи́ть]; **~or** [~rə] победи́тель(ница *f*) *m*; завоева́тель *m*, -ница *f*

conquest ['kɒŋkwest] завоева́ние; побе́да

conscience ['kɒnʃəns] со́весть *f*; ***have a guilty ~*** чу́вствовать угрызе́ния со́вести

conscientious [kɒnʃɪ'enʃəs] □ добросо́вестный

conscious ['kɒnʃəs] □ *effort, etc.* созна́тельный; (*aware*) сознаю́щий; **~ness** [~nɪs] созна́ние

conscript [kən'skrɪpt] призывни́к; **~ion** [kən'skrɪpʃn] во́инская пови́нность *f*

consecrate ['kɒnsɪkreɪt] *a church, etc.* освяща́ть [-яти́ть]

consecutive [kən'sekjʊtɪv] □ после́довательный

consent [kən'sent] **1.** согла́сие; **2.** соглаша́ться [-ласи́ться]

consequen|ce ['kɒnsɪkwens] (по-) сле́дствие; (*importance*) ва́жность *f*; **~t** [~kwənt] обусло́вленный; (*subsequent*) после́дующий; **~tly** [~kwəntlɪ] сле́довательно; поэ́тому

conserv|ation [kɒnsə'veɪʃn] сохране́ние; ***nature ~*** охра́на приро́ды; **~ative** [kən'sɜːvətɪv] **1.** □ консервати́вный; **2.** *pol.* консерва́тор; **~atory** [~trɪ] оранжере́я; *mus.* консервато́рия; **~e** [kən'sɜːv] сохраня́ть [-ни́ть]

consider [kən'sɪdə] *v/t.* обсужда́ть [-уди́ть]; (*think over*) обду́м(ыв)ать; (*regard*) полага́ть, счита́ть; (*take into account*) счита́ться с (Т); **~able** [~rəbl] □ значи́тельный; большо́й; **~ate** [~rət] внима́тельный (к Д); **~ation** [kənsɪdə'reɪʃn] обсужде́ние; факт; соображе́ние; внима́ние; ***take into ~*** принима́ть во внима́ние, учи́тывать; **~ing** [kən'sɪdərɪŋ] *prp.* учи́тывая (В), принима́я во внима́ние (В)

consign [kən'saɪn] перед(ав)а́ть; поруча́ть [-чи́ть]; *comm.* пос(ы-) ла́ть (груз) по а́дресу; **~ee** [kɒnsaɪ'niː] грузополуча́тель, адреса́т гру́за; **~ment** [~mənt] груз, па́ртия това́ров

consist [kən'sɪst] состоя́ть (***of*** из Р); заключа́ться (***in*** в П); **~ence, ~ency** [~əns, ~ənsɪ] логи́чность *f*; консисте́нция *f*; **~ent** [~ənt] □ после́довательный; согласу́ющийся (***with*** с Т)

consol|ation [kɒnsə'leɪʃn] утеше́ние; **~e** [kən'səʊl] утеша́ть [уте́шить]

consolidate [kən'sɒlɪdeɪt] *position, etc.* укрепля́ть [-пи́ть]; (*unite*) объединя́ть(ся) [-ни́ть(ся)]; *comm.* слива́ться [-и́ться]

consonant ['kɒnsənənt] □ (*in accord*) согла́сный, созву́чный

conspicuous [kən'spɪkjʊəs] □ заме́тный, броса́ющийся в глаза́

conspir|acy [kən'spɪrəsɪ] за́говор; **~ator** [~tə] загово́рщик *m*, -ица *f*; **~e** [kən'spaɪə] устра́ивать за́говор; сгова́риваться [сговори́ться]

constable ['kʌnstəbl] *hist.* конста́бль *m*; (*policeman*) полице́йский

constan|cy ['kɒnstənsɪ] постоя́нство; (*faithfulness*) ве́рность *f*; **~t** [~stənt] □ постоя́нный; ве́рный

consternation [kɒnstə'neɪʃn] смяте́ние; замеша́тельство (*от стра́ха*)

constipation [kɒnstɪ'peɪʃn] запо́р

constituen|cy [kən'stɪtjʊənsɪ] избира́тельный о́круг; (*voters*) избира́тели *m/pl.*; **~t** [~ənt] **1.** (*part*) составно́й; *pol.* учреди́тельный; **2.** избира́тель *m*; составна́я часть *f*

constitut|e ['kɒnstɪtjuːt] (*make up*) составля́ть [-а́вить]; (*establish*) осно́вывать [-нова́ть]; **~ion** [kɒnstɪ'tjuːʃn] (*makeup*) строе́ние; конститу́ция; учрежде́ние; физи́ческое *or* душе́вное здоро́вье; **~ional** [~ʃənl] □ конституцио́нный; *of body* органи́ческий

C

constrain [kən'streɪn] принуждáть [-нудить]; вынуждáть [вы́нудить]; (*limit*) сдéрживать [-жáть]; **~t** [~t] принуждéние; вы́нужденность *f*; *of feelings* скóванность *f*
constrict [kən'strɪkt] стя́гивать [стянýть]; сж(им)áть; **~ion** [~kʃn] сжáтие; стя́гивание
construct [kən'strʌkt] [по]стрóить; сооружáть [-удить]; *fig.* созд(а-в)áть; **~ion** [~kʃn] строи́тельство, стрóйка; (*building, etc.*) строéние; **~ *site*** стрóйка; **~ive** [~tɪv] конструкти́вный
construe [kən'struː] истолкóвывать [-ковáть]
consul ['kɒnsl] кóнсул; ***~ general*** генерáльный кóнсул; **~ate** ['kɒnsjʊlət] кóнсульство
consult [kən'sʌlt] *v/t.* спрáшивать совéта у (Р); *v/i.* [про]консульти́роваться, совещáться; ***~ a doctor*** пойти́ на консультáцию к врачý; **~ant** [~ənt] консультáнт; **~ation** [kɒnsl'teɪʃn] *specialist advice and advice bureau* консультáция, конси́лиум (врачéй)
consum|e [kən'sjuːm] *v/t.* съедáть [съесть]; (*use*) потребля́ть [-би́ть]; [из]расхóдовать; **~er** [~ə] потреби́тель *m*; ***~ goods*** потреби́тельские товáры
consummate [kən'sʌmɪt] □ совершéнный, закóнченный
consumption [kən'sʌmpʃn] потреблéние, расхóд; *med.* туберкулёз лёгких
contact ['kɒntækt] контáкт (*a. fig.*); ***business ~s*** деловы́е свя́зи
contagious [kən'teɪdʒəs] □ зарáзный, инфекциóнный
contain [kən'teɪn] содержáть (в себé), вмещáть [-ести́ть]; ***~ o.s.*** сдéрживаться [-жáться]; **~er** [~ə] контéйнер
contaminat|e [kən'tæmɪneɪt] *water, etc.* загрязня́ть [-ни́ть]; заражáть [зарази́ть]; *fig.* окáзывать [-зáть] пáгубное влия́ние; **~tion** [kəntæmɪ'neɪʃn]: ***radioactive ~*** радиоакти́вное загрязнéние
contemplat|e ['kɒntəmpleɪt] обдýм(ыв)ать; **~ion** [kɒntem'pleɪʃn] созерцáние; размышлéние
contempora|neous [kəntempə'reɪnɪəs] □ совпадáющий по врéмени, одновремéнный; **~ry** [kən'tempərərɪ] **1.** совремéнный; **2.** совремéнник *m*, -ица *f*
contempt [kən'tempt] презрéние (***for*** к Д); **~ible** [~əbl] □ презрéнный; **~uous** [~ʃʊəs] □ презри́тельный
contend [kən'tend] *v/i.* борóться; сопéрничать; *v/t.* утверждáть
content [kən'tent] **1.** довóльный; **2.** удовлетворя́ть [-ри́ть]; **3.** удовлетворéние; ***to one's heart's ~*** вдóволю; **4.** ['kɒntent] содержáние; ***table of ~s*** оглавлéние; **~ed** [kən'tentɪd] □ довóльный, удовлетворённый
contention [kən'tenʃn] *dissension* спор, ссóра; *assertion* утверждéние
contentment [kən'tentmənt] удовлетворённость *f*
contest **1.** ['kɒntest] кóнкурс; *sport* соревновáние; **2.** [kən'test] оспáривать [оспóрить]; *one's rights, etc.* отстáивать [отстоя́ть]; (*struggle*) борóться (за В); **~ant** учáстник (-ица) состязáния
context ['kɒntekst] контéкст
continent ['kɒntɪnənt] матери́к, континéнт; ***the*** ≈ *Brt.* (материкóвая) Еврóпа
contingen|cy [kən'tɪndʒənsɪ] случáйность *f*; непредви́денное обстоя́тельство; ***be prepared for every ~*** быть готóвым ко вся́ким случáйностям; **~t** [~dʒənt] □ **1.** случáйный, непредви́денный; **2.** грýппа; *mil.* контингéнт
continu|al [kən'tɪnjʊəl] □ непреры́вный, беспрестáнный; **~ation** [kəntɪnjʊ'eɪʃn] продолжéние; **~e** [kən'tɪnjuː] *v/t.* продолжáть [-дóлжить]; ***to be ~d*** продолжéние слéдует; *v/i.* продолжáться [-дóлжиться]; *of forest, road, etc.* простирáться, тянýться; **~ity** [kɒntɪ'njuːətɪ] непреры́вность *f*; **~ous** [kən'tɪnjʊəs] □ непреры́вный; (*unbroken*) сплошнóй
contort [kən'tɔːt] *of face* искажáть [искази́ть]
contour ['kɒntʊə] кóнтур, очертáние

contraband ['kɒntrəbænd] контрабáнда
contraceptive [kɒntrə'septɪv] противозачáточное срéдство
contract 1. [kən'trækt] *v/t. muscle* сокращáть [-рати́ть]; *alliance* заключáть [-чи́ть]; *v/i.* сокращáться [-рати́ться]; *of metal* сж(им)áть(ся); **2.** ['kɒntrækt] контрáкт, договóр; **~ion** [~ʃən] сжáтие; сокращéние; **~or** [~tə] подря́дчик
contradict [kɒntrə'dɪkt] противорéчить (Д); **~ion** [~kʃn] противорéчие; **~ory** [~tərɪ] □ противоречи́вый
contrary ['kɒntrərɪ] **1.** противополóжный; *person* упря́мый; **~ *to*** *prp.* вопреки́ (Д); **2.** обрáтное; ***on the ~*** наоборóт
contrast 1. ['kɒntrɑːst] противополóжность *f*; контрáст; **2.** [kən'trɑːst] *v/t.* сопоставля́ть [-áвить], срáвнивать [-ни́ть]; *v/i.* отличáться от (Р); контрасти́ровать с (Т)
contribut|e [kən'trɪbjuːt] (*donate*) [по]жéртвовать; *to a newspaper, etc.* сотрýдничать (***to*** в П); **~ion** [kɒntrɪ'bjuːʃn] вклад; взнос; **~or** [kən'trɪbjʊtə] áвтор; жéртвователь
contriv|ance [kən'traɪvəns] вы́думка; *mechanism, etc.* приспособлéние; **~e** [kən'traɪv] *v/t.* (*invent*) придýм(ыв)ать; (*scheme*) затевáть [-éять]; *v/i.* ухитря́ться [-ри́ться]; умудря́ться [-ри́ться]
control [kən'trəʊl] **1.** управлéние (*a. tech.*), регули́рование; контрóль *m*; **~ *desk*** пульт управлéния; ***lose ~ of o.s.*** потеря́ть самообладáние; ***under ~*** в поря́дке; **2.** управля́ть (Т); [про]контроли́ровать (*im*)*pf.*; *feelings, etc.* сдéрживать [-жáть]; **~ler** [~ə] контролёр, инспéктор; *ae., rail.* диспéтчер
controver|sial [kɒntrə'vɜːʃl] □ спóрный; **~sy** ['kɒntrəvɜːsɪ] спор, полéмика
convalesce [kɒnvə'les] выздорáвливать *impf.*; **~nce** [~ns] выздоровлéние; **~nt** [~nt] □ выздорáвливающий
convene [kən'viːn] *meeting, etc.* соз(ы)вáть; (*come together*) соб(и)рáть(ся)
convenien|ce [kən'viːnɪəns] удóбство; ***at your earliest ~*** как тóлько вы смóжете; ***public ~*** *euph.* убóрная; **~t** [~ɪənt] □ удóбный
convent ['kɒnvənt] монасты́рь *m*; **~ion** [kən'venʃn] съезд; (*agreement*) конвéнция, соглашéние; (*custom*) обы́чай, услóвность *f*
converge [kən'vɜːdʒ] сходи́ться [сойти́сь] (в однý тóчку)
convers|ation [kɒnvə'seɪʃn] разговóр, бесéда; **~ational** [~ʃənl] разговóрный; **~e** [kən'vɜːs] разговáривать, бесéдовать; **~ion** [kən'vɜːʃn] превращéние; *eccl., etc.* обращéние; *el.* преобразовáние; *stocks, etc.* конвéрсия
convert [kən'vɜːt] превращáть [-ати́ть]; *el.* преобразóвывать [-вáть]; *fin.* конверти́ровать; *eccl., etc.* обращáть [-рати́ть] (в другýю вéру); **~ible** [~əbl]: **~ *currency*** конверти́руемая валю́та
convey [kən'veɪ] *goods* перевози́ть [-везти́], переправля́ть [-прáвить]; *greetings, electricity, etc.* перед(ав)áть; **~ance** [~əns] перевóзка; достáвка; трáнспортное срéдство; **~or** [~ə] (**~ *belt***) конвéйер
convict 1. ['kɒnvɪkt] осуждённый; **2.** [kən'vɪkt] признавáть винóвным; **~ion** [kən'vɪkʃn] *law* осуждéние; (*firm belief*) убеждéние
convinc|e [kən'vɪns] убеждáть [убеди́ть] (***of*** в П); **~ing** [~ɪŋ] убеди́тельный
convoy ['kɒnvɔɪ] *naut.* конвóй; сопровождéние
convuls|e [kən'vʌls] содрогáться [-гнýться]; ***be ~d with laughter*** смея́ться до упáду; ***her face was ~d with pain*** её лицó искази́лось от бóли; **~ion** [~ʃn] *of ground* колебáние; *of muscles* сýдорога; **~ive** [~sɪv] сýдорожный
coo [kuː] ворковáть
cook [kʊk] **1.** пóвар; **2.** [при]готóвить едý; **~ery** ['kʊkərɪ] кулинáрия; приготовлéние еды́; **~ie, ~y** ['kʊkɪ] *Am.* печéнье
cool [kuːl] **1.** прохлáдный; *fig.* хладнокрóвный; (*imperturbable*) невозмути́мый; *pej.* дéрзкий, нахáль-

ный; ***keep ~!*** не горячи́сь! **2.** прохла́да; **3.** охлажда́ть(ся) [охлади́ть(ся)]; осты́(ва́)ть; **~headed** [ku:l'hedɪd] □ хладнокро́вный
coolness ['ku:lnɪs] холодо́к; прохла́да; хладнокро́вие
coop [ku:p] ~ ***up*** *или* ***in*** держа́ть взаперти́
cooperat|e [kəʊ'ɒpəreɪt] сотру́дничать; **~ion** [kəʊɒpə'reɪʃn] сотру́дничество; **~ive** [kəʊ'ɒpərətɪv] кооперати́вный; ~ ***society*** кооперати́в
coordinat|e [kəʊ'ɔ:dɪneɪt] координи́ровать *(im)pf.*; согласо́вывать [-ова́ть]; **~ion** [kəʊɔ:dɪ'neɪʃn] координа́ция
cope [kəʊp]: ~ ***with*** справля́ться [-а́виться] с (Т)
copier ['kɒpɪə] копирова́льный аппара́т
copious ['kəʊpɪəs] □ оби́льный
copper ['kɒpə] **1.** медь *f*; (*coin*) ме́дная моне́та; **2.** ме́дный
copy ['kɒpɪ] **1.** ко́пия; (*single example*) экземпля́р; **2.** перепи́сывать [-са́ть]; снима́ть [снять] ко́пию с (Р); **~book** тетра́дь *f*; **~right** а́вторское пра́во
coral ['kɒrəl] кора́лл
cord [kɔ:d] **1.** верёвка, шнур; ***vocal ~s*** голосовы́е свя́зки; **2.** свя́зывать [-за́ть] верёвкой
cordial ['kɔ:dɪəl] **1.** □ серде́чный, и́скренний; **2.** стимули́рующий напи́ток; **~ity** [kɔ:dɪ'ælətɪ] серде́чность *f*; раду́шие
cordon ['kɔ:dn] **1.** кордо́н; **2.** ~ ***off*** отгора́живать [-роди́ть]
corduroy ['kɔ:dərɔɪ] вельве́т в ру́бчик; **~s** *pl.* вельве́товые брю́ки *m/pl.*
core [kɔ:] сердцеви́на; *fig.* суть *f*; ***to the ~*** *fig.* до мо́зга косте́й
cork [kɔ:k] **1.** про́бка; **2.** затыка́ть про́бкой; **'~screw** што́пор
corn[1] [kɔ:n] зерно́; хлеба́ *m/pl.*; *Am., maize* кукуру́за
corn[2] [~] *on a toe* мозо́ль
corner ['kɔ:nə] **1.** у́гол; **2.** *fig.* загна́ть *pf.* в у́гол; припере́ть *pf.* к стене́
cornflakes корнфле́кс; кукуру́зные хло́пья
cornice ['kɔ:nɪs] *arch.* карни́з
coronary ['kɒrənərɪ] корона́рный; *su. coll.* инфа́ркт
coronation [kɒrə'neɪʃn] корона́ция
corpor|al ['kɔ:pərəl] **1.** □ теле́сный; **2.** *mil. approx.* ефре́йтор; **~ation** [kɔ:pə'reɪʃn] корпора́ция
corps [kɔ:]: ***diplomatic ~*** дипломати́ческий ко́рпус
corpse [kɔ:ps] труп
corpulen|ce ['kɔ:pjʊləns] ту́чность *f*; **~t** [~lənt] ту́чный
correct [kə'rekt] **1.** □ пра́вильный, ве́рный, то́чный; (*proper*) корре́ктный; **2.** *v/t.* исправля́ть [-а́вить], корректи́ровать; *manuscript* пра́вить; **~ion** [kə'rekʃn] (*act of correcting*) исправле́ние; (*the correction made*) попра́вка
correlat|e ['kɒrəleɪt] устана́вливать соотноше́ние; **~ion** [kɒrə'leɪʃn] соотноше́ние, взаимосвя́зь *f*
correspond [kɒrɪ'spɒnd] соотве́тствовать (***with***, ***to*** Д); *by letter* перепи́сываться (с Т); **~ence** [~əns] соотве́тствие, перепи́ска; **~ent** [~ənt] **1.** соотве́тствующий; **2.** корреспонде́нт *m*, -ка *f*; **~ing** [~ɪŋ] □ соотве́тствующий (Д)
corridor ['kɒrɪdɔ:] коридо́р
corroborate [kə'rɒbəreɪt] подтвержда́ть [-рди́ть]
corro|de [kə'rəud] разъеда́ть [-е́сть]; [за]ржаве́ть; **~sion** [kə'rəʊʒn] корро́зия, ржа́вчина; **~sive** [~sɪv] **1.** коррозио́нный; **2.** разъеда́ющее вещество́
corrugated ['kɒrəgeɪtɪd]: ~ ***iron*** рифлёное желе́зо
corrupt [kə'rʌpt] **1.** □ коррумпи́рованный, прода́жный; (*containing mistakes*) искажённый; (*depraved*) развращённый; **2.** *v/t.* искажа́ть [-зи́ть]; развраща́ть [-рати́ть]; подкупа́ть [-пи́ть]; *v/i.* [ис]по́ртиться; искажа́ться [-зи́ться]; **~ion** [~pʃn] искаже́ние; корру́пция, прода́жность *f*; развращённость *f*
corset ['kɔ:sɪt] корсе́т
cosmetic [kɒz'metɪk] **1.** космети́ческий; **2.** *pl.* косме́тика
cosmic ['kɒzmɪk] косми́ческий
cosmonaut ['kɒzmənɔ:t] космона́вт

C

cosmos ['kɒzmɒs] ко́смос
cost [kɒst] **1.** цена́, сто́имость *f*; *pl.* расхо́ды, изде́ржки; **~ *effectiveness*** рента́бельность *f*; **2.** [*irr.*] сто́ить
costly ['kɒstlɪ] дорого́й, це́нный
costume ['kɒstju:m] костю́м; **~ *jewel(le)ry*** бижуте́рия
cosy ['kəʊzɪ] □ ую́тный
cot [kɒt] де́тская крова́ть
cottage ['kɒtɪdʒ] котте́дж, небольшо́й дом (*обы́чно в дере́вне*); *Am.* ле́тняя да́ча; **~ *cheese*** тво́рог
cotton ['kɒtn] **1.** хло́пок; хлопчатобума́жная ткань; (*thread*) ни́тки; **2.** хлопчатобума́жный; **~ *wool*** ва́та; **3.**: **~ *on*** *coll.* понима́ть [-ня́ть]
couch [kaʊtʃ] дива́н, *Brt.* куше́тка
cough [kɒf] **1.** ка́шель *m*; ***a bad ~*** си́льный ка́шель; **2.** ка́шлять [ка́шлянуть]
could [kəd· *strong* kʊd] *pt. от* ***can***
council ['kaʊnsl] сове́т; ***Security*** ♀ Сове́т Безопа́сности; ***town ~*** городско́й сове́т, муниципалите́т; **~(l)or** [~sələ] член сове́та
counsel ['kaʊnsl] **1.** сове́т, совеща́ние; *law* адвока́т; **~ *for the prosecution*** обвини́тель *m*; **2.** дава́ть сове́т (Д); **~(l)or** [~ələ] *dipl., pol.* сове́тник
count¹ [kaʊnt] **1.** счёт; (*counting up*) подсчёт; **2.** *v/t.* [со]счита́ть; подсчи́тывать [-ита́ть]; (*include*) включа́ть [-чи́ть]; *v/i.* счита́ться; (*be of account*) име́ть значе́ние
count² [~] граф
countenance ['kaʊntənəns] **1.** лицо́; выраже́ние лица́; (*support*) подде́ржка; ***lose ~*** потеря́ть самооблада́ние; **2.** подде́рживать [-жа́ть], поощря́ть [-ри́ть]
counter¹ ['kaʊntə] прила́вок; *in bar, bank* сто́йка; *tech.* счётчик
counter² [~] **1.** противополо́жный (***to*** Д); встре́чный; **2.** *adv.* обра́тно; напро́тив; **3.** [вос]проти́виться (Д); *a blow* наноси́ть встре́чный уда́р
counteract [kaʊntər'ækt] противоде́йствовать (Д); нейтрализова́ть (*im*)*pf.*
counterbalance 1. ['kaʊntəbæləns] *mst. fig.* противове́с; **2.** [kaʊntə'bæləns] уравнове́шивать [-ве́сить]; служи́ть противове́сом (Д)
counterespionage [kaʊntər'espɪənɑ:ʒ] контрразве́дка
counterfeit ['kaʊntəfɪt] **1.** подде́льный; **2.** подде́лка; **3.** подде́л(ыв)ать
counterfoil ['kaʊntəfɔɪl] корешо́к (биле́та, квита́нции)
countermand [kaʊntə'mɑ:nd] *order* отменя́ть [-ни́ть]
countermove ['kaʊntəmu:v] *fig.* отве́тная ме́ра, контруда́р
counterpane ['kaʊntəpeɪn] покрыва́ло
counterpart ['kaʊntəpɑ:t] представи́тель друго́й стороны́ (*занима́ющий тот же пост, до́лжность и т.д.*); ***the English MPs met their Russian ~s*** англи́йские парламента́рии встре́тились со свои́ми ру́сскими колле́гами
countersign ['kaʊntəsaɪn] *v/t.* [по-] ста́вить втору́ю по́дпись (на П)
countess ['kaʊntɪs] графи́ня
countless ['kaʊntlɪs] бесчи́сленный, несчётный
country ['kʌntrɪ] **1.** страна́; ме́стность *f*; ***go to the ~*** пое́хать за́ город; ***live in the ~*** жить в се́льской ме́стности; **2.** дереве́нский; **~man** [~mən] се́льский жи́тель; земля́к, сооте́чественник; **~side** [~saɪd] се́льская ме́стность *f*
county ['kaʊntɪ] гра́фство; *Am.* о́круг
coup [ku:] уда́чный ход (*уда́р и т.п.*)
couple ['kʌpl] **1.** па́ра; **2.** соединя́ть [-ни́ть]; *zo.* спа́риваться
coupling ['kʌplɪŋ] *tech.* му́фта сцепле́ния
coupon ['ku:pɒn] купо́н, тало́н
courage ['kʌrɪdʒ] му́жество, сме́лость *f*, хра́брость *f*, отва́га; ***pluck up one's ~*** набра́ться *pf.* хра́брости; **~ous** [kə'reɪdʒəs] □ му́жественный, сме́лый, хра́брый
courier ['kʊrɪə] курье́р, на́рочный
course [kɔ:s] (*direction*) направле́ние, курс; *of events* ход; *of river* тече́ние; (*food*) блю́до; ***of ~*** коне́чно; ***in the ~ of*** в тече́ние
court [kɔ:t] **1.** двор (*a. fig.*); (*law ~*)

C

суд; *sport* площа́дка; ***tennis* ~** те́ннисный корт; **2.** (*woo*) уха́живать за (Т); (*seek favo[u]r of*) иска́ть расположе́ния (Р); **~eous** ['kɜːtɪəs] □ ве́жливый, учти́вый; **~esy** ['kɜːtəsɪ] учти́вость *f*, ве́жливость *f*; **~ martial** *mil.* **1.** вое́нный трибуна́л; **2.** суди́ть вое́нным трибуна́лом; **~ship** ['~ʃɪp] уха́живание; **~yard** двор

cousin ['kʌzn] *male* кузе́н, двою́родный брат; *female* кузи́на, двою́родная сестра́

cove [kəʊv] (ма́ленькая) бу́хта

cover ['kʌvə] **1.** (*lid*, *top*) кры́шка; *for bed*, *etc.* покрыва́ло; *of book* обло́жка; (*shelter*) укры́тие; *fig.* покро́в; ***send under separate* ~** посла́ть в отде́льном письме́, паке́те; **2.** покры́(ва́)ть (*a. comm.*); прикры́(ва́)ть; (*a.* **~ *up***) скры́(ва́)ть; **~ing** [~rɪŋ]: **~ *letter*** сопроводи́тельное письмо́

coverage ['kʌvərɪdʒ] репорта́ж; охва́т

covert ['kʌvət] □ скры́тый, та́йный

covet ['kʌvɪt] жа́ждать (Р); **~ous** [~əs] □ жа́дный, а́лчный; скупо́й

cow[1] [kaʊ] коро́ва

cow[2] [~] запу́гивать [-га́ть]; терроризова́ть (*im*)*pf.*

coward ['kaʊəd] трус *m*, -и́ха *f*; **~ice** [~ɪs] тру́сость *f*; малоду́шие; **~ly** [~lɪ] трусли́вый

cowboy ['kaʊbɔɪ] *Am.* ковбо́й

cower ['kaʊə] съёжи(ва)ться

cowl [kaʊl] капюшо́н

coy [kɔɪ] □ засте́нчивый

cozy ['kəʊzɪ] ую́тный

crab[1] [kræb] *zo.* краб

crab[2] [~] *bot.* ди́кая я́блоня; *coll.* ворчу́н

crack [kræk] **1.** (*noise*) треск; тре́щина; щель *f*; рассе́лина; *coll.* (*blow*) уда́р; *Am.* саркасти́ческое замеча́ние; ***at the* ~ *of dawn*** на заре́; **2.** *coll.* первокла́ссный; **3.** *v/t.* раска́лывать [-коло́ть], коло́ть; **~ *a joke*** отпусти́ть шу́тку; *v/i.* производи́ть треск, шум; [по]тре́скаться; раска́лываться [-коло́ться]; *of voice* лома́ться; **~ed** [~t] тре́снувший; *coll.* вы́живший из ума́; **~er** ['~ə] хлопу́шка; *Am.* кре́кер; **~le** ['~l] потре́скивание, треск

cradle ['kreɪdl] **1.** колыбе́ль *f*; *fig.* нача́ло; младе́нчество; **2.** бе́режно держа́ть в рука́х (как ребёнка)

craft [krɑːft] (*skill*) ло́вкость *f*, сноро́вка; (*trade*) ремесло́; (*boat*) су́дно (*pl.* суда́); **~sman** ['~smən] ма́стер; **~y** ['~ɪ] ло́вкий, хи́трый

crag [kræg] скала́, утёс; **~gy** ['~ɪ] скали́стый

cram [kræm] набива́ть [-би́ть]; впи́хивать [-хну́ть]; [на]пи́чкать; *coll.* [за]зубри́ть

cramp [kræmp] **1.** су́дорога; **2.** (*hamper*) стесня́ть [-ни́ть]; (*limit*) су́живать [су́зить]

cranberry ['krænbərɪ] клю́ква

crane [kreɪn] **1.** *bird* жура́вль *m*; *tech.* подъёмный кран; **2.** поднима́ть кра́ном; *neck* вытя́гивать [вы́тянуть] ше́ю

crank [kræŋk] **1.** *mot.* заводна́я ру́чка; *coll. person* челове́к с причу́дами; **2.** заводи́ть [-вести́] ру́чкой (автомаши́ну); **~shaft** *tech.* коле́нчатый вал; **~y** ['~ɪ] капри́зный; эксцентри́чный

cranny ['krænɪ] щель *f*; тре́щина

crape [kreɪp] креп

crash [kræʃ] **1.** гро́хот, гром; *ae.* ава́рия; *rail.* круше́ние; *fin.* крах; **2.** па́дать, ру́шиться с тре́ском; разби́(ва́)ться (*a. ae.*); *ae.* потерпе́ть *pf.* ава́рию; **~ helmet** защи́тный шлем; **~ landing** авари́йная поса́дка

crater ['kreɪtə] кра́тер; *mil.* воро́нка

crave [kreɪv] стра́стно жела́ть, жа́ждать (***for*** Р)

crawl [krɔːl] **1.** по́лзание; *swimming* кроль; **2.** по́лзать, [по]ползти́; *fig.* пресмыка́ться

crayfish ['kreɪfɪʃ] рак

crayon ['kreɪən] цветно́й каранда́ш; пасте́ль *f*, рису́нок пасте́лью *и́ли* цветны́м карандашо́м

craz|e [kreɪz] **1.** *coll.* ма́ния, пова́льное увлече́ние; ***be the* ~** быть в мо́де; **2.** своди́ть с ума́; **~y** ['kreɪzɪ] □ поме́шанный; *plan*, *etc.* безу́мный; ***be* ~ *about*** быть поме́шанным (на П)

creak [kriːk] **1.** скрип; **2.** [за]скрипе́ть

cream [kriːm] **1.** сли́вки *f/pl.*; крем; (*the best part*) са́мое лу́чшее; ***shoe ~*** крем для о́буви; ***sour ~*** смета́на; ***whipped ~*** взби́тые сли́вки; **2.** снима́ть сли́вки с (Р); **~y** ['kriːmɪ] □ (*containing cream*) сли́вочный

crease [kriːs] **1.** скла́дка; (*on paper*) сгиб; **2.** [по]мя́ть(ся); загиба́ть [загну́ть]; **~-proof** немну́щийся

creat|e [kriː'eɪt] [со]твори́ть; соз-д(ав)а́ть; **~ion** [~'eɪʃn] созда́ние; (со)творе́ние; **~ive** [~ɪv] тво́рческий; **~or** [~ə] созда́тель *m*, творе́ц; **~ure** ['kriːtʃə] созда́ние, существо́

creden|ce ['kriːdns] ве́ра, дове́рие; **~tials** [krɪ'denʃlz] *pl. dipl.* вери́тельные гра́моты *f/pl.*; удостовере́ние

credible ['kredəbl] □ заслу́живающий дове́рия; *story* правдоподо́бный; ***it's hardly ~ that*** маловероя́тно, что

credit ['kredɪt] **1.** дове́рие; хоро́шая репута́ция; *fin.* креди́т; **2.** ве́рить, доверя́ть (Д); *fin.* кредитова́ть (*im*)*pf.*; ***~ s.o. with s.th.*** счита́ть, что; **~able** ['~əbl] □ похва́льный; **~ card** креди́тная ка́рточка; **~or** [~ə] кредито́р; **~worthy** кредитоспосо́бный

credulous ['kredjʊləs] □ легкове́рный, дове́рчивый

creek [kriːk] бу́хта, небольшо́й зали́в; *Am.* руче́й

creep [kriːp] [*irr.*] по́лзать, [по]ползти́; *of plants* стла́ться, ви́ться; (*stealthily*) кра́сться; *fig.* ***~ in*** вкра́дываться [вкра́сться]; **~er** ['~ə] вью́щееся расте́ние

cremate [krə'meɪt] креми́ровать

crept [krept] *pt.* и *pt. p. om* ***creep***

crescent ['kresnt] полуме́сяц

crest [krest] *of wave, hill* гре́бень *m*; **~fallen** ['krestfɔːlən] упа́вший ду́хом; уны́лый

crevasse [krɪ'væs] рассе́лина

crevice ['krevɪs] щель *f*, расще́лина, тре́щина

crew[1] [kruː] *of train* брига́да; *naut.*, *ae.* экипа́ж, *mil.* кома́нда

crew[2] [~] *chiefly Brt. pt. om* ***crow***

crib [krɪb] *Am.* де́тская крова́тка; *educ.* шпарга́лка

cricket[1] ['krɪkɪt] *zo.* сверчо́к

cricket[2] [~] *game* краке́т; *coll.* ***not ~*** не по пра́вилам, нече́стно

crime [kraɪm] преступле́ние

criminal ['krɪmɪnl] **1.** престу́пник; **2.** престу́пный; кримина́льный, уголо́вный; ***~ code*** уголо́вный ко́декс

crimson ['krɪmzn] **1.** багро́вый, мали́новый; **2.** [по]красне́ть

cringe [krɪndʒ] пресмыка́ться

crinkle ['krɪŋkl] **1.** скла́дка; морщи́на; **2.** [с]мо́рщиться; [по]мя́ться

cripple ['krɪpl] **1.** кале́ка *m/f*, инвали́д; **2.** [ис]кале́чить, [из]уро́довать; *fig.* парализова́ть (*im*)*pf.*

crisis ['kraɪsɪs] кри́зис

crisp [krɪsp] **1.** *having curls* кудря́вый; *snow*, *etc.* хрустя́щий; *air* бодря́щий; **2.** ***potato ~s*** хрустя́щий карто́фель

crisscross ['krɪskrɒs] **1.** *adv.* крест-на́крест, вкось; **2.** перечёркивать крест-на́крест; ***~ed with roads*** покры́тый се́тью доро́г

criteri|on [kraɪ'tɪərɪən], *pl.* **~a** [~rɪə] крите́рий, мери́ло

criti|c ['krɪtɪk] кри́тик; **~cal** ['krɪtɪkl] крити́ческий; **~cism** [~sɪzəm], **~que** ['krɪtiːk] кри́тика; реце́нзия; **~cize** ['krɪtɪsaɪz] [рас]критикова́ть; (*judge severely*) осужда́ть [осуди́ть]

croak [krəʊk] [за]ка́ркать; [за]ква́кать

Croat ['krəʊæt] хорва́т, хорва́тка; **~ian** [krəʊ'eɪʃən] хорва́тский

crochet ['krəʊʃeɪ] **1.** вяза́ние (крючко́м); **2.** вяза́ть

crock [krɒk] гли́няный горшо́к; **~ery** ['krɒkərɪ] гли́няная/фая́нсовая посу́да

crony ['krəʊnɪ] *coll.* закады́чный друг

crook [krʊk] **1.** (*bend*) поворо́т; изги́б; *sl.* моше́нник; **2.** сгиба́ть(ся) [согну́ть(ся)]; **~ed** ['krʊkɪd] изо́гнутый; криво́й; *coll.* нече́стный

croon [kruːn] напева́ть вполго́лоса

crop [krɒp] **1.** урожа́й; посе́вы *m/pl.*; ***~ failure*** неурожа́й; **2.** (*bear a crop*) уроди́ться; *hair* подстрига́ть [-ри́чь]; ***~ up*** возника́ть [-и́кнуть]; обнару́житься

C

cross [krɒs] **1.** крест; **2.** □ (*transverse*) попере́чный; *fig.* серди́тый; **3.** *v/t. arms, etc.* скре́щивать [-ести́ть]; (*go across*) переходи́ть [перейти́], переезжа́ть [перее́хать]; *fig.* противоде́йствовать (Д); пере́чить; **~ o.s.** [пере]крести́ться; *v/i. of mail* размину́ться *pf.*; **~-bar** попере́чина; **~breed** по́месь *f*; (*plant*) гибри́д; **~-eyed** косогла́зый; **~ing** ['krɒsɪŋ] перекрёсток; перепра́ва; перехо́д; **~roads** *pl. или sg.* перекрёсток; **~-section** попере́чное сече́ние; **~wise** поперёк; крест-на́крест; **~word puzzle** кроссво́рд
crotchet ['krɒtʃɪt] *mus.* четвертна́я но́та; *caprice* фанта́зия
crouch [kraʊtʃ] нагиба́ться [нагну́ться]
crow [krəʊ] **1.** воро́на; пе́ние петуха́; **2.** кукаре́кать; **~bar** лом
crowd [kraʊd] **1.** толпа́; (*large number*) мно́жество, ма́сса; *coll.* толкотня́, да́вка; *coll.* компа́ния; **2.** собира́ться толпо́й, толпи́ться; набива́ться битко́м
crown [kraʊn] **1.** коро́на; *fig.* вене́ц; *of tree* кро́на; *of head* маку́шка; **2.** коронова́ть (*im*)*pf.*; *fig.* увенча́ть(ся); ***to ~ it all*** в доверше́ние всего́
cruci|al ['kru:ʃl] □ крити́ческий; реша́ющий; **~fixion** [kru:sɪ'fɪkʃn] распя́тие; **~fy** ['kru:sɪfaɪ] распина́ть [-пя́ть]
crude [kru:d] □ (*raw*) сыро́й; (*unrefined*) неочи́щенный; *statistics* гру́бый
cruel ['krʊəl] □ жесто́кий; *fig.* мучи́тельный; **~ty** [~tɪ] жесто́кость *f*
cruise [kru:z] **1.** *naut.* круи́з; **2.** крейси́ровать; соверша́ть ре́йсы; **~r** ['kru:zə] *naut.* кре́йсер
crumb [krʌm] кро́шка; **~le** ['krʌmbl] [рас-, ис]кроши́ть(ся)
crumple ['krʌmpl] [из-, по-, с]мя́ть(ся); [с]ко́мкать(ся)
crunch [krʌntʃ] жева́ть с хру́стом; хрусте́ть [хру́стнуть]
crusade [kru:'seɪd] кресто́вый похо́д; кампа́ния; **~r** [~ə] крестоно́сец; *fig.* боре́ц
crush [krʌʃ] **1.** да́вка; толкотня́; **2.** *v/t.* [раз]дави́ть; (~ *out*) выжима́ть [вы́жать]; *enemy* разбива́ть [-би́ть]
crust [krʌst] **1.** *of bread* ко́рка; *of earth* кора́; покрыва́ть(ся) ко́ркой; **~y** ['krʌstɪ] □ покры́тый ко́ркой
crutch [krʌtʃ] косты́ль *m*
crux [krʌks]: ***the ~ of the matter*** суть де́ла
cry [kraɪ] **1.** крик; вопль; плач; **2.** [за]пла́кать; (*exclaim*) восклица́ть [-и́кнуть]; (*shout*) крича́ть [кри́кнуть]; ***~ for*** [по]тре́бовать (Р)
cryptic ['krɪptɪk] (*mysterious*) таи́нственный; (*secret*) сокрове́нный
crystal ['krɪstl] *cut glass or rock* хруста́ль *m*; *tech.* криста́лл; *attr.* хруста́льный; **~lize** [~təlaɪz] кристаллизова́ть(ся) (*im*)*pf.*
cub [kʌb] детёныш
cub|e [kju:b] *math.* **1.** куб; ***~ root*** куби́ческий ко́рень *m*; **2.** возводи́ть в куб; **~ic(al)** ['kju:bɪk(l)] куби́ческий
cubicle ['kju:bɪkl] каби́нка
cuckoo ['kʊku:] куку́шка
cucumber ['kju:kʌmbə] огуре́ц
cuddle ['kʌdl] *v/t.* прижима́ть к себе́; *v/i.* приж(им)а́ться (друг к дру́гу)
cue [kju:] (билья́рдный) кий; (*hint*) намёк; *thea.* ре́плика
cuff [kʌf] **1.** манже́та, обшла́г; **2.** (*blow*) шлепо́к; дать затре́щину; **~links** за́понки
culminat|e ['kʌlmɪneɪt] достига́ть [-ти́гнуть] вы́сшей то́чки (*или* сте́пени); **~ion** [kʌlmɪ'neɪʃn] кульмина́ция
culprit ['kʌlprɪt] (*offender*) престу́пник; вино́вник
cultivat|e ['kʌltɪveɪt] обраба́тывать [-бо́тать], возде́л(ыв)ать; *plants* культиви́ровать; *friendship* стреми́ться завяза́ть дру́жеские отноше́ния; **~ion** [kʌltɪ'veɪʃn] *of soil* обрабо́тка, возде́лывание; *of plants* разведе́ние
cultural ['kʌltʃərəl] □ культу́рный
cultur|e ['kʌltʃə] культу́ра (*a. agric.*); **~ed** [~d] культу́рный; интеллиге́нтный
cumbersome ['kʌmbəsəm] громо́здкий; *fig.* обремени́тельный
cumulative ['kju:mjʊlətɪv] □ совоку́пный; накопи́вшийся

cunning ['kʌnɪŋ] **1.** ло́вкий; хи́трый; кова́рный; *Am. a.* привлека́тельный; **2.** ло́вкость *f*; хи́трость *f*; кова́рство
cup [kʌp] ча́шка; ча́ша; *as prize* ку́бок; **~board** ['kʌbəd] шка́ф(чик); **~ final** фина́л ро́зыгрыша ку́бка
cupola ['kju:pələ] ку́пол
curable ['kjʊərəbl] излечи́мый
curb [kɜ:b] **1.** узда́ (*a. fig.*); подгу́бный реме́нь; **2.** обу́здывать [-да́ть] (*a. fig.*)
curd [kɜ:d] простоква́ша; *pl.* творо́г; **~le** ['kɜ:dl] свёртываться [сверну́ться]
cure [kjʊə] **1.** лече́ние; сре́дство; **2.** [вы́]лечи́ть, излечивать [-чи́ть]; *meat* [за]копти́ть
curfew ['kɜ:fju:] коменда́нтский час
curio ['kjʊərɪəʊ] ре́дкая антиква́рная вещь *f*; **~sity** [kjʊərɪ'ɒsətɪ] любопы́тство; ре́дкая вещь; *f*; **~us** ['kjʊərɪəs] любопы́тный; пытли́вый; стра́нный; ***~ly enough*** как э́то ни стра́нно
curl [kɜ:l] **1.** ло́кон, завито́к; *pl.* ку́дри *f/pl.* **2.** ви́ться; *of smoke* клуби́ться; **~y** ['kɜ:lɪ] кудря́вый, выю́щийся
currant ['kʌrənt] сморо́дина; кори́нка
curren|cy ['kʌrənsɪ] *fin.* де́ньги *f/pl.*, валю́та; ***hard*** (***soft***) **~** конверти́руемая (неконверти́руемая) валю́та; **~t** [~ənt] **1.** □ теку́щий; *opinion, etc.* ходя́чий; **2.** пото́к; *in sea* тече́ние; *el.* ток
curriculum [kə'rɪkjələm] уче́бный план
curry[1] ['kʌrɪ] ка́рри *n*
curry[2] [~]: **~ *favo*(*u*)*r with*** зайскивать пе́ред (Т)
curse [kɜ:s] **1.** прокля́тие; руга́тельство; *fig.* бич, бе́дствие; **2.** проклина́ть [-кля́сть]; руга́ться; **~d** ['kɜ:sɪd] □ прокля́тый
cursory ['kɜ:sərɪ] бе́глый, бы́стрый; ***give a ~ glance*** пробежа́ть глаза́ми
curt [kɜ:t] *answer* ре́зкий
curtail [kɜ:'teɪl] укора́чивать [-роти́ть]; уре́з(ыв)ать; *fig.* сокраща́ть [сократи́ть]
curtain ['kɜ:tn] **1.** занаве́ска; *thea.* за́навес; **2.** занаве́шивать [-ве́сить]
curv|ature ['kɜ:vətʃə] кривизна́; **~e** [kɜ:v] **1.** *math.* крива́я; *of road, etc.* изги́б; **2.** повора́чивать [-верну́ть]; изгиба́ть(ся) [изогну́ть(ся)]; *of path, etc.* ви́ться
cushion ['kʊʃn] **1.** поду́шка; **2.** *on falling* смягча́ть [-чи́ть] уда́р
custody ['kʌstədɪ] опе́ка, попече́ние; ***take into ~*** задержа́ть, аресто́вать
custom ['kʌstəm] обы́чай; (*habit*) привы́чка; клиенту́ра; **~s** *pl.* тамо́жня; (*duties*) тамо́женные по́шлины *f/pl.*; **~ary** [~ərɪ] □ обы́чный; **~er** [~ə] покупа́тель *m*, -ница *f*; клие́нт *m*, -ка *f*; **~s examination** тамо́женный досмо́тр; **~s house** тамо́жня
cut [kʌt] **1.** разре́з, поре́з; *of clothes* покро́й; ***short ~*** коро́ткий путь *m*; **2.** [*irr.*] *v/t.* [от]ре́зать; разре́зать [-реза́ть]; *hair* [по]стри́чь; *precious stone* [от]шлифова́ть; *grass* [с]коси́ть; *teeth* проре́з(ыв)а́ться; ***~ short*** оборва́ть [обрыва́ть]; ***~ down*** сокраща́ть [-рати́ть]; ***~ out*** выреза́ть [вы́резать]; *dress* [с]крои́ть; *fig.* вытесня́ть [вы́теснить]; ***be ~ out for*** быть сло́вно со́зданным для (Р); *v/i.* ре́зать; ***~ in*** вмешиваться [-ша́ться]; ***it ~s both ways*** па́лка о двух конца́х
cute [kju:t] □ *coll.* хи́трый; *Am.* ми́лый, привлека́тельный
cutlery ['kʌtlərɪ] нож, ножевы́е изде́лия; столо́вые прибо́ры
cutlet ['kʌtlɪt] отбивна́я (котле́та)
cut|out *el.* автомати́ческий выключа́тель *m*, предохрани́тель *m*; **~ter** ['kʌtər] *cutting tool* резе́ц; *chopping knife* реза́к; *naut.* ка́тер; **~ting** ['kʌtɪŋ] **1.** □ о́стрый, ре́зкий; язви́тельный; **2.** ре́зание; *of clothes* кро́йка; *bot.* черено́к
cyber|netics [saɪbə'netɪks] киберне́тика; **~space** ['saɪbəspeɪs] виртуа́льная реа́льность
cycl|e ['saɪkl] **1.** цикл (*a. tech.*); круг; (*bicycle*) велосипе́д; **2.** е́здить на велосипе́де; **~ist** [~ɪst] велосипеди́ст *m*, -ка *f*
cyclone ['saɪkləʊn] цикло́н
cylinder ['sɪlɪndə] *geometry* ци-

ли́ндр
cymbal ['sɪmbl] *mus.* таре́лки *f/pl.*
cynic ['sɪnɪk] ци́ник; **~al** [~l] ци́ничный
cypress ['saɪprəs] *bot.* кипари́с
czar [zɑː] царь
Czech [tʃək] **1.** чех *m*, че́шка *f*; **2.** че́шский

D

dab [dæb] **1.** *with brush* мазо́к; *of colour* пятно́; **2.** слегка́ прикаса́ться, прикла́дывать (В); де́лать лёгкие мазки́ на (П)
dabble ['dæbl] плеска́ть(ся); *hands, feet etc.* болта́ть нога́ми *и т.д.* в воде́; занима́ться чем-л. пове́рхностно
dad [dæd], **~dy** ['dædɪ] *coll.* па́па
daffodil ['dæfədɪl] жёлтый нарци́сс
dagger ['dægə] кинжа́л; ***be at ~s drawn*** быть на ножа́х (с Т)
dahlia ['deɪlɪə] георги́н
daily ['deɪlɪ] **1.** *adv.* ежедне́вно; **2.** ежедне́вный; *cares etc.* повседне́вный; **3.** ежедне́вная газе́та
dainty ['deɪntɪ] **1.** □ ла́комый; изя́щный; изы́сканный; **2.** ла́комство, деликате́с
dairy ['deərɪ] *shop* магази́н моло́чных проду́ктов
daisy ['deɪzɪ] маргари́тка
dale [deɪl] доли́на, дол
dally ['dælɪ] зря теря́ть вре́мя
dam [dæm] **1.** да́мба, плоти́на; **2.** запру́живать [-уди́ть]
damage ['dæmɪdʒ] **1.** вред; повреждéние; (*loss*) уще́рб; **~s** *pl. law* уще́рб; компенса́ция (за причинённый уще́рб); **2.** поврежда́ть [-еди́ть], [ис]по́ртить
damn [dæm] проклина́ть [-ля́сть]; (*censure*) осужда́ть [осуди́ть]; (*swear at*) руга́ться
damnation [dæm'neɪʃn] *int.* прокля́тие; осужде́ние
damp [dæmp] **1.** сы́рость *f*, вла́жность *f*; **2.** вла́жный, сыро́й; **~en** ['dæmpən] [на]мочи́ть; *fig.* обескура́жи(ва)ть
danc|e [dɑːns] **1.** та́нец; та́нцы *m/pl.* **2.** танцева́ть; **~er** [~ə] танцо́р, танцо́вщик *m*, -и́ца *f*; **~ing** [~ɪŋ] та́нцы *m/pl.*; пля́ска; *attr.* танцева́льный; ***~ partner*** партнёр, да́ма
dandelion ['dændɪlaɪən] одува́нчик
dandle ['dændl] [по]кача́ть (на рука́х)
dandruff ['dændrʌf] пе́рхоть *f*
dandy ['dændɪ] **1.** щёголь *m*; **2.** *Am. sl.* первокла́ссный
Dane [deɪn] датча́нин *m*, -ча́нка *f*
danger ['deɪndʒə] опа́сность *f*; **~ous** ['deɪndʒrəs] □ опа́сный
dangle ['dæŋgl] висе́ть, свиса́ть [сви́снуть]; *legs* болта́ть (Т)
Danish ['deɪnɪʃ] да́тский
dar|e [deər] *v/i.* [по]сме́ть; отва́жи(ва)ться; *v/t.* пыта́ться подби́ть; **~edevil** смельча́к, сорвиголова́ *m*; **~ing** ['deərɪŋ] **1.** □ сме́лый, отва́жный; **2.** сме́лость *f*, отва́га
dark [dɑːk] **1.** тёмный; *skin* сму́глый; (*hidden*) та́йный; *look etc.* мра́чный; ***~ horse*** тёмная лоша́дка; **2.** темнота́, тьма; неве́дение; ***keep s.o. in the ~*** держа́ть кого́-л. в неве́дении; ***keep s.th. ~*** держа́ть в та́йне; **~en** ['dɑːkən] [с]темне́ть; [по]мрачне́ть; **~ness** ['dɑːknɪs] темнота́, тьма
darling ['dɑːlɪŋ] **1.** люби́мец (-мица); **2.** ми́лый, люби́мый
darn [dɑːn] [за]што́пать
dart [dɑːt] **1.** *in game* стрела́; (*sudden movement*) прыжо́к, рыво́к; **2.** *v/i. fig.* мча́ться стрело́й
dash [dæʃ] **1.** *of wave etc.* уда́р; (*rush*) стреми́тельное движе́ние; (*dart*) рыво́к; *fig.* при́месь *f*, чу́точка; *typ.* тире́ *n indecl.* **2.** *v/t.* броса́ть [бро́сить]; разби́(ва́)ть; *v/i.*

броса́ться [бро́ситься]; ***I'll have to*** **~** мне ну́жно бежа́ть; **~board** *mot.* прибо́рная доска́; **~ing** ['dæʃɪŋ] □ лихо́й

data ['deɪtə] *pl., Am. a. sg.* да́нные *n/pl.*; фа́кты *m/pl.*; **~ *bank*** банк да́нных; **~ *processing*** обрабо́тка да́нных

date¹ [deɪt] **1.** да́та, число́; *coll.* свида́ние; ***out of*** **~** устаре́лый; ***up to*** **~** нове́йший; совреме́нный; **2.** дати́ровать *(im)pf.*; *Am. coll.* усла́вливаться [-о́виться] с (T) (о встре́че); име́ть свида́ние

date² [~] *bot.* фи́ник

daub [dɔːb] **1.** [вы́-, из-, на]ма́зать; [на]малева́ть; **2.** мазня́

daughter ['dɔːtə] дочь *f*; **~-in-law** [~rɪnlɔː] неве́стка, сноха́

daunt [dɔːnt] устраша́ть [-ши́ть], запу́гивать [-га́ть]; **~less** ['dɔːntlɪs] неустраши́мый, бесстра́шный

dawdle ['dɔːdl] *coll.* безде́льничать

dawn [dɔːn] **1.** рассве́т, у́тренняя заря́; *fig.* заря́; **2.** света́ть

day [deɪ] день *m*; *(mst.* **~s** *pl.)* жизнь *f*; **~ *off*** выходно́й день *m*; ***every other*** **~** че́рез день; ***the*** **~ *after tomorrow*** послеза́втра; ***the other*** **~** на днях; неда́вно; **~break** рассве́т; **~dream** мечта́ть, гре́зить наяву́

daze [deɪz] ошеломля́ть [-ми́ть]

dazzle ['dæzl] ослепля́ть [-пи́ть]

dead [ded] **1.** мёртвый; *flowers* увя́дший; *(numbed)* онеме́вший; *silence etc.* по́лный; ***come to a*** **~ *stop*** ре́зко останови́ться; **~ *end*** тупи́к; **2.** *adv.* по́лно, соверше́нно; **~ *against*** реши́тельно про́тив; **3.** ***the*** **~** мёртвые *m/pl.*; ***in the*** **~ *of night*** глубо́кой но́чью; **~en** ['dedn] лиша́ть(ся) си́лы; *sound* заглуша́ть [-ши́ть]; **~lock** *fig.* тупи́к; **~ly** [~lɪ] смерте́льный; *weapon* смертоно́сный

deaf [def] □ глухо́й; **~en** [defn] оглуша́ть [-ши́ть]

deal [diːl] **1.** *(agreement)* соглаше́ние; *(business agreement)* сде́лка; ***a good*** **~** мно́го; ***a great*** **~** о́чень мно́го; **2.** *[irr.] v/t. (distribute)* разд(ав)а́ть; распределя́ть [-ли́ть]; *at cards* сдава́ть [сдать]; *v/i.* торгова́ть; **~ *with*** обходи́ться [обойти́сь] *or* поступа́ть [-пи́ть] с (T); име́ть де́ло с (T); **~er** ['diːlə] ди́лер, торго́вец; **~ing** ['diːlɪŋ] *(mst.* **~s** *pl.)*: ***have*** **~s *with*** вести́ дела́ (с T); **~t** [delt] *pt. и pt. p. от* **~**

dean [diːn] настоя́тель собо́ра; *univ.* дека́н

dear [dɪə] **1.** дорого́й *(a. = costly)*, ми́лый; *(in business letter)* (глубоко)уважа́емый; **2.** прекра́сный челове́к; **3.** *coll.* ***oh*** **~!**, **~ *me!*** Го́споди!

death [deθ] смерть *f*; **~ duty** нало́г на насле́дство; **~ly** [~lɪ]: **~ *pale*** бле́дный как смерть; **~ rate** сме́ртность *f*; **~ trap** опа́сное ме́сто

debar [dɪ'bɑː] [вос]препя́тствовать; не допуска́ть [-сти́ть]; *(exclude)* исключа́ть [-чи́ть]; *from voting etc.* лиша́ть пра́ва

debase [dɪ'beɪs] унижа́ть [-и́зить]; снижа́ть ка́чество (P), курс (валю́ты)

debat|able [dɪ'beɪtəbl] □ спо́рный; дискуссио́нный; **~e** [dɪ'beɪt] **1.** диску́ссия; пре́ния *n/pl.*, деба́ты *m/pl.*; **2.** обсужда́ть [-уди́ть]; [по]спо́рить; *(ponder)* обду́м(ыв)ать

debauch [dɪ'bɔːtʃ] **1.** развра́т; *(carouse)* попо́йка; **2.** развраща́ть [-рати́ть]

debilitate [dɪ'bɪlɪteɪt] *(weaken)* ослабля́ть [-а́бить]

debit ['debɪt] *fin.* **1.** де́бет; **2.** дебетова́ть *(im)pf.*, вноси́ть в де́бет

debris ['deɪbriː] разва́лины *f/pl.*; обло́мки *m/pl.*

debt [det] долг; **~or** ['detə] должни́к *m*, -и́ца *f*

decade ['dekeɪd] десятиле́тие; *of one's age* деся́ток

decadence ['dekədəns] упа́док; *in art* декаде́нтство

decant [dɪ'kænt] сце́живать [сцеди́ть]; **~er** [~ə] графи́н

decay [dɪ'keɪ] **1.** гние́ние; разложе́ние; *of teeth* разруше́ние; ка́риес; ***fall into*** **~** *of building* [об]ветша́ть; *fig.* приходи́ть [прийти́] в упа́док; **2.** [с]гнить; разлага́ться [-ложи́ться]

decease [dɪ'siːs] *part. law* смерть *f*, кончи́на; **~d** [~t] поко́йный

deceit [dɪ'siːt] обма́н; **~ful** [~fʊl]

лжи́вый; (*deceptive*) обма́нчивый
deceiv|e [dɪ'siːv] обма́нывать [-ну́ть]; **~er** [~ə] обма́нщик (-ица)
December [dɪ'sembə] дека́брь *m*
decen|cy ['diːsnsɪ] прили́чие; **~t** [~nt] □ прили́чный; *kind, well-behaved coll.* поря́дочный; *coll.* сла́вный; ***it's very ~ of you*** о́чень любе́зно с ва́шей стороны́
deception [dɪ'sepʃn] обма́н; ложь *f*
decide [dɪ'saɪd] реша́ть(ся) [решить(ся)]; принима́ть реше́ние; **~d** [~ɪd] (*clear-cut*) □ определённый; (*unmistakable*) бесспо́рный
decimal ['desɪml] **1.** десяти́чный; **2.** десяти́чная дробь *f*
decipher [dɪ'saɪfə] расшифро́вывать [-ова́ть]; *poor handwriting* разбира́ть [разобра́ть]
decisi|on [dɪ'sɪʒn] реше́ние (*a. law*); **~ve** [dɪ'saɪsɪv] *conclusive* реша́ющий; *resolute* реши́тельный; **~iveness** реши́тельность *f*
deck [dek] *naut.* па́луба; *Am. cards* коло́да; **~chair** шезло́нг
declar|able [dɪ'kleərəbl] подлежа́щий деклара́ции; **~ation** [deklə'reɪʃn] заявле́ние; деклара́ция (*a. fin.*); ***customs ~*** тамо́женная деклара́ция; **~e** [dɪ'kleər] объявля́ть [-ви́ть]; заявля́ть [-ви́ть]; выска́зываться [вы́сказаться] (***for*** за В, ***against*** про́тив Р); *to customs officials* предъявля́ть [-ви́ть]
decline [dɪ'klaɪn] **1.** (*fall*) паде́ние; *of strength* упа́док; *in prices* сниже́ние; *of health* ухудше́ние; *of life* зака́т; **2.** *v/t. an offer* отклоня́ть [-ни́ть]; *gr.* [про]склоня́ть; *v/i.* приходи́ть в упа́док; *of health etc.* ухудша́ться [уху́дшиться]
decode [diː'kəʊd] расшифро́вывать [-рова́ть]
decompose [diːkəm'pəʊz] разлага́ть(ся) [-ложи́ть(ся)]; [с]гнить
decorat|e ['dekəreɪt] украша́ть [укра́сить]; (*confer medal, etc. on*) награжда́ть [-ди́ть]; **~ion** [dekə'reɪʃn] украше́ние; о́рден, знак отли́чия; **~ive** ['dekərətɪv] декорати́вный
decor|ous ['dekərəs] □ присто́йный; **~um** [dɪ'kɔːrəm] этике́т
decoy [dɪ'kɔɪ] прима́нка (*a. fig.*)
decrease 1. ['diːkriːs] уменьше́ние, пониже́ние; **2.** [dɪ'kriːs] уменьша́ть(ся) [уме́ньшить(ся)], снижа́ть [-и́зить]
decree [dɪ'kriː] **1.** *pol.* ука́з, декре́т, постановле́ние; *law* реше́ние; **2.** постановля́ть [-ви́ть]
decrepit [dɪ'krepɪt] дря́хлый
dedicat|e ['dedɪkeɪt] посвяща́ть [-яти́ть]; **~ion** [dedɪ'keɪʃn] (*devotion*) пре́данность *f*; (*inscription*) посвяще́ние; ***work with ~*** по́лностью отдава́ть себя́ рабо́те
deduce [dɪ'djuːs] [с]де́лать вы́вод; заключа́ть [-чи́ть]
deduct [dɪ'dʌkt] вычита́ть [вы́честь]; **~ion** [dɪ'dʌkʃn] вы́чет; (*conclusion*) вы́вод, заключе́ние; *comm.* ски́дка
deed [diːd] **1.** де́йствие; посту́пок; *law* акт; ***~ of purchase*** догово́р ку́пли/прода́жи; **2.** *Am.* передава́ть по а́кту
deem [diːm] *v/t.* счита́ть [счесть]; *v/i.* полага́ть
deep [diːp] **1.** глубо́кий; *colo(u)r* густо́й; **2.** *poet.* мо́ре, океа́н; **~en** ['diːpən] углубля́ть(ся) [-би́ть(ся)]; уси́ливать(ся) [уси́лить(ся)]; **~-freeze** → ***freezer***; **~ness** [~nɪs] глубина́; **~-rooted** глубоко́ укорени́вшийся
deer [dɪə] оле́нь *m*
deface [dɪ'feɪs] обезобра́живать [-а́зить]
defam|ation [defə'meɪʃn] клевета́; **~e** [dɪ'feɪm] [о]клевета́ть
default [dɪ'fɔːlt] **1.** невыполне́ние обяза́тельств; не́явка; *comput.* автомати́ческий вы́бор; **2.** не выполня́ть обяза́тельства
defeat [dɪ'fiːt] **1.** пораже́ние; *of plans* расстро́йство; **2.** *mil., sport etc.* побежда́ть [-еди́ть]; расстра́ивать [-ро́ить]
defect [dɪ'fekt] недоста́ток; (*fault*) неиспра́вность *f*; дефе́кт, изъя́н; **~ive** [~tɪv] несоверше́нный, □ повреждённый; ***~ goods*** брако́ванные това́ры; ***mentally ~*** у́мственно отста́лый
defence → ***defense***
defend [dɪ'fend] обороня́ть(ся), [-ни́ть(ся)], защища́ть на суде́;

~ant [~ənt] *law* подсуди́мый; *civil* отве́тчик; **~er** [~ə] защи́тник
defense [dɪ'fens] оборо́на, защи́та; **~less** [~lɪs] беззащи́тный
defensive [dɪ'fensɪv] **1.** оборо́на; **2.** оборо́нный, оборони́тельный
defer [dɪ'fɜː] откла́дывать [отложи́ть]; отсро́чи(ва)ть
defian|ce [dɪ'faɪəns] (*challenge*) вы́зов; (*disobedience*) неповинове́ние; (*scorn*) пренебреже́ние; **~t** [~ənt] □ вызыва́ющий
deficien|cy [dɪ'fɪʃənsɪ] недоста́ток, нехва́тка; **~t** [~ənt] недоста́точный; несоверше́нный
deficit ['defɪsɪt] недочёт; недоста́ча; дефици́т
defile [dɪ'faɪl] загрязня́ть [-ни́ть]
defin|e [dɪ'faɪn] определя́ть [-ли́ть]; дава́ть характери́стику; (*show limits of*) оче́рчивать [-рти́ть], обознача́ть; **~ite** ['defɪnɪt] □ определённый; (*exact*) то́чный; **~ition** [defɪ'nɪʃn] определе́ние; **~itive** [dɪ'fɪnɪtɪv] □ (*final*) оконча́тельный
deflect [dɪ'flekt] отклоня́ть(ся) [-ни́ть(ся)]
deform|ed [dɪ'fɔːmd] изуро́дованный; искажённый; **~ity** [dɪ'fɔːmətɪ] уро́дство
defraud [dɪ'frɔːd] обма́нывать [-ну́ть]; выма́нивать (*of* В)
defray [dɪ'freɪ] опла́чивать [оплати́ть]
defrost [diː'frɒst] отта́ивать [-а́ять]; размора́живать [-ро́зить]
deft [deft] □ ло́вкий, иску́сный
defy [dɪ'faɪ] вызыва́ть [вы́звать]; броса́ть [бро́сить] вы́зов; вести́ себя́ вызыва́юще; (*flout*) пренебрега́ть [-бре́чь] (Т)
degenerate [dɪ'dʒenəreɪt] вырожда́ться [вы́родиться]
degrad|ation [degrə'deɪʃn] деграда́ция; **~e** [dɪ'greɪd] *v/t.* (*lower in rank*) понижа́ть [пони́зить]; (*abase*) унижа́ть [уни́зить]
degree [dɪ'griː] (*unit of measurement*) гра́дус; (*step or stage in a process*) у́ровень *m*; сте́пень *f*; (*a. univ.*) зва́ние; ***honorary ~*** почётное зва́ние; ***by ~s*** постепе́нно; ***in no ~*** ничу́ть, ниско́лько; ***to some ~*** в изве́стной сте́пени
deign [deɪn] снисходи́ть [снизойти́]; соизволя́ть [-о́лить]; *usu. iron.* удоста́ивать [-сто́ить]
deity ['diːɪtɪ] божество́
deject|ed [dɪ'dʒektɪd] □ удручённый; угнетённый; **~ion** [dɪ'dʒekʃn] уны́ние
delay [dɪ'leɪ] **1.** заде́ржка; отсро́чка; **2.** *v/t.* заде́рживать [-жа́ть]; откла́дывать [отложи́ть]; ме́длить с (Т); *v/i.* ме́длить, ме́шкать
delega|te 1. ['delɪgət] делега́т, представи́тель(ница *f*) *m*; **2.** [~geɪt] делеги́ровать (*im*)*pf.*, поруча́ть [-чи́ть]; **~tion** [delɪ'geɪʃn] делега́ция
deliberat|e 1. [dɪ'lɪbəreɪt] *v/t.* обду́м(ыв)ать; взве́шивать [-е́сить]; обсужда́ть [обсуди́ть]; *v/i.* совеща́ться; **2.** [~rət] □ преднаме́ренный, умы́шленный; **~ion** [dɪlɪbə'reɪʃn] размышле́ние; обсужде́ние; осмотри́тельность *f*; ***act with ~*** де́йствовать с осмотри́тельностью
delica|cy ['delɪkəsɪ] делика́тность *f*; *food* ла́комство; утончённость *f*; не́жность *f*; **~te** [~kɪt] □ делика́тный; (*fragile*) хру́пкий; изя́щный; *work* иску́сный; чувстви́тельный; щепети́льный; **~tessen** [delɪkə'tesn] магази́н деликате́сов, гастроно́м
delicious [dɪ'lɪʃəs] восхити́тельный; о́чень вку́сный
delight [dɪ'laɪt] **1.** удово́льствие; восто́рг; наслажде́ние; **2.** восхища́ть [-ити́ть]; наслажда́ться [-ди́ться]; доставля́ть удово́льствие (*in* Т); ***be ~ed with*** быть в восто́рге (от Р); ***~ to*** *inf.* име́ть удово́льствие (+ *inf.*); **~ful** [~fʊl] □ *girl etc.* очарова́тельный; восхити́тельный
delinquent [dɪ'lɪŋkwənt]: ***juvenile ~*** несовершенноле́тний престу́пник
deliri|ous [dɪ'lɪrɪəs] находя́щийся в бреду́, вне себя́, в исступле́нии; ***~ with joy*** вне себя́ от ра́дости; **~um** [~əm] бред
deliver [dɪ'lɪvə] *newspapers etc.* доставля́ть [-а́вить]; *a speech* произноси́ть [-нести́]; *order* сда́(ва́)ть; *a blow* наноси́ть [нанести́] (*уда́р*); ***be***

D

~ed *med.* роди́ть; **~ance** [~rəns] освобожде́ние; (*rescue*) спасе́ние
delude [dɪ'lu:d] вводи́ть в заблужде́ние; (*deceive*) обма́нывать [-ну́ть]
deluge ['delju:dʒ] **1.** наводне́ние; (*rain*) ли́вень; *fig.* пото́к; **2.** затопля́ть [-пи́ть]; наводня́ть [-ни́ть] *a. fig.*
delus|ion [dɪ'lu:ʒn] заблужде́ние; иллю́зия; **~ive** [~sɪv] □ обма́нчивый; иллюзо́рный
demand [dɪ'mɑ:nd] **1.** тре́бование; потре́бность *f*; *comm.* спрос; ***be in great ~*** по́льзоваться больши́м спро́сом; **2.** [по]тре́бовать (Р)
demilitarize [di:'mɪlɪtəraɪz] демилитаризова́ть (*im*)*pf.*
demobilize [di:'məʊbɪlaɪz] демобилизова́ть (*im*)*pf.*
democra|cy [dɪ'mɒkrəsɪ] демокра́тия; **~tic(al** □) [demə'krætɪk(əl)] демократи́ческий
demolish [dɪ'mɒlɪʃ] разруша́ть [-ру́шить]; (*pull down*) сноси́ть [снести́]
demon ['di:mən] де́мон, дья́вол
demonstrat|e ['demənstreɪt] [про-] демонстри́ровать; (*prove*) дока́зывать [-за́ть]; **~ion** [demən'streɪʃn] демонстра́ция; доказа́тельство; **~ive** [dɪ'mɒnstrətɪv] □ *person, behaviour* экспанси́вный; *gr.* указа́тельный
demoralize [dɪ'mɒrəlaɪz] деморализова́ть
demure [dɪ'mjʊə] □ скро́мный; *smile* засте́нчивый
den [den] ло́говище; берло́га; прито́н
denial [dɪ'naɪəl] отрица́ние; *official* опроверже́ние; (*refusal*) отка́з
denomination [dɪnɒmɪ'neɪʃn] *eccl.* вероиспове́дание; се́кта
denote [dɪ'nəʊt] означа́ть *impf.*, обознача́ть [-на́чить]
denounce [dɪ'naʊns] (*expose*) разоблача́ть [-чи́ть]; *to police* доноси́ть; *termination of a treaty, etc.* денонси́ровать (*im*)*pf.*
dens|e [dens] □ густо́й; пло́тный (*a. phys.*); *fig.* глу́пый, тупо́й; **~ity** ['densətɪ] густота́; пло́тность *f*
dent [dent] **1.** вмя́тина; **2.** вда́вливать [вдави́ть]; *v/i.* [по]гну́ться
dentist ['dentɪst] зубно́й врач
denture ['dentʃə] *mst. pl.* зубно́й проте́з
denunciation [dɪnʌnsɪ'eɪʃn] доно́с; обличе́ние, обвине́ние
deny [dɪ'naɪ] отрица́ть; отка́зываться [-за́ться] от (Р); (*refuse to give, allow*) отка́зывать [-за́ть] в (П); ***there is no ~ing*** сле́дует призна́ть
deodorant [di:'əʊdərənt] дезодора́нт
depart [dɪ'pɑ:t] *v/i.* уходи́ть [уйти́], уезжа́ть [уе́хать], отбы́(ва́)ть, отправля́ться [-а́виться]; отступа́ть [-пи́ть] (***from*** от Р); **~ment** [~mənt] *univ.* отделе́ние, факульте́т; *of science* о́бласть *f*, о́трасль; *in shop* отде́л; *Am.* министе́рство; ***State*** ♀ министе́рство иностра́нных дел; ***~ store*** универма́г; **~ure** [dɪ'pɑ:tʃə] отъе́зд; ухо́д; *rail.* отправле́ние; (*deviation*) отклоне́ние
depend [dɪ'pend]: ***~*** (***up***)***on*** зави́сеть от (Р); *coll.* ***it ~s*** смотря́ по обстоя́тельствам; ***you can ~ on him*** на него́ мо́жно положи́ться; **~able** [~əbl] надёжный; **~ant** [~ənt] иждиве́нец *m*, -нка *f*; **~ence** [~əns] зави́симость *f*; (*trust*) дове́рие; **~ent** [~ənt] □ (***on***) зави́сящий (от Р)
depict [dɪ'pɪkt] изобража́ть [-рази́ть]; *fig.* опи́сывать [-са́ть]
deplete [dɪ'pli:t] истоща́ть [-щи́ть]
deplor|able [dɪ'plɔ:rəbl] □ приско́рбный, заслу́живающий сожале́ния; *state* плаче́вный; **~e** [dɪ'plɔ:] (*disapprove of*) порица́ть; сожале́ть о (П)
deport [dɪ'pɔ:t] депорти́ровать
depose [dɪ'pəʊz] *from office* смеща́ть [смести́ть]; (*dethrone*) сверга́ть [све́ргнуть]
deposit [dɪ'pɒzɪt] **1.** *geol.* отложе́ние; за́лежь *f*; *fin.* вклад; депози́т; зада́ток; ***~ account*** депози́тный счёт; **2.** класть [положи́ть]; депони́ровать (*im*)*pf.*; дава́ть [дать] зада́ток; **~or** [dɪ'pɒzɪtə] вкла́дчик *m*, -ица *f*, депози́тор
depot 1. ['depəʊ] *rail.* депо́ *n indecl.*; *storage place* склад; **2.** ['di:pəʊ] *Am. rail.* железнодоро́жная ста́нция

deprave [dɪ'preɪv] развраща́ть [-ра-ти́ть]
depreciat|e [dɪ'priːʃɪeɪt] обесце́-ни(ва)ть; **~ion** [dɪpriːʃɪ'eɪʃn] сни-же́ние сто́имости; обесце́нение; амортиза́ция
depress [dɪ'pres] угнета́ть *impf.*; подавля́ть [-ви́ть]; **~ed** [~t] *fig.* уны́лый; **~ion** [dɪ'preʃn] угнетён-ное состоя́ние; *geogr.* впа́дина; *econ.* депре́ссия
deprive [dɪ'praɪv] лиша́ть [лиши́ть] (***of*** P)
depth [depθ] глубина́; ***be out of one's ~*** быть не под си́лу, быть недосту́пным понима́нию
deput|ation [depjʊ'teɪʃn] делега́-ция; **~y** ['depjʊtɪ] делега́т; депута́т; замести́тель(ница *f*) *m*
derange [dɪ'reɪndʒ] *plans etc.* рас-стра́ивать [-ро́ить]; (*put out of or-der*) приводи́ть в беспоря́док
derelict ['derəlɪkt] *ship* поки́нутый; *house* (за)бро́шенный
deri|de [dɪ'raɪd] осме́ивать [-ея́ть], высме́ивать [вы́смеять]; **~sion** [dɪ-'rɪʒn] высме́ивание; **~sive** [dɪ'raɪ-sɪv] □ издева́тельский; *scornful* насме́шливый
derive [dɪ'raɪv] (*originate*) происхо-ди́ть [-изойти́]; *benefit* извлека́ть [-вле́чь] (***from*** от P)
derogatory [dɪ'rɒgətrɪ] пренебре-жи́тельный
descend [dɪ'send] спуска́ться [спу-сти́ться]; сходи́ть [сойти́]; *ae.* сни-жа́ться [сни́зиться]; *from a person* происходи́ть [-изойти́] (***from*** из P); ***~ (up)on*** обру́ши(ва)ться на (B); **~ant** [~ənt] пото́мок
descent [dɪ'sent] спуск; сниже́ние; (*slope*) склон; происхожде́ние
describe [dɪ'skraɪb] опи́сывать [-са́ть]
description [dɪ'skrɪpʃn] описа́ние; ***of every ~*** са́мые ра́зные
desert[1] [dɪ'zɜːt]: ***get one's ~s*** получи́ть по заслу́гам
desert[2] **1.** ['dezət] пусты́ня; **2.** [dɪ-'zɜːt] *v/t.* (*leave*) броса́ть [бро́сить]; (*go away*) покида́ть [поки́нуть]; *v/i.* дезерти́ровать (*im*)*pf.*; **~ed** [~ɪd] *street* пусты́нный; (*neglected*) за-бро́шенный; (*abandoned*) поки́ну-тый; **~er** [~ə] дезерти́р; **~ion** [~ʃn] дезерти́рство; *spouse's* ухо́д
deserv|e [dɪ'zɜːv] заслу́живать [-жи́ть]; **~edly** [~ɪdlɪ] заслу́женно; **~ing** [~ɪŋ] заслу́живающий; дос-то́йный (***of*** P)
design [dɪ'zaɪn] **1.** (*intention*) за́мы-сел, наме́рение, план; *arch.* про-е́кт; *tech.* диза́йн; (*pattern*) узо́р; **2.** предназнача́ть [-зна́чить]; заду́-м(ыв)ать; [с]проекти́ровать; *ma-chinery* [с]конструи́ровать
designat|e ['dezɪgneɪt] определя́ть [-ли́ть]; (*mark out*) обознача́ть [-зна́чить]; (*appoint*) назнача́ть [-зна́чить]
designer [dɪ'zaɪnə] (*engineer*) конс-тру́ктор; диза́йнер; ***dress ~*** моде-лье́р
desir|able [dɪ'zaɪərəbl] □ жела́тель-ный; **~e** [dɪ'zaɪə] **1.** жела́ние; тре́-бование; **2.** [по]жела́ть (P); [по-] тре́бовать (P); ***leave much to be ~d*** оставля́ть жела́ть лу́чшего; **~ous** [~rəs] жела́ющий (***of*** P); ***be ~ of knowing*** стреми́ться/жела́ть узна́ть
desk [desk] пи́сьменный стол; ***~ diary*** насто́льный календа́рь; ***~top publishing*** насто́льное изда́тельст-во
desolat|e 1. ['desəleɪt] опустоша́ть [-ши́ть]; разоря́ть [-ри́ть]; **2.** [~lət] □ опустошённый; несча́стный; одино́кий; **~ion** [desə'leɪʃn] опус-тоше́ние; одино́чество
despair [dɪ'speə] **1.** отча́яние; ***drive s.o. to ~*** доводи́ть [-вести́] кого́-л. до отча́яния; **2.** отча́иваться [-ча́-яться]; теря́ть наде́жду (***of*** на B); **~ing** [~rɪŋ] □ отча́ивающийся
despatch → ***dispatch***
desperat|e ['despərət] □ *effort etc.* отча́янный; *state* безнадёжный; *adv.* отча́янно, стра́шно; **~ion** [des-pə'reɪʃn] отча́яние
despise [dɪ'spaɪz] презира́ть
despite [dɪ'spaɪt] *prp.* несмотря́ на (B)
despondent [dɪ'spɒndənt] □ по-да́вленный, удручённый
dessert [dɪ'zɜːt] десе́рт; *attr.* де-се́ртный
destin|ation [destɪ'neɪʃn] (*purpose,*

end) назначе́ние; ме́сто назначе́ния; **~e** ['destɪn] предназнача́ть [-зна́чить]; **be ~d** (*be fated*) предопределя́ть [-ли́ть]; **~y** [~tɪnɪ] судьба́
destitute ['destɪtjuːt] нужда́ющийся; лишённый (**of** Р)
D
destroy [dɪ'strɔɪ] уничтожа́ть [-о́жить]; истребля́ть [-би́ть]; *buildings, etc.* разруша́ть [-ру́шить]; **~er** [~ə] *warship* эсми́нец
destruct|ion [dɪ'strʌkʃn] разруше́ние; уничтоже́ние; **~ive** [~tɪv] □ разруши́тельный; па́губный; вре́дный
detach [dɪ'tætʃ] отделя́ть [-ли́ть]; разъединя́ть [-ни́ть]; (*tear off*) отрыва́ть [оторва́ть]; **~ed** [~t] отде́льный; *fig.* беспристра́стный; **~ment** [~mənt] *mil.* отря́д; *fig.* беспристра́стность *f*
detail ['diːteɪl] подро́бность *f*, дета́ль *f*; ***in ~*** дета́льно, подро́бно; ***go into ~s*** вника́ть (вдава́ться) в подро́бности
detain [dɪ'teɪn] заде́рживать [-жа́ть] (*a. by the police*); ***he was ~ed at work*** он задержа́лся на рабо́те
detect [dɪ'tekt] обнару́жи(ва)ть; (*notice*) замеча́ть [-е́тить]; **~ion** [dɪ'tekʃn] обнаруже́ние; *of crime* рассле́дование; **~ive** [~tɪv] **1.** детекти́в, операти́вник; **2.** детекти́вный
detention [dɪ'tənʃn] (*holding*) задержа́ние; (*custody*) содержа́ние под аре́стом; (*confinement*) заключе́ние
deter [dɪ'tɜː] уде́рживать [-жа́ть] (***from*** от Р)
deteriorat|e [dɪ'tɪərɪəreɪt] ухудша́ть(ся) [уху́дшить(ся)]; [ис]по́ртить(ся); **~ion** [dɪtɪərɪə'reɪʃn] ухудше́ние
determin|ation [dɪtɜːmɪ'neɪʃn] определе́ние; (*firmness*) реши́тельность *f*; **~e** [dɪ'tɜːmɪn] *v/t.* определя́ть [-ли́ть]; реша́ть [реши́ть]; *v/i.* реша́ться [реши́ться]; **~ed** [~d] реши́тельный
detest [dɪ'test] ненави́деть; пита́ть отвраще́ние к (Д); **~able** [~əbl] отврати́тельный
detonate ['detəneɪt] детони́ровать; взрыва́ть(ся) [взорва́ть(ся)]
detour ['diː'tʊə] око́льный путь *m*; объе́зд; ***make a ~*** сде́лать *pf.* крюк
detract [dɪ'trækt] умаля́ть [-ли́ть], уменьша́ть [уме́ньшить]
detriment ['detrɪmənt] уще́рб, вред
devalue [diː'væljuː] обесце́ни(ва)ть
devastat|e ['devəsteɪt] опустоша́ть [-ши́ть]; разоря́ть [-ри́ть]; **~ion** [devə'steɪʃn] опустоше́ние
develop [dɪ'veləp] разви́(ва́)ть(ся); *mineral resources* разраба́тывать [-бо́тать]; *phot.* проявля́ть [-ви́ть]; **~ment** [~mənt] разви́тие; разрабо́тка; (*event*) собы́тие
deviat|e ['diːvɪeɪt] отклоня́ться [-ни́ться]; **~ion** [diːvɪ'eɪʃn] отклоне́ние
device [dɪ'vaɪs] *tech.* приспособле́ние, устро́йство; (*way, method, trick*) приём; ***leave a p. to his own ~s*** предоставля́ть челове́ка самому́ себе́
devil ['devl] дья́вол, чёрт, бес; **~ish** [~əlɪʃ] □ дья́вольский, *coll.* черто́вский; **~ry** [~vlrɪ] чертовщи́на
devious ['diːvɪəs]: □ ***by ~ means*** нече́стным путём
devise [dɪ'vaɪz] приду́м(ыв)ать; изобрета́ть [-рести́]
devoid [dɪ'vɔɪd] (**of**) лишённый (Р)
devot|e [dɪ'vəʊt] посвяща́ть [-яти́ть] (В/Д); **~ed** [~ɪd] □ пре́данный, лю́бящий; **~ion** [dɪ'vəʊʃn] пре́данность *f*, привя́занность *f*
devour [dɪ'vaʊə] пож(и)ра́ть; ***be ~ed with curiosity*** сгора́ть от любопы́тства
devout [dɪ'vaʊt] □ *supporter, etc.* пре́данный; *relig.* благочести́вый
dew [djuː] роса́; **~y** [~ɪ] роси́стый, покры́тый росо́й
dexter|ity [dek'sterətɪ] ло́вкость *f*; **~ous** ['dekstrəs] ло́вкий
diabolic(al □) [daɪə'bɒlɪk(əl)] дья́вольский; *fig.* жесто́кий, злой
diagnosis [daɪəg'nəʊsɪs] диа́гноз
diagram ['daɪəgræm] диагра́мма; схе́ма
dial ['daɪəl] **1.** *of clock, etc.* цифербла́т; *tech.* шкала́ (цифербла́тного ти́па); *tel.* диск; **2.** *tel.* набира́ть [-бра́ть] но́мер; позвони́ть *pf.*
dialect ['daɪəlekt] диале́кт, наре́чие
dialogue ['daɪəlɒg] диало́г; разгово́р

diameter [daɪ'æmɪtə] диáметр
diamond ['daɪəmənd] алмáз; *precious stone* бриллиáнт; ромб; **~s** [~s] *pl. cards*: бýбны *f/pl.*
diaper ['daɪəpər] (*Brt.*: *nappy*) пелёнка
diaphragm ['daɪəfræm] *anat.* диафрáгма *a. optics*
diarrh(o)ea [daɪə'rɪə] понóс
diary ['daɪərɪ] дневни́к
dice [daɪs] (*pl. om* ***die²***) игрáльные кóсти *f/pl.*
dictat|e 1. ['dɪkteɪt] (*order*) предписáние; *of conscience* велéние; *pol.* диктáт; **2.** [dɪk'teɪt] [про]диктовáть (*a. fig.*); предпи́сывать [-сáть]; **~ion** [dɪk'teɪʃn] *educ.* диктóвка, диктáнт; предписáние; **~orship** [dɪk'teɪtəʃɪp] диктатýра
diction ['dɪkʃn] ди́кция; **~ary** [~rɪ] словáрь *m*
did [dɪd] *pt. om* ***do***
die¹ [daɪ] умирáть [умерéть], скончáться *pf.*; *coll.* стрáстно желáть; ***~ away***, ***~ down*** *of sound* замирáть [-мерéть]; *of wind* затихáть [-и́хнуть]; *of flowers* увядáть [-я́нуть]; *of fire* угасáть [угáснуть]
die² [~] (*pl.* **dice**) игрáльная кость *f*; ***the ~ is cast*** жрéбий брóшен
diet ['daɪət] **1.** *customary* пи́ща; *med.* диéта; **2.** *v/t.* держáть на диéте; *v/i.* быть на диéте
differ ['dɪfə] различáться, отличáться; (*disagree*) не соглашáться [-ласи́ться], расходи́ться [разойти́сь] (***from*** с Т, ***in*** в П); ***tastes ~*** о вкýсах не спóрят; **~ence** ['dɪfrəns] рáзница; разли́чие; разноглáсие; *math.* рáзность *f*; ***it makes no ~ to me*** мне всё равнó; **~ent** [~nt] □ рáзный; другóй, не такóй (***from*** как), инóй; **~entiate** [dɪfə'renʃɪeɪt] различáть(ся) [-чи́ть(-ся)], отличáться [-чи́ть(ся)]
difficult ['dɪfɪkəlt] □ трýдный; **~y** [~ɪ] трýдность *f*; затруднéние
diffiden|ce ['dɪfɪdəns] (*lack of confidence*) неувéренность *f*; (*shyness*) застéнчивость *f*; **~t** [~dənt] неувéренный; застéнчивый
diffus|e 1. [dɪ'fjuːz] *fig.* распространя́ть [-ни́ть]; **2.** [dɪ'fjuːs] распространённый; *light* рассéянный; **~ion** [dɪ'fjuːʒn] распространéние; рассéивание; *of gas*, *liquids* диффýзия
dig [dɪg] **1.** [*irr.*] копáться; [вы́]копать; ры́ться; [вы́]рыть; **2.** *coll.* (*a cutting remark*) толчóк
digest 1. [dɪ'dʒest] *food* переваривать [-ри́ть]; *information*, *etc.* усвáивать [усвóить] (*a. fig.*); *v/i.* перевáриваться [-ри́ться]; усвáиваться [усвóиться]; **2.** ['daɪdʒest] (*literary*) дайджéст; **~ible** [dɪ'dʒestəbl] *fig.* удобовари́мый; легкó усвáиваемый (*a. fig.*); **~ion** [~tʃən] *of food* пищеварéние; *of knowledge* усвоéние
digital ['dɪdʒɪtl] цифровóй
dignif|ied ['dɪgnɪfaɪd] преиспóлненный достóинства; **~y** [~faɪ] *fig.* облагорáживать [-рóдить]
dignit|ary ['dɪgnɪtərɪ] санóвник; лицó, занимáющее высóкий пóст; *eccl.* иерáрх; **~y** [~tɪ] достóинство
digress [daɪ'gres] отклоня́ться [-ни́ться]
dike [daɪk] дáмба; плоти́на; (*ditch*) канáва
dilapidated [dɪ'læpɪdeɪtɪd] вéтхий, стáрый
dilate [daɪ'leɪt] расширя́ть(ся) [-ши́рить(ся)]
diligen|ce ['dɪlɪdʒəns] прилежáние, усéрдие; **~t** □ прилéжный, усéрдный
dill [dɪl] укрóп
dilute [daɪ'ljuːt] разбавля́ть [-бáвить]; разводи́ть [-вести́]
dim [dɪm] **1.** □ *light* тýсклый; *outlines*, *details* неясный; *eyesight* слáбый; *recollections* смýтный; *coll.* (*stupid*) тупóй; **2.** [по]тускнéть; [за]тумáнить(ся); ***~ one's headlights*** включи́ть бли́жний свет
dime [daɪm] *Am.* монéта в дéсять цéнтов
dimension [dɪ'menʃn] размéр; объём; измерéние
dimin|ish [dɪ'mɪnɪʃ] уменьшáть(ся) [умéньшить(ся)]; убы́(ва)ть; **~utive** [dɪ'mɪnjʊtɪv] □ миниатю́рный
dimple ['dɪmpl] я́мочка (на щекé)
din [dɪn] шум; грóхот
dine [daɪn] [по]обéдать; [по]ýжинать; **~r** ['daɪnə] обéдающий; *rail.* (*part. Am.*) вагóн-ресторáн

dinghy ['dɪŋgɪ] ма́ленькая ло́дка
dingy ['dɪndʒɪ] □ гря́зный
dining | car *rail.* ваго́н-рестора́н; **~ room** столо́вая
dinner ['dɪnər] обе́д; ***at ~*** за обе́дом; ***formal ~*** официа́льный обе́д

D

dint [dɪnt]: ***by ~ of*** посре́дством (Р)
dip [dɪp] **1.** *v/t.* погружа́ть [-узи́ть], окуна́ть [-ну́ть]; *brush* обма́кивать [-кну́ть]; *into pocket* су́нуть; *v/i.* погружа́ться [-узи́ться], окуна́ться [-ну́ться]; *of flag* приспуска́ть [-сти́ть]; *of road* спуска́ться [-сти́ться]; **2.** (*slope*) укло́н; купа́ние; ***have a ~*** искупа́ться
diploma [dɪ'pləʊmə] дипло́м; **~cy** [~sɪ] диплома́тия; **~t** ['dɪpləmæt] диплома́т; **~tic(al** □) [dɪplə'mætɪk(əl)] дипломати́ческий
dire ['daɪə] ужа́сный
direct [dɪ'rekt, daɪ-] **1.** □ прямо́й; (*immediate*) непосре́дственный; (*straightforward*) я́сный; откры́тый; ***~ current*** *el.* постоя́нный ток; ***~ train*** прямо́й по́езд; **2.** *adv.* = **~ly**; **3.** руководи́ть (Т); управля́ть (Т); направля́ть [-а́вить]; ука́зывать доро́гу (Д); **~ion** [dɪ'rekʃən, daɪ-] направле́ние; руково́дство; указа́ние; инстру́кция; **~ive** [dɪ'rektɪv] директи́ва; **~ly** [~lɪ] **1.** *adv.* пря́мо, непосре́дственно; неме́дленно; **2.** *cj.* как то́лько
director [dɪ'rektər, daɪ-] дире́ктор; *cine.* режиссёр; ***board of ~s*** сове́т директоро́в; **~ate** [~rɪt] дире́кция; правле́ние; **~y** [~rɪ] (телефо́нный) спра́вочник
dirt [dɜːt] грязь *f*; **~ cheap** *coll.* о́чень дешёвый; *adv.* по дешёвке; **~y** ['dɜːtɪ] **1.** □ гря́зный; *joke* неприли́чный; *weather* нена́стный; ***~ trick*** по́длый посту́пок; **2.** [за]па́чкать
disability [dɪsə'bɪlətɪ] нетрудоспосо́бность *f*; бесси́лие; физи́ческий недоста́ток; ***~ pension*** пе́нсия по нетрудоспосо́бности
disabled [dɪs'eɪbld] искале́ченный; (*unable to work*) нетрудоспосо́бный; ***~ veteran*** инвали́д войны́
disadvantage [dɪsəd'vɑːntɪdʒ] недоста́ток; невы́годное положе́ние; уще́рб; неудо́бство
disagree [dɪsə'griː] расходи́ться во взгля́дах; противоре́чить друг дру́гу; (*quarrel*) [по]спо́рить; быть вре́дным (***with*** для Р); **~able** [~əbl] □ неприя́тный; **~ment** [~mənt] разногла́сие; несогла́сие
disappear [dɪsə'pɪə] исчеза́ть [-е́знуть]; пропада́ть [-па́сть]; *from sight* скры́(ва́)ться; **~ance** [~rəns] исчезнове́ние
disappoint [dɪsə'pɔɪnt] разочаро́вывать [-рова́ть]; *hopes etc.* обма́нывать [-ну́ть]; **~ment** [~mənt] разочарова́ние
disapprov|al [dɪsə'pruːvl] неодобре́ние; **~e** [dɪsə'pruːv] не одобря́ть [одо́брить] (Р); неодобри́тельно относи́ться (***of*** к Д)
disarm [dɪs'ɑːm] *v/t. mst. fig.* обезору́жи(ва)ть; разоружа́ть [-жи́ть]; *v/i.* разоружа́ться [-жи́ться]; **~ament** [dɪs'ɑːməmənt] разоруже́ние
disarrange [dɪsə'reɪndʒ] (*upset*) расстра́ивать [-ро́ить]; (*put into disorder*) приводи́ть в беспоря́док
disast|er [dɪ'zɑːstə] бе́дствие; катастро́фа; **~rous** [~trəs] □ бе́дственный; катастрофи́ческий
disband [dɪs'bænd] распуска́ть [-усти́ть]
disbelieve [dɪsbɪ'liːv] не [по]ве́рить; не доверя́ть (Д)
disc [dɪsk] диск
discard [dɪs'kɑːd] (*throw away*) выбра́сывать [-росить]; *hypothesis* отверга́ть [-е́ргнуть]
discern [dɪ'sɜːn] различа́ть [-чи́ть]; распозн(ав)а́ть *pf.*; отлича́ть [-чи́ть]; **~ing** [~ɪŋ] □ *person* проница́тельный
discharge [dɪs'tʃɑːdʒ] **1.** *v/t.* (*unload*) разгружа́ть [-узи́ть]; *prisoner* освобожда́ть [-боди́ть]; *from work* увольня́ть [уво́лить]; *duties* выполня́ть [вы́полнить]; *gun, etc.* разряжа́ть [-яди́ть]; *from hospital* выпи́сывать [вы́писать]; *v/i. of wound* гнои́ться; **2.** разгру́зка; (*shot*) вы́стрел; освобожде́ние; увольне́ние; *el.* разря́д; выполне́ние
disciple [dɪ'saɪpl] после́дователь (-ница *f*) *m*; *Bibl.* апо́стол
discipline ['dɪsɪplɪn] **1.** дисципли́на,

порядок; **2.** дисциплинировать *(im)pf.*
disclose [dɪs'kləʊz] обнаружи(ва)ть; раскры(ва)ть
disco ['dɪskəʊ] *coll.* дискотека
discolo(u)r [dɪs'kʌlə] обесцвечивать(ся) [-етить(ся)]
discomfort [dɪs'kʌmfət] **1.** неудобство; дискомфорт; *(uneasiness of mind)* беспокойство; **2.** причинять [-нить] неудобство (Д)
disconcert [dɪskən'sɜːt] [вз]волновать; смущать [смутить]; приводить в замешательство
disconnect [dɪskə'nekt] разъединять [-нить] *(a. el.)*; разобщать [-щить]; *(uncouple)* расцеплять [-пить]; **~ed** [~ɪd] □ *thoughts, etc.* бессвязный
disconsolate [dɪs'kɒnsələt] □ неутешный
discontent [dɪskən'tent] недовольство; неудовлетворённость *f*; **~ed** [~ɪd] □ недовольный; неудовлетворённый
discontinue [dɪskən'tɪnjuː] прер(ы)вать; прекращать [-ратить]
discord ['dɪskɔːd] разногласие; разлад
discotheque ['dɪskətek] → ***disco***
discount 1. ['dɪskaʊnt] *comm.* дисконт, учёт векселей; скидка; ***at a ~*** со скидкой; **2.** [dɪs'kaʊnt] дисконтировать *(im)pf.*, учитывать [учесть] (векселя); делать скидку
discourage [dɪs'kʌrɪdʒ] обескуражи(ва)ть; отбивать охоту (Д; ***from*** к Д)
discourse 1. [dɪs'kɔːs] рассуждение; речь *f*; беседа; **2.** ['dɪskɔːs] вести беседу
discourte|ous [dɪs'kɜːtɪəs] □ невежливый, неучтивый; **~sy** [~tɪsɪ] невежливость *f*, неучтивость *f*
discover [dɪs'kʌvə] делать открытие (P); обнаружи(ва)ть; **~y** [~rɪ] открытие
discredit [dɪs'kredɪt] **1.** дискредитация; **2.** дискредитировать *(im)pf.*; [о]позорить
discreet [dɪ'skriːt] □ *(careful)* осторожный, осмотрительный; тактичный
discrepancy [dɪs'krepənsɪ] *(lack of correspondence)* расхождение; противоречивость *f*; *(difference)* несходство
discretion [dɪ'skreʃn] благоразумие; осторожность *f*; усмотрение; ***at your ~*** на ваше усмотрение
discriminat|e [dɪs'krɪmɪneɪt] относиться по-разному; ***~ between*** отличать, различать; ***~ against*** дискриминировать; относиться предвзято (к Д); **~ing** [~ɪŋ] □ дискриминационный; *taste, etc.* разборчивый; **~ion** [~'neɪʃn] *(judgment, etc.)* проницательность *f*; *(bias)* дискриминация
discuss [dɪ'skʌs] обсуждать [-удить], дискутировать; **~ion** [~ʌʃən] обсуждение, дискуссия; *public* прения *n/pl.*
disdain [dɪs'deɪn] **1.** *(scorn)* презирать [-зреть]; *(think unworthy)* считать ниже своего достоинства; **2.** презрение; пренебрежение
disease [dɪ'ziːz] болезнь *f*; **~d** [~d] больной
disembark [dɪsɪm'bɑːk] высаживать(ся) [высадить(ся)]; сходить на берег; *goods* выгружать [выгрузить]
disengage [dɪsɪn'geɪdʒ] *(make free)* высвобождать(ся) [высвободить(ся)]; *tech.* *(detach)* разъединять [-нить]
disentangle [dɪsɪn'tæŋgl] распут(ыв)ать(ся); *fig.* выпутываться [выпутать(ся)]
disfavo(u)r [dɪs'feɪvə] **1.** немилость *f*; ***regard with ~*** относиться отрицательно; **2.** не одобрять [одобрить]
disfigure [dɪs'fɪgə] обезображивать [-разить], [из]уродовать
disgrace [dɪs'greɪs] **1.** *(loss of respect)* бесчестье; *(disfavour)* немилость *f*; *(cause of shame)* позор; **2.** [о]позорить; **~ful** [~fʊl] □ постыдный, позорный
disguise [dɪs'gaɪz] **1.** маскировка; переодевание; обманчивая внешность *f*, маска; ***in ~*** переодетый; **2.** [за]маскировать(ся); переоде(ва)ть(ся); *(hide)* скры(ва)ть
disgust [dɪs'gʌst] **1.** отвращение; **2.** внушать [-шить] отвращение (Д);

(*make indignant*) возмущáть [-ути́ть]; **~ing** [~ɪŋ] □ отврати́тельный
dish [dɪʃ] **1.** блю́до, тарéлка, ми́ска; ***the ~es*** *pl.* посу́да; (*food*) блю́до; **2.**: ***~ out*** расклáдывать на тарéлки
dishearten [dɪs'hɑːtn] приводи́ть [-вести́] в уны́ние
dishevel(l)ed [dɪ'ʃevld] растрёпанный, взъеро́шенный
dishonest [dɪs'ɒnɪst] □ нечéстный; недобросо́вестный; **~y** [~ɪ] нечéстность *f*; недобросо́вестность *f*; обмáн
dishono(u)r [dɪs'ɒnə] **1.** бесчéстье, позо́р; **2.** [о]позо́рить; *young girl* [о]бесчéстить; **~able** [~rəbl] □ бесчéстный, ни́зкий
disillusion [dɪsɪ'luːʒn] **1.** разочаровáние; **2.** разрушáть [-у́шить] иллю́зии (Р); **~ed** [~d] разочаро́ванный
disinclined [dɪsɪn'klaɪnd] нерасполо́женный
disinfect [dɪsɪn'fekt] дезинфици́ровать (*im*)*pf.*; **~ant** [~ənt] дезинфици́рующее срéдство
disintegrate [dɪs'ɪntɪgreɪt] распадáться [-пáсться]; разрушáться [-у́шиться]
disinterested [dɪs'ɪntrəstɪd] □ (*without self-interest*) бескоры́стный; (*without prejudice*) беспристрáстный
disk [dɪsk] диск; **~ drive** дисково́д
diskette [dɪ'sket] *comput.* дискéта
dislike [dɪs'laɪk] **1.** не люби́ть; **2.** нелюбо́вь *f* (***of*** к Д); антипáтия; ***take a ~ to*** невзлюби́ть (В)
dislocate ['dɪsləkeɪt] *med.* выви́хивать [вы́вихнуть]; (*put out of order*) нарушáть [нару́шить]
dislodge [dɪs'lɒdʒ] (*move*) смещáть [смести́ть]; *mil.* выбивáть [вы́бить]
disloyal [dɪs'lɔɪəl] □ *to state, etc.* нелоя́льный; *friend* невéрный
dismal ['dɪzməl] □ (*gloomy*) мрáчный; уны́лый; гнету́щий
dismantl|e [dɪs'mæntl] *tech.* разбирáть [разобрáть]; демонти́ровать (*im.*)*pf.*; **~ing** [~ɪŋ] демонтáж
dismay [dɪs'meɪ] **1.** смятéние, потрясéние; **2.** *v/t.* приводи́ть [-вести́] в смятéние
dismiss [dɪs'mɪs] *v/t.* (*allow to go*) отпускáть [-сти́ть]; *from work, service, etc.* увольня́ть [уво́лить]; ***~ all thoughts of*** отбро́сить дáже мысль (о П); **~al** [~l] увольнéние; отстранéние
dismount [dɪs'maʊnt] *v/i.* слезáть с ло́шади, с велосипéда
disobedien|ce [dɪsə'biːdɪəns] непослушáние, неповиновéние; **~t** [~t] □ непослу́шный
disobey [dɪsə'beɪ] не [по]слу́шаться (Р); *order* не подчиня́ться [-ни́ться] (Д)
disorder [dɪs'ɔːdə] беспоря́док; *med.* расстро́йство; **~s** *pl.* (*riots*) беспоря́дки *m/pl.*; ***throw into ~*** переверну́ть всё вверх дном; **~ly** [~lɪ] беспоря́дочный; неорганизо́ванный, бу́йный
disorganize [dɪs'ɔːgənaɪz] дезорганизовáть (*im*)*pf.*, расстрáивать [-ро́ить]
disown [dɪs'əʊn] не призн(ав)áть; откáзываться [-зáться] от (Р)
dispassionate [dɪ'spæʃənət] □ (*impartial*) беспристрáстный; (*cool*) бесстрáстный
dispatch [dɪ'spætʃ] **1.** отпрáвка; отправлéние; (*message*) сообщéние; **2.** пос(ы)лáть; отправля́ть [-áвить]
dispel [dɪ'spel] рассéивать [-сéять]; *crowd etc.* разгоня́ть [разогнáть]
dispensary [dɪ'spensərɪ] больни́чная аптéка; *in drugstore* рецепту́рный отдéл
dispense [dɪ'spens] *v/t. prescription* приготовля́ть; (*deal out*) раздавáть [-дáть]; ***~ justice*** отправля́ть [-áвить] правосу́дие; ***~ with*** обходи́ться [обойти́сь], откáзываться [-зáться]
disperse [dɪ'spɜːs] разгоня́ть [разогнáть]; рассéивать(ся) [-éять(ся)]; (*spread*) распространя́ть [-ни́ть]
dispirit [dɪ'spɪrɪt] удручáть [-чи́ть]; приводи́ть в уны́ние
displace [dɪs'pleɪs] (*take the place of*) заня́ть мéсто, замещáть [замести́ть]
display [dɪ'spleɪ] **1.** (*exhibit*) выставля́ть [вы́ставить]; *courage, etc.* проявля́ть [-яви́ть]; **2.** вы́ставка; проявлéние; *comput.* дисплéй
displeas|e [dɪs'pliːz] вызывáть [вы́звать] недово́льство, не [по]нрá-

виться (Д); быть не по вку́су (Д); **~ed** [~d] недово́льный; **~ure** [dɪs'pleʒə] недово́льство

dispos|al [dɪ'spəʊzl] *of troops, etc.* расположе́ние; (*removal*) удале́ние; ***put at s.o.'s ~*** предоста́вить в чьё-л. распоряже́ние; **~e** [dɪ'spəʊz] *v/t.* располага́ть [-ложи́ть] (В); *v/i.* ***~ of*** распоряжа́ться [-яди́ться] (Т); **~ed** [~d] располо́женный; настро́енный; (*be inclined to*) быть скло́нным; **~ition** [dɪspə'zɪʃn] расположе́ние; хара́ктер; предрасположе́ние (к Д), скло́нность (к Д)

disproportionate [dɪsprə'pɔːʃənət] □ непропорциона́льный, несоразме́рный

disprove [dɪs'pruːv] опроверга́ть [-ве́ргнуть]

dispute [dɪs'pjuːt] **1.** (*discuss*) обсужда́ть [-уди́ть]; (*call into question*) оспа́ривать [оспо́рить]; (*argue*) [по]спо́рить; **2.** ди́спут; деба́ты *m/pl.*; поле́мика; диску́ссия

disqualify [dɪs'kwɒlɪfaɪ] дисквалифици́ровать (*im*)*pf.*; лиша́ть пра́ва

disquiet [dɪs'kwaɪət] [о]беспоко́ить

disregard [dɪsrɪ'gɑːd] **1.** пренебреже́ние; игнори́рование; **2.** игнори́ровать (*im*)*pf.*; пренебрега́ть [-бре́чь] (Т)

disreput|able [dɪs'repjʊtəbl] □ *behavio(u)r* дискредити́рующий; по́льзующийся дурно́й репута́цией; **~e** [dɪsrɪ'pjuːt] дурна́я сла́ва

disrespect [dɪsrɪ'spekt] неуваже́ние; **~ful** [~fl] □ непочти́тельный

dissatis|faction [dɪsætɪs'fækʃn] недово́льство; неудовлетворённость *f*; **~factory** [~tərɪ] неудовлетвори́тельный; **~fy** [dɪs'sætɪsfaɪ] не удовлетворя́ть [-ри́ть]

dissect [dɪ'sekt] *anat.* вскры́(ва́)ть; *fig.* анализи́ровать

dissent [dɪ'sent] **1.** несогла́сие; **2.** расходи́ться во взгля́дах, мне́ниях

disservice [dɪs'sɜːvɪs]: ***he did her a ~*** он оказа́л ей плоху́ю услу́гу

dissimilar [dɪ'sɪmɪlə] □ непохо́жий, несхо́дный, разноро́дный

dissipat|e ['dɪsɪpeɪt] (*disperse*) рассе́ивать [-е́ять]; (*spend, waste*) растра́чивать [-тра́тить]; **~ion** [dɪsɪ'peɪʃn]: ***life of ~*** беспу́тный о́браз жи́зни

dissociate [dɪ'səʊʃɪeɪt] разобща́ть [-щи́ть] отмежёвываться [-ева́ться] (от Р)

dissolut|e ['dɪsəluːt] □ распу́щенный; беспу́тный; **~ion** [dɪsə'luːʃn] *of marriage, agreement* расторже́ние; *parl.* ро́спуск; *of firm, etc.* ликвида́ция, расформирова́ние

dissolve [dɪ'zɒlv] *v/t. parl. etc.* распуска́ть [-усти́ть]; *salt, etc.* растворя́ть [-ри́ть]; *marriage, agreement* расторга́ть [-о́ргнуть]; аннули́ровать (*im*)*pf.*; *v/i.* растворя́ться [-ри́ться]

dissonant ['dɪsənənt] нестро́йный, диссони́рующий

dissuade [dɪ'sweɪd] отгова́ривать [-вори́ть] (***from*** от Р)

distan|ce ['dɪstəns] расстоя́ние; *sport* диста́нция; даль *f*; *of time* промежу́ток, пери́од; ***in the ~*** вдали́; вдалеке́; ***keep s.o. at a ~*** держа́ть кого́-л. на расстоя́нии; **~t** [~t] □ да́льний, далёкий; отдалённый; *fig.* (*reserved*) сде́ржанный, холо́дный

distaste [dɪs'teɪst] отвраще́ние; **~ful** [~fl] □ неприя́тный (на В, ***to*** Д)

distend [dɪ'stend] разу́(ва́)ть(ся), наду́(ва́)ть(ся)

distil [dɪ'stɪl] *chem.* перегоня́ть [-гна́ть], дистиллирова́ть (*im*)*pf.*; ***~led water*** дистиллиро́ванная вода́; **~lery** [~ərɪ] перего́нный заво́д

distinct [dɪ'stɪŋkt] □ (*different*) разли́чный, осо́бый, индивидуа́льный; (*clear*) отчётливый; (*definite*) определённый; **~ion** [dɪs'tɪŋkʃn] разли́чие; (*hono(u)r*) честь; ***draw a ~ between*** де́лать разли́чие ме́жду (Т); ***writer of ~*** изве́стный писа́тель; **~ive** [~tɪv] □ отличи́тельный, характе́рный

distinguish [dɪ'stɪŋgwɪʃ] различа́ть [-чи́ть]; отлича́ть [-чи́ть]; ***~ o.s.*** отличи́ться; **~ed** [~t] выдаю́щийся, изве́стный; *guest* почётный

distort [dɪ'stɔːt] искажа́ть [исказ́ить] (*a. fig.*)

distract [dɪ'strækt] отвлека́ть [отвле́чь]; **~ion** [dɪ'strækʃn] отвлече́ние; (*amusement*) развлече́ние

D

distress [dɪ'stres] **1.** огорче́ние, го́ре; *naut.* бе́дствие; (*suffering*) страда́ние; (*poverty*) нужда́, нищета́; **~ signal** сигна́л бе́дствия; **2.** (*upset*) огорча́ть [-чи́ть]; расстра́ивать [-ро́ить]
distribut|e [dɪ'strɪbju:t] распределя́ть [-ли́ть]; (*hand out*) разд(ав)а́ть; *printed matter* распространя́ть [-ни́ть]; **~ion** [dɪstrɪ'bju:ʃn] распределе́ние; разда́ча; распростране́ние
district ['dɪstrɪkt] райо́н; о́круг; **election ~** избира́тельный о́круг
distrust [dɪs'trʌst] **1.** недове́рие; (*suspicion*) подозре́ние; **2.** не доверя́ть (Д); **~ful** [~fl] □ недове́рчивый; подозри́тельный; **~ of o.s.** неуве́ренный в себе́
disturb [dɪ'stɜ:b] [по]беспоко́ить; (*worry*) взволнова́ть; *peace, etc.* наруша́ть [-у́шить]; **~ance** [~əns] шум, трево́га, волне́ние; *pl.* волне́ния *n/pl.*
disuse [dɪs'ju:z] неупотребле́ние; **fall into ~** вы́йти из употребле́ния; *of law, etc.* не применя́ться, не испо́льзоваться
ditch [dɪtʃ] кана́ва, ров
dive [daɪv] **1.** ныря́ть [нырну́ть]; погружа́ться [-узи́ться]; пры́гать [-гнуть] в во́ду; *ae.* пики́ровать (*im*)*pf.*; **2.** прыжо́к в во́ду; погруже́ние; пики́рование; (*disreputable bar, etc.*) прито́н, погребо́к; **make a ~ for** броса́ться [бро́ситься]; **~r** ['daɪvə] водола́з; ныря́льщик *m*, -ица *f*; *sport* спортсме́н по прыжка́м в во́ду
diverge [daɪ'vɜ:dʒ] расходи́ться [разойти́сь] (*a. fig.*); (*turn away*) отклоня́ться [-ни́ться]; **~nce** [~əns] расхожде́ние; отклоне́ние; **~nt** [~ənt] □ расходя́щийся; **~ opinions** ра́зные мне́ния
divers|e [daɪ'vɜ:s] □ разли́чный, разнообра́зный; (*different*) ино́й; **~ion** [daɪ'vɜ:ʃən] (*amusement*) развлече́ние; (*turning away*) отклоне́ние; **~ity** [~sɪtɪ] разнообра́зие; разли́чие
divert [daɪ'vɜ:t] *attention* отвлека́ть [-е́чь]; (*amuse*) развлека́ть [-е́чь]
divid|e [dɪ'vaɪd] *v/t. math.* [раз]дели́ть; (*share out*) разделя́ть [-ли́ть]; *v/i.* [раз]дели́ться; разделя́ться [-ли́ться]; *math.* дели́ться без оста́тка; **~end** ['dɪvɪdend] *fin.* дивиде́нд; *math.* дели́мое
divine [dɪ'vaɪn] **1.** □ боже́ственный; **~ service** богослуже́ние; **2.** (*guess*) уга́дывать [-да́ть]
diving ['daɪvɪŋ] ныря́ние; *sport* прыжки́ в во́ду; **~ board** трампли́н
divinity [dɪ'vɪnɪtɪ] (*theology*) богосло́вие; (*a divine being*) божество́
divis|ible [dɪ'vɪzəbl] (раз)дели́мый; **~ion** [dɪ'vɪʒn] деле́ние; разделе́ние; (*department*) отде́л; *mil.* диви́зия; *math.* деле́ние
divorce [dɪ'vɔ:s] **1.** разво́д; **2.** (*dissolve a marriage*) расторга́ть брак (Р); разводи́ться [-вести́сь] с (Т); **be ~d** быть в разво́де
divulge [daɪ'vʌldʒ] разглаша́ть [-ласи́ть]
dizz|iness ['dɪzɪnɪs] головокруже́ние; **~y** ['dɪzɪ] □ головокружи́тельный; **I feel ~** у меня́ кру́жится голова́
do [du:] [*irr.*] **1.** *v/t.* [с]де́лать; *duty, etc.* выполня́ть [вы́полнить]; (*arrange*) устра́ивать [-ро́ить]; *homework etc.* приготовля́ть [-то́вить]; **~ London** осма́тривать Ло́ндон; **have done reading** ко́нчить чита́ть; *coll.* **~ in** (*exhaust*), *a. sl.* (*kill*) уби́(ва́)ть; **~ out** убира́ть [убра́ть]; **~ out of** выма́нивать [вы́манить] (обма́ном); **~ over** переде́л(ыв)ать; *with paint* покры́(ва́т)ь; **~ up** завора́чивать [заверну́ть]; [с]де́лать ремо́нт; *coat* застёгивать [-егну́ть]; (*tie*) завя́зывать [-за́ть]; **2.** *v/i.* [с]де́лать; поступа́ть [-пи́ть], де́йствовать; **~ so as to ...** устра́ивать так, что́бы ...; **that will ~** доста́точно, дово́льно; сойдёт; **how ~ you ~?** здра́вствуй(те)!; как вы пожива́ете?; **~ well** успева́ть; хорошо́ вести́ де́ло; **~ away with** уничтожа́ть [-о́жить]; **I could ~ with ...** мне мог бы пригоди́ться (И); **I could ~ with a shave** мне не помеша́ло бы побри́ться; **~ without** обходи́ться [обойти́сь] без (Р); **~ be quick!** поспеши́те!, скоре́й!; **~ you like**

London? – I ~ вам нра́вится Ло́ндон? – Да
docil|e ['dəʊsaɪl] послу́шный; (*easily trained*) поня́тливый; **~ity** [dəʊ'sɪlɪtɪ] послуша́ние; поня́тливость *f*
dock [dɑk] **1.** *naut.* док; *law* скамья́ подсуди́мых; **2.** *naut.* ста́вить су́дно в док; *of space vehicles* [со]стыкова́ться
dockyard ['dɒkjɑːd] верфь *f*
doctor ['dɒktə] *acad.* до́ктор; *med.* врач; **~ate** [~rət] сте́пень до́ктора
doctrine ['dɒktrɪn] уче́ние, доктри́на
document 1. ['dɒkjʊmənt] докуме́нт; **2.** [~ment] документи́ровать, подтвержда́ть докуме́нтами
dodge [dɒdʒ] **1.** увёртка, уло́вка, хи́трость *f*; **2.** уви́ливать [-льну́ть]; [с]хитри́ть; избега́ть [-ежа́ть] (Р)
doe [dəʊ] *mst.* са́мка оле́ня
dog [dɒg] **1.** соба́ка, пёс; **2.** ходи́ть по пята́м (Р); *fig.* пресле́довать; ***~ collar*** оше́йник
dogged ['dɒgɪd] □ упря́мый, упо́рный, насто́йчивый
dogma ['dɒgmə] до́гма; *specific* до́гмат; **~tic** [dɒg'mætɪk] *person* догмати́чный; **~tism** ['dɒgmətɪzəm] догмати́зм
dog-tired [dɒg'taɪəd] уста́лый как соба́ка
doings ['duːɪŋz] дела́ *n/pl.*, посту́пки *m/pl.*
do-it-yourself: ***~ kit*** набо́р инструме́нтов "сде́лай сам"
doleful ['dəʊlfʊl] □ ско́рбный, печа́льный
doll [dɒl] ку́кла
dollar ['dɒlə] до́ллар
domain [də'meɪn] (*estate*) владе́ние; (*realm*) сфе́ра; *fig.* о́бласть *f*
dome [dəʊm] ку́пол; (*vault*) свод
domestic [də'mestɪk] **1.** дома́шний; семе́йный; **2.** дома́шняя рабо́тница; слуга́ *m*; **~ate** [~tɪkeɪt] *animal* прируча́ть [-чи́ть]
domicile ['dɒmɪsaɪl] местожи́тельство
domin|ant ['dɒmɪnənt] госпо́дствующий, преоблада́ющий; **~ate** [~neɪt] госпо́дствовать, преоблада́ть; **~ation** [dɒmɪ'neɪʃn] госпо́дство, преоблада́ние; **~eer** [dɒmɪ'nɪə] вести́ себя́ деспоти́чески; **~eering** [~rɪŋ] □ деспоти́чный, вла́стный
don [dɒn] *univ.* преподава́тель
donat|e [dəʊ'neɪt] [по]же́ртвовать; **~ion** [~ʃn] поже́ртвование
done [dʌn] **1.** *pt. p. от* **do**; **2.** *adj.* гото́вый; ***~ in*** уста́лый; ***well ~(!)*** хорошо́ прожа́ренный; молоде́ц!
donkey ['dɒŋkɪ] осёл
donor ['dəʊnə] дари́тель(ница *f*) *m*; *of blood, etc.* до́нор
doom [duːm] **1.** рок, судьба́; (*ruin*) ги́бель; **2.** обрека́ть [-е́чь] (***to*** на В)
door [dɔː] дверь *f*; ***next ~*** ря́дом, в сосе́днем до́ме; ***out of ~s*** на откры́том во́здухе; **~handle** дверна́я ру́чка; **~keeper** швейца́р; **~way** вход, дверно́й проём
dope [dəʊp] нарко́тик; *sport* до́пинг; *coll.* (*blockhead*) о́лух
dormant ['dɔːmənt] *mst. fig.* безде́йствующий, спя́щий; ***~ capital*** мёртвый капита́л
dormitory ['dɔːmɪtrɪ] большо́е спа́льное помеще́ние (*в шко́лах, интерна́тах и т.д.*); *Am.* общежи́тие
dose [dəʊs] **1.** до́за; **2.** дози́ровать (*im*)*pf.*; дава́ть до́зами
dot [dɒt] **1.** то́чка; ***come on the ~*** прийти́ то́чно; **2.**: ***~ the i's*** ста́вить то́чки над i; **~ted line** пункти́р
dot|e [dəʊt]: ***~ (up)on*** души́ не ча́ять; **~ing** ['dəʊtɪŋ] о́чень любя́щий
double ['dʌbl] **1.** двойно́й; *fig.* двоя́кий; **2.** *person* двойни́к; двойно́е коли́чество; па́рная игра́; *thea.* (*understudy*) дублёр; **3.** *v/t.* удва́ивать [удво́ить]; скла́дывать вдво́е; ***~d up*** скрю́чившийся; *v/i.* удва́иваться [удво́иться]; **~-breasted** двубо́ртный; **~-dealing** двуру́шничество; **~-edged** обоюдоо́стрый
doubt [daʊt] **1.** *v/t.* сомнева́ться [усомни́ться] в (П); не доверя́ть (Д); *v/i.* име́ть сомне́ния; **2.** сомне́ние; ***no ~*** без сомне́ния; **~ful** ['daʊtfʊl] □ сомни́тельный; ***~ blessing*** па́лка о двух конца́х; **~less** ['daʊtlɪs] несомне́нно; вероя́тно

D

dough [dəʊ] тéсто; **~nut** ['dəʊnʌt] пóнчик
dove [dʌv] гóлубь *m*
down¹ [daʊn] пух; *dim.* пушóк
down² [~] **1.** *adv.* вниз, внизý; **~ *to*** вплоть до (Р); ***it suits me ~ to the ground*** меня́ э́то вполнé устрáивает; **2.** *prp.* вниз по (Д); вдоль по (Д); ***~ the river*** вниз по рекé; **3.** *adj.* напрáвленный вниз; ***prices are ~*** цéны снúзились; **4.** *v/t.* опускáть [опустúть]; *enemies* одолé(вá)ть; **~cast** удручённый; **~fall** падéние; **~hearted** [daʊn'hɑːtɪd] пáвший дýхом; **~hill** [daʊn'hɪl] вниз; под гóру; **~pour** лúвень *m*; **~right 1.** *adv.* совершéнно; пря́мо; **2.** *adj.* прямóй; (*frank*) откровéнный; (*honest*) чéстный; **~stairs** [daʊn'steəz] вниз, внизý; **~stream** [daʊn'striːm] вниз по течéнию; **~town** [daʊn'taʊn] *part. Am.* в цéнтре гóрода; **~ward(s)** [~wəd(z)] вниз, книзу
downy ['daʊnɪ] пушúстый, мя́гкий как пух
dowry ['daʊərɪ] придáное
doze [dəʊz] **1.** дремóта; ***have a ~*** вздремнýть; **2.** дремáть
dozen ['dʌzn] дю́жина
drab [dræb] тýсклый, однообрáзный
draft [drɑːft] **1.** = ***draught***; набросóк; черновúк; *fin.* чек; сýмма, полýченная по чéку; *mil.* призы́в, набóр; *arch.* эскúз; **2.** набрáсывать [-росáть]; призывáть [призвáть]
drag [dræg] **1.** обýза, брéмя *n*; **2.** *v/t.* [по]тянýть, [по]волочúть; ***I could hardly ~ my feet*** я éле волочúл нóги; *v/i.* [по]волочúться; ***~ on*** тянýться
dragon ['drægən] дракóн; **~fly** стрекозá
drain [dreɪn] **1.** дренáж; *pl.* канализáция; *from roof* водостóк; **2.** *v/t.* осушáть [-шúть]; *fig.* истощáть [-щúть]; **~age** ['dreɪnɪdʒ] дренáж; стóк; канализáция
drake [dreɪk] сéлезень *m*
drama|tic [drə'mætɪk] (***~ally***) драматúческий; театрáльный; драматúчный; **~tist** ['dræmətɪst] драматýрг; **~tize** [~taɪz] драматизúровать (*im*)*pf.*
drank [dræŋk] *pt. от* ***drink***
drape [dreɪp] [за]драпировáть; располагáть склáдками; **~ry** ['dreɪpərɪ] драпирóвка; (*cloth*) ткáни *f/pl.*
drastic ['dræstɪk] (***~ally***) решúтельный, крутóй; сильнодéйствующий
draught [drɑːft] *chiefly Brt.* тя́га; *in room* сквозня́к; (*drink*) глотóк; (*rough copy*) черновúк, набрóсок; **~s** *pl.* шáшки *f/pl.*; → ***draft***; ***~ beer*** бочковóе пúво; **~sman** [~smən] чертёжник; (*artist*) рисовáльщик *m*, -щица *f*
draw [drɔː] **1.** [*irr.*] [на]рисовáть; [по]тянýть; [по]тащúть; *tooth* вырывáть [вы́рвать]; *water* черпáть; *attention* привлекáть [-éчь]; *conclusion* приходúть [-ийтú] (к Д); *sport* закáнчивать [-кóнчить] (игрý) вничью́; ***~ near*** приближáться [-лúзиться]; ***~ out*** вытя́гивать [вы́тянуть]; ***~ up*** *paper* составля́ть [-áвить]; (*stop*) остана́вливаться [-новúться]; **2.** (*lottery*) жеребьёвка; *sport* ничья́; **~back** ['drɔːbæk] недостáток; **~er** [drɔː] выдвижнóй я́щик; **~s**: *a.* ***pair of ~*** *pl.* кальсóны *f/pl.*, *short* трусы́
drawing ['drɔːɪŋ] рисýнок; рисовáние; чертёж; ***~ board*** чертёжная доскá; ***~ room*** гостúная
drawn [drɔːn] *pt. p. от* ***draw***
dread [dred] **1.** боя́ться, страшúться (Р); **2.** страх, боя́знь *f*; **~ful** ['dredfl] □ ужáсный, стрáшный
dream [driːm] **1.** сон, сновидéние; (*reverie*) мечтá; **2.** [*a. irr.*] вúдеть во снé; мечтáть; ***~ up*** придýмывать [-мать]; воображáть [-разúть]; **~er** [~ə] мечтáтель(ница *f*) *m*, фантазёр(ка); **~y** [~ɪ] □ мечтáтельный
dreary ['drɪərɪ] □ тосклúвый; *weather* ненáстный; *work, etc.* скýчный
dredge [dredʒ] землечерпáлка
dregs [dregz] *pl.* осáдок; *of society* отбрóсы *m/pl.*; ***drink to the ~*** [вы́]пить до днá
drench [drentʃ] промокáть [-мóкнуть]; ***get ~ed*** промóкнуть до нúтки
dress [dres] **1.** плáтье; *collect.* одéжда; *thea.* ***~ rehearsal*** генерáльная

репети́ция; **2.** оде́(ва́)ть(ся); (*adorn*) украша́ть(ся) [укра́сить(ся)]; *hair* де́лать причёску; *med.* перевя́зывать [-за́ть]; **~ circle** *thea.* бельэта́ж; **~er** [~ə] ку́хонный шкаф; *Am. a.* комо́д, туале́тный сто́лик
dressing ['dresɪŋ] перевя́зочный материа́л; перевя́зка; *cul.* припра́ва; **~ *down*** головомо́йка; **~ gown** хала́т; **~ table** туале́тный сто́лик
dressmaker портни́ха
drew ['dru:] *pt. om* ***draw***
dribble ['drɪbl] ка́пать; пуска́ть слю́ни
dried [draɪd] сухо́й; вы́сохший
drift [drɪft] **1.** *naut.* дрейф; (*snow~*) сугро́б; *of sand* нано́с; *fig.* тенде́нция; ***did you get the ~ of what he said?*** ты улови́л смысл его́ слов?; **2.** *v/t.* сноси́ть [снести́]; наноси́ть [нанести́]; *leaves, snow* мести́; *v/i.* дрейфова́ть (*im*)*pf.*; намести́; *fig. of person* плыть по тече́нию
drill [drɪl] **1.** дрель; бу́рав; *tech.* бур; (*exercise*) упражне́ние; *sport* трениро́вка; **2.** [на]тренирова́ть
drink [drɪŋk] **1.** питьё; напи́ток; **2.** [*irr.*] [вы́]пить; пья́нствовать
drip [drɪp] ка́пать, па́дать ка́плями
drive [draɪv] **1.** езда́; пое́здка; подъе́зд (к до́му); *tech.* при́вод; *fig.* эне́ргия; си́ла; ***go for a ~*** пое́хать поката́ться на маши́не; **2.** [*irr.*] *v/t.* (*force along*) [по]гна́ть; *nail, etc.* вби(ва́)ть; (*convey*) вози́ть, [по]везти́; *v/i.* е́здить, [по]е́хать; ката́ться; [по]нести́сь; **~ *at*** намека́ть на (В)
drivel ['drɪvl] бессмы́слица, чепуха́
driven ['drɪvn] *pt. p. om* ***drive***
driver ['draɪvə] *mot.* води́тель *m*, шофёр; *rail.* машини́ст; ***racing ~*** го́нщик
drizzle ['drɪzl] **1.** и́зморось *f*; ме́лкий дождь *m*; **2.** мороси́ть
drone [drəʊn] **1.** *zo.* тру́тень *m*; **2.** жужжа́ть; *plane* гуде́ть
droop [dru:p] *v/t. head* опуска́ть [-сти́ть]; пове́сить; *v/i.* поника́ть [-и́кнуть]; *of flowers* увяда́ть [увя́нуть]
drop [drɒp] **1.** ка́пля; (*fruit ~*) леде-не́ц; *in prices, etc.* паде́ние, сниже́ние; *thea.* за́навес; **2.** *v/t.* роня́ть [урони́ть]; *smoking, etc.* броса́ть [бро́сить]; ***~ a p. a line*** черкну́ть кому́-л. слове́чко; *v/i.* ка́пать [ка́пнуть]; спада́ть [спасть]; па́дать [упа́сть]; понижа́ться [-и́зиться]; *of wind* стиха́ть [сти́хнуть]; **~ *in*** заходи́ть [зайти́], загля́дывать [загляну́ть]
drought [draʊt] за́суха
drove [drəʊv] **1.** (*herd*) ста́до; **2.** *pt. om* ***drive***
drown [draʊn] *v/t.* [у]топи́ть; *fig. sound* заглуша́ть [-ши́ть]; *v/i.* [у]тону́ть = ***be ~ed***; **~ *o.s.*** [у]топи́ться
drows|e [draʊz] [за]дрема́ть; **~y** ['draʊsɪ] со́нный
drudge [drʌdʒ] исполня́ть ску́чную, тяжёлую рабо́ту, тяну́ть ля́мку
drug [drʌg] лека́рство; *pl.* медикаме́нты *m/pl.*; нарко́тик; ***take ~s*** употребля́ть нарко́тики; **~ addict** наркома́н; **~gist** ['drʌgɪst] апте́карь *m*; **~store** *Am.* апте́ка
drum [drʌm] **1.** бараба́н; **2.** бить в бараба́н, бараба́нить
drunk [drʌŋk] **1.** *pt. p. om* ***drink***; **2.** пья́ный; ***get ~*** напива́ться пья́ным; **~ard** ['drʌŋkəd] пья́ница *m/f*; **~en** ['drʌŋkən] пья́ный
dry [draɪ] **1.** □ сухо́й, вы́сохший; ***~ as dust*** ску́чный; **2.** [вы́]суши́ть; [вы́]со́хнуть; ***~ up*** высу́шивать [вы́сушить]; *of river etc.* высыха́ть [вы́сохнуть], пересыха́ть [-со́хнуть]; **~ cleaner's** химчи́стка
dual ['dju:əl] □ двойно́й
dubious ['dju:bɪəs] □ сомни́тельный, подозри́тельный
duchess ['dʌtʃɪs] герцоги́ня
duck[1] [dʌk] у́тка; *fig.* ***a lame ~*** неуда́чник
duck[2] [~] ныря́ть [нырну́ть]; окуна́ться [-ну́ться]; (*move quickly*) увёртываться [уверну́ться]
duckling ['dʌklɪŋ] утёнок
due [dju:] **1.** до́лжный, надлежа́щий; **~ *to*** благодаря́; ***the train is ~ ...*** по́езд до́лжен прибы́ть ...; ***in ~ course*** в своё вре́мя; **2.** *adv. naut. east, etc.* то́чно, пря́мо; **3.** до́лжное; то, что причита́ется; ***give s.o. his ~*** отдава́ть до́лжное кому́-л.; *mst.* **~s** *pl.* сбо́ры *m/pl.*, нало́ги

D

m/pl.; пошлины *f/pl.*; членский взнос
duel ['dju:əl] **1.** дуэль *f*; **2.** драться на дуэли
duet [dju:'et] дуэт
dug [dʌg] *pt. u pt. p. от* **dig**
duke [dju:k] герцог
dull [dʌl] **1.** (**~y**) (*not sharp*) тупой (*a. fig.*); (*boring*) скучный; *comm.* вялый; *day* пасмурный; **2.** притуплять(ся) [-пить(ся)]; *fig.* делать(-ся) скучным; **~ness** ['dʌlnɪs] скука; вялость *f*; тупость *f*
duly ['dju:lɪ] должным образом
dumb [dʌm] □ немой; *Am.* глупый; **~found** [dʌm'faʊnd] ошеломлять [-мить]
dummy ['dʌmɪ] *tailor's* манекен; *mil.* макет; *Brt.* **baby's ~** (*Am. pacifier*) соска, пустышка
dump [dʌmp] **1.** свалка; **2.** сбрасывать [сбросить]; сваливать [-лить]; **~ing** *comm.* демпинг; **~s** *pl.*: **be down in the ~** плохое настроение
dunce [dʌns] тупица *m/f*
dune [dju:n] дюна
dung [dʌŋ] навоз
duplic|ate 1. ['dju:plɪkɪt] **a)** двойной; запасной; **b)** дубликат; копия; **in ~** в двух экземплярах; **2.** [~keɪt] снимать, делать копию с (Р); удваивать [удвоить]; **~ity** [dju:'plɪsɪtɪ] двуличность *f*
dura|ble ['djʊərəbl] □ прочный; длительный; **~tion** [djʊə'reɪʃn] продолжительность *f*
during ['djʊərɪŋ] *prp.* в течение (Р), во время (Р)
dusk [dʌsk] сумерки; **~y** ['dʌskɪ] □ сумеречный; *skin* смуглый
dust [dʌst] **1.** пыль *f*; **2.** (*wipe*) вытирать пыль; **~bin** *Brt.* (*Am. trash can*) мусорное ведро; **~er** ['dʌstə] тряпка для вытирания пыли; **~y** ['dʌstɪ] □ пыльный
Dutch [dʌtʃ] **1.** голландец *m*, -дка *f*; **2.** голландский; **the ~** голландцы *pl.*
duty ['dju:tɪ] долг, обязанность *f*; дежурство; *fin.* пошлина; **off ~** свободный от дежурства; **~-free** *adv.* беспошлинно
dwarf [dwɔ:f] **1.** карлик; **2.** [по]мешать росту; казаться маленьким (по сравнению с Т)
dwell [dwel] [*irr.*] жить; **~ (up)on** останавливаться [-новиться] на (П); **~ing** ['dwelɪŋ] жилище, дом
dwelt [dwelt] *pt. u pt. p. от* **dwell**
dwindle ['dwɪndl] уменьшаться [уменьшиться], сокращаться [-ратиться]
dye [daɪ] **1.** краска; краситель; *fig.* **of the deepest ~** отъявленный; **2.** [по-, вы]красить, окрашивать [окрасить]
dying ['daɪɪŋ] (*s.* **die**[1]) **1.** умирающий; *words* предсмертный; **2.** умирание; смерть
dynam|ic [daɪ'næmɪk] динамический; *fig.* динамичный; активный; энергичный; **~ics** [~ɪks] *mst. sg.* динамика; **~ite** ['daɪnəmaɪt] динамит

E

each [i:tʃ] каждый; **~ other** друг друга
eager ['i:gə] □ стремящийся; (*diligent*) усердный; энергичный; **~ness** [~nɪs] пыл, рвение
eagle ['i:gl] орёл, орлица
ear [ɪə] ухо (*pl.*: уши); *mus.* слух; **~drum** барабанная перепонка
earl [ɜ:l] граф (английский)
early ['ɜ:lɪ] **1.** ранний; (*premature*) преждевременный; **at the earliest** в лучшем случае; **it is too ~ to draw conclusions** делать выводы преждевременно; **2.** *adv.* рано; (*timely*) заблаговременно; **as ~ as** уже, ещё; как можно раньше

earmark ['ɪəmɑːk] (*set aside*) предназнача́ть [-зна́чить]
earn [ɜːn] зараба́тывать [-бо́тать]; *fig.* заслу́живать [-жи́ть]
earnest ['ɜːnɪst] **1.** □ серьёзный; убеждённый; и́скренний; **2.** серьёзность *f*; ***in ~*** серьёзно, всерьёз
earnings ['ɜːnɪŋz] за́работок
ear|phones ['ɪəfəʊnz] нау́шники *m./pl.*; **~ring** серьга́, серёжка; **~shot** преде́лы слы́шимости
earth [ɜːθ] **1.** земля́, земно́й шар; (*soil*) земля́, по́чва; **2.** *v/t.* (*~ up*) зары́(ва́)ть; зака́пывать [закопа́ть]; *el.* заземля́ть [-ли́ть]; **~en** [~n] земляно́й; **~enware** [~nweə] гли́няная посу́да; **~ly** [~lɪ] земно́й; **~quake** [~kweɪk] землетрясе́ние; **~worm** земляно́й червь *m.*, *coll.* червя́к
ease [iːz] **1.** лёгкость *f*; непринуждённость *f*; ***at ~*** свобо́дно, удо́бно; ***feel ill at ~*** чу́вствовать себя́ нело́вко; **2.** облегча́ть [-чи́ть]; успока́ивать [-ко́ить]
easel ['iːzl] мольбе́рт
easiness ['iːzɪnɪs] → ***ease 1***
east [iːst] **1.** восто́к; **2.** восто́чный; **3.** *adv.* на восто́к; к восто́ку (***of*** от Р)
Easter ['iːstə] Па́сха
easter|ly ['iːstəlɪ] с восто́ка; **~n** ['iːstən] восто́чный
eastward(s) ['iːstwəd(z)] на восто́к
easy ['iːzɪ] лёгкий; споко́йный; непринуждённый; ***take it ~!*** не торопи́(те)сь; споко́йнее!; **~ chair** кре́сло; **~going** *fig.* благоду́шный; беззабо́тный
eat [iːt] **1.** [*irr.*] [съ]есть; (*damage*) разъеда́ть [-е́сть] (*mst.* ***away***, ***into***) **2.** [et] *pt. от* ***eat 1***; **~able** ['iːtəbl] съедо́бный; **~en** ['iːtn] *pt. p. от* ***eat 1***
eaves [iːvz] *pl.* карни́з; **~drop** подслу́ш(ив)ать
ebb [eb] **1.** (*a.* **~-tide**) отли́в; *fig.* переме́на к ху́дшему; **2.** *of tide* убы́(ва́)ть; *fig.* ослабе́(ва́)ть
ebony ['ebənɪ] чёрное де́рево
eccentric [ɪk'sentrɪk] **1.** *fig.* эксцентри́чный; **2.** чуда́к
ecclesiastical [ɪkliːzɪ'æstɪkl] □ духо́вный, церко́вный
echo ['ekəʊ] **1.** э́хо; *fig.* отголо́сок; **2.** отдава́ться э́хом
eclair [ɪ'kleə] экле́р
eclipse [ɪ'klɪps] **1.** затме́ние; **2.** затмева́ть [-ми́ть] (*a. fig.*); заслоня́ть [-ни́ть]
ecology [ɪ'kɒlədʒɪ] эколо́гия
econom|ic [iːkə'nɒmɪk] экономи́ческий; **~al** [~l] эконо́мный, бережли́вый; **~ics** [~ɪks] *pl.* эконо́мика
econom|ist [ɪ'kɒnəmɪst] экономи́ст; **~ize** [~maɪz] [с]эконо́мить; **~y** [~mɪ] эконо́мия; бережли́вость *f*; ***national ~*** эконо́мика страны́
ecsta|sy ['ekstəsɪ] экста́з, восто́рг; **~tic** [ɪk'stætɪk] (***~ally***) восто́рженный
eddy ['edɪ] водоворо́т
edge [edʒ] **1.** край; *of knife* ле́звие, остриё; *of forest* опу́шка; *of cloth* кро́мка; *of road* обо́чина; ***be on ~*** быть в не́рвном состоя́нии; **2.** (*border*) окаймля́ть [-ми́ть]; ***~ one's way ...*** пробира́ться [-бра́ться]; **~ways** [~weɪz], **~wise** [~waɪz] кра́ем, бо́ком
edging ['edʒɪŋ] край, кайма́, бордю́р; *of photo*, *etc.* окантовка
edible ['edɪbl] съедо́бный
edit ['edɪt] [от]редакти́ровать; *film* [с]монти́ровать; **~ion** [ɪ'dɪʃn] изда́ние; **~or** ['edɪtə] реда́ктор; **~orial** [edɪ'tɔːrɪəl] **1.** реда́кторский; редакцио́нный; ***~ office*** реда́кция; **2.** передова́я статья́; **~orship** ['edɪtəʃɪp]: ***under the ~*** под реда́кцией
educat|e ['edjʊkeɪt] дава́ть образова́ние (Д); (*bring up*) воспи́тывать [-та́ть]; **~ion** [edjʊ'keɪʃn] образова́ние, воспита́ние; **~ional** [edjʊ'keɪʃnl] образова́тельный; педагоги́ческий; уче́бный
eel [iːl] у́горь *m*
effect [ɪ'fekt] **1.** (*result*) сле́дствие; результа́т; *phys.* эффе́кт; (*action*) де́йствие; (*impression*) эффе́кт, впечатле́ние; (*influence*) влия́ние; **~s** *pl.* иму́щество; ***come into ~*** вступа́ть в си́лу; ***in ~*** в су́щности; ***to no ~*** напра́сный; ***to the ~*** сле́дующего содержа́ния; **2.** производи́ть [-вести́]; выполня́ть [вы́полнить]; соверша́ть [-ши́ть]; **~ive** [~ɪv] эффекти́вный, действи́тель-

E

ный; *tech.* поле́зный; **~ual** [~ʃʊəl] *remedy, etc.* де́йственный, эффекти́вный
effeminate [ɪ'femɪnət] □ женоподо́бный
effervescent [efə'vesnt] **1.** шипу́чий; **2.** *fig.* брыз́жущий весе́льем
efficacy ['efɪkəsɪ] де́йственность *f*
efficien|cy [ɪ'fɪʃnsɪ] делови́тость *f*; эффекти́вность *f*; **~t** [~nt] □ делови́тый; уме́лый, продукти́вный; эффекти́вный
effort ['efət] уси́лие; попы́тка
effrontery [ɪ'frʌntərɪ] на́глость *f*
effusive [ɪ'fju:sɪv] □ экспанси́вный; несде́ржанный
egg[1] [eg] яйцо́; ***scrambled ~s*** *pl.* я́ичница-болту́нья; ***fried ~s*** *pl.* я́ичница-глазу́нья; ***hard-boiled*** (***soft-boiled***) **~** яйцо́ вкруту́ю (всмя́тку); **~shell** яи́чная скорлупа́
egg[2] [~] подстрека́ть [-кну́ть] (*mst.* ***~ on***)
egotism ['egəʊtɪzəm] эгои́зм, самомне́ние
Egyptian [ɪ'dʒɪpʃn] **1.** египтя́нин *m*, -я́нка *f*; **2.** еги́петский
eight [eɪt] **1.** во́семь; **2.** восьмёрка; **~een** [eɪ'ti:n] восемна́дцать; **~eenth** [eɪ'ti:nθ] восемна́дцатый; **~h** [eɪtθ] **1.** восьмо́й; **2.** восьма́я часть *f*; **~ieth** ['eɪtɪəθ] восьмидеся́тый; **~y** ['eɪtɪ] во́семьдесят
either ['aɪðə] **1.** *pron.* оди́н из двух; любо́й, ка́ждый; тот и́ли друго́й; и тот и друго́й, о́ба; **2.** *cj.* ***~ ... or ...*** и́ли ... и́ли ...; ли́бо ... ли́бо ...; ***not (...) ~*** та́кже не
ejaculate [ɪ'dʒækjʊleɪt] (*cry out*) восклица́ть [-ли́кнуть]; изверга́ть се́мя
eject [ɪ'dʒekt] (*throw out*) выгоня́ть [вы́гнать]; *from house* выселя́ть [вы́селить]; *lava* изверга́ть [-е́ргнуть]; *smoke* выпуска́ть [вы́пустить]
eke [i:k]: ***~ out*** восполня́ть [-по́лнить]; ***~ out a livelihood*** перебива́ться кое-ка́к
elaborat|e **1.** [ɪ'læbərət] □ сло́жный; тща́тельно разрабо́танный; **2.** [~reɪt] разраба́тывать [-бо́тать]; разви́(ва́)ть; **~ion** [ɪˌlæbə'reɪʃn] разрабо́тка; разви́тие; уточне́ние
elapse [ɪ'læps] проходи́ть [пройти́], протека́ть [проте́чь]
elastic [ɪ'læstɪk] **1.** (***~ally***) эласти́чный; упру́гий; **2.** рези́нка; **~ity** [elæ'stɪsətɪ] эласти́чность *f*, упру́гость *f*
elated [ɪ'leɪtɪd] □ в приподнятом настрое́нии
elbow ['elbəʊ] **1.** ло́коть *m*; *of pipe, etc.* коле́но; ***at one's ~*** под руко́й, ря́дом; **2.** прота́лкиваться [-толкну́ться]; ***~ out*** выта́лкивать [вы́толкнуть]; **~room** ме́сто, простра́нство; *fig.* свобо́да де́йствий
elder[1] ['eldə] *bot.* бузина́
elder[2] [~] **1.** ста́рец, ста́рший; **~ly** ['eldəlɪ] пожило́й
eldest ['eldɪst] са́мый ста́рший
elect [ɪ'lekt] **1.** *by vote* изб(и)ра́ть; (*choose, decide*) выбира́ть [вы́брать]; реша́ть [-ши́ть]; **2.** и́збранный; **~ion** [~kʃn] вы́боры *m/pl.*; **~or** [~tə] избира́тель *m*; **~oral** [~tərəl] избира́тельный; **~orate** [~tərət] избира́тели *m/pl.*
electri|c [ɪ'lektrɪk] электри́ческий; ***~ circuit*** электри́ческая цепь *f*; **~cal** [~trɪkl] □ электри́ческий; ***~ engineering*** электроте́хника; **~cian** [ɪlek'trɪʃn] электромонтёр
electri|city [ɪˌlek'trɪsətɪ] электри́чество; **~fy** [ɪ'lektrɪfaɪ] электрифици́ровать (*im*)*pf.*; [на]электризова́ть (*a. fig.*)
electron [ɪ'lektrɒn] электро́н; **~ic** [ɪlek'trɒnɪk] электро́нный; ***~ data processing*** электро́нная обрабо́тка да́нных; **~ics** электро́ника
elegan|ce ['elɪgəns] элега́нтность *f*; изя́щество; **~t** ['elɪgənt] □ элега́нтный, изя́щный
element ['elɪmənt] элеме́нт (*a. tech., chem.*); черта́; до́ля; ***the ~s*** стихи́я; **~s** *pl.* осно́вы *f/pl.*; ***in one's ~*** в свое́й стихи́и; ***there is an ~ of truth in this*** в э́том есть до́ля пра́вды; **~al** [elɪ'mentl] стихи́йный; **~ary** [~trɪ] □ элемента́рный; ***elementaries*** *pl.* осно́вы *f/pl.*
elephant ['elɪfənt] слон
elevat|e ['elɪveɪt] поднима́ть [-ня́ть]; повыша́ть [-вы́сить]; *fig.* возвыша́ть [-вы́сить]; **~ion** [elɪ'veɪʃn] возвыше́ние; (*elevated place*) воз-

вы́шенность *f*; (*height*) высота́; **~or** ['elɪveɪtə] *for grain* элева́тор, *for lifting loads* грузоподъёмник; *Am.* лифт

eleven [ɪ'levn] оди́ннадцать; **~th** [~θ] **1.** оди́ннадцатый; **2.** оди́ннадцатая часть *f*

elf [elf] эльф; прока́зник

elicit [ɪ'lɪsɪt]: **~ *the truth*** добива́ться [-би́ться] и́стины

eligible ['elɪdʒəbl] □ име́ющий пра́во быть и́збранным; (*suitable*) подходя́щий

eliminat|e [ɪ'lɪmɪneɪt] устраня́ть [-ни́ть]; уничтожа́ть [-то́жить]; (*exclude*) исключа́ть [-чи́ть]; **~ion** [ɪlɪmɪ'neɪʃn] устране́ние; уничтоже́ние; ***by a process of ~*** ме́тодом исключе́ния

elk [elk] *zo.* лось *m*

elm [elm] *bot.* вяз

eloquen|ce ['eləkwəns] красноре́чие; **~t** [~t] □ красноречи́вый

else [els] ещё; кро́ме; ина́че; ино́й, друго́й; ***or ~*** а то; и́ли же; **~where** [els'weə] где́-нибудь в друго́м ме́сте

elucidate [ɪ'lu:sɪdeɪt] разъясня́ть [-ни́ть]

elude [ɪ'lu:d] избега́ть [-ежа́ть] (P), уклоня́ться [-ни́ться] от (P); *of meaning* ускольза́ть [-зну́ть]

elusive [ɪ'lu:sɪv] неулови́мый

emaciated [ɪ'meɪʃɪeɪtɪd] истощённый, худо́й

email, E-mail ['i:meɪl] электро́нная по́чта

emanate ['eməneɪt] идти́ из (P); *rumours* исходи́ть (***from*** из, от P)

emancipat|e [ɪ'mænsɪpeɪt] освобожда́ть [освободи́ть]; **~ion** [ɪmænsɪ'peɪʃn] освобожде́ние, эманcипа́ция

embankment [ɪm'bæŋkmənt] на́сыпь *f*; *by river or sea* на́бережная

embargo [em'bɑ:gəʊ] эмба́рго *n indecl.*; запре́т; ***be under ~*** быть под запре́том

embark [ɪm'bɑ:k] *of goods* [по]грузи́ть(ся); *of passengers* сади́ться [сесть]; *fig.* **~** (***up***)***on*** бра́ться [взя́ться] (за В); предпринима́ть [-ня́ть]

embarrass [ɪm'bærəs] смуща́ть [смути́ть]; приводи́ть [-вести́] в замеша́тельство; стесня́ть [-ни́ть]; ***~ed by lack of money*** в стеснённом положе́нии; **~ing** [~ɪŋ] □ затрудни́тельный; неудо́бный; стеснённый; **~ment** [~mənt] (*difficulties*) затрудне́ние; смуще́ние; (*confusion*) замеша́тельство

embassy ['embəsɪ] посо́льство

embellish [ɪm'belɪʃ] украша́ть [укра́сить]

embers ['embəz] *pl.* тле́ющие у́гли *m/pl.*

embezzle [ɪm'bezl] растра́чивать [-а́тить]; **~ment** [~mənt] растра́та

embitter [ɪm'bɪtə] озлобля́ть [озло́бить], ожесточа́ть [-чи́ть]

emblem ['embləm] эмбле́ма; си́мвол; ***national ~*** госуда́рственный герб

embody [ɪm'bɒdɪ] воплоща́ть [-лоти́ть]; (*personify*) олицетворя́ть [-ри́ть]; (*include*) включа́ть [-чи́ть]

embrace [ɪm'breɪs] **1.** объя́тие; **2.** обнима́ть(ся) [-ня́ть(ся)]; (*accept*) принима́ть [-ня́ть]; (*include*) охва́тывать [охвати́ть]

embroider [ɪm'brɔɪdə] вы́ши(ва́)ть; **~y** [~rɪ] выши́вание; вы́шивка

embroil [ɪm'brɔɪl] запу́т(ыв)ать(ся); ввя́зываться [-за́ться]

emerald ['emərəld] изумру́д

emerge [ɪ'mɜ:dʒ] появля́ться [-ви́ться]; (*surface*) всплы(ва́)ть (*a. fig.*); **~ncy** [~ənsɪ] чрезвыча́йная (авари́йная) ситуа́ция; ***in an ~*** в слу́чае кра́йней необходи́мости; *attr.* запасно́й, вспомога́тельный; ***~ landing*** вы́нужденная поса́дка

emigra|nt ['emɪgrənt] эмигра́нт; **~te** [~greɪt] эмигри́ровать (*im*)*pf.*; **~tion** [emɪ'greɪʃn] эмигра́ция

eminen|ce ['emɪnəns] *geogr.* возвы́шенность *f*; *fig.* знамени́тость *f*; ***win ~ as a scientist*** стать *pf.* знамени́тым учёным; **~t** [~ənt] □ *fig.* выдаю́щийся; *adv.* чрезвыча́йно

emit [ɪ'mɪt] *sound, smell* изд(ав)а́ть, испуска́ть [-усти́ть]; *light* излуча́ть; *heat* выделя́ть [вы́делить]

emoti|on [ɪ'məʊʃn] чу́вство; возбужде́ние; волне́ние; эмо́ция *mst. pl.*; **~onal** [~ʃənl] □ эмоциона́льный; *voice* взволно́ванный; *music, etc.* волну́ющий

emperor ['empərə] импера́тор

empha|sis ['emfəsɪs] вырази́тельность *f*; ударе́ние, акце́нт; ***place ~ on s.th.*** подчёркивать [-еркну́ть] ва́жность чего́-л.; **~size** [~saɪz] подчёркивать [-черкну́ть]; **~tic** [ɪm'fætɪk] (**~ally**) *gesture etc.* вырази́тельный; *request* насто́йчивый

empire ['empaɪə] импе́рия

employ [ɪm'plɔɪ] употребля́ть [-би́ть], применя́ть [-ни́ть], испо́льзовать *(im)pf.*; предоставля́ть, нанима́ть на рабо́ту (Д); **~ee** [emplɔɪ'iː] слу́жащий [-щая], рабо́тник (-ица); **~er** [ɪm'plɔɪə] нанима́тель *m*, работода́тель *m*; **~ment** [~mənt] (*use*) примене́ние; рабо́та, заня́тие; ***~ agency*** бюро́ по трудоустро́йству; ***full ~*** по́лная за́нятость

empower [ɪm'paʊə] уполномо́чи(ва)ть

empress ['emprɪs] императри́ца

empt|iness ['emptɪnɪs] пустота́; **~y** [~tɪ] **1.** □ пусто́й, поро́жний; *coll.* голо́дный; ***I feel ~*** я го́лоден; **2.** опорожня́ть(ся) [-ни́ть(ся)]; [о]пусте́ть; *liquid* вылива́ть [вы́лить]; *sand, etc.* высыпа́ть [вы́сыпать]

enable [ɪ'neɪbl] дава́ть возмо́жность *f*; [с]де́лать возмо́жным (Д)

enact [ɪ'nækt] *law* постановля́ть [-ви́ть]; *thea.* игра́ть роль; ста́вить на сце́не

enamel [ɪ'næml] **1.** эма́ль *f*; *art* эма́ль, *obs.* фи́нифть; **2.** эмалирова́ть *(im)pf.*; покрыва́ть эма́лью

enamo(u)red [ɪ'næməd]: ***~ of*** влюблённый в (В)

enchant [ɪn'tʃɑːnt] очаро́вывать [-ова́ть]; **~ment** [~mənt] очарова́ние; **~ress** [~rɪs] *fig.* обворожи́тельная же́нщина, волше́бница

encircle [ɪn'sɜːkl] окружа́ть [-жи́ть]

enclos|e [ɪn'kləʊz] (*fence in*) огора́живать [-роди́ть]; *in letter, etc.* прилага́ть [-ложи́ть]; **~ure** [~ʒə] огоро́женное ме́сто; вложе́ние, приложе́ние

encompass [ɪn'kʌmpəs] окружа́ть [-жи́ть]

encore ['ɒŋkɔː] *thea.* **1.** бис!; **2.** крича́ть "бис"; вызыва́ть [вы́звать] на бис; (*give an encore*) биси́ровать

encounter [ɪn'kaʊntə] **1.** встре́ча; столкнове́ние; (*contest, competition*) состяза́ние; **2.** встреча́ть(ся) [-е́тить(ся)]; *difficulties etc.* ста́лкиваться [столкну́ться] (с Т); ната́лкиваться [натолкну́ться] (на В)

encourage [ɪn'kʌrɪdʒ] ободря́ть [-ри́ть]; поощря́ть [-ри́ть]; **~ment** [~mənt] ободре́ние; поощре́ние

encroach [ɪn'krəʊtʃ]: ***~ (up)on*** вторга́ться [вто́ргнуться] в (В); *rights* посяга́ть (на В); *time* отнима́ть [-ня́ть]; **~ment** [~mənt] вторже́ние

encumb|er [ɪn'kʌmbər] обременя́ть [-ни́ть]; (*cram*) загроможда́ть [-мозди́ть]; (*hamper*) затрудня́ть [-ни́ть]; [вос]препя́тствовать (Д); **~rance** [~brəns] бре́мя *n*; обу́за; *fig.* препя́тствие

encyclop(a)edia [ɪnsaɪklə'piːdɪə] энциклопе́дия

end [end] **1.** коне́ц, оконча́ние; цель *f*; ***no ~ of*** о́чень мно́го (Р); ***in the ~*** в конце́ концо́в; ***on ~*** стоймя́; *hair* ды́бом; беспреры́вно, подря́д; ***to that ~*** с э́той це́лью; **2.** конча́ть(ся) [ко́нчить(ся)]

endanger [ɪn'deɪndʒə] подверга́ть опа́сности

endear [ɪn'dɪə] внуша́ть любо́вь, заставля́ть полюби́ть; **~ment** [~mənt] ла́ска; ***words of ~*** ла́сковые слова́

endeavo(u)r [ɪn'devə] **1.** [по]пыта́ться, прилага́ть уси́лия, [по]стара́ться; **2.** попы́тка, стара́ние; ***make every ~*** сде́лать всё возмо́жное

end|ing ['endɪŋ] оконча́ние; **~less** ['endlɪs] □ бесконе́чный

endorse [ɪn'dɔːs] *fin.* индосси́ровать *(im)pf.*; (*approve*) одобря́ть [одо́брить]; **~ment** [ɪn'dɔːsmənt] индоссаме́нт, одобре́ние

endow [ɪn'daʊ] одаря́ть [-ри́ть]; (*give*) [по]же́ртвовать; **~ment** [~mənt] поже́ртвование, дар

endur|ance [ɪn'djʊərəns] *physical* про́чность *f*; *mental* выно́сливость

f; **~e** [ɪn'djʊə] выноси́ть [вы́нести], терпе́ть
enema ['enɪmə] кли́зма
enemy ['enəmɪ] враг; неприя́тель *m*; проти́вник
energ|etic [enə'dʒetɪk] (**~ally**) энерги́чный; **~y** ['enədʒɪ] эне́ргия
enfold [ɪn'fəʊld] (*embrace*) обнима́ть [обня́ть]; (*wrap up*) заку́тывать [-тать]
enforce [ɪn'fɔːs] заставля́ть [-а́вить], принужда́ть [-ди́ть]; *a law* вводи́ть [ввести́]; *strengthen* уси́ли(ва)ть
engage [ɪn'geɪdʒ] *v/t.* (*employ*) нанима́ть [наня́ть]; *rooms* заброни́ровать; *in activity* занима́ть [заня́ть]; (*attract*) привлека́ть [-е́чь]; завладе́(ва́)ть; *in conversation* вовлека́ть [-е́чь]; **be ~d** быть за́нятым; быть помо́лвленным; *v/i.* (*pledge*) обя́зываться [-за́ться]; занима́ться [заня́ться] (**in** Т); **~ment** [~mənt] обяза́тельство; встре́ча, свида́ние; помо́лвка
engaging [ɪn'geɪdʒɪŋ] □ очарова́тельный
engender [ɪn'dʒendə] *fig.* порожда́ть [породи́ть]
engine ['endʒɪn] *mot.* дви́гатель; мото́р; *rail.* парово́з; **~ driver** машини́ст
engineer [endʒɪ'nɪə] **1.** инжене́р; *naut.* меха́ник; *Am.* машини́ст; **2.** *fig.* подстра́ивать [-ро́ить]; **~ing** [~rɪŋ] машинострое́ние
English ['ɪŋglɪʃ] **1.** англи́йский; **2.** англи́йский язы́к; **the ~** англича́не *pl.*; **~man** [~mən] англича́нин; **~woman** [~ˌwʊmən] англича́нка
engrav|e [ɪn'greɪv] [вы́]гравирова́ть; *fig. in mind* запечатле́(ва́)ть; **~ing** [~ɪŋ] гравирова́ние; гравю́ра, эста́мп
engross [ɪn'grəʊs] поглоща́ть [-лоти́ть]; **~ing book** захва́тывающая кни́га
enhance [ɪn'hɑːns] *value, etc.* повыша́ть [повы́сить]; (*intensify*) уси́ли(ва)ть
enigma [ɪ'nɪgmə] зага́дка; **~tic** [enɪg'mætɪk] □ зага́дочный
enjoy [ɪn'dʒɔɪ] наслажда́ться [насла́ди́ться] (Т); получа́ть [-чи́ть] удово́льствие; **~ o.s.** развлека́ться [-ле́чься]; **~ good health** облада́ть хоро́шим здоро́вьем; **~able** [~əbl] прия́тный; **~ment** [~mənt] наслажде́ние, удово́льствие
enlarge [ɪn'lɑːdʒ] увели́чи(ва)ть(-ся); распространя́ться (**on** о П); **~ one's mind** расширя́ть [-ши́рить] кругозо́р; **~ment** [~mənt] расшире́ние; *of photo, etc.* увеличе́ние
enlighten [ɪn'laɪtn] просвеща́ть [-ети́ть]; разъясня́ть [-ни́ть]; **~ment** просвеще́ние; *of a person* просвещённость *f*
enlist [ɪn'lɪst] *v/i. mil.* поступа́ть [-пи́ть] на вое́нную слу́жбу; **~ help** привле́чь на по́мощь
enliven [ɪn'laɪvn] оживля́ть [-ви́ть]
enmity ['enmɪtɪ] вражда́, неприя́знь *f*
ennoble [ɪ'nəʊbl] облагора́живать [-ро́дить]
enorm|ity [ɪ'nɔːmətɪ] необъя́тность *f*; *pej.* чудо́вищность *f*; преступле́ние; **~ous** [~əs] □ огро́мный, грома́дный; чудо́вищный
enough [ɪ'nʌf] доста́точно, дово́льно
enquire [ɪn'kwaɪə] → **inquire**
enrage [ɪn'reɪdʒ] [вз]беси́ть, приводи́ть в я́рость
enrapture [ɪn'ræptʃə] восхища́ть [-ити́ть], очаро́вывать
enrich [ɪn'rɪtʃ] обогаща́ть [-гати́ть]
enrol(l) [ɪn'rəʊl] *v/t.* запи́сывать [-са́ть]; [за]регистри́ровать; *v/i.* запи́сываться [-са́ться]; **~ment** [~mənt] регистра́ция; за́пись *f*
en route [ˌɒn 'ruːt] по доро́ге
ensign ['ensaɪn] флаг; *Am. naut.* мла́дший лейтена́нт
ensue [ɪn'sjuː] (*follow*) [по]сле́довать; получа́ться в результа́те
ensure [ɪn'ʃʊə] обеспе́чивать [-чить]; (*guarantee*) руча́ться [поручи́ться] (за В)
entail [ɪn'teɪl] влечь за собо́й, вызыва́ть [вы́звать]
entangle [ɪn'tæŋgl] запу́тывать(ся), (*a. fig.*)
enter ['entə] *v/t. room, etc.* входи́ть [войти́] в (В); *university* поступа́ть [-пи́ть] в (В); *in book* вноси́ть

[внести́]; (*penetrate*) проника́ть [-ни́кнуть] в (В); *v/i.* входи́ть [войти́], вступа́ть [-пи́ть]
enterpris|e ['entəpraɪz] предприя́тие; (*quality*) предприи́мчивость *f*; **~ing** [~ɪŋ] □ предприи́мчивый
entertain [entə'teɪn] *guests* принима́ть [-ня́ть]; (*give food to*) угоща́ть [угости́ть]; (*amuse*) развлека́ть [-ле́чь], занима́ть [заня́ть]; **~ment** [~mənt] развлече́ние; приём
enthusias|m [ɪn'θju:zɪæzm] восто́рг; энтузиа́зм; **~t** [~æst] энтузиа́ст(ка); **~tic** [ɪnθju:zɪ'æstɪk] (**~ally**) восто́рженный; по́лный энтузиа́зма
entice [ɪn'taɪs] зама́нивать [-ни́ть]; (*tempt*) соблазня́ть [-ни́ть]; **~ment** [~mənt] собла́зн, прима́нка
entire [ɪn'taɪə] □ це́лый, весь; сплошно́й; **~ly** [~lɪ] всеце́ло; соверше́нно
entitle [ɪn'taɪtl] (*give a title to*) озагла́вливать [-ла́вить]; дава́ть пра́во (Д)
entity ['entɪtɪ] бытие́; су́щность *f*
entrails ['entreɪlz] *pl.* вну́тренности *f/pl.*
entrance ['entrəns] вход, въезд; *actor's* вы́ход; (*right to enter*) до́ступ; **~ *examinations*** вступи́тельные экза́мены
entreat [ɪn'tri:t] умоля́ть; **~y** [~ɪ] мольба́, про́сьба
entrench [ɪn'trentʃ] *fig.* укореня́ться [-ни́ться]
entrust [ɪn'trʌst] поруча́ть [-чи́ть]; доверя́ть [-ве́рить]
entry ['entrɪ] вход, въезд; *of an actor on stage* вход/вы́ход; *in book* за́пись; ***No*** ♀ вход (въезд) запрещён
enumerate [ɪ'nju:məreɪt] перечисля́ть [-и́слить]
envelop [ɪn'veləp] (*wrap*) заку́т(ыв)ать; *of mist, etc.* оку́т(ыв)ать; **~e** ['envələʊp] конве́рт
envi|able ['envɪəbl] □ зави́дный; **~ous** [~əs] □ зави́стливый
environ|ment [ɪn'vaɪərənmənt] окружа́ющая среда́; **~mental** окружа́ющий; **~ *protection*** охра́на окружа́ющей среды́; **~s** [ɪn'vaɪərənz] *pl.* окре́стности *f/pl.*
envisage [ɪn'vɪzɪdʒ] представля́ть себе́; (*anticipate*) предви́деть; (*consider*) рассма́тривать [-смотре́ть]
envoy ['envɔɪ] (*messenger*) посла́нец; (*diplomat*) посла́нник; полномо́чный представи́тель *m*
envy ['envɪ] **1.** за́висть *f*; **2.** [по]зави́довать (Д)
epic ['epɪk] **1.** эпи́ческая поэ́ма; **2.** эпи́ческий
epicenter (**-tre**) ['epɪsentə] эпице́нтр
epidemic [epɪ'demɪk] эпиде́мия
epilogue ['epɪlɒg] эпило́г
episode ['epɪsəʊd] слу́чай, эпизо́д, происше́ствие
epitome [ɪ'pɪtəmɪ] (*embodiment*) воплоще́ние
epoch ['i:pɒk] эпо́ха
equable ['ekwəbl] □ ро́вный; *fig.* уравнове́шенный
equal ['i:kwəl] **1.** □ ра́вный; одина́ковый; **~ *to*** *fig.* спосо́бный на (В); **2.** равня́ться (Д); **~ity** [ɪ'kwɒlətɪ] ра́венство; **~ization** [i:kwəlaɪ'zeɪʃn] ура́внивание; **~ize** [~aɪz] ура́внивать [-ня́ть]
equanimity [ekwə'nɪmətɪ] споко́йствие, душе́вное равнове́сие
equat|ion [ɪ'kweɪʒn] *math.* уравне́ние; **~or** [~tə] эква́тор
equilibrium [i:kwɪ'lɪbrɪəm] равнове́сие
equip [ɪ'kwɪp] *office, etc.* обору́довать; *expedition, etc.* снаряжа́ть [-яди́ть]; (*provide*) снабжа́ть [-бди́ть]; **~ment** [~mənt] обору́дование; снаряже́ние
equity ['ekwɪtɪ] справедли́вость *f*; беспристра́стность *f*; *fin. pl.* обыкнове́нные а́кции *f/pl.*
equivalent [ɪ'kwɪvələnt] **1.** эквивале́нт (***to*** Д); **2.** равноце́нный; равноси́льный
equivocal [ɪ'kwɪvəkəl] □ двусмы́сленный; (*questionable*) сомни́тельный
era ['ɪərə] э́ра; эпо́ха
eradicate [ɪ'rædɪkeɪt] искореня́ть [-ни́ть]
eras|e [ɪ'reɪz] стира́ть [стере́ть]; подчища́ть [-и́стить]; **~er** [~ə] *Am.* рези́нка
erect [ɪ'rekt] **1.** □ прямо́й; (*raised*) по́днятый; **2.** [по]стро́ить, воздви-

гáть [-и́гнуть]; **~ion** [ɪ'rekʃn] постро́йка, сооруже́ние, строе́ние
ermine ['ɜːmɪn] *zo.* горноста́й
erosion [ɪ'rəʊʒn] эро́зия
erotic [ɪ'rɒtɪk] эроти́ческий
err [ɜː] ошиба́ться [-би́ться], заблужда́ться
errand ['erənd] поруче́ние
errat|ic [ɪ'rætɪk] (**~ally**) неусто́йчивый; *player, behavio(u)r* неро́вный; **~um** [e'rɑːtəm], *pl.* **~a** [~tə] опеча́тка, опи́ска
erroneous [ɪ'rəʊnɪəs] □ оши́бочный
error ['erə] оши́бка, заблужде́ние; погре́шность *f* (*a. astr.*)
eruption [ɪ'rʌpʃn] изверже́ние; *on face, etc.* высыпа́ние (сы́пи); *of teeth* проре́зывание
escalator ['eskəleɪtə] эскала́тор
escapade ['eskəpeɪd] проде́лка; шальна́я вы́ходка
escape [ɪ'skeɪp] **1.** *v/i. from prison* бежа́ть; *from death* спаса́ться [спасти́сь]; *v/t. danger, etc.* избега́ть [-ежа́ть]; ускольза́ть [-зну́ть] (от Р); ***his name ~s me*** не могу́ припо́мнить его́ и́мени; **2.** побе́г, спасе́ние; (*leak*) уте́чка
escort 1. ['eskɔːt] сопровожде́ние, эско́рт; *mil.* конво́й; **2.** [ɪs'kɔːt, ~ɔːrt] сопровожда́ть, конвои́ровать
esoteric [esəʊ'terɪk] эзотери́ческий
especial [ɪ'speʃl] осо́бый; специа́льный; **~ly** [~ɪ] осо́бенно
espionage ['espɪənɑːʒ] шпиона́ж
essay ['eseɪ] о́черк, эссе́; (*attempt*) попы́тка; *educ.* сочине́ние
essen|ce ['esns] су́щность *f*; существо́; суть *f*; (*substance*) эссе́нция; **~tial** [ɪ'senʃl] **1.** □ суще́ственный (***to*** для Р), ва́жный; **2.** *pl.* всё необходи́мое
establish [ɪ'stæblɪʃ] *the truth, etc.* устана́вливать [-нови́ть]; (*set up*) учрежда́ть [-реди́ть], осно́вывать [-ова́ть]; **~ *o.s.*** поселя́ться [-ли́ться], устра́иваться [-ро́иться] (в П); **~ *order*** наводи́ть [-вести́] поря́док; **~ment** [~mənt] установле́ние; учрежде́ние; ***the*** **♀** истебли́шмент
estate [ɪ'steɪt] (*property*) иму́щество; (*land with a large house*) име́ние; ***real ~*** недви́жимость *f*
esteem [ɪ'stiːm] **1.** уваже́ние; **2.** уважа́ть
estimable ['estɪməbl] досто́йный уваже́ния
estimat|e 1. ['estɪmeɪt] оце́нивать [-ни́ть]; **2.** [~mɪt] сме́та, калькуля́ция; оце́нка; ***at a rough ~*** в гру́бом приближе́нии; **~ion** [estɪ'meɪʃn] оце́нка; (*opinion*) мне́ние
estrange [ɪ'streɪndʒ] отта́лкивать [-толкну́ть], сде́лать чужи́м
etching ['etʃɪŋ] *craft* гравиро́вка; *product* гравю́ра; травле́ние
etern|al [ɪ'tɜːnl] ве́чный; неизме́нный; **~ity** [~nɪtɪ] ве́чность *f*
ether ['iːθə] эфи́р
ethic|al ['eθɪkl] □ эти́чный, эти́ческий; **~s** ['eθɪks] э́тика
etiquette ['etɪket] этике́т
euro ['jʊrəʊ] е́вро
European [jʊərə'piːən] **1.** европе́ец *m*, -пе́йка *f*; **2.** европе́йский
Eurovision ['jʊərəvɪʒn] Еврови́дение
evacuate [ɪ'vækjʊeɪt] эвакуи́ровать (*im*)*pf.*
evade [ɪ'veɪd] (*avoid*) избега́ть [-ежа́ть] (Р); уклоня́ться [-ни́ться] от (Р); *law, etc.* обходи́ть [обойти́]
evaluat|e [ɪ'væljʊeɪt] оце́нивать [-ни́ть]; **~ion** [ɪvæljʊ'eɪʃn] оце́нка
evaporat|e [ɪ'væpəreɪt] испаря́ть (-ся) [-ри́ть(ся)]; *fig.* разве́иваться [-е́яться]; **~ion** [ɪvæpə'reɪʃn] испаре́ние
evasi|on [ɪ'veɪʒn] уклоне́ние, увёртка; **~ve** [~sɪv] □ укло́нчивый
eve [iːv] кану́н; ***on the ~ of*** накану́не (Р)
even ['iːvn] **1.** *adj.* □ (*level, smooth*) ро́вный, гла́дкий; (*equal*) ра́вный, одина́ковый; *number* чётный; **2.** *adv.* ро́вно; как раз; ***not ~*** да́же не; ***~ though, ~ if*** да́же е́сли; **3.** выра́внивать [вы́ровнять]; сгла́живать [сгла́дить]; **~ly** [~lɪ] ро́вно, по́ровну
evening ['iːvnɪŋ] ве́чер; вечери́нка; ***~ dress*** вече́рнее пла́тье; *man's* фрак
event [ɪ'vent] собы́тие, слу́чай; *sport* соревнова́ние; ***at all ~s*** во

всяком случае; ***be wise after the ~*** задним умом крепок; ***in the ~ of*** в случае (P); **~ful** [~fʊl] полный событий
eventual [ɪ'ventʃʊəl] возможный; конечный; **~ly** [~ɪ] в конце концов; со временем
ever ['evə] всегда; когда-нибудь, когда-либо; ***~ so*** очень; ***as soon as ~ I can*** как только я смогу; ***for ~*** навсегда; ***hardly ~*** почти не; **~green** вечнозелёный; **~lasting** [evə'lɑːstɪŋ] □ вечный; **~present** постоянный
every ['evrɪ] каждый; ***~ now and then*** время от времени; ***~ other day*** через день; ***have ~ reason*** иметь все основания; **~body** все *pl.*; каждый, всякий; **~day** ежедневный; **~one** каждый, всякий; все *pl.*; **~thing** всё; **~where** везде, всюду
evict [ɪ'vɪkt] выселять [выселить]
eviden|ce ['evɪdəns] доказательство; (*sign*) признак; (*data*) данные, факты; *law* улика; свидетельское показание; ***in ~*** в доказательство; **~t** [~nt] □ очевидный, явный
evil ['iːvl] **1.** □ злой; *influence* пагубный; дурной, плохой; **2.** зло
evince [ɪ'vɪns] проявлять [-вить]
evoke [ɪ'vəʊk] вызывать [вызвать]
evolution [iːvə'luːʃn] эволюция; развитие
evolve [ɪ'vɒlv] разви(ва)ться
ewe [juː] овца
exact [ɪg'zækt] **1.** □ точный, аккуратный; **2.** (*demand*) [по]требовать (P); взыскивать [-кать]; ***~ taxes*** взимать налоги; **~ing** [~ɪŋ] требовательный, взыскательный
exaggerate [ɪg'zædʒəreɪt] преувеличи(ва)ть
exalt [ɪg'zɔːlt] (*make higher*) повышать [повысить]; (*praise*) превозносить [-нести]; **~ation** [egzɔːl'teɪʃn] восторг
examin|ation [ɪgzæmɪ'neɪʃn] (*inspection*) осмотр; (*study*) исследование; *by experts* экспертиза; *in school*, *etc.* экзамен; **~e** [ɪg'zæmɪn] *patient*, *etc.* осматривать [-мотреть]; исследовать (*im*)*pf.*; [про]экзаменовать
example [ɪg'zɑːmpl] пример; (*sample*) образец; ***for ~*** например
exasperate [ɪg'zɑːspəreɪt] изводить [извести]; раздражать [-жить]; доводить до белого каления
excavate ['ekskəveɪt] выкапывать [выкопать]; *archaeology* вести раскопки
excavator ['ekskəveɪtə] экскаватор
exceed [ɪk'siːd] *speed*, *etc.* превышать [-высить]; (*be greater than*) превосходить [-взойти]; ***this ~s all limits!*** это переходит все границы!; **~ing** [~ɪŋ] □ превышающий
excel [ɪk'sel] *v/t.* преуспевать [-петь] (***in***, ***at*** T); *v/i.* выделяться [выделиться]; **~lence** ['eksələns] высокое качество; совершенство; **~lent** ['eksələnt] □ превосходный
except [ɪk'sept] **1.** исключать [-чить]; **2.** *prp.* исключая (B); кроме (P); ***~ for*** за исключением (P); **~ing** [~ɪŋ] *prp.* за исключением (P); **~ion** [ɪk'sepʃn] исключение; ***take ~ to*** возражать [-разить] (против P); **~ional** [~l] исключительный; *person* незаурядный
excess [ɪk'ses] избыток, излишек; эксцесс; ***~ fare*** доплата; ***~ luggage*** излишек багажа; багаж сверх нормы; ***~ profits*** сверхприбыль; **~ive** [~ɪv] □ чрезмерный
exchange [ɪks'tʃeɪndʒ] **1.** обмениваться [-няться] (T); обменивать [-нять] (***for*** на B); [по]меняться (T); **2.** обмен; (*a.* ♀) биржа; ***foreign ~*** иностранная валюта
exchequer [ɪks'tʃekə]: ***Chancellor of the*** ♀ министр финансов Великобритании
excise [ek'saɪz] *fin.* акциз, акцизный сбор
excit|able [ɪk'saɪtəbl] возбудимый; **~e** [ɪk'saɪt] возбуждать [-удить], [вз]волновать; **~ement** [~mənt] возбуждение, волнение
exclaim [ɪk'skleɪm] восклицать [-икнуть]
exclamation [ekskla'meɪʃn] восклицание
exclude [ɪk'skluːd] исключать [-чить]
exclusi|on [ɪk'skluːʒn] исключе-

ние; **~ve** [~sɪv] □ исключи́тельный; (*sole*) еди́нственный; **~ of** без; не счита́я; за исключе́нием (Р)
excrement ['ekskrɪmənt] экскре́менты *m/pl.*, испражне́ния *n/pl.*
excruciating [ɪk'skruːʃɪeɪtɪŋ] мучи́тельный
excursion [ɪk'skɜːʒn] экску́рсия; ***go on an ~*** отпра́виться (пое́хать) на экску́рсию
excus|able [ɪk'skjuːzəbl] □ прости́тельный; **~e 1.** [ɪk'skjuːz] извиня́ть [-ни́ть], проща́ть [прости́ть]; **2.** [ɪk'skjuːs] извине́ние; (*reason*) оправда́ние; (*pretext*) отгово́рка
execut|e ['eksɪkjuːt] (*carry out*) исполня́ть [-о́лнить]; (*fulfil*) выполня́ть [вы́]полнить); (*put to death*) казни́ть (*im*)*pf.*; **~ion** [eksɪ'kjuːʃn] исполне́ние; выполне́ние; (*capital punishment*) казнь *f*; **~ive** [ɪg'zekjʊtɪv] **1.** исполни́тельный; администрати́вный; **2.** исполни́тельная власть *f*; (*person*) администра́тор
exemplary [ɪg'zemplərɪ] образцо́вый, приме́рный
exemplify [ɪg'zemplɪfaɪ] (*illustrate by example*) поясня́ть приме́ром; (*serve as example*) служи́ть приме́ром (Р)
exempt [ɪg'zempt] **1.** освобожда́ть [-боди́ть] (от Р); **2.** освобождённый, свобо́дный (***of*** от Р)
exercise ['eksəsaɪz] **1.** упражне́ние; (*drill*) трениро́вка; (*walk*) прогу́лка; **2.** [на]тренирова́ть(ся); *patience, etc.* проявля́ть [-ви́ть]; (*use*) [вос]по́льзоваться
exert [ɪg'zɜːt] *strength, etc.* напряга́ть [-ря́чь]; *influence, etc.* ока́зывать [-за́ть]; ***~ o.s.*** прилага́ть [-ложи́ть] уси́лия; **~ion** [ɪg'zɜːʃn] напряже́ние, уси́лие
exhale [eks'heɪl] выдыха́ть [вы́дохнуть]
exhaust [ɪg'zɔːst] **1.** изнуря́ть [-ри́ть], истоща́ть [-щи́ть]; **2.** *pipe* выхлопна́я труба́; вы́хлоп; **~ion** [~ʃn] истоще́ние, изнуре́ние; **~ive** [~ɪv] □ (*very tiring*) изнуря́ющий; *study, etc.* всесторо́нний; *answer* исче́рпывающий
exhibit [ɪg'zɪbɪt] **1.** *interest etc.* проявля́ть [-ви́ть]; *at exhibition* выставля́ть [вы́ставить]; **2.** экспона́т; **~ion** [eksɪ'bɪʃn] проявле́ние; вы́ставка; **~or** [ɪg'zɪbɪtə] экспоне́нт
exhilarat|e [ɪg'zɪləreɪt] оживля́ть [-ви́ть]; [вз]бодри́ть; **~ing** [~ɪŋ] *weather, etc.* бодря́щий
exhort [ɪg'zɔːt] призыва́ть [-зва́ть]; увещева́ть; побужда́ть [-уди́ть] (к Д)
exigency ['eksɪdʒənsɪ] о́страя необходи́мость *f*
exile ['eksaɪl] **1.** *lit., hist.* изгна́ние, ссы́лка; изгна́нник, ссы́льный; **2.** ссыла́ть [сосла́ть]; *from a country* высыла́ть [вы́слать]
exist [ɪg'zɪst] существова́ть, жить; **~ence** [~əns] существова́ние, жизнь *f*; ***in ~*** = **~ent** [~ənt] существу́ющий
exit ['eksɪt] вы́ход; ***emergency ~*** запасно́й вы́ход
exodus ['eksədəs] ма́ссовый отъе́зд; *Bibl.* Исхо́д
exonerate [ɪg'zɒnəreɪt] опра́вдывать [-да́ть]; (*free from blame*) снима́ть [снять] обвине́ние; *from responsibility* снима́ть [снять] отве́тственность
exorbitant [ɪg'zɔːbɪtənt] □ непоме́рный, чрезме́рный
exotic [ɪg'zɒtɪk] экзоти́ческий
expan|d [ɪk'spænd] расширя́ть(ся) [-и́рить(ся)], увели́чи(ва)ть(ся); (*develop*) разви́(ва́)ть(ся); **~se** [ɪk'spæns] простра́нство; протяже́ние; **~sion** [~nʃn] расшире́ние; (*spread*) распростране́ние; разви́тие; **~sive** [~sɪv] □ обши́рный; *fig.* экспанси́вный
expect [ɪks'pekt] ожида́ть (Р); (*count on*) рассчи́тывать, наде́яться; (*think*) полага́ть, ду́мать; **~ant** [~ənt]: ***~ mother*** бере́менная же́нщина; **~ation** [ekspek'teɪʃn] ожида́ние; (*hope*) *mst. pl.* наде́жда
expedi|ent [ɪk'spiːdɪənt] **1.** подходя́щий, целесообра́зный, соотве́тствующий; **2.** сре́дство достиже́ния це́ли; приём; **~tion** [ekspɪ'dɪʃn] экспеди́ция; (*speed*) быстрота́
expel [ɪk'spel] *from school, etc.* исключа́ть [-чи́ть] (из Р)
expen|d [ɪk'spend] [ис]тра́тить; [из-]

расхо́довать; **~diture** [~ıtʃə] расхо́д, тра́та; **~se** [ık'spens] расхо́д, тра́та; ***at his ~*** за его́ счёт; ***travel ~s*** командиро́вочные; **~sive** [~sıv] □ дорого́й, дорогосто́ящий

experience [ık'spıərıəns] **1.** (*жи́зненный*) о́пыт; (*event*) слу́чай, приключе́ние; **2.** испы́тывать [испыта́ть]; (*suffer*) пережи́(ва́)ть; **~d** [~t] о́пытный; квалифици́рованный

experiment 1. [ık'sperımənt] о́пыт, экспериме́нт; **2.** [~ment] производи́ть о́пыты; **~al** [ıksperı'mentl] □ эксперимента́льный, о́пытный, про́бный

expert ['ekspɜːt] **1.** о́пытный, иску́сный; **2.** экспе́рт, знато́к, специали́ст; *attr.* высококвалифици́рованный

expir|ation [ekspı'reıʃn] (*end*) оконча́ние, истече́ние; **~e** [ık'spaıə] (*breathe out*) выдыха́ть [вы́дохнуть]; (*die*) умира́ть [умере́ть]; *fin.* истека́ть [-е́чь]

explain [ık'spleın] объясня́ть [-ни́ть]; (*justify*) опра́вдывать [-да́ть]

explanat|ion [eksplə'neıʃn] объясне́ние; (*justification*) оправда́ние; (*reason*) причи́на; **~ory** [ık'splænətrı] □ объясни́тельный

explicable [ık'splıkəbl] объясни́мый

explicit [ık'splısıt] □ я́сный, недвусмы́сленный, то́чный

explode [ık'spləʊd] (*blow up*) взрыва́ть(ся) [взорва́ть(ся)] (*a. fig.*); *of applause etc.* разража́ться [-рази́ться] (***with*** T)

exploit 1. ['eksplɔıt] по́двиг; **2.** [ık'splɔıt] эксплуати́ровать; *mining* разраба́тывать [-бо́тать]; **~ation** [eksplɔı'teıʃn] эксплуата́ция; разрабо́тка

explor|ation [eksplə'reıʃn] иссле́дование; **~e** [ık'splɔː] иссле́довать (*im*)*pf.*; *geol.* разве́д(ыв)ать; *problem, etc.* изуча́ть [-чи́ть]; **~er** [~rə] иссле́дователь(ница *f*) *m*

explosi|on [ık'spləʊʒn] взрыв; *of anger* вспы́шка; **~ve** [~sıv] **1.** □ взры́вчатый; *fig.* вспы́льчивый; **2.** взры́вчатое вещество́

exponent [ık'spəʊnənt] (*advocate*) сторо́нник, представи́тель *m*; *math.* показа́тель *m* сте́пени; (*interpreter*) толкова́тель *m*

export 1. ['ekspɔːt] э́кспорт, вы́воз; **2.** [ık'spɔːt] экспорти́ровать (*im*)*pf.*, вывози́ть [вы́везти]; **~er** [~ə] экспортёр

expos|e [ık'spəʊz] *to danger, etc.* подверга́ть [-е́ргнуть]; (*display*) выставля́ть [вы́ставить]; (*unmask*) разоблача́ть [-чи́ть]; *phot.* экспони́ровать (*im*)*pf.*; **~ition** [ekspə'zıʃn] вы́ставка; изложе́ние

exposure [ık'spəʊʒə] (*unmasking*) разоблаче́ние; *phot.* экспози́ция, вы́держка; возде́йствие вне́шней среды́; ***die of ~*** умере́ть от *переохлажде́ния и т.д.*

expound [ık'spaʊnd] излага́ть [изложи́ть]; (*explain*) разъясня́ть [-ни́ть]

express [ık'spres] **1.** □ (*clearly stated*) определённый, то́чно выраженный; (*urgent*) сро́чный; **2. ~** (***train***) экспре́сс; **3.** *adv.* спе́шно; **4.** выража́ть [вы́разить]; **~ion** [ık'spreʃn] выраже́ние; (*quality*) вырази́тельность *f*; **~ive** [~ıv] □ (*full of feeling*) вырази́тельный; (*~ of joy, etc.*) выража́ющий

expulsion [ık'spʌlʃn] изгна́ние; *from school, etc.* исключе́ние; *from country* вы́сылка

exquisite [ık'skwızıt] □ изы́сканный, утончённый; *sensibility* обострённый; *torture* изощрённый

extant [ek'stænt] сохрани́вшийся

extempor|aneous [ekstempə'reınıəs] □, **~ary** [ık'stempərərı] импровизи́рованный; **~e** [~pərı] *adv.* экспро́мтом

extend [ık'stend] *v/t.* протя́гивать [-тяну́ть]; (*spread*) распространя́ть [-ни́ть]; (*prolong*) продлева́ть [-ли́ть]; (*enlarge*) расширя́ть [-ши́рить]; *v/i.* простира́ться [простере́ться]

extensi|on [ık'stenʃn] (*enlargement*) расшире́ние; *of knowledge etc.* распростране́ние; (*continuance*) продле́ние; *arch.* пристро́йка; **~ve** [~sıv] □ обши́рный, простра́нный

extent [ık'stent] (*area, length*) протяже́ние; (*degree*) разме́р, сте́пень

f, мéра; ***to the ~ of*** в размéре (P); ***to some ~*** до извéстной стéпени
extenuate [ɪk'stenjʊeɪt] (*lessen*) уменьшáть [умéньшить]; (*find excuse for*) старáться найтú оправдáние; (*soften*) ослаблять [-áбить]
exterior [ek'stɪərɪə] **1.** внéшний, нарýжный; **2.** внéшняя сторонá
exterminate [ek'stɜːmɪneɪt] (*destroy*) истреблять [-бúть]; *fig.* искоренять [-нúть]
external [ek'stɜːnl] □ нарýжный, внéшний
extinct [ɪk'stɪŋkt] угáсший; *species, etc.* вы́мерший; *volcano etc.* потýхший
extinguish [ɪk'stɪŋgwɪʃ] [по]гасúть; [по]тушúть; *debt* погашáть [погасúть]
extol [ɪk'stəʊl] превозносúть [-нестú]
extort [ɪk'stɔːt] *money* вымогáть; *secret* выпы́тывать [вы́пытать]; **~ion** [ɪk'stɔːʃn] вымогáтельство
extra ['ekstrə] **1.** добáвочный, дополнúтельный; ***~ charges*** дополнúтельная (о)плáта; **2.** *adv.* осóбо; осóбенно; дополнúтельно; **3.** приплáта; **~s** *pl.* дополнúтельные расхóды; побóчные дохóды
extract **1.** ['ekstrækt] экстрáкт; *from text* вы́держка, отры́вок; **2.** [ɪk'strækt] *tooth* удалять [-лúть]; *bullet etc.* извлекáть [-éчь]; *chem.* экстрагúровать; **~ion** [~kʃn] экстрагúрование; (*ancestry, origin*) происхождéние
extraordinary [ɪk'strɔːdnrɪ] чрезвычáйный, необы́чный, экстраординáрный, выдаю́щийся
extrasensory [ekstrə'sensərɪ] внечýвственный, экстрасенсóрный
extravagan|ce [ɪk'strævəgəns] экстравагáнтность *f*; (*wastefulness*) расточúтельность *f*; (*excess*) излúшество; **~t** [~gənt] □ расточúтельный; сумасбрóдный, экстравагáнтный
extrem|e [ɪk'striːm] **1.** □ крáйний; предéльный; чрезвычáйный; **2.** крáйность *f*; ***go to ~*** пойтú на крáйние мéры; **~ity** [ɪk'stremətɪ] (*end*) оконéчность *f*, край; крáйность *f*; крáйняя нуждá; крáйняя мéра; **~ities** [~z] *pl.* конéчности *f/pl.*
extricate ['ekstrɪkeɪt] высвобождáть [вы́свободить], вы́зволить *mst. pl.*; ***~ o.s.*** выпýтываться [вы́путаться]
exuberan|ce [ɪg'zjuːbərəns] изобúлие, избы́ток; **~t** [~t] *vegetation* бýйный; *speech* обúльный, несдéржанный; (*full of life*) пóлный жúзни, экспансúвный
exult [ɪg'zʌlt] ликовáть; торжествовáть
eye [aɪ] **1.** глаз; *of needle* ýшко; ***with an ~ to*** с цéлью (+ *inf.*); ***catch s.o.'s ~*** поймáть чéй-л. взгляд; обратúть на себя внимáние; **2.** смотрéть на (В), прúстально разглядывать; **~ball** глазнóе яблоко; **~brow** бровь *f*; **...~d** [aɪd] ...глáзый; **~lash** реснúца; **~lid** вéко; **~sight** зрéние; **~ shadow** тéни для век; **~witness** свидéтель, очевúдец

F

fable ['feɪbl] бáсня; *fig.* вы́думка
fabric ['fæbrɪk] (*structure*) структýра; (*cloth*) ткань *f*; **~ate** ['fæbrɪkeɪt] (*mst. fig.*) выдýмывать [вы́думать]; (*falsify*) [с]фабриковáть
fabulous ['fæbjʊləs] □ баснослóвный; (*excellent*) великолéпный
face [feɪs] **1.** лицó, *joc. or pej.* физионóмия; *of cloth* лицевáя сторонá; *of watch* циферблáт; ***on the ~ of it*** с пéрвого взглядa; **2.** *v/t.* встречáть смéло; смотрéть в лицó

(Д); стоя́ть лицо́м к (Д); *of window*, *etc.* выходи́ть на (В); *tech.* облицо́вывать [-цева́ть]
facetious [fə'siːʃəs] □ шутли́вый
face value номина́льная сто́имость; ***take s.th. at (its) ~*** принима́ть [-ня́ть] за чи́стую моне́ту
facil|itate [fə'sɪlɪteɪt] облегча́ть [-чи́ть]; **~ity** [fə'sɪlətɪ] лёгкость *f*; спосо́бность *f*; *of speech* пла́вность *f*
facing ['feɪsɪŋ] *of wall*, *etc.* облицо́вка
F
fact [fækt] факт; ***as a matter of ~*** со́бственно говоря́; ***I know for a ~ that*** я то́чно зна́ю, что
faction ['fækʃn] фра́кция
factor ['fæktə] *math.* мно́житель; (*contributing cause*) фа́ктор; **~y** [~rɪ] фа́брика, заво́д
faculty ['fækəltɪ] спосо́бность *f*; *fig.* дар; *univ.* факульте́т
fad [fæd] (*craze*) увлече́ние; (*fancy*) при́хоть *f*, причу́да; (*fashion*) преходя́щая мо́да
fade [feɪd] увяда́ть [увя́нуть]; постепе́нно уменьша́ть [уме́ньшить]; *of colo(u)r* [по]линя́ть
fag [fæg] уста́лость, утомле́ние
fail [feɪl] **1.** *v/i.* (*grow weak*) ослабе́(ва́)ть; (*be wanting in*) недоста(ва́)ть; потерпе́ть *pf.* неуда́чу; *at examination* прова́ливаться [-ли́ться]; ***he ~ed to do*** ему́ не удало́сь сде́лать (В); забы́(ва́)ть; *v/t. of courage*, *etc.* покида́ть [-и́нуть]; **2.** *su.*: ***without ~*** наверняка́; непреме́нно; **~ing** ['feɪlɪŋ] недоста́ток; сла́бость *f*; **~ure** ['feɪljə] неуда́ча, неуспе́х; прова́л; банкро́тство; неуда́чник *m*, -ница *f*; *tech.* поврежде́ние, отка́з
faint [feɪnt] **1.** □ сла́бый; *light* ту́склый; **2.** [о]слабе́ть; потеря́ть созна́ние (***with*** от Р); **3.** о́бморок, поте́ря созна́ния; **~-hearted** [feɪnt'hɑːtɪd] трусли́вый, малоду́шный
fair[1] [feə] **1.** *adj.* прекра́сный, краси́вый; (*favo[u]rable*) благоприя́тный; *hair* белоку́рый; *weather* я́сный; (*just*) справедли́вый; **2.** *adv.* че́стно; пря́мо, я́сно; ***~ copy*** чистови́к; ***~ play*** че́стная игра́
fair[2] [~] я́рмарка
fair|ly ['feəlɪ] справедли́во; (*quite*) дово́льно; **~ness** ['feənɪs] справедли́вость *f*; красота́ (→ ***fair***[1]); ***in all ~*** со всей справедли́востью
fairy ['feərɪ] фе́я; **~land** ска́зочная страна́; **~ tale** ска́зка
faith [feɪθ] дове́рие, ве́ра, *a. relig.*; **~ful** ['feɪθfl] ве́рный, пре́данный; (*accurate*) то́чный, правди́вый; ***yours ~ly*** пре́данный Вам; **~less** ['feɪθlɪs] □ вероло́мный
fake [feɪk] *sl.* **1.** подде́лка, фальши́вка; **2.** подде́л(ыв)ать
falcon ['fɔːlkən] со́кол
fall [fɔːl] **1.** паде́ние; (*decline*) упа́док; (*declivity*, *slope*) обры́в, склон; *Am.* о́сень *f*; (*mst.* **~s** *pl.*) водопа́д; **2.** [*irr.*] па́дать [упа́сть]; спада́ть [спасть]; *of water* убы́(ва́)ть; ***~ back*** отступа́ть [-пи́ть]; ***~ ill*** *или* ***sick*** заболе́(ва́)ть; ***~ out*** [по]ссо́риться; ***~ short of*** не оправда́ть (ожида́ний); не достига́ть [-и́чь] *a.* [-и́гнуть] (це́ли); ***~ short*** уступа́ть в чём-л., не хвата́ть [-ти́ть]; ***~ to*** принима́ться [-ня́ться] за (В)
fallacious [fə'leɪʃəs] □ оши́бочный, ло́жный
fallacy ['fæləsɪ] заблужде́ние, оши́бочный вы́вод
fallen ['fɔːlən] *pt. p. от* ***fall***
falling ['fɔːlɪŋ] паде́ние; пониже́ние
fallout ['fɔːləʊt]: ***radioactive ~*** радиоакти́вные оса́дки
fallow ['fæləʊ] *adj.* вспа́ханный под пар
false [fɔːls] □ ло́жный, оши́бочный; *coin* фальши́вый; *friend* вероло́мный; *teeth* иску́сственный; **~hood** ['fɔːlshʊd] ложь *f*; (*falseness*) лжи́вость *f*
falsi|fication [fɔːlsɪfɪ'keɪʃn] подде́лка; *of theories*, *etc.* фальсифика́ция; **~fy** ['fɔːlsɪfaɪ] подде́л(ыв)ать; фальсифици́ровать
falter ['fɔːltə] *in walking* дви́гаться неуве́ренно; *in speech* запина́ться [запну́ться]; *fig.* колеба́ться
fame [feɪm] сла́ва; изве́стность *f*; **~d** [feɪmd] изве́стный, знамени́тый; ***be ~d for*** сла́виться (Т)
familiar [fə'mɪlɪə] □ бли́зкий, хорошо́ знако́мый; (*usual*) привы́чный; **~ity** [fəmɪlɪ'ærətɪ] (*of manner*) *a. pej.* фамилья́рность *f*; (*knowledge*) осведомлённость *f*; **~ize** [fə-

'mılıəraız] ознакомля́ть [-ко́мить]
family ['fæməlı] семья́, семе́йство; **~ tree** родосло́вное де́рево
fami|ne ['fæmın] го́лод; **~sh**: ***I feel ~ed*** я умира́ю от го́лода
famous ['feıməs] □ знамени́тый
fan¹ [fæn] **1.** ве́ер; *tech.* вентиля́тор; **2.**: **~ o.s.** обма́хивать(ся) [-хну́ть(ся)] ве́ером
fan² [~] *sport* боле́льщик *m*, -щица *f*, фана́т; (*admirer*) покло́нник *m*, -ница *f*
fanatic [fə'nætık] **1.** (*a.* **~al** [~ıkəl] □) фанати́чный; **2.** фана́тик *m*, -ти́чка *f*
fanciful ['fænsıfl] □ прихотли́вый, причу́дливый
fancy ['fænsı] **1.** фанта́зия, воображе́ние; (*whim*) при́хоть *f*; (*love*) пристра́стие; (*inclination*) скло́нность *f*; **2.** *prices* фантасти́ческий; **~ goods** *pl.* мо́дные това́ры *m/pl.*; **3.** вообража́ть [-рази́ть]; представля́ть [-а́вить] себе; [по]люби́ть; [за]хоте́ть; ***just ~!*** предста́вьте себе́!
fang [fæŋ] клык
fantas|tic [fæn'tæstık] (**~ally**) причу́дливый, фантасти́чный; *coll.* невероя́тный; потряса́ющий; **~y** ['fæntəsı] фанта́зия, воображе́ние
far [fɑː] *adj.* да́льний, далёкий, отдалённый; *adv.* далеко́; гора́здо; ***as ~ as*** до (Р); ***as ~ as I know*** наско́лько мне изве́стно; ***inso~*** (*Brt.* ***in so ~***) ***as*** поско́льку; ***~ away*** далеко́
fare [feə] пла́та за прое́зд; **~well** [fɛə'wel, feər~] **1.** проща́й(те)!; **2.** проща́ние
farfetched [fɑː'fetʃt] *fig.* притя́нутый за́ уши
farm [fɑːm] **1.** фе́рма; **2.** обраба́тывать зе́млю; **~er** ['fɑːmə] фе́рмер; **~house** жило́й дом на фе́рме; **~ing** заня́тие се́льским хозя́йством, фе́рмерство; **~-stead** ['fɑːmsted] уса́дьба
far-off ['fɑːrɔf] далёкий
farthe|r ['fɑːðə] **1.** *adv.* да́льше; **2.** *adj.* бо́лее отдалённый; **~st** [~ðıst] **1.** *adj.* са́мый далёкий, са́мый да́льний; **2.** *adv.* да́льше всего́
fascinat|e ['fæsıneıt] очаро́вывать [-ова́ть], пленя́ть [-ни́ть]; **~ion** [fæsı'neıʃn] очарова́ние
fashion ['fæʃn] **1.** (*prevailing style*) мо́да; стиль *m*; (*manner*) о́браз, мане́ра; ***in*** (***out of***) **~** (не)мо́дный; **2.** придава́ть фо́рму, вид (Д ***into*** Р); **~able** ['fæʃnəbl] мо́дный
fast¹ [fɑːst] (*fixed*, *firm*) про́чный, кре́пкий, твёрдый; (*quick*) бы́стрый; ***my watch is ~*** мои́ часы́ спеша́т
fast² [~] **1.** (*going without food*) пост; **2.** пости́ться
fasten ['fɑːsn] *v/t.* (*fix*) прикрепля́ть [-пи́ть]; (*tie*) привя́зывать [-за́ть]; *coat, etc.* застёгивать [-тегну́ть]; *door* запира́ть [-пере́ть]; *v/i.* запира́ться [запере́ться]; застёгивать(ся) [-тегну́ть(ся)]; **~ *upon*** *fig.* ухвати́ться за (В); **~er** [~ə] застёжка
fast food фаст-фу́д
fastidious [fæ'stıdıəs] □ разбо́рчивый; *about food* привере́дливый
fat [fæt] **1.** жи́рный; *person* ту́чный; **2.** жир; са́ло
fatal ['feıtl] рокова́й, фата́льный; (*causing death*) смерте́льный; **~ity** [fə'tælətı] (*doom*) обречённость *f*; (*destiny*) фата́льность *f*; (*caused by accident*) же́ртва; смерть *f*
fate [feıt] рок, судьба́
father ['fɑːðə] оте́ц; **~hood** [~hud] отцо́вство; **~-in-law** ['fɑːðərınlɔː] *husband's* свёкор; *wife's* тесть *m*; **~less** [~lıs] оста́вшийся без отца́; **~ly** [~lı] оте́ческий
fathom ['fæðəm] *fig.* вника́ть [вни́кнуть] в (В), понима́ть [поня́ть]
fatigue [fə'tiːg] **1.** утомле́ние, уста́лость *f*; **2.** утомля́ть [-ми́ть]
fat|ness ['fætnıs] жи́рность *f*; **~ten** ['fætn] *animal* отка́рмливать [откорми́ть]; [рас]толсте́ть
fatuous ['fætʃuəs] □ бессмы́сленный, глу́пый
faucet ['fɔːsıt] *esp. Am.* водопрово́дный кран
fault [fɔːlt] (*shortcoming*) недоста́ток; *tech.* неиспра́вность *f*, дефе́кт; (*blame*) вина́; ***find ~ with*** прид(и)ра́ться к (Д); ***be at ~*** быть вино́вным; **~finder** приди́ра *m/f*; **~less** ['fɔːltlıs] □ безупре́чный;

~y ['fɔ:ltɪ] □ *thing* с бра́ком, дефе́ктом; *method* поро́чный

favo(u)r ['feɪvə] **1.** благоскло́нность *f*; расположе́ние; одолже́ние, любе́зность *f*; ***do s.o. a ~*** оказа́ть *pf.* кому́-л. любе́зность; **2.** (*approve*) одобря́ть [-рить]; (*regard with goodwill*) хорошо́ относи́ться к (Д); **~able** [~rəbl] □ благоприя́тный; *opportunity* удо́бный; **~ite** ['feɪvərɪt] **1.** люби́мец *m*, -мица *f*; фавори́т; **2.** люби́мый

F

fawn [fɔ:n] све́тло-кори́чневый цвет

fax [fæks] **1.** факс; **2.** передава́ть [-да́ть] по фа́ксу

fear [fɪə] **1.** страх, боя́знь *f*; (*apprehension*) опасе́ние; **2.** боя́ться (Р); ***for ~ of*** из-за боя́зни; **~ful** ['fɪəfl] □ стра́шный, ужа́сный; **~less** ['fɪəlɪs] бесстра́шный

feasible ['fi:zəbl] (*capable of being done*) выполни́мый, осуществи́мый; возмо́жный

feast [fi:st] банке́т; пир, пи́ршество; *eccl.* церко́вный *или* престо́льный пра́здник

feat [fi:t] по́двиг

feather ['feðə] перо́; ***show the white ~*** *coll.* прояви́ть тру́сость *f*; **~brained** пустоголо́вый

feature ['fi:tʃə] **1.** черта́; осо́бенность *f*, сво́йство; *Am.* выдаю́щаяся газе́тная статья́; **~s** *pl.* черты́ лица́; **2.** *in story* фигури́ровать; *of a film* пока́зывать [-за́ть]; ***the film ~s a new actor as ...*** фильм с уча́стием но́вого актёра в ро́ли ...

February ['februərɪ] февра́ль *m*

fed [fed] *pt. u pt. p. om* ***feed***; ***I am ~ up with ...*** мне надое́л (-ла, -ло)

federa|l ['fedərəl] федера́льный; *in names of states* федерати́вный; **~tion** [fedə'reɪʃn] федера́ция

fee [fi:] *doctor's*, *etc.* гонора́р; *member's* взнос; *for tuition* пла́та

feeble ['fi:bl] □ сла́бый, хи́лый

feed [fi:d] **1.** *agric.* корм, фура́ж; *baby's* еда́, кормле́ние; *of a machine* пита́ние; **2.** [*irr.*] *v/t.* [по]корми́ть; пита́ть, подава́ть; *v/i.* пита́ться, корми́ться; (*graze*) пасти́сь; **~back** *tech.* обра́тная связь; **~ing-bottle** де́тский рожо́к

feel [fi:l] **1.** [*irr.*] [по]чу́вствовать (себя́); (*experience*) испы́тывать [-та́ть]; *by contact* ощуща́ть [ощути́ть]; (*touch*) [по]тро́гать; (*grope*) нащу́п(ыв)ать; ***~ like doing*** быть скло́нным сде́лать; **2.**: ***get the ~ of*** привыка́ть [-ы́кнуть]; **~ing** ['fi:lɪŋ] чу́вство, ощуще́ние

feet [fi:t] *pl. om* ***foot 1***

feign [feɪn] притворя́ться [-ри́ться], симули́ровать (*im*)*pf.*

feint [feɪnt] (*sham offensive*) финт, диве́рсия

fell [fel] **1.** *pt. om* ***fall***; **2.** *tree*, *etc.* [с]руби́ть

fellow ['feləʊ] па́рень; (*companion*) това́рищ; *professional* колле́га, сотру́дник; *of a college* член сове́та; **~-countryman** сооте́чественник; **~ship** [~ʃɪp] това́рищество

felt[1] [felt] *pt. u pt. p. om* ***feel***

felt[2] [~] во́йлок, фетр

female ['fi:meɪl] **1.** же́нский; **2.** же́нщина; *zo.* са́мка

feminine ['femɪnɪn] □ же́нский; же́нственный

fen [fen] боло́то, топь *f*

fence [fens] **1.** забо́р, и́згородь *f*, огра́да; ***sit on the ~*** занима́ть нейтра́льную пози́цию; **2.** *v/t.* отгора́живать [-роди́ть]; *v/i. sport* фехтова́ть

fencing ['fensɪŋ] **1.** и́згородь *f*, забо́р, огра́да; *sport* фехтова́ние; **2.** *attr.* фехтова́льный

fender ['fendə] (*fire screen*) ками́нная решётка; *of car*, *Am.* крыло́

ferment 1. ['fɜ:ment] заква́ска, ферме́нт; *chem.* броже́ние (*a. fig.*); **2.** [fə'ment] вызыва́ть броже́ние; броди́ть; **~ation** [fɜ:men'teɪʃn] броже́ние

fern [fɜ:n] па́поротник

feroci|ous [fə'rəʊʃəs] □ свире́пый; *dog* злой; **~ty** [fə'rɒsətɪ] свире́пость *f*

ferret ['ferɪt] **1.** *zo.* хорёк; **2.** [по-] ры́ться, [по]ша́рить; ***~ out*** вы́искивать [вы́искать]; *secret* разню́хивать [-хать]; вы́ведать *pf.*

ferry ['ferɪ] **1.** (*place for crossing river*, *etc.*) перево́з, перепра́ва; (*boat*) паро́м; **2.** перевози́ть [-вез-

ти́]; **~man** перево́зчик
fertil|e ['fɜ:taɪl] □ *soil* плодоро́дный; *humans, animals* плодови́тый (*a. fig.*); **~ *imagination*** бога́тое воображе́ние; **~ity** [fə'tɪlətɪ] плодоро́дие; плодови́тость *f*; **~ize** ['fɜ:tɪlaɪz] удобря́ть [удо́брить]; оплодотворя́ть [-ри́ть]; **~izer** ['fɜ:tɪlaɪzə] удобре́ние
fervent ['fɜ:vənt] горя́чий, пы́лкий
fervo(u)r ['fɜ:və] жар, пыл, страсть *f*
fester ['festə] гнои́ться
festiv|al ['festəvl] пра́здник; фестива́ль *m*; **~e** ['festɪv] □ пра́здничный; **~ity** [fe'stɪvətɪ] пра́зднество; торжество́
fetch [fetʃ] сходи́ть, съе́здить за (T); приноси́ть [-нести́]; **~ing** [~ɪŋ] □ привлека́тельный
fetter ['fetə] **1.** *mst.* **~*s*** *pl.* пу́ты *f/pl.*; *fig.* око́вы *f/pl.*, у́зы *f/pl.*; **2.** *fig.* свя́зывать [-за́ть] по рука́м и нога́м
feud [fju:d] *family* вражда́ *f*
feudal ['fju:dl] □ феода́льный
fever ['fi:və] лихора́дка, жар; **~ish** [~rɪʃ] □ лихора́дочный
few [fju:] немно́гие; немно́го, ма́ло (P); ***a ~*** не́сколько (P); ***a good ~*** дово́льно мно́го
fiancé(e) [fɪ'ɒnseɪ] жени́х (неве́ста)
fiasco [fɪ'æskəʊ] прова́л, по́лная неуда́ча, фиа́ско
fib [fɪb] **1.** вы́думка, непра́вда; **2.** прив(и)ра́ть
fiber, *Brt.* **fibre** ['faɪbə] волокно́, нить *f*
fickle ['fɪkl] непостоя́нный
fiction ['fɪkʃn] вы́мысел, вы́думка; худо́жественная литерату́ра, беллетри́стика; ***science ~*** нау́чная фанта́стика; **~al** [~l] □ вы́мышленный
fictitious [fɪk'tɪʃəs] □ подло́жный, фикти́вный; вы́мышленный
fiddle ['fɪdl] *coll.* **1.** скри́пка; *fig. a cheat* жу́льничество; **2.** игра́ть на скри́пке; *fig.* обма́нывать
fidelity [fɪ'delətɪ] ве́рность *f*, пре́данность *f*; (*accuracy*) то́чность *f*
fidget ['fɪdʒɪt] *coll.* **1.** непосе́да; **2.** ёрзать, верте́ться; **~y** [~ɪ] суетли́вый, беспоко́йный, не́рвный; *child* непосе́дливый
field [fi:ld] по́ле; (*meadow*) луг; *fig.* о́бласть; **~ events** лёгкая атле́тика; **~ glasses** полево́й бино́кль *m*; **~ of vision** по́ле зре́ния; **~-work** *geol., etc.* рабо́та в по́ле
fiend [fi:nd] дья́вол; *person* злоде́й; **~ish** ['fi:ndɪʃ] □ дья́вольский, жесто́кий, злой
fierce [fɪəs] □ свире́пый; *frost, etc.* лю́тый; *wind, etc.* си́льный; **~ness** ['fɪəsnɪs] свире́пость *f*, лю́тость *f*
fif|teen [fɪf'ti:n] пятна́дцать; **~teenth** [~θ] пятна́дцатый; **~th** [fɪfθ] **1.** пя́тый; **2.** пя́тая часть *f*; **~tieth** ['fɪftɪɪθ] пятидеся́тый; **~ty** ['fɪftɪ] пятьдеся́т
fig [fɪg] инжи́р
fight [faɪt] **1.** *mil.* сраже́ние, бой; *between persons* дра́ка; (*struggle*) борьба́; ***show ~*** быть гото́вым к борьбе́; **2.** [*irr.*] *v/t.* боро́ться про́тив (P); дра́ться (с T); *v/i.* сража́ться [срази́ться]; (*wage war*) воева́ть; боро́ться; **~er** ['faɪtər] бое́ц; *fig.* боре́ц; **~er plane** истреби́тель *m*; **~ing** ['faɪtɪŋ] сраже́ние, бой; дра́ка; *attr.* боево́й
figment ['fɪgmənt]: ***~ of imagination*** плод воображе́ния
figurative ['fɪgjʊrətɪv] □ перено́сный, метафори́ческий
figure ['fɪgə] **1.** фигу́ра; *math.* число́; ци́фра; (*diagram etc.*) рису́нок; *coll.* (*price*) цена́; **2.** *v/t.* представля́ть себе́; рассчи́тывать [-ита́ть]; *Am.* счита́ть, полага́ть; *v/i.* фигури́ровать
filch [fɪltʃ] [у]кра́сть; *coll.* [у-, с]тащи́ть (***from*** у P)
file[1] [faɪl] **1.** *tool* напи́льник; (*nail ~*) пи́лочка (для ногте́й); **2.** (*a. ~ down*) подпи́ливать [-ли́ть]
file[2] [~] **1.** (*folder*) па́пка; *of papers* подши́вка; *for reference* картоте́ка; *computer* файл; **2.** регистри́ровать (*im*)*pf.*; подшива́ть к де́лу
filial ['fɪlɪəl] □ сыно́вний, доче́рний
fill [fɪl] **1.** наполня́ть(ся) [-о́лнить(ся)]; *tooth* [за]пломбирова́ть; (*satisfy*) удовлетворя́ть [-ри́ть]; *Am. an order* выполня́ть [вы́полнить]; ***~ in*** заполня́ть [-о́лнить]; **2.** доста́точное коли́чество; ***eat one's ~*** нае́сться до́сыта

fillet ['fɪlɪt] *cul.* филé(й) *n indecl.*
filling ['fɪlɪŋ] наполнéние; (зубнáя) плóмба; *cul.* фарш, начи́нка; *mot.* ~ **station** бензозапрáвочная стáнция
film [fɪlm] **1.** (фото) плёнка; *cine.* фильм; (*thin layer*) плёнка; **2.** производи́ть киносъёмку (P); снимáть [снять]; экранизи́ровать (*im*)*pf.*
filter ['fɪltə] **1.** фильтр; **2.** [про-] фильтровáть; **~-tipped** с фи́льтром
filth [fɪlθ] грязь *f*; **~y** ['fɪlθɪ] □ гря́зный (*a. fig.*); ~ ***weather*** гнýсная погóда
fin [fɪn] *zo.* плавни́к
final ['faɪnl] **1.** □ заключи́тельный; окончáтельный; **2.** *sport* финáл; **~s** *univ.* выпускны́е экзáмены; **~ly** [~nəlɪ] в концé концóв; (*in conclusion*) в заключéние
financ|e ['faɪnæns] **1.** **~*s*** *pl.* финáнсы *m/pl.*; дéньги; **2.** *v/t.* финанси́ровать (*im*)*pf.*; **~ial** [faɪ'nænʃl] финáнсовый; **~ier** [~sɪə] финанси́ст
finch [fɪntʃ] *zo.* зя́блик
find [faɪnd] [*irr.*] **1.** находи́ть [найти́]; *by searching* оты́скивать [-кáть]; (*discover*) обнарýживать [-ить]; (*consider*) считáть [счесть]; *rhet.* обретáть [обрести́]; заст(ав)áть; **2.** нахóдка; **~ing** ['faɪndɪŋ] *law* решéние; *pl.* вы́воды
fine[1] [faɪn] □ тóнкий, изя́щный; прекрáсный; ***not to put too ~ a point on it*** говоря́ напрями́к
fine[2] [~] **1.** штраф; пéня; **2.** [о]штрафовáть
finesse [fɪ'nes] деликáтность *f*, утончённость *f*; *at cards*, *etc.* искýсный манёвр
finger ['fɪŋgə] **1.** пáлец; ***not to lift a ~*** пáлец о пáлец не удáрить; **2.** трóгать; *an instrument* перебирáть пáльцами; **~print** отпечáток пáльцев
finish ['fɪnɪʃ] **1.** *v/t.* кончáть [кóнчить]; (*complete*) завершáть [-ши́ть]; (*make complete*) отдéл(ыв)ать; *v/i.* кончáться [кóнчить(ся)]; *sport* финиши́ровать; **2.** конéц; (*polish*) отдéлка; *sport* фи́ниш
Finn [fɪn] финн, фи́нка; **~ish** **1.** фи́нский; **2.** фи́нский язы́к
fir [fɜː] ель *f*, пи́хта; **~cone** ['fɜːkəʊn] еловáя ши́шка
fire [faɪə] **1.** огóнь *m*; ***be on ~*** горéть; **2.** *v/t.* (*set fire to*) зажигáть [зажéчь], поджигáть [-жéчь]; *stove* [за]топи́ть; *fig.* воспламеня́ть [-ни́ть]; (*dismiss*) увольня́ть [уволить]; *v/i.* (*shoot*) стреля́ть [вы́стрелить]; **~ alarm** ['faɪərəlɑːm] пожáрная тревóга; **~brigade**, *Am.* **~department** пожáрная комáнда; **~ engine** ['faɪərendʒɪn] пожáрная маши́на; **~ escape** ['faɪərɪskeɪp] пожáрная лéстница; **~ extinguisher** ['faɪərɪkstɪŋgwɪʃə] огнетуши́тель *m*; **~fighter** пожáрный; **~place** ками́н; **~plug** пожáрный кран, гидрáнт; **~proof** огнеупóрный; **~side** мéсто óколо ками́на; **~ station** пожáрное депó; **~wood** дровá *n/pl.*; **~works** *pl.* фейервéрк
firing ['faɪərɪŋ] (*shooting*) стрельбá
firm[1] [fɜːm] фи́рма
firm[2] [~] □ крéпкий, плóтный, твёрдый; (*resolute*) устóйчивый; **~ness** ['fɜːmnɪs] твёрдость *f*
first [fɜːst] **1.** *adj.* пéрвый; ***at ~ sight*** с пéрвого взгля́да; ***in the ~ place*** во-пéрвых; **2.** *adv.* спервá, сначáла; впервы́е; скорéе; ***at ~*** сначáла; ***~ of all*** прéжде всегó; **3.** начáло; ***the ~*** пéрвое числó; ***from the ~*** с сáмого начáла; **~-born** пéрвенец; **~-class** *quality* первоклáссный; *travel* пéрвым клáссом; **~ly** ['fɜːstlɪ] во-пéрвых; **~-rate** превосхóдный; *int.* прекрáсно!
fiscal ['fɪskl] фискáльный, финáнсовый
fish [fɪʃ] **1.** ры́ба; *coll.* **odd** (*или* ***queer***) ~ чудáк; **2.** лови́ть ры́бу; ***~ for compliments*** напрáшиваться на комплимéнты; ***~ out*** вы́удить; **~bone** ры́бная кость *f*
fisherman ['fɪʃəmən] рыбáк, рыболóв
fishing ['fɪʃɪŋ] ры́бная лóвля; **~-line** лéса; **~ rod** ýдочка; (*without line*) уди́лище; **~ tackle** рыболóвные принадлéжности *f/pl.*
fiss|ion ['fɪʃn] *phys.* расщеплéние; **~ure** ['fɪʃə] трéщина, рассéлина
fist [fɪst] кулáк

fit¹ [fɪt] **1.** го́дный, подходя́щий; (*healthy*) здоро́вый; (*deserving*) досто́йный; **2.** *v/t.* подгоня́ть [-догна́ть] (***to*** к Д); (*be suitable for*) подходи́ть [подойти́] к (Д); приспособля́ть [-посо́бить] (***for, to*** к Д); **~ out** (*equip*) снаряжа́ть [-яди́ть]; (*supply*) снабжа́ть [-бди́ть]; *v/i.* (*suit*) годи́ться; *of dress* сиде́ть; приспособля́ться [приспосо́биться]
fit² [~] *med.* припа́док, при́ступ; *of generosity, etc.* поры́в; ***by ~s and starts*** уры́вками; ***give s.o. a ~*** потрясти́ *pf.*
fit|ful ['fɪtfl] □ су́дорожный, поры́вистый; **~ter** [~ə] меха́ник, монтёр; **~ting** [~ɪŋ] **1.** □ подходя́щий, го́дный; **2.** устано́вка; монта́ж; *of clothes* приме́рка; **~tings** *pl.* армату́ра
five [faɪv] **1.** пять; **2.** *in cards, bus number, etc.*; *school mark* пятёрка
fix [fɪks] **1.** устана́вливать [-нови́ть]; (*make fast*) укрепля́ть [-пи́ть]; *attention, etc.* сосредото́чивать [-то́чить], остана́вливать [-нови́ть] (на П); (*repair*) починя́ть [-ни́ть]; *Am.* (*prepare*) пригота́вливать [-то́вить]; *Am. hair etc.* приводи́ть в поря́док; **~ up** организова́ть (*im*)*pf.*; ула́живать [ула́дить]; (*arrange*) устра́ивать [-ро́ить]; *v/i.* затверде́(ва́)ть; остана́вливаться [-нови́ться] (***on*** на П); **2.** *coll.* диле́мма, затрудни́тельное положе́ние; **~ed** [fɪkst] (*adv.* **~edly** ['fɪksɪdlɪ]) неподви́жный; **~ture** ['fɪkstʃə] приспособле́ние; армату́ра; (*equipment*) обору́дование; ***lighting ~*** освети́тельное устро́йство
fizzle ['fɪzl] шипе́ть
flabby ['flæbɪ] □ вя́лый; *fig.* слабохара́ктерный
flag¹ [flæg] флаг, зна́мя *n*; ***~ of convenience*** *naut.* удо́бный флаг
flag² [~] **1.** (***~stone***) плита́; **2.** мости́ть пли́тами
flagrant ['fleɪgrənt] □ вопию́щий
flagstaff флагшто́к
flair [fleə] чутьё, нюх; (*ability*) спосо́бности *f/pl.*
flake [fleɪk] **1. ~s** *of snow* снежи́нки *f/pl.*; *pl.* хло́пья *m/pl.*; **2. *~ off*** [об]лупи́ться, шелуши́ться
flame [fleɪm] **1.** пла́мя *n*; ого́нь *m*; *fig.* страсть *f*; **2.** горе́ть, пламене́ть; пыла́ть
flan [flæn] откры́тый пиро́г; ола́дья
flank [flæŋk] **1.** бок, сторона́; *mil.* фланг; **2.** быть располо́женным сбо́ку, на фла́нге (Р); грани́чить (с Т), примыка́ть (к Д)
flannel ['flænl] шерстяна́я флане́ль *f*; **~s** [~z] *pl.* флане́левые брю́ки *f/pl.*
flap [flæp] **1.** *of wings* взмах; (*sound*) хло́панье; *of hat* у́хо; ***get into a ~*** засуети́ться *pf.*, паникова́ть; взма́хивать [-хну́ть]; **2.** *v/t.* (*give a light blow to*) шлёпать [-пну́ть]; легко́ ударя́ть; *v/i.* свиса́ть; *of flag* развева́ться [-ве́яться]
flare [fleə] **1.** горе́ть я́рким пла́менем; **~ *up*** вспы́хивать [-хнуть]; *fig.* вспыли́ть *pf.*; **2.** вспы́шка пла́мени; сигна́льная раке́та
flash [flæʃ] **1.** → ***flashy* 2.** вспы́шка; *fig.* про́блеск; ***in a ~*** мгнове́нно; **3.** сверка́ть [-кну́ть]; вспы́хивать [-хнуть]; пронести́сь *pf.* (*a.* **~ *by***); **~light** *phot.* вспы́шка; *Am.* карма́нный фона́рик *m*; **~y** показно́й; безвку́сный
flask [flɑːsk] фля́жка
flat [flæt] **1.** □ (*level*) пло́ский; (*smooth*) ро́вный; (*dull*) ску́чный; *voice* глухо́й; ***fall ~*** не вызыва́ть [вы́звать] интере́са; не име́ть успе́ха; ***~ tire*** (*Brt.* ***tyre***) спу́щенная ши́на; **2.** (*apartment*) кварти́ра; пло́скость *f*; *land* равни́на, низи́на; *mus.* бемо́ль *m.*; **~iron** утю́г; **~ten** ['flætn] де́лать(ся) пло́ским, ро́вным
flatter ['flætə] [по]льсти́ть (Д); ***I am ~ed*** я польщена́; **~er** [~rər] льстец *m*, льсти́ца *f*; **~ing** [~rɪŋ] ле́стный; **~y** [~rɪ] лесть *f*
flaunt [flɔːnt] выставля́ть [вы́ставить] на пока́з, афиши́ровать
flavo(u)r ['fleɪvə] **1.** (*taste*) вкус; *fig.* при́вкус; **2.** приправля́ть [-ра́вить]; придава́ть запах, при́вкус (Д); **~ing** [~rɪŋ] припра́ва; **~less** [~lɪs] безвку́сный
flaw [flɔː] (*crack*) тре́щина, щель *f*; *in character, etc.* недоста́ток; (*de-

fect) дефе́кт, изъя́н; **~less** ['flɔːlɪs] безупре́чный
flax [flæks] лён
flea [fliː] блоха́
fled [fled] *pt. и pt. p. от* ***flee***
flee [fliː] [*irr.*] бежа́ть, спаса́ться бе́гством
fleece [fliːs] **1.** ове́чья шерсть *f*; **2.** [о]стри́чь; *fig.* обдира́ть [ободра́ть]
fleet¹ [fliːt] □ бы́стрый
fleet² [~] флот
flesh [fleʃ] *soft or edible parts of animal bodies* мя́со; *body as opposed to mind or soul* плоть *f*; *of fruit or plant* мя́коть *f*; **~y** [~ɪ] мяси́стый; то́лстый
flew [fluː] *pt. от* ***fly***
flexib|ility [fleksə'bɪlətɪ] ги́бкость *f*; **~le** ['fleksəbl] □ ги́бкий; *fig.* пода́тливый, усту́пчивый
flicker ['flɪkə] **1.** *of light* мерца́ние; *of movement* трепета́ние; **2.** мерца́ть; трепета́ть *of smile* мелька́ть [-кну́ть]
flight¹ [flaɪt] полёт, перелёт; *of birds* стая; ***~ number*** но́мер ре́йса
flight² [~] бе́гство; ***put to ~*** обраща́ть в бе́гство
flighty ['flaɪtɪ] □ ве́треный
flimsy ['flɪmzɪ] (*not strong*) непро́чный; (*thin*) то́нкий; ***~ argument*** малоубеди́тельный до́вод
flinch [flɪntʃ] вздра́гивать [вздро́гнуть]; отпря́дывать [отпря́нуть]
fling [flɪŋ] **1.** бросо́к; весе́лье; ***have a ~*** кутну́ть, пожи́ть в своё удово́льствие; **2.** [*irr.*] *v/i.* кида́ться [ки́нуться], броса́ться [бро́ситься]; *v/t.* (*throw*) кида́ть [ки́нуть], броса́ть [бро́сить]; ***~ open*** распа́хивать [-хну́ть]
flint [flɪnt] кре́мень *m*
flippan|cy ['flɪpənsɪ] легкомы́слие; **~t** □ легкомы́сленный
flirt [flɜːt] **1.** коке́тка; **2.** флиртова́ть, коке́тничать; **~ation** [flɜː'teɪʃn] флирт
flit [flɪt] порха́ть [-хну́ть] (*a. fig.*); *of smile, etc.* пробежа́ть
float [fləʊt] **1.** *on fishing line* поплаво́к; **2.** *v/t. timber* сплавля́ть [-а́вить]; *fin.* вводи́ть [ввести́] пла́вающий курс; *v/i. of object* пла́вать, [по]плы́ть; держа́ться на воде́; *fig.* плыть по тече́нию
flock [flɒk] **1.** *of sheep* ста́до; *of birds* стая; **2.** стека́ться [сте́чься]; держа́ться вме́сте
flog [flɒg] [вы́]поро́ть; ***~ a dead horse*** стара́ться возроди́ть безнадёжно устаре́лое де́ло
flood [flʌd] **1.** (*a. **~ tide***) прили́в, подъём воды́; (*inundation*) наводне́ние, полово́дье, разли́в; *Bibl.* ***the*** **♀** всеми́рный пото́п; **2.** поднима́ться [-ня́ться], выступа́ть из берего́в; (*inundate*) затопля́ть [-пи́ть]; *the market* наводня́ть [-ни́ть]; **~gate** шлюз
floor [flɔː] **1.** пол; (*stor(e)y*) эта́ж; ***take the ~*** *parl.* взять *pf.* сло́во; **2.** настила́ть пол; *coll.* (*knock down*) сбива́ть [сбить] с ног; *fig.* (*nonplus*) [по]ста́вить в тупи́к; **~ing** ['flɔːrɪŋ] насти́лка поло́в; пол
flop [flɒp] **1.** шлёпаться [-пнуться]; плю́хать(ся) [-хнуть(-ся)]; *Am.* потерпе́ть *pf.* фиа́ско; **2.** *sl.* прова́л; **~py** [~ɪ]: ***~ disk*** *comput.* ги́бкий диск
florid ['flɒrɪd] □ цвети́стый (*a. fig.*)
florist ['flɒrɪst] продаве́ц цвето́в
flounce [flaʊns] *out of room* броса́ться [бро́ситься]
flounder¹ *zo.* ['flaʊndə] ка́мбала
flounder² [~] *esp. in water* бара́хтаться; *fig.* [за]пу́таться
flour [flaʊə] мука́
flourish ['flʌrɪʃ] *v/i.* пы́шно расти́; (*prosper*) процвета́ть, преуспева́ть; *v/t.* (*wave*) разма́хивать (Т)
flout [flaʊt] попира́ть [попра́ть]; пренебрега́ть [-ре́чь] (Т)
flow [fləʊ] **1.** тече́ние, пото́к; (*a. of speech*) струя́; *of sea* прили́в; **2.** течь; струи́ться; ли́ться
flower ['flaʊə] **1.** цвето́к; *fig.* цвет; ***in ~*** в цвету́; **2.** цвести́; **~y** [~rɪ] *fig.* цвети́стый
flown [fləʊn] *pt. p. от* ***fly***
flu [fluː] = ***influenza*** *coll.* грипп
fluctuat|e ['flʌktʃʊeɪt] колеба́ться; **~ion** [flʌktʃʊ'eɪʃn] колеба́ние
flue [fluː] дымохо́д
fluen|cy ['fluːənsɪ] *fig.* пла́вность *f*, бе́глость *f*; **~t** [~t] □ пла́вный, бе́г-

лый; ***she speaks ~ German*** она́ бе́гло говори́т по-неме́цки
fluff [flʌf] пух, пушо́к; **~y** ['flʌfɪ] пуши́стый
fluid ['flu:ɪd] **1.** жи́дкость *f*; **2.** жи́дкий; *fig.* неопределённый
flung [flʌŋ] *pt. и pt. p. от* **fling**
flurry ['flʌrɪ] волне́ние, сумато́ха
flush [flʌʃ] **1.** румя́нец; *of shame* кра́ска; *of feeling* прили́в; **2.** *v/t. toilet* спуска́ть [-сти́ть] во́ду (в убо́рной); (*rinse or wash clean*) промыва́ть [-мы́ть]; *v/i.* [по]красне́ть
fluster ['flʌstə] **1.** суета́, волне́ние; **2.** [вз]волнова́ть(ся)
flute [flu:t] *mus.* фле́йта
flutter ['flʌtə] **1.** порха́ние; *of leaves, a. fig.* тре́пет; *fig.* волне́ние; **2.** *v/i.* маха́ть [-хну́ть]; *in the wind* развева́ться; порха́ть [-хну́ть]
flux [flʌks] *fig.* тече́ние; пото́к; ***in a state of ~*** в состоя́нии непреры́вного измене́ния
fly [flaɪ] **1.** му́ха; ***a ~ in the ointment*** ло́жка дёгтя в бо́чке мёда; **2.** [*irr.*] лета́ть, [по]лете́ть; пролета́ть [-ете́ть]; (*hurry*) [по]спеши́ть; *of flag* поднима́ть [-ня́ть]; *ae.* пилоти́ровать; ***~ at*** набра́сываться [-ро́ситься] (с бра́нью) на (В); ***~ into a passion*** вспыли́ть *pf.*
flying ['flaɪɪŋ] лета́тельный; лётный; ***~ saucer*** лета́ющая таре́лка; ***~ visit*** мимолётный визи́т
fly|over путепро́вод; эстака́да; **~weight** *boxer* наилегча́йший вес; **~wheel** махови́к
foal [fəʊl] жеребёнок
foam [fəʊm] **1.** пе́на; ***~ rubber*** пенорези́на; **2.** [вс]пе́ниться; *of horse* взмы́ли(ва)ться; **~y** ['fəʊmɪ] пе́нящийся; взмы́ленный
focus ['fəʊkəs] **1.** *phot.*, *phys.* фо́кус; **2.** быть в фо́кусе; сосредото́чи(ва)ть (*a. fig.*)
fodder ['fɒdə] фура́ж, корм
foe [fəʊ] враг
fog [fɒg] **1.** тума́н; (*bewilderment*) замеша́тельство; **2.** [за]тума́нить; *fig.* напуска́ть [-сти́ть] тума́ну; озада́чи(ва)ть; **~gy** ['fɒgɪ] □ тума́нный
foible ['fɔɪbl] *fig.* сла́бость *f*
foil[1] [fɔɪl] (*thin metal*) фольга́; (*contrast*) противопоставле́ние
foil[2] [~] **1.** расстра́ивать пла́ны (Р); **2.** рапи́ра
fold [fəʊld] **1.** скла́дка, сгиб; **2.** *v/t.* скла́дывать [сложи́ть]; сгиба́ть [согну́ть]; *one's arms* скре́щивать [-ести́ть]; **~er** ['fəʊldə] *for papers* па́пка; брошю́ра
folding ['fəʊldɪŋ] складно́й; ***~ doors*** двуство́рчатые две́ри; **~ chair** складно́й стул; **~ umbrella** складно́й зо́нтик
foliage ['fəʊlɪɪdʒ] листва́
folk [fəʊk] наро́д, лю́ди *m/pl.*; **~lore** ['fəʊklɔ:] фолькло́р; **~song** наро́дная пе́сня
follow ['fɒləʊ] сле́довать (за Т *or* Д); (*watch*) следи́ть (за Т); (*pursue*) пресле́довать (В); (*engage in*) занима́ться [-ня́ться] (Т); (*understand*) понима́ть [-ня́ть]; ***~ suit*** сле́довать приме́ру; **~er** ['fɒləʊə] после́дователь(ница *f*) *m*; (*admirer*) покло́нник; **~ing** ['fɒləʊɪŋ] сле́дующий
folly ['fɒlɪ] безрассу́дство, глу́пость *f*, безу́мие
fond [fɒnd] □ не́жный, лю́бящий; ***be ~ of*** люби́ть (В)
fond|le ['fɒndl] [при]ласка́ть; **~ness** [~nɪs] не́жность *f*, любо́вь *f*
food [fu:d] пи́ща, еда́; **~stuffs** *pl.* (пищевы́е) проду́кты *m/pl.*
fool [fu:l] **1.** дура́к, глупе́ц; ***make a ~ of s.o.*** [o]дура́чить кого́-л.; **2.** *v/t.* обма́нывать [-ну́ть]; *v/i.* [по]дура́читься; ***~ about*** валя́ть дурака́
fool|ery ['fu:lərɪ] дура́чество; **~hardy** ['fu:lhɑ:dɪ] □ безрассу́дно хра́брый; **~ish** ['fu:lɪʃ] глу́пый, неразу́мный; **~ishness** [~nɪs] глу́пость *f*; **~proof** безопа́сный; безотка́зный
foot [fʊt] **1.** (*pl.* **feet**) нога́, ступня́; (*base*) основа́ние; *of furniture* но́жка; ***on ~*** пешко́м; **2.** *v/t.* (*mst.* ***~ up***) подсчи́тывать [-ита́ть]; ***~ the bill*** заплати́ть по счёту; ***~ it*** идти́ пешко́м; **~ball** футбо́л; **~fall** шаг; звук шаго́в; **~gear** *coll.* о́бувь *f*; **~hold** опо́ра (*a. fig.*)
footing ['fʊtɪŋ] опо́ра; ***on a friendly ~*** быть на дру́жеской ноге́; ***lose one's ~*** оступа́ться [-пи́ться]

foot|lights *pl. thea.* ра́мпа; **~path** тропи́нка; тропа́; **~print** след; **~sore** со стёртыми нога́ми; **~step** по́ступь *f*; шаг; ***follow in s.o.'s ~s*** идти́ по чьи́м-л. стопа́м; **~wear** о́бувь *f*

for [fə· *strong* fɔː] *prp. mst.* для (Р); ра́ди (Р); за (В); в направле́нии (Р), к (Д); из-за (Р), по причи́не (Р), вследствие; в тече́ние (Р); в продолже́ние (Р); ***~ three days*** в тече́ние трёх дней; уже́ три дня; вме́сто (Р); в обме́н на (В); ***~ all that*** несмотря́ на всё э́то; ***~ my part*** с моей стороны́; **2.** *cj.* так как, потому́ что, и́бо

forbad(e) [fəˈbæd] *pt. om* ***forbid***

forbear [fɔːˈbeə] *[irr.]* (*be patient*) быть терпели́вым; (*refrain from*) возде́рживаться [-жа́ться] (***from*** от Р)

forbid [fəˈbɪd] *[irr.]* запреща́ть [-ети́ть]; **~den** [~n] *pt. p. om* ***forbid***; **~ing** [~ɪŋ] □ (*threatening*) угрожа́ющий

forbor|e [fɔːˈbɔː] *pt. om* ***forbear***; **~ne** [~n] *pt. p. om* ***forbear***

force [fɔːs] **1.** си́ла; (*violence*) наси́лие; (*constraint*) принужде́ние; (*meaning*) смысл, значе́ние; **armed ~s** *pl.* вооружённые си́лы *f/pl.*; ***come into ~*** вступа́ть в си́лу; **2.** заставля́ть [-а́вить], принужда́ть [-уди́ть]; (*get by force*) брать си́лой; ***join ~s*** объединя́ть [-ни́ть] уси́лия; ***~ open*** взла́мывать [взлома́ть]; **~d** [~t]: ***~ landing*** вы́нужденная поса́дка; **~ful** [~fl] □ си́льный, де́йственный; *argument* убеди́тельный

forcible [ˈfɔːsəbl] □ (*using force*) наси́льственный; (*convincing*) убеди́тельный

ford [fɔːd] **1.** брод; **2.** переходи́ть вброд

fore [fɔː] **1.** *adv.* впереди́; **2.** *adj.* пере́дний; **~bode** [fɔːˈbəʊd] предвеща́ть; (*have a feeling*) предчу́вствовать; **~boding** предчу́вствие; **~cast 1.** [ˈfɔːkɑːst] предсказа́ние; ***weather ~*** прогно́з пого́ды; **2.** [fɔːˈkɑːst] *[irr.* (***cast***)*]* [с]де́лать (дава́ть [дать]) прогно́з; предска́зывать [-каза́ть]; **~father** пре́док; **~finger** указа́тельный па́лец; **~gone** [fɔːˈgɒn]: ***it's a ~ conclusion*** э́то предрешённый исхо́д; **~ground** пере́дний план; **~head** [ˈfɔːrɪd] лоб

foreign [ˈfɒrɪn] иностра́нный; *Brt.* ***the ♀ Office*** Министе́рство иностра́нных дел; ***~ policy*** вне́шняя поли́тика; **~er** [~ə] иностра́нец *m*, -нка *f*

fore|lock [ˈfɔːlɒk] прядь воло́с на лбу; **~man** бригади́р; ма́стер; **~most** пере́дний, передово́й; **~runner** предве́стник *m*, -ица *f*; **~see** [fɔːˈsiː] *[irr.* (***see***)*]* предви́деть; **~sight** [ˈfɔːsaɪt] предви́дение; (*provident care*) предусмотри́тельность *f*

forest [ˈfɒrɪst] лес

forestall [fɔːˈstɔːl] (*avert*) предупрежда́ть [-упреди́ть]; (*do s.th. first*) опережа́ть [-ди́ть]

forest|er [ˈfɒrɪstə] лесни́к, лесни́чий; **~ry** [~trɪ] лесни́чество, лесово́дство

fore|taste [ˈfɔːteɪst] **1.** предвкуше́ние; **2.** предвкуша́ть [-уси́ть]; **~tell** [fɔːˈtel] *[irr.* (***tell***)*]* предска́зывать [-за́ть]

forever [fəˈrevə] навсегда́

forfeit [ˈfɔːfɪt] **1.** штраф; *in game* фант; **2.** [по]плати́ться (Т); *right* утра́чивать [-а́тить]

forgave [fəˈgeɪv] *pt. om* ***forgive***

forge[1] [fɔːdʒ] (*mst.* ***~ ahead***) насто́йчиво продвига́ться вперёд

forge[2] [~] **1.** ку́зница; **2.** кова́ть; *signature, etc.* подде́л(ыв)ать; **~ry** [ˈfɔːdʒərɪ] подде́лка; *of document* подло́г

forget [fəˈget] *[irr.]* забы́(ва́)ть; **~ful** [~fl] □ забы́вчивый; **~-me-not** [~mɪnɒt] незабу́дка

forgiv|e [fəˈgɪv] *[irr.]* проща́ть [прости́ть]; **~en** [fəˈgɪvən] *pt. p. om* ***~e***; **~eness** [~nɪs] проще́ние; **~ing** [~ɪŋ] всепроща́ющий; □ великоду́шный, снисходи́тельный

forgo [fɔːˈgəʊ] *[irr.* (***go***)*]* возде́рживаться [-жа́ться] от (Р), отка́зываться [-за́ться] от (Р)

forgot, ~ten [fəˈgɒt(n)] *pt. a. pt. p. om* ***forget***

fork [fɔːk] ви́лка; *agric.* ви́лы *f/pl.*; *mus.* камерто́н; *of road* разветвле́ние

forlorn [fə'lɔːn] забро́шенный, несча́стный
form [fɔːm] **1.** фо́рма; фигу́ра; (*document*) бланк; *Brt. educ.* класс; ***matter of ~*** чи́стая форма́льность; **2.** образо́вывать(ся) [-ова́ть(ся)]; составля́ть [-а́вить]; (*create*) создава́ть [-а́ть]; (*organize*) организо́вывать [-ва́ть]; [с]формирова́ть
formal ['fɔːml] □ форма́льный; официа́льный; **~ity** [fɔː'mælətɪ] форма́льность *f*
formation [fɔː'meɪʃn] образова́ние; формирова́ние; *mil.* строй; (*structure*) строе́ние
former ['fɔːmə] пре́жний, бы́вший; предше́ствующий; ***the ~*** пе́рвый; **~ly** [~lɪ] пре́жде
formidable ['fɔːmɪdəbl] □ гро́зный; *size* грома́дный; (*difficult*) тру́дный
formula ['fɔːmjʊlə] фо́рмула; **~te** [~leɪt] формули́ровать (*im*)*pf.*, *pf. a.* [c-]
forsake [fə'seɪk] [*irr.*] оставля́ть [-а́вить], покида́ть [-и́нуть]
forswear [fɔː'sweə] [*irr.* (***swear***)] (*give up*) отка́зываться [-за́ться] от (P)
fort [fɔːt] *mil.* форт
forth [fɔːθ] *adv.* вперёд, да́льше; впредь; ***and so ~*** и так да́лее; **~coming** предстоя́щий
fortieth ['fɔːtɪɪθ] сорокова́й; сорокова́я часть *f*
forti|fication [fɔːtɪfɪ'keɪʃn] укрепле́ние; **~fy** ['fɔːtɪfaɪ] *mil.* укрепля́ть [-пи́ть]; *fig.* подкрепля́ть [-пи́ть]; ***~ o.s.*** подкрепля́ться [-пи́ться] (***with*** T); **~tude** [~tjuːd] си́ла ду́ха, сто́йкость *f*
fortnight ['fɔːtnaɪt] две неде́ли *f/pl.*
fortress ['fɔːtrɪs] кре́пость *f*
fortuitous [fɔː'tjuːɪtəs] □ случа́йный
fortunate ['fɔːtʃənət] счастли́вый, уда́чный; ***I was ~ enough*** мне посчастли́вилось; **~ly** *adv.* к сча́стью
fortune ['fɔːtʃən] судьба́; (*prosperity*) бога́тство, состоя́ние; ***good*** (***bad***) ***~*** (не)уда́ча; **~-teller** гада́лка
forty ['fɔːtɪ] со́рок
forward ['fɔːwəd] **1.** *adj.* пере́дний; (*familiar*) развя́зный, де́рзкий; *spring* ра́нний; **2.** *adv.* вперёд, да́льше; впредь; **3.** *sport* напада́ющий, фо́рвард; **4.** перес(ы-)ла́ть, направля́ть [-а́вить] (по но́вому а́дресу)
forwent [fɔː'went] *pt. om* ***forgo***
foster ['fɒstər] воспи́тывать [-ита́ть]; (*look after*) присма́тривать [-мотре́ть] (за T); *fig. hope etc.* пита́ть; (*cherish*) леле́ять; (*encourage*) поощря́ть [-ри́ть]; благоприя́тствовать (Д)
fought [fɔːt] *pt. u pt. p. om* ***fight***
foul [faʊl] **1.** □ (*dirty*) гря́зный; (*loathsome*) отврати́тельный (*a. weather*); нече́стный; **2.** *sport* наруше́ние пра́вил; **~ play** гру́бая игра́; **3.** [за]па́чкать(ся); (*pollute*) загрязня́ть [-ни́ть], допусти́ть *pf.* наруше́ние
found [faʊnd] **1.** *pt. u pt. p. om* ***find***; **2.** (*lay the foundation of*) закла́дывать [заложи́ть]; (*establish*) осно́вывать (основа́ть); учрежда́ть [-еди́ть]
foundation [faʊn'deɪʃn] фунда́мент, осно́ва; *for research, etc.* фонд
founder ['faʊndə] основа́тель(ница *f*) *m*; *of society* учреди́тель(ница *f*) *m*
foundry ['faʊndrɪ] *tech.* лите́йный цех
fountain ['faʊntɪn] фонта́н; **~ pen** автору́чка
four [fɔː] **1.** четы́ре; **2.** четвёрка (→ ***five 2.***); **~teen** [ˌfɔː'tiːn] четы́рнадцать; **~teenth** [~θ] четы́рнадцатый; **~th** [fɔːθ] **1.** четвёртый; **2.** че́тверть *f*
fowl [faʊl] дома́шняя пти́ца
fox [fɒks] **1.** лиси́ца, лиса́; **2.** [с]хитри́ть; обма́нывать [-ну́ть]; ***the question ~ed me*** вопро́с поста́вил меня́ в тупи́к; **~y** ['fɒksɪ] хи́трый
foyer ['fɔɪeɪ] фойе́ *n indecl.*
fraction ['frækʃn] *math.* дробь *f*; (*small part or amount*) части́ца
fracture ['fræktʃə] **1.** тре́щина, изло́м; *med.* перело́м; **2.** [с]лома́ть (*a. med.*)
fragile ['frædʒaɪl] хру́пкий (*a. fig.*), ло́мкий
fragment ['frægmənt] обло́мок, оско́лок; *of text* отры́вок; **~ary** [~ərɪ]

фрагмента́рный; (*not complete*) отры́вочный
fragran|ce ['freɪgrəns] арома́т; **~t** [~t] □ арома́тный
frail [freɪl] *in health* хру́пкий; хи́лый, боле́зненный; *morally* сла́бый
frame [freɪm] **1.** *anat.* скеле́т, о́стов; телосложе́ние; *of picture, etc.* ра́мка, ра́ма; *of spectacles* опра́ва; ***~ of mind*** настрое́ние; **2.** (*construct*) [по]стро́ить, выраба́тывать [вы́работать]; вставля́ть в ра́му; **~work** *tech.* ра́ма; карка́с; *fig.* структу́ра; ра́мки *f/pl.*
franchise ['fræntʃaɪz] пра́во уча́ствовать в вы́борах; *comm.* привиле́гия; лице́нзия
frank [fræŋk] □ и́скренний, открове́нный
frankfurter ['fræŋkfɜːtə] соси́ска
frankness ['fræŋknɪs] открове́нность *f*
frantic ['fræntɪk] (***~ally***) безу́мный; *efforts, etc.* отча́янный
fratern|al [frə'tɜːnl] □ бра́тский; *adv.* по-бра́тски; **~ity** [~nətɪ] бра́тство; *Am. univ.* студе́нческая организа́ция
fraud [frɔːd] обма́н, моше́нничество; **~ulent** ['frɔːdjʊlənt] □ обма́нный, моше́ннический
fray[1] [freɪ] дра́ка; (*quarrel*) ссо́ра
fray[2] [~] обтрепа́ться
freak [friːk] *of nature* капри́з, причу́да; *person, animal* уро́д; (*enthusiast*) фана́т; ***film ~*** кинома́н
freckle ['frekl] весну́шка; **~d** [~d] весну́шчатый
free [friː] **1.** □ *com.* свобо́дный, во́льный; (*not occupied*) неза́нятый; (*~ of charge*) беспла́тный; ***give s.o. a ~ hand*** предоста́вить по́лную свобо́ду де́йствий; ***he is ~ to*** он во́лен (+ *inf.*); ***make ~ to*** *inf.* позволя́ть себе́; ***set ~*** выпуска́ть на свобо́ду; **2.** освобожда́ть [-боди́ть]; **~dom** ['friːdəm] свобо́да; **~holder** свобо́дный со́бственник; **♀mason** масо́н; **~style** *sport* во́льный стиль; **~ trade area** свобо́дная экономи́ческая зо́на
freez|e [friːz] [*irr.*] *v/i.* замерза́ть [замёрзнуть]; (*congeal*) засты́(ва́)ть; мёрзнуть; *v/t.* замора́живать [-ро́зить]; **~er** ['friːzə] *domestic appliance* морози́льник; **~ing 1.** □ леденя́щий; **2.** замора́живание; замерза́ние; ***~ point*** то́чка замерза́ния
freight [freɪt] **1.** фрахт, груз; (*cost*) сто́имость перево́зки; **2.** [по]грузи́ть; [за]фрахтова́ть; **~ car** *Am. rail.* това́рный ваго́н; **~ train** *Am.* това́рный по́езд/соста́в
French [frentʃ] **1.** францу́зский; ***take ~ leave*** уйти́, не проща́ясь (*или* по-англи́йски); **2.** францу́зский язы́к; ***the ~*** францу́зы *pl.*; **~man** ['frentʃmən] францу́з; **~woman** ['frentʃwʊmən] францу́женка
frenz|ied ['frenzɪd] безу́мный, неи́стовый; **~y** [~zɪ] безу́мие, неи́стовство
frequen|cy ['friːkwənsɪ] частота́ (*a. phys.*); ча́стое повторе́ние; **~t 1.** [~t] □ ча́стый; **2.** [friː'kwənt] регуля́рно посеща́ть
fresh [freʃ] □ све́жий; но́вый; чи́стый; *Am.* развя́зный, де́рзкий; ***~ water*** пре́сная вода́; ***make a ~start*** нача́ть *pf.* всё снача́ла; **~en** ['freʃn] освежа́ть [-жи́ть]; *of the wind* [по]свеже́ть; **~man** [~mən] (*first-year student*) первоку́рсник; **~ness** [~nɪs] све́жесть *f*
fret [fret] **1.** волне́ние, раздраже́ние; **2.** беспоко́ить(ся), [вз]волнова́ть(ся); (*wear away*) подта́чивать [-точи́ть]
fretful ['fretfl] □ раздражи́тельный, капри́зный
friction ['frɪkʃn] тре́ние (*a. fig.*)
Friday ['fraɪdɪ] пя́тница
fridge [frɪdʒ] *coll.* холоди́льник
friend [frend] прия́тель(ница *f*) *m*, друг, подру́га; ***make ~s*** подружи́ться; **~ly** [~lɪ] дру́жеский; **~ship** [~ʃɪp] дру́жба
frigate ['frɪgət] фрега́т
fright [fraɪt] испу́г; *fig.* (*scarecrow*) пу́гало, страши́лище; **~en** ['fraɪtn] [ис]пуга́ть; (*~ away*) вспу́гивать [-гну́ть]; ***~ed at или of*** испу́ганный (T); **~ful** [~fl] □ стра́шный, ужа́сный
frigid ['frɪdʒɪd] □ холо́дный
frill [frɪl] обо́рка
fringe [frɪndʒ] **1.** бахрома́; *of hair*

чёлка; *of forest* опу́шка; **~ *benefits*** дополни́тельные льго́ты; **2.** отде́лывать бахромо́й; *with trees, etc.* окаймля́ть [-ми́ть]
frisk [frɪsk] резви́ться; **~y** ['frɪskɪ] □ ре́звый, игри́вый
fritter ['frɪtə]: **~ *away*** транжи́рить; растра́чиваться
frivol|ity [frɪ'vɒlətɪ] легкомы́слие; фриво́льность *f*; **~ous** ['frɪvələs] □ легкомы́сленный; несерьёзный
frizzle ['frɪzl] *of hair* завива́ть(ся) [-ви́ть(ся)]; *with a sizzle* жа́рить(ся) с шипе́нием
fro [frəʊ]: ***to and ~*** взад и вперёд
frock [frɒk] да́мское или де́тское пла́тье; *monk's habit* ря́са
frog [frɒg] лягу́шка
frolic ['frɒlɪk] **1.** ша́лость *f*; весе́лье; **2.** резви́ться; **~some** [~səm] □ игри́вый, ре́звый
from [frəm· *strong* frɒm] *prp.* от (Р); из (Р); с (Р); по (Д); ***defend ~*** защища́ть от (Р); ***~ day to day*** со дня на́ день
front [frʌnt] **1.** фаса́д; пере́дняя сторона́; *mil.* фронт; ***in ~ of*** пе́ред (Т); впереди́ (Р); **2.** пере́дний; **3.** (*face*) выходи́ть на (В) (*a.* **~ *on***); **~al** ['frʌntl] лобово́й; *anat.* ло́бный; *attack, etc.* фронта́льный; **~ier** ['frʌntɪə] **1.** грани́ца; **2.** пограни́чный
frost [frɒst] **1.** моро́з; **2.** *plants* поби́ть моро́зом; **~bite** обмороже́ние; **~y** ['frɒstɪ] □ моро́зный; *fig.* (*unfriendly*) ледяно́й
froth [frɒθ] **1.** пе́на; **2.** [вс-, за]пе́нить(ся); **~y** ['frɒθɪ] пе́нистый
frown [fraʊn] **1.** хму́рый взгляд; **2.** *v/i.* [на]хму́риться; **~ *on*** относи́ться [-нести́сь] неодобри́тельно
froze [frəʊz] *pt. om* ***freeze***; **~n** [~n] **1.** *pt. p. om* ***freeze***; **2.** замёрзший; *meat, etc.* заморо́женный
frugal ['fru:gl] □ *person* бережли́вый; *meal* скро́мный; *with money etc.* эконо́мный
fruit [fru:t] **1.** плод (*a. fig.*); фрукт *mst. pl.*; ***dried ~*** сухофру́кты; **2.** ***bear ~*** плодоно́сить, дава́ть плоды́; **~ful** ['fru:tfl] *fig.* плодотво́рный; **~less** [~lɪs] □ беспло́дный
frustrat|e [frʌ'streɪt] *plans* расстра́ивать [-ро́ить]; *efforts* де́лать тще́тным; **~ed** [~ɪd] обескура́женный, неудовлетворённый; **~ion** [frʌ'streɪʃn] расстро́йство, *of hopes* круше́ние
fry [fraɪ] [за-, под]жа́рить(ся); **~ing-pan** ['fraɪɪŋpæn] сковорода́
fudge [fʌdʒ] (*sweet*) пома́дка
fuel [fju:əl] **1.** то́пливо; **2.** *mot.* горю́чее; ***add ~ to the fire*** подлива́ть ма́сла в ого́нь
fugitive ['fju:dʒətɪv] (*runaway*) бегле́ц; *from danger, persecution, etc.* бе́женец *m*, -нка *f*
fulfil(l) [fʊl'fɪl] выполня́ть [вы́полнить], осуществля́ть [-ви́ть]; **~ment** [~mənt] осуществле́ние, выполне́ние
full [fʊl] **1.** □ по́лный; *hour* це́лый; **2.** *adv.* вполне́; как раз; о́чень; **3. *in ~*** по́лностью; ***to the ~*** в по́лной ме́ре; **~ dress** пара́дная фо́рма; **~-fledged** вполне́ опери́вшийся; *fig.* зако́нченный; полнопра́вный; **~-scale** [fʊl'skeɪl] в по́лном объёме
fumble ['fʌmbl] (*feel about*) ша́рить; (*rummage*) ры́ться; **~ *for words*** поды́скивать слова́
fume [fju:m] **1.** дым; (*vapour*) испаре́ние; **2.** дыми́ть(ся); *fig.* возмуща́ться
fumigate ['fju:mɪgeɪt] оку́ривать
fun [fʌn] весе́лье; заба́ва; ***have ~*** хорошо́ провести́ вре́мя; ***make ~ of*** высме́ивать [вы́смеять] (В)
function ['fʌŋkʃn] **1.** фу́нкция, назначе́ние; **2.** функциони́ровать, де́йствовать
fund [fʌnd] запа́с; *fin.* капита́л, фонд; **~s** *pl.* (*resources*) фо́нды *m/pl.*; ***public ~*** госуда́рственные сре́дства
fundament|al [fʌndə'mentl] □ основно́й, коренно́й, суще́ственный; **~als** *pl.* осно́вы *f/pl.*
funeral ['fju:nərəl] по́хороны *f/pl.*; *attr.* похоро́нный
funnel ['fʌnl] воро́нка; *naut.* дымова́я труба́
funny ['fʌnɪ] □ заба́вный, смешно́й; (*strange*) стра́нный
fur [fɜ:] мех; (*skin with ~*) шку́р(к)а; **~ *coat*** шу́ба; **~s** *pl.* меха́ *m/pl.*,

меховы́е това́ры *m/pl.*, пушни́на
furious ['fjʊərɪəs] □ (*violent*) бу́йный; (*enraged*) взбешённый
furl [fɜːl] *sails* свёртывать [сверну́ть]; *umbrella* скла́дывать [сложи́ть]
fur-lined ['fɜːlaɪnd] подби́тый ме́хом
furnace ['fɜːnɪs] горн; печь *f*
furnish ['fɜːnɪʃ] (*provide*) снабжа́ть [снабди́ть] (***with*** Т); *room, etc.* обставля́ть [-а́вить], меблирова́ть *(im)pf.*; **~ings** обстано́вка; дома́шние принадле́жности
furniture ['fɜːnɪtʃər] ме́бель *f*, обстано́вка
furrier ['fʌrɪə] скорня́к
furrow ['fʌrəʊ] *agric.* борозда́; (*groove*) коле́я
further ['fɜːðə] **1.** да́льше, да́лее; зате́м; кро́ме того́; **2.** соде́йствовать, спосо́бствовать (Д); **~ance** [~rəns] продвиже́ние (***of*** Р), соде́йствие (***of*** Д); **~more** [fɜːðə'mɔː] *adv.* к тому́ же, кро́ме того́
furthest ['fɜːðɪst] са́мый да́льний
furtive ['fɜːtɪv] □ скры́тый, та́йный; ***~ glance*** взгляд укра́дкой
fury ['fjʊərɪ] неи́стовство, я́рость *f*; ***fly into a ~*** прийти́ в я́рость
fuse[1] [fjuːz] *el.* пла́вкий предохрани́тель *m*, *coll.* про́бка
fuse[2] [~]: ***the lights have ~d*** про́бки перегоре́ли
fuss [fʌs] *coll.* **1.** суета́; (*row*) шум, сканда́л; ***make a ~*** подня́ть *pf.* шум; ***make a ~ of s.o.*** носи́ться с ке́м-л.; **2.** [за]суети́ться; [вз]волнова́ться (***about*** из-за Р)
futile ['fjuːtaɪl] бесполе́зный, тще́тный
future ['fjuːtʃə] **1.** бу́дущий; **2.** бу́дущее, бу́дущность *f*; ***in the near ~*** в ближа́йшее вре́мя; ***there is no ~ in it*** э́то бесперспекти́вно
fuzzy ['fʌzɪ] (*blurred*) сму́тный; (*fluffy*) пуши́стый

G

gab [gæb]: ***the gift of the ~*** хорошо́ подве́шенный язы́к
gabardine ['gæbədiːn] габарди́н
gabble ['gæbl] танато́рить
gable ['geɪbl] *arch.* фронто́н
gad [gæd]: ***~ about*** шля́ться, шата́ться
gadfly ['gædflaɪ] *zo.* сле́пень *m*
gadget ['gædʒɪt] приспособле́ние; *coll.* техни́ческая нови́нка
gag [gæg] **1.** *for stopping mouth* кляп; (*joke*) шу́тка, остро́та; **2.** затыка́ть рот (Д); заста́вить *pf.* замолча́ть
gaiety ['geɪətɪ] весёлость *f*
gaily ['geɪlɪ] *adv. om* ***gay*** ве́село; (*brightly*) я́рко
gain [geɪn] **1.** (*profit*) при́быль *f*; (*winnings*) вы́игрыш; (*increase*) приро́ст; **2.** выи́грывать [вы́играть]; приобрета́ть [-ести́]; ***~ weight*** [по]полне́ть
gait [geɪt] похо́дка
galaxy ['gæləksɪ] гала́ктика; *fig.* плея́да
gale [geɪl] шторм, си́льный ве́тер
gall [gɔːl] **1.** *med.* жёлчь *f*; *bitterness* жёлчность *f*; (*bad temper*) зло́ба; **2.** раздража́ть [-жи́ть]
gallant ['gælənt] **1.** гала́нтный; **2.** *adj.* ['gælənt] □ хра́брый, до́блестный
gall bladder жёлчный пузы́рь
gallery ['gælərɪ] галере́я; *thea.* балко́н; *coll.* галёрка
galley ['gælɪ] *naut.* ка́мбуз
gallon ['gælən] галло́н
gallop ['gæləp] **1.** гало́п; **2.** скака́ть гало́пом
gallows ['gæləʊz] *sg.* ви́селица
gamble ['gæmbl] **1.** аза́ртная игра́; риско́ванное предприя́тие; **2.** игра́ть в аза́ртные и́гры; *on stock exchange* игра́ть; **~r** [~ə] картёжник, игро́к

gambol ['gæmbl] **1.** прыжóк; **2.** прыгать, скакáть
game [geɪm] **1.** игрá; *of chess, etc.* пáртия; *of tennis* гейм; (*wild animals*) дичь *f*; **~s** *pl.* состязáния *n/pl.*, игры *f/pl.*; ***beat s.o. at his own ~*** бить когó-л. егó сóбственным орýжием; **2.** *coll.* охóтно готóвый (сдéлать чтó-л.); **3.** игрáть на дéньги; **~ster** [~stə] игрóк, картёжник
gander ['gændə] гусáк
gang [gæŋ] **1.** *of workers* бригáда; *of criminals* бáнда; **2. ~ up** объединúться *pf.*
gangster ['gæŋstə] гáнгстер
gangway [gæŋweɪ] *naut.* схóдни; *ae.* трап; (*passage*) прохóд
gaol [dʒeɪl] тюрьмá; → ***jail***
gap [gæp] *in text, knowledge* прóбел; (*cleft*) брешь *f*, щель *f*; *fig. between ideas, etc.* расхождéние
gape [geɪp] разевáть рот; [по]глазéть; зиять
garage ['gærɑːʒ] гарáж
garbage ['gɑːbɪdʒ] отбрóсы *m/pl.*; мýсор; **~ *chute*** мусоропрóвод
garden ['gɑːdn] **1.** сад; ***kitchen ~*** огорóд; **2.** занимáться садовóдством; **~er** [~ə] садóвник, садовóд; **~ing** [~ɪŋ] садовóдство
gargle ['gɑːgl] **1.** полоскáть гóрло; **2.** полоскáние для гóрла
garish ['geərɪʃ] брóский, кричáщий; яркий
garland ['gɑːlənd] гирлянда, венóк
garlic ['gɑːlɪk] чеснóк
garment ['gɑːmənt] предмéт одéжды
garnish ['gɑːnɪʃ] **1.** (*decoration*) украшéние, *mst. cul.*; **2.** украшáть [укрáсить]; гарнúровать
garret ['gærɪt] мансáрда
garrison ['gærɪsn] гарнизóн
garrulous ['gærʊləs] □ болтлúвый
gas [gæs] **1.** газ; *Am.* бензúн, горючее; **~bag** *coll.* болтýн; пустомéля; **2.** отравлять гáзом
gash [gæʃ] **1.** глубóкая рáна, разрéз; **2.** наносúть глубóкую рáну (Д)
gas lighter гáзовая зажигáлка
gasoline, gasolene ['gæsəliːn] *mot. Am.* бензúн
gasp [gɑːsp] задыхáться [задохнýться]; ловúть вóздух
gas station *Am.* автозапрáвочная стáнция; **~ stove** гáзовая плитá
gastri|c ['gæstrɪk] желýдочный; ***~ ulcer*** язва желýдка; **~tis** [gæ'straɪtɪs] гастрúт
gate [geɪt] ворóта *n/pl.*; *in fence* калúтка; **~way** ворóта *n/pl.*; вход; подворóтня
gather ['gæðə] *v/t.* соб(и)рáть; *harvest* снимáть [снять]; *flowers* [на-, со]рвáть; *fig.* дéлать вывод; ***~ speed*** набирáть скóрость; *v/i.* соб(и)рáться; **~ing** [~rɪŋ] собрáние; *social* встрéча; *med.* нарыв
gaudy ['gɔːdɪ] □ яркий, кричáщий, безвкýсный
gauge [geɪdʒ] **1.** *tech.* калúбр; измерúтельный прибóр; ***fuel ~*** *mot.* бензиномéр; **2.** измерять [-éрить]; градуúровать (*im*)*pf.*; *fig. person* оцéнивать [-нúть]
gaunt [gɔːnt] □ исхудáлый, измождённый; *place* забрóшенный, мрáчный
gauze [gɔːz] мáрля
gave [geɪv] *pt. om* ***give***
gawky ['gɔːkɪ] неуклюжий
gay [geɪ] □ весёлый; *colo(u)r* яркий, пёстрый; гомосексуáльный
gaze [geɪz] **1.** прúстальный взгляд; **2.** прúстально смотрéть
gazette [gə'zet] *official* бюллетéнь *m*, вéстник
gear [gɪə] **1.** механúзм; приспособлéния *n/pl.*; *tech.* шестерня; зубчáтая передáча; *mot.* передáча; скóрость *f*; (*equipment*) принадлéжности *f/pl.*; (*belongings*) вéщи *f/pl.*; ***change ~*** переключúть передáчу; ***in ~*** включённый, дéйствующий; **2.** приводúть в движéние; включáть [-чúть]
geese [giːs] *pl. om* ***goose***
gem [dʒem] драгоцéнный кáмень *m*; *fig.* сокрóвище
gender ['dʒendə] *gr.* род
gene [dʒiːn] *biol.* ген
general ['dʒenərəl] **1.** □ óбщий; обычный; (*in all parts*) повсемéстный; (*chief*) глáвный, генерáльный; ***~ election*** всеóбщие выборы *m/pl.*; **2.** *mil.* генерáл; **~ization** [dʒenrəlaɪ'zeɪʃn] обобщéние; **~ize**

['dʒenrəlaɪz] обобща́ть [-щи́ть]; **~ly** [~lɪ] вообще́; обы́чно
generat|e ['dʒenəreɪt] порожда́ть [-роди́ть]; производи́ть [-вести́]; *el.* выраба́тывать [вы́работать]; **~ion** [dʒenə'reɪʃn] поколе́ние; **~or** ['dʒenəreɪtə] генера́тор
gener|osity [dʒenə'rɒsətɪ] великоду́шие; *with money, etc.* ще́дрость *f*; **~ous** ['dʒenərəs] □ великоду́шный, ще́дрый
genetics [dʒɪ'netɪks] гене́тика
genial ['dʒi:nɪəl] □ *climate* тёплый, мя́гкий; до́брый, серде́чный
genius ['dʒi:nɪəs] ге́ний; тала́нт, гениа́льность *f*
genocide ['dʒenəsaɪd] геноци́д
genre ['ʒɑ:nrə] жанр
gentle ['dʒentl] □ мя́гкий; кро́ткий; ти́хий; не́жный; *animals* сми́рный; *breeze* лёгкий; **~man** джентельме́н; господи́н; **~manlike, ~manly** [~lɪ] воспи́танный; **~ness** [~nɪs] мя́гкость *f*; доброта́
genuine ['dʒenjʊɪn] □ (*real*) по́длинный; (*sincere*) и́скренний, неподде́льный
geography [dʒɪ'ɒgrəfɪ] геогра́фия
geology [dʒɪ'ɒlədʒɪ] геоло́гия
geometry [dʒɪ'ɒmətrɪ] геоме́трия
germ [dʒɜ:m] микро́б; (*embryo*) заро́дыш (*a. fig.*)
German ['dʒɜ:mən] **1.** герма́нский, неме́цкий; **~ *silver*** мельхио́р; **2.** не́мец, не́мка; неме́цкий язы́к
germinate ['dʒɜ:mɪneɪt] дава́ть ростки́, прораста́ть [-расти́]
gesticulat|e [dʒe'stɪkjʊleɪt] жестикули́ровать; **~ion** [~stɪkjʊ'leɪʃn] жестикуля́ция
gesture ['dʒestʃə] жест (*a. fig.*)
get [get] [*irr.*] **1.** *v/t.* (*obtain*) дост(ав)а́ть; (*receive*) получа́ть [-чи́ть]; (*earn*) зараба́тывать [-бо́тать]; (*buy*) покупа́ть, купи́ть; (*fetch*) приноси́ть [-нести́]; (*induce*) заставля́ть [-ста́вить]; ***I have got to ...*** мне ну́жно, я до́лжен; **~ *one's hair cut*** [по]стри́чься; **2.** *v/i.* (*become, be*) [с]де́латься, станови́ться [стать]; **~ *ready*** [при]гото́виться; **~ *about*** (*travel*) разъезжа́ть; *after illness* начина́ть ходи́ть; **~ *abroad*** *of rumo(u)rs* распространя́ться [-ни́ться]; **~ *across*** *fig.* заставля́ть [-а́вить] поня́ть; **~ *ahead*** продвига́ться вперёд; **~ *at*** доб(и)ра́ться до (Р); **~ *away*** уд(и)ра́ть, уходи́ть [уйти́]; **~ *down*** *from shelf* снима́ть [снять]; *from train* сходи́ть [сойти́]; **~ *in*** входи́ть [войти́]; **~ *on well with a p.*** хорошо́ ла́дить с ке́м-л.; **~ *out*** вынима́ть [вы́нуть]; **~ *to hear*** (***know, learn***) узн(ав)а́ть; **~ *up*** вст(ав)а́ть; **~up** ['getʌp] (*dress*) наря́д
geyser ['gi:zə] **1.** ге́йзер; **2.** *Brt.* га́зовая коло́нка
ghastly ['gɑ:stlɪ] ужа́сный
gherkin ['gɜ:kɪn] огу́рчик; ***pickled ~s*** корнишо́ны
ghost [gəʊst] при́зрак, привиде́ние; дух (*a. eccl.*); *fig.* тень *f*, лёгкий след; **~like** ['gəʊstlaɪk], **~ly** [~lɪ] похо́жий на привиде́ние, при́зрачный
giant ['dʒaɪənt] **1.** велика́н, гига́нт; **2.** гига́нтский
gibber ['dʒɪbə] говори́ть невня́тно; **~ish** [~rɪʃ] тараба́рщина
gibe [dʒaɪb] *v/i.* насмеха́ться (***at*** над Т)
gidd|iness ['gɪdɪnɪs] *med.* головокруже́ние; легкомы́слие; **~y** ['gɪdɪ] □ испы́тывающий головокруже́ние; (*not serious*) легкомы́сленный; ***I feel ~*** у меня́ кру́жится голова́; **~ *height*** головокружи́тельная высота́
gift [gɪft] дар, пода́рок; спосо́бность *f*, тала́нт (***of*** к Д); **~ed** ['gɪftɪd] одарённый, спосо́бный
gigantic [dʒaɪ'gæntɪk] (***~ally***) гига́нтский, грома́дный
giggle ['gɪgl] **1.** хихи́канье; **2.** хихи́кать [-кнуть]
gild [gɪld] [*irr.*] [по]золоти́ть
gill [gɪl] *zo.* жа́бра
gilt [gɪlt] **1.** позоло́та; **2.** позоло́ченный
gin [dʒɪn] (*machine or alcoholic beverage*) джин
ginger ['dʒɪndʒə] **1.** имби́рь *m*; **2. ~ up** *coll.* подстёгивать [-стегну́ть], оживля́ть [-ви́ть]; **~bread** имби́рный пря́ник; **~ly** [~lɪ] осторо́жный, ро́бкий
gipsy ['dʒɪpsɪ] цыга́н(ка)

giraffe [dʒɪ'rɑːf] жира́ф
girder ['gɜːdə] (*beam*) ба́лка
girdle ['gɜːdl] (*belt*) по́яс, куша́к; (*corset*) корсе́т
girl [gɜːl] де́вочка, де́вушка; **~friend** подру́га; **~hood** ['gɜːlhʊd] деви́чество; **~ish** □ деви́чий
giro ['dʒaɪrəʊ] *banking* безнали́чная опера́ция
girth [gɜːθ] обхва́т, разме́р; *for saddle* подпру́га
gist [dʒɪst] суть *f*
give [gɪv] [*irr.*] **1.** *v/t.* да(ва́)ть; *as gift* [по]дари́ть; (*hand over*) передава́ть [-да́ть]; (*pay*) [за]плати́ть; *pleasure* доставля́ть [-а́вить]; **~ *birth to*** роди́ть; **~ *away*** отд(ав)а́ть; *coll.* вы́да(ва́)ть, пред(ав)а́ть; **~ *in*** *application* под(ав)а́ть; **~ *off*** *smell* изд(ав)а́ть; **~ *up*** отка́зываться [-за́ться] от (Р); **2.** *v/i.* **~** (***in***) уступа́ть [-пи́ть]; **~ *into*** выходи́ть на (В); **~ *out*** конча́ться [ко́нчиться]; обесси́леть *pf.*; **~n** ['gɪvn] **1.** *pt. p. от* ***give***; **2.** *fig.* да́нный; (*disposed*) скло́нный (***to*** к Д)
glaci|al ['gleɪsɪəl] □ леднико́вый; **~er** ['glæsɪə] ледни́к
glad [glæd] □ дово́льный; ра́достный, весёлый; ***I am* ~** я ра́д(а); **~ly** охо́тно; **~den** ['glædn] [об]ра́довать
glade [gleɪd] поля́на
gladness ['glædnɪs] ра́дость *f*
glamo|rous ['glæmərəs] обая́тельный, очарова́тельный; **~(u)r** ['glæmə] очарова́ние
glance [glɑːns] **1.** бы́стрый взгляд; **2.** (*slip*) скользи́ть [-зну́ть] (*mst.* ***~ off***); **~ *at*** взгляну́ть на (В); **~ *back*** огля́дываться [-ну́ться]; **~ *through*** просма́тривать [-смо-тре́ть]
gland [glænd] же́леза
glare [gleə] **1.** ослепи́тельно сверка́ть; (*stare*) серди́то смотре́ть; **2.** серди́тый *or* свире́пый взгляд; ослепи́тельный блеск
glass [glɑːs] **1.** стекло́; стака́н; *for wine* рю́мка; (*looking* ~) зе́ркало; (***a pair of***) **~es** *pl.* очки́ *n/pl.*; **2.** *attr.* стекля́нный; **~house** *Brt.* (*greenhouse*) тепли́ца; *Am.* (*place where glass is made*) стеко́льный заво́д; **~y** ['glɑːsɪ] □ зерка́льный; *eyes* ту́склый
glaz|e [gleɪz] **1.** глазу́рь *f* **2.** глази́ровать (*im*)*pf.*; *windows* застекля́ть [-ли́ть]; **~ier** ['gleɪzɪə] стеко́льщик
gleam [gliːm] **1.** мя́гкий, сла́бый свет; про́блеск, луч; **2.** поблёскивать
glean [gliːn] *v/t. fig. information, etc.* тща́тельно собира́ть
glee [gliː] ликова́ние
glib [glɪb] □ *tongue* бо́йкий; **~ *excuse*** благови́дный предло́г
glid|e [glaɪd] **1.** скользи́ть, пла́вно дви́гаться; **2.** пла́вное движе́ние; **~er** ['glaɪdə] *ae.* планёр
glimmer ['glɪmə] **1.** мерца́ние, ту́склый свет; **2.** мерца́ть, ту́скло свети́ть
glimpse [glɪmps] **1.**: ***at a* ~** с пе́рвого взгля́да; ***catch a* ~** = *v.* ***glimpse*** **2.** [у]ви́деть ме́льком
glint [glɪnt] **1.** блеск; **2.** блесте́ть
glisten ['glɪsn], **glitter** ['glɪtə] блесте́ть, сверка́ть, сия́ть
gloat [gləʊt] злора́дствовать
global ['gləʊbl] глоба́льный, всеми́рный
globe [gləʊb] шар; земно́й шар; гло́бус; **~trotter** [~trɒtə] зая́длый путеше́ственник
gloom [gluːm] мрак; ***throw a* ~ *over ...*** поверга́ть [-ве́ргнуть] в уны́ние; **~y** ['gluːmɪ] □ мра́чный; угрю́мый
glori|fy ['glɔːrɪfaɪ] прославля́ть [-а́вить]; **~ous** ['glɔːrɪəs] □ великоле́пный, чуде́сный
glory ['glɔːrɪ] **1.** сла́ва; **2.** торжествова́ть; (*take pride*) горди́ться (***in*** Т)
gloss [glɒs] **1.** вне́шний блеск; гля́нец; (*explanatory comment*) поясне́ние, толкова́ние; **2.** наводи́ть гля́нец на (В); **~ *over*** приукра́шивать [-кра́сить]; обойти́ молча́нием
glossary ['glɒsərɪ] глосса́рий; *at end of book* слова́рь *m*
glossy ['glɒsɪ] □ *hair* блестя́щий; *photo, etc.* гля́нцевый
glove [glʌv] перча́тка; **~ *compartment*** *mot. coll.* бардачо́к
glow [gləʊ] **1.** (*burn*) горе́ть; *of coals*

тлеть; *with happiness* сиять; **2.** зарево; *on face* румянец; **~-worm** светлячок
glucose ['glu:kəʊs] глюкоза
glue [glu:] **1.** клей; **2.** [с]клеить; ***be ~d to*** быть прикованным (к Д)
glum [glʌm] мрачный, хмурый
glut [glʌt] избыток; затоваривание
glutton ['glʌtn] обжора *m/f*; **~y** [~ɪ] обжорство
gnash [næʃ] [за]скрежетать
gnat [næt] комар; (*midge*) мошка
gnaw [nɔ:] глодать; грызть (*a. fig.*)
gnome [nəʊm] гном, карлик
go [gəʊ] **1.** [*irr.*] ходить, идти; (*pass*) проходить [пройти]; (*leave*) уходить [уйти]; *by car, etc.* ездить, [по]ехать; (*become*) [с]делаться; (*function*) работать; ***let ~*** отпускать [отпустить]; выпускать из рук; ***~ to see*** заходить [зайти] к (Д), навещать [-естить]; ***~ at*** набрасываться [-роситься] на (В); ***~ by*** проходить [пройти] мимо; (*be guided by*) руководствоваться (Т); ***~ for*** идти [пойти] за (Т); ***~ for a walk*** пойти на прогулку; ***~ in for*** заниматься [-няться]; ***~ on*** продолжать [-должить]; идти дальше; ***~ through with*** доводить до конца (В); ***~ without*** обходиться (обойтись) без (Р); **2.** ходьба, движение; *coll.* энергия; ***on the ~*** на ходу; на ногах; ***no ~*** *coll.* не выйдет; не пойдёт; ***in one ~*** с первой попытки; в одном заходе; ***have a ~ at*** [по]пробовать (В)
goad [gəʊd] побуждать [побудить]; подстрекать [-кнуть]
goal [gəʊl] цель *f*; *sport* ворота *n/pl.*; гол; **~keeper** вратарь *m*
goat [gəʊt] козёл, коза
gobble ['gɒbl] есть жадно, быстро
go-between ['gəʊbɪtwi:n] посредник
goblin ['gɒblɪn] домовой
god [gɒd] (*deity*) бог; (*supreme being*) (***God***) Бог; божество; *fig.* кумир; ***thank God!*** слава Богу!; **~child** крестник *m*, -ница *f*; **~dess** ['gɒdɪs] богиня; **~father** крёстный отец; **~forsaken** ['~fəseɪkən] богом забытый; заброшенный; **~less** ['~lɪs] безбожный; **~mother** крёстная мать *f*
goggle ['gɒgl] **1.** таращить глаза; **2.** (***a pair of***) **~s** *pl.* защитные очки *n/pl.*
going ['gəʊɪŋ] **1.** действующий; ***be ~ to*** *inf.* намереваться, собираться (*+inf.*); ***~ concern*** процветающее предприятие; **2.** (*leave*) уход; отъезд; **~s-on** [gəʊɪŋz'ɒn]: ***what ~!*** ну и дела!
gold [gəʊld] **1.** золото; **2.** золотой; **~en** ['gəʊldən] золотой; **~finch** *zo.* щегол
golf [gɒlf] гольф
gondola ['gɒndələ] гондола
gone [gɒn] *pt. p. от* ***go***
good [gʊd] **1.** хороший; (*kind*) добрый; (*suitable*) годный, (*beneficial*) полезный; ***~ for colds*** помогает при простуде; ***Good Friday*** *relig.* Страстная пятница; ***be ~ at*** быть способным к (Д); **2.** добро, благо; польза; **~s** *pl.* товар; ***that's no ~*** это бесполезно; ***for ~*** навсегда; **~by(e)** [gʊd'baɪ] **1.** до свидания!, прощайте!; **2.** прощание; **~natured** добродушный; **~ness** ['~nɪs] доброта; *int.* Господи!; **~will** доб-рожелательность *f*
goody ['gʊdɪ] *coll.* конфета, лакомство
goose [gu:s], *pl.* **geese** [gi:s] гусь *m*
gooseberry ['gʊzbərɪ] крыжовник (*no pl.*)
goose|flesh, *a.* **~pimples** *pl. fig.* гусиная кожа, мурашки
gorge [gɔ:dʒ] (*ravine*) узкое ущелье
gorgeous ['gɔ:dʒəs] великолепный
gorilla [gə'rɪlə] горилла
gory ['gɔ:rɪ] □ окровавленный, кровавый
gospel ['gɒspəl] Евангелие
gossip ['gɒsɪp] **1.** сплетня; сплетник *m*, -ница *f*; **2.** [на]сплетничать
got [gɒt] *pt. и pt. p. от* ***get***
Gothic ['gɒθɪk] готический
gourmet ['gʊəmeɪ] гурман
gout [gaʊt] *med.* подагра
govern ['gʌvn] *v/t.* (*rule*) править, (*administer*) управлять (Т); **~ess** [~ənɪs] гувернантка; **~ment** [~ənmənt] правительство; управление;

attr. прави́тельственный; **~or** [~ənə] губерна́тор; *coll.* (*boss*) хозя́ин; шеф

gown [gaʊn] пла́тье; *univ.* ма́нтия

grab [græb] *coll.* хва́тывать [-ати́ть]

grace [greɪs] **1.** гра́ция, изя́щество; **2.** *fig.* украша́ть [укра́сить]; удоста́ивать [-сто́ить]; **~ful** ['greɪsfl] □ грацио́зный, изя́щный; **~fulness** [~nɪs] грацио́зность *f*, изя́щество

gracious ['greɪʃəs] □ любе́зный; благоскло́нный; (*merciful*) ми́лостивый; ***goodness ~!*** Го́споди!

gradation [grə'deɪʃn] града́ция, постепе́нный перехо́д

grade [greɪd] **1.** сте́пень *f*; (*rank*) ранг; (*quality*) ка́чество; *Am. educ.* класс; (*slope*) укло́н; **2.** [рас]сортирова́ть

gradient ['greɪdɪənt] укло́н; ***steep ~*** круто́й спуск *or* подъём

gradua|l ['grædʒʊəl] □ постепе́нный; **~te 1.** [~eɪt] градуи́ровать (*im*)*pf.*, наноси́ть деле́ния; конча́ть университе́т; *Am.* конча́ть (любо́е) уче́бное заведе́ние; **2.** [~ɪt] *univ.* выпускни́к университе́та; **~tion** [grædʒʊ'eɪʃn] градуиро́вка; *Am.* оконча́ние (вы́сшего) уче́бного заведе́ния

graft [grɑːft] **1.** *hort.* (*scion*) черено́к; приви́вка; **2.** приви́(ва́)ть; *med.* переса́живать ткань *f*

grain [greɪn] зерно́; (*cereals*) хле́бные зла́ки *m/pl.*; (*particle*) крупи́нка; *fig.* ***against the ~*** не по нутру́

gramma|r ['græmə] грамма́тика; **~tical** [grə'mætɪkəl] □ граммати́ческий

gram(me) [græm] грамм

granary ['grænərɪ] амба́р; жи́тница *a. fig.*

grand [grænd] **1.** □ *view, etc.* вели́чественный; *plans, etc.* грандио́зный; ***we had a ~ time*** мы прекра́сно провели́ вре́мя; **2.** *mus.* (*a.* ***~ piano***) роя́ль *m*; **~child** ['grænt-ʃaɪld] внук, вну́чка; **~eur** ['grændʒə] грандио́зность *f*; вели́чие

grandiose ['grændɪəʊs] □ грандио́зный

grandparents *pl.* де́душка и ба́бушка

grant [grɑːnt] **1.** предоставля́ть [-а́вить]; (*admit as true*) допуска́ть [-сти́ть]; **2.** дар; субси́дия; *student's* стипе́ндия; ***take for ~ed*** принима́ть [приня́ть] как само́ собо́й разуме́ющееся

granul|ated ['grænjʊleɪtɪd] гранули́рованный; **~e** ['grænjuːl] зёрнышко

grape [greɪp] *collect.* виногра́д; ***a bunch of ~s*** гроздь виногра́да; ***a ~*** виногра́дина; **~-fruit** грейп-фру́т

graph [grɑːf] гра́фик; **~ic** ['græfɪk] графи́ческий; нагля́дный; *description* я́ркий; ***~ arts*** *pl.* гра́фика; **~ite** ['græfaɪt] графи́т

grapple ['græpl]: ***~ with*** боро́ться с (T); *fig. difficulties* пыта́ться преодоле́ть

grasp [grɑːsp] **1.** хвата́ть [схвати́ть] (***by*** за B); *in one's hand* зажа(им)а́ть; хвата́ться [схвати́ться] (***at*** за B); **2.** понима́ть [поня́ть]; ***it's beyond my ~*** э́то вы́ше моего́ понима́ния; ***she kept the child's hand in her ~*** она́ кре́пко держа́ла ребёнка за́ руку

grass [grɑːs] трава́; (*pasture*) па́стбище; **~hopper** ['~hɒpə] кузне́чик; **~-widow** [~'wɪdəʊ] соло́менная вдова́; **~y** ['~ɪ] травяно́й

grate [greɪt] **1.** (*fireplace*) решётка; **2.** *cheese, etc.* [на]тере́ть; *teeth* [за-] скрежета́ть; ***~ on*** *fig.* раздража́ть [-жи́ть] (B)

grateful ['greɪtfl] □ благода́рный

grater ['greɪtə] тёрка

grati|fication [grætɪfɪ'keɪʃn] удовлетворе́ние; **~fy** ['grætɪfaɪ] удовлетворя́ть [-ри́ть]; (*indulge*) потака́ть (Д)

grating[1] ['greɪtɪŋ] □ скрипу́чий, ре́зкий

grating[2] [~] решётка

gratitude ['grætɪtjuːd] благода́рность *f*

gratuit|ous [grə'tjuːɪtəs] □ беспла́тный, безвозме́здный; **~y** [~ətɪ] посо́бие

grave[1] [greɪv] □ серьёзный, ве́ский; *illness, etc.* тяжёлый

grave[2] [~] моги́ла

gravel ['grævl] гра́вий

graveyard кла́дбище

gravitation [grævɪ'teɪʃn] притяже́-

G

ние; тяготе́ние (*a. fig.*)
gravity ['grævətɪ] серьёзность *f*; *of situation* тя́жесть *f*, опа́сность *f*
gravy ['greɪvɪ] (мясна́я) подли́вка
gray [greɪ] се́рый; → *Brt.* ***grey***
graze¹ [greɪz] пасти́(сь)
graze² [~] заде́(ва́)ть; (*scrape*) [по]цара́пать
grease [gri:s] **1.** жир; *tech.* конси́сте́нтная сма́зка; **2.** [gri:z] сма́з(ыв)ать
greasy ['gri:sɪ] □ жи́рный; *road* ско́льзкий
great [greɪt] □ вели́кий; большо́й; (*huge*) огро́мный; *coll.* великоле́пный; **~coat** *mil.* шине́ль *f*; **~-grandchild** [greɪt'græntʃaɪld] пра́внук *m*, -учка *f*; **~ly** [~lɪ] о́чень, си́льно; **~ness** [~nɪs] вели́чие
greed [gri:d] жа́дность *f*; **~y** ['gri:dɪ] □ жа́дный (***of, for*** к Д)
Greek [gri:k] **1.** грек *m*, греча́нка *f*; **2.** гре́ческий
green [gri:n] **1.** зелёный; (*unripe*) незре́лый; *fig.* нео́пытный; **2.** зелёный цвет, зелёная кра́ска; (*grassy plot*) лужа́йка; **~s** *pl.* зе́лень *f*, о́вощи *m/pl.*; **~grocery** овощно́й магази́н; **~house** тепли́ца, оранжере́я; **~ish** ['gri:nɪʃ] зеленова́тый
greet [gri:t] *guests, etc.* приве́тствовать; [по]здоро́ваться; **~ing** ['gri:tɪŋ] приве́тствие; приве́т
grenade [grɪ'neɪd] *mil.* грана́та
grew [gru:] *pt. om* ***grow***
grey [greɪ] **1.** се́рый; *hair* седо́й; **2.** се́рый цвет, се́рая кра́ска; **3.** посере́ть; ***turn ~*** [по]седе́ть; **~hound** борза́я
grid [grɪd] решётка
grief [gri:f] го́ре; ***come to ~*** потерпе́ть *pf.* неуда́чу, попа́сть *pf.* в беду́
griev|ance ['gri:vns] оби́да; (*complaint*) жа́лоба; ***nurse a ~*** затаи́ть оби́ду (***against*** на В); **~e** [gri:v] горева́ть; (*cause grief to*) огорча́ть [-чи́ть]; **~ous** ['gri:vəs] □ го́рестный, печа́льный
grill [grɪl] **1.** (электро)гри́ль; (*on cooker*) решётка; жа́реное на решётке (в гри́ле) мя́со; **2.** жа́рить на решётке (в гри́ле); **~room** гриль-ба́р
grim [grɪm] □ жесто́кий; *smile, etc.* мра́чный
grimace [grɪ'meɪs] **1.** грима́са, ужи́мка; **2.** грима́сничать
grim|e [graɪm] грязь *f*; **~y** ['graɪmɪ] □ запа́чканный, гря́зный
grin [grɪn] **1.** усме́шка; **2.** усмеха́ться [-хну́ться]
grind [graɪnd] [*irr.*] **1.** [с]моло́ть; разма́лывать [-моло́ть]; *to powder* растира́ть [растере́ть]; (*sharpen*) [на]точи́ть; *fig.* зубри́ть; **2.** разма́лывание; тяжёлая, ску́чная рабо́та; **~stone** точи́льный ка́мень *m*; ***keep one's nose to the ~*** труди́ться без о́тдыха
grip [grɪp] **1.** (*handle*) ру́чка, рукоя́тка; (*understanding*) понима́ние; *fig.* тиски́ *m/pl.*; **2.** (*take hold of*) схва́тывать [схвати́ть]; *fig.* овладева́ть внима́нием (Р)
gripe [graɪp] ворча́ние; (*colic pains*) ко́лики *f/pl.*
gripping ['grɪpɪŋ] захва́тывающий
grisly ['grɪzlɪ] ужа́сный
gristle ['grɪsl] хрящ
grit [grɪt] **1.** песо́к, гра́вий; *coll.* твёрдость хара́ктера; **~s** *pl.* овся́ная крупа́; **2.** [за]скрежета́ть (Т)
grizzly ['grɪzlɪ] **1.** се́рый; *hair* с про́седью; **2.** североамерика́нский медве́дь *m*, гри́зли *m indecl.*
groan [grəʊn] **1.** о́хать [о́хнуть]; *with pain, etc.* [за]стона́ть; **2.** стон
grocer|ies ['grəʊsərɪz] *pl.* бакале́я; **~y** [~rɪ] бакале́йный отде́л
groggy ['grɒgɪ] нетвёрдый на нога́х; *after illness* сла́бый
groin [grɔɪn] *anat.* пах
groom [gru:m] **1.** ко́нюх; (*bride~*) жени́х; **2.** уха́живать за (ло́шадью); хо́лить; ***well ~ed*** хоро-шо́ и тща́тельно оде́тый, опря́тный ухо́женный
groove [gru:v] желобо́к; *tech.* паз; *fig.* рути́на, привы́чка, колея́
grope [grəʊp] идти́ о́щупью; нащу́п(ыв)ать (*a. fig.*)
gross [grəʊs] **1.** □ (*flagrant*) вопию́щий; (*fat*) ту́чный; (*coarse*) гру́бый; *fin.* валово́й, бру́тто; **2.** ма́сса, гросс
grotesque [grəʊ'tesk] гроте́скный
grotto ['grɒtəʊ] грот

grouch [grautʃ] *Am. coll.* **1.** дурно́е настрое́ние; **2.** быть не в ду́хе; **~y** [~ı] ворчли́вый

ground¹ [graund] *pt. и pt. p. от* ***grind***; **~ *glass*** ма́товое стекло́

ground² [~] **1.** *mst.* земля́, по́чва; (*area of land*) уча́сток земли́; площа́дка; (*reason*) основа́ние; **~s** *pl. adjoining house* сад, парк; ***on the ~(s)*** на основа́нии (Р); ***stand one's ~*** уде́рживать свои́ пози́ции, прояви́ть твёрдость; **2.** обосно́вывать [-нова́ть]; *el.* заземля́ть [-ли́ть]; (*teach*) обуча́ть осно́вам предме́та; **~ floor** [graund'flɔː] *Brt.* пе́рвый эта́ж; **~less** [~lıs] □ беспричи́нный, необосно́ванный; **~nut** ара́хис; **~work** фунда́мент, осно́ва

group [gruːp] **1.** гру́ппа; **2.** соб(и)ра́ться; [с]группирова́ть(ся)

grove [grəuv] ро́ща, лесо́к

grovel ['grɒvl] *fig.* пресмыка́ться; заи́скивать

grow [grəu] [*irr.*] *v/i.* расти́; выраста́ть [вы́расти]; (*become*) [с]де́латься, станови́ться [стать]; *v/t. bot.* выра́щивать [вы́растить]; культиви́ровать (*im*)*pf.*

growl [graul] [за]рыча́ть

grow|n [grəun] *pt. p. от* ***grow***; **~n-up** ['grəunʌp] взро́слый; **~th** [grəuθ] рост; *med.* о́пухоль *f*

grub [grʌb] **1.** личи́нка; **2.** (*dig in dirt*) ры́ться (в П); **~by** ['grʌbı] гря́зный

grudge [grʌdʒ] **1.** неохо́та, недово́льство; (*envy*) за́висть *f*; **2.** [по-] зави́довать (Д, в П); неохо́тно дава́ть; [по]жале́ть

gruff [grʌf] □ ре́зкий; гру́бый; *voice* хри́плый

grumble ['grʌmbl] [за]ворча́ть; (*complain*) [по]жа́ловаться; *of thunder etc.* [за]грохота́ть; **~r** [~ə] *fig.* ворчу́н(ья *f* / *m*)

grunt [grʌnt] хрю́кать [-кнуть]; *of person* [про]бурча́ть

guarant|ee [gærən'tiː] **1.** гара́нтия; поручи́тельство; **2.** гаранти́ровать (*im*)*pf.*; руча́ться за (В); **~or** [gærən'tɔː] *law* поручи́тель (-ница *f*) *m*; **~y** ['gærəntı] гара́нтия

guard [gɑːd] **1.** охра́на; *mil.* карау́л; *rail.* проводни́к; **~s** *pl.* гва́рдия; ***be on one's ~*** быть начеку́; **2.** *v/t.* охраня́ть [-ни́ть]; сторожи́ть; (*protect*) защища́ть [защити́ть] (***from*** от Р); *v/i.* [по]бере́чься, остерега́ться [-ре́чься] (***against*** Р); **~ian** ['gɑːdıən] *law* опеку́н; **~ianship** [~ʃıp] *law* опеку́нство

guess [ges] **1.** дога́дка, предположе́ние; **2.** отга́дывать [-да́ть], уга́дывать [-да́ть]; *Am.* счита́ть, полага́ть

guest [gest] го́сть(я *f*) *m*; **~house** пансио́н

guffaw [gə'fɔː] хо́хот

guidance ['gaıdns] руково́дство

guide [gaıd] **1.** *for tourists* экскурсово́д, гид; **2.** направля́ть [-ра́вить]; руководи́ть (Т); **~book** путеводи́тель *m*

guile [gaıl] хи́трость *f*, кова́рство; **~ful** ['gaılfl] □ кова́рный; **~less** [~lıs] □ простоду́шный

guilt [gılt] вина́, вино́вность *f*; **~less** ['gıltlıs] невино́вный; **~y** ['gıltı] □ вино́вный, винова́тый

guise [gaız]: ***under the ~ of*** под ви́дом (Р)

guitar [gı'tɑː] гита́ра

gulf [gʌlf] зали́в; *fig.* про́пасть *f*

gull¹ [gʌl] ча́йка

gull² [~] обма́нывать [-ну́ть]; [о]дура́чить

gullet ['gʌlıt] пищево́д; (*throat*) гло́тка

gullible ['gʌlıbl] легкове́рный

gulp [gʌlp] **1.** жа́дно глота́ть; **2.** глото́к; ***at one ~*** за́лпом

gum¹ [gʌm] десна́

gum² [~] **1.** клей; ***chewing ~*** жева́тельная рези́нка; **2.** скле́и(ва)ть

gun [gʌn] ору́дие, пу́шка; (*rifle*) ружьё; (*pistol*) пистоле́т; **~boat** каноне́рка; **~man** банди́т; **~ner** *mil., naut.* ['gʌnə] артиллери́ст, канони́р, пулемётчик; **~powder** по́рох

gurgle ['gɜːgl] *of water* [за]бу́лькать

gush [gʌʃ] **1.** си́льный пото́к; **~ *of enthusiasm*** взрыв энтузиа́зма; **2.** хлы́нуть *pf.*; ли́ться пото́ком; *fig.* бу́рно излива́ть чу́вства

gust [gʌst] *of wind* поры́в

gusto ['gʌstəu] смак; ***with ~*** с больши́м энтузиа́змом

gut [gʌt] кишка́; **~s** *pl.* вну́тренности *f/pl.*; *coll.* ***he has plenty of ~s*** он мужественный (*or* волевой) человек

gutter ['gʌtə] сточная канава; *on roof* жёлоб; ***~ press*** бульварная пресса

guy [gaɪ] *chiefly Brt.* (*person of grotesque appearance*) чучело; *Am. coll.* (*fellow, person*) малый; парень *m*

guzzle ['gʌzl] жадно пить; (*eat*) есть с жадностью

gymnas|ium [dʒɪm'neɪzɪəm] спортивный зал; **~tics** [dʒɪm'næstɪks] *pl.* гимнастика

gypsy ['dʒɪpsɪ] *esp. Am.* цыган(ка)

gyrate [dʒaɪ'reɪt] двигаться по кругу, вращаться

H

haberdashery ['hæbədæʃərɪ] (*goods*) галантерея; (*shop*) галантерейный магазин

habit ['hæbɪt] привычка; **~able** ['hæbɪtəbl] годный для жилья; **~ation** [hæbɪ'teɪʃn] жильё

habitual [hə'bɪtʃʊəl] обычный; (*done by habit*) привычный

hack[1] [hæk] [на-, с]рубить

hack[2] [~] (*horse*) наёмная лошадь *f*, кляча; (*writer*) халтурщик; *coll.* писака

hackneyed ['hæknɪd] *fig.* избитый

had [d, əd, həd· *strong* hæd] *pt. u pt. p. om* ***have***

haddock ['hædək] пикша

h(a)emoglobin [hiːmə'gləʊbɪn] гемоглобин

h(a)emorrhage ['hemərɪdʒ] кровоизлияние

haggard ['hægəd] □ измождённый, осунувшийся

haggle ['hægl] (*bargain*) торговаться

hail[1] [heɪl]: ***~ a taxi*** подозвать такси

hail[2] [~] **1.** град; **2.** ***it ~ed today*** сегодня был град; **~stone** градина

hair [heə] волос; ***keep your ~ on!*** спокойно!; **~cut** стрижка; **~do** причёска; **~dresser** парикмахер; **~dryer** фен; **~pin** шпилька; **~-raising** страшный; **~'s-breadth** минимальное расстояние; **~splitting** крохоборство; **~y** [~rɪ] волосатый

hale [heɪl] здоровый, крепкий

half [hɑːf, hæf] **1.** половина; ***~ past two*** половина третьего; ***one and a ~*** полтора *n/m*, полторы *f*; ***go halves*** делить пополам; ***not ~!*** *Brt. coll.* ещё бы!; а как же!; **2.** полу...; половинный; **3.** почти; наполовину; **~-caste** метис; **~hearted** □ равнодушный, вялый; **~-length** (*a.* ***~ portrait***) поясной портрет; **~penny** ['heɪpnɪ] полпенни *n indecl.*; **~-time** *sport* конец тайма; **~way** на полпути; **~-witted** полоумный

halibut ['hælɪbət] палтус

hall [hɔːl] зал; холл, вестибюль *m*; (*entrance ~*) прихожая; *college* (*residence*) общежитие для студентов

hallow ['hæləʊ] освящать [-ятить]

halo ['heɪləʊ] *astr.* ореол (*a. fig.*); *of saint* нимб

halt [hɔːlt] **1.** (*temporary stop*) привал; остановка; ***come to a ~*** остановиться *pf.*; **2.** останавливать(ся) [-новить(ся)]; делать привал; *mst. fig.* (*hesitate*) колебаться; запинаться [запнуться]

halve [hɑːv] **1.** делить пополам; **2.** **~s** [hɑːvz, hævz] *pl. om* ***half***

ham [hæm] (*pig thigh*) окорок, (*meat of pig thigh*) ветчина

hamburger ['hæmbɜːgə] булочка с котлетой, гамбургер

hamlet ['hæmlɪt] деревушка

hammer ['hæmə] **1.** молоток; ***sledge ~*** молот; **2.** ковать молотом; бить молотком; (*knock*) [по-]

стучáть; (*form by ~ing*) выкóвывать [вы́ковать]; **~ into s.o.'s head** вбивáть [вбить] комý-л. в гóлову
hammock ['hæmək] гамáк
hamper[1] ['hæmpə] корзи́на с кры́шкой
hamper[2] [~] [вос]препя́тствовать; [по]мешáть (Д)
hand [hænd] **1.** рукá; (*writing*) пóчерк; *of watch* стрéлка; (*worker*) рабóчий; **at ~** под рукóй; **a good (poor) ~ at** (не-)искýсный в (П); **change ~s** переходи́ть [-ейти́] из рук в рýки; **~ and glove** в тéсной свя́зи; **lend a ~** помогáть [-мóчь]; **off ~** экспрóмтом; **on ~** *comm.* имéющийся в продáже; в распоряжéнии; **on the one ~** с однóй стороны́; **on the other ~** с другóй стороны́; **~-to-~** рукопáшный; **come to ~** попадáться [-пáсться] пóд руку; **2. ~ down** оставля́ть потóмству; **~ in** вручáть [-чи́ть]; **~ over** перед(ав)áть; **~bag** дáмская сýмочка; **~brake** *mot.* ручнóй тóрмоз; **~cuff** нарýчник; **~ful** ['hændfl] горсть *f*; *coll.* "наказáние"; **she's a real ~** онá сýщее наказáние
handicap ['hændıkæp] **1.** помéха; *sport* гандикáп; **2.** стáвить в невы́годное положéние; **~ped**: **physically ~** с физи́ческим недостáтком; **mentally ~** ýмственно отстáлый
handi|craft ['hændıkrɑːft] ручнáя рабóта; ремеслó; **~work** ручнáя рабóта; **is this your ~ ?** *fig.* э́то твои́х рук дéло?
handkerchief ['hæŋkətʃıf] носовóй платóк
handle ['hændl] **1.** рýчка; *of tool, etc.* рукоя́тка; **2.** держáть в рукáх, трóгать или брать рукáми; (*deal with*) обходи́ться [обойти́сь] с (Т); обращáться с (Т)
hand|made [hænd'meıd] ручнóй рабóты; **~shake** рукопожáтие; **~some** ['hænsəm] краси́вый; (*generous*) щéдрый; (*large*) поря́дочный; **~writing** пóчерк; **~y** ['hændı] удóбный; (*nearby*) бли́зкий
hang [hæŋ] **1.** [*irr.*] *v/t.* вéшать [повéсить]; *lamp, etc.* подвéшивать [-вéсить]; (*pt. и pt. p.* **~ed**) вéшать [повéсить]; *v/i.* висéть; **~ about, ~ around** слоня́ться, околáчиваться; **~ on** держáть(ся) (за В); *fig.* упóрствовать; **~ on !** подождите минýтку!; **2.**: **get the ~ of** понимáть [-ня́ть]; разобрáться [разбирáться]
hangar ['hæŋə] ангáр
hanger ['hæŋə] *for clothes* вéшалка
hangings ['hæŋıŋz] *pl.* драпирóвки *f/pl.*, занавéски *f/pl.*
hangover ['hæŋəʊvə] *from drinking* похмéлье; *survival* пережи́ток
haphazard [hæp'hæzəd] **1.** наудáчу, наобýм; **2.** □ случáйный
happen ['hæpən] случáться [-чи́ться], происходи́ть [произойти́]; откáзываться [-зáться]; **he ~ed to be at home** он оказáлся дóма; **it so ~ed that ...** случи́лось так, что ...; **~ (up)on** случáйно встрéтить; **~ing** ['hæpənıŋ] слýчай, собы́тие
happi|ly ['hæpılı] счастли́во, к счáстью; **~ness** [~nıs] счáстье
happy ['hæpı] □ *com.* счастли́вый; (*fortunate*) удáчный; **~-go-lucky** беспéчный
harangue [hə'ræŋ] разглагóльствовать
harass ['hærəs] [за]трави́ть; (*pester*) изводи́ть [-вести́]; [из]мýчить
harbo(u)r ['hɑːbər] **1.** гáвань *f*, порт; **~ duties** портóвые сбóры; **2.** (*give shelter to*) дать убéжище (Д), приюти́ть; *fig.* затáивать [-и́ть]
hard [hɑːd] **1.** *adj. com.* твёрдый, жёсткий; (*strong*) крéпкий; (*difficult*) трýдный; тяжёлый; **~ cash** нали́чные *pl.* (дéньги); **~ currency** твёрдая валю́та; **~ of hearing** тугóй на ýхо; **2.** *adv.* твёрдо; крéпко; си́льно; упóрно; с трудóм; **~ by** бли́зко, ря́дом; **~ up** в затрудни́тельном финáнсовом положéнии; **~-boiled** [hɑːd'bɔıld] → **egg**; *fig.* бесчýвственный, чёрствый; *Am.* хладнокрóвный; **~ disk** жёсткий диск; **~en** ['hɑːdn] затвердевáть, [за]твердéть; *fig.* закаля́ть(ся) [-ли́ть(ся)]; **~-headed** [hɑːd'hedıd] □ практи́чный, трéзвый; **~-hearted** [hɑːd'hɑːtıd] бесчýвственный; **~ly** ['hɑːdlı] с тру-дóм, едвá, едвá ли; **~ship** [~ʃıp] невзгóды; трýд-

H

ности; (*lack of money*) нуждá; **~ware** *comput.* аппа-рáтное обеспéчение; **~y** ['hɑːdɪ] □ смéлый, отвáжный; (*able to bear hard work, etc.*) вынóсливый

hare [heə] зáяц; **~-brained** опромéтчивый; (*foolish*) глýпый

harm [hɑːm] **1.** вред, зло; (*damage*) ущéрб; **2.** [по]вредить (Д); **~ful** ['hɑːmfl] □ врéдный, пáгубный; **~less** [~lɪs] □ безврéдный, безобидный

harmon|ious [hɑː'məʊnɪəs] □ гармони́чный, стрóйный; **~ize** ['hɑːmənaɪz] *v/t.* гармонизи́ровать (*im*)*pf.*; приводи́ть в гармóнию; *v/i.* гармони́ровать; **~y** [~nɪ] гармóния, созвýчие; (*agreement*) соглáсие

harness ['hɑːnɪs] **1.** ýпряжь *f*, сбрýя; **2.** запрягáть [запря́чь]

harp [hɑːp] **1.** áрфа; **2.** игрáть на áрфе; **~** (***up***)***on*** твердить, завести́ *pf.* волы́нку о (П)

harpoon [hɑː'puːn] гарпýн, острогá

harrow ['hærəʊ] *agric.* **1.** боронá; **2.** [вз]борони́ть; *fig.* [из]мýчить; **~ing** [~ɪŋ] *fig.* мучи́тельный

harsh [hɑːʃ] □ рéзкий; жёсткий; (*stern*) стрóгий, сурóвый; *to taste* тéрпкий

harvest ['hɑːvɪst] **1.** *of wheat, etc.* жáтва, убóрка; *of apples, etc.* сбор; урожáй; ***bumper* ~** небывáлый урожáй; **2.** собирáть урожáй

has [z, əz, həz˙, *strong* hæz] 3rd *p. sg. pres. om* ***have***

hash [hæʃ] рýбленое мя́со; *fig.* пýтаница

hast|e [heɪst] спéшка, поспéшность *f*, торопли́вость *f*; ***make* ~** [по]спеши́ть; **~en** ['heɪsn] спеши́ть, [по-] тороπи́ться; (*speed up*) ускоря́ть [-óрить]; **~y** ['heɪstɪ] □ поспéшный; необдýманный

hat [hæt] шля́па; *without brim* шáпка; ***talk through one's* ~** нести́ чушь *f*

hatch [hætʃ] *naut.*, *ae.* люк

hatchet ['hætʃɪt] топóрик

hat|e [heɪt] **1.** нéнависть *f*; **2.** ненави́деть; **~eful** ['heɪtfl] ненави́стный; **~red** ['heɪtrɪd] нéнависть *f*

haught|iness ['hɔːtɪnɪs] надмéнность *f*; высокомéрие; **~y** [~tɪ] □ надмéнный, высокомéрный

haul [hɔːl] **1.** перевóзка; (*catch*) улóв; **2.** тянýть; перевози́ть [-везти́]; **~age** [~ɪdʒ] транспортирóвка, достáвка

haunch [hɔːntʃ] бедрó

haunt [hɔːnt] **1.** *of ghost* появля́ться [-ви́ться] в (П); (*frequent*) чáсто посещáть; **2.** люби́мое мéсто; *of criminals, etc.* притóн; ***~ed look*** затрáвленный вид

have [v, əv, həv˙, *strong* hæv] **1.** [*irr.*] *v/t.* имéть; ***I ~ to do*** я дóлжен сдéлать; ***~ one's hair cut*** [по-] стри́чься; ***he will ~ it that ...*** он настáивает на том, чтóбы (+ *inf.*); ***I had better go*** мне лýчше уйти́; ***I had rather go*** я предпочёл бы уйти́; ***~ about one*** имéть при себé; ***~ it your own way*** поступáй как знáешь; *opinion* дýмай, что хóчешь; **2.** *v/aux. вспомогáтельный глагóл для образовáния перфéктной фóрмы*: ***I ~ come*** я пришёл

havoc ['hævək] опустошéние; (*destruction*) разрушéние; ***play ~ with*** вноси́ть [внести́] беспоря́док/хаóс в (В); разрýшить *pf.*

hawk [hɔːk] (*a. pol.*) я́стреб

hawker ['hɔːkə] ýличный торгóвец

hawthorn ['hɔːθɔːn] боя́рышник

hay [heɪ] сéно; ***~ fever*** сéнная лихорáдка; **~loft** сеновáл; **~stack** стог сéна

hazard ['hæzəd] **1.** риск; (*danger*) опáсность *f*; **2.** рисковáть [-кнýть]; **~ous** ['hæzədəs] □ рискóванный

haze [heɪz] ды́мка, тумáн

hazel ['heɪzl] **1.** (*tree*) орéшник; **2.** (*colo[u]r*) кáрий; **~nut** леснóй орéх

hazy ['heɪzɪ] □ тумáнный; *fig.* смýтный

H-bomb водорóдная бóмба

he [ɪ, hɪ˙, *strong* hiː] **1.** *pron. pers.* он; ***~ who ...*** тот, кто ...; **2. *~-...*** *пéред назвáнием живóтного обозначáет самцá*

head [hed] **1.** *com.* головá; *of government, etc.* главá; *of department, etc.* руководи́тель *m*, начáльник; *of bed* изголóвье; *of coin* лицевáя сторонá, орёл; ***come to a ~*** *fig.* дости́гнуть *pf.* крити́ческой стáдии; ***get it into one's ~ that ...***

вбить себе́ в го́лову, что ...; **2.** гла́вный; **3.** *v/t.* возглавля́ть; **~ off** (*prevent*) предотвраща́ть [-ати́ть]; **~ for** *v/i.* направля́ться [-а́виться]; держа́ть курс на (В); **~ache** ['hedeɪk] головна́я боль *f*; **~dress** головно́й убо́р; **~ing** ['~ɪŋ] загла́вие; **~land** мыс; **~light** *mot.* фа́ра; **~line** (газе́тный) заголо́вок; **~long** *adj.* опроме́тчивый; *adv.* опроме́тчиво; очертя́ го́лову; **~master** дире́ктор шко́лы; **~phone** нау́шник; **~quarters** *pl.* штаб; *of department, etc.* гла́вное управле́ние; **~strong** своево́льный, упря́мый; **~way**: ***make ~*** де́лать успе́хи, продвига́ться; **~y** ['hedɪ] □ опьяня́ющий; *with success* опьянённый

heal [hiːl] зале́чивать [-чи́ть], исцеля́ть [-ли́ть]; (*a.* **~ up**) зажи́(ва́)ть

health [helθ] здоро́вье; **~ful** [~fl] □ целе́бный; **~-resort** куро́рт; **~y** ['helθɪ] □ здоро́вый; (*good for health*) поле́зный

heap [hiːp] **1.** ку́ча, гру́да; *fig.* ма́сса, у́йма; **2.** нагроможда́ть [-мозди́ть]; *of food, etc.* накла́дывать [-ложи́ть]

hear [hɪə] [*irr.*] [у]слы́шать; [по-] слу́шать; **~ *s.o. out*** вы́слушать *pf.*; **~d** [hɜːd] *pt. и pt. p. от* ***hear***; **~er** ['hɪərə] слу́шатель(ница *f*) *m*; **~ing** [~ɪŋ] слух; *law* слу́шание де́ла; ***within ~*** в преде́лах слы́шимости; **~say** ['hɪəseɪ] слу́хи, то́лки

heart [hɑːt] се́рдце; му́жество; (*essence*) суть *f*; (*innermost part*) сердцеви́на; *of forest* глубина́; **~s** *pl.* че́рви *f/pl.*; *fig.* се́рдце, душа́; ***by ~*** наизу́сть; ***lose ~*** па́дать ду́хом; ***take ~*** воспря́нуть ду́хом; ***take to ~*** принима́ть бли́зко к се́рдцу; **~ attack** серде́чный при́ступ; **~broken** уби́тый го́рем; **~burn** изжо́га; **~en** ['hɑːtn] ободря́ть [-ри́ть]; **~felt** душе́вный, и́скренний

hearth [hɑːθ] оча́г (*a. fig.*)

heart|less ['hɑːtlɪs] □ бессерде́чный; **~rending** [~rendɪŋ] душераздира́ющий; **~-to-~** дру́жеский; **~y** ['hɑːtɪ] □ дру́жеский, серде́чный; (*healthy*) здоро́вый

heat [hiːt] **1.** *com.* жара́, жар; *fig.* пыл; *sport* забе́г, заплы́в, зае́зд; **2.** нагре́(ва́)ть(ся); *fig.* [раз]горячи́ть; **~er** ['hiːtə] обогрева́тель

heath [hiːθ] ме́стность *f*, поро́сшая ве́реском; (*waste land*) пу́стошь *f*; *bot.* ве́реск

heathen ['hiːðn] **1.** язы́чник; **2.** язы́ческий

heating ['hiːtɪŋ] обогрева́ние; отопле́ние

heave [hiːv] **1.** подъём; **2.** [*irr.*] *v/t.* (*haul*) поднима́ть [-ня́ть]; *v/i. of waves* вздыма́ться; (*strain*) напряга́ться [-я́чься]

heaven ['hevn] небеса́ *n/pl.*, не́бо; ***move ~ and earth*** [с]де́лать всё возмо́жное; **~ly** [~lɪ] небе́сный; *fig.* великоле́пный

heavy ['hevɪ] □ *com.* тяжёлый; *crop* оби́льный; *sea* бу́рный; *sky* мра́чный; неуклю́жий; **~weight** *sport* тяжелове́с

heckle ['hekl] прерыва́ть замеча́ниями; задава́ть ка́верзные вопро́сы

hectic ['hektɪk] *activity* лихора́дочный; **~ *day*** напряжённый день *m*

hedge [hedʒ] **1.** жива́я и́згородь *f*; **2.** *v/t.* огора́живать и́згородью; *v/i.* (*evade*) уклоня́ться от прямо́го отве́та; увíливать [увильну́ть]; **~hog** *zo.* ёж

heed [hiːd] **1.** внима́ние, осторо́жность *f*; ***take no ~ of*** не обраща́ть внима́ния на (В); **2.** обраща́ть внима́ние на (В); **~less** [~lɪs] □ небре́жный; необду́манный; **~ *of danger*** не ду́мая об опа́сности

heel [hiːl] **1.** *of foot* пя́тка; *of shoe* каблу́к; ***head over ~s*** вверх торма́шками; ***down at ~*** *fig.* неря́шливый; **2.** поста́вить *pf.* набо́йку (на В)

hefty ['heftɪ] *fellow* здорове́нный; *blow* си́льный

height [haɪt] высота́; *person's* рост; (*high place*) возвы́шенность *f*; *fig.* верх; **~en** ['haɪtn] *interest* повыша́ть [повы́сить]; (*make more intense*) уси́ли(ва)ть

heir [eə] насле́дник; **~ess** ['eərɪs, 'eərəs] насле́дница

held [held] *pt. и pt. p. от* ***hold***

helicopter ['helɪkɒptə] вертолёт

hell [hel] ад; *attr.* а́дский; ***raise ~***

поднять ужасный крик; **~ish** [~ɪʃ] адский
hello [hə'ləʊ] *coll.* привет; *tel.* алло!
helm [helm] *naut.* штурвал; *fig.* кормило
helmet ['helmɪt] шлем
helmsman ['helmzmən] *naut.* рулевой
help [help] **1.** *com.* помощь *f*; ***there is no ~ for it !*** ничего не поделаешь!; **2.** *v/t.* помогать [помочь] (Д); ***~ yourself to fruit*** берите фрукты; ***I could not ~ laughing*** я не мог не рассмеяться; *v/i.* помогать [-мочь]; **~er** ['helpə] помощник (-ица); **~ful** ['helpfl] полезный; **~ing** ['helpɪŋ] *of food* порция; ***have another ~*** взять *pf.* ещё (***of*** P); **~less** ['helplɪs] □ беспомощный; **~lessness** ['helplɪsnɪs] беспомощность *f*
hem [hem] **1.** рубец; *of skirt* подол; **2.** подрубать [-бить]; ***~ in*** окружать [-жить]
hemisphere ['hemɪsfɪə] полушарие
hemlock ['hemlɒk] *bot.* болиголов
hemp [hemp] конопля; (*fibre*) пенька
hen [hen] курица
hence [hens] отсюда; следовательно; ***a year ~*** через год; **~forth** [hens'fɔːθ], **~forward** [hens'fɔːwəd] с этого времени, впредь
henpecked ['henpekt] находящийся под башмаком у жены
her [ə, hə˞, *strong* hɜː] *pers. pron.* (*косвенный падеж от* **she**) её; ей
herb [hɜːb] (целебная) трава; (пряное) растение
herd [hɜːd] **1.** стадо; *fig.* толпа; **2.** *v/t.* пасти (скот); *v/i.*: ***~ together*** [с]толпиться; **~sman** ['hɜːdzmən] пастух
here [hɪə] здесь, тут; сюда; вот; ***~'s to you !*** за ваше здоровье!
here|after [hɪər'ɑːftə] в будущем; **~by** этим, настоящим; таким образом
heredit|ary [hɪ'redɪtrɪ] наследственный; **~y** [~tɪ] наследственность *f*
here|upon [hɪərə'pɒn] вслед за этим; **~with** при сём
heritage ['herɪtɪdʒ] наследство; наследие (*mst. fig.*)
hermetic [hɜː'metɪk] (**~ally**) герметический
hermit ['hɜːmɪt] отшельник
hero ['hɪərəʊ] герой; **~ic** [~'rəʊɪk] (**~ally**) героический, геройский; **~ine** ['herəʊɪn] героиня; **~ism** [~ɪzəm] героизм
heron ['herən] *zo.* цапля
herring ['herɪŋ] сельдь *f*; *cul.* селёдка
hers [hɜːz] *pron. poss.* её
herself [hɜː'self] сама; себя, -ся, -сь
hesitat|e ['hezɪteɪt] [по]колебаться; *in speech* запинаться [запнуться]; **~ion** [hezɪ'teɪʃn] колебание; запинка
hew [hjuː] [*irr.*] рубить; разрубать [-бить]; (*shape*) высекать [высечь]
hey [heɪ] эй!
heyday ['heɪdeɪ] *fig.* зенит, расцвет
hicc|up, ~ough ['hɪkʌp] **1.** икота; **2.** икать [икнуть]
hid [hɪd], **hidden** ['hɪdn] *pt. и pt. p. от* ***hide***
hide [haɪd] [*irr.*] [с]прятать(ся); (*conceal*) скры(ва)ть; **~-and-seek** [haɪdn'siːk] прятки
hideous ['hɪdɪəs] □ отвратительный, уродливый
hiding-place потаённое место, укрытие
hi-fi ['haɪfaɪ] высокая точность воспроизведения звука
high [haɪ] **1.** □ *adj. com.* высокий; (*lofty*) возвышенный; *wind* сильный; *authority* высший, верховный; *meat* с душком; ***it's ~ time*** давно пора; ***~ spirits*** *pl.* приподнятое настроение; **2.** *adv.* высоко; сильно; ***aim ~*** высоко метить; **~-brow** интеллектуал; **~-class** первоклассный; **~-grade** высокого качества; **~-handed** своевольный; властный; **~lands** *pl.* гористая местность *f*
high|light выдающийся момент; **~ly** ['haɪlɪ] очень, весьма; ***speak ~ of*** высоко отзываться о (П); **~-minded** возвышенный, благородный; **~-rise building** высотное здание;

~-strung óчень чувстви́тельный; напряжённый; **~way** гла́вная доро́га, шоссе́; *fig.* прямо́й путь *m*; **~ code** пра́вила доро́жного движе́ния
hijack ['haɪdʒæk] *plane* угоня́ть [-на́ть]; *train, etc.* соверша́ть [-ши́ть] налёт; **~er** [~ə] уго́нщик
hike [haɪk] *coll.* **1.** прогу́лка; похо́д; **2.** путеше́ствовать пешко́м; **~r** ['haɪkə] пе́ший тури́ст
hilarious [hɪ'leərɪəs] □ весёлый, смешно́й; *coll.* умори́тельный
hill [hɪl] холм; **~billy** *Am.* ['hɪlbɪlɪ] челове́к из глуби́нки; **~ock** ['hɪlək] хо́лмик; **~side** склон холма́; **~y** [~ɪ] холми́стый
hilt [hɪlt] рукоя́тка (*са́бли и т.д.*)
him [ɪm, *strong* hɪm] *pers. pron.* (*ко́свенный паде́ж от* **he**) его́, ему́; **~self** [hɪm'self] сам; себя́, -ся, -сь
hind [haɪnd] за́дний; **~ leg** за́дняя нога́
hinder ['hɪndə] **1.** препя́тствовать (Д); **2.** *v/t.* [по]меша́ть
hindrance ['hɪndrəns] поме́ха, препя́тствие
hinge [hɪndʒ] **1.** *of door* пе́тля; шарни́р; *fig.* сте́ржень *m*, суть *f*; **2. ~ upon** *fig.* зави́сеть от (Р)
hint [hɪnt] **1.** намёк; **2.** намека́ть [-кну́ть] (**at** на В)
hip[1] [hɪp] бе́дро; **~ pocket** за́дний карма́н
hip[2] [~] я́года шипо́вника
hippopotamus [hɪpə'pɒtəməs] гиппопота́м, бегемо́т
hire ['haɪə] **1.** *worker* наём; *car, TV, etc.* прока́т; **2.** нанима́ть [наня́ть]; *room, etc.* снима́ть [снять]; брать [взять] напрока́т; **~ out** сдава́ть в прока́т; **~ purchase** поку́пка в рассро́чку
his [ɪz, *strong* hɪz] *poss. pron.* его́, свой
hiss [hɪs] *v/i.* [за-, про]шипе́ть; *v/t.* осви́стывать [-ста́ть]
histor|ian [hɪ'stɔːrɪən] исто́рик; **~ic(al** □) [hɪs'tɒːrɪk(l)] истори́ческий; **~y** ['hɪstərɪ] исто́рия
hit [hɪt] **1.** уда́р; попада́ние; *thea., mus.* успе́х; **direct ~** прямо́е попада́ние; **2.** [*irr.*] ударя́ть [уда́рить]; поража́ть [порази́ть]; *target* попада́ть [попа́сть] в (В); **~ town, the beach, etc.** *Am. coll.* (*arrive*) прибы́(ва́)ть в, на (В); *coll.* **~ it off with** [по]ла́дить с (Т); **~ (up)on** находи́ть [найти́] (В); **~ in the eye** *fig.* броса́ться [бро́ситься] в глаза́
hitch [hɪtʃ] **1.** толчо́к, рыво́к; *fig.* препя́тствие; **2.** зацепля́ть(ся) [-пи́ть(ся)], прицепля́ть(ся) [-пи́ть(ся)]; **~-hike** *mot.* е́здить автосто́пом
hither ['hɪðər] *lit.* сюда́; **~to** [~'tuː] *lit.* до сих пор
hive [haɪv] **1.** у́лей; (*of bees*) рой пчёл; *fig.* людско́й мураве́йник; **2.** жить вме́сте
hoard [hɔːd] **1.** (скры́тый) запа́с, склад; **2.** накопля́ть [-пи́ть]; запаса́ть [-сти́] (В); *secretly* припря́т(ыв)ать
hoarfrost ['hɔːfrɒst] и́ней
hoarse [hɔːs] □ хри́плый, си́плый
hoax [həʊks] **1.** обма́н, ро́зыгрыш; **2.** подшу́чивать [-ути́ть] над (Т), разы́грывать [-ра́ть]
hobble ['hɒbl] *v/i.* прихра́мывать
hobby ['hɒbɪ] *fig.* хо́бби *n indecl.*, люби́мое заня́тие
hock [hɒk] (*wine*) рейнве́йн
hockey ['hɒkɪ] хокке́й
hoe [həʊ] *agric.* **1.** ца́пка; **2.** ца́пать
hog [hɒg] свинья́ (*a. fig.*); бо́ров
hoist [hɔɪst] **1.** *for goods* подъёмник; **2.** поднима́ть [-ня́ть]
hold [həʊld] **1.** *naut.* трюм; **catch** (*or* **get, lay, take**) **~ of** схва́тывать [схвати́ть] (В); **keep ~ of** уде́рживать [-жа́ть] (В); **2.** [*irr.*] *v/t.* держа́ть; (*sustain*) выде́рживать [вы́держать]; (*restrain*) остана́вливать [-нови́ть]; *meeting, etc.* проводи́ть [-вести́]; *attention* завладе́(ва́)ть; занима́ть [-ня́ть]; (*contain*) вмеща́ть [вмести́ть]; (*think*) счита́ть; **~ one's own** отста́ивать свою́ пози́цию; **~ talks** вести́ перегово́ры; **~ the line!** *tel.* не ве́шайте тру́бку; **~ over** откла́дывать [отложи́ть]; **~ up** (*support*) подде́рживать [-жа́ть]; (*delay*) заде́рживать [-жа́ть]; останови́ть с це́лью грабежа́; **3.** *v/i.* остана́вливаться [-нови́ться]; *of weather* держа́ться; **~ forth** разгла-

го́льствовать; **~ *good*** (*or* ***true***) име́ть си́лу; **~ *off*** держа́ться по́одаль; **~ *on*** де́ржиться за (В); **~ *to*** приде́рживаться (Р); **~er** [~ə] аренда́тор; владе́лец; **~ing** [~ɪŋ] уча́сток зе́мли; владе́ние; **~-up** *Am.* налёт, ограбле́ние

hole [həʊl] дыра́, отве́рстие; *in ground* я́ма; *of animals* нора́; *coll. fig.* затрудни́тельное положе́ние; ***pick ~s in*** находи́ть недоста́тки в (П); придира́ться [придра́ться]

holiday ['hɒlədɪ] пра́здник, официа́льный день о́тдыха; о́тпуск; **~s** *pl. educ.* кани́кулы *f/pl.*

hollow ['hɒləʊ] **1.** □ пусто́й, по́лый; *cheeks* ввали́вшийся; *eyes* впа́лый; **2.** по́лость *f*; *in tree* дупло́; (*small valley*) лощи́на; **3.** выда́лбливать [вы́долбить]

holly ['hɒlɪ] остроли́ст, па́дуб

holster ['həʊlstə] кобура́

holy ['həʊlɪ] свято́й, свяще́нный; ♀ ***Week*** Страстна́я неде́ля

homage ['hɒmɪdʒ] уваже́ние; ***do*** (*or* ***pay***, ***render***) **~** отдава́ть дань уваже́ния (***to*** Д)

home [həʊm] **1.** дом, жили́ще; ро́дина; ***at ~*** до́ма; ***maternity ~*** роди́льный дом; **2.** *adj.* дома́шний; вну́тренний; оте́чественный; **~ *industry*** оте́чественная промы́шленность *f*; ♀ ***Office*** министе́рство вну́тренних дел; ♀ ***Secretary*** мини́стр вну́тренних дел; **3.** *adv.* домо́й; ***hit*** (*or* ***strike***) **~** попа́сть *pf.* в цель *f*; **~less** [~lɪs] бездо́мный; **~like** ую́тный; непринуждённый; **~ly** [~lɪ] *fig.* просто́й, обы́денный; дома́шний; *Am.* (*plain-looking*) некраси́вый; **~made** дома́шнего изготовле́ния; **~sickness** тоска́ по ро́дине; **~ward(s)** [~wəd(z)] домо́й

homicide ['hɒmɪsaɪd] уби́йство; уби́йца *m/f*

homogeneous [hɒmə'dʒiːnɪəs] □ одноро́дный, гомоге́нный

honest ['ɒnɪst] □ че́стный; **~y** [~ɪ] че́стность *f*

honey ['hʌnɪ] мёд; (*mode of address*) дорога́я; **~comb** ['hʌnɪkəʊm] со́ты; **~moon 1.** медо́вый ме́сяц; **2.** проводи́ть медо́вый ме́сяц

honorary ['ɒnərərɪ] почётный

hono(u)r ['ɒnə] **1.** честь *f*; (*respect*) почёт; *f*; *mil., etc.* по́честь; **2.** чтить, почита́ть; *fin. check/Brt. cheque* опла́чивать [-лати́ть]; **~able** ['ɒnərəbl] □ почётный, благоро́дный; (*upright*) че́стный

hood [hʊd] (*covering for head*) капю-шо́н; *Am.* (*for car engine*) капо́т

hoodwink ['hʊdwɪŋk] обма́нывать [-ну́ть]

hoof [huːf] копы́то

hook [huːk] **1.** крюк, крючо́к; ***by ~ or by crook*** пра́вдами и непра́вдами, так и́ли ина́че; **2.** зацепля́ть [-пи́ть]; *dress. etc.* застёгивать(ся) [-стегну́ть(ся)]

hoop [huːp] о́бруч; ***make s.o. jump through ~s*** подверга́ть кого́-л. тяжёлому испыта́нию

hoot [huːt] **1.** ши́канье; *mot.* сигна́л; **2.** *v/i.* оши́кивать [-кать]; дава́ть сигна́л, сигна́лить; *v/t.* (*a.* **~ *down***) осви́стывать [-иста́ть]

hop¹ [hɒp] *bot.* хмель *m*

hop² [~] **1.** прыжо́к; ***keep s.o. on the ~*** не дава́ть кому́-л. поко́я; **2.** на одно́й ноге́

hope [həʊp] **1.** наде́жда; ***past ~*** безнадёжный; ***raise ~*** обнадё-жи(ва)ть; **2.** наде́яться (***for*** на В); **~ful** [~fl] (*promising*) подаю́щий на де́жды; (*having hope*) наде́ющийся; **~less** [~lɪs] безнадёжный

horde [hɔːd] орда́; по́лчища; *pl.* то́лпы *f/pl.*

horizon [hə'raɪzn] горизо́нт; *fig.* кругозо́р

hormone ['hɔːməʊn] гормо́н

horn [hɔːn] *animal's* рог; звуково́й сигна́л; *mus* рожо́к; **~ *of plenty*** рог изоби́лия

hornet ['hɔːnɪt] *zo.* ше́ршень *m*

horny ['hɔːnɪ] *hands* мозо́листый

horoscope ['hɒrəskəʊp] гороско́п; ***cast a ~*** составля́ть [-а́вить] гороско́п

horr|ible ['hɒrəbl] □ стра́шный, ужа́сный; **~id** ['hɒrɪd] ужа́сный; (*repelling*) проти́вный; **~ify** ['hɒrɪfaɪ] ужаса́ть [-сну́ть]; шоки́ровать; **~or** ['hɒrə] у́жас

hors d'œuvres [ɔː'dɜːv] *pl.* заку́ски *f/pl.*

H

horse [hɔːs] лóшадь *f*, конь *m*; ***get on a ~*** сесть *pf.* на лóшадь; ***dark ~*** тёмная лошáдка; **~back: *on ~*** верхóм; **~ laugh** *coll.* грýбый, грóмкий хóхот; **~man** всáдник; **~power** лошади́ная си́ла; **~ race** скáчки; **~radish** хрен; **~shoe** подкóва
horticulture ['hɔːtɪkʌltʃə] садовóдство
hose [həʊz] (*pipe*) шланг
hosiery ['həʊzɪərɪ] чулóчные издéлия *n/pl.*
hospice ['hɒspɪs] *med.* хóспис
hospitable [hɒs'pɪtəbl] □ гостеприи́мный
hospital ['hɒspɪtl] больни́ца; *mil.* гóспиталь *m*; **~ity** [hɒspɪ'tælətɪ] гостеприи́мство; **~ize** ['hɒspɪtəlaɪz] госпитализи́ровать
host[1] [həʊst] хозя́ин; ***act as ~*** быть за хозя́ина
host[2] [~] мнóжество, *coll.* мáсса, тьмá
hostage ['hɒstɪdʒ] залóжник *m*, -ница *f*
hostel ['hɒstl] общежи́тие; (*youth ~*) турбáза
hostess ['həʊstɪs] хозя́йка (→ ***host***)
hostil|e ['hɒstaɪl] враждéбный; **~ity** [hɒ'stɪlətɪ] враждéбность *f*; враждéбный акт; *pl. mil.* воéнные дéйствия
hot [hɒt] горя́чий; *summer* жáркий; *fig.* пы́лкий; **~bed** парни́к; ***~ dog*** *fig.* бýлочка с горя́чей соси́ской
hotchpotch ['hɒtʃpɒtʃ] *fig.* вся́кая вся́чина, смесь *f*
hotel [həʊ'tel] отéль *m*, гости́ница
hot|headed опромéтчивый; **~house** оранжерéя, тепли́ца; **~ spot** *pol.* горя́чая тóчка; **~-water bottle** грéлка
hound [haʊnd] **1.** гóнчая; **2.** *fig.* [за]трави́ть
hour [aʊə] час; врéмя; ***24 ~s*** сýтки; ***rush ~*** часы́ пик; **~ly** [~lɪ] ежечáсный
house [haʊs] **1.** *com.* дом; здáние; *parl.* палáта; ***apartment ~*** многоквarти́рный дом; **2.** [haʊz] *v/t.* поселя́ть [-ли́ть]; помещáть [-ести́ть]; (*give shelter to*) приюти́ть *pf.*; *v/i.* помещáться [-ести́ться]; **~hold** домáшний круг; семья́; **~holder** домовладéлец; **~keeper** экономка; домáшняя хозя́йка; **~keeping**: ***do the ~*** вести́ домáшнее хозя́йство; **~-warming** новосéлье; **~wife** домохозя́йка
housing ['haʊzɪŋ] обеспéчение жильём; ***~ conditions*** жили́щные услóвия
hove [həʊv] *pt. и pt. p. от* ***heave***
hovel ['hɒvl] лачýга, хибáрка
hover ['hɒvə] *of bird* пари́ть; *ae.* кружи́ть(ся); **~ craft** сýдно на воздýшной подýшке
how [haʊ] как?, каки́м óбразом?; ***~ about ...?*** как насчёт (Р) ...?; **~ever** [haʊ'evə] **1.** *adv.* как бы ни; **2.** *cj.* однáко, и всё же
howl [haʊl] **1.** вой, завывáние; **2.** [за]вы́ть; **~er** ['haʊlə] *sl.* грýбая оши́бка; ля́псус
hub [hʌb] *of wheel* ступи́ца; *fig. of activity* центр; *of the universe* пуп земли́
hubbub ['hʌbʌb] шум; *coll.* гóмон, гам
huddle ['hʌdl] **1.** *of things* [с]вали́ть в кýчу; ***~ together*** *of people* сби́ться *pf.* в кýчу; **2.** кýча; *of people* сýтолока, суматóха
hue[1] [hjuː] оттéнок
hue[2] [~]: ***~ and cry*** крик, шум
huff [hʌf] раздражéние; ***get into a ~*** оби́деться
hug [hʌg] **1.** объя́тие; **2.** обнимáть [-ня́ть]; *fig.* быть привéрженным; ***~ o.s.*** поздравля́ть [-áвить] себя́
huge [hjuːdʒ] □ огрóмный, громáдный
hulk [hʌlk] *fig.* ýвалень
hull [hʌl] *bot.* шелухá, скорлупá; *naut.* кóрпус
hum [hʌm] [за]жужжáть; (*sing*) напевáть; *coll.* ***make things ~*** вноси́ть оживлéние в рабóту
human ['hjuːmən] **1.** человéческий; **2.** *coll.* человéк; **~e** [hjuː'meɪn] гумáнный, человéчный; **~eness** гумáнность *f*; **~itarian** [hjuːmænɪ'teərɪən] гумани́ст; гумáнный; **~ity** [hjuː'mæ-nətɪ] человéчество; **~kind** [hjuː-mən'kaɪnd] род человéческий; **~ly** по-человéчески
humble ['hʌmbl] **1.** □ (*not self-im-*

portant) смире́нный, скро́мный; (*lowly*) просто́й; **2.** унижа́ть [уни́зить]; смиря́ть [-ри́ть]
humbug ['hʌmbʌg] (*deceit*) надува́тельство; (*nonsense*) чепуха́
humdrum ['hʌmdrʌm] однообра́зный, ску́чный
humid ['hju:mɪd] сыро́й, вла́жный; **~ity** [hju:'mɪdətɪ] вла́жность *f*
humiliat|e [hju:'mɪlɪeɪt] унижа́ть [уни́зить]; **~ion** [hju:mɪlɪ'eɪʃn] униже́ние
humility [hju:'mɪlətɪ] смире́ние
humorous ['hju:mərəs] □ юмористи́ческий
humo(u)r ['hju:mə] **1.** ю́мор, шутли́вость *f*; (*mood*) настрое́ние; ***out of ~*** не в ду́хе; **2.** (*indulge*) потака́ть (Д); ублажа́ть [-жи́ть]
hump [hʌmp] **1.** горб; **2.** [с]го́рбить(ся)
hunch [hʌntʃ] **1.** горб; (*intuitive feeling*) чутьё, интуи́ция; ***have a ~ that*** у меня́ тако́е чу́вство, что ...; **2.** [с]го́рбить(ся) (*a.* ***up***); **~back** горбу́н(ья)
hundred ['hʌndrəd] **1.** сто; **2.** со́тня; **~th** [~θ] со́тый; со́тая часть *f*; **~weight** це́нтнер
hung [hʌŋ] *pt. и pt. p. от* ***hang***
Hungarian [hʌŋ'geərɪən] **1.** венгр *m*, -ге́рка *f*; **2.** венге́рский
hunger ['hʌŋgə] **1.** го́лод; *fig.* жа́жда; **2.** *v/i.* голода́ть; быть голо́дным; *fig. desire* жа́ждать (***for*** Р)
hungry ['hʌŋgrɪ] □ голо́дный; ***get ~*** проголода́ться
hunk [hʌŋk] ломо́ть *m*; *of meat* большо́й кусо́к
hunt [hʌnt] **1.** охо́та; (*search*) по́иски *m/pl.* (***for*** Р); **2.** охо́титься на (В) *or* за (Т); ***~ out*** *or* ***up*** оты́скивать [-ка́ть]; ***~ for*** *fig.* охо́титься за (Т), иска́ть (Р *or* В); **~er** ['hʌntə] охо́тник; **~ing grounds** охо́тничьи уго́дья
hurdle ['hɜ:dl] барье́р; **~s** ска́чки с препя́тствиями; бег с препя́тствиями
hurl [hɜ:l] **1.** си́льный бросо́к; **2.** швыря́ть [-рну́ть], мета́ть [метну́ть]
hurricane ['hʌrɪkən] урага́н
hurried ['hʌrɪd] торопли́вый
hurry ['hʌrɪ] **1.** торопли́вость *f*, поспе́шность *f*; ***be in no ~*** не спеши́ть; ***what's the ~?*** заче́м спеши́ть?; **2.** *v/t.* [по]торопи́ть; *v/i.* [по]спеши́ть (*a.* ***~ up***)
hurt [hɜ:t] [*irr.*] (*injure*) ушиба́ть [-би́ть] (*a. fig.*); причиня́ть боль *f*; боле́ть
husband ['hʌzbənd] муж; (*spouse*) супру́г
hush [hʌʃ] **1.** тишина́, молча́ние; **2.** ти́ше!; **3.** установи́ть *pf.* тишину́; ***~ up*** *facts* скры(ва́)ть; ***the affair was ~ed up*** де́ло замя́ли
husk [hʌsk] **1.** *bot.* шелуха́; **2.** очища́ть от шелухи́, [об]лущи́ть; **~y** ['hʌskɪ] □ (*hoarse*) си́плый; охри́плый; (*burly*) ро́слый
hustle ['hʌsl] **1.** *v/t.* (*push*) толка́ть [-кну́ть]; пиха́ть [пихну́ть]; (*hurry*) [по]торопи́ть; *v/i.* толка́ться; [по]торопи́ться; **2.** толкотня́; ***~ and bustle*** шум и толкотня́
hut [hʌt] хи́жина
hutch [hʌtʃ] *for rabbits, etc.* кле́тка
hyacinth ['haɪəsɪnθ] гиаци́нт
hybrid ['haɪbrɪd] гибри́д; *animal* по́месь *f*
hydro ['haɪdrə] водо...; **~-electric power station** гидро(электро-)ста́нция; **~foil** су́дно на подво́дных кры́льях; **~gen** ['haɪdrədʒən] водоро́д; **~phobia** ['haɪdrə'fəʊbɪə] бе́шенство; **~plane** ['haɪdrəpleɪn] гидропла́н
hygiene ['haɪdʒi:n] гигие́на
hymn [hɪm] (церко́вный) гимн
hyphen ['haɪfn] дефи́с; **~ate** [~fəneɪt] писа́ть через чёрточку
hypnotize ['hɪpnətaɪz] [за]гипнотизи́ровать
hypo|chondriac [haɪpə'kɒndrɪæk] ипохо́ндрик; **~crisy** [hɪ'pɒkrəsɪ] лицеме́рие; **~crite** ['hɪpəkrɪt] лицеме́р; **~critical** [hɪpə'krɪtɪkl] лицеме́рный; нейскренний; **~thesis** [haɪ'pɒθəsɪs] гипо́теза, предположе́ние
hysterical [hɪ'sterɪkl] истери́чный; **~ics** [hɪ'sterɪks] *pl.* исте́рика

I

I [aɪ] *pers. pron.* я; **~ *feel cold*** мне хо́лодно; ***you and*** **~** мы с ва́ми
ice [aɪs] **1.** лёд; **2.** замора́живать [-ро́зить]; *cul.* глазирова́ть *(im)pf.*; **~ *over*** покрыва́ть(ся) льдом; **~ age** леднико́вый пери́од; **~box** *Am.* холоди́льник; **~breaker** ледоко́л; **~ cream** моро́женое; **~d** охлаждённый; *cake* глазиро́ванный; **~ hockey** хокке́й; **~ rink** като́к
icicle ['aɪsɪkl] сосу́лька
icing ['aɪsɪŋ] *cul.* са́харная глазу́рь *f*
icon ['aɪkən] ико́на
icy ['aɪsɪ] □ ледяно́й (*a. fig.*)
idea [aɪ'dɪə] (*concept*) иде́я; (*notion*) поня́тие, представле́ние; (*thought*) мысль *f*; **~l** [~l] **1.** □ идеа́льный; **2.** идеа́л
identi|cal [aɪ'dentɪkl] □ тот (же) са́мый; тожде́ственный; иденти́чный, одина́ковый; **~fication** [aɪ'dentɪfɪ'keɪʃn] определе́ние; опозна́(ва́)ние; установле́ние ли́чности; **~fy** [~faɪ] определя́ть [-ли́ть]; опозн(ав)а́ть; устана́вливать ли́чность *f* (Р); **~ty** [~tɪ]: ***prove s.o.'s*** **~** установи́ть *pf.* ли́чность *f*; **~ card** удостовере́ние ли́чности
idiom ['ɪdɪəm] идио́ма; (*language*) наре́чие, го́вор, язы́к
idiot ['ɪdɪət] идио́т *m*, -ка *f*; **~ic** [ɪdɪ'ɒtɪk] **(-ally)** идио́тский
idle ['aɪdl] **1.** неза́нятый; безрабо́тный; лени́вый; *question* пра́здный; (*futile*) тще́тный; *tech.* безде́йствующий, холосто́й; **2.** *v/t.* проводи́ть (вре́-мя) без де́ла (*mst.* **~ *away***); *v/i.* лени́ться, безде́льничать; **~ness** [~nɪs] пра́здность *f*; безде́лье; **~r** [~ə] безде́льник *m*, -ица *f*, лентя́й *m*, -ка *f*
idol ['aɪdl] и́дол; *fig.* куми́р; **~ize** ['aɪdəlaɪz] боготвори́ть
idyl(l) ['ɪdɪl] иди́ллия
if [ɪf] *cj.* е́сли; е́сли бы; (= ***whether***) ли: ***I don't know*** **~ *he knows*** не зна́ю, зна́ет ли он ...; **~ *I were you ...*** на ва́шем ме́сте
ignit|e [ɪg'naɪt] зажига́ть [-же́чь]; загора́ться [-ре́ться], воспламеня́ться [-ни́ться]; **~ion** [ɪg'nɪʃn] *mot.* зажига́ние
ignoble [ɪg'nəʊbl] □ ни́зкий, неблагоро́дный
ignor|ance ['ɪgnərəns] неве́жество; *of intent, etc.* неве́дение; **~ant** [~rənt] неве́жественный; несве́дущий; **~e** [ɪg'nɔː] игнори́ровать
ill [ɪl] **1.** *adj.* больно́й; дурно́й; **~ *omen*** дурно́е предзнамено́вание; **2.** *adv.* едва́ ли; пло́хо; **3.** зло, вред
ill|-advised неблагоразу́мный; **~-bred** невоспи́танный
illegal [ɪ'liːgl] □ незако́нный
illegible [ɪ'ledʒəbl] □ неразбо́рчивый
illegitimate [ɪlɪ'dʒɪtɪmət] □ незако́нный; *child* незаконнорождённый
ill|-fated злосча́стный, злополу́чный; **~-founded** необосно́ванный; **~-humo(u)red** раздражи́тельный
illiterate [ɪ'lɪtərət] □ негра́мотный
ill|-mannered невоспи́танный, гру́бый; **~-natured** □ зло́бный, недоброжела́тельный
illness ['ɪlnɪs] боле́знь *f*
ill|-timed несвоевре́менный, неподходя́щий; **~-treat** пло́хо обраща́ться с (Т)
illumin|ate [ɪ'luːmɪneɪt] освеща́ть [-ети́ть], озаря́ть [-ри́ть]; (*enlighten*) просвеща́ть [-ети́ть]; (*cast light on*) пролива́ть свет на (В); **~ating** [~neɪtɪŋ] поучи́тельный, освети́тельный; **~ation** [ɪluːmɪ'neɪʃn] освеще́ние; (*display*) иллюмина́ция
illus|ion [ɪ'luːʒn] иллю́зия, обма́н чувств; **~ive** [~sɪv], **~ory** [~sərɪ] □ при́зрачный, иллюзо́рный
illustrat|e ['ɪləstreɪt] иллюстри́ровать *(im)pf.*; (*explain*) поясня́ть [-ни́ть]; **~ion** [ɪlə'streɪʃn] иллюстра́ция; **~ive** ['ɪləstrətɪv] иллюстрати́вный
illustrious [ɪ'lʌstrɪəs] □ просла́вленный, знамени́тый
ill-will недоброжела́тельность *f*
image ['ɪmɪdʒ] о́браз; изображе́ние; (*reflection*) отраже́ние; (*likeness*) подо́бие, ко́пия

I

imagin|able [ɪ'mædʒɪnəbl] □ вообрази́мый; **~ary** [~nərɪ] воображáемый; мни́мый; **~ation** [ɪmædʒɪ'neɪʃn] воображéние, фантáзия; **~ative** [ɪ'mædʒɪnətɪv] □ одарённый воображéнием; **~e** [ɪ'mædʒɪn] воображáть [-рази́ть], представля́ть [-áвить] себé

imbecile ['ɪmbəsi:l] **1.** слабоу́мный; **2.** *coll.* глупéц

imbibe [ɪm'baɪb] (*absorb*) впи́тывать [впитáть] (*a. fig.*); *fig. ideas, etc.* усвáивать [усвóить]

imita|te ['ɪmɪteɪt] подражáть (Д); (*copy, mimic*) передрáзнивать [-ни́ть]; поддéл(ыв)ать; **~tion** [ɪmɪ'teɪʃn] подражáние; имитáция, поддéлка; *attr.* искýсственный

immaculate [ɪ'mækjʊlət] безукори́зненный, безупрéчный

immaterial [ɪmə'tɪərɪəl] (*unimportant*) несущéственный, невáжный; (*incorporeal*) невещéственный, нематериáльный

immature [ɪmə'tjʊə] незрéлый

immediate [ɪ'mi:djət] □ непосрéдственный; ближáйший; (*urgent*) безотлагáтельный; **~ly** [~lɪ] *adv. of time, place* непосрéдственно; немéдленно

immemorial [ɪmə'mɔ:rɪəl]: ***from time ~*** испокóн векóв

immense [ɪ'mens] □ огрóмный

immerse [ɪ'mɜ:s] погружáть [-узи́ть], окунáть [-нýть]; *fig.* ***~ o.s. in*** погружáться [-узи́ться]

immigra|nt ['ɪmɪgrənt] иммигрáнт *m*, -ка *f*; **~te** [~greɪt] иммигри́ровать (*im*)*pf.*; **~tion** [ɪmɪ'greɪʃn] иммигрáция

imminent ['ɪmɪnənt] грозя́щий, нави́сший; ***a storm is ~*** надвигáется бýря

immobile [ɪ'məʊbaɪl] неподви́жный

immoderate [ɪ'mɒdərət] непомéрный, чрезмéрный

immodest [ɪ'mɒdɪst] □ нескрóмный

immoral [ɪ'mɒrəl] □ безнрáвственный

immortal [ɪ'mɔ:tl] бессмéртный

immun|e [ɪ'mju:n] невосприи́мчивый (***from*** к Д); **~ity** [~ɪtɪ] *med.* иммуни́тéт, невосприи́мчивость *f* (***from*** к Д); *dipl.* иммуни́тéт

imp [ɪmp] дьяволёнок, бесёнок; шалуни́шка *m/f*

impact ['ɪmpækt] удáр; (*collision*) столкновéние; *fig.* влия́ние, воздéйствие

impair [ɪm'peə] (*weaken*) ослабля́ть [-áбить]; *health* подрывáть [-дорвáть], (*damage*) повреждáть [-ди́ть]

impart [ɪm'pɑ:t] (*give*) прид(ав)áть; (*make known*) сообщáть [-щи́ть]

impartial [ɪm'pɑ:ʃl] □ беспристрáстный, непредвзя́тый

impassable [ɪm'pɑ:səbl] □ непроходи́мый; *for vehicles* непроéзжий

impassive [ɪm'pæsɪv] □ спокóйный, бесстрáстный

impatien|ce [ɪm'peɪʃns] нетерпéние; **~t** [~nt] □ нетерпели́вый

impeccable [ɪm'pekəbl] (*flawless*) безупрéчный

impede [ɪm'pi:d] [вос]препя́тствовать (Д)

impediment [ɪm'pedɪmənt] помéха

impel [ɪm'pel] (*force*) вынуждáть [вы́нудить]; (*urge*) побуждáть [-уди́ть]

impending [ɪm'pendɪŋ] предстоя́щий, надвигáющийся

impenetrable [ɪm'penɪtrəbl] □ непроходи́мый; непроницáемый (*a. fig.*); *fig.* непостижи́мый

imperative [ɪm'perətɪv] □ *manner, voice* повели́тельный, влáстный; (*essential*) крáйне необходи́мый

imperceptible [ɪmpə'septəbl] неощути́мый; незамéтный

imperfect [ɪm'pɜ:fɪkt] □ несовершéнный; (*faulty*) дефéктный

imperial [ɪm'pɪərɪəl] □ импéрский; (*majestic*) вели́чественный

imperil [ɪm'perəl] подвергáть [-вéргнуть] опáсности

imperious [ɪm'pɪərɪəs] □ (*commanding*) влáстный; (*haughty*) высокомéрный

impermeable [ɪm'pɜ:mɪəbl] непроницáемый

impersonal [ɪm'pɜ:sənl] *gr.* безли́чный; безли́кий; объекти́вный

impersonate [ɪm'pɜ:səneɪt] исполня́ть роль *f* (Р), выдавáть себя́ за; изображáть [-ази́ть]

impertinen|ce [ɪm'pɜ:tɪnəns] дéр-

зость *f.*; **~t** [~nənt] □ дерзкий
imperturbable [ɪmpə'tɜːbəbl] □ невозмутимый
impervious [ɪm'pɜːvɪəs] → ***impermeable***; *fig.* глухой (***to*** к Д)
impetu|ous [ɪm'petjʊəs] □ стремительный; (*done hastily*) необдуманный; **~s** ['ɪmpɪtəs] импульс, толчок
impinge [ɪm'pɪndʒ]: **~** (***up***)***on*** [по-] влиять, отражаться [-зиться]
implacable [ɪm'plækəbl] □ (*relentless*) неумолимый; (*unappeasable*) непримиримый
implant [ɪm'plɑːnt] *ideas, etc.* насаждать [насадить]; внушать [-шить]
implausible [ɪm'plɔːzəbl] неправдоподобный, невероятный
implement ['ɪmplɪmənt] **1.** (*small tool*) инструмент; *agric.* орудие; **2.** выполнять [выполнить]
implicat|e ['ɪmplɪkeɪt] вовлекать [-ечь], впут(ыв)ать; **~ion** [ɪmplɪ'keɪʃn] вовлечение; скрытый смысл, намёк
implicit [ɪm'plɪsɪt] □ (*unquestioning*) безоговорочный; (*suggested*) подразумеваемый; (*implied*) недосказанный
implore [ɪm'plɔː] умолять [-лить]
imply [ɪm'plaɪ] подразумевать; (*insinuate*) намекать [-кнуть] на (В); значить
impolite [ɪmpə'laɪt] □ невежливый
impolitic [ɪm'pɒlətɪk] □ нецелесообразный; неблагоразумный
import 1. ['ɪmpɔːt] ввоз, импорт; **~s** *pl.* ввозимые товары *m/pl.*; **2.** [ɪm'pɔːt] ввозить [ввезти], импортировать *(im)pf.*; **~ance** [ɪm'pɔːtns] значение, важность *f*; **~ant** [~tnt] важный, значительный
importunate [ɪm'pɔːtʃʊnət] □ назойливый
impos|e [ɪm'pəʊz] *v/t.* навязывать [-зать]; *a tax* облагать [обложить]; **~ *a fine*** наложить штраф; *v/i.* **~ *upon*** злоупотреблять [-бить] (Т); **~ing** [~ɪŋ] внушительный, впечатляющий
impossib|ility [ɪmpɒsə'bɪlətɪ] невозможность *f*; **~le** [ɪm'pɒsəbl] □ невозможный; (*unbearable*) *coll.* несносный
impostor [ɪm'pɒstə] шарлатан; самозванец
impoten|ce ['ɪmpətəns] бессилие, слабость *f*; *med.* импотенция; **~t** [~tənt] бессильный, слабый; импотентный
impoverish [ɪm'pɒvərɪʃ] доводить до нищеты; *fig.* обеднять [-нить]
impracticable [ɪm'præktɪkəbl] □ неисполнимый, неосуществимый
impractical [ɪm'præktɪkl] □ непрактичный
impregnate ['ɪmpregneɪt] (*saturate*) пропитывать [-питать]; (*fertilize*) оплодотворять [-творить]
impress [ɪm'pres] отпечат(ыв)ать; (*fix*) запечатле(ва)ть; (*bring home*) внушать [-шить] (***on*** Д); производить впечатление на (В); **~ion** [ɪm'preʃn] впечатление; *typ.* оттиск; ***I am under the ~ that*** у меня такое впечатление, что ...; **~ionable** [ɪm'preʃənəbl] впечатлительный; **~ive** [ɪm'presɪv] □ внушительный, впечатляющий
imprint [ɪm'prɪnt] **1.** *in memory, etc.* запечатле(ва)ть; **2.** отпечаток
imprison [ɪm'prɪzn] сажать [посадить]/заключать [-чить] в тюрьму; **~ment** [~mənt] тюремное заключение
improbable [ɪm'prɒbəbl] □ невероятный, неправдоподобный
improper [ɪm'prɒpə] неуместный; (*indecent*) непристойный; (*incorrect*) неправильный
improve [ɪm'pruːv] *v/t.* улучшать [улучшить]; [у]совершенствовать; *v/i.* улучшаться [улучшиться]; [у]совершенствоваться; **~ *upon*** улучшать [улучшить] (В); **~ment** [~mənt] улучшение; усовершенствование
improvise ['ɪmprəvaɪz] импровизировать *(im)pf.*
imprudent [ɪm'pruːdnt] □ неблагоразумный; неосторожный
impuden|ce ['ɪmpjʊdəns] наглость *f*; дерзость *f*; **~t** [~dənt] наглый; дерзкий
impulse ['ɪmpʌls] импульс, толчок; (*sudden inclination*) порыв
impunity [ɪm'pjuːnətɪ] безнаказанность *f*; ***with ~*** безнаказанно

impure [ɪm'pjʊə] нечи́стый; гря́зный (*a. fig.*); (*indecent*) непристо́йный; *air* загрязнённый; (*mixed with s.th.*) с при́месью
impute [ɪm'pjuːt] припи́сывать [-са́ть] (Д/В)
in [ɪn] **1.** *prp.* в, во (П *or* В); **~ number** в коли́честве (Р), числом в (В); **~ itself** само́ по себе́; **~ 1949** в 1949-ом (в ты́сяча девятьсо́т со́рок девя́том) году́; **cry out ~ alarm** закрича́ть в испу́ге (*or* от стра́ха); **~ the street** на у́лице; **~ my opinion** по моему́ мне́нию, помо́ему; **~ English** по-англи́йски; **a novel ~ English** рома́н на англи́йском языке́; **~ thousands** ты́сячами; **~ the circumstances** в э́тих усло́виях; **~ this manner** таки́м о́бразом; **~ a word** одни́м сло́вом; **be ~ power** быть у вла́сти; **be engaged ~ reading** занима́ться чте́нием; **2.** *adv.* внутри́; внутрь; **she's ~ for an unpleasant surprise** её ожида́ет неприя́тный сюрпри́з; *coll.*; **be ~ with** быть в хоро́ших отноше́ниях с (Т)
inability [ɪnə'bɪlətɪ] неспосо́бность *f*
inaccessible [ɪnæk'sesəbl] □ недосту́пный; непристу́пный
inaccurate [ɪn'ækjərət] □ нето́чный
inactiv|e [ɪn'æktɪv] □ безде́ятельный; безде́йствующий; **~ity** [ɪnæk'tɪvətɪ] безде́ятельность *f*; ине́ртность *f*
inadequate [ɪn'ædɪkwɪt] □ (*insufficient*) недоста́точный; (*not capable*) неспосо́бный; *excuse* неубеди́тельный
inadmissible [ɪnəd'mɪsəbl] недопусти́мый, неприе́млемый
inadvertent [ɪnəd'vɜːtənt] □ невнима́тельный; неумы́шленный; (*unintentional*) ненаме́ренный
inalienable [ɪn'eɪlɪənəbl] □ неотъе́млемый
inane [ɪ'neɪn] □ (*senseless*) бессмы́сленный; (*empty*) пусто́й
inanimate [ɪn'ænɪmət] □ неодушевлённый; (*lifeless*) безжи́зненный
inappropriate [ɪnə'prəʊprɪət] неуме́стный, несоотве́тствующий
inapt [ɪn'æpt] □ неспосо́бный; (*not suitable*) неподходя́щий
inarticulate [ɪnɑː'tɪkjʊlət] □ нечленоразде́льный, невня́тный
inasmuch [ɪnəz'mʌtʃ]: **~ as** *adv.* так как; в виду́ того́, что; поско́льку
inattentive [ɪnə'tentɪv] невнима́тельный
inaugura|te [ɪ'nɔːgjʊreɪt] *launch* откры́(ва́)ть; (*install as president*) вводи́ть в до́лжность; **~tion** [ɪnɔːgjʊ'reɪʃn] вступле́ние в до́лжность, инаугура́ция; (торже́ственное) откры́тие
inborn [ɪn'bɔːn] врождённый, прирождённый
incalculable [ɪn'kælkjʊləbl] □ неисчисли́мый, бессчётный; *person* капри́зный, ненадёжный
incapa|ble [ɪn'keɪpəbl] □ неспосо́бный (**of** к Д *or* на В); **~citate** [ɪnkə'pæsɪteɪt] де́лать неспосо́бным, неприго́дным
incarnate [ɪn'kɑːnɪt] воплощённый, олицетворённый
incautious [ɪn'kɔːʃəs] □ неосторо́жный, опроме́тчивый
incendiary [ɪn'sendɪərɪ] *mil.*, *fig.* зажига́тельный
incense[1] ['ɪnsens] ла́дан
incense[2] [ɪn'sens] приводи́ть в я́рость
incentive [ɪn'sentɪv] сти́мул
incessant [ɪn'sesnt] □ непреры́вный
inch [ɪntʃ] дюйм; *fig.* пядь *f*; **by ~es** ма́ло-пома́лу
inciden|ce ['ɪnsɪdəns]: **high ~ of** большо́е коли́чество слу́чаев; **~t** [~t] слу́чай; происше́ствие; *mil.*, *dipl.* инциде́нт; **~tal** [ɪnsɪ'dentl] □ случа́йный; побо́чный; прису́щий (Д); *pl.* непредви́денные расхо́ды *m/pl.*; **~tally** случа́йно; ме́жду про́чим; попу́тно
incinerate [ɪn'sɪnəreɪt] испепеля́ть [-ли́ть]; сжига́ть [сжечь]
incis|ion [ɪn'sɪʒn] разре́з, надре́з; **~ive** [ɪn'saɪsɪv] □ о́стрый; *criticism*, *etc.* ре́зкий
incite [ɪn'saɪt] (*instigate*) подстрека́ть [-кну́ть]; (*move to action*) побужда́ть [-уди́ть]
inclement [ɪn'klemənt] суро́вый, холо́дный
inclin|ation [ɪnklɪ'neɪʃn] (*slope*) на-

клóн, уклóн; (*mental leaning*) склóнность *f*; **~e** [ɪn'klaɪn] **1.** *v/i.* склоня́ться [-ни́ться]; **~ *to*** *fig.* быть склóнным к (Д); *v/t.* наклоня́ть [-ни́ть]; склоня́ть [-ни́ть] (*a. fig.*); **2.** наклóн

inclose [ɪn'kləʊz] → ***enclose***

inclu|de [ɪn'klu:d] включа́ть [-чи́ть]; содержа́ть; **~sive** [~sɪv] □ включа́ющий в себя́, содержа́щий; ***from Monday to Friday ~*** с понедéльника до пя́тницы включи́тельно

incoheren|ce [ɪnkəʊ'hɪərəns] несвя́зность *f*; непослéдовательность *f*; **~t** [~t] □ несвя́зный; (*not consistent*) непослéдовательный

income ['ɪŋkʌm] дохóд

incomparable [ɪn'kɒmprəbl] □ (*not comparable*) несравни́мый; *matchless* несравнéнный

incompatible [ɪŋkəm'pætəbl] несовмести́мый

incompetent [ɪn'kɒmpɪtənt] □ несвéдущий, неумéлый; *specialist* некомпетéнтный; *law* недееспосóбный

incomplete [ɪŋkəm'pli:t] □ непóлный; (*unfinished*) незакóнченный

incomprehensible [ɪŋkɒmprɪ'hensəbl] □ непоня́тный, непостижи́мый

inconceivable [ɪŋkən'si:vəbl] □ невообрази́мый

incongruous [ɪn'kɒŋgrʊəs] □ (*out of place*) неумéстный; (*absurd*) нелéпый; (*incompatible*) несовмести́мый

inconseqential [ɪn'kɒnsɪkwəntʃl] □ несущéственный

inconsidera|ble [ɪŋkən'sɪdərəbl] □ незначи́тельный, нева́жный; **~te** [-rɪt] □ невнима́тельный (***to*** к Д); (*rash*) необду́манный

inconsisten|cy [ɪnkən'sɪstənsɪ] непослéдовательность *f*, противорéчие; **~t** [~tənt] □ непослéдовательный, противоречи́вый

inconsolable [ɪnkən'səʊləbl] □ безутéшный

inconvenien|ce [ɪŋkən'vi:nɪəns] **1.** неудóбство; **2.** причиня́ть [-ни́ть] неудóбство; [по]беспокóить; **~t** [~nɪənt] □ неудóбный, затрудни́тельный

incorporat|e [ɪn'kɔ:pəreɪt] объединя́ть(ся) [-ни́ть(ся)]; включа́ть [-чи́ть] (***into*** в В); **~ed** [~reɪtɪd] зарегистри́рованный в ка́честве юриди́ческого лица́

incorrect [ɪŋkə'rekt] □ непра́вильный

incorrigible [ɪn'kɒrɪdʒəbl] □ неисправи́мый

increase [ɪn'kri:s] **1.** увели́чи(ва)ть(ся); [вы́]расти́; *of wind, etc.* уси́ли(ва)ть(ся); **2.** ['ɪnkri:s] рост; увеличéние; прирóст

incredible [ɪn'kredəbl] □ невероя́тный; неимовéрный

incredul|ity [ɪnkrɪ'dju:lətɪ] недовéрчивость *f*; **~ous** [ɪn'kredjʊləs] □ недовéрчивый

increment ['ɪŋkrəmənt] прирóст

incriminate [ɪn'krɪmɪneɪt] инкрими́нировать (*im*)*pf.*; *law* обвиня́ть в преступлéнии

incrustation [ɪnkrʌ'steɪʃn] инкруста́ция

incubator ['ɪŋkʊbeɪtə] инкуба́тор

incur [ɪn'kɜ:] навлека́ть [-вле́чь] на себя́; **~ *losses*** понести́ *pf.* убы́тки

incurable [ɪn'kjʊərəbl] неизлечи́мый; *fig.* неисправи́мый

indebted [ɪn'detɪd] *for money* в долгу́ (*a. fig.*); *fig.* обя́занный

indecen|cy [ɪn'di:snsɪ] непристóйность *f*; неприли́чие; **~t** [~snt] неприли́чный

indecisi|on [ɪndɪ'sɪʒn] нереши́тельность *f*; (*hesitation*) колеба́ние; **~ve** [~'saɪsɪv] нереши́тельный; не реша́ющий; **~ *evidence*** недоста́точно убеди́тельные доказа́тельства

indecorous [ɪn'dekərəs] □ неприли́чный; некоррéктный

indeed [ɪn'di:d] в са́мом дéле, действи́тельно; неужéли!

indefensible [ɪndɪ'fensəbl] □ *mil.* незащити́мая пози́ция; (*unjustified*) не имéющий оправда́ния; *fig.* несостоя́тельный

indefinite [ɪn'defɪnət] □ неопределённый (*a. gr.*); неограни́ченный

indelible [ɪn'deləbl] □ неизглади́мый

indelicate [ɪn'delɪkət] □ неделика́т-

ный; нескро́мный; *remark* бестáктный
indemnity [ɪn'demnətɪ] гара́нтия возмеще́ния убы́тков; компенса́ция
indent [ɪn'dent] *v/t. typ.* нач(ин)а́ть с кра́сной строки́; *v/i. comm.* [с]де́лать зака́з на (В)
independen|ce [ɪndɪ'pendəns] незави́симость *f*, самостоя́тельность *f*; **~t** [~t] □ незави́симый, самостоя́тельный
indescribable [ɪndɪs'kraɪbəbl] □ неопису́емый
indestructible [ɪndɪ'strʌktəbl] □ неразруши́мый
indeterminate [ɪndɪ'tɜːmɪnət] □ неопределённый; (*vague, not clearly seen*) нея́сный
index ['ɪndeks] и́ндекс, указа́тель *m*; показа́тель *m*; **~ finger** указа́тельный па́лец
India ['ɪndɪə]: **~ rubber** каучу́к; рези́на; **~n** [~n] **1.** *of India* инди́йский; *of North America* инде́йский; ***~ corn*** кукуру́за; ***~ summer*** ба́бье ле́то; **2.** инди́ец, индиа́нка; *of North America* инде́ец, индиа́нка
indicat|e ['ɪndɪkeɪt] ука́зывать [-за́ть]; (*show*) пока́зывать [-за́ть]; (*make clear*) д(ав)а́ть поня́ть; означа́ть *impf.*; **~ion** [ɪndɪ'keɪʃn] (*sign*) знак, при́знак; **~or** ['ɪndɪkeɪtə] стре́лка; *mot.* сигна́л поворо́та, *coll.* мига́лка
indifferen|ce [ɪn'dɪfrəns] равноду́шие, безразли́чие; **~t** [~t] равноду́шный, безразли́чный; ***~ actor*** посре́дственный актёр
indigenous [ɪn'dɪdʒɪnəs] тузе́мный; ме́стный
indigest|ible [ɪndɪ'dʒestəbl] □ *fig.* неудобовари́мый; **~ion** [~tʃən] расстро́йство желу́дка
indign|ant [ɪn'dɪgnənt] □ негоду́ющий; **~ation** [ɪndɪg'neɪʃn] негодова́ние; **~ity** [ɪn'dɪgnɪtɪ] униже́ние, оскорбле́ние
indirect ['ɪndɪrekt] □ непрямо́й; *route* око́льный; *answer* укло́нчивый; ***~ taxes*** ко́свенные нало́ги
indiscre|et [ɪndɪ'skriːt] □ нескро́мный; (*tactless*) беста́ктный; **~tion** [~'skreʃn] нескро́мность *f*; беста́ктность *f*
indiscriminate [ɪndɪ'skrɪmɪnət] □ неразбо́рчивый
indispensable [ɪndɪ'spensəbl] □ необходи́мый, обяза́тельный
indispos|ed [ɪndɪ'spəʊzd] (*disinclined*) нерасполо́женный; нездоро́вый; **~ition** ['ɪndɪspə'zɪʃn] нежела́ние; недомога́ние
indisputable [ɪndɪ'spjuːtəbl] неоспори́мый, бесспо́рный
indistinct [ɪndɪ'stɪŋkt] □ нея́сный, неотчётливый; *speech* невня́тный
individual [ɪndɪ'vɪdjʊəl] **1.** □ индивидуа́льный; характе́рный; (*separate*) отде́льный; **2.** индиви́дуум, ли́чность *f*; **~ity** [~vɪdjʊ'ælətɪ] индивидуа́льность *f*
indivisible [ɪndɪ'vɪzəbl] недели́мый
indolen|ce ['ɪndələns] лень *f*; **~t** [~t] лени́вый
indomitable [ɪn'dɒmɪtəbl] □ неукроти́мый
indoor ['ɪndɔː] вну́тренний; **~s** [ɪn'dɔːz] в до́ме
indorse → ***endorse***
indubitable [ɪn'djuːbɪtəbl] □ несомне́нный
induce [ɪn'djuːs] заставля́ть [-а́вить]; (*bring about*) вызыва́ть [вы́звать]; **~ment** [~mənt] сти́мул, побужде́ние
indulge [ɪn'dʌldʒ] *v/t.* доставля́ть удово́льствие (Д ***with*** Т); (*spoil*) балова́ть; потво́рствовать (Д); *v/i.* ***~ in*** увлека́ться [-е́чься] (Т); пред(ав)а́ться (Д); **~nce** [~əns] потво́рство; **~nt** [~ənt] □ снисходи́тельный; нетре́бовательный; потво́рствующий
industri|al [ɪn'dʌstrɪəl] □ промы́шленный; произво́дственный; **~alist** [~ɪst] промы́шленник; **~ous** [ɪn'dʌstrɪəs] трудолюби́вый
industry ['ɪndəstrɪ] промы́шленность *f*, индустри́я; трудолю́бие
inedible [ɪn'edɪbl] несъедо́бный
ineffect|ive [ɪnɪ'fektɪv], **~ual** [~tʃʊəl] □ безрезульта́тный; неэффекти́вный
inefficient [ɪnɪ'fɪʃnt] □ *person* неспосо́бный, неуме́лый; *method, etc.* неэффекти́вный
inelegant [ɪn'elɪgənt] □ неэлега́нтный

ineligible [ɪn'elɪdʒəbl]: ***be ~ for*** не имéть прáва (на В)
inept [ɪ'nept] □ неумéстный, неподходя́щий; неумéлый
inequality [ɪnɪ'kwɒlətɪ] нерáвенство
inert [ɪ'nɜːt] □ инéртный; (*sluggish*) вя́лый; **~ia** [ɪ'nɜːʃə], **~ness** [ɪ'nɜːtnɪs] инéрция; вя́лость *f*
inescapable [ɪnɪ'skeɪpəbl] □ неизбéжный
inessential [ɪn'əsenʃl] □ несущéственный
inestimable [ɪn'estɪməbl] □ неоценúмый
inevitable [ɪn'evɪtəbl] □ неизбéжный, неминýемый
inexact [ɪnɪg'zækt] □ нетóчный
inexhaustible [ɪnɪg'zɔːstəbl] □ неистощúмый, неисчерпáемый
inexorable [ɪn'eksərəbl] □ неумолúмый, непреклóнный
inexpedient [ɪnɪk'spiːdɪənt] □ нецелесообрáзный
inexpensive [ɪnɪk'spensɪv] □ недорогóй, дешёвый
inexperience [ɪnɪk'spɪərɪəns] неóпытность *f*; **~d** [~t] неóпытный
inexplicable [ɪnɪk'splɪkəbl] □ необъяснúмый, непоня́тный
inexpressible [ɪnɪk'spresəbl] □ невыразúмый, неописýемый
inextinguishable [ɪnɪk'stɪŋgwɪʃəbl] □ неугасúмый
inextricable [ɪnɪk'strɪkəbl] □ запýтанный
infallible [ɪn'fæləbl] □ безошúбочный, непогрешúмый; *method* надёжный
infam|ous ['ɪnfəməs] □ посты́дный, позóрный, бесчéстный; **~y** [~mɪ] бесчéстье, позóр; (*infamous act*) нúзость *f*; пóдлость *f*
infan|cy ['ɪnfənsɪ] младéнчество; **~t** [~t] младéнец
infantile ['ɪnfəntaɪl] младéнческий; *behaviour* инфантúльный
infantry ['ɪnfəntrɪ] пехóта
infatuated [ɪn'fætjʊeɪtɪd]: ***be ~ with*** быть без умá от (Р)
infect [ɪn'fekt] заражáть [-разúть]; **~ion** [ɪn'fekʃn] инфéкция; **~ious** [~ʃəs] □, **~ive** [~tɪv] инфекциóнный, зарáзный; *fig.* заразúтельный
infer [ɪn'fɜː] дéлать вы́вод; (*imply*) подразумевáть; **~ence** ['ɪnfərəns] вы́вод, заключéние
inferior [ɪn'fɪərɪə] **1.** (*subordinate*) подчинённый; (*worse*) хýдший, неполноцéнный; *goods* нúзкого кáчества; **2.** подчинённый; **~ity** [ɪnfɪərɪ'ɒrətɪ] нúзкое кáчество (положéние); неполноцéнность *f*; ***~ complex*** кóмплекс неполноцéнности
infernal [ɪn'fɜːnl] □ *mst. fig.* áдский
infertile [ɪn'fəːtaɪl] бесплóдный (*a. fig.*); неплодорóдный
infest [ɪn'fest]: ***be ~ed*** кишéть (Т)
infidelity [ɪnfɪ'delətɪ] невéрность *f* (***to*** Д)
infiltrate ['ɪnfɪltreɪt] (*enter secretly*) проникáть [-úкнуть]; просáчиваться [-сочúться]
infinit|e ['ɪnfɪnət] □ бесконéчный, безгранúчный; **~y** [ɪn'fɪnətɪ] бесконéчность *f*; безгранúчность *f*
infirm [ɪn'fɜːm] □ нéмощный, дря́хлый; **~ary** [~ərɪ] больнúца; **~ity** [~ətɪ] нéмощь *f*
inflam|e [ɪn'fleɪm] воспламеня́ть (-ся) [-úть(ся)]; *med.* воспаля́ть(ся) [-лúть(ся)]; **~ed** [~d] воспалённый
inflamma|ble [ɪn'flæməbl] □ воспламеня́ющийся; **~tion** [ɪnflə'meɪʃn] *med.* воспалéние; **~tory** [ɪn'flæmətrɪ] *speech* подстрекáтельский; *med.* воспалúтельный
inflat|e [ɪn'fleɪt] надý(вá)ть; *tyre* накáчивать [-чáть]; *prices* взвúнчивать [-нтúть]; **~ion** [ɪn'fleɪʃn] *of balloon*, *etc.* надувáние; *econ.* инфля́ция
inflexible [ɪn'fleksəbl] □ негúбкий; *fig.* непреклóнный, непоколебúмый
inflict [ɪn'flɪkt] *a blow*, *etc.* наносúть [-нестú]; *pain* причиня́ть [-нúть]; *views*, *etc.* навя́зывать(ся)
influen|ce ['ɪnflʊəns] **1.** влия́ние, воздéйствие; **2.** [по]влия́ть на (В); воздéйствовать на (В) (*im*)*pf.*; **~tial** [ɪnflʊ'enʃl] влия́тельный
influenza [ɪnflʊ'enzə] грипп
influx ['ɪnflʌks] притóк; *of visitors* наплы́в
inform [ɪn'fɔːm] *v/t.* информúро-

вать (*im*)*pf.*, уведомля́ть [уве́домить] (***of*** о П); *v/i.* доноси́ть [-нести́] (***against*** на В); ***keep s.o. ~ed*** держа́ть в ку́рсе де́л

informal [ɪn'fɔːml] □ неофициа́льный; *conversation* непринуждённый; **~ality** [ɪnfɔː'mælətɪ] несоблюде́ние форма́льностей; непринуждённость *f*

inform|ation [ɪnfə'meɪʃn] информа́ция, све́дения *n/pl.*; спра́вка; **~ative** [ɪn'fɔːmətɪv] информи́рующий; содержа́тельный; (*educational*) поучи́тельный

infrequent [ɪn'friːkwənt] □ ре́дкий

infringe [ɪn'frɪndʒ] наруша́ть [-ру́шить] (*a.* ~ ***upon***)

infuriate [ɪn'fjʊərɪeɪt] [вз]беси́ть

ingen|ious [ɪn'dʒiːnɪəs] □ изобрета́тельный; **~uity** [ɪndʒɪ'njuːətɪ] изобрета́тельность *f*; **~uous** [ɪn'dʒenjʊəs] □ (*frank*) чистосерде́чный; (*lacking craft or subtlety*) простоду́шный; просто́й, бесхи́тростный

ingratitude [ɪn'grætɪtjuːd] неблаго́дарность *f*

ingredient [ɪn'griːdɪənt] составна́я часть *f*, ингредие́нт (*a. cul.*)

inhabit [ɪn'hæbɪt] населя́ть; обита́ть, жить в (П); **~ant** [~ɪtənt] жи́тель(ница *f*) *m*, обита́тель(ница *f*) *m*

inhal|ation [ɪnhə'leɪʃn] *med.* ингаля́ция; **~e** [ɪn'heɪl] вдыха́ть [вдохну́ть]

inherent [ɪn'hɪərənt] □ прису́щий

inherit [ɪn'herɪt] насле́довать (*im*)*pf.*; *fig.* унасле́довать *pf.*; **~ance** [~ɪtəns] насле́дство (*a. fig.*)

inhibit [ɪn'hɪbɪt] сде́рживать [сдержа́ть], [вос]препя́тствовать (Д); **~ion** [ɪnhɪ'bɪʃn] *med.* торможе́ние

inhospitable [ɪn'hɒspɪtəbl] □ негостеприи́мный

inhuman [ɪn'hjuːmən] □ бесчелове́чный; античелове́ческий

inimitable [ɪ'nɪmɪtəbl] □ неподража́емый; (*peerless*) несравне́нный

initia|l [ɪ'nɪʃl] **1.** □ нача́льный, первонача́льный; **2.** нача́льная бу́ква; **~s** *pl.* инициа́лы *m/pl.*; **~te** [~ɪeɪt] вводи́ть [ввести́]; *into a secret* посвяща́ть [-вяти́ть]; (*start*) положи́ть *pf.* нача́ло (Д); **~tive** [ɪ'nɪʃətɪv] инициати́ва; **~tor** [~ʃɪəɪtə] инициа́тор

inject [ɪn'dʒekt] *med.* [с]де́лать инъе́кцию; **~ion** [~ʃn] инъе́кция, впры́скивание, уко́л

injur|e ['ɪndʒə] [по]вреди́ть, повреждать [-еди́ть]; *in war, etc.* ра́нить (*im*)*pf.*; (*wrong*) обижа́ть [-и́деть]; **~ious** [ɪn'dʒʊərɪəs] □ вре́дный; **~y** ['ɪndʒərɪ] оскорбле́ние; поврежде́ние, ра́на; *sport* тра́вма

injustice [ɪn'dʒʌstɪs] несправедли́вость *f*

ink [ɪŋk] черни́ла *n/pl.*

inkling ['ɪŋklɪŋ] намёк (на В); (*suspicion*) подозре́ние

inland ['ɪnlənd] **1.** вну́тренняя террито́рия страны́; **2.** вну́тренний; **3.** [ɪn'lænd] внутрь, внутри́ (страны́)

inlay [ɪn'leɪ] инкруста́ция

inlet ['ɪnlet] у́зкий зали́в, бу́хта; впускно́е отве́рстие

inmate ['ɪnmeɪt] *of hospital* больно́й, пацие́нт, обита́тель; *of prison* заключённый

inmost ['ɪnməʊst] глубоча́йший, *thoughts* сокрове́ннейший

inn [ɪn] гости́ница, тракти́р

innate [ɪ'neɪt] □ врождённый, приро́дный

inner ['ɪnə] вну́тренний; **~most** [~məʊst] → ***inmost***

innocen|ce ['ɪnəsns] *law* невино́вность *f*; неви́нность *f*; простота́; **~t** [~snt] □ неви́нный; *law* невино́вный

innocuous [ɪ'nɒkjʊəs] □ безвре́дный; *remark* безоби́дный

innovation [ɪnə'veɪʃn] нововведе́ние, но́вшество

innuendo [ɪnjuː'endəʊ] ко́свенный намёк, инсинуа́ция

innumerable [ɪ'njuːmərəbl] □ бесчётный, бесчи́сленный

inoculate [ɪ'nɒkjʊleɪt] [с]де́лать приви́вку (Д от Р)

inoffensive [ɪnə'fensɪv] безоби́дный, безвре́дный

inopportune [ɪn'ɒpətjuːn] □ несвоевре́менный, неподходя́щий

inordinate [ɪ'nɔːdɪnət] непоме́рный, чрезме́рный

in-patient ['ɪnpeɪʃnt] стациона́рный больно́й

inquest ['ınkwest] *law* рассле́дование, выясне́ние причи́н сме́рти
inquir|e [ın'kwaıə] *v/t.* спра́шивать [-роси́ть]; *v/i.* узн(ав)а́ть; наводи́ть [-вести́] спра́вки (***about***, ***after***, ***for*** о П; ***of*** у Р); **~ *into*** выясня́ть, рассле́довать *(im)pf*; **~ing** [~rıŋ] □ *mind* пытли́вый; **~y** [~rı] рассле́дование, сле́дствие; *(question)* вопро́с; ***make ~ies*** наводи́ть спра́вки
inquisitive [ın'kwızıtıv] □ любозна́тельный; любопы́тный
insan|e [ın'seın] □ психи́чески больно́й; *fig.* безу́мный; **~ity** [ın'sænətı] психи́ческое заболева́ние; безу́мие
insatiable [ın'seıʃəbl] □ ненасы́тный; *(greedy)* жа́дный
inscribe [ın'skraıb] *(write)* надпи́сывать [-са́ть] (***in***, ***on*** В/Т *or* В на П)
inscription [ın'skrıpʃn] на́дпись *f*
inscrutable [ın'skru:təbl] □ непостижи́мый, зага́дочный
insect ['ınsekt] насеко́мое; **~icide** [ın'sektısaıd] инсектици́д
insecure [ınsı'kjʊə] □ ненадёжный; *(not safe)* небезопа́сный
insens|ible [ın'sensəbl] □ *to touch, etc.* нечувстви́тельный; потеря́вший созна́ние; *(unsympathetic)* бесчу́вственный; **~itive** [~ıtıv] нечувстви́тельный; невосприи́мчивый
inseparable [ın'seprəbl] □ неразлу́чный; неотдели́мый (***from*** от Р)
insert [ın'sɜ:t] вставля́ть [-а́вить]; *advertisement* помеща́ть [-ести́ть]; **~ion** [ın'sɜ:ʃn] *of lace, etc.* вста́вка; *(announcement)* объявле́ние
inside [ın'saıd] **1.** вну́тренняя сторона́; вну́тренность *f*; *of clothing* изна́нка; ***turn ~ out*** вы́вернуть *pf.* на изна́нку; ***he knows his subject ~ out*** он зна́ет свой предме́т назубо́к; **2.** *adj.* вну́тренний; **3.** *adv.* внутрь, внутри́; **4.** *prp.* внутри́ (Р)
insidious [ın'sıdıəs] □ преда́тельский, кова́рный
insight ['ınsaıt] проница́тельность *f*; интуи́ция
insignificant [ınsıg'nıfıkənt] незначи́тельный, малова́жный
insincere [ınsın'sıə] неи́скренний
insinuat|e [ın'sınjʊeıt] намека́ть [-кну́ть] на (В); **~ *o.s.*** *fig.* вкра́дываться [вкра́сться]; **~ion** [ınsınjʊ'eıʃn] инсинуа́ция
insipid [ın'sıpıd] безвку́сный, пре́сный
insist [ın'sıst]: **~ (*up*)*on*** наста́ивать [-стоя́ть] на (П); **~ence** [~əns] насто́йчивость *f*; **~ent** [~ənt] насто́йчивый
insolent ['ınsələnt] □ высокоме́рный; на́глый
insoluble [ın'sɒljʊbl] нераствори́мый; *fig.* неразреши́мый
insolvent [ın'sɒlvənt] неплатёжеспособный
insomnia [ın'sɒmnıə] бессо́нница
inspect [ın'spekt] осма́тривать [осмотре́ть]; производи́ть [-вести́] инспе́кцию; **~ion** [ın'spekʃn] осмо́тр; инспе́кция
inspir|ation [ınspə'reıʃn] вдохнове́ние; воодушевле́ние; **~e** [ın'spaıə] *fig.* вдохновля́ть [-ви́ть]; *hope* вселя́ть [-ли́ть]; *fear* внуша́ть [-ши́ть]
install [ın'stɔ:l] устана́вливать [-нови́ть]; *tech.* [с]монти́ровать; **~ation** [ınstə'leıʃn] устано́вка
instalment [ın'stɔ:lmənt] очередно́й взнос (при поку́пке в рассро́чку); часть рома́на *и т.д.*, публику́емого в не́скольких номера́х
instance ['ınstəns] слу́чай; приме́р; ***for ~*** наприме́р
instant ['ınstənt] **1.** □ неме́дленный, безотлага́тельный; **2.** мгнове́ние; моме́нт; **~aneous** [ınstən'teınıəs] мгнове́нный; **~ly** ['ınstəntlı] неме́дленно, то́тчас
instead [ın'sted] взаме́н, вме́сто; **~ *of*** вме́сто (Р)
instep ['ınstep] подъём (ноги́)
instigat|e ['ınstıgeıt] *(urge on)* побужда́ть (-уди́ть); *(incite)* подстрека́ть [-кну́ть]; **~or** [~ə] подстрека́тель(ница *f*) *m*
instil(l) [ın'stıl] *fig.* внуша́ть [-ши́ть] (***into*** Д)
instinct ['ınstıŋkt] инсти́нкт; **~ive** [ın'stıŋktıv] □ инстинкти́вный
institut|e ['ınstıtju:t] нау́чное учрежде́ние, институ́т; **2.** *(set up)* учрежда́ть [-еди́ть]; *(found)* осно́вывать [-ва́ть]; **~ion** [ınstı'tju:ʃn] уч-

I

реждéние; ***educational ~*** учéбное заведéние

instruct [ɪn'strʌkt] обучáть [-чи́ть], [на]учи́ть; [про]инструкти́ровать (*im*)*pf.*; **~ion** [ɪn'strʌkʃn] обучéние; инстру́кция; **~ive** [~tɪv] □ поучи́тельный; **~or** [~tə] руководи́тель *m*, инстру́ктор; (*teacher*) преподавáтель *m*

instrument ['ɪnstrʊmənt] инструмéнт; *fig.* ору́дие; прибóр, аппарáт; **~al** [ɪnstrʊ'mentl] □ слу́жащий срéдством; *gr.* твори́тельный

insubordinate [ɪnsə'bɔːdɪnət] (*not submissive*) непокóрный

insufferable [ɪn'sʌfrəbl] □ невыноси́мый, нестерпи́мый

insufficient [ɪnsə'fɪʃnt] недостáточный

insula|r ['ɪnsjʊlə] □ островнóй; *fig.* зáмкнутый; **~te** [~leɪt] *el.* изоли́ровать (*im*)*pf.*; **~tion** [ɪnsjʊ'leɪʃn] *el.* изоля́ция; ***~ tape*** изоляциóнная лéнта

insulin ['ɪnsjʊlɪn] инсули́н

insult 1. ['ɪnsʌlt] оскорблéние; **2.** [ɪn'sʌlt] оскорбля́ть [-би́ть]

insur|ance [ɪn'ʃʊərəns] страховáние; (*sum insured*) су́мма страховáния, *coll.* страхóвка; ***~ company*** страховáя компáния; **~e** [ɪn'ʃʊə] [за]страховáть(ся)

insurgent [ɪn'sɜːdʒənt] повстáнец; мятéжник

insurmountable [ɪnsə'maʊntəbl] непреодоли́мый

insurrection [ɪnsə'rekʃn] восстáние

intact [ɪn'tækt] цéлый, невреди́мый

intangible [ɪn'tændʒəbl] □ неосязáемый; *fig.* неулови́мый

integ|ral ['ɪntɪgrəl] □ неотъéмлемый; (*whole*) цéлый, цéлостный; ***~ part*** неотъéмлемая часть; **~rate** [~greɪt] объединя́ть [-ни́ть]; *math.* интегри́ровать (*im*)*pf.*; **~rity** [ɪn'tegrɪtɪ] чéстность *f*; (*entireness*) цéлостность *f*

intellect ['ɪntəlekt] ум, интеллéкт; **~ual** [ɪntɪ'lektjʊəl] **1.** □ интеллектуáльный, у́мственный; ***~ property*** интеллектуáльная сóбственность; **2.** интеллигéнт *m*, -ка *f*; **~s** *pl.* интеллигéнция

intelligence [ɪn'telɪdʒəns] ум, рассу́док, интеллéкт; *mil.* ***~ service*** развéдывательная слу́жба, развéдка

intellig|ent [ɪn'telɪdʒənt] у́мный; *coll.* смышлёный; **~ible** [~dʒəbl] □ поня́тный

intend [ɪn'tend] намеревáться, собирáться; (*mean*) имéть в виду́; ***~ for*** (*destine for*) предназначáть [-знá-чить] для (Р)

intense [ɪn'tens] □ си́льный; интенси́вный, напряжённый

intensify [ɪn'tensɪfaɪ] уси́ли(ва)ть-(ся); интенсифици́ровать (*im*)*pf.*

intensity [ɪn'tensətɪ] интенси́вность *f*, си́ла; *of colo*(*u*)*r* я́ркость *f*

intent [ɪn'tent] **1.** □ погружённый (***on*** в В); поглощённый (***on*** Т); *look* внимáтельный, при́стальный; **2.** намéрение, цель *f*; ***to all ~s and purposes*** в су́щности, на сáмом дéле; **~ion** [ɪn'tenʃn] намéрение; **~ional** [~ʃənl] □ (пред)намéренный, умы́шленный

inter... ['ɪntə] *pref.* меж..., между...; пере...; взаимо...

interact [ɪntər'ækt] взаимодéйствовать

intercede [ɪntə'siːd] [по]ходáтайствовать; *in order to save* заступáться [-пи́ться]

intercept [ɪntə'sept] *letter, etc.* перехвáтывать [-хвати́ть]; (*listen in on*) подслу́шивать [-шать]

intercession [ɪntə'seʃn] ходáтайство

interchange [ɪntə'tʃeɪndʒ] **1.** *v/t.* обмéниваться [-ня́ться] (Т); **2.** обмéн

intercom ['ɪntəkɒm] вну́тренняя телефóнная связь, селéктор

intercourse ['ɪntəkɔːs] *social* общéние; *sexual* половы́е сношéния *n/pl.*

interest ['ɪntrəst] **1.** интерéс; заинтересóванность *f* (***in*** в П); (*advantage, profit*) пóльза, вы́года; *fin.* процéнты *m/pl.* ***~ rate*** стáвка процéнта; **2.** интересовáть; заинтересóвывать [-совáть]; **~ing** [~ɪŋ] □ интерéсный

interface [ɪntə'feɪs] стык; *comput.* интерфéйс; *fig.* взаимосвя́зь *f*

interfere [ɪntə'fɪə] вме́шиваться [-ша́ться] (***in*** в В); (*hinder*) [по]меша́ть (***with*** Д); **~nce** [~rəns] вмеша́тельство; поме́ха
interim ['ɪntərɪm] **1.** промежу́ток вре́мени; ***in the ~*** тем вре́менем; **2.** вре́менный, промежу́точный
interior [ɪn'tɪərɪə] **1.** вну́тренний; ***~ decorator*** оформи́тель интерье́ра; **2.** вну́тренняя часть *f*; *of house* интерье́р; вну́тренние о́бласти страны́; *pol.* вну́тренние дела́ *n/pl.*
interjection [ɪntə'dʒekʃn] восклица́ние; *gr.* междоме́тие
interlace [ɪntə'leɪs] переплета́ть(ся) [-плести́(сь)]
interlock [ɪntə'lɒk] сцепля́ть(ся) [-пи́ть(ся)]; соединя́ть(ся) [-ни́ть(ся)]
interlocutor [ɪntə'lɒkjʊtə] собесе́дник
interlude ['ɪntəlu:d] *thea.* антра́кт; *mus.*, *fig.* интерлю́дия
intermedia|ry [ɪntə'mi:dɪərɪ] **1.** посре́днический; **2.** посре́дник; **~te** [~'mi:dɪət] □ промежу́точный
interminable [ɪn'tɜ:mɪnəbl] □ бесконе́чный
intermingle [ɪntə'mɪŋgl] сме́шивать(ся) [-ша́ть(ся)]; обща́ться
intermission [ɪntə'mɪʃn] переры́в, па́уза
intermittent [ɪntə'mɪtənt] □ преры́вистый
intern [ɪn'tɜ:n] интерни́ровать (*im*)*pf.*
internal [ɪn'tɜ:nl] □ вну́тренний
international [ɪntə'næʃnl] □ междунаро́дный, интернациона́льный; ***~ law*** междунаро́дное пра́во; ***♀ Monetary Fund*** Междунаро́дный валю́тный фонд
Internet ['ɪntənet] *comput.* Интерне́т
interplanetary [ɪntə'plænətrɪ] межплане́тный
interpose [ɪntə'pəʊz] *v/t.* *remark* вставля́ть [-а́вить], вкли́ни(ва)ться (ме́жду Т); *v/i.* станови́ться [стать] (***between*** ме́жду Т); (*interfere*) вме́шиваться [-ша́ться] (в В)
interpret [ɪn'tɜ:prɪt] объясня́ть [-ни́ть], истолко́вывать [-кова́ть]; переводи́ть [-вести́] (у́стно); **~ation** [ɪntɜ:prɪ'teɪʃn] толкова́ние, интерпрета́ция, объясне́ние; **~er** [ɪn'tɜ:prɪtə] перево́дчик (-ица *f*) *m*
interrogat|e [ɪn'terəgeɪt] допра́шивать [-роси́ть]; **~ion** [ɪnterə'geɪʃn] допро́с; **~ive** [ɪntə'rɒgətɪv] □ вопроси́тельный (*a. gr.*)
interrupt [ɪntə'rʌpt] прер(ы)ва́ть; **~ion** [~'rʌpʃn] переры́в
intersect [ɪntə'sekt] пересека́ть(ся) [-се́чь(ся)]; **~ion** [~kʃn] пересече́ние
intersperse [ɪntə'spɜ:s] разбра́сывать [-броса́ть], рассыпа́ть; ***~ with jokes*** пересыпа́ть шу́тками
intertwine [ɪntə'twaɪn] сплета́ть(ся) [-ести́(сь)]
interval ['ɪntəvl] *of time* интерва́л, промежу́ток; *of space* расстоя́ние; *thea.* антра́кт; *in school* переме́на
interven|e [ɪntə'vi:n] вме́шиваться [-ша́ться]; вступа́ться [-пи́ться]; **~tion** [~'venʃn] интерве́нция; вмеша́тельство
interview ['ɪntəvju:] **1.** интервью́ *n indecl.*; *for a job* собесе́дование; **2.** брать [взять] интервью́; проводи́ть [-вести́] собесе́дование
intestine [ɪn'testɪn] кишка́; **~s** *pl.* кишки́ *f/pl.*, кише́чник
intima|cy ['ɪntɪməsɪ] инти́мность *f*, бли́зость *f*; **~te** **1.** [~meɪt] сообща́ть [-щи́ть]; (*hint*) намека́ть [-кну́ть] на (В); **2.** [~mɪt] □ инти́мный, ли́чный; бли́зкий; **~tion** [ɪntɪ'meɪʃn] сообще́ние; намёк
intimidate [ɪn'tɪmɪdeɪt] [ис]пуга́ть; *by threats* запу́гивать [-га́ть]
into ['ɪntʊ, ɪntə] *prp.* в, во (В); ***translate ~ English*** переводи́ть [-вести́] на англи́йский язы́к
intolera|ble [ɪn'tɒlərəbl] □ (*unbearable*) невыноси́мый, нестерпи́мый; **~nt** [~rənt] □ (*lacking forbearance, bigoted*) нетерпи́мый
intonation [ɪntə'neɪʃn] интона́ция
intoxica|te [ɪn'tɒksɪkeɪt] опьяня́ть [-ни́ть] (*a. fig.*); **~tion** [ɪntɒksɪ'keɪʃn] опьяне́ние
intractable [ɪn'træktəbl] □ упря́мый; неподатливый
intravenous [ɪntrə'vi:nəs] □ внутриве́нный
intrepid [ɪn'trepɪd] бесстра́шный, отва́жный

intricate ['ɪntrɪkɪt] □ сло́жный, запу́танный
intrigu|e [ɪn'tri:g] **1.** интри́га; (*love affair*) любо́вная связь *f*; **2.** интригова́ть; [за]интригова́ть, [за]интересова́ть; **~ing** [~ɪŋ] интригу́ющий; *coll.* интере́сный
intrinsic [ɪn'trɪnsɪk] (**~ally**) вну́тренний; (*inherent*) сво́йственный, прису́щий
introduc|e [ɪntrə'dju:s] вводи́ть [ввести́]; (*acquaint*) представля́ть [-а́вить]; **~tion** [~'dʌkʃn] (*preface*) введе́ние, предисло́вие; представле́ние; *mus.* интроду́кция; **~tory** [~'dʌktərɪ] вступи́тельный, вво́дный
intru|de [ɪn'tru:d] *into s.o.'s private life* вторга́ться [вто́ргнуться]; появля́ться [-ви́ться] некста́ти; **~der** [~ə] челове́к, прише́дший некста́ти; навя́зчивый челове́к; **~sion** [~u:ʒn] вторже́ние; появле́ние без приглаше́ния; ***sorry for the ~*** прости́те за беспоко́йство
intrust [ɪn'trʌst] → ***entrust***
intuition [ɪntju:'ɪʃn] интуи́ция
inundate ['ɪnʌndeɪt] затопля́ть [-пи́ть], наводня́ть [-ни́ть]
invade [ɪn'veɪd] *mil.* вторга́ться [вто́ргнуться]; *of tourists, etc.* наводня́ть [-ни́ть]; ***~ s.o.'s privacy*** нару́шить чьё-л. уедине́ние; **~r** [~ə] захва́тчик
invalid 1. [ɪn'vælɪd] недействи́тельный, не име́ющий зако́нной си́лы; *argument* несостоя́тельный; **2.** ['ɪnvəlɪd] инвали́д; **~ate** [ɪn'vælɪdeɪt] сде́лать недействи́тельным
invaluable [ɪn'væljuəbl] □ неоцени́мый
invariable [ɪn'veərɪəbl] □ неизме́нный
invasion [ɪn'veɪʒn] вторже́ние
invent [ɪn'vent] (*create*) изобрета́ть [-брести́]; *story* выду́мывать [вы́думать]; **~ion** [ɪn'venʃn] изобрете́ние; вы́думка; (*faculty*) изобрета́тельность *f*; **~ive** [~tɪv] □ изобрета́тельный; **~or** [~tə] изобрета́тель *m*; **~ory** ['invəntrɪ] инвента́рная о́пись *f*
inverse [ɪn'vɜ:s] обра́тный; ***in ~ order*** в обра́тном поря́дке
invert [ɪn'vɜ:t] перевора́чивать [-верну́ть]; (*put in the opposite position*) переставля́ть [-а́вить]; ***~ed commas*** кавы́чки
invest [ɪn'vest] *money* вкла́дывать [вложи́ть]; *fig. with authority, etc.* облека́ть [обле́чь] (***with*** Т); инвести́ровать
investigat|e [ɪn'vestɪgeɪt] рассле́довать (*im*)*pf.*; (*study*) иссле́довать (*im*)*pf.*; **~ion** [ɪnvestɪ'geɪʃn] (*inquiry*) рассле́дование; *law* сле́дствие; иссле́дование
invest|ment [ɪn'vestmənt] вложе́ние де́нег, инвести́рование; (*sum*) инвести́ция, вклад; **~or** [ɪn'vestə] вкла́дчик, инве́стор
inveterate [ɪn'vetərət] (*deep-rooted*) закорене́лый; *coll. smoker, etc.* зая́длый; ***~ prejudices*** глубоко́ укорени́вшиеся предрассу́дки
invidious [ɪn'vɪdɪəs] □ вызыва́ющий оби́ду, за́висть; *remark* оби́дный
invigorate [ɪn'vɪgəreɪt] дава́ть си́лы (Д); бодри́ть
invincible [ɪn'vɪnsəbl] непобеди́мый
inviolable [ɪn'vaɪələbl] □ неруши́мый; неприкоснове́нный; ***~ right*** неруши́мое пра́во
invisible [ɪn'vɪzəbl] неви́димый
invit|ation [ɪnvɪ'teɪʃn] приглаше́ние; **~e** [ɪn'vaɪt] приглаша́ть [-ласи́ть]
invoice ['ɪnvɔɪs] *comm.* накладна́я, счёт-факту́ра
invoke [ɪn'vəʊk] взыва́ть [воззва́ть] о (П)
involuntary [ɪn'vɒləntrɪ] □ (*forced*) вы́нужденный; (*contrary to choice*) нево́льный; (*done unconsciously*) непроизво́льный
involve [ɪn'vɒlv] вовлека́ть [-е́чь]; впу́т(ыв)ать
invulnerable [ɪn'vʌlnərəbl] □ неуязви́мый
inward ['ɪnwəd] **1.** вну́тренний; **2.** *adv.* (*mst.* **~s** [~z]) внутрь; вну́тренне
iodine ['aɪədi:n] йод
irascible [ɪ'ræsəbl] □ раздражи́тельный
irate [aɪ'reɪt] гне́вный
iridescent [ɪrɪ'desnt] ра́дужный

iris ['aıərıs] *anat.* ра́дужная оболо́чка; *bot.* и́рис
Irish ['aıərıʃ] **1.** ирла́ндский; **2.** ***the ~*** ирла́ндцы *m/pl.*
irksome ['ɜːksəm] надое́дливый; раздража́ющий
iron ['aıən] **1.** желе́зо; утю́г; ***have many ~s in the fire*** бра́ться сра́зу за мно́го дел; **2.** желе́зный; **3.** [вы́]утю́жить, [вы́]гла́дить
ironic(al □) [aı'rɒnık(l)] ирони́ческий
iron|ing ['aıənıŋ] **1.** гла́женье; ве́щи для гла́женья; **2.** глади́льный; **~board** глади́льная доска́; **~mongery** ['aıənmʌŋgərı] металлоизде́лия; **~works** *mst. sg.* металлурги́ческий заво́д
irony ['aıərənı] иро́ния
irrational [ı'ræʃənl] неразу́мный; иррациона́льный (*a. math.*)
irreconcilable [ı'rekənsaıləbl] □ непримири́мый; *ideas, etc.* несовмести́мый
irrecoverable [ırı'kʌvərəbl] □: ***~ losses*** невосполни́мые поте́ри
irrefutable [ırı'fjuːtəbl] □ неопровержи́мый
irregular [ı'regjʊlə] □ непра́вильный (*a. gr.*); (*disorderly*) беспоря́дочный; (*not regular*) нерегуля́рный; ***~ features*** непра́вильные черты́ лица́
irrelevant [ı'reləvənt] □ не относя́щийся к де́лу; не име́ющий значе́ния
irreparable [ı'repərəbl] □ непоправи́мый
irreplaceable [ırı'pleısəbl] незамени́мый
irreproachable [ırı'prəʊtʃəbl] □ безукори́зненный, безупре́чный
irresistible [ırı'zıstəbl] □ неотрази́мый; *desire, etc.* непреодоли́мый
irresolute [ı'rezəluːt] □ нереши́тельный
irrespective [ırı'spektıv] безотноси́тельный (***of*** к Д); незави́симый (***of*** от Р)
irresponsible [ırı'spɒnsəbl] □ безотве́тственный
irreverent [ı'revərənt] □ непочти́тельный
irrevocable [ı'revəkəbl] □ безвозвра́тный, бесповоро́тный
irrigate ['ırıgeıt] ороша́ть [ороси́ть]
irrita|ble ['ırıtəbl] □ раздражи́тельный; **~te** [~teıt] раздража́ть [-жи́ть]; **~tion** [ırı'teıʃn] раздраже́ние
Islam [ız'lɑːm] исла́м; **~ic** [ız'læmık] исла́мский
is [ız] *3rd p. sg. pres. от* **be**
island ['aılənd] о́стров; **~er** [~ə] островитя́нин *m*, -тя́нка *f*
isle [aıl] о́стров; **~t** [aı'lıt] острово́к
isolat|e ['aısəleıt] изоли́ровать (*im*)*pf.*; (*separate*) отделя́ть [-ли́ть]; **~ed**: ***in ~ cases*** в отде́льных слу́чаях; **~ion** [aısə'leıʃn] изоля́ция; уедине́ние
issue ['ıʃuː] **1.** (*a. flowing out*) вытека́ние; *law* (*offspring*) пото́мство; (*publication*) вы́пуск, изда́ние; (*outcome*) исхо́д, результа́т; *of money* эми́ссия; ***be at ~*** быть предме́том спо́ра; ***point at ~*** предме́т обсужде́ния; **2.** *v/i. of blood* [по]те́чь (***from*** из Р); вытека́ть [вы́течь] (***from*** из Р); *of sound* изд(ав)а́ть; *v/t. book, etc.* выпуска́ть [вы́пустить], изд(ав)а́ть
isthmus ['ısməs] перешéек
it [ıt] *pers. pron.* он, она́, оно́; э́то; ***~ is cold*** хо́лодно; ***~ is difficult to say ...*** тру́дно сказа́ть
Italian [ı'tælıən] **1.** италья́нский; **2.** италья́нец *m*, -нка *f*; **3.** италья́нский язы́к
italics [ı'tælıks] *typ.* курси́в
itch [ıtʃ] **1.** чесо́тка; зуд (*a. fig.*); **2.** чеса́ться; ***be ~ing to*** *inf.* горе́ть жела́нием (+ *inf.*)
item ['aıtem] **1.** (*single article*) пункт, пара́граф; *on agenda* вопро́с; *on programme* но́мер; (*object*) предме́т
itinerary [aı'tınərərı] маршру́т
its [ıts] *poss. pron. от* ***it*** его́, её, свой
itself [ıt'self] (сам *m*, сама́ *f*) само́; себя́, -с, -сь; себе́; ***in ~*** само по себе́; само́ собо́й; (*separately*) отде́льно
ivory ['aıvərı] слоно́вая кость *f*
ivy ['aıvı] плющ

I

J

jab [dʒæb] *coll.* **1.** толка́ть [-кну́ть]; ты́кать [ткнуть]; (*stab*) пыря́ть [-рну́ть]; **2.** тычо́к, пино́к; (*prick*) уко́л (*a. coll. injection*)
jabber ['dʒæbə] болта́ть, тарато́рить
jack [dʒæk] **1.** *cards* вале́т; *mot.* домкра́т; ***Union*** ♀ госуда́рственный флаг Соединённого короле́вства; **2.** **~ *up*** поднима́ть домкра́том; **~ass** осёл; дурак
jackdaw ['dʒækdɔː] га́лка
jacket ['dʒækɪt] *lady's* жаке́т; *man's* пиджак; *casual* ку́ртка
jack|knife складно́й нож; *fig.* (*dive*) прыжо́к в во́ду согну́вшись; ***~-of-all-trades*** ма́стер на все ру́ки
jade [dʒeɪd] *min.* нефри́т
jagged ['dʒægɪd] зу́бчатый; ***~ rocks*** о́стрые ска́лы
jail [dʒeɪl] **1.** тюрьма́; тюре́мное заключе́ние; **2.** *v/t.* заключа́ть [-чи́ть] в тюрьму́; **~er** ['dʒeɪlə] тюре́мный надзира́тель
jam[1] [dzæm] варе́нье, джем, пови́дло
jam[2] [~] **1.** да́вка, сжа́тие; ***traffic ~*** зато́р, про́бка; ***be in a ~*** быть в затрудни́тельном положе́нии; **2.** заж(им)а́ть; (*pinch*) защемля́ть [-ми́ть]; (*push into confined space*) набива́ть битко́м; (*block*) загромажда́ть [-мозди́ть]; *v/i.* закли́ни(ва)ть
jangle ['dʒæŋgl] издава́ть [-да́ть] ре́зкий звук
janitor ['dʒænɪtə] дво́рник
January ['dʒænjʊərɪ] янва́рь *m*
Japanese [dʒæpə'niːz] **1.** япо́нский; **2.** япо́нец *m*, -нка *f*; ***the ~*** *pl.* япо́нцы *pl.*
jar[1] [dʒɑː] (*vessel, usu. of glass*) ба́нка
jar[2] [~] **1.** *v/t.* толка́ть [-кну́ть]; *v/i.* ре́зать слух; **2.** толчо́к; (*shock*) потрясе́ние
jaundice ['dʒɔːndɪs] *med.* желту́ха; *fig.* жёлчность *f*; **~d** [~t] желту́шный; *fig.* зави́стливый
jaunt [dʒɔːnt] пое́здка, прогу́лка; ***let's go for a ~ to London*** дава́й-ка съе́здим в Ло́ндон; **~y** ['dʒɔːntɪ] □ беспе́чный; бо́йкий
javelin ['dʒævlɪn] *sport* копьё
jaw [dʒɔː] че́люсть *f*; **~s** *pl.* рот; *animal's* пасть *f*; **~bone** че́люстная кость *f*
jazz [dʒæz] джаз
jealous ['dʒeləs] □ ревни́вый; зави́стливый; **~y** [~ɪ] ре́вность *f*; за́висть *f*
jeans [dʒiːnz] *pl.* джи́нсы *pl.*
jeep® [dʒiːp] *mil.* джип, вездехо́д
jeer [dʒɪə] **1.** насме́шка, издёвка; **2.** насмеха́ться, глуми́ться (***at*** над T)
jelly ['dʒelɪ] **1.** желе́ *n indecl.*; (*aspic*) сту́день *m*; **2.** засты́(ва́)ть; **~fish** меду́за
jeopardize ['dʒepədaɪz] подверга́ть опа́сности, [по]ста́вить под угро́зу
jerk [dʒɜːk] **1.** рыво́к; толчо́к; ***the car stopped with a ~*** маши́на ре́зко останови́лась; **2.** ре́зко толка́ть или дёргать; дви́гаться толчка́ми; **~y** ['dʒɜːkɪ] □ отры́вистый; *movement* су́дорожный; (*bumpy*) тря́ский; **~ily** *adv.* рывка́ми
jersey ['dʒɜːzɪ] *fabric, garment* дже́рси *indecl.*
jest [dʒest] **1.** шу́тка; ***in ~*** в шу́тку; **2.** [по]шути́ть
jet [dʒet] **1.** *of water, gas, etc.* струя́; **2.** бить струёй; **3.** *ae.* реакти́вный самолёт; *attr.* реакти́вный;
jetty ['dʒetɪ] *naut.* при́стань *f*
Jew [dʒuː] евре́й(-ка *f*) *m*
jewel ['dʒuːəl] драгоце́нный ка́мень *m.*; **~(l)er** [~ə] ювели́р; **~(le)ry** [~rɪ] драгоце́нности *f/pl.*
Jew|ess ['dʒuːɪs] евре́йка; **~ish** [~ɪʃ] евре́йский
jiffy ['dʒɪfɪ] *coll.* миг, мгнове́ние
jigsaw ['dʒɪgsɔː]: **~ (*puzzle*)** соста́вная карти́нка-зага́дка
jilt [dʒɪlt] бро́сить *pf.*
jingle ['dʒɪŋgl] **1.** звон, звя́канье; **2.** [за]звене́ть, звя́кать [-кнуть]
jitters ['dʒɪtəz] не́рвное возбужде́ние; ***she's got the ~*** она трясётся от стра́ха
job [dʒɒb] рабо́та, труд; де́ло; ***by the ~*** сде́льно; ***it's a good ~ ...***

хорошо́, что ...; ***it's just the ~*** э́то то, что ну́жно; ***know one's ~*** знать своё де́ло; **~ber** ['dʒɒbə] занима́ющийся случа́йной рабо́той; бро́кер, ма́клер
jockey ['dʒɒkɪ] жоке́й
jocose [dʒəʊ'kəʊs] шутли́вый; *mood* игри́вый
jocular ['dʒɒkjʊlə] шутли́вый
jog [dʒɔg] **1.** толчо́к (*a. fig.*); тря́ская езда́; **2.** *v/t.* толка́ть [-кну́ть]; *v/i.* (*mst.* ***~ along,***) бе́гать (бежа́ть) трусцо́й; трясти́сь; *fig.* понемно́гу продвига́ться; **~ger** люби́тель *m* оздорови́тельного бе́га
join [dʒɔɪn] **1.** *v/t.* (*connect*) соединя́ть [-ни́ть], присоединя́ть [-ни́ть]; *a company* присоединя́ться [-ни́ться] к (Д); всупи́ть в чле́ны (Р); ***~ hands*** объединя́ться [-ни́ться]; бра́ться за́ руки; *v/i.* соединя́ться [-ни́ться]; (*unite*) объединя́ться [-ни́ться]; ***~ in with*** присоединя́ться [-ни́ться] к (Д); ***~ up*** поступа́ть [-и́ть] на вое́нную слу́жбу; **2.** соедине́ние; *tech.* шов
joiner ['dʒɔɪnə] сто́ляр
joint [dʒɔɪnt] **1.** *tech.* соедине́ние; стык; *anat.* суста́в; *of meat* кусо́к мя́са для жа́рения; ***put out of ~*** вы́вихнуть *pf.*; **2.** □ объединённый; о́бщий; ***~ owners*** совладе́льцы; ***~ venture*** совме́стное предприя́тие; **~-stock** акционе́рный капита́л; ***~ company*** акционе́рное о́бщество
jok|e [dʒəʊk] **1.** шу́тка, остро́та; **2.** *v/i.* [по]шути́ть; *v/t.* поддра́знивать [-ни́ть]; ***~ing apart ...*** е́сли говори́ть серьёзно; шу́тки в сто́рону; **~er** ['dʒəʊkə] шутни́к *m*, -ни́ца *f*
jolly ['dʒɒlɪ] **1.** весёлый, ра́достный; **2.** *adv.* о́чень; ***it's ~ hard ...*** черто́вски тру́дно ...
jolt [dʒəʊlt] **1.** трясти́ [тряхну́ть], встря́хивать [-хну́ть]; **2.** толчо́к; *fig.* встря́ска
jostle ['dʒɒsl] **1.** толка́ть(ся); тесни́ть(ся); **2.** толчо́к; *in crowd* толкотня́, да́вка
jot [dʒɒt] **1.** ничто́жное коли́чество, йо́та; ***not a ~ of truth*** ни ка́пли пра́вды; **2.** ***~ down*** бе́гло набро-са́ть *pf.*, кра́тко записа́ть *pf.*
journal ['dʒɜːnl] журна́л; дневни́к; **~ism** ['dʒɜːnəlɪzəm] журнали́стика; **~ist** [~ɪst] журнали́ст
journey ['dʒɜːnɪ] **1.** пое́здка, путеше́ствие; ***go on a ~*** отпра́виться *pf.* в путеше́ствие; **2.** путеше́ствовать
jovial ['dʒəʊvɪəl] весёлый, общи́тельный
joy [dʒɔɪ] ра́дость *f*, удово́льствие; **~ful** ['dʒɔɪfl] □ ра́достный, весёлый; **~less** [~lɪs] □ безра́достный; **~ous** [~əs] □ ра́достный, весёлый
jubil|ant ['dʒuːbɪlənt] лику́ющий; **~ee** ['dʒuːbɪliː] юбиле́й
judge [dʒʌdʒ] **1.** судья́ *m* (*a. sport*); *art* знато́к, цени́тель *m*; *in competition* член жюри́, *pl.* жюри́ *pl. indecl.*; **2.** *v/i.* суди́ть; быть арби́тром в спо́ре; ***~ for yourself ...*** посуди́ сам ...; *v/t.* суди́ть о (П); (*decide the merit of*) оце́нивать [-ни́ть]; (*condemn*) осужда́ть [осуди́ть], порица́ть
judg(e)ment ['dʒʌdʒmənt] *law* пригово́р, реше́ние суда́; сужде́ние; (*good sense*) рассуди́тельность *f*; (*opinion*) мне́ние, взгляд
judicial [dʒuː'dɪʃl] □ суде́бный
judicious [dʒuː'dɪʃəs] □ здравомы́слящий, рассуди́тельный; **~ness** [~nɪs] рассуди́тельность *f*
judo ['dʒuːdəʊ] дзюдо́ *n indecl.*
jug [dʒʌg] (*vessel*) кувши́н; *sl.* (*prison*) тюрьма́
juggle ['dʒʌgl] **1.** фо́кус, трюк; **2.** жонгли́ровать (*a. fig.*); **~r** [~ə] жонглёр
juic|e [dʒuːs] сок; **~y** ['dʒuːsɪ] □ со́чный; *gossip, etc.* сма́чный, пика́нтный
July [dʒu'laɪ] ию́ль *m*
jumble ['dʒʌmbl] **1.** пу́таница, беспоря́док; **2.** толка́ться; переме́шивать(ся); дви́гаться беспоря́дочным о́бразом; *chiefly Brt.* ***~ sale*** благотвори́тельная распрода́жа
jump [dʒʌmp] **1.** прыжо́к; скачо́к (*a. fig.*); **2.** *v/i.* пры́гать [-гнуть]; скака́ть; ***~ at** an offer, etc.* охо́тно приня́ть *pf.*, ухва́тываться [ухвати́ться] за (В); ***~ to conclusions*** де́лать поспе́шные вы́воды; ***~ to one's feet*** вскочи́ть *pf.* (на́ ноги); ***the strange noise made me ~*** э́тот стра́нный звук заста́вил меня́

J

вздрóгнуть; *v/t.* перепрыгивать [-гнуть]
jumper[1] ['dʒʌmpə] (*horse, athlete*) прыгýн
jumper[2] [~] (*garment*) джéмпер
jumpy ['dʒʌmpɪ] нéрвный
junct|ion ['dʒʌŋkʃn] соединéние (*a. el.*); *rail.* железнодорóжный ýзел; (*crossroads*) перекрёсток; **~ure** [~ktʃə]: ***at this ~*** в э́тот момéнт
June [dʒu:n] ию́нь *m*
jungle ['dʒʌŋgl] джýнгли *f/pl.*; густы́е зáросли *f/pl.*
junior ['dʒu:nɪə] **1.** *in age, rank* млáдший; молóже (***to*** Р *or* чем И); **2.** (*person*) млáдший
junk [dʒʌŋk] рýхлядь *f*, хлам, от - брóсы *m/pl.*
junta ['dʒʌntə] хýнта
juris|diction [dʒʊərɪs'dɪkʃn] отправлéние правосýдия; юрисдúкция; **~prudence** [dʒʊərɪs'pru:dəns] юриспрудéнция
juror ['dʒʊərə] *law* присяжный
jury ['dʒʊrɪ] *law* присяжные *m/pl.*; *in competition* жюри́ *n indecl.*; **~man** присяжный; член жюри́
just [dʒʌst] **1.** □ *adj.* справедли́вый; (*exact*) вéрный, тóчный; **2.** *adv.* тóчно, как раз, и́менно; тóлько что; прямо; ***~ now*** сейчáс, сию́ минýту; тóлько что
justice ['dʒʌstɪs] справедли́вость *f*; *law* правосýдие; судья́ *m*
justifiable ['dʒʌstɪ'faɪəbl] оправданный
justification [dʒʌstɪfɪ'keɪʃn] оправдáние; (*ground*) основáние
justify ['dʒʌstɪfaɪ] оправдывать [-дать]
justly ['dʒʌstlɪ] справедли́во
justness ['dʒʌstnɪs] справедли́вость *f*
jut [dʒʌt] (*a.* ***~ out***) выступáть, вы́да(вá)ться
juvenile ['dʒu:vənaɪl] ю́ный, ю́ношеский; *delinquent* несовершеннолéтний

K

kaleidoscope [kə'laɪdəskəʊp] калейдоскóп (*a. fig.*)
kangaroo [kæŋgə'ru:] кенгурý *m/f indecl.*
karate [kə'rɑ:tɪ] каратé
keel [ki:l] **1.** киль *m*; **2.** ***~ over*** опроки́дывать(ся) [-и́нуть(ся)]
keen [ki:n] □ (*sharp*) óстрый (*a. fig.*); (*acute*) проницáтельный; (*intense*) си́льный; (*enthusiastic*) стрáстный; ***be ~ on*** óчень люби́ть (В), стрáстно увлекáться (Т)
keep [ki:p] **1.** содержáние; (*food*) пропитáние; ***for ~s*** *coll.* навсегдá; **2.** [*irr.*] *v/t. com* держáть; сохраня́ть [-ни́ть], храни́ть; (*manage*) содержáть; *diary* вести́; *word* [с]держáть; ***~ company with*** поддéрживать знакóмство с (Т); ухáживать за (Т); ***~ waiting*** заставля́ть ждать; ***~ away*** не подпускáть (***from*** к Д); ***~ in*** не выпускáть; *hat, etc.* ***~ on*** не снимáть; ***~ up*** поддéрживать [-жáть]; **3.** *v/i.* держáться; удéрживаться (-жáться) (***from*** от Р); (*remain*) ост(ав)áться; *of food* не пóртиться; ***~ doing*** продолжáть дéлать; ***~ away*** держáться в отдалéнии; ***~ from*** воздéрживаться [-жáться] от (Р); ***~ off*** держáться в сторонé от (Р); ***~ on*** (*talk*) продолжáть говори́ть; ***~ to*** придéрживаться (Р); ***~ up*** держáться бóдро; ***~ up with*** держáться наравнé с (Т), идти́ в нóгу с (Т)
keep|er ['ki:pə] (*custodian*) храни́тель *m*; **~ing** ['ki:pɪŋ] хранéние; содержáние; ***be in*** (***out of***) ***~ with ...*** (не) соотвéтствовать (Д); **~sake** ['ki:pseɪk] сувени́р, подáрок на пáмять

keg [keg] бочо́нок
kennel ['kenl] конура́
kept [kept] *pt. и pt. p. от* ***keep***
kerb(stone) ['kɜːb(stəʊn)] поре́брик
kerchief ['kɜːtʃɪf] (головно́й) плато́к; косы́нка
kernel ['kɜːnl] зерно́, зёрнышко; *of nut* ядро́; *fig.* суть *f*
kettle ['ketl] ча́йник; ***that's a different ~ of fish*** э́то совсе́м друго́е де́ло; **~drum** лита́вра
key [kiː] **1.** ключ (*a. fig.*); код; *mus., tech.* кла́виш(а); *mus.* ключ, тона́льность *f*; *fig.* тон; **2.** *mus.* настра́ивать [-ро́ить]; ***~ up*** *fig.* придава́ть реши́мость (Д); ***be ~ed up*** быть в взви́нченном состоя́нии; **~board** клавиату́ра; **~hole** замо́чная сква́жина; **~note** основна́я но́та ключа́; *fig.* основна́я мысль *f*; **~stone** *fig.* краеуго́льный ка́мень *m*
kick [kɪk] **1.** *with foot* уда́р; пино́к; *coll.* (*stimulus, pleasure*) удово́льствие; **2.** *v/t.* ударя́ть [уда́рить]; *horse* брыка́ть [-кну́ть]; ***~ out*** (*eject, dismiss*) выгоня́ть [вы́гнать]; вышвы́ривать [вы́швырнуть]; *v/i.* брыка́ться [-кну́ться], ляга́ться [ля́гнуться]; (*complain, resist*) [вос-]проти́виться
kid [kɪd] **1.** козлёнок; (*leather*) ла́йка; *coll.* ребёнок; **2.** *coll.* (*pretend*) притворя́ться [-ри́ться]; (*deceive as a joke*) шутли́во обма́нывать [-ну́ть]
kidnap ['kɪdnæp] похища́ть [-хи́тить]; **~(p)er** [~ə] похити́тель *m*; (*extortionist*) вымога́тель *m*
kidney ['kɪdnɪ] *anat.* по́чка; **~ bean** фасо́ль *f*; **~ machine** *аппарат:* иску́сственная по́чка
kill [kɪl] уби́(ва́)ть; (*slaughter*) заби́(ва́)ть; *fig.* [по]губи́ть; ***~ time*** убива́ть вре́мя; **~er** ['kɪlə] уби́йца *m/f.*; **~ing** [~ɪŋ] (*exhausting*) уби́йственный; (*amusing*) умори́тельный; ***the work is really ~*** рабо́та про́сто на изно́с
kin [kɪn] родня́; ***next of ~*** ближа́йшие ро́дственники
kind [kaɪnd] **1.** □ до́брый, серде́чный; **2.** сорт, разнови́дность *f*; род; ***nothing of the ~*** ничего́ подо́бного; ***pay in ~*** плати́ть нату́рой; *fig.* отблагодари́ть; *for bad deed* [от-] плати́ть той же моне́той; **~-hearted** добросерде́чный
kindle ['kɪndl] разжига́ть [-же́чь]; воспламеня́ть [-ни́ть]; *interest* возбужда́ть [-ди́ть]
kindling ['kɪndlɪŋ] расто́пка
kind|ly ['kaɪndlɪ] до́брый; **~ness** [~nɪs] доброта́; до́брый посту́пок; ***do s.o. a ~*** ока́з(ыв)а́ть кому́-л. любе́зность *f*
kindred ['kɪndrɪd] **1.** ро́дственный; **2.** родня́; ро́дственники
king [kɪŋ] коро́ль *m*; **~dom** ['kɪŋdəm] короле́вство; *bot. zo.* (расти́тельное, живо́тное) ца́рство; **~ly** [~lɪ] короле́вский, ца́рственный
kink [kɪŋk] *in metal* изги́б; *fig., in character* стра́нность *f*; причу́да
kin|ship ['kɪnʃɪp] родство́; **~sman** ['kɪnzmən] ро́дственник
kiosk ['kiːɒsk] кио́ск; *Brt.* ***telephone ~*** телефо́нная бу́дка
kip [kɪp] *chiefly Brt. coll.* (*bed*) ко́йка; (*sleep*) сон; ***~ down*** [по]кема́рить; устро́иться; вздремну́ть *pf.*
kiss [kɪs] **1.** поцелу́й; **2.** [по]целова́ть(ся)
kit [kɪt] *mil.* ли́чное снаряже́ние; ***first-aid ~*** апте́чка; ***tool ~*** набо́р инструме́нтов; компле́кт принадле́жностей
kitchen ['kɪtʃɪn] ку́хня
kite [kaɪt] (бума́жный) змей
kitten ['kɪtn] котёнок
knack [næk] уме́ние, сноро́вка; ***get the ~*** научи́ться *pf.* (***of*** Д), приобрести́ *pf.* на́вык
knapsack ['næpsæk] ра́нец, рюкза́к
knave [neɪv] *cards* вале́т
knead [niːd] [с]меси́ть
knee [niː] коле́но; **~cap** *anat.* коле́нная ча́шка; **~l** [niːl] [*irr.*] станови́ться на коле́ни; стоя́ть на коле́нях (***to*** пе́ред Т)
knelt [nelt] *pt. и pt. p. от* ***kneel***
knew [njuː] *pt. от* ***know***
knickknack ['nɪknæk] безделу́шка
knife [naɪf] **1.** (*pl.* **knives**) нож; **2.** зака́лывать [заколо́ть] ножо́м
knight [naɪt] **1.** ры́царь *m*; *chess* конь *m*; **2.** *modern use* жа́ловать

ти́тул; **~ly** [~lı] ры́царский (*a. fig.*)
knit [nıt] [*irr.*] [с]вяза́ть; (*~ together*) *med.* сраста́ться [срасти́сь]; **~ *one's brows*** хму́рить бро́ви; **~ting** ['nıtıŋ] **1.** вяза́ние; **2.** вяза́льный
knives [naıvz] *pl. om* ***knife***
knob [nɒb] (*swelling*) ши́шка; (*door ~*) ру́чка; *on radio, etc.* кно́пка
knock [nɒk] **1.** стук; *on the head, etc.* уда́р; **2.** ударя́ть(ся) [уда́рить(ся)]; [по]стуча́ть(ся); *coll.* ***~ about*** разъезжа́ть по све́ту; ***~ down*** сбива́ть с ног; *mot.* сбить *pf.* маши́ной; ***be ~ed down*** быть сби́тым маши́ной; ***~ off work*** прекраща́ть рабо́ту; ***~ off*** стря́хивать [-хну́ть], сма́хивать [-хну́ть]; ***~ out*** вы́би(ва́)ть, выкола́чивать [вы́колотить]; *sport.* нокаути́ро-вать (*im*)*pf.*; ***~ over*** сбива́ть [сбить] с ног; *object* опроки́дывать [-ки́нуть]; **~-out** нока́ут (*a.* ***~ blow***)
knoll [nəʊl] холм, бугóр
knot [nɒt] **1.** у́зел; *in wood* сук, сучо́к; ***get tied up in ~s*** запу́тываться [-таться]; **2.** завя́зывать у́зел (*or* узло́м); спу́т(ыв)ать; **~ty** ['nɒtı] узлова́тый; сучкова́тый; *fig.* тру́дный
know [nəʊ] [*irr.*] знать; быть знако́мым с (Т); (*recognize*) узн(ава́)ть; ***~ French*** говори́ть по-францу́зски; ***be in the ~*** быть в ку́рсе де́ла; ***come to ~*** узн(ав)а́ть; **know-how** уме́ние; *tech.* но́у-ха́у; **~ing** ['nəʊıŋ] □ ло́вкий, хи́трый; *look* многозначи́тельный; **~ledge** ['nɒlıdʒ] зна́ние; ***to my ~*** по мои́м све́дениям; **~n** [nəʊn] *pt. p. om* ***know***; ***come to be ~*** сде́латься *pf.* изве́стным; ***make ~*** объявля́ть [-ви́ть]
knuckle ['nʌkl] **1.** суста́в па́льца руки́; **2.** ***~ down***, ***~ under*** уступа́ть [-пи́ть]; подчиня́ться [-ни́ться]
Koran [kə'rɑːn] Кора́н

L

label ['leıbl] **1.** ярлы́к (*a. fig.*); этике́тка; *tie-on* би́рка; *stick-on* накле́йка; **2.** накле́ивать/привя́зывать ярлы́к на (В)/к (Д) (*a. fig.*)
laboratory [lə'bɒrətrı] лаборато́рия; ***~ assistant*** лабора́нт *m*, -ка *f*
laborious [lə'bɔːrıəs] □ тру́дный
labo(u)r ['leıbə] **1.** труд; рабо́та; (*childbirth*) ро́ды *pl.*; ***forced ~*** принуди́тельные рабо́ты *f/pl.*; ***~ exchange*** би́ржа труда́; **2.** рабо́чий; **3.** *v/i.* труди́ться, рабо́тать; прилага́ть уси́лия; **~ed** [~d] вы́мученный; тру́дный; **~er** [~rə] рабо́чий; **~-intensive** трудоёмкий
lace [leıs] **1.** кру́жево; (*shoe ~*) шнуро́к; **2.** [за]шнурова́ть]
lacerate ['læsəreıt] раздира́ть [разодра́ть]; (*cut*) разреза́ть [-ре́зать]
lack [læk] **1.** недоста́ток, нехва́тка; отсу́тствие (Р); **2.** испы́тывать недоста́ток, нужду́ в (П); не хвата́ть [-ти́ть], недостава́ть; ***he ~s courage*** у него́ не хвата́ет му́жества
lacquer ['lækə] **1.** лак; **2.** [от]лакирова́ть, покрыва́ть [-ы́ть] ла́ком
lad [læd] (*boy*) ма́льчик; (*fellow*) па́рень *m*; (*youth*) ю́ноша *m*
ladder ['lædə] приставна́я ле́стница, стремя́нка; *in stocking* спусти́вшаяся петля́
laden ['leıdn] нагружённый; *fig.* обременённый
ladies, ladies (room), the ladies' ['leıdız] же́нский туале́т; *coll.* (*lavatory*) же́нская убо́рная
ladle ['leıdl] **1.** *tech.* ковш; черпа́к; *for soup* поло́вник; **2.** отче́рпывать [отчерпну́ть]; *soup* разли́(-ва́)ть (*a.* ***~ out***)
lady ['leıdı] да́ма; *title* ле́ди *f indecl.*; **~bird** бо́жья коро́вка
lag [læg] (*trail*) тащи́ться (сза́ди); отст(ав)а́ть (*a.* ***~ behind***)

laggard ['lægəd] медли́тельный, вя́лый челове́к; отстаю́щий
lagoon [lə'gu:n] лагу́на
laid [leɪd] *pt.* и *pt. p. от* ***lay***
lain [leɪn] *pt. p. от* ***lie***²
lair [leə] ло́говище, берло́га
lake [leɪk] о́зеро
lamb [læm] **1.** ягнёнок; (*food*) бара́нина; **2.** [о]ягни́ться; **~skin** овчи́на, ове́чья шку́ра
lame [leɪm] **1.** □ хромо́й; *fig. excuse* сла́бый, неубеди́тельный; **2.** [из]уве́чить, [ис]кале́чить
lament [lə'ment] **1.** сетова́ние, жа́лоба; **2.** [по]се́товать; опла́к(ив)ать; **~able** ['læməntəbl] жа́лкий; печа́льный; **~ation** [læmən'teɪʃn] жа́лоба, плач
lamp [læmp] ла́мпа; *in street* фона́рь *m*
lampoon [læm'pu:n] па́сквиль *m*
lamppost фона́рный столб
lampshade абажу́р
land [lænd] **1.** земля́; (*not sea*) су́ша; (*soil*) земля́, по́чва; (*country*) страна́; **~ *register*** земе́льный рее́стр; ***travel by ~*** е́хать (е́здить) су́шей/назе́мным тра́нспортом; **2.** *of ship passengers* выса́живать(ся) [вы́садить(ся)]; *of aircraft* приземля́ться [-ли́ться]
landing ['lændɪŋ] вы́садка; *ae.* приземле́ние, поса́дка; при́стань *f*
land|lady хозя́йка; **~lord** хозя́ин; **~mark** ориенти́р; *fig.* (*turning point*) ве́ха; **~-owner** землевладе́лец; **~scape** ['lændskeɪp] ландша́фт, пейза́ж; **~slide** о́ползень *m*
lane [leɪn] тропи́нка; *in town* переу́лок; *of traffic* ряд
language ['læŋgwɪdʒ] язы́к (речь); ***strong ~*** си́льные выраже́ния *n/pl.*, брань *f*
languid ['læŋgwɪd] □ то́мный
languish ['læŋgwɪʃ] (*lose strength*) [за]ча́хнуть; (*pine*) тоскова́ть, томи́ться
languor ['læŋgə] апати́чность *f*; томле́ние; то́мность *f*
lank ['læŋk] □ высо́кий и худо́й; *hair* прямо́й; **~y** ['læŋkɪ] □ долговя́зый
lantern ['læntən] фона́рь *m*
lap¹ [læp] **1.** по́ла; *anat.* коле́ни *n/pl*; *fig.* ло́но; *sport.* круг; **2.** перекры́(ва́)ть
lap² [~] *v/t* (*drink*) [вы́]лака́ть; жа́дно пить; *v/i.* плеска́ться
lapel [lə'pel] ла́цкан
lapse [læps] **1.** *of time* ход; (*slip*) оши́бка, про́мах; *moral* паде́ние; **2.** [в]пасть; приня́ться *pf.* за ста́рое; (*expire*) истека́ть [-е́чь]; ***~ into silence*** умолка́ть [умо́лкнуть]
larceny ['lɑ:sənɪ] кра́жа, воровство́
lard [lɑ:d] топлёное свино́е са́ло
larder ['lɑ:də] кладова́я
large [lɑ:dʒ] □ большо́й; (*substantial*) кру́пный; (*too big*) вели́к; ***at ~*** на свобо́де; **~ly** ['lɑ:dʒlɪ] в значи́тельной сте́пени; в основно́м, гла́вным о́бразом; **~-scale** кру́пный, крупномасшта́бный
lark [lɑ:k] жа́воронок; *fig.* шу́тка, прока́за, заба́ва
larva ['lɑ:və] *zo.* личи́нка
laryngitis [lærɪn'dʒaɪtɪs] ларинги́т
larynx ['lærɪŋks] горта́нь *f*
lascivious [lə'sɪvɪəs] □ похотли́вый
laser ['leɪzə] ла́зер
lash [læʃ] **1.** плеть *f*; (*whip*) кнут; (*blow*) уда́р; (*eye ~*) ресни́ца; **2.** хлеста́ть [-ну́ть]; (*fasten*) привя́зывать [-за́ть]; *fig.* бичева́ть
lass, **lassie** [læs, 'læsɪ] де́вушка, де́вочка
lassitude ['læsɪtju:d] уста́лость *f*
last¹ [lɑ:st] **1.** *adj.* после́дний; про́шлый; кра́йний; ***~ but one*** предпосле́дний; ***~ night*** вчера́ ве́чером; **2.** коне́ц; ***at ~*** наконе́ц; ***at long ~*** в конце́ концо́в; **3.** *adv.* в после́дний раз; по́сле всех; в конце́
last² [~] продолжа́ться [-до́лжиться]; [про]дли́ться; (*suffice*) хвата́ть [-ти́ть]; (*hold out*) сохраня́ться [-ни́ться]
lasting ['lɑ:stɪŋ] □ дли́тельный; *peace* про́чный
lastly ['lɑ:stlɪ] наконе́ц
latch [lætʃ] **1.** щеко́лда, задви́жка; замо́к с защёлкой; **2.** запира́ть [запере́ть]
late [leɪt] по́здний; (*delayed*) запозда́лый; (*former*) неда́вний; (*deceased*) поко́йный; *adv.* по́здно; ***at (the) ~st*** не поздне́е; ***of ~*** после́днее вре́мя; ***be ~*** опа́здывать [опозда́ть]; **~ly** ['leɪtlɪ] неда́вно; в по-

L

сле́днее вре́мя

latent ['leɪtnt] скры́тый

lateral ['lætərəl] □ боково́й

lathe [leɪð] тока́рный стано́к

lather ['lɑːðə] **1.** мы́льная пе́на; **2.** *v/t.* намы́ли(ва)ть; *v/i.* мы́литься, намы́ли(ва)ться

Latin ['lætɪn] **1.** лати́нский язы́к; **2.** лати́нский; ~ **American** латино-америка́нец, -нский

latitude ['lætɪtjuːd] *geogr., astr.* широта́; *fig.* свобо́да де́йствий

latter ['lætə] после́дний; второ́й; **~ly** [~lɪ] в после́днее вре́мя

lattice ['lætɪs] решётка (*a.* **~work**)

laudable ['lɔːdəbl] □ похва́льный

laugh [lɑːf] **1.** смех; **2.** смея́ться; ***~ at a p.*** высме́ивать [вы́смеять] (В), смея́ться над (Т); **~able** ['lɑːfəbl] □ смешно́й; **~ter** ['lɑːftə] смех

launch [lɔːntʃ] **1.** ка́тер; мото́рная ло́дка; **2.** *rocket* запуска́ть [-сти́ть]; *boat* спуска́ть [-сти́ть]; *fig.* пуска́ть в ход; **~ing** [~ɪŋ] → ***launch 2***; ~ **pad** пускова́я устано́вка; ~ **site** пускова́я площа́дка

laundry ['lɔːndrɪ] пра́чечная; бельё для сти́рки *or* из сти́рки

laurel ['lɒrəl] лавр

lavatory ['lævətrɪ] убо́рная

lavender ['lævəndə] лава́нда

lavish ['lævɪʃ] **1.** □ ще́дрый, расточи́тельный; **2.** расточа́ть [-чи́ть]

law [lɔː] зако́н; пра́вило; *law* пра́во; юриспруде́нция; ***lay down the ~*** кома́ндовать; **~-abiding** законопослу́шный, соблюда́ющий зако́н; ~ **court** суд; **~ful** ['lɔːfl] □ зако́нный; **~less** ['lɔːlɪs] □ *person* непоко́рный; *state* анархи́чный

lawn[1] [lɔːn] (*linen*) бати́ст

lawn[2] [~] (*grassy area*) лужа́йка, газо́н; **~chair** *Am.* шезло́нг; ~ **mower** газонокоси́лка

law|suit ['lɔːsuːt] суде́бный проце́сс; **~yer** ['lɔːjə] юри́ст; адвока́т

lax [læks] □ вя́лый; ры́хлый; (*careless*) небре́жный; (*not strict*) нестро́гий; **~ative** ['læksətɪv] слаби́тельное

lay[1] [leɪ] **1.** *pt. от* ***lie***[2]; **2.** (*secular*) све́тский

lay[2] [~] **1.** положе́ние, направле́ние; **2.** [*irr.*] *v/t.* класть [положи́ть]; *blame* возлага́ть [-ложи́ть]; *table* накры́(ва́)ть; ***~ in stocks*** запаса́ться [запасти́сь] (***of*** Т); ***~ low*** (*knock down*) повали́ть *pf.*; ***I was laid low by a fever*** меня свали́ла лихора́дка; ***~ off*** увольня́ть [-лить]; ***~ out*** выкла́дывать [вы́ложить]; *park, etc.* разби́(ва́)ть; ***~ up*** (*collect and store*) [на]копи́ть; прико́вывать к посте́ли; *v/i. of hen* [с]нести́сь; держа́ть пари́ (*a.* ***~ a wager***)

layer ['leɪə] слой, пласт, наслое́ние

layman ['leɪmən] миря́нин; (*amateur*) неспециали́ст, люби́тель *m*

lay|-off сокраще́ние ка́дров; **~out** планиро́вка

lazy ['leɪzɪ] лени́вый

lead[1] [led] свине́ц

lead[2] [liːd] **1.** руково́дство; инициати́ва; *sport.* ли́дерство; (*first place*) пе́рвое ме́сто; *thea.* гла́вная роль *f*; *el.* про́вод; **2.** [*irr.*] *v/t.* води́ть, [по-] вести́; приводи́ть [-вести́] (***to*** к Д); (*direct*) руководи́ть (Т); *cards* ходи́ть [пойти́] с (Р *pl.*); ***~ on*** соблазня́ть [-ни́ть]; *v/t.* вести́; быть пе́рвым; ***~ off*** отводи́ть; *v/i.* нач(ин)а́ть

leaden ['ledn] свинцо́вый (*a. fig.*)

leader ['liːdə] руководи́тель(ница *f*) *m*; ли́дер; *in newspaper* передова́я статья́

leading ['liːdɪŋ] **1.** руководя́щий; веду́щий; (*outstanding*) выдаю́щийся; ***~ question*** наводя́щий вопро́с; **2.** руково́дство; веде́ние

leaf [liːf] (*pl.*: **leaves**) лист (*bot. pl.*: ли́стья); (*leafage*) листва́; ***turn over a new ~*** нача́ть но́вую жизнь; **~let** ['liːflɪt] листо́вка

league [liːg] ли́га; ***in ~ with*** в сою́зе с (Т)

leak [liːk] **1.** течь *f*; *of gas, etc.* уте́чка (*a. fig.*); **2.** дава́ть течь, пропуска́ть во́ду; ***~ out*** проса́чиваться [-сочи́ться] (*a. fig.*); **~age** ['liːkɪdʒ] проса́чивание; **~y** ['liːkɪ] протека́ющий, с те́чью

lean[1] [liːn] [*irr.*] прислоня́ть(ся) [-ни́ть(ся)] (***against*** к Д); опира́ться [опере́ться] (***on*** на В) (*a. fig.*); наклоня́ть(ся) [-ни́ть(ся)] (*a. **~ forward***)

lean² [~] то́щий, худо́й; *meat* нежи́рный
leant [lent] *chiefly Brt. pt. p. от **lean***
leap [liːp] **1.** прыжо́к, скачо́к; **2.** [*a. irr.*] пры́гать [-гнуть], скака́ть *once* [скакну́ть]; **~t** [lept] *pt. p. от **leap***; **~ year** високо́сный год
learn [lɜːn] [*a. irr.*] изуча́ть [-чи́ть], [на]учи́ться (Д); ***~ from*** узн(ав)а́ть от (Р); **~ed** ['lɜːnɪd] □ учёный; **~ing** [~ɪŋ] уче́ние; учёность *f*, эруди́ция; **~t** [lɜːnt] *chiefly Brt. pt. p. от **learn***
lease [liːs] **1.** аре́нда; (*period*) срок аре́нды; ***long-term ~*** долгосро́чная аре́нда, ли́зинг; **2.** сдава́ть в аре́нду; брать в аре́нду
leash [liːʃ] поводо́к, при́вязь *f*
least [liːst] *adj.* мале́йший; наиме́ньший; *adv.* ме́нее всего́, в наиме́ньшей сте́пени; ***at*** (***the***) ***~*** по кра́йней ме́ре; ***not in the ~*** ничу́ть, ниско́лько; ***to say the ~*** мя́гко говоря́
leather ['leðə] **1.** ко́жа; **2.** ко́жаный
leave [liːv] **1.** разреше́ние, позволе́ние; (*absence, holiday*) о́тпуск; **2.** [*irr.*] *v/t.* оставля́ть [-а́вить]; (*abandon*) покида́ть [поки́нуть]; предоставля́ть [-а́вить]; (*bequeath, etc.*) оставля́ть; завеща́ть *im*(*pf*); ***~ it to me*** предоста́вь(те) э́то мне; ***~ off*** броса́ть [бро́сить]; *v/i.* уезжа́ть [уе́хать]; уходи́ть [уйти́]
leaves [liːvz] *pl. от **leaf***
leavings ['liːvɪŋz] оста́тки *m/pl.*
lecture ['lektʃə] **1.** ле́кция; (*reproof*) нота́ция; **2.** *v/i.* чита́ть ле́кции; *v/t.* чита́ть нота́цию; отчи́тывать [-ита́ть]; **~r** [~rə] (*speaker*) докла́дчик; *professional* ле́ктор; *univ.* преподава́тель *m*
led [led] *pt. и pt. p. от **lead***
ledge [ledʒ] вы́ступ, усту́п
ledger ['ledʒə] *fin.* гроссбу́х, бухга́лтерская кни́га
leech [liːtʃ] *zo.* пия́вка
leer [lɪə] смотре́ть и́скоса (***at*** на В); де́лать гла́зки кому́-нибу́дь; кри́во улыба́ться [улыбну́ться]
leeway ['liːweɪ] *naut.* дрейф; *fig.* ***make up ~*** навёрстывать упу́щенное
left¹ [left] *pt. и pt. p. от **leave***; ***be ~*** ост(ав)а́ться
left² [~] **1.** ле́вый; **2.** ле́вая сторона́; **~-hander** левша́ *m/f*
left-luggage| locker *rail. Brt.* автомати́ческая ка́мера хране́ния; **~ office** ка́мера хране́ния
leg [leg] нога́; *of table, etc.* но́жка; *of trousers* штани́на
legacy ['legəsɪ] (*bequest*) насле́дство; *fig.* (*heritage*) насле́дие
legal ['liːgl] □ зако́нный, лега́льный; правово́й; **~ize** [~gəlaɪz] узако́ни(ва)ть, легализова́ть (*im*)*pf.*
legend ['ledʒənd] леге́нда; **~ary** [~drɪ] легенда́рный
legible ['ledʒəbl] □ разбо́рчивый
legislat|ion [ledʒɪs'leɪʃn] законода́тельство; **~ive** ['ledʒɪslətɪv] законода́тельный; **~or** [~leɪtə] законода́тель *m*
legitima|cy [lɪ'dʒɪtɪməsɪ] зако́нность *f*; **~te 1.** [~meɪt] узако́ни(ва)ть; **2.** [~mɪt] зако́нный
leisure ['leʒə] досу́г; ***at your ~*** когда́ вам удо́бно; **~ly** *adv.* не спеша́, споко́йно; *adj.* неторопли́вый
lemon ['lemən] лимо́н; **~ade** [lemə'neɪd] лимона́д
lend [lend] [*irr.*] ода́лживать [одолжи́ть]; *money* дава́ть взаймы́; *fig.* д(ав)а́ть, прид(ав)а́ть; ***~ a hand*** помога́ть [-мо́чь]
length [leŋð] длина́; расстоя́ние; *of time* продолжи́тельность *f*; *of cloth* отре́з; ***at ~*** наконе́ц; *speak* подро́бно; ***go to any ~s*** быть гото́вым на всё; **~en** ['leŋθən] удлиня́ть(ся) [-ни́ть(ся)]; **~wise** [~waɪz] в длину́; вдоль; **~y** [~ɪ] дли́нный; *time* дли́тельный; *speech* растя́нутый; многосло́вный
lenient ['liːnɪənt] □ мя́гкий; снисходи́тельный
lens [lenz] ли́нза; *phot.* объекти́в; *anat.* хруста́лик; ***contact ~*** конта́ктная ли́нза
lent [lent] *pt. и pt. p. от **lend***
Lent [lent] вели́кий пост
lentil ['lentɪl] чечеви́ца
leopard ['lepəd] леопа́рд
less [les] **1.** (*comp. от **little***) ме́ньший; **2.** *adv.* ме́ньше, ме́нее; **3.** *prp.* ми́нус (Р); ***none the ~*** тем не ме́нее
lessen ['lesn] *v/t.* уменьша́ть

L

[умéньшить]; *v/i.* уменьшáться [умéньшиться]
lesser ['lesə] мéньший
lesson ['lesn] урóк; *fig.* **teach s.o. a ~** проучи́ть (В) *pf.*; **let this be a ~ to you** пусть э́то послу́жит тебé урóком
lest [lest] чтóбы не, как бы не
let [let] [*irr.*] оставля́ть [-áвить]; сдавáть внаём; позволя́ть [-вóлить] (Д), пускáть [пусти́ть]; **~ be** остáвить *pf.* в покóе; **~ alone** *adv.* не говоря́ ужé о ... (П); **~ down** опускáть [-сти́ть]; *fig.* подводи́ть [-вести́]; **~ go** выпускáть из рук; **~ o.s. go** дать *pf.* вóлю чу́вствам; увлекáться [увлéчься]; **~ into** *a secret, etc.* посвящáть [-яти́ть] в; **~ off** *gun* стреля́ть [вы́стрелить] из (Р); *steam mst. fig.* выпускáть [вы́пустить] пар; **~ out** выпускáть [вы́пустить]; **~ up** *Am.* ослабé(вá)ть
lethal ['li:θl] смертéльный, летáльный
lethargy ['leθədʒɪ] летарги́я; вя́лость *f*
letter ['letə] бу́ква; письмó; **capital (small) ~** заглáвная, прописнáя (стрóчная) бу́ква; **to the ~** буквáльно; **man of ~s** литерáтор; **registered ~** заказнóе письмó; **~ box** почтóвый я́щик; **~ing** [~rɪŋ] *f on gravestone, etc.* нáдпись *f*; *in book* размéр и фóрма букв
lettuce ['letɪs] салáт
level ['levl] **1.** горизонтáльный; (*even*) рóвный; (*equal*) одинáковый, рáвный, равномéрный; **draw ~ with** поравня́ться *pf.* с (Т); **keep a ~ head** сохраня́ть [-ни́ть] хладнокрóвие; **2.** у́ровень *m*; *fig.* масштáб; **~ of the sea** у́ровень мóря; **on the ~** чéстно, правди́во; **3.** *v/t.* вырáвнивать [вы́ровнять]; уравнивать [-вня́ть]; **~ to the ground** сровня́ть *pf.* с землёй; **~ up** повышáть урáвнивая; *v/i.* **~ at** прицéли(ва)ться в (В); **~ crossing** переéзд; **~headed** рассуди́тельный
lever ['li:və] рычáг
levy ['levɪ]: **~ taxes** взимáть налóги
lewd [lju:d] □ похотли́вый
liability [laɪə'bɪlətɪ] ответственность *f* (*a. law*); (*obligation*) обязáтельство; (*debt*) задóлженность *f*; *fig.* привéрженность *f*, склóнность *f*; **liabilities** *pl.* обязáтельства *n/pl.*; *fin.* долги́ *m/pl.*
liable ['laɪəbl] □ отвéтственный (за В); обя́занный; (*subject to*) подвéрженный; **be ~ to** быть предрасполóженным к (Д)
liar ['laɪə] лгун *m*, -ья *f*
libel ['laɪbəl] **1.** клеветá; **2.** [на]клеветáть на (В), оклеветáть (В) *pf.*
liberal ['lɪbərəl] **1.** □ (*generous*) щéдрый; (*ample*) оби́льный; *mst. pol.* либерáльный; **2.** либерáл(ка)
liberat|e ['lɪbəreɪt] освобождáть [-боди́ть]; **~ion** [lɪbə'reɪʃn] освобождéние; **~or** ['lɪbəreɪtə] освободи́тель *m*
liberty ['lɪbətɪ] свобóда; (*familiar or presumptuous behavio(u)r*) бесцеремóнность *f*; **be at ~** быть свобóдным; **take the ~ of** брать [взять] на себя́ смéлость; **take liberties with s.o.** позволя́ть себé вóльности с кем-л.
librar|ian [laɪ'breərɪən] библиотéкарь *m*; **~y** ['laɪbrərɪ] библиотéка
lice [laɪs] *pl. om* **louse**
licen|ce, *Am. also* **~se** ['laɪsəns] **1.** разрешéние; *comm.* лицéнзия; (*freedom*) вóльность *f*; **driving ~** води́тельские правá *n/pl.*; **2.** разрешáть [-ши́ть]; давáть прáво (В)
licentious [laɪ'senʃəs] □ распу́щенный
lick [lɪk] **1.** обли́зывание; **2.** лизáть [лизну́ть]; обли́зывать [-зáть]; *coll.* (*thrash*) [по]би́ть, [по]колоти́ть; **~ into shape** привести́ *pf.* в поря́док
lid [lɪd] кры́шка; (*eye ~*) вéко
lie¹ [laɪ] **1.** ложь *f*; **give the ~ to** обличáть во лжи; **2.** [со]лгáть
lie² [~] **1.** положéние; направлéние; **explore the ~ of the land** *fig.* зонди́ровать пóчву; **2.** [*irr.*] лежáть; быть располóженным, находи́ться; (*consist*) заключáться; **~ ahead** предстоя́ть (Д); **~ down** ложи́ться [лечь]; **~ in wait for** поджидáть (В) (спря́тавшись)
lieu [lju:]: **in ~ of** вмéсто (Р)
lieutenant [lef'tenənt] лейтенáнт
life [laɪf] жизнь *f*; (*way of ~*) óбраз

жи́зни; биогра́фия; (*vitality*) жи́вость *f*; **for ~** пожи́зненный; на всю жизнь; **~ sentence** пригово́р к пожи́зненному заключе́нию; **~boat** спаса́тельная шлю́пка; **~guard** спаса́тель *m*; **~ insurance** страхова́ние жи́зни; **~ jacket** спаса́тельный жиле́т; **~less** □ бездыха́нный, безжи́зненный; **~like** реалисти́чный; сло́вно живо́й; **~long** всю жизнь; **~time** вся жизнь *f*, це́лая жизнь *f*

lift [lɪft] **1.** лифт; *for goods*, *etc.* подъёмник; *fig.* (*high spirits*) воодушевле́ние; **give s.o. a ~** подвози́ть [-везти́] кого́-л.; **2.** *v/t.* поднима́ть [-ня́ть]; возвыша́ть [-вы́сить]; *sl.* [у]кра́сть; *v/i.* возвыша́ться [вы́ситься]; *of mist*, *etc.* поднима́ться [-ня́ться]

ligament ['lɪgəmənt] *anat.* свя́зка

light[1] [laɪt] **1.** свет; (*lighting*) освеще́ние; ого́нь *m*; *fig.* (*luminary*) свети́ло; **come to ~** стать изве́стным; обнару́живаться [-жится]; **will you give me a ~?** да́йте мне прикури́ть; **put a ~ to** зажига́ть [заже́чь]; **2.** све́тлый, я́сный; **3.** [*a. irr.*] *v/t.* зажига́ть [заже́чь]; освеща́ть [-ети́ть]; *v/i.* (*mst.* **~ up**) загора́ться [-ре́ться]; освеща́ться [-ети́ться]

light[2] [~] **1.** □ *adj.* лёгкий (*a. fig.*); **make ~ of** относи́ться несерьёзно к (Д); **travel ~** путеше́ствовать налегке́; **2. ~ on** неожи́данно натолкну́ться *pf.* на (В)

lighten ['laɪtn] освеща́ть [-ети́ть]; (*become brighter*) [по]светле́ть

lighter ['laɪtə] *for cigarettes*, *etc.* зажига́лка

light|-headed легкомы́сленный; **~-hearted** □ беззабо́тный; весёлый; **~house** мая́к

lighting ['laɪtɪŋ] освеще́ние

lightness лёгкость *f*

lightning [laɪtnɪŋ] мо́лния; **with ~ speed** молниено́сно; **~ conductor**, **~ rod** громоотво́д

lightweight *sport* боксёр лёгкого ве́са; легкове́сный (*a. fig.*)

like [laɪk] **1.** похо́жий, подо́бный; ра́вный; **as ~ as two peas** похо́жи как две ка́пли воды́; **such~** подо́бный тому́, тако́й; *coll.* **feel ~** хоте́ть (+ *inf.*); **what is he ~?** что он за челове́к?; **2.** не́что подо́бное; **~s** *pl.* скло́нности *f/pl.*, влече́ния *n/pl.*; **his ~** ему́ подо́бные; **3.** люби́ть; [за]хоте́ть; **how do you ~ London?** как вам нра́вится Ло́ндон?; **I should ~ to know** я хоте́л бы знать

likeable ['laɪkəbl] симпати́чный

like|lihood ['laɪklɪhʊd] вероя́тность *f*; **~ly** ['laɪklɪ] вероя́тный; (*suitable*) подходя́щий; **he is ~ to die** он вероя́тно умрёт; **as ~ as not** вполне́ возмо́жно

like|n ['laɪkən] уподобля́ть [-о́бить]; (*compare*) сра́внивать [-ни́ть]; **~ness** ['laɪknɪs] схо́дство; **~wise** [~waɪz] то́же, та́кже; подо́бно

liking ['laɪkɪŋ] расположе́ние (**for** к Д); **take a ~ to** полюби́ть *pf.* (В)

lilac ['laɪlək] **1.** сире́нь *f*; **2.** сире́невый, лило́вый

lily ['lɪlɪ] ли́лия; **~ of the valley** ла́ндыш

limb [lɪm] коне́чность *f*; *of tree* ве́тка

lime[1] [laɪm] *tree* ли́па

lime[2] [~] и́звесть *f*; **~light** свет ра́мпы; *fig.* центр внима́ния

limit ['lɪmɪt] преде́л, грани́ца; **be ~ed to** ограни́чивать(ся) (Т); **speed ~** преде́льная ско́рость *f*; **time ~** ограниче́ние во вре́мени; преде́льный срок; **~ation** [lɪmɪ'teɪʃn] ограниче́ние; **~ed** ['lɪmɪtɪd]: **~ (liability) company** компа́ния с ограни́ченной отве́тственностью; **~less** ['lɪmɪtlɪs] □ безграни́чный

limp[1] [lɪmp] **1.** [за]хрома́ть; **2.** прихра́мывание, хромота́

limp[2] [~] вя́лый; сла́бый; **her body went ~** те́ло её обмя́кло

limpid ['lɪmpɪd] прозра́чный

line [laɪn] **1.** ли́ния (*a. rail.*, *tel.*, *ae*); *typ.* строка́; *in drawing* черта́, штрих; (*fishing ~*) леса́; специа́льность *f*, заня́тие; **~s** *pl.* стро́ки; **~ of conduct** ли́ния поведе́ния; **hard ~s** *pl.* неуда́ча; **in ~ with** в согла́сии с (Т); **stand in ~** *Am.* стоя́ть в о́череди; **that's not in my ~** э́то не по мое́й ча́сти; **2.** *v/t.* разлино́вывать [-нова́ть]; *sew.* класть на

L

подкла́дку; *of trees, etc.* тяну́ться вдоль (Р); *v/i.* **~ up** выстра́иваться [вы́строиться] (в ряд)
linear ['lɪnɪə] лине́йный
linen ['lɪnɪn] **1.** полотно́; бельё; **2.** льняно́й
liner ['laɪnə] *naut.* ла́йнер; *ae.* возду́шный ла́йнер
linger ['lɪŋgə] [по]ме́длить; **~ over** заде́рживаться [-жа́ться] на (П)
lingerie ['læːnʒəriː] да́мское бельё
lining ['laɪnɪŋ] *of garment* подкла́дка; *tech.* оби́вка, облицо́вка
link [lɪŋk] **1.** звено́; связь *f* (*a. fig.*); соедине́ние; **2.** соединя́ть [-ни́ть]
linoleum [lɪ'nəʊlɪəm] лино́леум
linseed ['lɪnsiːd]: **~ oil** льняно́е ма́сло
lion ['laɪən] лев; **~ess** [~es] льви́ца
lip [lɪp] губа́; (*edge*) край; *coll.* (*impudence*) де́рзость *f*; **~stick** губна́я пома́да
liquid ['lɪkwɪd] **1.** жи́дкий; **2.** жи́дкость *f*
liquidat|e ['lɪkwɪdeɪt] ликвиди́ровать *im(pf.)*; *debt* выпла́чивать [вы́платить]; **~ion** [lɪkwɪ'deɪʃn] ликвида́ция; вы́плата до́лга
liquor ['lɪkə] спиртно́й напи́ток
lisp [lɪsp] **1.** шепеля́вость *f*; **2.** шепеля́вить
list¹ [lɪst] **1.** спи́сок, пе́речень *m*; **2.** вноси́ть в спи́сок; составля́ть спи́сок (Р)
list² [~] **1.** *naut.* крен; **2.** [на]крени́ться
listen ['lɪsn] [по]слу́шать; (*heed*) прислу́ш(ив)аться (**to** к Д); **~ in** (*eavesdrop*) подслу́ш(ив)ать (**to** В); слу́шать ра́дио; **~er** [~ə] слу́шатель(ница *f*) *m*
listless ['lɪstlɪs] апати́чный, вя́лый
lit [lɪt] *pt. и pt. p. om* **light¹**
literacy ['lɪtərəsɪ] гра́мотность *f*
literal ['lɪtərəl] □ буква́льный, досло́вный
litera|ry ['lɪtərərɪ] литерату́рный; **~te** [~rət] гра́мотный; **~ture** ['lɪtrətʃə] литерату́ра
lithe [laɪð] ги́бкий
lithography [lɪ'θɒgrəfɪ] литогра́фия
litre, *Am.* **liter** ['liːtə] литр
litter¹ ['lɪtə] **1.** помёт (припло́д); **2.** [о]щени́ться, [о]пороси́ться *и т. д.*
litter² [~] **1.** му́сор; **2.** [на]му́сорить, [на]сори́ть
little ['lɪtl] **1.** *adj.* ма́ленький, небольшо́й; *time* коро́ткий; **a ~ one** малы́ш; **2.** *adv.* немно́го, ма́ло; **3.** пустя́к; ме́лочь *f*; **a ~** немно́го; **~ by ~** ма́ло-пома́лу, постепе́нно; **not a ~** нема́ло
liturgy ['lɪtədʒɪ] *eccl.* литурги́я
live [lɪv] **1.** *com.* жить; существова́ть; **~ to see** дожи́(ва́)ть до (Р); **~ down**: **I'll never ~ it down** мне э́того никогда́ не забу́дут; **~ out** пережи́(ва́)ть; **~ up to expectations** опра́вдывать [-да́ть] (В); **2.** [laɪv] живо́й; *coals, etc.* горя́щий; *el.* под напряже́нием; **~lihood** ['laɪvlɪhʊd] сре́дства к существова́нию; **~liness** [~nɪs] жи́вость *f*; оживле́ние; **~ly** ['laɪvlɪ] живо́й; оживлённый
liver ['lɪvə] *anat.* пе́чень *f*; *cul.* печёнка
live|s [laɪvz] *pl. om* **life**; **~-stock** ['laɪvstɒk] дома́шний скот
livid ['lɪvɪd] ме́ртвенно-бле́дный; **~ with rage** взбешённый
living ['lɪvɪŋ] **1.** живо́й; живу́щий, существу́ющий; **2.** сре́дства существова́ния; жизнь *f*, о́браз жи́зни; **~ room** гости́ная
lizard ['lɪzəd] я́щерица
load [ləʊd] **1.** груз; но́ша; (*weight of cares, etc.*) бре́мя *n*; *tech.* нагру́зка; **2.** [на]грузи́ть; *gun* заряжа́ть [-ряди́ть]; *fig.* обременя́ть [-ни́ть]; **~ing** [ləʊdɪŋ] погру́зка; груз
loaf¹ [ləʊf] (*pl.* **loaves**) (*white*) бато́н; (*mst. brown*) буха́нка
loaf² [~] безде́льничать; шата́ться, слоня́ться без де́ла
loafer ['ləʊfə] безде́льник
loan [ləʊn] **1.** заём; *from bank* ссу́да; **the book is on ~** кни́га на рука́х; **2.** дава́ть взаймы́; дава́ть [дать] ссу́ду
loath [ləʊθ] (*reluctant*) несклóнный; **~e** [ləʊð] пита́ть отвраще́ние к (Д); **~some** ['ləʊðsəm] □ отврати́тельный
loaves [ləʊvz] *pl. om* **loaf**
lobby ['lɒbɪ] **1.** *in hotel* вестибю́ль *m*; *parl.* кулуа́ры *m/pl.*; (*group*) ло́бби; *thea.* фойе́ *n indecl.*; **2.** *parl.* пыта́ться возде́йствовать на

членов конгресса
lobe [ləʊb] *of ear* мочка
lobster ['lɒbstə] омар
local ['ləʊkəl] **1.** □ местный; **~ government** местные органы власти; **2.** местный житель *m*; (*a.* **~ train**) пригородный поезд; **~ity** [ləʊ'kælətɪ] местность *f*, район; (*neighbo(u)rhood*) окрестность *f*; **~ize** ['ləʊkəlaɪz] локализовать (*im*)*pf*.
locat|e [ləʊ'keɪt] *v/t.* определять место (P); располагать в определённом месте; назначать место для (P); **be ~d** быть расположенным; **~ion** [~ʃn] место; *Am.* местонахождение
lock¹ [lɒk] *of hair* локон
lock² [~] **1.** замок; *on canal* шлюз; **2.** *v/t.* запирать [запереть]; **~ in** запирать [запереть]; *v/i.* запираться [запереться]
lock|er ['lɒkə] запирающийся шкафчик; **~et** ['lɒkɪt] медальон; **~-out** локаут; **~smith** слесарь *m*
locomotive ['ləʊkəməʊtɪv] (*или* **~ engine**) локомотив, паровоз, тепловоз, электровоз
locust ['ləʊkəst] саранча
lodg|e [lɒdʒ] **1.** сторожка; (*mst.* **hunting ~**) охотничий домик; **2.** *v/t.* да(ва)ть помещение (Д); *v/i.* снимать комнату; *of bullet, etc.* застревать [-рять]; **~er** ['lɒdʒə] квартирант *m*, -ка *f*; **~ing** ['lɒdʒɪŋ]: **live in ~s** снимать комнату
loft [lɒft] чердак; **hay ~** сеновал; **~y** ['lɒftɪ] □ (*haughty*) высокомерный; *building* величественный; *style* возвышенный
log [lɒg] колода; бревно; **~ cabin** бревенчатая хижина
loggerhead ['lɒgəhed]: **be at ~s** быть в ссоре, ссориться (**with** с Т)
logic ['lɒdʒɪk] логика; **~al** [ˌlɒdʒɪkl] □ логический
loin [lɔɪn] филейная часть *f*; **~s** *pl.* поясница
loiter ['lɔɪtə] слоняться без дела; (*linger*) мешкать
loll [lɒl] сидеть/стоять развалясь
lone|liness ['ləʊnlɪnɪs] одиночество; **~ly** [~lɪ], **~some** [~səm] одинокий
long¹ [lɒŋ] **1.** долгий срок, долгое время *n*; **before ~** вскоре; **for ~** надолго; **2.** *adj.* длинный; долгий; медленный; **in the ~ run** в конце концов; **be ~** долго длиться; **3.** *adv.* долго; **as ~ ago as ...** ещё ...; **~ ago** давно; **so ~!** пока (до свидания)!; **~er** дольше; больше
long² [~] страстно желать, жаждать (**for** P), тосковать (по Д)
long-distance *attr.* дальний; *sport* на длинные дистанции; *tel.* междугородний
longing ['lɒŋɪŋ] **1.** □ тоскующий; **2.** сильное желание, стремление (к Д), тоска (по Д)
longitude ['lɒndʒɪtjuːd] *geogr.* долгота
long|-sighted дальнозоркий; **~-suffering** многострадальный; **~-term** долгосрочный; **~-winded** □ многословный
look [lʊk] **1.** взгляд; *in face, eyes* выражение; (*appearance*) вид, наружность *f* (*a.* **~s** *pl.*); **have a ~ at a th.** посмотреть *pf.* на (B); ознакомляться [-комиться] с (T); **2.** *v/i* [по]смотреть (**at** на B); выглядеть; **~ for** искать (B *or* P); **~ forward to** предвкушать [-усить] (B); с радостью ожидать (P); **~ into** рассматривать [-мотреть], разбираться [-зобраться]; **~ out!** берегись!; **~ (up)on** *fig.* смотреть как на (B); считать (за B); **~ with disdain** смотреть с презрением; **~ over** не замечать [-етить]; **~ through** просматривать [-мотреть]; **~ up** *in dictionary, etc.* [по]искать; (*visit*) навещать [-естить]
looker-on [lʊkər'ɒn] зритель *m*; (невольный) свидетель *m*
looking glass зеркало
lookout ['lʊkaʊt] (*view*) вид; (*prospects*) виды *m/pl.*, шансы *m/pl.*; **that is my ~** это моё дело
loom¹ [luːm] ткацкий станок
loom² [~] маячить, неясно вырисовываться
loop [luːp] **1.** петля; **2.** делать петлю; закреплять петлёй; **~hole** *mst. fig.* лазейка
loose [luːs] □ *com.* свободный; (*vague*) неопределённый; (*not*

close-fitting) просто́рный; (*not tight*)болта́ющийся, шата́ющийся; (*licentious*) распу́щенный; *earth* ры́хлый; **~n** ['luːsn] (*make loose*) ослабля́ть(ся) [-а́бить(ся)]; (*untie*) развя́зывать [-яза́ть]; разрыхля́ть [-ли́ть]; расша́тывать [-шата́ть]

loot [luːt] **1.** [о]гра́бить; **2.** добы́ча, награ́бленное добро́

lopsided [lɒp'saɪdɪd] кривобо́кий; кособо́кий

loquacious [lə'kweɪʃəs] болтли́вый

lord [lɔːd] лорд; (*ruler, master*) повели́тель *m*; ***the*** ♎ Госпо́дь *m*; ***my*** **~** [mɪ'lɔːd] мило́рд; ***the*** ♎***'s Prayer*** Отче наш; ***the*** ♎***'s Supper*** Та́йная ве́черя; **~ly** ['lɔːdlɪ] высокоме́рный

lorry ['lɒrɪ] *mot.* грузови́к

lose [luːz] [*irr.*] *v/t.* [по]теря́ть; *a chance, etc.* упуска́ть [-сти́ть]; *game, etc.* прои́грывать [-ра́ть]; **~ *o.s.*** заблуди́ться *pf.*; *v/i.* [по]теря́ть; *sport* прои́грывать [-ра́ть]; *of watch* отст(ав)а́ть

loss [lɒs] поте́ря, утра́та; *comm.* уще́рб, убы́ток; ***at a*** **~** в расте́рянности; ***with no*** **~** ***of time*** не теряя вре́мени

lost [lɒst] *pt. и pt. p. от* **lose**; ***be*** **~** пропада́ть [-па́сть]; (*perish*) погиба́ть [-ги́бнуть]; *fig.* растеря́ться *pf.*; **~** ***property office*** стол нахо́док

lot [lɒt] (*destiny*) жре́бий; у́часть *f*, до́ля; *comm.* (*consignment*) па́ртия това́ров; уча́сток земли́; *coll.* ма́сса, у́йма; ***draw*** **~s** броса́ть жре́бий; ***fall to a p.'s*** **~** вы́пасть *pf.* на чью-л. до́лю

lotion ['ləʊʃn] лосьо́н

lottery ['lɒtərɪ] лотере́я

loud [laʊd] □ гро́мкий, зву́чный; (*noisy*) шу́мный; *colo(u)r* крикли́вый, крича́щий

lounge [laʊndʒ] **1.** (*loll*) сиде́ть разваля́сь; (*walk idly*) слоня́ться; **2.** пра́здное времяпрепровожде́ние; *thea.* фойе́ *n indecl.*; *at airport* зал ожидания; *in house* гости́ная

lous|e [laʊs] (*pl.*: **lice**) вошь *f* (*pl.*: вши); **~y** ['laʊzɪ] вши́вый (*a. coll. fig.*); *sl.* парши́вый

lout [laʊt] ха́мский, неотёсанный челове́к

lovable ['lʌvəbl] □ привлека́тельный, ми́лый

love [lʌv] **1.** любо́вь *f*; влюблённость *f*; предме́т любви́; ***give*** (*or* ***send***) ***one's*** **~** ***to a p.*** передава́ть, посыла́ть приве́т (Д); ***in*** **~** ***with*** влюблённый в (В); ***make*** **~** ***to*** быть бли́зкими; занима́ться любо́вью; ***not for*** **~** ***or money*** ни за что (на све́те); **2.** люби́ть; **~** ***to do*** де́лать с удово́льствием; **~** ***affair*** любо́вная свя́зь; *coll.* рома́н; **~ly** ['lʌvlɪ] прекра́сный, чу́дный; **~r** ['lʌvə] (*a paramour*) любо́вник *m*, -ница *f*; возлю́бленный; (*one fond of s.th.*) люби́тель(ница *f*) *m*

loving ['lʌvɪŋ] □ лю́бящий

low¹ [ləʊ] ни́зкий, невысо́кий; *fig.* сла́бый; *voice, sound, etc.* ти́хий; *behavio(u)r* ни́зкий, непристо́йный; ***feel*** **~** быть в плохо́м настрое́нии; пло́хо себя́ чу́вствовать

low² [~] **1.** мыча́ние; **2.** [за]мыча́ть

lower¹ ['ləʊə] **1.** *comp. от* **low¹**; ни́зший; ни́жний; **2.** *v/t. sails, etc.* спуска́ть [-сти́ть]; *eyes* опуска́ть [-сти́ть]; *prices, voice, etc.* снижа́ть [-и́зить]; *v/i.* снижа́ться [-и́зиться]

lower² ['laʊə] смотре́ть угрю́мо; (*scowl*) [на]хму́риться

low|-grade ни́зкого со́рта, плохо́го ка́чества; **~land** ни́зменность *f*; **~-necked** с глубо́ким вы́резом; **~-paid** низкоопла́чиваемый; **~-spirited** пода́вленный, уны́лый

loyal ['lɔɪəl] □ ве́рный, пре́данный, лоя́льный; **~ty** [~tɪ] ве́рность *f*, пре́данность *f*, лоя́льность *f*

lubric|ant ['luːbrɪkənt] сма́зочное вещество́, сма́зка; **~ate** [~keɪt] сма́з(ыв)ать; **~ation** [luːbrɪ'keɪʃn] сма́зывание

lucid ['luːsɪd] □ я́сный; (*transparent*) прозра́чный

luck [lʌk] уда́ча, сча́стье; ***good*** **~** счастли́вый слу́чай, уда́ча; ***bad*** **~**, ***hard*** **~**, ***ill*** **~** неуда́ча; **~ily** ['lʌkɪlɪ] к/по сча́стью; **~y** ['lʌkɪ] □ счастли́вый, уда́чный; приноси́щий уда́чу

lucrative ['luːkrətɪv] □ при́быльный, вы́годный

ludicrous ['luːdɪkrəs] □ неле́пый, смешно́й

lug [lʌg] [по]тащи́ть; *coll.* [по]воло́чи́ть
luggage ['lʌgɪdʒ] бага́ж
lukewarm ['lu:kwɔ:m] чуть тёплый; *fig.* прохла́дный
lull [lʌl] **1.** (~ *to sleep*) убаю́к(ив)ать; *fig.* успока́ивать [-ко́ить]; усыпля́ть [-пи́ть]; **2.** *in fighting, storm, etc.* вре́менное зати́шье
lullaby ['lʌləbaɪ] колыбе́льная (пе́сня)
lumber ['lʌmbə] *esp. Brt.* (*junk*) хлам; *esp. Am.* пиломатериа́лы *m/pl.*
lumin|ary ['lu:mɪnərɪ] *mst. fig.* свети́ло; **~ous** [~nəs] □ светя́щийся, све́тлый
lump [lʌmp] **1.** глы́ба, ком; *person* чурба́н; *of sugar, etc.* кусо́к; (*swelling*) ши́шка; *~ sum* о́бщая су́мма; *a ~ in the throat* комо́к в го́рле; **2.** *v/t.*: *~ together* [с]вали́ть в ку́чу; *v/i.* сбива́ться в ко́мья
lunatic ['lu:nətɪk] *mst. fig.* сумасше́дший
lunch ['lʌntʃ] обе́д в по́лдень, ленч; *have ~* [по]обе́дать
lung [lʌŋ] лёгкое; **~s** *pl.* лёгкие *n/pl.*
lunge [lʌndʒ] **1.** *mst. in fencing* вы́пад, уда́р; **2.** *v/i.* наноси́ть уда́р (*at* Д)
lurch¹ [lɜ:tʃ] *naut.* [на]крени́ться; идти́ шата́ясь
lurch² [~]: *leave a. p. in the ~* бро́сить *pf.* кого́-л. в беде́
lure [ljʊə] **1.** (*bait*) прима́нка; *fig.* собла́зн; **2.** прима́нивать [-ни́ть]; *fig.* соблазня́ть [-ни́ть]
lurid ['lʊərɪd] (*glaring*) крича́щий; о́чень я́ркий; (*shocking*) жу́ткий, ужа́сный; (*gaudy*) аляпова́тый
lurk [lɜ:k] ждать притаи́вшись; скрыва́ться в заса́де; таи́ться
luscious ['lʌʃəs] □ со́чный
lust [lʌst] (*sexual desire*) по́хоть *f*; (*craving*) жа́жда
lust|er, *Brt.* **lustre** ['lʌstə] блеск; (*pendant*) лю́стра; **~rous** ['lʌstrəs] □ блестя́щий
lute [lu:t] *mus.* лю́тня
Lutheran ['lu:θərən] лютера́нин *m*, -анка *f*; лютера́нский
luxur|iant [lʌg'ʒʊərɪənt] бу́йный, пы́шный; **~ious** [~rɪəs] роско́шный, пы́шный; **~y** ['lʌkʃərɪ] ро́скошь *f*; предме́т ро́скоши
lying ['laɪɪŋ] **1.** *pr. p. от* **lie¹** *и* **lie²**; **2.** *adj.* от *lie* (*telling lies*) лжи́вый
lymph [lɪmf] ли́мфа
lynch [lɪntʃ] линчева́ть
lynx [lɪŋks] *zo.* рысь *f*
lyric ['lɪrɪk], **~al** [~ɪkəl] □ лири́ческий; **~s** *pl.* ли́рика

M

M

macabre [mə'kɑ:brə] мра́чный; *~ humour* чёрный ю́мор
macaroni [mækə'rəʊnɪ] макаро́ны *f/pl.*
macaroon [mækə'ru:n] минда́льное пече́нье
machination [mækɪ'neɪʃn] (*usu. pl.*) махина́ции, ко́зни *f/pl.*; интри́га
machine [mə'ʃi:n] стано́к; маши́на; механи́зм; *attr.* маши́нный; *~ translation* маши́нный перево́д; *~-made* маши́нного произво́дства; **~ry** [~ərɪ] маши́нное обору́дование, маши́ны
mackerel ['mækrəl] макре́ль, ску́мбрия
mad [mæd] □ сумасше́дший, поме́шанный; *animals* бе́шеный; *be ~ about* быть без ума́ от (Д); *be ~ with s.o.* серди́ться на (В); *go ~* сходи́ть с ума́; *drive ~* своди́ть с ума́
madam ['mædəm] мада́м *f indecl.*; суда́рыня
mad|cap сорвиголова́ *m/f*; **~den** ['mædn] [вз]беси́ть; своди́ть с ума́; раздража́ть [-жи́ть]
made [meɪd] *pt. и pt. p. от* **make**

mad|house *fig.* сумасше́дший дом; **~man** сумасше́дший; *fig.* безу́мец **~ness** ['mædnɪs] сумасше́ствие; безу́мие

magazine [mægə'ziːn] (*journal*) жур-на́л

maggot ['mægət] личи́нка

magic ['mædʒɪk] **1.** (*a.* **~al** ['mædʒɪkəl] □) волше́бный; **2.** волшебство́; **~ian** [mə'dʒɪʃn] волше́бник

magistrate ['mædʒɪstreɪt] судья́

magnanimous [mæg'nænɪməs] □ великоду́шный

magnet ['mægnɪt] магни́т; **~ic** [mæg'netɪk] (**~ally**) магни́тный; *fig.* притяга́тельный

magni|ficence [mæg'nɪfɪsns] великоле́пие; **~ficent** [~snt] великоле́пный; **~fy** ['mægnɪfaɪ] увели́чи(ва)ть; **~fying glass** лу́па; **~tude** ['mægnɪtjuːd] величина́; ва́жность *f*; **~ *of the problem*** масшта́бность пробле́мы

mahogany [mə'hɒgənɪ] кра́сное де́рево

maid [meɪd] *in hotel* го́рничная; (*house* ~) домрабо́тница; ***old*** **~** ста́рая де́ва

maiden ['meɪdn] **1.** де́вушка; **2.** незаму́жняя; *fig. voyage, etc.* пе́рвый; **~ *name*** де́вичья фами́лия; **~ly** [~lɪ] де́вичий

mail [meɪl] **1.** по́чта; *attr.* почто́вый; **2.** отправля́ть [-а́вить] по по́чте; посыла́ть по́чтой; **~box** *Am.* почто́вый я́щик; **~man** *Am.* почтальо́н; **~-order** зака́з по по́чте

maim [meɪm] [ис]кале́чить

main [meɪn] **1.** гла́вная часть *f*; **~s** *pl. el., etc.* магистра́ль *f*; ***in the*** **~** в основно́м; **2.** гла́вный, основно́й; **~land** ['meɪnlənd] матери́к; **~ly** ['meɪnlɪ] гла́вным о́бразом; бо́льшей ча́стью; **~ road** шоссе́ *n indecl.*, магистра́ль *f*; **~spring** *fig.* дви́жущая си́ла; **~stay** *fig.* гла́вная опо́ра

maintain [meɪn'teɪn] подде́рживать [-жа́ть]; (*support*) содержа́ть *impf.*; утвержда́ть [-рди́ть]; (*preserve*) сохраня́ть [-ни́ть]; **~ *that*** утвержда́ть, что ...; **~ *the status quo*** сохраня́ть ста́тус-кво́

maintenance ['meɪntənəns] (*upkeep*) поддержа́ние; (*preservation*) сохране́ние; *tech.* техни́ческое обслу́живание; (*child support, etc.*) содержа́ние

maize [meɪz] кукуру́за

majest|ic [mə'dʒestɪk] (**~ally**) величественный; **~y** ['mædʒəstɪ] вели́чественность *f*; ***His*** (***Her***) **~** его (её) вели́чество

major ['meɪdʒə] **1.** бо́льший; кру́пный; *mus.* мажо́рный; **~ *key*** мажо́рная тона́льность; **2.** майо́р; *Am. univ.* о́бласть/предме́т специализа́ция; **~ general** генера́л-майо́р; **~ity** [mə'dʒɒrətɪ] соверше́ннолетие; большинство́; ***in the*** **~ *of cases*** в большинстве́ слу́чаев

make [meɪk] **1.** [*irr.*] *v/t. com.* [с]де́лать; (*manufacture*) производи́ть [-вести́]; (*prepare*) [при]гото́вить; (*constitute*) составля́ть [-а́вить]; *peace, etc.* заключа́ть [-чи́ть]; (*compel, cause to*) заставля́ть [-ста́вить]; **~ *good*** выполня́ть [вы́полнить]; *loss* возмеща́ть [-мести́ть]; **~ *sure of*** удостоверя́ться [-ве́риться] в (П); **~ *way*** уступа́ть доро́гу (***for*** Д); **~ *into*** превраща́ть [-рати́ть], переде́л(ыв)ать в (В); **~ *out*** разбира́ть [разобра́ть]; *cheque* выпи́сывать [вы́писать]; **~ *over*** перед(ав)а́ть; **~ *up*** составля́ть [-а́вить]; *a quarrel* ула́живать [ула́дить]; сде́лать макия́ж; *time* навёрстывать [наверста́ть]; = **~ *up for*** (*v/i.*); **~ *up one's mind*** реша́ться [-ши́ться]; **2.** *v/i.* направля́ться [-а́виться] (***for*** к Д); **~ *off*** сбежа́ть *pf.* (***with*** с Т); **~ *for*** направля́ться [-а́виться]; **~ *up for*** возмеща́ть [-мести́ть]; *grief caused, etc.* сгла́живать [-дить], искупа́ть [-пи́ть]; **3.** моде́ль *f*; (*firm's*) ма́рка; ***of British*** **~** произво́дства Великобрита́нии; **~-believe** фанта́зия; **~shift** заме́на; подру́чное/вре́менное сре́дство; *attr.* вре́менный; **~up** соста́в; *thea.* грим; косме́тика

maladjusted [mælə'dʒʌstɪd] пло́хо приспосо́бленный; **~ *child*** тру́дновоспиту́емый ребёнок

malady ['mælədɪ] боле́знь *f* (*a. fig.*)

male [meɪl] **1.** мужско́й; **2.** *person*

M

мужчи́на; *animal* саме́ц
malevolen|ce [mə'levələns] (*rejoicing in s.o.'s misfortune*) злора́дство; (*wishing evil*) недоброжела́тельность *f*; **~t** [~lənt] □ злора́дный; недоброжела́тельный
malice ['mælɪs] *of person* злой; *of act, thought, etc.* зло́ба; ***bear s.o.*** **~** затаи́ть *pf.* зло́бу на (В)
malicious [mə'lɪʃəs] □ зло́бный
malign [mə'laɪn] **1.** □ па́губный, вре́дный; **2.** [на]клевета́ть на (В), оклевета́ть (В); **~ant** [mə'lɪgnənt] □ зло́бный; *med.* злока́чественный
malinger [mə'lɪŋgə] притворя́ться, симули́ровать; **~er** [~rə] симуля́нт *m*, -ка *f*
mallet ['mælɪt] деревя́нный молото́к
malnutrition ['mælnjuː'trɪʃn] недоеда́ние; непра́вильное пита́ние
malt [mɔːlt] со́лод
maltreat [mæl'triːt] пло́хо обраща́ться с (Т)
mammal ['mæml] млекопита́ющее
mammoth ['mæməθ] ма́монт
man [mæn] (*pl.* **men**) челове́к; мужчи́на *m*; (*~kind*) челове́чество; *chess* фигу́ра; ***the ~ in the street*** обы́чный челове́к
manage ['mænɪdʒ] *v/i.* руководи́ть; управля́ть (Т), заве́довать (Т); *problem, etc.* справля́ться [-а́виться] с (Т); обходи́ться [обойти́сь] (***without*** без Р); **~ *to*** (+ *inf.*) [с]уме́ть ...; **~able** [~əbl] □ *person* послу́шный; сгово́рчивый; *task etc.* выполни́мый; **~ment** [~mənt] (*control*) управле́ние; (*governing body*) правле́ние; (*managerial staff*) администра́ция; (*senior staff*) дире́кция; **~r** [~ə] ме́неджер; дире́ктор
managing ['mænɪdʒɪŋ] руководя́щий; **~ *director*** замести́тель дире́ктора
mandat|e ['mændeɪt] (*authority*) полномо́чие; *for governing a territory* манда́т; *given by voters* нака́з; *law* прика́з суда́; **~ory** ['mændətərɪ] обяза́тельный
mane [meɪn] гри́ва; *man's* копна́ воло́с
manful ['mænfl] □ му́жественный
mangle ['mæŋgl] [ис]кале́чить; [из-]уро́довать; *text, etc.* искажа́ть [искази́ть]
man|handle ['mænhændl] гру́бо обраща́ться, избива́ть [-би́ть]; **~hood** ['mænhʊd] возмужа́лость *f*, зре́лый во́зраст
mania ['meɪnɪə] ма́ния; **~c** ['meɪnæk] манья́к *m*, -я́чка *f*
manicure ['mænɪkjʊə] **1.** маникю́р; **2.** де́лать маникю́р (Д)
manifest ['mænɪfest] **1.** □ очеви́дный, я́вный; **2.** *v/t.* обнару́жи(-ва)ть; проявля́ть [-ви́ть]; **~ation** ['mænɪfe'steɪʃn] проявле́ние
manifold ['mænɪfəʊld] □ (*various*) разнообра́зный, разноро́дный; (*many*) многочи́сленный
manipulat|e [mə'nɪpjʊleɪt] манипули́ровать; **~ion** [mənɪpjʊ'leɪʃn] манипуля́ция; *of facts* подтасо́вка
man|kind [mæn'kaɪnd] челове́чество; **~ly** [~lɪ] му́жественный; **~made** иску́сственный
mannequin ['mænɪkɪn] (*person*) манеке́нщица; (*dummy*) манеке́н
manner ['mænə] спо́соб, ме́тод; мане́ра; о́браз де́йствий; **~s** *pl.* уме́ние держа́ть себя́; мане́ры *f/pl.*; обы́чаи *m/pl.*; ***all ~ of*** вся́кого ро́да; са́мые ра́зные; ***in a ~*** в не́которой сте́пени; ***in this ~*** таки́м о́бразом; ***in such a ~ that*** таки́м о́бразом, что ...; **~ed** [~d] (*displaying a particular manner*) мане́рный; (*precious*) вы́чурный; **~ly** [~lɪ] ве́жливый
maneuver; *Brt.* **manœuvre** [mə'nuːvə] **1.** манёвр; махина́ция; интри́га; **2.** маневри́ровать
manor ['mænə] поме́стье
manpower ['mænpaʊə] рабо́чая си́ла
mansion ['mænʃn] большо́й дом; *in town* особня́к
manslaughter ['mænslɔːtə] непредумы́шленное уби́йство
mantelpiece ['mæntlpiːs] по́лка ками́на
manual ['mænjʊəl] **1.** ручно́й; **~ *labo(u)r*** физи́ческий труд; **2.** (*handbook*) руково́дство; (*textbook*) уче́бник; (*reference book*)

M

справоч-ник; *tech.* инстру́кция (по эксплуата́ции)
manufactur|e [mænjʊ'fæktʃə] **1.** изготовле́ние; *on large scale* произво́дство; **2.** производи́ть [-вести́]; **~er** [~rə] производи́тель *m*, изготови́тель *m*; **~ing** [~rɪŋ] произво́дство; *attr.* промы́шленный
manure [mə'njʊə] **1.** (*dung*) наво́з; **2.** унаво́живать
many ['menɪ] **1.** мно́гие, многочи́сленные; мно́го; ***~ a time*** мно́го раз; **2.** мно́жество; ***a good ~*** большо́е коли́чество; ***a great ~*** грома́дное коли́чество; **~sided** многосторо́нний
map [mæp] **1.** ка́рта; **2.** наноси́ть на ка́рту; ***~ out*** [с]плани́ровать
maple ['meɪpl] клён
mar [mɑː] [ис]по́ртить
marathon ['mærəθən] марафо́н (*a. fig.*)
marble ['mɑːbl] мра́мор
March[1] [mɑːtʃ] март
march[2] [~] **1.** *mil.* марш; похо́д; *fig. of events* разви́тие; **2.** марширо-ва́ть; *fig.* идти́ вперёд (*a.* ***~ on***)
mare [meə] кобы́ла; ***~'s nest*** иллю́зия
margarine [mɑːdʒə'riːn] маргари́н
margin ['mɑːdʒɪn] край; *of page* поля́ *n/pl.*; *of forest* опу́шка; ***~ of profit*** чи́стая при́быль *f*; **~al** [~l] □ находя́щийся на краю́; ***~ notes*** заме́тки на поля́х страни́цы
marigold ['mærɪgəʊld] ноготки́ *m/pl.*
marine [mə'riːn] **1.** морско́й; **2.** солда́т морско́й пехо́ты; **~r** ['mærɪnə] морепла́ватель *m*; моря́к, матро́с
marital ['mærɪtl] □ *of marriage* бра́чный; *of married persons* супру́жеский
maritime ['mærɪtaɪm] морско́й
mark[1] [mɑːk] *currency* ма́рка
mark[2] [~] **1.** ме́тка, знак; (*school ~*) балл, отме́тка; (*trade ~*) фабри́чная ма́рка; (*target*) мише́нь *f*; (*stain*) пятно́; (*trace*) след; ***a man of ~*** выдаю́щийся челове́к; ***hit the ~*** *fig.* попа́сть *pf.* в цель; ***up to the ~*** *fig.* на до́лжной высоте́; **2.** *v/t.* отмеча́ть [-е́тить] (*a. fig.*); ста́вить отме́тку в (П); ***~ off*** отделя́ть [-ли́ть]; ***~ time*** топта́ться на ме́сте; **~ed** [mɑːkt] □ отме́ченный; (*readily seen*) заме́тный
marker ['mɑːkə] *comput.* ма́ркер
market ['mɑːkɪt] **1.** ры́нок; *comm.* сбыт; ***on the ~*** в прода́же; ***~ economy*** ры́ночная эконо́мика; **2.** прода́(ва)ть; **~able** [~əbl] хо́дкий; **~ing** [~ɪŋ] (*trade*) торго́вля; (*sale*) сбыт; ма́ркетинг
marksman ['mɑːksmən] ме́ткий стрело́к
marmalade ['mɑːməleɪd] (апельси́новое) варе́нье
marquee [mɑː'kiː] большо́й шатёр
marriage ['mærɪdʒ] брак; (*wedding*) сва́дьба; бракосочета́ние; ***civil ~*** гражда́нский брак; **~able** [~əbl] бра́чного во́зраста; ***~ certificate*** свиде́тельство о бра́ке
married ['mærɪd] *man* жена́тый; *woman* заму́жняя; ***~ couple*** супру́ги *pl.*
marrow[1] ['mærəʊ] ко́стный мозг; ***be chilled to the ~*** продро́гнуть *pf.* до мо́зга косте́й
marrow[2] [~] *bot.* кабачо́к
marry ['mærɪ] *v/t. of parent* (*give son in marriage*) жени́ть; (*give daughter in marriage*) вы́дать *pf.* за́муж; *relig.* [об]венча́ть; *civil* сочета́ть бра́-ком; *of man* жени́ться на (П); *v/i.* жени́ться; *of woman* выходи́ть [вы́йти] за́муж
marsh [mɑːʃ] боло́то
marshal ['mɑːʃl] **1.** ма́ршал; *Am. also* суде́бное/полице́йское должностно́е лицо́; **2.**: ***~ one's thoughts*** привести́ *pf.* свои́ мы́сли в систе́му
marshy ['mɑːʃɪ] боло́тистый, то́пкий
marten ['mɑːtɪn] *zo.* куни́ца
martial ['mɑːʃl] □ вое́нный; войнственный; ***~ law*** вое́нное положе́ние
martyr ['mɑːtə] му́ченик *m*, -ница *f*; *mst. fig.* страда́лец *m*, -лица *f*
marvel ['mɑːvl] **1.** чу́до; **2.** удивля́ться [-ви́ться]; **~(l)ous** ['mɑːvələs] □ изуми́тельный
mascot ['mæskət] талисма́н
masculine ['mɑːskjʊlɪn] мужско́й; (*manly*) му́жественный
mash [mæʃ] **1.** *cul.* пюре́ *n indecl.*; **2.**

размина́ть [-мя́ть]; **~ed potatoes** *pl.* карто́фельное пюре́ *n indecl.*
mask [mɑːsk] **1.** ма́ска; **2.** [за]маскирова́ть; (*conceal*) скры́(ва́)ть; **~ed** [~t]: **~ ball** маскара́д
mason ['meɪsn] ка́менщик; масо́н; **~ry** [~rɪ] ка́менная (*or* кирпи́чная) кла́дка
masquerade [mæskə'reɪd] маскара́д
mass¹ [mæs] *relig.* ме́сса
mass² [~] **1.** ма́сса; **2.** соб(и)ра́ться
massacre ['mæsəkə] **1.** резня́; **2.** зве́рски убива́ть [уби́ть]
massage ['mæsɑːʒ] **1.** масса́ж; **2.** масси́ровать
massive ['mæsɪv] масси́вный; кру́пный
mass media *pl.* сре́дства ма́ссовой информа́ции
mast [mɑːst] *naut.* ма́чта
master ['mɑːstə] **1.** хозя́ин; (*teacher*) учи́тель *m*; (*expert*) ма́стер; **♀ of Arts** маги́стр иску́сств; **2.** (*overcome*) одоле́(ва́)ть; (*gain control of*) справля́ться [-а́виться]; (*acquire knowledge of*) овладе́(ва́)ть (Т); **~ful** ['mɑːstəfl] вла́стный, ма́стерский; **~ key** отмы́чка; универса́льный ключ; **~ly** [~lɪ] мастерско́й; **~piece** шеде́вр; **~y** ['mɑːstərɪ] госпо́дство, власть *f*; (*skill*) мастерство́
masticate ['mæstɪkeɪt] жева́ть
mastiff ['mæstɪf] масти́ф
mat [mæt] **1.** цино́вка; *of fabric* ко́врик; *sport.* мат; **2.** *hair* слипа́ться [сли́пнуться]
match¹ [mætʃ] спи́чка
match² [~] **1.** ро́вня *m/f*; *sport.* матч, состяза́ние; (*marriage*) брак, па́ртия; **be a ~ for** быть ро́вней (Д); **2.** *v/t.* [с]равня́ться с (Т); *colo(u)rs, etc.* подбира́ть; **well ~ed couple** хоро́шая па́ра; *v/i.* соотве́тствовать; сочета́ться; **to ~ in colour**, *etc.* подходя́щий; **~less** ['mætʃlɪs] несравне́нный, бесподо́бный
mate [meɪt] **1.** това́рищ; *coll. address* друг; *of animal* саме́ц (са́мка); *naut.* помо́щник капита́на; **2.** *of animals* спа́ривать(ся)
material [mə'tɪərɪəl] **1.** □ материа́льный; *evidence* веще́ственный; **2.** материа́л (*a. fig.*); (*cloth*) мате́рия
matern|al [mə'tɜːnl] □ матери́нский; **~ity** [~nɪtɪ] матери́нство; **~ hospital** роди́льный дом
mathematic|ian [mæθəmə'tɪʃn] матема́тик; **~s** [~'mætɪks] (*mst. sg.*) матема́тика
matinee ['mætɪneɪ] *thea.*, *cine.* дневно́е представле́ние
matriculate [mə'trɪkjʊleɪt] быть при́нятым в университе́т
matrimon|ial [mætrɪ'məʊnɪəl] □ бра́чный; супру́жеский; **~y** ['mætrɪmənɪ] супру́жество, брак
matrix ['meɪtrɪks] ма́трица
matron ['meɪtrən] матро́на; *in hospital approx.* сестра́-хозя́йка
matter ['mætə] **1.** (*substance*) вещество́, материа́л; (*content*) содержа́ние; (*concern*) вопро́с, де́ло; **what's the ~?** что случи́лось?, в чём де́ло?; **no ~ who ...** всё равно́, кто ...; **~ of course** само́ собо́й разуме́ющееся де́ло; **for that ~** что каса́ется э́того; **~ of fact** факт; **as a ~ of fact** вообще́-то; **2.** име́ть значе́ние; **it does not ~** ничего́; **~-of-fact** практи́чный, делово́й
mattress ['mætrɪs] матра́с
matur|e [mə'tjʊə] **1.** □ зре́лый; *wine* вы́держанный; **2.** созре́(ва́)ть; достига́ть [-ти́чь] зре́лости; **~ity** [~rɪtɪ] зре́лость *f*
maudlin ['mɔːdlɪn] □ плакси́вый
maul [mɔːl] [рас]терза́ть; *fig.* жесто́ко критикова́ть
mauve [məʊv] розова́то-лило́вый
mawkish ['mɔːkɪʃ] □ сентимента́льный
maxim ['mæksɪm] афори́зм; при́нцип
maximum ['mæksɪməm] **1.** ма́ксимум; **2.** максима́льный
May¹ [meɪ] май
may² [~] [*irr.*] (*мода́льный глаго́л без инфинити́ва*) [с]мочь; **~ I come in?** мо́жно войти́? **you ~ want to ...** возмо́жно вы [за]хоти́те ...
maybe ['meɪbɪː] мо́жет быть
May Day ['meɪdeɪ] Первома́йский пра́здник
mayonnaise [meɪə'neɪz] майоне́з

mayor [meə] мэр
maze [meɪz] лабири́нт; *fig.* пу́таница; ***be in a ~*** быть в замеша́тельстве, в расте́рянности
me [mi:, mɪ] *ко́свенный паде́ж от* **I**: мне, меня́; *coll.* я
meadow ['medəʊ] луг
meager; *Brt.* **meagre** ['mi:gə] худо́й, то́щий; *meal, etc.* ску́дный
meal [mi:l] еда́ (за́втрак, обе́д, у́жин)
mean¹ [mi:n] □ по́длый, ни́зкий; (*stingy*) скупо́й; (*shabby*) убо́гий, жа́лкий
mean² [~] **1.** сре́дний; → ***meantime***; **2.** середи́на; **~s** *pl.* состоя́ние, бога́тство; (*a. sg.*) (*way to an end*) сре́дство; спо́соб; ***by all ~s*** обяза́тельно; коне́чно; ***by no ~s*** ниско́лько; отню́дь не ...; ***by ~s of*** с по́мощью (Р); посре́дством
mean³ [~] [*irr.*] (*intend*) намерева́ться; име́ть в виду́; хоте́ть сказа́ть, подразумева́ть; (*destine*) предназнача́ть [-зна́чить]; зна́чить; ***~ well*** име́ть до́брые наме́рения
meaning [mi:nɪŋ] значе́ние; смысл; **~less** [~lɪs] бессмы́сленный
meant [ment] *pt. и pt. p. от* **mean**
mean|time, ~while тем вре́менем; ме́жду тем
measles ['mi:zlz] *pl.* корь *f*
measure ['meʒə] **1.** ме́ра; ***beyond ~*** сверх ме́ры; ***in great ~*** в большо́й сте́пени; ***made to ~*** сде́ланный на зака́з; ***~ for ~*** *approx.* о́ко за о́ко; ***take ~s*** принима́ть [-ня́ть] ме́ры; **2.** ме́рить, измеря́ть [-е́рить]; [с]ме́рить; *sew.* снима́ть ме́рку с (Р); ***~ one's words*** взве́шивать слова́; **~ment** [~mənt] разме́р; измере́ние
meat [mi:t] мя́со; *fig.* суть *f*; **~ball** фрикаде́лька; **~s** (*pl.*) те́фтели (*pl.*)
mechanic [mɪ'kænɪk] меха́ник; **~al** [~nɪkəl] □ механи́ческий; *fig.* машина́льный; **~al engineering** машинострое́ние; **~s** (*mst. sg.*) меха́ника
medal [medl] меда́ль *f*
meddle [medl] (***with***, ***in***) вме́шиваться [-ша́ться] (в В); **~some** [~səm] □ надое́дливый
mediat|e ['mi:dɪeɪt] посре́дничать; **~ion** [mi:dɪ'eɪʃn] посре́дничество; **~or** ['mi:dɪeɪtə] посре́дник
medical ['medɪkəl] □ медици́нский; враче́бный; ***~ certificate*** больни́чный листо́к; медици́нское свиде́тельство; ***~ examination*** медици́нский осмо́тр
medicin|al [me'dɪsɪnl] □ лека́рственный; целе́бный; **~e** ['medsɪn] медици́на; лека́рство
medieval [medɪ'i:vəl] □ средневеко́вый
mediocre [mi:dɪ'əʊkə] посре́дственный
meditat|e ['medɪteɪt] *v/i.* размышля́ть; *v/t.* обду́м(ыв)ать (В); **~ion** [medɪ'teɪʃn] размышле́ние, медита́ция
medium ['mi:dɪəm] **1.** (*middle position or condition*) середи́на; (*means of effecting or transmitting*) сре́дство; (*phys., surrounding substance*) среда́; **2.** сре́дний
medley ['medlɪ] смесь *f*
meek [mi:k] □ кро́ткий, мя́гкий; **~ness** ['mi:knɪs] кро́тость *f*
meet [mi:t] [*irr.*] *v/t.* встреча́ть [-е́тить]; (*become aquainted with*) [по]знако́миться с (Т); (*satisfy*) удовлетворя́ть [-ри́ть]; *debt* опла́чивать [-лати́ть]; ***go to ~ a p.*** встреча́ть [-е́тить] (В); ***there is more to it than ~s the eye*** э́то де́ло не так про́сто; *v/i.* [по]знако́миться; (*get together*) соб(и)ра́ться; ***~ with*** испы́тывать [-пыта́ть] (В), подверга́ться [-вергну́ться]; **~ing** ['mi:tɪŋ] заседа́ние; встре́ча; ми́тинг, собра́ние
melancholy ['melənkɒlɪ] **1.** уны́ние; грусть *f*; **2.** *of person* уны́лый; *of something causing sadness* гру́стный, печа́льный
mellow ['meləʊ] *person* смягча́ть (-ся) [-чи́ть(ся)]; *fruit* созре́(ва́)ть
melo|dious [mɪ'ləʊdɪəs] □ мелоди́чный; **~dy** ['melədɪ] мело́дия
melon ['melən] ды́ня
melt [melt] [рас]та́ять; *metal* [рас-] пла́вить(ся); *fat* растапливать [-топи́ть]; *fig.* смягча́ть(ся) [-чи́ть(ся)]
member ['membə] член (*a. parl.*); **~ship** [~ʃɪp] чле́нство

memoirs ['memwɑːz] *pl.* мемуа́ры *m/pl.*
memorable ['memərəbl] □ (досто)па́мятный
memorandum [memə'rændəm] запи́ска; *dipl.* мемора́ндум
memorial [mɪ'mɔːrɪəl] **1.** (*commemorative object, monument, etc.*) па́мятник; (*written record, athletic tournament, etc.*) мемориа́л; **2.** мемориа́льный
memorize ['meməraɪz] запомина́ть [запо́мнить]; (*learn by heart*) зау́чивать наизу́сть
memory ['memərɪ] па́мять *f* (*a. of computer*); воспомина́ние
men [men] (*pl. om* ***man***) мужчи́ны *m/pl.*
menace ['menəs] **1.** угрожа́ть, грози́ть (Д; ***by***, ***with*** Т); **2.** угро́за; опа́сность *f*; (*annoying person*) зану́да
mend [mend] **1.** *v/t.* [по]чини́ть; ~ ***one's ways*** исправля́ться [-а́виться]; *v/i.* (*improve*) улучша́ться [улу́чшиться]; *of health* поправля́ться [-а́виться]; **2.** почи́нка; ***on the*** ~ на попра́вку
mendacious [men'deɪʃəs] □ лжи́вый
meningitis [menɪn'dʒaɪtɪs] менинги́т
menstruation [menstrʊ'eɪʃn] менструа́ция
mental ['mentl] □ *of the mind* у́мственный; *illness* психи́ческий; ***make a ~ note of*** отме́тить *pf.* в уме́ (В); ~ ***hospital*** психиатри́ческая больни́ца; **~ity** [men'tælətɪ] склад ума́; у́мственная спосо́бность; пси́хика
mention ['menʃn] **1.** упомина́ние; **2.** упомина́ть [-мяну́ть] (В *or* о П); ***don't ~ it!*** не́ за что!; ***not to ~*** не говоря́ уж (о П)
menu ['menjuː] меню́ *n indecl.*
meow, *Brt.* **miaow** [mɪ'aʊ] [за]мяу́кать
mercenary ['mɜːsɪnərɪ] □ коры́стный
merchandise ['mɜːtʃəndaɪz] това́ры *m/pl.*
merchant ['mɜːtʃənt] торго́вец; *chiefly Brt.* ~ **bank** комме́рческий банк
merci|ful ['mɜːsɪfʊl] □ милосе́рдный; **~less** [~lɪs] □ беспоща́дный
mercury ['mɜːkjʊrɪ] ртуть *f*
mercy ['mɜːsɪ] милосе́рдие; поща́да; ***be at the ~ of*** быть во вла́сти (Р); по́лностью зави́сеть от (Р)
mere [mɪə] просто́й; ***a ~ child*** всего́ лишь ребёнок; **~ly** то́лько, про́сто
merge [mɜːdʒ] сли́(ва́)ть(ся) (***in*** с Т); объединя́ться [-ни́ться]; **~r** ['mɜːdʒə] *comm.* слия́ние, объедине́ние
meridian [mə'rɪdɪən] *geogr.* меридиа́н
meringue [mə'ræŋ] *cul.* мере́нга
merit ['merɪt] **1.** заслу́га; (*worth*) досто́инство; ***judge s.o. on his ~s*** оце́нивать кого́-л. по заслу́гам; **2.** заслу́живать [-ужи́ть]
mermaid ['mɜːmeɪd] руса́лка
merriment ['merɪmənt] весе́лье
merry ['merɪ] □ весёлый, ра́достный; ***make ~*** весели́ться; **~-go-round** карусе́ль *f*; **~-making** весе́лье; пра́зднество
mesh [meʃ] (*one of the spaces in net, etc.*) ячейка; **~es** *pl.* се́ти *f/pl.*
mess[1] [mes] **1.** беспоря́док; (*confusion*) пу́таница; (*trouble*) неприя́тность *f*; ***make a ~ of a th.*** прова́ливать де́ло; **2.** *v/t.* приводи́ть в беспоря́док; *v/i. coll.* ~ ***about*** рабо́тать ко́е-как; (*tinker*) копа́ться, вози́ться
mess[2] [~] *mil.* столо́вая
message ['mesɪdʒ] сообще́ние; *dipl., a. coll.* посла́ние; ***did you get the ~?*** поня́тно? усекли́?
messenger ['mesɪndʒə] курье́р
messy ['mesɪ] неу́бранный; гря́зный; в беспоря́дке
met [met] *pt. u pt. p. om* ***meet***
metal ['metl] мета́лл; (*road-~*) ще́бень *m*; *attr.* металли́ческий; **~lic** [mɪ'tælɪk] металли́ческий; **~lurgy** [mɪ'tælədʒɪ] металлу́ргия
metaphor ['metəfə] мета́фора
meteor ['miːtɪə] метео́р; **~ology** [miːtɪə'rɒlədʒɪ] метеороло́гия
meter ['miːtə] счётчик; ~ ***reading*** показа́ние счётчика
meter, *Brt.* **metre** ['miːtə] метр
method ['meθəd] ме́тод, спо́соб; систе́ма, поря́док; **~ical** [mɪ'θɒ-

M

dıkl] систематический, методический; (*orderly*) методичный
meticulous [mɪˈtɪkjʊləs] □ тщательный
metric [ˈmetrɪk] (**~ally**): **~ system** метрическая система
metropoli|s [məˈtrɒpəlɪs] столица; метрополия; **~tan** [metrəˈpɒlɪtən] **1.** *eccl.* митрополит; **2.** *adj.* (*of a capital*) столичный
mettle [ˈmetl] сила характера; храбрость *f*; бодрость *f*; (*endurance*) выносливость *f*
Mexican [ˈmeksɪkən] **1.** мексиканский; **2.** мексиканец *m*, -нка *f*
mice [maɪs] *pl.* мыши *f/pl.*
micro... [ˈmaɪkrəʊ] микро...
microbe [ˈmaɪkrəub] микроб
micro|phone [ˈmaɪkrəfəʊn] микрофон; **~scope** [ˈmaɪkrəskəʊp] микроскоп; **~wave oven** микроволновая печь *f*
mid [mɪd] средний; срединный; **~air**: **in ~** высоко в воздухе; **~day** **1.** полдень *m*; **2.** полуденный
middle [ˈmɪdl] **1.** середина; **2.** средний; **♀ Ages** *pl.* средневековье; **~-aged** [~ˈeɪdʒd] средних лет; **~-class** буржуазный; **~man** посредник; **~weight** боксёр среднего веса
middling [ˈmɪdlɪŋ] (*mediocre*) посредственный; (*medium*) средний
midge [mɪdʒ] мошка; **~t** [ˈmɪdʒɪt] карлик; *attr.* карликовый
mid|land [ˈmɪdlənd] центральная часть страны; **~night** полночь *f*; **~riff** [ˈmɪdrɪf] *anat.* диафрагма; **~st** [mɪdst]: ***in the ~ of*** среди (P); ***in our ~*** в нашей среде; **~summer** [~ˈsʌmə] середина лета; **~way** [~ˈweɪ] на полпути; **~wife** акушерка; **~winter** [~ˈwɪntə] середина зимы
might¹ [maɪt] *pt. om* **may**
might² [~] мощь *f*; могущество; ***with ~ and main*** изо всех сил; **~y** [ˈmaɪtɪ] могущественный; *blow* мощный; *adv. coll. Am.*: ***that's ~ good of you*** очень мило с вашей стороны
migrat|e [maɪˈgreɪt] мигрировать; **~ion** [~ʃn] миграция; *of birds* перелёт

mike [maɪk] *coll.* микрофон
mild [maɪld] □ мягкий; *drink, tobacco* слабый; (*slight*) лёгкий
mildew [ˈmɪldjuː] *bot.* милдью *n indecl.*; *on bread* плесень *f*
mile [maɪl] миля
mil(e)age [ˈmaɪlɪdʒ] расстояние в милях
milieu [ˈmiːljɜː] среда, окружение
milit|ary [ˈmɪlɪtrɪ] **1.** □ военный; воинский; **~ service** военная служба; **2.** военные; военные власти *f/pl.*; **~ia** [mɪˈlɪʃə] милиция
milk [mɪlk] **1.** молоко; ***condensed ~*** сгущённое молоко; ***powdered ~*** сухое молоко; ***whole ~*** цельное молоко; **2.** [по]доить; **~maid** доярка; **~y** [ˈmɪlkɪ] молочный; **♀ Way** Млечный путь *m*
mill [mɪl] **1.** мельница; (*factory*) фабрика, завод; **2.** [с]молоть
millennium [mɪˈlenɪəm] тысячелетие
millepede [ˈmɪlɪpiːd] *zo.* многоножка
miller [ˈmɪlə] мельник
millet [ˈmɪlɪt] просо
millinery [ˈmɪlɪnərɪ] ателье дамских шляп
million [ˈmɪljən] миллион; **~aire** [mɪljəˈneə] миллионер; **~th** [ˈmɪljənθ] **1.** миллионный; **2.** миллионная часть *f*
millstone жёрнов; ***be a ~ round s.o.'s neck*** камень на шее; тяжёлая ответственность *f*
milt [mɪlt] молоки *f/pl.*
mimic [ˈmɪmɪk] **1.** имитатор; **2.** пародировать (*im*)*pf.*; подражать (Д); **~ry** [~rɪ] подражание; *zo.* мимикрия
mince [mɪns] **1.** *v/t. meat* пропускать [-стить] через мясорубку; ***he does not ~ matters*** он говорит без обиняков; *v/i.* говорить жеманно; **2.** мясной фарш (*mst.* **~d meat**); **~meat** фарш из изюма, яблок *и т. п.*; **~ pie** пирожок (→ ***mincemeat***)
mincing machine мясорубка
mind [maɪnd] **1.** ум, разум; (*opinion*) мнение; (*intention*) намерение; желание; память *f*; ***to my ~*** на мой взгляд; ***be out of one's ~*** быть без ума; ***change one's ~*** передум(ы-

в)ать; ***bear in ~*** иметь в виду; ***have a ~ to*** хотеть (*+inf.*); ***have s.th. on one's ~*** беспокоиться о чём-л.; ***be in two ~s*** колебаться, быть в нерешительности; ***make up one's ~*** решаться [-шиться]; ***set one's ~ to ...*** твёрдо решить; **2.** (*look after*) присматривать [-мотреть] за (T); (*heed*) остерегаться [-речься] (P); ***never ~!*** ничего!; ***I don't ~*** (***it***) я ничего не имею против; ***would you ~ taking off your hat?*** будьте добры, снимите шляпу; **~ful** ['maɪndfʊl] (***of***) внимательный к (Д); заботливый

mine¹ [maɪn] *pron.* мой *m*, моя *f*, моё *n*, мои *pl.*

mine² [~] **1.** рудник; (*coal ~*) шахта; *fig.* источник; *mil.* мина; **2.** добы(ва)ть; **~r** ['maɪnə] шахтёр, *coll.* горняк

mineral ['mɪnərəl] **1.** минерал; **2.** минеральный; ***~ resources*** полезные ископаемые

mingle ['mɪŋgl] смешивать(ся) [-шать(ся)]

miniature ['mɪnətʃə] **1.** миниатюра; **2.** миниатюрный

minibus микроавтобус

minim|ize ['mɪnɪmaɪz] доводить [довести] до минимума; *fig.* преуменьшать [-еньшить]; **~um** [~ɪməm] **1.** минимум; **2.** минимальный

mining ['maɪnɪŋ] горнодобывающая промышленность *f*

minister ['mɪnɪstə] *pol.* министр; *eccl.* священник

ministry ['mɪnɪstrɪ] *pol.*, *eccl.* министерство

mink [mɪŋk] *zo.* норка

minor ['maɪnə] **1.** (*inessential*) несущественный; (*inferior in importance*) второстепенный; *mus.* минорный; **2.** несовершеннолетний; **~ity** [maɪ'nɒrətɪ] меньшинство

mint¹ [mɪnt] **1.** (*place*) монетный двор; ***a ~ of money*** большая сумма; **2.** [от]чеканить

mint² [~] *bot.* мята

minuet [mɪnjʊ'et] менуэт

minus ['maɪnəs] **1.** *prp.* без (P), минус; ***it's ~ 10° now*** сейчас (на улице) минус десять градусов; **2.** *adj.* отрицательный

minute **1.** [maɪ'nju:t] □ мелкий; (*slight*) незначительный; (*detailed*) подробный, детальный; **2.** ['mɪnɪt] минута; момент; **~s** *pl.* протокол

mirac|le ['mɪrəkl] чудо; ***work ~s*** творить чудеса; **~ulous** [mɪ'rækjʊləs] □ чудесный

mirage ['mɪrɑ:ʒ] мираж

mire ['maɪə] трясина; (*mud*) грязь *f*

mirror ['mɪrə] **1.** зеркало; **2.** отражать [отразить]

mirth [mɜ:θ] веселье, радость *f*; **~ful** [~fl] □ весёлый, радостный; **~less** [~lɪs] □ безрадостный

miry ['maɪərɪ] топкий

misadventure ['mɪsəd'ventʃə] несчастье; несчастный случай

misapply ['mɪsə'plaɪ] неправильно использовать

misapprehend [mɪsæprɪ'hend] понимать [-нять] превратно

misbehave [mɪsbɪ'heɪv] плохо вести себя

miscalculate [mɪs'kælkjʊleɪt] ошибаться в расчёте, подсчёте

miscarr|iage [mɪs'kærɪdʒ] (*failure*) неудача; *med.* выкидыш; ***~ of justice*** судебная ошибка; **~y** [~rɪ] терпеть неудачу; иметь выкидыш

miscellaneous [mɪsə'leɪnɪəs] □ разный, смешанный

mischief ['mɪstʃɪf] озорство; проказы *f/pl.*; (*harm*) вред; зло; ***do s.o. a ~*** причинять [-нить] кому-л. зло

mischievous ['mɪstʃɪvəs] □ (*injurious*) вредный; *mst. child* озорной; шаловливый

misconceive [mɪskən'si:v] неправильно понять *pf.*

misconduct **1.** [mɪs'kɒndʌkt] плохое поведение; **2.** [~kən'dʌkt]: ***~ o.s.*** дурно вести себя

misconstrue [mɪskən'stru:] неправильно истолковывать

misdeed [mɪs'di:d] проступок

misdirect [mɪsdɪ'rekt] неверно направить; *mail* неправильно адресовать

miser ['maɪzə] скупец, скряга *m/f*

miserable ['mɪzrəbl] □ (*wretched*) жалкий; (*unhappy*) несчастный; (*squalid*) убогий; *meal* скудный

miserly ['maɪzəlɪ] скупой

misery ['mɪzərɪ] невзго́да, несча́стье, страда́ние; (*poverty*) нищета́
misfortune [mɪs'fɔːtʃən] неуда́ча, несча́стье, беда́
misgiving [mɪs'gɪvɪŋ] опасе́ние, предчу́вствие дурно́го
misguide [mɪs'gaɪd] вводи́ть в заблужде́ние; дава́ть [дать] непра́вильный сове́т
mishap ['mɪshæp] неприя́тное происше́ствие, неуда́ча
misinform [mɪsɪn'fɔːm] непра́вильно информи́ровать, дезинформи́ровать
misinterpret [mɪsɪn'tɜːprɪt] неве́рно поня́ть *pf.*, истолко́вывать
mislay [mɪs'leɪ] [*irr.* (***lay***)] положи́ть не на ме́сто; *lose* затеря́ть; ***I've mislaid my pipe somewhere*** я куда́-то дел свою́ тру́бку
mislead [mɪs'liːd] [*irr.* (***lead***)] вести́ по непра́вильному пути́; вводи́ть в заблужде́ние
mismanage [mɪs'mænɪdʒ] пло́хо вести́ дела́
misplace [mɪs'pleɪs] положи́ть не на ме́сто; *p. pt.* **~d** *fig.* неуме́стный
misprint [mɪs'prɪnt] опеча́тка
misread [mɪs'riːd] [*irr.* (***read***)] непра́вильно проче́сть *pf.*; непра́вильно истолко́вывать
misrepresent [mɪsreprɪ'zent] представля́ть в ло́жном све́те; искажа́ть [-кази́ть]
miss¹ [mɪs] де́вушка; (*as title*) мисс
miss² [~] **1.** про́мах; ***give s.th. a ~*** пропусти́ть *pf.*, не сде́лать *pf.* чего́-л.; **2.** *v/t. chance* упуска́ть [-сти́ть]; *train* опа́здывать [-да́ть] на (В); (*fail to notice*) не заме́тить *pf.*; (*not find*) не заста́ть *pf.* до́ма; (*long for*) тоскова́ть по (Т, Д); *v/i.* (*fail to hit*) прома́хиваться [-хну́ться]
missile ['mɪsaɪl] раке́та; ***guided ~*** управля́емая раке́та
missing ['mɪsɪŋ] отсу́тствующий, недостаю́щий; *mil.* пропа́вший бе́з вести; ***be ~*** отсу́тствовать
mission ['mɪʃn] ми́ссия, делега́ция; (*task*) зада́ча; (*calling*) призва́ние
misspell [mɪs'spel] [*a. irr.* (***spell***)] [с]де́лать орфографи́ческую оши́бку; непра́вильно написа́ть
mist [mɪst] тума́н; ды́мка
mistake [mɪ'steɪk] **1.** [*irr.* (***take***)] ошиба́ться [-би́ться]; (*understand wrongly*) непра́вильно понима́ть [-ня́ть]; непра́вильно принима́ть [-ня́ть] (***for*** за (В); ***be ~n*** ошиба́ться [-би́ться]; **2.** оши́бка; заблужде́ние; ***by ~*** по оши́бке; **~n** [~ən] оши́бочный, непра́вильно по́нятый; (*ill-judged*) неосмотри́тельный; неуме́стный
mister ['mɪstə] ми́стер, господи́н
mistletoe ['mɪsltəʊ] оме́ла
mistress ['mɪstrɪs] *of household, etc.* хозя́йка до́ма; (*school ~*) учи́тельница; (*a paramour*) любо́вница
mistrust [mɪs'trʌst] **1.** не доверя́ть (Д); **2.** недове́рие; **~ful** [~fʊl] □ недове́рчивый
misty ['mɪstɪ] □ тума́нный; (*obscure*) сму́тный
misunderstand [mɪsʌndə'stænd] [*irr.* (***stand***)] непра́вильно понима́ть; **~ing** [~ɪŋ] недоразуме́ние; (*disagreement*) размо́лвка
misuse **1.** [mɪs'juːz] злоупотребля́ть [-би́ть] (Т); (*treat badly*) ду́рно обраща́ться с (Т); **2.** [~'juːs] злоупотребле́ние
mite [maɪt] (*small child*) малю́тка *m/f*
mitigate ['mɪtɪgeɪt] смягча́ть [-чи́ть]; (*lessen*) уменьша́ть [уме́ньшить]
mitten ['mɪtn] рукави́ца
mix [mɪks] [с]меша́ть(ся); переме́шивать [-ша́ть]; (*mingle with*) обща́ться; **~ed** переме́шанный, сме́шанный; (*of different kind*) разноро́дный; ***~ up*** перепу́т(ыв)ать; ***be ~ed up in*** быть заме́шанным в (П); **~ture** ['mɪkstʃə] смесь *f*
moan [məʊn] **1.** стон; **2.** [за]стона́ть
mob [mɒb] **1.** толпа́; **2.** (*throng*) [с]толпи́ться; (*besiege*) осажда́ть [-ди́ть]
mobil|e ['məʊbaɪl] *person, face, mind* живо́й, подви́жный; *mil.* моби́льный; ***~ phone*** моби́льный телефо́н; **~ization** [məʊbɪlaɪ'zeɪʃn] *mil., etc.* мобилиза́ция; **~ize** ['məʊbɪlaɪz] (*a. fig.*) мобилизова́ть (*im*)*pf.*
moccasin ['mɒkəsɪn] мокаси́н

mock [mɒk] **1.** насме́шка; **2.** подде́льный; *v/t.* осме́ивать [-ея́ть]; *v/i.*: **~ *at*** насмеха́ться [-ея́ться] над (Т); **~ery** [~ərɪ] издева́тельство, осмея́ние

mode [məʊd] ме́тод, спо́соб; *tech.* режи́м; **~ *of life*** о́браз жи́зни

model ['mɒdl] **1.** моде́ль *f*; *fashion* манеке́нщица; *art* нату́рщик *m*, -ица *f*; *fig.* приме́р; образе́ц; *attr.* образцо́вый; **2.** *sculpture* вы́лепить; (**~ *after***, [***up***]***on***) брать приме́р

modem ['məʊdem] мо́дем

moderat|e 1. ['mɒdərət] □ уме́ренный; **2.** ['mɒdəreɪt] умеря́ть [уме́рить]; смягча́ть(ся) [-чи́ть(ся)]; *wind* стиха́ть [сти́хнуть]; **~ion** [mɒdə'reɪʃn] уме́ренность *f*

modern ['mɒdən] совреме́нный; **~ize** [~aɪz] модернизи́ровать (*im*)*pf.*

modest ['mɒdɪst] □ скро́мный; **~y** [~ɪ] скро́мность *f*

modi|fication [mɒdɪfɪ'keɪʃn] видоизмене́ние; *mst. tech.* модифика́ция; **~fy** ['mɒdɪfaɪ] видоизменя́ть [-ни́ть]; (*make less severe*) смягча́ть [-чи́ть]; модифици́ровать

modul|ate ['mɒdjʊleɪt] модули́ровать; **~e** ['mɒdjuːl] *math.* мо́дуль *m*; (*separate unit*) блок, се́кция; (*spacecraft*) мо́дульный отсе́к; ***lunar*** **~** лу́нная капсула

moist [mɔɪst] вла́жный; **~en** ['mɔɪsn] увлажня́ть(ся) [-ни́ть(ся)]; **~ure** ['mɔɪstʃə] вла́га

molar ['məʊlə] коренно́й зуб

mold[1] [məʊld] (*Brt.* **mould**) (*fungus*) пле́сень *f*

mold[2] [~] (*Brt.* **mould**) **1.** (лите́йная) фо́рма; **2.** *tech.* отлива́ть [-ли́ть]; *fig.* [с]формирова́ть

moldy ['məʊldɪ] (*Brt.* **mouldy**) запле́сневелый

mole[1] [məʊl] *zo.* крот; (*secret agent*) «крот»

mole[2] [~] (*breakwater*) мол

mole[3] [~] *on skin* ро́динка

molecule ['mɒlɪkjuːl] моле́кула

molest [mə'lest] приста́(ва́)ть к (Д)

mollify ['mɒlɪfaɪ] успока́ивать [-ко́ить], смягча́ть [-чи́ть]

molt [məʊlt] (*Brt.* **moult**) *zo.* [по]линя́ть

moment ['məʊmənt] моме́нт, миг, мгнове́ние; ***at the*** **~** в да́нное вре́мя; ***a great*** **~** ва́жное собы́тие; **~ary** [~trɪ] (*instantaneous*) мгнове́нный; (*not lasting*) кратковре́менный; **~ous** [mə'mentəs] □ ва́жный; **~um** [~təm] *phys.* ине́рция; дви́жущая си́ла; ***gather*** **~** набира́ть ско́рость *f*; разраста́ться [-ти́сь]

monarch ['mɒnək] мона́рх; **~y** [~ɪ] мона́рхия

monastery ['mɒnəstrɪ] монасты́рь *m*

Monday ['mʌndɪ] понеде́льник

monetary ['mʌnɪtrɪ] валю́тный; *reform, etc.* де́нежный

money ['mʌnɪ] де́ньги *f/pl.*; ***ready*** **~** нали́чные де́ньги *f/pl.*; ***be out of*** **~** не име́ть де́нег; **~box** копи́лка; **~-order** де́нежный перево́д

mongrel ['mʌŋgrəl] *dog* дворня́жка

monitor ['mɒnɪtə] *in class* ста́роста; *tech.* монито́р

monk [mʌŋk] мона́х

monkey ['mʌŋkɪ] **1.** обезья́на; **2.** *coll.* дура́читься; **~ *with*** вози́ться с (Т); **~ wrench** *tech.* разводно́й га́ечный ключ

mono|logue ['mɒnəlɒg] моноло́г; **~polist** [mə'nɒpəlɪst] монополи́ст; **~polize** [~laɪz] монополизи́ровать (*im*)*pf.*; **~poly** [~lɪ] монопо́лия (Р); **~tonous** [mə'nɒtənəs] □ моното́нный; **~tony** [~tənɪ] моното́нность *f*

monsoon [mɒn'suːn] муссо́н

monster ['mɒnstə] чудо́вище; *fig.* монстр; *attr.* (*huge*) гига́нтский

monstro|sity [mɒn'strɒsətɪ] чудо́вищность *f*; **~us** ['mɒnstrəs] □ чудо́вищный; безобра́зный

month [mʌnθ] ме́сяц; **~ly** ['mʌnθlɪ] **1.** (еже)ме́сячный; **~ *season ticket*** ме́сячный проездно́й биле́т; **2.** ежеме́сячный журна́л

monument ['mɒnjʊmənt] па́мятник; монуме́нт; **~al** [mɒnjʊ'mentl] □ монумента́льный

mood [muːd] настрое́ние

moody ['muːdɪ] (*gloomy*) угрю́мый; (*in low spirits*) не в ду́хе; пере-

M

ме́нчивого настрое́ния; капри́зный
moon [muːn] луна́, ме́сяц; ***reach for the ~*** жела́ть невозмо́жного; **~light** лу́нный свет; **~lit** за́литый лу́нным све́том
moor¹ [muə] торфяни́стая ме́стность *f*, поро́сшая ве́реском
moor² [~] *naut.* [при]швартова́ться
moot [muːt]: **~ *point*** спо́рный вопро́с
mop [mɒp] **1.** шва́бра; **~ *of hair*** копна́ воло́с; **2.** мыть, протира́ть шва́брой
mope [məʊp] хандри́ть
moped ['məʊped] мопе́д
moral ['mɒrəl] **1.** □ мора́льный, нра́вственный; **2.** мора́ль *f*; **~s** *pl.* нра́вы *m/pl.*; **~e** [mə'rɑːl] *part. mil.* мора́льное состоя́ние; **~ity** [mə'rælətɪ] мора́ль *f*, э́тика; **~ize** ['mɒrəlaɪz] морализи́ровать
moratorium [mɒrə'tɔːrɪəm] *pl.*, **~ria** [~rɪə] *comm., pol., mil.* морато́рий
morbid ['mɔːbɪd] боле́зненный
more [mɔː] бо́льше; бо́лее; ещё; **~ *or less*** бо́лее и́ли ме́нее; ***once ~*** ещё раз; ***no ~*** бо́льше не ...; ***the ~ so as ...*** тем бо́лее, что ...; **~over** [mɔː'rəʊvə] кро́ме того́, бо́лее того́
morning ['mɔːnɪŋ] у́тро; ***in the ~*** у́тром; ***tomorrow ~*** за́втра у́тром
morose [mə'rəʊs] □ мра́чный
morphia ['mɔːfɪə], **morphine** ['mɔːfiːn] мо́рфий
morsel ['mɔːsl] кусо́чек
mortal ['mɔːtl] **1.** □ сме́ртный; *wound* смерте́льный; **2.** сме́ртный; ***ordinary ~*** просто́й сме́ртный; **~ity** [mɔː'tælətɪ] (*being mortal*; *a.* **~** *rate*) сме́ртность *f*
mortar ['mɔːtə] известко́вый раство́р
mortgage ['mɔːgɪdʒ] **1.** ссу́да (под недви́жимость); закладна́я; **2.** закла́дывать [заложи́ть]
morti|fication [mɔːtɪfɪ'keɪʃn] чу́вство стыда́; ***to my ~*** к моему́ стыду́; **~fy** ['mɔːtɪfaɪ] (*shame, humiliate*) обижа́ть [оби́деть]; унижа́ть [уни́зить]; (*cause grief*) оскорбля́ть [-би́ть]
mortuary ['mɔːtʃərɪ] морг
mosaic [məʊ'zeɪɪk] моза́ика
Moslem ['mɒzləm] = **Muslim**
mosque [mɒsk] мече́ть *f*
mosquito [məs'kiːtəʊ] кома́р; *in tropics* моски́т
moss [mɒs] мох; **~y** ['~ɪ] мши́стый
most [məʊst] **1.** *adj.* □ наибо́льший; **2.** *adv.* бо́льше всего́; **~ *beautiful*** са́мый краси́вый; **3.** наибо́льшее коли́чество; бо́льшая часть *f*; ***at*** (***the***) **~** са́мое бо́льшее, не бо́льше чем; ***make the ~ of ...*** наилу́чшим о́бразом испо́льзовать; ***the ~ I can do*** всё, что я могу́ сде́лать; **~ly** ['məʊstlɪ] по бо́льшей ча́сти; гла́вным о́бразом; ча́ще всего́
motel [məʊ'tel] моте́ль *m*
moth [mɒθ] моль *f*; мотылёк; **~-eaten** изъе́денный мо́лью
mother ['mʌðə] **1.** мать *f*; **2.** относи́ться по-матери́нски к (Д); **~hood** ['mʌðəhʊd] матери́нство; **~-in-law** [~rɪnlɔː] (*wife's mother*) тёща; (*husband's mother*) свекро́вь *f*; **~ly** [~lɪ] матери́нский; **~-of-pearl** [~rəv'pɜːl] перламу́тровый; **~ tongue** родно́й язы́к
motif [məʊ'tiːf] моти́в
motion ['məʊʃn] **1.** движе́ние; *of mechanism* ход; (*proposal*) предложе́ние; **2.** *v/t.* пока́зывать же́стом; *v/i.* кива́ть [кивну́ть] (***to*** на В); **~less** [~lɪs] неподви́жный; **~-picture** *Am.* (кино)фи́льм
motiv|ate ['məʊtɪveɪt] мотиви́ровать; **~e** ['məʊtɪv] **1.** *of power* дви́жущий; **2.** (*inducement*) по́вод, моти́в
motley ['mɒtlɪ] пёстрый
motor ['məʊtə] **1.** дви́гатель *m*, мото́р; **2.** мото́рный; **~ mechanic, ~ fitter** автомеха́ник; **3.** е́хать (везти́) на автомаши́не; **~boat** мото́рная ло́дка; **~car** автомаши́на, *coll.* маши́на; **~cycle** мотоци́кл; **~ing** ['məʊtərɪŋ] автомоби́льный спорт; автотури́зм; **~ist** [~rɪst] автомобили́ст *m*, -ка *f*; **~ scooter** моторо́ллер; **~ way** автостра́да
mottled ['mɒtld] кра́пчатый
mound [maʊnd] (*hillock*) холм; (*heap*) ку́ча
mount¹ [maʊnt] возвы́шенность *f*; гора́; **♀ *Everest*** гора́ Эвере́ст

mount² [~] *v/i.* поднима́ться [-ня́ться]; сади́ться на ло́шадь *f*; *v/t. radio, etc.* устана́вливать [-нови́ть], [с]монти́ровать; (*frame*) вставля́ть в ра́му (в опра́ву)
mountain ['maʊntɪn] **1.** гора́; **2.** го́рный, наго́рный; **~eer** [maʊntɪ'nɪə] альпини́ст(ка); **~ous** ['maʊntɪnəs] гори́стый
mourn [mɔːn] горева́ть; *s.b.'s death* опла́к(ив)ать; **~er** ['mɔːnə] скорбя́щий; **~ful** ['mɔːnfl] □ печа́льный, ско́рбный; **~ing** ['mɔːnɪŋ] тра́ур
mouse [maʊs] (*pl.* ***mice***) мышь *f*
moustache [mə'stɑːʃ] = ***mustache***
mouth [maʊθ], *pl.* **~s** [~z] рот; *of river* у́стье; *of cave, etc.* вход; **~organ** губна́я гармо́ника; **~piece** *of pipe, etc.* мундшту́к; *fig.* ру́пор
move [muːv] **1.** *v/t. com.* дви́гать [дви́нуть]; передвига́ть [-и́нуть]; (*touch*) тро́гать [тро́нуть]; (*propose*) вноси́ть [внести́]; *v/i.* дви́гаться [дви́нуться]; (*change residence*) переезжа́ть [перее́хать]; *of events* разви́(ва́)ться; *of affairs* идти́ [пойти́]; *fig. in artistic circles, etc.* враща́ться; ***~ in*** въезжа́ть [въе́хать]; ***~ on*** дви́гаться вперёд; **2.** движе́ние; перее́зд; *in game pf.* ход; *fig.* шаг; ***on the ~*** на ходу́; ***make a ~*** сде́лать ход; **~ment** ['muːvmənt] движе́ние; *of symphony, etc.* часть *f*
movies ['muːvɪz] *pl.* кино́ *n indecl.*
moving ['muːvɪŋ] □ дви́жущийся; (*touching*) тро́гательный; ***~ staircase*** эскала́тор
mow [məʊ] [*irr.*] [с]коси́ть; **~n** *pt. p. om* ***mow***
Mr. ['mɪstə] → ***mister***
Mrs. ['mɪsɪz] ми́ссис, госпожа́
much [mʌtʃ] *adj.* мно́го; *adv.* о́чень; ***I thought as ~*** я так и ду́мал; ***make ~ of*** придава́ть [прида́ть] большо́е значе́ние; окружи́ть внима́нием; ба́ловать (В); ***I am not ~ of a dancer*** я нева́жно танцу́ю
muck [mʌk] наво́з; *fig.* дрянь *f*
mucus ['mjuːkəs] слизь *f*
mud [mʌd] грязь *f*
muddle ['mʌdl] **1.** *v/t.* перепу́т(ывать; [с]пу́тать (*a.* ***~ up***); **2.** *coll.* пу́таница, неразбери́ха; (*disorder*) беспоря́док
mud|dy ['mʌdɪ] гря́зный; **~guard** крыло́
muffin ['mʌfɪn] сдо́бная бу́лочка
muffle ['mʌfl] *of voice, etc.* глуши́ть, заглуша́ть [-ши́ть]; (*envelop*) заку́т(ыв)ать; **~r** [~ə] (*device for deadening sound; Am. esp. mot.*) глуши́тель *m*
mug [mʌg] кру́жка
muggy ['mʌgɪ] ду́шный, вла́жный
mulberry ['mʌlbərɪ] (*tree*) ту́товое де́рево, шелкови́ца; (*fruit*) ту́товая я́года
mule [mjuːl] мул; ***stubborn as a ~*** упря́мый как осёл
mull [mʌl]: ***~ over*** обду́м(ыв)ать; размышля́ть [-мы́слить]
mulled [mʌld]: ***~ wine*** глинтве́йн
multi|ple ['mʌltɪpl] **1.** *math.* кра́тный; **2.** *math.* кра́тное число́; (*repeated*) многокра́тный; *interests. etc.* разнообра́зный; **~plication** [mʌltɪplɪ'keɪʃn] умноже́ние; увеличе́ние; ***~ table*** табли́ца умноже́ния; **~plicity** [~'plɪsətɪ] многочи́сленность *f*; (*variety*) разнообра́зие; **~ply** ['mʌltɪplaɪ] увели́чи(ва)ть(-ся); *math.* умножа́ть [-о́жить]; **~purpose** многоцелево́й; **~tude** [~tjuːd] мно́жество, ма́сса; толпа́
mum [mʌm]: ***keep ~*** пома́лкивать
mumble ['mʌmbl] [про]бормота́ть
mummy ['mʌmɪ] му́мия
mumps [mʌmps] *sg.* сви́нка
mundane ['mʌndeɪn] земно́й, мирско́й; □ бана́льный; *life* прозаи́чный
municipal [mjuː'nɪsɪpl] □ муниципа́льный; **~ity** [~nɪsɪ'pælətɪ] муниципалите́т
mural ['mjʊərəl] фре́ска; стенна́я ро́спись *f*
murder ['mɜːdə] **1.** уби́йство; **2.** уби́(ва́)ть; **~er** [~rə] уби́йца *m/f*; **~ous** [~rəs] □ уби́йственный
murky ['mɜːkɪ] □ тёмный; *day* па́смурный
murmur ['mɜːmə] **1.** *of brook* журча́ние; *of voices* ти́хие зву́ки голосо́в; шёпот; **2.** [за]журча́ть; шепта́ть; (*grumble*) ворча́ть
musc|le ['mʌsl] му́скул, мы́шца;

M

~ular ['mʌskjʊlə] (*brawny*) мускули́стый; му́скульный
muse¹ [mju:z] му́за
muse² [~] заду́м(ыв)аться (***about***, ***on*** над Т)
museum [mju:'zɪəm] музе́й
mushroom ['mʌʃrʊm] **1.** гриб; ***pick ~s*** собира́ть грибы́; **2.** (*grow rapidly*) расти́ как грибы́
music ['mju:zɪk] му́зыка; музыка́льное произведе́ние; (*notes*) но́ты *f/pl.*; ***face the ~*** расхлёбывать ка́шу; ***set to ~*** положи́ть *pf.* на му́зыку; **~al** ['mju:zɪkl] □ музыка́льный; мелоди́чный; **~-hall** мю́зик-холл; эстра́дный теа́тр; **~ian** [mju:'zɪʃn] музыка́нт
Muslim ['mʊzlɪm] мусульма́нский
muslin ['mʌzlɪn] мусли́н
musquash ['mʌskwɒʃ] онда́тра; мех онда́тры
mussel ['mʌsl] ми́дия
must [mʌst]: ***I ~*** я до́лжен (+ *inf.*); ***I ~ not*** мне нельзя́; ***he ~ still be there*** он должно́ быть всё ещё там
mustache [mə'stɑ:ʃ] усы́ *m/pl.*
mustard ['mʌstəd] горчи́ца
muster ['mʌstə] (*gather*) собира́ться [-бра́ться]; **~** (***up***) ***one's courage*** набра́ться *pf.* хра́брости, собра́ться *pf.* с ду́хом
musty ['mʌstɪ] за́тхлый
mutation [mju:'teɪʃn] *biol.* мута́ция
mut|e [mju:t] **1.** □ немо́й; **2.** немо́й; **~ed** ['~ɪd] приглушённый
mutilat|e ['mju:tɪleɪt] [из]уве́чить; **~ion** [~'eɪʃn] уве́чье
mutin|ous ['mju:tɪnəs] □ мяте́жный (*a. fig.*); **~y** [~nɪ] бунт, мяте́ж
mutter ['mʌtə] **1.** бормота́нье; (*grumble*) ворча́ние; **2.** [про]бормота́ть; [про]ворча́ть
mutton ['mʌtn] бара́нина; ***leg of ~*** бара́нья нога́; **~ *chop*** бара́нья отбивна́я
mutual ['mju:tʃʊəl] □ обою́дный, взаи́мный; о́бщий; **~ *friend*** о́бщий друг
muzzle ['mʌzl] **1.** мо́рда, ры́ло; *of gun* ду́ло; (*for dog*) намо́рдник; **2.** надева́ть намо́рдник (Д); *fig.* заста́вить *pf.* молча́ть
my [maɪ] *poss. pron.* мой *m*, моя́ *f*, моё *n*; мои́ *pl.*
myrtle ['mɜ:tl] мирт
myself [maɪ'self] *refl. pron.* **1.** себя́, меня́ самого́; -ся, -сь; **2.** *pron. emphatic* сам; ***I did it ~*** я сам э́то сде́лал
myster|ious [mɪ'stɪərɪəs] □ зага́дочный, таи́нственный; **~y** ['mɪstərɪ] та́йна; ***it's a ~ to me ...*** остаётся для меня́ зага́дкой
mysti|c ['mɪstɪk] (*a.* **~al** [~kl] □) мисти́ческий; **~fy** [~tɪfaɪ] мистифици́ровать (*im*)*pf.*; (*bewilder*) озада́чи(ва)ть
myth [mɪθ] миф

N

nab [næb] *coll.* (*arrest*) накрыва́ть [-ы́ть]; (*take unawares*) застига́ть [-и́гнуть]
nag [næg] *coll.* пили́ть
nail [neɪl] **1.** *anat.* но́готь *m*; гвоздь *m*; **~ *file*** пи́лка для ногте́й; **2.** заби́(ва́)ть гвоздя́ми; приби́(ва́)ть; **~ *s.b. down*** заста́вить *pf.* раскры́ть свои́ ка́рты; прижа́ть *pf* к стене́
naïve [naɪ'i:v] *or* **naive** □ наи́вный; безыску́сный
naked ['neɪkɪd] □ наго́й, го́лый; (*evident*) я́вный; ***with the ~ eye*** невооружённым гла́зом; **~ness** [~nɪs] нагота́
name [neɪm] **1.** и́мя *n*; (*surname*) фами́лия; *of things* назва́ние; ***of*** (*coll.* ***by***) ***the ~ of*** по и́мени (И); ***in the ~ of*** во и́мя (Р); от и́мени (Р); ***call a p. ~s*** [об]руга́ть (В); **2.** наз(ы)ва́ть; дава́ть и́мя (Д); **~less**

['neımlıs] □ безымя́нный; **~ly** ['~lı] и́менно; **~-plate** табли́чка с фами́лией; **~-sake** тёзка *m/f*
nap¹ [næp] **1.** коро́ткий/лёгкий сон; **2.** дрема́ть [вздремну́ть]; ***catch s.b. ~ping*** заст(ав)а́ть кого́-л. врасплох
nap² [~] *on cloth* ворс
nape [neıp] заты́лок
napkin ['næpkın] салфе́тка; *baby's* пелёнка
narcotic [nɑː'kɒtık] **1.** (***~ally***) наркоти́ческий; **2.** нарко́тик
narrat|e [nə'reıt] расска́зывать [-за́ть]; **~ion** [~ʃn] расска́з; **~ive** ['nærətıv] повествова́ние
narrow ['nærəʊ] **1.** □ у́зкий; (*confined*) те́сный; *person, mind* ограни́ченный, недалёкий; **2. ~s** *pl.* проли́в; **3.** су́живать(ся) [су́зить (-ся)]; уменьша́ть(ся) [уме́ньшить (-ся)]; *of chances, etc.* ограни́чи(ва)ть; **~-minded** у́зкий; с предрассу́дками
nasal ['neızl] □ носово́й; *voice* гнуса́вый
nasty ['nɑːstı] □ (*offensive*) проти́вный; неприя́тный; гря́зный; (*spiteful*) зло́бный
nation ['neıʃn] на́ция
national ['næʃnl] **1.** □ национа́льный, наро́дный; госуда́рственный; **2.** (*citizen*) по́дданный; **~ity** [næʃə'nælətı] национальность *f*; гражда́нство, по́дданство; **~ize** ['næʃnəlaız] национализи́ровать (*im*)*pf.*
native ['neıtıv] **1.** □ родно́й; (*indigenous*) тузе́мный, ме́стный, коренно́й; ***~ language*** родно́й язы́к; **2.** уроже́нец *m*, -нка *f*; ме́стный жи́тель
natural ['nætʃrəl] □ есте́ственный; *leather, etc.* натура́льный; ***~ sciences*** есте́ственные нау́ки *f/pl.*; **~ize** [~aız] предоставля́ть [-а́вить] гражда́нство
nature ['neıtʃə] приро́да; хара́ктер
naught [nɔːt] ничто́; ноль *m*; ***set at ~*** ни во что не ста́вить; пренебрега́ть [-бре́чь] (Т)
naughty ['nɔːtı] □ непослу́шный, капри́зный
nause|a ['nɔːzıə] тошнота́; (*disgust*) отвраще́ние; **~ate** ['nɔːzıeıt] *v/t.* тошни́ть; ***it ~s me*** меня́ тошни́т от э́того; вызыва́ть [вы́звать] отвраще́ние; ***be ~d*** испы́тывать отвраще́ние
nautical ['nɔːtıkl] морско́й
naval ['neıvl] (вое́нно-)морско́й
nave [neıv] *arch.* неф
navel ['neıvl] пуп, пупо́к
naviga|ble ['nævıgəbl] □ судохо́дный; **~te** [~geıt] *v/i. naut., ae.* управля́ть; *v/t. ship, plane* вести́; **~tion** [nævı'geıʃn] навига́ция; ***inland ~*** речно́е судохо́дство; **~tor** ['nævıgeıtə] шту́рман
navy ['neıvı] вое́нно-морски́е си́лы; вое́нно-морско́й флот; **~(blue)** тёмно-си́ний
near [nıə] **1.** *adj.* бли́зкий; бли́жний; (*stingy*) скупо́й; ***in the ~ future*** в ближа́йшее вре́мя; ***~ at hand*** под руко́й; **2.** *adv.* ря́дом; бли́зко, недалеко́; почти́; ско́ро; **3.** *prp.* о́коло (Р), у (Р); **4.** приближа́ться [-ли́зиться] к (Д); **~by** [nıə'baı] близлежа́щий; ря́дом; **~ly** ['nıəlı] почти́; **~-sighted** [nıə'saıtıd] близору́кий
neat [niːt] □ чи́стый, опря́тный; *figure* изя́щный; стро́йный; *workmanship* иску́сный; (*undiluted*) неразба́вленный; **~ness** ['niːtnıs] опря́тность *f*
necess|ary ['nesəsərı] **1.** □ необходи́мый, ну́жный; **2.** необходи́мое; **~itate** [nı'sesıteıt] [по]тре́бовать; вынужда́ть [вы́нудить]; **~ity** [~tı] необходи́мость *f*, нужда́
neck [nek] ше́я; *of bottle, etc.* го́рлышко; ***~ of land*** перешеек; ***risk one's ~*** рискова́ть голово́й; ***stick one's ~ out*** рискова́ть; [по]ле́зть в пе́тлю; **~band** во́рот; **~lace** ['~lıs] ожере́лье; **~tie** га́лстук
née [neı] урождённая
need [niːd] **1.** на́добность *f*, потре́бность *f*; необходи́мость *f*; (*poverty*) нужда́; ***be in ~ of*** нужда́ться в (П); **2.** нужда́ться в (П); ***I ~ it*** мне э́то ну́жно; ***if ~ be*** в слу́чае необходи́мости; **~ful** [~fl] □ ну́жный
needle ['niːdl] игла́, иго́лка; (*knitting ~*) спи́ца
needless ['niːdlıs] □ нену́жный; ***~ to say*** разуме́ется

N

needlework вы́шивка
needy ['ni:dɪ] □ нужда́ющийся
negat|ion [nɪ'geɪʃn] отрица́ние; **~ive** ['negətɪv] **1.** □ отрица́тельный; негати́вный; **2.** *phot.* негати́в; ***answer in the ~*** дава́ть [дать] отрицательный ответ
neglect [nɪ'glekt] **1.** пренебреже́ние; (*carelessness*) небре́жность *f*; **2.** пренебрега́ть [-бре́чь] (Т); **~ed** [~ɪd] забро́шенный; **~ful** [~fʊl] небре́жный
negligen|ce ['neglɪdʒəns] небре́жность *f*; (*attitude*) хала́тность *f*; **~t** [~t] □ небре́жный; хала́тный
negligible ['neglɪdʒəbl] ничто́жный, незначи́тельный
negotia|te [nɪ'gəʊʃɪeɪt] вести́ перегово́ры; догова́риваться [-вори́ться] о (П); *obstacles, etc.* преодоле́(ва́)ть; **~tion** [nɪgəʊʃɪ'eɪʃn] перегово́ры *m/pl.*; **~tor** [nɪ'gəʊʃɪeɪtə] лицо́, веду́щее перегово́ры
Negr|ess ['ni:grɪs] *contemptuous* афроамерика́нка, негритя́нка; **~o** ['ni:grəʊ], *pl.* **~es** [~z] афроамерика́нец, негр
neigh [neɪ] **1.** ржа́ние; **2.** [за]ржа́ть
neighbo(u)r ['neɪbə] сосе́д(ка); **~hood** [~hʊd] окру́га, райо́н; **~ing** [~rɪŋ] сосе́дний
neither ['naɪðə] **1.** ни тот, ни друго́й; **2.** *adv.* та́кже не; ***~ ... nor ...*** ни ... ни ...

N

nephew ['nevju:] племя́нник
nerve [nɜ:v] **1.** нерв; (*courage*) му́жество, хладнокро́вие; на́глость *f*; ***get on s.b.'s ~s*** де́йствовать на не́рвы; ***have the ~ to ...*** име́ть на́глость *f*; **2.** придава́ть си́лы (хра́брости) (Д)
nervous ['nɜ:vəs] □ не́рвный; (*highly strung, irritable*) нерво́зный; **~ness** [~nɪs] не́рвность *f*, нерво́зность *f*
nest [nest] **1.** гнездо́ (*a. fig.*); **2.** вить гнездо́; **~le** ['nesl] *v/i.* удо́бно устро́иться *pf.*; приж(им)а́ться (***to, on, against*** к Д); *v/t. one's head* приж(им)а́ть (го́лову)
net[1] [net] **1.** сеть *f*; **2.** расставля́ть се́ти; пойма́ть *pf.* се́тью
net[2] [~] **1.** не́тто *adj. indecl.*, *weight*, *profit* чи́стый; **2.** приноси́ть (получа́ть) чи́стый дохо́д
nettle ['netl] **1.** *bot.* крапи́ва; **2.** обжига́ть крапи́вой; *fig.* раздража́ть, [рас]серди́ть
network ['netwɜ:k] *tech., rail, etc.* сеть *f*
neuralgia [njʊə'rældʒə] невралги́я
neurosis [njʊə'rəʊsɪs] невро́з
neuter ['nju:tə] *gr.* сре́дний род
neutral ['nju:trəl] **1.** □ нейтра́льный; **2.** нейтра́льное госуда́рство; **~ity** [nju:'trælətɪ] нейтралите́т; **~ize** ['nju:trəlaɪz] нейтрализова́ть (*im*)*pf.*
never ['nevə] никогда́; совсе́м не; **~ ending** бесконе́чный, несконча́емый; **~more** никогда́ бо́льше; **~theless** [nevəðə'les] тем не ме́нее; несмотря́ на э́то
new [nju:] но́вый; *vegetables, moon* молодо́й; *bread, etc.* све́жий; **~born** новоро́жденный; **~comer** вновь прибы́вший; новичо́к; **~fangled** ['~fæŋgld] новомо́дный; **~ly** ['nju:lɪ] за́ново, вновь; неда́вно
news [nju:z] но́вости *f/pl.*, изве́стия *n/pl.*; ***what's the ~?*** что но́вого?; **~agent** продаве́ц газе́т; **~paper** газе́та; **~print** газе́тная бума́га; **~reel** киножурна́л; **~stall, ~-stand** газе́тный кио́ск
New Testament Но́вый заве́т
New Year Но́вый год; ***~'s Eve*** кану́н Но́вого го́да; ***Happy ~!*** С Но́вым Го́дом!
next [nekst] **1.** *adj.* сле́дующий; ближа́йший; ***~ door to*** в сле́дующем до́ме; *fig.* чуть (ли) не, почти́; ***~ to*** во́зле (Р); вслед за (Т); **2.** *adv.* пото́м, по́сле, зате́м; в сле́дующий раз; **~ of kin** ближа́йший (-шая) ро́дственник (-ица)
nibble ['nɪbl] *v/t.* обгры́з(а́)ть
nice [naɪs] □ прия́тный, ми́лый, сла́вный; (*fine, delicate*) то́нкий; **~ty** ['naɪsətɪ] (*delicate point, detail*) то́нкости *f/pl.*, дета́ли *f/pl.*
niche [nɪtʃ] ни́ша
nick [nɪk] **1.** (*notch*) зару́бка; ***in the ~ of time*** как раз во́время; **2.** сде́лать *pf.* зару́бку в (П); *Am.* (*cheat*) обма́нывать [-ну́ть]; *Brt. coll.* (*steal*) стащи́ть *pf.*
nickel ['nɪkl] **1.** *min.* ни́кель *m*; *Am.*

монéта в 5 цéнтов; **2.** [от]никели́ровать
nickname ['nɪkneɪm] **1.** прóзвище; **2.** прозывáть [-звáть]; да(вá)ть прóзвище (Д)
nicotine ['nɪkəti:n] никоти́н
niece [ni:s] племя́нница
niggard ['nɪgəd] скупéц; **~ly** [~lɪ] скупóй; *sum, etc.* жáлкий
night [naɪt] ночь *f*, вéчер; ***by ~, at ~*** нóчью; ***stay the ~*** переночевáть; **~club** ночнóй клуб; **~fall** сýмерки *f/pl.*; **~dress, ~gown** ночнáя рубáшка; **~ingale** ['naɪtɪŋgeɪl] соловéй; **~ly** ['naɪtlɪ] ночнóй; *adv.* нóчью; кáждую ночь; **~mare** кошмáр
nil [nɪl] *sport* ноль *m or* нуль *m*; ничегó
nimble ['nɪmbl] □ провóрный, лóвкий; *mind* живóй
nimbus ['nɪmbəs] *eccl., art* нимб
nine [naɪn] дéвять; девя́тка; → ***five***; **~pins** *pl.* кéгли *f/pl.*; **~teen** [naɪn'ti:n] девятнáдцать; **~ty** ['naɪntɪ] девянóсто
ninny ['nɪnɪ] *coll.* простофи́ля *m/f*
ninth [naɪnθ] **1.** девя́тый; **2.** девя́тая часть *f*
nip [nɪp] **1.** щипóк; (*bite*) укýс; (*frost*) морóз; ***there is a ~ in the air*** вóздух морóзный; **2.** щипáть [щипнýть]; *finger* прищемля́ть [-ми́ть]; *flowers* поби́ть *pf.* морóзом; ***~ in the bud*** пресекáть в зарóдыше
nipper ['nɪpə] (***a pair of***) **~s** *pl.* клéщи *pl.*; *coll.* малы́ш
nipple ['nɪpl] сосóк
nitrate ['naɪtreɪt] нитрáт
nitrogen ['naɪtrədʒən] азóт
no [nəʊ] **1.** *adj.* никакóй; ***in ~ time*** в мгновéние óка; ***~ one*** никтó; **2.** *adv.* нет; **3.** отрицáние
Nobel prize [nəʊ'bel] Нóбелевская прéмия
nobility [nəʊ'bɪlətɪ] дворя́нство; благорóдство
noble ['nəʊbl] **1.** □ благорóдный; (*highborn*) знáтный; ***~ metal*** благорóдный метáлл; **2.** = **~man** титулóванное лицó, дворяни́н
nobody ['nəʊbədɪ] *pron.* никтó; *su.* ничтóжный человéк
nocturnal [nɒk'tɜ:nl] ночнóй
nod [nɒd] **1.** кивáть головóй; (*doze*) дремáть; *coll.* (*drowse*) клевáть нóсом; **2.** кивóк головóй
noise [nɔɪz] шум; (*din*) грóхот; ***make a ~*** *fig.* поднимáть [-ня́ть] шум; **~less** ['nɔɪzlɪs] □ бесшýмный
noisy ['nɔɪzɪ] □ шýмный; *child* шумли́вый
nomin|al ['nɒmɪnl] □ номинáльный; *gr.* именнóй; ***~ value*** номинáльная ценá; **~ate** ['nɒmɪneɪt] (*appoint*) назначáть [-знáчить]; *candidate* выдвигáть ['-инуть]; **~ation** [nɒmɪ'neɪʃn] выдвижéние; назначéние
non [nɒn] *prf.* не..., бес..., без...
nonalcoholic безалкогóльный
nonchalance ['nɒnʃələns] беззабóтность *f*
noncommittal [nɒnkə'mɪtl] уклóнчивый
nondescript ['nɒndɪskrɪpt] (*dull*) невзрáчный; *colo(u)r* неопределённый
none [nʌn] **1.** ничтó, никтó; ни оди́н; никакóй; **2.** нискóлько, совсéм не ...; ***~theless*** тем не мéнее
nonentity [nɒ'nentətɪ] *person* ничтóжество
nonexistent несуществýющий
nonpayment *mst. fin.* неплатёж, неуплáта
nonplus [nɒn'plʌs] приводи́ть в замешáтельство, озадáчи(ва)ть
nonpolluting [nɒnpə'lu:tɪŋ] не загрязня́ющий средý
nonprofit некоммéрческий
nonresident не проживáющий в дáнном мéсте
nonsens|e ['nɒnsəns] вздор, бесмы́слица; **~ical** [nɒn'sensɪkl] бесмы́сленный
nonsmoker *person* некуря́щий; *Brt. rail* вагóн для некуря́щих
nonstop безостанóвочный; *ae.* беспосáдочный
noodle ['nu:dl]: **~s** *pl.* лапшá
nook [nʊk] укрóмный уголóк; закоýлок; ***search every ~ and cranny*** обшáрить *pf.* все углы́ и закоýлки
noon [nu:n] пóлдень *m*
noose [nu:s] петля́; (*lasso*) аркáн
nor [nɔ:] и не; тáкже не; ни

N

norm [nɔːm] но́рма; **~al** ['nɔːml] □ норма́льный; **~alize** [~əlaɪz] приводи́ть [-вести́] в но́рму; нормализова́ть (*im*)*pf.*
north [nɔːθ] **1.** се́вер; **2.** се́верный; **3.** *adv.*: **~ of** к се́веру от (Р); **~-east** **1.** се́веро-восто́к; **2.** се́веро-восто́чный (*a.* **~-eastern**; **~erly** ['nɔːðəlɪ], **~ern** ['nɔːðən] се́верный; **~ward(s)** ['nɔːθwəd(z)] *adv.* на се́вер; к се́веру; **~-west** **1.** се́веро-за́пад; *naut.* норд-вест; **2.** се́веро-за́падный (*a.* **~-western**)
nose [nəʊz] **1.** нос; (*sense of smell*, *a. fig.*) чутьё; *of boat*, *etc.* нос; **2.** *v/t.* [по]ню́хать; *information* разню́х(ив)ать; **~gay** буке́т цвето́в
nostril ['nɒstrəl] ноздря́
nosy ['nəʊzɪ] *coll.* любопы́тный
not [nɒt] не
notable ['nəʊtəbl] □ примеча́тельный, знамена́тельный; *person* выдаю́щийся
notary ['nəʊtərɪ] нота́риус (*a.* **public ~**)
notation [nəʊ'teɪʃn] *mus.* нота́ция; за́пись *f*
notch [nɒtʃ] **1.** зару́бка; (*mark*) ме́тка; **2.** [с]де́лать зару́бку
note [nəʊt] **1.** заме́тка; за́пись *f*; (*comment*) примеча́ние; (*bank note*) банкно́т; (*denomination*) де́нежная купю́ра; *dipl.* но́та; *mus.* но́та; **man of ~** знамени́тость *f*; **worthy of ~** досто́йный внима́ния; **2.** замеча́ть [-е́тить]; (*mention*) упомина́ть [-мяну́ть]; (*a.* **~ down**) де́лать заме́тки, запи́сывать [-са́ть]; (*make a mental note*) отмеча́ть [-е́тить]; **~book** записна́я кни́жка; **~d** [~ɪd] хорошо́ изве́стный; **~worthy** примеча́тельный
nothing ['nʌθɪŋ] ничто́, ничего́; **for ~** зря, да́ром; **come to ~** ни к чему́ не привести́ *pf.*; **to say ~ of** не говоря́ уже́ о (П); **there is ~ like ...** нет ничего́ лу́чшего, чем ...
notice ['nəʊtɪs] **1.** внима́ние; извеще́ние, уведомле́ние; (*warning*) предупрежде́ние; (*announcement*) объявле́ние; **at short ~** без предупрежде́ния; **give ~** предупрежда́ть об увольне́нии (*or* об ухо́де); извеща́ть [-ести́ть]; **2.** замеча́ть [-е́тить]; обраща́ть внима́ние на (В); **~able** [~əbl] □ досто́йный внима́ния; заме́тный; **~ board** доска́ объявле́ний
notification [nəʊtɪfɪ'keɪʃn] извеще́ние, сообще́ние
notify ['nəʊtɪfaɪ] извеща́ть [-ести́ть], уведомля́ть [уве́домить]
notion ['nəʊʃn] поня́тие, представле́ние
notorious [nəʊ'tɔːrɪəs] □ общеизве́стный; *pej.* пресловутый
notwithstanding [nɒtwɪθ'stændɪŋ] несмотря́ на (В), вопреки́ (Д)
nought [nɔːt] ничто́; *math.* ноль *m or* нуль *m*; **bring to ~** своди́ть [свести́] на нет
nourish ['nʌrɪʃ] пита́ть (*a. fig.*); [на-, по]корми́ть; *fig. hope*, *etc.* леле́ять; **~ing** [~ɪŋ] пита́тельный; **~ment** [~mənt] пита́ние; пи́ща (*a. fig.*)
novel ['nɒvl] **1.** но́вый; (*unusual*) необы́чный; **2.** рома́н; **~ist** [~ɪst] писа́тель *m*, -ница *f*; романи́ст; **~ty** [~tɪ] нови́нка; новизна́; (*method*) но́вшество
November [nəʊ'vembə] ноя́брь *m*
novice ['nɒvɪs] новичо́к; *eccl.* послу́шник *m*, -ница *f*
now [naʊ] **1.** тепе́рь, сейча́с; то́тчас; **just ~** то́лько что; **~ and again** (*или* **then**) вре́мя от вре́мени; **2.** *cj.* когда́, раз
nowadays ['naʊədeɪz] ны́нче; в на́ши дни; в на́ше вре́мя
nowhere ['nəʊweə] нигде́, никуда́
noxious ['nɒkʃəs] □ вре́дный
nozzle ['nɒzl] *of hose* наконе́чник; *tech.* со́пло
nucle|ar ['njuːklɪə] я́дерный; **~ pile** я́дерный реа́ктор; **~ power plant** а́томная электроста́нция; **~us** [~s] ядро́
nude [njuːd] го́лый, наго́й; *art.* **~ figure** обнажённая фигу́ра
nudge [nʌdʒ] *coll.* **1.** подта́лкивать [-толкну́ть]; **2.** лёгкий толчо́к ло́ктем
nuisance ['njuːsns] неприя́тность *f*; доса́да; *fig.* надое́дливый челове́к
null [nʌl] недействи́тельный; **become ~ and void** утра́чивать [утра́тить] зако́нную си́лу; **~ify**

N

['nʌlıfaı] аннули́ровать (*im*)*pf.*; расторга́ть [-то́ргнуть]
numb [nʌm] *with terror* онеме́вший, оцепене́вший; *with cold* окочене́вший
number ['nʌmbə] **1.** число́; но́мер; (*figure*) ци́фра; **2.** нумерова́ть; (*be in number*) насчи́тывать; **~less** [~lıs] бесчи́сленный; **~ plate** *mot.* номерно́й знак
numeral ['nju:mərəl] **1.** *gr.* и́мя числи́тельное; (*figure*) ци́фра; **2.** цифрово́й
numerical [nju:'merıkəl] □ числово́й; чи́сленный
numerous ['nju:mərəs] □ многочи́сленный; ***in ~ cases*** во мно́гих слу́чаях
nun [nʌn] мона́хиня
nunnery ['nʌnərı] же́нский монасты́рь *m*
nurse [nɜ:s] **1.** ня́ня (*a.* ***~-maid***); медици́нская сестра́, медсестра́; **2.** (*breast-feed*) [на]корми́ть гру́дью; (*take nourishment from the breast*) соса́ть грудь *f*; (*rear*) вска́рмливать; (*look after*) уха́живать за (Т); **~ry** ['nɜ:sərı] де́тская (ко́мната); *agric.* пито́мник; ***~ school*** де́тский сад
nursing ['nɜ:sıŋ]: ***~ home*** ча́стная лече́бница; ***~ staff*** медсёстры
nurture ['nɜ:tʃə] (*bring up*) воспи́тывать [-та́ть]
nut [nʌt] opéx; *tech.* га́йка; ***a hard ~ to crack*** кре́пкий оре́шек; **~cracker** щипцы́ для оре́хов; **~meg** ['nʌtmeg] муска́тный оре́х
nutri|tion [nju:'trıʃn] пита́ние; **~tious** [~ʃəs], **~tive** ['nju:trətıv] □ пита́тельный
nut|shell оре́ховая скорлупа́; ***in a ~*** кра́тко, в двух слова́х; **~ty** ['nʌtı] *taste* име́ющий вкус оре́ха; *coll. idea, etc.* бредово́й; *person* безу́мный, психо́ванный
nylon ['naılɒn] нейло́н
nymph [nımf] ни́мфа

O

oaf [əʊf] дура́к; у́валень *m*
oak [əʊk] дуб; *attr.* дубо́вый
oar [ɔ:] **1.** весло́; **2.** *poet.* грести́; **~sman** ['ɔ:zmən] гребе́ц
oasis [əʊ'eısıs] оа́зис
oat [əʊt] овёс (*mst.* ***~s*** *pl.*)
oath [əʊθ] кля́тва; *mil.*, *law* прися́га; (*curse*) руга́тельство
oatmeal ['əʊtmi:l] овся́нка
obdurate ['ɒbdjʊərət] □ (*stubborn*) упря́мый; (*unrepentant*) нераска́янный
obedien|ce [ə'bi:dıəns] повинове́ние; **~t** [~t] □ послу́шный
obelisk ['ɒbəlısk] обели́ск
obese [əʊ'bi:s] ту́чный
obesity [əʊ'bi:sətı] ту́чность *f*
obey [ə'beı] повинова́ться (*im*)*pf.* (Д); [по]слу́шаться (Р)
obituary [ə'bıtʃʊərı] некро́лог
object 1. ['ɒbdʒıkt] предме́т, вещь *f*; объе́кт; *fig.* цель *f*; наме́рение; **2.** [əb'dʒekt] (*disapprove*) не одобря́ть (Р), протестова́ть; возража́ть [-рази́ть] (***to*** про́тив Р); ***if you don't ~*** е́сли вы не возража́ете
objection [əb'dʒekʃn] возраже́ние; проте́ст; **~able** [~əbl] □ нежела́тельный; (*distasteful*) неприя́тный
objective [əb'dʒektıv] **1.** □ объекти́вный; **2.** объе́кт, цель *f*
obligat|ion [ɒblı'geıʃn] (*promise*) обяза́тельство; (*duty*) обя́занность *f*; **~ory** [ə'blıgətrı] □ обяза́тельный
oblig|e [ə'blaıdʒ] (*require*) обя́зывать [-за́ть]; (*compel*) вынужда́ть [-нудить]; ***I was ~d to ...*** я был вы́нужден ...; ***~ a p.*** де́лать одолже́ние кому́-либо; ***much ~d*** о́чень благода́рен (-рна); **~ing** [~ıŋ] □

услу́жливый, любе́зный
oblique [ə'bli:k] □ косо́й; *gr.* ко́свенный
obliterate [ə'blɪtəreɪt] (*efface*) изгла́живать(ся) [-ла́дить(ся)]; (*destroy*) уничтожа́ть [-о́жить]; (*expunge*) вычёркивать [вы́черкнуть]
oblivi|on [ə'blɪvɪən] забве́ние; **~ous** [~əs] □ забы́вчивый
obnoxious [əb'nɒkʃəs] проти́вный, несно́сный
obscene [əb'si:n] □ непристо́йный
obscur|e [əb'skjʊə] **1.** □ тёмный; (*not distinct*) нея́сный; *author, etc.* малоизве́стный; *meaning, etc.* непоня́тный; **2.** *sun, etc.* заслоня́ть [-ни́ть]; **~ity** [~rətɪ] неизве́стность *f*; *in text* нея́сное ме́сто
obsequious [əb'si:kwɪəs] □ подобостра́стный
observ|able [əb'zɜ:vəbl] □ заме́тный; **~ance** [~vəns] *of law, etc.* соблюде́ние; *of anniversary, etc.* пра́зднование; **~ant** [~vənt] □ наблюда́тельный; **~ation** [ɒbzə'veɪʃn] наблюде́ние; наблюда́тельность *f*; (*comment*) замеча́ние; **~atory** [əb'zɜ:vətrɪ] обсервато́рия; **~e** [əb'zɜ:v] *v/t.* наблюда́ть; *fig.* соблюда́ть [-юсти́]; (*notice*) замеча́ть [-е́тить] (В); *v/i.* замеча́ть [-е́тить]; **~er** [~ə] наблюда́тель *m*
obsess [əb'ses]: **~ed by**, *a.* **with** одержи́мый (Т); **~ion** [əb'seʃn] навя́зчивая иде́я; одержи́мость *f*
obsolete ['ɒbsəli:t] устаре́лый; *words, etc.* устаре́вший
obstacle ['ɒbstəkl] препя́тствие
obstinate ['ɒbstənət] упря́мый; насто́йчивый
obstruct [əb'strʌkt] [по]меша́ть (Д), затрудня́ть [-ни́ть]; (*block*) загражда́ть [-ади́ть] загора́живать [-роди́ть]; **~ion** [əb'strʌkʃn] препя́тствие, поме́ха; загражде́ние; *law* обстру́кция; **~ive** [~tɪv] препя́тствующий; обструкцио́нный
obtain [əb'teɪn] *v/t.* (*receive*) получа́ть [-чи́ть]; (*procure*) добы́(ва́)ть; (*acquire*) обрета́ть [-ести́]; **~able** [~əbl] досту́пный; *result, etc.* достижи́мый
obtru|de [əb'tru:d] навя́зывать(ся) [-за́ть(ся)] (**on** Д); **~sive** [~sɪv] навя́зчивый
obvious ['ɒbvɪəs] □ очеви́дный, я́сный, я́вный
occasion [ə'keɪʒn] **1.** слу́чай; возмо́жность *f*; (*reason*) по́вод, причи́на; (*special event*) собы́тие; ***on that ~*** в тот раз; ***on the ~ of*** по слу́чаю (Р); ***rise to the ~*** оказа́ться *pf.* на высоте́ положе́ния; **2.** причиня́ть [-ни́ть]; дава́ть по́вод к (Д); **~al** [~ʒnl] □ случа́йный; ре́дкий
occult [ɒ'kʌlt] □ окку́льтный
occup|ant ['ɒkjʊpənt] (*inhabitant*) жи́тель *m*, -ница *f*; (*tenant*) жиле́ц; ***the ~s of the car*** е́хавшие (*or* сидя́щие) в маши́не; **~ation** [ɒkjʊ'peɪʃn] *mil.* оккупа́ция; (*work, profession*) заня́тие, профе́ссия; **~y** ['ɒkjʊpaɪ] *seat, etc.* занима́ть [заня́ть]; (*take possession of*) завладе́(ва́)ть (Т); оккупи́ровать (*im*)*pf.*
occur [ə'kɜ:] (*take place*) случа́ться [-чи́ться]; (*be met with*) встреча́ться [-е́титься]; ***~ to a p.*** приходи́ть в го́лову; **~rence** [ə'kʌrəns] происше́ствие, слу́чай
ocean ['əʊʃn] океа́н
o'clock [ə'klɒk]: ***five ~*** пять часо́в
ocul|ar ['ɒkjʊlə] глазно́й; **~ist** ['ɒkjʊlɪst] окули́ст, глазно́й врач
odd [ɒd] □ нечётный; *sock, etc.* непа́рный; (*extra*) ли́шний; *of incomplete set* разро́зненный; (*strange*) стра́нный; **~ity** ['ɒdɪtɪ] чудакова́тость *f*; **~s** [ɒdz] ша́нсы *m/pl.*; ***be at ~ with*** не ла́дить с (Т); ***~ and ends*** оста́тки *m/pl.*; вся́кая вся́чина
odious ['əʊdɪəs] ненави́стный; (*repulsive*) отврати́тельный
odo(u)r ['əʊdə] за́пах; арома́т
of [ɒv; *mst.* əv, v] *prp.* о, об (П); из (Р); от (Р); *denoting cause, affiliation, agent, quality, source; often corresponds to the genitive case in Russian*; ***think ~ s.th.*** ду́мать о (П); ***out ~ charity*** из милосе́рдия; ***die ~*** умере́ть *pf.* от (Р); ***cheat ~*** обсчи́тывать на (В); ***the battle ~ Quebec*** би́тва под Квебе́ком; ***proud ~*** го́рдый (Т); ***the roof ~ the house*** кры́ша до́ма
off [ɔ:f, ɒf] **1.** *adv.* прочь; ***far ~*** дале-

O

кó; *translated into Russian mst. by verbal prefixes*: **go ~** (*leave*) уходи́ть [уйти́]; **switch ~** выключа́ть [вы́клю-чить]; **take ~** (*remove*) снима́ть [снять]; **on and ~**, **~ and on** вре́мя от вре́мени; **be well ~** быть обеспе́ченным; **2.** *prp.* с (Р), со (Р) *indicates removal from a surface*; от (Р) *indicates distance*; **3.** *adj.*: **day ~** выходно́й день; **~side** *Brt.* пра́вая сторона́; *Am.* ле́вая сторона́; **the ~ season** мёртвый сезо́н

offal ['ɒfl] потроха́ *m/pl.*

offend [ə'fend] *v/t.* обижа́ть [оби́деть]; *feelings* оскорбля́ть [-би́ть]; *v/i.* наруша́ть [-у́шить] (**against** В); **~er** [~ə] оби́дчик; *law* правонару-ши́тель(ница *f*) *m*; **first ~** человек, суди́мый (соверши́вший преступле́ние) впервы́е

offen|se, *Brt.* **~ce** [ə'fens] (*transgression*) просту́пок; оби́да, оскорбле́ние; *mil.* наступле́ние

offensive [ə'fensɪv] **1.** □ (*insulting*) оскорби́тельный, оби́дный; (*disagreeable*) проти́вный; **2.** *mil.* наступле́ние

offer ['ɒfə] **1.** предложе́ние; **2.** *v/t.* предлага́ть [-ложи́ть]; **~ an explanation** дава́ть [дать] объясне́ние; **~ resistance** оказа́ть [-а́зывать] сопротивле́ние

offhand [ɒf'hænd] *manner* бесцеремо́нный; развя́зный; *adv.* без подгото́вки; **he couldn't tell me ~ ...** он не смог мне сра́зу отве́тить ...

office ['ɒfɪs] (*position*) до́лжность *f*; слу́жба; (*premises*) конто́ра; канцеля́рия; *of doctor, dentist, etc.* кабине́т; **~** министе́рство; **~ hours** часы́ рабо́ты, приёмные часы́

officer ['ɒfɪsə] *mil.* офице́р

official [ə'fɪʃl] **1.** □ официа́льный; служе́бный; **through ~ channels** по официа́льным кана́лам; **2.** должностно́е лицо́, слу́жащий; *hist., a. pej.* чино́вник

officious [ə'fɪʃəs] □ назо́йливый, навя́зчивый

off|set возмеща́ть [-ести́ть]; **~shoot** побе́г; ответвле́ние; **~spring** о́тпрыск, пото́мок; **~-the-record** конфиденциа́льный

often ['ɒfn] ча́сто, мно́го раз; **more ~ than not** бо́льшей ча́стью; в большинстве́ слу́чаев

ogle ['əʊgl] стро́ить гла́зки (Д)

oil [ɔɪl] **1.** (*vegetable ~*) ма́сло; (*petroleum*) нефть *f*; **diesel ~** соля́рка; **fuel ~** жи́дкое то́пливо; **2.** сма́з(ыв)ать; **~cloth** клеёнка; **~field** нефтяно́е месторожде́ние; **~well** нефтяна́я сква́жина; **~y** ['ɔɪlɪ] масляни́стый, ма́сляный; *fig.* еле́йный

ointment ['ɔɪntmənt] мазь *f*

OK, okay [əʊ'keɪ] *coll.* **1.** *pred.* в поря́дке, хорошо́; **2.** *int.* хорошо́!, ла́дно!, идёт!; слушаюсь!

old [əʊld] *com.* ста́рый; (**in times**) **of ~** в старину́; **~ age** ста́рость *f*; **~-fashioned** [~'fæʃnd] старомо́дный

olfactory [ɒl'fæktərɪ] обоня́тельный

olive ['ɒlɪv] *fruit* масли́на; *colo(u)r* оли́вковый цвет

Olympic [ə'lɪmpɪk]: **the ~ Games** Олимпи́йские и́гры

omelet(te) ['ɒmlɪt] омле́т

ominous ['ɒmɪnəs] □ злове́щий

omission [ə'mɪʃn] (*oversight*) упуще́ние; (*leaving out*) про́пуск

omit [ə'mɪt] пропуска́ть [-сти́ть]; (*on purpose*) опуска́ть [-сти́ть]

on [ɒn] **1.** *prp. mst.* на (П *or* В); **~ the wall** на стене́; **~ good authority** из достове́рного исто́чника; **~ the 1st of April** пе́рвого апре́ля; **~ his arrival** по его́ прибы́тии; **talk ~ a subject** говори́ть на те́му; **~ hearing it** услы́шав э́то; **2.** *adv.* да́льше; вперёд; да́лее; **keep one's hat ~** остава́ться в шля́пе; **have a coat ~** быть в пальто́; **and so ~** и так да́лее (и т.д.); **be ~** быть запу́щенным в ход, включённым (*и т. п.*)

once [wʌns] **1.** *adv.* раз; не́когда; когда́-то; **at ~** сейча́с же; **~ and for all** раз (и) навсегда́; **~ in a while** и́зредка; **this ~** на э́тот раз; **2.** *cj.* как то́лько

one [wʌn] **1.** оди́н; еди́ный; еди́нственный; како́й-то; **~ day** одна́жды; **~ never knows** никогда́ не зна́ешь; **2.** (число́) оди́н; едини́ца; **the little ~s** малыши́ *m/pl.*; **~ another** друг дру́га; **at ~** заодно́; **~ by ~** оди́н за

O

другим; ***I for*** ~ я со своей стороны
onerous ['ɒnərəs] □ обременительный
one|self [wʌn'self] *pron. refl.* -ся, -сь, (самого) себя; **~-sided** □ односторонний; **~-way**: ~ ***street*** улица с односторонним движением
onion ['ʌnjən] лук, луковица
onlooker ['ɒnlʊkə] → ***looker-on***
only ['əʊnlɪ] **1.** *adj.* единственный; **2.** *adv.* единственно; только, лишь; исключительно; ~ ***yesterday*** только вчера; **3.** *cj.* но; ~ ***that ...*** если бы не то, что ...
onset ['ɒnset] начало
onslaught ['ɒnslɔːt] атака, нападение
onward ['ɒnwəd] **1.** *adj.* продвигающий; ~ ***movement*** движение вперёд; **2.** *adv.* вперёд; впереди
ooze [uːz] [про]сочиться
opaque [əʊ'peɪk] □ непрозрачный
open ['əʊpən] **1.** □ *com.* открытый; (*frank*) откровенный; ~ ***to*** доступный (Д); ***in the ~ air*** на открытом воздухе; **2.** ***bring into the*** ~ сделать *pf.* достоянием общественности; **3.** *v/t.* откры(ва)ть; нач(ин)ать; *v/i.* откры(ва)ться; нач(ин)аться; ~ ***into*** *of door* откры(ва)ться в (В); ~ ***on to*** выходить на *or* в (В); **~-handed** щедрый; **~ing** [~ɪŋ] отверстие; начало; *of exhibition* открытие; **~-minded** *fig.* непредубеждённый
opera ['ɒpərə] опера; ~ **glasses** *pl.* театральный бинокль *m*
operat|e ['ɒpəreɪt] *v/t.* управлять (Т); *part. Am.* приводить в действие; *v/i. med.* оперировать (*im*)*pf.*; работать; действовать; **~ion** [ɒpə'reɪʃn] действие; *med.*, *mil.*, *comm.* операция; процесс; ***be in*** ~ быть в действии; **~ive** ['ɒpərətɪv] □ *having force* действительный; *effective* действенный; *working* действующий; **~or** ['ɒpəreɪtə] *of a machine* управляющий; *tel.* оператор; телеграфист(ка *f*) *m*
opinion [ə'pɪnjən] мнение; взгляд; ***in my*** ~ по-моему
opponent [ə'pəʊnənt] оппонент, противник
opportun|e ['ɒpətjuːn] □ благоприятный, подходящий; *timely* своевременный; **~ity** [ɒpə'tjuːnətɪ] удобный случай, возможность *f*
oppos|e [ə'pəʊz] противопоставлять [-ставить]; (*be against*) [вос-] противиться (Д); **~ed** [~d] противопоставленный; ***as ~ to*** в отличие от (Р); ***be*** ~ быть против (Р); **~ite** ['ɒpəzɪt] **1.** □ противоположный; **2.** *prp.*, *adv.* напротив, против (Р); **3.** противоположность *f*; **~ition** [ɒpə'zɪʃn] противопоставление; сопротивление; оппозиция
oppress [ə'pres] притеснять [-нить], угнетать; **~ion** [~ʃn] притеснение, угнетение; **~ive** [~sɪv] □ гнетущий; *weather* душный
optic ['ɒptɪk] глазной, зрительный; **~al** [~l] □ оптический; **~ian** [ɒp'tɪʃn] оптик
optimism ['ɒptɪmɪzəm] оптимизм
optimistic [ɒptɪ'mɪstɪk] *person* оптимистичный; *prognosis*, *etc.* оптимистический
option ['ɒpʃn] выбор, право выбора; **~al** ['ʃənl] □ необязательный, факультативный
opulence ['ɒpjʊləns] богатство
or [ɔː] или; ~ ***else*** иначе; или же
oracle ['ɒrəkl] оракул
oral ['ɔːrəl] □ устный; словесный
orange ['ɒrɪndʒ] **1.** апельсин; оранжевый цвет; **2.** оранжевый
orator ['ɒrətə] оратор
orbit ['ɔːbɪt] орбита; ***put into*** ~ выводить [-вести] на орбиту
orchard ['ɔːtʃəd] фруктовый сад
orchestra ['ɔːkɪstrə] оркестр
ordain [ɔː'deɪn] посвящать в духовный сан
ordeal [ɔː'diːl] *fig.* испытание
order ['ɔːdə] **1.** порядок; (*command*) приказ; *comm.* заказ; ***take*** (***holy***) **~s** принимать духовный сан; ***in ~ to*** чтобы; ***in ~ that*** с тем, чтобы; ***make to*** ~ делать на заказ; ***out of*** ~ неисправный; **2.** приказывать [-зать]; *comm.* заказывать [-зать]; **~ly** [~lɪ] (*well arranged*, *tidy*) аккуратный; дисциплинированный
ordinary ['ɔːdənrɪ] обыкновенный; заурядный; ***out of the*** ~ необычный

ore ['ɔː] руда́
organ ['ɔːgən] о́рган; *mus.* орга́н; **~ic** [ɔː'gænɪk] (**~ally**) органи́ческий; *fig.* органи́чный
organ|ization [ɔːgənaɪ'zeɪʃn] организа́ция; **~ize** ['ɔːgənaɪz] организова́ть *(im)pf.*; **~izer** [~ə] организа́тор
orgy ['ɔːdʒɪ] о́ргия
orient ['ɔːrɪənt] **1.**: ***the*** ♎ Восто́к, восто́ч-ные стра́ны *f/pl.*; **2.** ориенти́ро-вать *(im)pf.*; **~al** [ɔːrɪ'entl] □ восто́чный, азиа́тский; **~ate** ['ɔːrɪənteɪt] ориенти́ровать *(im)pf.*
orifice ['ɒrɪfɪs] (*opening*) отве́рстие
origin ['ɒrɪdʒɪn] (*source*) исто́чник; (*derivation*) происхожде́ние; (*beginning*) нача́ло
original [ə'rɪdʒənl] **1.** □ (*first*) первонача́льный; *ideas, etc.* оригина́льный; (*not a copy*) по́длинный; **2.** оригина́л, по́длинник; (*eccentric*) чуда́к; ***in the ~*** в оригина́ле; **~ity** [ərɪdʒə'nælətɪ] оригина́льность *f*
originat|e [ə'rɪdʒɪneɪt] *v/t.* дава́ть нача́ло (Д), порожда́ть [породи́ть]; *v/i.* происходи́ть [-изойти́] (***from*** от Р); **~or** [~ə] инициа́тор
ornament 1. ['ɔːnəmənt] украше́ние (*a. fig.*), орна́мент; **2.** [~ment] украша́ть [укра́сить]; **~al** [ɔːnə'mentl] □ декорати́вный
ornate [ɔː'neɪt] □ бога́то укра́шенный; *style* витиева́тый
orphan ['ɔːfn] **1.** сирота́ *m/f.*; **2.** осироте́вший (*a.* **~ed**); **~age** ['ɔːfənɪdʒ] сиро́тский дом; прию́т для сиро́т
orthodox ['ɔːθədɒks] □ ортодокса́льный; *eccl.* правосла́вный
oscillate ['ɒsɪleɪt] *swing* кача́ться; (*fluctuate*), *a. fig.* колеба́ться
ostensible [ɒ'stensəbl] □ слу́жащий предло́гом; мни́мый; очеви́дный
ostentatious [ɒsten'teɪʃəs] □ показно́й
ostrich ['ɒstrɪtʃ] *zo.* стра́ус
other ['ʌðə] друго́й; ино́й; ***the ~ day*** на днях; ***the ~ morning*** неда́вно у́тром; ***every ~ day*** че́рез день; ***in ~ words*** други́ми слова́ми; **~wise** [~waɪz] ина́че; и́ли же
otter ['ɒtə] *zo.* вы́дра
ought [ɔːt]: ***I ~ to*** мне сле́довало бы; ***you ~ to have done it*** вам сле́довало э́то сде́лать
ounce [aʊns] у́нция
our ['aʊə] *poss. adj.*; **~s** ['aʊəz] *pron. & pred. adj.* наш, на́ша, на́ше; на́ши *pl.*; **~selves** [aʊə'selvz] *pron.* **1.** *refl.* себя́, -ся, -сь; **2.** *for emphasis* (мы) са́ми
oust [aʊst] выгоня́ть [вы́гнать], вытесня́ть [вы́теснить]
out [aʊt] *adv.* нару́жу; вон; в, на; *often translated by the prefix* вы-: ***take ~*** вынима́ть [вы́нуть]; ***have it ~ with s.o.*** объясни́ться *pf.* с ке́м-л.; ***~ and ~*** соверше́нно; ***a/the way ~*** вы́ход; ***~ size*** разме́р бо́льше норма́льного; *prp.* **~ *of***: из (Р); вне (Р); из-за (Р)
out|... [aʊt] пере...; вы...; рас...; про...; воз..., вз...; из...; **~balance** [~'bæləns] переве́шивать [-ве́сить]; **~break** ['aʊtbreɪk] *of anger, etc.* вспы́шка; *of war, etc.* (внеза́пное) нача́ло; **~building** ['aʊtbɪldɪŋ] надво́рное строе́ние; **~burst** [~bɜːst] взрыв, вспы́шка; **~cast** [~kɑːst] отве́рженный; **~come** [~kʌm] результа́т; **~cry** [~kraɪ] кри́ки, шум; проте́ст; **~do** [aʊt'duː] [*irr.* (**do**)] превосходи́ть [-взойти́]; **~door** ['aʊtdɔː] *adj.* (находя́щийся) на откры́том во́здухе; *clothes* ве́рхний; **~doors** [~'dɔːz] *adv.* на откры́том во́здухе; ***it's cold ~*** на у́лице хо́лодно
outer ['aʊtə] вне́шний, нару́жный; **~most** [~məʊst] кра́йний; са́мый да́льний от це́нтра
out|fit ['aʊtfɪt] (*equipment*) снаряже́ние; (*clothes*) костю́м; **~going** [~gəʊɪŋ] уходя́щий; *letters, etc.* исходя́щий; *person* общи́тельный; ужи́вчивый; **~grow** [aut'grəʊ] [*irr.* (**grow**)] *clothes* выраста́ть [вы́расти] из (Р); **~house** [~haʊs] надво́рное строе́ние; *Am.* убо́рная во дворе́
outing ['aʊtɪŋ] (за́городная) прогу́лка, экску́рсия
out|last [aʊt'lɑːst] *mst. of person* пережи́(ва́)ть; *of things* служи́ть (носи́ться) до́льше, чем...; **~law** ['aʊtlɔː] **1.** челове́к вне зако́на; **2.**

объявля́ть вне зако́на; **~lay** [~leɪ] расхо́ды *m/pl.*; **~let** [~let] выпускно́е отве́рстие; вы́ход; **~line** [~laɪn] **1.** (*a. pl.*) очерта́ние, ко́нтур; **2.** де́лать набро́сок (P); **~live** [aʊt'lɪv] пережи́(ва́)ть; **~look** ['aʊtlʊk] вид, перспекти́ва; то́чка зре́ния, взгляд; **~lying** [~laɪɪŋ] отдалённый; **~number** [aʊt'nʌmbə] превосходи́ть чи́сленностью; **~patient** амбулато́рный больно́й; **≈patient Department** поликли́ника при больни́це; **~pouring** ['~pɔːrɪŋ] *mst. pl.* излия́ние (чувств); **~put** [~pʊt] (*production*) вы́пуск; проду́кция; (*productivity*) производи́тельность *f*

outrage ['aʊtreɪdʒ] **1.** наруше́ние прили́чий; безобра́зие; возмути́тельное явле́ние; **2.** оскорбля́ть [-би́ть] возмуща́ть [-ути́ть]; изнаси́ловать; **~ous** [aʊt'reɪdʒəs] □ возмути́тельный; безобра́зный; сканда́льный

out|right ['aʊtraɪt] откры́то, пря́мо, реши́тельно; **~run** [aʊt'rʌn] [*irr.* (***run***)] перегоня́ть [-гна́ть], опережа́ть [-реди́ть]; **~set** ['aʊtset] нача́ло; ***from the ~*** с са́мого нача́ла; **~shine** [aʊt'ʃaɪn] [*irr.* (***shine***)] затмева́ть [-ми́ть]; **~side** ['aʊtsaɪd] нару́жная сторона́; (*surface*) пове́рхность *f*; вне́шний вид; ***at the ~*** са́мое бо́льшее; **2.** ['aʊtsaɪd] нару́жный, вне́шний; кра́йний; **3.** *adv.* нару́жу; снару́жи; на (откры́том) во́здухе; **4.** *prp.* вне (P); **~sider** [aʊt'saɪdə] посторо́нний (челове́к); **~skirts** ['aʊtskɜːts] *pl.* окра́ина; **~spoken** [aʊt'spəʊkən] □ открове́нный; **~standing** [aʊt'stændɪŋ] *fig.* выдаю́щийся; *bill* неопла́ченный; **~stretch** [aʊt'stretʃ] протя́гивать [-тяну́ть]; **~strip** [~'strɪp] опережа́ть [-реди́ть]; (*surpass*) превосходи́ть [-взойти́]

outward ['aʊtwəd] **1.** вне́шний, нару́жный; ***during the ~ journey*** (***to*** ***...***) во вре́мя пое́здки туда́ (в B); **2.** *adv.* (*mst.* **~s** [~z]) нару́жу; за преде́лы

outweigh [aʊt'weɪ] превосходи́ть ве́сом; переве́шивать [переве́сить]

oven ['ʌvn] *in bakery, industry, etc.* печь *f*; *in stove* духо́вка

over ['əʊvə] **1.** *adv. usually translated by verbal prefixes*: пере...; вы...; про...; сно́ва; вдоба́вок; сли́шком; ***~ and above*** в добавле́ние, к тому́же; (***all***) ***~ again*** сно́ва, ещё раз; ***~ and ~*** (***again***) сно́ва и сно́ва; ***read ~*** перечи́тывать [-чита́ть]; ***it's all ~*** всё ко́нчено; **2.** *prp.* над (T); по (Д); за (B); свы́ше (P); сверх (P) че́рез (B); о(б) (П); ***all ~ the town*** по всему́ го́роду

over|... ['əʊvə] *pref.* сверх...; над...; пере...; чрезме́рно; **~act** [əʊvə'ækt] переи́грывать [-гра́ть]; **~all** ['əʊvərɔːl] *working clothes* хала́т; **~s** комбинезо́н, *coll.* спецо́вка; **~awe** [əʊvər'ɔː] внуша́ть [-ши́ть] благогове́йный стра́х; **~balance** [əʊvə'bæləns] теря́ть равнове́сие; *fig.* переве́шивать [-ве́сить]; **~bearing** [əʊvə'beərɪŋ] □ вла́стный; **~board** ['əʊvəbɔːd] *naut.* за́ борт, за бо́ртом; **~cast** ['əʊvəkɑːst] покры́тый облака́ми; па́смурный; **~charge** [əʊvə'tʃɑːdʒ] брать [взять] сли́шком мно́го (***for*** за B); **~coat** ['əʊvəkəʊt] пальто́ *n indecl.*; **~come** [əʊvə'kʌm] [*irr.* (***come***)] (*surmount*) преодоле́(ва́)ть, (*defeat*) побежда́ть [-еди́ть]; **~crowd** [əʊvə'kraʊd] переполня́ть [-по́лнить]; **~do** [əʊvə'duː] [*irr.* (***do***)] *meat, etc.* пережа́ри(ва)ть; (*go too far*) переусе́рдствовать (*im*)*pf.*; **~draw** [əʊvə'drɔː] [*irr.* (***draw***)]: ***~ one's account*** превы́сить *pf.* креди́т в ба́нке; **~dress** [əʊvə'dres] оде́(ва́)ться; сли́шком наря́дно; **~due** [əʊvə'djuː] *payment* просро́ченный; ***the bus is 5 minutes ~*** авто́бус опа́здывает на пять мину́т; **~eat** [əʊvər'iːt] перееда́ть [-е́сть]; **~flow 1.** [əʊvə'fləʊ] [*irr.* (***flow***)] *v/t.* затопля́ть [-пи́ть]; *v/i.* перели́(ва́)ться; **2.** ['əʊvəfləʊ] наводне́ние; разли́в; **~grow** [əʊvə'grəʊ] [*irr.* (***grow***)] *with weeds* зараста́ть [-ти́]; **~hang** [əʊvə'hæŋ] [*irr.* (***hang***)] *v/i.* нависа́ть [-и́снуть]; **~haul** [əʊvə'hɔːl] (*repair*) (капита́льно) [от]ремонти́ровать; **~head 1.** [əʊvə'hed] *adv.* над голово́й, наверху́; **2.** ['əʊvəhed] *adj.* ве́рхний; **3. ~s** ['əʊvəhedz] *pl. comm.* накладны́е расхо́ды *m/pl.*; **~hear** [əʊvə'hɪə] [*irr.* (***hear***)] подслу́ш(ив)ать; нечáянно услы́шать; **~lap** [əʊvə'læp] *v/i.* заходи́ть оди́н за друго́й; *fig.* совпада́ть; **~lay** [əʊvə'leɪ] [*irr.* (***lay***)] *tech.* покры́(ва́)ть; **~load** [əʊvə'ləʊd] перегружа́ть [-узи́ть]; **~look** [əʊvə'lʊk] *of windows, etc.* выходи́ть на (В); (*not notice*) про-пуска́ть [-сти́ть]; упуска́ть [-сти́ть]; **~pay** [əʊvə'peɪ] [*irr.* (***pay***)] пере-пла́чивать [-лати́ть]; **~power** [əʊvə'paʊə] переси́ли(ва)ть; **~rate** ['əʊvə'reɪt] переоце́нивать [-ни́ть]; **~reach** [əʊvə'ri:tʃ] перехитри́ть *pf.*; **~ *o.s.*** брать сли́шком мно́го на себя́; **~ride** [əʊvə'raɪd] [*irr.* (***ride***)] *fig.* отверга́ть [-е́ргнуть]; **~run** [əʊvə'rʌn] [*irr.* (***run***)] перелива́ться че́рез край; **~seas** [əʊvə'si:z] **1.** иностра́нный, заграни́чный; **2.** за рубежо́м, за грани́цей; **~seer** ['əʊvəsɪə] надсмо́трщик; **~shadow** [əʊvə'ʃædəʊ] *fig.* затмева́ть [-ми́ть]; **~sight** [~saɪt] недосмо́тр; **~sleep** [əʊvə'sli:p] [*irr.* (***sleep***)] прос(ы)па́ть; **~state** [əʊvə'steɪt] преувели́чи(ва)ть; **~statement** преувеличе́ние; **~strain** [əʊvə'streɪn] **1.** переутомле́ние; **2.** переутомля́ть [-ми́ть]; **~take** [əʊvə'teɪk] [*irr.* (***take***)] обгоня́ть [обогна́ть]; *of events* засти́гнуть *pf.* врасплóх; **~tax** [əʊvə'tæks] облага́ть чрезме́рным нало́гом; *fig. strength, etc.* перенапряга́ть [-ря́чь]; ***don't ~ my patience*** не испы́тывай моё терпе́ние; **~throw** [əʊvə'θrəʊ] [*irr.* (***throw***)] сверга́ть [све́ргнуть]; **~time** ['əʊvətaɪm] **1.** сверхуро́чная рабо́та; **2.** *adv.* сверхуро́чно

overture ['əʊvətjʊə] *mus.* увертю́ра

over|turn [əʊvə'tɜ:n] опроки́дывать [-и́нуть]; **~whelm** [əʊvə'welm] (*crush*) подавля́ть [-ви́ть]; переси́ли(ва)ть; ***~ed with grief*** уби́тый го́рем; **~work** ['əʊvəwɜ:k] **1.** переутомле́ние; **2.** [əʊvə'wɜ:k] переутомля́ть(ся) [-ми́ть(ся)]; **~wrought** [əʊvə'rɔ:t] в состоя́нии кра́йнего возбужде́ния; *nerves* перенапряжённый

owe [əʊ] быть до́лжным (Д/В); быть обя́занным (Д/Т)

owing ['əʊɪŋ] до́лжный; неупла́ченный; **~ *to*** *prp.* благодаря́ (Д)

owl [aʊl] сова́

own [əʊn] **1.** свой, со́бственный; родно́й; **2.** ***my ~*** моя́ со́бственность *f*; ***a house of one's ~*** со́бственный дом; ***hold one's ~*** не сдава́ть свой пози́ции; **3.** владе́ть (Т); (*admit, confess*) призна(ва́)ть (В); **~ *to*** призна́(ва́)ться в (П)

owner ['əʊnə] владе́лец *m*, -лица *f*; хозя́ин; **~ship** [~ʃɪp] со́бственность *f*

ox [ɒks], *pl.* **oxen** ['ɒksn] вол, бык

oxid|e ['ɒksaɪd] о́кись *f*; **~ize** ['ɒksɪdaɪz] окисля́ть(ся) [-ли́ть(ся)]

oxygen ['ɒksɪdʒən] кислоро́д

oyster ['ɔɪstə] у́стрица

P

P

pace [peɪs] **1.** (*step*) шаг; (*speed*) темп, ско́рость *f*; **2.** *v/t.* ме́рить шага́ми; *v/i.* [за]шага́ть; *room* ходи́ть взад и вперёд; ***set the ~*** задава́ть темп

pacify ['pæsɪfaɪ] (*calm*) умиротворя́ть [-ри́ть]; *rebellion* усмиря́ть [-ри́ть]

pack [pæk] **1.** *of cigarettes, etc.*, па́чка; *of papers* ки́па; *cards* коло́да; *of dogs* сво́ра; *of wolves* стая́; **2.** *v/t.* (*often ~ up*) упако́вывать [-кова́ть]; укла́дываться [уложи́ться]; (*fill*) заполня́ть [запо́лнить]; наби́(ва́)ть; (*a.* ~ **off**) выпрова́живать [вы́проводить]; отгружа́ть [отгрузи́ть]; ~**age** ['pækɪdʒ] (*parcel*) паке́т, свёрток, упако́вка; ~ **tour** туристи́ческая пое́здка, ко́мплексное турне́; ~**er** ['pækə] упако́вщик *m*, -ица *f*; ~**et** ['pækɪt] паке́т; па́чка; **small** ~ *mail* бандеро́ль *f*

pact [pækt] пакт, догово́р

pad [pæd] **1.** мя́гкая прокла́дка; (*writing* ~) блокно́т; **2.** подби́(ва́)ть, наби́(ва́)ть (ва́той *и т. д.*); *fig.* ~ **out** перегружа́ть [-узи́ть]

paddle ['pædl] **1.** гребо́к; байда́рочное весло́; **2.** грести́; плыть на байда́рке

paddling pool ['pædlɪŋ] *coll.* лягуша́тник

paddock ['pædək] вы́гон

padlock ['pædlɒk] вися́чий замо́к

pagan ['peɪgən] **1.** язы́чник; **2.** язы́ческий

page [peɪdʒ] страни́ца

pageant ['pædʒənt] карнава́льное (пра́здничное) ше́ствие; пы́шное зре́лище

paid [peɪd] *pt. и pt. p. от* **pay**

pail [peɪl] ведро́

pain [peɪn] **1.** боль *f*; ~**s** *pl.* (*often sg.*) страда́ния *n/pl.*; **on** ~ **of** под стра́хом (P); **be in** ~ испы́тывать боль; **spare no** ~**s** приложи́ть все уси́лия; **take** ~**s** [по]стара́ться; **2.** причиня́ть боль (Д); ~**ful** ['peɪnfl] □ боле́зненный; мучи́тельный; ~**less** ['~lɪs] □ безболе́зненный; ~**staking** ['peɪnzteɪkɪŋ] усе́рдный, стара́тельный

paint [peɪnt] **1.** кра́ска; "**Wet** ♀" Осторо́жно, окра́шено; **2.** [по]кра́сить; ~**brush** кисть *f*; ~**er** ['peɪntə] *art* худо́жник; (*decorator*) маля́р; ~**ing** ['peɪntɪŋ] (*art or occupation*) жи́вопись *f*; (*work of art*) карти́на

pair [peə] **1.** па́ра; **a** ~ **of scissors** но́жницы *f/pl.*; **2.** (~ *off*) соединя́ть(ся) по дво́е; раздели́ть *pf.* на па́ры; *biol.* спа́ривать(ся)

pal [pæl] прия́тель(ница *f*) *m*; *coll.* ко́реш

palace ['pælɪs] дворе́ц

palate ['pælət] *anat.* нёбо; *fig.* вкус

pale [peɪl] **1.** □ бле́дный; ~ **ale** све́тлое пи́во; **2.** [по]бледне́ть

paleness ['peɪlnɪs] бле́дность *f*

palette ['pælət] пали́тра

pall [pɔːl] *v/i.* приеда́ться [-е́сться]

palliate ['pælɪeɪt] *pain* облегча́ть [-чи́ть]

pall|id ['pælɪd] □ бле́дный; ~**or** [~lə] бле́дность *f*

palm[1] [pɑːm] **1.** *of hand* ладо́нь *f*; **2.** ~ **off on s.b.** *coll.* подсо́вывать [подсу́нуть]; *fig. pej.* всу́чивать [-чи́ть] (Д)

palm[2] [~], ~**tree** па́льма; ♀ **Sunday** Ве́рбное воскресе́нье

palpable ['pælpəbl] □ осяза́емый; ощути́мый; *fig.* очеви́дный, я́вный

palpitat|e ['pælpɪteɪt] *with fear, etc.* трепета́ть; *of heart* си́льно би́ться; ~**ion** [pælpɪ'teɪʃn] сердцебие́ние

paltry ['pɔːltrɪ] □ пустяко́вый, ничто́жный

pamper ['pæmpə] [из]ба́ловать

pamphlet ['pæmflɪt] памфле́т

pan [pæn] (*saucepan*) кастрю́ля; (*frying* ~) сковорода́, (-ро́дка)

pan... [~] *pref.* пан...; обще...

panacea [pænə'sɪə] панаце́я

pancake ['pænkeɪk] блин; *without yeast* бли́нчик; *small and thick* ола́дья

pandemonium [pændɪ'məʊnɪəm] смяте́ние; *fig.* столпотворе́ние

pander ['pændə] потво́рствовать (**to** Д)

pane [peɪn] (око́нное) стекло́

panel ['pænl] **1.** *arch.* пане́ль *f*; *mot.* прибо́рная доска́; **2.** обшива́ть пане́лями

pang [pæŋ] внеза́пная о́страя боль *f*; ~**s of conscience** угрызе́ния со́вести

panic ['pænɪk] **1.** пани́ческий; **2.** па́ника; ~**-stricken** [~strɪkən] охва́ченный па́никой

pansy ['pænzɪ] *bot.* аню́тины гла́зки *m/pl.*

pant [pænt] задыха́ться; тяжело́ дыша́ть; вздыха́ть; стра́стно жела́ть (**for**, **after** P)

panties ['pæntɪz] (**a pair of** ~) *women's* тру́сики; *children's* штани́шки

pantry ['pæntrɪ] кладова́я

pants [pænts] *pl.* (***a pair of ~***) трусы́; *Am.* брю́ки *m/pl.*
papal ['peɪpəl] □ па́пский
paper ['peɪpə] **1.** бума́га; (*news~*) газе́та; (*wall~*) обо́и *m/pl.*; нау́чный докла́д; докуме́нт; **2.** окле́ивать [окле́ить] обо́ями; **~back** кни́га в мя́гком переплёте; **~ bag** кулёк; **~ clip** скре́пка; **~work** канцеля́рская рабо́та
paprika ['pæprɪkə] кра́сный пе́рец
par [pɑː] ра́венство; (*recognized or face value*) номина́льная сто́имость *f*; ***at ~*** по номина́лу; ***be on a ~ with*** быть наравне́, на одно́м у́ровне с (Т)
parable ['pærəbl] при́тча
parachut|e ['pærəʃuːt] парашю́т; **~ist** [~ɪst] парашюти́ст
parade [pə'reɪd] **1.** *mil.* пара́д; ***make a ~ of*** выставля́ть напока́з; **2.** щеголя́ть
paradise ['pærədaɪs] рай
paradox ['pærədɒks] парадо́кс; **~ical** [~ɪkl] парадокса́льный
paraffin ['pærəfɪn] *chiefly Brt.* кероси́н; (*~ wax*) парафи́н
paragon ['pærəgən] образе́ц; ***~ of virtue*** образе́ц доброде́тели
paragraph ['pærəgrɑːf] абза́ц; газе́тная заме́тка
parallel ['pærəlel] **1.** паралле́льный; **2.** паралле́ль *f* (*a. fig.*); *geogr.* паралле́ль *f*; ***without ~*** несравни́мый; **3.** быть паралле́льным с (Т), (*compare*) проводи́ть [-вести́] паралле́ль ме́жду; сра́внивать [-ни́ть]
paraly|se *Am.* **~ze** ['pærəlaɪz] парализова́ть (*im*)*pf.* (*a. fig.*); **~sis** [pə'ræləsɪs] *med.* парали́ч
paramount ['pærəmaʊnt]: ***of ~ importance*** первостепе́нной ва́жности
parapet ['pærəpɪt] парапе́т
paraphernalia [pærəfə'neɪlɪə] *pl.* ли́чные ве́щи *f/pl.*, принадле́жности
parasite ['pærəsaɪt] парази́т (*a. fig.*)
paratroops ['pærətruːps] *pl.* парашю́тно-деса́нтные войска́ *n/pl.*
parcel ['pɑːsl] **1.** паке́т; *mail* посы́лка; **2.** (*mst.* ***~ out***) *land* дели́ть на уча́стки; (*mst.* ***~ up***) упако́вывать [-ова́ть]
parch [pɑːtʃ] иссуша́ть [-ши́ть]; *of sun* опаля́ть [-ли́ть]; ***my throat is ~ed*** у меня́ пересо́хло в го́рле
parchment [pɑːtʃmənt] перга́мент
pardon ['pɑːdn] **1.** проще́ние; *law* поми́лование; **2.** проща́ть [прости́ть]; поми́ловать *pf.*; **~able** [~əbl] □ прости́тельный
pare [peə] (*peel*) [по]чи́стить; (*cut*) обреза́ть [-ре́зать]; *fig.* [о-, по-] стри́чь; *fig. expenses* уре́з(ыв)ать
parent ['peərənt] *mst. pl.* роди́тели *m/pl.*; **~age** [~ɪdʒ] происхожде́ние; **~al** [pə'rentl] □ роди́тельский
parenthe|sis [pə'renθəsɪs], *pl.* **~ses** [~siːz] вво́дное сло́во *or* предложе́ние; *pl. typ.* (кру́глые) ско́бки *f/pl.*
paring ['peərɪŋ] кожура́, ко́рка, шелуха́; **~s** *pl.* обре́зки *m/pl.*; *of vegetables, fruit* очи́стки *f/pl.*
parish ['pærɪʃ] **1.** церко́вный прихо́д; **2.** прихо́дский; **~ioners** [pə'rɪʃənəz] прихожа́не *pl.*
parity ['pærətɪ] ра́венство; равноце́нность *f*; *fin.* парите́т
park [pɑːk] **1.** (*public garden*) парк; *for vehicles* стоя́нка; **2.** *mot.* паркова́ть, ста́вить на стоя́нку; **~ing** ['pɑːkɪŋ] автостоя́нка; ***No ~ing*** стоя́нка запрещена́
parlance ['pɑːləns]: ***in common ~*** в обихо́дной ре́чи
parliament ['pɑːləmənt] парла́мент; **~ary** [pɑːlə'mentərɪ] парла́ментский
parlo(u)r ['pɑːlə] *in house* гости́ная; *Am., for services* ателье́ *n indecl.*; ***~ games*** ко́мнатные и́гры
parody ['pærədɪ] паро́дия
parole [pə'rəʊl] че́стное сло́во; усло́вно-досро́чное освобожде́ние
parquet ['pɑːkeɪ] парке́т
parrot ['pærət] **1.** попуга́й; **2.** повторя́ть как попуга́й
parry ['pærɪ] (*ward off*) отража́ть [-рази́ть], пари́ровать (*a. fig.*)
parsimonious [pɑːsɪ'məʊnɪəs] □ скупо́й
parsley ['pɑːslɪ] петру́шка
parsnip ['pɑːsnɪp] пастерна́к
parson ['pɑːsn] приходско́й свяще́нник, па́стор
part [pɑːt] **1.** часть *f*, до́ля; уча́стие;

thea. a. fig. роль *f*; мéстность *f*, край; *mus.* пáртия; ***in these ~s*** в э́тих краях; ***take in good ~*** не оби́деться *pf.*, приня́ть *pf.* спокóйно; ***take ~*** принимáть [-ня́ть] учáстие; ***for my*** (***own***) ***~*** с моéй стороны́; ***in ~*** части́чно; ***on the ~ of*** со стороны́ (Р); **2.** *adv.* чáстью, отчáсти; **3.** *v/t.* разделя́ть [-ли́ть]; ***~ the hair*** дéлать пробóр; *v/i.* разлучáться [-чи́ться], расст(ав)áться (***with***, ***from*** с Т)

partial ['pɑːʃl] □ части́чный; (*not indifferent*) пристрáстный; неравноду́шный (***to*** к Д); ***I'm ~ to peaches*** я люблю́ пéрсики

particip|ant [pɑː'tɪsɪpənt] учáстник *m*, -ица *f*; **~ate** [~peɪt] учáствовать (***in*** в П); **~ation** [~'peɪʃn] учáстие

particle ['pɑːtɪkl] части́ца

particular [pə'tɪkjʊlə] **1.** □ осóбенный; осóбый; (*hard to satisfy*) разбóрчивый; ***in this ~ case*** в дáнном слу́чае; ***for no ~ reason*** без осóбой причи́ны; **2.** подрóбность *f*, детáль *f*; ***in ~*** в осóбенности; **~ly** [pə'tɪkjʊləlɪ] осóбенно

parting ['pɑːtɪŋ] **1.** (*separation*) разлу́ка; (*farewell*) прощáние; *in hair* пробóр; **2.** прощáльный

partisan [pɑːtɪ'zæn] **1.** (*adherent*) сторóнник *m*, -ица *f*; *mil.* партизáн; **2.** партизáнский

partition [pɑː'tɪʃn] **1.** (*division*) раздéл; (*separating structure*) перегорóдка; **2.**: ***~ off*** отгорáживать [-роди́ть]

partly ['pɑːtlɪ] чáстью, отчáсти

partner ['pɑːtnə] **1.** *in crime* соучáстник *m*, -ица *f*; *comm.* компаньóн, партнёр; *sport, etc.* партнёр; **2.** быть партнёром; **~ship** [~ʃɪp] парнёрство; (*marriage*) сою́з, товáрищество, компáния

part-owner совладéлец

partridge ['pɑːtrɪdʒ] куропáтка

part-time непóлный рабóчий день; *attr.* не пóлностью зáнятый; ***~ worker*** рабóчий, зáнятый непóлный рабóчий день

party ['pɑːtɪ] *pol.* пáртия; (*team*) отря́д; (*group*) гру́ппа, компáния, *law* сторонá; учáстник (***to*** в П); (*social gathering*) вечери́нка

pass ['pɑːs] **1.** прохóд; *mountain* перевáл; (*permit*) прóпуск; бесплáтный билéт; *univ.* посрéдственная сдáча экзáмена; *cards, sport* пас; **2.** *v/i.* проходи́ть [пройти́]; (*drive by*) проезжáть [-éхать]; переходи́ть (***from ... to ...*** из (Р) ... в (В) ...); *cards* пасовáть; ***~ as***, ***for*** считáться (Т), слыть (Т); ***~ away*** умирáть [умерéть]; ***~ by*** проходи́ть ми́мо; ***~ into*** переходи́ть [перейти́] в (В); ***~ off*** *of pain, etc.* проходи́ть [пройти́]; ***~ on*** идти́ дáльше; ***~ out*** (*faint*) [по]теря́ть сознáние; **3.** *v/t.* проходи́ть [пройти́]; проезжáть [-éхать]; миновáть (*im*)*pf.*; *exam* сдать *pf.*; обгоня́ть [обогнáть], опережáть [-реди́ть]; переправля́ть(ся) [-áвить(ся)] чéрез (В); (*a.* ***~ on***) перед(ав)áть; *sentence* выноси́ть [вы́нести]; *time* проводи́ть [-вести́]; *law* принимáть [-ня́ть]; **~able** ['pɑːsəbl] *road, etc.* проходи́мый; (*tolerable*) снóсный

passage ['pæsɪdʒ] прохóд; *of time* течéние; переéзд, переправа; *ae.* перелёт; *crossing by ship* плáвание, рейс; (*corridor*) коридóр; *from book* отры́вок

passenger ['pæsɪndʒə] пассажи́р; ***~-train*** пассажи́рский пóезд

passer-by [pɑːsə'baɪ] прохóжий

passion ['pæʃn] *strong emotion, desire* страсть *f*; (*anger*) гнев; **♀ *Week*** Страстнáя недéля; **~ate** [~ɪt] □ стрáстный, пы́лкий

passive ['pæsɪv] □ пасси́вный; *gr.* ***the ~ voice*** страдáтельный залóг

passport ['pɑːspɔːt] пáспорт

password ['pɑːswɜːd] парóль *m*

past [pɑːst] **1.** *adj.* прóшлый; мину́вший; ***for some time ~*** за послéднее врéмя; **2.** *adv.* ми́мо; **3.** *prp.* за (Т); пóсле (Р); ми́мо (Р); свы́ше (Р); ***half ~ two*** полови́на трéтьего; ***~ endurance*** нестерпи́мый; ***~ hope*** безнадёжный; **4.** прóшлое

paste [peɪst] **1.** (*glue*) клей; **2.** клéить, приклé(ва)ть

pastel ['pæstl] (*crayon*) пастéль *f*

pasteurize ['pæstəraɪz] пастеризовáть (*im*)*pf.*

pastime ['pɑːstaɪm] времяпрепро-

вожде́ние
pastor ['pɑːstə] па́стор *m*; **~al** [~rəl] *of shepherds or country life* пастора́льный; *of clergy* па́сторский
pastry ['peɪstrɪ] (*dough*) те́сто; (*tart*) пиро́жное; **~ cook** конди́тер
pasture ['pɑːstʃə] **1.** па́стбище; вы́гон; **2.** пасти́(сь)
pat [pæt] **1.** похло́пывание; **2.** *on back* похло́п(ыв)ать; [по]гла́дить; **3.** кста́ти; как раз подходя́щий; ***a ~ answer*** гото́вый отве́т (*a. fig.* шабло́нный)
patch [pætʃ] **1.** *on clothes* запла́та; *of colo(u)r* пятно́; клочо́к земли́; **2.** [за]лата́ть; [по]чини́ть; ***~ up a quarrel*** ула́живать [-а́дить] ссо́ру
patent ['peɪtnt] **1.** (*obvious*) я́вный; запатенто́ванный; ***~ leather*** лакиро́ванная ко́жа; **2.** (*a. letters ~ pl.*) пате́нт; **3.** [за]патентова́ть; **~ee** [peɪtn'tiː] владе́лец пате́нта
patern|al [pə'tɜːnl] □ отцо́вский; (*fatherly*) оте́ческий; **~ity** [~nətɪ] отцо́вство
path [pɑːθ], *pl.* **~s** [pɑːðz] тропи́нка, доро́жка
pathetic [pə'θetɪk] жа́лкий; печа́льный; тро́гательный
patien|ce ['peɪʃns] терпе́ние; **~t** [~nt] **1.** □ терпели́вый; **2.** больно́й *m*, -на́я *f*, пацие́нт *m*, -тка *f*
patriot ['pætrɪət] патрио́т; **~ism** ['~ɪzəm] патриоти́зм
patrol [pə'trəʊl] *mil.* **1.** патру́ль *m*; **2.** патрули́ровать
patron ['peɪtrən] (*supporter, sponsor*) покрови́тель *m*; (*customer*) клие́нт, покупа́тель *m*; **~age** ['pætrənɪdʒ] *support* покрови́тельство; **~ize** [~naɪz] покрови́тельствовать; (*be condescending*) снисходи́тельно относи́ться к (Д)
patter ['pætə] говори́ть скорогово́ркой; [про]бормота́ть: *of rain* бараба́нить; *of feet* топота́ть
pattern ['pætn] **1.** образе́ц; (*way*) о́браз; (*design*) узо́р; **2.** де́лать по образцу́ (***on*** P)
paunch [pɔːntʃ] брюшко́
pauper ['pɔːpə] ни́щий *m*, -щая *f*
pause [pɔːz] **1.** па́уза, переры́в; **2.** [с]де́лать па́узу
pave [peɪv] [вы́]мости́ть; ***~ the way for*** *fig.* прокла́дывать [проложи́ть] путь; **~ment** ['peɪvmənt] тротуа́р
pavilion [pə'vɪlɪən] павильо́н
paw [pɔː] **1.** ла́па (*coll a.* = ***hand***); **2.** тро́гать ла́пой
pawn¹ [pɔːn] *chess* пе́шка
pawn² [~] **1.** зало́г, закла́д; ***in ~*** в закла́де; **2.** закла́дывать [заложи́ть]; **~broker** владе́лец ломба́рда; ростовщи́к; **~shop** ломба́рд
pay [peɪ] **1.** (о)пла́та, упла́та; *wages* зарпла́та; **2.** [*irr.*] *v/t.* [за]плати́ть; *bill, etc.* опла́чивать [оплати́ть]; ***~ a visit*** посеща́ть [-ети́ть], (*official*) наноси́ть [-нести́] визи́т; ***~ attention to*** обраща́ть внима́ние на (В); ***~ down*** плати́ть нали́чными; *v/i.* (*be profitable*) окупа́ться [-пи́ться] (*a. fig.*); ***~ for*** [у-, за]плати́ть за (В), опла́чивать; *fig.* [по]плати́ться за (В); **~able** ['peɪəbl] опла́чиваемый подлежа́щий упла́те; **~-day** день зарпла́ты; *coll.* получка; **~ing** ['peɪɪŋ] вы́годный; **~ment** ['~mənt] упла́та, опла́та, платёж
pea [piː] *bot.* горо́х; горо́шина; **~s** *pl.* горо́х; *attr.* горо́ховый
peace [piːs] мир; споко́йствие; **~able** ['piːsəbl] □ миролюби́вый, ми́рный; **~ful** ['~fl] □ ми́рный, споко́йный; **~maker** миротво́рец
peach [piːtʃ] пе́рсик
peacock ['piːkɒk] павли́н
peak [piːk] *of mountain* верши́на (*a. fig.*); *of cap* козырёк; ***~ of summer*** разга́р ле́та; *attr.* максима́льный; вы́сший
peal [piːl] **1.** звон колоколо́в; *of thunder* раска́т; ***~ of laughter*** взрыв сме́ха; **2.** звони́ть
peanut ['piːnʌt] ара́хис
pear [peə] гру́ша
pearl [pɜːl] *collect.* же́мчуг; жемчу́жина *a. fig.*; *attr.* жемчу́жный; ***~ barley*** перло́вая крупа́, *coll.* перло́вка
peasant ['peznt] **1.** крестья́нин *m*, -янка *f*; **2.** крестья́нский; **~ry** [~ri] крестья́нство
peat [piːt] торф
pebble ['pebl] га́лька
peck [pek] клева́ть [клю́нуть]

peckish ['pekɪʃ] *coll.* голо́дный; ***feel ~*** хоте́ть есть
peculiar [pɪ'kjuːlɪə] □ (*distinctive*) своеобра́зный; осо́бенный; (*strange*) стра́нный; (*characteristic*) сво́йственный (Д); **~ity** [pɪkjuːlɪ'ærətɪ] осо́бенность *f*; стра́нность *f* сво́йство
peddler *or Brt.* **pedlar** ['pedlə] разно́счик; у́личный торго́вец
pedal ['pedl] **1.** педа́ль *f*; **2.** е́хать на велосипе́де
pedest|al ['pedɪstl] пьедеста́л (*a. fig.*); **~rian** [pɪ'destrɪən] **1.** пешехо́д; **2.** пешехо́дный; **~rian crossing** перехо́д
pedigree ['pedɪgriː] родосло́вная; происхожде́ние
peek [piːk] → ***peep***
peel [piːl] **1.** ко́рка, ко́жица, шелуха́; **2.** (*a.* ***~ off***) *v/t.* снима́ть ко́жицу, ко́рку, шелуху́ с (Р); *fruit, vegetables* [по]чи́стить; *v/i.* [об]лупи́ться; *of skin* сходи́ть [сойти́]
peep[1] [piːp] [про]пища́ть
peep[2] [~] **1.** взгляд укра́дкой; ***have a ~*** взгляну́ть *pf.*; **2.** взгляну́ть *pf.* укра́дкой; ***~ in*** загля́дывать [-яну́ть]; **~hole** *in door* глазо́к
peer[1] [pɪə]: ***~ at*** всма́триваться [всмотре́ться]
peer[2] [~] ро́вня *m/pf.*; пэр; **~less** ['pɪəlɪs] несравне́нный
peevish ['piːvɪʃ] □ брюзгли́вый
peg [peg] **1.** ко́лышек; *for coats, etc.* ве́шалка; (*clothes ~*) прище́пка; *fig.* ***take a p. down a ~*** сбива́ть спесь с кого́-л.; **2.** прикрепля́ть ко́лышком; отмеча́ть ко́лышками; ***~ away*** *impf. only, coll.* вка́лывать; упо́рно рабо́тать
pellet ['pelɪt] ша́рик; (*pill*) пилю́ля; *collect.* дробь *f*
pell-mell [pel'mel] вперемéшку
pelt[1] [pelt] ко́жа, шку́ра
pelt[2] [~] (*throw at*) забра́сывать [-роса́ть]; *v/i. of rain, etc.* бараба́нить
pelvis ['pelvɪs] *anat.* таз
pen [pen] **1.** ру́чка; ***ballpoint ~*** ша́риковая ру́чка; ***fountain ~*** авторучка; **2.** [на]писа́ть
penal ['piːnl] уголо́вный; ***~ offence***, *Am.* **-se** уголо́вное преступле́ние; **~ize** ['piːnəlaɪz] нака́зывать [-за́ть]; **~ty** ['penəltɪ] наказа́ние; *sport.* пена́льти; *attr.* штрафно́й
pence [pens] *pl. om* ***penny***
pencil ['pensl] **1.** каранда́ш; ***in ~*** карандашо́м; **2.** (*draw*) [на]рисова́ть; писа́ть карандашо́м
pendant ['pendənt] куло́н; брело́к
pending ['pendɪŋ] **1.** *law* ожида́ющий реше́ния; **2.** *prp.* (вплоть) до (Р)
pendulum ['pendjʊləm] ма́ятник
penetra|ble ['penɪtrəbl] □ проница́емый; **~te** [~treɪt] проника́ть [-ни́кнуть] в (В); (*pervade*) прони́зывать [-за́ть]; *fig.* вника́ть [вни́кнуть] в (В); **~ting** ['~treɪtɪŋ] (*acute*) проница́тельный; *sound, etc.* пронзи́тельный; **~tion** [penɪ'treɪʃn] проникнове́ние; проница́тельность *f*
peninsula [pə'nɪnsjʊlə] полуо́стров
peniten|ce ['penɪtəns] раска́яние; покая́ние; **~t** [~nt] □ ка́ющийся; **~tiary** [penɪ'tenʃərɪ] исправи́тельный дом; тюрьма́
penknife ['pennaɪf] перочи́нный нож
pen name псевдони́м
pennant ['penənt] вы́мпел
penniless ['penɪlɪs] без копе́йки
penny ['penɪ] пе́нни *n indecl.*, пенс; ***cost a pretty ~*** влете́ть *pf.* в копе́ечку
pen pal друг по перепи́ске
pension 1. ['penʃn] пе́нсия; (*disability ~*) пе́нсия по инвали́дности; **2.** *v/t.* назна́чить *pf.* пе́нсию; (***~ off***) увольня́ть на пе́нсию; **~er** ['penʃənə] пенсионе́р(ка)
pensive ['pensɪv] □ заду́мчивый
pent [pent] заключённый; **~-up** *anger, etc.* накопи́вшийся; пода́вленный
penthouse ['penthaʊs] кварти́ра; вы́строенная на кры́ше до́ма
people ['piːpl] **1.** (*race, nation*) наро́д; (*persons generally*) лю́ди *m/pl.*; (*inhabitants*) населе́ние; **2.** заселя́ть [-ли́ть]; *country* населя́ть [-ли́ть]
pepper ['pepə] **1.** пе́рец; **2.** [по-, на]перчи́ть; **~mint** *bot.* пе́речная мя́та; **~y** [~rɪ] напе́рченный; *fig.* вспы́льчивый, раздражи́тельный

per [pɜː] по (Д), че́рез (В), посре́дством (Р); за (В); ~ ***annum*** в год, ежего́дно; **~cent** проце́нт
perambulator [pəˈræmbjʊleɪtə] де́тская коля́ска
perceive [pəˈsiːv] (*visually*) замеча́ть [-е́тить]; (*discern*) различа́ть [-чи́ть]; *mentally* понима́ть [-ня́ть]; осозн(ав)а́ть; *through senses* [по-] чу́вствовать; ощуща́ть [-ути́ть]
percentage [pəˈsentɪdʒ] проце́нт
percepti|ble [pəˈseptəbl] □ ощути́мый, различи́мый; **~on** [~ʃn] восприя́тие
perch¹ [pɜːtʃ] *zo.* о́кунь *m*
perch² [~] сади́ться [сесть]; уса́живаться [усе́сться]
percolator [ˈpɜːkəleɪtə] кофева́рка
percussion [pəˈkʌʃn] уда́р; *mus. collect.* уда́рные инструме́нты
peremptory [pəˈremptərɪ] безапелляцио́нный, категори́чный, (*manner*) вла́стный
perennial [pəˈrenɪəl] □ *fig.* ве́чный, неувяда́емый; *bot.* многоле́тний
perfect [ˈpɜːfɪkt] **1.** □ соверше́нный; (*exact*) то́чный; **2.** [pəˈfekt] [у]соверше́нствовать; **~ion** [~ʃn] соверше́нство
perfidious [pəˈfɪdɪəs] □ *lit.* вероло́мный
perforate [ˈpɜːfəreɪt] перфори́ровать *(im)pf.*
perform [pəˈfɔːm] исполня́ть [-о́лнить] (*a. thea.*); *thea., mus.* игра́ть [сыгра́ть]; **~ance** [~əns] исполне́ние (*a. thea.*); *thea.* спекта́кль *m*; *sport.* достиже́ние; **~er** [~ə] исполни́тель(ница *f*) *m*
perfume [ˈpɜːfjuːm] *liquid* духи́ *m/pl.*; (*smell, bouquet*) арома́т, (*fragrance*) благоуха́ние
perfunctory [pəˈfʌŋktərɪ] □ (*automatic*) машина́льный; *fig.* (*careless*) небре́жный; (*superficial*) пове́рхностный
perhaps [pəˈhæps] мо́жет быть
peril [ˈperəl] опа́сность *f*; **~ous** [~əs] □ опа́сный
period [ˈpɪərɪəd] пери́од; эпо́ха; (*full stop*) то́чка, коне́ц; **~ic** [pɪərɪˈɒdɪk] периоди́ческий; **~ical** [~dɪkl] **1.** → ***periodic*** **2.** периоди́ческое изда́ние
periphery [pəˈrɪferɪ] окру́жность *f*; *fig.* перифери́я
perish [ˈperɪʃ] погиба́ть [-и́бнуть]; **~able** [ˈperɪʃəbl] □ *food* скоропо́ртящийся; **~ing** [~ɪŋ]: ***it's ~ here*** здесь жу́тко хо́лодно
perjur|e [ˈpɜːdʒə]: **~ *o.s.*** лжесвиде́тельствовать; **~y** [~rɪ] лжесвиде́тельство
perk [pɜːk] *coll.*: *mst.* **~ *up*** *v/i.* оживля́ться [-ви́ться]; **~y** [ˈpɜːkɪ] □ живо́й; (*self-assured*) самоуве́ренный
permanen|ce [ˈpɜːmənəns] постоя́нство; **~t** [~nt] постоя́нный, неизме́нный; **~ *address*** постоя́нный а́дрес; **~ *wave*** зави́вка «перманéнт»
permea|ble [ˈpɜːmɪəbl] проница́емый; **~te** [~mɪeɪt] проника́ть [-и́кнуть]; пропи́тывать [-ита́ть]
permissi|ble [pəˈmɪsəbl] □ допусти́мый; **~on** [~ʃn] разреше́ние
permit **1.** [pəˈmɪt] разреша́ть [-ши́ть], позволя́ть [-во́лить]; допуска́ть [-усти́ть]; ***weather ~ting*** е́сли пого́да позво́лит; **2.** [ˈpɜːmɪt] разреше́ние; (*document*) про́пуск
pernicious [pəˈnɪʃəs] □ па́губный, вре́дный
perpendicular [pɜːpənˈdɪkjʊlə] □ перпендикуля́рный
perpetrate [ˈpɜːpɪtreɪt] соверша́ть [-ши́ть]
perpetu|al [pəˈpetʃʊəl] □ постоя́нный, ве́чный; **~ate** [~ʃʊeɪt] увекове́чи(ва)ть
perplex [pəˈpleks] озада́чи(ва)ть, сбива́ть с то́лку; **~ity** [~ətɪ] озада́ченность *f*; недоуме́ние
perquisite [ˈpɜːkwɪzɪt] побо́чное преиму́щество; льго́та
persecut|e [ˈpɜːsɪkjuːt] пресле́довать; **~ion** [pɜːsɪˈkjuːʃn] пресле́дование
persever|ance [pɜːsɪˈvɪərəns] насто́йчивость *f*, упо́рство; **~e** [~ˈvɪə] *v/i.* упо́рно продолжа́ть (***in*** В)
persist [pəˈsɪst] упо́рствовать (***in*** в П); **~ence** [~əns] насто́йчивость *f*; **~ent** [~ənt] □ насто́йчивый; (*unceasing*) беспреста́нный
person [ˈpɜːsn] лицо́, ли́чность *f*; персо́на, осо́ба; ***pleasant ~*** прия́тный челове́к; **~age** [~ɪdʒ] ва́жная

P

персóна; *lit.* персонáж; **~al** [~l] □ ли́чный, персонáльный; **~ality** [pɜːsəˈnælətɪ] ли́чность *f*; **~ify** [pəˈsɒnɪfaɪ] (*give human qualities*) олицетворя́ть [-ри́ть]; (*embody, exemplify*) воплощáть [-лоти́ть]; **~nel** [pɜːsəˈnel] персонáл, штат; **~ *department*** отдéл кáдров
perspective [pəˈspektɪv] перспекти́ва; (*view*) вид
perspir|ation [pɜːspəˈreɪʃn] потéние; пот; **~e** [pəˈspaɪə] [вс]потéть
persua|de [pəˈsweɪd] убеждáть [убеди́ть]; **~sion** [~ʒn] убеждéние; убеди́тельность *f*; **~sive** [~sɪv] □ убеди́тельный
pert [pɜːt] □ дéрзкий
pertain [pəˈteɪn] (*relate*) имéть отношéние (к Д); (*belong*) принадлежáть
pertinacious [pɜːtɪˈneɪʃəs] □ упря́мый; (*determined*) настóйчивый
pertinent [ˈpɜːtɪnənt] умéстный; относя́щийся к дéлу
perturb [pəˈtɜːb] [вз]волновáть, [о]беспокóить
perusal [pəˈruːzl] внимáтельное прочтéние; рассмотрéние
pervade [pəˈveɪd] *of smell, etc.* распространя́ться [-ни́ться] по (Д)
pervers|e [pəˈvɜːs] □ преврáтный, отклоня́ющийся от нóрмы; извращённый; **~ion** [ʃn] *med.* извращéние
pervert 1. [pəˈvɜːt] извращáть [-рати́ть]; совращáть [-рати́ть]; **2.** [ˈpɜːvɜːt] извращéнец
pest [pest] *fig.* я́зва, бич; *zo.* вреди́тель *m*; **~er** [ˈ~ə] докучáть (Д); надоедáть [-éсть] (Д); **~icide** [ˈ~tɪsaɪd] пестици́д
pet [pet] **1.** домáшнее живóтное; (*favourite*) люби́мец, бáловень *m*; **2.** люби́мый; **~ *name*** ласкáтельное и́мя; **3.** бáловать; ласкáть
petal [ˈpetl] *bot.* лепестóк
petition [pəˈtɪʃn] **1.** прошéние, ходáтайство; **2.** обращáться [-ати́ться] с прошéнием; ходáтайствовать
petrol [ˈpetrəl] *chiefly Brt.* бензи́н
petticoat [ˈpetɪkəʊt] ни́жняя ю́бка; комбинáция
petty [ˈpetɪ] □ мéлкий; (*small-minded*) мéлочный
petulant [ˈpetjʊlənt] раздражи́тельный, капри́зный
pew [pjuː] церкóвная скамья́
phantom [ˈfæntəm] фантóм, при́зрак; иллю́зия
pharmacy [ˈfɑːməsɪ] фармаци́я; (*drugstore*) аптéка
phase [feɪz] фáза; пери́од, этáп
phenomen|on [fəˈnɒmɪnən], *pl.* **~a** [~nə] явлéние; фенóмен
phial [ˈfaɪəl] пузырёк
philologist [fɪˈlɒlədʒɪst] филóлог
philosoph|er [fɪˈlɒsəfə] филóсоф; **~ize** [~faɪz] философóфствовать; **~y** [~fɪ] филосóфия
phlegm [flem] мокрóта; (*sluggishness*) флегмати́чность *f*
phone [fəʊn] → ***telephone***
phonetics [fəˈnetɪks] *pl.* фонéтика
phon(e)y [ˈfəʊnɪ] *coll.* (*false*) фальши́вый, неестéственный
phosphorus [ˈfɔsfərəs] фóсфор
photograph [ˈfəʊtəgrɑːf] **1.** фотогрáфия, сни́мок; **2.** [с]фотографи́ровать; **~er** [fəˈtɒgrəfə] фотóграф; **~y** [~fɪ] фотогрáфия
phrase [freɪz] **1.** фрáза, выражéние; **2.** выражáть [вы́разить]; [с]формули́ровать
physic|al [ˈfɪzɪkəl] □ физи́ческий; материáльный; **~ian** [fɪˈzɪʃn] врач; **~ist** [ˈ~sɪst] фи́зик; **~s** [ˈfɪzɪks] *sg.* фи́зика
physique [fɪˈziːk] телосложéние
pianist [ˈpɪənɪst] пиани́ст
piano [pɪˈænəʊ] *upright* пиани́но; ***grand ~*** роя́ль *m*; ***~ concerto*** концéрт для роя́ля с оркéстром
pick [pɪk] **1.** вы́бор; (*tool*) киркá; **2.** выбирáть [вы́брать]; *nose* ковыря́ть в (П); *flowers, fruit* соб(и-)рáть; (*pluck*) срывáть [сорвáть]; ***~ out*** выбирáть [вы́брать]; ***~ up*** подбирáть [подобрáть]; поднимáть [-ня́ть]; (*collect s.o.*) заезжáть [заéхать] за (Т); **~-a-back** [ˈpɪkəbæk], = ***piggy-back*** [ˈpɪgɪbæk], на спинé; на закóрках; ***give me a ~*** посади́ меня́ на плéчи; **~axe** киркá
picket [ˈpɪkɪt] **1.** (*stake*) кол; *mil.* застáва; пост; *of strikers, etc.* пикéт; **2.** пикети́ровать
picking [ˈpɪkɪŋ] *of fruit* сбор; **~s** *pl.* остáтки *m/pl.*, объéдки *m/pl.*

P

pickle ['pɪkl] **1.** марина́д; *pl.* пи́кули *f/pl.*; *coll.* беда́; неприя́тности *f/pl.*; ***be in a ~*** вли́пнуть *pf.*; **2.** [за-] маринова́ть; ***~d herring*** марино́ванная селёдка
pickup (*van*) пика́п
pictorial [pɪk'tɔ:rɪəl] иллюстри́рованный; *art* изобрази́тельный
picture ['pɪktʃə] **1.** карти́на; ***~s*** *pl.* (*generally*) жи́вопись *f*; *chiefly Brt.* кино́ *indecl.*; ***put in the ~*** вводи́ть [ввести́] в курс де́ла; ***~ gallery*** карти́нная галере́я; ***~ (post)card*** откры́тка с ви́дом; **2.** (*depict*) изобража́ть [-рази́ть]; (*describe*) опи́сывать [-са́ть]; (*imagine*) вообража́ть [-рази́ть]; ***~ to o.s.*** представля́ть [-а́вить] себе́; ***~sque*** [pɪktʃə'resk] живопи́сный
pie [paɪ] пиро́г; *small* пирожо́к
piece [pi:s] **1.** кусо́к, часть *f*; (*fragment*) обры́вок, обло́мок; (*single article*) вещь *f*; предме́т; шту́ка; ***~ of advice*** сове́т; ***~ of news*** но́вость *f*; ***by the ~*** пошту́чно; ***give a ~ of one's mind*** выска́зывать своё мне́ние; ***take to ~s*** разбира́ть на ча́сти; **2.**: ***~ together*** соединя́ть в одно́ це́лое, собира́ть из кусо́чков; **~meal** по частя́м, уры́вками; **~ work** сде́льная рабо́та
pier [pɪə] *naut.* пирс; мол; *of bridge* усто́й, бык; (*breakwater*) волноло́м; (*wharf*) при́стань *f*
pierce [pɪəs] пронза́ть [-зи́ть]; прока́лывать [-коло́ть]; *of cold* пронизывать [-за́ть]
piety ['paɪətɪ] благоче́стие; набо́жность *f*
pig [pɪg] свинья́
pigeon ['pɪdʒɪn] го́лубь *m*; **~-hole** **1.** отделе́ние (пи́сьменного стола́ *u m. n.*); **2.** раскла́дывать по я́щикам; *fig.* откла́дывать в до́лгий я́щик
pig|headed [pɪg'hedɪd] упря́мый; **~skin** свина́я ко́жа; **~sty** свина́рник; **~tail** коси́чка, коса́
pike [paɪk] (*fish*) щу́ка
pile [paɪl] **1.** ку́ча, гру́да; (*stack*) шта́бель *m*; **2.** скла́дывать [сложи́ть]; сва́ливать в ку́чу
piles *pl. med.* геморро́й
pilfer ['pɪlfə] ворова́ть; стяну́ть *pf.*
pilgrim ['pɪlgrɪm] пало́мник; **~age** ['pɪlgrɪmɪdʒ] пало́мничество
pill [pɪl] табле́тка; ***bitter ~*** *fig.* го́рькая пилю́ля
pillage ['pɪlɪdʒ] мародёрство
pillar ['pɪlə] столб, коло́нна; *Brt.* **~-box** почто́вый я́щик
pillion ['pɪljən] *on motorcycle* за́днее сиде́нье
pillow ['pɪləʊ] поду́шка; **~case**, **~-slip** на́волочка
pilot ['paɪlət] **1.** *ae.* пило́т; *naut.* ло́цман; **2.** *naut.* проводи́ть [-вести́]; *ae.* пилоти́ровать
pimple ['pɪmpl] пры́щик
pin [pɪn] **1.** була́вка; ***hair ~*** шпи́лька; *Brt.* ***drawing ~*** (*Am. thumbtack*) кно́пка; **2.** прика́лывать [-коло́ть]; ***~ down*** припере́ть *pf.* к сте́нке; ***~ one's hopes on*** возлага́ть [-ложи́ть] наде́жды на (В)
pinafore ['pɪnəfɔ:] пере́дник
pincers ['pɪnsəz] *pl.* кле́щи *f/pl.*; (*tweezers*) пинце́т
pinch [pɪntʃ] **1.** щипо́к; *of salt, etc.* щепо́тка; *fig.* стеснённое положе́ние; ***at a ~*** в кра́йнем слу́чае; **2.** *v/t.* щипа́ть [щипну́ть]; (*squeeze*) прищемля́ть [-ми́ть]; *v/i.* [по]скупи́ться; *of shoes* жать
pine[1] [paɪn]: ***~ away*** [за]ча́хнуть; ***~ for*** тоскова́ть по (П)
pine[2] [~] *bot.* сосна́; **~apple** анана́с; **~ cone** сосно́вая ши́шка
pinion ['pɪnjən] *tech.* (*cogwheel*) шестерня́
pink [pɪŋk] **1.** *bot.* гвозди́ка; ро́зовый цвет; **2.** ро́зовый
pinnacle ['pɪnəkl] *arch.* остроконе́чная ба́шенка; *of mountain* верши́на; *fig.* верх
pint [paɪnt] пи́нта
pioneer [paɪə'nɪə] **1.** пионе́р; первопрохо́дец *m*; **2.** прокла́дывать путь *m* (***for*** Д)
pious ['paɪəs] □ на́божный
pip [pɪp] *of fruit* ко́сточка, зёрнышко
pipe [paɪp] труба́; *smoker's* тру́бка; *mus.* ду́дка; **2.**: ***~ down*** замолча́ть *pf.*; **~ dream** несбы́точная мечта́; **~line** трубопрово́д; нефтепрово́д; **~r** ['paɪpə] *mst.* волы́нщик
piping ['paɪpɪŋ]: ***~ hot*** о́чень горя́чий

piquant ['pi:kənt] пика́нтный (*a. fig.*)
pique [pi:k] **1.** доса́да; **2.** (*nettle*) раздража́ть; вызыва́ть доса́ду; (*wound*) уязвля́ть [-ви́ть] заде́(ва́)ть
pira|cy ['paɪərəsɪ] пира́тство (*a. in publishing*); **~te** [~rət] **1.** пира́т
pistol ['pɪstl] пистоле́т
piston ['pɪstən] *tech.* по́ршень *m*; **~ stroke** ход по́ршня
pit [pɪt] я́ма; *mining* ша́хта; *thea.* оркестро́вая я́ма
pitch[1] [pɪtʃ] смола́; (*tar*) дёготь *m*; ***as black as ~*** чёрный как смоль
pitch[2] [~] (*degree*) сте́пень *f*; *mus.* высота́ то́на; *naut.* ки́левая ка́чка; *tech.* (*slope*) накло́н; *tech.* (*thread*) шаг резьбы́; *sport* по́ле, площа́дка; **2.** *v/t.* (*set up camp, tent, etc.*) раз-би́(ва́)ть; (*throw*) броса́ть [бро́сить]; *naut.* кача́ть; *fig.* **~ *into*** набра́сываться [-ро́ситься] на (В)
pitcher ['pɪtʃə] (*jug*) кувши́н; (*sport*) подаю́щий
pitchfork ['pɪtʃfɔ:k] ви́лы *f/pl.*
pitfall ['pɪtfɔ:l] *fig.* лову́шка
pith [pɪθ] *bot.* сердцеви́на; *fig.* су́щ-ность *f*, суть *f*; **~y** ['pɪθɪ] *fig.* сжа́тый; содержа́тельный
pitiable ['pɪtɪəbl] □ (*arousing pity*) несча́стный; (*arousing contempt*) жа́лкий
pitiful ['pɪtɪfl] □ (*arousing compassion*) жа́лостливый; (*arousing contempt*) жа́лкий
pitiless ['pɪtɪlɪs] □ безжа́лостный
pittance ['pɪtəns] гроши́
pity ['pɪtɪ] **1.** жа́лость *f* (***for*** к Д), ***it is a ~*** жаль; **2.** [по]жале́ть
pivot ['pɪvət] **1.** ось *f* враще́ния; *fig.* сте́ржень *m*; **2.** враща́ться ([***up***]***on*** вокру́г Р)
pizza ['pi:tsə] пи́цца
placard ['plækɑ:d] плака́т
placate [plə'keɪt] умиротворя́ть [-ри́ть]
place [pleɪs] **1.** ме́сто; го́род, селе́-ние; дом; (*station*) до́лжность *f*; ***give ~ to*** уступа́ть ме́сто (Д); ***in ~ of*** вме́сто (Р); ***in ~s*** места́ми; ***out of ~*** неуме́стный; **2.** [по]ста́вить, класть [положи́ть]; *orders, etc.* раз-меща́ть [-ести́ть]; *article, etc.* поме-ща́ть [-ести́ть]; ***I can't ~ her*** не могу́ вспо́мнить, отку́да я её зна́ю
placid ['plæsɪd] □ споко́йный
plagiar|ism ['pleɪdʒərɪzəm] плаги-а́т; **~ize** [~raɪz] занима́ться пла-гиа́том
plague [pleɪg] **1.** (*pestilence*) чума́ *fig.* (*calamity*) бе́дствие; (*scourge*) бич; **2.** [из]му́чить; *coll.* надоеда́ть [-е́сть] (Д)
plaice [pleɪs] ка́мбала
plaid [plæd] шотла́ндка; плед
plain [pleɪn] **1.** □ просто́й; поня́т-ный, я́сный; (*obvious*) очеви́дный; обыкнове́нный; (*smooth, level*) гла́дкий, ро́вный; **2.** *adv.* я́сно; открове́нно; **3.** *geogr.* равни́на; **~-*spoken*** прямо́й
plaint|iff ['pleɪntɪf] исте́ц *m*, исти́ца *f*; **~ive** ['pleɪntɪv] □ жа́лобный, за-уны́вный
plait [plæt] **1.** коса́; **2.** заплета́ть [-ести́]
plan [plæn] **1.** план, прое́кт; **2.** [за]плани́ровать; составля́ть план; *fig.* намеча́ть [-е́тить]; (*intend*) на-мерева́ться
plane[1] [pleɪn] **1.** пло́ский; **2.** пло́с-кость *f*, *math.* прое́кция; *ae.* само-лёт; *fig.* у́ровень *m*
plane[2] [~] **1.** (*tool*) руба́нок; **2.** [вы́]строга́ть
planet ['plænɪt] плане́та
plank [plæŋk] **1.** доска́; **2.** настила́ть *or* обшива́ть до́сками
plant [plɑ:nt] **1.** расте́ние; *tech.* за-во́д, фа́брика; **2.** *tree* сажа́ть [по-сади́ть]; [по]ста́вить; **~ation** [plæn-'teɪʃən] планта́ция; насажде́ние
plaque [plɑ:k] (*wall ornament*) та-ре́лка; *on door, etc.* доще́чка, таб-ли́чка; ***memorial ~*** мемориа́льная доска́
plasma ['plæzmə] пла́зма
plaster ['plɑ:stə] **1.** *for walls* штукату́рка; *med.* пла́стырь *m*; (*mst.* **~ *of Paris***) гипс; ***sticking ~*** *med.* лейкопла́стырь; **2.** [о]штука-ту́рить; накла́дывать пла́стырь на (В)
plastic ['plæstɪk] (**~*ally***) **1.** пласти́-ческий; **2.** пластма́сса, пла́стик; **~ *surgery*** пласти́ческая хирурги́я
plate [pleɪt] **1.** (*dish*) таре́лка;

(*metal tableware*) посу́да; (*sheet of glass, metal, etc.*) лист; *on door* доще́чка; ***silver ~*** столо́вое серебро́; **2.** покрыва́ть мета́ллом
plateau ['plætəʊ] плато́ *n indecl.*
platform ['plætfɔ:m] *rail.* перро́н, платфо́рма; *for speakers* трибу́на; *on bus, etc.* площа́дка; *pol.* полити́ческая програ́мма
platinum ['plætɪnəm] пла́тина; *attr.* пла́тиновый
platitude ['plætɪtju:d] бана́льность *f*; иста́сканное выраже́ние
platoon [plə'tu:n] *mil.* взвод
platter ['plætə] блю́до
plausible ['plɔ:zəbl] □ правдоподо́бный; *of excuse, argument, etc.* благови́дный
play [pleɪ] **1.** игра́; пье́са; ***fair ~*** че́стная игра́; **2.** игра́ть [сыгра́ть] (в В, *mus.* на П); (*direct*) направля́ть [-́вить]; ***~ off*** *fig.* разы́грывать [-ра́ть]; стра́вливать [страви́ть] (***against*** с Т); ***~ed out*** вы́дохшийся; **~bill** театра́льная афи́ша; **~er** ['pleɪə] игро́к; актёр; **~-mate** това́рищ по и́грам, друг де́тства; **~ful** ['pleɪfl] □ игри́вый; **~goer** ['~gəʊə] театра́л; **~-ground** де́тская площа́дка; **~-house** теа́тр; **~pen** де́тский мане́ж; **~thing** игру́шка; **~wright** ['~raɪt] драмату́рг
plea [pli:] про́сьба, мольба́; *law* заявле́ние в суде́; ***on the ~*** (***of*** *или* ***that ...***) под предло́гом (Р *or* что ...)
plead [pli:d] *v/i.*: ***~ for*** вступа́ться [-пи́ться] за (В); говори́ть за (В); ***~ guilty*** признава́ть себя́ вино́вным; *v/t. in court* защища́ть [-ити́ть]; приводи́ть в оправда́ние
pleasant ['pleznt] □ прия́тный
please [pli:z] [по]нра́виться (Д); угожда́ть [угоди́ть] (Д); ***if you ~*** с ва́шего позволе́ния; изво́льте!; ***~ come in!*** войди́те, пожа́луйста!; доставля́ть удово́льствие (Д); ***be ~d to do*** де́лать с удово́льствием; ***be ~d with*** быть дово́льным (Т); **~d** [pli:zd] дово́льный
pleasing ['pli:zɪŋ] □ прия́тный
pleasure ['pleʒə] удово́льствие, наслажде́ние; *attr.* развлека́тельный, увесели́тельный; ***at your ~*** по ва́шему жела́нию
pleat [pli:t] **1.** скла́дка; **2.** де́лать скла́дки на (П)
pledge [pledʒ] **1.** зало́г, закла́д; (*promise*) обеща́ние; **2.** закла́дывать [заложи́ть]; обеща́ть; (*vow*) [по]кля́сться; обя́зываться [-за́ть-ся]; ***he ~d himself*** он связа́л себя́ обеща́нием
plenary ['pli:nərɪ] плена́рный
plenipotentiary [plenɪpə'tenʃərɪ] полномо́чный представи́тель *m*
plentiful ['plentɪfl] □ оби́льный
plenty ['plentɪ] **1.** изоби́лие; ***~ of*** мно́го (Р); **2.** *coll.* вполне́; дово́льно
pleurisy ['plʊərəsɪ] плеври́т
pliable ['plaɪəbl] □ ги́бкий; *fig.* пода́тливый, мя́гкий
pliancy ['plaɪənsɪ] ги́бкость *f*
pliers ['plaɪəz] *pl.* плоскогу́бцы *m/pl.*
plight [plaɪt] плохо́е положе́ние, состоя́ние
plod [plɒd] (*a.* ***~ along, on***) [по]тащи́ться; корпе́ть (***at*** над Т)
plot [plɒt] **1.** уча́сток земли́, деля́нка; (*conspiracy*) за́говор; *lit.* фа́була, сюже́т; **2.** *v/i.* гото́вить за́говор; *v/t. on map* наноси́ть [нанести́]; замышля́ть [-ы́слить]; интригова́ть
plow, *Brt.* **plough** [plaʊ] **1.** плуг; **2.** [вс]паха́ть; *fig.* [из]борозди́ть; **~land** пахо́тная земля́; па́шня
pluck [plʌk] **1.** *coll.* сме́лость *f*, му́жество; **2.** *flowers* срыва́ть [сорва́ть]; *fowl* ощи́пывать [-па́ть]; ***~ at*** дёргать [дёрнуть] (В); хвата́ть(ся) [схвати́ть(ся)] за (В); ***~ up courage*** собра́ться *pf.* с ду́хом; **~y** ['plʌkɪ] сме́лый, отва́жный
plug [plʌg] **1.** заты́чка; *in bath, etc.* про́бка; *el.* ште́псель *m*; ***~ socket*** ште́псельная розе́тка; **2.** *v/t. stop up* затыка́ть [заткну́ть]; ***~ in*** включа́ть [-чи́ть]
plum [plʌm] сли́ва; *attr.* сли́вовый
plumage ['plu:mɪdʒ] опере́ние
plumb [plʌm] *adv.* (*exactly*) то́чно; пря́мо, как раз
plumb|er ['plʌmə] санте́хник, *coll.* водопрово́дчик; **~ing** [~ɪŋ] *in house*

P

водопрово́д и канализа́ция
plummet ['plʌmɪt] свинцо́вый отве́с; *on fishing line* грузи́ло
plump¹ [plʌmp] (*chubby*) пу́хлый; (*somewhat fat*) по́лный; *poultry* жи́рный
plump² [~] **1.** □ *coll.* реши́тельный; **2.** бу́хаться [-хнуться]; **3.** *adv. coll.* пря́мо, без обиняко́в
plunder ['plʌndə] [о]гра́бить
plunge [plʌndʒ] **1.** (*dive*) ныря́ть [нырну́ть]; *hand, etc.* окуна́ть [-ну́ть]; **2.** ныря́ние; погруже́ние; ***take the ~*** [с]де́лать реши́тельный шаг
plural ['plʊərəl] *gr.* мно́жественное число́; (*multiple*) многочи́сленный
plush [plʌʃ] плюш
ply¹ [plaɪ] *v/t. with questions* засыпа́ть [засы́пать], забра́сывать [-роса́ть]; *v/i.* курси́ровать
ply² [~] слой; **~wood** фане́ра
pneumatic [nju:'mætɪk] (***~ally***) пневмати́ческий
pneumonia [nju:'məʊnɪə] воспале́ние лёгких, пневмони́я
poach¹ [pəʊtʃ] браконье́рствовать
poach² [~]: ***~ed egg*** яйцо́-пашо́т
poacher ['pəʊtʃə] браконье́р
PO Box (= *Post Office Box*) почто́вый я́щик (п/я)
pocket ['pɒkɪt] **1.** карма́н; (*air ~*) возду́шная я́ма; **2.** класть в карма́н; *fig. appropriate* прикарма́ни(ва)ть; *pride* подавля́ть [-ви́ть]; *insult* прогла́тывать [-лоти́ть]; **3.** карма́нный
pod [pɒd] **1.** *of seed* стручо́к; **2.** *shell v/t.* лу́щить
poem ['pəʊɪm] поэ́ма; стихотворе́ние
poet ['pəʊɪt] поэ́т; **~ess** [~əs] поэте́сса; **~ic(al** □) [pəʊ'etɪk(əl)] поэти́ческий; поэти́чный; **~ry** ['pəʊɪtrɪ] поэ́зия
poignan|cy ['pɔɪnjənsɪ] острота́; **~t** [~nt] о́стрый; тро́гательный; *fig.* мучи́тельный
point [pɔɪnt] **1.** (*dot*) то́чка; (*item*) пункт; *on thermometer* гра́дус, деле́ние; (*essence*) смысл; суть де́ла; *sport* очко́; (*sharp end*) остриё, о́стрый коне́ц; *rail* стре́лка; ***~ of view*** то́чка зре́ния; ***the ~ is that ...*** де́ло в том, что ...; ***make a ~ of*** + *ger.* поста́вить себе́ зада́чей (+ *inf.*); ***in ~ of*** в отноше́нии (Р); ***off the ~*** не (относя́щийся) к де́лу; ***be on the ~ of*** + *ger.* соб(и)ра́ться (+ *inf.*); ***win on ~s*** выи́грывать по очка́м; ***to the ~*** к де́лу (относя́щийся); ***a sore ~*** больно́й вопро́с; ***that's beside the ~*** э́то не при чём; **2.** *v/t.*: ***~ one's finger*** пока́зывать па́льцем (***at*** на В); заостря́ть [-ри́ть]; (*often ~* ***out***) ука́зывать [-за́ть]; ***~ a weapon at*** направля́ть [-ра́вить] ору́жие на (В); *v/i.*: ***~ at*** ука́зывать [-за́ть] на (В); ***~ to*** быть напра́вленным на (В); **~-blank**: ***ask ~*** спра́шивать в упо́р; ***refuse ~*** категори́чески отказа́ть(ся) *pf.*; **~ed** ['pɔɪntɪd] □ остроконе́чный; о́стрый; *fig.* ко́лкий; **~er** ['pɔɪntə] стре́лка *m*; *teacher's* ука́зка; *dog* по́йнтер; **~less** ['~lɪs] бессмы́сленный
poise [pɔɪz] **1.** равнове́сие; *carriage* оса́нка; **2.** *v/i.* баланси́ровать
poison ['pɔɪzn] **1.** яд, отра́ва; **2.** отравля́ть [-ви́ть]; **~ous** [~əs] (*fig. a.*) ядови́тый
poke [pəʊk] **1.** толчо́к, тычо́к; **2.** *v/t.* (*prod*) ты́кать [ткнуть]; толка́ть [-кну́ть]; сова́ть [су́нуть]; *fire* меша́ть кочерго́й; ***~ fun at*** подшу́чивать [-шути́ть] над (Т); *v/i.* сова́ть нос (***into*** в В); (*grope for*) иска́ть о́щупью (***for*** В *or* Р)
poker ['pəʊkə] кочерга́
poky ['pəʊkɪ] те́сный; убо́гий
polar ['pəʊlə] поля́рный; ***~ bear*** бе́лый медве́дь *m*; **~ity** [pəʊ'lærətɪ] поля́рность *f*
pole¹ [pəʊl] (*of planet*; *a. elec.*) по́люс
pole² [~] (*post*; *a. in sport*) шест
Pole³ [~] поля́к *m*, по́лька *f*
polemic [pə'lemɪk] (*a.* **~al** [~mɪkl] □) полеми́чный, полеми́ческий; **~s** [~s] поле́мика
police [pə'li:s] **1.** поли́ция; **2.** соде́рживать поря́док в (П); **~man** полице́йский; ***~ station*** полице́йский уча́сток
policy¹ ['pɒləsɪ] поли́тика; ли́ния поведе́ния
policy² [~]: ***insurance ~*** страхово́й по́лис

Polish[1] ['pəʊlɪʃ] по́льский
polish[2] ['pɒlɪʃ] **1.** полиро́вка; *fig.* лоск; **2.** [от]полирова́ть; *floor* натира́ть [-ере́ть]; *shoes* почи́стить; *fig.* наводи́ть [-вести́] лоск
polite [pə'laɪt] □ ве́жливый; **~ness** [~nɪs] ве́жливость *f*
politic|al [pə'lɪtɪkl] □ полити́ческий; **~ian** [pɒlɪ'tɪʃən] поли́тик, полити́ческий де́ятель; **~s** ['pɒlətɪks] *pl.* поли́тика
poll [pəʊl] **1.** голосова́ние; (*elections*) вы́боры; ***opinion*** **~** опро́с обще́ственного мне́ния; **2.** *v/t. receive votes* получа́ть [-чи́ть]; *v/i.* [про]голосова́ть
pollen ['pɒlən] пыльца́
polling ['pəʊlɪŋ] **1.** → ***poll***; **2.**: **~ *station*** избира́тельный уча́сток
pollute [pə'lu:t] загрязня́ть [-ни́ть]; оскверня́ть [-ни́ть]
pollution [pə'lu:ʃn] загрязне́ние
polyethylene [pɒlɪ'eθɪli:n] *or Brt.* **polythene** ['pɒlɪθi:n] полиэтиле́н
polyp ['pɒlɪp] *zo.*, **~us** [~əs] *med.* поли́п
pomegranate ['pɒmɪgrænɪt] грана́т
pommel ['pɒml] *of sword* голо́вка; *of saddle* лука́; *v/t.* = ***pummel***
pomp [pɒmp] по́мпа; великоле́пие
pompous ['pɒmpəs] □ напы́щенный, помпе́зный
pond [pɒnd] пруд
ponder ['pɒndə] *v/t.* обду́м(ыв)ать; *v/i.* заду́м(ыв)аться; **~ous** [~rəs] □ *fig.* тяжелове́сный
pontoon [pɒn'tu:n] понто́н; **~ bridge** понто́нный мост
pony ['pəʊnɪ] *horse* по́ни *m indecl.*
poodle ['pu:dl] пу́дель *m*
pool [pu:l] **1.** (*puddle*) лу́жа; (*pond*) пруд; (*swimming* ~) пла́вательный бассе́йн; **2.** *cards* банк; *billards* пул; *comm.* фонд; *v/t.* объединя́ть в о́бщий фонд; скла́дываться [сложи́ться] (***with*** с Т)
poor [pʊə] □ бе́дный; неиму́щий; (*unfortunate*) несча́стный; (*scanty*) ску́дный; (*bad*) плохо́й; **~ly** ['pʊəlɪ] *adj.* нездоро́вый
pop [pɒp] **1.** (*explosive sound*) хлопо́к; *coll.* (*fizzy drink*) шипу́чка; **2.** *v/t.* (*put*) сова́ть [су́нуть]; *of cork v/i.* хло́пать [-пнуть]; **~ *across*** *to a shop, etc.* сбе́гать; **~ *in*** заскочи́ть, забежа́ть
popcorn ['pɒpkɔ:n] попко́рн; возду́шная кукуру́за
pope [pəʊp] (ри́мский) па́па *m*
poplar ['pɒplə] то́поль *m*
poppy ['pɒpɪ] мак
popula|ce ['pɒpjʊləs] (*the masses*) ма́ссы; (*the common people*) просто́й наро́д; населе́ние; **~r** [~lə] (*of the people*) наро́дный; (*generally liked*) популя́рный; **~rity** [~'lærətɪ] популя́рность *f*
populat|e ['pɒpjʊleɪt] населя́ть [-ли́ть]; **~ion** [pɒpjʊ'leɪʃn] населе́ние
populous ['pɒpjʊləs] □ многолю́дный
porcelain ['pɔ:səlɪn] фарфо́р
porch [pɔ:tʃ] крыльцо́; по́ртик; *Am.* вера́нда
pore[1] [pɔ:] по́ра
pore[2] [~] *problem* размышля́ть, *book* корпе́ть (***over*** над Т)
pork [pɔ:k] свини́на
pornography [pɔ:'nɒgrəfɪ] порногра́фия
porous ['pɔ:rəs] □ по́ристый
porridge ['pɒrɪdʒ] овся́ная ка́ша
port[1] [pɔ:t] га́вань *f*, порт; *naut.* (*left side*) ле́вый борт
port[2] [~] портве́йн
portable ['pɔ:təbl] портати́вный
portal [pɔ:tl] *arch.* порта́л
portend [pɔ:'tend] предвеща́ть
portent ['pɔ:tent] предве́стник, предзнаменова́ние
porter ['pɔ:tə] вахтёр; *in hotel* швейца́р; *rail, etc.* носи́льщик; *Am. on train* проводни́к
portion ['pɔ:ʃn] **1.** часть *f*; *of food, etc.* по́рция; **2.** (*share out*) [раз-]дели́ть
portly ['pɔ:tlɪ] доро́дный
portrait ['pɔ:trɪt] портре́т; **~ist** [~ɪst] портрети́ст
portray [pɔ:'treɪ] рисова́ть (писа́ть) портре́т с (Р); изобража́ть [-рази́ть]; (*describe*) опи́сывать [-са́ть]; **~al** [~əl] изображе́ние; описа́ние
pose [pəʊz] **1.** по́за; **2.** *for an artist* пози́ровать; *question* (по)ста́вить; **~ *as*** выдава́ть себя́ за (В)
position [pə'zɪʃn] ме́сто; положе́-

P

ние; пози́ция; состоя́ние; то́чка зре́ния
positive ['pɒzətɪv] **1.** □ положи́тельный, позити́вный; (*sure*) уве́ренный; (*definite*) определённый; **2.** *phot.* позити́в
possess [pə'zes] *quality* облада́ть (T); *things* владе́ть (T); *fig.* овладе́(ва́)ть (T); ***be ~ed*** быть одержи́мым; **~ion** [~zeʃn] владе́ние; ***take ~ of*** завладе́(ва́)ть (T); облада́ние; *fig.* одержи́мость *f*; **~or** [~zesə] владе́лец; облада́тель *m*
possib|ility [pɒsə'bɪlətɪ] возмо́жность *f*; **~le** ['pɒsəbl] возмо́жный; **~ly** [~ɪ] возмо́жно; ***if I ~ can*** е́сли у меня́ бу́дет возмо́жность *f*
post[1] [pəʊst] столб
post[2] [~] **1.** (*mail*) по́чта; *mil.* (*duty station*) пост; (*appointment, job*) до́лжность *f*; **2.** *v/t.* отправля́ть по по́чте
postage ['pəʊstɪdʒ] почто́вая опла́та; **~ stamp** почто́вая ма́рка
postal ['pəʊstl] □ почто́вый; ***~ order*** де́нежный почто́вый перево́д
post|card откры́тка; **~code** почто́вый и́ндекс
poster ['pəʊstə] афи́ша, плака́т
poste restante [pəʊst'rɪstænt] *chiefly Brt.* до востре́бования
posterior [pɒ'stɪərɪə] (*subsequent*) после́дующий; (*behind*) за́дний; (*buttocks*) зад
posterity [pə'sterətɪ] пото́мство
post-free *chiefly Brt.* → **postpaid**
postgraduate [pəʊst'grædʒʊət] аспира́нт(ка); (*not working for degree*) стажёр; ***~ study*** аспиранту́ра
posthumous ['pɒstjʊməs] посме́ртный; *child* рождённый по́сле сме́рти отца́
post|man почтальо́н; **~mark 1.** почто́вый ште́мпель *m*; **2.** [за]штемпелева́ть; **~master** нача́льник почто́вого отделе́ния
postmortem [pəʊst'mɔːtəm] вскры́тие, аутопси́я
post|office отделе́ние свя́зи, *coll.* по́чта; **~box** абонеме́нтный почто́вый я́щик; ***general ~ office*** (гла́вный) почта́мт; **~paid** опла́ченный отправи́телем
postpone [pəʊs'pəʊn] отсро́чи(-ва)ть; откла́дывать [отложи́ть]; **~ment** [~mənt] отсро́чка
postscript ['pəʊsskrɪpt] постскри́птум
postulate 1. ['pɒstjʊlət] постула́т; **2.** [~leɪt] постули́ровать (*im*)*pf.*
posture ['pɒstʃə] (*attitude*) по́за; (*carriage*) оса́нка
postwar [pəʊst'wɔː] послевое́нный
posy ['pəʊzɪ] буке́т цвето́в
pot [pɒt] **1.** горшо́к; котело́к; ***~s of money*** ку́ча де́нег; **2.** *plants* сажа́ть в горшо́к; *jam, etc.* заготовля́ть впрок, [за]консерви́ровать
potato [pə'teɪtəʊ] (*single*) карто́фелина; **~es** [~z] *pl.* карто́фель *m*; *coll.* карто́шка; ***~ crisps*** хрустя́щий карто́фель
pot-belly брю́хо, пу́зо
poten|cy ['pəʊtnsɪ] эффекти́вность *f*; (*sexual*) поте́нция; *of drink* кре́пость *f*; **~t** [~tnt] □ эффекти́вный; кре́пкий; **~tial** [pə'tenʃl] **1.** потенциа́льный, возмо́жный; **2.** потенциа́л
pothole ['pɒthəʊl] вы́боина, ры́твина
potion ['pəʊʃn] зе́лье; ***love ~*** любо́вный напи́ток
pottery ['pɒtərɪ] керами́ческие (*or* гонча́рные) изде́лия *n/pl.*
pouch [paʊtʃ] су́мка (*a. biol.*); мешо́чек
poultry ['pəʊltrɪ] дома́шняя пти́ца
pounce [paʊns] **1.** прыжо́к; **2.** набра́сываться [-ро́ситься] (**[*up*]*on*** на B)
pound [paʊnd] (*weight*) фунт; (*money*) **~** (***sterling***) фунт сте́рлингов (*abbr.* £)
pound[2] [~] [ис-, рас]толо́чь; (*strike*) колоти́ть; ***~ to pieces*** разби́ть *pf.*
pour [pɔː] *v/t.* лить; ***~ out*** нали́(ва́)ть; *dry substance* сы́пать, насыпа́ть [насы́пать]; *v/i.* ли́ться; [по]сы́паться **~ing** [~rɪŋ]: ***~ rain*** проливно́й дождь *m*
pout [paʊt] *v/i.* [на]ду́ться; ***~ one's lips*** наду́(ва́)ть гу́бы
poverty ['pɒvətɪ] бе́дность *f*
powder ['paʊdə] **1.** порошо́к; (*face ~*) пу́дра; (*gun~*) по́рох; **2.** [ис]толо́чь; [на]пу́дрить(ся); посыпа́ть

[посы́пать]; ~ **compact** пу́дреница

power ['paʊə] си́ла; мощь *f*; *tech.* мо́щность *f*; *atomic, etc.* эне́ргия; *pol.* держа́ва; власть *f*; *law* полномо́чие; *math* сте́пень *f*; ***mental ~s*** у́мственные спосо́бности; **~ful** [~fl] мо́щный, могу́щественный; си́льный; **~less** [~lɪs] бесси́льный; ~ **plant**, ~ **station** электроста́нция

powwow ['paʊwaʊ] совеща́ние, собра́ние

practica|ble ['præktɪkəbl] □ реа́льный, осуществи́мый; **~l** [~kl] практи́ческий; *mind, person, etc.* практи́чный; факти́ческий; ~ ***joke*** ро́зыгрыш

practice ['præktɪs] пра́ктика; (*training*) упражне́ние, трениро́вка; (*habit*) привы́чка; (*custom*) обы́чай; ***in ~*** факти́чески; ***put into ~*** осуществля́ть [-ви́ть]

practice, *Brt.* **practise** [~] *v/t.* применя́ть [-ни́ть]; *medicine, etc.* занима́ться [-ня́ться] (Т); упражня́ться в (П); практикова́ть; *v/i.* упражня́ться; **~d** [~t] о́пытный

practitioner [præk'tɪʃənə]: ***general ~*** врач-терапе́вт

praise [preɪz] **1.** похвала́; **2.** [по]хвали́ть

praiseworthy ['preɪzwɜːðɪ] досто́йный похвалы́

prance [prɑːns] *of child* пры́гать; *of horse* гарцева́ть

prank [præŋk] вы́ходка, прока́за

prattle ['prætl] болта́ть; *of baby* лепета́ть

prawn [prɔːn] *zo.* креве́тка

pray [preɪ] [по]моли́ться; [по]проси́ть

prayer [preə] моли́тва; ***Lord's*** ♀ О́тче наш; ~ **book** моли́твенник

pre... [priː, pri] до...; пред...

preach [priːtʃ] пропове́довать; **~er** ['priːtʃə] пропове́дник

precarious [prɪ'keərɪəs] (*uncertain*) ненадёжный; (*dangerous*) опа́сный

precaution [prɪ'kɔːʃn] предосторо́жность *f*; ***take ~s*** принима́ть [-ня́ть] ме́ры предосторо́жности

precede [prɪ'siːd] предше́ствовать (Д); **~nce** ['presɪdəns] первоочерёдность, приорите́т; **~nt** ['presɪdənt] прецеде́нт

precept ['priːsept] наставле́ние

precinct ['priːsɪŋkt] преде́л; *Am.* (*electoral ~*) избира́тельный о́круг; **~s** *pl.* окре́стности *f/pl.*

precious ['preʃəs] **1.** □ драгоце́нный; ~ ***metals*** благоро́дные мета́ллы; **2.** *coll. adv.* о́чень

precipi|ce ['presɪpɪs] про́пасть *f*; **~tate 1.** [prɪ'sɪpɪteɪt] вверга́ть [-е́ргнуть]; (*hasten*) ускоря́ть [-о́рить]; **2.** [~tɪt] **a)** □ (*rash*) опроме́тчивый; (*violently hurried*) стреми́тельный; **b)** *chem.* оса́док; **~tous** [prɪ'sɪpɪtəs] □ (*steep*) круто́й; обры́вистый

precis|e [prɪ'saɪs] □ то́чный; *tech.* прецизио́нный; **~ion** [~'sɪʒn] то́чность *f*

preclude [pri'kluːd] исключа́ть зара́нее; (*prevent*) предотвраща́ть [-рати́ть] (В); (*hinder*) [по]меша́ть (Д)

precocious [prɪ'kəʊʃəs] □ не по года́м развито́й

preconceive ['priːkən'siːv] представля́ть себе́ зара́нее; **~d** [~d] предвзя́тый

preconception [priːkən'sepʃn] предвзя́тое мне́ние

precondition [priːkən'dʃn] предвари́тельное усло́вие

predatory ['predətrɪ] хи́щный

predecessor ['priːdɪsesə] предше́ственник [-ица]

predestine [priː'destɪn] предопределя́ть [-ли́ть]; ***~d*** предопределённый

predetermine [priːdɪ'tɜːmɪn] предопределя́ть [-ли́ть]

predicament [prɪ'dɪkəmənt] нело́вкое положе́ние; серьёзное затрудне́ние

predicate ['predɪkət] *gr.* сказу́емое; утвержда́ть [-ди́ть]

predict [prɪ'dɪkt] предска́зывать [-за́ть]; **~ion** [~kʃn] предсказа́ние

predilection [priːdɪ'lekʃn] скло́нность *f*, пристра́стие (***for*** к Д)

predispose [priːdɪs'pəʊz] предрасполага́ть [-ложи́ть]

predomina|nce [prɪ'dɒmɪnəns] госпо́дство, преоблада́ние; **~nt**

P

[~nənt] □ преоблада́ющий, домини́рующий; **~te** [~neɪt] госпо́дствовать, преоблада́ть (***over*** над T)
preeminent [priː'emɪnənt] превосходя́щий; выдаю́щийся
prefabricated [priː'fæbrɪkeɪtɪd]: **~ *house*** сбо́рный до́м
preface ['prefɪs] **1.** предисло́вие; **2.** начина́ть [-ча́ть] (B ***with***, с P); снабжа́ть предисло́вием
prefect ['priːfekt] префе́кт
prefer [prɪ'fɜː] предпочита́ть [-почесть]; (*put forward*) выдвига́ть [вы́двинуть]; **~able** ['prefrəbl] □ предпочти́тельный; **~ence** [~rəns] предпочте́ние; **~ential** [prefə'renʃl] □ предпочти́тельный; *econ.* льго́тный
prefix ['priːfɪks] пре́фикс, приста́вка
pregnan|cy ['pregnənsɪ] бере́менность *f*; **~t** [~nənt] □ бере́менная; *fig.* чрева́тый; **~ *pause*** многозначи́тельная па́уза
prejudice ['predʒʊdɪs] **1.** предрассу́док; предубежде́ние; **2.** предубежда́ть [-ди́ть]; (*harm*) [по]вреди́ть, наноси́ть уще́рб (Д)
preliminary [prɪ'lɪmɪnərɪ] **1.** □ предвари́тельный; **2.** подготови́тельное мероприя́тие
prelude ['preljuːd] *mus.* прелю́дия (*a. fig.*)
prematur|e ['premətjʊə] преждевре́менный; **~ *baby*** недоно́шенный ребёнок
premeditation [priːmedɪ'teɪʃn] преднаме́ренность *f*
premier ['premɪə] пе́рвый, гла́вный; премье́р-мини́стр
première ['premɪeə] премье́ра
premises ['premɪsɪz] *pl.* помеще́ние
premium ['priːmɪəm] (*reward*) награ́да; *payment* пре́мия; ***at a ~*** вы́ше номина́льной сто́имости; в большо́м спро́се
premonition [preːmə'nɪʃn] предчу́вствие
preoccup|ied [prɪː'ɒkjʊpaɪd] озабо́ченный; **~y** [~paɪ] поглоща́ть внима́ние (P); занима́ться [-ня́ться] (***with*** T)
prepaid [priː'peɪd] зара́нее опла́ченный; ***carriage ~*** доста́вка опла́чена
preparat|ion [prepə'reɪʃn] приготовле́ние; подгото́вка; *med.* препара́т; **~ory** [prɪ'pærətrɪ] предвари́тельный; подготови́тельный; ***~ to leaving*** пе́ред тем как уйти́
prepare [prɪ'peə] *v/t. of surprise, etc.* пригота́вливать [-то́вить]; *of dinner, etc.* [при]гото́вить; (*for an exam, etc.*) подгота́вливать [-то́вить]; *v/i.* [при]гото́виться; подгота́вливаться [-то́виться] (***for*** к Д); **~d** [~d] □ гото́вый; подгото́вленный
prepondera|nce [prɪ'pɒndərəns] переве́с; **~nt** [~rənt] име́ющий переве́с; **~ntly** [~lɪ] преиму́щественно
prepossessing [priːpə'zesɪŋ] □ располага́ющий; привлека́тельный
preposterous [prɪ'pɒstərəs] неле́пый, абсу́рдный
prerequisite [priː'rekwɪzɪt] предпосы́лка, непреме́нное усло́вие
presage ['presɪdʒ] предвеща́ть; предчу́вствовать
preschool [priː'skuːl] дошко́льный
prescribe [prɪ'skraɪb] предпи́сывать [-писа́ть]; *med.* прописывать [-писа́ть]
prescription [prɪ'skrɪpʃn] предпи́сывание; распоряже́ние; *med.* реце́пт
presence ['prezns] прису́тствие; ***~ of mind*** прису́тствие ду́ха
present[1] ['preznt] **1.** □ прису́тствующий; (*existing now*) тепе́решний, настоя́щий; (*given*) да́нный; **2.** настоя́щее вре́мя; ***at ~*** сейча́с; в да́нное вре́мя; ***for the ~*** пока́; на э́тот раз
present[2] [prɪ'zent] (*introduce, etc.*) представля́ть [-а́вить]; *gift* преподноси́ть [-нести́]; *petition* под(ав)а́ть (проше́ние); *a play* [по]ста́вить; *ticket* предъявля́ть [-ви́ть]
present[3] ['preznt] пода́рок
presentation [prezn'teɪʃn] представле́ние, презента́ция; (*exposition*) изложе́ние
presentiment [prɪ'zentɪmənt] предчу́вствие
presently ['prezntlɪ] вско́ре; сейча́с

preservati|on [prezə'veɪʃn] охрáна, сохранéние; сохрáнность *f*; **~ve** [prɪ'zɜːvətɪv] консервáнт
preserve [prɪ'zɜːv] **1.** сохранять [-нить]; предохранять [-нить]; *vegetables, etc.* консервировать; **2.** (*mst. pl.*) консéрвы *m/pl.*; варéнье; (**game ~**) заповéдник
preside [prɪ'zaɪd] председáтельствовать (**over** на П)
presiden|cy ['prezɪdənsɪ] президéнтство; **~t** [~dənt] президéнт
press [pres] **1.** печáть *f*, прéсса; (*crowd*) толпá; *coll.* дáвка; *tech.* пресс; **2.** *v/t.* жать; давить; *button* наж(им)áть; (*force*) навязывать [-зáть] (**on** Д); ***I am ~ed for time*** меня поджимáют срóки; у меня мáло врéмени; **~ *for*** настáивать [настоять] на (П); **~ *on*** двигаться дáльше; **~ card** журналистское удостоверéние; **~ing** ['presɪŋ] срóчный, неотлóжный; (*insistent*) настоятельный; **~ure** ['preʃə] давлéние (*a. fig.*); сжáтие
prestig|e [pre'stiːʒ] престиж; **~ious** [pre'stɪdʒəs] (*having prestige*) влиятельный; *hono(u)red* уважáемый
presum|able [prɪ'zjuːməbl] предположительный; **~e** [prɪ'zjuːm] *v/t.* предполагáть [-ложить]; *v/i.* полагáть; (*dare*) осмéли(ва)ться; **~ (*up*)*on*** злоупотреблять [-бить] (Т); ***he ~s too much*** он слишком мнóго себé позволяет
presumpt|ion [prɪ'zʌmpʃn] предположéние; *law* презýмпция; **~uous** [~tʃʊəs] самонадéянный, переступáющий границы чегó-то
presuppos|e [priːsə'pəʊz] предполагáть [-ложить]; **~ition** [priːsʌpə'zɪʃn] предположéние
pretend [prɪ'tend] притворяться [-риться]; [с]дéлать вид
pretense, *Brt.* **pretence** [prɪ'tens] (*false show*) притвóрство; (*pretext*) предлóг
preten|sion [prɪ'tenʃn] претéнзия, притязáние (**to** на В); **~tious** [~ʃəs] претенциóзный
pretext ['priːtekst] предлóг
pretty ['prɪtɪ] **1.** □ красивый; приятный; хорóшенький; **2.** *adv.* довóльно, весьмá; ***be sitting ~*** хорошó устрóился
prevail [prɪ'veɪl] одолевáть [-лéть] (**over** В); преобладáть; превалировать; (**over** над Т *or* средú Р); **~ (*up*)*on s.b. to do s.th.*** убедить *pf.* когó-л. чтó-л. сдéлать; **~ing** [~ɪŋ] госпóдствующий, преобладáющий
prevalent ['prevələnt] □ распространённый
prevaricate [prɪ'værɪkeɪt] уклоняться от прямóго отвéта, увиливать [-льнýть]
prevent [prɪ'vent] предотвращáть [-атить]; (*hinder*) [по]мешáть (Д); *crime* предупреждáть [-упредить]; **~ion** [prɪ'venʃn] предупреждéние; предотвращéние; **~ive** [~tɪv] **1.** □ предупредительный; профилактический; **2.** *med.* профилактическое срéдство
pre|view ['priːvjuː] *of film, etc* предварительный просмóтр
previous ['priːvɪəs] □ предыдýщий; (*premature*) преждеврéменный; **~ *to*** до (Р); **~ly** [~lɪ] прéжде (Р); пéред (Т)
prewar [priː'wɔː] довоéнный
prey [preɪ] **1.** добыча; (*fig.*, *victim*) жéртва; ***beast*** (***bird***) ***of ~*** хищный зверь *m.* (хищная птица); **2.**: **~ (*up*)*on*** охóтиться (на В); *fig.* терзáть
price [praɪs] **1.** ценá; **2.** (*value*) оцéнивать [-нить]; назначáть цéну (Д); **~less** ['~lɪs] бесцéнный
prick [prɪk] **1.** укóл; шип; *of conscience* угрызéния *n/pl.*; **2.** *v/t.* колóть [кольнýть]; **~ *up one's ears*** навострить ýши; *v/i.* колóться; **~le** ['prɪkl] шип, колючка; **~ly** ['~lɪ] (*having prickles or thorns*) колючий; (*causing stinging sensation*) кóлкий; (*touchy*) обидчивый
pride [praɪd] **1.** гóрдость *f*; ***take ~ in*** гордиться (Т); **2.**: **~ *o.s.*** гордиться ([***up***]***on*** Т)
priest [priːst] свящéнник
prim [prɪm] □ чóпорный
prima|cy ['praɪməsɪ] пéрвенство; **~ry** [~rɪ] первоначáльный; *colours, etc.* основнóй; начáльный; *geol.* первичный; ***of ~ importance*** первостепéнной вáжности

P

prime [praɪm] **1.** □ (*main*) гла́вный, основно́й; (*original*) первонача́льный; перви́чный; (*excellent*) превосхо́дный; ***~ minister*** премье́р-мини́стр; **2.** *fig.* расцве́т; ***in one's ~*** в расцве́те сил; **3.** *v/t.* снабжа́ть информа́цией; ната́скивать
primer ['prɪmə] (*schoolbook*) буква́рь *m*; (*paint*) грунто́вка
primeval [praɪ'miːvl] □ первобы́тный
primitive ['prɪmɪtɪv] первобы́тный; примити́вный
primrose ['prɪmrəʊz] при́мула
prince [prɪns] (*son of royalty*) принц; князь *m*; **~ss** [prɪn'ses] (*daughter of sovereign*) принце́сса; (*wife of nonroyal prince*) княги́ня; (*daughter of nonroyal prince and princess*) княжна́
principal ['prɪnsəpl] **1.** □ гла́вный, основно́й; **2.** *univ.* ре́ктор; *of school* дире́ктор шко́лы; *fin.* основно́й капита́л; *thea.* веду́щий актёр
principle ['prɪnsəpl] при́нцип; пра́вило; ***on ~*** из при́нципа; ***a matter of ~*** де́ло при́нципа
print [prɪnt] **1.** *typ.* печа́ть *f*; о́ттиск; (*type*) шрифт; (*imprint*) след, отпеча́ток (*a. photo*); *art* гравю́ра; ***out of ~*** тира́ж распро́дан; **2.** [на]печа́тать; *phot.* отпеча́т(ыв)ать; *fig.* запечатле́(ва́)ть (***on*** на П); **~er** ['prɪntə] печа́тник; *comput.* при́нтер
printing ['prɪntɪŋ] печа́тание; печа́тное де́ло; ***~ of 50,000 copies*** тира́ж в 50 000 экземпля́ров; *attr.* печа́тный; **~ office** типогра́фия
prior ['praɪə] **1.** предше́ствующий (***to*** Д); **2.** *adv.*: ***~ to*** до (Р); **~ity** [praɪ'ɒrətɪ] приорите́т; очерёдность *f*; ***of top ~*** первостепе́нной ва́жности
prism ['prɪzəm] при́зма
prison ['prɪzn] тюрьма́; **~er** [~ə] заключённый; (*~ of war*) военнопле́нный
privacy ['praɪvəsɪ] (*seclusion*) уедине́ние; ли́чная/ча́стная жизнь
private ['praɪvɪt] **1.** □ ча́стный; (*personal*) ли́чный; (*secluded*) уединённый; *conversation* с гла́зу на глаз; **2.** *mil.* рядово́й; ***in ~*** конфиденциа́льно; ***keep s.th. ~*** держа́ть в та́йне
privation [praɪ'veɪʃn] лише́ние, нужда́
privatize ['praɪvɪtaɪz] приватизи́ровать
privilege ['prɪvəlɪdʒ] привиле́гия; льго́та; **~d** привилегиро́ванный
privy ['prɪvɪ]: ***~ to*** посвящённый в (В)
prize[1] [praɪz]: ***~ open*** вскрыва́ть [-ры́ть], взла́мывать [-лома́ть]
prize[2] [~] **1.** пре́мия, приз; трофе́й; *in lottery* вы́игрыш; **2.** удосто́енный пре́мии; **3.** высоко́ цени́ть; **~-fighter** боксёр-профессиона́л; **~ winner** призёр; лауреа́т
pro [prəʊ] *pl.* **pros**: ***the ~s and cons*** до́воды за и про́тив
probab|ility [prɒbə'bɪlətɪ] вероя́тность *f*; **~le** ['prɒbəbl] вероя́тный
probation [prə'beɪʃn] испыта́тельный срок; *law* усло́вное освобожде́ние
probe [prəʊb] *med.* **1.** зонд; **2.** зонди́ровать; *into problem* глубоко́ изуча́ть [-чи́ть]
problem ['prɒbləm] пробле́ма; вопро́с; (*difficulty*) тру́дность *f*; *math.* зада́ча; **~atic(al** □) [prɒblə'mætɪk(əl)] проблемати́чный
procedure [prə'siːdʒə] процеду́ра
proceed [prə'siːd] отправля́ться да́льше; приступа́ть [-пи́ть] (***to*** к Д); (*act*) поступа́ть [-пи́ть]; продолжа́ть [-до́лжить] (***with*** В); ***~ from*** исходи́ть (из Р); **~ing** [~ɪŋ] посту́пок; **~s** *pl. law* судопроизво́дство; (*scientific publication*) запи́ски *f/pl.*, труды́ *m/pl.*; **~s** ['prəʊsiːdz] дохо́д, вы́ручка
process ['prəʊses] **1.** проце́сс (*a. law*); ***in the ~*** в хо́де; ***in the ~ of construction*** стро́ящийся; **2.** *tech.* обраба́тывать [-бо́тать]; **~ing** [~ɪŋ] *of data, etc.* обрабо́тка; *of food* перерабо́тка; **~ion** [~ʃn] проце́ссия; **~or** [~ə] *comput.* проце́ссор
proclaim [prə'kleɪm] провозглаша́ть [-ласи́ть]; *war, etc.* объявля́ть [-ви́ть]
proclamation [prɒklə'meɪʃn] объ-

P

явле́ние, провозглаше́ние
procrastinate [prəʊ'kræstɪneɪt] (*delay*) *v/i.* оття́гивать [-яну́ть], (*put off*) откла́дывать [отложи́ть]; (*drag out*) тяну́ть
procure [prə'kjʊə] *v/t.* дост(ав)а́ть
prod [prɒd] **1.** тычо́к, толчо́к; **2.** ты́кать (ткнуть); толка́ть [-кну́ть]; *fig.* подстрека́ть [-кну́ть]
prodigal ['prɒdɪgl] расточи́тельный; ***the ♀ Son*** блу́дный сын
prodig|ious [prə'dɪdʒəs] □ удиви́тельный; (*huge*) грома́дный; **~y** ['prɒdɪdʒɪ] чу́до; ***child ~*** вундерки́нд
produc|e **1.** [prə'djuːs] (*show*) предъявля́ть [-ви́ть]; (*proof*, *etc.*) представля́ть [-а́вить]; производи́ть [-вести́]; *film*, *etc.* [по]ста́вить; *sound* изд(ав)а́ть; **2.** ['prɔdjuːs] проду́кция; проду́кт; **~er** [prə'djuːsə] *of goods* производи́тель *m*; *thea.* режиссёр; *cine.* продю́сер
product ['prɒdʌkt] проду́кт; изде́лие; **~ion** [prə'dʌkʃn] произво́дство; проду́кция; *thea.* постано́вка; ***mass ~*** ма́ссовое произво́дство; **~ive** [prə'dʌktɪv] □ производи́тельный, *fig.* продукти́вный; *soil* плодоро́дный; *writer* плодови́тый; **~ivity** [prɒdʌk'tɪvətɪ] (*efficiency*) продукти́вность *f*, (*rate of production*) производи́тельность *f*
profane [prə'feɪn] (*desecrate*) оскверня́ть [-ни́ть]
profess [prə'fes] (*declare*) заявля́ть [-ви́ть]; (*claim*) претендова́ть на (В); ***I don't ~ to be an expert on this subject*** я не счита́ю себя́ специали́стом в э́той о́бласти; **~ion** [prə'feʃn] профе́ссия; **~ional** [~ənl] **1.** □ профессиона́льный; **2.** специали́ст; профессиона́л (*a. sport*); **~or** [~sə] профе́ссор
proffer ['prɒfə] предлага́ть [-ложи́ть]
proficien|cy [prə'fɪʃnsɪ] овладе́ние; о́пытность *f*; уме́ние; **~t** [~ʃnt] □ уме́лый, иску́сный
profile ['prəʊfaɪl] про́филь *m*
profit ['prɒfɪt] **1.** *comm.* при́быль *f*; вы́года, по́льза; ***gain ~ from*** извле́чь *pf.* по́льзу из (Р); **2.** *v/t.* приноси́ть по́льзу (Д); *v/i.* ***~ by*** [вос]по́льзоваться (Т); извлека́ть по́льзу из (Р); **~able** [~əbl] при́быльный; вы́годный; поле́зный; **~eer** [prɒfɪ'tɪə] спекуля́нт; **~-sharing** уча́стие в при́были
profound [prə'faʊnd] □ глубо́кий; (*thorough*) основа́тельный; **~ly** о́чень, глубоко́
profus|e [prə'fjuːs] □ оби́льный; ще́дрый; **~ion** [prə'fjuːʒn] изоби́лие
progeny ['prɒdʒənɪ] пото́мство
prognosis [prɒg'nəʊsɪs] прогно́з
program(me) ['prəʊgræm] **1.** програ́мма; **2.** программи́ровать; *comput.* **~er** [~ə] программи́ст
progress **1.** ['prəʊgres] прогре́сс; продвиже́ние; *in studies* успе́хи *m/pl.*; ***be in ~*** развива́ться; вести́сь; **2.** [prə'gres] продвига́ться вперёд; [с]де́лать успе́хи; **~ive** [~sɪv] □ передово́й, прогресси́вный; *illness*, *disease* прогресси́рующий; ***~ taxation*** прогресси́вный нало́г
prohibit [prə'hɪbɪt] запреща́ть [-ети́ть]; **~ion** [prəʊɪ'bɪʃn] запреще́ние; **~ive** [prə'hɪbətɪv] □ запрети́тельный
project **1.** ['prɒdʒekt] прое́кт (*a. arch.*); план; **2.** [prə'dʒekt] *v/t. light* броса́ть [бро́сить]; (*plan*) [с-, за]проекти́ровать; *v/i.* (*jut out*) вы́да(ва́)ться; **~ile** [prə'dʒektaɪl] снаря́д
prolific [prə'lɪfɪk] (**~*ally***) *writer*, *etc.* плодови́тый
prolix ['prəʊlɪks] □ многосло́вный
prologue ['prəʊlɒg] проло́г
prolong [prə'lɒŋ] продлева́ть [-ли́ть]; *law* пролонги́ровать
promenade [prɒmə'nɑːd] **1.** прогу́лка; ме́сто для прогу́лки; *along waterfront* на́бережная; *in park* алле́я; **2.** прогу́ливаться [-ля́ться]
prominent ['prɒmɪnənt] (*conspicuous*) □ ви́дный, заме́тный; (*jutting out*) выступа́ющий; *fig.* (*outstanding*) выдаю́щийся
promiscuous [prə'mɪskjʊəs] □ неразбо́рчивый; огу́льный; *sexually* сексуа́льно распу́щенный
promis|e ['prɒmɪs] **1.** обеща́ние; ***make a ~*** [по]обеща́ть; ***show great ~*** подава́ть больши́е на-

де́жды; **2.** обеща́ть (*im*)*pf.*, *pf. a.* [по-]; **~ing** [~ɪŋ] □ *fig.* перспекти́вный; подаю́щий наде́жды
promontory ['prɒməntrɪ] мыс
promot|e [prə'məʊt] (*further*) спосо́бствовать (*im*)*pf.*, *pf. a.* [по-] (Д); соде́йствовать (*im*)*pf.*, *pf. a.* [по-] (Д); (*establish*) учрежда́ть [-ди́ть]; (*advance in rank, station, etc.*) повыша́ть по слу́жбе; *mil.* присво́ить (очередно́е) зва́ние (Р); **~ion** [prə'məʊʃn] *in position* повыше́ние; продвиже́ние
prompt [prɒmpt] **1.** □ бы́стрый; *reply* неме́дленный; **2.** побужда́ть [-уди́ть]; внуша́ть [-ши́ть]; (*suggest*) подска́зывать [-за́ть] (Д); **~ness** ['prɒmptnɪs] быстрота́; прово́рство
promulgate ['prɒmlgeɪt] обнаро́довать; провозглаша́ть [-аси́ть]
prone [prəʊn] □ (*face down*) (лежа́щий) ничко́м; **~ to** скло́нный к (Д); ***he is ~ to colds*** он легко́ простужа́ется
prong [prɒŋ] *agric.* **~s** *pl.* ви́лы *f/pl.*
pronounce [prə'naʊns] (*articulate*) произноси́ть [-нести́]; (*proclaim*) объявля́ть [-ви́ть]; (*declare*) заявля́ть [-ви́ть]
pronunciation [prənʌnsɪ'eɪʃn] произноше́ние
proof [pru:f] **1.** доказа́тельство; (*test*) испыта́ние; прове́рка; *typ.* корректу́ра; **2.** (*impervious*) непроница́емый; **~-reader** корре́ктор
prop [prɒp] **1.** подпо́рка; *fig.* опо́ра; **2.** подпира́ть [-пере́ть]; **~ *against*** приста́влять [-вить] к (Д); прислони́ть
propagate ['prɒpəgeɪt] размножа́ть(ся) [-о́жить(ся)]; (*spread*) распространя́ть(ся) [-ни́ть(ся)]
propel [prə'pel] продвига́ть вперёд; ***~ s.o. towards ...*** подтолкну́ть *pf.* кого́-л. к (Д); **~ler** [~ə] пропе́ллер; *naut.* гребно́й винт
propensity [prə'pensətɪ] предрасполо́женность *f*; скло́нность *f*
proper ['prɒpə] □ (*own, peculiar*) сво́йственный, прису́щий; подходя́щий; пра́вильный; (*decent, seemly*) прили́чный; **~ty** [~tɪ] иму́щество, со́бственность *f*; (*quality*) сво́йство; ***intellectual ~*** интеллектуа́льная со́бственность
prophe|cy ['prɒfəsɪ] проро́чество; **~sy** [~saɪ] [на]проро́чить
prophet ['prɒfɪt] проро́к
prophylactic [prɒfɪ'læktɪk] **1.** профилакти́ческий; **2.** профила́ктика
proportion [prə'pɔ:ʃn] **1.** пропо́рция; соразме́рность *f*; (*size*) до́ля, часть *f*; **~s** *pl.* разме́ры *m/pl*; **2.** соразмеря́ть [-ме́рить]; **~al** [~l] пропорциона́льный
propos|al [prə'pəʊzl] предложе́ние; **~e** [prə'pəʊz] *v/t.* предлага́ть [-ложи́ть]; *v/i. marriage* сде́лать *pf.* предложе́ние; (*intend*) намерева́ться, предполага́ть; **~ition** [prɒpə'zɪʃn] (*offer*) предложе́ние
propound [prə'paʊnd] предлага́ть на обсужде́ние, выдвига́ть [-́винуть]
propriet|ary [prə'praɪətrɪ]: ***~ rights*** права́ со́бственности; ***~ name*** фи́рменное назва́ние; **~or** [~ətə] владе́лец *m*, -лица *f*; **~y** [~ətɪ] уме́стность *f*, присто́йность *f*
propulsion [prə'pʌlʃn] движе́ние вперёд
prosaic [prə'zeɪk] (***~ally***) *fig.* прозаи́чный
prose [prəʊz] **1.** про́за; **2.** прозаи́ческий; *fig.* прозаи́чный
prosecut|e ['prɒsɪkju:t] пресле́довать в суде́бном поря́дке; **~ion** [prɒsɪ'kju:ʃn] суде́бное разбира́тельство; **~or** ['prɒsɪkju:tə] *law* обвини́тель *m*; ***public ~*** прокуро́р
prospect 1. ['prɒspekt] перспекти́ва, вид (*a. fig.*); **2.** [prə'spekt] *geol.* разве́д(ыв)ать (***for*** на В); **~ive** [prə'spektɪv] □ бу́дущий, ожида́емый; **~us** [~təs] проспе́кт
prosper ['prɒspə] *v/i.* процвета́ть; преуспева́ть; **~ity** [prɒ'sperətɪ] процвета́ние; благополу́чие; *fig.* расцве́т; **~ous** ['prɒspərəs] состоя́тельный; процвета́ющий
prostitute ['prɒstɪtju:t] проститу́тка
prostrat|e ['prɒstreɪt] (*lying flat*) распростёртый; (*without srength*) обесси́ленный; ***~ with grief*** сло́мленный го́рем; **~ion** [~ʃn] *fig.* из-

неможе́ние

prosy ['prəʊzɪ] □ *fig.* прозаи́чный; бана́льный

protect [prə'tekt] защища́ть [-ити́ть]; [пред]охраня́ть [-ни́ть] (***from*** от P); **~ion** [prə'tekʃn] защи́та; **~ive** [~tɪv] защи́тный; предохрани́тельный; **~or** [~tə] защи́тник; (*patron*) покрови́тель *m*

protest 1. ['prəʊtest] проте́ст; **2.** [prə'test] *v/t.* (*declare*) заявля́ть [-ви́ть], утвержда́ть; *v/i.* [за]протестова́ть

Protestant ['prɒtɪstənt] **1.** протеста́нт *m*, -ка *f*; **2.** протеста́нтский

protestation [prɒtə'steɪʃn] торже́ственное заявле́ние

protocol ['prəʊtəkɒl] протоко́л (*a. dipl.*)

prototype ['prəʊtətaɪp] прототи́п

protract [prə'trækt] тяну́ть (B *or* c T); продолжа́ть [-до́лжить]; **~ed** затяжно́й

protru|de [prə'tru:d] выдава́ться нару́жу, торча́ть; **~ing** [~ɪŋ] выступа́ющий; **~ *eyes*** глаза́ навы́кате; **~sion** [~ʒn] вы́ступ

protuberance [prə'tju:bərəns] вы́пуклость *f*

proud [praʊd] □ го́рдый (***of*** T)

prove [pru:v] *v/t.* дока́зывать [-за́ть]; *v/i.*: **~ *o.s. to be*** ока́зываться [-за́ться]

proverb ['prɒvз:b] посло́вица

provide [prə'vaɪd] *v/t.* снабжа́ть [-бди́ть]; предоставля́ть [-а́вить]; *law* ста́вить усло́вием; предусма́тривать [-мотре́ть]; *v/i.*: **~ *for one's family*** обеспе́чивать [-чить] свою́ семью́; **~*d*** (***that***) при усло́вии (что)

providen|ce ['prɒvɪdəns] провиде́ние; (*prudence*) предусмотри́тельность *f*; **~t** [~dənt] □ предусмотри́тельный

provin|ce ['prɒvɪns] о́бласть *f*; прови́нция; *fig.* сфе́ра де́ятельности; **~cial** [prə'vɪnʃl] **1.** провинциа́льный; **2.** провинциа́л *m*, -ка *f*

provision [prə'vɪʒn] снабже́ние; обеспече́ние; *law of contract*, *etc.* положе́ние; **~*s*** *pl.* проду́кты; **~al** [~ʒənl] □ предвари́тельный; ориентиро́вочный; вре́менный

proviso [prə'vaɪzəʊ] усло́вие

provocat|ion [prɒvə'keɪʃn] вы́зов; провока́ция; **~ive** [prə'vɒkətɪv] *behaviour* вызыва́ющий; *question*, *etc.* провокацио́нный

provoke [prə'vəʊk] (с)провоци́ровать; (*stir up*) возбужда́ть [-буди́ть]; (*cause*) вызыва́ть [вы́звать]; (*make angry*) [рас]серди́ть

prowl [praʊl] кра́сться; броди́ть

proximity [prɒk'sɪmətɪ] бли́зость *f*

proxy ['prɒksɪ] (*authorization*) полномо́чие; (*substitute*) замести́тель; **~ vote** голосова́ние по дове́ренности; дове́ренность *f*

prude [pru:d] ханжа́

pruden|ce ['pru:dns] благоразу́мие; (*forethought*) предусмотри́тельность *f*; осторо́жность *f*; **~t** [~nt] □ благоразу́мный; осторо́жный; **~ *housekeeper*** бережли́вая хозя́йка

prudery ['pru:dərɪ] ха́нжество

prune[1] [pru:n] черносли́в

prune[2] [~] *agric.* подреза́ть [-ре́зать], обреза́ть [обре́зать]; *fig.* сокраща́ть [-рати́ть]

pry[1] [praɪ] подгля́дывать [-яде́ть]; **~ *into*** сова́ть нос в (B)

pry[2] [~]: *Am.* **~ *open*** → ***prize***[1]

psalm [sɑ:m] псало́м

pseudonym ['sju:dənɪm] псевдони́м

psychiatrist [saɪ'kaɪətrɪst] психиа́тр

psychic ['saɪkɪk], **~al** [~kɪkl] □ психи́ческий

psycholog|ical [saɪkə'lɒdʒɪkl] психологи́ческий; **~ist** [saɪ'kɒlədʒɪst] психо́лог; **~y** [~dʒɪ] психоло́гия

pub [pʌb] паб, пивно́й бар

puberty ['pju:bətɪ] полова́я зре́лость *f*

public ['pʌblɪk] **1.** □ публи́чный, обще́ственный; госуда́рственный; коммуна́льный; **~ *convenience*** обще́ственный туале́т; **~ *figure*** госуда́рственный де́ятель; **~ *opinion*** обще́ственное мне́ние; **~ *house*** пивна́я; **~ *spirit*** обще́ственное созна́ние; **2.** пу́блика; обще́ственность *f*; **~ation** [pʌblɪ'keɪʃn] опубликова́ние; изда́ние; ***monthly* ~** ежеме́сячник; **~ity**

P

[pʌb'lɪsətɪ] гла́сность *f*; (*advertising*) рекла́ма
publish ['pʌblɪʃ] [о]публикова́ть, изд(ав)а́ть; оглаша́ть [огласи́ть]; ***~ing house*** изда́тельство; **~er** [~ə] изда́тель *m*; **~s** *pl.* изда́тельство
pucker ['pʌkə] **1.** [с]мо́рщить(ся); *frown* [на]су́пить(ся); **2.** морщи́на
pudding ['pʊdɪŋ] пу́динг; ***black ~*** кровяна́я колбаса́
puddle ['pʌdl] лу́жа
puff [pʌf] **1.** *of wind* дунове́ние; *of smoke* клуб; **2.** *v/t.* (*~ out*) наду́(ва́)ть; ***~ed eyes*** распу́хшие глаза́ *m/pl.*; *v/i.* дуть поры́вами; пыхте́ть; ***~ away at*** попы́хивать (Т); ***~ out*** наду́(ва́)ться; **~ paste** слоёное те́сто; **~y** ['pʌfɪ] запыха́вшийся; *eyes* отёкший; *face* одутлова́тый
pug [pʌg]: ***~ dog*** мопс
pugnacious [pʌg'neɪʃəs] драчли́вый
pug-nosed ['pʌgnəʊzd] курно́сый
puke [pju:k] **1.** рво́та; **2.** *v/i.* [вы́]рвать
pull [pʊl] **1.** тя́га (*a. fig.*); (*inhalation of smoke*) затя́жка; **2.** [по]тяну́ть; (*drag*) таска́ть, [по]тащи́ть; (*~ out*) выдёргивать [вы́дернуть]; (*tug*) дёргать [-рнуть]; ***~ down*** (*demolish*) сноси́ть [снести́]; ***~ out*** (*move away*) отходи́ть [отойти́]; *med.* ***~ through*** *fig.* спаса́ть [-сти́]; (*recover*) поправля́ться [-а́виться]; ***~ o.s. together*** взять *pf.* себя́ в ру́ки; ***~ up*** подтя́гивать [-яну́ть]; *car, etc.* остана́вливать(ся) [-нови́ть(ся)]
pulley ['pʊlɪ] *tech.* блок; шкив
pullover ['pʊləʊvə] пуло́вер
pulp [pʌlp] *of fruit* мя́коть *f*; *of wood* древе́сная ма́сса; *fig.* бесфо́рменная ма́сса
pulpit ['pʊlpɪt] ка́федра
puls|ate [pʌl'seɪt] пульси́ровать; би́ться; **~e** [pʌls] пульс; *tech.* и́мпульс
pumice ['pʌmɪs] пе́мза
pummel ['pʌml] [по]колоти́ть, [по]бить
pump [pʌmp] **1.** насо́с; **2.** кача́ть; ***~ out*** выка́чивать [вы́качать]; ***~ up*** нака́чивать [-ча́ть]
pumpkin ['pʌmpkɪn] ты́ква
pun [pʌn] **1.** каламбу́р; игра́ слов; **2.** [с]каламбу́рить
punch [pʌntʃ] **1.** *tech.* пробо́йник; *for perforating* компо́стер; (*blow with fist*) уда́р кулако́м; **2.** *~ hole* проби́(ва́)ть; [про]компости́ровать; (*hit with fist*) бить кулако́м
punctilious [pʌŋk'tɪlɪəs] педанти́чный; щепети́льный до мелоче́й
punctual ['pʌŋktʃʊəl] □ пунктуа́льный; **~ity** [pʌŋktʃʊ'ælətɪ] пунктуа́льность *f*
punctuat|e ['pʌŋktʃʊeɪt] ста́вить зна́ки препина́ния; *fig.* прерыва́ть [-рва́ть]; **~ion** [pʌŋktʃʊ'eɪʃn] пунктуа́ция; ***~ mark*** знак препина́ния
puncture ['pʌŋktʃə] **1.** *tyre* проко́л; *med.* пу́нкция; **2.** прока́лывать [-коло́ть]
pungen|cy ['pʌndʒənsɪ] острота́, е́дкость *f*; **~t** [~nt] о́стрый, е́дкий (*a. fig.*)
punish ['pʌnɪʃ] нака́зывать [-за́ть]; **~able** [~əbl] наказу́емый; **~ment** [~mənt] наказа́ние
puny ['pju:nɪ] кро́хотный; тщеду́шный
pupil[1] ['pju:pl] *of eye* зрачо́к
pupil[2] [~] учени́к *m*, -и́ца *f*
puppet ['pʌpɪt] ку́кла, марионе́тка (*a. fig.*); **~ show** ку́кольное представле́ние
puppy ['pʌpɪ] щено́к; *coll.* (*greenhorn*) молокосо́с
purchas|e ['pɜ:tʃəs] **1.** поку́пка, заку́пка; **2.** покупа́ть [купи́ть]; приобрета́ть [-рести́]; **~er** [~ə] покупа́тель *m*, -ница *f*; **~ing** [~ɪŋ]: ***~ power*** покупа́тельная спосо́бность
pure [pjʊə] □ чи́стый; **~bred** ['pjʊəbred] чистокро́вный, поро́дистый
purgat|ive ['pɜ:gətɪv] слаби́тельное; **~ory** [~trɪ] чисти́лище
purge [pɜ:dʒ] очища́ть [очи́стить]
purify ['pjʊərɪfaɪ] очища́ть [очи́стить]
purity ['pjʊərɪtɪ] чистота́
purl [pɜ:l] *of water* журча́ть
purple ['pɜ:pl] **1.** пурпу́рный; багро́вый; **2.** ***turn ~*** [по]багрове́ть
purport ['pɜ:pət] смысл, суть *f*
purpose ['pɜ:pəs] **1.** наме́рение, цель *f*; целеустремлённость *f*; ***on ~*** наме́ренно, наро́чно; ***to the ~*** кста́ти; к де́лу; ***to no ~*** напра́сно; **2.**

P

име́ть це́лью; намерева́ться [наме́риться]; **~ful** [~fl] □ целенапра́вленный; целеустремлённый; **~less** [~lıs] □ бесце́льный; **~ly** [~lı] наро́чно
purr [pɜː] [за]мурлы́кать
purse [pɜːs] **1.** кошелёк; *Am.* (*handbag*) су́мочка; ***public ~*** казна́; **2.** *lips* подж(им)а́ть
pursuance [pə'sjuːəns]: выполне́ние; ***in*** (***the***) ***~ of one's duty*** при исполне́нии свои́х обя́занностей
pursu|e [pə'sjuː] (*go after*) пресле́довать (В); (*work at*) занима́ться [заня́ться] (Т); (*continue*) продолжа́ть [-до́лжить]; **~er** [~ə] пресле́дователь *m*, -ница *f*; **~it** [pə'sjuːt] пресле́дование; пого́ня *f*; *mst.* **~s** *pl.* заня́тие
pus [pʌs] *med.* гной
push [pʊʃ] **1.** толчо́к; (*pressure*) давле́ние; напо́р; (*effort*) уси́лие; *of person* напо́ристость *f*; ***at a ~*** при необходи́мости; **2.** толка́ть [-кну́ть]; наж(им)а́ть (на В); продвига́ть(ся) [-ви́нуть(ся)] (*a.* ***~ on***); ***~ into*** *fig.* заставля́ть [-а́вить]; ***~ one's way*** прота́лкиваться [протолка́ться]; **~-button** *el.* нажимна́я кно́пка; **~chair** де́тская *or* прогу́лочная (*invalid's* инвали́дная) коля́ска
puss(y) ['pʊs(ı)] ко́шечка, ки́ска
put [pʊt] [*irr.*] **1.** класть [положи́ть]; [по]ста́вить; сажа́ть [посади́ть]; *question, etc.* зад(ав)а́ть; *into pocket, etc.* сова́ть [су́нуть]; (*express*) выража́ть [-азить]; (*explain*) объясня́ть [-ни́ть]; ***~ across a river****, etc.* перевози́ть [-везти́]; ***~ back*** ста́вить на ме́сто; ста́вить наза́д; ***~ by money*** откла́дывать [отложи́ть]; ***~ down*** (*rebellion*) подавля́ть [-ви́ть]; (*write down*) запи́сывать [-са́ть]; (*set down*) положи́ть, [по]ста́вить; (*attribute*) припи́сывать [-са́ть] (***to*** Д); ***~ forth*** проявля́ть [-ви́ть]; *shoots* пуска́ть [пусти́ть]; ***~ in*** вставля́ть [-а́вить]; всо́вывать [всу́нуть]; ***~ off*** (*defer*) откла́дывать [отложи́ть]; ***~ on*** *dress, etc.* наде́(ва́)ть; (*feign*) притворя́ться; (*exaggerate*) преувели́чивать [-чить]; *weight* прибавля́ть [-а́вить]; ***~ out*** выкла́дывать [вы́ложить]; (*extend*) протя́гивать [-тяну́ть]; *fire* [по]туши́ть; ***~ through*** *tel.* соединя́ть [-ни́ть] (***to*** с Т); ***~ to*** прибавля́ть [-ба́вить]; ***~ to death*** казни́ть (*im*)*pf.*; ***~ up*** *building* [по]стро́ить, возводи́ть [-вести́]; *prices* повыша́ть [-ы́сить]; дава́ть [дать] приста́нище; **2.** *v/i.*: ***~ to sea*** [вы]ходи́ть в мо́ре; ***~ in*** *naut.* заходи́ть в порт; ***~ up at*** остана́вливаться [останови́ться] в (П); ***~ up with*** *fig.* мири́ться с (Т)
putrefy ['pjuːtrıfaı] [с]гнить; разлага́ться [-ложи́ть]
putrid ['pjuːtrıd] □ гнило́й; (*ill-smelling*) воню́чий
putty ['pʌtı] **1.** зама́зка; **2.** зама́з(ыв)ать
puzzle ['pʌzl] **1.** недоуме́ние; зага́дка, головоло́мка; ***crossword ~*** кроссво́рд; **2.** *v/t.* озада́чи(ва)ть; ста́вить в тупи́к; ***~ out*** разгада́ть распу́т(ыв)ать; *v/i.* би́ться (***over*** над Т); **~r** [~ə] *coll.* головоло́мка, кре́пкий оре́шек
pygmy ['pıgmı] пигме́й
pyjamas [pə'dʒɑːməz] *pl.* пижа́ма
pyramid ['pırəmıd] пирами́да
python ['paıθn] пито́н

Q

Q

quack[1] [kwæk] кря́кать [-кнуть]
quack[2] [~] (*sham doctor*) шарлата́н
quadrangle ['kwɒdræŋgl] четырёху́гольник
quadru|ped ['kwɒdrʊped] четверо-

но́гое живо́тное; **~ple** ['kwɒdrʊpl] □ учетверённый
quagmire ['kwægmaɪə] трясина
quail [kweɪl] (*falter*) дро́гнуть *pf.*; (*funk*) [с]тру́сить
quaint [kweɪnt] причу́дливый, стра́нный, курьёзный
quake [kweɪk] [за]трясти́сь; [за-] дрожа́ть; дро́гнуть *pf.*; *stronger* содрога́ться [-гну́ться]
quali|fication [kwɒlɪfɪ'keɪʃn] квалифика́ция; (*restriction*) огово́рка, ограниче́ние; **~fy** ['kwɒlɪfaɪ] *v/t.* квалифици́ровать (*im*)*pf.*; огова́ривать [-вори́ть]; ограни́чи(ва)ть; (*modify*) уточня́ть [-ни́ть]; (*describe*) оце́нивать [-ни́ть] (**as** Т); *v/i.* подгота́вливаться [-гото́виться] (**for** к Д); **~ty** [~tɪ] ка́чество; сво́йство
qualm [kwɑːm] сомне́ние
quandary ['kwɒndərɪ]: ***be in a ~*** не знать как поступи́ть
quantity ['kwɒntətɪ] коли́чество; *math.* величина́; мно́жество
quarantine ['kwɒrəntiːn] **1.** каранти́н; **2.** подверга́ть каранти́ну; содержа́ть в каранти́не
quarrel ['kwɒrəl] **1.** ссо́ра, перебра́нка; **2.** [по]ссо́риться; **~some** □ [~səm] сварли́вый
quarry ['kwɒrɪ] **1.** карье́р, каменоло́мня; **2.** добы́(ва́)ть, разраба́тывать
quart [kwɔːt] ква́рта
quarter ['kwɔːtə] **1.** че́тверть *f*, четвёртая часть; (*three months*) ква́ртал; (*place*) ме́сто, сторона́; **~s** *pl. mil.* каза́рмы *f/pl.*; *fig.* исто́чники *m/pl.*; ***from all ~s*** со всех сторо́н; ***~ past two*** че́тверть тре́тьего; **2.** дели́ть на четы́ре ча́сти; (*give lodgings*) *a. mil.* расквартиро́вывать [-ирова́ть]; **~ly** [~lɪ] **1.** кварта́льный; **2.** (*periodical*) ежекварта́льный журна́л
quartet(te) [kwɔː'tet] *mus.* кварте́т
quartz [kwɒːts] кварц; *attr.* ква́рцевый
quash [kwɒʃ] (*cancel*) отменя́ть, аннули́ровать (*im*)*pf.*; (*crush*) подавля́ть [-дави́ть]
quaver ['kweɪvə] **1.** дрожь *f*; *mus.* восьма́я но́та; **2.** говори́ть дрожа́щим го́лосом
quay [kiː] при́стань *f*
queasy ['kwiːzɪ]: □ ***I feel ~*** меня́ тошни́т
queen [kwiːn] короле́ва; *chess* ферзь *m*; *cards* да́ма
queer [kwɪə] стра́нный, эксцентри́чный; *sl.* (*a. su.*) гомосексуа́льный; гомосексуали́ст
quench [kwentʃ] *thirst* утоля́ть [-ли́ть]; *fire* [по]туши́ть; (*cool*) охлажда́ть [охлади́ть]
querulous ['kwerʊləs] □ ворчли́вый
query ['kwɪərɪ] **1.** вопро́с; (*doubt*) сомне́ние; вопроси́тельный знак; **2.** спра́шивать [спроси́ть]; выража́ть ['-рази́ть] сомне́ние
quest [kwest] по́иски *m/pl.*; ***in ~ of*** в по́исках
question ['kwestʃən] **1.** вопро́с; сомне́ние; пробле́ма; ***beyond*** (***all***) ***~*** вне вся́кого сомне́ния; ***in ~*** о кото́ром идёт речь; ***call into ~*** подверга́ть сомне́нию; ***settle a ~*** реши́ть *pf.* вопро́с; ***that is out of the ~*** об э́том не мо́жет быть и ре́чи; **2.** расспра́шивать [-роси́ть]; задава́ть вопро́с (Д); (*interrogate*) допра́шивать [-роси́ть]; подверга́ть сомне́нию; **~able** [~əbl] сомни́тельный; **~naire** [kwestʃə'neə] анке́та; *for polls, etc.* вопро́сник
queue [kjuː] **1.** о́чередь *f*, хвост; **2.** (*mst.* ***~ up***) станови́ться в о́чередь
quibble ['kwɪbl] **1.** (*evasion*) увёртка; спор из-за пустяко́в; **2.** (*evade*) уклоня́ться [-ни́ться]; (*argue*) спо́рить из-за пустяко́в
quick [kwɪk] **1.** (*lively*) живо́й; (*fast*) бы́стрый, ско́рый; *hands, etc.* прово́рный; *ear* о́стрый; *eye* зо́ркий; **2.** чувстви́тельное ме́сто; ***cut to the ~*** задева́ть за живо́е; **~en** ['kwɪkən] *v/t.* ускоря́ть [-о́рить]; (*liven*) оживля́ть [-ви́ть]; *v/i.* ускоря́ться [-о́риться]; оживля́ться [-ви́ться]; **~ness** ['kwɪknɪs] быстрота́; оживлённость *f*; *of mind* сообрази́тельность *f*; **~sand** зыбу́чий песо́к *m/pl.*; **~silver** ртуть *f*; **~-witted** [~'wɪtɪd] нахо́дчивый
quiet ['kwaɪət] **1.** □ (*calm*) споко́йный, ти́хий; (*noiseless*) бесшу́м-

ный; ***keep s.th.* ~** умáлчивать [умолчáть] (о П); **2.** покóй; тишинá; ***on the* ~** тайкóм, втихомóлку; **3.** успокáивать(ся) [-кóить(ся)]
quill [kwɪl] пти́чье перó; *of porcupine, etc.* иглá
quilt [kwɪlt] **1.** стёганое одея́ло; **2.** [вы́]стегáть; **~ed** ['~ɪd] стёганый
quince [kwɪns] *fruit, tree* айвá
quinine [kwɪ'niːn] *pharm.* хини́н
quintuple ['kwɪntjʊpl] пятикрáтный
quip [kwɪp] острота́; кóлкость *f*
quirk [kwɜːk] причу́да
quit [kwɪt] **1.** покидáть [-и́нуть]; оставля́ть [-áвить]; (*stop*) прекращáть [-ати́ть]; ***give notice to* ~** под(ав)áть заявлéние об ухóде; **2.** свобóдный, отдéлавшийся (***of*** от Р)
quite [kwaɪt] вполнé, совершéнно, совсéм; (*rather*) довóльно; **~ *a hero*** настоя́щий герóй; **~ (*so*)*!*** так!, совершéнно вéрно!
quits [kwɪts]: ***we are* ~** мы с вáми кви́ты
quiver ['kwɪvə] [за]дрожáть, [за-] трепетáть
quiz [kwɪz] **1.** (*interrogation*) опрóс; (*written or oral test*) провéрка знáний; *entertainment* виктори́на; **2.** расспрáшивать [-роси́ть], опрáшивать [опроси́ть]
quizzical ['kwɪzɪkl] *look* насмéшливый
quorum ['kwɔːrəm] *parl.* квóрум
quota ['kwəʊtə] дóля, часть *f*, квóта
quotation [kwəʊ'teɪʃn] цитáта; цити́рование
quote [kwəʊt] [про]цити́ровать

R

rabbi ['ræbaɪ] равви́н
rabbit ['ræbɪt] крóлик
rabble ['ræbl] сброд; чернь *f*
rabid ['ræbɪd] □ неистовый, я́ростный; бéшеный
rabies ['reɪbiːz] бéшенство
race[1] [reɪs] рáса; (*breed*) порóда
race[2] [~] **1.** состязáние в скóрости; бег; гóнки *f/pl.*; ***horse* ~s** *pl.* скáчки *f/pl.*; бегá *m/pl.*; **2.** (*move at speed*) [по]мчáться; *compete* состязáться в скóрости; учáствовать в скáчках *и т.п.*; **~course** ипподрóм; **~track** *sport* трек; *for cars, etc.* автомотодром
racial ['reɪʃl] рáсовый
rack [ræk] **1.** вéшалка; *for dishes* суши́лка; (*shelves*) стеллáж, пóлка; *rail.* ***luggage* ~** сéтка для вещéй; ***go to* ~ *and ruin*** пойти́ прáхом; погибáть [-и́бнуть]; разоря́ться [-ри́ться]; **2. ~ *one's brains*** ломáть себé гóлову
racket[1] ['rækɪt] тéннисная ракéтка
racket[2] [~] шум, гам; *Am.* рэ́кет; **~eer** [rækə'tɪə] афери́ст; *Am.* вымогáтель *m*, рэкети́р
racy ['reɪsɪ] □ пикáнтный; колори́тный; рискóванный
radar ['reɪdɑː] радáр; радиолокáтор
radian|ce ['reɪdɪəns] сия́ние; **~t** [~nt] □ (*transmitted by radiation*) лучи́стый; (*shining, resplendent*) сия́ющий, лучезáрный
radiat|e ['reɪdɪeɪt] излучáть [-чи́ть]; **~ion** [reɪdɪ'eɪʃn] излучéние; **~or** ['reɪdɪeɪtə] излучáтель *m*; *mot.* радиáтор; *for heating* батарéя, радиáтор
radical ['rædɪkl] **1.** □ *pol.* радикáльный; (*fundamental*) кореннóй; **2.** *math.* кóрень *m*; *pol.* радикáл
radio ['reɪdɪəʊ] **1.** рáдио *n indecl.*; **~ *show*** радиопостанóвка; **~ *set*** радиоприёмник; **~ *therapy*** рентгенотерапи́я **2.** передавáть по рáдио; **~active** радиоакти́вный; **~ *waste*** радиоакти́вные отхóды; **~-activity** радиоакти́вность *f*; **~-**

R

graph [~grɑːf] рентге́новский сни́мок
radish ['rædɪʃ] ре́дька; (***red***) ~ реди́ска; **~es** *pl.* реди́с *collect.*
radius ['reɪdɪəs] ра́диус; ***within a ~ of*** в ра́диусе (P)
raffle ['ræfl] **1.** *v/t.* разы́грывать в лотере́е; *v/i.* уча́ствовать в лотере́е; **2.** лотере́я
raft [rɑːft] **1.** плот; **2.** *timber* сплавля́ть [-а́вить]; **~er** [~ə] *arch.* стропи́ло
rag [ræg] тря́пка; **~s** *pl.* тряпьё, ве́тошь *f*; лохмо́тья *m/pl.*
ragamuffin ['rægəmʌfɪn] оборва́нец; у́личный мальчи́шка
rage [reɪdʒ] **1.** я́рость *f*, гнев; (*vogue*) пова́льное увлече́ние; ***it is all the ~*** э́то после́дний крик мо́ды; **2.** [вз]беси́ться; *of storm, etc.* бушева́ть
ragged ['rægɪd] □ неро́вный; *clothes* рва́ный
ragout ['ræguː] *cul.* рагу́
raid [reɪd] **1.** *mil* налёт; *by police* обла́ва; **2.** соверша́ть [-ши́ть] налёт на (B); *mil.* вторга́ться [вто́ргнуться] в (B)
rail[1] [reɪl] **1.** (*hand~*) пери́ла *n/pl.*; (*fence*) огра́да; *rail* рельс; *naut.* по́ручень *m*; ***go off the ~s*** сойти́ *pf.* с ре́льсов; *fig.* сби́ться с *pf.* пути́; **2.** е́хать по желе́зной доро́ге
rail[2] [~] [вы́]руга́ть, [вы́]брани́ть (***at***, ***against*** B)
railing ['reɪlɪŋ] огра́да; пери́ла *n/pl.*
railroad ['reɪlrəʊd] *chiefly Am.*, **railway** [~weɪ] желе́зная доро́га
rain [reɪn] **1.** дождь *m*; **2. *it's ~ing*** идёт дождь; *fig.* [по]сы́паться; **~bow** ра́дуга; **~coat** *Am.* дождеви́к, плащ; **~fall** коли́чество оса́дков; **~y** ['reɪnɪ] дождли́вый; *fig.* ***for a ~ day*** на чёрный день *m*
raise [reɪz] (*often* ***~ up***) поднима́ть [-ня́ть]; *monument* воздвига́ть [-ви́гнуть]; (*elevate*) возвыша́ть [-вы́сить]; (*bring up*) воспи́тывать [-ита́ть]; *laughter, suspicion, etc.* вызыва́ть [вы́звать]; *money* добы́(ва́)ть, собира́ть; *increase* повыша́ть [-вы́сить]
raisin ['reɪzn] изю́минка; *pl.* изю́м *collect.*
rake[1] [reɪk] **1.** *agric.* гра́бли *f/pl.*; **2.** *v/t.* сгреба́ть [-ести́]; разгреба́ть [-ести́]; *fig.* **~ *for*** тща́тельно иска́ть (B *or* P)
rake[2] [~] пове́са, распу́тник
rally ['rælɪ] **1.** (*gather*) собира́ть(ся) [собра́ть(ся)]; *fig.* собра́ться *pf.* с си́лами; овладе́(ва́)ть собо́й; (*rouse*) воодушевля́ть [-шеви́ть]; (*recover*) оправля́ться [опра́виться]; **2.** *Am.* ма́ссовый ми́тинг; *sport* ра́лли
ram [ræm] **1.** бара́н; *astr.* Ове́н; **2.** [про]тара́нить; заби́(ва́)ть; **~ *home*** вдолби́ть *pf.* в го́лову
rambl|e ['ræmbl] **1.** прогу́лка; **2.** (*wander*) броди́ть; (*speak incoherently*) говори́ть бессвя́зно; **~er** [~ə] праздношата́ющийся; (*plant*) ползу́чее расте́ние; **~ing** [~ɪŋ] бродя́чий; бессвя́зный; *town* беспоря́дочно разбро́санный; ползу́чий
ramify ['ræmɪfaɪ] разветвля́ться [-етви́ться]
ramp [ræmp] скат, укло́н; **~ant** ['ræmpənt] *plants* бу́йный; *sickness, etc.* свире́пствующий; *fig.* (*unrestrained*) необу́зданный
rampart ['ræmpɑːt] крепостно́й вал
ramshackle ['ræmʃækl] ве́тхий; обветша́лый
ran [ræn] *pt. om* ***run***
ranch [ræntʃ] ра́нчо *n indecl.* фе́рма
rancid ['rænsɪd] □ прого́рклый
ranco(u)r ['ræŋkə] зло́ба
random ['rændəm] **1. *at ~*** науга́д, наобу́м; **2.** сде́ланный (вы́бранный *и т.д.*) науда́чу; случа́йный
rang [ræŋ] *pt. om* ***ring***
range [reɪndʒ] **1.** ряд; *of mountains* цепь *f*; (*extent*) преде́л, амплиту́да; диапазо́н (*a. mus.*); *mil.* (*shooting ~*) стре́льбище; **2.** *v/t.* выстра́ивать в ряд; располага́ть [-ложи́ть]; *v/i.* выстра́иваться в ряд, располага́ться [-ложи́ться]; *of land* простира́ться; (*wander*) броди́ть
rank [ræŋk] **1.** ряд; *mil.* шере́нга; (*status*) зва́ние, чин; катего́рия; ***~ and file*** рядово́й соста́в; *fig.* обыкнове́нные лю́ди; **2.** *v/t.* стро́ить в шере́нгу; выстра́ивать в ряд; классифици́ровать (*im*)*pf.*; (*consider*)

считáть; *v/i.* стрóиться в шерéнгу; равня́ться (**with** Д); **3.** *vegetation* бýйный
rankle ['ræŋkl] (*fester*) гнои́ться; причиня́ть [-ни́ть] гнев, боль *f*
ransack ['rænsæk] (*search*) [по-] ры́ться в (П); (*plunder*) [о]грáбить
ransom ['rænsəm] вы́куп
rant [rænt] разглагóльствовать
rap [ræp] **1.** лёгкий удáр; *at door, etc.* стук; *fig.* **not a ~** ни грóша; **2.** ударя́ть [удáрить]; [по]стучáть
rapaci|ous [rə'peɪʃəs] □ жáдный; *animal* хи́щный; **~ty** [rə'pæsɪtɪ] жáдность *f*; хи́щность *f*
rape [reɪp] **1.** изнаси́лование; **2.** [из]наси́ловать
rapid ['ræpɪd] **1.** □ бы́стрый, скóрый; **2. ~s** *pl.* порóги *m/pl.*; **~ity** [rə'pɪdətɪ] быстротá скóрость *f*
rapt [ræpt] (*carried away*) восхищённый; (*engrossed*) поглощённый; **~ure** ['ræptʃə] востóрг, экстáз; **go into ~s** приходи́ть в востóрг
rare [reə] □ рéдкий; *air* разрежённый; *undercooked* недожáренный; **at ~ intervals** рéдко
rarity ['reərətɪ] рéдкость *f*; *thing* раритéт
rascal ['rɑːskl] мошéнник; *child coll.* плути́шка
rash[1] [ræʃ] □ опромéтчивый; необдýманный
rash[2] [~] *med.* сыпь *f*
rasp [rɑːsp] **1.** (*grating sound*) скрéжет; **2.** скрежетáть; **~ing voice** скрипýчий гóлос
raspberry ['rɑːzbrɪ] мали́на
rat [ræt] кры́са; **smell a ~** [по]чýять недóброе
rate[1] [reɪt] **1.** нóрма; стáвка; (*tax*) мéстный налóг; разря́д; (*speed*) скóрость *f*; **at any ~** во вся́ком слýчае; **~ of exchange** (валю́тный) курс; **~ of profit** нóрма при́были; **interest ~** процéнтная стáвка; **birth ~** рождáемость *f*; **death ~** смéртность *f*; **2.** оцéнивать [-ни́ть]; расцéнивать [-ни́ть]; *fin.* облагáться налóгом; **~ among** считáться среди́ (Р)
rate[2] [~] (*scold*) брани́ть [вы́бранить] [от]ругáть
rather ['rɑːðə] скорéе; предпочти́тельно; вернéе; довóльно; **I had ~...** я предпочёл бы ...; *int.* ещё бы!
ratify ['rætɪfaɪ] ратифици́ровать (*im*)*pf.*; утверждáть [-рди́ть]
rating ['reɪtɪŋ] (*valuing*) оцéнка; сýмма налóга; класс; *in opinion poll* рéйтинг
ratio ['reɪʃɪəʊ] соотношéние, пропóрция; коэффициéнт
ration ['ræʃn] **1.** рациóн; паёк; **2.** норми́ровать вы́дачу (Р)
rational ['ræʃnl] □ рационáльный; разýмный; **~ity** [ræʃə'nælətɪ] рационáльность *f*; разýмность *f*; **~ize** ['ræʃnəlaɪz] (*give reasons for*) опрáвдывать [-дáть]; (*make mare efficient*) рационализи́ровать (*im*)*pf.*
rattle ['rætl] **1.** треск; *of window* дребезжáние; *of talk* трескотня́; (*baby's toy*) погремýшка; **2.** [за]-дребезжáть; *of train, etc.* [про]громыхáть; *of pots, etc.* [за]гремéть (Т); говори́ть без ýмолку; **~ off** отбарабáнить *pf.*; **~snake** гремýчая змея́
ravage ['rævɪdʒ] **1.** опустошéние; **2.** опустошáть [-ши́ть], разоря́ть [-ри́ть]
rave [reɪv] брéдить (*a. fig.*), говори́ть бессвя́зно; (*rage*) неи́стовствовать; **~ about** быть без умá от (Р)
ravel ['rævl] *v/t.* запýт(ыв)ать; распýт(ыв)ать; *v/i.* запýт(ыв)аться; (*a.* **~ out**) расползáться по швам
raven ['reɪvn] вóрон
ravenous ['rævənəs] прожóрливый; **feel ~** быть голóдным как волк
ravine [rə'viːn] оврáг, лощи́на
raving ['reɪvɪŋ]: **he's ~ mad** он совсéм спя́тил
ravish ['rævɪʃ] приводи́ть в востóрг; **~ing** [~ɪŋ] восхити́тельный
raw [rɔː] □ сырóй; *hide, etc.* необрабóтанный; (*inexperienced*) неóпытный; *knee, etc.* обóдранный; **~-boned** худóй, костля́вый; **~ material** сырьё
ray [reɪ] луч; *fig.* прóблеск
rayon ['reɪɒn] искýсственный шёлк, вискóза

R

raze [reɪz]: **~ *to the ground*** разруша́ть до основа́ния
razor ['reɪzə] бри́тва; **~-blade** ле́звие бри́твы
re... [riː] *pref.* (*придаёт сло́ву значе́ния*:) сно́ва, за́ново, ещё раз, обра́тно
reach [riːtʃ] **1.** ***beyond ~*** вне преде́лов досяга́емости; ***within easy ~*** поблизости; под руко́й; ***within ~*** *financially* досту́пный; **2.** *v/t.* достига́ть [-и́гнуть] (Р); доезжа́ть [дойти́] до (Р); *of forest, land, etc.* простира́ться [-стере́ться] до (Р); (*pass*) протя́гивать [-яну́ть]; (*get to*) дост(ав)а́ть до (Р); *v/i.* протя́гивать ру́ку (***for*** за Т)
react [rɪ'ækt] реаги́ровать; **~ *against*** *idea, plan, etc.* возража́ть [-зи́ть] (про́тив Р)
reaction [rɪ'ækʃn] реа́кция; **~ary** [~ʃənrɪ] **1.** реакцио́нный; **2.** реакционе́р
read 1. [riːd] [*irr.*] [про]чита́ть; (*study*) изуча́ть [-чи́ть]; (*interpret*) истолко́вывать [-кова́ть]; *of instrument* пока́зывать [-за́ть]; *of text* гласи́ть; **~ *to s.o.*** чита́ть кому́-л. вслух; **2.** [red] **a**) *pt. и pt. p. от* ***read 1.***; **b**) *adj.*: ***well ~*** начи́танный; **~able** ['~əbl] разбо́рчивый; интере́сный; (*legible*) чёткий; **~er** ['~ə] чита́тель(ница *f*) *m*; (*reciter*) чтец; *univ.* ле́ктор
readi|ly ['redɪlɪ] *adv.* охо́тно; без труда́; легко́; **~ness** [~nɪs] гото́вность *f*; подгото́вленность *f*
reading ['riːdɪŋ] чте́ние; (*interpretation*) толкова́ние, понима́ние; *parl.* чте́ние (законопрое́кта); **~ lamp** насто́льная ла́мпа; **~ room** чита́льный зал
readjust [riːə'dʒʌst] *tech.* отрегули́ровать; приспоса́бливать [-со́бить]; *of attitude situation, etc.* пересма́тривать [-смотре́ть]; **~ment** [~mənt] регулиро́вка; приспособле́ние
ready ['redɪ] □ гото́вый; *money* нали́чный; ***make*** (*или* ***get***) **~** [при-] гото́вить(ся); **~-made** гото́вый
reaffirm [riːə'fɜːm] вновь подтвержда́ть
reagent [riː'eɪdʒənt] *chem.* реакти́в
real [rɪəl] □ действи́тельный; реа́льный; настоя́щий; **~ *estate*** недви́жимость *f*; **~ity** [rɪ'ælətɪ] действи́тельность *f*; **~ization** [rɪəlaɪ'zeɪʃn] понима́ние, осозна́ние; (*implementation*) осуществле́ние, реализа́ция (*a. comm.*); **~ize** ['rɪəlaɪz] представля́ть себе́; осуществля́ть [-ви́ть]; осозн(ав)а́ть; соobража́ть [-ази́ть]; реализова́ть (*im*)*pf.*
realm [relm] короле́вство; ца́рство; *fig.* сфе́ра; ***be in the ~ of fantasy*** из о́бласти фанта́зии
reanimate [riː'ænɪmeɪt] оживля́ть [-ви́ть]; воскреша́ть, [-еси́ть]
reap [riːp] [с]жать; *fig.* пож(ин)а́ть; **~er** ['~ə] *machine* жа́тка
reappear ['riːə'pɪə] сно́ва появля́ться
reappraisal [riːə'preɪzl] переоце́нка
rear [rɪə] **1.** *v/t.* воспи́тывать [-та́ть]; (*breed*) выра́щивать [вы́растить]; *v/i. of horse* станови́ться на дыбы́; **2.** за́дняя сторона́; *mil.* тыл; ***at the ~ of, in the ~ of*** позади́ (Р); **3.** за́дний; ты́льный; **~-admiral** контрадмира́л
rearm [riː'ɑːm] переворужа́ть(ся) [-жи́ть(ся)]
rearrange [riːə'reɪndʒ] перестра́ивать [-стро́ить]; *timetable, etc.* изменя́ть [-ни́ть], переде́лывать [-лать]; *furniture* переставля́ть [-ста́вить]
reason ['riːzn] **1.** (*intellectual capability*) ра́зум, рассу́док; (*cause*) основа́ние, причи́на; (*sense*) смысл; ***by ~ of*** по причи́не (Р); ***for this ~*** поэ́тому; ***it stands to ~ that ...*** я́сно, что ..., очеви́дно, что ...; **2.** *v/i.* рассужда́ть [-уди́ть]; **~ *out*** разга́дывать [-да́ть]; проду́мать *pf.* до конца́; **~ *out of*** разубежда́ть [-еди́ть] в (П); **~able** [~əbl] □ (благо)разу́мный; (*moderate*) уме́ренный; **~ing** [~ɪŋ] рассужде́ние
reassure [riːə'ʃʊə] успока́ивать [-ко́ить], ободря́ть [-ри́ть]
rebate ['riːbeɪt] *comm.* ски́дка; вы́чет
rebel 1. ['rebl] бунтовщи́к *m*, -и́ца *f*; (*insurgent*) повста́нец; *fig.* бунта́рь *m*; **2.** [~] (*a.* **~lious** [rɪ'beljəs]) мяте́жный; **3.** [rɪ'bel] восст(ав)а́ть;

R

бунтова́ть [вз-ся]; **~lion** [rɪ'beljən] восста́ние; (*riot*) бунт

rebirth [riː'bɜːθ] возрожде́ние

rebound [rɪ'baʊnd] **1.** отска́кивать [-скочи́ть]; **~ *on*** *fig.* обора́чиваться [оберну́ться] (про́тив Р); **2.** рикоше́т; отско́к

rebuff [rɪ'bʌf] **1.** отпо́р; ре́зкий отка́з; **2.** дава́ть о́тпор (Д)

rebuild [riː'bɪld] [*irr.* (***build***)] сно́ва [по] стро́ить; реконструи́ровать; перестра́ивать [-стро́ить]

rebuke [rɪ'bjuːk] **1.** упрёк; вы́говор; **2.** упрека́ть [-кну́ть], де́лать вы́говор (Д)

recall [rɪ'kɔːl] **1.** *of diplomat, etc.* о́тзыв; ***beyond ~*** безвозвра́тно, бесповоро́тно; **2.** отзыва́ть [отозва́ть]; (*revoke*) отменя́ть [-ни́ть]; (*remind*) напомина́ть [-о́мнить]; (*call to mind*) вспомина́ть [-о́мнить] (В)

recapture [riː'kæptʃe] *territory* взять обра́тно; освобожда́ть [-боди́ть]; ***~ the atmosphere*** воссоздава́ть [-да́ть] атмосфе́ру

recede [rɪ'siːd] (*move back*) отступа́ть [-пи́ть]; (*move away*) удаля́ться [-ли́ться]

receipt [rɪ'siːt] (*document*) распи́ска, квита́нция; (*receiving*) получе́ние; *cul.* реце́пт; **~s** *pl.* прихо́д

receive [rɪ'siːv] получа́ть [-чи́ть]; *guests, etc.* принима́ть [-ня́ть]; *news, ideas* воспринима́ть [-ня́ть]; **~er** [~ə] получа́тель *m*, -ница *f*; *tel.* телефо́нная тру́бка; *radio* приёмник

recent ['riːsnt] □ неда́вний; све́жий; но́вый; ***in ~ years*** в после́дние го́ды; **~ly** [~lɪ] неда́вно

receptacle [rɪ'septəkl] вмести́лище

reception [rɪ'sepʃn] получе́ние; приём; ***~ desk*** *in hotel* регистра́ция; *in hospital* регистрату́ра; **~ist** [~ənɪst] регистра́тор

receptive [rɪ'septɪv] □ восприи́мчивый (к Д)

recess [rɪ'ses] *parl.* кани́кулы *f/pl.*; (*break*) переры́в; *arch.* ни́ша; **~es** *pl. fig.* глуби́ны *f/pl.*; **~ion** [~ʃn] *econ.* спад

recipe ['resəpɪ] *cul.* реце́пт

recipient [rɪ'sɪpɪənt] получа́тель *m*, -ница *f*

reciproc|al [rɪ'sɪprəkl] взаи́мный; обою́дный; **~ate** [~keɪt] отвеча́ть [-ве́тить] взаи́мностью; (*interchange*) обме́ниваться [-ня́ться]; **~ity** [resɪ'prɒsətɪ] взаи́мность *f*

recit|al [rɪ'saɪtl] чте́ние, деклама́ция; (*account*) повествова́ние, расска́з; *mus.* со́льный; **~ation** [resɪ'teɪʃn] деклама́ция; **~e** [rɪ'saɪt] [про]деклами́ровать

reckless ['reklɪs] □ безрассу́дный; опроме́тчивый; беспе́чный

reckon ['rekən] *v/t.* счита́ть; причисля́ть [-чи́слить] (***among*** к Д); счита́ть [счесть] за (В); ***~ up*** подсчита́ть *pf.*; *v/i.* (*consider*) счита́ть, ду́мать, предполага́ть [-ложи́ть]; **~ (*up*)*on*** *fig.* рассчи́тывать на (В); ***a man to be ~ed with*** челове́к, с кото́рым сле́дует счита́ться; **~ing** [~ɪŋ] подсчёт, счёт; распла́та

reclaim [rɪ'kleɪm] [по]тре́бовать обра́тно; *waste* утилизи́ровать; *land* осва́ивать [-во́ить]; *neglected land* рекультиви́ровать

recline [rɪ'klaɪn] отки́дывать(ся) [-и́нуть(ся)]; полулежа́ть

recluse [rɪ'kluːs] отше́льник *m*, -ница *f*

recogni|tion [rekəg'nɪʃn] (*realization*) осозна́ние; узнава́ние; призна́ние (Р); ***change beyond ~*** изменя́ться [-ни́ться] до неузнава́емости; ***gain ~*** доби́ться *pf.* призна́ния; **~ze** ['rekəgnaɪz] узн(ав)а́ть; призн(ав)а́ть

recoil [rɪ'kɔɪl] **1.** *mil.* отда́ча; **2.** отска́кивать [-скочи́ть], отпря́нуть *pf.*; *of gun* отдава́ть [-да́ть]

recollect [rekə'lekt] вспомина́ть [вспо́мнить] (В); ***as far as I can ~*** наско́лько я по́мню; **~ion** [rekə'lekʃn] воспомина́ние, па́мять *f* (***of*** о П)

recommend [rekə'mend] рекомендова́ть (*im*)*pf.*, *pf. a.* [по-], [по]сове́товать; **~ation** [rekəmen'deɪʃn] рекоменда́ция

recompense ['rekəmpens] **1.** вознагражде́ние; компенса́ция; ***as or in ~*** в ка́честве компенса́ции (***for*** за В); **2.** вознагражда́ть [-ради́ть]; отпла́чивать [отплати́ть] (Д); *for a*

R

loss, *etc.* компенси́ровать, возмеща́ть [-мести́ть]
reconcil|e ['rekənsaɪl] примиря́ть [-ри́ть] (***to*** с Т); ула́живать [ула́дить]; **~ *o.s.*** примиря́ться [-ри́ться]; **~iation** [rekənsɪlɪ'eɪʃn] примире́ние; ула́живание
recon|aissance [rɪ'kɒnəsns] *mil.* разве́дка; **~oitre** [rekə'nɔɪtə] производи́ть разве́дку; разве́д(ыв)ать
reconsider [riːkən'sɪdə] пересма́тривать [-мотре́ть]
reconstruct [riːkəns'trʌkt] восстана́вливать [-нови́ть]; перестра́ивать [-стро́ить]; **~ion** [~'strʌkʃn] реконстру́кция; восстановле́ние
record 1. ['rekɔːd] за́пись *f*; *sport* реко́рд; *of meeting* протоко́л; ***place on ~*** запи́сывать [-са́ть]; граммофо́нная пласти́нка, диск; репута́ция; **~ *library*** фоноте́ка; **~ *office*** госуда́рственный архи́в; ***off the ~*** неофициа́льно; ***on ~*** зарегистри́рованный; *attr.* реко́рдный; ***in ~ time*** в реко́рдно коро́ткое вре́мя; **2.** [rɪ'kɔːd] [за]пи́сывать [-са́ть], [за]регистри́ровать; **~er** [rɪ'kɔːdə] регистра́тор; (*instrument*) самопи́сец; **~ing** [~ɪŋ] за́пись *f* (*a. mus.*)
recount [rɪ'kaʊnt] расска́зывать [-за́ть]
recourse [rɪ'kɔːs]: ***have ~ to*** прибега́ть [-бе́гнуть] к (Р)
recover [rɪ'kʌvə] *v/t.* получа́ть обра́тно; верну́ть *pf.*; *waste* утилизи́ровать, регенери́ровать; *v/i. from illness* оправля́ться [-а́виться]; **~y** [~rɪ] восстановле́ние; выздоровле́ние; ***economic ~*** восстановле́ние наро́дного хозя́йства
recreation [rekrɪ'eɪʃn] о́тдых; развлече́ние
recrimination [rɪkrɪmɪ'neɪʃn] контрообвине́ние
recruit [rɪ'kruːt] **1.** *mil.* новобра́нец; *fig.* новичо́к; **2.** брать [взять] на вое́нную слу́жбу; *new players* наб(и)ра́ть; *for work* [за]вербова́ть
rectangle ['rektæŋgl] прямоуго́льник
recti|fy ['rektɪfaɪ] (*put right*) исправля́ть [-а́вить]; **~tude** ['rektɪtjuːd] прямота́, че́стность *f*
rector ['rektə] *univ.* ре́ктор; *eccl.* па́стор, свяще́нник; **~y** [~rɪ] дом свяще́нника
recumbent [rɪ'kʌmbənt] лежа́чий
recuperate [rɪ'kjuːpəreɪt] восстана́вливать си́лы; оправля́ться [опра́виться]
recur [rɪ'kɜː] (*be repeated*) повторя́ться [-и́ться]; (*go back to s.th.*) возраща́ться [-рати́ться] (***to*** к Д); *of ideas*, *event* приходи́ть сно́ва на ум, на па́мять; (*happen again*) происходи́ть вновь; **~rence** [rɪ'kʌrəns] повторе́ние; **~rent** [~rənt] □ повторя́ющийся; периоди́ческий; *med.* возвра́тный
recycling [riː'saɪklɪŋ] перерабо́тка; повто́рное испо́льзование
red [red] **1.** кра́сный; **~ *herring*** *fig.* отвлече́ние внима́ния; **≈ *Cross*** Кра́сный Крест; **~ *tape*** волоки́та, бюрократи́зм; **2.** кра́сный цвет
red|breast ['redbrest] мали́новка; **~den** ['redn] [по]красне́ть
redeem [rɪ'diːm] (*make amends*) искупа́ть [-пи́ть]; (*get back*) выкупа́ть [вы́купить]; спаса́ть [-сти́]; **~er** [~ə] спаси́тель *m*
red-handed [red'hændɪd]: ***catch a p. ~*** пойма́ть *pf.* кого́-л. на ме́сте преступле́ния
red-hot [red'hɒt] накалённый докрасна́; горя́чий; *fig.* взбешённый
redirect [riːdɪ'rekt] *letter* переадресо́вывать [-ва́ть]
red-letter [red'letə]: **~ *day*** счастли́вый день; кра́сный день календаря́
redness ['rednɪs] краснота́
redouble [riː'dʌbl] удва́ивать(ся) [удво́ить(ся)]
redress [rɪ'dres] **1.** *errors*, *etc.* исправле́ние; *law* возмеще́ние; **2.** исправля́ть [-а́вить]; возмеща́ть [-ести́ть]
reduc|e [rɪ'djuːs] *in size* понижа́ть [-и́зить]; *prices*, *etc.* снижа́ть [-и́зить]; доводи́ть [довести́] (***to*** до Р); *pain* уменьша́ть [уме́ньшить]; (*lessen*) сокраща́ть [-рати́ть]; уре́з(ыв)ать; **~tion** [rɪ'dʌkʃn] сниже́ние, ски́дка; уменьше́ние; сокраще́ние; *of picture*, *etc.* уме́ньшенная ко́пия

R

redundant [rɪ'dʌndənt] □ изли́шний; ***be made ~*** быть уво́ленным
reed [riːd] тростни́к; камы́ш
reeducation [riːedjʊ'keɪʃn] переобуче́ние
reef [riːf] *geogr. naut.* риф
reek [riːk] **1.** вонь *f*; за́тхлый за́пах; **2.** *v/i.* дыми́ться; (неприя́тно) па́хнуть (***of*** Т)
reel [riːl] **1.** кату́шка; *for film, etc.* боби́на; **2.** *v/i.* [за]кружи́ться, [за]верте́ться; (*stagger*) шата́ться [шатну́ться]; ***my head ~ed*** у меня́ закружи́лась голова́; *v/t.* [на]мота́ть; ***~ off*** разма́тывать [-мота́ть]; *fig.* отбараба́нить *pf.*
reelect [riːɪ'lekt] переизб(и)ра́ть
reenter [riː'entə] сно́ва входи́ть в (В)
reestablish [riːɪ'stæblɪʃ] восстана́вливать [-нови́ть]
refer [rɪ'fɜː]: ***~ to*** *v/t.* относи́ть [отнести́] (к Д); (*direct*) направля́ть [-ра́вить], отсыла́ть [отосла́ть] (к Д); (*hand over*) передава́ть на рассмотре́ние (Д); (*attribute*) припи́сывать [-са́ть]; *v/i.* (*allude to*) ссыла́ться [сосла́ться] на (В); (*relate*) относи́ться [отнести́сь] к (Д); **~ee** [refə'riː] *sport* судья́ *m*; *football* арби́тр (*a. fig.*); *boxing* ре́фери *m indecl.*; **~ence** ['refrəns] спра́вка; *in book* ссы́лка; (*testimonial*) рекоменда́ция; (*allusion*) упомина́ние; (*relationship*) отноше́ние; ***in ~ to*** относи́тельно (Р); ***~ book*** спра́вочник; ***~ library*** спра́вочная библиоте́ка; ***make ~ to*** ссыла́ться [сосла́ться] на (В)
referendum [refə'rendəm] рефере́ндум
refill [riː'fɪl] наполня́ть сно́ва; пополня́ть(ся) [-по́лнить(ся)]
refine [rɪ'faɪn] *tech.* очища́ть [очи́стить]; *sugar* рафини́ровать (*im*)*pf.*; *fig.* де́лать(ся) бо́лее утончённым; ***~ (up)on*** [у]соверше́нствовать; **~d** [~d] *person* рафини́рованный; *style, etc.* изы́сканный, утончённый; очи́щенный; **~ry** [~ərɪ] *for sugar* са́харный заво́д
reflect [rɪ'flekt] *v/t.* отража́ть [отрази́ть]; *v/i.* ***~ (up)on***: броса́ть тень на (В); (*meditate on*) размышля́ть [-ы́слить] о (П); (*tell on*) отража́ться [-рази́ться] на (В); **~ion** [rɪ'flekʃn] отраже́ние; отсве́т; размышле́ние, обду́мывание; *fig.* тень *f*
reflex ['riːfleks] рефле́кс
reforest [riː'fɒrɪst] восстана́вливать [-нови́ть] лес
reform [rɪ'fɔːm] **1.** рефо́рма; **2.** реформи́ровать (*im*)*pf.*; *of person* исправля́ть(ся); **~ation** [refə'meɪʃən] преобразова́ние; исправле́ние; *hist.* ***the*** ♀ Реформа́ция; **~er** [~mə] рефо́рматор
refraction [rɪ'frækʃn] *phys.* рефра́кция, преломле́ние
refrain[1] [rɪ'freɪn] *v/i.* возде́рживаться [-жа́ться] (***from*** от Р)
refrain[2] [~] припе́в, рефре́н
refresh [rɪ'freʃ] освежа́ть [-жи́ть]; *with food or drink* подкрепля́ть(ся) [-пи́ться]; **~ment** [~mənt] еда́; питьё
refrigerat|e [rɪ'frɪdʒəreɪt] замора́живать [-ро́зить]; (*cool*) охлажда́ть(ся) [охлади́ть(ся)]; **~ion** [rɪfrɪdʒə'reɪʃn] замора́живание; охлажде́ние; **~or** [rɪ'frɪdʒəreɪtə] холоди́льник; *of van, ship, etc.* рефрижера́тор
refuel [riː'fjʊəl] *mot.* заправля́ться [-а́виться] (горю́чим)
refuge ['refjuːdʒ] убе́жище; ***take ~*** укрыва́ться [-ы́ться]; **~e** [refjʊ'dʒiː] бе́женец *m*, -нка *f*
refund [rɪ'fʌnd] возмеща́ть расхо́ды (Д); возвраща́ть [-рати́ть]
refusal [rɪ'fjuːzl] отка́з
refuse 1. [rɪ'fjuːz] *v/t.* отка́зываться [-за́ться] от (Р); отка́зывать [-за́ть] в (П); (*deny*) отверга́ть [отве́ргнуть]; *v/i.* отка́зываться [-за́ться]; **2.** ['refjuːs] отбро́сы *m/pl.*; му́сор; ***~ dump*** сва́лка
refute [rɪ'fjuːt] опроверга́ть [-ве́ргнуть]
regain [rɪ'geɪn] получа́ть обра́тно; сно́ва достига́ть; *strength* восстана́вливать [-нови́ть]
regal ['riːgəl] □ короле́вский, ца́рственный
regale [rɪ'geɪl] *v/t.* угоща́ть [угости́ть]; *v/i.* наслажда́ться [-ди́ться]
regard [rɪ'gɑːd] **1.** внима́ние; ува-

R

же́ние; ***with ~ to*** по отноше́нию к (Д); ***kind ~s*** серде́чный приве́т; **2.** [по]смотре́ть на (В); (*consider*) счита́ть, рассма́тривать (***as*** как); (*concern*) каса́ться; относи́ться [отнести́сь] к (Д); ***as ~s ...*** что каса́ется (Р); **~ing** [~ɪŋ] относи́тельно (Р); **~less** [~lɪs] *adv.*: ***~ of*** несмотря́ на (В), незави́симо от (Р)

regent ['riːdʒənt] ре́гент

regime [reɪ'ʒiːm] режи́м

regiment ['redʒɪmənt] полк

region ['riːdʒən] о́бласть *f* (*a. administrative*); райо́н; *large* регио́н; **~al** [~l] □ областно́й; райо́нный; региона́льный

register ['redʒɪstə] **1.** журна́л; (*written record*) за́пись *f*; *tech.*, *mus.* реги́стр; **2.** регистри́ровать(ся) (*im*)*pf.*, *pf. a.* [за-]; заноси́ть в спи́сок; *mail* посыла́ть заказны́м; (*show*) пока́зывать [-за́ть]

registr|ar [redʒɪ'strɑː] регистра́тор; слу́жащий регистату́ры; **~ation** [redʒɪ'streɪʃn] регистра́ция; **~y** [redʒɪ'strɪ]: ***~ office*** загс

regret [rɪ'gret] **1.** сожале́ние; **2.** [по]жале́ть (***that ...*** что ...); сожале́ть о (П); **~ful** [~fl] □ по́лный сожале́ния; опеча́ленный; **~table** [~əbl] □ приско́рбный

regular ['regjʊlə] □ пра́вильный; регуля́рный (*army a.*), постоя́нный); **~ity** [regjʊ'lærətɪ] регуля́рность *f*

regulat|e ['regjʊleɪt] [у]регули́ровать, упоря́дочи(ва)ть; *tech.* [от-] регули́ровать; **~ion** [regjʊ'leɪʃn] регули́рование; (*rule*) пра́вило

rehabilitation [riːəbɪlɪ'teɪʃn] реабилита́ция; трудоустро́йство; перевоспита́ние

rehears|al [rɪ'hɜːsl] *thea.*, *mus.* репети́ция; **~e** [rɪ'hɜːs] *thea.* [про]репети́ровать

reign [reɪn] **1.** ца́рствование; *fig.* власть *f*; **2.** ца́рствовать; *fig.* цари́ть

reimburse [riːɪm'bɜːs] возвраща́ть [-рати́ть]; возмеща́ть [-мести́ть] расхо́ды (Д)

rein [reɪn] вожжа́; *fig.* узда́

reindeer ['reɪndɪə] се́верный оле́нь *m*

reinforce [riːɪn'fɔːs] уси́ливать [уси́лить]; укрепля́ть [-пи́ть]; *mil.* подкрепля́ть [-пи́ть] (*a. fig.*); **~ment** [~mənt] усиле́ние; *mil.* подкрепле́ние

reinstate [riːɪn'steɪt] восстана́вливать [-нови́ть] (*в права́х и т.д.*)

reiterate [riː'ɪtəreɪt] повторя́ть [-ри́ть]

reject [rɪ'dʒekt] **1.** *idea*, *etc.* отверга́ть [отве́ргнуть]; (*refuse to accept*) отка́зываться [-за́ться] от (Р); *proposal* отклоня́ть [-ни́ть]; *goods* бракова́ть; **2.** ['riːdʒekt] брак; **~s** брако́ванный това́р; **~ion** [rɪ'dʒekʃn] отка́з; брако́вка

rejoic|e [rɪ'dʒɔɪs] *v/t.* [об]ра́довать; *v/i.* [об]ра́доваться (***at***, ***in*** Д); **~ing** [~ɪŋ] (*часто ~s pl.*) весе́лье

rejoin [rɪ'dʒɔɪn] возража́ть [-рази́ть]; **~der** [~də] отве́т; возраже́ние

rejuvenate [rɪ'dʒuːvəneɪt] омола́живать(ся) [омолоди́ть(ся)]

relapse [rɪ'læps] **1.** *law*, *med.* рециди́в; **2.** *into bad habits*, *etc.* верну́ться *pf.*; ***~ into silence*** (сно́ва) умолка́ть

relate [rɪ'leɪt] *v/t.* расска́зывать [-за́ть]; (*connect*) свя́зывать [-за́ть], соотноси́ть; *v/i.* относи́ться [отнести́сь]; **~d** [~ɪd] (*connected*) свя́занный; состоя́щий в родстве́ (***to*** с Т)

relation [rɪ'leɪʃn] отноше́ние; связь *f*; родство́; ро́дственник *m*, -ица *f*; ***in ~ to*** по отноше́нию к (Д); **~ship** [~ʃɪp] связь; родство́

relative ['relətɪv] **1.** □ относи́тельный; (*comparative*) сравни́тельный; ***~ to*** относя́щийся к (Д); **2.** ро́дственник *m*, -ица *f*

relax [rɪ'læks] *v/t.* ослабля́ть [-а́бить]; *muscles* расслабля́ть [-а́бить]; *v/i.* [о]сла́бнуть; расслабля́ться [-а́биться]; **~ation** [rɪlæk'seɪʃn] ослабле́ние; расслабле́ние; (*amusement*) развлече́ние

relay ['rɪːleɪ] **1.** сме́на; *sport* эстафе́та; *attr.* эстафе́тный; *el.* реле́ *n indecl.*; **2.** *radio* ретрансли́ровать (*im*)*pf.*

release [rɪ'liːs] **1.** освобожде́ние; высвобожде́ние; избавле́ние; *of*

R

film вы́пуск; **2.** (*set free*) освобожда́ть [-боди́ть]; высвобожда́ть [вы́свободить]; (*relieve*) избавля́ть [-а́вить]; (*issue*) выпуска́ть [вы́пустить]; (*let go*) отпуска́ть [-сти́ть]
relegate ['relɪgeɪt] отсыла́ть [отосла́ть], низводи́ть [-вести́]; направля́ть [-ра́вить] (**to** к Д); *sport* переводи́ть [-вести́]
relent [rɪ'lent] смягча́ться [-чи́ться]; **~less** [~lɪs] □ безжа́лостный
relevant ['reləvənt] уме́стный; относя́щийся к де́лу
reliab|ility [rɪlaɪə'bɪlətɪ] надёжность *f*; достове́рность *f*; **~le** [rɪ'laɪəbl] надёжный; достове́рный
reliance [rɪ'laɪəns] дове́рие; уве́ренность *f*
relic ['relɪk] пережи́ток; рели́квия
relief [rɪ'li:f] облегче́ние; (*assistance*) по́мощь *f*; посо́бие; подкрепле́ние; *in shiftwork* сме́на; *geogr* релье́ф; ***to my ~*** к моему́ облегче́нию; ***~ fund*** фонд по́мощи
relieve [rɪ'li:v] облегча́ть [-чи́ть]; (*free*) освобожда́ть [-боди́ть]; (*help*) ока́зывать по́мощь *f* (Д), выруча́ть [вы́ручить]; *of shift* сменя́ть [-ни́ть]; (*soften*) смягча́ть [-чи́ть]; ***~ one's feelings*** отвести́ *pf.* ду́шу
religion [rɪ'lɪdʒən] рели́гия
religious [rɪ'lɪdʒəs] □ религио́зный; (*conscientious*) добросо́вестный
relinquish [rɪ'lɪŋkwɪʃ] *hope, etc.* оставля́ть [-а́вить]; *habit* отка́зываться [-за́ться]; ***~ one's rights*** уступа́ть [-пи́ть] права́
relish ['relɪʃ] **1.** вкус; при́вкус; *cul.* припра́ва; **2.** наслажда́ться [-лади́ться] (Т); получа́ть удово́льствие от (Р); придава́ть вкус (Д); ***eat with ~*** есть с аппети́том
reluctan|ce [rɪ'lʌktəns] нежела́ние; неохо́та, нерасположе́ние; **~t** [~nt] □ неохо́тный; (*offering resistance*) сопротивля́ющийся
rely [rɪ'laɪ]: **~ (*up*)*on*** полага́ться [-ложи́ться] на (В), наде́яться на (В); (*depend on*) зави́сеть от (Р)
remain [rɪ'meɪn] ост(ав)а́ться; ***it ~s to be seen*** э́то ещё вы́яснится; ещё посмо́трим; **~der** [~də] оста́ток
remark [rɪ'mɑ:k] **1.** замеча́ние; ***I made no ~*** я ничего́ не сказа́ла; **2.** (*notice, say*) замеча́ть [-е́тить]; выска́зываться [вы́сказаться] (***on*** о П); **~able** [rɪ'mɑ:kəbl] (*of note*) замеча́тельный; (*extraordinary*) удиви́тельный
remedy ['remədɪ] **1.** сре́дство, лека́рство; ме́ра (***for*** про́тив Р); **2.** (*put right*) исправля́ть [-а́вить]
rememb|er [rɪ'membə] по́мнить; (*recall*) вспомина́ть [-о́мнить]; ***~ me to ...*** переда́й(те) приве́т (Д); **~rance** [~brəns] (*recollection*) па́мять *f*, воспомина́ние; (*memento*) сувени́р
remind [rɪ'maɪnd] напомина́ть [-о́мнить] (Д; ***of*** о П *or* В); **~er** [~ə] напомина́ние
reminiscence [remɪ'nɪsns] воспомина́ние
remiss [rɪ'mɪs] □ неради́вый; небре́жный; хала́тный; **~ion** [rɪ'mɪʃn] (*forgiveness*) проще́ние; освобожде́ние от до́лга; (*abatement*) уменьше́ние; *med.* реми́ссия
remit [rɪ'mɪt] *goods* перес(ы)ла́ть; *money* переводи́ть [-вести́]; (*abate*) уменьша́ть(ся) [уме́ньшить(ся)]; **~tance** [~əns] де́нежный перево́д
remnant ['remnənt] *of cloth* оста́ток; *of food* оста́тки
remodel [ri:'mɒdl] перестра́ивать [-стро́ить]
remonstrate ['remənstreɪt] протестова́ть; увещева́ть (***with*** В)
remorse [rɪ'mɔ:s] угрызе́ния (*n/pl.*) со́вести; раска́яние; **~less** [~lɪs] □ безжа́лостный
remote [rɪ'məʊt] □ отдалённый; да́льний; ***~ control*** дистанцио́нное управле́ние; ***I haven't got the ~st idea*** не име́ю ни мале́йшего поня́тия
remov|al [rɪ'mu:vl] перее́зд; *of threat, etc.* устране́ние; *from office* смеще́ние; ***~ van*** фурго́н для перево́зки ме́бели; **~e** [rɪ'mu:v] *v/t.* удаля́ть [-ли́ть]; уноси́ть [унести́]; передвига́ть [-и́нуть]; (*take off*) снима́ть [снять]; (*take away*) уб(и-)ра́ть; (*dismiss*) снима́ть [снять]; *v/i.* переезжа́ть [перее́хать]; **~ers** [~əz]

R

firm трансаге́нтство; *personnel* перево́зчики
remunerat|e [rɪ'mjuːnəreɪt] вознагражда́ть [-ради́ть]; (*pay*) опла́чивать [оплати́ть]; **~ive** [rɪ'mjuːnərətɪv] □ (*profitable*) вы́годный
Renaissance [rɪ'neɪsns] эпо́ха Возрожде́ния; Ренесса́нс; ♀ (*revival*) возрожде́ние
render ['rendə] (*service*) ока́зывать [оказа́ть]; (*represent*) изобража́ть [-рази́ть]; *mus.* исполня́ть [-о́лнить]; (*translate*) переводи́ть [перевести́]; (*give as due*) возд(ав)а́ть
renew [rɪ'njuː] возобновля́ть [-нови́ть]; **~al** [~əl] возобновле́ние
renounce [rɪ'naʊns] отка́зываться [-за́ться] от (Р); (*disown*) отрека́ться [отре́чься] от (Р)
renovate ['renəveɪt] восстана́вливать [-нови́ть]; обновля́ть [обнови́ть]
renown [rɪ'naʊn] сла́ва; изве́стность *f*; **~ed** [~d] □ просла́вленный, изве́стный
rent[1] [rent] проре́ха; дыра́
rent[2] [~] **1.** *for land* аре́ндная пла́та; *for apartment* кварти́рная пла́та; **2.** (*occupy for* ~) взять в наём; (*let for* ~) сдать в наём; **~al** [rentl] (*rate of rent*) аре́ндная пла́та
renunciation [rɪnʌnsɪ'eɪʃn] отрече́ние; отка́з (***of*** от Р)
reopen [riː'əʊpən] открыва́ть [-ры́ть] вновь; ***~ negotiations*** возобновля́ть [-нови́ть] перегово́ры
repair [rɪ'peə] **1.** почи́нка, ремо́нт; ***in good ~*** в испра́вном состоя́нии; **2.** [по]чини́ть, [от]ремонти́ровать; (*make amends for*) исправля́ть [-а́вить]
reparation [repə'reɪʃn] возмеще́ние; *pol.* репара́ция
repartee [repɑː'tiː] остроу́мный отве́т
repay [*irr.* (***pay***)] [rɪ'peɪ] (*reward*) отблагодари́ть (***for*** за В); отдава́ть долг (Д); возмеща́ть [-ести́ть]; **~ment** [~mənt] *of money* возвра́т; возмеще́ние
repeal [rɪ'piːl] аннули́ровать (*im*)*pf.*; отменя́ть [-ни́ть]
repeat [rɪ'piːt] **1.** повторя́ть(ся) [-ри́ть(ся)]; **2.** повторе́ние; **~ed** [~ɪd]: ***~ efforts*** неоднокра́тные уси́лия
repel [rɪ'pel] отта́лкивать [оттолкну́ть]; *mil.* отража́ть [-рази́ть], отбива́ть [-би́ть]
repent [rɪ'pent] раска́иваться [-ка́яться] (***of*** в П); **~ance** [~əns] раска́яние; **~ant** [~ənt] ка́ющийся
repercussion [riːpə'kʌʃn] *of sound* отзвук; *fig.* после́дствие
repertoire ['repətwɑː] реперту́ар
repetition [repɪ'tɪʃn]повторе́ние
replace [rɪ'pleɪs] ста́вить, класть обра́тно; (*change for another*) заменя́ть [-ни́ть]; (*take place of*) замеща́ть [-ести́ть], заменя́ть [-ни́ть]; **~ment** [~mənt] замеще́ние, заме́на
replenish [rɪ'plenɪʃ] пополня́ть [-о́лнить]; **~ment** [~mənt] пополне́ние (*a. mil.*)
replete [rɪ'pliːt] напо́лненный; насы́щенный
replica ['replɪkə] то́чная ко́пия
reply [rɪ'plaɪ] **1.** отве́т (***to*** на В); **2.** отвеча́ть [-е́тить]; (*retort*) возража́ть [-рази́ть]
report [rɪ'pɔːt] **1.** (*account*) отчёт сообще́ние; *mil.* донесе́ние; *official* докла́д; (*hearsay*) молва́, слух; (***on*** о П); **2.** сообща́ть [-щи́ть] (В *or* о П); *mil.* доноси́ть [-нести́] о (П); сде́лать *pf.* докла́д; докла́дывать [доложи́ть]; ***~ for work*** яви́ться *pf.* на рабо́ту; **~er** [~ə] репортёр
repos|e [rɪ'pəʊz] о́тдых; переды́шка; **~itory** [rɪ'pɒsɪtrɪ] склад; храни́лище
represent [reprɪ'zent] представля́ть [-а́вить]; изобража́ть [-рази́ть]; *thea.* исполня́ть роль *f* (Р); **~ation** [~zən'teɪʃn] изображе́ние; *parl.* представи́тельство; *thea.* представле́ние; постано́вка; **~ative** [reprɪ'zentətɪv] **1.** □ (*typical*) характе́рный; *parl.* представи́тельный; **2.** представи́тель *m*, -ница *f*; ***House of ♀s*** *pl. Am. parl.* пала́та представи́телей
repress [rɪ'pres] подавля́ть [-ви́ть]; **~ion** [rɪ'preʃn] подавле́ние
reprimand ['reprɪmɑːnd] **1.** вы́говор; **2.** де́лать вы́говор (Д)
reprint [riː'prɪnt] **1.** перепеча́тка; **2.**

перепеча́тывать [-тать]
reprisal [rɪ'praɪzl] отве́тное де́йствие
reproach [rɪ'prəʊtʃ] **1.** упрёк, уко́р; **2.** (*~ a p. with a th.*) упрека́ть [-кну́ть] (кого́-л. в чём-л.)
reprobate ['reprəbeɪt] негодя́й, распу́тник
reproduc|e [riːprə'djuːs] воспроизводи́ть [-извести́]; (*beget*) размножа́ться [-о́житься]; **~tion** [~'dʌkʃn] воспроизведе́ние; *of offspring* размноже́ние; (*copy*) репроду́кция
reproof [rɪ'pruːf] вы́говор; порица́ние
reprove [rɪ'pruːv] де́лать вы́говор (Д)
reptile ['reptaɪl] пресмыка́ющееся
republic [rɪ'pʌblɪk] респу́блика; **~an** [~lɪkən] **1.** республика́нский; **2.** республика́нец *m*, -нка *f*
repudiate [rɪ'pjuːdɪeɪt] (*disown*) отрека́ться [-ре́чься] от (Р); (*reject*) отверга́ть [-ве́ргнуть]
repugnan|ce [rɪ'pʌgnəns] отвраще́ние; **~t** [~nənt] □ отта́лкивающий, отврати́тельный
repuls|e [rɪ'pʌls] *mil.* отбива́ть [-би́ть], отража́ть [отрази́ть]; (*alienate*) отта́лкивать [оттолкну́ть]; **~ive** [~ɪv] □ отта́лкивающий; омерзи́тельный
reput|able ['repjʊtəbl] □ уважа́емый; почте́нный; *company*, *firm*, *etc.* соли́дный; **~ation** [repjʊ'teɪʃn] репута́ция; **~e** [ri'pjuːt] репута́ция; **~ed** [rɪ'pjuːtɪd] изве́стный; (*supposed*) предполага́емый; ***be ~ (to be ...)*** слыть за (В)
request [rɪ'kwest] **1.** тре́бование; про́сьба; **2.** [по]проси́ть (В *or* Р *or* о П)
require [rɪ'kwaɪə] (*need*) нужда́ться в (П); (*demand*) [по]тре́бовать (Р); **~d** [~d] ну́жный; (*compulsory*) обяза́тельный; **~ment** [~mənt] нужда́; тре́бование; потре́бность *f*; ***meet the ~s*** отвеча́ть тре́бованиям
requisit|e ['rekwɪzɪt] **1.** необходи́мый; **2. ~es** *pl.* всё необходи́мое, ну́жное; ***sports ~*** спорти́вное снаряже́ние; **~ion** [rekwɪ'zɪʃn] зая́вка, тре́бование
requital [rɪ'kwaɪtl] (*recompense*) вознагражде́ние; (*avenging*) возме́здие
requite [rɪ'kwaɪt] отпла́чивать [-лати́ть] (Д ***for*** за В); (*avenge*) [ото]мсти́ть за (В)
rescue ['reskjuː] **1.** освобожде́ние; спасе́ние; ***come to s.o.'s ~*** прийти́ кому́-л. на по́мощь *f*; **2.** освобожда́ть [-боди́ть]; спаса́ть [-сти́]; ***~ party*** гру́ппа спаса́телей
research [rɪ'sɜːtʃ] иссле́дование
resembl|ance [rɪ'zembləns] схо́дство (***to*** с Т); **~e** [rɪ'zembl] походи́ть на (В), име́ть схо́дство с (Т)
resent [rɪ'zent] возмуща́ться [-мути́ться]; негодовать на (В); обижа́ться [оби́деться] за (В); ***I ~ his familiarity*** меня́ возмуща́ет его́ фамилья́рность; **~ful** [~fl] □ оби́женный; возмущённый; **~ment** [~mənt] негодова́ние; чу́вство оби́ды
reservation [rezə'veɪʃn] огово́рка; *for game* запове́дник; *for tribes* резерва́ция; (*booking*) предвари́тельный зака́з; ***without ~*** без вся́ких огово́рок, безогово́рочно
reserve [rɪ'zɜːv] **1.** запа́с; *fin.* резе́рвный фонд; резе́рв; (*reticence*) сде́ржанность *f*, скры́тность *f*; **2.** сберега́ть [-ре́чь]; (*keep back*) прибераге́ть [-ре́чь]; откла́дывать [отложи́ть]; (*book*) зака́зывать [-за́ть]; *for business purposes* [за]брони́ровать; оставля́ть за собо́й; ***I ~ the right to ...*** я оставля́ю за собо́й пра́во ...; **~d** [~d] □ скры́тный; зака́занный зара́нее
reside [rɪ'zaɪd] жить, прожива́ть; **~nce** ['rezɪdəns] местожи́тельство; *official* резиде́нция; **~nt** [~dənt] **1.** прожива́ющий, живу́щий; **2.** постоя́нный жи́тель *m*; *in hotel* постоя́лец
residu|al [rɪ'zɪdjʊəl] оста́точный; **~e** ['rezɪdjuː] оста́ток; (*sediment*) оса́док
resign [rɪ'zaɪn] *v/t. right*, *etc.* отка́зываться [-за́ться] от; *hope* оставля́ть [-а́вить]; *rights* уступа́ть [-пи́ть]; ***~ o.s. to*** покоря́ться [-ри́ться] (Д); *v/i.* уходи́ть в отста́вку; **~ation** [rezɪg'neɪʃn] отста́вка; ухо́д с рабо́ты

resilien|ce [rɪ'zɪlɪəns] упру́гость *f*, эласти́чность *f*; **~t** [~nt] упру́гий, эласти́чный; *person* жизнесто́йкий
resin ['rezɪn] смола́
resist [rɪ'zɪst] сопротивля́ться (Д); противостоя́ть (Д); **~ance** [~əns] сопротивле́ние; *to colds*, *etc.* сопротивля́емость *f*; **~ant** [~ənt] сопротивля́ющийся; ***heat ~*** жаросто́йкий; ***fire ~*** огнеупо́рный
resolut|e ['rezəluːt] □ реши́тельный; **~ion** [rezə'luːʃn] (*motion*) резолю́ция, реши́тельность *f*, реши́мость *f*; ***make a ~*** реша́ть [-ши́ть]
resolve [rɪ'zɒlv] **1.** *v/t. fig.* реша́ть [реши́ть]; *problem*, *etc.* разреша́ть [-ши́ть]; *v/i.* реша́ть(ся) [реши́ть(-ся)]; **~ (*up*)*on*** реша́ться [-ши́ться] на (В); **2.** реше́ние; **~d** [~d] по́лный реши́мости
resonance ['rezənəns] резона́нс
resonant ['rezənənt] □ звуча́щий; резони́рующий; ***be ~ with*** быть созву́чным
resort [rɪ'zɔːt] **1.** (*health ~*) куро́рт; (*expedient*) наде́жда; ***in the last ~*** в кра́йнем слу́чае; **2. *~ to***: прибега́ть [-е́гнуть] к (Д); обраща́ться [-ати́ться] к (Д)
resound [rɪ'zaʊnd] [про]звуча́ть; оглаша́ть(ся) [огласи́ть(ся)]
resource [rɪ'sɔːs]: **~*s*** *pl.* ресу́рсы *m/pl.*; возмо́жность *f*; нахо́дчивость *f*; **~ful** [~fl] □ нахо́дчивый
respect [rɪ'spekt] **1.** (*esteem*) уваже́ние; (*relation*) отноше́ние; ***in this ~*** в э́том отноше́нии; **~*s*** *pl.* приве́т; **2.** *v/t.* уважа́ть, почита́ть; ***you must ~ his wishes*** вы обя́заны счита́ться с его́ пожела́ниями; **~able** [~əbl] □ прили́чный, поря́дочный; респекта́бельный; *part. comm.* соли́дный; **~ful** [~fl] □ ве́жливый, почти́тельный; **~ing** [~ɪŋ] относи́тельно (Р); **~ive** [~ɪv] □ соотве́тствующий; ***we went to our ~ places*** мы разошли́сь по свои́м места́м; **~ively** [~ɪvlɪ] соотве́тственно
respirat|ion [respə'reɪʃn] дыха́ние; вдох и вы́дох; **~or** ['respəreɪtə] респира́тор
respite ['respaɪt] переды́шка; (*reprieve*) отсро́чка
respond [rɪ'spɒnd] отвеча́ть [-е́тить]; **~ *to*** реаги́ровать на; отзыва́ться [отозва́ться] на (В)
response [rɪ'spɒns] отве́т; *fig.* о́тклик; реа́кция
responsi|bility [rɪspɒnsɪ'bɪlətɪ] отве́тственность *f*; **~ble** [rɪ'spɒnsəbl] отве́тственный (***for*** за В, ***to*** пе́ред Т)
rest[1] [rest] **1.** о́тдых, поко́й; (*stand*) подста́вка; опо́ра; **2.** *v/i.* отдыха́ть [отдохну́ть]; (*remain*) остава́ться; (*lean*) опира́ться [опере́ться] (***on*** на В); **~ *against*** прислоня́ть [-ни́ть]; *fig.* **~ (*up*)*on*** осно́вываться [-ова́ться] на (П); *v/t.* дава́ть о́тдых (Д)
rest[2] [~] оста́ток
restaurant ['restrɒnt] рестора́н; **~ car** ваго́н-рестора́н
restful ['restfl] споко́йный
restive ['restɪv] □ стропти́вый, упря́мый
restless ['restlɪs] непосе́дливый, неугомо́нный; *night*, *etc.* беспоко́йный
restoration [restə'reɪʃn] *arch.*, *hist.* реставра́ция; восстановле́ние
restore [rɪ'stɔː] восстана́вливать [-нови́ть]; (*return*) возвраща́ть [-рати́ть]; (*reconvert*) реставри́ровать (*im*)*pf.*; **~ *to health*** вы́лечивать [вы́лечить]
restrain [rɪ'streɪn] сде́рживать [-жа́ть]; уде́рживать; *feelings* подавля́ть [-ви́ть]; **~t** [~t] сде́ржанность *f*; (*restriction*) ограниче́ние; (*check*) обузда́ние
restrict [rɪ'strɪkt] ограни́чи(ва)ть; **~ion** [rɪ'strɪkʃn] ограниче́ние
result [rɪ'zʌlt] **1.** результа́т, исхо́д; (*consequence*) сле́дствие; **2.** явля́ться [яви́ться] сле́дствием (***from*** Р); **~ *in*** приводи́ть [-вести́] к (Д), конча́ться ['-читься]
resum|e [rɪ'zjuːm] (*renew*) возобновля́ть [-ви́ть]; (*continue*) продолжа́ть [-лжить]; **~ *one's seat*** верну́ться на своё ме́сто; **~ *classes*** возобнови́ть *pf.* заня́тия
resurrection [rezə'rekʃn] *of custom*, *etc.* воскреше́ние; ***the*** ♀ Воскре-

се́ние
resuscitate [rɪ'sʌsɪteɪt] *med.* приводи́ть [-вести́] в созна́ние
retail ['ri:teɪl] **1.** ро́зничная прода́жа; ***goods sold by ~*** това́ры, продаю́щиеся в ро́зницу; *attr.* ро́зничный; **2.** продава́ть(ся) в ро́зницу
retain [rɪ'teɪn] (*preserve*) сохраня́ть [-ни́ть]; (*hold*) уде́рживать [-жа́ть]
retaliat|e [rɪ'tælɪeɪt] отпла́чивать [-лати́ть] (тем же); **~ion** [rɪtælɪ'eɪʃn] отпла́та, возме́здие; ***in ~ for*** в отве́т на
retard [rɪ'tɑ:d] (*check*) заде́рживать [-жа́ть]; замедля́ть [-е́длить]; **~ed** [~ɪd]: ***mentally ~ child*** у́мственно отста́лый ребёнок
retention [rɪ'tenʃn] удержа́ние; сохране́ние
retentive [rɪ'tentɪv]: ***~ memory*** хоро́шая па́мять *f*
reticent ['retɪsnt] скры́тный; молчали́вый
retinue ['retɪnju:] сви́та, сопровожда́ющие ли́ца
retir|e [rɪ'taɪə] *v/t.* увольня́ть с рабо́ты; *v/i.* выходи́ть в отста́вку; *because of age* уходи́ть [уйти́] на пе́нсию; (*withdraw*) удаля́ться [-ли́ться]; (*seclude o.s.*) уединя́ться [-ни́ться]; **~ed** [~d] (*secluded*) уединённый; отставно́й, в отста́вке; **~ement** [~mənt] отста́вка; ухо́д на пе́нсию; уедине́ние; ***~ age*** пенсио́нный во́зраст; **~ing** [-rɪŋ] скро́мный, засте́нчивый
retort [rɪ'tɔ:t] **1.** ре́зкий (*or* нахо́дчивый) отве́т; возраже́ние; **2.** *to a biting remark* [от]пари́ровать; возража́ть [-рази́ть]
retrace [ri:'treɪs] просле́живать [-еди́ть]; ***~ one's steps*** возвраща́ться тем же путём
retract [rɪ'trækt] отрека́ться [отре́чься] от (Р); *one's words, etc.* брать наза́д; (*draw in*) втя́гивать [втяну́ть]
retraining [ri:'treɪnɪŋ] переподгото́вка
retreat [rɪ'tri:t] **1.** отступле́ние (*part. mil.*); (*place of privacy or safety*) приста́нище; **2.** (*walk away*) уходи́ть [уйти́]; удаля́ться [-ли́ться]; *part. mil.* отступа́ть [-пи́ть]
retrench [rɪ'trentʃ] сокраща́ть [-рати́ть]; [с]эконо́мить
retrieve [rɪ'tri:v] (*get back*) брать [взять] обра́тно; (*restore*) восстана́вливать [-нови́ть]; (*put right*) исправля́ть [-а́вить]
retro... ['retrəʊ] обра́тно...; **~active** [retrəʊ'æktɪv] име́ющий обра́тную си́лу; **~grade** ['retrəʊgreɪd] реакцио́нный; **~spect** ['retrəʊspekt] ретроспекти́ва; **~spective** [retrəʊ'spektɪv] □ ретроспекти́вный; *law* име́ющий обра́тную си́лу
return [rɪ'tɜ:n] **1.** возвраще́ние; возвра́т; *fin.* оборо́т; дохо́д, при́быль *f*; результа́т вы́боров; ***many happy ~s of the day*** поздравля́ю с днём рожде́ния; ***in ~*** в обме́н (***for*** на В); в отве́т; ***by ~*** *of post* с обра́тной по́чтой; ***tax ~*** нало́говая деклара́ция; ***~ ticket*** обра́тный биле́т; **2.** *v/i.* возвраща́ться [-рати́ться]; верну́ться *pf.*; *v/t.* возвраща́ть [-рати́ть]; верну́ть *pf.*; присыла́ть наза́д; (*reply*) отвеча́ть [-е́тить]; ***~ s.o.'s kindness*** отблагодари́ть за доброту́
reunion [ri:'ju:nɪən] *of friends, etc.* встре́ча; *of family* сбор всей семьи́; (*reuniting*) воссоедине́ние
revaluation [ri:vælјʊ'eɪʃn] переоце́нка; *of currency* ревальва́ция
reveal [rɪ'vi:l] обнару́жи(ва)ть; *secret, etc.* откры́(ва́)ть; **~ing** [~ɪŋ] *fig.* показа́тельный
revel ['revl] пирова́ть; упи́(ва́)ться (***in*** Т)
revelation [revə'leɪʃn] открове́ние (*a. eccl.*); (*disclosure*) разоблаче́ние; откры́тие
revelry ['revəlrɪ] разгу́л; (*binge*) пиру́шка; кутёж
revenge [rɪ'vendʒ] **1.** месть *f*; *sport* рева́нш; отме́стка; ***in ~ for*** в отме́стку за (В); **2.** [ото]мсти́ть за (В); **~ful** [~fl] мсти́тельный
revenue ['revənju:] дохо́д; *of state* госуда́рственные дохо́ды; ***Internal***, (*Brt.*) ***Inland ~*** Нало́говое управле́ние
reverberate [rɪ'vɜ:bəreɪt] отража́ть(ся) [отрази́ть(ся)]
revere [rɪ'vɪə] уважа́ть, почита́ть;

R

~nce ['revərəns] почтéние
reverent ['revərənt] почтúтельный; пóлный благоговéния
reverie ['revərɪ] мечты́ *f/pl.*; мечтáние
revers|al [rɪ'vɜːsl] изменéние; обрáтный ход; *of judg(e)ment* отмéна; **~e** [rɪ'vɜːs] **1.** обрáтная сторонá; *of paper* оборóт, оборóтная сторонá (*a. fig.*); (*opposite*) противополóжное; **~s** *pl.* преврáтности *f/pl.*; **2.** обрáтный; противополóжный; **3.** изменя́ть [-ни́ть]; повoрáчивать назáд; *mot.* давáть зáдний ход; *law* отменя́ть [-ни́ть]
revert [rɪ'vɜːt] *to former state or question* возвращáться [-рати́ться]
review [rɪ'vjuː] **1.** (*survey*) обзóр; *law* пересмóтр; (*journal*) обозрéние; *of book* рецéнзия; **2.** пересмáтривать [-смотрéть]; писáть рецéнзию о (П)
revis|e [rɪ'vaɪz] пересмáтривать [-смотрéть]; (*correct*) исправля́ть [-áвить]; **~ion** [rɪ'vɪʒn] пересмóтр; (*reworking*) переработка; исправленное издáние
reviv|al [rɪ'vaɪvl] возрождéние; *of trade, etc.* оживлéние; **~e** [rɪ'vaɪv] приходи́ть *or* приводи́ть в чу́вство; (*liven up*) оживля́ть(ся) [-ви́ть(ся)]; ожи(вá)ть
revoke [rɪ'vəʊk] *v/t.* (*repeal*) отменя́ть [-ни́ть]; *promise* брать [взять] назáд
revolt [rɪ'vəʊlt] **1.** восстáние; бунт; **2.** *v/i.* восстá(вá)ть (*a. fig.*); *v/t. fig.* оттáлкивать [оттолкну́ть]
revolution [revə'luːʃn] (*revolving*) вращéние; (*one complete turn*) оборóт; *pol.* революция; **~ary** [~ʃənərɪ] **1.** революциóнный; **2.** революционéр *m*, -ка *f*; **~ize** [~aɪz] революционизи́ровать (*im*)*pf.*
revolv|e [rɪ'vɒlv] *v/i.* вращáться; *v/t.* вращáть; обду́м(ыв)ать; **~ *a problem in one's mind*** всесторóнне обду́мывать проблéму; **~er** [~ə] револьвéр; **~ing** [~ɪŋ] вращáющийся; **~ *door*** вращáющаяся дверь *f*
reward [rɪ'wɔːd] **1.** нагрáда; вознаграждéние; **2.** вознаграждáть [-радúть]; награждáть [-ради́ть]; **~ing** [~ɪŋ]: **~ *work*** благодáрная рабóта
rewrite [riː'raɪt] [*irr.* (***write***)] перепи́сывать [-сáть]
rhapsody ['ræpsədɪ] рапсóдия
rheumatism ['ruːmətɪzəm] ревмати́зм
rhinoceros ['raɪnɒsərəs] носорóг
rhubarb ['ruːbɑːb] ревéнь *m*
rhyme [raɪm] **1.** ри́фма; (рифмóванный) стих; ***without ~ or reason*** нет никакóго смы́сла; ни с тогó, ни с сегó; **2.** рифмовáть(ся) (***with*** с Т)
rhythm ['rɪθəm] ритм; **~ic(al)** [~mɪk(l)] ритми́чный, ритми́ческий
rib [rɪb] ребрó
ribald ['rɪbəld] гру́бый; непристóйный; скабрёзный
ribbon ['rɪbən] лéнта; *mil.* óрденская лéнта; ***tear to ~s*** изорвáть в клóчья
rice [raɪs] рис; *attr.* ри́совый
rich [rɪtʃ] □ богáтый (***in*** Т); (*splendid*) роскóшный; *soil* плодорóдный; *food* жи́рный; *colo(u)r* сóчный; ***get ~*** разбогатéть; **~es** ['rɪtʃɪz] *pl.* богáтство; сокрóвища *n/pl.*
rick [rɪk] *agric.* скирдá
ricket|s ['rɪkɪts] *pl.* рахи́т; **~y** [~ɪ] рахи́тичный; *chair. etc.* шáткий
rid [rɪd] [*irr.*] избавля́ть [-áвить] (***of*** от Р); ***get ~ of*** отдéл(ыв)аться от (Р), избавля́ться [-áвиться] от (Р)
ridden ['rɪdn] *pt. p. om* ***ride***
riddle¹ ['rɪdl] загáдка; ***ask a ~*** задавáть загáдку
riddle² [~] (*sieve*) **1.** си́то, решетó; **2.** изрешéчивать [-шети́ть]
ride [raɪd] **1.** *on horseback* ездá верхóм; *for pleasure* прогу́лка; **2.** [*irr.*] *v/i. in car, on horseback, etc.* éздить, [по]éхать; катáться верхóм; *v/t.* [по]éхать на (П); **~r** [~ə] всáдник *m*, -ица *f*; *in circus* наéздник *m*, -ица *f*
ridge [rɪdʒ] гóрный кряж, хребéт; *on rooftop* конёк
ridicul|e ['rɪdɪkjuːl] **1.** осмея́ние, насмéшка; **2.** высмéивать [вы́смеять]; **~ous** [rɪ'dɪkjʊləs] □ нелéпый, смешнóй; ***don't be ~!*** не говори́ ерунду́!

riding ['raɪdɪŋ] верховáя ездá
rife [raɪf]: ~ ***with*** изобúлующий (Т)
riffraff ['rɪfræf] подóнки, отбрóсы (óбщества) *m/pl.*
rifle [raɪfl] винтóвка; *for hunting* ружьё; **~man** *mil.* стрелóк
rift [rɪft] трéщина, рассéлина; *fig.* разры́в; *geol.* разлóм
rig [rɪg] **1.** *naut.* оснáстка; *coll.* нарýд; (*oil* ~) буровáя вы́шка; **2.** оснащáть [оснастúть]; *coll.* наряжáть [-ядúть]; **~ging** ['rɪgɪŋ] *naut.* такелáж, снáсти *f/pl.*
right [raɪt] **1.** □ (*correct*) прáвильный, вéрный; (*suitable*) подходя́щий, нýжный; прáвый; ***be*** ~ быть прáвым; ***put*** ~ приводúть в порядок; **2.** *adv.* прямо; прáвильно; справедлúво; как раз; ~ ***away*** срáзу, сейчáс же; ~ ***on*** прямо вперёд; **3.** прáво; справедлúвость *f*; прáвда; ***by*** ~ ***of*** на основáнии (Р); ***on*** (*or* ***to***) ***the*** ~ напрáво; **4.** приводúть в поря́док; (*correct*) исправля́ть [-́вить]; **~eous** ['raɪtʃəs] □ прáведный; **~ful** [~fl] □ справедлúвый; закóнный; **~ly** [~lɪ] прáвильно; справедлúво
rigid ['rɪdʒɪd] □ негнýщийся, негúбкий, жёсткий; *fig.* сурóвый; непреклóнный; ***be*** ~ ***with fear*** оцепенéть от стрáха; **~ity** [rɪ'dʒɪdətɪ] жёсткость *f*; непреклóнность *f*
rigo(u)r ['rɪgə] сурóвость *f*, стрóгость *f*
rigorous ['rɪgərəs] □ *climate* сурóвый; *measures* стрóгий
rim [rɪm] ободóк; (*edge*) край; *of wheel* обод; *of glasses* опрáва
rind [raɪnd] *of fruit* кожурá; *of cheese, etc.* кóрка
ring[1] [rɪŋ] **1.** (*of bells*) звон; звонóк; **2.** [*irr.*] [за]звучáть; *at door* [по-] звонúть; ~ ***s.o. up*** позвонúть *pf.* комý-л. по телефóну; ***that*** **~*s a bell*** это мне чтó-то напоминáет
ring[2] [~] **1.** кольцó; круг; *sport* ринг; **2.** (*mst.* ~ ***in***, ***round***, ***about***) окружáть [-жúть]; **~leader** зачúнщик *m*, -ица *f*; **~let** ['rɪŋlɪt] колéчко; лóкон; ~ **road** кольцевáя дорóга
rink [rɪŋk] катóк
rinse [rɪns] [вы]полоскáть; *dishes* сполоснýть *pf.*
riot ['raɪət] **1.** беспоря́дки *m/pl.*; *of colo(u)rs* бýйство; ***run*** ~ шýмно веселúться, разгуля́ться *pf.*; **2.** принимáть учáстие в беспоря́дках, волнéниях; бýйствовать
rip [rɪp] **1.** (*tear*) [по]рвáть; **2.** прорéха
ripe [raɪp] □ зрéлый (*a. fig.*); спéлый; готóвый; ***the time is*** ~ ***for ...*** пришлó врéмя ...; **~n** ['~ən] созрé(вá)ть, [по]спéть
ripple ['rɪpl] **1.** рябь *f*, зыбь *f*; (*sound*) журчáние; **2.** покрывáть(ся) ря́бью, журчáть
rise [raɪz] **1.** повышéние; *of sun* восхóд; *of road, etc.* подъём; *geogr.* возвы́шенность *f*; *of river* истóк; **2,** [*irr.*] поднимáться [-ня́ться]; всходúть; *of river* брать началó; ~ ***to*** быть в состоя́нии, спрáвиться с (Т); **~n** ['rɪzn] *pt. p. om* ***rise***
rising ['raɪzɪŋ] возвышéние; восстáние; восхóд
risk [rɪsk] **1.** риск; ***run a*** (*or* ***the***) ~ рисковáть [-кнýть]; **2.** (*venture*) отвáжи(ва)ться на (В); рисковáть [-кнýть] (Т); **~y** ['~ɪ] □ рискóванный
rit|e [raɪt] обря́д, церемóния; **~ual** ['rɪtʃʊəl] **1.** ритуáльный; **2.** ритуáл
rival ['raɪvəl] **1.** сопéрник *m*, -ница *f*; *comm.* конкурéнт; **2.** сопéрничающий; **3.** сопéрничать с (Т); **~ry** [~rɪ] сопéрничество; соревновáние
river ['rɪvə] рекá; **~bed** рýсло рекú; **~mouth** ýстье рекú; **~side** бéрег рекú; *attr.* прибрéжный
rivet ['rɪvɪt] **1.** заклёпка; **2.** заклёпывать [-лепáть]; *fig. attention* прикóвывать [-овáть] (В к Д)
road [rəʊd] дорóга; путь *m*; ~ ***accident*** дорóжное происшéствие, авáрия; **~side** обóчина; **~sign** дорóжный знак
roam [rəʊm] *v/t.* бродúть по (Д); *v/i.* стрáнствовать
roar [rɔː] **1.** *of storm, lion* [за]ревéть; *of cannon* [за]грохотáть; ~ ***with laughter*** покáтываться сó смеху; **2.** рёв; грóхот
roast [rəʊst] **1.** [из]жáрить(ся); **2.** жáреный; ~ ***meat*** жаркóе
rob [rɒb] [о]грáбить; *fig.* лишáть

[-ши́ть] (*of* P); **~ber** ['~ə] грабитель *m*; **~bery** ['~ərɪ] грабёж
robe [rəʊb] *magistrate's* ма́нтия; (*bath* ~) хала́т
robin ['rɒbɪn] мали́новка
robot ['rəʊbɒt] ро́бот
robust [rəʊ'bʌst] □ кре́пкий, здоро́вый
rock¹ [rɒk] скала́; утёс; го́рная поро́да; **~ *crystal*** го́рный хруста́ль *m*
rock² [~] **1.** *mus.* рок; **2.** *v/t.* кача́ть [-чну́ть]; *strongly* [по]шатну́ть; *to sleep* убаю́к(ив)ать; *v/i.* кача́ться; **~ *with laughter*** трясти́ от сме́ха
rocket ['rɒkɪt] раке́та; *attr.* раке́тный
rocking chair кача́лка
rocky ['rɒkɪ] (*full of rocks*) камени́стый; скали́стый
rod [rɒd] *tech.* сте́ржень *m*; прут *m*; *for fishing* уди́лище; ***piston*** **~** шток
rode [rəʊd] *pt. om* ***ride***
rodent ['rəʊdənt] грызу́н
roe¹ [rəʊ] *zo.* косу́ля
roe² [~] икра́; ***soft*** **~** моло́ки *f/pl.*
rogu|e [rəʊg] моше́нник; плут; **~ish** ['rəʊgɪʃ] плутова́тый
role [rəʊl] *thea.* роль *f* (*a. fig.*)
roll [rəʊl] **1.** *of cloth, paper, etc.* руло́н; (*list*) спи́сок; *of thunder* раска́т; (*bread* ~) бу́лочка; *naut.* бортова́я ка́чка; **2.** *v/t.* ката́ть, [по]кати́ть; *dough* раска́тывать [-ката́ть]; *metal* прока́тывать [-ката́ть]; **~ *up*** свёртывать [сверну́ть]; ска́тывать; *v/i.* ката́ться, [по]кати́ться; валя́ться (***in*** в П); *of thunder* грохота́ть; **~er** ['rəʊlə] ро́лик; вал; **~ *skates*** ро́ликовые коньки́
rollick ['rɒlɪk] шу́мно весели́ться
rolling ['rəʊlɪŋ] (*hilly*) холми́стый; **~ *mill*** *tech.* прока́тный стан; **~ *pin*** скалка́; **~ *stone*** *person* перекати́-по́ле
Roman ['rəʊmən] **1.** ри́мский; **~ *numeral*** ри́мская ци́фра; **2.** ри́млянин *m*, -янка *f*
romance [rəʊ'mæns] **1.** *mus.* рома́нс; (*tale*) рома́н (*a. love affair*); **2.** *fig.* приукра́шивать действи́тельность; фантази́ровать; стро́ить возду́шные за́мки; **3.** ♀ рома́нский
romantic [rəʊ'mæntɪk] (**~*ally***) **1.** романти́чный; **2.** **~ist** [~tɪsɪst] рома́нтик; **~ism** [~tɪsɪzəm] романти́зм, рома́нтика
romp [rɒmp] вози́ться, шу́мно игра́ть
roof [ru:f] кры́ша; **~ *of the mouth*** нёбо; **~ing** [~ɪŋ] **1.** кро́вельный материа́л; **2.** кро́вля; **~*ing felt*** толь *m*
rook¹ [rʊk] *bird* грач
rook² [~] *coll.* **1.** моше́нник; **2.** обма́нывать [-ну́ть]
rook³ [~] *chess* ладья́
room [ru:m, rʊm] ко́мната; ме́сто; простра́нство; ***make*** **~ *for*** освободи́ть ме́сто для (Р); **~mate** това́рищ по ко́мнате; **~y** ['ru:mɪ] □ просто́рный
roost [ru:st] **1.** насе́ст; **2.** уса́живаться на насе́ст; *fig.* устра́иваться на́ ночь; **~er** ['~ə] пету́х
root [ru:t] **1.** ко́рень *m*; ***get to the*** **~ *of*** добра́ться *pf.* до су́ти (Р); ***take*** **~** пуска́ть ко́рни; укореня́ться [-ни́ться]; **2.** **~ *out*** вырыва́ть с ко́рнем (*a. fig.*); (*find*) разы́скивать [-ка́ть]; ***stand*** **~*ed to the spot*** стоя́ть как вко́панный; **~ed** ['ru:tɪd] укорени́вшийся
rope [rəʊp] **1.** кана́т; верёвка; *mst. naut.* трос; *of pearls* ни́тка; ***know the*** **~*s*** *pl.* знать все ходы́ и вы́ходы; ***show the*** **~*s*** *pl.* вводи́ть [ввести́] в суть де́ла; **2.** свя́зывать верёвкой; привя́зывать кана́том; (*mst.* **~ *off***) отгороди́ть кана́том
rosary ['rəʊzərɪ] *eccl.* чётки *f/pl.*
rose¹ [rəʊz] ро́за; ро́зовый цвет
rose² [~] *pt. om* ***rise***
rosin ['rɒzɪn] канифо́ль *f*
rostrum ['rɒstrəm] ка́федра; трибу́на
rosy ['rəʊzɪ] □ ро́зовый; румя́ный; *fig.* ра́дужный
rot [rɒt] **1.** гние́ние; гниль *f*; **2.** *v/t.* [с]гнои́ть; *v/i.* сгни(ва́)ть, [с]гнить
rota|ry ['rəʊtərɪ] враща́тельный; **~te** [rəʊ'teɪt] враща́ть(ся); (*alternate*) чередова́ть(ся); **~tion** [rəʊ'teɪʃn] враще́ние; чередова́ние
rotten ['rɒtn] □ гнило́й; испо́рченный; *a. sl.* отврати́тельный
rouge [ru:ʒ] румя́на *n/pl.*
rough [rʌf] **1.** □ (*crude*) гру́бый; (*uneven*) шерша́вый; шерохова́тый; (*violent*) бу́рный; (*inexact*) приблизи́тельный; **~ *and ready***

сде́ланный кое-как, на́спех; грубова́тый; **2.**: **~ it** обходи́ться без обы́чных удо́бств; **~en** ['rʌfn] де́лать(ся) гру́бым, шерохова́тым; **~ly** ['~lı] гру́бо, приблизи́тельно; **~ speaking** гру́бо говоря́; **~ness** ['~nıs] шерохова́тость *f*; гру́бость *f*

round [raʊnd] **1.** □ кру́глый; кругово́й; **~ trip** пое́здка в о́ба конца́; **2.** *adv.* круго́м, вокру́г; обра́тно; (*often* **~ about**) вокру́г да о́коло; **all year ~** кру́глый год; **3.** *prp.* вокру́г, круго́м (Р); за (В *or* Т); по (Д); **4.** круг; цикл; *of talks* тур; *sport* ра́унд; *doctor's* обхо́д; **5.** *v/t.* закругля́ть [-ли́ть]; огиба́ть [обогну́ть]; **~ up** окружа́ть [-жи́ть]; *v/i.* закругля́ться [-ли́ться]; **~about** ['raʊndəbaʊt] **1.** *way* око́льный; **2.** *mot.* кольцева́я тра́нспортная развя́зка; *at fair* карусе́ль *f*; **~ish** ['raʊndıʃ] круглова́тый; **~up** *of cattle* заго́н скота́; обла́ва

rous|e [raʊz] *v/t.* (*waken*) [раз]буди́ть; *fig.* возбужда́ть [-уди́ть]; воодушевля́ть [-ви́ть]; **~ o.s.** встряхну́ться *pf.*; *v/i.* просыпа́ться [-сну́ться]; **~ing** ['raʊzıŋ] возбужда́ющий; *cheers* бу́рный

rout [raʊt] обраща́ть в бе́гство

route [ru:t] путь *m*; маршру́т

routine [ru:'ti:n] **1.** режи́м, поря́док; рути́на; **2.** рути́нный

rove [rəʊv] скита́ться; броди́ть

row[1] [rəʊ] ряд

row[2] [raʊ] *coll.* гвалт; (*quarrel*) ссо́ра

row[3] [rəʊ] грести́; **~boat** гребна́я ло́дка; **~er** ['rəʊə] гребе́ц

royal ['rɔıəl] □ короле́вский; великоле́пный; **~ty** [~tı] член(ы) короле́вской семьи́; а́вторский гонора́р

rub [rʌb] *v/t.* тере́ть; протира́ть [-тере́ть]; натира́ть [натере́ть]; **~ in** втира́ть [втере́ть]; **~ out** стира́ть [стере́ть]; **~ up** [от]полирова́ть; (*freshen*) освежа́ть [-жи́ть]; *v/i.* тере́ться (**against** о В); *fig.* **~ along** проби́(ва́)ться с трудо́м

rubber ['rʌbə] каучу́к; рези́на; (*eraser*) рези́нка; (*contraceptive*) противозача́точное сре́дство; презервати́в; *cards* ро́ббер; *attr.* рези́новый

rubbish ['rʌbıʃ] му́сор, хлам; *fig.* вздор; глу́пости *f/pl.*

rubble ['rʌbl] (*debris*) обло́мки; ще́бень *m*

ruby ['ru:bı] руби́н; руби́новый цвет

rucksack ['rʌksæk] рюкза́к

rudder ['rʌdə] *naut.* руль *m*

ruddy ['rʌdı] я́рко-кра́сный; *cheeks* румя́ный

rude [ru:d] □ неотёсанный; гру́бый; невё́жливый; *fig. health* кре́пкий; **~ awakening** неприя́тное откры́тие; го́рькое разочарова́ние

rudiment ['ru:dımənt] *biol.* руди́ме́нт; **~s** *pl.* осно́вы *f/pl.*; **~s of knowledge** элемента́рные зна́ния

rueful ['ru:fl] □ печа́льный

ruffian ['rʌfıən] громи́ла, хулига́н

ruffle ['rʌfl] **1.** *sew.* сбо́рка; *on water* рябь *f*; **2.** *hair* [взъ]еро́шить; *water* ряби́ть; *fig.* наруша́ть споко́йствие (Р), [вс]трево́жить

rug [rʌg] плед; *on floor* ковёр, ко́врик; **~ged** ['rʌgıd] неро́вный; шерохова́тый; *terrain* пересечённый; *features* гру́бые, ре́зкие

ruin ['ru:ın] **1.** ги́бель *f*, разоре́ние; *of hopes, etc.* круше́ние; *mst.* **~s** *pl.* разва́лины *f/pl.*, руи́ны *f/pl.*; **2.** [по]губи́ть; разоря́ть [-ри́ть]; разруша́ть [-у́шить]; *dishono(u)r* [о]бесче́стить; **~ous** ['ru:ınəs] □ губи́тельный; разори́тельный; разру́шенный

rul|e [ru:l] **1.** пра́вило; правле́ние; власть *f*; *for measuring* лине́йка; **as a ~** обы́чно; **2.** *v/t.* управля́ть (Т); (*give as decision*) постановля́ть [-ви́ть]; **~ out** исключа́ть [-чи́ть]; *v/i.* ца́рствовать; **~er** ['ru:lə] прави́тель *m*

rum [rʌm] ром

Rumanian [ru:'meınıən] **1.** румы́нский; **2.** румы́н *m*, -ка *f*

rumble ['rʌmbl] **1.** громыха́ние; гро́хот; **2.** [за]громыха́ть; [за]грохота́ть; *of thunder* [за]греме́ть

rumina|nt ['ru:mınənt] жва́чное; **~te** [~neıt] *fig.* размышля́ть

rummage ['rʌmıdʒ] *v/t.* перерыва́ть; *v/i.* ры́ться; **~ sale** благотвори́тельная распрода́жа

rumo(u)r ['ru:mə] **1.** слух; молва́; **2.**: **it is ~ed that ...** хо́дят слу́хи, что ...

R

rump [rʌmp] огу́зок
rumple ['rʌmpl] (с)мять; *hair* [взъ]еро́шить
run [rʌn] **1.** [*irr.*] *v/i. com.* бе́гать, [по]бежа́ть; [по]те́чь; *of colo*(*u*)*rs, etc.* расплы́(ва́)ться; *of engine* рабо́тать; *text* гласи́ть; **~ across a p.** случа́йно встре́тить (В); **~ away** убега́ть [убежа́ть]; **~ down** сбега́ть [сбежа́ть]; *of watch, etc.* остана́вливаться [-ови́ться]; истоща́ться [-щи́ться]; **~ dry** иссяка́ть [-я́кнуть]; **~ for** *parl.* выставля́ть свою́ кандидату́ру на (В); **~ into** впада́ть в (В); *debt* залеза́ть [-ле́зть]; *person* встреча́ть [-е́тить]; **~ on** продолжа́ться [-до́лжиться]; говори́ть без умо́лку; **~ out**, **~ short** конча́ться [ко́нчиться]; **~ through** прочита́ть бе́гло *pf.*; *capital* прома́тывать [-мота́ть]; **~ to** (*reach*) достига́ть [-и́гнуть]; **~ up to** доходи́ть [дойти́] до (Р); **2.** *v/t.* пробега́ть [-бежа́ть] (расстоя́ние); *water* нали́(ва́)ть; *business* вести́; (*drive in*) вонза́ть [-зи́ть]; *department, etc.* руководи́ть; проводи́ть [-вести́] (Т, **over** по Д); *car* сбива́ть [сбить]; **~ down** *fig.* поноси́ть (В); (*tire*) переутомля́ть [-ми́ть]; **~ over** переезжа́ть [-е́хать], сби(ва́)ть; прочита́ть бе́гло *pf.*; **~ up** *prices* взду(ва́)ть; *building* возводи́ть [-вести́]; **~ up a bill at** [за]должа́ть (Д); **3.** бег; пробе́г; *of mechanism* рабо́та, де́йствие; *of time* тече́ние, ход; ряд; (*outing*) пое́здка, прогу́лка; руково́дство; **the common ~** обыкнове́нные лю́ди *m/pl.*; *thea.* **have a ~ of 20 nights** идти́ два́дцать вечеро́в подря́д; **in the long ~** со вре́менем; в конце́ концо́в
run|about ['rʌnəbaʊt] *mot.* малолитра́жка; **~away** бегле́ц
rung[1] [rʌŋ] *pt. p. от* **ring**
rung[2] [~] ступе́нька стремя́нки
runner ['rʌnə] бегу́н; *of sledge* по́лоз; *of plant* побе́г; **~-up** [~'rʌp] *sport* занима́ющий второ́е ме́сто
running ['rʌnɪŋ] **1.** бегу́щий; *track* бегово́й; **two days ~** два дня подря́д; **2.** бе́ганье; *of person* бег; *of horses* бега́ *m/pl.*; **~ board** подно́жка; **~ water** *in nature* проточная вода́; *in man-made structures* водопрово́д
runway ['rʌnweɪ] *ae.* взлётно-поса́дочная полоса́
rupture ['rʌptʃə] **1.** разры́в; (*hernia*) гры́жа; **2.** разрыва́ть [разорва́ть] (*a. fig.*); прор(ы)ва́ть
rural ['rʊərəl] □ се́льский, дереве́нский
rush[1] [rʌʃ] **1.** *bot.* тростни́к, камы́ш; **~ mat** цино́вка
rush[2] [~] **1.** (*influx*) наплы́в; **~ hours** *pl.* часы́ пик; **2.** *v/i.* мча́ться; броса́ться [бро́ситься]; носи́ться, [по-] нести́сь; **~ into** броса́ться необду́манно в (В); *v/t.* мчать
rusk [rʌsk] суха́рь *m*
Russian ['rʌʃn] **1.** ру́сский; **2.** ру́сский, ру́сская; ру́сский язы́к
rust [rʌst] **1.** ржа́вчина; **2.** [за]ржаве́ть
rustic ['rʌstɪk] (**~ally**) дереве́нский; (*simple*) просто́й; (*rough*) гру́бый
rustle ['rʌsl] **1.** [за]шелесте́ть; **2.** ше́лест, шо́рох
rust|proof ['rʌstpru:f] нержаве́ющий; **~y** ['rʌstɪ] заржа́вленный, ржа́вый
rut [rʌt] коле́я (*a. fig.*)
ruthless ['ru:θlɪs] безжа́лостный
rye [raɪ] *bot.* рожь *f*; **~ bread** ржано́й хлеб

R

S

sabbatical [sə'bætɪkl]: **~ *leave*** *univ.* академический отпуск
saber, *Brt.* **sabre** ['seɪbə] сабля, шашка
sable ['seɪbl] соболь *m*; (*fur*) соболий мех
sabotage ['sæbətɑːʒ] **1.** саботаж; **2.** саботировать (В)
sack¹ [sæk] **1.** разграбление; **2.** [раз]грабить
sack² [~] **1.** мешок; **2.** класть, ссыпать в мешок; *coll.* (*dismiss*) увольнять [-лить]; **~cloth, ~ing** ['sækɪŋ] мешковина
sacrament ['sækrəmənt] *act or rite* таинство; (*Eucharist*) причастие
sacred ['seɪkrɪd] □ святой; священный; *mus.* духовный
sacrifice ['sækrɪfaɪs] **1.** жертва; (*offering to a deity*) жертвоприношение; ***at a ~*** с убытками; **2.** [по-] жертвовать
sacrilege ['sækrɪlɪdʒ] святотатство, кощунство
sad [sæd] □ печальный, грустный; ***in a ~ state*** в плачевном состоянии
sadden ['sædn] [о]печалить(ся)
saddle ['sædl] **1.** седло; **2.** [о]седлать; *fig.* взваливать [-лить] (***s.o. with sth.*** что-нибудь на кого-нибудь); обременять [-нить]
sadism ['seɪdɪzəm] садизм
sadness ['sædnɪs] печаль *f*, грусть *f*
safe [seɪf] **1.** □ невредимый; надёжный; безопасный; ***~ and sound*** цел и невредим; ***in ~ hands*** в надёжных руках; **2.** сейф; **~guard 1.** гарантия; **2.** охранять [-нить]; гарантировать
safety ['seɪftɪ] **1.** безопасность *f*, надёжность *f*; **2.** безопасный; **~ belt** ремень *m* безопасности, привязной ремень *m*; **~ pin** английская булавка; **~ razor** безопасная бритва; **~ valve** предохранительный клапан
saffron ['sæfrən] шафран
sag [sæg] *of roof, etc.* оседать [-сесть], прогибаться [-гнуться]; *of cheeks, etc.* обвисать [-иснуть]; ***her spirits ~ged*** она упала духом
sage¹ [seɪdʒ] мудрец
sage² [~] *bot.* шалфей
said [sed] *pt. и pt. p. om* **say**
sail [seɪl] **1.** парус; плавание под парусами; **2.** *v/i.* идти под парусами; (*travel over*) плавать, [по]плыть, отплы(ва)ть; *v/t.* (*control navigation of*) управлять; плавать по (Д); **~boat** парусная лодка; **~ing** [~ɪŋ] плавание; ***it wasn't plain ~*** всё было не так просто; **~or** [~ə] моряк, матрос; ***be a*** (***good***) ***bad ~*** (не) страдать морской болезнью; **~plane** планёр
saint [seɪnt] святой; **~ly** ['seɪntlɪ] *adj.* святой
sake [seɪk]: ***for the ~ of*** ради (Р); ***for my ~*** ради меня
sal(e)able ['seɪləbl] ходкий (товар)
salad ['sæləd] салат
salary ['sælərɪ] оклад, заработная плата
sale [seɪl] продажа; (*clearance ~*) распродажа; аукцион; ***be for ~, be on ~*** иметься в продаже
sales|man ['seɪlzmən] продавец; *door-to-door* коммивояжёр; **~woman** продавщица
saline ['seɪlaɪn] соляной; солёный
saliva [sə'laɪvə] слюна
sallow ['sæləʊ] *complexion* нездоровый; желтоватый
salmon ['sæmən] лосось *m*; *flesh* лососина
salon ['sælɒn]: ***beauty ~*** косметический салон
saloon [sə'luːn] зал; *naut.* салон; бар, пивная; *Brt.* (*car*) седан
salt [sɔːlt] **1.** соль *f*, *fig.* остроумие; ***take s.th. with a grain of ~*** относиться к чему-л. скептически; **2.** солёный; **3.** [по]солить; засаливать [-солить]; **~cellar** солонка; **~y** ['sɔːltɪ] солёный
salutary ['sæljʊtrɪ] □ благотворный; полезный для здоровья
salut|ation [sæljuː'teɪʃn] приветст-

вие; **~e** [sə'lu:t] **1.** *mil.* отдáние чéсти; вóинское привéтствие; *with weapons* салю́т; **2.** привéтствовать; отдавáть честь *f* (Д)

salvage ['sælvɪdʒ] **1.** *of ship, property, etc.* спасéние; (*what is saved*) спасённое имýщество; (*scrap*) ути́ль *m*; *paper* макулатýра; *naut.* подъём; **2.** спасáть [спасти́]

salvation [sæl'veɪʃn] спасéние; ♀ ***Army*** Áрмия спасéния

salve [sælv] **1.** успокои́тельное срéдство; **2.** *conscience* успокáивать [-кóить]

salvo ['sælvəʊ] *of guns* залп; *fig.* взрыв аплодисмéнтов

same [seɪm]: ***the ~*** тот же сáмый; та же сáмая; то же сáмое; ***all the ~*** тем не мéнее, всё-таки; ***it is all the ~ to me*** мне всё равнó

sample ['sɑːmpl] **1.** прóба; образчик, образéц; *fig.* примéр; **2.** [по-] прóбовать; отбирáть образцы́ (Р); *wine, etc.* дегусти́ровать

sanatorium [sænə'tɔːrɪəm] санатóрий

sanction ['sæŋkʃn] **1.** (*permission*) разрешéние; (*approval*) одобрéние; *official* сáнкция; ***apply ~s against*** применя́ть [-ни́ть] сáнкции прóтив (Р); **2.** санкциони́ровать (*im*)*pf.*; давáть [дать] соглáсие, разрешéние; **~uary** [~tʃʊərɪ] (*holy place*) святи́лище; (*refuge*) убéжище

sand [sænd] **1.** песóк; (*~ bank*) óтмель *f*; *of desert* пески́ *m/pl.* **~s** *pl.* песчáный пляж; **2.** (*sprinkle with ~*) посыпáть пескóм; (*polish*) протирáть [-ерéть] пескóм

sandal ['sændl] сандáлия; (*lady's a.*) босонóжки *f/pl.*

sandpaper наждáчная бумáга

sandwich ['sænwɪdʒ] **1.** бутербрóд, сáндвич; **2.**: ***~ between*** вти́скивать [-нуть] мéжду (Т)

sandy ['sændɪ] песчáный; песóчный; песóчного цвéта

sane [seɪn] нормáльный; *fig.* здрáвый, разýмный; здравомы́слящий

sang [sæŋ] *pt. om* ***sing***

sanguine ['sæŋgwɪn] жизнерáдостный, сангвини́ческий

sanitary ['sænɪtrɪ] □ санитáрный; гигиени́ческий; ***~ napkin*** гигиени́ческая проклáдка

sanitation [sænɪ'teɪʃn] санитáрные услóвия; *for sewage* канализáция

sanity ['sænətɪ] психи́ческое здорóвье; здрáвый ум

sank [sæŋk] *pt. om* ***sink***

sap [sæp] **1.** *of plants* сок; *fig.* жи́зненные си́лы *f/pl.*; **2.** истощáть [-щи́ть]; *confidence* подрывáть [подорвáть]; **~less** ['sæplɪs] истощённый; **~ling** ['sæplɪŋ] молодóе деревцó

sapphire ['sæfaɪə] *min.* сапфи́р

sappy ['sæpɪ] сóчный; *fig.* пóлный сил

sarcasm ['sɑːkæzəm] саркáзм

sardine [sɑː'diːn] сарди́н(к)а; ***packed like ~s*** как сéльди в бóчке

sardonic [sɑ'dɒnɪk] (***~ally***) сардони́ческий

sash [sæʃ] кушáк, пóяс

sash window подъёмное окнó

sat [sæt] *pt. и pt. p. om* ***sit***

satchel ['sætʃəl] сумка, рáнец

sateen [sə'tiːn] сати́н

satellite ['sætəlaɪt] *celestial* спýтник (*a. spacecraft*)

satiate ['seɪʃɪeɪt] пресыщáть [-ы́тить]; насыщáть [-ы́тить]; **~ed** [~ɪd] сы́тый

satin ['sætɪn] атлáс

satir|e ['sætaɪə] сати́ра; **~ical** [sə'tɪrɪkl] сатири́ческий; **~ist** ['sætərɪst] сати́рик; **~ize** [~raɪz] высмéивать [вы́смеять]

satisfaction [sætɪs'fækʃn] удовлетворéние

satisfactory [sætɪs'fæktərɪ] удовлетвори́тельный

satisfy ['sætɪsfaɪ] удовлетворя́ть [-ри́ть]; *hunger, etc.* утоля́ть [-ли́ть]; *obligations* выполня́ть [вы́полнить]; (*convince*) убеждáть [убеди́ть]

saturate ['sætʃəreɪt] *chem.* насыщáть [-ы́тить]; пропи́тывать [-итáть]; ***we came home ~ed*** покá мы добежáли дó дому, мы промóкли

Saturday ['sætədɪ] суббóта

sauce [sɔːs] сóус; (*gravy*) подли́вка; *coll.* (*impudence*) дéрзость *f*; **~pan** кастрю́ля; **~r** ['sɔːsə] блю́дце

saucy ['sɔːsɪ] *coll.* дéрзкий
sauerkraut ['sauəkraut] кислая капýста
sauna ['sɔːnə] сáуна
saunter ['sɔːntə] **1.** прогýливаться; **2.** прогýлка
sausage ['sɒsɪdʒ] (*frankfurter*) сосиска; (*salami, etc.*) колбасá; (*polony, saveloy*) сардéлька
savage ['sævɪdʒ] **1.** □ дикий; (*cruel*) жестóкий; (*ferocious*) свирéпый; **2.** дикáрь *m*, -арка *f*; *fig.* зверь *m*; **~ry** [~rɪ] дикость *f*; жестóкость *f*
save [seɪv] спасáть [спасти]; избавлять [-бáвить] (***from*** от Р); *strength, etc.* сберегáть [-рéчь]; (*put by*) [с]копить, откладывать [отложить]; *time, money, etc.* [с]эконóмить
saving ['seɪvɪŋ] **1.** □ (*redeeming*) спасительный; **2.** (*rescue*) спасéние; **~s** *pl.* сбережéния *n/pl.*
savings bank сберегáтельная кáсса
savio(u)r ['seɪvɪə] спаситель *m*; ***the*** ♀ Спаситель *m*
savo(u)r ['seɪvə] **1.** (*taste*) вкус; *fig.* привкус; **2.** (*enjoy*) смаковáть; **~ *of*** пáхнуть (Т); *fig.* отдавáть (Т); **~y** [~rɪ] вкýсный; пикáнтный, óстрый
saw[1] [sɔː] *pt. от* ***see***
saw[2] [~] **1.** пилá; **2.** [*irr.*] пилить; **~dust** опилки *f/pl.*; **~mill** лесопилка; лесопильный завóд; **~n** [sɔːn] *pt. p. от* ***saw***
say [seɪ] **1.** [*irr.*] говорить [сказáть]; ***that is to ~*** тó есть, т.е.; ***you don't ~!*** неужéли!; ***I ~!*** послýшай(те)!; ***he is said to be ...*** говорят, что он ...; ***I dare ~ ...*** навéрно (вполнé) возмóжно ...; ***they ~ ...*** говорят ...; **2.** ***have one's ~*** высказать *pf.* своё мнéние, сказáть *pf.* своё слóво; **~ing** ['seɪɪŋ] поговóрка
scab [skæb] *on a sore* струп
scaffolding ['skæfəldɪŋ] *arch.* лесá *m/pl.*
scald [skɔːld] **1.** ожóг; **2.** [о]шпáрить; обвáривать [-рить]
scale[1] [skeɪl] **1.** *of fish, etc.* чешýйка (*collect.*: чешуя); *inside kettles, etc.* нáкипь *f*; **2.** *fish* [по]чистить; *of skin* шелушиться
scale[2] [~] (***a pair of***) **~s** *pl.* весы *m/pl.*
scale[3] [~] **1.** масштáб; (*size*) размéр; *in grading* шкалá; *mus.* гáмма; **2.**: **~ *up*** постепéнно увеличивать; **~ *down*** постепéнно уменьшáть в масштáбе
scallop ['skɒləp] *mollusk* гребешóк
scalp [skælp] кóжа головы; *hist.* скальп
scamp [skæmp] **1.** шалýн; бездéльник; **2.** рабóтать кóе-как; **~er** [~ə] бежáть поспéшно; **~ *away*, *off*** уд(и)рáть
scandal ['skændl] скандáл; позóр; (*gossip*) сплéтни *f/pl.*; ***it's a ~!*** позóр!; **~ize** [~dəlaɪz] возмущáть [-тить]; шокировать *impf.*; **~ous** [~ləs] □ позóрный; скандáльный; (*defamatory*) клеветнический; (*shocking*) ужáсный
scant, scanty [skænt, 'skæntɪ] скýдный; недостáточный
scapegoat ['skeɪpgəut] козёл отпущéния
scar [skɑː] **1.** шрам; рубéц; **2.** *v/t.* покрывáться рубцáми; ***his face was ~red*** лицó егó было покрыто шрáмами; *v/i.* [за]рубцевáться
scarc|e [skeəs] недостáточный; скýдный; (*rare*) рéдкий; *goods* дефицитный; ***make o.s. ~*** убирáться [убрáться]; **~ely** ['~lɪ] едвá ли; как тóлько; едвá; **~ity** ['~sətɪ] нехвáтка; рéдкость *f*
scare [skeə] **1.** [на-, ис]пугáть; отпýгивать [-гнýть] (*a.* **~ *away***); **2.** испýг; пáника; **~crow** пýгало; *a. fig.* чýчело
scarf [skɑːf] шарф; (*head~*) платóк, косынка
scarlet ['skɑːlɪt] **1.** áлый цвет; **2.** áлый; **~ *fever*** скарлатина
scathing ['skeɪðɪŋ] рéзкий; язвительный
scatter ['skætə] разбрáсывать [-бросáть] (*a.* **~ *about*, *around***); рассыпáть(ся) [-ыпать(ся)]; *clouds, etc.* рассéивать(ся) [-éять(ся)]; *crowd* разбегáться [-ежáться]
scenario [sɪ'nɑːrɪəu] сценáрий
scene [siːn] сцéна; вид; мéсто дéйствия; ***behind the ~s*** за кулисами (*a. fig.*); ***make a ~*** устрóить *pf.* сцéну, скандáл; **~ry** ['siːnərɪ] *thea.* декорáции *f/pl.*; пейзáж

S

scent [sent] **1.** аромáт, зáпах; (*perfume*) духи́ *m/pl.*; *hunt.* след; чутьё; нюх; ***follow the wrong ~*** идти́ по лóжному слéду; **2.** *danger, etc.* [по]чу́ять; [на]души́ть
schedule ['ʃedjuːl] **1.** *of charges* спи́сок, пéречень *m*; *of work* грáфик, план; (*timetable*) расписáние; ***a full ~*** большáя прогрáмма; **2.** составля́ть расписáние (Р); (*plan*) назначáть [назнáчить], намечáть [-éтить]
scheme [skiːm] **1.** схéма; план; проéкт; (*plot*) интри́га; **2.** *v/t.* [за]проекти́ровать; *v/i.* плести́ интри́ги
schnitzel ['ʃnɪtzl] шни́цель *m*
scholar ['skɒlə] учёный; (*holder of scholarship*) стипендиáт; **~ly** [~lɪ] *adj.* учёный; **~ship** [~ʃɪp] учёность *f*, эруди́ция; (*grant-in-aid*) стипéндия
school [skuːl] **1.** шкóла; ***at ~*** в шкóле; ***secondary*** (*Am.* ***high***) **~** срéдняя шкóла; **2.** [на]учи́ть; приучáть [-чи́ть]; **~boy** шкóльник; **~fellow** шкóльный товáрищ; **~girl** шкóльница; **~ing** ['skuːlɪŋ] обучéние в шкóле; **~master** учи́тель *m*; **~mate** → ***schoolfellow***; **~mistress** учи́тельница; **~room** клáссная кóмната
science ['saɪəns] наýка
scientific [saɪən'tɪfɪk] (***~ally***) наýчный
scientist ['saɪəntɪst] учёный
scintillate ['sɪntɪleɪt] и́скриться; сверкáть [-кнýть]; мерцáть; ***scintillating wit*** блестя́щее остроýмие
scissors ['sɪzəz] *pl.* (*a* ***pair of ~***) нóжницы *f/pl.*
sclerosis [sklə'rəʊsɪs] *med.* склерóз
scoff [skɒf] **1.** насмéшка; **2.** смея́ться (***at*** над Т)
scold [skəʊld] [вы́-, от]ругáть, [вы́-]брани́ть; отчи́тывать [-читáть]
scone [skɒn] бýлочка
scoop [skuːp] **1.** совóк; *for liquids* черпáк, ковш; *in newspaper* сенсациóнная нóвость *f*; **2.** зачéрпывать [-пнýть]
scooter ['skuːtə] *child's* самокáт; *mot.* моторóллер
scope [skəʊp] кругозóр; размáх; охвáт; простóр; *of activity* сфéра; ***outside the ~*** за предéлами (***of*** Р)
scorch [skɔːtʃ] *v/t.* обжигáть [обжéчь]; [с]пали́ть; *coll.* бéшено нести́сь; **~er** ['~ə] *coll.* (*hot day*) знóйный день
score [skɔː] **1.** (*cut*) зарýбка; *sport* счёт; *mus.* партитýра; **~s** *pl.* мнóжество; ***on the ~ of*** по причи́не (Р); ***on that ~*** на э́тот счёт, по э́тому пóводу; ***what's the ~?*** какóй счёт?; **2.** отмечáть [-éтить]; засчи́тывать [-итáть]; вы́игрывать [вы́играть]; забивáть гол; *mus.* оркестровáть (*im*)*pf.*; *chiefly Am.* [вы́]брани́ть; **~board** таблó *n indecl.*
scorn [skɔːn] **1.** презрéние; **2.** презирáть [-зрéть]; *advice* пренебрегáть [-рéчь]; **~ful** ['skɔːnfl] □ *pers.* надмéнный; *look, etc.* презри́тельный
Scotch [skɒtʃ] **1.** шотлáндский; **2.** шотлáндский диалéкт; (*whiskey*) шотлáндское ви́ски; ***the ~*** шотлáндцы *m/pl.*; **~man** шотлáндец; *trademark* **~ tape** клéйкая лéнта, скотч; **~woman** шотлáндка
scot-free [skɒt'friː] невреди́мый; (*unpunished*) безнакáзанный
scoundrel ['skaʊndrəl] негодя́й, подлéц
scour[1] ['skaʊə] *v/t.* [вы́]чи́стить; *pan* начищáть [начи́стить]; *with water* промывáть [про]мы́ть
scour[2] ['~] *area* прочёсывать [-чесáть] (В); *v/i.* ры́скать (*a.* ***about***)
scourge [skɜːdʒ] **1.** бич (*a. fig.*); бéдствие; **2.** [по]карáть
scout [skaʊt] **1.** развéдчик (*a. ae.*); ***Boy ~s*** *pl.* скáуты *m/pl.*; **2.** производи́ть развéдку; ***~ about for*** [по]искáть (В)
scowl [skaʊl] **1.** хмýрый вид; **2.** [на]хмýриться; ***~ at*** хмýро посмотрéть *pf.* на (В)
scraggy ['skrægɪ] тóщий
scram [skræm] *coll.*: ***~!*** убирáйся!
scramble ['skræmbl] **1.** [вс]карáбкаться; борóться (***for*** за В); **~d eggs** *pl.* я́ичница-болтýнья; **2.** свáлка, борьбá; карáбканье
scrap [skræp] **1.** *of paper* клочóк, кусóчек; *of cloth* лоскутóк; (*cut-*

S

ting) вы́резка; (*waste*) лом; втори́чное сырьё; **~s** *pl.* оста́тки *m/pl.*; *of food* объе́дки *m/pl.*; **2.** (*throw away*) выбра́сывать [вы́бросить]
scrap|e [skreɪp] **1.** скобле́ние; *on knee, etc.* цара́пина; (*predicament*) затрудне́ние; **2.** скобли́ть; скрести́(сь); соскреба́ть [-ести́] (*mst.* **~ off**); отчища́ть [-и́стить]; (*touch*) заде́(ва́)ть; **~ *together*** *money* наскрести́
scrap iron желе́зный лом
scrappy ['skræpɪ] отры́вочный
scratch [skrætʃ] цара́пина; ***start from ~*** начина́ть всё с нуля́; [о]цара́пать; **~ *out*** (*erase*) вычёркивать [вы́черкнуть]
scrawl [skrɔːl] **1.** кара́кули *f/pl.*; **2.** написа́ть *pf.* неразбо́рчиво
scream [skriːm] **1.** вопль *m*; крик; ***~s of laughter*** взры́вы сме́ха; **2.** пронзи́тельно крича́ть
screech [skriːtʃ] **1.** крик; визг; **2.** пронзи́тельно крича́ть; взвизгивать [-гнуть]
screen [skriːn] **1.** ши́рма; экра́н (*a. cine*); **~ *adaptation*** экраниза́ция; ***adapt for the ~*** экранизи́ровать; ***the ~*** кино́ *n indecl.*; **2.** (*protect*) прикры́(ва́)ть; заслоня́ть [-ни́ть]; *film* пока́зывать на экра́не; просе́ивать [-е́ять]; (*investigate*) проверя́ть [-е́рить]
screw [skruː] **1.** шуру́п; винт; **2.** приви́нчивать [-нти́ть] (*mst.* **~ *on***); **~ *together*** скрепля́ть винта́ми; **~ *up*** зави́нчивать [-нти́ть]; *one's face* [с]мо́рщить; **~driver** отвёртка
scribble ['skrɪbl] **1.** кара́кули *f/pl.*; **2.** написа́ть *pf.* небре́жно
scrimp [skrɪmp]: **~ *and save*** вся́чески эконо́мить
script [skrɪpt] *cine.* сцена́рий; **~writer** сценари́ст
Scripture ['skrɪptʃə]: ***Holy ~*** Свяще́нное писа́ние
scroll [skrəʊl] сви́ток; (*list*) спи́сок
scrub[1] [skrʌb] куст; **~s** *pl.* куста́рник; за́росль *f*
scrub[2] [~] мыть [вы́мыть]
scrubby ['skrʌbɪ] *plant* (*stunted*) ча́хлый
scruffy ['skrʌfɪ] гря́зный; неопря́тный
scrup|le ['skruːpl] сомне́ния *n/pl.*; **~ulous** ['skruːpjʊləs] □ щепети́льный; (*thorough*) скрупулёзный; (*conscientious*) добросо́вестный
scrutin|ize ['skruːtɪnaɪz] внима́тельно рассма́тривать [-мотре́ть]; *case, etc.* тща́тельно изуча́ть [-чи́ть]; **~y** ['skruːtɪnɪ] испыту́ющий взгляд; всесторо́нняя прове́рка; внима́тельное изуче́ние
scud [skʌd] *of clouds* нести́сь; *of yacht* скользи́ть
scuffle ['skʌfl] **1.** потасо́вка, дра́ка; **2.** [по]дра́ться
sculptor ['skʌlptə] ску́льптор
sculpture ['skʌlptʃə] **1.** скульпту́ра; **2.** [из]ва́ять; *in stone* высека́ть [вы́сечь]; *in wood* ре́зать [вы́резать]
scum [skʌm] пе́на; *fig.* подо́нки *m/pl.*
scurf [skɜːf] пе́рхоть *f*
scurry ['skʌrɪ] бы́стро бе́гать; суетли́во дви́гаться; снова́ть (туда́ и сюда́); ***they scurried for shelter*** они́ бро́сились в укры́тие
scurvy ['skɜːvɪ] *med.* цинга́
scythe [saɪð] коса́
sea [siː] мо́ре; *attr.* морско́й; ***be at ~*** *fig.* не знать, что де́лать; недоумева́ть; **~faring** ['siːfeərɪŋ] морепла́вание; **~going** ['siːgəʊɪŋ] *ship* морехо́дный
seal[1] [siːl] *zo.* тюле́нь *m*
seal[2] [~] **1.** печа́ть *f*; (*leaden ~*) пло́мба; **2.** *letter* запеча́т(ыв)ать; скрепля́ть печа́тью; *room* опеча́т(ыв)ать
sea level у́ровень *m* мо́ря
sealing ['siːlɪŋ] *tech.* уплотне́ние; **~ wax** сургу́ч
seam [siːm] **1.** шов (*a. tech*); рубе́ц; *geol.* пласт; **2.** сши(ва́)ть
sea|man моря́к; матро́с; **~plane** гидросамолёт
searing ['sɪərɪŋ]: **~ *pain*** жгу́чая боль *f*
search [sɜːtʃ] **1.** по́иски *m/pl.*; *by police* о́быск; ро́зыск; ***in ~ of*** в по́исках (P); **~ *party*** поиско́вая гру́ппа; **2.** *v/t.* иска́ть; обы́скивать [-ка́ть]; **~ *me!*** не име́ю поня́тия; *v/i.* разы́скивать [-ка́ть] (***for*** В); **~ing** [~ɪŋ] тща́тельный; *look* ис-

S

пыту́ющий; **~light** проже́ктор; **~ warrant** о́рдер на о́быск
sea|shore морско́й бе́рег; **~sick** страда́ющий морско́й боле́знью; **~side** побере́жье; взмо́рье; ***go to the ~*** пое́хать *pf.* на мо́ре; *attr.* примо́рский; ***~ resort*** морско́й куро́рт
season ['siːzn] **1.** вре́мя го́да; пери́од; сезо́н; ***holiday ~*** пери́од отпуско́в; ***apricots are in ~ now*** абрико́сы сейча́с созре́ли; ***with the compliments of the ~*** с лу́чшими пожела́ниями к пра́зднику; **2.** *v/t. food* приправля́ть [-а́вить]; *wood* выде́рживать [вы́держать]; **~able** [~əbl] □ своевре́менный; по сезо́ну; **~al** [~zənl] □ сезо́нный; **~ing** [~zənɪŋ] припра́ва; **~ ticket** сезо́нный биле́т
seat [siːt] **1.** *in car* сиде́нье; (*garden ~*) скамья́; *thea., etc.* ме́сто; ***take a ~*** сесть *pf.*; ***take one's ~*** занима́ть [-ня́ть] своё ме́сто; **2.** уса́живать [усади́ть]; (*hold*) вмеща́ть [вмести́ть]; **~ed** [~ɪd] сидя́щий; ***be ~ed*** сиде́ть, сади́ться [сесть]
sea|weed морска́я во́доросль *f*; **~-worthy** го́дный к пла́ванию
secede [sɪ'siːd] отделя́ться [-ли́ться]; отка́лываться [отколо́ться]
seclu|de [sɪ'kluːd] изоли́ровать (***from*** от Р); **~ *o.s.*** уединя́ться [-ни́ться]; **~d** [~ɪd] уединённый; изоли́рованный; **~sion** [~'kluːʒn] уедине́ние
second ['sekənd] **1.** □ второ́й; втори́чный; уступа́ющий (***to*** Д); ***on ~ thoughts*** по зре́лому размышле́нию; **2.** секу́нда; ***a split ~*** до́ля секу́нды; мгнове́ние **3.** (*support*) подде́рживать [-жа́ть]; **~ary** [~rɪ] □ втори́чный; второстепе́нный; побо́чный; ***~ education*** сре́днее образова́ние; **~-hand** поде́ржанный; *information* из вторы́х рук; ***~ bookshop*** букинисти́ческий магази́н; **~ly** [~lɪ] во-вторы́х; **~-rate** второсо́ртный; *hotel* второразря́дный; *writer, etc.* посре́дственный
secre|cy ['siːkrəsɪ] *of person* скры́тность *f*; секре́тность *f*; **~t** ['siːkrɪt] **1.** □ та́йный, секре́тный; **2.** та́йна, секре́т; ***in ~*** секре́тно, тайко́м; ***be in on the ~*** быть посвящённым в секре́т; ***keep a ~*** храни́ть та́йну
secretary ['sekrətrɪ] секрета́рь *m*, *coll.* секрета́рша; мини́стр
secret|e [sɪ'kriːt] *med.* выделя́ть [вы́делить]; **~ion** [~'kriːʃn] выделе́ние
secretive ['siːkrətɪv] скры́тный
section ['sekʃn] (*cut*) сече́ние, разре́з; (*part*) часть *f*; *of orange* до́лька; *in newspaper* отде́л; *of book* разде́л; **~al** [~ʃənl] разбо́рный, секцио́нный
sector ['sektə] се́ктор
secular ['sekjʊlə] □ *noneccl.* све́тский; *of this world* мирско́й
secur|e [sɪ'kjʊə] **1.** □ (*safe*) безопа́сный; (*reliable*) надёжный; (*firm*) про́чный; уве́ренный; ***I feel ~ about my future*** я уе́рена в своём бу́дущем; **2.** (*make fast*) закрепля́ть [-пи́ть]; обеспе́чи(ва)ть; (*make safe*) обезопа́сить *pf*; (*get*) дост(ав)а́ть; **~ity** [~rətɪ] безопа́сность *f*; надёжность *f*; обеспе́чение; зало́г; **~ities** *pl.* це́нные бума́ги *f/pl.*
sedate [sɪ'deɪt] □ степе́нный
sedative ['sedətɪv] *mst. med.* успока́ивающее сре́дство
sedentary ['sedntrɪ] □ сидя́чий
sediment ['sedɪmənt] оса́док
seduc|e [sɪ'djuːs] соблазня́ть [-ни́ть]; **~tive** [sɪ'dʌktɪv] □ соблазни́тельный
see [siː] [*irr.*] *v/i.* [у]ви́деть; ***I ~*** я понима́ю; ***~ about a th.*** [по]забо́титься о (П); ***~ through a p.*** ви́деть кого́-л. насквозь; *v/t.* [у]ви́деть; *film, etc.* [по]смотре́ть; замеча́ть [-е́тить]; понима́ть [-ня́ть]; посеща́ть [-ети́ть]; ***~ a p. home*** провожа́ть кого́-нибудь домо́й; ***~ off*** провожа́ть [-води́ть]; ***~ to*** позабо́титься (о П); заня́ться *pf.* (Т); ***~ a th. through*** доводи́ть [довести́] что́-нибудь до конца́; ***live to ~*** дожи́(ва́)ть до (Р)
seed [siːd] **1.** се́мя *n* (*a. fig*); *of grain* зерно́; *collect.* семена́ *n/pl.*; *of apple, etc.* зёрнышко; (*offspring*) *mst. Bibl.* пото́мство; **2.** *v/t.* засева́ть [засе́ять]; [по]се́ять; **~ling** ['siːdlɪŋ] *agric.* се́янец; (*tree*) са́женец; **~s** *pl.* расса́да *collect.*; **~y** ['siːdɪ] напол-

ненный семена́ми; (*shabby*) потрёпанный, обноси́вшийся; *coll.* не в фо́рме; нездоро́вый
seek [siːk] [*irr.*] *mst. fig.* иска́ть (Р); **~ *advice*** обраща́ться за сове́том; **~ *after*** добива́ться (Р); **~ *out*** разы́скивать [-ыска́ть]; оты́скивать [-ка́ть]
seem [siːm] [по]каза́ться; **~ing** ['~ɪŋ] □ ка́жущийся; мни́мый; **~ingly** ['~ɪŋlɪ] пови́димому; **~ly** ['~lɪ] подоба́ющий; присто́йный
seen [siːn] *pt. p. от* ***see***
seep [siːp] проса́чиваться [-сочи́ться]
seesaw ['siːsɔː] доска́-каче́ли *f/pl.*
seethe [siːð] бурли́ть; *fig.* кипе́ть
segment ['segmənt] *math.* сегме́нт, отре́зок; *of orange* до́лька; (*part*) кусо́к, часть *f*
segregate ['segrɪgeɪt] отделя́ть [-ли́ть]
seismic ['saɪzmɪk] сейсми́ческий
seiz|e [siːz] (*take hold of*) хвата́ть [схвати́ть]; (*take possession of*) *of* захва́тывать [захвати́ть]; ухвати́ться за (В) *pf.* (*a. fig.*); *property* конфискова́ть (*im*)*pf.*; *fig. of feeling* охва́тывать [-ти́ть]; **~ure** ['siːʒə] *med.* при́ступ
seldom ['seldəm] *adv.* ре́дко, почти́ никогда́
select [sɪ'lekt] **1.** отбира́ть [отобра́ть]; *s.th. to match* подбира́ть [подобра́ть]; **2.** отбо́рный; (*exclusive*) и́збранный; **~ion** [sɪ'lekʃn] вы́бор; подбо́р; отбо́р
self [self] **1.** *pron.* сам; себя́; *coll.* = ***myself*** *etc.* я сам *и т.д.*; **2.** *su.* (*pl.* **selves** [selvz]) ли́чность *f*; **~-assured** самоуве́ренный; **~-centered**, *Brt.* ***-centred*** эгоцентри́чный; **~-command** самооблада́ние; **~-conceit** самомне́ние; **~-conscious** засте́нчивый; **~-contained** *person* самостоя́тельный; *lodgings, etc.* отде́льный; *fig.* за́мкнутый; **~-control** самооблада́ние; **~-defence** (**-nse**): ***in ~*** при самозащи́те; **~-determination** самоопределе́ние; **~-evident** очеви́дный; **~-interest** своекоры́стие; **~ish** ['selfɪʃ] эгоисти́чный; **~-possession** самооблада́ние; **~-reliant** полага́ющийся на самого́ себя́; **~-seeking** своекоры́стный; **~-service** самообслу́живание; **~-willed** своево́льный
sell [sel] [*irr.*] прод(ав)а́ть; торгова́ть; ***~ off***, ***~ out*** распрод(ав)а́ть; **~er** ['selə] продаве́ц (-вщи́ца)
semblance ['sembləns] подо́бие; вид; ***put on a ~ of ...*** притворя́ться [-ри́ться]
semi... ['semɪ...] полу...; **~final** полуфина́л
seminary ['semɪnərɪ] семина́рия
semolina [semə'liːnə] ма́нная крупа́; *cooked* ма́нная ка́ша
senate ['senɪt] сена́т; *univ.* сове́т
senator ['senətə] сена́тор
send [send] [*irr.*] пос(ы)ла́ть; отправля́ть [-а́вить]; ***~ for*** пос(ы-)ла́ть за (Т); ***~ out*** *signal, etc.* посыла́ть [-сла́ть]; *invitations* разосла́ть [рассыла́ть]; ***~ up*** вызыва́ть повыше́ние (Р); ***~ word*** сообща́ть [-щи́ть]; **~er** [~ə] отправи́тель *m*
senile ['siːnaɪl] ста́рческий
senior ['siːnɪə] **1.** ста́рший; ***~ partner*** *comm.* глава́ фи́рмы; **2.** ста́рше; ***he is my ~ by a year*** он ста́рше меня́ на́ год; **~ity** [siːnɪ'ɒrətɪ] старшинство́
sensation [sen'seɪʃn] ощуще́ние; чу́вство; сенса́ция; ***cause a ~*** вызыва́ть ['-звать] сенса́цию; **~al** [~ʃənl] □ сенсацио́нный
sense [sens] **1.** чу́вство; ощуще́ние; смысл; значе́ние; ***common ~*** здра́вый смысл; ***bring a p. to his ~s*** *pl. fig.* образу́мить *pf.* кого́-л.; ***make ~*** име́ть смысл; быть поня́тным; **2.** ощуща́ть [ощути́ть], [по]чу́вствовать
senseless ['senslɪs] □ бессмы́сленный; (*unconscious*) без созна́ния
sensibility [sensə'bɪlətɪ] чувстви́тельность *f*
sensible ['sensəbl] □ (благо)разу́мный; здравомы́слящий; (*that can be felt*) ощути́мый, заме́тный; ***be ~ of*** созн(ав)а́ть (В)
sensitiv|e ['sensətɪv] □ чувстви́тельный (***to*** к Д); **~ity** [sensə'tɪvətɪ] чувстви́тельность *f* (***to*** к Д)
sensual ['senʃʊəl] □ чу́вственный
sent [sent] *pt. и pt. p. от* ***send***

S

sentence ['sentəns] **1.** *law* пригово́р; *gr.* предложе́ние; ***serve one's ~*** отбыва́ть наказа́ние; **2.** пригова́ривать [-говори́ть]
sententious [sen'tenʃəs] дидакти́чный; нравоучи́тельный
sentiment ['sentɪmənt] чу́вство; (*opinion*) мне́ние; → ***~ality***; **~al** [sentɪ'mentl] сентимента́льный; **~ality** [sentɪmen'tælətɪ] сентимента́льность *f*
sentry ['sentrɪ] *mil.* часово́й
separa|ble ['sepərəbl] □ отдели́мый; **~te 1.** □ ['seprɪt] отде́льный; осо́бый; *pol.* сепара́тный; **2.** ['sepəreɪt] отделя́ть(ся) [-ли́ть(ся)]; (*part*) разлуча́ть(ся) [-чи́ть(ся)]; (*go different ways*) расходи́ться [разойти́сь]; **~tion** [sepə'reɪʃn] разлу́ка; расстава́ние; **~tism** ['sepərətɪzəm] сепарати́зм; **~tist** ['sepərətɪst] сепарати́ст
September [sep'tembə] сентя́брь *m*
sequel ['si:kwəl] *of story* продолже́ние; (*result, consequence*) после́дствие
sequence ['si:kwəns] после́довательность *f*; (*series*) ряд, цикл
serenade [serə'neɪd] серена́да
seren|e [sɪ'ri:n] □ безо́блачный (*a. fig.*); я́сный; безмяте́жный; споко́йный; **~ity** [sɪ'renətɪ] споко́йность; безмяте́жность *f*; безо́блачность *f*
serf [sɜ:f] *hist.* крепостно́й
sergeant ['sɑ:dʒənt] *mil.* сержа́нт
serial ['sɪərɪəl] □ поря́дковый; сери́йный; после́довательный; ***~ number*** сери́йный но́мер
series ['sɪəri:z] *sg. a. pl.* се́рия; (*number*) ряд; *of goods* па́ртия
serious ['sɪərɪəs] □ серьёзный; ***be ~*** серьёзно говори́ть; **~ness** [~nɪs] серьёзность *f*
sermon ['sɜ:mən] про́поведь *f*
serpent ['sɜ:pənt] змея́; **~ine** [~aɪn] изви́листый
servant ['sɜ:vənt] слуга́ *m*; служа́нка; прислу́га; ***civil ~*** госуда́рственный слу́жащий
serve [sɜ:v] **1.** *v/t.* [по]служи́ть (Д); *dinner, ball in tennis, etc.* под(ав)а́ть; *in shops, etc.* обслу́живать [-жи́ть]; *law* вруча́ть [-чи́ть] (***on*** Д); *sentence* отбы́(ва́)ть; (***it***) ***~s him right*** так ему́ и на́до; ***~ out*** вы́да(ва́)ть, разд(ав)а́ть; *v/i.* [по]служи́ть (*a. mil.*) (*as* Т); **2.** *tennis*: пода́ча
service ['sɜ:vɪs] **1.** слу́жба; *in hotel, etc.* обслу́живание; услу́га; (*a.* ***divine ~***) богослуже́ние; (*train, etc.* ~) сообще́ние; *tennis*: пода́ча; *tech.* техобслу́живание; ***the ~s*** *pl.* а́рмия, флот и вое́нная авиа́ция; ***be at a p.'s ~*** быть к чьи́м-либо услу́гам; ***~ station*** ста́нция техобслу́живания; **2.** *Am. tech.* [от]ремонти́ровать; **~able** ['sɜ:vɪsəbl] □ поле́зный; про́чный
serviette [sɜ:vɪ'et] салфе́тка
servile ['sɜ:vaɪl] подобостра́стный
servitude ['sɜ:vɪtju:d] ра́бство; ***penal ~*** ка́торжные рабо́ты, отбы́тие сро́ка наказа́ния
session ['seʃn] *parl.* се́ссия; *law, etc.* заседа́ние
set [set] **1.** [*irr.*] *v/t.* (*adjust*) [по]ста́вить; *place* класть [положи́ть]; помеща́ть (-ести́ть); *homework, etc.* зад(ав)а́ть; *cine.* вставля́ть в ра́му; уса́живать [усади́ть] (***to*** за В); *med.* вправля́ть [-а́вить]; ***~ a p. laughing*** [рас]смеши́ть кого́-л.; ***~ sail*** отпра́виться *pf.* в пла́вание; ***~ aside*** откла́дывать [отложи́ть]; ***~ store by*** высоко́ цени́ть (В); счита́ть ва́жным (В); ***~ forth*** излага́ть [изложи́ть]; ***~ off*** отправля́ться [-́виться]; ***~ up*** учрежда́ть [-еди́ть]; устра́ивать **2.** *v/i. astr.* заходи́ть [зайти́], сади́ться [сесть]; *of jelly* засты́(ва́)ть; ***~ about a th.*** принима́ться [-ня́ться] за что́-л.; ***~ out*** → ***~ off***; ***~ to work*** бра́ться [взя́ться] за рабо́ту; ***~ o.s. up as*** выдава́ть себя́ за (В); **3.** неподви́жный; *time* определённый; *rules* устано́вленный; *smile* засты́вший; (*rigid*) твёрдый; ***hard ~*** нужда́ющийся; **4.** набо́р; компле́кт; *of furniture* гарниту́р; (*tea ~, etc.*) серви́з; (радио-) приёмник; (*group*) круг; *tennis*: сет; *thea.* декора́ции
setback ['setbæk] заде́ржка; неуда́ча; *in production* спад
settee [se'ti:] куше́тка
setting ['setɪŋ] *of jewels* опра́ва; *thea.* декора́ции; *fig.* окружа́ющая

S

обстано́вка; *of sun* захо́д
settle ['setl] *v/t.* поселя́ть [-ли́ть]; приводи́ть в поря́док; *nerves*; успока́ивать [-ко́ить]; *question* реша́ть [-и́ть]; (*arrange*) устра́ивать [-ро́ить], ула́живать [-а́дить]; заселя́ть [-ли́ть]; *bill* опла́чивать [-ати́ть]; *v/i.* (*often* **~ down**) поселя́ться [-ли́ться]; устра́иваться [-ро́иться]; уса́живаться [усе́сться]; приходи́ть к соглаше́нию; *of dust, etc.* оседа́ть [осе́сть]; *of weather* устана́вливаться [-нови́ться]; **~d** ['setld] постоя́нный; усто́йчивый; **~ment** ['setlmənt] (*agreement*) соглаше́ние; (*act*) урегули́рование; (*village, etc.*) поселе́ние; ***reach a ~*** достига́ть [-ти́чь] соглаше́ния; **~r** ['setlə] поселе́нец
set-to ['settu] сва́тка; *coll.* потасо́вка; *verbal* перепа́лка
seven ['sevn] семь; семёрка → ***five***; **~teen(th)** [sevn'tiːn(θ)] семна́дцать [-тый]; **~th** ['sevnθ] **1.** □ седьмо́й; **2.** седьма́я часть *f*; **~tieth** ['sevntɪɪθ] семидеся́тый; **~ty** ['sevntɪ] се́мьдесят
sever ['sevə] *v/t.* (*cut*) разреза́ть [-е́зать]; разрыва́ть [-зорва́ть] (*a. fig.*); *v/i.* [по]рва́ть(ся)
several ['sevrəl] не́сколько (Р); (*some*) не́которые *pl.*; □ отде́льный; ***they went their ~ ways*** ка́ждый пошёл свое́й доро́гой; **~ly** по отде́льности
sever|e [sɪ'vɪə] (*strict, stern*) стро́гий, суро́вый (*a. of climate*); (*violent, strong*) си́льный; *competition* жесто́кий; *losses* кру́пный; **~ity** [sɪ'verətɪ] стро́гость *f*, суро́вость *f*
sew [səʊ] [*irr.*] [с]шить; ***~ on*** пришива́ть [-ши́ть]
sewer ['sjuːə] канализацио́нная труба́; **~age** ['sjuːərɪdʒ] канализа́ция
sew|ing ['səʊɪŋ] шитьё; *attr.* шве́йный; **~n** [səʊn] *pt. p. om* ***sew***
sex [seks] пол; секс; **~ual** ['sekʃʊəl] □ полово́й; сексуа́льный
shabby ['ʃæbɪ] □ *clothes* потёртый; *building, etc.* убо́гий; *behavio(u)r* по́длый; *excuse* жа́лкий
shack [ʃæk] *Am.* лачу́га, хиба́рка
shackle ['ʃækl]: **~s** *pl.* (*fetters*) око́вы *f/pl.*
shade [ʃeɪd] **1.** тень *f*; (*hue*) отте́нок; (*lamp ~*) абажу́р; *fig.* нюа́нс; *paint* те́ни *f/pl.*; **2.** заслоня́ть [-ни́ть]; затеня́ть [-ни́ть]; [за-] штрихова́ть
shadow ['ʃædəʊ] **1.** тень *f*; (*ghost*) при́зрак; **2.** (*follow*) та́йно следи́ть за (Т); **~y** [~ɪ] тени́стый; (*indistinct*) сму́тный, нея́сный
shady ['ʃeɪdɪ] тени́стый; *coll.* тёмный, сомни́тельный; *side* теново́й
shaft [ʃɑːft] *tech.* вал
shaggy ['ʃægɪ] косма́тый
shake [ʃeɪk] **1.** [*irr.*] *v/t.* трясти́ (В *or* Т); тряхну́ть (Т) *pf.*; встря́хивать [-хну́ть]; *of explosion* потряса́ть [-сти́] (*a. fig.*); *faith* [по]колеба́ть; *finger, fist* [по]грози́ть; ***~ hands*** пожа́ть ру́ку друг дру́гу, обменя́ться рукопожа́тием; ***~ one's head*** покача́ть *pf.* голово́й; *v/i.* [за]трясти́сь; [за]дрожа́ть (***with, at*** от Р); **2.** дрожь *f*; потрясе́ние; **~n** ['ʃeɪkən] **1.** *p. pt. om* ***shake***; **2.** *adj.* потрясённый
shaky ['ʃeɪkɪ] □ *on one's legs* нетвёрдый; *hands* трясу́щийся; (*not firm*) ша́ткий; ***my German is ~*** я пло́хо зна́ю неме́цкий язы́к
shall [ʃæl] [*irr.*] *v/aux. вспом. глаго́л, образу́ющий бу́дущее (1-е лицо́ еди́нственного и мно́жественного числа́:)* ***I ~ do*** я бу́ду де́лать, я сде́лаю
shallow ['ʃæləʊ] **1.** ме́лкий; *fig.* пове́рхностный; **2.**: ***the ~s*** мелково́дье
sham [ʃæm] **1.** притво́рный; подде́льный; **2.** притво́рство; подде́лка; притво́рщик *m*; **3.** *v/t.* симули́ровать (*im*)*pf.*; *v/i.* притворя́ться [-ри́ться]
shamble ['ʃæmbl] волочи́ть но́ги
shambles ['ʃæmblz] (*disorder*) беспоря́док
shame [ʃeɪm] **1.** стыд; позо́р; ***for ~!*** сты́дно!; ***what a ~!*** кака́я жа́лость!; ***it's a ~ that ...*** жаль, что ...; ***put to ~*** [при]стыди́ть; **2.** [при]стыди́ть; [о]срами́ть; **~-faced** ['ʃeɪmfeɪst] □ пристыжённый, винова́тый вид; **~ful** ['ʃeɪmfl] □

постыдный; позорный; **~less** ['ʃeɪmlɪs] □ бесстыдный
shampoo [ʃæm'puː] **1.** шампунь *m*; мытьё головы; **2.** мыть шампунем
shamrock ['ʃæmrɒk] трилистник
shank [ʃæŋk] *anat.* голень *f*
shape [ʃeɪp] **1.** форма; (*outline*) очертание; **2.** *v/t.* созд(ав)ать; придавать форму, вид (Д); *v/i.* [с]формироваться; **~less** [~lɪs] бесформенный; **~ly** [~lɪ] хорошо сложённый
share [ʃeə] **1.** доля, часть *f*; (*participation*) участие; *fin.* акция; ***go ~s*** *pl.* платить поровну; ***have no ~ in*** не иметь отношения (к Д); **2.** *v/t.* [по]делиться (Т); *v/i.* участвовать (***in*** в П); **~holder** акционер
shark [ʃɑːk] акула (*a. fig.*)
sharp [ʃɑːp] **1.** □ *com.* острый (*a. fig.*); *fig.* (*clear in shape*) отчётливый; *turn* крутой; (*biting*) едкий; *pain* резкий; *voice* пронзительный; *remark* колкий; *coll.* продувной; **2.** *adv.* круто; точно; ***at 2 o'clock ~*** ровно в два часа; ***look ~!*** живо!; **3.** *mus.* диез; **~en** ['ʃɑːpən] [на]точить; заострять [-рить]; **~ener** ['ʃɑːpənə] (*pencil ~*) точилка; **~ness** ['ʃɑːpnɪs] острота; резкость *f*; **~-sighted** зоркий; **~-witted** остроумный
shatter ['ʃætə] разбивать вдребезги; *hope* разрушать [-рушить]; *health* расстраивать [-роить]
shave [ʃeɪv] **1.** [*irr.*] [по]брить(ся); *plank* [вы]строгать; **2.** бритьё; ***have a ~*** [по]бриться; ***have a close ~*** едва избежать опасности; **~n** ['ʃeɪvn] бритый
shaving ['ʃeɪvɪŋ] **1.** бритьё; **~s** *pl.* стружки *f/pl.*; **~ cream** крем для бритья
shawl [ʃɔːl] шаль *f*, головной платок
she [ʃiː] **1.** она; **2.** женщина; **she-...** самка: ***she-wolf*** волчица
sheaf [ʃiːf] *agric.* сноп; *of paper* связка
shear [ʃɪə] **1.** [*irr.*] *sheep* [о]стричь; *fig.* обдирать как липку; **2. ~s** *pl.* (большие) ножницы *f/pl.*
sheath [ʃiːθ] ножны *f/pl.*; **~e** [ʃiːð] вкладывать в ножны
sheaves [ʃiːvz] *pl. от* ***sheaf***
shed[1] [ʃed] [*irr*] *hair, etc.* [по]терять; *tears, blood* проли(ва)ть; *clothes, skin* сбрасывать [сбросить]; ***~ new light on s.th.*** проливать [-лить] свет (на В)
shed[2] [~] сарай
sheen [ʃiːn] блеск; *reflected* отблеск
sheep [ʃiːp] овца; **~dog** овчарка; **~ish** ['ʃiːpɪʃ] глуповатый; робкий; **~skin** овчина; ***~ coat, ~ jacket*** дублёнка, полушубок
sheer [ʃɪə] (*absolute*) полнейший; (*diaphanous*) прозрачный; (*steep*) отвесный; ***by ~ chance*** по чистой случайности; ***~ nonsense*** абсолютная чепуха; ***~ waste of time*** бесполезная трата времени
sheet [ʃiːt] простыня; *of paper, metal* лист; *of water, snow* широкая полоса; **~ iron** листовое железо; **~ lightning** зарница
shelf [ʃelf] полка; *of rock* уступ; *sea* шельф
shell [ʃel] **1.** (*nut ~*) скорлупа; *of mollusc* раковина; *of tortoise* панцирь *m*; *tech.* корпус; **2.** *eggs* очищать [очистить] от скорлупы; *peas* лущить; *mil.* обстреливать [-лять]; **~fish** моллюск
shelter ['ʃeltə] **1.** *bulding, etc.* приют (*a. fig.*), кров; убежище (*a. mil.*); **2.** *v/t.* приютить *pf.*; *v/i.* (*a.* ***take ~***) укры(ва)ться; приютиться *pf.*
shelve [ʃelv] *fig.* откладывать в долгий ящик
shelves [ʃelvz] *pl. от* ***shelf***
shepherd ['ʃepəd] **1.** пастух; **2.** *sheep* пасти; *people* [про]вести
sherry ['ʃerɪ] херес
shield [ʃiːld] **1.** щит; защита; ***ozone ~*** озонный слой; **2.** заслонять [-нить] (***from*** от Р)
shift [ʃɪft] **1.** *at work* смена; (*change*) изменение; (*move*) сдвиг; ***make ~ to*** ухитряться [-риться]; довольствоваться (***with*** Т); **2.** *v/t.* [поменять; перемещать [-местить]; *v/i.* изворачиваться [извернуться]; перемещаться [-меститься]; ***~ for o.s.*** обходиться без помощи; **~y** ['ʃɪftɪ] скользкий, *fig.* изворотливый,

ло́вкий; ~ ***reply*** укло́нчивый отве́т
shilling [ˈʃɪlɪŋ] ши́ллинг
shin [ʃɪn] *anat.* го́лень *f*
shine [ʃaɪn] **1.** сия́ние; свет; блеск, гля́нец; **2.** [*irr.*] сия́ть; свети́ть; блесте́ть; (*polish*) [от]полирова́ть; *shoes* [по]чи́стить; *fig.* блиста́ть
shingle [ˈʃɪŋgl] (*gravel*) га́лька
shiny [ˈʃaɪnɪ] □ (*polished*) начи́щенный; *through wear* лосня́щийся; (*bright*) блестя́щий
ship [ʃɪp] **1.** су́дно, кора́бль *m*; **2.** (*carry*) перевози́ть [-везти́]; **~board**: *naut.* ***on*** ~ на корабле́; **~building** судострое́ние; **~ment** [ˈʃɪpmənt] груз; погру́зка; **~owner** судовладе́лец; **~ping** [ˈʃɪpɪŋ] (*loading*) погру́зка; (*transport*) перево́зка; торго́вый флот, суда́ *n/pl.*; (*ship traffic*) судохо́дство; **~wreck 1.** кораблекруше́ние; **2.** потерпе́ть *pf.* кораблекруше́ние; **~yard** верфь *f*
shirk [ʃɜːk] увиливать [-льну́ть] от (Р); **~er** [ˈʃɜːkə] ло́дырь *m*; уви́ливающий (от Р)
shirt [ʃɜːt] руба́шка, соро́чка; *woman's also* блу́зка; **~sleeves**: ***in one's*** ~ без пиджака́
shiver [ˈʃɪvə] **1.** дрожь *f*; **2.** [за]дрожа́ть
shoal[1] [ʃəʊl] мелково́дье; мель *f*
shoal[2] [~] *of fish* ста́я, кося́к
shock [ʃɒk] **1.** *fig.* потрясе́ние; *med.* шок; **2.** *fig.* потряса́ть [-ясти́]; шоки́ровать; ~ ***absorber*** *mot.* амортиза́тор; **~ing** [ˈʃɒkɪŋ] □ сканда́льный; ужа́сный; потряса́ющий
shod [ʃɒd] *pt. и pt. p. от* ***shoe***
shoddy [ˈʃɒdɪ] *goods, etc.* дрянно́й
shoe [ʃuː] **1.** ту́фля; *heavy* башма́к; *above ankle* полуботи́нок; (*horse* ~) подко́ва; **2.** [*irr.*] обу́(ва́)ть; подко́вывать [-кова́ть]; **~horn** рожо́к; **~lace** шнуро́к для боти́нок; **~maker** сапо́жник; ~ **polish** крем для о́буви
shone [ʃɒn] *pt. и pt. p. от* ***shine***
shook [ʃʊk] *pt. от* ***shake***
shoot [ʃuːt] **1.** *bot.* росто́к, побе́г; **2.** [*irr.*] *v/t.* стреля́ть; (*kill*) [за]стрели́ть *pf.*; (*execute by shooting*) расстре́ливать [-ля́ть]; *cine.* снима́ть [снять], засня́ть *pf.*; *v/i.* стреля́ть [вы́стрелить]; *of pain* дёргать; (*a.* ~ ***along***, ***past***) проноси́ться [-нести́сь]; промелькну́ть *pf.*; промча́ться *pf.*; ~ ***ahead*** ри́нуться вперёд; **~er** [ˈʃuːtə] стрело́к
shooting [ˈʃuːtɪŋ] стрельба́; *hunt.* охо́та; *cine.* съёмка; ~ ***star*** па́дающая звезда́
shop [ʃɒp] **1.** магази́н; (*work* ~) мастерска́я; ***talk*** ~ говори́ть о рабо́те со свои́ми колле́гами; **2.** де́лать поку́пки (*mst.* ***go ~ping***); **~keeper** владе́лец магази́на; **~per** [ˈ~ə] покупа́тель *m*; **~ping** [ˈ~ɪŋ]: ~ ***center***(***-tre***) торго́вый центр; ~ **window** витри́на
shore [ʃɔː] бе́рег; взмо́рье; побере́жье; ***on the*** ~ на́ берег, на берегу́
shorn [ʃɔːn] *pt. p. от* ***shear***
short [ʃɔːt] коро́ткий; (*brief*) кра́ткий; *in height* невысо́кий; (*insufficient*) недоста́точный; (*not complete*) непо́лный; *answer* ре́зкий, сухо́й; *pastry* песо́чный; ***in*** ~ коро́че говоря́; вкра́тце; ***fall ~ of*** уступа́ть в чём-л.; *expectations, etc.* не опра́вдывать [-да́ть]; ***cut*** ~ пре́р(ы)ва́ть; ***run*** ~ иссяка́ть [-я́кнуть]; ***stop ~ of*** не доезжа́ть [дое́хать], не доходи́ть [дойти́] до (Р) (*a. fig.*); **~age** [ˈʃɔːtɪdʒ] нехва́тка, дефици́т; **~-circuit** коро́ткое замыка́ние; **~-coming** недоста́ток; изъя́н; **~cut** кратча́йший путь *m*; **~en** [ˈʃɔːtn] *v/t.* сокраща́ть [-рати́ть]; укора́чивать [-роти́ть]; *v/i.* сокраща́ться [-рати́ться]; укора́чиваться [-роти́ться]; **~hand** стеногра́фия; **~ly** [ˈʃɔːtlɪ] *adv.* вско́ре; **~s** [~s] *pl.* шо́рты; **~-sighted** близору́кий; **~-term** краткосро́чный; ~ **wave** коротково́лновый; **~-winded** страда́ющий оды́шкой
shot [ʃɒt] **1.** *pt. и pt. p. от* ***shoot***; **2.** вы́стрел; *collect.* дробь *f*, дроби́нка (*mst.* ***small*** ~); *pers.* стрело́к; *sport* ядро́; *stroke, in ball games* уда́р; *phot.* сни́мок; *med.* инъе́кция; ***have a*** ~ сде́лать *pf.* попы́тку; *coll.* ***not by a long*** ~ отню́дь не; **~gun** дробови́к
should [ʃʊd, ʃəd] *pt. от* ***shall***

S

shoulder ['ʃəʊldə] **1.** плечо́; **2.** взва́ливать на пле́чи; *fig.* брать на себя́; ~ **blade** *anat.* лопа́тка; ~ **strap** брете́лька; *mil.* пого́н
shout [ʃaʊt] **1.** крик; во́зглас; **2.** [за]крича́ть [кри́кнуть]; [на]крича́ть (***at*** на В)
shove [ʃʌv] **1.** толчо́к; **2.** толка́ть [-кну́ть]; ~ ***off*** ста́лкивать [столкну́ть]; отта́лкивать [оттолкну́ть]
shovel ['ʃʌvl] **1.** (*spade*) лопа́та; *for use in home* сово́к; **2.** сгреба́ть лопа́той
show [ʃəʊ] **1.** [*irr.*] *v/t.* (*manifest*) ока́зывать [-за́ть]; (*exhibit*) выставля́ть [вы́ставить]; *interest, etc.* проявля́ть [-ви́ть]; (*prove*) дока́зывать [-за́ть]; ~ ***in*** вводи́ть [ввести́]; ~ ***up*** (*expose*) разоблача́ть [-ачи́ть]; *v/i. coll.* (*appear*) появля́ться [-ви́ться]; ~ ***off*** [по]щеголя́ть; пуска́ть пыль в глаза́; **2.** (*spectacle*) зре́лище; (*exhibition*) вы́ставка; (*outward appearance*) ви́димость *f*; *thea.* спекта́кль *m*; **~case** витри́на
shower ['ʃaʊə] **1.** ли́вень *m*; душ; ***take a*** ~ принима́ть [-ня́ть] душ; **2.** ли́ться ли́внем; *fig.* осыпа́ть [осы́пать]; *questions* засыпа́ть [-пать]; **~y** ['ʃaʊərɪ] дождли́вый
show|n [ʃəʊn] *pt. p. om* ***show***; **~room** вы́ставочный зал; ~ **window** *Am.* витри́на; **~y** ['ʃəʊɪ] показно́й
shrank [ʃræŋk] *pt. om* ***shrink***
shred [ʃred] **1.** *of cloth* лоскуто́к; *of paper* клочо́к; ***tear to ~s*** разорва́ть [разрыва́ть] в кло́чья; **2.** [*irr.*] ре́зать, рвать на клочки́; *cul.* [на]шинкова́ть
shrewd [ʃruːd] проница́тельный; *in business* де́льный, расчётливый
shriek [ʃriːk] **1.** визг, крик, вопль *m*; **2.** [за]вопи́ть, [за]визжа́ть
shrill [ʃrɪl] □ пронзи́тельный, ре́зкий
shrimp [ʃrɪmp] *zo.* креве́тка; *coll. pers.* сморчо́к
shrine [ʃraɪn] святы́ня
shrink [ʃrɪŋk] [*irr.*] (*become smaller*) сокраща́ться [-рати́ться]; *of wood, etc.* усыха́ть [усо́хнуть]; *of cloth* сади́ться [сесть]; *recoil* отпрянуть
shrivel ['ʃrɪvl] смо́рщи(ва)ть(ся); съёжи(ва)ться
shroud [ʃraʊd] **1.** са́ван; *fig.* покро́в; **2.** оку́т(ыв)ать (*a. fig.*)
shrub [ʃrʌb] куст; ***~s*** *pl.* куста́рник
shrug [ʃrʌg] пож(им)а́ть плеча́ми
shrunk [ʃrʌŋk] *pt. u pt. p. om* ***shrink*** (*a.* ***~en***)
shudder ['ʃʌdə] **1.** дрожа́ть *impf.*; содрога́ться [-гну́ться]; ***I ~ to think*** я содрога́юсь при мы́сли об э́том; **2.** дрожь *f*
shuffle ['ʃʌfl] **1.** ша́ркать; *cards* [пере]тасова́ть; ~ ***off*** *responsibility* перекла́дывать [переложи́ть] отве́тственность на други́х; **2.** ша́рканье; тасо́вка
shun [ʃʌn] избега́ть [-ежа́ть] (Р)
shunt [ʃʌnt] *fig. coll.* (*postpone*) откла́дывать [отложи́ть]
shut [ʃʌt] [*irr.*] **1.** закры́(ва́)ть(ся), затворя́ть(ся) [-ри́ть(ся)]; ~ ***down*** (*close*) закрыва́ть [-ры́ть]; ~ ***up!*** замолчи́!; **2.** закры́тый; **~ter** ['ʃʌtə] ста́вень *m*; *phot.* затво́р
shuttle ['ʃʌtl] (*device for weaving*) челно́к; ~ ***service*** челно́чные ре́йсы; при́городный по́езд
shy [ʃaɪ] *animal* пугли́вый; *person* засте́нчивый
shyness ['ʃaɪnɪs] засте́нчивость *f*
Siberian [saɪ'bɪərɪən] **1.** сиби́рский; **2.** сибиря́к *m*, -я́чка *f*
sick [sɪk] **1.** больно́й (***of*** Т); чу́вствующий тошноту́; уста́вший (***of*** от П); ***I am ~ of ...*** мне надое́ло (+ *inf.*, И); ***I feel ~*** меня́ тошни́т; **~en** ['sɪkən] *v/i.* заболе́(ва́)ть; [за]ча́хнуть; ~ ***at*** чу́вствовать отвраще́ние к (Д); *v/t.* де́лать больны́м; вызыва́ть тошноту́ у (Р)
sickle ['sɪkl] серп
sick|-leave: ***I am on ~*** я на больни́чном; **~ly** ['sɪklɪ] боле́зненный; (*causing nausea*) тошнотво́рный; (*puny*) хи́лый; **~ness** ['sɪknɪs] боле́знь *f*; тошнота́; ~ **pay** вы́плата по больни́чному листу́
side [saɪd] **1.** *com.* сторона́; бок; (*edge*) край; ***~ by ~*** бок о́ бок; ***to be on the safe ~*** на вся́кий слу́чай; ***on the one ~ ... on the other ~*** с одно́й стороны́ ... с друго́й стороны́; ***take the ~ of*** примыка́ть к той и́ли

S

ино́й стороне́ (P); **2.** *attr.* боково́й; *effect, etc.* побо́чный; **3.** **~ *with*** встать *pf.* на сто́рону (P); **~board** буфе́т, серва́нт; **~car** *mot.* коля́ска мотоци́кла; **~light** *mot.* подфа́рник; **~-long**: **~ *glance*** взгляд и́скоса; **~-walk** *Am.* тротуа́р
siding ['saɪdɪŋ] *rail.* запа́сный путь *m*
sidle ['saɪdl] подходи́ть бочко́м
siege [siːdʒ] оса́да; ***lay ~ to*** осажда́ть [осади́ть]
sieve [sɪv] си́то
sift [sɪft] просе́ивать [-е́ять]; *fig.* [про]анализи́ровать
sigh [saɪ] **1.** вздох; **2.** вздыха́ть [вздохну́ть]
sight [saɪt] **1.** зре́ние; вид; взгля́д; (*spectacle*) зре́лище; *of gun* прице́л; **~s** *pl.* достопримеча́тельности *f/pl.*; ***catch ~ of*** ви́деть, заме́тить *pf.*; ***lose ~ of*** потеря́ть из ви́ду; **2.** уви́деть *pf.*; **~seeing** ['saɪtsiːɪŋ] осмо́тр достопримеча́тельностей
sign [saɪn] **1.** знак; при́знак; симпто́м; *over a shop* вы́веска; ***as a ~ of*** в знак (P); **2.** *v/i.* подава́ть знак (Д); *v/t.* подпи́сывать [-са́ть]
signal ['sɪgnəl] **1.** сигна́л; **2.** [по]дава́ть сигна́л; подава́ть [-да́ть] знак; [про]сигна́лить
signature ['sɪgnətʃə] по́дпись *f*
sign|board вы́веска; **~er** ['saɪnə] лицо́, подписа́вшее како́й-либо докуме́нт
signet ['sɪgnɪt]: **~ *ring*** кольцо́ с печа́ткой
signific|ance [sɪg'nɪfɪkəns] значе́ние; **~ant** [~kənt] значи́тельный; *look* многозначи́тельный; ва́жный
signify ['sɪgnɪfaɪ] зна́чить, означа́ть
signpost доро́жный указа́тель *m*
silence ['saɪləns] **1.** молча́ние; тишина́; безмо́лвие; **~!** ти́хо!; **2.** заста́вить *pf.* молча́ть; заглуша́ть [-ши́ть]; **~r** [~ə] *mot.* глуши́тель *m*
silent ['saɪlənt] безмо́лвный; молчали́вый; (*noiseless*) бесшу́мный
silk [sɪlk] **1.** шёлк; **2.** (*made of silk*) шёлковый; **~en** ['sɪlkən] (*resembling silk*) шелкови́стый; **~worm** шелкови́чный червь *m*; **~y** ['sɪlkɪ] шелкови́стый
sill [sɪl] *of window* подоко́нник
silly ['sɪlɪ] □ глу́пый; ***don't be ~*** не валя́й дурака́
silt [sɪlt] **1.** ил; **2.** заи́ливаться (*mst.* **~ *up***)
silver ['sɪlvə] **1.** серебро́; **2.** (*made of silver*) сере́бряный; **~y** [~rɪ] серебри́стый
similar ['sɪmɪlə] □ схо́дный (с T), похо́жий (на B); подо́бный, аналоги́чный; **~ity** [sɪmə'lærətɪ] схо́дство; подо́бие
simile ['sɪmɪlɪ] сравне́ние
simmer ['sɪmə] ме́дленно кипе́ть; держа́ть на ме́дленном огне́
simple ['sɪmpl] просто́й; несло́жный; **~hearted** простоду́шный; на́ивный; **~ton** [~tən] проста́к
simpli|city [sɪm'plɪsətɪ] простота́; простоду́шие; **~fy** ['sɪmplɪfaɪ] упроща́ть [-ости́ть]
simply ['sɪmplɪ] про́сто
simulate ['sɪmjʊleɪt] симули́ровать (*im*)*pf.*; притворя́ться [-ори́ться]
simultaneous [sɪml'teɪnɪəs] □ одновре́менный; **~ *interpretation*** синхро́нный перево́д; **~ *interpreter*** перево́дчик-синхрони́ст
sin [sɪn] **1.** грех; **2.** согреша́ть [-ши́ть], [по]греши́ть
since [sɪns] **1.** *prp.* с (P); **2.** *adv.* с тех пор; ... тому́ наза́д; **3.** *cj.* с тех пор, как; так как; поско́льку
sincer|e [sɪn'sɪə] □ и́скренний; **~ely**: ***yours ~*** и́скренне Ваш, *formal* с глубо́ким уваже́нием; **~ity** [sɪn'serətɪ] и́скренность *f*
sinew ['sɪnjuː] сухожи́лие; **~y** [~ɪ] жи́листый
sinful ['sɪnfl] □ гре́шный
sing [sɪŋ] [*irr.*] [с]петь; **~ *s.o.'s praises*** петь кому-л. дифира́мбы
singe [sɪndʒ] опаля́ть [-ли́ть]
singer ['sɪŋgə] пев́ец *m*, певи́ца *f*
single ['sɪŋgl] **1.** □ еди́нственный; одино́чный; (*alone*) одино́кий; (*not married*) холосто́й, незаму́жняя; ***in ~ file*** гусько́м; **2.**: **~ *out*** отбира́ть [отобра́ть]; **~-breasted** однобо́ртный; **~-handed** самостоя́тельно, без посторо́нней по́мощи; **~-minded** целеустремлённый; **~t** ['sɪŋglɪt] ма́йка
singular ['sɪŋgjʊlə] необыча́йный;

S

стра́нный; *gr.* еди́нственный; **~ity** [sıŋgjʊ'lærətı] осо́бенность *f*, необыча́йность *f*
sinister ['sınıstə] злове́щий
sink [sıŋk] **1.** [*irr.*] *v/i.* (*fall*) опуска́ться [-сти́ться] (*a. of sun, etc.*); [за-, по-, у]тону́ть; *fig.* погружа́ться [-узи́ться]; (*subside*) оседа́ть [осе́сть]; **~ or swim** будь что бу́дет; *v/t.* затопля́ть [-пи́ть]; **2.** *in kitchen* ра́ковина
sinless ['sınlıs] безгре́шный
sinner ['sınə] гре́шник *m*, -ица *f*
sip [sıp] пить ма́ленькими глотка́ми
siphon ['saıfn] сифо́н
sir [sɜː] *form of adress* су́дарь *m*; ♀ сэр
siren ['saıərən] сире́на
sirloin ['sɜːlɔın] филе́йная часть
sister ['sıstə] сестра́; **~-in-law** [~rınlɔː] сестра́ му́жа (жены́); **~ly** [~lı] се́стринский
sit [sıt] [*irr.*] *v/i.* сиде́ть; *of assembly* заседа́ть; **~ down** сади́ться [сесть]; **~ for** *paint.* пози́ровать; **~ for an examination** сдава́ть экза́мен
site [saıt] ме́сто, местоположе́ние; **building ~** строи́тельная площа́дка
sitting ['sıtıŋ] заседа́ние; **~ room** гости́ная
situat|ed ['sıtjʊeıtıd] располо́женный; **~ion** [sıtʃʊ'eıʃn] положе́ние; ситуа́ция; (*job*) ме́сто
six [sıks] **1.** шесть; **2.** шестёрка; **~teen** [sık'stiːn] шестна́дцать; **~teenth** [sık'stiːnθ] шестна́дцатый; **~th** [sıksθ] **1.** шесто́й; **2.** шеста́я часть *f*; **~tieth** ['sıkstııəθ] шестидеся́тый; **~ty** ['sıkstı] шестьдеся́т
size [saız] **1.** величина́; *of books, etc.* форма́т; (*dimension*) разме́р (*a. of shoes, clothing*); **2. ~ up** определи́ть взве́сить *fig.* оцени́ть *pf.*, поня́ть *pf.*
siz(e)able ['saızəbl] поря́дочного разме́ра
sizzle ['sızl] шкворча́ть, шипе́ть
skat|e [skeıt] **1.** конёк (*pl.*: коньки́); **2.** ката́ться на конька́х; **~er** ['skeıtə] конькобе́жец *m*, -жка *f*
skein [skeın] мото́к пря́жи
skeleton ['skelıtn] *anat.* скеле́т; *tech.* о́стов, карка́с; **~ key** отмы́чка
skeptic, *Brt.* **sceptic** ['skeptık] скéптик; **~al** [~tıkl] □ скепти́ческий
sketch [sketʃ] **1.** эски́з, набро́сок; **2.** де́лать набро́сок, эски́з (P); **~y** ['~ı] пове́рхностный
ski [skiː] **1.** (*pl.* **~** *или* **~s**) лы́жа; **2.** ходи́ть на лы́жах
skid [skıd] **1.** *mot.* юз, зано́с; *of wheels* буксова́ние; **2.** *v/i.* буксова́ть; идти́ [пойти́] ю́зом; *of person* скользи́ть
skillful, *Brt.* **skilful** ['skılfl] □ иску́сный, уме́лый
skill [skıl] мастерство́, уме́ние; **~ed** [~d] квалифици́рованный, иску́сный
skim [skım] *cream, scum, etc.* снима́ть [снять]; (*glide*) скользи́ть [-зну́ть] по (Д); (*read*) просма́тривать [-смотре́ть]; **~ over** бе́гло прочи́тывать; **~med milk** сня́тое молоко́
skimp [skımp] эконо́мить; [по]скупи́ться (**on** на В); **~y** ['skımpı] □ ску́дный
skin [skın] **1.** ко́жа; (*hide*) шку́ра; *of apricot, etc.* кожура́; **2.** *v/t.* сдира́ть ко́жу, шку́ру с (Р); **~-deep** пове́рхностный; **~ diver** аквалангист; **~flint** скря́га *m*; **~ny** ['skını] то́щий; **~ tight** в обтя́жку
skip [skıp] **1.** прыжо́к, скачо́к; **2.** *v/i.* [по]скака́ть; *fig.* переска́кивать [-скочи́ть] (**from** с [Р]), (**to** на [В]); *v/t.* (*omit*) пропуска́ть [-сти́ть]
skipper ['skıpə] капита́н
skirmish ['skɜːmıʃ] *mil.* сты́чка (*a. fig.*)
skirt [skɜːt] **1.** (*waist-down garment or part of a dress*) ю́бка; *of coat* пола́; (*edge*) край, окра́ина; **2.** *v/t.* обходи́ть [обойти́]; объезжа́ть [-е́хать]
skit [skıt] сати́ра, паро́дия
skittle ['skıtl] ке́гля; **play (at) ~s** *pl.* игра́ть в ке́гли; **~ alley** кегельба́н
skulk [skʌlk] кра́сться
skull [skʌl] че́реп
sky [skaı] не́бо (небеса́ *pl.*); **praise to the skies** расхва́ливать до небе́с; **out of a clear ~** как гром среди́ я́сного не́ба; **~lark 1.** жа́воронок; **2.** выки́дывать шту́чки;

~light световóй люк; **~line** горизóнт; *of buildings, etc.* очертáние; **~scraper** небоскрёб; **~ward(s)** ['skaɪwəd(z)] к нéбу
slab [slæb] плитá
slack [slæk] **1.** (*remiss*) нерадúвый; *behavio(u)r* расхля́банный; (*loose*) слáбый; (*slow*) мéдленный; *rope, etc.* слáбо натя́нутый; (*a. comm.*) вя́лый; **2.** *naut. of rope* слабúна; **~s** *pl.* брю́ки *f/pl.*; **3.** = **~en** ['slækn] ослабля́ть [-áбить]; [о]слáбнуть; замедля́ть [-éдлить]
slain [sleɪn] *p. pt. от* ***slay***
slake [sleɪk] *thirst* утоля́ть [-лúть]
slalom ['slɑːləm] слалóм
slam [slæm] **1.** хлóпанье; **2.** хлóпать [-пнуть] (T); захлóпывать(ся) [-пнуть(ся)]
slander ['slɑːndə] **1.** клеветá; **2.** [на]клеветáть; **~ous** [~rəs] □ клеветнúческий
slang [slæŋ] сленг; жаргóн
slant [slɑːnt] склон, уклóн (*a. fig.*); тóчка зрéния; **~ed** [~ɪd] (*biased*) тенденциóзный; **~ing** [~ɪŋ] □ *adj.* наклóнный; косóй
slap [slæp] **1.** шлепóк; ***~ in the face*** пощёчина; **2.** шлёпать [-пнуть]; *on back, etc.* хлóпать [-пнуть]
slash [slæʃ] **1.** разрéз; **2.** (*wound*) [по]рáнить; *with whip, etc.* [ис]полосовáть [полоснýть]
slate [sleɪt] слáнец; *for roof* шúфер
slattern ['slætən] неря́ха
slaughter ['slɔːtə] **1.** убóй (скотá); *fig.* резня́, кровопролúтие; **2.** [за-] рéзать; забивáть [-бúть]; **~house** бóйня
Slav [slɑːv] **1.** славянúн *m*, -я́нка *f*; **2.** славя́нский
slave [sleɪv] **1.** раб *m*, -ы́ня *f*; *attr.* рáбский; **2.** рабóтать как кáторжник
slav|ery ['sleɪvərɪ] рáбство; **~ish** [~vɪʃ] □ рáбский
slay [sleɪ] [*irr.*] убú(вá)ть
sled [sled], **sledge**[1] [sledʒ] сáни *f/pl.*; *child's* сáнки *f/pl.*
sledge[2] [~] (*~ hammer*) кузнéчный мóлот
sleek [sliːk] **1.** □ *animal's coat* глáдкий и блестя́щий; *manner* вкрáдчивый
sleep [sliːp] **1.** [*irr.*] *v/i.* [по]спáть; ***~ like a log*** спать мёртвым сном; ***~ on it*** отложúть *pf.* до зáвтра; *v/t.* давáть (комý-нибудь) ночлéг; ***put to ~*** *animal* усыпля́ть [-пúть]; **2.** сон; **~er** ['~ə] спя́щий; *rail* спáльный вагóн; **~ing** ['~ɪŋ]: ***~ bag*** спáльный мешóк; ***~ pill*** таблéтка снотвóрного; ***~ing car*** *rail.* спáльный вагóн; **~less** ['~lɪs] □ бессóнный; **~-walker** лунáтик; **~y** ['~ɪ] □ сóнный, *coll.* зáспанный
sleet [sliːt] мóкрый снег; **~y** ['sliːtɪ] сля́котный
sleeve [sliːv] рукáв; *tech.* мýфта; втýлка
sleigh [sleɪ] сáни *f/pl.*
sleight [slaɪt] (*mst.* ***~ of hand***) лóвкость *f* (рук)
slender ['slendə] □ стрóйный; тóнкий; (*scanty*) скýдный
slept [slept] *pt. и pt. p. от* ***sleep***
sleuth [sluːθ] *joc.* сы́щик, детектúв
slew [sluː] *pt. от* ***slay***
slice [slaɪs] **1.** лóмоть *m*, *dim.* лóмтик; (*part*) часть *f*; **2.** [на]рéзать лóмтиками
slick [slɪk] *coll.* глáдкий; *Am.* хúтрый, скóльзкий
slid [slɪd] *pt. и pt. p. от* ***slide***
slide [slaɪd] **1.** [*irr.*] скользúть [-знýть]; катáться по льдý; вдвигáть [-úнуть], всóвывать [всýнуть] (*into* в В); ***let things ~*** относúться ко всемý спустя́ рукавá; **2.** *photo.* диапозитúв, слайд; **3.** скольжéние; *for children* дéтская гóрка; *land~* óползень *m*; **~ rule** логарифмúческая линéйка
slight [slaɪt] **1.** □ (*thin and delicate*) тóнкий, хрýпкий; незначúтельный; слáбый; ***not the ~est idea*** ни малéйшего представлéния; **2.** (*disrespect*) пренебрежéние; **3.** обижáть [-úдеть]; унижáть [-úзить]
slim [slɪm] (*slender*) тóнкий, тóненький; *person* стрóйный; ***~ hope*** слáбая надéжда
slim|e [slaɪm] (*mud*) жúдкая грязь *f*; (*silt*) ил; **~y** ['slaɪmɪ] слúзистый, скóльзкий
sling [slɪŋ] **1.** *bandage* пéревязь; **2.** *throw* [*irr.*] швыря́ть [швырнýть]
slink [slɪŋk] [*irr.*] крáсться; ***~ off***

S

потихо́ньку отходи́ть [отойти́]

slip [slɪp] **1.** [*irr.*] *v/i.* скользи́ть; поскользну́ться *pf.*; *out of hands* выскольза́ть [вы́скользнуть]; *of wheels* буксова́ть; *v/t.* сова́ть [су́нуть]; *one's attention* ускольза́ть [-зну́ть]; **~ a p.'s memory** вылететь из головы́ (Р); **~ on** (**off**) наде́(ва́)ть, сбра́сывать [сбро́сить]; **2.** скольже́ние; *of paper* поло́ска; про́мах; оши́бка; *in writing* опи́ска; (*petticoat*) комбина́ция; (*pillowcase*) на́волочка; **give a p. the ~** ускольза́ть [-зну́ть] от (Р); **~ of the tongue** огово́рка; **~per** ['slɪpə] ко́мнатная ту́фля; **~pery** ['slɪpərɪ] ско́льзкий; (*not safe*) ненадёжный; **~shod** ['slɪpʃɒd] неря́шливый; (*careless*) небре́жный; **~t** [slɪpt] *pt. u p. pt. om* **slip**

slit [slɪt] **1.** разре́з; щель *f*; **2.** [*irr.*] разре́зать в длину́

sliver ['slɪvə] *of wood* ще́пка; *of glass* оско́лок

slogan [sləʊgən] ло́зунг

slop [slɒp] **1.**: **~s** *pl.* помо́и *m/pl.*; **2.** (*spill*) проли́(ва́)ть; расплёскивать (-ся) [-еска́ть(ся)]

slop|e [sləʊp] **1.** накло́н, склон, скат; **2.** клони́ться; име́ть накло́н; **~ing** ['~ɪŋ] пока́тый

sloppy ['slɒpɪ] (*slovenly*) неря́шливый; (*careless*) небре́жный; сентимента́льный

slot [slɒt] щель *f*; про́резь *f*; паз; (*place or job*) ме́сто

sloth [sləʊθ] лень *f*, ле́ность *f*; *zo.* лени́вец

slot machine иго́рный (торго́вый) автома́т

slouch [slaʊtʃ] **1.** [с]суту́литься; *when sitting* [с]го́рбиться; **~ about, around** слоня́ться без де́ла; **2.** суту́лость *f*

slovenly ['slʌvnlɪ] неря́шливый

slow [sləʊ] **1.** ме́дленный; медли́тельный; (*dull in mind*) тупо́й; *trade* вя́лый; *watch* отст(ав)а́ть; **2.** (*a.* **~ down, up**) замедля́ть(ся) [заме́длить(ся)]; **~poke** (*or chiefly Brt.* **~coach**) копу́ша; **~-witted** тупо́й, тупова́тый

slug [slʌg] слизня́к

slugg|ard ['slʌgəd] лежебо́ка *m/f.*; **~ish** ['slʌgɪʃ] ме́дленный, вя́лый

sluice [slu:s] шлюз

slum [slʌm] *mst.* **~s** *pl.* трущо́бы

slumber ['slʌmbə] **1.** дремо́та; сон; **2.** дрема́ть; спать

slump [slʌmp] **1.** *of prices, demand* ре́зкое паде́ние; **2.** ре́зко па́дать; *into a chair, etc.* тяжело́ опуска́ться

slung [slʌŋ] *pt. u pt. p. om* **sling**

slunk [slʌŋk] *pt. u pt. p. om* **slink**

slur [slɜ:] **1.** *in speech* невня́тная речь; *on reputation, etc.* пятно́; **2.** *v/t.* говори́ть невня́тно; **~ over** ума́лчивать [-молча́ть], опуска́ть [-сти́ть]; *fig. coll.* сма́зывать [сма́зать]

slush [slʌʃ] сля́коть *f*; та́лый снег

sly [slaɪ] □ хи́трый; лука́вый; **on the ~** тайко́м

smack[1] [smæk]: **~ of** име́ть (при́-) вкус; па́хнуть (Т)

smack[2] [~] **1.** (*kiss*) зво́нкий поцелу́й; (*slap*) шлепо́к; **2.** *lips* чмо́кать [-кнуть]; хло́пать [-пнуть] (Т); шлёпать [-пнуть]

small [smɔ:l] *com.* ма́ленький, небольшо́й; *mistakes, etc.* ме́лкий; незначи́тельный; **~ change** ме́лочь *f*; **~ fry** ме́лкая рыбёшка; **~ of the back** *anat.* поясни́ца; **in the ~ hours** под у́тро; в предрассве́тные часы́; **~ arms** *pl.* стре́лковое ору́жие; **~pox** *med.* о́спа; **~ talk** лёгкий, бессодержа́тельный разгово́р; све́тская болтовня́

smart [smɑ:t] **1.** □ *blow* ре́зкий, си́льный; (*clever*) ло́вкий; у́мный; (*stylish*) элега́нтный; (*witty*) остроу́мный; (*fashionable*) мо́дный; **2.** боль *f*; **3.** боле́ть, садни́ть; *fig.* страда́ть; **~ness** ['smɑ:tnɪs] наря́дность *f*, элега́нтность *f*, ло́вкость *f*

smash [smæʃ] **1.** *v/t. enemy* сокруша́ть [-ши́ть] *a. fig.*; разбива́ть вдре́безги; *v/i.* разби́(ва́)ться; ста́лкиваться [столкну́ться] (**into** с Т); **~-up** (*collision*) столкнове́ние; катастро́фа

smattering ['smætərɪŋ] пове́рхностное зна́ние; небольшо́е коли́чество чего́-то

smear [smɪə] **1.** пятно́; мазо́к (*a. med.*); **2.** [на]ма́зать, изма́з(ыв)ать

S

smell [smel] **1.** зáпах; *sense* обоня́ние; **2.** [*irr.*] [по]чу́вствовать зáпах; *of animal* [по]чу́ять (В); (*a.* **~ *at***) [по]ню́хать (В); **~ *of*** пáхнуть (Т)

smelt[1] [smelt] *pt. и pt. p. om* ***smell***

smelt[2] [~] выплавля́ть [вы́плавить]

smile [smaɪl] **1.** улы́бка; **2.** улыбáться [-бну́ться]

smirk [smɜːk] ухмыля́ться [-льну́ться]

smite [smaɪt] [*irr.*] (*afflict*) поражáть [-рази́ть]; ***she was smitten with sorrow*** онá былá уби́та гóрем

smith [smɪθ]: ***black~*** кузнéц

smithereens ['smɪðə'riːnz]: ***break into ~*** разбивáть [-би́ть] вдрéбезги

smithy ['smɪðɪ] ку́зница

smitten ['smɪtn] *pt. p. om* ***smite***

smock [smɒk] *child's* дéтский халáтик; *woman's* жéнская [крестья́нская) блу́за

smoke [sməʊk] **1.** дым; ***have a ~*** покури́ть *pf.*; ***go up in ~*** кóнчиться *pf.* ничéм; **2.** кури́ть; [на]дыми́ть; (*emit ~*) [за]дыми́ться; *tobacco, etc.* выку́ривать [вы́курить] (*a.* **~ *out***); **~dried** копчёный; **~less** ['~lɪs] безды́мный; **~r** ['~ə] куря́щий; *rail coll.* вагóн для куря́щих; **~stack** дымовáя трубá

smoking ['sməʊkɪŋ] куря́щий; **~ compartment** *rail.* купé для куря́щих; **~ room** кóмната для курéния

smoky ['sməʊkɪ] ды́мный; наку́ренный

smolder, *Brt.* **smoulder** ['sməʊldə] тлеть

smooth [smuːð] **1.** □ глáдкий; *takeoff, etc.* плáвный; (*calm*) спокóйный; (*ingratiating*) вкрáдчивый; (*flattering*) льсти́вый; **2.** приглáживать [-лáдить]; **~ *out*** разглáживать [-лáдить]; *fig.* (*a.* **~ *over***) смягчáть [-чи́ть]; *differences* сглáживать [-áдить]

smote [sməʊt] *pt. om* ***smite***

smother ['smʌðə] [за]души́ть; *anger, etc.* подави́ть *pf.*

smudge [smʌdʒ] **1.** [за]пáчкать(ся); **2.** гря́зное пятнó

smug [smʌg] самодовóльный

smuggle ['smʌgl] занимáться контрабáндой; провози́ть контрабáндой; **~r** [~ə] контрабанди́ст *m*, -ка *f*

smut [smʌt] **1.** (*soot*) сáжа, кóпоть *f*; (*fungus, crop disease*) головня́; (*obscene language*) непристóйность *f*; ***a talk ~*** нести́ похабщину

smutty ['smʌtɪ] □ гря́зный

snack [snæk] лёгкая заку́ска; ***have a ~*** перекуси́ть; **~-bar** заку́сочная

snag [snæg] *fig.* препя́тствие; ***there's a ~*** в э́том загвóздка

snail [sneɪl] *zo.* ули́тка; ***at a ~'s pace*** мéдленно как черепáха

snake [sneɪk] *zo.* змея́

snap [snæp] **1.** (*noise*) щелчóк; треск; (*fastener*) кнóпка, застёжка; *coll.* (*photo*) сни́мок; *fig.* (*zest*) живость; ***cold ~*** внезáпное похолодáние; **2.** *v/i.* (*break*) [с]ломáться; (*make a sharp noise*) щёлкать [-кнуть]; (*snatch*) ухвáтываться [ухвати́ться] (***at*** за В); *of a dog, a. fig.* огрызáться [-зну́ться] (***at*** на В); (*break, as a string, etc.*) [по-] рвáться; (*close, as a fastener*) защёлкивать [защёлкнуть]; *phot.* дéлать сни́мок (Р); **~ *out of it!*** брóсь(те)!, встряхни́тесь!; **~** *up* (*buy up*) раскупáть [-пи́ть]; **~dragon** льви́ный зев; **~ fastener** кнóпка (застёжка); **~pish** ['snæpɪʃ] □ раздражи́тельный; **~py** ['snæpɪ] *coll.* энерги́чный; живóй; ***make it ~!*** поживée; **~shot** *phot.* сни́мок

snare [sneə] **1.** силóк; *fig.* лову́шка, западня́; **2.** лови́ть [поймáть] силкáми *m/pl.*

snarl [snɑːl] **1.** рычáние; **2.** [про-] рычáть; *fig.* огрызáться [-зну́ться]

snatch [snætʃ] **1.** рывóк; (*a grab*) хватáние; (*fragment*) обры́вок; кусóчек; **2.** хватáть [схвати́ть]; (**~** *away*) вырывáть [-рвать]; **~ *at*** хватáться [схвати́ться] за (В); **~ *up*** подхвáтывать [-хвати́ть]

sneak [sniːk] **1.** *v/i.* (*move stealthily*) крáсться; **~ *up*** подкрáдываться [-рáсться]; *v/t.* (*take in a furtive way, as a look, a smoke, etc.*) стащи́ть *pf.*, укрáсть *pf.*; **2.** (*telltale*) я́бедник *m*, -ица *f*; **~ers** ['sniːkəz] *pl. Am.* полукéды *f/pl.*; (*running shoes*) кроссóвки *f/pl.*

S

sneer [snɪə] **1.** (*contemptuous smile*) презри́тельная усме́шка; насме́шка; **2.** насме́шливо улыба́ться; насмеха́ться, глуми́ться (***at*** над Т)
sneeze [sniːz] **1.** чиха́нье; **2.** чиха́ть [чихну́ть]
snicker ['snɪkə] хихи́кать [-кнуть]; *of horses* ржать
sniff [snɪf] *v/t.* [по]ню́хать; *of dog* учу́ять; *v/i.* шмы́гать [-гну́ть] но́сом
snigger ['snɪgə] → ***snicker***
snip [snɪp] **1.** (*piece cut off*) обре́зок; кусо́к; (*cut*) надре́з; **2.** (*trim*) подреза́ть [-ре́зать]; (*cut out*) выре́зывать [вы́резать]
sniper ['snɑɪpə] сна́йпер
snivel ['snɪvl] хны́кать; (*after crying*) всхли́пывать [-пнуть]; *coll.* распуска́ть со́пли
snob [snɒb] сноб; **~bery** ['snɒbərɪ] снобі́зм
snoop [snuːp] подгля́дывать, выню́хивать, чужи́е та́йны
snooze [snuːz] *coll.* **1.** лёгкий, коро́ткий сон; **2.** дрема́ть, вздремну́ть *pf.*
snore [snɔː] [за]храпе́ть
snorkel ['snɔːkl] шно́ркель *m*
snort [snɔːt] фы́ркать [-кнуть]; *of horse* [за]храпе́ть
snout [snaʊt] *pig's* ры́ло; *dog's, etc.* мо́рда
snow [snəʊ] **1.** снег; **2.** ***it is ~ing*** идёт снег; ***be covered with ~*** быть занесённым сне́гом; ***be ~ed under with work*** быть зава́ленным рабо́той; **~ball** снежо́к; **~drift** сугро́б; **~fall** снегопа́д; **~flake** снежи́нка; **~ plow**, *Brt.* **~ plough** снегоочисти́тель *m*; **~storm** вью́га; **~-white** белосне́жный; **~y** ['snəʊɪ] □ сне́жный
snub [snʌb] **1.** *fig.* оса́живать [осади́ть]; **2.** пренебрежи́тельное обхожде́ние; **~-nosed** курно́сый
snug [snʌg] □ ую́тный; **~gle** ['snʌgl] (ла́сково) приж(им)а́ться (***up to*** к Д)
so [səʊ] так; ита́к; таки́м о́бразом; ***I hope ~*** я наде́юсь, что да; ***Look, it's raining. ~ it is.*** Смотри́, идёт дождь. Да, действи́тельно; ***you are tired***, **~ *am I*** вы уста́ли и я то́же; **~** ***far*** до сих пор
soak [səʊk] *v/t.* [за]мочи́ть; (*draw in*) впи́тывать [впита́ть]; *v/i.* промока́ть; **~ *in*** пропи́тываться [-пита́ться]; **~ *through*** проса́чиваться [-сочи́ться]; ***get ~ed to the skin*** промо́кнуть до ни́тки
soap [səʊp] **1.** мы́ло; **2.** намы́ли(ва)ть; **~ dish** мы́льница; **~-suds** мы́льная пе́на; **~y** ['səʊpɪ] □ мы́льный
soar [sɔː] (*fly high*) пари́ть; *of birds* взмыва́ть [-ыть]; *of prices* подска́кивать [-кочи́ть]
sob [sɒb] **1.** всхлип; рыда́ние; **2.** [за]рыда́ть; разрыда́ться *pf.*
sober ['səʊbə] **1.** □ тре́звый (*a. fig.*); **2.** *fig.* отрезвля́ть [-ви́ть]; ***have a ~ing effect*** [по]де́йствовать отрезвля́юще; **~ *up*** протрезвля́ться [-ви́ться]
so-called [səʊ'kɔːld] так называ́емый
sociable ['səʊʃəbl] □ обще́ительный
social ['səʊʃl] **1.** □ обще́ственный; социа́льный; **~ *security*** социа́льное обеспе́чение; **2.** вечери́нка
socialism ['səʊʃəlɪzəm] социали́зм
society [sə'saɪətɪ] о́бщество; *comm.* компа́ния; (*the public, the community*) обще́ственность *f*; (*association*) объедине́ние
sociology [səʊsɪ'ɒlədʒɪ] социоло́гия
sock [sɒk] носо́к
socket ['sɒkɪt] *of eye* впа́дина; *for bulb* патро́н; *for wall* розе́тка; *tech.* ште́псельное гнездо́
soda ['səʊdə] со́да; (*drink*) газиро́ванная вода́
sodden ['sɒdn] промо́кший
soft [sɒft] □ *com.* мя́гкий; не́жный; ти́хий; нея́ркий; (*unmanly*) изне́женный; (*weak in mind*) *coll.* придуркова́тый; **~ *drink*** безалкого́льный напи́ток; **~en** ['sɒfn] смягча́ть(ся) [-чи́ть(ся)]; **~hearted** мягкосерде́чный; **~ware** *comput.* програ́ммное обеспе́чение
soggy ['sɒgɪ] сыро́й; пропи́танный водо́й
soil [sɔɪl] **1.** (*earth*) по́чва, земля (*a. fig. country*); **2.** (*dirty*) [за]па́чкать(ся)

S

solace ['sɒlɪs] утешéние
solar ['səʊlə] сóлнечный; ~ ***eclipse*** сóлнечное затмéние
sold [səʊld] *pt. и pt. p. от* ***sell***
solder ['sɒldə] **1.** припóй; **2.** паять; запáивать [запаять]
soldier ['səʊldʒə] солдáт
sole[1] [səʊl] □ единственный; (*exclusive*) исключи́тельный
sole[2] [~] **1.** *of foot* ступня́; *of shoe* подмётка; **2.** стáвить подмётку на (В)
sole[3] [~] *zo.* кáмбала
solely ['səʊllɪ] исключи́тельно, еди́нственно
solemn ['sɒləm] □ *event, etc.* торжéственный; серьёзный; (*pompous*) напы́щенный; **~ity** [sə'lemnətɪ] торжéственность *f*; **~ize** ['sɒləmnaɪz]: ~ ***a marriage*** сочетáть брáком
solicit [sə'lɪsɪt] *help, etc.* проси́ть; **~or** [~ə] *law Brt.* адвокáт, юрискóнсульт; **~ous** [~əs] □ (*considerate*) забóтливый; ~ ***of*** стремя́щийся к (Д); **~ude** [~juːd] забóтливость *f*, забóта
solid ['sɒlɪd] **1.** □ твёрдый; (*firm*) прóчный; (*unbroken*) сплошнóй; масси́вный; (*sound, reliable*) соли́дный; (*dependable*) надёжный; (*unanimous*) единоглáсный; (*united*) сплочённый; ***a*** ~ ***hour*** цéлый час; ***on*** ~ ***ground*** *fig.* на твёрдой пóчве; ~ ***gold*** чи́стое зóлото; **2.** *phys.* твёрдое тéло; **~arity** [sɒlɪ'dærətɪ] солидáрность *f*
soliloquy [sə'lɪləkwɪ] монолóг
solit|ary ['sɒlɪtrɪ] □ (*lonely*) одинóкий; (*secluded*) уединённый; **~ude** [~tjuːd] одинóчество, уединéние
solo ['səʊləʊ] сóло *n indecl.*; **~ist** ['səʊləʊɪst] соли́ст *m*, -ка *f*
solu|ble ['sɒljʊbl] раствори́мый; *fig.* (*solvable*) разреши́мый; **~tion** [sə'luːʃn] (*process*) растворéние; (*result of process*) раствóр
solv|e [sɒlv] решáть [реши́ть], разрешáть [-ши́ть]; **~ent** ['~vənt] **1.** *fin.* платёжеспособный; *chem.* растворя́ющий; **2.** раствори́тель *m*
somb|er, *Brt.* **~re** ['sɒmbə] □ мрáчный; угрю́мный; *clothes* тёмный
some [sʌm, səm] нéкий; какóй-то; какóй-нибудь; нéсколько; нéкоторые; óколо (Р); ~ ***20 miles*** миль двáдцать; ***in*** ~ ***degree, to*** ~ ***extent*** до извéстной стéпени; **~body** ['sʌmbədɪ] ктó-то; ктó-нибудь; **~how** ['sʌmhaʊ] кáк-то; кáк-нибудь; ~ ***or other*** так или инáче; **~one** ['sʌmwʌn] → ***somebody***
somersault ['sʌməsɔːlt] кувыркáние; *in air* сáльто *n indecl.*; ***turn*** **~s** *pl.* кувыркáться, [с]дéлать сáльто, ***turn a*** ~ кувыркнýться *pf.*
some|thing ['sʌmθɪŋ] чтó-то; чтó-нибудь; кое-чтó; ~ ***like*** приблизи́тельно; чтó-то врóде (Р): ***is*** ~ ***the matter?*** чтó-нибудь не в поря́дке?; **~time** когдá-то, когдá-нибудь, когдá-либо; **~times** иногдá; **~what** слегкá, немнóго; до нéкоторой стéпени; **~where** гдé-то, кудá-то; гдé-нибудь, кудá-нибудь
son [sʌn] сын, *dim.* сынóк; (*pl.*: сыновья́; *rhet.*: сыны́)
sonata [sə'nɑːtə] сонáта
song [sɒŋ] песня, *dim.* пéсенка; ромáнс; *coll.* ***for a*** ~ за бесцéнок; **~bird** пéвчая пти́ца
son-in-law зять *m*
sonorous ['sɒnərəs] □ звýчный
soon [suːn] скóро, вскóре; рáно; ***as*** ~ ***as*** как тóлько; **~er** ['suːnə] скорée; ***no*** ~ ***... than*** едвá ..., как; ***no*** ~ ***said than done*** скáзано – сдéлано; ***the*** ~ ***the better*** чем скорée, тем лýчше
soot [sʊt] сáжа; кóпоть *f*
soothe [suːð] успокáивать [-кóить] (*a. fig.*); *fig.* утешáть [утéшить]
sooty ['sʊtɪ] □ закопчённый; чёрный как сáжа
sophist|icated [sə'fɪstɪkeɪtɪd] изы́сканный; *person* свéтский, искушённый; *machinery* слóжный; *argument* изощрённый
soporific [sɒpə'rɪfɪk] снотвóрное
sordid ['sɔːdɪd] □ *condition* убóгий; *behavio(u)r, etc.* гнýсный
sore [sɔː] **1.** □ (*tender*) чувстви́тельный; *point* болéзненный; (*painful*) больнóй, воспалённый; (*aggrieved*) оби́женный; ***she has a*** ~ ***throat*** у неё боли́т гóрло; **2.** боля́чка; *from rubbing* натёртое

ме́сто; (*running* ~) гноя́щаяся ра́н(к)а
sorrel ['sɒrəl] *bot.* ща́вель *m*
sorrow ['sɒrəʊ] го́ре, печа́ль *f*; (*regret*) сожале́ние; ***to my great*** ~ к моему́ вели́кому сожале́нию; **~ful** ['sɔrəʊfʊl] печа́льный, ско́рбный
sorry ['sɒrɪ] □ по́лный сожале́ния; **~?** *mst. Brt.* прости́те, не расслы́шал(а), *coll.* что?; (***I am***) (***so***) **~!** мне о́чень жаль! винова́т!; ***I feel*** ~ ***for you*** мне вас жаль; ***I'm*** ~ ***to say that ...*** к сожале́нию, я ...; ***say*** ~ извиня́ться [-ни́ться]
sort [sɔːt] **1.** род, сорт; ***people of all*** **~*s*** *pl.* лю́ди вся́кого разбо́ра; ~ ***of*** *coll.* как бу́дто; ***be out of*** **~*s*** *pl.* быть не в ду́хе; пло́хо чу́вствовать себя́; **2.** сортирова́ть; ~ ***out*** разбира́ть [разобра́ть]; рассортиро́вывать [-ирова́ть]
so-so ['səʊsəʊ] *coll.* так себе́, нева́жно
SOS [esəʊ'es] СОС: сигна́л бе́дствия в а́збуке мо́рзе
souffle ['suːfleɪ] суфле́ *n indecl.*
sought [sɔːt] *pt. и pt. p. от* **seek**
soul [səʊl] душа́ (*a. fig.*); (*person*) челове́к, душа́
sound[1] [saʊnd] □ (*healthy*) здоро́вый, кре́пкий, (*firm*) про́чный; (*sensible*) здра́вый; *in mind* норма́льный; *comm.* надёжный; *sleep* глубо́кий: ***be*** ~ ***asleep*** кре́пко спать
sound[2] [~] **1.** звук, шум; *mus.* звуча́ние; **2.** звуча́ть (*a. fig.*); раз-д(ав)а́ться; *fig.* [про]зонди́ровать; *patient's chest* выслу́шивать [вы́слушать]; ~ ***barrier*** звуково́й барье́р; **~ing** ['saundɪŋ] *naut.* проме́р глубины́ воды́; **~less** [~lɪs] □ беззву́чный; **~-proof** звуконепроница́емый; **~ track** звуково́е сопровожде́ние
soup [suːp] суп; **~plate** глубо́кая таре́лка; **~ spoon** столо́вая ло́жка
sour ['saʊə] □ ки́слый; (*bad-tempered*) раздражи́тельный; ~ ***cream*** смета́на; *fig.* угрю́мый; ***turn*** ~ закиса́ть [-и́снуть]; прокиса́ть [-и́снуть]
source [sɔːs] исто́к; исто́чник (*mst. fig.*)
south [saʊθ] **1.** юг; **2.** ю́жный; **~-east 1.** ю́го-восто́к; **2.** ю́го-восто́чный (*a.* **~*eastern***)
souther|ly ['sʌðəlɪ], **~n** ['sʌðən] ю́жный; **~ner** ['sʌðənə] южа́нин, южа́нка
southernmost са́мый ю́жный
southward, **~ly** ['saʊθwəd, ~lɪ], **~s** [~dz] *adv.* к ю́гу, на юг
south|west 1. ю́го-за́пад; **2.** ю́го-за́падный (*a.* **~*-westerly***, **~*-western***); **~wester** ю́го-за́падный ве́тер
souvenir [suːvə'nɪə] сувени́р
sovereign ['sɒvrɪn] **1.** сувере́нный; **2.** госуда́рь *m*; мона́рх; (*coin*) сове́рен; **~ty** [~tɪ] суверените́т
Soviet ['səʊvɪet] **1.** сове́т; **2.** сове́тский
sow[1] [saʊ] *zo.* свинья́; (*breeding* ~) свинома́тка
sow[2] [səʊ] [*irr.*] [по]се́ять; засева́ть [засе́ять]; **~n** [səʊn] *pt. p. от* **sow**[2]
soya beans ['sɔɪə] со́евые бобы́ *m/pl.*
spa [spɑː] куро́рт с минера́льными исто́чниками
space [speɪs] простра́нство; ме́сто; промежу́ток; *of time* срок; *attr.* косми́ческий; **~craft** косми́ческий кора́бль *m*
spacing ['speɪsɪŋ]: ***type s.th. in double*** ~ печа́тать че́рез два интерва́ла
spacious ['speɪʃəs] просто́рный; обши́рный; вмести́тельный
spade [speɪd] лопа́та; **~*s*** *cards* пи́ки *f/pl.*; **~work** предвари́тельная (кропотли́вая) рабо́та
spaghetti [spə'getɪ] *pl.* спаге́тти *indecl.*
span [spæn] **1.** *of bridge* пролёт; коро́ткое расстоя́ние и́ли вре́мя; **2.** перекрыва́ть [-кры́ть] стро́ить мост че́рез (В); измеря́ть [-е́рить]
spangle ['spæŋgl] **1.** блёстка; **2.** украша́ть блёстками; *fig.* усе́ивать [усе́ять] пядя́ми
Spaniard ['spænjəd] испа́нец *m*, -нка *f*
spaniel ['spænjəl] спание́ль *m*
Spanish ['spænɪʃ] испа́нский
spank [spæŋk] *coll.* **1.** шлёпать [-пнуть]; отшлёпать; **2.** шлепо́к

spanking ['spæŋkɪŋ] *breeze* свéжий
spare [speə] **1.** □ (*reserve*) запаснóй; (*surplus*) ли́шний, свобóдный; (*thin*) худощáвый; **~ *time*** свобóдное врéмя *n*; **2.** (**~** *part*) запаснáя часть *f*; **3.** *life* [по]щади́ть; (*grudge*) [по]жалéть; (*save*) [с]берéчь; *time* уделя́ть [-ли́ть]; (*save from*) избавля́ть [-áвить] от (Р)
sparing ['speərɪŋ] □ эконóмный; (*frugal*) скýдный; ***he is ~ of praise*** он скуп на похвалы́
spark [spɑːk] **1.** и́скра (*a. fig.*); **2.** [за]искри́ться; **~(ing) plug** *mot.* зажигáтельная свечá
sparkle ['spɑːkl] **1.** и́скра; (*process*) сверкáние; **2.** [за]и́скриться, [за]сверкáть; ***sparkling wine*** игри́стое винó
sparrow ['spærəʊ] воробéй
sparse [spɑːs] □ рéдкий; (*scattered*) разбрóсанный; **~ly** [~lɪ]: **~ *populated*** малонаселённый
spasm [spæzəm] спáзма, сýдорога; **~ *of coughing*** при́ступ кáшля; **~odic(al** □) [spæz'mɒdɪk(əl)] сýдорожный
spat [spæt] *pt. и pt. p. от* ***spit***
spatter ['spætə] бры́згать [-знуть]; *with mud* забры́згать, обры́згать гря́зью; (*spill*) расплёскивать [-плескáть]
spawn [spɔːn] **1.** икрá; **2.** метáть икрý; *multiply* [рас]плоди́ться
speak [spiːk] [*irr.*] *v/i.* говори́ть; [по]говори́ть (***with***, ***to*** с Т); разговáривать; **~ *out*** выскáзываться [вы́сказаться] откровенно; **~ *up*** говори́ть грóмко; (*express, as opinion, etc.*) выскáзывать [вы́сказать]; *v/t. the truth, etc.* говори́ть [сказáть]; **~er** ['spiːkə] выступáющий; доклáдчик; орáтор; *parl.* спи́кер
spear [spɪə] **1.** копьё; острогá; **2.** пронзáть копьём; *fish* бить острогóй
special ['speʃl] □ специáльный; (*exceptional*) осóбенный; осóбый; **~ *delivery*** срóчная достáвка; **~ *powers*** чрезвычáйные полномóчия; **~ist** [~ʃəlɪst] специали́ст; **~ity** [speʃɪ'ælətɪ] → ***specialty***; **~ize** ['speʃəlaɪz] специализи́ровать(ся) (*im*)*pf.* (в П *or* по Д); ***specialty*** ['speʃəltɪ] осóбенность *f*; специáльность *f*
species ['spiːʃiːz] вид; разнови́дность *f*; ***human ~*** человéческий род
speci|fic [spə'sɪfɪk] (**~*ally***) харáктерный; специфи́ческий; осóбый; (*definite*) определённый; **~*fic gravity*** удéльный вес; **~fy** ['spesɪfaɪ] оговáривать [-вори́ть]; тóчно определя́ть; (*stipulate*) предусмáтривать [-мотрéть], обуслáвливать [-слóвить]; **~men** ['spesɪmən] образéц, обрáзчик; экземпля́р
specious ['spiːʃəs] □ *excuse* благови́дный; показнóй
speck [spek] *of dirt, dust, etc.* пя́тнышко; *of colo(u)r* крáпинка
spectacle ['spektəkl] (*show*) зрéлище; **~s** [~z] *pl.* (*glasses*) очки́ *n/pl.*
spectacular [spek'tækjʊlə] □ эффéктный; *coll.* потрясáющий
spectator [spek'teɪtə] зри́тель *m*, -ница *f*
spect|er, *Brt.* **~re** ['spektə] при́зрак
spectrum ['spektrəm] спектр
speculat|e ['spekjʊleɪt] (*consider*) размышля́ть [-мы́слить]; *fin.* спекули́ровать (***in*** Т); **~ion** [spekjʊ'leɪʃn] размышлéние; (*supposition*) предположéние; *fin.* спекуля́ция; **~ive** ['spekjʊlətɪv] (*given to theory*) умозри́тельный; *fin.* спекуляти́вный; **~or** ['spekjʊleɪtə] спекуля́нт
sped [sped] *pt. и pt. p. от* ***speed***
speech [spiːtʃ] речь *f*; **~less** ['spiːtʃlɪs]: немóй; онемéвший; ***I was ~*** я лиши́лся дара рéчи
speed [spiːd] **1.** скóрость *f*, быстротá; *mot.* скóрость *f*; ***at full ~*** на пóлной скóрости; **2.** [*irr.*] *v/i.* [по-] спеши́ть; бы́стро идти́; **~ *by*** промчáться *pf.* мимо; *v/t.* **~ *up*** ускоря́ть [-óрить]; **~ing** ['~ɪŋ] *mot.* превышéние скóрости; **~ limit** разрешáемая скóрость *f*; **~ometer** [spiː'dɒmɪtə] *mot.* спидóметр; **~y** ['spiːdɪ] □ бы́стрый
spell[1] [spel] **1.** (корóткий) перúод; ***a cold ~*** перúод холóдной погóды; ***for a ~*** на врéмя; ***rest for a ~*** немнóго передохнýть *pf.*
spell[2] [~] писáть, произноси́ть по бýквам; *fig.* (*signify, bode*) сули́ть

S

spell³ [~] ча́ры *f/pl.*; очарова́ние; **~bound** очаро́ванный
spelling ['spelɪŋ] правописа́ние; орфогра́фия
spelt [spelt] *chiefly Brt. pt. и pt. p. от* ***spell***
spend [spend] [*irr.*] *money* [по]тра́тить, [из]расхо́довать; *time* проводи́ть [-вести́]; **~thrift** ['spendθrɪft] мот, расточи́тель *m*, -ница *f*
spent [spent] **1.** *pt. и pt. p. от* ***spend***; **2.** *adj.* (*exhausted*) истощённый; измо́танный
sperm [spɜːm] спе́рма
spher|e [sfɪə] шар; сфе́ра; *celestial* небе́сная сфе́ра; *fig.* о́бласть *f*, сфе́ра; по́ле де́ятельности; **~ical** ['sferɪkl] □ сфери́ческий
spice [spaɪs] **1.** спе́ция, пря́ность *f*; *fig.* при́вкус; при́месь *f*; **2.** приправля́ть [-а́вить]
spick and span ['spɪkən'spæn] (*spotlessly clean*) сверка́ющий чистото́й; с иго́лочки
spicy ['spaɪsɪ] □ пря́ный; *fig.* пика́нтный
spider ['spaɪdə] *zo.* пау́к
spike [spaɪk] **1.** (*point*) остриё; *on shoe* шип; *bot.* ко́лос; **2.** снабжа́ть шипа́ми; (*pierce*) пронза́ть [-зи́ть]
spill [spɪl] [*irr.*] *v/t.* проли́(ва́)ть; *powder* рассыпа́ть [-ы́пать]; *v/i.* проли́(ва́)ться
spilt [spɪlt] *pt. и pt. p. от* ***spill***
spin [spɪn] **1.** [*irr.*] *yarn* [с]прясть; (*~ round*) крути́ться; [за]кружи́ть(ся); верте́ться; ***~ when fishing*** лови́ть ры́бу спи́ннингом; ***my head is ~ning*** у меня́ кру́жится голова́; ***~ a yarn*** расска́зывать исто́рию/небыли́цы; ***~ round*** оберну́ться *pf.*; **2.** круже́ние; бы́страя езда́
spinach ['spɪnɪdʒ] шпина́т
spinal ['spaɪnl] спинно́й; ***~ column*** позвоно́чный столб, спинно́й хребе́т; ***~ cord*** спинно́й мозг
spine [spaɪn] *anat.* позвоно́чник; *bot.* колю́чка; **~less** ['~lɪs] *fig.* бесхребе́тный
spinning| mill пряди́льная фа́брика; **~ wheel** пря́лка
spinster ['spɪnstə] (*old maid*) ста́рая де́ва; *law* (*unmarried woman*) незаму́жняя же́нщина
spiny ['spaɪnɪ] (*prickly*) колю́чий
spiral ['spaɪərəl] **1.** □ спира́льный; ***~ staircase*** винтова́я ле́стница; **2.** спира́ль *f*
spire ['spaɪə] *arch.* шпиль *m*
spirit ['spɪrɪt] **1.** *com.* дух, душа́; (*ghost*) привиде́ние; (*enthusiasm*) воодушевле́ние; (*alcohol*) спирт; ***~s*** *pl.* (***high*** припо́днятое, ***low*** пода́вленное) настрое́ние; спиртны́е напи́тки *m/pl.*; **2. *~ away, off*** та́йно похища́ть; **~ed** [~ɪd] (*lively*) живо́й; (*courageous*) сме́лый; (*energetic*) энерги́чный; ***~ argument*** жа́ркий спор; **~less** [~lɪs] вя́лый; ро́бкий; безжи́зненный
spiritual ['spɪrɪtʃʊəl] □ духо́вный; **~ism** [~ɪzəm] спирити́зм
spit¹ [spɪt] **1.** (*spittle*) слюна́; плево́к; *fig.* подо́бие; **2.** [*irr.*] плева́ть [плю́нуть]; *of fire* рассыпа́ть и́скры; *of cat* шипе́ть; *of rain* мороси́ть; ***the ~ting image of s.o.*** то́чная ко́пия кого́-л.
spit² [~] *geogr.* коса́, о́тмель *f*; *cul.* ве́ртел
spite [spaɪt] **1.** зло́ба, злость *f*; ***in ~ of*** не смотря́ на (В); **2.** досажда́ть [досади́ть]; **~ful** ['spaɪtfʊl] зло́бный
spitfire ['spɪtfaɪə] вспы́льчивый челове́к
spittle ['spɪtl] слюна́; плево́к
splash [splæʃ] **1.** бры́зги *f/pl.* (*mst. ~es pl.*); плеск; **2.** бры́згать [-знуть]; забры́згать *pf.*; плеска́ть(ся) [-сну́ть]
spleen [spliːn] *anat.* селезёнка; *fig.* раздраже́ние
splend|id ['splendɪd] □ великоле́пный, роско́шный; **~o(u)r** [~də] блеск, великоле́пие
splice [splaɪs] *rope* сплета́ть [сплести́]; *wood* соединя́ть [-ни́ть]; *tape, etc.* скле́ивать [-ить]
splint [splɪnt] *med.* ши́на; ***put an arm in a ~*** накла́дывать ши́ну на (В); **~er** ['splɪntə] **1.** *of stone* оско́лок; *of wood* ще́пка; *in skin* зано́за; **2.** расщепля́ть(ся) [-пи́ть(ся)]; раска́лываться [-коло́ться]
split [splɪt] **1.** (*crack, fissure*) тре́щина; щель *f*; *fig.* раско́л; **2.** рас-

S

щеплённый; раско́лотый; **3.** [*irr.*] *v/t.* раска́лывать [-коло́ть]; расщепля́ть (-пи́ть); (*divide*) [по]дели́ть; **~ hairs** вдава́ться в то́нкости; спо́рить о пустяка́х; **~ one's sides laughing** надрыва́ться от сме́ха; *v/i.* раска́лываться [-коло́ться]; раздели́ться *pf.*; (*burst*) ло́паться [ло́пнуть]; **~ting** ['splɪtɪŋ] *headache* ужа́сный

splutter ['splʌtə] → **sputter**

spoil¹ [spɔɪl] **1.** (*a.* **~s** *pl.*) добы́ча

spoil² [~] [*irr.*] [ис]по́ртить; *food* [ис]по́ртиться; *child* [из]балова́ть

spoke¹ [spəʊk] *of wheel* спи́ца; *of ladder* ступе́нька, перекла́дина

spoke² [~] *pt. от* **speak**; **~n** ['spəʊkən] *pt. p. от* **speak**; **~sman** ['spəʊksmən] представи́тель *m*

sponge [spʌndʒ] **1.** гу́бка; **2.** *v/t.* вытира́ть или мыть гу́бкой; **~ up** впи́тывать гу́бкой; *v/i. fig.* парази́т; жить на чужо́й счёт; **~ cake** бискви́т; **~r** ['spʌndʒə] нахле́бник (-ница)

spongy ['spʌndʒɪ] гу́бчатый

sponsor ['spɒnsə] **1.** спо́нсор; (*guarantor*) поручи́тель *m*, -ница *f*; **2.** руча́ться [поручи́ться] за (В); рекомендова́ть; финанси́ровать

spontaneous [spɒn'teɪnɪəs] □ *behavio(u)r, talk* непосре́дственный, непринуждённый; спонта́нный; **~ generation** самозарожде́ние

spook [spu:k] привиде́ние; **~y** ['~ɪ] жу́ткий

spool [spu:l] *in sewing machine* шпу́лька; *in tape-recorder* боби́на; *of film, etc.* кату́шка

spoon [spu:n] **1.** ло́жка; **2.** черпа́ть ло́жкой; **~ful** ['spu:nfl] ло́жка (ме́ра)

spore [spɔ:] спо́ра

sport [spɔ:t] **1.** спорт; *attr.* спорти́вный; (*amusement, fun*) развлече́ние, заба́ва; (*good* **~**) *sl.* молоде́ц; **~s** *pl.* спорти́вные и́гры *f/pl.*; **~s ground** спорти́вная площа́дка; **2.** *v/i.* игра́ть, весели́ться, резви́ться; *v/t. coll.* щеголя́ть (Т); **~sman** ['spɔ:tsmən] спортсме́н

spot [spɒt] **1.** *com.* пятно́; *small* кра́пинка; (*place*) ме́сто; *coll.* (*small quantity*) немно́жко; **be in a ~** быть в тру́дном положе́нии; **on the ~** на ме́сте; сра́зу, неме́дленно; **2.** [за-, пере]па́чкать; (*detect*) обнару́жи(ва)ть; *coll.* (*identify*) опозн(ав)а́ть; **~less** ['spɒtlɪs] □ безупре́чный; незапя́тнанный; **~ light** проже́ктор; *fig.* центр внима́ния; **~ty** ['spɒtɪ] пятни́стый; *face* прыщева́тый

spouse [spaʊz] супру́г *m*, -а *f*

spout [spaʊt] **1.** *water* струя́; *of teapot, etc.* но́сик; **2.** ли́ться струёй; бить струёй; *coll.* (*speak*) разглаго́льствовать

sprain [spreɪn] **1.** *med.* растяже́ние; **2.** растя́гивать [-тяну́ть]

sprang [spræŋ] *pt. от* **spring**

sprawl [sprɔ:l] (*a.* **~ out**) растя́гивать(ся) [-яну́ть(ся)]; *in a chair* разва́ливаться [-ли́ться]; *bot.* бу́йно разраста́ться

spray¹ [spreɪ] **1.** водяна́я пыль *f*; бры́зги *f/pl.*; (*instrument*) пульвериза́тор, распыли́тель *m* (*a.* **~er**); **2.** распыля́ть [-ли́ть]; опры́скивать [-скать], обры́зг(ив)ать

spray² [~] (*cluster, bunch*) кисть *f*, гроздь *f*

spread [spred] **1.** [*irr.*] *v/t.* (*a.* **~ out**) расстила́ть [разостла́ть]; *news* распространя́ть [-ни́ть]; *butter* нама́з(ыв)ать (Т); *wings* расправля́ть [-а́вить]; **~ the table** накры́(ва́)ть на стол; *v/i. of fields* простира́ться; *of fire, etc.* распространя́ться [-ни́ться]; **2.** *pt. и pt. p. от* **spread 1.**; **3.** распростране́ние; протяже́ние

spree [spri:] весе́лье; (*drinking*) кутёж; **go on a shopping ~** отпра́виться по магази́нам; накупи́ть вся́кой вся́чины

sprig [sprɪg] ве́точка, побе́г

sprightly ['spraɪtlɪ] (*lively*) живо́й, оживлённый, (*cheerful*) весёлый; бо́дрый

spring [sprɪŋ] **1.** (*leap*) прыжо́к, скачо́к; (*mineral* **~**, *etc.*) родни́к, ключ; (*a.* **~time**) весна́; *tech.* пружи́на; *of vehicle* рессо́ра; *fig.* моти́в; **2.** [*irr.*] *v/t.* (*explode*) взрыва́ть [взорва́ть]; **~ a leak** дава́ть течь *f*; *v/i.* (*jump*) пры́гать [-гнуть]; *to one's feet* вска́кивать [вскочи́ть];

bot. появля́ться [-ви́ться]; ~ ***aside*** отскочи́ть *pf.* в сто́рону; ~ ***up*** *fig.* возника́ть [-ни́кнуть]; ~ **board** трампли́н; ~ **tide** весна́; **~y** ['sprɪŋɪ] □ упру́гий

sprinkl|e ['sprɪŋkl] *liquid* бры́згать [-знуть]; обры́згивать [-знуть]; *sand, sugar* посыпа́ть [-ы́пать]; **~ing** [~ɪŋ]: ***a*** ~ немно́го

sprint [sprɪnt] *sport* **1.** спринт; **2.** *sport* бежа́ть с максима́льной ско́ростью на коро́ткую диста́нцию; ***he ~ed past us*** он промча́лся ми́мо

sprout [spraʊt] **1.** *of plant* пуска́ть ростки́; *of seeds* прораста́ть [-расти́]; **2.** *bot.* росто́к, побе́г

spruce¹ [spru:s] □ (*neat*) опря́тный; (*smart*) наря́дный

spruce² [~] *bot.* ель *f*

sprung [sprʌŋ] *pt. u pt. p. om* **spring**

spry [spraɪ] (*lively*) живо́й; (*nimble*) подви́жный

spun [spʌn] *pt. u pt. p. om* **spin**

spur [spɜ:] **1.** шпо́ра; *fig.* побужде́ние; ***act on the ~ of the moment*** де́йствовать не разду́мывая; **2.** пришпо́ривать; побужда́ть [-уди́ть]; ~ ***on*** спеши́ть; *fig.* подстёгивать [-егну́ть]

spurious ['spjʊərɪəs] □ подде́льный; фальши́вый

spurn [spɜ:n] отверга́ть, отказа́ться *pf.* с презре́нием

spurt [spɜ:t] **1.** *of liquid* бить струёй; *of flame* выбра́сывать [вы́бросить]; **2.** *water* струя́; (*gust*) поры́в ве́тра; *sport* рыво́к (*a. fig.*)

sputter ['spʌtə] **1.** бры́зги *f/pl.*; шипе́ние; **2.** *of fire* [за]треща́ть, [за]шипе́ть; бры́згаться слюно́й при разгово́ре; говори́ть бы́стро и бессвя́зно

S

spy [spaɪ] **1.** шпио́н *m*, -ка *f*; **2.** шпио́нить, следи́ть (***on*** за Т); (*notice*) заме́тить *pf.*

squabble ['skwɒbl] **1.** перебра́нка, ссо́ра; **2.** [по]вздо́рить

squad [skwɒd] *of workers* брига́да; отря́д; (*a. mil.*) гру́ппа, кома́нда (*a. sport*); ~ **car** *Am.* патру́льная маши́на; **~ron** ['skwɒdrən] *mil.* эскадро́н; *ae.* эскадри́лья; *naut.* эска́дра

squalid ['skwɒlɪd] □ убо́гий

squall [skwɔ:l] **1.** *of wind* шквал; вопль *m*, крик; **2.** [за]вопи́ть

squander ['skwɒndə] прома́тывать [-мота́ть], [рас]транжи́рить

square [skweə] **1.** □ квадра́тный; *shoulders, right angles, etc.* прямо́й; (*fair, honest*) прямо́й, че́стный; **2.** квадра́т; (*town* ~) пло́щадь *f*; **3.** *v/t.* де́лать прямоуго́льным; (*pay*) опла́чивать [оплати́ть]; (*bring into accord*) согласо́вывать [-сова́ть]; *v/i.* согласо́вываться [-сова́ться]

squash [skwɒʃ] **1.** фрукто́вый напи́ток; (*crush*) да́вка, толчея́; **2.** разда́вливать [-дави́ть]

squat [skwɒt] **1.** призе́мистый; **2.** сиде́ть на ко́рточках; ~ ***down*** присе́сть *pf.* на ко́рточки

squawk [skwɒ:k] **1.** *bird's* пронзи́тельный крик; **2.** пронзи́тельно крича́ть

squeak [skwi:k] [про]пища́ть; *of shoes, etc.* скрипе́ть

squeal [skwi:l] [за]визжа́ть; *sl.* доноси́ть [донести́]

squeamish ['skwi:mɪʃ] □ (*too scrupulous*) щепети́льный; оби́дчивый; *about food, etc.* привере́дливый; (*fastidious*) брезгли́вый

squeeze [skwi:z] **1.** сж(им)а́ть; (*clench*) сти́скивать [-снуть]; *lemon, etc.* выжима́ть [вы́жать]; *fig. money* вымога́ть (***from*** у Р); **2.** сжа́тие; пожа́тие; давле́ние; да́вка; **~r** ['skwi:zə] выжима́лка

squelch [skweltʃ] хлю́пать

squint [skwɪnt] коси́ть; *at the sun* [со]щу́риться

squirm [skwɜ:m] изви́(ва́)ться, [с]ко́рчиться

squirrel [skwɪrəl] бе́лка

squirt [skwɜ:t] **1.** струя́; *coll.* (*a nobody*) вы́скочка *m/f.*; **2.** бры́згать [-знуть]; бить то́нкой струёй

stab [stæb] **1.** уда́р; **2.** *v/t. to death* зака́лывать [заколо́ть]; *v/i.* (*wound*) наноси́ть уда́р (***at*** Д)

stabili|ty [stə'bɪlətɪ] усто́йчивость *f*, *fin.* стаби́льность *f*; про́чность *f*; **~ze** ['steɪbəlaɪz] стабилизи́ровать (*im*)*pf.*; **~er** ['steɪbəlaɪzə] *tech.* стабилиза́тор

stable¹ ['steɪbl] □ усто́йчивый; *situation, etc.* стаби́льный

stable² [~] конюшня
stack [stæk] **1.** *of hay* стог; *of wood* шта́бель *m*; *of books* сто́пка; ку́ча; **2.** скла́дывать [сложи́ть]
stadium ['steɪdɪəm] *sport* стадио́н
staff [stɑ:f] **1.** (*flag* ~) дре́вко; (*body of employees*) штат, персона́л; ***editorial*** **~** редколле́гия; **2.** набира́ть [-ра́ть] персона́л; укомплекто́вывать [-това́ть]
stag [stæg] *zo.* оле́нь-саме́ц
stage [steɪdʒ] **1.** сце́на, подмо́стки *m/pl.*; *for singer, etc.* эстра́да; *fig.* ста́дия, эта́п; **2.** [по]ста́вить; **~ manager** режиссёр
stagger ['stægə] *v/i.* шата́ть(ся) [(по)шатну́ться]; *v/t. fig.* потряса́ть [-ясти́]; поража́ть [порази́ть]; **~ing** [~ɪŋ] потряса́ющий
stagna|nt ['stægnənt] □ *water* стоя́чий; **~te** [stæg'neɪt] заста́иваться [застоя́ться]; *fig. mst. econ.* быть в состоя́нии засто́я
staid [steɪd] □ уравнове́шенный, степе́нный; сде́ржанный
stain [steɪn] **1.** пятно́ (*a. fig.*); **2.** [за]па́чкать; *fig.* [за]пятна́ть; ***~ed glass*** цветно́е стекло́; ***~ed glass window*** витра́ж; **~less** ['steɪnlɪs] *steel* нержаве́ющий
stair [steə] ступе́нька; **~s** *pl.* ле́стница; **~case, ~way** ле́стница; ле́стничная кле́тка
stake [steɪk] **1.** *wooden* кол; (*bet*) ста́вка; ***be at*** **~** *fig.* быть поста́вленным на ка́рту; **2.** *money* ста́вить (***on*** на В)
stale [steɪl] □ несве́жий; *air* спёртый; *joke* изби́тый; *bread* чёрствый; *news* устаре́вший
stalemate ['steɪlmeɪt] *chess* пат; *fig.* тупи́к
stalk [stɔ:k] **1.** сте́бель *m*; *of leaf* черено́к; **2.** *v/i.* ва́жно ше́ствовать, го́рдо выступа́ть
stall [stɔ:l] **1.** *for animals* сто́йло; *in market mst. Brt.* прила́вок; кио́ск, ларёк; *thea.* ме́сто в парте́ре; **2.**: ***the engine ~ed*** мото́р загло́х
stallion ['stælɪən] жеребе́ц
stalwart ['stɔ:lwət] ро́слый, кре́пкий; *supporter* сто́йкий
stamina ['stæmɪnə] выно́сливость *f*
stammer ['stæmə] **1.** заика́ться [-кну́ться]; запина́ться [запну́ться]; **2.** заика́ние
stamp [stæmp] **1.** штамп, ште́мпель *m*, печа́ть *f*; *fig.* отпеча́ток, печа́ть *f*; *for letter* ма́рка; *of feet* то́панье; **~ *collector*** филатели́ст; **2.** [про]штампова́ть; [по]ста́вить ште́мпель *m*, печа́ть *f*; то́пать ного́й
stampede [stæm'pi:d] **1.** пани́ческое бе́гство; **2.** обраща́ть(ся) в пани́ческое бе́гство
stand [stænd] **1.** [*irr.*] *v/i. com.* стоя́ть; проста́ивать [-стоя́ть]; (~ *still*) остана́вливаться [-нови́ться]; (~ *fast*) держа́ться; устоя́ть *pf.*; **~ *against*** [вос]проти́виться, сопротивля́ться (Д); **~ *aside*** [по]сторони́ться; **~ *by*** прису́тствовать; *fig.* быть нагото́ве; подде́рживать [-жа́ть]; **~ *for*** быть кандида́том (Р); стоя́ть за (В); зна́чить; **~ *out*** выделя́ться [вы́делиться] (***against*** на П); **~ *over*** остава́ться нерешённым; **~ *up*** вст(ав)а́ть, поднима́ться [-ня́ться]; **~ *up for*** защища́ть [-ити́ть]; **2.** *v/t.* [по]ста́вить; (*bear*) выде́рживать [вы́держать], выноси́ть [вы́нести]; *coll* (*treat*) угоща́ть [угости́ть] (Т); **3.** остано́вка; сопротивле́ние; то́чка зре́ния; стенд; кио́ск; пози́ция; ме́сто; (*support*) подста́вка; (*rostrum*) трибу́на; ***make a ~ against*** сопротивля́ться (Д)
standard ['stændəd] **1.** зна́мя *n*, флаг; но́рма, станда́рт; образе́ц *m*; **~ *of living*** жи́зненный у́ровень *m*; **2.** станда́ртный; образцо́вый; **~ize** [~aɪz] стандартизи́ровать (*im*)*pf.*
standby ['stændbaɪ] **1.** опо́ра; **2.** *tech.*, *fin.* резе́рвный
standing ['stændɪŋ] **1.** (*posture, etc.*) стоя́чий; *permanent* постоя́нный; **2.** (*rank, reputation*) положе́ние; (*duration*) продолжи́тельность *f*
stand|offish [stænd'ɒfɪʃ] за́мкнутый; надме́нный; **~point** то́чка зре́ния; **~still** остано́вка; ***the work came to a*** **~** рабо́та останови́лась; ***bring to a*** **~** останови́ть, засто́порить

S

stank [stæŋk] *pt. от* **stink**
stanza ['stænzə] строфа́
staple ['steɪpl] основно́й; **~ diet** осно́ва пита́ния
star [stɑː] **1.** звезда́ (*a. fig.*); *fig.* судьба́; **the ꝸs and Stripes** *pl. Am.* национа́льный флаг США; **thank one's lucky ~s** благодари́ть судьбу́; **2.** игра́ть гла́вную роль *f*
starboard ['stɑːbəd] *naut.* пра́вый борт
starch [stɑːtʃ] **1.** крахма́л; **2.** [на-] крахма́лить
stare [steə] **1.** при́стальный взгляд; **2.** смотре́ть при́стально; уста́виться *pf.*; (**at** на В)
stark [stɑːk] (*stiff*) окочене́лый; (*utter*) соверше́нный; *adv.* соверше́нно
starling ['stɑːlɪŋ] скворе́ц
starry ['stɑːrɪ] звёздный
start [stɑːt] **1.** нача́ло; *of train, etc.* отправле́ние; *sport* старт; **give a ~** вздро́гнуть *pf.*; **give s.o. a ~** испуга́ть кого́-л.; **give s.o. a ~ in life** помо́чь *pf.* кому́-л. встать на́ ноги; **2.** *v/i. at a sound, etc.* вздра́гивать [-ро́гнуть]; *from one's seat, etc.* вска́кивать [вскочи́ть]; отправля́ться в путь; *sport* стартова́ть (*im*)*pf.*; нач(ин)а́ться; *v/t.* (*set going*) пуска́ть (пусти́ть); *sport* дава́ть старт (Д); *fig.* нач(ин)а́ть; учрежда́ть [-еди́ть]; побужда́ть [-уди́ть] (**~ a p. doing** кого́-л. де́лать); **~er** ['stɑːtə] *mot.* стартёр
startl|e [stɑːtl] (*alarm*) трево́жить (*take aback*) поража́ть [порази́ть]; [ис-, на]пуга́ть; **~ing** ['stɑːtlɪŋ] порази́тельный
starv|ation [stɑː'veɪʃən] го́лод; голода́ние; **~e** [stɑːv] голода́ть; умира́ть с го́лоду; мори́ть го́лодом; **~ for** *fig.* жа́ждать (Р)
state [steɪt] **1.** состоя́ние; (*station in life*) положе́ние; госуда́рство (*pol. a.* ꝸ); (*member of federation*) штат; *attr.* госуда́рственный; **get into a ~** разне́рвничаться *pf.*, разволнова́ться *pf.*; **~ of emergency** чрезвыча́йное положе́ние; **2.** заявля́ть [-ви́ть]; констати́ровать (*im*)*pf.*; [с]формули́ровать; (*set forth*) излага́ть (изложи́ть); **~ly** [~lɪ] вели́чественный; **~ment** [~mənt] утвержде́ние; официа́льное заявле́ние; *fin.* отчёт; **~room** *naut.* отде́льная каю́та; **~sman** ['steɪtsmən] госуда́рственный де́ятель *m*
static ['stætɪk] *el.* стати́ческий; неподви́жный; (*stable*) стаби́льный
station ['steɪʃn] **1.** *radio, el., rail.* ста́нция; (*building*) вокза́л; **2.** размеща́ть [-ести́ть] (*a. mil.*); **~ary** ['steɪʃənrɪ] неподви́жный; стациона́рный; **~ery** [~] канцеля́рские това́ры *m/pl.*
statistics [stə'tɪstɪks] стати́стика
statue ['stætʃuː] ста́туя
stature ['stætʃə] рост; масшта́б, кали́бр
status ['steɪtəs] положе́ние; **~ quo** ста́тус-кво
statute ['stætʃuːt] стату́т; зако́н; законода́тельный акт; *pl.* уста́в
staunch [stɔːntʃ] *supporter* ве́рный; непоколеби́мый
stay [steɪ] **1.** пребыва́ние, визи́т; *law* отсро́чка; **2.** *v/t. law* приостана́вливать [-нови́ть]; *v/i.* (*remain*) ост(ав)а́ться; *as guest at hotel, etc.* остана́вливаться [-нови́ться], жить (**at** в П), [по]гости́ть
stead [sted]: **in a person's ~** вме́сто кого́-нибудь; **~fast** ['stedfɑːst] сто́йкий, непоколеби́мый
steady ['stedɪ] **1.** □ (*balanced*) усто́йчивый; *look, etc.* при́стальный; (*regular*) постоя́нный; равноме́рный; (*stable*) уравнове́шенный; **2.** де́лать(ся) усто́йчивым; приводи́ть в равнове́сие; *adv.* **~!** осторо́жно!
steak [steɪk] *of beef* бифште́кс; (*fillet ~*) вы́резка
steal [stiːl] [*irr.*] *v/t.* [с]ворова́ть, [у]кра́сть; *v/i.* кра́сться, прокра́дываться [-ра́сться]
stealth [stelθ]: **by ~** укра́дкой, тайко́м; **~y** ['stelθɪ] □ та́йный; бесшу́мный; **~ glance** взгляд укра́дкой; **~ steps** краду́щиеся шаги́
steam [stiːm] **1.** пар; **2.** *attr.* парово́й; **3.** *v/i.* (*move by steam*) *of train* идти́; *of ship* пла́вать; [по]плы́ть; **get ~ed up** запоте́ть *pf.*; *fig.* [вз]волнова́ться; *v/t.* вари́ть

S

на пару́; пари́ть; выпа́ривать [вы́парить]; **~er** ['sti:mə] *naut.* парохо́д; *cul.* скорова́рка; **~y** ['sti:mɪ] насы́щенный па́ром; *glass* запоте́вший

steel [sti:l] **1.** сталь *f*; **2.** стально́й (*a.* **~y**); **~ o.s. for** собра́ть всё своё му́жество; ожесточа́ться [-чи́ть-ся]; **~works** сталелите́йный заво́д

steep [sti:p] круто́й; *coll. price* сли́шком высо́кий

steeple ['sti:pl] шпиль *m*; *with bell* колоко́льня; **~chase** ска́чки с препя́тствиями

steer [stɪə] пра́вить рулём; *naut., etc.* управля́ть (T); **~ing** ['~ɪŋ]: **~ wheel** *naut.* штурва́л; *mot.* рулево́е колесо́, *coll.* бара́нка; **~sman** ['stɪəzmən] рулево́й

stem[1] [stem] **1.** *bot.* сте́бель *m*; *gr.* осно́ва; **2.** *v/i.* (*arise*) происходи́ть [-изойти́]

stem[2] [~] (*stop, check*) заде́рживать [-жа́ть]

stench [stentʃ] злово́ние

stencil ['stensl] трафаре́т

stenographer [ste'nɒgrəfə] стено-гра́фист *m*, -ка *f*

step[1] [step] **1.** шаг (*a. fig.*); похо́дка; *of stairs* ступе́нька; (*footboard*) подно́жка; *fig.* ме́ра; ***it's only a ~ from here*** отсю́да руко́й пода́ть; **~ *by* ~** постепе́нно; ***a rushed ~*** необ-ду́манный шаг; ***take ~s*** принима́ть [-ня́ть] ме́ры; ***tread in the ~s of*** *fig.* идти́ по стопа́м (P); **~s** *pl.* стремя́н-ка; **2.** *v/i.* шага́ть [шагну́ть], ступа́ть [-пи́ть]; ходи́ть, идти́ [пойти́]; **~ *aside*** посторони́ться *pf.*; **~ *back*** отступи́ть *pf.* наза́д, отойти́ *pf.*; **~ *up*** *v/t.* (*increase*) по-выша́ть [-ы́сить]

step[2] [~]: **~daughter** па́дчерица; **~father** о́тчим; **~mother** ма́чеха

steppe [step] степь *f*

stepping-stone ка́мень *m* для перехо́да через руче́й; **~ *to suc-cess*** ступе́нь к успе́ху

stepson па́сынок

stereo ['sterɪəʊ] стереофони́чес-кий (прои́грыватель *m or* радио-приёмник)

stereotype ['sterɪətaɪp] стереоти́п

steril|e ['steraɪl] беспло́дный; (*free from germs*) стери́льный; **~ity** [ste'rɪlətɪ] беспло́дие; стери́ль-ность *f*; **~ize** ['sterəlaɪz] стерили-зова́ть (*im*)*pf.*

sterling ['stɜ:lɪŋ]: ***the pound ~*** фунт сте́рлингов

stern[1] [stɜ:n] □ стро́гий, суро́вый

stern[2] [~] *naut.* корма́

stevedore ['sti:vədɔ:] до́кер; пор-то́вый гру́зчик

stew [stju:] **1.** [с]туши́ть(ся); **2.** ту-шёное мя́со; ***be in a ~*** волно-ва́ться, беспоко́иться

steward ['stjʊəd] *naut., ae.* стю́ард, бортпроводни́к; **~ess** ['stjʊədɪs] стюарде́сса, бортпроводни́ца

stick[1] [stɪk] па́лка; (*walking ~*) трость *f*; **~s** *for fire* хво́рост

stick[2] [~] [*irr.*] *v/i.* прикле́и(ва)ться, прилипа́ть [-ли́пнуть]; (*become fixed*) застрева́ть [-ря́ть]; завяза́ть [-я́знуть]; *at home* торча́ть; **~ *to*** приде́рживаться [-жа́ться] (P); **~ *at nothing*** не остана́вливаться ни пе́ред чем; **~ *out*, ~ *up*** торча́ть; стоя́ть торчко́м; *v/t.* вка́лывать [вколо́ть]; *fork, etc.* втыка́ть [вот-кну́ть]; *stamp* накле́ивать [-е́ить]; прикле́и(ва)ть; *coll.* (*bear*) тер-пе́ть, вы́терпеть *pf.*; **~ *ing plaster*** лейкопла́стырь *m*

sticky ['stɪkɪ] ли́пкий, кле́йкий; ***come to a ~ end*** пло́хо ко́нчить *pf.*

stiff [stɪf] □ жёсткий, неги́бкий; *lock, etc.* туго́й; тру́дный; *relations* натя́нутый; **~ *with cold*** окочене́ть *pf.* от хо́лода; **~en** ['stɪfn] *of starch, etc.* [за]густе́ть

stifle ['staɪfl] задыха́ться [задох-ну́ться]; *rebellion* подавля́ть [-ви́ть]

stigma ['stɪgmə] *fig.* пятно́, клеймо́

still [stɪl] **1.** *adj.* ти́хий; неподви́ж-ный; **2.** *adv.* ещё, всё ещё; **3.** *cj.* всё же, одна́ко; **4.** (*make calm*) успо-ка́ивать [-ко́ить]; **~born** мертво-рождённый; **~ life** натюрмо́рт; **~ness** ['stɪlnɪs] тишина́

stilted ['stɪltɪd] *style* высокопа́рный

stimul|ant ['stɪmjʊlənt] *med.* воз-бужда́ющее сре́дство; *fig.* сти́мул; **~ate** [~leɪt] (*excite*) возбужда́ть [-уди́ть]; стимули́ровать (*a. fig.*); поощря́ть [-ри́ть]; **~ating** стимули́рующий, вдохновля́ющий; **~us** [~ləs] сти́мул

sting [stɪŋ] **1.** (*organ*) жа́ло; (*bite*) уку́с; о́страя боль *f*; *fig.* ко́лкость *f*; **2.** [*irr.*] [у]жа́лить; *of nettle* жечь(ся); (*smart, burn*) садни́ть; *fig.* уязвля́ть [-ви́ть]

sting|iness ['stɪndʒɪnɪs] ска́редность *f*; **~y** ['stɪndʒɪ] скупо́й

stink [stɪŋk] **1.** вонь *f*; **2.** [*irr.*] воня́ть

stint [stɪnt] **1.** (*fixed amount*) но́рма; **2.** (*keep short*) ограни́чи(ва)ть; [по]скупи́ться на (В); ***she doesn't ~ herself*** она́ себе́ ни в чём не отка́зывает

stipulat|e ['stɪpjʊleɪt] ста́вить усло́вия; обусло́вливать [-вить]; ***the ~ed sum*** оговорённая су́мма; **~ion** [stɪpjʊ'leɪʃn] усло́вие

stir [stɜː] **1.** шевеле́ние; (*excitement*) суета́, сумато́ха; движе́ние; *fig.* оживле́ние; ***create a ~*** наде́лать *pf.* мно́го шу́ма; **2.** *leaves, etc.* шевели́ть(ся) [-льну́ть(ся)]; *tea, etc.* [по]меша́ть; [вз]волнова́ть; ***~ up*** (*excite*) возбужда́ть [-уди́ть]; разме́шивать [-ша́ть]

stirrup ['stɪrəp] стре́мя *n* (*pl.*: стремена́)

stitch [stɪtʃ] **1.** *sew.* стежо́к; *in knitting* петля́; *med.* шов; **2.** [с]шить, проши́(ва́)ть

stock [stɒk] **1.** (*supply*) запа́с; ***live ~*** поголо́вье скота́, скот; ***capital ~*** уставно́й капита́л; ***take ~ of*** де́лать переучёт (Р), производи́ть инвентариза́цию; *fig.* крити́чески оце́нивать; **2.** *size* станда́ртный; *joke, etc.* изби́тый; **3.** (*supply*) снабжа́ть [-бди́ть]

stock|breeder животново́д; **~broker** биржево́й ма́клер; бро́кер; **~ exchange** фо́ндовая би́ржа; **~holder** *Am.* акционе́р

stocking ['stɔkɪŋ] чуло́к

stock|taking переучёт, инвентариза́ция; **~y** ['stɒkɪ] корена́стый

stoic ['stəʊɪk] **1.** сто́ик; **2.** стои́ческий

stole [stəʊl] *pt. от* ***steal***; **~n** ['stəʊlən] *pt. p. от* ***steal***

stolid ['stɒlɪd] □ флегмати́чный

stomach ['stʌmək] **1.** желу́док; живо́т; ***it turns my ~*** от э́того меня́ тошни́т; **2.** *fig.* переноси́ть [-нести́]

stone [stəʊn] **1.** ка́мень *m*; *of fruit* ко́сточка; ***leave no ~ unturned*** [с]де́лать всё возмо́жное; **2.** ка́менный; **3.** броса́ть ка́мни, броса́ться камня́ми; *fruit* вынима́ть ко́сточки из (Р); **~-deaf** соверше́нно глухо́й; **~ware** гонча́рные изде́лия *n/pl.*

stony ['stəʊnɪ] камени́стый; *fig.* ка́менный

stood [stʊd] *pt. и pt. p. от* ***stand***

stool [stuːl] (*seat*) табуре́тка; (*f(a)eces*) стул

stoop [stuːp] **1.** *v/i.* наклоня́ться [-ни́ться], нагиба́ться [нагну́ться]; (*be bent*) [с]суту́литься; *fig.* унижа́ться [уни́зиться] (***to*** до Р); *v/t.* суту́лить; **2.** суту́лость *f*

stop [stɔp] **1.** *v/t.* затыка́ть [заткну́ть] (*a.* ***~ up***), заде́л(ыв)ать; *tooth* [за]пломбирова́ть; (*prevent*) уде́рживать [-жа́ть]; (*cease*) прекраща́ть [-крати́ть]; (*halt*) остана́вливать [-нови́ть]; ***~ it!*** прекрати́!; *v/i.* перест(ав)а́ть; (*stay*) остана́вливаться [-нови́ться]; (*finish*) прекраща́ться [-рати́ться]; конча́ться [ко́нчиться]; **2.** остано́вка; па́уза; заде́ржка; *tech.* упо́р; *gr.* (*a.* ***full ~***) то́чка; **~page** ['stɒpɪdʒ] остано́вка, прекраще́ние рабо́ты; *tech.* про́бка, засоре́ние; **~per** ['stɒpə] про́бка; **~ping** ['stɒpɪŋ] (зубна́я) пло́мба

storage ['stɔːrɪdʒ] хране́ние; *place* склад

store [stɔː] **1.** запа́с; склад; *Am.* магази́н; (*department ~*) универма́г; ***in ~*** нагото́ве; про запа́с; **2.** храни́ть на скла́де; (*put by*) запаса́ть [-сти́]; **~house** склад; *fig.* сокро́вищница; **~keeper** *Am.* хозя́ин магази́на

stor(e)y ['stɒrɪ] эта́ж

stork [stɔːk] а́ист

storm [stɔːm] **1.** бу́ря; *at sea* шторм; *mil.* штурм; ***a ~ in a teacup*** бу́ря в стака́не воды́; **2.** бушева́ть; *mil.* штурмова́ть (*a. fig.*); **~y** ['~ɪ] □ бу́рный (*a. fig.*); штормово́й

story ['stɔːrɪ] (*account*) расска́з, исто́рия; *lit.* расска́з; *longer* по́весть *f*; *cine.* сюже́т; *in newspaper* статья́

stout [staʊt] **1.** □ *thing* кре́пкий, про́чный; (*sturdy*) пло́тный; (*fat*) ту́чный; (*brave*) отва́жный; **2.** кре́пкое тёмное пи́во

stove [stəʊv] печь *f*, пе́чка; (ку́хонная) плита́

stow [stəʊ] (*pack*) укла́дывать [уложи́ть]; **~away** *naut.* безбиле́тный пассажи́р

straggl|e ['strægl] *of houses* быть разбро́санным; (*drop behind*) отст(ав)а́ть; **~ing** [~ɪŋ] разбро́санный; беспоря́дочный

straight [streɪt] **1.** *adj.* прямо́й; че́стный; (*undiluted*) неразба́вленный; ***put ~*** приводи́ть в поря́док; **2.** *adv.* пря́мо; сра́зу; **~en** ['streɪtn] выпрямля́ть(ся) [вы́прямить(ся)]; ***~ out*** приводи́ть в поря́док; **~forward** [~'fɔːwəd] □ че́стный, прямо́й, открове́нный

strain¹ [streɪn] поро́да; сорт; черта́ хара́ктера

strain² [~] напряже́ние; *tech.* (*force*) нагру́зка; растяже́ние (*a. med.*); *mus. mst.* **~s** *pl.* напе́в, мело́дия; **2.** *v/t.* натя́гивать [натяну́ть]; напряга́ть [-я́чь]; (*filter*) проце́живать [-еди́ть]; (*exhaust*) переутомля́ть [-ми́ть]; *med.* растя́гивать [-яну́ть]; *v/i.* напряга́ться [-я́чься]; тяну́ться (***after*** за Т); тяну́ть изо всех сил (***at*** В); [по]стара́ться; **~er** ['streɪnə] (*colander*) дуршла́г; (*sieve*) си́то; цеди́лка

strait [streɪt] проли́в; **~s** *pl.* затрудни́тельное положе́ние; **~ened** ['streɪtnd]: ***be in ~ circumstances*** оказа́ться *pf.* в стеснённом положе́нии

strand [strænd] *of hair* прядь *f*; *of cable* жи́ла; **~ed** [~ɪd]: ***be ~*** *fig.* оказа́ться *pf.* без средств

strange [streɪndʒ] □ стра́нный; (*alien*) чужо́й; (*unknown*) незнако́мый; **~r** ['streɪndʒə] незнако́мец *m*, -мка *f*; посторо́нний (челове́к)

strangle ['strængl] [за]души́ть

strap [stræp] **1.** *on watch, etc.* ремешо́к; (*shoulder ~*) брете́лька; *mil.* пого́н; **2.** стя́гивать ремнём

stratagem ['strætədʒəm] уло́вка; хи́трость *f*

strateg|ic [strə'tiːdʒɪk] (**~*ally***) страте́ги́ческий; **~y** ['strætədʒɪ] страте́гия

strat|um ['strɑːtəm], *pl.* **~a** [~tə] *geol.* пласт; *social* слой

straw [strɔː] **1.** соло́ма; соло́минка; ***the last ~*** после́дняя ка́пля; **2.** соло́менный; **~berry** ['~brɪ] клубни́ка; (*a.* ***wild ~***) земляни́ка

stray [streɪ] **1.** сбива́ться с пути́, заблуди́ться *pf.*; забрести́ *pf.*; *of thoughts, affections* блужда́ть; **2.** (*a.* **~*ed***) заблуди́вшийся; бездо́мный; *dog, cat* бродя́чий; *bullet* шальна́я пу́ля

streak [striːk] поло́ска; *fig.* черта́; ***~s of grey*** про́седь *f*

stream [striːm] **1.** пото́к (*a. fig.*); (*brook*) руче́й; (*jet*) струя́; **2.** *v/i.* [по]те́чь; *poet.* струи́ться; *of flag, etc.* развева́ться

streamline *v/t.* придава́ть [прида́ть] обтека́емую фо́рму; упроща́ть [упрости́ть]; *fig.* рационализи́ровать

street [striːt] у́лица; *attr.* у́личный; ***not up my ~*** не по мое́й ча́сти; ***~ lamp*** у́личный фона́рь *m*; **~car** *Am.* трамва́й

strength [streŋθ] си́ла; *of cloth, etc.* про́чность *f*; *of alcohol, etc.* кре́пость *f*; ***on the ~ of*** на основа́нии (Р); **~en** ['streŋθən] *v/t.* уси́ли(ва)ть; укрепля́ть [-пи́ть]; *v/i.* уси́ли(ва)ться

strenuous ['strenjʊəs] энерги́чный; *day, work* напряжённый, тяжёлый

stress [stres] **1.** напряже́ние (*a. tech.*); (*accent*) ударе́ние; **2.** подчёркивать [-черкну́ть]; ста́вить ударе́ние на (П)

stretch [stretʃ] **1.** *v/t.* (*~ tight*) натя́гивать [-яну́ть]; (*make wider or longer*) растя́гивать [-яну́ть]; *neck* вытя́гивать [вы́тянуть]; протя́гивать [-яну́ть]; (*mst.* ***~ out***); ***~ a point*** допуска́ть [-сти́ть] натя́жку, преувели́чи(ва)ть; *v/i.* тяну́ться; растя́гиваться [-яну́ться]; **2.** растя́гивание; напряже́ние; *of road* отре́зок; натя́жка; преувеличе́ние; (*level area*) простра́нство; промежу́ток вре́мени; **~er** ['stret-

S

ʃə] носилки *f/pl.*
strew [struː] [*irr.*] посыпать [посыпать]; (*litter, scatter*) разбрасывать [-росать]
stricken ['strɪkən] *pt. p. от* ***strike***
strict [strɪkt] (*exact*) точный; (*severe*) строгий
stride [straɪd] **1.** [*irr.*] шагать [шагнуть]; ~ ***over*** перешагивать [-нуть]; **2.** большой шаг; ***take (s.th.) in one's*** ~ *fig.* легко добиваться своего; легко переносить [-нести]
strident ['straɪdnt] □ резкий, скрипучий; пронзительный
strike [straɪk] **1.** забастовка; ***be on*** ~ бастовать; **2.** [*irr.*] *v/t.* ударять [ударить]; *coins, etc.* [от]чеканить; *fig.* поражать [поразить]; находить [найти]; *a bargain* заключать [-чить]; *a pose* принимать [-нять]; ~ ***up*** *acquaintance* познакомиться; *v/i. of clock* [про]бить; [за]бастовать; ~ ***home*** *fig.* попадать в самую точку; **~r** ['straɪkə] забастовщик (-ица)
striking ['straɪkɪŋ] □ поразительный; ~ ***changes*** разительные перемены
string [strɪŋ] **1.** верёвка; бечёвка; *mus.* струна; *of pearls* нитка; **~s** *pl. mus.* струнные инструменты *m/pl.*; ***pull*** **~s** использовать свои связи; **2.** [*irr.*] *beads* нанизывать [-зать]; ~ **band** струнный оркестр
stringent ['strɪndʒənt] *rules* строгий; (*which must be obeyed*) обязательный
strip [strɪp] **1.** сдирать [содрать] (*a.* ~ ***off***); *bark* обдирать [ободрать]; разде(ва)ть(ся); *of rank, etc.* лишать [лишить] (***of*** P); (*rob*) [о]грабить; **2.** полоса, полоска; ***landing*** ~ взлётно-посадочная полоса
stripe [straɪp] полоса; *mil.* нашивка
strive [straɪv] [*irr.*] [по]стараться; стремиться (***for, after*** к Д); **~n** ['strivn] *pt. p. от* ***strive***
strode [strəʊd] *pt. от* ***stride***
stroke [strəʊk] **1.** удар (*a. med.*); *of pen, etc.* штрих; *of brush* мазок; ***at one*** ~ одним махом; ~ ***of luck*** удача; **2.** [по-] гладить
stroll [strəʊl] **1.** прогуливаться [-ляться]; **2.** прогулка
strong [strɒŋ] □ *com.* сильный; прочный; *tea, etc.* крепкий; *cheese* острый; *argument* убедительный; ***a*** ~ ***point*** сильная сторона; **~hold** *fig.* оплот; **~-willed** решительный; упрямый
strove [strəʊv] *pt. от* ***strive***
struck [strʌk] *pt. и pt. p. от* ***strike***
structure ['strʌktʃə] структура (*a. phys.*); *social* строй; *arch.* строение (*a. phys.*), сооружение
struggle ['strʌgl] **1.** бороться; всячески стараться; биться (***with*** над Т); ~ ***through*** с трудом пробиваться; **2.** борьба
strung [strʌŋ] *pt. и pt. p. от* ***string***
stub [stʌb] **1.** *of cigarette* окурок; *of pencil* огрызок; **2.** *one's toe* удариться [удариться] (***against*** о В)
stubble ['stʌbl] стерня; *of beard* щетина
stubborn ['stʌbən] □ упрямый; неподатливый; *efforts, etc.* упорный
stuck [stʌk] *pt. и pt. p. от* ***stick***; **~-up** *coll.* высокомерный; заносчивый
stud [stʌd] **1.** (*collar*~) запонка; (*press*-~) кнопка; *on boots* шип; **2.** усеивать [усеять] (Т)
student ['stjuːdnt] студент *m*, -ка *f*
studied ['stʌdɪd] *answer, remark* обдуманный; *insult* преднамеренный; умышленный
studio ['stjuːdɪəʊ] студия; *artist's* ателье *n indecl.*, мастерская
studious ['stjuːdɪəs] □ нарочитый; прилежный
study ['stʌdɪ] **1.** изучение; (*research*) исследование; (*room*) кабинет; *paint.* этюд, эскиз; **2.** учиться (Д); изучать [-чить]; исследовать (*im*)*pf.*
stuff [stʌf] **1.** материал; вещество; (*cloth*) ткань *f*, материя; ~ ***and nonsense*** чепуха; **2.** *v/t.* (*fill*) наби(ва)ть; *cul.* фаршировать; начинять [-нить]; (*shove into*) засовывать [засунуть]; (*overeat*) объедаться [объесться]; **~ing** ['stʌfɪŋ] набивка; *cul.* начинка; **~y** ['stʌfɪ] □ спёртый, душный

S

stumble ['stʌmbl] спотыка́ться [-ткну́ться]; *in speech* запина́ться [запну́ться]; ~ ***upon*** натыка́ться [наткну́ться] на (В)
stump [stʌmp] **1.** *of tree* пень *m*; *of tail, etc.* обру́бок; *of cigarette* оку́рок; **2.** *v/t. coll.* ста́вить в тупи́к; *v/i.* тяжело́ ступа́ть; **~y** ['stʌmpɪ] призе́мистый
stun [stʌn] оглуша́ть [-ши́ть] (*a. fig.*); *fig.* ошеломля́ть [-ми́ть]
stung [stʌŋ] *pt. и pt. p. от* ***sting***
stunk [stʌŋk] *pt. и pt. p. от* ***stink***
stunning ['stʌnɪŋ] *coll.* сногсшиба́тельный
stunt [stʌnt] трюк
stup|efy ['stju:pɪfaɪ] ошеломля́ть [-ми́ть]; поража́ть [порази́ть]; *with drug* одурма́нить; **~id** ['stju:pɪd] □ глу́пый, тупо́й; **~idity** [stju:'pɪdətɪ] глу́пость *f*
sturdy ['stɜ:dɪ] си́льный, кре́пкий; здоро́вый; *thing* про́чный
sturgeon [stɜ:dʒən] осётр; *cul.* осетри́на
stutter ['stʌtə] заика́ться
stye [staɪ] *on eyelid* ячме́нь *m*
style [staɪl] стиль *m*; (*fashion*) мо́да; фасо́н; ***life*** ~ о́браз жи́зни
stylish ['staɪlɪʃ] □ мо́дный; элега́нтный, *coll.* сти́льный
suave [swɑ:v] гла́дкий; обходи́тельный; мя́гкий в обраще́нии
sub... [sʌb] *mst.* под...; суб...
subconscious [sʌb'kɒnʃəs] **1.** подсозна́тельный; **2.** подсозна́ние; подсознательное
subdivision [sʌbdɪ'vɪʒn] подразделе́ние; *of a group a.* се́кция
subdue [səb'dju:] (*conquer, subjugate*) покоря́ть [-ри́ть]; подавля́ть [-ви́ть] (*reduce*) уменьша́ть [уме́ньшить]
subject ['sʌbdʒɪkt] **1.** подчинённый; подвла́стный; *fig.* ~ ***to*** подлежа́щий (Д); ***she is*** ~ ***to colds*** она́ подве́ржена просту́дам; **2.** *adv.*: ~ ***to*** при усло́вии (Р); **3.** *pol.* по́дданный; *in school* предме́т; *of novel* сюже́т; (*a.* ~ ***matter***) те́ма; ***drop the*** ~ перевести́ *pf.* разгово́р на другу́ю те́му; **4.** [səb'dʒekt] подчиня́ть [-ни́ть]; *fig.* подверга́ть [-е́ргнуть]
subjugate ['sʌbdʒʊgeɪt] (*entral(l)*) поработи́ть [-бори́ть]; покоря́ть [-ри́ть]
sublease [sʌb'li:s] субаре́нда
sublime [sə'blaɪm] □ возвы́шенный
submachine [sʌbmə'ʃi:n]: ~ ***gun*** автома́т
submarine [sʌbmə'ri:n] *naut.* подво́дная ло́дка, субмари́на
submerge [səb'mɜ:dʒ] погружа́ть(ся) [-узи́ть(ся)]; затопля́ть [-пи́ть]
submiss|ion [səb'mɪʃn] подчине́ние; поко́рность *f*; *of documents, etc.* представле́ние; **~ive** [səb'mɪsɪv] □ поко́рный
submit [səb'mɪt] (*give in*) покоря́ться [-ри́ться] (Д); (*present*) представля́ть [-а́вить]
subordinate 1. [sə'bɔ:dɪnət] подчинённый; *gr.* прида́точный; **2.** [~] подчинённый (-ённая); **3.** [sə'bɔ:dineit] подчиня́ть [-ни́ть]
subscribe [səb'skraɪb] *v/t.* (*donate*) [по]же́ртвовать; *v/i.* подде́рживать [-жа́ть] (***to*** В); *magazine, etc.* подпи́сываться [-са́ться] (***to*** на В); **~r** [~ə] подпи́счик *m*, -чица *f*; *tel.* абоне́нт
subscription [səb'skrɪpʃn] подпи́ска; *to series of concerts, etc.* абонеме́нт; *to club* чле́нские взно́сы
subsequent ['sʌbsɪkwənt] □ после́дующий; **~ly** впосле́дствии
subservient [səb'sɜ:vɪənt] подобостра́стный; (*serving to promote*) соде́йствующий (***to*** Д)
subsid|e [səb'saɪd] *of temperature* спада́ть [спасть]; *of water* убы́(ва́)ть; *of wind* утиха́ть [ути́хнуть]; *of passions* уле́чься *pf.*; **~iary** [səb'sɪdɪərɪ] **1.** □ вспомога́тельный; **2.** филиа́л, доче́рняя компа́ния; **~ize** ['sʌbsɪdaɪz] субсиди́ровать (*im*)*pf.*; **~y** ['sʌbsɪdɪ] субси́дия
subsist [səb'sɪst] (*exist*) существова́ть; жить (***on*** на В); (*eat*) пита́ться (***on*** Т); **~ence** [~əns] существова́ние; ***means of*** ~ сре́дства к существова́нию
substance ['sʌbstəns] вещество́; (*gist*) су́щность *f*, суть *f*; (*content*) содержа́ние

S

substantial [səb'stænʃl] □ существенный, важный; (*strongly made*) прочный; (*considerable*) значительный; *meal* сытный
substantiate [səb'stænʃɪeɪt] обосновывать [-новать]; доказывать справедливость (Р); (*confirm*) подтверждать [-рдить]
substitut|e ['sʌbstɪtjuːt] **1.** заменять [-нить]; *at work* замещать [-естить] (***for*** В); **2.** замена; (*thing*) суррогат; **~ion** [sʌbstɪ'tjuːʃn] замена
subterfuge ['sʌbtəfjuːdʒ] увёртка, уловка
subterranean [sʌbtə'reɪnɪən] □ подземный
subtle ['sʌtl] □ тонкий; утончённый; (*elusive*) неуловимый
subtract [səb'trækt] *math.* вычитать [вычесть]
suburb ['sʌbɜːb] пригород; предместье; (*outskirts*) окраина; **~an** [sə'bɜːbən] пригородный
subvention [səb'venʃn] субвенция, дотация
subversive [sʌb'vɜːsɪv] *fig.* подрывной
subway ['sʌbweɪ] подземный переход; *Am. rail.* метро(политен) *n indecl.*
succeed [sək'siːd] [по]следовать за (Т); (*take the place of*) быть преемником (Р); достигать цели; (*do well*) преуспе(ва)ть
success [sək'ses] успех; (*good fortune*) удача; **~ful** [sək'sesfl] □ успешный; удачный; *person* удачливый; *businessman* преуспевающий; **~ion** [~'seʃn] последовательность *f*; (*series*) ряд; ***in ~*** один за другим; подряд; **~ive** [~'sesɪv] □ последующий, следующий; **~or** [~'sesə] *at work* преемник *m*, -ница *f*; *to throne* наследник *m*, -ница *f*
succinct [sək'sɪnkt] краткий, сжатый
succulent ['sʌkjʊlənt] сочный
succumb [sə'kʌm] *to temptation, etc.* подд(ав)аться (***to*** Д); *to pressure, etc.* не выдерживать [выдержать] (***to*** Р)
such [sʌtʃ] такой; *pred.* таков, -á *и т.д.*; ***~ a man*** такой человек; ***~ as*** такой, как ...; как например
suck [sʌk] сосать; высасывать [высосать] (*a.* ***~ out***); всасывать [всосать] (*a.* ***~ in***); **~er** ['sʌkə] *Am. coll.* простак; **~le** ['sʌkl] кормить грудью; **~ling** ['sʌklɪŋ] грудной ребёнок; *animal* сосун(ок)
suction ['sʌkʃn] **1.** *tech.* всасывание; **2.** *attr.* всасывающий
sudden ['sʌdn] □ внезапный; ***all of a ~*** внезапно, вдруг
suds [sʌdz] *pl.* мыльная пена
sue [sjuː] *v/t.* предъявлять [-вить] иск кому-л.; *v/i.* возбуждать дело (***for*** о П)
suede [sweɪd] замша
suffer ['sʌfə] *v/i.* [по]страдать (***from*** от Р *or* Т); *v/t.* (*undergo, endure*) [по]терпеть; **~er** [~rə] страдалец *m*, -лица *f*; **~ing** [~rɪŋ] страдание
suffice [sə'faɪs] хватать [-тить], быть достаточным; ***~ it to say that*** достаточно сказать, что ...
sufficient [sə'fɪʃnt] □ достаточный
suffocate ['sʌfəkeɪt] *v/t.* [за]душить; *v/i.* задыхаться [задохнуться]
suffrage ['sʌfrɪdʒ] избирательное право
sugar ['ʃʊgə] **1.** сахар; ***granulated ~*** сахарный песок; ***lump ~*** (сахар-) рафинад; **2.** сахарный; **3.** *tea, etc.* положить сахар; **~y** [~rɪ] *fig.* приторный, слащавый
suggest [sə'dʒest] (*propose*) предлагать [-ложить]; *solution* подсказывать [-зать]; наводить на мысль *f* о (П); [по]советовать; **~ion** [~ʃən] совет, предложение; (*hint*) намёк; **~ive** [~ɪv] □ (*giving food for thought*) наводящий на размышление; (*improper*) непристойный; *joke* двусмысленный
suicide ['suːɪsaɪd] самоубийство; ***commit ~*** покончить *pf.* с собой
suit [suːt] **1.** (*a.* ***~ of clothes***) костюм; *cards* масть *f*; *law* судебное дело, иск; **2.** *v/t.* (*adapt*) приспосабливать [-особить] (***to, with*** к Д); соответствовать (Д); удовлетворить; (*be convenient or right*) устраивать [-роить]; подходить [подойти] (Д); ***~ yourself*** поступай

S

как зна́ешь; *v/i.* (*be appropriate*) подходи́ть, годи́ться; **~able** ['su:təbl] □ подходя́щий; соотве́тствующий; **~case** чемода́н
suite [swi:t] *mus.* сю́ита; *in hotel* но́мер-люкс; *of furniture* гарниту́р
suited ['sʊ:tɪd] подходя́щий
sulfur, *Brt.* **sulphur** ['sʌlfə] *chem.* се́ра; **~ic** [sʌl'fjuərɪk] се́рный
sulk [sʌlk] **1.** [на]ду́ться; быть не в ду́хе; **2.**: **~s** [~s] *pl.* плохо́е настрое́ние; **~y** ['sʌlkɪ] □ наду́тый
sullen ['sʌlən] угрю́мый, мра́чный; *sky* па́смурный
sultry ['sʌltrɪ] □ ду́шный, зно́йный
sum [sʌm] **1.** су́мма; итог; *in* **~** ко́ротко говоря́; **~s** *pl.* арифме́тика; **2.** (*a.* **~ up**) *math.* скла́дывать [сложи́ть]; *fig.* подводи́ть ито́г
summar|ize ['sʌməraiz] сумми́ровать (*im*)*pf.*; подводи́ть [-вести́] ито́г; написа́ть *pf.* резюме́; **~y** [~rɪ] сво́дка; аннота́ция, резюме́ *n indecl.*
summer ['sʌmə] ле́то; *in* **~** ле́том; **~y** [~ri] ле́тний
summit ['sʌmɪt] верши́на (*a. fig.*); *pol.* са́ммит, встре́ча в верха́х; *fig.* преде́л
summon ['sʌmən] соз(ы)ва́ть (собра́ние *и т. п.*); *law* вызыва́ть [вы́звать]; **~s** [~z] вы́зов в суд; *law* суде́бная пове́стка
sumptuous ['sʌmptʃʊəs] роско́шный; пы́шный
sun [sʌn] **1.** со́лнце; **2.** со́лнечный; **3.** гре́ть(ся) на со́лнце; **~bathe** загора́ть; **~burn** зага́р; *painful* со́лнечный ожо́г
Sunday ['sʌndɪ] воскресе́нье
sundown захо́д со́лнца
sundry ['sʌndrɪ] ра́зный; ***all and*** **~** все без исключе́ния
sunflower ['sʌnflaʊə] подсо́лнечник
sung [sʌŋ] *pt. p. om* ***sing***
sunglasses *pl.* тёмные очки́ *n/pl.*
sunk [sʌŋk] *pt. p. om* ***sink***
sunken [sʌŋkən] *fig.* впа́лый
sun|ny ['sʌnɪ] □ со́лнечный; **~rise** восхо́д со́лнца; **~set** захо́д со́лнца, зака́т; **~shade** зо́нт(ик) от со́лнца; **~shine** со́лнечный свет; ***in the*** **~** на со́лнце; **~stroke** *med.* со́лнечный уда́р; **~tan** зага́р; **~tanned** загоре́лый
super... ['su:pə] *pref.*: пе́ре..., пре...; сверх...; над...; су́пер...
super ['su:pə] замеча́тельный; **~!** здо́рово!
superb [su:'pɜ:b] великоле́пный, превосхо́дный
super|cilious [su:pə'sɪlɪəs] □ высокоме́рный; **~ficial** [su:pə'fɪʃl] □ пове́рхностный; **~fluous** [su:'pɜ:flʊəs] ли́шний, изли́шний; **~human** сверхчелове́ческий; **~intend** [su:pərɪn'tend] (*watch*) надзира́ть за (Т); (*direct*) руководи́ть (Т); **~intendent** [~ənt] руководи́тель *m*
superior [su:'pɪərɪə] **1.** □ *in rank* вы́сший, ста́рший; *in quality* превосхо́дный; превосходя́щий (***to*** В); **~ *smile*** надме́нная улы́бка; **2.** нача́льник; *eccl.* настоя́тель *m*, -ница *f*; *of a convent* ***mother/father*** **♀** игу́менья/игу́мен; **~ity** [su:pɪərɪ'ɒrətɪ] *of quality, quantity, etc.* превосхо́дство; *of rank* старшинство́
super|lative [su:'pɜ:lətɪv] **1.** □ высоча́йший; велича́йший; **2.** *gr.* превосхо́дная сте́пень *f*; **~man** ['su:pəmæn] суперме́н; **~market** ['su:pəmɑ:kɪt] универса́м (= *универса́льный магази́н самообслу́живания*); **~sede** [su:pə'si:d] (*replace*) заменя́ть [-ни́ть]; (*displace*) вытесня́ть [вы́теснить]; *fig.* (*overtake*) обгоня́ть [обогна́ть]; **~sonic** [su:pə'sɒnɪk] сверхзвуково́й; **~stition** [su:pə'stɪʃn] суеве́рие; **~stitious** [~'stɪʃəs] суеве́рный; **~vene** [~'vi:n] сле́довать за че́м-либо; **~vise** ['su:pəvaiz] надзира́ть (Т); **~vision** [su:pə'vɪʒn] надзо́р; **~visor** ['su:pəvaɪzə] надзира́тель *m*, -ница *f*
supper ['sʌpə] у́жин; ***the Last*** **♀** Та́йная Ве́черя
supplant [sə'plɑ:nt] вытесня́ть [вы́теснить] (В)
supple ['sʌpl] ги́бкий (*a. fig.*)
supplement **1.** ['sʌplɪmənt] (*addition*) дополне́ние; *to a periodical* приложе́ние; **2.** [~'ment] дополня́ть [допо́лнить]; **~ary** [sʌlɪ'mentərɪ] дополни́тельный, доба́вочный

S

supplier [sə'plaɪə] поставщи́к
supply [sə'plaɪ] **1.** снабжа́ть [-бди́ть] (***with*** Т); *goods* поставля́ть [-а́вить]; *information, etc.* предоставля́ть [-а́вить]; **2.** снабже́ние; поста́вка; (*stock*) запа́с; **supplies** *pl.* (*food*) продово́льствие; ***~ and demand*** спрос и предложе́ние
support [sə'pɔːt] **1.** подде́ржка; *phys., tech.* опо́ра (*a. fig.*); **2.** подпира́ть [-пере́ть]; *a candidature, etc.* подде́рживать [-жа́ть]; *one's family, etc.* содержа́ть
suppose [sə'pəʊz] (*assume*) предполага́ть [-ложи́ть]; (*imagine*) полага́ть; *coll.* ***~ we do so?*** а е́сли мы э́то сде́лаем?; ***he's ~d to be back today*** он до́лжен сего́дня верну́ться
supposed [sə'pəʊzd] □ предполага́емый; **~ly** [sə'pəʊzɪdlɪ] предположи́тельно; я́кобы
supposition [sʌpə'zɪʃn] предположе́ние
suppress [sə'pres] *uprising, yawn, etc.* подавля́ть [-ви́ть]; (*ban*) запреща́ть [-ети́ть]; *laugh, anger, etc.* сде́рживать [-жа́ть]; **~ion** [sə'preʃn] подавле́ние
suprem|acy [suː'preməsɪ] превосхо́дство; **~e** [suː'priːm] □ *command, etc.* верхо́вный; (*greatest*) высоча́йший
surcharge ['sɜːtʃɑːdʒ] (*extra charge*) припла́та, допла́та
sure [ʃʊə] □ *com.* ве́рный; (*certain*) уве́ренный; (*safe*) безопа́сный; надёжный; *Am.* **~!** коне́чно; ***make ~ that ...*** вы́яснить *pf.*, убеди́ться *pf.*, прове́рить *pf.*; **~ly** ['ʃʊəlɪ] несомне́нно
surf [sɜːf] прибо́й
surface ['sɜːfɪs] пове́рхность *f*; ***on the ~*** *fig.* чи́сто вне́шне; на пе́рвый взгляд; ***~ mail*** обы́чной по́чтой
surfing ['sɜːfɪŋ] се́рфинг
surge [sɜːdʒ] **1.** волна́; **2.** *of waves* вздыма́ться; *of crowd* подава́ться [-да́ться] вперёд; *of emotions* [на-] хлы́нуть *pf.*
surg|eon ['sɜːdʒən] хиру́рг; **~ery** ['sɜːdʒərɪ] хирурги́я; опера́ция; *Brt.* приёмная (врача́); ***~ hours*** приёмные часы́
surgical ['sɜːdʒɪkl] □ хирурги́ческий
surly ['sɜːlɪ] □ неприве́тливый; хму́рый; угрю́мый
surmise [sə'maɪz] **1.** предположе́ние; **2.** предполага́ть [-ложи́ть]
surmount [sə'maʊnt] преодоле́(ва́)ть, превозмога́ть [-мо́чь]
surname ['sɜːneɪm] фами́лия
surpass [sə'pɑːs] *expectations, etc.* превосходи́ть [-взойти́]
surplus ['sɜːpləs] **1.** изли́шек; (*remainder*) оста́ток; **2.** изли́шний; ли́шний
surprise [sə'praɪz] **1.** удивле́ние; *event, present, etc.* неожи́данность *f*, сюрпри́з; *attr.* неожи́данный; **2.** удивля́ть [-ви́ть]; (*take unawares*) застава́ть врасплóх
surrender [sə'rendə] **1.** сда́ча; капитуля́ция; **2.** *v/t.* сда(ва́)ть; *one's rights* отка́зываться [-за́ться] от (Р); *v/i.* сд(ав)а́ться
surround [sə'raʊnd] окружа́ть [-жи́ть]; **~ing** [~ɪŋ] окружа́ющий; **~ings** [~ɪŋz] *pl.* окре́стности *f/pl.*; (*environment*) среда́, окруже́ние
survey [sɜː'veɪ] **1.** (*look at, examine*) обозре́(ва́)ть; осма́тривать [осмотре́ть]; производи́ть [-вести́] топографи́ческую съёмку; **2.** ['sɜːveɪ] осмо́тр; (*study*) обзо́р; топографи́ческая съёмка; *attr.* обзо́рный; **~or** [sə'veɪə] землеме́р; топо́граф
surviv|al [sə'vaɪvl] выжива́ние; (*relic*) пережи́ток; **~e** [sə'vaɪv] *v/t.* пережи́(ва́)ть *mst. pf.*; *v/i.* остава́ться в живы́х, вы́жи(ва́)ть; *of custom* сохраня́ться [-ни́ться]; **~or** [sə'vaɪvə] оста́вшийся в живы́х
susceptible [sə'septəbl] □ восприи́мчивый (***to*** к Д); (*sensitive*) чувстви́тельный; (*easily enamo(u)red*) влю́бчивый
suspect [səs'pekt] **1.** подозрева́ть, запода́зривать [-до́зрить] (***of*** в П); *the truth of, etc.* сомнева́ться [усомни́ться] в (П); (*think*) предполага́ть; **2.** ['sʌspekt] подозри́тельный; подозрева́емый
suspend [sə'spend] подве́шивать [-е́сить]; (*stop for a time*) приостана́вливать [-нови́ть]; вре́менно

S

прекраща́ть; **~ed** [~ɪd] подвесно́й; **~ers** [~əz] *pl. Am.* подтя́жки *f/pl.*
suspens|e [sə'spens] напряжённое внима́ние; (*uneasy uncertainty*) состоя́ние неизве́стности, неопределённости; ***in ~*** напряжённо, в напряже́нии; **~ion** [sə'spenʃn] прекраще́ние; ***~ bridge*** вися́чий мост
suspici|on [sə'spɪʃn] подозре́ние; *trace, nuance* отте́нок; **~ous** [~ʃəs] □ подозри́тельный
sustain [sə'steɪn] (*support*) подпира́ть [-пере́ть], подде́рживать [-жа́ть] (*a. fig.*); *law* подтвержда́ть [-рди́ть]; выде́рживать [вы́держать]; (*suffer*) выноси́ть [вы́нести], испы́тывать [испыта́ть]
sustenance ['sʌstɪnəns] пи́ща; сре́дства к существова́нию
swaddle ['swɒdl] [c-, за]пелена́ть
swagger ['swægə] ходи́ть с ва́жным ви́дом; (*brag*) [по]хва́стать (*a.* -ся)
swallow[1] ['swɒləʊ] *zo.* ла́сточка
swallow[2] [~] глото́к; глота́ть; прогла́тывать [-лоти́ть]
swam [swæm] *pt. om* **swim**
swamp [swɒmp] **1.** боло́то, топь *f*; **2.** затопля́ть [-пи́ть], залива́ть; **~y** ['swɒmpɪ] боло́тистый
swan [swɒn] ле́бедь *m*
swap [swɒp] *coll.* **1.** обме́нивать(ся) [-ня́ть(ся)]; [по]меня́ть(ся); **2.** обме́н
swarm [swɔːm] **1.** *of bees* рой; *of birds* ста́я; толпа́; **2.** *of bees* рои́ться; кише́ть (***with*** T); ***crowds ~ed into the cinema*** толпа́ хлы́нула в кинотеа́тр
swarthy ['swɔːðɪ] сму́глый
sway [sweɪ] **1.** кача́ние; (*influence*) влия́ние; **2.** кача́ть(ся) [качну́ть(ся)]; *fig.* [по]влия́ть, склони́ть на свою́ сто́рону
swear [sweə] [*irr.*] (*take an oath*) [по]кля́сться (***by*** T); (*curse*) [вы́-]руга́ться; **~word** руга́тельство
sweat [swet] **1.** пот; **2.** [*irr.*] *v/i.* [вс]поте́ть; исполня́ть тяжёлую рабо́ту; *v/t.* заставля́ть поте́ть; ***~ blood*** *coll.* рабо́тать как вол; **~er** ['swetə] сви́тер; **~y** ['swetɪ] по́тный
Swede [swiːd] шве́д *m*, -ка *f*
swede [~] *bot.* брю́ква
Swedish ['swiːdɪʃ] шве́дский
sweep [swiːp] **1.** [*irr.*] мести́, подмета́ть [-ести́]; *chimney* [по]чи́стить; (*rush*) проноси́ться [-нести́сь] (*a.* ***~ past, along***); ***~ s.o. off his feet*** вскружи́ть кому́-л. го́лову; **2.** *of arm* взмах; (*curve*) изги́б; ***make a clean ~*** (***of***) отде́л(ыв)аться (от P); **~er** ['swiːpə]: ***road ~*** подмета́тельная маши́на; **~ing** ['swiːpɪŋ] □ *gesture* широ́кий; *accusation* огу́льный; *changes* радика́льный, широкомасшта́бный; **~ings** [~z] *pl.* му́сор
sweet [swiːt] **1.** □ сла́дкий; *air* све́жий; *water* пре́сный; *person* ми́лый; ***have a ~ tooth*** быть сластёной; **2.** конфе́та; **~s** *pl.* сла́сти *f/pl.*; **~en** ['swiːtn] подсла́щивать [-ласти́ть]; ***~ the pill*** позолоти́ть *pf.* пилю́лю; **~heart** возлю́бленный (-енная)
swell [swel] **1.** [*irr.*] *v/i.* [о-, при-, рас]пу́хнуть; *of cheek* разду́(ва́)ться; *of wood* набуха́ть [-у́хнуть]; *of sound* нараста́ть [-сти́]; *v/t.* (*increase*) увели́чи(ва)ть; **2.** *coll.* (*fashionable*) шика́рный; (*excellent*) великоле́пный; **3.** *coll.* франт; **~ing** ['swelɪŋ] о́пухоль *f*; *slight* припу́хлость *f*
swelter ['sweltə] изнемога́ть от жары́
swept [swept] *pt. u pt. p. om* **sweep**
swerve [swɜːv] свора́чивать [сверну́ть] в сто́рону; *of car, etc.* ре́зко сверну́ть *pf.*
swift [swɪft] □ бы́стрый, ско́рый; **~ness** ['~nɪs] быстрота́
swill [swɪl] **1.** (*slops*) помо́и *m/pl.*; **2.** [про]полоска́ть, опола́скивать [-лосну́ть] (*a.* ***~ out***)
swim [swɪm] **1.** [*irr.*] пла́вать, [по-]плы́ть; перепл(ыв)а́ть (*a.* ***~ across***); ***my head ~s*** у меня́ голова́ кру́жится; **2.** пла́вание; ***be in the ~*** быть в ку́рсе де́л; **~mer** ['~ə] плове́ц *m*, -вчи́ха *f*; **~ming** ['~ɪŋ] пла́вание; ***~ pool*** пла́вательный бассе́йн; ***~ trunks*** пла́вки; **~suit** купа́льный костю́м
swindle ['swɪndl] **1.** обма́нывать

S

[-ну́ть], наду́(ва́)ть; **2.** обма́н, надува́тельство; **~r** [~ə] моше́нник
swine [swaɪn] *coll. fig.* свинья́
swing [swɪŋ] **1.** [*irr.*] кача́ть(ся) [качну́ть(ся)]; *hands* разма́хивать; *feet* болта́ть; (*hang*) висе́ть; **2.** кача́ние; разма́х; взмах; ритм; каче́ли *f/pl.*; ***in full ~*** в по́лном разга́ре; ***go with a ~*** проходи́ть о́чень успе́шно; **~ door** дверь *f*, открыва́ющаяся в любу́ю сто́рону
swipe [swaɪp] уда́рить; *joc.* (*steal*) стащи́ть
swirl [swɜːl] **1.** *in dance*, *etc.* кружи́ть(ся); *of dust*, *etc.* клуби́ться; *of water* крути́ться; **2.** водоворо́т
Swiss [swɪs] **1.** швейца́рский; **2.** швейца́рец *m*, -рка *f*; ***the ~*** *pl.* швейца́рцы *m/pl.*
switch [swɪtʃ] **1.** *el.* выключа́тель *m*; *radio*, *TV* переключа́тель *m*; **2.** (*whip*) хлеста́ть [-стну́ть]; *el.* переключа́ть [-чи́ть] (*often* ***~ over***) (*a. fig.*); *fig.* ***~ the conversation*** переводи́ть [-вести́] разгово́р (на В); ***~ on*** *el.* включа́ть [-чи́ть]; ***~ off*** выключа́ть [вы́ключить]; **~board** *tel.* коммута́тор
swollen ['swəʊlən] *pt. p. от* ***swell***
swoon [swuːn] **1.** о́бморок; **2.** па́дать в о́бморок
swoop [swuːp] (*a.* ***~ down***), ри́нуться; (*suddenly attack*) налета́ть [-ете́ть] (***on*** на В)
sword [sɔːd] шпа́га; меч
swore [swɔː] *pt. от* ***swear***
sworn [swɔːn] *pt. p. от* ***swear***; *adj. enemy* закля́тый
swum [swʌm] *pt. p. от* ***swim***
swung [swʌŋ] *pt. и pt. p. от* ***swing***
syllable ['sɪləbl] слог
syllabus ['sɪləbəs] уче́бный план
symbol ['sɪmbl] си́мвол, усло́вное обозначе́ние; **~ic(al)** [sɪm'bɒlɪk(l)] символи́ческий; **~ism** ['sɪmbəlɪzəm] символи́зм
symmetr|ical [sɪ'metrɪkl] □ симметри́чный; **~y** ['sɪmətrɪ] симметри́я
sympath|etic [sɪmpə'θetɪk] (***~ally***) сочу́вственный; **~ize** ['sɪmpəθaɪz] [по]сочу́вствовать (***with*** Д); **~y** ['sɪmpəθɪ] сочу́вствие (***with*** к Д)
symphony ['sɪmfənɪ] симфо́ния
symptom ['sɪmptəm] симпто́м
synchron|ize ['sɪŋkrənaɪz] *v/i.* совпада́ть по вре́мени; *v/t. actions* синхронизи́ровать (*im*)*pf.*; **~ous** [~nəs] □ синхро́нный
syndicate ['sɪndɪkət] синдика́т
synonym ['sɪnənɪm] сино́ним; **~ous** [sɪ'nɒnɪməs] синоними́ческий
synopsis [sɪ'nɒpsɪs] кра́ткое изложе́ние, сино́псис
synthe|sis ['sɪnθesɪs] си́нтез; **~tic** [sɪn'θetɪk] синтети́ческий
syringe [sɪ'rɪndʒ] шприц
syrup ['sɪrəp] сиро́п
system ['sɪstəm] систе́ма; **~atic** [sɪstə'mætɪk] (***~ally***) системати́ческий

T

tab [tæb] *for hanging garment* ве́шалка; *mil.* наши́вка, петли́ца
table ['teɪbl] стол; (*list of data*, *etc.*) табли́ца; ***~ of contents*** оглавле́ние; **~cloth** ска́терть *f*; **~ d'hôte** ['tɑːbl'dout] табльдо́т; о́бщий стол; **~ lamp** насто́льная ла́мпа; **~spoon** столо́вая ло́жка
tablet ['tæblɪt] *med.* табле́тка; *of soap* кусо́к; мемориа́льная доска́
table tennis насто́льный те́ннис
taboo [tə'buː] табу́ *n indecl.*
tacit ['tæsɪt] □ подразумева́емый; молчали́вый; **~urn** ['tæsɪtɜːn] □ неразгово́рчивый
tack [tæk] **1.** гво́здик с широ́кой шля́пкой; (*thumb~*) *Am.* кно́пка; **~ing** *sew.* намётка; **2.** *v/t.* прикрепля́ть гво́здиками и́ли кно́пками; *sewing* смётывать [смета́ть]

tackle ['tækl] **1.** (*equipment*) принадлéжности *f/pl.*; *for fishing* снасть *f*; **2.** (*deal with*) энерги́чно брáться за (В); *problem* би́ться над (Т)
tact [tækt] такт, такти́чность *f*; **~ful** ['tæktfʊl] такти́чный
tactics ['tæktɪks] *pl.* тáктика
tactless ['tæktlɪs] □ бестáктный
tag [tæg] **1.** би́рка, этикéтка; *fig.* изби́тое выражéние; ***price ~*** цéнник; **2.**: ***~ along*** слéдовать по пятáм; тащи́ться сзáди
tail [teɪl] **1.** хвост; *of coat* фáлда; полá; *of coin* обрáтная сторонá; ***heads or ~s?*** орёл или рéшка?; **2.** *v/t.* (*follow*) слéдовать, тащи́ться (***after*** за Т); *Am. coll. of police* вы́слéживать [вы́следить]; *v/i.* тянýться верени́цей; ***~ off*** (*fall behind*) отст(ав)áть; **~coat** фрак; **~light** *mot.* зáдний фонарь *m*/свет
tailor ['teɪlə] портнóй; **~-made** сдéланный по закáзу
take [teɪk] **1.** [*irr.*] *v/t.* брать [взять]; *medicine, etc.* принимáть [-ня́ть]; [съ]есть; [вы́]пить; *seat* занимáть [заня́ть]; *phot.* снимáть [снять]; *time* отнимáть [-ня́ть]; ***I ~ it that*** я полагáю, что ...; ***~ in hand*** взять *pf.* в свои́ рýки; ***~ o.s. in hand*** взять *pf.* себя́ в рýки; ***~ pity on*** сжáлиться *pf.* над (Т); ***~ place*** случáться [-чи́ться], происходи́ть (произойти́); ***~ a rest*** отдыхáть (отдохнýть); ***~ a hint*** поня́ть *pf.* намёк; ***~ a seat*** сади́ться [сесть]; ***~ a taxi*** брать [взять] такси́; ***~ a view*** вы́скáзывать свою́ тóчку зрéния; ***~ a walk*** [по]гуля́ть, прогýливаться [-ля́ться]; ***~ down*** снимáть [снять]; запи́сывать [-сáть]; ***~ for*** принимáть [-ня́ть] за (В); ***~ from*** брать [взять] у Р; ***~ in*** (*deceive*) обмáнывать [-нýть]; (*understand*) поня́ть *pf.*; ***~ off*** *coat, etc.* снимáть [снять]; ***~ out*** вынимáть [вы́нуть]; ***~ to pieces*** разбирáть [разобрáть]; ***~ up*** брáться [взя́ться] за (В); *space, time* занимáть [заня́ть], отнимáть [отня́ть]; **2.** *v/i.* (*have the intended effect*) [по]дéйствовать; (*be a success*) имéть успéх; ***~ after*** походи́ть на (В); ***~ off*** *ae.* взлетáть [-етéть]; ***~ over*** принимáть делá (***from*** от Р); ***~ to*** пристрасти́ться к (Д) *pf.*; привязáться к (Д) *pf.*; **~n** ['teɪkən] *pt. p. om* ***take***; ***be ~ ill*** заболé(вá)ть; **~-off** ['teɪ'kɔf] (*impersonation*) подражáние; *ae.* взлёт
takings ['teɪkɪŋz] *pl. comm.* вы́ручка; сбор
tale [teɪl] расскáз, пóвесть *f*; (*false account*) вы́думка; (*unkind account*) сплéтня; ***tell ~s*** сплéтничать
talent ['tælənt] талáнт; **~ed** [~ɪd] талáнтливый
talk [tɔːk] **1.** разговóр, бесéда; **~s** *pl. pol.* переговóры; ***there is ~ that ...*** говоря́т, что ...; **2.** [по]говори́ть; разговáривать; [по]бесéдовать; **~ative** ['tɔːkətɪv] разговóрчивый; **~er** ['tɔːkə] **1.** говоря́щий; говорли́вый человéк
tall [tɔːl] высóкий; ***~ order*** чрезмéрное трéбование; ***~ story*** *coll.* небыли́ца; неправдоподóбная истóрия
tally ['tælɪ] соотвéтствовать (***with*** Д)
tame [teɪm] **1.** □ *animal* ручнóй, прирýчённый; (*submissive*) покóрный; (*dull*) скýчный; **2.** приручáть [-чи́ть]
tamper ['tæmpə]: ***~ with*** трóгать; копáться; *document* поддéл(ывать) (В); ***someone has ~ed with my luggage*** ктó-то копáлся в моём багажé
tan [tæn] **1.** (*sun~*) загáр; **2.** загорáть
tang [tæŋ] (*taste*) рéзкий при́вкус; (*smell*) зáпах
tangent ['tændʒənt] *math.* касáтельная; ***go*** (*a.* ***fly***) ***off at a ~*** рéзко отклони́тся *pf.*
tangerine [tændʒə'riːn] мандари́н
tangible ['tændʒəbl] □ осязáемый, ощути́мый
tangle ['tæŋgl] **1.** пýтаница, неразбери́ха; **2.** запýт(ыв)ать(ся)
tank [tæŋk] цистéрна; бак; *mil.* танк, *attr.* тáнковый; ***gas(oline) ~***, *Brt.* ***petrol ~*** бензобáк
tankard ['tæŋkəd] высóкая крýжка
tanker ['tæŋkə] *naut.* тáнкер; *mot.* автоцистéрна

tantalize ['tæntəlaɪz] дразни́ть; [за-, из]му́чить
tantrum ['tæntrəm] *coll.* вспы́шка гне́ва *или* раздраже́ния; ***throw a ~*** закати́ть *pf.* исте́рику
tap[1] [tæp] **1.** *for water, gas* кран; **2.:** ***~ for money*** выпра́шивать де́ньги у P; ***~ for information*** выу́живать [-удить] информа́цию
tap[2] [~] **1.** [по]стуча́ть; [по]хло́пать; **2.** лёгкий стук; **~-dance** чечётка
tape [teɪp] тесьма́; *sport* фи́нишная ле́нточка; магни́тная ле́нта; ***sticky ~*** ли́пкая ле́нта; **~ measure** ['teɪpmeʒə] руле́тка; *of cloth* санти́метр
taper ['teɪpə] *v/i.* су́живаться к концу́; *v/t.* заостря́ть [-ри́ть]
tape recorder магнитофо́н
tapestry ['tæpəstrɪ] гобеле́н
tar [tɑː] **1.** дёготь *m*; *for boats* смола́; **2.** [вы́]смоли́ть
tardy ['tɑːdɪ] □ (*slow-moving*) медли́тельный; (*coming or done late*) запозда́лый
target ['tɑːgɪt] цель *f* (*a. fig.*); мише́нь *f* (*a. fig.*)
tariff ['tærɪf] тари́ф
tarnish ['tɑːnɪʃ] *fig.* [о]поро́чить; *v/i. of metal* [по]тускне́ть; ***~ed reputation*** запя́тнанная репута́ция
tarpaulin [tɑː'pɔːlɪn] брезе́нт
tart[1] [tɑːt] откры́тый пиро́г с фру́ктами; сла́дкая ватру́шка
tart[2] [~] ки́слый, те́рпкий; *fig.* ко́лкий
tartan ['tɑːtn] шотла́ндка
task [tɑːsk] (*problem*) зада́ча; (*job*) зада́ние; ***set a ~*** дать *pf.* зада́ние; ***take to ~*** отчи́тывать [-ита́ть]; **~ force** *mil.* операти́вная гру́ппа
taste [teɪst] **1.** вкус; ***have a ~ for*** люби́ть, знать толк (в П); **2.** [по]про́бовать; *fig.* испы́тывать [-пыта́ть]; ***~ sweet*** быть сла́дким на вкус; **~ful** ['teɪstfl] □ (сде́ланный) со вку́сом; изя́щный; **~less** [~lɪs] безвку́сный
tasty ['teɪstɪ] □ вку́сный
tatter|ed ['tætəd] изно́шенный, изо́рванный; **~s** *pl.* лохмо́тья *n/pl.*; ***tear to ~s*** разорва́ть в кло́чья; *fig.* разбива́ть [-би́ть] в пух и прах
tattle ['tætl] болтовня́
tattoo [tə'tuː] (*design on skin*) татуиро́вка
taught [tɔːt] *pt. и pt. p. от* ***teach***
taunt [tɔːnt] **1.** насме́шка, ко́лкость *f*; **2.** говори́ть ко́лкости (Д), дразни́ть
taut [tɔːt] (*stretched tight*) ту́го натя́нутый; *nerves* взви́нченный
tawdry ['tɔːdrɪ] □ безвку́сный; крича́щий
tawny ['tɔːnɪ] рыжева́то-кори́чневый
tax [tæks] **1.** нало́г (***on*** на В); ***income ~*** подохо́дный нало́г; ***~ evasion*** уклоне́ние от упла́ты нало́га; ***value added ~*** нало́г на доба́вочную сто́имость *f*; **2.** облага́ть нало́гом; *one's strength* чрезме́рно напряга́ть; ***~ s.o.'s patience*** испы́тывать чьё-л. терпе́ние; ***~ a p. with a th.*** обвиня́ть [-ни́ть] кого́-л. в чём-л.; **~ation** [tæk'seɪʃn] обложе́ние нало́гом; взима́ние нало́га
taxi ['tæksɪ] = **~cab** такси́ *n indecl.*
taxpayer ['tækspeɪə] налогоплате́льщик
tea [tiː] чай; ***make*** (***the***) ***~*** зава́ривать [-ри́ть] чай
teach [tiːtʃ] [*irr.*] [на]учи́ть, обуча́ть [-чи́ть]; *a subject* препода́ва́ть; **~er** ['tiːtʃə] учи́тель *m*, -ница *f*; *univ.* преподава́тель *m*, -ница *f*
teacup ['tiːkʌp] ча́йная ча́шка
team [tiːm] **1.** *sport* кома́нда; *of workers* брига́да; ***~ spirit*** чу́вство ло́ктя; **2.:** ***~ up*** сотру́дничать; **~work** совме́стная рабо́та
teapot ['tiːpɒt] ча́йник (для зава́рки)
tear[1] [teə] **1.** [*irr.*] дыра́, проре́ха; **2.** [по]рва́ться; разрыва́ть(ся) [разорва́ть(ся)]; *fig.* раздира́ть(ся); (*go at great speed*) [по]мча́ться; ***country torn by war*** страна́, раздира́емая войно́й
tear[2] [tɪə] слеза́ (*pl.* слёзы)
tearful ['tɪəfl] □ слезли́вый; *eyes* по́лный слёз
tease [tiːz] **1.** челове́к, лю́бящий поддра́знивать; **2.** *coll.* дразни́ть; подшу́чивать; **~r** [~ə] *coll.* головоло́мка
teat [tiːt] сосо́к
technic|al ['teknɪkl] □ техни́ческий;

T

~ality [teknɪ'kælətɪ] техни́ческая дета́ль *f*; форма́льность *f*; **~ian** [tek'nɪʃn] те́хник
technique [tek'ni:k] те́хника; ме́тод, спо́соб
technology [tek'nɒlədʒɪ] техноло́гия; технологи́ческие нау́ки *f/pl.*
tedious ['ti:dɪəs] □ ску́чный, утоми́тельный
tedium ['ti:dɪəm] утоми́тельность *f*; ску́ка
teem [ti:m] изоби́ловать, кише́ть (***with*** Т)
teenager ['ti:neɪdʒə] подро́сток; ю́ноша *m* / де́вушка *f* до двадцати́ лет
teeth [ti:θ] *pl. от* ***tooth***; **~e** [ti:ð]: ***the child is teething*** у ребёнка проreза́ются зу́бы
teetotal(l)er [ti:'təʊtlə] тре́звенник
telecommunications [telɪkəmju:nɪ'keɪʃnz] *pl.* сре́дства да́льней свя́зи
telegram ['telɪgræm] телегра́мма
telegraph ['telɪgrɑ:f] **1.** телегра́ф; **2.** телеграфи́ровать *(im)pf.*; **3.** *attr.* телегра́фный
telephone ['telɪfəʊn] **1.** телефо́н; **2.** звони́ть по телефо́ну; **~ booth** телефо́н-автома́т; **~ directory** телефо́нный спра́вочник
telescop|e ['telɪskəʊp] телеско́п; **~ic** [telɪs'kɒpɪk] телескопи́ческий; ***~ aerial*** выдвижна́я анте́нна
teletype ['telɪtaɪp] телета́йп
televis|ion ['telɪvɪʒn] телеви́дение
telex ['teleks] те́лекс
tell [tel] *[irr.] v/t.* говори́ть [сказа́ть]; (*relate*) расска́зывать [-за́ть]; (*distinguish*) отлича́ть [-чи́ть]; ***~ a p. to do a th.*** веле́ть кому́-л. что́-л. сде́лать; ***~ off*** *coll.* [вы́]брани́ть; *v/i.* (*affect*) ска́зываться [сказа́ться]; (*know*) знать; ***how can I ~?*** отку́да мне знать?; **~er** ['telə] *esp. Am.* касси́р (в ба́нке); **~ing** ['telɪŋ] □ многоговоря́щий, многозначи́тельный; **~tale** ['telteɪl] я́беда *m & f*
telly ['telɪ] *chiefly Brt. coll.* те́лик
temper ['tempə] **1.** *steel* закаля́ть [-ли́ть] (*a. fig.*); **2.** нрав; (*mood*) настрое́ние; (*irritation, anger*) раздраже́ние, гнев; ***he has a quick ~*** он вспы́льчив; **~ament** ['temprəmənt] темпера́мент; **~amental** [temprə'mentl] □ темпера́ментный; **~ate** ['tempərət] □ *climate* уме́ренный; *behavio(u)r* сде́ржанный; **~ature** ['temprətʃə] температу́ра
tempest ['tempɪst] бу́ря; **~uous** □ [tem'pestʃʊəs] бу́рный (*a. fig.*)
temple[1] [templ] храм
temple[2] [~] *anat.* висо́к
tempo ['tempəʊ] темп
tempor|ary ['temprərɪ] □ вре́менный; **~ize** [~raɪz] стара́ться вы́играть вре́мя, тяну́ть вре́мя
tempt [tempt] искуша́ть [-уси́ть], соблазня́ть [-ни́ть]; (*attract*) привлека́ть [-е́чь]; **~ation** [temp'teɪʃn] искуше́ние, собла́зн; **~ing** ['~tɪŋ] □ зама́нчивый, соблазни́тельный
ten [ten] **1.** де́сять; **2.** деся́ток
tenable ['tenəbl]: ***not a ~ argument*** аргуме́нт, не выде́рживающий кри́тики
tenaci|ous [tɪ'neɪʃəs] □ це́пкий; ***~ memory*** хоро́шая па́мять *f*; **~ty** [tɪ'næsətɪ] це́пкость *f*, насто́йчивость *f*
tenant ['tenənt] *of land* аренда́тор; *of flat* квартира́нт
tend [tend] *v/i.* быть скло́нным (***to*** к Д); *v/t.* ***prices ~ to rise during the holiday season*** в пери́од отпуско́в це́ны обы́чно повыша́ются; уха́живать за (Т); присма́тривать [-мотре́ть]; *tech.* обслу́живать [-и́ть]; **~ency** ['tendənsɪ] тенде́нция; *of person* скло́нность *f*
tender ['tendə] **1.** □ *com.* не́жный; ***~ spot*** больно́е (уязви́мое) ме́сто; **2.** *comm.* те́ндер; **3.** предлага́ть [-ложи́ть]; *documents* представля́ть [-а́вить]; *apologies, etc.* приноси́ть [-нести́]; **~hearted** [~'hɑ:tɪd] мягкосерде́чный; **~ness** [~nɪs] не́жность *f*
tendon ['tendən] *anat.* сухожи́лие
tendril ['tendrəl] *bot.* у́сик
tenement ['tenəmənt]: ***~ house*** многокварти́рный дом
tennis ['tenɪs] те́ннис
tenor ['tenə] *mus.* те́нор; (*general course*) тече́ние, направле́ние; *of life* укла́д; (*purport*) о́бщий смысл

T

tens|e [tens] **1.** *gr.* вре́мя *n*; **2.** натя́нутый; *muscles, atmosphere, etc.* напряжённый; **~ion** ['tenʃn] напряже́ние; натяже́ние; *pol.* напряжённость *f*

tent [tent] пала́тка, шатёр

tentacle ['tentəkl] *zo.* щу́пальце

tentative ['tentətɪv] □ (*trial*) про́бный; (*provisional*) предвари́тельный

tenterhooks ['tentəhuks]: ***be on ~*** сиде́ть как на иго́лках; ***keep s.o. on ~*** держа́ть кого́-л. в неизве́стности

tenth [tenθ] **1.** деся́тый; **2.** деся́тая часть *f*

tenure ['tenjuə] пребывание в должности; пра́во владе́ния землёй; срок владе́ния

tepid ['tepɪd] □ теплова́тый; *fig.* прохла́дный

term [tɜːm] **1.** (*period*) срок; *univ.* семе́стр; *ling.* те́рмин; *school* че́тверть; **~s** *pl.* усло́вия; ***be on good*** (***bad***) ***~s*** быть в хоро́ших (плохи́х) отноше́ниях; ***come to ~s*** прийти́ *pf.* к соглаше́нию; **2.** (*call*) наз(ы)ва́ть; (*name*) [на]именова́ть

termina|l ['tɜːmɪnl] **1.** □ коне́чный; **2.** *el.* кле́мма, зажи́м; *Am. rail.* коне́чная ста́нция; **air ~** аэровокза́л; **bus ~** автовокза́л; **~te** [~neɪt] конча́ть(ся) [ко́нчить(ся)]; ***~ a contract*** расто́ргнуть *pf.* контра́кт; **~tion** [tɜːmɪ'neɪʃn] оконча́ние; коне́ц

terminus ['tɜːmɪnəs] *rail., bus* коне́чная ста́нция

terrace ['terəs] терра́са; **~s** *pl. sport* трибу́ны стадио́на; **~d** [~t] располо́женный терра́сами

terrestrial [te'restrɪəl] □ земно́й

terrible ['terəbl] □ ужа́сный, стра́шный

terri|fic [tə'rɪfɪk] (***~ally***) *coll.* потряса́ющий, великоле́пный; **~fy** ['terɪfaɪ] *v/t.* ужаса́ть [-сну́ть]

territor|ial [terɪ'tɔːrɪəl] □ территориа́льный; **~y** ['terətrɪ] террито́рия

terror ['terə] у́жас; (*violence*) терро́р; **~ize** [~raɪz] терроризова́ть (*im*)*pf.*

terse [tɜːs] □ (*concise*) сжа́тый

test [test] **1.** испыта́ние (*a. fig.*); про́ба; контро́ль *m*; *in teaching* контро́льная рабо́та; (*check*) прове́рка; *attr.* испыта́тельный; про́бный; ***nuclear ~s*** я́дерные испыта́ния; **2.** подверга́ть испыта́нию, прове́рке

testament ['testəmənt] *law* завеща́ние; ***Old*** (***New***) ♀ Ве́тхий (Но́вый) заве́т

testify ['testɪfaɪ] *law* дава́ть показа́ние (***to*** в по́льзу Р, ***against*** про́тив Р); свиде́тельствовать (***to*** о П)

testimon|ial [testɪ'məunɪəl] рекоменда́ция, характери́стика; **~y** ['testɪmənɪ] *law* свиде́тельские показа́ния; *fig.* свиде́тельство

test pilot лётчик-испыта́тель *m*

test tube *chem.* проби́рка

tête-à-tête [teɪtɑː'teɪt] с гла́зу на́ глаз

tether ['teðə]: ***come to the end of one's ~*** дойти́ *pf.* до ру́чки

text [tekst] текст; **~book** уче́бник

textile ['tekstaɪl] **1.** тексти́льный; **2.** **~s** *coll.* тексти́ль *m*

texture ['tekstʃə] *of cloth* тексту́ра; *of mineral, etc.* структу́ра

than [ðæn, ðən] чем, не́жели; ***more ~ ten*** бо́льше десяти́

thank [θæŋk] **1.** [по]благодари́ть (В); ***~ you*** благодарю́ вас; **2.** **~s** *pl.* спаси́бо!; ***~s to*** благодаря́ (Д); **~ful** ['~fl] □ благода́рный; **~less** ['~lɪs] □ неблагода́рный

that [ðæt, ðət] **1.** *pron.* тот, та, то; те *pl.*; (*a.* э́тот *и т. д.*); кото́рый *и т. д.*; **2.** *cj.* что; что́бы

thatch [θætʃ]: ***~ed roof*** соло́менная кры́ша

thaw [θɔː] **1.** о́ттепель *f*; (*melting*) та́яние; **2.** *v/i.* [рас]та́ять; (*a.* ***~ out***) отта́ивать [отта́ять]

the [ðə, … ðɪ, … ðiː] [ðiː *пе́ред гла́сными* ði, *пе́ред согла́сными* ðə] **1.** *определённый арти́кль*; **2.** *adv.* ***~ … ~ …*** чем ..., тем ...

theat|er, *Brt.* **theatre** ['θɪətə] теа́тр; *fig.* аре́на; ***operating ~*** операцио́нная; ***~ of war*** теа́тр вое́нных де́йствий; **~rical** □ [θɪ'ætrɪkl] театра́льный (*a. fig.*); сцени́ческий

theft [θeft] воровство́; кра́жа

their [ðeə] *poss. pron.* (*om* ***they***) их;

T

свой, своя́, своё, свои́ *pl.*; **~s** [ðeəz] *poss. pron. pred.* их, свой *и т.д*
them [ðəm, ðem] *pron.* (*ко́свенный паде́ж от* **they**) их, им
theme [θiːm] те́ма
themselves [ðəm'selvz] *pron. refl.* себя́, -ся; *emphatic* са́ми
then [ðen] **1.** *adv.* тогда́; пото́м, зате́м; ***from ~ on*** с тех пор; ***by ~*** к тому́ вре́мени; **2.** *cj.* тогда́, в тако́м слу́чае; зна́чит; **3.** *adj.* тогда́шний
thence *lit* [ðens] отту́да; с того́ вре́мени; *fig.* отсю́да, из э́того
theology [θɪ'ɒlədʒɪ] богосло́вие
theor|etic(al) □ [θɪə'retɪk(l)] теорети́ческий; **~ist** ['θɪərɪst] теоре́тик; **~y** ['θɪərɪ] тео́рия
there [ðeə] там, туда́; ***~!*** (ну) вот!; ***~ she is*** вон она́; ***~ is, ~ are*** [ðə'rɪz, ðə'rɑː] есть, име́ется, име́ются; **~about(s)** [ðeərə'baʊt(s)] побли́зости; (*approximately*) о́коло э́того, приблизи́тельно; **~after** [ðeər'ɑːftə] по́сле того́; **~by** ['ðeə'baɪ] посре́дством э́того, таки́м о́бразом; **~fore** ['ðeəfɔː] поэ́тому; сле́довательно; **~upon** ['ðeərə'pɒn] сра́зу же; тут; всле́дствие того́
thermo|meter [θə'mɒmɪtə] термо́метр, гра́дусник; **~nuclear** [θɜːməʊ'njʊklɪə] термоя́дерный; **~s** ['θɜːməs] (*or* ***~ flask***) те́рмос
these [ðiːz] *pl. от* **this**
thes|is ['θiːsɪs], *pl.* **~es** [~siːz] те́зис; диссерта́ция
they [ðeɪ] *pers. pron.* они́
thick [θɪk] **1.** □ *com.* то́лстый; *fog, hair, etc.* густо́й; *voice* хри́плый; *coll.* (*stupid*) глу́пый; ***that's a bit ~*** э́то уж сли́шком; **2.** *fig.* гу́ща; ***in the ~ of*** в са́мой гу́ще Р; **~en** ['θɪkən] утолща́ть(ся) [утолщи́ть(ся)]; *of darkness, fog, etc.* сгуща́ть(ся) [сгусти́ть(ся)]; **~et** ['θɪkɪt] ча́ща; *of bushes* за́росли *f/pl.*; **~headed** тупоголо́вый, тупоу́мный; **~ness** ['θɪknɪs] толщина́; (*density*) густота́; **~set** [θɪk'set] *person* корена́стый; **~-skinned** (*a. fig.*) толстоко́жий
thie|f [θiːf], *pl.* **~ves** [θiːvz] вор; **~ve** [θiːv] *v/i.* ворова́ть
thigh [θaɪ] бедро́
thimble ['θɪmbl] напёрсток
thin [θɪn] **1.** □ *com.* то́нкий; *person* худо́й, худоща́вый; *hair* ре́дкий; *soup* жи́дкий; **2.** де́лать(ся) то́нким, утонча́ть(ся) [-чи́ть(ся)]; [по]реде́ть; [по]худе́ть
thing [θɪŋ] вещь *f*; предме́т; де́ло; **~s** *pl.* (*belongings*) ве́щи *f/pl.*; (*luggage*) бага́ж; (*clothes*) оде́жда; *for painting, etc.* принадле́жности *f/pl.*; ***the ~ is that*** де́ло в том, что ...; ***the very ~*** как раз то, что ну́жно; ***~s are getting better*** положе́ние улучша́ется
think [θɪŋk] [*irr.*] *v/i.* [по]ду́мать (***of, about*** о П); *abstractly* мы́слить; (*presume*) полага́ть; (*remember*) вспомина́ть [вспо́мнить] (***of*** о П); (*intend*) намерева́ться (+ *inf.*); (*devise*) приду́м(ыв)ать (***of*** В); *v/t.* счита́ть [счесть]; ***~ a lot of*** высоко́ цени́ть; быть высо́кого мне́ния о (П)
third [θɜːd] **1.** тре́тий; **2.** треть *f*
thirst [θɜːst] **1.** жа́жда (*a. fig.*); **2.** жа́ждать (***for, after*** Р) (*part. fig.*); **~y** ['~ɪ]: ***I am ~*** я хочу́ пить
thirt|een [θɜː'tiːn] трина́дцать; **~eenth** [θɜː'tiːnθ] трина́дцатый; **~ieth** ['θɜːtɪɪθ] тридца́тый; **~y** ['θɜːtɪ] три́дцать
this [ðɪs] *demonstrative pron.* (*pl.* ***these***) э́тот, э́та, э́то; э́ти *pl.*; ***~ morning*** сего́дня у́тром; ***one of these days*** как-нибу́дь, когда́-нибудь
thistle ['θɪsl] чертополо́х
thorn [θɔːn] *bot.* шип, колю́чка; **~y** ['θɔːnɪ] колю́чий; *fig.* тяжёлый, терни́стый
thorough ['θʌrə] □ основа́тельный, тща́тельный; (*detailed*) дета́льный, подро́бный; **~ly** *adv.* основа́тельно, доскона́льно; **~bred** чистокро́вный; **~fare** у́лица, магистра́ль *f*; "***No ~***" "Прое́зда нет"
those [ðəʊz] *pl. от* **that**
though [ðəʊ] *conj.* хотя́; да́же е́сли бы, хотя́ бы; *adv.* тем не ме́нее, одна́ко; всё-таки; ***as ~*** как бу́дто, сло́вно
thought [θɔːt] **1.** *pt. и pt. p. от* ***think***; **2.** мысль *f*, мышле́ние; (*contemplation*) размышле́ние; (*care*) забо́та; внима́тельность *f*; **~ful**

['θɔːtfl] □ заду́мчивый; (*considerate*) забо́тливый; внима́тельный (***of*** к Д); **~less** ['θɔːtlɪs] □ (*careless*) беспе́чный; необду́манный; невнима́тельный (***of*** к Д)
thousand ['θaʊznd] ты́сяча; **~th** ['θaʊznθ] **1.** ты́сячный; **2.** ты́сячная часть *f*
thrash [θræʃ] [вы́]поро́ть; избива́ть [-би́ть]; *fig.* (*defeat*) побежда́ть [-еди́ть]; **~ *out*** тща́тельно обсужда́ть [-уди́ть]; **~ing** ['θræʃɪŋ]: ***give s.o. a good ~*** основа́тельно поколоти́ть *pf.* кого́-л.
thread [θred] **1.** ни́тка, нить *f*; *fig.* нить *f*; *of a screw*, *etc.* резьба́; **2.** *needle* продева́ть ни́тку в (В); *beads* нани́зывать [-за́ть]; **~bare** ['θredbeə] потёртый, изно́шенный; потрёпанный; *fig.* (*hackneyed*) изби́тый
threat [θret] угро́за; **~en** ['θretn] *v/t.* (при)грози́ть, угрожа́ть (Д ***with*** Т); *v/i.* грози́ть
three [θriː] **1.** три; **2.** тро́йка → ***five***; **~fold** ['θriːfəʊld] тройно́й; *adv.* втройне́; **~-*ply*** трёхслойный
thresh [θreʃ] *agric.* обмолоти́ть *pf.*
threshold ['θreʃhəʊld] поро́г
threw [θruː] *pt. om* ***throw***
thrice [θraɪs] три́жды
thrift [θrɪft] бережли́вость *f*, эконо́мность *f*; **~y** ['θrɪftɪ] □ эконо́мный, бережли́вый
thrill [θrɪl] **1.** *v/t.* [вз]волнова́ть; приводи́ть в тре́пет, [вз]будора́жить; *v/i.* (за)трепета́ть (***with*** от Р); [вз]волнова́ться; **2.** тре́пет; глубо́кое волне́ние; не́рвная дрожь *f*; **~er** ['θrɪlə] детекти́вный *or* приключе́нческий рома́н *or* фильм, три́ллер; **~ing** ['θrɪlɪŋ] захва́тывающий; *news* потряса́ющий
thrive [θraɪv] [*irr.*] *of business* процвета́ть; *of person* преуспева́ть; *of plants* разраста́ться; **~n** ['θrɪvn] *pt. p. om* ***thrive***
throat [θrəʊt] го́рло; ***clear one's ~*** отка́шливаться [-ляться]
throb [θrɒb] **1.** пульси́ровать; си́льно би́ться; **2.** пульса́ция; бие́ние, *fig.* тре́пет
throes [θrəʊz]: ***be in the ~ of*** в хо́де, в проце́ссе
throne [θrəʊn] трон, престо́л
throng [θrɒŋ] **1.** толпа́; **2.** [с]толпи́ться; (*fill*) заполня́ть [-о́лнить]; ***people ~ed to the square*** наро́д толпо́й вали́л на пло́щадь *f*
throttle ['θrɒtl] (*choke*) [за]души́ть; (*regulate*) дроссели́ровать
through [θruː] **1.** че́рез (В); сквозь (В); по (Д); *adv.* насквозь; от нача́ла до конца́; **2.** *train*, *etc.* прямо́й; ***be ~ with s.o.*** порва́ть с ке́м-л.; ***put ~*** *tel.* соедини́ть *pf.* (с Т); **~out** [θruː'aʊt] **1.** *prp.* че́рез (В); по всему́, всей ...; **2.** повсю́ду; во всех отноше́ниях
throve [θrəʊv] *pt. om* ***thrive***
throw [θrəʊ] **1.** [*irr.*] броса́ть [бро́сить], кида́ть [ки́нуть]; *discus*, *etc.* мета́ть [метну́ть]; **~ *away*** выбра́сывать ['-росить]; (*forgo*) упуска́ть [-сти́ть]; **~ *over*** перебра́сывать [-бро́сить]; **~ *light on s.th.*** пролива́ть [-ли́ть] свет на (В); **2.** бросо́к; броса́ние; **~n** [~n] *pt. p. om* ***throw***
thru *Am.* = ***through***
thrush [θrʌʃ] дрозд
thrust [θrʌst] **1.** толчо́к; *mil.* уда́р; **2.** [*irr.*] (*push*) толка́ть [-кну́ть]; (*poke*) ты́кать [ткнуть]; **~ *o.s. into*** *fig.* втира́ться [втере́ться] в (В); **~ *upon a p.*** навя́зывать [-за́ть] (Д)
thud [θʌd] глухо́й звук *or* стук
thug [θʌg] головоре́з
thumb [θʌm] **1.** большо́й па́лец (руки́); **2.** *book* перели́стывать [-ста́ть]; **~ *a lift*** *coll.* голосова́ть (на доро́ге)
thump [θʌmp] **1.** глухо́й стук; тяжёлый уда́р; **2.** стуча́ть [-у́кнуть]
thunder ['θʌndə] **1.** гром; **2.** [за]греме́ть; *fig.* мета́ть гро́мы и мо́лнии; **~bolt** уда́р мо́лнии; **~clap** уда́р гро́ма; **~ous** ['θʌndərəs] □ (*very loud*) громово́й, оглуша́ющий; **~storm** гроза́; **~struck** *fig.* как гро́мом поражённый
Thursday ['θɜːzdɪ] четве́рг
thus [ðʌs] так, таки́м о́бразом
thwart [θwɔːt] *plans*, *etc.* меша́ть, расстра́ивать [-ро́ить]; ***be ~ed at every turn*** встреча́ть препя́тствия на ка́ждом шагу́

tick[1] [tɪk] *zo.* клещ
tick[2] [~] **1.** *of clock* ти́канье; **2.** *v/i.* ти́кать
tick[3] [~] *mark* га́лочка; ***~ off*** отмеча́ть га́лочкой
ticket ['tɪkɪt] **1.** биле́т; ***price ~*** этике́тка с ценóй; ***cloakroom ~*** номеро́к; ***round trip*** (*Brt.* ***return***) ***~*** обра́тный биле́т; ***~ office*** биле́тная ка́сса
tickl|e ['tɪkl] (по)щекота́ть; ***~ish*** [~ɪʃ] □ *fig.* щекотли́вый
tidal ['taɪdl]: ***~ wave*** прили́вная волна́
tidbit [tɪdbɪt], *Brt.* **titbit** ['tɪtbɪt] ла́комый кусо́чек; *fig.* пика́нтная но́вость *f*
tide [taɪd] **1.** ***low ~*** отли́в; ***high ~*** прили́в; *fig.* тече́ние; направле́ние; **2.** *fig.* ***~ over***: ***will this ~ you over till Monday?*** Э́то вам хва́тит до понеде́льника?
tidy ['taɪdɪ] **1.** опря́тный; аккура́тный; *sum* значи́тельный; **2.** уб(и)ра́ть; приводи́ть в поря́док
tie [taɪ] **1.** га́лстук; *sport* ничья́; ***~s*** *pl.* (*bonds*) у́зы *f/pl.*; **2.** *v/t. knot, etc.* завя́зывать [-за́ть]; *together* свя́зывать [-за́ть]; *v/i.* сыгра́ть *pf.* вничью́
tier [tɪə] я́рус
tiff [tɪf] *coll.* размо́лвка
tiger ['taɪgə] тигр
tight [taɪt] □ туго́й; ту́го натя́нутый; (*fitting too closely*) те́сный; *coll.* (*drunk*) подвы́пивший; *coll.* ***~ spot*** *fig.* затрудни́тельное положе́ние; ***~en*** ['taɪtn] стя́гивать(ся) [стяну́ть(ся)] (*a.* ***~ up***); *belt, etc.* затя́гивать [-яну́ть]; *screw* подтя́гивать [-яну́ть]; ***~fisted*** скупо́й; ***~s*** [taɪts] *pl.* колго́тки
tigress ['taɪgrɪs] тигри́ца
tile [taɪl] **1.** *for roof* черепи́ца; *for walls, etc.* облицо́вочная пли́тка, *decorative* изразе́ц; **2.** покрыва́ть черепи́цей; облицо́вывать пли́ткой
till[1] [tɪl] ка́сса
till[2] [~] **1.** *prp.* до Р; **2.** *cj.* пока́
till[3] [~] *agric.* возде́л(ыв)ать (В); [вс]паха́ть
tilt [tɪlt] **1.** накло́нное положе́ние, накло́н; ***at full ~*** на по́лной ско́рости; **2.** наклоня́ть(ся) [-ни́ть(ся)]
timber ['tɪmbə] лесоматериа́л, строево́й лес
time [taɪm] **1.** *com.* вре́мя *n*; (*suitable ~*) пора́; (*term*) срок; ***at the same ~*** в то же вре́мя; ***beat ~*** отбива́ть такт; ***for the ~ being*** пока́, на вре́мя; ***in*** (*or* ***on***) ***~*** во́время; ***next ~*** в сле́дующий раз; ***what's the ~?*** кото́рый час?; **2.** (уда́чно) выбира́ть вре́мя для Р; ***~ limit*** преде́льный срок; ***~r*** ['taɪmə] та́ймер; ***~ly*** ['taɪmlɪ] своевре́менный; ***~saving*** эконо́мящий вре́мя; ***~table*** *rail* расписа́ние
timid ['tɪmɪd] □ ро́бкий
tin [tɪn] **1.** о́лово; (*container*) консе́рвная ба́нка; **2.** консерви́ровать
tinfoil ['tɪnfɔɪl] фольга́
tinge [tɪndʒ] **1.** слегка́ окра́шивать; *fig.* придава́ть отте́нок (Д); **2.** лёгкая окра́ска; *fig.* отте́нок
tingle ['tɪŋgl] испы́тывать *или* вызыва́ть пока́лывание (в онеме́вших коне́чностях), пощи́пывание (на моро́зе), звон в уша́х *и т. п.*
tinker ['tɪŋkə] вози́ться (***with*** с Т)
tinkle ['tɪŋkl] звя́кать [-кнуть]
tin|ned [tɪnd] консерви́рованный; ***~ opener*** консе́рвный нож
tinsel ['tɪnsl] мишура́
tint [tɪnt] **1.** кра́ска; (*shade*) отте́нок; **2.** слегка́ окра́шивать; *hair* подкра́шивать
tiny ['taɪnɪ] □ о́чень ма́ленький, кро́шечный
tip[1] [tɪp] (то́нкий) коне́ц, наконе́чник; *of finger, etc.* ко́нчик
tip[2] [~] **1.** информа́ция; (*hint*) намёк; (*advice*) рекоменда́ция, осно́ванная на малодосту́пной информа́ции; **2.** дава́ть на чай (Д); дава́ть информа́цию (Д), рекоменда́цию
tip[3] [~] опроки́дывать [-и́нуть]
tipple ['tɪpl] *coll.* вы́пи(ва́)ть, пить
tipsy ['tɪpsɪ] подвы́пивший
tiptoe ['tɪptəʊ]: ***on ~*** на цы́почках
tire[1] (*Brt.* ***tyre***) ши́на; ***flat ~*** спу́щенная ши́на
tire[2] [taɪə] утомля́ть [-ми́ть]; уста́(ва́)ть; ***~d*** [~d] уста́лый; ***~less*** ['~lɪs] неутоми́мый; ***~some*** ['~səm] утоми́тельный; (*pesky*) надое́дливый; (*boring*) ску́чный

T

tissue ['tɪʃuː] ткань *f* (*a. biol.*); ~ **paper** папиро́сная бума́га
title ['taɪtl] загла́вие, назва́ние; (*person's status*) ти́тул; зва́ние; ~ **holder** *sport* чемпио́н; ~ **page** ти́тульный лист
titter ['tɪtə] **1.** хихи́канье; **2.** хихи́кать [-кнуть]
tittle-tattle ['tɪtltætl] спле́тни *f/pl.*, болтовня́
to [tə, ... tʊ, ... tuː] *prp. indicating direction, aim* к (Д); в (В); на (В); *introducing indirect object, corresponds to the Russian dative case*: ~ **me** *etc.* мне *и т. д.*; ~ ***and fro*** *adv.* взад и вперёд; *показатель инфинитива*: ~ ***work*** рабо́тать; ***I weep ~ think of it*** я пла́чу, ду́мая об э́том
toad [təʊd] жа́ба; **~stool** пога́нка
toast [təʊst] **1.** гре́нок; (*drink*) тост; **2.** де́лать гре́нки; поджа́ри(ва)ть; *fig.* (*warm o.s.*) гре́ть(ся); пить за (В); **~er** [~ə] то́стер
tobacco [tə'bækəʊ] таба́к; **~nist's** [tə'bækənɪsts] таба́чный магази́н
toboggan [tə'bɒgən] **1.** са́ни *f/pl.*; *children's* са́нки; **2.** ката́ться на саня́х, са́нках
today [tə'deɪ] сего́дня; настоя́щее вре́мя; ***from ~*** с сего́дняшнего дня; ***a month ~*** че́рез ме́сяц
toe [təʊ] па́лец (на ноге́); *of boot, sock* носо́к
toffee ['tɒfɪ] ири́ска; *soft* тяну́чка
together [tə'geðə] вме́сте
togs [tɒgs] *pl. coll.* оде́жда
toil [tɔɪl] **1.** тяжёлый труд; **2.** уси́ленно труди́ться; тащи́ться, идти́ с трудо́м
toilet ['tɔɪlɪt] туале́т; ~ **paper** туале́тная бума́га
token ['təʊkən] знак; ***as a ~ of*** в знак чего́-то; ~ ***payment*** символи́ческая пла́та
told [təʊld] *pt. u pt. p. от* ***tell***
tolera|ble ['tɒlərəbl] □ терпи́мый; (*fairly good*) сно́сный; **~nce** [~rəns] терпи́мость *f*; **~nt** [~rənt] □ терпи́мый; **~te** [~reɪt] [вы-, по]терпе́ть, допуска́ть [-сти́ть]
toll [təʊl] (*tax*) по́шлина, сбо́р; *fig.* дань *f*; **~gate** ме́сто, где взима́ются сбо́ры; заста́ва
tom [tɒm]: ~ ***cat*** кот
tomato [tə'mɑːtəʊ], *pl.* **~es** [~z] помидо́р, тома́т
tomb [tuːm] моги́ла
tomboy ['tɒmbɔɪ] сорване́ц (о де́вочке)
tomfoolery [tɒm'fuːlərɪ] дура́чество
tomorrow [tə'mɒrəʊ] за́втра
ton [tʌn] *metric* то́нна
tone [təʊn] **1.** *mus.*, *paint.*, *fig.* тон; интона́ция; **2.**: ~ ***down*** смягча́ть(ся) [-чи́ть]; ~ ***in with*** гармони́ровать (с Т)
tongs [tɒŋz] *pl.* щипцы́ *m/pl.*, кле́щи, *a.* клещи́ *f/pl.*
tongue [tʌŋ] язы́к; ***hold your ~!*** молчи́(те)!
tonic ['tɒnɪk] *med.* тонизи́рующее сре́дство; ~ **water** то́ник
tonight [tə'naɪt] сего́дня ве́чером
tonnage ['tʌnɪdʒ] *naut.* тонна́ж; (*freight carrying capacity*) грузоподъёмность *f*; (*duty*) тонна́жный сбор
tonsil ['tɒnsl] *anat.* гла́нда, минда́лина
too [tuː] та́кже, то́же; *of degree* сли́шком; о́чень; (*moreover*) бо́лее того́; к тому́ же; ***there was ground frost last night, and in June ~!*** вчера́ но́чью – за́морозки на по́чве, и э́то ию́не!
took [tʊk] *pt. от* ***take***
tool [tuːl] (рабо́чий) инструме́нт; *fig.* ору́дие
toot [tuːt] **1.** гудо́к; **2.** дать гудо́к; *mot.* просигна́ли(зи́рова)ть
tooth [tuːθ] (*pl.* **teeth**) зуб; **~ache** зубна́я боль *f*; **~brush** зубна́я щётка; **~less** ['tuːθlɪs] □ беззу́бый; **~paste** зубна́я па́ста
top [tɒp] **1.** ве́рхняя часть *f*; верх; *of mountain* верши́на; *of head, tree* маку́шка; (*lid*) кры́шка; *leafy top of root vegetable* ботва́; ***at the ~ of one's voice*** во весь го́лос; ***on ~*** наверху́; ***on ~ of all this*** в доверше́ние всего́; в доба́вок ко всему́; **2.** вы́сший, пе́рвый; *speed, etc.* максима́льный; **3.** (*cover*) покры́(ва́)ть; *fig.* (*surpass*) превыша́ть [-ы́сить]
topic ['tɒpɪk] те́ма; **~al** [~kl] ак-

T

туáльный, злободнéвный

top-level: **~ *negotiations*** переговоры на вы́сшем у́ровне

topple ['tɒpl] [с]вали́ть; опроки́дывать(ся) [-и́нуть(ся)] (*a.* **~ *over***)

topsy-turvy ['tɒpsɪ'tɜːvɪ] □ (перевёрнутый) вверх дном

torch [tɔːtʃ] фа́кел; ***electric*** **~** электри́ческий фона́рь *m*; *chiefly Brt.* (*flashlight*) карма́нный фона́рик

tore [tɔː] *pt. om* ***tear***

torment 1. ['tɔːment] муче́ние, му́ка; **2.** [tɔː'ment] [из-, за]му́чить

torn [tɔːn] *pt. p. om* ***tear***

tornado [tɔː'neɪdəʊ] торна́до (*indecl.*); смерчь *m*; (*hurricane*) урага́н

torpedo [tɔː'piːdəʊ] **1.** торпе́да; **2.** торпеди́ровать (*im*)*pf.* (*a. fig.*)

torpid ['tɔːpɪd] □ (*inactive, slow*) вя́лый, апати́чный

torrent ['tɒrənt] пото́к (*a. fig.*)

torrid ['tɒrɪd] жа́ркий, зно́йный

tortoise ['tɔːtəs] *zo.* черепа́ха

tortuous ['tɔːtʃʊəs] (*winding*) изви́листый; *fig.* (*devious*) укло́нчивый, нейскренний

torture ['tɔːtʃə] **1.** пы́тка (*a. fig.*); **2.** пыта́ть; [из-, за]му́чить

toss [tɒs] (*fling*) броса́ть [бро́сить]; *in bed* беспоко́йно мета́ться; *head* вски́дывать [-и́нуть]; *coin* подбра́сывать [-ро́сить] (*mst.* **~ *up***)

tot [tɒt] (*child*) малы́ш

total ['təʊtl] **1.** □ (*complete*) по́лный, абсолю́тный; *war* тота́льный; *number* о́бщий; **2.** су́мма; ито́г; ***in*** **~** в ито́ге; **3.** подводи́ть ито́г, подсчи́тывать [-ита́ть]; (*amount to*) составля́ть в ито́ге; (*equal*) равня́ться (Д); **~itarian** [təʊtælɪ'teərɪən] тоталита́рный; **~ly** [~lɪ] по́лностью, соверше́нно

totter ['tɒtə] идти́ нéтвёрдой похо́дкой; (*shake*) шата́ться [(по)шатну́ться]; (*be about to fall*) разруша́ться

touch [tʌtʃ] **1.** (*sense*) осяза́ние; (*contact*) прикоснове́ние; *fig.* конта́кт, связь *f*; ***a*** **~** (*a little*) чу́точка; (*a trace*) при́месь *f*; *of illness* лёгкий при́ступ; штрих; **2.** тро́гать [тро́нуть] (В) (*a. fig.*); прикаса́ться [-косну́ться], притра́гиваться [-тро́нуться] к (Д); *fig. subject, etc.* каса́ться [косну́ться] (Р); затра́гивать [-ро́нуть]; ***be*** **~*ed*** *fig.* быть тро́нутым; **~ *up*** подправля́ть [-а́вить]; **~ing** ['tʌtʃɪŋ] тро́гательный; **~y** ['tʌtʃɪ] □ оби́дчивый

tough [tʌf] **1.** *meat, etc.* жёсткий (*a. fig.*); (*strong*) про́чный; *person* выно́сливый; *job, etc.* тру́дный; **2.** хулига́н; **~en** ['tʌfn] де́лать(ся) жёстким

tour [tʊə] **1.** пое́здка, экску́рсия, тур; *sport, thea.* турне́ *n indecl.*; *a. thea.* гастро́ли *f/pl.*; **2.** соверша́ть путеше́ствие *или* турне́ по (Д); путеше́ствовать (***through*** по Д); гастроли́ровать; **~ist** ['tʊərɪst] тури́ст *m*, -ка *f*; **~ *agency*** туристи́ческое аге́нтство

tournament ['tʊənəmənt] турни́р

tousle ['taʊzl] взъеро́ши(ва)ть, растрёпывать (-репа́ть)

tow [təʊ] *naut* **1.** букси́р; ***take in*** **~** брать на букси́р; ***with all her kids in*** **~** со все́ми детьми́; **2.** букси́ровать

toward(s) [tə'wɔːdz, twɔːdʒ] *prp.* (*direction*) по направле́нию к (Д); (*relation*) к (Д), по отноше́нию к (Д); (*purpose*) для (Р), на (В)

towel ['taʊəl] полоте́нце

tower ['taʊə] **1.** ба́шня; **2.** возвыша́ться (***above***, ***over*** над Т) (*a. fig.*)

town [taʊn] **1.** го́род; **2.** *attr.* городско́й; **~ *council*** городско́й сове́т; **~ *hall*** ра́туша; **~ dweller** горожа́нин *m*, -нка *f*; **~sfolk** ['taʊnzfəʊk], **~speople** ['taʊnzpiːpl] *pl.* горожа́не *m/pl.*

toxic ['tɒksɪk] токси́ческий

toy [tɔɪ] **1.** игру́шка; **2.** *attr.* игру́шечный; **3.** игра́ть, забавля́ться; **~ *with*** (*consider*) поду́мывать

trace [treɪs] **1.** след; (*very small quantity*) следы́, незначи́тельное коли́чество; **2.** (*draw*) [на]черти́ть; (*locate*) высле́живать [вы́следить] (В); (*follow*) просле́живать [-еди́ть] (В)

track [træk] **1.** след; (*rough road*) просёлочная доро́га; (*path*) тропи́нка; *for running* бегова́я доро́жка; *for motor racing* трек; *rail* колея́; ***be on the right*** (***wrong***) **~**

T

быть на пра́вильном (ло́жном) пути́; **2.** следи́ть за (T); просле́живать [-еди́ть] (B); ~ ***down*** высле́живать [вы́следить] (B)
tract [trækt] простра́нство, полоса́ земли́; *anat.* тракт; ***respiratory*** ~ дыха́тельные пути́
tractable ['træktəbl] *person* сгово́рчивый
tract|ion ['trækʃn] тя́га; ~ ***engine*** тяга́ч; **~or** ['træktə] тра́ктор
trade [treɪd] **1.** профе́ссия; ремесло́; торго́вля; **2.** торгова́ть (***in*** T; ***with*** с T); (*exchange*) обме́нивать [-ня́ть] (***for*** на B); ~ ***on*** испо́льзовать (*im*)*pf.*; **~mark** фабри́чная ма́рка; **~r** ['treɪdə] торго́вец; **~sman** ['treɪdzmən] торго́вец; (*shopkeeper*) владе́лец магази́на; **~(s) union** [treɪd(z)'juːnɪən] профсою́з
tradition [trə'dɪʃn] (*custom*) тради́ция, обы́чай; (*legend*) преда́ние; **~al** [~ʃənl] □ традицио́нный
traffic [træfɪk] **1.** движе́ние (у́личное, железнодоро́жное *и т. д.*); (*vehicles*) тра́нспорт; (*trading*) торго́вля; ~ ***jam*** зато́р у́личного движе́ния; ~ **lights** *pl.* светофо́р; ~ **police** ГАИ (госуда́рственная автомоби́льная инспе́кция)
tragedy ['trædʒədɪ] траге́дия
tragic(al) □ ['trædʒɪk(l)] траги́ческий, траги́чный
trail [treɪl] **1.** след; (*path*) тропа́; **2.** *v/t.* (*pull*) тащи́ть, волочи́ть; (*track*) идти́ по сле́ду (P); *v/i.* тащи́ться, волочи́ться; *bot.* ви́ться; **~er** ['treɪlə] *mot.* прице́п, тре́йлер
train [treɪn] **1.** по́езд; (*retinue*) сви́та; *film star's* толпа́ (покло́нников); ***by*** ~ по́ездом; ***freight*** ~ това́рный соста́в; ***suburban*** ~ при́городный по́езд, *coll.* электри́чка; ~ ***of thought*** ход мы́слей; **2.** (*bring up*) воспи́тывать [-та́ть]; приуча́ть [-чи́ть]; (*coach*) [на]трениро-ва́ть(ся); обуча́ть [-чи́ть]; *lions, etc.* [вы́]дрессирова́ть
trait [treɪt] (характе́рная) черта́
traitor ['treɪtə] преда́тель *m*, изме́нник
tram [træm], **~car** ['træmkɑː] трамва́й, ваго́н трамва́я
tramp [træmp] **1.** (*vagrant*) бродя́га *m*; (*hike*) путеше́ствие пешко́м; *of feet* то́пот; звук тяжёлых шаго́в; **2.** тяжело́ ступа́ть; тащи́ться с трудо́м; то́пать; броди́ть; **~le** ['træmpl] (*crush underfoot*) топта́ть; тяжело́ ступа́ть; ~ ***down*** зата́птывать [-топта́ть]
trance [trɑːns] транс
tranquil ['træŋkwɪl] □ споко́йный; **~(l)ity** [træŋ'kwɪlətɪ] споко́йствие; **~(l)ize** ['træŋkwɪlaɪz] успока́ивать(ся) [-ко́ить(ся)]; **~(l)izer** ['træŋkwɪlaɪzə] транквилиза́тор
transact [træn'zækt] заключа́ть [-чи́ть] сде́лку, вести́ дела́ с (T); **~ion** [~'zækʃn] сде́лка; **~s** *pl.* (*proceedings*) труды́ *m/pl.* нау́чного о́бщества
transatlantic [trænzət'læntɪk] трансатланти́ческий
transcend [træn'send] выходи́ть [вы́йти] за преде́лы; *expectations, etc.* превосходи́ть [-взойти́], превыша́ть [-ы́сить]
transfer 1. [træns'fɜː] *v/t.* переноси́ть [-нести́], перемеща́ть [-мести́ть]; *ownership* перед(ав)а́ть; *to another job, town, team, etc.* переводи́ть [-вести́]; *v/i. Am., of passengers* переса́живаться [-се́сть]; **2.** ['trænsfəː] перено́с; переда́ча; *comm.* трансфе́рт; перево́д; *Am.* переса́дка; **~able** [træns'fɜːrəbl] с пра́вом переда́чи; переводи́мый
transfigure [træns'fɪgə] видоизменя́ть [-ни́ть]; *with joy, etc.* преобража́ть [-рази́ть]
transfixed [træns'fɪkst]: ~ ***with fear*** ско́ванный стра́хом
transform [træns'fɔːm] превраща́ть [-врати́ть]; преобразо́вывать [-зова́ть]; **~ation** [~fə'meɪʃn] преобразова́ние; превраще́ние; **~er** [~'fɔːmə] трансформа́тор
transfusion [træns'fjuːʒn]: ***blood*** ~ перелива́ние кро́ви
transgress [trænz'gres] *v/t. law, etc.* преступа́ть [-пи́ть]; *agreement* наруша́ть [-у́шить]; *v/i.* (*sin*) [со]греши́ть; **~ion** [~'greʃn] просту́пок; *of law, etc.* наруше́ние
transient ['trænzɪənt] → ***transitory***; *Am., a.* (*temporary guest/lodger*)

T

вре́менный жиле́ц; челове́к/скита́лец, и́щущий себе́ рабо́ту
transit ['trænzɪt] прое́зд; *of goods* перево́зка; транзи́т; ***he is here in ~*** он здесь прое́здом
transition [træn'zɪʃn] перехо́д; перехо́дный пери́од
transitory ['trænsɪtrɪ] □ мимолётный; преходя́щий
translat|e [træns'leɪt] переводи́ть [-вести́] (***from*** с Р, ***into*** на В); *fig.* (*interpret*) [ис]толкова́ть; объясня́ть [-ни́ть]; **~ion** [~'leɪʃn] перево́д; **~or** [~leɪtə] перево́дчик *m*, -чица *f*
translucent [trænz'lu:snt] полупрозра́чный
transmission [trænz'mɪʃn] переда́ча (*a. radio & tech.*); *radio*, *TV* трансля́ция
transmit [trænz'mɪt] перед(ав)а́ть (*a. radio*, *TV*, *a.* трансли́ровать); *heat* проводи́ть *impf.*; **~ter** [~ə] переда́тчик (*a. radio*, *TV*)
transparent [træns'pærənt] □ прозра́чный (*a. fig.*)
transpire [træn'spaɪə] *fig.* вы́ясниться *pf.*, оказа́ться *pf.*; *coll.* случа́ться [-чи́ться]
transplant [træns'plɑ:nt] **1.** переса́живать [-сади́ть]; *fig. people* переселя́ть [-ли́ть]; **2.** ['trænsplɑ:nt] *med.* переса́дка
transport **1.** [træn'spɔ:t] перевози́ть [-везти́]; транспорти́ровать *im*(*pf.*); *fig.* увлека́ть [-е́чь]; восхища́ть [-ити́ть]; **2.** ['trænspɔ:t] тра́нспорт; перево́зка; *of joy*, *delight*, *etc.* ***be in ~s*** быть вне себя́ (***of*** от Р); **~ation** [trænspɔ:'teɪʃn] перево́зка, транспортиро́вка
transverse ['trænzvɜ:s] □ попере́чный; **~ly** попе́рёк
trap [træp] **1.** лову́шка, западня́ (*a. fig.*); капка́н; **2.** *fig.* (*lure*) замани́ть *pf.* в лову́шку; ***fall into a ~*** попа́сть *pf.* в лову́шку; (*fall for the bait*) попа́сться *pf.* на у́дочку; **~door** опускна́я дверь *f*
trapeze [trə'pi:z] трапе́ция
trappings ['træpɪŋz] *pl.* (*harness*) сбру́я; *fig.* ***the ~ of office*** вне́шние атрибу́ты служе́бного положе́ния
trash [træʃ] хлам; (*waste food*) отбро́сы *m/pl.*; *fig.* дрянь *f*; *book* макулату́ра; (*nonsense*) вздор, ерунда́; **~y** ['træʃɪ] □ дрянно́й
travel ['trævl] **1.** *v/i.* путеше́ствовать; е́здить, [по]е́хать; (*move*) передвига́ться [-и́нуться]; *of light*, *sound* распространя́ться (-ни́ться); *v/t.* объезжа́ть [-е́здить, -е́хать]; проезжа́ть [-е́хать] (... *км в час и т. п.*); **2.** путеше́ствие; *tech.* ход; (пере)движе́ние; **~(l)er** [~ə] путеше́ственник *m*, -ица *f*
traverse [trə'vɜ:s] **1.** пересека́ть [-се́чь]; (*pass through*) проходи́ть [пройти́] (В); **2.** попере́чина
travesty ['trævəstɪ] паро́дия
trawler ['trɔ:lə] тра́улер
tray [treɪ] подно́с
treacher|ous ['tretʃərəs] □ (*disloyal*) преда́тельский, вероло́мный; (*unreliable*) ненадёжный; ***~ weather*** кова́рная пого́да; **~y** [~rɪ] преда́тельство, вероло́мство
treacle ['tri:kl] па́тока; (*chiefly Brt.*, *molasses*) мела́сса
tread [tred] **1.** [*irr.*] ступа́ть [-пи́ть]; ***~ down*** зата́птывать [затопта́ть]; ***~ lightly*** *fig.* де́йствовать осторо́жно, такти́чно; **2.** по́ступь *f*, похо́дка; *of stairs* ступе́нька; *of tire*, *Brt. tyre* проте́ктор
treason ['tri:zn] (госуда́рственная) изме́на
treasure ['treʒə] **1.** сокро́вище; **2.** храни́ть; (*value greatly*) дорожи́ть; **~r** [~rə] казначе́й
treasury ['treʒərɪ]; сокро́вищница; *Brt.* ***the*** ♀ Казначе́йство
treat [tri:t] **1.** *v/t. chem.* обраба́тывать [-бо́тать]; *med.* лечи́ть; (*stand a drink*, *etc.*) угоща́ть [угости́ть] (***to*** Т); (*act towards*) обраща́ться [обрати́ться] с (Т), обходи́ться [обойти́сь] с (Т); *v/i.* ***~ of*** рассма́тривать [-мотре́ть], обсужда́ть [-уди́ть] (В); ***~ for ... with*** лечи́ть (от Р, Т); **2.** (*pleasure*) удово́льствие, наслажде́ние; ***this is my ~*** за всё плачу́ я!; я угоща́ю!
treatise ['tri:tɪz] нау́чный труд
treatment ['tri:tmənt] *chem.*, *tech.* обрабо́тка (Т); *med.* лече́ние; (*handling*) обраще́ние (***of*** с Т)
treaty ['tri:tɪ] догово́р

T

treble ['trebl] **1.** □ тройно́й, утро́енный; **2.** тройно́е коли́чество; *mus.* ди́скант; **3.** утра́ивать(ся) [утро́ить(ся)]
tree [tri:] де́рево; ***family ~*** родосло́вное де́рево
trellis ['trelɪs] решётка; шпале́ра
tremble ['trembl] [за]дрожа́ть, [за]трясти́сь (***with*** от Р)
tremendous [trɪ'mendəs] □ грома́дный; стра́шный; *coll.* огро́мный, потряса́ющий
tremor ['tremə] дрожь *f*; **~s** *pl.* подзе́мные толчки́
tremulous ['tremjʊləs] □ дрожа́щий; (*timid*) тре́петный, ро́бкий
trench [trentʃ] кана́ва; *mil.* транше́я, око́п
trend [trend] **1.** направле́ние (*a. fig.*); *fig.* (*course*) тече́ние; (*style*) стиль *m*; (*tendency*) тенде́нция; **2.** име́ть тенде́нцию (***towards*** к Д); склоня́ться
trendy ['trendɪ] *coll.* сти́льный; мо́дный
trespass ['trespəs] зайти́ *pf.* на чужу́ю террито́рию; (*sin*) соверша́ть просту́пок; (*encroach*) злоупотребля́ть [-би́ть] (***on*** Т); ***~ on s.o.'s time*** посяга́ть на чьё-л. вре́мя
trial ['traɪəl] (*test*, *hardship*) испыта́ние, про́ба; *law* суде́бное разбира́тельство; суд; *attr.* про́бный, испыта́тельный; ***on ~*** под судо́м; ***give a. p. a ~*** взять кого́-л. на испыта́тельный срок
triang|le ['traɪæŋgl] треуго́льник; **~ular** [traɪ'æŋgjʊlə] □ треуго́льный
tribe [traɪb] пле́мя *n*; *pej.* компа́ния; братва́
tribune ['trɪbju:n] (*platform*) трибу́на; (*person*) трибу́н
tribut|ary ['trɪbjʊtərɪ] *geogr.* прито́к; **~e** ['trɪbju:t] дань *f* (*a. fig.*); ***pay ~ to*** *fig.* отдава́ть до́лжное (Д)
trice [traɪs]: ***in a ~*** вмиг, ми́гом
trick [trɪk] **1.** (*practical joke*) шу́тка, *child's* ша́лость *f*; *done to amuse* фо́кус, трюк; уло́вка; (*special skill*) сноро́вка; ***do the ~*** поде́йствовать *pf.*, дости́чь *pf.* це́ли; **2.** (*deceive*) обма́нывать [-ну́ть]; наду́(ва́)ть; **~ery** ['trɪkərɪ] надува́тельство, обма́н
trickle ['trɪkl] течь стру́йкой; (*ooze*) сочи́ться
trick|ster ['trɪkstə] обма́нщик; **~y** ['trɪkɪ] □ (*sly*) хи́трый; (*difficult*) сло́жный, тру́дный; ***~ customer*** ско́льзкий тип
tricycle ['traɪsɪkl] трёхколёсный велосипе́д
trifl|e ['traɪfl] **1.** пустя́к; ме́лочь *f*; ***a ~*** *fig.*, *adv.* немно́жко; **2.** *v/i.* занима́ться пустяка́ми; относи́ться несерьёзно к (Д); ***he is not to be ~ed with*** с ним шу́тки пло́хи; *v/t.* ***~ away*** зря тра́тить; **~ing** ['traɪflɪŋ] пустя́чный, пустяко́вый
trigger ['trɪgə] **1.** *mil.* спусково́й крючо́к; **2.** (*start*) дава́ть [дать] нача́ло; вызыва́ть ['-звать] (В)
trill [trɪl] **1.** трель *f*; **2.** выводи́ть трель
trim [trɪm] **1.** *figure* аккура́тный, ла́дный; *garden* приведённый в поря́док; **2.** *naut.* (у́гол наклоне́ния су́дна) диффере́нт; ***in good ~*** в поря́дке; **3.** *hair*, *etc.* подреза́ть [-е́зать], подстрига́ть [-и́чь]; *dress* отде́л(ыв)ать; *hedge* подра́внивать [-ровня́ть]; **~ming** ['trɪmɪŋ] *mst.* **~s** *pl.* отде́лка; *cul.* припра́ва, гарни́р
trinket ['trɪŋkɪt] безделу́шка
trip [trɪp] **1.** пое́здка; экску́рсия; **2.** *v/i.* идти́ легко́ и бы́стро; (*stumble*) спотыка́ться [споткну́ться] (*a. fig.*); *v/t.* подставля́ть подно́жку (Д)
tripartite [traɪ'pɑ:taɪt] *agreement* трёхсторо́нний; состоя́щий из трёх часте́й
tripe [traɪp] *cul.* рубе́ц
triple ['trɪpl] тройно́й; утро́енный; **~ts** ['trɪplɪts] *pl.* тро́йня *sg.*
tripper [trɪpə] *coll.* экскурса́нт
trite [traɪt] □ бана́льный, изби́тый
triumph ['traɪəmf] **1.** триу́мф; торжество́; **2.** (*be victorious*) побежда́ть [-ди́ть]; (*celebrate victory*) торжествова́ть, восторжествова́ть *pf.* (***over*** над Т); **~al** [traɪ'ʌmfl] триумфа́льный; **~ant** [traɪ'ʌmfənt] победоно́сный; торжеству́ющий
trivial ['trɪvɪəl] □ ме́лкий, пустяко́вый; тривиа́льный

T

trod [trɒd] *pt. от* ***tread***; **~den** ['trɔdn] *pt. p. от* ***tread***
trolley ['trɒlɪ] теле́жка; *Am. streetcar* трамва́й; ***~ bus*** тролле́йбус
trombone [trɒm'bəʊn] *mus.* тромбо́н
troop [tru:p] **1.** (*group*) гру́ппа, толпа́; **2.** дви́гаться толпо́й; ***~ away***, ***~ off*** удаля́ться [-ли́ться]; ***we all ~ed to the museum*** мы всей гру́ппой пошли́ в музе́й; ***~s*** *pl.* войска́ *n/pl.*
trophy ['trəʊfɪ] трофе́й
tropic ['trɒpɪk] тро́пик; ***~s*** *pl.* тро́пики *m/pl.*; **~al** □ [~pɪkəl] тропи́ческий
trot [trɒt] **1.** *of horse* рысь *f*; бы́стрый шаг; ***keep s.o. on the ~*** не дава́ть кому́-л. поко́я; **2.** бежа́ть трусцо́й
trouble ['trʌbl] **1.** (*worry*) беспоко́йство; (*anxiety*) волне́ние; (*cares*) забо́ты *f/pl.*, хло́поты *f/pl.*; (*difficulties*) затрудне́ния *n/pl.*; беда́; ***get into ~*** попа́сть *pf.* в беду́; ***take the ~*** стара́ться, прилага́ть уси́лия; **2.** [по]беспоко́ить(ся); трево́жить; [по]проси́ть; утружда́ть; ***don't ~!*** не утружда́й(те) себя́!; **~some** [~səm] тру́дный, причиня́ющий беспоко́йство; **~-shooter** [~ʃu:tə] авари́йный монтёр; уполномо́ченный по урегули́рованию конфли́ктов
troupe [tru:p] *thea.* тру́ппа
trousers ['traʊzəz] *pl.* брю́ки *f/pl.*
trout [traʊt] форе́ль *f*
truant ['tru:ənt] *pupil* прогу́льщик; ***play ~*** прогу́ливать уро́ки
truce [tru:s] переми́рие
truck [trʌk] **1.** (*barrow*) теле́жка; *Am.* (*motorvehicle*) грузови́к; *Brt. rail.* грузова́я платфо́рма; **2.** *mst. Am.* перевози́ть на грузовика́х
truculent ['trʌkjʊlənt] (*fierce*) свире́пый; (*cruel*) жесто́кий; агресси́вный
trudge [trʌdʒ] идти́ с трудо́м; таска́ться, [по]тащи́ться; ***I had to ~ to the station on foot*** пришло́сь тащи́ться на ста́нцию пешко́м
true [tru:] ве́рный, пра́вильный; (*real*) настоя́щий; ***it is ~*** э́то пра́вда; ***come ~*** сбы́(ва́)ться; ***~ to life*** реалисти́ческий; (*genuine*) правди́вый; *portrait, etc.* как живо́й
truism ['tru:ɪzəm] трюи́зм
truly ['tru:lɪ] ***he was ~ grateful*** он был и́скренне благода́рен; ***Yours ~*** (*at close of letter*) пре́данный Вам
trump [trʌmp] **1.** (*card*) ко́зырь *m*; **2.** бить козырно́й ка́ртой
trumpet ['trʌmpɪt] **1.** труба́; ***blow one's own ~*** расхва́ливать себя́; **2.** [за-, про]труби́ть; *fig.* раструби́ть *pf.*; **~er** [~ə] труба́ч
truncheon ['trʌntʃən] *policeman's* дуби́нка
trunk [trʌŋk] *of tree* ствол; *anat.* ту́ловище; *elephant's* хо́бот; *Am. mot.* бага́жник; (*large suitcase*) чемода́н; ***pair of ~s*** трусы́; ***~ call*** *tel.* вы́зов по междугоро́дному телефо́ну; ***~ road*** магистра́ль *f*
trust [trʌst] **1.** дове́рие; ве́ра; *comm.* конце́рн, трест; ***on ~*** на ве́ру; в креди́т; ***position of ~*** отве́тственное положе́ние; **2.** *v/t.* [по]ве́рить (Д); доверя́ть [-е́рить] (Д ***with*** В); *v/i.* полага́ться [положи́ться] (***in***, ***to*** на В); наде́яться (***in***, ***to*** на В); ***I ~ they will agree*** наде́юсь, они́ согася́тся; **~ee** [trʌs'ti:] опеку́н; попечи́тель *m*; довери́тельный со́бственник; **~ful** ['trʌstfl] □, **~ing** ['trʌstɪŋ] □ дове́рчивый; **~worthy** [~wɜ:ðɪ] заслу́живающий дове́рия; надёжный
truth [tru:θ] пра́вда; (*verity*) и́стина; **~ful** ['tru:θfl] □ *person* правди́вый; *statement, etc. a.* ве́рный
try [traɪ] **1.** (*sample*) [по]про́бовать; (*attempt*) [по]пыта́ться; [по]стара́ться; (*tire, strain*) утомля́ть [-ми́ть]; *law* суди́ть; (*test*) испы́тывать [испыта́ть]; ***~ on*** примеря́ть [-е́рить]; ***~ one's luck*** попыта́ть *pf.* сча́стья; **2.** попы́тка; **~ing** ['traɪɪŋ] тру́дный; тяжёлый; (*annoying*) раздража́ющий
T-shirt ['ti:ʃɜ:t] ма́йка (с коро́ткими рукава́ми), футбо́лка
tub [tʌb] (*barrel*) ка́дка; (*wash~*) лоха́нь *f*; *coll.* (*bath ~*) ва́нна
tube [tju:b] труба́, тру́бка; *Brt.* (*subway*) метро́ *n indecl.*; *of paint, etc.* тю́бик; ***inner ~*** *mot.* ка́мера

tuber ['tju:bə] *bot.* клу́бень *m*
tuberculosis [tju:bɜ:kjʊ'ləʊsɪs] туберкулёз
tubular ['tju:bjʊlə] □ тру́бчатый
tuck [tʌk] **1.** *on dress* скла́дка, сбо́рка; **2.** де́лать скла́дки; засо́вывать [-су́нуть]; (*hide*) [с]пря́тать; **~ *in*** *shirt* запра́вить *pf.*; *to food* упи́сывать; **~ *up*** *sleeves* засу́чивать [-чи́ть]
Tuesday ['tju:zdɪ] вто́рник
tuft [tʌft] *of grass* пучо́к; *of hair* хохо́л
tug [tʌg] **1.** (*pull*) рыво́к; *naut.* букси́р; **2.** тащи́ть [тяну́ть]; (*a.* ***tug at***) дёргать [дёрнуть]
tuition [tju:'ɪʃn] обуче́ние
tulip ['tju:lɪp] тюльпа́н
tumble ['tʌmbl] **1.** *v/i.* (*fall*) па́дать [упа́сть]; (*overturn*) опроки́дываться [-и́нуться]; *into bed* повали́ться; **~ *to*** (*grasp*, *realize*) разгада́ть *pf.*, поня́ть *pf.*; **2.** паде́ние; **~*down*** полуразру́шенный; **~*r*** [~ə] (*glass*) стака́н
tummy ['tʌmɪ] *coll.* живо́т; *baby's* живо́тик
tumo(u)r ['tju:mə] о́пухоль *f*
tumult ['tju:mʌlt] (*uproar*) шум и кри́ки; сумато́ха; си́льное волне́ние; **~*uous*** [tju:'mʌltʃʊəs] шу́мный, бу́йный; взволно́ванный
tuna ['tju:nə] туне́ц
tune [tju:n] **1.** мело́дия, моти́в; ***in ~*** *piano* настро́енный; ***in ~ with*** сочета́ющийся, гармони́рующий; ***out of ~*** расстро́енный; ***sing out of ~*** фальши́вить; **2.** настра́ивать [-ро́ить]; (*a.* **~ *in***) *radio* настра́ивать (***to*** на В); **~*ful*** ['tju:nfl] □ мелоди́чный
tunnel ['tʌnl] **1.** тунне́ль *m* (*a.* тонне́ль *m*); **2.** проводи́ть тунне́ль (под Т, сквозь В)
turbid ['tɜ:bɪd] (*not clear*) му́тный; *fig.* тума́нный
turbot ['tɜ:bət] па́лтус
turbulent ['tɜ:bjʊlənt] бу́рный (*a. fig.*); *mob*, *etc.* бу́йный
tureen [tə'ri:n] су́пница
turf [tɜ:f] дёрн; (*peat*) торф; (*races*) ска́чки *f/pl.*; ***the ~*** ипподро́м
Turk [tɜ:k] ту́рок *m*, турча́нка *f*
turkey ['tɜ:kɪ] индю́к *m*, инде́йка *f*
Turkish ['tɜ:kɪʃ] **1.** туре́цкий; **~ *delight*** раха́т-луку́м; **2.** туре́цкий язы́к
turmoil ['tɜ:mɔɪl] смяте́ние; волне́ние; беспоря́док
turn [tɜ:n] **1.** *v/t.* (*round*) враща́ть, верте́ть; *head*, *etc.* повора́чивать [поверну́ть]; (*change*) превраща́ть [-рати́ть]; (*direct*) направля́ть [-ра́вить]; **~ *a corner*** заверну́ть *pf.* за у́гол; **~ *down*** *suggestion* отверга́ть [-е́ргнуть]; (*fold*) загиба́ть [загну́ть]; **~ *off*** *tap* закры́(ва́)ть; *light*, *gas*, *etc.* выключа́ть [вы́ключить]; **~ *on*** *tap* откры́(ва́)ть; включа́ть [-чи́ть]; **~ *out*** выгоня́ть [вы́гнать]; *of job*, *etc.* увольня́ть [уво́лить]; *goods* выпуска́ть (вы́пустить); **~ *over*** перевёртывать [-верну́ть]; *fig.* перед(ав)а́ть; **~ *up*** *collar*, *etc.* поднима́ть; **2.** *v/i.* враща́ться, верте́ться; повора́чиваться [поверну́ться]; станови́ться [стать]; превраща́ться [-рати́ться]; **~ *pale*, *red*, *etc.*** побледне́ть *pf.*, покрасне́ть *pf.*, *и т. д.*; **~ *about*** обора́чиваться [оберну́ться]; **~ *in*** (*inform on*) доноси́ть [-нести́]; (*go to bed*) ложи́ться спать; **~ *out*** ока́зываться [-за́ться]; **~ *to*** принима́ться [-ня́ться] за (В); обраща́ться [обрати́ться] к (Д); **~ *up*** появля́ться [-ви́ться]; **~ *upon*** обраща́ться [обрати́ться] про́тив (Р); **3.** *su.* поворо́т; изги́б; переме́на; услу́га; *of speech* оборо́т; *coll.* (*shock*) испу́г; ***at every ~*** на ка́ждом шагу́, постоя́нно; ***in ~s*** по о́череди; ***it is my ~*** моя́ о́чередь *f*; ***take ~s*** де́лать поочерёдно; ***in his ~*** в свою́ о́чередь; ***do s.o. a good ~*** оказа́ть *pf.* кому́-л. услу́гу; **~*er*** ['tɜ:nə] то́карь *m*
turning ['tɜ:nɪŋ] *of street*, *etc.* поворо́т; **~ *point*** *fig.* поворо́тный пункт; перело́м; *fig.* кри́зис
turnip ['tɜ:nɪp] *bot.* ре́па
turnout ['tɜ:naʊt] *econ.* вы́пуск, проду́кция; число́ уча́ствующих на собра́нии, голосова́нии, и. т. д.; **~*over*** ['tɜ:nəʊvə] *comm.* оборо́т; *of goods* товарооборо́т; **~*stile*** ['tɜ:nstaɪl] турнике́т
turpentine ['tɜ:pəntaɪn] скипида́р

T

turquoise ['tɜːkwɔɪz] *min.* бирюза́; бирюзо́вый цвет
turret ['tʌrɪt] ба́шенка
turtle ['tɜːtl] *zo.* черепа́ха
tusk [tʌsk] *zo.* би́вень *m*
tussle ['tʌsl] потасо́вка; дра́ка
tussock ['tʌsək] ко́чка
tutor ['tjuːtə] **1.** (*private teacher*) репети́тор; *Brt. univ.* преподава́тель *m*, -ница *f*; **2.** дава́ть ча́стные уро́ки; обуча́ть [-чи́ть]; **~ial** [tjuː'tɔːrɪəl] *univ.* консульта́ция
tuxedo [tʌk'siːdəʊ] *Am.* смо́кинг
twaddle ['twɒdl] **1.** пуста́я болтовня́; **2.** пустосло́вить
twang [twæŋ] **1.** *of guitar* звон; (*mst. **nasal** ~*) гнуса́вый го́лос; **2.** звене́ть
tweak [twiːk] **1.** щипо́к; **2.** ущипну́ть
tweed [twiːd] твид
tweezers ['twiːzəz] *pl.* пинце́т
twelfth [twelfθ] двена́дцатый
twelve [twelv] двена́дцать
twent|ieth ['twentɪɪθ] двадца́тый; **~y** ['twentɪ] два́дцать
twice [twaɪs] два́жды; вдво́е; ***think ~*** хорошо́ обду́мать
twiddle ['twɪdl] *in hands* верте́ть; (*play*) игра́ть (Т); ***~ one's thumbs*** *fig.* безде́льничать
twig [twɪg] ве́точка, прут
twilight ['twaɪlaɪt] су́мерки *f/pl.*
twin [twɪn] близне́ц; ***~ towns*** города́-побрати́мы
twine [twaɪn] **1.** бечёвка, шпага́т; **2.** [с]вить; *garland* [с]плести́; *of plants* обви́(ва́)ть(ся)
twinge [twɪndʒ] при́ступ бо́ли; ***~ of conscience*** угрызе́ния со́вести *f/pl.*
twinkle ['twɪŋkl] **1.** мерца́ние, мига́ние; *of eyes* и́скорки; **2.** [за]мерца́ть; мига́ть; искри́ться; **~ling** [~ɪŋ]: ***in the ~ of an eye*** в мгнове́ние о́ка
twirl [twɜːl] верте́ть, крути́ть
twist [twɪst] **1.** круче́ние; (*~ together*) скру́чивание; *of road, etc.* изги́б; *fig.* (*change*) поворо́т; *of ankle* вы́вих; **2.** [с]крути́ть; повора́чивать [-верну́ть], [с]ви́ться; сплета́ть(ся) [-ести́(сь)]; ***~ the facts*** искажа́ть [-ази́ть] фа́кты
twit [twɪt] *coll.* болва́н
twitch [twɪtʃ] **1.** подёргивание; **2.** подёргиваться
twitter ['twɪtə] **1.** щёбет; **2.** [за]щебета́ть (*a. of little girls*), чири́кать [-кнуть]; ***be in a ~*** дрожа́ть
two [tuː] **1.** два, две; дво́е; па́ра; ***in ~*** на́двое, попола́м; ***put ~ and ~ together*** смекну́ть в чём де́ло *pf.*; ***the ~ of them*** они́ о́ба; **2.** дво́йка; → ***five***; ***in ~s*** попа́рно; **~-faced** [~'feɪst] *fig.* двули́чный; **~fold** ['tuːfəʊld] **1.** двойно́й; **2.** *adv.* вдво́е; **~pence** ['tʌpəns] два пе́нса; **~-stor(e)y** двухэта́жный; **~-way** двусторо́нний
type [taɪp] **1.** тип; *of wine, etc.* сорт; *typ.* шрифт; ***true to ~*** типи́чный; **2.** печа́тать на маши́нке; **~writer** пи́шущая маши́нка
typhoid ['taɪfɔɪd] (*a. **~ fever***) брюшно́й тиф
typhoon [taɪ'fuːn] тайфу́н
typhus ['taɪfəs] сыпно́й тиф
typi|cal ['tɪpɪkl] типи́чный; **~fy** [~faɪ] служи́ть типи́чным приме́ром для (Р)
typist ['taɪpɪst] машини́стка; ***shorthand ~*** (машини́стка-)стенографи́ст(ка)
tyrann|ical [tɪ'rænɪkəl] □ тирани́ческий; **~ize** ['tɪrənaɪz] тира́нить; **~y** ['tɪrənɪ] тирани́я
tyrant ['taɪrənt] тира́н
tyre ['taɪə] → ***tire***
tzar [zɑː] → ***czar***

T

U

ubiquitous [juːˈbɪkwɪtəs] □ вездесу́щий *a. iro.*
udder [ˈʌdə] вы́мя *n*
UFO [ˈjuːfəʊ] НЛО
ugly [ˈʌglɪ] □ уро́дливый, безобра́зный (*a. fig.*); **~ customer** мёрзкий/опа́сный тип
ulcer [ˈʌlsə] я́зва
ulterior [ʌlˈtɪərɪə]: **~ motive** за́дняя мысль *f*
ultimate [ˈʌltɪmɪt] □ после́дний; коне́чный; (*final*) оконча́тельный; **~ly** [~lɪ] в конце́ концо́в
ultra... [ˈʌltrə] *pref.* сверх..., у́льтра...
umbrage [ˈʌmbrɪdʒ]: **take ~ at** обижа́ться [оби́деться] на (В)
umbrella [ʌmˈbrelə] зо́нтик; **telescopic ~** складно́й зо́нтик
umpire [ˈʌmpaɪə] **1.** *sport* судья́ *m*, арби́тр; **2.** суди́ть
un... [ʌn] *pref.* (*придаёт отрица́тельное или противополо́жное значе́ние*) не..., без...
unable [ʌnˈeɪbl] неспосо́бный; **be ~** быть не в состоя́нии, не [с]мочь
unaccountabl|e [ʌnəˈkaʊntəbl] □ необъясни́мый, непостижи́мый; **~y** [~blɪ] по непоня́тной причи́не
unaccustomed [ʌnəˈkʌstəmd] не привы́кший; (*not usual*) непривы́чный
unacquainted [ʌnəˈkweɪntɪd]: **~ with** незнако́мый с (Т); не зна́ющий (Р)
unaffected [ʌnəˈfektɪd] □ (*genuine*) непритво́рный, и́скренний; (*not affected*) не(за)тро́нутый (**by** Т)
unaided [ʌnˈeɪdɪd] без посторо́нней по́мощи
unalterable [ʌnˈɔːltərəbl] □ неизме́нный
unanimous [juːˈnænɪməs] □ единоду́шный; *in voting* единогла́сный
unanswerable [ʌnˈɑːnsərəbl] □ *argument* неопровержи́мый
unapproachable [ʌnəˈprəʊtʃəbl] □ (*physically inaccessible*) непристу́пный; *person* недосту́пный
unasked [ʌnˈɑːskt] непро́шеный; **I did this ~** я э́то сде́лал по свое́й инициати́ве
unassisted [ʌnəˈsɪstɪd] без посторо́нней по́мощи, самостоя́тельно
unassuming [ʌnəˈsjuːmɪŋ] скро́мный, непритяза́тельный
unattractive [ʌnəˈtræktɪv] непривлека́тельный
unauthorized [ʌnˈɔːθəraɪzd] неразрешённый; *person* посторо́нний
unavail|able [ʌnəˈveɪləbl] не име́ющийся в нали́чии; отсу́тствующий; **these goods are ~ at present** э́тих това́ров сейча́с нет; **~ing** [~lɪŋ] бесполе́зный
unavoidable [ʌnəˈvɔɪdəbl] неизбе́жный
unaware [ʌnəˈweə] не зна́ющий, не подозрева́ющий (**of** Р); **be ~ of** ничего́ не знать о (П); не замеча́ть [-е́тить] (Р); **~s** [~z]: **catch s.o. ~** застава́ть [-ста́ть] кого́-л. врасплох
unbalanced [ʌnˈbælənst] неуравнове́шенный (*a. mentally*)
unbearable [ʌnˈbeərəbl] □ невыноси́мый, нестерпи́мый
unbecoming [ʌnbɪˈkʌmɪŋ] □ (*inappropriate*) неподходя́щий; (*unseemly*) неподоба́ющий; *clothes* не иду́щий к лицу́
unbelie|f [ʌnbɪˈliːf] неве́рие; **~vable** [ˈʌnbɪˈliːvəbl] □ невероя́тный
unbend [ʌnˈbend] [*irr.* (**bend**)] выпрямля́ть(ся) [вы́прямить(ся)]; *fig.* станови́ться непринуждённым; **~ing** [~ɪŋ] □ *fig.* чи́стый; *fig.* непреклóнный
unbias(s)ed [ʌnˈbaɪəst] □ беспристра́стный
unbind [ʌnˈbaɪnd] [*irr.* (**bind**)] развя́зывать [-за́ть]
unblemished [ʌnˈblemɪʃt] чи́стый; *fig.* незапя́тнанный
unblushing [ʌnˈblʌʃɪŋ] беззастéнчивый
unbolt [ʌnˈbəʊlt] отпира́ть [-пере́ть]
unbounded [ʌnˈbaʊndɪd] □ неограни́ченный; беспреде́льный

unbroken [ʌn'brəʊkn] (*whole*) неразби́тый; *record* непоби́тый; (*uninterrupted*) непреры́вный
unburden [ʌn'bɜːdn]: ~ ***o.s.*** излива́ть [-ли́ть] ду́шу
unbutton [ʌn'bʌtn] расстёгивать [расстегну́ть]
uncalled-for [ʌn'kɔːldfɔː] непро́шенный; неуме́стный
uncanny [ʌn'kænɪ] □ сверхъесте́ственный; жу́ткий, пуга́ющий
uncared [ʌn'keəd]: **~-for** забро́шенный
unceasing [ʌn'siːsɪŋ] □ непрекраща́ющийся, беспреры́вный
unceremonious [ʌnserɪ'məʊnɪəs] бесцеремо́нный
uncertain [ʌn'sɜːtn] неуве́ренный; *plans, etc.* неопределённый; неизве́стный; ***it is ~ whether he will be there*** неизве́стно, бу́дет ли он там; ~ ***weather*** переме́нчивая пого́да; **~ty** [~tɪ] неуве́ренность *f*; неизве́стность *f*; неопределённость *f*
unchanging [ʌn'tʃeɪndʒɪŋ] □ неизме́нный
uncharitable [ʌn'tʃærɪtəbl] □ немилосе́рдный; ~ ***words*** жесто́кие слова́
unchecked [ʌn'tʃekt] беспрепя́тственный; (*not verified*) непрове́ренный
uncivil [ʌn'sɪvl] неве́жливый; **~ized** [ʌn'sɪvɪlaɪzd] нецивилизо́ванный
uncle ['ʌŋkl] дя́дя *m*
unclean [ʌn'kliːn] □ нечи́стый
uncomfortable [ʌn'kʌmfətəbl] неудо́бный; *fig.* нело́вкий
uncommon [ʌn'kɒmən] □ (*remarkable*) необыкнове́нный; (*unusual*) необы́чный; (*rare*) ре́дкий
uncommunicative [ʌnkə'mjuːnɪkətɪv] неразгово́рчивый, сде́ржанный; скры́тный
uncomplaining [ʌnkəm'pleɪnɪŋ] безро́потный
uncompromising [ʌn'kɒmprəmaɪzɪŋ] □ бескомпроми́ссный
unconcerned [ʌnkən'sɜːnd]: ***be ~ about*** относи́ться равноду́шно, безразли́чно (к Д)
unconditional [ʌnkən'dɪʃənl] □ безогово́рочный, безусло́вный
unconquerable [ʌn'kɒŋkrəbl] □ непобеди́мый
unconscious [ʌn'kɒnʃəs] □ (*not intentional*) бессозна́тельный; потеря́вший созна́ние; ***be ~ of*** не созн(ав)а́ть Р; ***the ~*** подсозна́ние; **~ness** [~nɪs] бессозна́тельное состоя́ние
unconstitutional [ʌnkɒnstɪ'tjuːʃnl] □ противоре́чащий конститу́ции; неконституцио́нный
uncontrollable [ʌnkən'trəʊləbl] □ неудержи́мый; неуправля́емый
unconventional [ʌnkən'venʃənl] □ (*free in one's ways*) чу́ждый усло́вности; (*unusual*) необы́чный; эксцентри́чный; (*original*) нешабло́нный
uncork [ʌn'kɔːk] отку́пори(ва)ть
uncount|able [ʌn'kaʊntəbl] бесчи́сленный; **~ed** [~tɪd] несчётный
uncouth [ʌn'kuːθ] (*rough*) гру́бый
uncover [ʌn'kʌvə] *face, etc.* откры́(ва́)ть; снима́ть кры́шку с (Р); *head* обнажа́ть [-жи́ть]; *fig. plot, etc.* раскрыва́ть [-ы́ть]
uncult|ivated [ʌn'kʌltɪveɪtɪd] *land* невозде́ланный; *plant* ди́кий; *person* неразвито́й; некульту́рный
undamaged [ʌn'dæmɪdʒd] неповреждённый
undaunted [ʌn'dɔːntɪd] □ (*fearless*) неустраши́мый
undecided [ʌndɪ'saɪdɪd] □ нерешённый; (*in doubt*) нереши́тельный
undeniable [ʌndɪ'naɪəbl] □ неоспори́мый; несомне́нный
under ['ʌndə] **1.** *adv.* ни́же; внизу́; вниз; **2.** *prp.* под (В, Т); ни́же (Р); ме́ньше (Р); при (П); **3.** *pref.* ни́же..., под..., недо...; **4.** ни́жний; ни́зший; **~bid** [ʌndə'bɪd] [*irr.* (***bid***)] предлага́ть бо́лее ни́зкую це́ну, чем (И); **~brush** [~brʌʃ] подле́сок; **~carriage** [~kærɪdʒ] шасси́ *n indecl.*; **~clothing** [~kləʊðɪŋ] ни́жнее бельё; **~cut** [~kʌt] сбива́ть це́ну; **~done** [ʌndə'dʌn] недожа́ренный; *cake* непропечённый; **~estimate** [ʌndər'estɪmeɪt] недооце́нивать [-и́ть]; **~fed** [~fed] недоко́рмленный, истощённый от недоеда́ния; **~go** [ʌndə'gəʊ] [*irr.*

(***go***)] испы́тывать [испыта́ть]; *criticism*, *etc.* подверга́ться [-е́ргнуться] (Д); **~graduate** [ʌndə'grædʒʊət] студе́нт *m*, -ка *f*; **~ground** [~graʊnd] **1.** подзе́мный; *pol.* подпо́льный; **2.** метро́(полите́н) *n indecl.*; (*movement*) подпо́лье; **~hand** [ʌndə'hænd] **1.** та́йный, закули́сный; **2.** *adv.* та́йно, за спино́й; **~lie** [ʌndə'laɪ] [*irr.* (***lie***)] лежа́ть в осно́ве (Р); **~line** [ʌndə'laɪn] подчёркивать [-черкну́ть]; **~mine** [ʌndə'maɪn] подрыва́ть [подорва́ть]; **~neath** [ʌndə'ni:θ] **1.** *prp.* под (Т/В); **2.** *adv.* вниз, внизу́; **~rate** [ʌndə'reɪt] недооце́нивать [-и́ть]; **~ secretary** [ʌndə'sekrətrɪ] замести́тель *m*, помо́щник мини́стра (в А́нглии и США); **~signed** [ʌndə'saɪnd] нижеподписа́вшийся; **~stand** [ʌndə'stænd] [*irr.* (***stand***)] *com.* понима́ть [поня́ть]; подразумева́ть (***by*** под Т); ***make o.s. understood*** уме́ть объясни́ться; **~-standable** [ʌndə'stændəbl] поня́тный; **~-standing** [ʌndə'stændɪŋ] понима́ние; взаимопонима́ние; (*agreement*) договорённость *f*; ***come to an ~*** договори́ться *pf.*; **~state** [ʌndə'steɪt] преуменьша́ть [-ме́ньшить]; **~stood** [ʌndə'stʊd] *pt. и pt. p. от* ***understand***; **~take** [ʌndə'teɪk] [*irr.* (***take***)] предпринима́ть [-ня́ть]; (*make o.s. responsible for*) брать на себя́; обя́зываться (-за́ться); **~taker** [~teɪkə] содержа́тель *m* похоро́нного бюро́; **~taking** [ʌndə'teɪkɪŋ] предприя́тие; **~tone** [~təʊn]: ***in an ~*** вполго́лоса; **~value** [ʌndə'vælju:] недооце́нивать [-и́ть]; **~wear** [~weə] ни́жнее бельё; **~write** [ʌndə'raɪt] [*irr.* (***write***)] [за]страхова́ть; **~writer** [~raɪtə] поруча́тель-гара́нт; страхова́тель *m*

undeserved [ʌndɪ'zз:vd] □ незаслу́женный

undesirable [ʌndɪ'zaɪərəbl] □ нежела́тельный; *moment*, *etc.* неудо́бный, неподходя́щий

undisciplined [ʌn'dɪsɪplɪnd] недисциплини́рованный

undiscriminating [ʌndɪs'krɪmɪneɪtɪŋ] неразбо́рчивый

undisguised [ʌndɪs'gaɪzd] □ откры́тый, я́вный; незамаскиро́ванный

undivided [ʌndɪ'vaɪdɪd] □ неразделённый; *attention* по́лный

undo [ʌn'du:] [*irr.* (***do***)] *string*, *etc.* развя́зывать [-за́ть]; *buttons*, *zip* расстёгивать [расстегну́ть]; (*destroy*) погуби́ть *pf.*; **~ing** [~ɪŋ]: ***that was my ~*** это погуби́ло меня́

undoubted [ʌn'daʊtɪd] несомне́нный, бесспо́рный

undreamed-of, undreamt-of [ʌn'dremtɒv] невообрази́мый, неожи́данный

undress [ʌn'dres] разде́(ва́)ть(ся); **~ed** [~st] неоде́тый

undue [ʌn'dju:] □ (*excessive*) чрезме́рный

undulating ['ʌndjʊleɪtɪŋ] *geogr.* холми́стый

unduly [ʌn'dju:lɪ] чересчу́р, чрезме́рно

unearth [ʌn'з:θ] вырыва́ть из земли́; *fig.* (*discover*) раска́пывать [-копа́ть]; **~ly** [ʌn'з:θlɪ] (*not terrestrial*) неземно́й; (*supernatural*) сверхъесте́ственный; (*weird*) стра́нный; *time* чересчу́р ра́нний (час)

uneas|iness [ʌn'i:zɪnɪs] беспоко́йство, трево́га; **~y** [ʌn'i:zɪ] □ беспоко́йный, трево́жный

uneducated [ʌn'edjʊkeɪtɪd] необразо́ванный

unemotional [ʌnɪ'məʊʃənl] бесстра́стный; неэмоциона́льный

unemploy|ed [ʌnɪm'plɔɪd] безрабо́тный; **~ment** [~mənt] безрабо́тица

unending [ʌn'endɪŋ] □ несконча́емый, бесконе́чный

unendurable [ʌnɪn'djʊərəbl] нестерпи́мый

unequal [ʌn'i:kwəl] □ нера́вный; *length*, *weight* разли́чный; ***be ~ to*** не в си́лах; *task*, *etc.* не по плечу́; **~led** [~d] непревзойдённый

unerring [ʌn'з:rɪŋ] □ безоши́бочный

uneven [ʌn'i:vn] □ неро́вный; *temper* неуравнове́шенный

uneventful [ʌnɪ'ventfl] □ без осо́-

U

бых собы́тий/приключе́ний
unexpected [ʌnɪks'pektɪd] □ неожи́данный
unexposed [ʌnɪk'spəʊzd] *film* неэкспони́рованный
unfailing [ʌn'feɪlɪŋ] □ ве́рный, надёжный; *interest* неизме́нный; *patience*, *etc.* неистощимый, беспреде́льный
unfair [ʌn'feə] □ несправедли́вый; *play*, *etc.* нече́стный
unfaithful [ʌn'feɪθfl] □ неве́рный; (*violating trust*) вероло́мный; *to the original* нето́чный
unfamiliar [ʌnfə'mɪlɪə] незнако́мый; *surroundings* непривы́чный
unfasten [ʌn'fɑːsn] *door* открыва́ть [-ы́ть]; *buttons*, *etc.* расстёгивать [расстегну́ть]; *knot* развя́зывать [-за́ть]; **~ed** [~d] расстёгнутый; *door* неза́пертый
unfavo(u)rable [ʌn'feɪvərəbl] □ неблагоприя́тный; *reports*, *etc.* отрица́тельный
unfeeling [ʌn'fiːlɪŋ] □ бесчу́вственный
unfinished [ʌn'fɪnɪʃt] незако́нченный
unfit [ʌn'fɪt] него́дный, неподходя́щий; **~ *for service*** него́ден к вое́нной слу́жбе
unflagging [ʌn'flægɪŋ] □ неослабева́ющий
unfold [ʌn'fəʊld] развёртывать(ся) [-верну́ть(ся)]; *plans*, *secret*, *etc.* раскры́(ва́)ть
unforeseen [ʌnfɔː'siːn] непредви́денный
unforgettable [ʌnfə'getəbl] □ незабыва́емый
unfortunate [ʌn'fɔːtʃənɪt] несча́стный; неуда́чный; (*unlucky*) неуда́чливый; **~ly** [~lɪ] к несча́стью; к сожале́нию
unfounded [ʌn'faʊndɪd] необосно́ванный
unfriendly [ʌn'frendlɪ] недружелю́бный; неприве́тливый
unfruitful [ʌn'fruːtfl] □ неплодоро́дный; *fig.* беспло́дный
unfurl [ʌn'fɜːl] развёртывать [разверну́ть]
ungainly [ʌn'geɪnlɪ] нескла́дный
ungodly [ʌn'gɔdlɪ]: нечести́вый; ***he woke us up at an ~ hour*** он разбуди́л нас безбо́жно ра́но
ungovernable [ʌn'gʌvənəbl] □ неуправля́емый; *temper*, *etc.* неукроти́мый, необу́зданный
ungracious [ʌn'greɪʃəs] □ (*not polite*) неве́жливый
ungrateful [ʌn'greɪtfl] □ неблагода́рный
unguarded [ʌn'gɑːdɪd] □ неохраня́емый, незащищённый; *fig.* неосторо́жный
unhampered [ʌn'hæmpəd] беспрепя́тственный
unhappy [ʌn'hæpɪ] □ несча́стный
unharmed [ʌn'hɑːmd] *thing* неповреждённый; *person* невреди́мый
unhealthy [ʌn'helθɪ] □ нездоро́вый, боле́зненный; *coll.* (*harmful*) вре́дный
unheard-of [ʌn'hɜːdɒv] неслы́ханный
unhesitating [ʌn'hezɪteɪtɪŋ] □ реши́тельный; **~ly** [~lɪ] не коле́блясь
unholy [ʌn'həʊlɪ] поро́чный; *coll.* жу́ткий, ужа́сный
unhoped-for [ʌn'həʊptfɔː] неожи́данный
unhurt [ʌn'hɜːt] невреди́мый, це́лый
uniform ['juːnɪfɔːm] **1.** □ одина́ковый; (*alike all over*) единообра́зный, одноро́дный; **2.** фо́рма, фо́рменная оде́жда; **~ity** [juːnɪ'fɔːmətɪ] единообра́зие, одноро́дность *f*
unify ['juːnɪfaɪ] объединя́ть [-ни́ть]; унифици́ровать (*im*)*pf.*
unilateral [juːnɪ'lætrəl] односторо́нний
unimaginable [ʌnɪ'mædʒɪnəbl] □ невообрази́мый
unimportant [ʌnɪm'pɔːtənt] □ нева́жный
uninhabit|able [ʌnɪn'hæbɪtəbl] неприго́дный для жилья́; **~ed** [~tɪd] *house* нежило́й; необита́емый
uninjured [ʌn'ɪndʒəd] непострада́вший; невреди́мый
unintelligible [ʌnɪn'telɪdʒəbl] □ непоня́тный; *hand writing* неразбо́рчивый, нево́льный
unintentional [ʌnɪn'tenʃənl] □ ненаме́ренный, неумы́шленный

uninteresting [ʌn'ɪntrəstɪŋ] □ неинтере́сный
uninterrupted [ʌnɪntə'rʌptɪd] □ непреры́вный, беспреры́вный
uninvit|ed [ʌnɪn'vaɪtɪd] неприглашённый; *pej.* незва́ный; ***come ~*** прийти́ *pf.* без приглаше́ния; **~ing** [~tɪŋ] непривлека́тельный; *food* неаппети́тный
union ['juːnɪən] сою́з; (*trade ~*) профсою́з; **♀ *Jack*** брита́нский национа́льный флаг
unique ['juːniːk] еди́нственный в своём ро́де, уника́льный
unison ['juːnɪzn] унисо́н; гармо́ния; в по́лном согла́сии; ***act in ~*** де́йствовать сла́женно
unit ['juːnɪt] *mil.* часть *f*, подразделе́ние; *math.* едини́ца; *tech.* агрега́т; **~ *furniture*** секцио́нная ме́бель; **~e** [juː'naɪt] *in marriage* сочета́ть у́зами бра́ка; соединя́ть(ся) [-ни́ть(ся)]; объединя́ть(ся) [-ни́ть(ся)]; **~y** ['juːnətɪ] еди́нство
univers|al [juːnɪ'vɜːsl] □ *agreement, etc.* всео́бщий; всеми́рный; *mst. tech.* универса́льный; **~e** ['juːnɪvɜːs] мир, вселе́нная; **~ity** [juːnɪ'vɜːsətɪ] университе́т
unjust [ʌn'dʒʌst] □ несправедли́вый; **~ified** [ʌn'dʒʌstɪfaɪd] неопра́вданный
unkempt [ʌn'kempt] (*untidy*) беспоря́дочный; неопря́тный; *hair* растрёпанный
unkind [ʌn'kaɪnd] □ недо́брый
unknown [ʌn'nəʊn] неизве́стный; ***~ to me*** *adv.* без моего́ ве́дома
unlace [ʌn'leɪs] расшнуро́вывать [-ова́ть]
unlawful [ʌn'lɔːfl] □ незако́нный
unless [ən'les, ʌn'les] *cj.* е́сли не
unlike [ʌn'laɪk] **1.** непохо́жий на (В); ***it's quite ~ her*** э́то совсе́м на неё не похо́же; **2.** *prp.* в отли́чие от (Р); **~ly** [ʌn'laɪklɪ] неправдоподо́бный, невероя́тный; маловероя́тный; ***his arrival today is ~*** маловероя́тно, что он прие́дет сего́дня
unlimited [ʌn'lɪmɪtɪd] неограни́ченный
unload [ʌn'ləʊd] выгружа́ть [вы́грузить], разгружа́ть [-узи́ть]; *mil. a weapon* разряжа́ть [-яди́ть]
unlock [ʌn'lɒk] отпира́ть [отпере́ть]; **~ed** [~t] неза́пертый
unlooked-for [ʌn'lʊktfɔː] неожи́данный, непредви́денный
unlucky [ʌn'lʌkɪ] □ неуда́чный, несчастли́вый; ***I was ~*** мне не повезло́; ***be ~*** (*bring ill-luck*) приноси́ть несча́стье
unmanageable [ʌn'mænɪdʒəbl] □ неуправля́емый; *child, problem* тру́дный
unmanly [ʌn'mænlɪ] нему́жественный; не по-мужски́; трусли́вый
unmarried [ʌn'mærɪd] нежена́тый, холосто́й; *woman* незаму́жняя
unmask [ʌn'mɑːsk] *fig.* разоблача́ть [-чи́ть]
unmatched [ʌn'mætʃt] не име́ющий себе́ ра́вного, непревзойдённый
unmerciful [ʌn'mɜːsɪfl] безжа́лостный
unmerited [ʌn'merɪtɪd] незаслу́женный
unmistakable [ʌnmɪs'teɪkəbl] □ ве́рный, очеви́дный; несомне́нный; (*clearly recognizable*) легко́ узнава́емый
unmitigated [ʌn'mɪtɪgeɪtɪd] несмягчённый; *fig.* отъя́вленный, по́лный, абсолю́тный
unmoved [ʌn'muːvd] оста́вшийся равноду́шным; бесчу́вственный; ***he was ~ by her tears*** её слёзы не тро́нули его́
unnatural [ʌn'nætʃrəl] □ неесте́ственный; (*contrary to nature*) противоесте́ственный
unnecessary [ʌn'nesəsrɪ] □ нену́жный, ли́шний; (*excessive*) изли́шний
unnerve [ʌn'nɜːv] обесси́ливать; лиша́ть прису́тствия ду́ха, реши́мости
unnoticed [ʌn'nəʊtɪst] незаме́ченный
unobserved [ʌnəb'zɜːvd] незаме́ченный
unobtainable [ʌnəb'teɪnəbl]: **~ *thing*** недосту́пная вещь *f*
unobtrusive [ʌnəb'truːsɪv] ненавя́зчивый

U

unoccupied [ʌn'ɒkjʊpaɪd] неза́нятый
unoffending [ʌnə'fendɪŋ] безоби́дный
unofficial [ʌnə'fɪʃl] неофициа́льный
unopened [ʌn'əʊpənd] неоткры́тый; *letter* нераспеча́танный
unopposed [ʌnə'pəʊzd] не встреча́ющий сопротивле́ния
unpack [ʌn'pæk] распако́вывать [-ова́ть]
unpaid [ʌn'peɪd] *debt* неупла́ченный; *work* неопла́ченный
unparalleled [ʌn'pærəleld] беспримéрный; *success, kindness* необыкнове́нный
unpardonable [ʌn'pɑːdɔnəbl] □ непрости́тельный
unperturbed [ʌnpə'tɜːbd] невозмути́мый
unpleasant [ʌn'pleznt] □ неприя́тный; **~ness** [~nɪs] неприя́тность *f*
unpopular [ʌn'pɒpjʊlə] □ непопуля́рный; ***make o.s. ~*** лиша́ть [-ши́ть] себя́ популя́рности
unpractical [ʌn'præktɪkəl] непракти́чный
unprecedented [ʌn'presɪdəntɪd] □ беспрецеде́нтный; *courage* беспримéрный
unprejudiced [ʌn'predʒʊdɪst] □ непредубеждённый; непредвзя́тый
unprepared [ʌnprɪ'peəd] □ неподгото́вленный; без подгото́вки
unpretentious [ʌnprɪ'tenʃəs] □ скро́мный, без претéнзий
unprincipled [ʌn'prɪnsəpld] беспринци́пный
unprofitable [ʌn'prɒfɪtəbl] невы́годный; *enterprise* нерента́бельный
unpromising [ʌn'prɒmɪsɪŋ] малообеща́ющий; ***the crops look ~*** вряд ли бу́дет хоро́ший урожа́й
unproved [ʌn'pruːvd] недока́занный
unprovoked [ʌnprə'vəʊkt] неспровоци́рованный
unqualified [ʌn'kwɒlɪfaɪd] неквалифици́рованный; некомпете́нтный; *denial, etc.* безоговоро́чный; *success, etc.* реши́тельный; безграни́чный
unquestionable [ʌn'kwestʃənəbl] несомне́нный, неоспори́мый
unravel [ʌn'rævəl] распу́т(ыв)ать (*a. fig.*); (*solve*) разга́дывать [-да́ть]
unreal [ʌn'rɪəl] нереа́льный
unreasonable [ʌn'riːznəbl] □ не(благо)разу́мный; безрассу́дный; *price, etc.* чрезме́рный
unrecognizable [ʌn'rekəgnaɪzəbl] □ неузнава́емый
unrelated [ʌnrɪ'leɪtɪd] *people* не ро́дственники; *ideas, facts, etc.* не име́ющий отноше́ния; не свя́занные (ме́жду собо́й)
unrelenting [ʌnrɪ'lentɪŋ] □ неумоли́мый; ***it was a week of ~ activity*** всю неде́лю мы рабо́тали без переды́шки
unreliable [ʌnrɪ'laɪəbl] ненадёжный
unrelieved [ʌnrɪ'liːvd]: ***~ boredom*** необлегчённая ску́ка; ***~ sadness*** неизбы́вная грусть *f*
unremitting [ʌnrɪ'mɪtɪŋ] □ беспреры́вный; *pain, etc.* неослабева́ющий
unreserved [ʌnrɪ'zɜːvd] □ *seat, etc.* незаброни́рованный; *support, etc.* безоговоро́чный
unrest [ʌn'rest] *social, political* волне́ния, беспоря́дки; (*disquiet*) беспоко́йство
unrestrained [ʌnrɪs'treɪnd] □ *behavio(u)r* несдéржанный; *anger, etc.* необу́зданный
unrestricted [ʌnrɪs'trɪktɪd] □ неограни́ченный
unrewarding [ʌnrɪ'wɔːdɪŋ] неблаго́дарный
unripe [ʌn'raɪp] незре́лый, неспе́лый
unrival(l)ed [ʌn'raɪvld] непревзойдённый; не име́ющий сопе́рников
unroll [ʌn'rəʊl] развёртывать [-верну́ть]
unruffled [ʌn'rʌfld] *sea, etc.* гла́дкий; *person* невозмути́мый
unruly [ʌn'ruːlɪ] непослу́шный; непоко́рный; бу́йный
unsafe [ʌn'seɪf] □ (*not dependable*) ненадёжный; (*dangerous*) опа́сный
unsal(e)able [ʌn'seɪləbl] *goods* нехо́дкий

unsanitary [ʌn'sænɪtərɪ] антисанитáрный
unsatisfactory [ʌnsætɪs'fæktərɪ] □ неудовлетвори́тельный
unsavo(u)ry [ʌn'seɪvərɪ] невкýсный; неприя́тный; (*offensive*) отврати́тельный
unscathed [ʌn'skeɪðd] невреди́мый
unscrew [ʌn'skru:] отви́нчивать (-ся) [-нти́ть(ся)]; вывёртывать [-вернуть]
unscrupulous [ʌn'skru:pjʊləs] □ беспринци́пный; неразбóрчивый в срéдствах
unseasonable [ʌn'si:zənəbl] □ (*ill-timed*) несвоеврéменный; не по сезóну
unseemly [ʌn'si:mlɪ] неподобáющий; (*indecent*) непристóйный
unseen [ʌn'si:n] (*invisible*) неви́димый; (*not seen*) неви́данный
unselfish [ʌn'selfɪʃ] □ бескоры́стный
unsettle [ʌn'setl] *person* расстрáивать [-рóить]; **~d** [~d] *weather* неустóйчивый; *problem, etc.* нерешённый; *bill* неоплáченный
unshaken [ʌn'ʃeɪkən] непоколеби́мый
unshaven [ʌn'ʃeɪvn] небри́тый
unshrinkable [ʌn'ʃrɪŋkəbl] безусáдочный
unsightly [ʌn'saɪtlɪ] непригля́дный
unskil(l)|ful [ʌn'skɪlfl] □ неумéлый, неискýсный; **~ed** [ʌn'skɪld] неквалифици́рованный
unsociable [ʌn'səʊʃəbl] необщи́тельный
unsolicited [ʌnsə'lɪsɪtɪd] непрóшенный
unsophisticated [ʌnsə'fɪstɪkeɪtɪd] безыскýсный, бесхи́тростный; простóй, простодýшный
unsound [ʌn'saʊnd] □ *health* нездорóвый; *views* не(достáточно) обоснóванный; *judg(e)ment* шáткий; лишённый прóчности
unsparing [ʌn'speərɪŋ] □ (*unmerciful*) беспощáдный; (*profuse*) щéдрый; **~ *efforts*** неустáнные уси́лия
unspeakable [ʌn'spi:kəbl] □ невырази́мый; (*terrible*) ужáсный
unstable [ʌn'steɪbl] □ неустóйчивый; *phys., chem.* нестóйкий
unsteady [ʌn'stedɪ] □ → ***unstable***; *hand* трясýщийся; *steps* нетвёрдый; шáткий; непостоя́нный
unstudied [ʌn'stʌdɪd] невы́ученный; естéственный, непринуждённы
unsuccessful [ʌnsək'sesfl] □ неудáчный, безуспéшный; неудáчливый
unsuitable [ʌn'su:təbl] □ неподходя́щий
unsurpassed [ʌnsə'pɑ:st] непревзойдённый
unsuspect|ed [ʌnsəs'pektɪd] □ неожи́данный; **~ing** [~ɪŋ] неподозревáемый (***of*** о П)
unsuspicious [ʌnsə'spɪʃəs] □ *person* неподозревáющий; довéрчивый
unswerving [ʌn'swɜ:vɪŋ] □ неуклóнный
untangle [ʌn'tæŋgl] распýт(ыв)ать
untarnished [ʌn'tɑ:nɪʃt] *reputation* незапя́тнанный
untenable [ʌn'tenəbl] *theory etc.* несостоя́тельный
unthink|able [ʌn'θɪŋkəbl] немы́слимый; **~ing** [~ɪŋ] □ бездýмный; опромéтчивый
untidy [ʌn'taɪdɪ] □ неопря́тный, неаккурáтный; *room* неýбранный
untie [ʌn'taɪ] развя́зывать [-зáть]; *one thing from another* отвя́зывать [-зáть]
until [ən'tɪl] **1.** *prp.* до (Р); ***not ~ Sunday*** не рáнее воскресéнья; **2.** *cj.* (до тех пор) покá ... (не) ...
untimely [ʌn'taɪmlɪ] несвоеврéменный; **~ *death*** безврéменная кончи́на
untiring [ʌn'taɪərɪŋ] □ неутоми́мый
untold [ʌn'təʊld] (*not told*) нерасскáзанный; (*incalculable*) несмéтный, несчётный
untouched [ʌn'tʌtʃt] нетрóнутый
untroubled [ʌn'trʌbld]: необеспокóенный; **~ *life*** безмятéжная жизнь *f*
untrue [ʌn'tru:] □ невéрный; ***this is ~*** это непрáвда
untrustworthy [ʌn'trʌstwɜ:ðɪ] не заслýживающий довéрия

U

unus|ed 1. [ʌn'ju:zd] (*new*) не бы́вший в употребле́нии; (*not used*) неиспо́льзованный; **2.** [ʌn'ju:st] непривы́кший (**to** к Д); **~ual** [ʌn'ju:ʒʊəl] □ необыкнове́нный, необы́чный
unvarnished [ʌn'vɑ:nɪʃt] *fig.* неприкра́шенный
unvarying [ʌn'veərɪɪŋ] □ неизменя́ющийся, неизме́нный
unveil [ʌn'veɪl] *statute, monument* откры́(ва́)ть
unwanted [ʌn'wɒntɪd] *child* нежела́нный; нену́жный
unwarranted [ʌn'wɒrəntɪd] □ неразрешённый; неопра́вданный; *criticism, etc.* незаслу́женный
unwavering [ʌn'weɪvərɪŋ] □ непоколеби́мый; **~ look** при́стальный взгляд
unwell [ʌn'wel]: нездоро́вый; ***he is ~*** ему́ нездоро́вится; ***feel ~*** нева́жно (пло́хо) себя́ чу́вствовать
unwholesome [ʌn'həʊlsəm] неблаготво́рный; (*harmful*) вре́дный
unwieldy [ʌn'wi:ldɪ] □ *carton, etc.* громо́здкий
unwilling [ʌn'wɪlɪŋ] □ несклóнный, нежела́ющий; нерасполо́женный; ***be ~ to do s.th.*** не хоте́ть что́-то сде́лать
unwise [ʌn'waɪz] □ неразу́мный
unwittingly [ʌn'wɪtɪŋlɪ] нево́льно, непреднаме́ренно
unworthy [ʌn'wɜ:ðɪ] □ недосто́йный
unwrap [ʌn'ræp] развёртывать(ся) [-верну́ть(ся)]
unyielding [ʌn'ji:ldɪŋ] □ неподатливый, неусту́пчивый
unzip [ʌn'zɪp] расстёгивать [-егну́ть]; ***come ~ped*** расстегну́ться *pf.*
up [ʌp] **1.** *adv.* вверх, наве́рх; вверху́, наверху́; вы́ше; *fig.* ***be ~ to the mark*** быть в фо́рме, на высоте́; ***be ~ against a task*** стоя́ть перед зада́чей; ***~ to*** вплоть до (Р); ***it is ~ to me*** (***to do***) мне прихо́дится (де́лать); ***what's ~?*** *coll.* что случи́лось?, в чём де́ло?; ***what is he ~ to?*** чем он занима́ется?; **2.** *prp.* вверх по (Д); по направле́нию к (Д); ***~ the river*** вверх по реке́; **3.** *su.* ***the ~s and downs*** *fig.* превра́тности судьбы́; **4.** *vb. coll.* поднима́ть [-ня́ть]; *prices* повыша́ть [-ы́сить]
up|braid [ʌp'breɪd] [вы́]брани́ть; **~bringing** ['ʌpbrɪŋɪŋ] воспита́ние; **~date** [ʌp'deɪt] модернизи́ровать; *person* держа́ть в ку́рсе де́ла; **~heaval** [ʌp'hi:vl] *earthquake, etc.* сдвиг; *fig.* глубо́кие (революцио́нные) переме́ны; **~hill** [ʌp'hɪl] (иду́щий) в го́ру; *fig.* тяжёлый; **~hold** [ʌp'həʊld] *irr. support* подде́рживать [-жа́ть]; **~holster** [ʌp'həʊlstə] оби́(ва́)ть; **~holstery** [~stərɪ] оби́вка
up|keep ['ʌpki:p] содержа́ние; *cost* сто́имость *f* содержа́ния; **~lift 1.** ['ʌplɪft] душе́вный подъём; **2.** [ʌp'lɪft] поднима́ть [-ня́ть]
upon [ə'pɒn] → ***on***
upper ['ʌpə] ве́рхний; вы́сший; ***gain the ~ hand*** одéрживать [одержа́ть] верх (над Т); **~most** [~məʊst] са́мый ве́рхний; наивы́сший; ***be ~ in one's mind*** стоя́ть на пе́рвом ме́сте, быть гла́вным
uppish ['ʌpɪʃ] *coll.* надме́нный
upright ['ʌpraɪt] □ прямо́й (*a. fig.*), вертика́льный; *adv. a.* стоймя́; **~ piano** пиани́но *n indecl.*
up|rising ['ʌpraɪzɪŋ] восста́ние; **~roar** ['ʌprɔ:] шум, *coll.* гам; **~roarious** [ʌp'rɔ:rɪəs] □ (*noisy*) шу́мный; (*funny*) ужа́сно смешно́й
up|root [ʌp'ru:t] вырыва́ть с ко́рнем; *fig.* ***I don't want to ~ myself again*** я не хочу́ сно́ва переезжа́ть; **~set** [ʌp'set] [*irr.* (***set***)] (*knock over*) опроки́дывать(ся) [-и́нуть(ся)]; *person, plans, etc.* расстра́ивать [-ро́ить]; **~shot** ['ʌpʃɒt] ито́г, результа́т; ***the ~ of it was that ...*** ко́нчилось тем, что ...; **~side: ~ down** [ʌpsaɪd'daʊn] вверх дном; **~stairs** [ʌp'steəz] вверх (по ле́стнице), наве́рх(у́); **~start** ['ʌpstɑ:t] вы́скочка *m/f*; **~stream** [ʌp'stri:m] вверх по тече́нию; **~-to-date** [ʌptə'deɪt] совреме́нный; ***bring s.o. ~*** вводи́ть [ввести́] кого́-л. в курс де́ла; **~turn** [ʌp'tɜ:n] сдвиг к лу́чшему; улучше́ние; **~ward(s)**

['ʌpwədz] вверх, наве́рх; **~ *of*** свы́ше, бо́льше
urban ['ɜːbən] городско́й; **~e** [ɜːb'eɪn] ве́жливый; (*refined*) изы́сканный; (*suave*) обходи́тельный
urchin ['ɜːtʃɪn] мальчи́шка *m*
urge [ɜːdʒ] **1.** (*try to persuade*) убежда́ть [-еди́ть]; подгоня́ть [подогна́ть] (*often* **~ *on***); **2.** стремле́ние, жела́ние, толчо́к *fig.*; **~ncy** ['ɜːdʒənsɪ] (*need*) настоя́тельность *f*; (*haste*) сро́чность *f*; насто́йчивость *f*; **~nt** ['ɜːdʒənt] □ сро́чный; настоя́тельный, насто́йчивый
urin|al ['jʊərɪnl] писсуа́р; **~ate** [~rɪneɪt] [по]мочи́ться; **~e** [~rɪn] моча́
urn [ɜːn] у́рна
us [əs, ... ʌs] *pers. pron.* (*ко́свенный паде́ж от* **we**) нас, нам, на́ми
usage ['juːzɪdʒ] употребле́ние; (*custom*) обы́чай
use 1. [juːs] употребле́ние; примене́ние; по́льзование; (*usefulness*) по́льза; (*habit*) привы́чка; **(*of*) *no* ~** бесполе́зный; ***come into* ~** войти в употребле́ние; ***for general* ~** для о́бщего по́льзования; ***what's the* ~ ...?** како́й смысл ...?, что то́лку ...?; **2.** [juːz] употребля́ть [-би́ть]; по́льзоваться (Т); воспо́льзоваться (Т) *pf.*; испо́льзовать (*im*)*pf.*; (*treat*) обраща́ться с (Т), обходи́ться [обойти́сь] с (Т); ***I* ~*d to do*** я, быва́ло, ча́сто де́лал; **~d** [juːst]: **~ *to*** привы́кший к (Д); **~ful** ['juːsfl] □ поле́зный; приго́дный; ***come in* ~** пригоди́ться; **~less** ['juːslɪs] □ бесполе́зный; неприго́дный, него́дный; **~r** ['juːzə] по́льзователь *m*; (*customer*) потреби́тель *m*; *of library*, *etc.* чита́тель *m*
usher ['ʌʃə] (*conduct*) проводи́ть [-вести́]; (**~ *in***) вводи́ть [ввести́]; **~ette** [~'ret] билетёрша
usual ['juːʒʊəl] □ обыкнове́нный, обы́чный
usurp [juː'zɛːp] узурпи́ровать (*im*)*pf.*; **~er** [juː'zɜːpə] узурпа́тор
utensil [juː'tensl] (*mst. pl.* **~s**) инструме́нт; посу́да; ***kitchen* ~*s*** ку́хонные принадле́жности *f/pl.*
utility [juː'tɪlətɪ] (*usefulness*) поле́зность *f*; ***public utilities*** коммуна́льные услу́ги/предприя́тия
utiliz|ation [juːtəlaɪ'zeɪʃn] испо́льзование, утилиза́ция; **~e** ['juːtəlaɪz] испо́льзовать (*im*)*pf.*, утилизи́ровать (*im*)*pf.*
utmost ['ʌtməʊst] кра́йний, преде́льный; ***do one's* ~** сде́лать *pf.* всё возмо́жное; ***at the* ~** са́мое бо́льшее
utter ['ʌtə] **1.** □ *fig.* по́лный; соверше́нный; **2.** *sounds* изд(ав)а́ть; *words* произноси́ть [-нести́]; **~ance** [~ərəns] выска́зывание; ***give* ~ *to*** выска́зывать [-сказа́ть]; *emotion* дать вы́ход (Д)
U-turn ['juːtɜːn] *mot.* разворо́т

V

vacan|cy ['veɪkənsɪ] (*emptiness*) пустота́; (*unfilled job*) вака́нсия; *in hotel* свобо́дная ко́мната; **~t** ['veɪkənt] □ неза́нятый, вака́нтный; пусто́й; *look*, *mind*, *etc.* отсу́тствующий
vacat|e [və'keɪt] *house*, *hotel room*, *etc.* освобожда́ть [-боди́ть]; **~ion** [və'keɪʃn, *Am.* veɪ'keɪʃən] *univ.* кани́кулы *f/pl.*; *Am.* (*holiday*) о́тпуск; ***be on* ~** быть в о́тпуске
vaccin|ate ['væksɪneɪt] *med.* [с]де́лать приви́вку; **~ation** [væksɪ'neɪʃn] приви́вка; **~e** ['væksiːn] вакци́на
vacillate ['væsəleɪt] колеба́ться
vacuum ['vækjʊəm] *phys.* ва́куум (*a. fig.*); **~ cleaner** пылесо́с; **~ flask** те́рмос; **~-packed** в ва́куумной упако́вке

vagabond ['vægəbɒnd] бродя́га *m*
vagrant ['veɪgrənt] бродя́га *m*
vague [veɪg] неопределённый, нея́сный, сму́тный; ***I haven't the ~st idea of ...*** я не име́ю ни мале́йшего представле́ния о (П)
vain [veɪn] □ (*useless*) тще́тный, напра́сный; (*conceited*) тщесла́вный; ***in ~*** напра́сно, тще́тно; **~glorious** [veɪn'glɒːrɪəs] тщесла́вный; (*boastful*) хвастли́вый
valet ['vælɪt, 'væleɪ] камерди́нер
valiant ['vælɪənt] *rhet.* хра́брый, до́блестный
valid ['vælɪd] *law* действи́тельный (*a. ticket, etc.*), име́ющий си́лу; *argument, etc.* ве́ский, обосно́ванный
valley ['vælɪ] доли́на
valo(u)r ['vælə] *rhet.* до́блесть *f*
valuable ['væljuəbl] **1.** це́нный; **2. ~s** *pl.* це́нности *f/pl.*
valuation [vælju'eɪʃn] оце́нка
value ['væljuː] **1.** це́нность *f*; *comm.* сто́имость *f*; *math.* величина́; ***put*** (*or* ***set***) ***little ~ on*** невысоко́ цени́ть; **2.** оце́нивать [-и́ть] (В); цени́ть (В); дорожи́ть (Т); **~less** ['væljuːlɪs] ничего́ не сто́ящий
valve ['vælv] *tech.* ве́нтиль *m*, кла́пан (*a. anat.*)
van [væn] автофурго́н; *rail.* бага́жный *or* това́рный ваго́н *f*
vane [veɪn] (*weathercock*) флю́гер; *of propeller* ло́пасть *f*
vanguard ['vængɑːd]: ***be in the ~*** быть в пе́рвых ряда́х; *fig.* аванга́рд
vanilla [və'nɪlə] вани́ль *f*
vanish ['vænɪʃ] исчеза́ть [-е́знуть]
vanity ['vænətɪ] тщесла́вие; **~ bag** (су́мочка-)космети́чка
vanquish ['væŋkwɪʃ] побежда́ть [-еди́ть]
vantage ['vɑːntɪdʒ]: ***~ point*** удо́бное для обзо́ра ме́сто; вы́годная пози́ция
vapid ['væpɪd] □ пло́ский; пре́сный; *fig.* неинтере́сный
vaporize ['veɪpəraɪz] испаря́ть(ся) [-ри́ть(ся)]
vapo(u)r ['veɪpə] пар
varia|ble ['veərɪəbl] **1.** □ непостоя́нный, изме́нчивый; **2.** *math.* переме́нная величина́; **~nce** [~rɪəns]: ***be at ~*** расходи́ться во мне́ниях; быть в противоре́чии; **~nt** [~rɪənt] вариа́нт; **~tion** [veərɪ-'eɪʃn] измене́ние; *mus.* вариа́ция
varie|d ['veərɪd] → ***various***; **~gated** ['veərɪgeɪtɪd] разноцве́тный, пёстрый; **~ty** [və'raɪətɪ] разнообра́зие; (*sort*) сорт, разнови́дность *f*; ряд, мно́жество; ***for a ~ of reasons*** по ря́ду причи́н; ***~ show*** варьете́; эстра́дное представле́ние
various ['veərɪəs] ра́зный; (*of different sorts*) разли́чный; разнообра́зный; **~ly** [~lɪ] по-ра́зному
varnish ['vɑːnɪʃ] **1.** лак; *fig.* (*gloss*) лоск; **2.** покрыва́ть ла́ком
vary ['veərɪ] (*change*) изменя́ть(ся) [-ни́ть(ся)]; (*be different*) разни́ться; *of opinion* расходи́ться [разойти́сь]; (*diversify*) разнообра́зить
vase [vɑːz] ва́за
vast [vɑːst] □ обши́рный, грома́дный
vat [væt] чан; бо́чка, ка́дка
vault [vɔːlt] **1.** свод; (*tomb*, *crypt*) склеп; (*cellar*) подва́л, по́греб; **2.** (*a. **~ over***) перепры́гивать [-гнуть]
veal [viːl] теля́тина; *attr.* теля́чий
veer [vɪə] *of wind* меня́ть направле́ние; *of views, etc.* изменя́ть [-ни́ть]; ***the car ~ed to the right*** маши́ну занесло́ впра́во
vegeta|ble ['vedʒtəbl] **1.** о́вощ; **~s** *pl.* зе́лень *f*, о́вощи *m/pl.*; *attr. oil* расти́тельный; овощно́й; ***~ garden*** огоро́д; ***~ marrow*** кабачо́к; **~rian** [vedʒɪ'teərɪən] **1.** вегетариа́нец *m*, -нка *f*; **2.** вегетариа́нский; **~tion** [vedʒɪ'teɪʃn] расти́тельность *f*
vehemen|ce ['viːəməns] си́ла; стра́стность *f*; **~t** [~t] си́льный; стра́стный; *protests, etc.* бу́рный
vehicle ['viːɪkl] автомаши́на, авто́бус *и т. д.* (*любо́е тра́нспортное сре́дство*); *fig.* сре́дство; *med.* перено́счик
veil [veɪl] **1.** вуа́ль *f*; *of mist* пелена́; *fig.* заве́са; ***bridal ~*** фата́; **2.** закрыва́ть вуа́лью; *fig.* завуали́ровать; *in mist* оку́тывать

vein [veɪn] ве́на; *geol.* жи́ла; *fig.* жи́лка; (*mood*) настрое́ние
velocity [vɪ'lɒsətɪ] ско́рость *f*

velvet ['velvɪt] бáрхат; *attr.* бáрхатный; **~y** [~ɪ] бáрхатный (*fig.*); бархати́стый
vendor ['vendə] (ýличный) продавéц *m*, -вщица *f*
veneer [və'nɪə] фанéра; *fig.* фасáд
venerable ['venərəbl] □ почтéнный; *eccl. title* преподóбный
venereal [və'nɪərɪəl] венери́ческий
Venetian [və'niːʃn] венециáнский; **~ blinds** *pl.* жалюзи́ *n indecl.*
vengeance ['vendʒəns] месть *f*
venom ['venəm] (*part.* змеи́ный) яд (*a. fig.*); *fig.* злóба; **~ous** [~əs] □ ядови́тый (*a. fig.*)
vent [vent] **1.** вентиляциóнное отвéрстие; (*air ~*) отдýшина; ***give ~ to*** изли́(вá)ть (В); **2.** *fig.* изли́(вá)ть (В), давáть вы́ход (Д)
ventilat|e ['ventɪleɪt] провéтри(ва)ть; *fig.*, *of question* обсуждáть [-уди́ть], выясня́ть [вы́яснить]; **~ion** [ventɪ'leɪʃn] вентиля́ция
venture ['ventʃə] **1.** рискóванное предприя́тие; ***at a ~*** наугáд; ***joint ~*** совмéстное предприя́тие; **2.** рисковáть [-кнýть] (Т); отвáжи(ва)ться на (В) (*a.* ***~ upon***)
veracious [və'reɪʃəs] правди́вый
veranda(h) [və'rændə] верáнда
verb|al ['vɜːbl] □ словéсный; (*oral*) ýстный; *gr.* отглагóльный; **~atim** [vɜː'beɪtɪm] дослóвно, слóво в слóво; **~ose** [vɜː'bəʊs] □ многослóвный
verdict ['vɜːdɪkt] *law* верди́кт; ***what's your ~, doctor?*** каковó Вáше мнéние, дóктор?
verdure ['vɜːdʒə] зéлень *f*
verge [vɜːdʒ] **1.** (*edge*) край; *of forest* опýшка; *of flower bed* бордю́р; *fig.* грань *f*; ***on the ~ of*** на грáни (П); **2.**: ***~ (up)on*** грани́чить с (Т)
veri|fy ['verɪfaɪ] проверя́ть [-éрить]; (*bear out*) подтверждáть [-рди́ть]; **~table** ['verɪtəbl] □ настоя́щий, и́стинный
vermin ['vɜːmɪn] *coll.* вреди́тели *m/pl.*; (*lice, etc.*) парази́ты *m/pl.*
vermouth ['vɜːməθ] вéрмут
vernacular [və'nækjʊlə] *language* роднóй; мéстный диалéкт
versatile ['vɜːsətaɪl] разносторóнний; (*having ma ny uses*) универсáльный
verse [vɜːs] стихи́ *m/pl.*; (*line*) строкá; (*stanza*) строфá; **~d** [vɜːst] óпытный, свéдущий; ***she is well ~ in English history*** онá хорошó знáет англи́йскую истóрию
version ['vɜːʃn] вариáнт; (*account of an event, etc.*) вéрсия; (*translation*) перевóд
vertebral ['vɜːtɪbrəl]: ***~ column*** позвонóчник
vertical ['vɜːtɪkəl] □ вертикáльный; *cliff, etc.* отвéсный
vertigo ['vɜːtɪgəʊ] головокружéние
verve [vɜːv] энтузиáзм; подъём
very ['verɪ] **1.** *adv.* óчень; ***the ~ best*** сáмое лýчшее; **2.** *adj.* настоя́щий, сýщий; *emphatic* сáмый; ***the ~ same*** тот сáмый; ***the ~ thing*** и́менно то, что нýжно; ***the ~ thought*** ужé однá мысль *f*, самá мысль *f*; ***the ~ stones*** дáже кáмни *m/pl.*
vessel ['vesl] сосýд (*a. anat.*); *naut.* сýдно, корáбль *m*
vest [vest] жилéт; *chiefly Brt.* мáйка
vestibule ['vestɪbjuːl] вестибю́ль *m*
vestige ['vestɪdʒ] (*remains*) след, остáток; ***there is not a ~ of truth in this*** в э́том нет и дóли прáвды
veteran ['vetərən] **1.** ветерáн; **2.** *attr.* стáрый; (*experienced*) óпытный
veterinary ['vetrɪnərɪ] **1.** ветеринáр (*mst.* ***~ surgeon***); **2.** ветеринáрный
veto ['viːtəʊ] **1.** вéто *n indecl*; **2.** налагáть [-ложи́ть] вéто на (В)
vex [veks] досаждáть [досади́ть], раздражáть [-жи́ть]; **~ation** [vek'seɪʃn] досáда, неприя́тность *f*; **~atious** [vek'seɪʃəs] досáдный; **~ed** ['vekst] *person* раздосáдованный; *question* спóрный; больнóй
via ['vaɪə] чéрез (В)
viable ['vaɪəbl] жизнеспосóбный
vial ['vaɪəl] пузырёк
vibrat|e [vaɪ'breɪt] вибри́ровать; **~ion** [~ʃn] вибрáция
vice[1] [vaɪs] порóк
vice[2] [~] *chiefly Brt.* → ***vise***
vice[3] [~] *pref.* ви́це...; ***~ president*** ви́це-президéнт
vice versa [vaɪsɪ'vɜːsə] наоборóт
vicinity [vɪ'sɪnətɪ] (*neighbo[u]rhood*)

окре́стность *f*; бли́зость *f*; ***in the ~*** недалеко́ (***of*** от P)
vicious ['vɪʃəs] □ поро́чный; злой; ***~ circle*** поро́чный круг
vicissitude [vɪ'sɪsɪtju:d]: *mst.* ***~s*** *pl.* превра́тности *f/pl.*
victim ['vɪktɪm] же́ртва; **~ize** [~tɪmaɪz] (*for one's views, etc.*) пресле́довать
victor ['vɪktə] победи́тель *m*; **~ious** [vɪk'tɔ:rɪəs] □ победоно́сный; **~y** ['vɪktərɪ] побе́да
video ['vɪdɪəʊ] ви́део; **~ camera** видеока́мера; **~ cassette** видеокассе́та; **~ recorder** видеомагнитофо́н, *coll.* ви́дик
vie [vaɪ] сопе́рничать
view [vju:] **1.** вид (***of*** на B); по́ле зре́ния; (*opinion*) взгляд; (*intention*) наме́рение; ***in ~ of*** ввиду́ P; ***on ~*** (вы́ставленный) для обозре́ния; ***with a ~ to*** + *ger.* с наме́рением (+ *inf.*); ***have in ~*** име́ть в виду́; **2.** (*examine*) осма́тривать [осмотре́ть]; (*consider*) рассма́тривать [-мотре́ть]; (*look at*) [по]смотре́ть на (B); **~point** то́чка зре́ния
vigil|ance ['vɪdʒɪləns] бди́тельность *f*; **~ant** [~lənt] □ бди́тельный
vigo|rous ['vɪgərəs] □ си́льный, энерги́чный; **~(u)r** ['vɪgə] си́ла, эне́ргия
vile [vaɪl] □ ме́рзкий, ни́зкий
villa ['vɪlə] ви́лла
village ['vɪlɪdʒ] село́, дере́вня; *attr.* се́льский, дереве́нский; **~r** [~ə] се́льский (-кая) жи́тель *m* (-ница *f*)
villain ['vɪlən] злоде́й, негодя́й
vim [vɪm] эне́ргия, си́ла
vindic|ate ['vɪndɪkeɪt] (*prove*) дока́зывать [-за́ть]; (*justify*) опра́вдывать [-да́ть]; **~tive** [vɪn'dɪktɪv] □ мсти́тельный
vine [vaɪn] виногра́дная лоза́; **~gar** ['vɪnɪgə] у́ксус; **~-growing** виногра́дарство; **~yard** ['vɪnjəd] виногра́дник
vintage ['vɪntɪdʒ] сбор виногра́да; вино́ урожа́я определённого го́да; ***~ wine*** ма́рочное вино́
violat|e ['vaɪəleɪt] *law, promise, etc.* наруша́ть [-у́шить]; (*rape*) [из]наси́ловать; **~ion** [vaɪə'leɪʃn] наруше́ние
violen|ce ['vaɪələns] си́ла; наси́лие; ***outbreak of ~*** беспоря́дки *m/pl.*; **~t** [~nt] □ (*strong*) си́льный, мо́щный, неи́стовый; *quarrel, etc.* я́ростный; *death* наси́льственный
violet ['vaɪələt] фиа́лка; фиоле́товый цвет
violin [vaɪə'lɪn] скри́пка
viper ['vaɪpə] гадю́ка
virgin ['vɜ:dʒɪn] **1.** де́вственница; ***the Blessed ♀*** Де́ва Мари́я, Богоро́дица; **2.** де́вственный (*a.* **~al**); **~ity** [və'dʒɪnətɪ] де́вственность *f*
Virgo ['vɜ:gəʊ] *in the zodiac* Де́ва
viril|e ['vɪraɪl] (*sexually potent*) ви́рильный; по́лный эне́ргии, му́жественный; **~ity** [vɪ'rɪlətɪ] му́жественность *f*; (*potency*) мужска́я си́ла
virtu|al ['vɜ:tʃʊəl] □ факти́ческий; **~e** ['vɜ:tju:] доброде́тель *f*; (*advantage*) досто́инство; ***by ~ of*** благодаря́; в си́лу (P); **~ous** ['vɜ:tʃʊəs] □ доброде́тельный; (*chaste*) целому́дренный
virulent ['vɪrʊlənt] *poison* смерте́льный; *illness* свире́пый; опа́сный; *fig.* зло́бный
virus ['vaɪərəs] ви́рус; *attr.* ви́русный
visa ['vi:zə] ви́за; ***entry*** (***exit***) **~** въездна́я (выездна́я) ви́за
viscount ['vaɪkaʊnt] вико́нт
viscous ['vɪskəs] □ вя́зкий; *liquid* тягу́чий, густо́й
vise [vaɪs] *tech.* тиски́ *m/pl.*
visibility [vɪzə'bɪlətɪ] ви́димость *f*
visible ['vɪzəbl] □ (*apparent, evident*) ви́димый; (*conspicuous, prominent*) ви́дный; *fig.* (*obvious*) я́вный, очеви́дный
vision ['vɪʒn] (*eyesight*) зре́ние; (*mental picture*) ви́дение; *fig.* проница́тельность *f*; ***field of ~*** по́ле зре́ния; **~ary** ['vɪʒənərɪ] прови́дец *m*, -дица *f*; (*one given to reverie*) мечта́тель *m*, -ница *f*
visit ['vɪzɪt] **1.** *v/t. person* навеща́ть [-ести́ть]; *museum, etc.* посеща́ть [-ети́ть]; *v/i.* ходи́ть в го́сти; (*stay*) гости́ть; **2.** посеще́ние, визи́т; **~ing** [~ɪŋ]: ***~ card*** визи́тная ка́рточка; ***~ hours*** приёмные часы́; **~or** ['vɪzɪtə] посети́тель *m*, -ница *f*, гость *m*, -я *f*

vista ['vɪstə] перспекти́ва (*a. fig.*); (*view*) вид
visual ['vɪʒʊəl] зри́тельный; нагля́дный; ~ ***aids*** нагля́дные посо́бия; **~ize** [~aɪz] представля́ть себе́, мы́сленно ви́деть
vital ['vaɪtl] □ жи́зненный; (*essential*) насу́щный, существе́нный; *person*, *style* живо́й; **~s**, ~ ***parts*** *pl.* жи́зненно ва́жные о́рганы *m/pl.*; **~ity** [vaɪ'tælətɪ] жи́зненная си́ла; эне́ргия; жи́вость *f*; ***the child is full of*** ~ ребёнок по́лон жи́зни
vitamin ['vaɪtəmɪn, *Brt.* 'vɪtəmɪn] витами́н; ~ ***deficiency*** авитамино́з
vivaci|ous [vɪ'veɪʃəs] живо́й, темпера́ментный; **~ty** [vɪ'væsətɪ] жи́вость *f*
vivid ['vɪvɪd] □ *fig.* живо́й, я́ркий
vixen ['vɪksn] лиса́, лиси́ца
vocabulary [və'kæbjʊlərɪ] слова́рь *m*, спи́сок слов; *person's* запа́с слов
vocal ['vəʊkl] □ голосово́й; (*talkative*) разгово́рчивый; *mus.* вока́льный; ~ ***cords*** голосовы́е свя́зки
vocation [vəʊ'keɪʃn] призва́ние; профе́ссия; **~al** [~l] □ профессиона́льный
vogue [vəʊg] мо́да; популя́рность *f*; ***be in*** ~ быть в мо́де
voice [vɔɪs] **1.** го́лос; ***at the top of one's*** ~ во весь го́лос; ***give*** ~ ***to*** выража́ть [вы́разить] (В); **2.** выража́ть [вы́разить]
void [vɔɪd] **1.** пусто́й; лишённый (***of*** Р); *law* недействи́тельный; **2.** пустота́; пробе́л
volatile ['vɒlətaɪl] *chem.* лету́чий; *fig.* изме́нчивый
volcano [vɒl'keɪnəʊ] (*pl.*: ***volcanoes***) вулка́н
volition [və'lɪʃn] во́ля
volley ['vɒlɪ] *of shots* залп; *fig. of questions*, *etc.* град; **~ball** волейбо́л
voltage ['vəʊltɪdʒ] *el.* напряже́ние
voluble ['vɒljʊbl] разгово́рчивый, говорли́вый
volum|e ['vɒljuːm] объём; (*book*) том; (*capacity*) ёмкость *f*, вмести́тельность *f*; *fig. of sound*, *etc.* си́ла, полнота́; ~ ***control*** *radio*, *T.V.* регуля́тор зву́ка; **~inous** [və'luːmɪnəs] □ объёмистый; обши́рный
volunt|ary ['vɒləntrɪ] □ доброво́льный; **~eer** [vɒlən'tɪə] **1.** доброво́лец; **2.** *v/i.* вызыва́ться [вы́зваться] (***for*** на В); идти́ доброво́льцем; *v/t. help*, *etc.* предлага́ть [-ложи́ть]
voluptu|ary [və'lʌptʃʊərɪ] сласто-лю́бец; **~ous** [~ʃʊəs] сладостра́стный
vomit ['vɒmɪt] **1.** рво́та; **2.** [вы́]рвать: ***he is ~ing*** его́ рвёт
voraci|ous [və'reɪʃəs] □ прожо́рливый, жа́дный; ~ ***reader*** ненасы́тный чита́тель *m*; **~ty** [və'ræsətɪ] прожо́рливость *f*
vortex ['vɔːteks] *mst. fig.* водоворо́т; *of wind* вихрь *m*
vote [vəʊt] **1.** голосова́ние; (*vote cast*) го́лос; пра́во го́лоса; во́тум; (*decision*) реше́ние; ***cast a*** ~ отдава́ть го́лос (***for*** за В; ***against*** про́тив Р); ~ ***of no confidence*** во́тум недове́рия; ***put to the*** ~ поста́вить *pf.* на голосова́ние; **2.** *v/i.* голосова́ть (*im*)*pf.*, *pf. a.* [про-] (***for*** за В; ***against*** про́тив Р); *v/t.* голосова́ть (*im*)*pf.*, *pf. a.* [про-]; **~r** ['vəʊtə] избира́тель *m*, -ница *f*
voting ['vəʊtɪŋ] **1.** голосова́ние; **2.** избира́тельный
vouch [vaʊtʃ]: ~ ***for*** руча́ться [поручи́ться] за (В); **~er** ['vaʊtʃə] (*receipt*) распи́ска; *fin.* ва́учер
vow [vaʊ] **1.** обе́т, кля́тва; **2.** *v/t.* [по]кля́сться в (П)
vowel ['vaʊəl] гла́сный
voyage [vɔɪɪdʒ] **1.** путеше́ствие (морско́е), пла́вание; **2.** путеше́ствовать мо́рем
vulgar ['vʌlgə] □ (*unrefined*) вульга́рный; (*low*) по́шлый; (*common*) широко́ распространённый
vulnerable ['vʌlnərəbl] □ *fig. position* уязви́мый; *person* рани́мый
vulture ['vʌltʃə] *zo.* гриф; *fig.* стервя́тник

W

wad [wɒd] *of cotton, paper* комо́к; *of banknotes* па́чка
waddle ['wɒdl] ходи́ть вперева́лку
wade [weɪd] *v/t.* переходи́ть вброд; *v/i.* проб(и)ра́ться (***through*** по Д *or* че́рез В)
wafer ['weɪfə] *eccl.* обла́тка; ва́фля
waffle ['wɒfl] *cul.* ва́фля
waft [wɒft, wɑːft] **1.** *of wind* дунове́ние; *of air* струя́; **2.** доноси́ться [-нести́сь]
wag [wæg] **1.** (*joker*) шутни́к; **2.** маха́ть [махну́ть] (Т); *of dog* виля́ть [вильну́ть] хвосто́м; **~ *one's finger*** грози́ть па́льцем
wage[1] [weɪdʒ]: **~ *war*** вести́ войну́
wage[2] *mst.* **~s** [weɪdʒɪz] *pl.* за́работная пла́та, зарпла́та; **~ *freeze*** замора́живание за́работной пла́ты
wag(g)on ['wægən] пово́зка, теле́га; *Brt. rail.* това́рный ваго́н; *open* ваго́н-платфо́рма
waif [weɪf] *homeless* бездо́мный ребёнок; безпризо́рник; *neglected* безнадзо́рный ребёнок
wail [weɪl] **1.** вопль *m*; вой; (*lament*) причита́ние; *of wind* завыва́ние; **2.** [за]вопи́ть; выть, завы́(ва́)ть; причита́ть
waist [weɪst] та́лия; ***stripped to the ~*** го́лый по по́яс; **~coat** ['weɪskəʊt, 'weskət] *chiefly Brt.* (*vest*) жиле́т
wait [weɪt] *v/i.* ждать (***for*** В *or* Р), ожида́ть (***for*** Р), подожда́ть *pf.* (***for*** В *or* Р); (*ча́сто*: **~ *at table***) обслу́живать [-жи́ть] (В); ***well, we'll have to ~ and see*** что ж, поживём-уви́дим; ***I'll ~ up for you*** я не ля́гу, подожду́ тебя́; *v/t.* выжида́ть [вы́ждать] (В); **~er** ['weɪtə] официа́нт
waiting ['weɪtɪŋ] ожида́ние; **~ room** приёмная; *rail.* зал ожида́ния
waitress ['weɪtrɪs] официа́нтка
waive [weɪv] *a claim, right, etc.* отка́зываться [-за́ться] от (Р)
wake [weɪk] **1.**: ***hunger brought disease in its ~*** го́лод повлёк за собо́й эпиде́мию; **2.** [*irr.*] *v/i.* бо́дрствовать; (*mst.* **~ *up***) просыпа́ться [просну́ться]; *fig.* пробужда́ться [-уди́ться]; *v/t.* [раз]буди́ть; *fig.* пробужда́ть [-уди́ть]; *desire, etc.* возбужда́ть [-уди́ть]; **~ful** ['weɪkfl] □ бессо́нный; (*vigilant*) бди́тельный; **~n** ['weɪkən] → ***wake 2***
walk [wɔːk] **1.** *v/i.* ходи́ть, идти́ [пойти́]; (*stroll*) гуля́ть, прогу́ливаться; **~ *away*** отходи́ть [отойти́]; **~ *in*(*to*)** входи́ть [войти́]; **~ *off*** уходи́ть [уйти́]; **~ *out*** выходи́ть [вы́йти]; **~ *over*** (*cross*) переходи́ть (перейти́); **~ *up*** подходи́ть [-дойти́]; **2.** ходьба́; (*gait*) похо́дка; прогу́лка пешко́м; (*path*) тропа́, алле́я; **~ *of life*** сфе́ра де́ятельности; профе́ссия
walking ['wɔːkɪŋ] **1.** ходьба́; **2.**: **~ *dictionary*** ходя́чая энциклопе́дия; **~ stick** трость *f*
walk|out ['wɔːk'aʊt] забасто́вка; **~over** лёгкая побе́да
wall [wɔːl] **1.** стена́; (*side, unit*) сте́нка; ***drive s.o. up the ~*** доводи́ть кого́-л. до исступле́ния; **2.** обноси́ть стено́й; **~ *up*** заде́л(ыв)ать (*дверь и т. п.*)
wallet ['wɒlɪt] бума́жник
wallflower желтофио́ль *f*; *fig.* де́вушка, оста́вшаяся без партнёра (на та́нцах, и т. д.)
wallop ['wɒləp] *coll.* [по]би́ть, [по-, от]колоти́ть
wallow ['wɒləʊ] валя́ться
wallpaper обо́и *m/pl.*
walnut ['wɔːlnʌt] *bot.* гре́цкий оре́х
walrus ['wɔːlrəs] *zo.* морж
waltz [wɔːls] **1.** вальс; **2.** танцева́ть вальс
wan [wɒn] □ бле́дный, ту́склый
wander ['wɒndə] броди́ть; блужда́ть (*a. of gaze, thoughts, etc.*)
wane [weɪn]: ***be on the ~*** *of moon* убы́(ва́)ть, быть на ущёрбе; *of popularity, etc.* уменьша́ться [-ши́ться], снижа́ться [-и́зиться]
wangle ['wæŋgl] заполучи́ть хи́тростью; *coll.* вы́клянчить
want [wɒnt] **1.** (*lack*) недоста́ток

(***of*** Р *or* в П); (*powerty*) нужда́; (*need*) потре́бность *f*; **2.** *v/i.* ***be ~ing***: ***he is ~ing in patience*** ему́ недостаёт терпе́ния; ***~ for*** нужда́ться в (П); *v/t.* [за]хоте́ть (Р *a.* В); [по]жела́ть (Р *a.* В); нужда́ться в (Д); ***he ~s energy*** ему́ недостаёт эне́ргии; ***what do you ~?*** что вам ну́жно?; ***you ~ to see a doctor*** вам сле́дует обрати́ться к врачу́; **~ed** ['~ɪd] (в объявле́ниях) тре́буется; *law* разы́скивается

wanton ['wɒntən] □ (*debauched*) распу́тный; *cruelty* бессмы́сленный

war [wɔː] **1.** война́; *fig.* борьба́; ***be at ~*** воева́ть с (Т); ***make ~*** вести́ войну́ ([***up***]***on*** с Т); **2.** *attr.* вое́нный; ***~ memorial*** па́мятник солда́там, поги́бшим на войне́

warble ['wɔːbl] *of birds* издава́ть тре́ли; *of person* залива́ться пе́сней

ward [wɔːd] **1.** находя́щийся под опе́кой; *in hospital* пала́та; **2. ~** (***off***) *blow* отража́ть [отрази́ть], *danger, illness* отвраща́ть [-рати́ть]; **~er** ['wɔːdə] *in prison* надзира́тель *m*; тюре́мщик; **~robe** ['wɔːdrəʊb] платяно́й шкаф; (*clothes*) гардеро́б

ware [weə] *in compds.* посу́да; **~s** *pl.* това́р(ы *pl.*) изде́лия

warehouse ['weəhaʊs] склад

war|fare ['wɔːfeə] война́, спо́собы веде́ния войны́; **~head** [~hed] боеголо́вка

warm [wɔːm] **1.** □ тёплый (*a. fig.*); *fig.* горя́чий; *person* серде́чный; **2.** тепло́; **3.** [на-, ото-, со]гре́ть, нагре́(ва́)ть(ся), согре́(ва́)ться (*a.* ***~ up***); ***his words ~ed my heart*** его́ слова́ согре́ли мою́ ду́шу; **~th** [~θ] тепло́; теплота́ (*a. fig.*)

warn [wɔːn] предупрежда́ть [-реди́ть] (***of, against*** о П); (*caution*) предостерега́ть [-стере́чь] (***of, against*** от Р); **~ing** ['wɔːnɪŋ] предупрежде́ние; предостереже́ние

warp [wɔːp] *of wood* [по]коро́бить(ся); *fig.* извраща́ть [-рати́ть]; (*distort*) искажа́ть [искази́ть]; ***~ed mind*** извращённый ум

warrant ['wɒrənt] **1.** (*justification*) оправда́ние; *fin.* гара́нтия, руча́тельство; (*arrest ~*) о́рдер на аре́ст; **2.** опра́вдывать [-да́ть]; руча́ться [поручи́ться] за (В); (*guarantee*) гаранти́ровать (*im*)*pf.*; **~y** [~ɪ] гара́нтия; руча́тельство

warrior ['wɒrɪə] *poet.* во́ин

wart [wɔːt] борода́вка

wary ['weərɪ] □ осторо́жный

was [wəz, ... wɒz] *pt. om* ***be***

wash [wɒʃ] **1.** *v/t. floor, dishes* [вы́-, по]мы́ть; *face* умы́ть *pf.*; *wound, etc.* промы́(ва́)ть; *clothes* [вы́]стира́ть; *v/i.* [вы́]мы́ться, умы́ться *pf.*; стира́ться; ***that won't ~*** *coll.* не пройдёт; э́тому никто́ не пове́рит; **2.** мытьё; сти́рка; (*articles for washing*) бельё; *of waves* прибо́й; ***mouth ~*** полоска́ние; **~-basin** ра́ковина; **~er** ['wɒʃə] (*washing machine*) стира́льная маши́на; *tech.* ша́йба, прокла́дка; **~ing** ['wɒʃɪŋ] **1.** мытьё; сти́рка; (*articles*) бельё; **2.** стира́льный; ***~ing powder*** стира́льный порошо́к

washroom ['wɒʃrʊm] *Am. euph.* (*lavatory*) убо́рная

wasp [wɒsp] оса́

waste [weɪst] **1.** (*loss*) поте́ря; (*wrong use*) изли́шняя тра́та; (*domestic*) отбро́сы *m/pl.*; *tech.* отхо́ды *m/pl.*; ***lay ~*** опустоша́ть [-ши́ть]; ***~ of time*** напра́сная тра́та вре́мени; **2.**: ***~ land*** пусты́рь *m*; *plot of ground* пу́стошь *f*; **3.** *v/t. money, etc.* [по-, рас]тра́тить зря; *time* [по]теря́ть; *resources* истоща́ться [-щи́ться]; **~ful** ['weɪstfl] □ расточи́тельный; **~ paper** испо́льзованная/нену́жная бума́га; *for pulping* макулату́ра; **~paper basket** корзи́на для нену́жных бума́г

watch[1] [wɒtʃ] (*wrist ~*) нару́чные часы́ *m/pl.*; ва́хта

watch[2] [~] *v/i.*: ***~ for*** *chance, etc.* выжида́ть [вы́ждать] (В); ***~ out!*** осторо́жно!; *v/t.* (*look at*) смотре́ть; (*observe*) наблюда́ть, следи́ть за (Т); **~dog** сторожева́я соба́ка; **~ful** [~fl] бди́тельный; **~maker** часовщи́к; **~man** [~mən] вахтёр

water ['wɔːtə] **1.** вода́; **~s** *pl.* во́ды *f/pl.*; ***drink the ~s*** пить минера́ль-

W

ные во́ды; ***throw cold ~ on s.o.*** охлади́ть *pf.* пыл, отрезви́ть *pf.*; *attr.* водяно́й; во́дный; водо...; **2.** *v/t.* поли́(ва́)ть; *animals* [на]пои́ть; (*a.* ***~ down***) разбавля́ть водо́й; *fig.* чересчу́р смягча́ть; *v/i.* *of eyes* слези́ться; ***it makes my mouth ~*** от э́того у меня́ слю́нки теку́т; **~colo(u)r** акваре́ль *f*; **~fall** водопа́д; **~ heater** (*kettle*) кипяти́льник

watering ['wɔːtərɪŋ]: **~can** ле́йка; **~place** *for animals* водопо́й; (*spa*) куро́рт на во́дах

water| level у́ровень *m* воды́; **~ lily** водяна́я ли́лия, кувши́нка; **~ main** водопрово́дная магистра́ль *f*; **~melon** арбу́з; **~ polo** во́дное по́ло *n indecl.*; **~proof 1.** непромока́емый; **2.** непромока́емый плащ *m*; **~ supply** водоснабже́ние; **~tight** водонепроница́емый; *fig. alibi, etc.* неопровержи́мый; **~-way** во́дный путь *m*; фарва́тер; **~works** *pl. a., sg.* систе́ма водоснабже́ния; **~y** ['wɔːtərɪ] водяни́стый

wave [weɪv] **1.** волна́; *of hand* знак, взмах; **2.** *v/t.* [по]маха́ть, де́лать знак (Т); *hair* зави́(ва́)ть; ***~ a p. away*** де́лать знак кому́-либо удали́ться; отстраня́ть [-ни́ть] же́стом; ***~ aside*** *fig.* отма́хиваться [-хну́ться] от (Р); *v/i. of flags* развева́ться; *of hair* ви́ться; *of corn, grass* колыха́ться; *of boughs* кача́ться; **~length** длина́ волны́

waver ['weɪvə] [по]колеба́ться; *of flames* колыха́ться [-хну́ться]; *of troops, voice* дро́гнуть *pf.*

wavy ['weɪvɪ] волни́стый

wax[1] [wæks] воск; *in ear* се́ра; *attr.* восково́й

wax[2] [~] [*irr.*] *of moon* прибы́(ва́)ть

way [weɪ] *mst.* доро́га, путь *m*; (*direction*) сторона́, направле́ние; ме́тод, спо́соб; (*custom, habit*) обы́чай, привы́чка; (*a.* **~s** *pl.*) о́браз жи́зни; поведе́ние; ***~ in*** вход; ***out*** вы́ход; ***in a ~*** в изве́стном смы́сле; ***in many ~s*** во мно́гих отноше́ниях; ***this ~*** сюда́; ***by the ~*** кста́ти, ме́жду про́чим; ***by ~ of*** в ка́честве (Р); (*through*) че́рез; ***in the ~*** *fig.* поперёк доро́ги; ***on the ~*** в пути́; по доро́ге; ***out of the ~*** находя́щийся в стороне́; (*unusual*) необы́чный; необыкнове́нный; ***under ~*** на ходу́; в пути́; ***give ~*** уступа́ть [-пи́ть] (Д); ***have one's ~*** добива́ться своего́; наста́ивать на своём; ***keep out of s.o.'s ~*** избега́ть кого́-л.; ***lead the ~*** идти́ впереди́, [по]вести́; ***lose the ~*** заблуди́ться *pf.*; **~lay** [weɪ'leɪ] [*irr.* (***lay***)] подстерега́ть [-ре́чь]; **~side 1.** обо́чина; **2.** придоро́жный; **~ward** ['weɪwəd] □ своенра́вный

we [wɪ, ... wiː] *pers. pron.* мы

weak [wiːk] □ сла́бый; **~en** ['wiːkən] *v/t.* ослабля́ть [-а́бить]; *v/i.* [о]слабе́ть; **~ling** ['wiːklɪŋ] физи́чески сла́бый *or* слабово́льный челове́к; **~ly** [~lɪ] *adv.* сла́бо; **~ness** [~nɪs] сла́бость *f*

wealth [welθ] бога́тство; (*profusion*) изоби́лие; **~y** ['welθɪ] □ бога́тый

wean [wiːn] отнима́ть от груди́; отуча́ть [-чи́ть] (***from, off*** от Р)

weapon ['wepən] ору́жие (*a. fig.*)

wear [weə] **1.** [*irr.*] *v/t. hat, glasses, etc.* носи́ть; (*a.* ***~ away, down, off***) стира́ть [стере́ть]; изна́шивать (*fig.* изнуря́ть [-ри́ть] *mst.* ***~ out***); *v/i.*: ***~ on*** ме́дленно тяну́ться; **2.** (*a.* ***~ and tear***, *part. tech.*) изно́с; ***men's (ladies') ~*** мужска́я (же́нская) оде́жда

wear|iness ['wɪərɪnɪs] уста́лость *f*; утомлённость *f*; **~isome** [~səm] □ (*tiring*) утоми́тельный; (*boring*) ску́чный; **~y** ['wɪərɪ] **1.** утомлённый; **2.** утомля́ть(ся) [-ми́ть(ся)]; *v/i.* наску́чить *pf.*

weasel ['wiːzl] *zo.* ла́ска

weather ['weðə] **1.** пого́да; ***be a bit under the ~*** нева́жно себя́ чу́вствовать; быть в плохо́м настрое́нии; **2.** *v/t. rocks* изна́шивать [-носи́ть]; *a storm* выде́рживать [вы́держать] (*a. fig.*); *v/i.* выве́триваться [вы́ветриться]; **~-beaten** *face* обве́тренный; *person* пострада́вший от непого́ды; **~ forecast** прогно́з пого́ды

weav|e [wiːv] [*irr.*] [со]тка́ть; [с]плести́; *fig. story* сочиня́ть [-ни́ть]; **~er** ['wiːvə] ткач *m*, ткачи́ха *f*

web [web] *spider's* паути́на; ***a ~ of lies*** паути́на лжи
wed [wed] *of woman* выходи́ть за́муж (за В); *of man* жени́ться (*im*)*pf.* (на П); сочета́ться бра́ком; **~ding** ['wedɪŋ] **1.** сва́дьба; **2.** сва́дебный; **~ring** обруча́льное кольцо́
wedge [wedʒ] **1.** клин; ***drive a ~ between*** *fig.* вби(ва́)ть клин ме́жду (T); **2.** (*a.* ***~ in***) вкли́нивать(ся) [-нить(ся)]; ***~ o.s. in*** вти́скиваться [вти́снуться]
wedlock ['wedlɒk] брак
Wednesday ['wenzdɪ] среда́
wee [wiː] кро́шечный, малю́сенький; ***~ hours*** предрассве́тные часы́
weed [wiːd] **1.** сорня́к; **2.** [вы́]поло́ть; **~killer** гербици́д; **~y** ['wiːdɪ] заро́сший сорняко́м; *coll. fig. person* то́щий, долговя́зый
week [wiːk] неде́ля; ***by the ~*** понеде́льно; ***for ~s on end*** це́лыми неде́лями; ***this day ~*** неде́лю тому́ наза́д; че́рез неде́лю; **~day** бу́дний день *m*; **~end** [wiːk'end] суббо́та и воскресе́нье, уике́нд; **~ly** ['wiːklɪ] **1.** еженеде́льный; **2.** еженеде́льник
weep [wiːp] [*irr.*] [за]пла́кать; **~ing** ['wiːpɪŋ] *person* пла́чущий; *willow* плаку́чий
weigh [weɪ] *v/t.* взве́шивать [-е́сить] (*a. fig.*); ***~ anchor*** поднима́ть я́корь *m*; ***~ed down*** отягощённый; *v/i.* ве́сить; взве́шиваться [-е́ситься]; *fig.* име́ть вес, значе́ние; ***~ (up)on*** тяготе́ть над (T)
weight [weɪt] **1.** вес; (*heaviness*) тя́жесть *f*; (*object for weighing*) ги́ря; *sport* шта́нга; *of responsibility* бре́мя *n*; влия́ние; **2.** отягоща́ть [-готи́ть]; *fig.* обременя́ть [-ни́ть]; **~y** ['weɪtɪ] □ тяжёлый; тру́дный; *fig.* ва́жный, ве́ский
weird [wɪəd] (*uncanny*) таи́нственный; стра́нный
welcome ['welkəm] **1.** приве́тствие; ***you are ~ to*** + *inf.* мо́жете (+ *inf.*); ***you are ~*** не́ за что!; ***~!*** добро́ пожа́ловать!; **2.** (*wanted*) жела́нный; (*causing gladness*) прия́тный; **3.** (*greet*) приве́тствовать (*a. fig.*); (*receive*) раду́шно принима́ть
weld [weld] *tech.* сва́ривать [-и́ть]
welfare ['welfeə] *of nation* благосостоя́ние; *of person* благополу́чие; *Am.* социа́льная по́мощь *f*
well[1] [wel] коло́дец; *fig.* исто́чник; (*stair~*) пролёт; *tech.* бурова́я сква́жина; **2.** хлы́нуть *pf.*
well[2] [~] **1.** хорошо́; ***~ off*** состоя́тельный; ***I am not ~*** мне нездоро́вится; **2.** *int.* ну! *or* ну, ...; **~being** [~'biːɪŋ] благополу́чие; **~-bred** [~'bred] (хорошо́) воспи́танный; **~-built** [~'bɪlt] хорошо́ сложённый; **~-founded** [~'faʊndɪd] обосно́ванный; **~-kept** [~'kept] *garden* ухо́женный; *secret* тща́тельно храни́мый; **~-read** [~'red] начи́танный; *in history, etc.* хорошо́ зна́ющий; **~-timed** [~'taɪmd] своевре́менный; **~-to-do** [~tə'duː] состоя́тельный, зажи́точный; **~-worn** [~'wɔːn] поно́шенный; *fig.* изби́тый
Welsh [welʃ] **1.** уэ́льский, валли́йский; **2.** валли́йский язы́к; ***the ~*** валли́йцы *m/pl.*
welter ['weltə] *of ideas* сумбу́р
went [went] *pt. om* **go**
wept [wept] *pt. u pt. p. om* **weap**
were [wə, wɜː] *pt. pl. om* **be**
west [west] **1.** за́пад; **2.** за́падный; **3.** *adv.* к за́паду, на за́пад; ***~ of*** к за́паду от (P); **~erly** ['westəlɪ], **~ern** ['westən] за́падный; **~ward(s)** ['westwəd(z)] на за́пад
wet [wet] **1.** дождли́вая пого́да; ***don't go out in the ~*** не выходи́ под дождь *m*; **2.** мо́крый; *weather* сыро́й; дождли́вый; "**~ *Paint***" "окра́шено"; ***get ~ through*** наскво́зь промо́кнуть *pf.*; **3.** [*irr.*] [на]мочи́ть, нама́чивать [-мочи́ть]
whale [weɪl] кит
wharf [wɔːf] прича́л, при́стань *f*
what [wɒt] **1.** что?; ско́лько ...?; **2.** то, что; что; ***~ about ...?*** что но́вого о ...?; ну как ...?; ***~ for?*** заче́м?; ***~ a pity ...*** кака́я жа́лость ...; **3.** ***~ with ...*** из-за (P), отча́сти от (P); **4.** како́й; **~(so)ever** [wɒt(sou)'evə] како́й бы ни; что бы ни; ***there is no doubt ~*** нет никако́го сомне́ния

W

wheat [wi:t] пшени́ца

wheel [wi:l] **1.** колесо́; *mot.* руль *m*; **2.** *pram, etc.* ката́ть, [по]кати́ть; **~ *into*** вка́тывать [-ти́ть]; **~ *round*** повора́чивать(ся) [поверну́ть(ся)]; **~-barrow** та́чка; **~chair** инвали́дная коля́ска

wheeze [wi:z] хрипе́ть; дыша́ть с при́свистом

when [wen] **1.** когда́?; **2.** *conj.* когда́, в то вре́мя как, как то́лько; тогда́ как

whenever [wen'evə] вся́кий раз когда́; когда́ бы ни

where [weə] где, куда́; ***from* ~** отку́да; **~about(s) 1.** [weərə'baʊt(s)] где?; **2.** ['weərəbaʊt(s)] местонахожде́ние; **~as** [weər'æz] тогда́ как; поско́льку; **~by** [weə'baɪ] посре́дством чего́; **~in** [weər'ɪn] в чём; **~of** [weər'ɒv] из кото́рого; о кото́ром; о чём; **~upon** [weərə'pɒn] по́сле чего́

wherever [weər'evə] где бы ни; куда́ бы ни

wherewithal [weəwɪ'ðɔ:l] необходи́мые сре́дства *n/pl.*

whet [wet] [на]точи́ть; *fig.* возбужда́ть [-уди́ть]

whether ['weðə] … ли; **~ *or not*** так и́ли ина́че; в любо́м слу́чае

which [wɪtʃ] **1.** кото́рый?; како́й?; **2.** кото́рый; что; **~ever** [~'evə] како́й уго́дно, како́й бы ни ...

whiff [wɪf] *of air* дунове́ние, струя́; (*smell*) за́пах; *of pipe, etc.* затя́жка

while [waɪl] **1.** вре́мя *n*, промежу́ток вре́мени; ***after a* ~** че́рез не́которое вре́мя; ***a little*** (***long***) **~ *ago*** неда́вно (давно́); ***in a little* ~** ско́ро; ***for a* ~** на вре́мя; *coll.* ***worth* ~** сто́ящий затра́ченного труда́; **2. ~ *away*** *time* проводи́ть [-вести́]; **3.** (*a.* ***whilst*** [waɪlst]) пока́, в то вре́мя как; тогда́ как

whim [wɪm] при́хоть *f*, капри́з

whimper ['wɪmpə] [за]хны́кать

whim|sical ['wɪmzɪkl] □ прихотли́вый, причу́дливый; **~sy** ['wɪmzɪ] при́хоть *f*; причу́да

whine [waɪn] [за]скули́ть; [за]хны́кать

whip [wɪp] **1.** *v/t.* хлеста́ть [-стну́ть]; (*punish*) [вы́]сечь; *eggs, cream* сби(ва́)ть; **~ *out*** *gun, etc.* выхва́тывать ['-хватить]; **~ *up*** расшеве́ливать [-ли́ть]; подстёгивать [-стегну́ть]; *v/i.*: ***I'll just* ~ *round to the neighbo(u)rs*** я то́лько сбе́гаю к сосе́дям; **2.** плеть *f*; кнут, (*a.* ***riding* ~**) хлыст

whippet ['wɪpɪt] *zo.* го́нчая

whipping ['wɪpɪŋ] (*punishment*) по́рка

whirl [wɜ:l] **1.** *of dust* вихрь *m*; круже́ние; ***my head is in a* ~** у меня́ голова́ идёт кру́гом; **2.** кружи́ть(ся); **~pool** водоворо́т; **~wind** смерч

whisk [wɪsk] **1.** (*egg* ~) муто́вка; **2.** *v/t.* *cream, etc.* сби(ва́)ть; (*remove*) сма́хивать [-хну́ть]; *v/i.* *of mouse, etc.* ю́ркать [ю́ркнуть]; **~ers** ['wɪskəz] *pl. zo.* усы́ *m/pl.*; (*side* ~) бакенба́рды *f/pl.*

whiskey, *Brt.* **whisky** ['wɪskɪ] ви́ски *n indecl.*

whisper ['wɪspə] **1.** шёпот; **2.** шепта́ть [шепну́ть]

whistle ['wɪsl] **1.** свист; свисто́к (*a. instrument*); **2.** свисте́ть [сви́стнуть]

white [waɪt] **1.** *com.* бе́лый; (*pale*) бле́дный; **~ *coffee*** ко́фе с молоко́м; **~ *lie*** ложь *f* во спасе́ние; неви́нная ложь *f*; **2.** бе́лый цвет; *of eye, egg* бело́к; **~n** ['waɪtn] [по]бели́ть; (*turn white*) [по]беле́ть; **~ness** ['waɪtnɪs] белизна́; **~wash 1.** побе́лка; **2.** [по]бели́ть; *fig.* обеля́ть [-ли́ть]

whitish ['waɪtɪʃ] бел(ес)ова́тый

Whitsun ['wɪtsn] *eccl.* Тро́ица

whiz(z) [wɪz] *of bullets, etc.* свисте́ть; **~ *past*** промча́ться *pf.* ми́мо

who [hu:] *pron.* **1.** кто?; **2.** кото́рый; кто; тот, кто ...; *pl.*: те, кто

whoever [hu:'əvə] *pron.* кто бы ни ...; (*who ever*) кто то́лько; кото́рый бы ни ...

whole [həʊl] **1.** □ (*complete, entire*) це́лый, весь; (*intact, undamaged*) це́лый; **~ *milk*** це́льное молоко́; **~ *number*** це́лое число́; **2.** це́лое; всё *n*; ито́г; ***on the* ~** в це́лом; **~-hearted** □ и́скренний, от всего́ се́рдца; **~sale 1.** (*mst.* **~ *trade***) о́птовая торго́вля; **2.** о́птовый; *fig.* (*indis-*

W

criminate) огу́льный; **~ *dealer*** о́птовый торго́вец; **3.** о́птом; **~some** ['həʊlsəm] □ поле́зный, здра́вый

wholly ['həʊlɪ] *adv.* целико́м, всеце́ло, по́лностью

whom [hu:m] *pron.* (*вини́тельный паде́ж от* **who**) кого́ *и т. д.*; кото́рого *и т. д.*

whoop [hu:p]: **~ *of joy*** ра́достный во́зглас; **~ing cough** ['hu:pɪŋ kɒf] *med.* коклю́ш

whose [hu:z] (*роди́тельный паде́ж от* **who**) чей *m*, чья *f*, чьё *n*, чьи *pl.*; *relative pron. mst.*: кото́рого, кото́рой: **~ *father*** оте́ц кото́рого

why [waɪ] **1.** *adv.* почему́?, отчего́?, заче́м?; **2.** *int.* да ведь ...; что ж...

wick [wɪk] фити́ль *m*

wicked ['wɪkɪd] □ (*malicious*) злой, зло́бный; (*depraved*) бессо́вестный; (*immoral*) безнра́вственный

wicker ['wɪkə]: **~ *basket*** плетёная корзи́нка; **~ *chair*** плетёный стул

wide [waɪd] *a.* □ *and adv.* широ́кий; обши́рный; широко́; далеко́, далёко (***of*** от Р); **~ *awake*** бди́тельный; осмотри́тельный; ***three feet* ~** шириной в три фу́та; **~ *of the mark*** далёкий от и́стины; не по существу́; **~n** ['waɪdn] расширя́ть(ся) [-и́рить(ся)]; **~-spread** распространённый

widow ['wɪdəʊ] вдова́; ***grass* ~** соло́менная вдова́; *attr.* вдо́вий; **~er** [~ə] вдове́ц

width [wɪdθ] ширина́; (*extent*) широта́

wield [wi:ld] *lit.* владе́ть (Т); держа́ть в рука́х

wife [waɪf] жена́; (*spouse*) супру́га

wig [wɪg] пари́к

wild [waɪld] **1.** □ ди́кий; *flowers* полево́й; *sea* бу́рный; *behavio*(*u*)*r* бу́йный; ***be* ~ *about s.o.*** *or* ***s.th.*** быть без ума́/в ди́ком восто́рге от кого́-л. *or* чего́-л.; ***run* ~** расти́ без присмо́тра; ***talk* ~** говори́ть не ду́мая; **2.** **~**, **~s** [~z] ди́кая ме́стность *f*; де́бри *f/pl.*; **~cat strike** неофициа́льная забасто́вка; **~erness** ['wɪldənɪs] пусты́ня, ди́кая ме́стность *f*; **~fire**: ***like* ~** с быстрото́й мо́лнии; **~fowl** дичь *f*

wile [waɪl] *mst.* **~s** *pl.* хи́трость *f*; уло́вка

wil(l)ful ['wɪlfl] упря́мый, своево́льный; (*intentional*) преднаме́ренный

will [wɪl] **1.** во́ля; (*willpower*) си́ла во́ли; (*desire*) жела́ние; *law* (*testament*) завеща́ние; ***with a* ~** энерги́чно; **2.** [*irr.*] *v/aux.*: ***he* ~ *come*** он придёт; **3.** завеща́ть (*im*)*pf.*; [по]жела́ть, [за]хоте́ть; **~ *o.s.*** (*compel o.s.*) заставля́ть [-ста́вить] себя́

willing ['wɪlɪŋ] □ *to help, etc.* гото́вый (***to*** на В *or* + *inf.*); **~ness** [~nɪs] гото́вность *f*

willow ['wɪləʊ] *bot.* и́ва

wilt [wɪlt] *of flowers* [за]вя́нуть; *of person* [по]ни́кнуть; раскиса́ть [-ки́снуть]

wily ['waɪlɪ] □ хи́трый, кова́рный

win [wɪn] [*irr.*] *v/t.* побежда́ть [-еди́ть]; выи́грывать; *victory* оде́рживать [-жа́ть]; *prize* получа́ть [-чи́ть]; **~ *a p. over*** угова́ривать [-вори́ть]; склони́ть кого́-л. на свою́ сто́рону; *v/i.* выи́грывать [вы́играть]; оде́рживать побе́ду

wince [wɪns] вздра́гивать [вздро́гнуть]

winch [wɪntʃ] лебёдка; во́рот

wind¹ [wɪnd] ве́тер; (*breath*) дыха́ние; *of bowels, etc.* га́зы *m/pl.*; *mus.* духовы́е инструме́нты *m/pl.* ***let me get my* ~ *back*** подожди́, я отдышу́сь; ***get* ~ *of*** *s.th.* [по]чу́ять; узна́ть *pf.*, пронюха́ть *pf.*; ***second* ~** второ́е дыха́ние

wind² [waɪnd] [*irr.*] *v/t.* нама́тывать [намота́ть]; обма́тывать [обмота́ть]; *plant* обви́(ва́)ть; **~ *up*** *watch* заводи́ть [завести́]; *comm.* ликвиди́ровать (*im*)*pf.*; *discussion, etc.* зака́нчивать [зако́нчить]; *v/i.* нама́тываться [намота́ться]; обви́(ва́)ться

wind|bag ['wɪndbæg] *sl.* болту́н; пустозво́н; **~fall** па́данец; *fig.* неожи́данное сча́стье

winding ['waɪndɪŋ] **1.** изги́б, изви́лина; (*act of* ~) нама́тывание; *el.* обмо́тка; **2.** изви́листый; **~ *stairs*** *pl.* винтова́я ле́стница

wind instrument духово́й инструме́нт

windmill ветряна́я ме́льница

window ['wɪndəʊ] окно́; (*shop* ~) витри́на; ~ **dressing** оформле́ние витри́ны; *fig.* показу́ха *coll.*; ~**sill** [~sɪl] подоко́нник

wind|pipe ['wɪndpaɪp] *anat.* трахе́я; ~**shield**, *Brt.* ~**screen** *mot.* ветрово́е стекло́

windy ['wɪndɪ] □ ве́треный; *fig.* (*wordy*) многосло́вный; *chiefly Brt. coll.* ***get*** ~ стру́сить *pf.*

wine [waɪn] вино́; ~ **glass** бокал; рю́мка

wing [wɪŋ] (*a. arch.*) крыло́; *thea.* ~***s*** *pl.* кули́сы *f/pl.*; ***take*** ~ полете́ть *pf.*; ***on the*** ~ в полёте; ***take s.o. under one's*** ~ взять *pf.* кого́-л. под своё кры́лышко

wink [wɪŋk] **1.** (*moment*) миг; *coll.* ***not get a*** ~ ***of sleep*** не сомкну́ть *pf.* глаз; **2.** морга́ть [-гну́ть], мига́ть [мигну́ть]; ~ ***at*** подми́гивать [-гну́ть] (Д); *fig.* смотре́ть сквозь па́льцы на (В)

win|ner ['wɪnə] победи́тель *m*, -ница *f*; *in some competitions* призёр; лауреа́т; ***Nobel Prize*** ♀ лауреа́т Но́белевской пре́мии; ~**ning** ['wɪnɪŋ] **1.** (*in the lead*) выи́грывающий; побежда́ющий; (*having won*) вы́игравший, победи́вший; *fig.* (*attractive, persuasive*) обая́тельный (*a.* ~ ***some*** [~səm]); **2.**: ~***s*** *pl.* вы́игрыш

wint|er ['wɪntə] **1.** зима́; *attr.* зи́мний; **2.** проводи́ть зи́му, [пере-, про]зимова́ть; ~**ry** ['wɪntrɪ] зи́мний

wipe [waɪp] вытира́ть [вы́тереть]; *tears* утира́ть [утере́ть]; ~ ***off*** стира́ть [стере́ть]; ~ ***out*** (*destroy*) уничтожа́ть [-о́жить]; ~**er** ['waɪpə] (*windshield* ~, *Brt. windscreen* ~) стеклоочисти́тель *m*; *coll.* дво́рник

wire ['waɪə] **1.** про́волока; *el.* про́вод; *coll.* телегра́мма; **2.** [с]де́лать прово́дку; телеграфи́ровать (*im*)*pf.*; ~ **netting** про́волочная се́тка

wiry ['waɪərɪ] *person* жи́листый; *hair* жёсткий

wisdom ['wɪzdəm] му́дрость *f*; ~ ***tooth*** зуб му́дрости

wise[1] [waɪz] му́дрый; благоразу́мный; ~**crack** *coll.* остро́та

wise[2] [~]: ***in no*** ~ нико́им о́бразом

wish [wɪʃ] **1.** жела́ние; пожела́ние; **2.** [по]жела́ть (Р) (*a.* ~ ***for***); ~ ***well*** (***ill***) жела́ть добра́ (зла); ~**ful** ['wɪʃfl]: ~ ***thinking*** *in context* принима́ть жела́емое за действи́тельное

wisp [wɪsp] *of smoke* стру́йка; *of hair* прядь *f*

wistful ['wɪstfl] □ заду́мчивый, тосկли́вый

wit [wɪt] (*verbal felicity*) остроу́мие; (*mental astuteness*) ум, ра́зум (*a.* ~***s*** *pl.*); остросло́в; ***be at one's*** ~***s' end*** в отча́янии; ***I'm at my*** ~***s' end*** пря́мо ум за ра́зум захо́дит; ***be scared out of one's*** ~***s*** испуга́ться до́ смерти

witch [wɪtʃ] колду́нья; ве́дьма; ~**craft** колдовство́; ~**hunt** охо́та за ве́дьмами

with [wɪð] с (Т), со (Т); (*because of*) от (Р); у (Р); при (П); ~ ***a knife*** ножо́м, ~ ***a pen*** ру́чкой

withdraw [wɪð'drɔː] [*irr.* (***draw***)] *v/t.* убира́ть; *quickly* одёргивать [-рнуть]; *money from banks* брать [взять]; брать наза́д; *from circulation* изыма́ть [изъя́ть]; *troops* выводи́ть [-вести]; *v/i.* удаля́ться [-ли́ться]; *mil.* отходи́ть [отойти́]; ~**al** [~əl] изъя́тие; удале́ние; *mil.* отхо́д; вы́вод; ~**n** *person* за́мкнутый

wither ['wɪðə] *v/i.* [за]вя́нуть; *v/t. crops* погуби́ть *pf.*

with|hold [wɪð'həʊld] [*irr.* (***hold***)] (*refuse to give*) отка́зывать [-за́ть] в (П); *information* скры(ва́)ть (***from*** от Р); ~**in** [~'ɪn] **1.** *lit. adv.* внутри́; **2.** *prp.* в (П), в преде́лах (Р); внутри́ (Р); ~ ***call*** в преде́лах слы́шимости; ~**out** [~'aʊt] **1.** *lit. adv.* вне, снару́жи; **2.** *prp.* без (Р); вне (Р); ***it goes*** ~ ***saying ...*** само́ собо́й разуме́ется; ~**stand** [~'stænd] [*irr.* (***stand***)] выде́рживать [вы́держать]; противостоя́ть (Д)

witness ['wɪtnɪs] **1.** свиде́тель *m*, -ница *f*; очеви́дец *m*, -дица *f*; ***bear*** ~ свиде́тельствовать (***to*** о П); **2.**

свидéтельствовать о (П); быть свидéтелем (Р); *signature*, *etc.* заверя́ть [-éрить]
wit|ticism ['wɪtɪsɪzəm] острóта; **~ty** ['wɪtɪ] □ остроу́мный
wives [waɪvz] *pl. от* ***wife***
wizard ['wɪzəd] волшéбник, маг
wizened ['wɪznd] *old lady* вы́сохший; *apple*, *etc.* смóрщенный
wobble ['wɒbl] качáться, шатáться
woe [wəʊ] гóре; **~begone** ['wəʊbɪgɒn] удручённый
woke [wəʊk] *pt. от* ***wake***; **~n** ['wəʊkən] *pt. p. от* ***wake***
wolf [wʊlf] **1.** волк; **2.** ***~ down*** éсть бы́стро и с жáдностью; нáспех проглоти́ть
wolves [wʊlvz] *pl. от* ***wolf***
woman ['wʊmən] жéнщина; ***old ~*** стару́ха; ***~ doctor*** жéнщина-врач; **~ish** [~ɪʃ] □ женоподóбный, бáбий; **~kind** [~'kaɪnd] *collect.* жéнщины *f/pl.*; **~ly** [~lɪ] жéнственный
womb [wu:m] *anat.* мáтка; чрéво; утрóба мáтери
women ['wɪmɪn] *pl. от* ***woman***; **~folk** [~fəʊk] жéнщины *f/pl.*
won [wʌn] *pt.* и *pt. p. от* ***win***
wonder ['wʌndə] **1.** удивлéние, изумлéние; (*miracle*) чу́до; **2.** удивля́ться [-ви́ться] (***at*** Д); ***I ~*** интерéсно, хотéлось бы знать; **~ful** [~fl] □ удиви́тельный, замечáтельный
won't [wəʊnt] не бу́ду *и т. д.*; не хочу́ *и т. д.*
wont [~]: ***be ~*** имéть обыкновéние
woo [wu:] ухáживать за (Т)
wood [wʊd] лес; (*material*) дéрево, лесоматериáл; (*fire ~*) дровá *n/pl.*; ***dead ~*** сухостóй; *fig.* баллáст; *attr.* леснóй, деревя́нный; дровянóй; **~cut** гравю́ра на дéреве; **~cutter** дровосéк; **~ed** ['wʊdɪd] леси́стый; **~en** ['wʊdn] деревя́нный; *fig.* безжи́зненный; **~pecker** [~pekə] дя́тел; **~winds** [~wɪndz] деревя́нные духовы́е инструмéнты *m/pl.*; **~work** деревя́нные издéлия *n/pl.*; *of building* деревя́нные чáсти *f/pl.*; **~y** ['wʊdɪ] леси́стый
wool [wʊl] шерсть *f*; *attr.* шерстянóй; **~gathering** ['wʊlgæðərɪŋ] *fig.* мечтáтельность; витáние в облакáх; **~(l)en** ['wʊlɪn] шерстянóй; **~ly** ['wʊlɪ] **1.** (*like wool*) шерсти́стый; *thoughts* неясный; **2.** ***woollies*** *pl.* шерстяны́е издéлия *n/pl.*; *esp.* бельё
word [wɜ:d] **1.** *mst.* слóво; разговóр; (*news*) извéстия, нóвости; (*promise*) обещáние, слóво; **~s** *pl. mus.* словá *n/pl.*; *fig.* (*angry argument*) кру́пный разговóр; ***in a ~*** одни́м слóвом; ***in other ~s*** други́ми словáми; ***~ of hono(u)r*** чéстное слóво; **2.** формули́ровать (*im*)*pf.*, *pf. a.* [с-]; **~ing** ['wɜ:dɪŋ] формулирóвка
wordy ['wɜ:dɪ] □ многословный
wore [wɔ:] *pt. от* ***wear 1***
work [wɜ:k] **1.** рабóта; труд; дéло; заня́тие; *art*, *lit.* произведéние, сочинéние; *attr.* рабóто...; рабóчий; **~s** *pl.* механи́зм; (*construction*) строи́тельные рабóты *f/pl.*; (*mill*) завóд; (*factory*) фáбрика; ***all in a day's ~*** дéло привы́чное; ***be out of ~*** быть безрабóтным; ***I'm sure it's his ~*** увéрен, э́то дéло егó рук; ***set to ~*** брáться за рабóту; **2.** *v/i.* рабóтать; занимáться [-ня́ться] (*have effect*) дéйствовать; *v/t.* [*irr.*] *land*, *etc.* обрабáтывать [-бóтать]; [*regular vb.*] *mine*, *etc.* разрабáтывать [-бóтать]; *machine*, *etc.* приводи́ть в дéйствие; ***~ one's way*** *through crowd* пробú(вá)ться, с трудóм пробивáть себé дорóгу (*both a. fig.*); ***~ off*** *debt* отрабáтывать [-бóтать]; *anger* успокáиваться [-кóиться]; ***~ out*** *problem* решáть [реши́ть]; *plan* разрабáтывать [-бóтать]; *agreement* составля́ть [-вить]; [*a. irr.*]; ***~ up*** (*excite*) возбуждáть; *coll.* взбудорáжи(ва)ть; ***don't get ~ed up*** спокóйно
work|able ['wɜ:kəbl] осуществи́мый; пригóдный; пригóдный для обрабóтки; **~aday** бу́дний; повседнéвный; **~day** (*time worked for payment*) трудодéнь *m*; **~er** ['wɜ:kə] *manual* рабóчий; рабóтник (-ица); **~ing** ['wɜ:kɪŋ] рабóчий; рабóтающий; дéйствующий; ***in ~ order*** в рабóчем состоя́нии; ***~ capital*** оборóтный капитáл

W

workman ['wɜːkmən] рабо́тник; **~ship** мастерство́; (*signs of skill*) отде́лка
workshop ['wɜːkʃɒp] мастерска́я; *in factory* цех
world [wɜːld] *com.* мир, свет; *attr.* миров*о́*й, всеми́рный; *fig.* ***a ~ of difference*** огро́мная ра́зница; ***come into the ~*** роди́ться, появи́ться *pf.* на свет; ***come up in the ~*** преуспе́(ва́)ть (в жи́зни); сде́лать карье́ру; ***it's a small ~*** мир те́сен; ***~ champion*** чемпио́н ми́ра
wordly ['wɜːldlɪ] све́тский
world power мирова́я держа́ва
worldwide ['wɜːldwaɪd] всеми́рный
worm [wɜːm] **1.** червя́к, червь *m*; *med.* глист; **2.** выве́дывать (вы́ведать), выпы́тывать [вы́пытать] (***out of*** у Р); ***~ o.s.*** *fig.* вкра́дываться [вкра́сться] (***into*** в В)
worn [wɔːn] *pt. p. от* ***wear***; **~-out** [wɔːn'aʊt] изно́шенный; *fig.* изму́ченный
worry ['wʌrɪ] **1.** беспоко́йство; трево́га; (*care*) забо́та; **2.** беспоко́ить(ся); (*bother with questions, etc.*) надоеда́ть [-е́сть] (Д); (*pester*) пристава́ть к (Д); [за]му́чить; ***she'll ~ herself to death!*** она́ совсе́м изведёт себя́!
worse [wɜːs] ху́дший; *adv.* ху́же; *pain, etc.* сильне́е; ***from bad to ~*** всё ху́же и ху́же; **~n** ['wɜːsn] ухудша́ть(ся) [уху́дшить(ся)]
worship ['wɜːʃɪp] **1.** *eccl.* богослуже́ние; **2.** поклоня́ться (Д); (*love*) обожа́ть; **~per** [~ə] покло́нник *m*, -ица *f*
worst [wɜːst] (самый) ху́дший, наиху́дший; *adv.* ху́же всего́; ***if the ~ comes to the ~*** в са́мом ху́дшем слу́чае; ***the ~ of it is that ...*** ху́же всего́ то, что ...
worth [wɜːθ] **1.** сто́ящий; заслу́живающий; ***be ~*** заслу́живать, сто́ить; **2.** цена́; сто́имость *f*; це́нность *f*; ***idea of little ~*** иде́я, не име́ющая осо́бой це́нности; **~less** [wəːθlis] ничего́ не сто́ящий; не име́ющий це́нности; **~-while** [wəːθ'waɪl] *coll.* сто́ящий; ***be ~*** име́ть смысл; ***be not ~*** не сто́ить труда́; **~y** ['wɜːðɪ] □ досто́йный (***of*** Р); заслу́живающий (***of*** В)
would [wʊd] (*pt. от* ***will***) *v/aux.*: ***he ~ do it*** он сде́лал бы э́то; он обы́чно э́то де́лал
wound[1] [wuːnd] **1.** ра́на, ране́ние; **2.** ра́нить (*im*)*pf.*; заде́(ва́)ть
wound[2] [waʊnd] *pt. и pt. p. от* ***wind***
wove ['wəʊv] *pt. от* ***weave***; **~n** ['wəʊvn] *pt. p. от* ***weave***
wrangle ['ræŋgl] **1.** препрека́ния *n/pl.*, **2.** препрека́ться
wrap [ræp] *v/t.* (*ча́сто* ***~ up***) завёртывать [заверну́ть]; *in paper* обёртывать [оберну́ть]; заку́т(ывать)ать; *fig.* оку́т(ыв)ать; ***be ~ped up in*** *thought, etc.* быть погружённым в (В); *v/i.* ***~ up*** заку́т(ыв)аться; **~per** ['ræpə] обёртка; **~ping** ['ræpɪŋ] упако́вка; обёртка
wrath [rɔːθ] гнев
wreath [riːθ], *pl.* **~s** [riːðz] *placed on coffin* вено́к; гирля́нда; *fig. of smoke* кольцо́, коле́чко
wreck [rek] **1.** (*destruction*) *esp. of ship* круше́ние; ава́рия; катастро́фа; *involving person, vehicle, etc.* разва́лина; **2.** *building, plans* разруша́ть [-у́шить]; *car* разби́ть *pf.*; ***be ~ed*** потерпе́ть *pf.* круше́ние; **~age** ['rekɪdʒ] (*remains*) обло́мки
wrench [rentʃ] **1.** (*spanner*) га́ечный ключ; ***give a ~*** дёрнуть *pf.*; **2.** вырыва́ть [-рвать]; *joint* выви́хивать [вы́вихнуть]; *fig.*, (*distort*) искажа́ть [искази́ть]; ***~ open*** взла́мывать [взлома́ть]
wrest [rest] вырыва́ть [вы́рвать] (***from*** у Р) (*a. fig.*); **~le** ['resl] *mst. sport* боро́ться; **~ling** ['~lɪŋ] борьба́
wretch [retʃ]: ***poor ~*** бедня́га
wretched ['retʃɪd] □ несча́стный; (*pitiful*) жа́лкий
wriggle ['rɪgl] *of worm, etc.* изви́(ва́)ться; ***~ out of*** уклоня́ться [-ни́ться] от (Р), выкру́чиваться [вы́крутиться] из (Р)
wring [rɪŋ] [*irr.*] скру́чивать [-ути́ть]; *one's hands* лома́ть; (*a.* ***~ out***) *washing, etc.* выжима́ть [вы́жать]; *money* вымога́ть (***from*** у Р); *confession* вы́рвать *pf.* (***from*** у Р)

W

wrinkle ['rɪŋkl] **1.** *in skin* морщи́на; *in dress* скла́дка; **2.** [с]мо́рщить(ся)
wrist [rɪst] запя́стье; ~ ***watch*** ручны́е (*or* нару́чные) часы́ *m/pl.*
write [raɪt] [*irr.*] [на]писа́ть; ~ ***down*** запи́сывать [-са́ть]; ~ ***out*** *check, Brt. cheque, etc.* выпи́сывать [вы́писать]; ~ **off** (*cancel*) спи́сывать [-са́ть]; **~r** ['raɪtə] писа́тель *m*, -ница *f*
writhe [raɪð] *with pain* [с]ко́рчиться
writing ['raɪtɪŋ] **1.** *process* писа́ние; (*composition*) письмо́; (литерату́рное) произведе́ние, сочине́ние; (*a.* ***hand~***) по́черк; ***in*** ~ пи́сьменно; **2.** пи́сьменный; ~ **paper** пи́счая бума́га
written ['rɪtn] **1.** *pt. p. от* ***write***; **2.** пи́сьменный
wrong [rɒŋ] **1.** □ (*not correct*) непра́вильный, оши́бочный; не тот (кото́рый ну́жен); ***be*** ~ быть непра́вым; ***go*** ~ *of things* не получа́ться [-чи́ться], срыва́ться [сорва́ться]; (*make a mistake*) сде́лать *pf.* оши́бку; ***come at the ~ time*** прийти́ *pf.* не во́время; *adv.* непра́вильно, не так; **2.** неправота́; непра́вильность *f*; (*injustice, unjust action*) оби́да; несправедли́вость *f*; зло; ***know right from*** ~ отлича́ть добро́ от зла; **3.** поступа́ть несправедли́во с (Т); обижа́ть [оби́деть]; **~doer** ['rɒŋdu:ə] гре́шник *m*, -ница*f*; престу́пник *m*, -ница *f*; правонаруши́тель *m*; **~ful** ['rɒŋfl] □ (*unlawful*) незако́нный; (*unjust*) несправедли́вый
wrote [rəʊt] *pt. от* ***write***
wrought [rɔ:t] *pt. и pt. p. от* ***work 2*** [*irr.*]: ~ ***iron*** ко́ваное желе́зо
wrung [rʌŋ] *pt. и pt. p. от* ***wring***
wry [raɪ] □ *smile* криво́й; *remark* переко́шенный; ирони́ческий

X

xerox ['zɪərɒks] **1.** ксе́рокс; **2.** ксерокопи́ровать
Xmas ['krɪsməs, 'eksməs] → ***Christmas***
X-ray ['eksreɪ] **1.** рентге́новские лучи́ *m/pl.*; рентгеногра́мма; **2.** просве́чивать [просвети́ть] рентге́новскими лу́чами; [с]де́лать рентге́н
xylophone ['zaɪləfəʊn] ксилофо́н

Y

yacht [jɒt] **1.** я́хта; **2.** плыть на я́хте; **~ing** ['jɒtɪŋ] па́русный спорт
yankee ['jæŋkɪ] *coll.* я́нки *m indecl.*
yap [jæp] **1.** тя́вкать [-кнуть]; болта́ть
yard[1] [jɑ:d] двор
yard[2] [~] ярд; измери́тельная лине́йка; **~stick** *fig.* мери́ло, ме́рка
yarn [jɑ:n] пря́жа; *coll. fig.* расска́з; ***spin a*** ~ плести́ небыли́цы
yawn [jɔ:n] **1.** зево́та; **2.** зева́ть [зевну́ть]; *fig.* (*be wide open*) зия́ть
year [jɪə, jɜ:] год (*pl.* года́, го́ды, лета́ *n/pl.*); ***he is six ~s old*** ему́ шесть лет; **~ly** ['~lɪ] ежего́дный
yearn [jɜ:n] тоскова́ть (***for*** по Д)

yeast [ji:st] дрóжжи *f/pl.*
yell [jel] **1.** пронзи́тельный крик; **2.** пронзи́тельно кричáть, (*howl*) [за]вопи́ть
yellow ['jeləʊ] **1.** жёлтый; *coll.* (*cowardly*) трусли́вый; **~ press** жёлтая прéсса; **2.** [по]желтéть; **~ed** [~d] пожелтéвший; **~ish** [~ɪʃ] желтовáтый
yelp [jelp] **1.** лай, визг; **2.** [за]визжáть, [за]лáять
yes [jes] да; нет: ***don't you like tea? – Yes, I do*** Вы не лю́бите чай? – Нет, люблю́
yesterday ['jestədɪ] вчерá
yet [jet] **1.** *adv.* ещё, всё ещё; ужé; до сих пор; дáже; тем не мéнее; ***as ~*** покá, до сих пор; ***not ~*** ещё не(т); **2.** *cj.* однáко, всё же, несмотря́ на э́то
yield [ji:ld] **1.** *v/t.* (*give*) приноси́ть [-нести́]; (*surrender*) сдa(вá)ть; *v/i.* уступáть [-пи́ть] (***to*** Д); подд(ав)áться; сд(ав)áться; **2.** *agric.* урожáй; *fin.* дохóд; **~ing** ['ji:ldɪŋ] □ *fig.* усту́пчивый
yog|a ['jəʊgə] (*system*) йóга; **~i** [~gɪ] йог
yog(h)urt [jɒgət] йóгурт
yoke [jəʊk] ярмó (*a. fig.*); и́го; *for carrying buckets, pails, etc.* коромы́сло
yolk [jəʊk] желтóк
you [jə, ... jʊ, ... ju:] *pron. pers.* ты, вы; тебя́, вас; тебé, вам (*чáсто* ***to ~***) *и т. д.*; ***~ and I*** (***me***) мы с вáми
young [jʌŋ] **1.** □ молодóй; *person* ю́ный; **2. *the ~*** молодёжь *f*; *zo.* детёныши *m/pl.*; **~ster** ['jʌŋstə] подрóсток, ю́ноша *m*
your [jə, ... jɔ:] *pron. poss.* твой *m*, твоя́ *f*, твоё *n*, твои́ *pl.*; ваш *m*, вáша *f*, вáше *n*, вáши *pl.*; **~s** [jɔ:z] *pron. poss. absolute form* твой *m*, твоя́ *f и т. д.*; **~self** [jɔ:'self], *pl.* **~selves** [~'selvz] сам *m*, самá *f*, самó *n*, сáми *pl.*; себя́, -ся
youth [ju:θ] *collect.* молодёжь *f*; (*boy*) ю́ноша *m*, мóлодость *f*; ***in my ~*** в мóлодости (*or* в ю́ности); **~ful** ['ju:θfl] □ ю́ношеский; (*looking young*) моложáвый

Z

zeal [zi:l] рвéние, усéрдие; **~ous** ['zeləs] □ рья́ный, усéрдный, рéвностный
zenith ['zenɪθ] зени́т (*a. fig.*)
zero ['zɪərəʊ] нуль *m* (*a.* ноль *m*); ***10° below*** (***above***) **~** дéсять грáдусов морóза (теплá) *or* ни́же (вы́ше) нуля́
zest [zest] (*gusto*) жар; ***~ for life*** жизнерáдостность *f*; любóвь к жи́зни
zigzag ['zɪgzæg] зигзáг
zinc [zɪŋk] цинк; *attr.* ци́нковый
zip [zɪp] (*sound of bullets*) свист; *coll.* энéргия; ***~ code*** почтóвый и́ндекс; ***~ fastener*** = **~per** ['zɪpə] (застёжка-)мóлния
zone [zəʊn] зóна (*a. pol.*); *geogr.* пóяс; (*region*) райóн
zoo [zu:] зоосáд, зоопáрк
zoolog|ical [zu:ə'lɒdʒɪkl] □ зоологи́ческий; ***~ gardens*** → ***zoo***; **~y** [zu:'ɒlədʒɪ] зоолóгия
zoom [zu:m] **1.** (*hum, buzz*) жужжáние; *ae.*, (*vertical climb*) свечá, гóрка; **2.** [про]жужжáть; *ae.* [с]дéлать свечу́/гóрку; ***~ lens*** объекти́в с перемéнным фóкусным расстоя́нием

Appendix

Important Russian Abbreviations

авт. ***автóбус*** bus
АЗС ***автозапрáвочная стáнция*** filling station
акад. ***акадéмик*** academician
АТС ***автоматíческая телефóнная стáнция*** telephone exchange
АЭС ***áтомная электростáнция*** nuclear power station

б-ка ***библиотéка*** library
б. ***бывший*** former, ex-
БСЭ ***Большáя совéтская энциклопéдия*** Big Soviet Encyclopedia

в. ***век*** century
вв. ***векá*** centuries
ВВС ***воéнно-воздýшные сíлы*** Air Forces
ВИЧ ***вíрус имунодефицíта человéка*** HIV (human immunodeficiency virus)
вм. ***вмéсто*** instead of
ВОЗ ***Всемíрная организáция здравоохранéния*** WHO (World Health Organization)
ВС ***Верхóвный Совéт*** *hist.* Supreme Soviet; ***вооружённые сíлы*** the armed forces
вуз ***вы́сшее учéбное заведéние*** university, college

г ***грамм*** gram(me)
г. 1. ***год*** year; **2.** ***гóрод*** city
га ***гектáр*** hectare
ГАИ ***Государственная автомобíльная инспéкция*** traffic police
ГАТТ ***Генерáльное соглашéние по тамóженным тарíфам и торгóвле*** GATT (General Agreement on Tariffs and Trade)
гг. ***гóды*** years
г-жа ***госпожá*** Mrs
глав... *in compounds* ***глáвный*** chief, main
главврáч ***глáвный врач*** head physician
г-н ***господíн*** Mr
гос... *in compounds* ***госудáрственный*** state, public
гр. ***граждани́н*** citizen
ГУМ ***Госудáрственный универсáльный магазíн*** department store

дир. ***дирéктор*** director
ДК ***Дом культýры*** House of Culture
доб. ***добáвочный*** additional
доц. ***доцéнт*** lecturer, reader, assistant professor
д-р ***дóктор*** doctor

ЕС ***Европéйский сою́з*** EU (European Union)
ЕЭС ***Европéйское экономíческое соóбщество*** EEC (European Economic Community)

ж.д. ***желéзная дорóга*** railroad, railway

зав. ***завéдующий*** head of ...
загс ***отдéл зáписей граждáнского состоя́ния*** registrar's (registry) office
зам. ***заместíтель*** deputy, assistant

и др. ***и другíе*** etc.
им. ***íмени*** called
и мн. др. ***и мнóгие другíе*** and many (much) more
ИНТЕРПОЛ ***Междунарóдная организáция уголóвной полíции*** INTERPOL
и пр., и проч. ***и прóчее*** etc
ИТАР ***Информациóнное телегрáфное агéнтство Россíи*** ITAR (Information Telegraph Agency of Russia)
и т.д. ***и так дáлее*** and so on
и т.п. ***и томý подóбное*** etc.

к. ***копéйка*** kopeck
кг ***килогрáмм*** kg (kilogram[me])
кв. 1. ***квадрáтный*** square; **2.** ***квартíра*** apartment, flat
км/час ***киломéтров в час*** km/h (kilometers per hour)
колхóз ***коллектíвное хозя́йство*** collective farm, kolkhoz
коп. ***копéйка*** kopeck
к.п.д. ***коэффициéнт полéзного дéйствия*** efficiency

КПСС *Коммунистическая партия Советского Союза* *hist.* C.P.S.U. (Communist Party of the Soviet Union)
куб. *кубический* cubic

л.с. *лошадиная сила* h.p. (horse power)

МАГАТЭ *Международное агентство по атомной энергии* IAEA (International Atomic Energy Agency)
МБР *Министерство безопасности России* Ministry of Security of Russia
МВД *Министерство внутренних дел* Ministry of Internal Affairs
МВФ *Международный валютный фонд* IMF (International Monetary Fund)
МГУ *Московский государственный университет* Moscow State University
МИД *Министерство иностранных дел* Ministry of Foreign Affairs
МО *Министерство обороны* Ministry of Defence
МОК *Международный олимпийский комитет* IOC (International Olympic Committee)
МОТ *Международная организация труда* ILO (International Labor Organization)
м.пр. *между прочим* by the way, incidentally; among other things
МХАТ *Московский художественный академический театр* Academic Artists' Theater, Moscow

напр. *например* for instance
№ *номер* number
НАТО *Североатлантический союз* NATO (North Atlantic Treaty Organization)
НЛО *неопознанный летающий объект* UFO (unidentified flying object)
н.э. *нашей эры* A.D.

о. *остров* island
обл. *область* region
ОБСЕ *Организация по безопасности и сотрудничеству в Европе* OSCE (Organisation on Security and Cooperation in Europe)
о-во *общество* society
оз. *озеро* lake
ОНО *отдел народного образования* Department of Popular Education
ООН *Организация Объединённых Наций* UNO (United Nations Organization)
отд. *отдел* section, ***отделение*** department
ОПЕК *Организация стран-экспортёров нефти* OPEC (Organization of Petroleum Exporting Countries)

п. *пункт* point, paragraph
пер. *переулок* lane
ПК *персональный компьютер* PC (personal computer)
пл. *площадь* *f* square; area (*a. math.*)
проф. *профессор* professor

р. 1. *река* river; **2. *рубль*** *m* r(o)uble
райком *районный комитет* district committee (*Sov.*)
РИА *Российское информационное агентство* Information Agency of Russia
РФ *Российская Федерация* Russian Federation

с.г. *сего года* (of) this year
след. *следующий* following
см *сантиметр* cm. (centimeter)
с.м. *сего месяца* (of) this month
см. *смотри* see
СНГ *Содружество независимых государств* CIS (Commonwealth of Independent States)
СП *совместное предприятие* joint venture
СПИД *синдром преобретённого имунодефицита* AIDS (acquired immune deficiency syndrome)
ср. *сравни* cf. (compare)
СССР *Союз Советских Социалистических Республик* *hist.* U.S.S.R. (Union of Soviet Socialist

Republics)
ст. ***ста́нция*** station
стенгазе́та ***стенна́я газе́та*** wall newspaper
с., стр. ***страни́ца*** page
с.х. ***се́льское хозя́йство*** agriculture
с.-х. ***сельскохозя́йственный*** agricultural
США ***Соединённые Шта́ты Аме́рики*** U.S.A (United States of America)

т ***то́нна*** ton
т. 1. ***това́рищ*** comrade; **2**. ***том*** volume
ТАСС ***Телегра́фное аге́нтство Сове́тского Сою́за*** *hist.* TASS (Telegraph Agency of the Soviet Union)
т-во ***това́рищество*** company, association
т. е. ***то есть*** i.e. (that is)
тел. ***телефо́н*** telephone
т.к. ***так как*** cf. ***так***
т. наз. ***так называ́емый*** so-called
тов. → ***т. 1***
торгпре́дство ***торго́вое представи́тельство*** trade agency
тт. ***тома́*** volumes
тыс. ***ты́сяча*** thousand

ул. ***у́лица*** street

ФБР ***Федера́льное бюро́ рассле́дований*** FBI (Federal Bureau of Investigation)
ФИФА ***Междунаро́дная ассоциа́ция футбо́льных о́бществ*** FIFA (Fédération Internationale de Football)
ФРГ ***Федерати́вная Респу́блика Герма́ния*** Federal Republic of Germany

ЦБР ***Центра́льный банк Росси́и*** Central Bank of Russia
ЦПКиО ***Цени́ральный парк культу́ры и о́тдыха*** Central Park for Culture and Recreation
ЦРУ ***Центра́льное разве́дывательное управле́ние*** CIA (Central Intelligence Agency)

ЮАР ***Ю́жно-Африка́нская Респу́блика*** South African Republic
ЮНЕСКО ***Организа́ция Объединённых на́ций по вопро́сам образова́ния, нау́ки и культу́ры*** UNESCO (United Nations Educational, Scientific and Cultural Organization)

Important American and British Abbreviations

AC ***alternating current*** переме́нный ток
A/C ***account (current)*** теку́щий счёт
acc(t). ***account*** отчёт; счёт
AEC ***Atomic Energy Commission*** Коми́ссия по а́томной эне́ргии
AFL-CIO ***American Federation of Labor & Congress of Industrial Organizations*** Америка́нская федера́ция труда́ и Конгре́сс произво́дственных профсою́зов, АФТ/КПП
AL, Ala. ***Alabama*** Алаба́ма (штат в США)
Alas. ***Alaska*** Аля́ска (штат в США)
a.m. ***ante meridiem (= before noon)*** до полу́дня
AP ***Associated Press*** Ассоши'йтед пресс
AR ***Arkansas*** Арка́нзас (штат в США)
ARC ***American Red Cross*** Америка́нский Кра́сный Крест
Ariz. ***Arizona*** Аризо́на (штат в США)
ATM ***automated teller machine*** банкома́т
AZ ***Arizona*** Аризо́на (штат в США)

BA ***Bachelor of Arts*** бакала́вр иску́сств
BBC. ***British Broadcasting Corporation*** Брита́нская радиовеща́тельная корпора́ция
B/E ***Bill of Exchange*** ве́ксель *m*, тра́тта
BL ***Bachelor of Law*** бакала́вр пра́ва
B/L ***bill of lading*** коносаме́нт; тра́нспортная накладна́я
BM ***Bachelor of Medicine*** бакала́вр медици́ны
BOT ***Board of Trade*** министе́рство торго́вли (Великобрита́нии)
BR ***British Rail*** Брита́нская желе́зная доро́га
Br(it). ***Britain*** Великобрита́ния; ***British*** брита́нский, англи́йский
Bros. ***brothers*** бра́тья *pl.* (в назва́ниях фирм)

c. 1. ***cent(s)*** цент (америка́нская моне́та); **2.** ***circa*** приблизи́тельно, о́коло; **3.** ***cubic*** куби́ческий
CA ***California*** Калифо́рния (штат в США)
C/A ***current account*** теку́щий счёт
Cal(if). ***California*** Калифо́рния (штат в США)
Can. ***Canada*** Кана́да; ***Canadian*** кана́дский
CIA ***Central Intelligence Agency*** Центра́льное разве́дывательное управле́ние, ЦРУ
CID ***Criminal Investigation Department*** кримина́льная поли́ция
c.i.f. ***cost, insurance, freight*** цена́, включа́ющая сто́имость, расхо́ды по страхова́нию и фрахт
CIS ***Commonwealth of Independent States*** содру́жество незави́симых госуда́рств, СНГ
c/o ***care of*** че́рез, по а́дресу (на́дпись на конве́ртах)
Co. ***Company*** о́бщество, компа́ния
COD ***cash*** (*am. collect*) ***on delivery*** нало́женный платёж, упла́та при доста́вке
Colo. ***Colorado*** Колора́до (штат в США)
Conn. ***Connecticut*** Конне́ктикут (штат в США)
cwt ***hundredweight*** хандредвейт

DC 1. ***direct current*** посто́янный ток; **2.** ***District of Columbia*** федера́льный о́круг Колу́мбия (с америка́нской столи́цей)
Del. ***Delaware*** Де́лавэр (штат в США)
dept. ***Department*** отде́л; управле́ние; министе́рство; ве́домство
disc. ***discount*** ски́дка; ди́сконт, учёт векселе́й
div. ***dividend*** дивиде́нд
DJ 1. ***disc jockey*** диск-жоке́й; **2.** ***dinner jacket*** смо́кинг
dol. ***dollar*** до́ллар
DOS ***disk operating system*** ди́сковая операцио́нная систе́ма
doz. ***dozen*** дю́жина

dpt. ***Department*** отде́л; управле́ние; министе́рство; ве́домство

E 1. ***East*** восто́к; ***Eastern*** восто́чный; **2.** ***English*** англи́йский
E. & O.E. ***errors and omissions excepted*** исключа́я оши́бки и про́пуски
EC ***European Community*** Европе́йское Соо́бщество, ЕС
ECOSOC ***Economic and Social Council*** Экономи́ческий и социа́льный сове́т, ООН
ECU ***European Currency Unit*** Европе́йская де́нежная едини́ца, ЭКЮ
EEC ***European Economic Community*** Европе́йское экономи́ческое соо́бщество, ЕЭС
e.g. ***exempli gratia*** (лат. = ***for instance***) напр. (наприме́р)
Enc. ***enclosure(s)*** приложе́ние (-ния)
Esq. ***Esquire*** эскваи́р (ти́тул дворяни́на, должностно́го лица́; обы́чно ста́вится в письме́ по́сле фами́лии)
etc. & c. ***et cetera, and so on*** и так да́лее
EU ***European Union*** Европе́йский сою́з

f ***feminine*** же́нский; *gram.* же́нский род; ***foot*** фут, ***feet*** фу́ты; ***following*** сле́дующий
FBI ***Federal Bureau of Investigation*** федера́льное бюро́ рассле́дований (в США)
FIFA ***Fédération Internationale de Football Association*** Междунаро́дная федера́ция футбо́льных о́бществ, ФИФА
Fla. ***Florida*** флори́да (штат в США)
F.O. ***Foreign Office*** министе́рство иностра́нных дел
fo(l) ***folio*** фо́лио *indecl. n* (форма́т в пол-листа́); лист (бухга́лтерской кни́ги)
f.o.b. ***free on board*** франко-борт, ФОБ
fr. ***franc(s)*** фра́нк(и)
FRG ***Federal Republic of Germany*** Федерати́вная Респу́блика Герма́ния, ФРГ
ft. ***foot*** фут, ***feet*** фу́ты

g. ***gram(me)*** грамм
GA (Ga.) ***Georgia*** Джо́рджия (штат в США)
GATT ***General Agreement on Tariffs and Trade*** Генера́льное соглаше́ние по тамо́женным тари́фам и торго́вле
GB ***Great Britain*** Великобрита́ния
GI ***government issue*** *fig.* америка́нский солда́т
GMT ***Greenwich Mean Time*** сре́днее вре́мя по гри́нвичскому меридиа́ну
gr. ***gross*** бру́тто
gr.wt. ***gross weight*** вес бру́тто

h. ***hour(s)*** час(ы́)
HBM. ***His (Her) Britannic Majesty*** Его́ (Её) Брита́нское Вели́чество
H.C. ***House of Commons*** Пала́та о́бщин (в Великобрита́нии)
hf. ***half*** полови́на
HIV ***human immunodeficiency virus*** ВИЧ
HL ***House of Lords*** пала́та ло́рдов (в Великобрита́нии)
HM ***His (Her) Majesty*** Его́ (Её) Вели́чество
HMS ***His (Her) Majesty's Ship*** кора́бль англи́йского вое́нно-морско́го фло́та
HO ***Home Office*** министе́рство вну́тренних дел (в А́нглии)
HP, hp ***horsepower*** лошади́ная си́ла (едини́ца мо́щности)
HQ, Hq ***Headquarters*** штаб
HR ***House of Representatives*** пала́та представи́телей (в США)
HRH ***His (Her) Royal Highness*** Его́ (Её) Короле́вское Высо́чество
hrs. ***hours*** часы́

IA, Ia. ***Iowa*** Айо́ва (штат в США)
IAEA ***International Atomic Energy Agency*** Междунаро́дное аге́нтство по а́томной эне́ргии, МАГАТЭ
ID ***identification*** удостовере́ние ли́чности
Id(a). ***Idaho*** А́йдахо (штат в США)
i.e., ie ***id est*** (лат. = ***that is to say***) т.е. (то есть)
IL, Ill. ***Illinois*** Иллино́йс (штат в США)

IMF ***International Monetary Fund*** Междунаро́дный валю́тный фонд ООН
in. ***inch(es)*** дю́йм(ы)
Inc., inc. ***incorporated*** объединённый; зарегистри́рованный как корпора́ция
incl. ***inclusive, including*** включи́тельно
Ind. ***Indiana*** Индиа́на (штат в США)
inst. ***instant*** с.м. (сего́ ме́сяца)
INTERPOL ***International Criminal Police Organization*** Междунаро́дная организа́ция уголо́вной поли́ции, ИНТЕРПОЛ
IOC ***International Olympic Committee*** Междунаро́дный олимпи́йский комите́т, МОК
IQ ***intelligence quotient*** коэффицие́нт у́мственных спосо́бностей
Ir. ***Ireland*** Ирла́ндия; ***Irish*** ирла́ндский

JP ***Justice of the Peace*** мирово́й судья́
Jnr, Jr, jun., junr ***junior*** мла́дший

Kan(s). ***Kansas*** Канза́с (штат в США)
KB ***kilobyte*** килоба́йт
kg ***kilogram(me)s.*** килогра́мм, кг
km ***kilometer, -tre*** киломе́тр
kW, kw ***kilowatt*** килова́тт
KY, Ky ***Kentucky*** Кенту́кки (штат в США)

l. ***litre*** литр
L pound sterling фунт сте́рлингов
La. ***Louisiana*** Луизиа́на (штат в США)
LA *1.* ***Los Angeles*** Лос-Анджелес; **2.** ***Australian pound*** австрали́йский фунт (де́нежная едини́ца)
lb., lb ***pound*** фунт (ме́ра ве́са)
L/C ***letter of credit*** аккредити́в
LP ***Labour Party*** лейбори́стская па́ртия
Ltd, ltd ***limited*** с ограни́ченной отве́тственностью

m. 1. ***male*** мужско́й; **2.** ***meter, -tre*** метр; **3.** ***mile*** ми́ля; **4.** ***minute*** мину́та
MA ***Master of Arts*** маги́стр иску́сств
Mass. ***Massachusetts*** Массачу́сетс (штат в США)
max. ***maximum*** ма́ксимум
MD ***medicinae doctor*** (лат. = ***Doctor of Medicine***) до́ктор медици́ны
Md. ***Maryland*** Мэ́риленд (штат в США)
ME, Me. ***Maine*** Мэн (штат в США)
mg. ***milligram(me)(s)*** миллигра́мм
Mich. ***Michigan*** Мичига́н (штат в США)
Minn. ***Minnesota*** Миннесо́та (штат в США)
Miss. ***Mississippi*** Миссиси́пи (штат в США)
mm. ***millimeter*** миллиме́тр
MO 1. ***Missouri*** Миссу́ри (штат в США); **2.** ***money order*** де́нежный перево́д по по́чте
Mont. ***Montana*** Монта́на (штат в США)
MP 1. ***Member of Parliament*** член парла́мента; **2.** ***military police*** вое́нная поли́ция
mph ***miles per hour*** (сто́лько-то) миль в час
Mr ***Mister*** ми́стер, господи́н
Mrs *originally* ***Mistress*** ми́ссис, госпожа́
MS 1. ***Mississippi*** Миссиси́пи (штат в США); **2.** ***manuscript*** ру́копись *f*; **3.** ***motorship*** теплохо́д

N ***north*** се́вер; ***northern*** се́верный
NATO ***North Atlantic Treaty Organization*** Североатланти́ческий сою́з, НАТО
NC, N.C. ***North Carolina*** Се́верная Кароли́на (штат в США)
ND, ND. ***North Dakota*** Се́верная Дако́та (штат в США)
NE 1. ***Nebraska*** Небра́ска (штат в США); **2.** ***northeast*** се́веро-восто́к
Neb(r). ***Nebraska*** Небра́ска (штат в США)
Nev. ***Nevada*** Нева́да (штат в США)
NH, N.H ***New Hampshire*** Нью-Хэ́мпшир (штат в США)
NJ, N.J ***New Jersey*** Нью-Дже́рси (штат в США)
NM, N.M(ex). ***New Mexico*** Нью-Ме́ксико (штат в США)
nt.wt. ***net weight*** вес не́тто, чи́стый вес

NW ***northwestern*** се́веро-за́падный
NY, N.Y. ***New York*** Нью-Йо́рк (штат в США)
NYC, N.Y.C. ***New York City*** Нью-Йо́рк (го́род)

OH ***Ohio*** Ога́йо (штат в США)
OHMS ***On His (Her) Majesty's Service*** состоя́щий на короле́вской (госуда́рственной или вое́нной) слу́жбе; служе́бное де́ло
OK 1. ***okay*** всё в поря́дке, всё пра́вильно; утверждено́, согласо́вано; **2.** ***Oklahoma*** Оклахо́ма (штат в США)
Okla. ***Oklahoma*** Оклахо́ма (штат в США)
OR, Ore(g). ***Oregon*** Орего́н (штат в США)
OSCE ***Organisation on Security and Cooperation in Europe*** Организа́ция по безопа́сности и сотру́дничеству в Евро́пе, ОБСЕ

p *Brt* ***penny, pence*** пе́нни, пенс
p. ***page*** страни́ца; ***part*** часть, ч.
PA, Pa. ***Pennsylvania*** Пенсильва́ния (штат в США)
p.a. ***per annum*** (лат.) в год; ежего́дно
PC 1. ***personal computer*** персона́льный компью́тер; **2.** ***police constable*** полице́йский
p.c. ***per cent*** проце́нт, проце́нты
pd. ***paid*** упла́чено; опла́ченный
Penn(a). ***Pennsylvania*** Пенсильва́ния (штат в США)
per pro(c). ***per procurationem (= by proxy)*** по дове́ренности
p.m., pm ***post meridiem (= after noon)*** ...часов (часа) дня
PO 1. ***post office*** почто́вое отделе́ние; **2.** ***postal order*** де́нежный перево́д по по́чте
POB ***post office box*** почто́вый абонеме́нтный я́щик
POD ***pay on delivery*** нало́женный платёж
Pres. ***president*** президе́нт
Prof. ***professor*** проф. профе́ссор
PS ***Postscript*** постскри́птум, припи́ска
PTO., p.t.o. ***please turn over*** см. н/об. (смотри́ на оборо́те)

RAF ***Royal Air Force*** вое́нно-возду́шные си́лы Великобрита́нии
RAM ***random access memory*** операти́вное запомина́ющее устро́йство, ОЗУ
ref. ***reference*** ссы́лка, указа́ние
regd ***registered*** зарегистри́рованный; заказно́й
reg.ton ***register ton*** реги́стровая то́нна
Rev., Revd ***Reverend*** преподо́бный
RI, R.I. ***Rhode Island*** Род-А́йленд (штат в США)
RN ***Royal Navy*** вое́нно-морско́й флот Великобрита́нии
RP ***reply paid*** отве́т опла́чен

S ***south*** юг; ***southern*** ю́жный
s 1. ***second*** секу́нда; **2.** *hist.* ***shilling*** ши́ллинг
SA 1. ***South Africa*** Ю́жная А́фрика; **2.** ***Salvation Army*** А́рмия спасе́ния
SC, S.C. ***South Carolina*** Ю́жная Кароли́на (штат в США)
SD, S.D(ak). ***South Dakota*** Ю́жная Дако́та (штат в США)
SE 1. ***southeast*** юго-восто́к; ***southeastern*** юго-восто́чный; **2.** ***Stock Exchange*** фо́ндовая би́ржа (в Ло́ндоне)
Soc. ***society*** о́бщество
Sq. ***Square*** пло́щадь *f*
sq. ***square...*** квадра́тный
SS ***steamship*** парохо́д
stg. ***sterling*** фунт сте́рлингов
suppl. ***supplement*** дополне́ние, приложе́ние
SW ***southwest*** юго-за́пад; ***southwestern*** юго-за́падный

t ***ton*** то́нна
TB ***tuberculosis*** туберкулёз, ТБ
tel. ***telephone*** телефо́н, тел.
Tenn. ***Tennessee*** Те́ннесси (штат в США)
Tex. ***Texas*** Теха́с (штат в США)
TU ***trade(s) union*** тред-ю́нион профессиона́льный сою́з
TUC ***Trade Unions Congress*** конгре́сс (брита́нских) тред-юнио́нов

UK ***United Kingdom*** Соединённое Короле́вство (Англия, Шотла́н-

дия, Уэльс и Се́верная Ирла́ндия)
UFO ***unidentified flying object*** неопо́знанные лета́ющие объе́кты, НЛО
UN ***United Nations*** Объединённые На́ции
UNESCO ***United Nations Educational, Scientific, and Cultural Organization*** Организа́ция Объединённых На́ций по вопро́сам просвеще́ния, нау́ки и культу́ры, ЮНЕСКО
UNSC ***United Nations Security Council*** Сове́т Безопа́сности ООН
UP ***United Press*** телегра́фное аге́нтство „Ю́на́йтед Пресс"
US(A) ***United States (of America)*** Соединённые Шта́ты (Аме́рики)
USW ***ultrashort wave*** у́льтрако́роткие во́лны, УКВ
UT, Ut. ***Utah*** Ю́та (штат в США)

V ***volt(s)*** во́льт(ы) В
VA, Va. ***Virginia*** Вирджи́ния (штат в США)
VCR ***video cassette recorder*** видеомагнитофо́н
viz. ***videlicet*** (лат.) а и́менно
vol. ***volume*** том
vols ***volumes*** тома́ *pl*
VT, Vt. ***Vermont*** Вермо́нт (штат в США)

W 1. ***west*** за́пад; ***western*** за́падный; **2.** ***watt*** ватт, Вт
WA, Wash. ***Washington*** Вашингто́н (штат в США)
W.F.T.U. ***World Federation of Trade Unions*** Всеми́рная федера́ция профессиона́льных сою́зов, ВФП
WHO ***World Health Organization*** Всеми́рная организа́ция здравоохране́ния, ВОЗ
Wis(c). ***Wisconsin*** Виско́нсин (штат в США)
wt., wt ***weight*** вес
WV, W Va. ***West Virginia*** За́падная Вирги́ния (штат в США)
WWW ***World-Wide Web*** всеми́рная паýтина
WY, Wyo. ***Wyoming*** Вайо́минг (штат в США)

Xmas ***Christmas*** Рождество́

yd(s) ***yard(s)*** ярд(ы)
YMCA ***Young Men's Christian Association*** Христиа́нская ассоциа́ция молоды́х люде́й
YWCA ***Young Women's Christian Association*** Христиа́нская ассоциа́ция молоды́х (де́вушек)

Russian Geographical Names

Австра́лия *f* Australia
А́встрия *f* Austria
Азербайджа́н *m* Azerbaijan
А́зия *f* Asia
Алба́ния *f* Albania
А́льпы *pl. the* Alps
Аля́ска *f* Alaska
Аме́рика *f* America
А́нглия *f* England
Антаркти́да *f the* Antarctic Continent, Antarctica
Анта́рктика *f* Antarctic
Аргенти́на *f* Argentina
А́рктика *f* Arctic (Zone)
Арме́ния *f* Armenia
Атла́нтика *f*, **Атланти́ческий океа́н** *m the* Atlantic (Ocean)
Афганиста́н *m* Afghanistan
Афи́ны *pl.* Athens
А́фрика *f* Africa

Байка́л *m* (Lake) Baikal
Балти́йское мо́ре *the* Baltic Sea
Ба́ренцево мо́ре *the* Barents Sea
Белору́ссия *f* Byelorussia
Бе́льгия *f* Belgium
Бе́рингово мо́ре *the* Bering Sea
Бе́рингов проли́в *the* Bering Straits
Болга́рия *f* Bulgaria
Бо́сния *f* Bosnia
Брита́нские острова́ *the* British Isles
Брюссе́ль *m* Brussels
Будапе́шт *m* Budapest
Бухаре́ст *m* Bucharest

Варша́ва *f* Warsaw
Вашингто́н *m* Washington
Великобрита́ния *f* Great Britain
Ве́на *f* Vienna
Ве́нгрия *f* Hungary
Вене́ция *f* Venice
Во́лга *f the* Volga

Гаа́га *f the* Hague
Герма́ния *f* Germany
Гимала́и *pl. the* Himalayas
Гонко́нг *m* Hong Kong
Гренла́ндия *f* Greenland
Гре́ция *f* Greece
Гру́зия *f* Georgia (Caucasus)

Да́ния *f* Denmark
Днепр *m* Dniepr
Донба́сс *m* (Доне́цкий бассе́йн) *the* Donbas, *the* Donets Basin
Дуна́й *m the* Danube

Евро́па *f* Europe
Еги́пет *m* [-пта] Egypt
Енисе́й *m the* Yenisei

Иерусали́м *m* Jerusalem
Изра́иль *m* Israel
И́ндия *f* India
Ира́к *m* Iraq
Ира́н *m* Iran
Ирла́ндия *f* Ireland; Eire
Исла́ндия *f* Iceland
Испа́ния *f* Spain
Ита́лия *f* Italy

Кавка́з *m the* Caucasus
Казахста́н *m* Kasakhstan
Каи́р *m* Cairo
Камча́тка *f* Kamchatka
Кана́да *f* Canada
Каре́лия *f* Karelia
Карпа́ты *pl. the* Carpathians
Каспи́йское мо́ре *the* Caspian Sea
Кёльн *m* Cologne
Ки́ев *m* Kiev
Кипр *m* Cyprus
Коре́я *f* Korea
Крым *m* [в -ý] *the* Crimea
Кузба́сс *m* Кузне́цкий бассе́йн *the* Kuzbas, *the* Kuznetsk Basin

Ла́дожское о́зеро Lake Ladoga
Ла-Ма́нш *m the* English Channel
Ленингра́д *m* Leningrad (*hist.*)
Лива́н *m* Lebanon
Литва́ *f* Lithuania
Ла́твия *f* Latvia

Ме́ксика *f* Mexico
Молдо́ва *f* Moldova
Монго́лия *f* Mongolia
Москва́ *f* Moscow

Нева́ *f the* Neva
Нидерла́нды *pl. the* Netherlands
Норве́гия *f* Norway

Нью-Йо́рк *m* New York

Палести́на *f* Palestine
Пари́ж *m* Paris
По́льша *f* Poland
Пра́га *f* Prague

Рейн *m* Rhine
Рим *m* Rome
Росси́йская Федера́ция *f* Russian Federation
Росси́я *f* Russia
Румы́ния *f* Romania

Санкт-Петербу́рг *m* St. Petersburg
Се́верный Ледови́тый океа́н *the* Arctic Ocean
Сиби́рь *f* Siberia
Стокго́льм *m* Stockholm
Соединённые Шта́ты Аме́рики *pl. the* United States of America

Те́мза *f* the Thames
Таджикиста́н *m* Tajikistan
Туркмениста́н *f* Turkmenistan
Ту́рция *f* Turkey

Узбекиста́н *m* Uzbekistan
Украи́на *f the* Ukraine
Ура́л *m the* Urals

Финля́ндия *f* Finland
Фра́нция *f* France

Чёрное мо́ре *the* Black Sea
Чечня́ *f* Chechnia
Че́шская Респу́блика *f the* Czech Republic

Швейца́рия *f* Switzerland
Шве́ция *f* Sweden

Эдинбу́рг *m* Edinburgh
Эсто́ния *f* Estonia

Ю́жно-Африка́нская Респу́блика *f the* South African Republic

English Geographical Names

Afghanistan [æf'gænɪstɑːn] Афганистáн
Africa ['æfrɪkə] Áфрика
Alabama [ˌælə'bæmə] Алабáма (штат в США)
Alaska [ə'læskə] Аля́ска (штат в США)
Albania [æl'beɪnjə] Албáния
Alps [ælps] *the* Áльпы
Amazon ['æməzn] *the* Амазóнка
America [ə'merɪkə] Амéрика
Antarctica [ænt'ɑːktɪkə] *the* Антáртика
Arctic ['ɑːktɪk] *the* Áрктика
Argentina [ˌɑːdʒən'tiːnə] Аргенти́на
Arizona [ˌærɪ'zəʊnə] Аризóна (штат в США)
Arkansas ['ɑːkənsɔː] Аркáнзас (штат и рекá в США)
Asia ['eɪʃə] Áзия; ***Middle* ~** Срéдняя Áзия
Athens ['æθɪnz] г. Афи́ны
Atlantic Ocean [ətˌlæntɪk'əʊʃn] *the* Атланти́ческий океáн
Australia [ɒ'streɪljə] Австрáлия
Austria ['ɒstrɪə] Áвстрия

Baikal [baɪ'kæl] óзеро Байкáл
Balkans ['bɔːlkənz] *the* Балкáны
Baltic Sea [ˌbɔːltɪk'siː] *the* Балти́йское мóре
Barents Sea ['bæːrəntsiː] *the* Бáренцево мóре
Belfast [ˌbel'fɑːst] г. Бéлфаст
Belgium ['beldʒəm] Бéльгия
Bering Sea [ˌbeərɪŋ'siː] *the* Бéрингово мóре
Berlin [bɜː'lɪn] г. Берли́н
Birmingham ['bɜːmɪŋəm] г. Би́рмингем
Black Sea [ˌblæk'siː] *the* Чёрное мóре
Bosnia ['bɒznɪə] Бóсния
Boston ['bɒstən] г. Бостóн
Brazil [brə'zɪl] Брази́лия
Britain ['brɪtn] (***Great*** Велико) Британия
Brussels ['brʌslz] г. Брюссель
Bucharest [ˌbuːkə'rest] г. Бухарéст
Bulgaria [bʌl'geərɪə] Болгáрия
Byelorussia [bɪˌeləʊ'rʌʃə] Белорýссия, Беларýсь

Cairo ['kaɪrəʊ] г. Каи́р
Calcutta [kæl'kʌtə] г. Калькýтта
California [ˌkʌlɪ'fɔːnjə] Калифóрния (штат в США)
Cambridge ['keɪmbrɪdʒ] г. Кéмбридж
Canada ['kænədə] Канáда
Cape Town ['keɪptaʊn] г. Кéйптаун
Carolina [ˌkærə'laɪnə] Кароли́на (***North*** Сéверная, ***South*** Óжная)
Caspian Sea [ˌkæspɪən'siː] *the* Каспи́йское мóре
Caucasus ['kɔːkəsəs] *the* Кавкáз
Ceylon [sɪ'lɒn] о. Цéйлон
Chechnia ['tʃetʃnɪə] Чечня́
Chicago [ʃɪ'kɑːgəʊ, *Am.* ʃɪ'kɔːgəʊ] г. Чикáго
Chile ['tʃɪlɪ] Чи́ли
China ['tʃaɪnə] Китáй
Colorado [ˌkɒlə'rɑːdəʊ] Колорáдо (штат в США)
Columbia [kə'lʌmbɪə] Колýмбия (рекá, гóрод, админ. округ)
Connecticut [kə'netɪkət] Коннектикут (рекá и штат в США)
Copenhagen [ˌkəʊpn'heɪgən] г. Копенгáген
Cordilleras [ˌkɔːdɪ'ljeərəz] *the* Кордильеры (горы)
Croatia [krəʊ'eɪʃə] Хорвáтия
Cuba ['kjuːbə] Кýба
Cyprus ['saɪprəs] о. Кипр
Czech Republic [ˌtʃek rɪ'pʌblɪk] *the* Чéшская Респýблика

Dakota [də'kəʊtə] Дакóта ***North*** Сéверная, ***South*** Óжная (штáты в США)
Danube ['dænjuːb] р. Дунáй
Delaware ['deləweə] Дéлавер (штат в США)
Denmark ['denmɑːk] Дáния
Detroit [də'trɔɪt] г. Детрóйт
Dover ['dəʊvə] г. Дувр
Dublin ['dʌblɪn] г. Дýблин

Edinburgh ['edɪnbərə] г. Э́динбург
Egypt ['iːdʒɪpt] Еги́пет
Eire ['eərə] Э́йре
England ['ɪŋglənd] Áнглия
Europe ['jʊərəp] Еврóпа

Finland ['fɪnlənd] Финля́ндия
Florida ['flɒrɪdə] Фло́рида
France [frɑːns] Фра́нция

Geneva [dʒɪ'niːvə] г. Жене́ва
Georgia ['dʒɔːdʒjə] Джо́рджия (штат в США); Гру́зия
Germany ['dʒɜːmənɪ] Герма́ния
Gibraltar [dʒɪ'brɔːltə] Гибра́лтар
Glasgow ['glɑːzgəʊ] г. Гла́зго
Greece ['griːs] Гре́ция
Greenwich ['grenɪtʃ] г. Гри́н(в)ич

Hague ['heɪg] *the* г. Га́ага
Harwich ['hærɪdʒ] г. Ха́ридж
Hawaii [hə'waiiː] Гава́йи (о́стров, штат в США)
Helsinki ['helsɪŋkɪ] г. Хе́льсинки
Himalaya [ˌhɪmə'leɪə] *the* Гимала́и
Hiroshima [hɪ'rɒʃɪmə] г. Хиро́сима
Hollywood ['hɒlɪwʊd] г. Го́лливуд
Hungary ['hʌŋgərɪ] Ве́нгрия

Iceland ['aɪslənd] Исла́ндия
Idaho ['aɪdəhəʊ] А́йдахо (штат в США)
Illinois [ˌɪlə'nɔɪ] И́ллинойс (штат в США)
India ['ɪndjə] И́ндия
Indiana [ˌɪndɪ'ænə] Индиа́на (штат в США)
Indian Ocean [ˌɪndjən'əʊʃən] *the* Инди́йский океа́н
Iowa ['aɪəʊə] А́йова (штат в США)
Iran [ɪ'rɑːn] Ира́н
Iraq [ɪ'rɑːk] Ира́к
Ireland ['aɪələnd] Ирла́ндия
Israel ['ɪzreɪəl] Изра́иль
Italy ['ɪtəlɪ] Ита́лия

Japan [dʒə'pæn] Япо́ния
Jersey ['dʒɜːzɪ] о. Дже́рси
Jerusalem [dʒə'ruːsələm] г. Иерусалим

Kansas ['kænzəs] Ка́нзас (штат в США)
Kentucky [ken'tʌkɪ] Кенту́кки (штат в США)
Kiev ['kiːev] г. Ки́ев
Korea [kə'rɪə] Коре́я
Kosovo ['kɒsəvəʊ] Ко́сово
Kremlin ['kremlɪn] Кремль
Kuwait [kʊ'weɪt] Куве́йт

Latvia ['lætvɪə] Ла́твия
Libya ['lɪbɪə] Ли́вия
Lithuania [ˌlɪθjuː'eɪnjə] Литва́
Lisbon ['lɪzbən] г. Лиссабо́н
Liverpool ['lɪvəpuːl] г. Ли́верпул
London ['lʌndən] г. Ло́ндон
Los Angeles [lɒs'ændʒɪliːz] г. Лос-А́нджелес
Louisiana [luːˌiːzɪ'ænə] Луизиа́на (штат в США)
Luxembourg ['lʌksəmbɜːg] г. Люксембу́рг

Madrid [mə'drɪd] г. Мадри́д
Maine [meɪn] Мэн (штат в США)
Malta ['mɔːltə] Ма́льта (о. и госуда́рство)
Manitoba [ˌmænɪ'təʊbə] Манитоба
Maryland ['meərɪlənd] Мэ́риленд (штат в США)
Massachusetts [ˌmæsə'tʃuːsɪts] Массачу́сетс (штат в США)
Melbourne ['melbən] г. Мельбурн
Mexico ['meksɪkəʊ] Ме́ксика
Michigan ['mɪʃɪgən] Ми́чиган (штат в США)
Minnesota [ˌmɪnɪ'səʊtə] Миннесо́та (штат в США)
Minsk [mɪnsk] г. Минск
Mississippi [ˌmɪsɪ'sɪpɪ] Миссиси́пи (река́ и штат в США)
Missouri [mɪ'zʊərɪ] Миссу́ри (река́ и штат в США)
Moldova [mɒl'dəʊvə] Молдо́ва
Montana [mɒn'tænə] Монта́на (штат в США)
Montreal [ˌmɒntrɪ'ɔːl] г. Монреа́ль
Moscow ['mɒskəʊ] г. Москва́
Munich ['mjuːnɪk] г. Мю́нхен

Nebraska [nə'bræskə] Небра́ска (штат в США)
Netherlands ['neðələndz] *the* Нидерла́нды
Nevada [nə'vɑːdə] Нева́да (штат в США)
Newfoundland ['njuːfəndlənd] о. Ньюфа́ундленд
New Hampshire [ˌnjuː'hæmpʃə] Нью-Хэ́мпшир (штат в США)
New Jersey [ˌnjuː'dʒɜːzɪ] Нью-Дже́рси (штат в США)
New Mexico [ˌnjuː'meksɪkəʊ] Нью-Ме́ксико (штат в США)

New Orleans [ˌnjuːˈɔːlıənz] г. Нóвый Орлеáн
New York [ˌnjuːˈjɔːk] Нью-Йóрк (город и штат в США)
New Zealand [ˌnjuːˈziːlənd] Нóвая Зелáндия
Niagara [naıˈægərə] *the* р. Ниагáра, Ниагáрские водопáды
Nile [naıl] *the* р. Нил
North Sea [ˌnɔːθˈsiː] *the* Сéверное мóре
Norway [ˈnɔːweı] Норвéгия

Ohio [əʊˈhaıəʊ] Огáйо (рекá и штат в США)
Oklahoma [ˌəʊkləˈhəʊmə] Оклахóма (штат в США)
Oregon [ˈɒrıgən] Орегóн (штат в США)
Oslo [ˈɒzləʊ] г. Осло
Ottawa [ˈɒtəwə] г. Оттáва
Oxford [ˈɒksfəd] г. Óксфорд

Pacific Ocean [pəˌsıfıkˈəʊʃn] Тíхий океáн
Pakistan [ˌpɑːkıˈstɑːn] Пакистáн
Paris [ˈpærıs] г. Парíж
Pennsylvania [ˌpensılˈveınjə] Пенсильвáния (штат в США)
Philippines [ˈfılıpiːnz] *the* Филиппíны
Poland [ˈpəʊlənd] Пóльша
Portugal [ˈpɔːtʃʊgl] Португáлия
Pyrenees [ˌpırəˈniːz] *the* Пиренéйские гóры

Quebec [kwıˈbek] г. Квебéк

Rhine [raın] *the* р. Рейн
Rhode Island [ˌrəʊdˈaılənd] Род-Áйленд (штат в США)
Rome [rəʊm] г. Рим
Romania [ruːˈmeınjə] Румы́ния
Russia [ˈrʌʃə] Россíя

Saudi Arabia [ˌsaʊdıəˈreıbıə] Саýдовская Арáвия
Scandinavia [ˌskændıˈneıvjə] Скандинáвия
Scotland [ˈskɒtlənd] Шотлáндия
Seoul [səʊl] г. Сеул
Serbia [ˈsɜːbıə] Сéрбия
Siberia [saıˈbıərıə] Сибíрь
Singapore [ˌsıŋəˈpɔː] Сингапýр
Spain [speın] Испáния
Stockholm [ˈstɒkhəʊm] г. Стокгóльм
St Petersburg [sntˈpiːtəzbɜːg] г. Санкт-Петербýрг
Stratford [ˈstrætfəd] -on-Avon [ˈeivən] г. Стрáтфорд-на-Э́йвоне
Sweden [swiːdn] Швéция
Switzerland [ˈswıtsələnd] Швейцáрия
Sydney [ˈsıdnı] г. Сíдней

Taiwan [ˌtaıˈwɑːn] Тайвáнь
Teh(e)ran [ˌteəˈrɑːn] г. Тегерáн
Tennessee [ˌtenəˈsiː] Теннесí (рекá и штат в США)
Texas [ˈteksəs] Тéхас (штат в США)
Thames [temz] *the* р. Тéмза
Turkey [ˈtɜːkı] Тýрция

Ukraine [juːˈkreın] *the* Украйна
Urals [ˈjʊərəlz] *the* Урáльские гóры
Utah [ˈjuːtɑː] Ю́та (штат в США)

Venice [ˈvenıs] г. Венéция
Vermont [vɜːˈmɒnt] Вермонт (штат в США)
Vienna [vıˈenə] г. Вéна
Vietnam [ˌviːetˈnæm] Вьетнáм
Virginia [vəˈdʒınjə] ***West*** Зáпадная Вирджíния (штат в США)

Warsaw [ˈwɔːsɔː] г. Варшáва
Washington [ˈwɒʃıŋtən] Вáшингтон (город и штат в США)
Wellington [ˈwelıŋtən] г. Вéллингтон (столица Новой Зеландии)
White Sea [ˌwaıtˈsiː] *the* Бéлое мóре
Wimbledon [ˈwımbldən] г. Уимблдон
Wisconsin [wısˈkɒnsın] Вискóнсин (рекá и штат в США)
Worcester [ˈwʊstə] г. Вýстер
Wyoming [waıˈəʊmıŋ] Вайóминг (штат в США)

Yugoslavia [ˌjuːgəʊˈslɑːvjə] Югослáвия

Zurich [ˈzʊərık] г. Цю́рих

Numerals

Cardinals

0 ноль & нуль *m* naught, zero
1 оди́н *m*, одна́ *f*, одно́ *n* one
2 два *m*/*n*, две *f* two
3 три three
4 четы́ре four
5 пять five
6 шесть six
7 семь seven
8 во́семь eight
9 де́вять nine
10 де́сять ten
11 оди́ннадцать eleven
12 двена́дцать twelve
13 трина́дцать thirteen
14 четы́рнадцать fourteen
15 пятна́дцать fifteen
16 шестна́дцать sixteen
17 семна́дцать seventeen
18 восемна́дцать eighteen
19 девятна́дцать nineteen
20 два́дцать twenty
21 два́дцать оди́н *m* (одна *f*, одно *n*) twenty-one
22 два́дцать два *m*/*n* (две *f*) twenty-two
23 два́дцать три twenty-three
30 три́дцать thirty
40 со́рок forty
50 пятьдеся́т fifty
60 шестьдеся́т sixty
70 се́мьдесят seventy
80 во́семьдесят eighty
90 девяно́сто ninety
100 сто (а *или* one) hundred
200 две́сти two hundred
300 три́ста three hundred
400 четы́реста four hundred
500 пятьсо́т five hundred
600 шестьсо́т six hundred
700 семьсо́т seven hundred
800 восемьсо́т eight hundred
900 девятьсо́т nine hundred
1000 (одна́) ты́сяча *f* (а *или* one) thousand
60140 шестьдеся́т ты́сяч сто со́рок sixty thousand one hundred and forty
1 000 000 (оди́н) миллио́н *m* (а *или* one) million
1 000 000 000 (оди́н) миллиа́рд *m* milliard, *Am.* billion

Ordinals

1st пе́рвый first
2nd второ́й second
3rd тре́тий third
4th четвёртый fourth
5th пя́тый fifth
6th шесто́й sixth
7th седьмо́й seventh
8th восьмо́й eighth
9th девя́тый ninth
10th деся́тый tenth
11th оди́ннадцатый eleventh
12th двена́дцатый twelfth
13th трина́дцатый thirteenth
14th четы́рнадцатый fourteenth
15th пятна́дцатый fifteenth
16th шестна́дцатый sixteenth
17th семна́дцатый seventeenth
18th восемна́дцатый eighteenth
19th девятна́дцатый nineteenth
20th двадца́тый twentieth
21st два́дцать пе́рвый twenty-first
22nd два́дцать второ́й twenty-second
23rd два́дцать тре́тий twenty-third
30th тридца́тый thirtieth
40th сороково́й fortieth
50th пятидеся́тый fiftieth
60th шестидеся́тый sixtieth
70th семидеся́тый seventieth
80th восьмидеся́тый eightieth
90th девяно́стый ninetieth
100th со́тый (one) hundredth
200th двухсо́тый two hundredth
300th трёхсо́тый three hundredth
400th четырёхсо́тый four hundredth

500th пятисо́тый five hundredth
600th шестисо́тый six hundredth
700th семисо́тый seven hundredth
800th восьмисо́тый eight hundredth
900th девятисо́тый nine hundredth
1000th ты́сячный (one) thousandth
60 140th шестьдесят ты́сяч сто сороково́й sixty thousand one hundred and fortieth
1 000 000th миллио́нный millionth

American and British Weights and Measures

1. Linear Measure

1 inch (in.) дюйм = 2,54 см
1 foot (ft) фут = 30,48 см
1 yard (yd) ярд = 91,44 см

2. Nautical Measure

1 fathom (fm) морска́я саже́нь = 1,83 м
1 cable('s) length ка́бельтов = 183 м, в США = 120 морски́м саже́ням = 219 м
1 nautical mille (n. m.) *or* **1 knot** морска́я ми́ля = 1852 м

3. Square Measure

1 square inch (sq. in.) квадра́тный дюйм = 6,45 кв. см
1 square foot (sq. ft) квадра́тный фут = 929,03 кв. см
1 square yard (sq. yd) квадра́тный ярд = 8361,26 кв. см
1 square rod (sq. rd) квадра́тный род = 25,29 кв. м
1 rood (ro.) руд = 0,25 а́кра
1 acre (a.) акр = 0,4 га
1 square mile (sq. ml, *Am.* **sq. mi.)** квадра́тная ми́ля = 259 га

4. Cubic Measure

1 cubic inch (cu. in.) куби́ческий дюйм = 16,387 куб. см
1 cubic foot (cu. ft) куби́ческий фут = 28 316,75 куб. см
1 cubic yard (cu. yd) куби́ческий ярд = 0,765 куб. м
1 register ton (reg. tn) реги́стровая то́нна = 2,832 куб. см

5. British Measure of Capacity

Dry and Liquid Measure

Ме́ры жи́дких и сыпу́чих тел
1 imperial gill (gl, gi.) станда́ртный джилл = 0,142 л
1 imperial pint (pt) станда́ртная пи́нта = 0,568 л
1 imperial quart (qt) станда́ртная ква́рта = 1,136 л
1 imperial gallon (Imp. gal.) станда́ртный галло́н = 4,546 л

Dry Measure

1 imperial peck (pk) станда́ртный пек = 9,092 л
1 imperial bushel (bu., bsh.) станда́ртный бу́шель = 36,36 л
1 imperial quarter (qr) станда́ртная че́тверть = 290,94 л

Liquid Measure

1 imperial barrel (bbl., bl) станда́ртный ба́ррель = 1,636 гл

6. American Measure of Capacity

Dry Measure

1 U.S. dry pint америка́нская суха́я пи́нта = 0,551 л
1 U.S. dry quart америка́нская суха́я ква́рта = 1,1 л
1 U.S. dry gallon америка́нский сухо́й галло́н = 4,4 л
1 U.S. peck америка́нский пек = 8,81 л
1 U.S. bushel америка́нский бу́шель = 35,24 л

Liquid Measure

1 U.S. liquid gill америка́нский джилл (жи́дкости) = 0,118 л
1 U.S. liquid pint америка́нская пи́нта (жи́дкости) = 0,473 л
1 U.S. liquid quart америка́нская ква́рта (жи́дкости) = 0,946 л
1 U.S. gallon америка́нский галло́н (жи́дкости) = 3,785 л
1 U.S. barrel америка́нский ба́ррель = 119 л
1 U.S. barrel petroleum америка́нский ба́ррель не́фти = 158,97 л

7. Avoirdupois Weight

1 grain (gr.) гран = 0,0648 г
1 dram (dr.) дра́хма = 1,77 г
1 ounce (oz) у́нция = 28,35 г
1 pound (lb.) фунт = 453,59 г

1 quarter (**qr**) че́тверть = 12,7 кг, в США = 11,34 кг

1 hundredweight (**cwt**) це́нтнер = 50,8 кг, в США = 45,36 кг

1 stone (**st.**) стон = 6,35 кг

1 ton (**tn, t**) = 1016 кг (тж long ton: tn. l.), в США = 907,18 кг (тж short ton: tn. sh.)

Some Russian First Names

Алекса́ндр *m*, Alexander
dim: Са́ня, Са́ша, Шу́ра, Шу́рик
Алекса́ндра *f*, Alexandra
dim: Са́ня, Са́ша, Шу́ра
Алексе́й *m*, Alexis
dim: Алёша, Лёша
Анастаси́я *f*, *coll.* Наста́сья, Anastasia
dim: На́стя, Настёна, Та́ся
Анато́лий *m* Anatoly
dim: То́лик, То́ля
Андре́й *m* Andrew
dim: Андре́йка, Андрю́ша
А́нна *f* Ann, Anna
dim: А́ннушка, Аню́та, Аня, Ню́ра, Ню́ша, Ню́ся
Анто́н *m* Antony
dim: Анто́ша, То́ша
Антони́на *f* Antoni(n)a
dim: То́ня
Арка́дий *m* Arcady
dim: Арка́ша, Адик
Арсе́ний *m* Arseny
dim: Арсю́ша
Бори́с *m* Boris
dim: Бо́ря, Бори́ска
Вади́м *m* Vadim
dim: Ди́ма, Ва́дик, Ва́дя
Валенти́н *m* Valentine
dim: Ва́ля
Валенти́на *f* Valentine
dim: Ва́ля, Валю́ша, Ти́на
Вале́рий *m* Valery
dim: Вале́ра, Ва́ля, Вале́рик
Вале́рия *f* Valeria
dim: Ле́ра, Леру́ся
Варва́ра *f* Barbara
dim: Ва́ря, Варю́ша
Васи́лий *m* Basil
dim: Ва́ся, Василёк
Ве́ра *f* Vera
dim: Веру́ся, Веру́ша
Ви́ктор *m* Victor
dim: Ви́тя, Витю́ша
Викто́рия *f* Victoria
dim: Ви́ка
Влади́мир *m* Vladimir
dim: Во́ва, Воло́дя
Владисла́в *m* Vladislav
dim: Вла́дя, Вла́дик, Сла́ва, Сла́вик
Все́волод *m* Vsevolod
dim: Се́ва
Вячесла́в *m* Viacheslav
dim: Сла́ва, Сла́вик
Гали́на *f* Galina
dim: Га́ля, Га́лочка
Генна́дий *m* Gennady
dim: Ге́на, Ге́ня, Ге́ша
Гео́ргий *m* **Его́р** *m* George, Egor
dim: Го́ша, Жо́ра/Его́рка
Григо́рий *m* Gregory
dim: Гри́ша, Гри́ня
Да́рья *f* Daria
dim: Да́ша, Дашу́ля, Да́шенька
Дени́с *m* Denis
dim: Дени́ска
Дми́трий *m* Dmitry
dim: Ди́ма, Ми́тя, Митю́ша
Евге́ний *m* Eugene
dim: Же́ня
Евге́ния *f* Eugenia
dim: Же́ня
Екатери́на *f* Catherine
dim: Ка́тя, Катю́ша
Еле́на *f* Helen
dim: Ле́на, Алёнка, Алёна, Алёнушка, Лёля
Елизаве́та *f* Elizabeth
dim: Ли́за, Ли́занька
Заха́р *m* Zachary
dim: Заха́рка
Зинаида *f* Zinaida
dim: Зи́на, Зину́ля
Зо́я *f* Zoe
dim: Зо́енька
Ива́н *m* John
dim: Ва́ня, Ваню́ша
И́горь *m* Igor
dim: Игорёк, Га́рик
Илья *m* Elijah, Elias
dim: Илю́ша
Инноке́нтий *m* Innokenty
dim: Ке́ша
Ио́сиф *m* **О́сип** *m* Joseph
dim: О́ся
Ири́на *f* Irene
dim: И́ра, Ири́нка, Ири́ша, Иру́ся
Кири́лл *m* Cyril
dim: Кири́лка, Кирю́ша
Кла́вдия *f* Claudia
dim: Кла́ва, Кла́ша, Кла́вочка
Константи́н *m* Constantine
dim: Ко́ка, Ко́стя
Ксе́ния *f* **Акси́нья** *f* Xenia

dim: Ксéня, Ксю́ша
Кузьмá *m* Cosmo
dim: Кýзя
Ларúса *f* Larisa
dim: Ларúска, Лáра, Лóра
Лев *m* Leo
dim: Лёва, Лёвушка
Леонúд *m* Leonid
dim: Лёня
Лúдия *f* Lydia
dim: Лúда, Лидýся, Лидýша
Любóвь *f* Lubov (Charity)
dim: Лю́ба, Любáша
Людмúла *f* Ludmila
dim: Лю́да, Лю́ся, Мúла
Макáр *m* Macar
dim: Макáрка, Макáрушка
Максúм *m* Maxim
dim: Максúмка, Макс
Маргарúта *f* Margaret
dim: Рúта, Маргó(ша)
Марúна *f* Marina
dim: Марúнка, Марúша
Марúя *f* **Мáрья** *f* Maria
dim: Марúйка, Марýся, Мáня, Мáша, Мáшенька
Марк *m* Mark
dim: Маркýша, Маркýся
Матвéй *m* Mathew
dim: Матвéйка, Матю́ша, Мóтя
Михаúл *m* Michael
dim: Михáлка, Мúша, Мишýля
Надéжда *f* Nadezhda (Hope)
dim: Нáдя, Надю́ша
Натáлия *f coll.* **Натáлья** *f* Natalia
dim: Натáша, Нáта, Натýля, Натýся, Тáта
Никúта *m* Nikita
dim: Нúка, Никúтка, Никúша
Николáй *m* Nicholas
dim: Нúка, Николáша, Кóля
Нúна *f* Nina
dim: Нинýля, Нинýся
Оксáна *f* Oxana
dim: Ксáна
Олéг *m* Oleg
dim: Олéжка
Óльга *f* Olga
dim: Óля, Óлюшка, Олю́ша
Пáвел *m* Paul
dim: Пáвлик, Павлýша, Пáша
Пётр *m* Peter
dim: Петрýша, Пéтя
Полúна *f* Pauline
dim: Полúнка, Пóля, Пáша
Раúса *f* Raisa
dim: Рáя, Раю́ша
Ростислáв *m* Rostislav
dim: Рóстик, Рóся, Слáва, Слáвик
Руслáн *m* Ruslan
dim: Руслáнка, Рýсик
Светлáна *f* Svetlana
dim: Светлáнка, Свéта
Святослáв *m* Sviatoslav
dim: Слáва
Семён *m* Simeon, Simon
dim: Сёма, Сéня
Сергéй *m* Serge
dim: Сергýня, Серёжа, Серж
Станислáв *m* Stanislav
dim: Стáсик, Слáва
Степáн *m* Stephen
dim: Степáша, Стёпа
Степанúда *f* Stephanie
dim: Стёша
Тамáра *f* Tamara
dim: Тóма
Татьяна *f* Tatiana
dim: Тáня, Таню́ша, Тáта
Тимофéй *m* Timothy
dim: Тúма, Тимóша
Фёдор *m* Theodore
dim: Фéдя, Федю́ля(ня)
Фéликс *m* Felix
dim: Фéля
Филúпп *m* Philip
dim: Фúля, филю́ша
Эдуáрд *m* Edward
dim: Э́дик, Э́дя
Э́мма *f* Emma
dim: Э́ммочка
Ю́лия *f* Julia
dim: Ю́ля
Ю́рий *m* Yuri
dim: Ю́ра, Ю́рочка, Юрáша
Я́ков *m* Jacob
dim: Я́ша, Я́шенька, Яшýня
Ярослáв *m* Yaroslav
dim: Слáва (ик)

Grammatical Tables

Conjugation and Declension

The following two rules relative to the spelling of endings in Russian inflected words must be observed:

1. Stems terminating in г, к, х, ж, ш, ч, щ are never followed by ы, ю, я, but by **и, у, а**.

2. Stems terminating in ц are never followed by и, ю, я, but by **ы, у, а**.

Besides these, a third spelling rule, dependent on phonetic conditions, i.e. the position of stress, is likewise important:

3. Stems terminating in ж, ш, ч, ц can be followed by an o in the ending only if the syllable in question bears the stress; otherwise, i.e. in unstressed position, **e** is used instead.

A. Conjugation

Prefixed forms of the perfective aspect are represented by adding the prefix in angle brackets, e.g.: <про>чита́ть = чита́ть *impf.*, прочита́ть *pf.*

Personal endings of the present (and perfective future) tense:

1st conjugation:	-ю (-у)	-ешь	-ет	-ем	-ете	-ют (-ут)
2nd conjugation:	-ю (-у)	-ишь	-ит	-им	-ите	-ят (-ат)

Reflexive:

1st conjugation:	-юсь (-усь)	-ешься	-ется	-емся	-етесь	-ются (-утся)
2nd conjugation:	-юсь (-усь)	-ишься	-ится	-имся	-итесь	-ятся (-атся)

Suffixes and endings of the other verbal forms:

imp.	-й(те)	-и(те)	-ь(те)	
reflexive	-йся (-йтесь)	-ись (-итесь)	-ься (-ьтесь)	
	m	*f*	*n*	*pl.*
p. pr. a.	-щий(ся)	-щая(ся)	-щее(ся)	-щие(ся)
g. pr.	-я(сь)	-а(сь)		
p. pr. p.	-мый	-мая	-мое	-мые
short form	-м	-ма	-мо	-мы
pt.	-л	-ла	-ло	-ли
	-лся	-лась	-лось	-лись
p. pt. a.	-вший(ся)	-вшая(ся)	-вшее(ся)	-вшие(ся)
g. pt.	-в(ши)	-вши(сь)		
p. pt. p.	-нный	-нная	-нное	-нные
	-тый	-тая	-тое	-тые
short form	-н	-на	-но	-ны
	-т	-та	-то	-ты

Stress:

a) There is *no change of stress unless the final syllable of the infinitive is stressed*, i. e. in all forms of the verb stress remains invariably on the root syllable accentuated in the infinitive, e.g.: пла́кать. The forms of пла́кать correspond to paradigm [3], except for the stress, which is always on пла́-. The imperative of such verbs also differs from the paradigms concerned: it is in **-ь**(**те**) provided their stem ends in **one consonant** only, e.g.: пла́кать – пла́чь(те), ве́рить – ве́рь(те); and in **-и**(**те**) (unstressed!) in cases of **two and more consonants** preceding the imperative ending, e.g.: по́мнить – по́мни(те). Verbs with a vowel stem termination, however, generally form their imperative in **-й**(**те**): успоко́ить – успоко́й(те).

b) The prefix вы- in perfective verbs always bears the stress: вы́полнить (but *impf.*: выполня́ть). Imperfective (iterative) verbs with the suffix -ыв-/-ив- are always stressed on the syllable preceding the suffix: пока́зывать (but *pf.* показа́ть), спра́шивать (but *pf.* спроси́ть).

c) In the past participle passive of verbs in **-а́ть** (**-я́ть**), there is usually a shift of stress back onto the root syllable as compared with the infinitive (see paradigms [1]–[4], [6], [7], [28]). With verbs in **-е́ть** and **-и́ть** such a shift may occur as well, very often in agreement with a parallel accent shift in the 2nd p.sg. present tense, e.g.: [про]смотре́ть: [про]смотрю́, смо́тришь – просмо́тренный; see also paradigms [14]–[16] as against [13]: [по]мири́ть: [по]мирю́, -и́шь – помирённый. In this latter case the short forms of the participles are stressed on the last syllable throughout: -ённый: -ён, -ена́, -ено́, -ены́. In the former examples, however, the stress remains on the same root syllable as in the long form: -'енный: -'ен, -'ена, -'ено, -'ены.

(*a*) present, (*b*) future, (*c*) imperative, (*d*) present participle active, (*e*) present participle passive, (*f*) present gerund, (*g*) preterite, (*h*) past participle active, (*i*) past participle passive, (*j*) past gerund.

Verbs in **-ать**

1	<про>**чита́ть**
(*a*), <(*b*)>	<про>чита́ю, -а́ешь, -а́ют
(*c*)	<про>чита́й(те)!
(*d*)	чита́ющий
(*e*)	чита́емый
(*f*)	чита́я
(*g*)	<про>чита́л, -а, -о, -и
(*h*)	<про>чита́вший
(*i*)	прочи́танный
(*j*)	прочита́в

2	<по>**трепа́ть** (with л after б, в, м, п, ф)
(*a*), <(*b*)>	<по>треплю́, -е́плешь, -е́плют
(c)	<по>трепли́(те)!
(*d*)	тре́плющий
(*e*)	–
(*f*)	трепля́
(*g*)	<по>трепа́л, -а, -о, -и
(*h*)	<по>трепа́вший
(i)	<по>трёпанный
(j)	потрепа́в

3	<об>**глода́ть** (with changing consonant: г, д, з > ж; к, т > ч; х, с > ш; ск, ст > щ)
(*a*), <(*b*)>	<об>гложу́, -о́жешь, -о́жут
(*c*)	<об>гложи́(те)!
(*d*)	гло́жущий
(*e*)	–
(*f*)	гложа́
(*g*)	<об>глода́л, -а, -о, -и
(*h*)	<об>глода́вший
(*i*)	обгло́данный
(*j*)	обглода́в

4 <по>**держа́ть**
(with preceding ж, ш, ч, щ)
(*a*), <(*b*)> <по>держу́, -е́ржишь, -е́ржат
(*c*) <по>держи́(те)!
(*d*) держа́щий
(*e*) –
(*f*) держа́
(*g*) <по>держа́л, -а, -о, -и
(*h*) <по>держа́вший
(*i*) поде́ржанный
(*j*) подержа́в

Verbs in **-авать**

5 **дава́ть**
(*a*) даю́, даёшь, даю́т
(*c*) дава́й(те)!
(*d*) даю́щий
(*e*) дава́емый
(*f*) дава́я
(*g*) дава́л, -а, -о, -и
(*h*) дава́вший
(*i*) –
(*j*) –

Verbs in **-евать**

(*e.* = -ю́, -ёшь, *etc.*)
6 <на>**малева́ть**
(*a*), <(*b*)> <на>малю́ю, -ю́ешь, -ю́ют
(*c*) <на>малю́й(те)!
(*d*) малю́ющий
(*e*) малю́емый
(*f*) малю́я
(*g*) <на>малева́л, -а, -о, -и
(*h*) <на>малева́вший
(*i*) намалёванный
(*j*) намалева́в

Verbs in **-овать**

(and in **-евать** with preceding ж, ш, ч, щ, ц)
7 <на>**рисова́ть**
(*e.* = -ю́, -ёшь, *etc.*)
(*a*), <(*b*)> <на>рису́ю, -у́ешь, -у́ют
(*c*) <на>рису́й(те)!
(*d*) рису́ющий
(*e*) рису́емый
(*f*) рису́я
(*g*) <на>рисова́л, -а, -о, -и
(*h*) <на>рисова́вший
(*i*) нарисо́ванный
(*j*) нарисова́в

Verbs in **-еть**

8 <по>**жале́ть**
(*a*), <(*b*)> <по>жале́ю, -е́ешь, -е́ют
(*c*) <по>жале́й(те)!
(*d*) жале́ющий
(*e*) жале́емый
(*f*) жале́я
(*g*) <по>жале́л, -а, -о, -и
(*h*) <по>жале́вший
(*i*) ...ённый (*e.g.*: одолённый)
(*j*) пожале́в

9 <по>**смотре́ть**
(*a*), <(*b*)> <по>смотрю́, -о́тришь, -о́трят
(*c*) <по>смотри́(те)!
(*d*) смо́трящий
(*e*) –
(*f*) смотря́
(*g*) <по>смотре́л, -а, -о, -и
(*h*) <по>смотре́вший
(*i*) ...о́тренный (*e.g.*: просмо́тренный)
(*j*) посмотре́в

10 <по>**терпе́ть**
(with л after б, в, м, п, ф)
(*a*), <(*b*)> <по>терплю́, -е́рпишь, -е́рпят
(*c*) <по>терпи́(те)!
(*d*) терпя́щий
(*e*) терпи́мый
(*f*) терпя́
(*g*) <по>терпе́л, -а, -о, -и
(*h*) <по>терпе́вший
(*i*) ...ённый (*e.g.*: претерпенный)
(*j*) потерпе́в

11 <по>**лете́ть**
(with changing consonant:
г, з > ж
к, т > ч
х, с > ш
ск, ст > щ)
(*a*), <(*b*)> <по>лечу́, -ети́шь, -етя́т
(*c*) <по>лети́(те)
(*d*) летя́щий

(*e*)	–
(*f*)	летя́
(*g*)	<по>лете́л, -а, -о, -и
(*h*)	<по>лете́вший
(*i*)	...енный (*e.g.*: ве́рченный)
(*j*)	полете́в(ши)

Verbs in **-ереть**

12	<по>**тере́ть**
	(*st.* = -ешь, -ет, *etc.*)
(*a*), <(*b*)>	<по>тру́, -трёшь, -тру́т
(*c*)	<по>три́(те)!
(*d*)	тру́щий
(*e*)	–
(*f*)	–
(*g*)	<по>тёр, -ла, -ло, -ли
(*h*)	<по>тёрший
(*i*)	потёртый
(*j*)	потере́в

Verbs in **-ить**

13	<по>**мири́ть**
(*a*), <(*b*)>	<по>мирю́, -ри́шь, -ря́т
(*c*)	<по>мири́(те)!
(*d*)	миря́щий
(*e*)	мири́мый
(*f*)	миря́
(*g*)	<по>мири́л, -а, -о, -и
(*h*)	<по>мири́вший
(*i*)	помирённый
(*j*)	помири́в(ши)

14	<по>**люби́ть**
	(with л after б, в, м, п, ф)
(*a*), <(*b*)>	<по>люблю́, -ю́бишь, -ю́бят
(*c*)	<по>люби́(те)!
(*d*)	лю́бящий
(*e*)	люби́мый
(*f*)	любя́
(*g*)	<по>люби́л, -а, -о, -и
(*h*)	<по>люби́вший
(*i*)	...лю́бленный (*e.g.*: возлю́бленный)
(*j*)	полюби́в

15	<по>**носи́ть**
	(with changing consonant see No 11)
(*a*), <(*b*)>	<по>ношу́, -о́сишь, -о́сят
(*c*)	<по>носи́(те)!
(*d*)	но́сящий
(*e*)	носи́мый
(*f*)	нося́
(*g*)	<по>носи́л, -а, -о, -и
(*h*)	<по>носи́вший
(*i*)	поно́шенный
(*j*)	поноси́в

16	<на>**кроши́ть**
	(with preceding ж, ш, ч, щ)
(*a*), <(*b*)>	<на>крошу́, -о́шишь, -о́шат
(*c*)	<на>кроши́(те)!
(*d*)	кроша́щий
(*e*)	кроши́мый
(*f*)	кроша́
(*g*)	<на>кроши́л, -а, -о, -и
(*h*)	<на>кроши́вший
(*i*)	накро́шенный
(*j*)	накроши́в

Verbs in **-оть**

17	<за>**коло́ть**
(*a*), <(*b*)>	<за>колю́, -о́лешь, -о́лют
(*c*)	<за>коли́(те)!
(*d*)	ко́лющий
(*e*)	–
(*f*)	–
(*g*)	<за>коло́л, -а, -о, -и
(*h*)	<за>коло́вший
(*i*)	зако́лотый
(*j*)	заколо́в

Verbs in **-уть**

18	<по>**ду́ть**
(*a*), <(*b*)>	<по>ду́ю, -у́ешь, -у́ют
(*c*)	<по>ду́й(те)!
(*d*)	ду́ющий
(*e*)	–
(*f*)	ду́я
(*g*)	<по>ду́л, -а, -о, -и
(*h*)	<по>ду́вший
(*i*)	...ду́тый (*e.g.*: разду́тый)
(*j*)	поду́в

19	<по>**тяну́ть**
(*a*), <(*b*)>	<по>тяну́, -я́нешь, -я́нут
(*c*)	<по>тяни́(те)!
(*d*)	тя́нущий
(*e*)	–
(*f*)	–
(*g*)	<по>тяну́л, -а, -о, -и
(*h*)	<по>тяну́вший

(*i*)	потя́нутый
(*j*)	потяну́в

20	<со>**гну́ть**
	(*st.* = -ешь, -ет, *etc.*)
(*a*), <(*b*)>	<со>гну́, -нёшь, -ну́т
(*c*)	<со>гни́(те)!
(*d*)	гну́щий
(*e*)	–
(*f*)	–
(*g*)	<со>гну́л, -а, -о, -и
(*h*)	<со>гну́вший
(*i*)	со́гнутый
(*j*)	согну́в

21	<за>**мёрзнуть**
(*a*), <(*b*)>	<за>мёрзну, -нешь, -нут
(*c*)	<за>мёрзни(те)!
(*d*)	мёрзнущий
(*e*)	–
(*f*)	–
(*g*)	<за>мёрз, -зла, -о, -и
(*h*)	<за>мёрзший
(*i*)	...нутый (*e.g.*: воздви́гнутый)
(*j*)	замёрзши

Verbs in **-ыть**

22	<по>**кры́ть**
(*a*), <(*b*)>	<по>кро́ю, -о́ешь, -о́ют
(*c*)	<по>кро́й(те)!
(*d*)	кро́ющий
(*e*)	–
(*f*)	кро́я
(*g*)	<по>кры́л, -а, -о, -и
(*h*)	<по>кры́вший
(*i*)	<по>кры́тый
(*j*)	покры́в

23	<по>**плы́ть**
	(*st.* = -ешь, -ет, *etc.*)
(*a*), <(*b*)>	<по>плыву́, -вёшь, -ву́т
(*c*)	<по>плыви́(те)!
(*d*)	плыву́щий
(*e*)	–
(*f*)	плывя́
(*g*)	<по>плы́л, -а́, -о, -и
(*h*)	<по>плы́вший
(*i*)	...плы́тый (*e.g.*: проплы́тый)
(*j*)	поплы́в

Verbs in **-зти́, -зть (-сти)**

24	<по>**везти́**
	(-с[т]- = -с[т]-instead of -з- throughout)
	(*st.* = -ешь, -ет, *etc.*)
(*a*), <(*b*)>	<по>везу́, -зёшь, -зу́т
(*c*)	<по>вези́(те)!
(*d*)	везу́щий
(*e*)	везо́мый
(*f*)	везя́
(*g*)	<по>вёз, -везла́, -о́, -и́
(*h*)	<по>вёзший
(*i*)	повезённый
(*j*)	повезя́

Verbs in **-сти́, -сть**

25	<по>**вести́**
	(-т- = -т- instead of -д- throughout)
	(*st.* = -ешь, -ет, *etc.*)
(*a*), <(*b*)>	<по>веду́, -дёшь, -ду́т
(*c*)	<по>веди́(те)!
(*d*)	веду́щий
(*e*)	ведо́мый
(*f*)	ведя́
(*g*)	<по>вёл, -вела́, -о́, -и́
(*h*)	<по>ве́дший
(*i*)	поведённый
(*j*)	поведя́

Verbs in **-чь**

26	<по>**влечь**
(*a*), <(*b*)>	<по>влеку́, -ечёшь, -еку́т
(*c*)	<по>влеки́(те)!
(*d*)	влеку́щий
(*e*)	влеко́мый
(*f*)	–
(*g*)	<по>влёк, -екла́, -о́, -и́
(*h*)	<по>влёкший
(*i*)	...влечённый (*e.g.*: увлечённый)
(*j*)	повлёкши

Verbs in **-ять**

27	<рас>**та́ять**
	(*e.* = -ю́, -ёшь, -ёт, *etc.*)
(*a*), <(*b*)>	<рас>та́ю, -а́ешь, -а́ют
(*c*)	<рас>та́й(те)!
(*d*)	та́ющий
(*e*)	–
(*f*)	та́я

(*g*) <рас>та́ял, -а, -о, -и
(*h*) <рас>та́явший
(*i*) ...а́янный (*e.g.*: обла́янный)
(*j*) раста́яв

28 <по>**теря́ть**
(*a*), <(*b*)> <по>теря́ю, -я́ешь, -я́ют
(*c*) <по>теря́й(те)!
(*d*) теря́ющий
(*e*) теря́емый
(*f*) теря́я
(*g*) <по>теря́л, -а, -о, -и
(*h*) <по>теря́вший
(*i*) поте́рянный
(*j*) потеря́в

B. Declension

Noun

a) Succession of the six cases (horizontally): nominative, genitive, dative, accusative, instrumental and prepositional in the singular and (thereunder) the plural. *With nouns denoting animate beings (persons and animals) there is a coincidence of endings in the accusative and genitive both singular and plural of the masculine, but only in the plural of the feminine and neuter genders.* This rule also applies, of course, to adjectives as well as various pronouns and numerals that must in syntactical connections agree with their respective nouns.

b) Variants of the following paradigms are pointed out in notes added to the individual declension types or, if not, mentioned after the entry word itself.

Masculine nouns:

		N	*G*	*D*	*A*	*I*	*P*
1	ви́д	-	-а	-у	-	-ом	-е
		-ы	-ов	-ам	-ы	-ами	-ах

Note: Nouns in -ж, -ш, -ч, -щ have in the *g/pl.* the ending -ей.

		N	*G*	*D*	*A*	*I*	*P*
2	реб	**-ёнок**	-ёнка	-ёнку	-ёнка	-ёнком	-ёнке
		-я́та	-я́т	-я́там	-я́т	-я́тами	-я́тах
3	слу́ча	**-й**	-я	-ю	-й	-ем	-е
		-и	-ев	-ям	-и	-ями	-ях

Notes: Nouns in -ий have in the *prpos/sg.* the ending -ии.
When *e.*, the ending of the *instr/sg.* is -ём, and of the *g/pl.* -ёв.

		N	*G*	*D*	*A*	*I*	*P*
4	про́фил	**-ь**	-я	-ю	-ь	-ем	-е
		-и	-ей	-ям	-и	-ями	-ях

Note: When *e.*, the ending of the *instr/sg.* is -ём.

Feminine nouns:

		N	*G*	*D*	*A*	*I*	*P*
5	рабо́т	**-а**	-ы	-е	-у	-ой	-е
		-ы	-	-ам	-ы	-ами	-ах
6	неде́л	**-я**	-и	-е	-ю	-ей	-е
		-и	-ь	-ям	-и	-ями	-ях

Notes: Nouns in -ья have in the *g/pl.* the ending -ий (unstressed) or -éй (stressed), the latter being also the ending of nouns in -éя. Nouns in -я with preceding vowel terminate in the *g/pl.* in -й (for -ий see also No. 7). When *e.*, the ending of the *instr/sg.* is -ёй (-ёю).

7	áрм**и**	**-я**	-и	-и	-ю	-ей	-и
		-и	-й	-ям	-и	-ями	-ях
8	тетрáд	**-ь**	-и	-и	-ь	-ью	-и
		-и	-ей	-ям	-и	-ями	-ях

Neuter nouns:

9	блю́д	**-о**	-а	-у	-о	-ом	-е
		-а	-	-ам	-а	-ами	-ах
10	пóл	**-е**	-я	-ю	-е	-ем	-е
		-я́	-éй	-я́м	-я́	-я́ми	-я́х

Note: Nouns in -ье have in the *g/pl.* the ending -ий. In addition, they do not shift their stress.

11	учи́ли**щ**	**-е**	-а	-у	-е	-ем	-е
		-а	-	-ам	-а	-ами	-ах
12	желáн**и**	**-е**	-я	-ю	-е	-ем	-и
		-я	-й	-ям	-я	-ями	-ях
13	врé**м**	**-я**	-ени	-ени	-я	-енем	-ени
		-енá	-ён	-енáм	-енá	-енáми	-енáх

Adjective

also ordinal numbers, etc.

Notes

a) Adjectives in **-ский** have no predicative (short) forms.

b) Variants of the following paradigms have been recorded with the individual entry words.

		m	*f*	*n*	*pl.*	
14	бéл	**-ый(-óй)**	**-ая**	**-ое**	**-ые**	long form
		-ого	-ой	-ого	-ых	
		-ому	-ой	-ому	-ым	
		-ый	-ую	-ое	-ые	
		-ым	-ой	-ым	-ыми	
		-ом	-ой	-ом	-ых	
		-	-á	-о (*a.* -ó)	-ы (*a.* -ы́)	short form

15	си́н	**-ий**	**-яя**	**-ее**	**-ие**	long form
		-его	-ей	-его	-их	
		-ему	-ей	-ему	-им	
		-ий	-юю	-ее	-ие	
		-им	-ей	-им	-ими	
		-ем	-ей	-ем	-их	
		-(ь)	-я́	-е	-и	short form
16	стро́г	**-ий**	**-ая**	**-ое**	**-ие**	long form
		-ого	-ой	-ого	-их	
		-ому	-ой	-ому	-им	
		-ий	-ую	-ое	-ие	
		-им	-ой	-им	-ими	
		-ом	-ой	-ом	-их	
		-	-а́	-о	-и (*а.* -й)	short form
17	то́щ	**-ий**	**-ая**	**-ее**	**-ие**	long form
		-его	-ей	-его	-их	
		-ему	-ей	-ему	-им	
		-ий	-ую	-ее	-ие	
		-им	-ей	-им	-ими	
		-ем	-ей	-ем	-их	
		-	-а	-е (-о́)	-и	short form
18	оле́н	**-ий**	**-ья**	**-ье**	**-ьи**	
		-ьего	-ьей	-ьего	-ьих	
		-ьему	-ьей	-ьему	-ьим	
		-ий	-ью	-ье	-ьи	
		-ьим	-ьей	-ьим	-ьими	
		-ьем	-ьей	-ьем	-ьих	
19	дя́дин	**-**	**-а**	**-о**	**-ы**	
		-а	-ой	-а	-ых	
		-у	-ой	-у	-ым	
		-	-у	-о	-ы	
		-ым	-ой	-ым	-ыми	
		-ом[1]	-ой	-ом	-ых	

[1]) Masculine surnames in -ов, -ев, -ин, -ын have the ending -е.

Pronoun

20	**я**	меня́	мне	меня́	мной (мно́ю)	мне
	мы	нас	нам	нас	на́ми	нас
21	**ты**	тебя́	тебе́	тебя́	тобо́й (тобо́ю)	тебе́
	вы	вас	вам	вас	ва́ми	вас
22	**он**	его́	ему́	его́	им	нём
	она́	её	ей	её	е́ю (ей)	ней
	оно́	его́	ему́	его́	им	нём
	они́	их	им	их	и́ми	них

Note: After prepositions the oblique forms receive an н-prothesis, e.g.: для него́, с не́ю (ней).

23	**кто**	кого́	кому́	кого́	кем	ком
	что	чего́	чему́	что	чем	чём

Note: In combinations with ни-, не- a preposition separates such compounds, e.g. ничто́: ни от чего́, ни к чему́.

24	**мой**	моего́	моему́	мой	мои́м	моём
	моя́	моє́й	моє́й	мою́	моє́й	моє́й
	моё	моего́	моему́	моё	мои́м	моём
	мои́	мои́х	мои́м	мои́	мои́ми	мои́х
25	**наш**	на́шего	на́шему	наш	на́шим	на́шем
	на́ша	на́шей	на́шей	на́шу	на́шей	на́шей
	на́ше	на́шего	на́шему	на́ше	на́шим	на́шем
	на́ши	на́ших	на́шим	на́ши	на́шими	на́ших
26	**чей**	чьего́	чьему́	чей	чьим	чьём
	чья	чьей	чьей	чью	чьей	чьей
	чьё	чьего́	чьему́	чьё	чьим	чьём
	чьи	чьих	чьим	чьи	чьи́ми	чьих
27	**э́тот**	э́того	э́тому	э́тот	э́тим	э́том
	э́та	э́той	э́той	э́ту	э́той	э́той
	э́то	э́того	э́тому	э́то	э́тим	э́том
	э́ти	э́тих	э́тим	э́ти	э́тими	э́тих
28	**тот**	того́	тому́	тот	тем	том
	та	той	той	ту	той	той
	то	того́	тому́	то	тем	том
	те	тех	тем	те	те́ми	тех
29	**сей**	сего́	сему́	сей	сим	сём
	сия́	сей	сей	сию́	сей	сей
	сие́	сего́	сему́	сие́	сим	сём
	сии́	сих	сим	сии́	си́ми	сих
30	**сам**	самого́	самому́	самого́	сами́м	само́м
	сама́	само́й	само́й	саму́, само́ё	само́й	само́й
	само́	самого́	самому́	само́	сами́м	само́м
	са́ми	сами́х	сами́м	сами́х	сами́ми	сами́х
31	**весь**	всего́	всему́	весь	всем	всём
	вся	всей	всей	всю	всей	всей
	всё	всего́	всему́	всё	всем	всём
	все	всех	всем	все	все́ми	всех
32	**не́сколько**	не́скольких	не́скольким	не́сколько	не́сколькими	не́скольких

Numeral

33	**оди́н**	одного́	одному́	оди́н	одни́м	одно́м
	одна́	одно́й	одно́й	одну́	одно́й	одно́й
	одно́	одного́	одному́	одно́	одни́м	одно́м
	одни́	одни́х	одни́м	одни́	одни́ми	одни́х

34	**два**	**две**	**три**	**четы́ре**	
	двух	двух	трёх	четырёх	
	двум	двум	трём	четырём	
	два	две	три	четы́ре	
	двумя́	двумя́	тремя́	четырьмя́	
	двух	двух	трёх	четырёх	
35	**пять**	**пятна́дцать**	**пятьдеся́т**	**сто**	**со́рок**
	пяти́	пятна́дцати	пяти́десяти	ста	сорока́
	пяти́	пятна́дцати	пяти́десяти	ста	сорока́
	пять	пятна́дцать	пятьдеся́т	сто	со́рок
	пятью	пятна́дцатью	пятью́десятью	ста	сорока́
	пяти́	пятна́дцати	пяти́десяти	ста	сорока́
36	**две́сти**	**три́ста**	**четы́реста**	**пятьсо́т**	
	двухсо́т	трёхсо́т	четырёхсо́т	пятисо́т	
	двумста́м	трёмста́м	четырёмста́м	пятиста́м	
	две́сти	три́ста	четы́реста	пятьсо́т	
	двумяста́ми	тремяста́ми	четырьмяста́ми	пятьюста́ми	
	двухста́х	трёхста́х	четырёхста́х	пятиста́х	
37	**о́ба**	**о́бе**	**дво́е**	**че́тверо**	
	обо́их	обе́их	двои́х	четверы́х	
	обо́им	обе́им	двои́м	четверы́м	
	о́ба	о́бе	дво́е	че́тверо	
	обо́ими	обе́ими	двои́ми	четверы́ми	
	обо́их	обе́их	двои́х	четверы́х	